THE OXFORD HANDBOOK OF

CONTEMPORARY BRITISH AND IRISH POETRY

OXFORD HANDBOOKS OF LITERATURE

The Oxford Handbooks of Literature are envisaged as volumes on an ambitious scale offering around forty newly written chapters in key fields of literary and cultural study. The series aims to represent the latest research and to indicate current trends, with a view to providing a readership of faculty, postgraduate scholars, and senior undergraduates, with both an overview and orientation across a wide range of rubrics, to point up the latest thinking and research among leading specialists and to indicate where significant new departures are in progress.

THE OXFORD HANDBOOK OF

CONTEMPORARY BRITISH AND IRISH POETRY

Edited by
PETER ROBINSON

OXFORD
UNIVERSITY PRESS

OXFORD
UNIVERSITY PRESS

Great Clarendon Street, Oxford, OX2 6DP,
United Kingdom

Oxford University Press is a department of the University of Oxford.
It furthers the University's objective of excellence in research, scholarship,
and education by publishing worldwide. Oxford is a registered trade mark of
Oxford University Press in the UK and in certain other countries

© Oxford University Press 2013

The moral rights of the authors have been asserted

First Edition published in 2013

Impression: 1

All rights reserved. No part of this publication may be reproduced, stored in
a retrieval system, or transmitted, in any form or by any means, without the
prior permission in writing of Oxford University Press, or as expressly permitted
by law, by licence or under terms agreed with the appropriate reprographics
rights organization. Enquiries concerning reproduction outside the scope of the
above should be sent to the Rights Department, Oxford University Press, at the
address above

You must not circulate this work in any other form
and you must impose this same condition on any acquirer

Published in the United States of America by Oxford University Press
198 Madison Avenue, New York, NY 10016, United States of America

British Library Cataloguing in Publication Data

Data available

Library of Congress Control Number: 2013945912

ISBN 978-0-19-959680-5

Printed and bound in Great Britain by
CPI Group (UK) Ltd, Croydon, CR0 4YY

Links to third party websites are provided by Oxford in good faith and
for information only. Oxford disclaims any responsibility for the materials
contained in any third party website referenced in this work.

Preface

When Jacqueline Baker at Oxford University Press invited me to edit a Handbook dedicated to contemporary British and Irish poetry I was grateful for the opportunity to reflect upon what it had felt like in early 2007 to re-enter a poetry scene I had contributed to from the middle of the 1970s, one I'd then been obliged to leave and keep up with from a distance at the end of the following decade. On repatriation after living and working in Japan, and holidaying mostly in Italy, for the previous eighteen years, I encountered at close quarters conditions in the British and Irish poetry world that were quite different to those I had left: some of the most active publishers were new, a number of the prominent figures were from a younger generation or two, the possibilities for becoming involved, for reading and publishing, were more various and extensive, as were the kinds of opportunity to teach and encourage poetry that opened up before me. Though initially daunted by the challenge of editing a volume that would include approximately forty contributions, which were to contribute original research to an indefinite and rapidly evolving area, I have found the process of doing so immensely informative and educative, and would like to thank Jacqueline for suggesting that I take on the project and then for supporting and guiding me through its various intricacies.

One of the things that hadn't changed, and appeared in some lights to have darkened, was a sense of factionalizing and division, of local, disconnected activity, overlapping circles, exclusivities and the like, which could occasionally erupt into conflict so vociferous that it would reach the daily news-sheets, and always in a manner to feed the intermittent media sideline of disparaging the contemporary arts. Such a state of affairs, which indicates a degree of inattention to poetry, even among poets and readers, has the cultural drawback of preventing development through an appreciation and critical understanding of what has been achieved and where it might be imitated, adapted, added to, or evolved. Thus, while there have been volumes of criticism dedicated to some of the poets whose work is addressed here, and while there have been a number of attempts to argue for directions of development, or to criticize failures to so develop, there is, it would appear, no one volume that attempts to offer at least a partial understanding of the range and variety of poetry being written now and simultaneously in these islands. The way to approach this, I believed, was to allow poets and critics from a range of constituencies the occasion to inhabit the pages of an extensive single volume.

What then came to be called *The Oxford Handbook of Contemporary British and Irish Poetry* needed first to be planned and given an outline structure, not least so that it could be reported on and evaluated, and this before any of the contributors to the eventual book were contacted. The volume's shape and sequencing is my own, as is the conception of what might be a sort of anthropological fieldwork as the best approach to such complex contemporary conditions—ones which, as I argue, can never be more than partially known by any of its individual participants, participant-observers, or interested onlookers. My first thanks must thus go to those commissioned and anonymous reviewers, whose comments, mostly positive but also constructively negative, were without exception helpful in refining the finally accepted proposal.

However much editors may plan volumes that they hope will do such-and-such beneficial things for the field of study to which they are addressed, the fulfilment of those hopes is then more or less entirely dependent on the intelligence, energy, organization, dedication, and commitment of the invited contributors who deliver on their promises to write. Their input helped revise by filling out the bare outlines of a projected contents list, their chapters giving nuance and individuality to, as well as calling for some reconsideration or reshaping of, that editorial armature. I am extremely grateful to all of my writers for their collaborative contributions, and their willingness to respond assiduously when in receipt of editorial suggestions and encouragements.

Though these large gatherings of chapters can of course be read by picking out topics that particularly engage the reader, this Handbook has been planned to create a cumulatively informed and informative sequence. It can be read from the Introduction through to the final chapter, and the five parts into which its chapters are grouped have been conceived to move from accounts of the contemporary period in poetry itself, through to a series of enduring ethical, political, and cultural problems around which much contemporary poetry has variously circled. Thus readers may go from beginning to end, may read single parts, and may pick out individual chapters. Detail of the rationale in planning and sequencing what is much larger than a standard monograph are given in the final section of my 'Introduction: The Limits and Openness of the Contemporary'.

One characteristic of the contemporary period and recent past of poetry is the increase in the number of poets who are employed in higher education and who also publish literary criticism. As a result, the contributors to this Handbook are often themselves poets, and some of their writing is that of parties who are interested in ways that differ from those of literary critics and historians who do not themselves attempt to contribute poetry to the contemporary. Occasionally they are, and I am, the subject of comment in their roles as poets, poet-critics, or, as I prefer to call them, poets who also write criticism. This may seem an unusual feature of a volume of commentary on what for other books in this series can appropriately be called an academic field; but it is an inevitability of writing on contemporary literature, and especially in so theoretically and culturally self-conscious a field as that of contemporary poetry. It would be misleading to pretend that the object of study in this area can be clearly and simply separated from those studying it. This can only begin to seem a fact of the subject when the inquirers are of so much later generations than those of the poets studied, that they, along with their contemporaneous critics, supporters and detractors, are dead. As a result, this Handbook, while contributing to the study of contemporary poetry, also changes—as is the case with all such inquiry, but more directly so here because issues and persons are alive—the object of their remarks in the very process of characterizing it. *The Oxford*

Handbook of Contemporary British and Irish Poetry is thus a volume that has been produced as much for the poetry world as for the academy, and it aims to be one that helps inform and explicate the concerns of each to the other.

Editors of collective volumes such as this usually contribute an introduction and one, or more, chapters. Doing so, they too find themselves in need of editorial advice. In my case, I would like to thank Adam Piette, Natalie Pollard, Stephen Romer, and Helen Small for their kind and helpful comments on one or other of my contributions. I would especially like to acknowledge John Kerrigan's generous, and repeated, input into all four.

I would also like to thank my wife, Ornella Trevisan, and our daughters Matilde and Giulia, for their patience and support over the years that I have been involved in this Handbook and, simultaneously, other publications, all of them produced alongside the various and time-consuming aspects of my work at the University of Reading. Without their company and generosity through life I would not have been able so happily to complete this volume or indeed any other piece of my writing, translating, and editing.

Finally, then, let me conclude with a salutation to the poets who are writing now, to the readers who follow their work, and the students of this endlessly fascinating ancient and modern art form. I hope you find as much stimulus from reading and thinking about the subjects explored in these chapters as has been provided to me.

Peter Robinson
17 June 2012

Contents

List of Contributors … xiii

Introduction: The Limits and Openness of the Contemporary … 1
PETER ROBINSON

PART I MOVEMENTS OVER TIME

1. Modernist Survivors … 21
   EDWARD LARRISSY

2. The Thirties Bequest … 38
   MICHAEL O'NEILL

3. The Unburied Past: Walking with Ghosts of the 1940s … 57
   LEO MELLOR

4. 'Obscure and Doubtful': Stevie Smith, F. T. Prince, and Legacy … 77
   WILLIAM MAY

5. The Movement: Never and Always … 94
   MARTIN DODSWORTH

6. 'In different voices': Modernism since the 1960s … 111
   JEREMY NOEL-TOD

7. Two Poetries?: A Re-examination of the 'Poetry Divide' in 1970s Britain … 130
   HELEN BAILEY

8. A Dog's Chance: The Evolution of Contemporary Women's Poetry? … 151
   DERYN REES-JONES

9. CAT-scanning the Little Magazine … 173
   RICHARD PRICE

10. Books and the Market: Trade Publishers, State Subsidies, and Small Presses — 191
   MATTHEW SPERLING

PART II SENSES OF FORM AND TECHNIQUE

11. 'Space available': A Poet's Decisions — 215
    JEFFREY WAINWRIGHT

12. Contemporary Poetry and Close Reading — 230
    ADAM PIETTE

13. 'All livin language is sacred': Poetry and Varieties of English in these Islands — 246
    SIMON DENTITH

14. Misremembered Lyric and Orphaned Music — 266
    ZOË SKOULDING

15. 'The degree of power exercised': Recent Ekphrasis — 286
    CONOR CARVILLE

16. Cinema Mon Amour: How British Poetry Fell in Love with Film — 303
    SOPHIE MAYER

17. Singing Schools and Beyond: The Roles of Creative Writing — 322
    PETER CARPENTER

PART III POETRY IN PLACES

18. Historical and Archaeological: The Poetry of Recovery and Memory — 341
    HEATHER O'DONOGHUE

19. London, Albion — 359
    JOHN KERRIGAN

20. The 'London Cut': Poetry and Science — 384
    PETER MIDDLETON

21. 'Dafter than we care to own': Some Poets of the North of England — 407
    DAVID WHEATLEY

22. Auden in Ireland 424
    JOHN REDMOND

23. 'Other Modes of Being': Nuala ní Dhomhnaill, Paul Muldoon, and Translation 442
    MARIA JOHNSTON

24. Writing [W]here: Gender and Cultural Positioning in Ireland and Wales 461
    ALICE ENTWISTLE

25. The Altered Sublime: Raworth, Crozier, Prynne 481
    ROD MENGHAM

PART IV BORDER CROSSINGS

26. Dislocating Country: Post-War English Poetry and the Politics of Movement 497
    DAVID HERD

27. Multi-ethnic British Poetries 517
    OMAAR HENA

28. European Affinities 538
    STEPHEN ROMER

29. Scottish Poetry in the Wider World 558
    IAIN GALBRAITH

30. The View from the USA 576
    ROMANA HUK

31. Audience and Awkwardness: Personal Poetry in Britain and New Zealand 596
    ANNA SMAILL

PART V RESPONSIBILITIES AND VALUES

32. Speech Acts, Responsibility, and Commitment in Poetry 617
    MAXIMILIAN DE GAYNESFORD

33. 'Is a chat with me your fancy?': Address in Contemporary British Poetry 638
    NATALIE POLLARD

34. 'There Again': Composition, Revision, and Repair 657
    PETER ROBINSON

35. Reparation, Atonement, and Redress 676
    PIERS PENNINGTON

36. Contemporary Poetry and Belief 694
    MICHAEL SYMMONS ROBERTS

37. The Loneliness of the Long-Distance Poet 707
    ANDREA BRADY

38. Contemporary Poetry and Value 727
    PETER ROBINSON

Index 749

List of Contributors

Helen Bailey is a postgraduate researcher and teaching assistant at the University of Reading. Her undergraduate degree was obtained from the University of Durham in 2008 and she was awarded a Master's degree from the University of Reading in 2009. She has written on 1970s British poetry, as well as various aspects of narrative theory in the works of Samuel Beckett, Lawrence Durrell, and Laurence Sterne. She also presented a paper at the Bernard Spencer Centenary Conference in 2009. Her doctoral research explores the connection between music and the concept of 'spirit' in the writing of Samuel Beckett.

Andrea Brady is Senior Lecturer at Queen Mary University of London, where she teaches both early modern and contemporary poetry. She is the author of *English Funerary Elegy in the Seventeenth Century* (Palgrave Macmillan, 2006), as well as several books of poetry: *Mutability* (Seagull, 2012), *Wildfire: A Verse Essay on Obscurity and Illumination* (Krupskaya, 2010), *Embrace* (Object Permanence, 2005), and *Vacation of a Lifetime* (Salt, 2001). She is Director of the *Archive of the Now* (<http://www.archiveofthenow.org/>), an online repository of contemporary poetry, and co-editor of the small press Barque.

Peter Carpenter has taught English and Creative Writing since 1980; he currently works at Tonbridge School, was made a Visiting Fellow at the University of Warwick in 2000, and was Creative Writing Fellow at the University of Reading during 2007–8. *Just Like That: New and Selected Poems* was published by Smith Doorstop in autumn 2012, following five previous collections of poetry, and poems featured in many literary journals including the *TLS*, *Poetry Review*, *Poetry Ireland Review*, and *The Independent*. He has been a co-director of Worple Press since 1997, publishing works from a range of authors including Iain Sinclair, Peter Robinson, and Peter Kane Dufault; he has given talks, and tutored and run writing workshops for many organizations including the Arvon Foundation, Poetry Ireland, the Poetry Trust, and Survivors' Poetry. He is literary executor to William Hayward and is a regular essayist and reviewer for a number of literary journals including *Agenda*, *The North*, and the *London Magazine*.

Conor Carville is a Lecturer in English and Creative Writing at the University of Reading. He is the author of *The Ends of Ireland: Criticism, Subjectivity, History* (Manchester University Press, 2012) as well as many essays on Irish poetry, fiction, and criticism. His first collection of poetry was published by Dedalus Press in 2012.

Maximilian de Gaynesforde is Professor of Philosophy at the University of Reading, having previously been a Fellow of Lincoln College, Oxford. He has written a number of articles on the relationship between philosophy and poetry, as well as on the philosophy of mind and language. He is the author of *I: The Meaning of the First Person Term* (Clarendon Press, 2006), *Hilary Putnam* (McGills-Queens University Press/Acumen, 2006), and *John McDowell* (Blackwell/Polity Press, 2004), and has edited a volume of essays on the philosophy of action, *Agents and Their Actions* (Blackwell, 2011).

Simon Dentith is Professor of English at the University of Reading. He has written widely on Victorian topics, and also has interests in contemporary Scottish writing, and contemporary poetry. His most recent book is *Epic and Empire in Nineteenth-Century Britain* (Cambridge University Press, 2006), and he has also recently edited Trollope's *Phineas Finn* for Oxford World's Classics.

Martin Dodsworth is Emeritus Professor of English Literature, Royal Holloway, University of London. He has written on poetry for *The Review*, the *London Magazine*, *The Listener*, and *The Guardian*, and edited *The Survival of Poetry* (Faber, 1970).

Alice Entwistle is Principal Lecturer in English at the University of Glamorgan. She has published *Contemporary Women Poets Writing in and out of Wales* (Seren, 2013). Current projects include a critical study of Gwyneth Lewis (University of Wales Press: Writers of Wales), an anthology of modernist and innovative poetries in Wales, edited with John Goodby, and a creative-critical study of Ciaran Carson, co-authored with Kevin Mills.

Iain Galbraith was born in Glasgow and now lives in Wiesbaden, Germany. His work as a poet, translator, and essayist has been widely published in journals and books in the UK and abroad. His most recent book publications include a substantial edited anthology of Scottish poetry in German translation, *Bereder Norden: Schottische Lyrik seit 1900* (Edition Rugerup, 2011), and two translated editions of poetry, John Burnside's *Versuch über das Licht* (Hanser Verlag, 2011), and W. G. Sebald's *Across the Land and the Water: Selected Poems 1964–2001* (Hamish Hamilton, 2011).

Omaar Hena is an Assistant Professor of English at Wake Forest University where he researches and teaches world anglophone literature with an emphasis on poetry and poetics. He has published in *Contemporary Literature, Minnesota Review*, and *The Princeton Encyclopedia of Poetry and Poetics*. His book manuscript examines contemporary postcolonial poetry and the politics of globality in the work of Paul Muldoon, Derek Walcott, Ingrid de Kok, and Daljit Nagra.

David Herd is the author of two critical works published by Manchester University Press, *John Ashbery and American Poetry* (2000) and *Enthusiast! Essays on Modern American Literature* (2007). His collections of poetry include *All Just* (Carcanet Press, 2012) and *Outwith* (BookThug, 2012). His recent writings on poetry and politics have appeared in *PN Review, Parallax*, and *Almost Island*. He is Professor of Modern Literature at the University of Kent, where he directs the Centre for Modern Poetry.

Romana Huk is co-editor of *Contemporary British Poetry: Essays in Theory and Criticism* (SUNY Press, 1996), editor of *Assembling Alternatives: Reading Postmodern Poetries Transnationally* (Wesleyan University Press, 2003), and author of *Stevie Smith: Between the Lines* (Palgrave, 2005). Her thirty-plus essays on contemporary poetry and poetics have appeared in journals and critical collections on either side of the Atlantic. To date, her research interests have ranged from working-class writing to race and performance poetries to, most recently, philosophy and theology as processed by the transatlantic avant-garde. Having taught in both the US and the UK, she returned in 2002 as a senior professor to her alma mater, the University of Notre Dame.

Maria Johnston has been the Christopher Tower Lecturer in Poetry in the English Language at Christ Church College, Oxford. She is a regular reviewer of contemporary poetry for a variety of publications in Ireland, the UK, and the United States, and has most recently co-edited (with Philip Coleman) *Reading Pearse Hutchinson: From Findrum to Fisterra* (Irish Academic Press, 2011).

John Kerrigan is Professor of English 2000 at the University of Cambridge. Among his publications are *Revenge Tragedy: Aeschylus to Armageddon* (Clarendon Press, 1996) and *Archipelagic English: Literature, History, and Politics 1603–1707* (Oxford University Press, 2008). He is completing a book about British and Irish poetry since 1960.

Edward Larrissy is Professor of Poetry and Head of the School of English at Queen's University, Belfast, where he is affiliated to the Seamus Heaney Centre for Poetry. Before that he was Professor of English at the University of Leeds, where he led the AHRC project 'Leeds Poetry 1950–1980'. His books include *Reading Twentieth Century Poetry: The Language of Gender and Objects* (Blackwell, 1990), *Yeats the Poet: The Measures of Difference* (Harvester, 1994), and *Blake and Modern Literature* (Palgrave Macmillan, 2006). He has edited *Romanticism and Postmodernism* (Cambridge University Press, 1999) and *W. B. Yeats: The Major Works* (Oxford World's Classics, 2000). Professor Larrissy is a Member of the Royal Irish Academy.

William May is a Lecturer in English at the University of Southampton. Recent publications include *Stevie Smith and Authorship* (Oxford University Press, 2010), and *Postwar Literature: 1950–1990* (Longman, 2010). He has also guest-edited an issue of *Contemporary Music Review* (Routledge) on collaborations between contemporary poets and musicians.

Sophie Mayer is the author of *The Cinema of Sally Potter: A Politics of Love* (Wallflower, 2009), co-editor of *There She Goes: Feminist Filmmaking and Beyond*, author of two volumes of poetry, *Her Various Scalpels* (Shearsman Books, 2009) and *The Private Parts of Girls* (Salt Publishing, 2011), and a chapbook *Kiss Off* (Oystercatcher, 2011). Her academic writing on film and poetry has appeared in *Screen, SubStance, Studies in Canadian Literature*, and *Studies in American Indian Literature*. She is a regular contributor to *Sight & Sound, Eyewear, Hand + Star, Horizon Review*, and *Sound and Music*.

Leo Mellor is the Roma Gill Fellow at Murray Edwards College, University of Cambridge. He works on modernism, contemporary poetry, post-pastoral nature writing, and war literature. His book *Reading the Ruins: Modernism, Bombsites and British Culture* was published by Cambridge University Press in 2011. His own poetry includes *Things Settle* and *Marsh Fear/Fen Tiger*.

Rod Mengham is Reader in Modern English Literature at the University of Cambridge, where he is also Curator of Works of Art at Jesus College. He has written books on Charles Dickens, Emily Brontë, Thomas Hardy, and Henry Green, as well as *The Descent of Language* (Bloomsbury, 1993). He has edited collections of essays on contemporary fiction, violence and avant-garde art, and the fiction of the 1940s. He is also editor of the Equipage series of poetry pamphlets and co-editor and co-translator of *Altered State: the New Polish Poetry* (Arc Publications, 2003) and co-editor of *Vanishing Points: New Modernist Poems* (Salt Publishing, 2005). He has curated numerous exhibitions, most recently, Jake and Dinos Chapman, *In the Realm of the Senseless* (Rondo Sztuki, Katowice, 2011). His own poems have been published under the titles *Unsung: New and Selected Poems* (Folio/Salt, 1996; 2nd edn., 2001) and *Parleys and Skirmishes* with photographs by Marc Atkins (Ars Cameralis, 2007).

Peter Middleton is the author of *Distant Reading: Performance, Readership, and Consumption in Contemporary Poetry* (Alabama University Press), a book of poems, *Aftermath* (Salt), co-author with Tim Woods of *Literatures of Memory* (Manchester University Press), and is currently writing a book on science and poetry. He teaches at the University of Southampton.

Jeremy Noel-Tod is a Lecturer in Literature and Creative Writing at the University of East Anglia. His poetry criticism has been published widely over the last ten years, and includes essays on J. H. Prynne and W. H. Auden. He is the new editor of *The Oxford Companion to Modern Poetry* (formerly *The Oxford Companion to Twentieth Century Poetry*, ed. Ian Hamilton).

Heather O'Donoghue is Reader in Old Norse at the University of Oxford, and a Professorial Fellow of Linacre College. She has published on various aspects of Old Norse-Icelandic literature, including saga narratology and the afterlife of Old Norse myth. She is working at present on a history of the influence of Old Norse myth on poetry in English, from the medieval period to the present day.

Michael O'Neill is a Professor of English at Durham University. He has written widely on Romantic and post-Romantic poetry, and his books include *The All-Sustaining Air: Romantic Legacies in British, American, and Irish Poetry since 1900* (Oxford University Press, paperback 2012). With Michael D. Hurley, he is the author of *The Cambridge Introduction to Poetic Form* (2012). He is also the author of two collections of poetry, *The Stripped Bed* (Collins Harvill, 1990) and *Wheel* (Arc, 2008).

Piers Pennington is completing a doctoral thesis on modern poetry at Corpus Christi College, Oxford. He is editor of *Geoffrey Hill and His Contexts* (with Matthew Sperling), (Peter Lang, 2011).

Adam Piette is a Professor of Modern Literature at the University of Sheffield. He is the author of *Remembering and the Sound of Words: Mallarmé, Proust, Joyce, Beckett* (Clarendon Press, 1996) and *Imagination at War: British Fiction and Poetry 1939–1945* (Papermac, 1995). *The Literary Cold War: 1945 to Vietnam* appeared from Edinburgh University Press in 2009. He is co-editor with Alex Houen of the poetry journal *Blackbox Manifold*.

Natalie Pollard is a British Academy Research Fellow at the Department of English Literature at the University of Reading. She specializes in contemporary British poetry, and has published on Geoffrey Hill, W. S. Graham, and Don Paterson. Her book, *Speaking to You: Contemporary Poetry and Public Address,* published by Oxford University Press, focuses on how post-1960s poetry uses intimate speech to *you* to negotiate public tastes and expectations.

Richard Price is Head of Content and Research Strategy at the British Library. His books include *The Fabulous Matter of Fact: The Poetics of Neil M. Gunn* (Edinburgh University Press) and, with David Miller, *British Poetry Magazines 1914–2000* (British Library). He has written on Edward Thomas, Basil Bunting, Ford Madox Ford, Margaret Tait, and Roy Fisher, and curated the exhibitions *Ted Hughes: The Page is Printed* and *Migrant: The Possibility of Poetry* at the British Library. His poetry collections include *Lucky Day*, *Rays*, and *Small World* (Carcanet Press). His latest work of fiction is *The Island* (Two Ravens). He has edited little magazines over several decades, currently *Painted, spoken*.

John Redmond is a Senior Lecturer at the University of Liverpool. He is the author of two collections of poetry published by Carcanet, *Thumb's Width* (2001) and *MUDe* (2008). He has also written a Creative Writing textbook, *How to Write a Poem* (Blackwell, 2005) and has edited the *Selected Poems of James Liddy* (Arlen House, 2011). His critical book, *Poetry and Privacy: Questioning Public Interpretations of Contemporary British and Irish Poetry* is forthcoming from Seren in 2013.

Deryn Rees-Jones is Reader in English Literature at the University of Liverpool. A poet and a critic, she was named as one of the 20 Next Generation poets by the Poetry Book Society. Her most recent books include *Consorting with Angels: Modern Women Poets* (Bloodaxe Books, 2005), a new edition of Marie Stopes' novel *Love's Creation* (Sussex Academic, 2012), and *Burying the Wren* (Seren, 2012).

Peter Robinson, the editor of this *Handbook*, is Professor of English and American Literature at the University of Reading, an award-winning poet, translator from the Italian, and poetry editor for Two Rivers Press. His recent publications include *Poetry & Translation: The Art of the Impossible* (Liverpool University Press, 2010), *Poems by*

Antonia Pozzi (Oneworld Classics, 2011), and *The Returning Sky* (Shearsman Books, 2012), a Poetry Book Society Recommendation. He has also edited *An Unofficial Roy Fisher* (Shearsman Books, 2010), Bernard Spencer's *Complete Poetry, Translations & Selected Prose* (Bloodaxe Books, 2011), and the anthologies *Reading Poetry* (Two Rivers Press, 2011) and *A Mutual Friend: Poems for Charles Dickens* (Two Rivers Press, 2012). His poetry is the subject of *The Salt Companion to Peter Robinson*, ed. Adam Piette and Katy Price (2007).

Stephen Romer is a poet, editor, and translator. His most recent collection of poems, *Yellow Studio*, was shortlisted for the T. S. Eliot Prize 2008. He edited *20th Century French Poems* for Faber (2002) and *Into the Deep Street: 7 Modern French Poets* for Anvil (2009). His translation of Yves Bonnefoy's *The Arrière-pays* is published by Seagull (2012) and an anthology of *fin-de-siècle* stories, *Decadent French Tales*, by Oxford World's Classics (2013). He is Maître de Conférences at Tours University, and lives in the Loire Valley. He was made a Fellow of the Royal Society of Literature in 2011.

Zoë Skoulding lectures in the School of English at Bangor University, and has been Editor of the international quarterly *Poetry Wales* since 2008. Her most recent collection of poems is *Remains of a Future City* (Seren, 2008), longlisted for Wales Book of the Year 2009. She is a member of Parking Non-Stop, whose CD *Species Corridor*, combining experimental soundscape with poetry and song, was released by Klangbad in 2008.

Anna Smaill is a lecturer in Creative Writing at the University of Hertfordshire. She is the author of *The Violinist in Spring* (Victoria University Press, 2005) and has written widely on contemporary New Zealand literature, including articles on the novelist Janet Frame. Her poetry has been published in journals and anthologies in both the UK and NZ.

Matthew Sperling is a Leverhulme Early Career Fellow at the University of Reading, researching poetry publishing in Britain and Ireland since 1960. He is co-editor of *Geoffrey Hill and His Contexts* (Peter Lang, 2011), has published essays on contemporary poets including Roy Fisher and J. H. Prynne, and completed a monograph on Hill and philology. Before coming to Reading, he was Fellow by Special Election at Keble College, Oxford, from 2009 to 2012.

Michael Symmons Roberts was born in 1963 in Preston, Lancashire. His poetry has won the Whitbread Poetry Award, and been shortlisted for the Griffin International Poetry Prize, the Forward Prize, and twice for the T. S. Eliot Prize. He has received major awards from the Arts Council and the Society of Authors. His continuing collaboration with composer James MacMillan has led to two BBC Proms choral commissions, song cycles, music theatre works and operas for the Royal Opera House, Scottish Opera, Boston Lyric Opera, and Welsh National Opera. Their WNO commission, *The Sacrifice*, won the RPS Award for opera. He has also published two novels, and is Professor of Poetry at Manchester Metropolitan University.

Jeffrey Wainwright's *Selected Poems* (1985), *The Red-Headed Pupil* (1994), *Out of the Air* (1999), and *Clarity or Death!* (2008) are all published by Carcanet Press. His new book of poems, *The Reasoner*, appeared in autumn 2012. The second edition of his book on the purposes and styles of poetry, *Poetry: the Basics*, came out from Routledge in 2011. Manchester University Press published *Acceptable Words: Essays on the Poetry of Geoffrey Hill* in 2006. Until 2008 he was Professor of English at Manchester Metropolitan University. He lives in Manchester, and has a website at <www.jeffreywainwright.co.uk>.

David Wheatley is a Senior Lecturer at the University of Aberdeen. He is the author of four collections of poetry with Gallery Press and features in *The Penguin Book of Irish Poetry*. He has edited the *Poems of James Clarence Mangan* (Gallery Press, 2003) and Samuel Beckett's *Selected Poems 1930–1989* (Faber, 2009).

INTRODUCTION: THE LIMITS AND OPENNESS OF THE CONTEMPORARY

PETER ROBINSON

I

'There is one thing to be said for contemporary poetry that can't be said of any other', T. S. Eliot averred in a piece of film footage, 'and that is that it is written by our contemporaries.'[1] He prefaces this with a reminiscence of the argument in his 1919 essay 'Tradition and the Individual Talent', saying that it is 'no more use trying to be traditional than it is trying to be original'. And this must be true too of trying to be contemporary. 'Il faut être absolument moderne', Arthur Rimbaud wrote in 1873,[2] but, doubtless, it would be a mistake to *try* and be that too. Yet while it may be foolish to attempt to be traditional or original or modern or contemporary, finding that your work is, or can't help being, a combination of these things may produce puzzling states of affairs, not least because you can't, strictly speaking, have either willed it, or fully intended the exact combination of qualities that it manifests. The limits and openness of the contemporary mean that it is always also a terra incognita into which we can't but stray, and in which we are forever attempting to take our bearings or draw a map—metaphors for the activity of reading, interpreting, and understanding poetry that have been used before. *The Oxford Handbook of Contemporary British and Irish Poetry* is a collaborative effort at sketching a map of the always partially unknown.

---

[1] T. S. Eliot, a filmed remark on a BBC *Arena* profile shown on Thursday, 8 Oct. 2009.
[2] Arthur Rimbaud, *Une saison en enfer*, in *Œuvres complètes,* ed. Antoine Adam (Paris: Gallimard, 1972), 116.

Eliot's observation about contemporary poetry should not be mistaken for his damning of it with faint praise. After all, when he spoke, he was alive and a poet himself. Rather it is suggesting that if you are interested in past poetry, if you read Rimbaud or Eliot, for example, then really to understand them now you might also have to take a look at contemporary poetry, for, according to Eliot's own theory, the significance of past works is forever being altered by the addition of works in the present which retain value for those who read in the future. Poetry, and literature as a whole, is, in this sense, either a living process—or on the way to becoming an inert exhibit in a lost-world museum. So his one thing to be said in favour of contemporary poetry, that our contemporaries write it, may, implicitly, not be the only thing to be said for it. Contemporary poetry is essential to the continuing life of poetry and literature. Even the poetry of dead languages requires the existence of living languages to have its value and significance. But how does the poetic-looking writing being produced by people living now reach the category, by no means a neutral one, of 'contemporary poetry' and what, precisely, do the geographical and political adjectives in the title of this *Handbook* add to the aesthetic and cultural distinctions that it appears explicitly to make? When did what is currently considered the 'contemporary' begin? When does recent poetry stop being contemporary?

Though a majority of the poets whose work is referred to and discussed in the following chapters are alive as I write, they are joined by poets from the generations of the living who died, as we say, before their time, and, in living memory, by the parental and grandparental generations of those still living. For a person of my age (b. 1953), this will take us back to poets born in the 1880s, that's to say the generation of Marianne Moore and T. S. Eliot—though even this notion ought to be flexible enough to include those who had children later in life, allowing for the presence of poets born in the 1860s, such as Charlotte Mew and W. B. Yeats, and the 1870s, such as Wallace Stevens. And, at a stretch, a case might still be made for the contemporaneity of the long-living Thomas Hardy, born in 1840, a great-grandparental figure whose poetry was being published alongside that of the generation of my grandparents, and whose poetic significance emerged as something of a polemical issue during the 1960s and 1970s, decades in which the youngest poets whose work is discussed here were being born. These presences, and ones from further back in history too, may also be considered part of the contemporary, because the present is also shaped by poetry from the recent or more remote past freshly brought to bear as significant within it, and especially by present acts of revival that invite contemporaries to look again at the poetry of—among poets recently brought back into print—Kenneth Allott, Hope Mirrlees, Lynette Roberts, Bernard Spencer, A. S. J. Tessimond, and Sylvia Townsend Warner.

So to put some parenthetical dates into the chronology of this *Handbook*, it might be proposed that since the oldest living contemporary poets, those such as Mairi MacInnes (b. 1925), were born midway through the decade of the 1920s, and were thus beginning to publish visibly some thirty years later, the word 'contemporary' here refers to poetry published over the last approximately sixty years. However, those poets, some of them born when Hardy was still to publish his final collection, *Winter Words* (1928), lived and worked through years in which the generation of my grandparents were very much alive and present as formative influences. This is why the first part of the *Handbook*, one called 'Movements over Time', begins by exploring the continuing significance of poets publishing their major works in the 1920s and in subsequent decades until we enter the 'contemporary' proper, namely, the last some sixty years. This *Handbook* has, though, taken a number of years to bring from initial conception to publication, and the work it contains has been in the press for about twelve months. This suggests, as does the fugitive nature of the present moment, that the contemporary and its notional parentheses are in perpetual forward movement, and from this fact also arises further forms of limit and openness implied in the title to this introductory chapter. Everything published is instantly dated, on its copyright page if nowhere else, most of it shifting helplessly back into the forgotten or all but forgotten, and the challenge for those interested in contemporary poetry will not only involve keeping a weather eye on the new poetry being published, but also finding a continuing readership for work believed to be valuable but suddenly and unexpectedly considered passé, for the now out-of-fashion that still constitutes the immediately contemporary's most recent past.

The continuing addition of poetic works in the present which may retain value in the future does, of course, beg the great question for contemporary poetry and literature, and adds a further air of the terra incognita to the subject of this *Handbook*—namely that we cannot know for certain which works, however admired at present, will retain value in the future by continuing to be read and to influence what future poets may write. The vitality of contemporary poetry also depends upon the limit and openness of this uncertainty, for if we knew for sure which works will survive and which won't, then the work we knew it about would not, in exactly this sense, be contemporary any more. It is also sobering to bear in mind that poetry by our contemporaries the future will take to heart may be work which, though written now, remains as yet unpublished, or has appeared in print but is neglected or unnoticed. Unlike Handbook gatherings of chapters on earlier periods, the contemporary has only a sketchy and forming canon to revise or expand, it can't by its nature have a firmly established one. The individual poems and poets focused on by this volume's contributors were chosen by them to illustrate their concerns. Though being included in discussions here does mean something, it doesn't mean elevation to a canon of the contemporary—for, as I say, if it's contemporary it can't be canonical. Those undecided questions of value hovering over works by the living and recently dead are only still floating in the air above, for instance, Shakespeare's oeuvre in its apocryphal manifestations and as regards the debatable qualities it variously displays. This doesn't of course mean his works cannot be revalued, and they are thus not altogether removed from the whirligig of time. Rather, the conditions for revaluing, say, *Hamlet*, as T. S. Eliot attempted and significantly failed to do, are of a different order to those of contemporary poets in their lifetimes with at least one foot in oblivion and aspiring to obscurity.

II

Broadcast during 2009, the BBC *Arena* programme devoted to T. S. Eliot which included his remark about contemporary poetry, began with opening credits not accompanied by 'Macavity' from *Cats*, or the poet's solemn voice reading 'Let us go then, you and I, | When the evening is spread out against the sky'.[3] Rather, the titles rolled to the sound of a different voice, acoustic guitar, bass, and Spanish arpeggio accompaniment to the words: 'Ezra Pound and T. S. Eliot fighting in the captain's tower'. Bob Dylan (for it was he) doesn't merely name-drop these two high modernist poets into the penultimate verse of his long song 'Desolation Row' from *Highway 61 Revisited* (1965). Eliot settled in England in 1914, joined Faber & Gwyer in 1925, set up the company's poetry list, and eventually helped establish the Poetry Book Society, contributing thus to what is now optimistically and mistakenly called the 'mainstream', while Pound, who gave up on London literary life and went to Paris in 1920, became modernist father-figure for the Beats and Black Mountaineers, re-emerging in British poetry via their influence about the time Dylan's song was released and Eliot died with a wave of so-called 'alternative' or 'underground' neo-experimental poetry whose exponents are now among the scene's senior citizens. 'Which side are you on?' Dylan's song asks; but it puts that question into bleak perspective with the chorus, for what may be Eliot's own 'mermaids flow' where 'nobody has to think too much | about Desolation Row'. This not only made me think, just a few years after its release, about what 'nobody' might be overlooking, but also wonder how many possible things Eliot and Pound could have been fighting about, and how not to get caught between the pass and fell of mighty opposites.

The contemporary period, its parameters covering the last approximately sixty years, is one of enormous change in the varieties of spoken and written English, in the accents of authority and power, the vocabularies of technical and technological innovation, the terms for evaluation and appreciation—and poetry in these years has registered and responded, both critically and creatively, to these developments. The changing values associated with individualism and choice have been exploited and explored in the near-compulsory distinctiveness of poetic 'signature styles', the plurality and variety of what counts as a poem being never so unpredictable as now. The contemporary has witnessed various species of free and syllabic verse, alongside numerous revivals of poetry's formal and formalist resources. It has been a time too when transformations in sexual relations, the rebalancing of gender authority, the renegotiation of the public and private spheres, have created unprecedented opportunities for the subject matter, style, and vocabulary of poetry. It is a period in which the democratization of politics and international relations, and the decline of deference, has increased the ubiquity of protest and authorized commentary, one in which the physical environment, whether natural

---

[3] T. S. Eliot, 'The Love Song of J. Alfred Prufrock', in *Collected Poems 1909–1962* (London: Faber & Faber, 1963), 13.

or urban, has experienced dramatic changes of appearance and usage. I might thus further interpret Eliot's claim on our attention of contemporary poetry that not only is it written by those alive when we are, but also by those inevitably engaged with the concerns that press upon us, its immediate target readers. Whether we are fighting over similar things to Ezra Pound and T. S. Eliot in the captain's tower of a symbolic *Titanic*, or looking elsewhere to see other subjects considered more appropriate to the issues and conflicts of our day, the poetry wars have been fought out so urgently because they have involved in emblematically contested terms the intractable problems that our cultures and societies have had to face and endure. Similar claims might be made for other forms of literature and the arts more widely. The claim of poetry is that its intimacy with the language of individual utterance and singular subjectivity allows it to register, render, and respond to contemporary conditions with a distinctively nuanced, articulate immediacy of emotion and insight. Writing on modern British art, T. J. Clark has noted that 'Poetry, with its bizarre contest between Americans-in-London and cultivated lower-middle "provincial" bathos, took its own unpredictable path'.[4] Yet the unpredictability of its contested roads taken or not includes fighting between the influence of those Americans-in-London, and between exponents of what Clark calls 'provincial' bathos, while, as his adjectives imply, the poetry wars were felt to be fought over a territory of acutely conflicted cultural crisis. And they still are.

I was myself made more intimately aware of that fought-over divide between the 'mainstream' and the 'underground' a decade after Dylan's album was released when instructed in it, and its further balkanized intricacies, by a co-editor on the little magazine *Perfect Bound* (1976–9). Based in Cambridge and aligned with a fraction of the poetry scene that, however reluctantly, takes its name from the university town, it was identified as such in spite of attempts to loosen the confines of the identity definition by including work by various non- or less-received poets, including the then latest generation. One problem for me with the divisions of that moment in the poetry wars was I found myself unable to regulate appetites, instincts, and reading needs sufficiently to establish poems I could, but more often couldn't, write, clearly within identity criteria which appeared as complexly shifting and yet prone to fixing as are ethnic discriminations, class and gender markers, or national and political allegiances within the British Isles. Nor would attempts to belong have struck me as prudent or dignified, being yet another instance, like traditional, original, modern, or contemporary, of the things that it's no use *trying* to be.

Yet drifting and shifting within the debatable terrain of that division between a great many then current modes also served to help perceive what contributed to a poetic work's being unacceptable to one or other of those crudely defined factions. Attempts to articulate differences between these fractious groupings have seen the so-called 'mainstream' poetry focused on the achievement of end product, which it exhibits in the form of discrete poems, while the 'alternative' poetry is thought to privilege writing process

---

[4] T. J. Clark, 'False Moderacy', *London Review of Books*, 34/6 (22 Mar. 2012), 11.

and to exhibit the precipitates of such explorations.[5] Similarly interdependent contrasts are then made between 'closed' and 'open' form, 'regular' metres and 'free' verse, and the employment or eschewal of rhyme. Such characteristics can extend even to the use of initial capital letters in verse lines, or capital letters at all, of ampersands or the spelled-out 'and', and of completed or pointedly incomplete syntactic units. Some of these features, in the weakest cases worn as identity markers, have turned out to be ambiguous indicators, for the thus distinguished kinds frequently share characteristics, converging or diverging, in their particular colloquial or dialect speech-forms, their use of specialist vocabularies or technical jargons. Such selected characteristics are then associated (by the practitioners themselves and their first circles of reception) with political allegiance, such as the idea that paratactic syntax is believed to be egalitarian, while hypotaxis is by contrast thought to be hierarchical in its subordination of clauses. This series of binary contrasts organizing the identity criteria for the two supposed factions seemed then, and does now, inhibiting—especially for those starting out—of a verbal imagination. Such discriminations and attempted identifications are, as I have suggested, simultaneously the terms for deadly serious attempts at articulations of poetics and politicized aesthetics, particularly valuable if formulated in response to perceived changes in practice; but those group-formations and tribal warring also contribute to a discrediting and marginalizing of such efforts at self-definition and clarification.[6] Closer acquaintance with the poems attributed to any faction quickly reveal sub-factionalizing, and infighting, making for yet further inhibition and dismay—felt as a feedback effect from the expectations of imagined modernist or mainstream audiences, the availability and control of publication outlets, and other constraints upon the achievement of even minimal visibility.

Conflict in the area of poetry may derive, then, from a series of associations of ideas. Aesthetic judgements, such as the handling of enjambments or the fitting of phrases to rhythmic patterns, are associated with ethical values—respect for others, belief in forms of community, political loyalties and allegiances; then these associated compounds of aesthetics and ethics are appropriated or attributed to particular interest groups in society. Simultaneously, the associations may run the other way round: values espoused by particular interest groups in society are associated with a kind of poetry, and this kind is identified by particular aesthetic features of poems, preferably ones easy to recognize, even by inexperienced readers. Such processes of association can be promoted and maintained so long as the agents of the institutions function under near-monopoly

---

[5] For a case against poetry from metropolitan trade publishers, see 'Resting on Laurels', in *An Andrew Crozier Reader*, ed. Ian Brinton (Manchester: Carcanet Press, 2012), 247–59; for a case against poetry associated with experiment, see the introduction to Charles Simic and Don Paterson (eds.), *New British Poetry* (Saint Paul, Minn.: Graywolf Press, 2004).

[6] For anthologies that represent, all but exclusively, the supposed two poetries, see Sean O'Brien, *The Firebox: Poetry in Britain and Ireland after 1945* (London: Picador, 1998), and Richard Caddel and Peter Quartermain (eds.), *Other: British and Irish Poetry since 1970* (Hanover, NH: Wesleyan University Press, 1999).

conditions, a small number of poetry magazines and literary journals, a limited number of poetry lists, just a few well-endowed prizes, and a tiny number of celebrity poets.

But what is the cultural consequence of definition by contrasts being taken for a fixing of differences in kind? The critical assertion of a distinction between two poems, or types of poem, the assertion that one is different from the other in such-and-such ways, can be construed as a claim that they have nothing in common, that there is a fracture or break between these distinct ways of proceeding in writing, or it can be perceived as a mutual definition that binds the two works together in their difference. Just as contrast may be a higher form of comparison, so poems and poets may be linked by the distinctions between them. If you describe yourself as 'a mainstream poet', and some have, the adjective suggests, whatever it is taken to mean, that there are other kinds of poet it is possible to be, and that if you do not have any sense of this stated or unstated contrastingly adjectival condition, then you have little chance of identifying what 'mainstream-ness' could be. The same can be said about 'alternative' poetries, which have to be alternatives to something, or of 'underground' poetry, where there has to be a contrastive overground, and this is likely to be the case for any and every 'ourselves alone' definitional gambit.

Furthermore, by substituting superficial indicators (however cunningly theorized) of inclusion or exclusion from supposedly autonomous bodies for the far more difficult and patience-requiring task of pondering over time which verbal artefacts continue to sustain and reward attention with value attributed to them, and which ones perhaps don't, means failing at the same time to ask what it is about these artworks which fascinates or fails to do so. The substitution of superficial indicators of allegiance or belonging for reading of this order indicates that it is not only the creative imagination that is being hampered, but the critical imagination too. The combined undermining of these human capacities from within is an unhappier aspect of the contemporary poetry field as experienced over the last four decades and more. One purpose of this *Oxford Handbook of Contemporary British and Irish Poetry* is to sketch a space for curiosity and mutually enhancing accuracy of distinction that may help to mitigate the widespread self-confusion by means of other-denigration witnessed on all sides.

III

The resulting factionalized state of affairs has tended to be interpreted from too close up, and, as it were, on a darkling plain by night. Mimicking embedded structures at work in the culture at large, it has played itself out as the seeming endgame of a centre and periphery model founded upon the growth of the nation state whose greatest triumph was the centralization of power in a capital city and the reduction of the rest of the country, or, in the case of the United Kingdom, countries, to the status of provinces. It is noticeable, for instance, in Great Britain and Northern Ireland, that while the intellectual support for experimental, vanguard writing has tended to focus itself in or nearer the capital, and advocacy for traditional poetic models has outposts in a number of provincial centres, nevertheless, the commercial publishers and the reviewing organs of the book trade, drawing a form of authenticity from those provinces, tend to ignore, if not openly to denigrate, the self-consciously innovative and unorthodox in their midst. The centralization of preferring power in the capital extended to the control of the print culture too, and it is for this reason that at the beginning of the twentieth century it was felt to be incumbent upon Ezra Pound and then T. S. Eliot to establish themselves at the global centre of anglophone publishing might; and it remains the case today that, to an unusually large extent, and despite various countervailing tendencies, the creation of reputation is achieved by the publishers, editors, journalists, prize judges, grant awarders, and such like figures in London, and, to a much lesser extent, Oxbridge, where many of those figures will have been educated.

Yet the period covered by this *Handbook* has also seen dramatic reductions in this achieved centralization of publishing, the power to use economic capital to constitute and distribute what is now called, in acknowledgement of its monetary infiltration, cultural capital. The primary reason for this has been the inability, broadly speaking, of commercial metropolitan publishers to sustain a viable book-trade market for their poetry products. There have been fluctuations in this state of affairs, and exceptions to the rule, such as the success of John Betjeman's *Collected Poems*, or the sales figures achieved by Faber & Faber for Seamus Heaney's collections of poetry; but, by and large, the numbers achieved for the sales of most poetry books do not make them, in the commercial terms required by trade publishers, viable as marketable units. In the pre-1970s world of autonomous publishing houses, such as Jonathan Cape, Secker & Warburg, or André Deutsch, it was possible for relatively benign and culturally sensitive gentlemen publishers, as they had been called, to subsidize their poetry lists from more directly and successfully commercial publishing, on the grounds, as it might have been, that the cultural kudos of having a poetry list could be offset against weaknesses on the balance sheet. Cultural capital could then, to a certain extent, trump actual money. The rise in production costs that occurred during the 1970s, encouraging a number of publishers to abandon poetry, the multiple takeover and combining of these old independent houses, and the dominance of accountancy concerns in an ever more global trading environment, led to the decimation of trade publishers' poetry lists. When, for example, Random House, itself absorbed by Bertelsmann in 1998, bought both Secker and Cape it made commercial sense to combine their lists under the Cape imprint, keeping on a few poets from both lists and dropping others. In the United States such a process, which might be called the aggravated de-commercialization of poetry, has been mitigated by support to poetic culture provided by well-founded university presses—California, Chicago, Pittsburgh, Princeton, and Wesleyan, for instance, which all have poetry lists. The solitary UK instance, Oxford University Press, was itself discontinued for what were said to be commercial reasons in the late 1990s.

The presses that evidently benefited from London's relative and Oxford's near complete abandonment of the field were the specialist small imprints set up in the 1970s, two of which, Bloodaxe Books and Carcanet Press, now have the largest poetry lists of any UK publisher. While a few of the let-go poets with an edge of cultural capital to sell were taken on by surviving trade publishers in London, the specialist firms, their books being subsidized by Arts Council grants and, sometimes, benefactor owners, came to the rescue of many others; and though a couple of these surviving smaller presses, Anvil and Enitharmon, are located in the capital, the vast majority of the new specialist presses were not, saving on costs by being housed in much cheaper office space or private dwellings in the provinces. They were able to rival and indeed quickly surpass the metropolitan trade publishers in the range and artistic commitment of their lists; but they were not able wholly to solve the initial problem of how to make units of poetry sell in large enough numbers to be commercially viable. It was also an uphill struggle for them to achieve for their lists the kinds of cultural capital that the metropolitan publishers, Faber & Faber supreme among them, had achieved, and retained at the level of book trade market penetration and media attention, if not ubiquitously in the minds of poetry readers. The specialist presses have remained dependent on Arts Council grants for their continuance, and their vulnerability to changing economic climates is illustrated in the wake of the 2008 credit crunch and its consequences for government funding of the arts as I write.

That free market capitalism post-1980s style has not thoroughly de-commercialized poetry and driven it into complete invisibility may be a result of two technological and three cultural developments, both of them running in parallel to the way in which developments in global capitalist business models have tended to suck power away from independent companies in metropolitan centres. The two technological developments are the Internet and print-on-demand, while the cultural developments are the growth of public poetry readings, of poetry competitions, and the rise of creative writing as a subject taught in school and university. Poetry readings developed alongside the popular cultural events of the 1960s, and, though experiencing vicissitudes, are surviving resolutely a half-century later. Poetry competitions emerged in the 1980s alongside the free-market commercial models, and Roy Fisher's satire 'A Modern Story', subtitled 'A prophesy (1981)', saw what was happening almost before it did.[7] Superficially like an updated form of the discredited vanity publishing of poetry, they thrive on the willingness of aspirant poets to pay entry fees—helping to fund, in lottery fashion, the arts organ or organization that hosts them, paying a judging fee to poets with some kudos to advertise, and contributing prize money to the few. Yet, despite all that might be said against this feeding on gullibility and attention-seeking, the multiplying popularity of such competitions and the ways in which emerging poets have used them to advertise their own growing capital has underlined the capacity of this near-costless, not to say priceless, art form to seed itself across the ground and burst into flower.

Alongside such widespread activity and its visibility, echoed in the annual poetry book prizes that began to proliferate in the 1990s, are the creative writing courses that have multiplied first outside and now almost ubiquitously within UK universities. Curiously enough, the two genres of creative writing best suited to this workshop and

---

[7] Roy Fisher, *The Long and the Short of It: Poems 1955–2005* (Tarset: Bloodaxe Books, 2005), 144–5.

teacher-led format are lyric poetry and the short story, two of the forms most difficult to convert into commercially viable units for a mass market. Once again, whatever may be said against the idea that writing poetry or short fiction is teachable, it appears to be a fact of the large capitalist democracies (in anglophone countries at least) that a distinct proportion of their populations are inspired to seek identity and expression in such imaginative composition. While creative writing courses, both inside and outside institutions of education, are expensively fee-paying, indicating the commitment of participants to this form of life, there are also innumerable workshops, poetry cafes, slams, reading groups, and other social points of contact which involve much smaller or no outlay and have their constituencies in cities, towns, and villages throughout the United Kingdom's three-and-a-third countries, and Eire's one. The contemporary situation resembles some of the diagnostic and prognostic utterances in Guy Debord's 'Situationist Manifesto' (1960) where he sees artists 'separated from society' and 'separated from each other by competition', while foreseeing that 'everyone will become an artist' and that this development will 'help the rapid dissolution of the linear criteria of novelty'.[8] Contemporary poetry has shown itself to be so simultaneously vulnerable and resilient within the consumerist spectacle, caught, as it is, in a prize and competition scene that, in principle, presupposes the ability of all to write and create, that it may thus model in acute form the contradictions through which we are now obliged to live.

The two technological developments I mentioned earlier have also contributed to movements away from the dictation of taste, the compounding of cultural capital, in metropolitan centres. The Internet has proved itself so ideally compatible with bookselling that it's difficult to recall the rarity-value of, for instance, the cloth-bound and at that time only edition of Frank O'Hara's *Collected Poems* (New York: Knopf, 1971) in mid-1970s Britain. Nowadays, practically any poetry book you can imagine yourself wanting to buy is one click away. This fact, with the development of print-on-demand technologies, by which a single copy of a collection can be produced and dispatched to its purchaser from the same point in space at a remarkably small unit cost, has meant that niche publishing by dedicated people with some page-making design software on their portable computers is more than viable. If they are also well linked into the Internet's innumerable bookselling outlets, including their own websites, they can achieve global reach for the sale of a particular poet's books to his or her following with a very low risk margin. Though retaining a large share of cultural capital and access to actual money, trade presses with metropolitan ground rents and company overheads have not been able to monopolize and cartel these small-scale publishing activities out of existence.

The institutions for the publication, reception, and promotion of poetry were, historically, formed by editors of little magazines, quarterlies, well-founded literary journals, anthologies, publishers' editors, book reviewers, academics, senior poets, and other arbiters of taste. The story of Seamus Heaney's emergence from provincial academic, a

---

[8] Alex Danchev (ed.), *100 Artists' Manifestos* (London: Penguin Books, 2011), 350.

member of Philip Hobsbaum's Belfast outpost of The Group, in 1963, to Faber & Faber author with the publication of *Death of a Naturalist* in 1966 is an almost textbook illustration of the workings of the metropolitan institutions of poetic art in their heyday.[9] But is he any good? Though this may seem an impertinent question, it is worth asking whether the various players who belong to or operate the institutions have good reasons—good art reasons, that is—for their decisions. The relevance of this question, and the consequences of its answer, run as follows: if the answer is 'no', then the only explanation for why Heaney received his Nobel Prize is because powerful people, including economically powerful people, of course, made decisions in favour of his work throughout his career, and the one reason why we need, cravenly, to believe them and read him is because their power is able to make such decisions have consequences within the institutions of publishing, literary journalism, and other forms of media promotion in the societies to which we can't help but belong.

If, on the other hand, the answer is 'yes', they do have reasons, which means reasons that others such as ourselves can understand and appreciate (even if we don't agree that they are decisive for us), then the institutions drop out of the picture. They don't drop out in so far as they are the means by which the reasons are made manifest in social life, but they do drop out in that they are not, in themselves, the significant and decisive factor in the accumulation of cultural capital. The circumstances of premature or belated canonization are also part of a poem's history in the world, and they stick to the work, inflecting its meaning, but its longer-term survival will require argued-for evaluations that carry conviction. The necessary condition is that informed readers of poetry can appreciate, even if they don't happen to find finally convincing, the reasons given for the evaluation of a particular poem. This latter being the case, it would be as unreal to assert that Heaney's poetry isn't any good as to say that his work is unquestionably the best—because sufficient critical evidence supports the former being untrue, while that same evidence has meaning because located in evaluative contexts that are necessarily relational, plural, open to revision, and, his work being contemporary, not yet so decisively settled.

Poetry, like music, is an art form and a way of life that manifests itself in a great many ways—and to exclude the most marginal and amateur of performers from the art form is neither possible nor healthy. Just as the poorest street singer and Jessye Norman are both performing music, so the simplest and least appreciated piece of lyrical writing that has individually decided returns for its right margins may, just like, for instance, Tomas Tranströmer, the 2011 Nobel Laureate's works, be allowed the name of poetry. Given the technological and cultural developments, and, in addition, the new social networks, the recently still active near-monopoly conditions for the establishment and promotion of cultural capital among poets have not disappeared, but can appear marginal to the daily activities of those who keep the art alive. Those attempted monopolies of power have, nevertheless, been weakened both because of that de-commercialization

---

[9] See Dennis O'Driscoll, *Stepping Stones: Interviews with Seamus Heaney* (London: Faber & Faber, 2008), 73–87.

of poetry and because the people who like it, want to read, write it, and write about it, are, for better or worse, now able to do it at nearly no cost. And they can, occasionally, achieve the reception that characterized Philip Larkin's unpredicted breakthrough with the Marvell Press's edition of *The Less Deceived* (1955) when, though beginning to receive attention through the coincident publicity activities associated with the rise of the Movement, his early fiction publisher had not initially been interested in publishing the same writer's verse.

This sketched description of the recent past and the current situation in poetry could be considered an account of why the contemporary remains a cloudy and unknowing temporal space. In that realm it is not then possible to say definitively what is the best poetry of this period, the current contemporary situation being one in which there isn't a single cultural taste shaping what the poetry of this moment is like. There are, rather, a number of different sets of associated values and ideas about what poetry is and may be, and there are many individuals, small groups, and sections of the reading public who have invested time and money and attributed value to the different kinds of poetry currently being produced, much of it almost entirely under the radar of literary journalism and the media. A poet's asking in the late 1990s who's in charge here suggests that the de-commercialization of the art could create disorientation in those who hoped to pass definitively through the portals of institutions which may have appeared more intact then than now. Yet if the answer is that no one person or group of people is in charge, then the deregulation associated with such a situation has to distinguish within itself between what might be the processes of community self-management, and the law of an economic jungle in action.[10] However, though the current situation may seem an improvement in the natural democracy of art by which the good comes to the fore because it is argued for by those interested, who, through the curiosity and appetite driven by such interest, are best placed to know, I turn now to how such a plural community of writing may be viewed and interpreted.

IV

The then Poet Laureate Andrew Motion offered an indicative summary of such a new pluralism in his Foreword to Peter Barry's *Poetry Wars: British Poetry of the 1970s and the Battle of Earls Court* (2006) when noting 'the comparatively well-tempered acceptance that we live in a culture of poetries, not in one dominated by an Establishment'.[11] Motion's use of 'poetries' here, the plural form of an uncountable abstraction, whose use is by no means restricted to concession-granting established figures, looks like a

---

[10] See Sean O'Brien, 'Introduction: Who's in Charge Here?', in *The Deregulated Muse: Essays on Contemporary British & Irish Poetry* (Newcastle upon Tyne: Bloodaxe Books, 1998), 13–20.

[11] Andrew Motion, Foreword to Peter Barry's *Poetry Wars: British Poetry of the 1970s and the Battle of Earls Court* (Cambridge: Salt Publishing, 2006), p. xii.

bet-hedging device flinching before the possibility that all these various phenomena are still and nevertheless parts of a singular 'poetry'. John Lucas's polemic in a recent article[12] argues that faced with such balkanizing of the art and the multiplication of the constituencies whose interests are expressed in making value claims, we have instead a form of non-benign tolerance in which all are free to ignore the existence of those parts of the field that don't happen to interest them. In this version of contemporary poetry, rather than vociferously opposing the work of what has been characterized as radical obscurity, or, for that matter, the poetry of what some describe as reader-cultivating anecdote, we have opted for a form of Internet-era market-multiculturalism in which anyone can buy into anything they want, while free to be indifferently uncurious about the values and activities and ways of life around us which do not happen to tickle our consumerist fancies. Such a state of affairs is less dissimilar to the 'poetry wars' of previous decades than might first appear, for the attitudes of prejudice and incuriosity remain entrenched. As the two 'sides' have multiplied into a multi-directional civil strife, the exhausted combatants of earlier and later skirmishes have withdrawn to lick their wounds—some of us, doubtless, continuing to publish through the new outlets, while unexpectedly finding it possible to occupy positions as teachers in an academy which lately discovered it could benefit from encouraging verbal creativity.

The planning and design of this *Handbook* have been undertaken with the desire to dispel both the divide-and-rule poverty of the two-poetries moment as equally the ignorantly non-benign tolerance of highly fragmented and indifferent fractions. In place of the embattled ultra-ism to be encountered in some quarters, and the fragmentation of interest groups and other clans to be noted everywhere, this volume proposes an anthropological approach to contemporary poetry motivated by an unprejudiced—or as unprejudiced as possible—curiosity. In any area of human activity definition is relational, and one thing that was evidently wrong with the two-poetries divide was that it required mutually reductive definitions of the opposing party. Yet, as I have suggested, one problem with such denigrating definition of others is that it inflicts a reciprocally falsified back-formed definition on those doing the denigrating. Running down those you see as opposing you is not a route to self-knowledge. The anthropologically unprejudiced curiosity advocated in this *Handbook* is offered as a means for improving self-knowledge in readers and writers of poetry by better understanding the other poetry and poetic activity that is going on all around. By this means it may be possible to discern the outlines of a poetic culture through the ruins of a market.

W. H. Auden made a telling point about how 'Time that is intolerant | Of the brave and innocent' nevertheless 'Worships language and forgives | Everyone by whom it lives.'[13] It may then seem that while living contemporary poets are, however bravely and innocently, engaged in career formation, composing oeuvres by issuing pamphlets and collections, praising and criticizing, accepting and rejecting, neglecting and awarding, and all the other

---

[12] See John Lucas, 'The Anthology Business', *The Dark Horse*, 25 (Summer–Autumn 2010), 22.
[13] W. H. Auden, 'In Memory of W. B. Yeats', in *The English Auden: Poems, Essays, & Dramatic Writings, 1927–1939*, ed. Edward Mendelson (London: Faber & Faber, 1977), 242.

activities that go along with writing poems in the current state of human culture, they are also, haplessly even, contributing to the continuing life of literature and poetry, and maintaining the life of the language. Poetry contributes to keeping alive and extending for current circumstances the capacity of readers and people at large to articulate and express what they may understandably call their own ideas and feelings. The question to ask of poets and their works may then be and should perhaps continue to be, as W. S. Graham put it in one of his poems: 'What is the language using us for?'[14] Active contributions to the social processes of language use in poetry are thus, as I have been arguing and Graham's question underlines, simultaneously within and beyond the control of individual wills.

V

As already noted, this *Handbook*'s first part, 'Movements over Time', presents an overview and articulates changes in the current processes and developments of poetry during the approximately sixty-year period I have outlined. The model here is the one readers coming to this series of chapters will likely be most familiar with, a linear history of one thing after another. The contributors to this part touch on the processes by which these senses of movement and periodic change are instigated, the extent to which they may or may not be factitious, and the possibility that the decades covered by the *Handbook* have seen the emergence of a multi-linear, or even a non-linear, or a perhaps cross-sectional model for a poetic culture. This part of the book also sets out to see reputations emerging from social groupings and from such affinities and antipathies as have been already considered. Thus the part serves as an introduction to this field, and as a setting for the variety of approaches and issues that follow.

In Part Two, 'Senses of Form and Technique', some crucial features of poetry as formed language are explored. It thus considers the relationship between individual decisions in the marked forming of poems and the contribution that those creative acts make to the reading of significance in their thematic materials. The part serves thus to underline the interactive formation of writing and reading techniques. Further chapters explore relations between this art form and others such as song, painting, and film. The time frame of the *Handbook* is one in which experiments that were instituted during the modernist period in the first part of the twentieth century were resisted, revived, evolved, and have exfoliated into an unprecedented range of verbal objects that can lay claim to the name of 'poem'. The part casts light on developments in some of these phenomena, and helps to account for a multiplicity ranging from CDs of sound recordings for text-less performances through to print-only verbal objects and artists' books featuring texts produced by poets.

---

[14] W. S. Graham, *New Collected Poems*, ed. Matthew Francis (London: Faber & Faber, 2004), 199.

Part Three, 'Poetry in Places', addresses the *Handbook*'s subject from its currently evolving geographical and geopolitical perspectives, ones that naturally imply and include the ecological and environmental. It considers changes that have occurred in the poetry connected to this archipelago's various national movements and the simultaneous commitments and resistances to such movements in poets aligned with or marginal to those political ambitions. It addresses, overtly and implicitly, the conflict between the provinces and the capital, the emergence of poems and poetry associated with particular cities, and the continuing commitment to the natural environment, both as source for metaphor and as political pressure point. Contributors address these various means for locating poets in territories, and thus of associating them with social and political issues, in ways that include acknowledgement of different languages and dialects, there being more languages spoken in Britain and Ireland than English—though by its nature this anglophone volume can do little more than acknowledge them by, for instance, the study of indigenous poetic translation. Contributors also question the extent to which such forms of geographical and political location can support essentialist credentials, and thus take into account the kinds of transits and transitions that mark a group of cultures which has been ever more subject to the practical possibilities of travel, resettlement, and hybrid evolution.

The purpose of Part Four, 'Border Crossings', is to sketch locations and transits for contemporary British and Irish poetry in the larger context of world poetry. There have been conferences and publications on the fraught question of a special relationship with poetry from the United States, and this topic may also be understood in terms of the Cold War stand-off between the poetry of the West and an interest in that of Russia's Silver Age. The existence of less prominent relationships between poets during this period and other poetries in European languages are explored, as is the under-considered issue of relations between poetry from these islands and the anglophone poetries from the independent countries that formed the Commonwealth during the early years of the *Handbook*'s time frame. This is one of the places where questions of ethnic identity and post-colonialism make their significance most directly felt. Beside these relations are those that poetry in English has with writings from other continents and, beyond the anglophone, the challenges presented by poetry in translation.

A fifth and final part, 'Responsibilities and Values', explores the complex connections that have been articulated between poetry and some of the pressing concerns during these decades. This part includes relations between poetry and philosophical ethics, poetry and political commitments, as well as the quasi-religious roles that poetry has been called upon to perform. These forms of social and cultural commitment are considered in the context of counter-arguments offered to that most memorable formulation ('poetry makes nothing happen'[15]) made by Auden not many years before the beginning of the decades covered by this *Handbook*. Supporting his view of the matter,

---

[15] Auden, 'In Memory of W. B. Yeats', 242.

with different inflections, there have also been returns to the claim that poetry will best serve culture and society if wedded to an uncommitted aesthetic autonomy—this being, of course, another idea of poetry's responsibility. The volume concludes with an attempt to explore further how the openness and limits of the contemporary and its poetry may be shaped and facilitated by the unpredictable processes of evaluation involved in the composition, reading, and reception of a poem.

The writing and reading of poetry now involves a complex of activities undertaken, usually for very small or no monetary reward, by people devoted to it. That you have read as far as the final paragraph in this introductory chapter may mean that you already are, or are in the process of becoming, one of them. I have here offered a guide to what you can expect from the following chapters in the volume, and have sketched a way of holding their various contents in relations with each other, even on those occasions when the book's contributors tacitly or explicitly offer these contents as distinctly different kinds of poetry. I have thus invited you not only to take an interest in the poetry and poets that you are drawn to from across this field, but also to appreciate how that work and its writers are involved in larger networks of activity by patterns of tacitly comparative definition through drawn distinctions and staged contrasts.

But I would like to conclude by offering an idea of what all these poets and their poetry might have in common, and what young poets coming to this art might attempt to achieve, in association with their older contemporaries, and before them, with the entire tradition to which the present is attached. *The Oxford Handbook of Contemporary British and Irish Poetry* explores throughout its length how, granted their 'essential technical complexity and inescapable self-consciousness', the various poems discussed may 'address, express and restructure real emotions in ways that neither evade them with formalism nor degrade them into kitsch'.[16]

Select Bibliography

Auden, W. H., *The English Auden: Poems, Essays, & Dramatic Writings, 1927–1939*, ed. Edward Mendelson (London: Faber & Faber, 1977).
Caddel, Richard and Quartermain, Peter (eds.), *Other: British and Irish Poetry since 1970* (Hanover, NH: Wesleyan University Press, 1999).
Clark, T. J., 'False Moderacy', *London Review of Books,* 34/6 (22 Mar. 2012), 11.
Danchev, Alex (ed.), *100 Artists' Manifestos* (London: Penguin Books, 2011).
Eliot, T. S., *Collected Poems 1909–1962* (London: Faber & Faber, 1963).
Fisher, Roy, *The Long and the Short of It: Poems 1955–2005* (Tarset: Bloodaxe Books, 2005).

---

[16] Bernard Williams, *On Opera* (New Haven and London: Yale University Press, 2006), 120.

Graham, W. S., *New Collected Poems,* ed. Matthew Francis (London: Faber & Faber, 2004).

Lucas, John, 'The Anthology Business', *The Dark Horse,* 25 (Summer–Autumn 2010), 22.

Motion, Andrew, Foreword to Peter Barry's *Poetry Wars: British Poetry of the 1970s and the Battle of Earls Court* (Cambridge: Salt Publishing, 2006).

O'Brien, Sean, 'Introduction: Who's in Charge Here?', in *The Deregulated Muse: Essays on Contemporary British & Irish Poetry* (Newcastle upon Tyne: Bloodaxe Books, 1998), 13–20.

O'Brien, Sean, *The Firebox: Poetry in Britain and Ireland after 1945* (London: Picador, 1998).

O'Driscoll, Dennis, *Stepping Stones: Interviews with Seamus Heaney* (London: Faber & Faber, 2008).

Rimbaud, Arthur, *Une saison en enfer,* in *Œuvres complètes,* ed. Antoine Adam (Paris: Gallimard, 1972).

Williams, Bernard, *On Opera* (New Haven and London: Yale University Press, 2006).

PART I
MOVEMENTS OVER TIME

CHAPTER 1

MODERNIST SURVIVORS

EDWARD LARRISSY

The years after the Second World War ('the Emergency', in Ireland) did not provide fertile ground for British or Irish poets who wished to continue or develop the innovations of modernism, at least the formal ones. Yet there were those who persisted with that impetus, and their works, often in the manner of a distinctive regional or national modernism, are the subject of this chapter. In fact, though relegated to an inferior position in the discussion of poetry in that period, it was, as Charles Tomlinson pointed out in the third edition of *The Pelican Guide to English Literature*, 'precisely in the fifties that David Jones, Hugh MacDiarmid, Austin Clarke and Basil Bunting were beginning a re-emergence'.[1] The present essay will exclude Clarke, on the grounds that his impressive adaptation of Irish poetic metres is not truly modernist, despite his frankness and lack of sentimentality. On the other hand, MacDiarmid is included on the grounds that, by the fifties, he was working in an undeniably modernist mode. Nor were echoes of an heroic past wanting: Pound's *Cantos* kept emerging, and one should not underestimate also the abiding influence of his translation, *The Classic Anthology Defined by Confucius*, published in Britain in 1955.[2]

In Britain, the dominant mode of forties poetry is usually identified as 'neo-Romantic'. And with all deference to the fact that Dylan Thomas is profoundly indebted to Eliot— and to Eliot's promotion of the virtues of Donne—this does seem an appropriate term for poets such as Thomas himself, or George Barker, or Kathleen Raine. Even the decadent classicism of Lawrence Durrell reveals its late Romantic affiliations in its erotic languor. As for Thomas himself, indebtedness to Eliot and a taste for myth are not enough to affirm a modernist identity for his recurring cycles of birth, flourishing, decline, death,

---

[1] Charles Tomlinson, 'Poetry Today', in Boris Ford (ed.), *The Pelican Guide to English Literature*, vii. *The Modern Age* (3rd edn., Harmondsworth: Penguin Books, 1973), 471–89 (472).

[2] Ezra Pound, *The Classic Anthology Defined by Confucius* (London: Faber & Faber, 1955). First published in America the previous year by Harvard University Press.

and renewal, which have obvious sources in aspects of Blake and Wordsworth. The most coherent account of Thomas's surrealism would also link it to these Romantic ideas.

As one moves into the fifties, the Movement reaction against neo-Romanticism is anything but friendly towards a revival of modernism. Larkin told Ian Hamilton in 1964 that the poetry he had been influenced by was not 'Eliot or Pound or anybody who is normally regarded as "modern"—which is a sort of technique word, isn't it?' The poetry he prized was by 'people to whom technique seems to matter less than content, people who accept the forms they have inherited but use them to express their own content'.[3] It was this kind of view, expressed in various ways by Robert Conquest and the contributors to the *New Lines* anthology (1956) that had already been castigated by Charles Tomlinson in his review of the book for *Essays in Criticism*. His critique is summed up in his title: 'The Middlebrow Muse'.[4]

I

Despite these unfriendly currents, the post-war period had begun with the completion of a major poem by one of the pioneers of modernist poetry, H.D., who had been part of the Imagist grouping in London before the First World War. Her three-volume poem, *Trilogy*, was rounded off in 1946 with the publication of its final section, *The Flowering of the Rod*.[5] She had spent the years of the Second Word War in London, a fact that provides the basis for substantial parts of the thought and imagery of the poem. All three sections were published by Oxford University Press, then regarded as a significant publisher of new British poetry. If recourse to the myth-kitty was sufficient to make one a modernist, the forties would be full of modernists. But about *Trilogy* there can be little doubt: it is an ambitious extension of the modernist aim to reinterpret ancient myths and traditions through the medium of an innovative poetic technique. The poem seeks to demonstrate that the modern age of mechanized warfare, inspired by habits of thought that run counter to poetic imagination, cannot prevail, and that the poetic imagination itself has the resources to reinvigorate civilization on a new and creative basis. This message is particularly clear in the first volume, *The Walls Do Not Fall* (1944), the title of which is a figurative comment on the Blitz. In a characteristically modernist move, renewal gathers insight and strength from an ancient past whose lineaments are not clearly discernible except to the initiate, the one who has faith in the poetic imagination. For the ancient truths are the truths of spiritual death and resurrection understood by ancient Egypt,

---

[3] Ian Hamilton, 'Four Conversations: Thom Gunn, Philip Larkin, Christopher Middleton and Charles Tomlinson', *London Magazine*, 4/6 [=4/8] (4 Nov. 1964), 64–85 (71).

[4] Charles Tomlinson, 'The Middlebrow Muse', *Essays in Criticism*, 7 (Apr. 1957), 208–17.

[5] H.D. [Hilda Doolittle], *Trilogy: The Walls Do Not Fall; Tribute to the Angels; The Flowering of the Rod* (Manchester: Carcanet, 1973). References will be given in the main text as *T* followed by page number. The three parts of *Trilogy* were not brought together between the covers of one book until this edition appeared in 1973.

and, indeed, by subsequent generations: poetic and sacred traditions are a 'palimpsest' of stories written over each other in layers and encoding the same message. We may read that message with fresh insight at the stage where a civilization is about to be renewed on the ashes of its former structures: for 'the ancient rubrics reveal that we are back at the beginning' (*T* 14). Thus, although there is 'ruin everywhere', nevertheless, 'through our desolation | thoughts stir, inspiration stalks us [...] || unaware, Spirit announces the Presence' (*T* 3). The Egyptian gods Osiris and, most of all, Thoth (Hermes in Greek), are associated with 'the palette, the pen, the quill' (*T* 16), and there is a notable thematic concentration on the craft of writing: this connects at the stylistic level to a certain tough musicality which is highly reminiscent of Pound, a fact that is, presumably, no accident:

bone, stone, marble
hewn from within by that craftsman,

[...]

is master-mason planning
the stone marvel (*T* 8)

This passage is characteristic in the way that it links its concepts by means of a network of alliteration, assonance and internal rhyme: 'marble', 'marvel', 'master-mason'. Rachel Blau du Plessis characterizes the whole range of effects in her work, linking them to H.D.'s undoubted interest in psychoanalysis: 'anagram-based phonemic play and metonymic chains, revealing why Freud's tactics of free association became important in her work'.[6] At the thematic level, the craftsman idea associated with the mason (another touch of Pound) is nevertheless also identified with the production of organic form, for the marble of the sculptor is equated with the naturally developing hardness of the seashell: a kind of having it both ways (organicism plus controlling craft) which is also quite common in modernist aesthetics, not least in those of Pound. For all the latter's invoking of the idea of poet as sculptor, he remains wedded to the revelation of 'the thing', whether objective or subjective, as required by the Imagist aesthetic: this idea is subject to complication in his work, but not abandoned.

While Egyptian mythology is given pride of place in *The Walls Do Not Fall*, other belief-systems are brought in aid of the idea of spiritual rebirth, most of all the Judaeo-Christian. Angels become symbols of the visitation of creativity in *Tribute to the Angels* (1945). In *The Flowering of the Rod* (1946), Kaspar, the wise man who brings myrrh to the baby Jesus, represents patriarchal presumption, a symbolism deriving from his gift, which is associated with death and embalming. Yet, in an apt enactment of the kind of resurrection H. D. has in mind, Mary Magdalene adroitly challenges his view, becoming in the process the prime representative of feminine wisdom and inspiration, associated in the poem's palimpsestic method with Isis and other figures of

---

[6] Rachel Blau du Plessis, 'H.D. and Revisionary Myth-Making', in Alex Davis and Lee M. Jenkins (eds.), *The Cambridge Companion to Modernist Poetry* (Cambridge: Cambridge University Press, 2007), 114–25 (119).

female power. Yet for H. D. she is the most appropriate symbol because she had been condemned as immoral by a patriarchal code of laws.

H. D. was to leave London for Switzerland, never to return. The departure has a kind of symbolic appropriateness, as if marking the end of a cosmopolitan period in the history of poetry in Britain. Yet, as we have already noted, some of the pioneers of modernist poetry in Britain and Ireland were to enjoy a late flowering in the years after the war. Despite the international consciousness and connections which seem inseparable from modernist art, post-war modernist poetry in the British Isles exhibits a characteristic concentration on the local and the national, a phenomenon which is worth standing back from and examining.

II

Modernist writing offers new representations of the self. By implication, and often deliberately, it also offers hints for the renewal of the self and, as part of the same process, of society. For it may be that the exploration of long-ignored aspects of the psyche reveals that they have been repressed, and that the work of representing them is itself revolutionary. In Yeats, in Pound, in Lawrence, in H.D., this rediscovery of the self is also the rediscovery of types of humanity that existed in the past: in Celtic society, in archaic Greece, in ancient China, in the age of the troubadours, in Etruria, in ancient Egypt. There are traces of a similar belief-structure in Eliot, for his engagement with Jessie L. Weston's *From Ritual to Romance* was by no means superficial, nor was it mainly intended for mock-heroic purposes. Eliot's desire for the spiritual renewal of Europe always encompassed a sense that this would have to incorporate ritual, in a sanctified transformation of the savage mind. Even for a writer such as Virginia Woolf, who did not employ mythological machinery, the radically original depiction of mental process was linked to a profound social critique. The obviousness of such a point becomes merely banal when one considers also Wyndham Lewis, or the early work of Auden. Whether or not linked to revisionist accounts of the past, modernism tended to be a project for the radical reordering of society, and whatever other merits it may have, the account given of it by Georg Lukács, most clearly and concisely in *The Meaning of Contemporary Realism*, is on this matter quite superficial: Lukács stresses modernism's concentration on isolated subjectivity, as if this *ipso facto* excluded any means of implying an interesting view about society in general.[7] But Adorno's critique of Lukács stresses modernism's potential for the illuminating representation of social reality through formal experimentation, and this is surely how its practitioners understood the matter.[8]

---

[7] Georg Lukács, *The Meaning of Contemporary Realism* (1957), trans. John and Necke Maunder (London: Merlin Press, 1963), 39.

[8] Theodor Adorno, *Aesthetic Theory* (1970), ed. Gretel Adorno and Rolf Tiedemann, ed. and trans. Robert Hullot-Kentor (2nd edn., London: Continuum, 2007), 187.

It is in this light, at least in part, that the cosmopolitanism of many modernist texts needs to be understood: that is to say, while it might in some instances be part of a subversive reordering of provincial narrowness, it was often, also, an exploration of alternative ways of being human, alternative forms of human culture. Where it issues in a concern for what Eliot called 'the mind of Europe', this is an example of seriousness about the historical nature of society. Another version of socio-historical awareness is to be found in the reinvestigation of national traditions and identity. Alex Davis and Lee M. Jenkins have offered a salutary critique of 'the tendency of accepting too quickly and uncritically the commonplace that modernism is a transnational or even supranational entity'.[9] As they point out, 'that modernism and nationalism need not be mutually incompatible is vividly demonstrated by the example of the Irish Literary Revival'.[10] Referring to 'Ireland's lack of a developed industrial base (with the exception of Belfast)', they quote a piece of analysis by Terry Eagleton in order to illuminate the nature of the Irish Revival: 'Both nationalism and modernism eclipse the prosaic time of modernity, placing this whole epoch in brackets by the power of a thought which, in striving for some pre-bourgeois form of life, finds its models for this in a pre-bourgeois world.'[11] However, it is not sufficient merely to note the parallel between modernism and nationalism, real though this is: a more intimate link, and one which reinforces the parallel, is to be found in modernism's tendency to discover traces of a vital, anti-bourgeois tradition in its own locality, since that is the place where one may be able to effect something that actually connects with one's own existence. One version of locality is nation. Even where there are few traces of mystical nationalism, as in Virginia Woolf or D. H. Lawrence, what we have are 'Condition of England' novels, representing a radical reinterpretation of that nineteenth-century genre.

Another way to revive local tradition is to think in terms of the region, especially if the traditions are distinctive. In this light, the regional can offer, in Robert Crawford's words, 'a sense of empowering marginality'.[12] This is the topic to which Crawford gives the useful title, 'Modernism as Provincialism'.[13] Talk of regionalism should not obscure what is in fact a related phenomenon: the potent attractions of representing the small nation. While Basil Bunting's Northumbria may fit the regional description, it is more illuminating to assign some of the energy of Hugh MacDiarmid's poetry to the idea of reviving a neglected national tradition, a position sharing some similarity to that of the Irish Revival. Nor is Bunting's own regionalism to be entirely separated from the idea of nation: the echoes in *Briggflatts* of Old Welsh, of Anglo-Saxon, of Norse, make Northumbria seem more like a repository of ancient layers contributing to an English

---

[9] Alex Davis and Lee M. Jenkins (eds.), *Locations of Literary Modernism: Region and Nation in British and American Modernist Poetry* (Cambridge: Cambridge University Press, 2000), 4.

[10] Davis and Jenkins (eds.), *Locations*, 5.

[11] Davis and Jenkins (eds.), *Locations*, 5. For the quotation from Eagleton, *Heathcliff and the Great Hunger* (London: Verso, 1995), 285.

[12] Robert Crawford, 'MacDiarmid in Montrose', in Davis and Jenkins (eds.), *Locations*, 35–56 (55).

[13] Robert Crawford, *Devolving English Literature* (2nd edn., Edinburgh: Edinburgh University Press, 2000), 216–70.

nationhood, rather than a marginal and idiosyncratic entity. In none of this, though, should one neglect the modernist interest in other cultures. For Irish modernists of the thirties, French modernist poetry provides ways of representing aspects of their culture which are obscured by the modes of the Revival; while for Bunting, Persian poetry—as interpreted, for instance, in his *The Spoils* (1965)—offers an example of a clear registering of sensuous delight for which he finds analogues in the less probable-seeming context of Northumbria.

III

H.D.'s husband, from whom she divorced, was also part of the Imagist group, and was the subject of a biography—*Richard Aldington: An Englishman* (1931)—by the Irish modernist poet Thomas MacGreevy. MacGreevy was one of a loose association of Irish poets who looked to modern European poetry, including its contemporary manifestations, and sought a modern poetic language. Apart from MacGreevy, the poets still remembered are Samuel Beckett, Denis Devlin, and Brian Coffey. The international interests of these poets do not imply that they shy away from the fashioning of a distinctive Irish modernist poetry, though admittedly this description seems inappropriate to Beckett, for while his sensibility can arguably be related to a distinctively Irish vein of black humour and extreme speculation, he does not even toy with ideas of national essence. Devlin and Coffey both write on Irish subjects, and Devlin's early work includes translations of Rimbaud, Baudelaire, Mallarmé, and Apollinaire into Irish, a gesture that cannot be summarized as submission to the French, but rather, considering that he is a poet who normally wrote in English, a work of grafting one sensibility onto another.

MacGreevy, who belonged to an earlier generation, not only included Irish subjects in his slender poetic oeuvre, but also attempted to connect with Irish tradition in poems such as 'Crón Tráth na nDéithe' (Irish: 'Twilight of the Gods') and 'Aodh Ruadh O Domhnaill' (Red Hugh O'Donnell).[14] The former, dated Easter Sunday 1923, and apparently influenced by Eliot's *The Waste Land*, is a fragmentary and despairing reflection on the pale green of Ireland's new nationhood, written on the seventh anniversary of the Easter Rising, and in the latter stages of the brutal and debilitating civil war which followed independence for the twenty-six counties of the Irish Free State. The other poem recounts the author's attempt to find the grave near Valladolid of the Gaelic chieftain Red Hugh O'Donnell who had fled to Spain from the forces of the English crown in the early seventeenth century. O'Donnell was a committed Catholic as well as a remarkably doughty leader of the Gaelic cause who defeated the English forces on several occasions.

[14] Thomas MacGreevy, *Collected Poems of Thomas MacGreevy: An Annotated Edition* (Dublin: Anna Livia Press; Washington DC: Catholic University of America Press, 1991), 14–24, 34–5. Subsequent quotations given in the text as *CPTM* followed by page number.

In their different ways, each of these poems asserts an international connection to a specifically Irish experience.

MacGreevy, never prolific, produced only four poems between 1934 and his death in 1967. This sporadic return of the muse appears to be celebrated in 'Moments Musicaux' (*CPTM* 65–7). The elated and springy rhythm of this lyrical expression of gratitude encompasses also moments of sadness for those who could 'stay | With you gone' (*CPTM* 66). John Goodby interprets these as MacGreevy's comrades of European days, Devlin and Coffey, who did not, like himself, return to Ireland.[15] The lyrical sweetness of this poem prompts one to register a useful distinction drawn by Goodby, with a little assistance from Alex Davis and Marjorie Perloff: namely, that MacGreevy and Devlin are in the line of the post-symbolist modernism of Eliot, while Coffey belongs to the open poetics of Pound and his disciples.[16] This is a good point, so far as it goes, but further discrimination would also register that Devlin's clotted textures owe more to symbolism than does the gnomic fragmentariness of MacGreevy's lines.

The style is not inappropriate to the mystical Celtic nationalism MacGreevy entertained by this point in his life. 'Breton Oracles' and 'Homage to Vercingetorix' both celebrate the Celtic heritage of France, the latter referring to the great Gallic chieftain who came close to defeating Julius Caesar (*CPTM* 68–70, 63–4). 'Breton Oracles' shows the speaker exploring an Irish kinship with the mystical Catholicism of Celtic Brittany: 'Over years, and from farther and nearer, | I had thought I knew you—| in spirit—I am of Ireland' (*CPTM* 68). 'Homage to Vercingetorix' straightforwardly compares Caesar to a 'Black-and-Tan', despite the fact that he is conceded to possess 'reserves | Of literary talent | And polite manners' (*CPTM* 64). Ireland, it is implied, is at one with a mystical European tradition and at odds both with militant Roman authority, and with the modern Anglo-Saxon world that inherits its rational organization of dominion. Here, Eagleton's remark—quoted above—about modernism, nationalism, and the pre-bourgeois, seems as apt as anywhere. Stan Smith makes a related comment with specific reference to MacGreevy: 'The cosmopolitanism of MacGreevy's forms and sensibility nevertheless works to express a traditional, strangely anachronistic content.'[17]

Denis Devlin undertakes a comparable manoeuvre, albeit one that is less explicit, in his thirties translations of French poets. Placed alongside other features of his work—all his 'strange landscapes of language' (in the apt words of Alan Gillis)—one is entitled to entertain the hypothesis that he at least thinks Ireland can find a kindred spirit in the imaginative adventurousness of French symbolism.[18] This seems to be borne out in a poem published in *Lough Derg and Other Poems* (1946): 'Encounter' shows the poet

---

[15] John Goodby, *Irish Poetry Since 1950: From Stillness Into History* (Manchester: Manchester University Press, 2000), 50.

[16] Goodby, *Irish Poetry Since 1950*, 49–50.

[17] Stan Smith, *Irish Poetry and the Construction of Modern Identity: Ireland Between Fantasy and History* (Dublin: Irish Academic Press, 2005), 49.

[18] Alan Gillis, *Irish Poetry of the 1930s* (Oxford: Oxford University Press, 2005), 96–7.

sitting out at a café in France with an Englishman, and with François from Touraine.[19] The Englishman convicts the Celt of allowing the poor to remain poor by praising them and praising God for 'standing still'. But the poet answers: 'Milton and Marvell, like the toady Horace, | Praised the men of power'. The point is very close to that which is implied in MacGreevy's 'Vercingetorix'. Meanwhile, a poetic interjection from François has succinctly evoked another view of the world: 'Patience, listen to the world's | Growth, resulting in fire and childlike water'. The poem concludes with an evocative description of the surrounding evening. The poetry of being, of the wonder of being, is at odds with an instrumental rationality wielded in common by the pagan Roman Empire and the British Empire.

The title poem, 'Lough Derg', offers a perfect example of the inadequacy of referring Devlin's work to the model of an Eliotic modernism. Its regular 'Venus and Adonis' stanzas are handled in orthodox enough fashion, with some ringing pentameter lines. The debt to the innovations of modernism resides partly in these 'strange landscapes of language'—surreal confections of exotic imagery and unexpected abstract adjectives that bear a dim resemblance to the work of Dylan Thomas:

Bolder than the peasant tiger whose autumn beauty
Sags in the expletive kill, or the sacrifice
Of death puffed positive in the stance of duty (*CPDD* 133)

These lines describe the 'first geometer', thus identified as superior to the mentality of the peasants who prefer their pilgrimage, divided between the 'stance of duty' and an innocent but potentially unrestrained tiger which is dying. The whole poem, in this respect reminiscent of Patrick Kavanagh's 'Lough Derg Pilgrimage', convicts the Irish Catholic Church of inculcating guilt and contempt for the body in a manner comparable to Jansenism (Devlin refers, wittily enough, to 'Clan Jansen' (*CPDD* 132)), the stern Catholic tendency whose tenets have been compared to those of Calvin. In the same volume is to be found a poem that presents the Buddha in a positive light: a light that, from its presence in the same volume, must be similar to that cast by the early Irish Christianity of the 'monks in convents of coracles' ('Lough Derg', *CPDD* 134). These, with their 'grace to give without demand', are praised for qualities similar to those of the Buddha. The Buddha 'Blesses without obliging | Loves without condescension'. There is a certain 'Irish Orientalism' in this (to use Joseph Lennon's phrase) that resides in the well-known equation of Celtic sensibility and traditions with various forms of 'oriental' belief.[20] By contrast, St Teresa, in 'Meditation at Avila', is aligned with the destructive element in Catholicism: 'Covetous, burning virgin! | Scorning to nourish body's | Farmland's with soul's | Modulating rains' (*CPDD* 163–4). It is in 'Est Prodest', again from

---

[19] Denis Devlin, *Collected Poems of Denis Devlin*, ed. J. C. C. Mays (Dublin: The Dedalus Press, 1989), 136. Future references are given in the text as *CPDD* followed by page number.

[20] Joseph Lennon, *Irish Orientalism: A Literary and Intellectual History* (Syracuse, NY: Syracuse University Press, 2004).

the same volume, that we are offered the closest thing to a coherent account of Devlin's positive beliefs, for here, as J. C. C. Mays points out, we encounter the central truth that 'love of justice, love of God, love of woman are aspects of the same love' (*CPDD* 33). The poem draws to a close with an ecstatic sense of potential union with God: 'And he will move breathing | Through us wing-linked | Proleptic of what Eden'. The beloved woman may be, as in the work of Eugenio Montale, a modern Beatrice. This topic is developed at length in *The Heavenly Foreigner*, a long poem first published in 1950 (*CPDD* 260–74). Like 'Lough Derg', it deploys the trope of the pilgrim, the speaker who moves from one sacred site to another: the poem is divided into sections bearing the names of cathedral cities and of other sites which resonate with the idea of sacred love.

Brian Coffey's poetry is indeed more securely in the modernist line that descends from Pound and Williams via Olson to the neo-modernist poetries of our own day. Phrasing is often clipped, though not always, it must be said, with a short line-length. His is a style of terse lyricism: the definite article is frequently dropped; images are juxtaposed, but bound together by a strain of meditative thought. Rhyme may be used, though as part of a network of sound-textures that in general avoids regular pattern. The idea governing the actual shape of the poem is rather the venerable post-Romantic one of thought finding its own organic shape. In less experimental poems, such as *Missouri Sequence* (1962), the reflective mind is shown responding to its immediate setting: 'Our children have eaten supper, | play Follow-my-leader, | make songs from room to room | around and around; | once each minute | past my desk they go'.[21] At the other extreme is a poem such as 'The Prayers' (from *Chanterelles* (1985)) that bears comparison with some late modernist poetry such as that of J. H. Prynne in its attempt to construct a tough, linguistically self-conscious, but still lyrical mode for an unforgivingly radical depiction of mental association:

One had not known oneself
They had known one frail
Theirs   lump   theirs

Close of action   Query none
Eyes matt   Heart matt

No stage needs setting
In hope failed at void. (*P&V* 222)

The themes that lurk within these gnomic utterances are, though, perhaps easier to identify than Prynne's: they offer themselves for 'naturalization' (to use a formalist term) as representations of moments of fundamental existential questioning about life's purpose, and are reminiscent in this respect of Coffey's friend Beckett. The preceding fragment, for instance, offers a brief gloss on despair, comprising an avowal of inauthentic existence (acquiescence in others' judgement of one's being). This point might provide access

---

[21] Brian Coffey, *Poems and Versions 1929–1990* (Dublin: The Dedalus Press, 1991), 69. Subsequent references are given in the text as *P&V* followed by page number.

to what is arguably Coffey's best poem, *Death of Hektor* (1979). A striking piece of modernist neoclassicism, this poem is for the most part (at least after its first section) cast in rolling five- to six-beat lines which mirror the capaciousness, if not always the length, of Homer's hexameters. In clear, classically inspired outline, it delineates in newly minted form the timeless in Homer and in the character of Hektor:

he had been fatherly husbandly to friends just
could ask for equal treatment from equal foe
yet not forget worst fears might come to pass (*P&V* 163)

Despite the deliberate avoidance of punctuation, the combination of style and subject is oddly reminiscent of a number of classically inspired poems ('Ceasefire', for instance) by another Irish poet, Michael Longley.

Samuel Beckett is the odd man out in this company. He had welcomed the poetry of Coffey and Devlin in his review article, 'Recent Irish Poetry', written under the pseudonym 'Andrew Belis' for a special Irish number of *The Bookman* in August 1934.[22] He compared their work to that of Thomas MacGreevy, to whom he was particularly close. The review is aggressively contemptuous of those it sees as inheriting the modes and themes of the Revival. But Beckett himself was not prolific in poetry in the post-war period, and what little he wrote was often in French, most notably in the *Mirlitonnades* of the late 1970s.[23] Derek Mahon, though, has translated eight of these short poems, and David Wheatley has written about them.[24] Beckett, however, is not a figure much invoked even by those who espouse a modernist turn in Irish poetry.

IV

The phrase 'modernist survivor' does not seem quite appropriate for Hugh MacDiarmid, who before the Second World War was chiefly associated with the Scots Revival, and who wrote often in traditional forms derived from song and ballad. Nor can his post-war work be properly understood without an awareness of that past. His great poem of the fifties, *In Memoriam James Joyce*, is plausibly modernist, and its title is instructive not merely about the encyclopedic range of reference he presumed to share with Joyce, nor only about the sense of the work as object on the page, which the poem might broadly be said to share with *Ulysses*. It also points to MacDiarmid's desire to identify his Scottish nationalism with an international outlook capable of bypassing the English. Joyce may not have been a nationalist, but he certainly wished to write for his 'race', and believed

---

[22] Andrew Belis [Samuel Beckett], 'Recent Irish Poetry', *The Bookman*, 86 (Aug. 1934), 235–6.
[23] Samuel Beckett, *Poèmes [suivi de Mirlitonnades]* (Paris: Éditions de Minuit, 1978).
[24] Derek Mahon, 'Burbles (after Samuel Beckett)', *Hermathena*, 156 (Summer 1994), 59–60; David Wheatley, 'Labours Unfinished: Beckett's *mirlitonnades* and the Poetics of Incompletion', *Fulcrum: An Annual of Poetry and Aesthetics*, 6 (2007), 500–6.

that he could best do so by identifying the traditions and modes of writing that Ireland shared, or could share, with Europe, rather than England. In the case of MacDiarmid one can draw the various implications together: England could not offer the context in which a lengthy philosophical poem, drawing on science, political discourse, economics, and philology, and composed in a frankly intellectual register, could prosper. *In Memoriam James Joyce* is that poem. It can certainly be written by a Scot, but written in English, rather than Scots, in the same spirit as Joyce assuming proprietorship of the English language. The aspect of the poem that suggests the word as object—the lengthy footnotes and epigraphs, the sense of the poem itself as encompassing different types of text—is both a way of demystifying the flexibility of language (for expression is only possible under different modes of discourse), and a way of trying not to look like the well-made English poem. These qualities are also those which establish its title to the description 'modernist', since it exhibits a foregrounding of textuality which bears comparison to aspects of Joyce's *Ulysses,* while in its decidedly un-mellifluous discursiveness it bears a remote resemblance to parts of Pound's *Cantos.*

Some of the most cogent lines in *In Memoriam James Joyce* self-reflexively relate MacDiarmid's artistic methods to his theory of language as marvellous in its capacity to fit itself variously to the perception of things, the demands of argument and philosophical exposition, or the expression of mood. The marvellousness resides in the fitness, and this is a quality that MacDiarmid would celebrate in verse intended to exhibit the flexible powers of language, its capacity to embody and express a lucid, rational, but wondering and myriad-minded view of life:

So this is what our lives have been given to find,
A language that can serve our purposes,
A marvellous lucidity, a quality of fiery aery light [25]

By way of discouraging this wonder, 'English official criticism has erected | A stone-heap, a dead load of moral qualities' (*MCP* 865). These lines come from a section entitled 'England Is Our Enemy' (*MCP* 858–70), in which MacDiarmid proceeds to enumerate the timorous and uncommitted character, as he sees it, of English thought: 'A middle-class standard of morality, | As much religion as, say, St Paul had, | As much atheism as Shelley had' (*MCP* 865). The whole miserable spectacle is summarized as 'an immense load | Of self-neutralising moral and social qualities' (*MCP* 865). Not that the summary is entirely MacDiarmid's own. These lines, with those about St Paul and Shelley, are borrowed wholesale from an essay by Ford Madox Ford.[26] Yet in a sense it seems appropriate that, here and elsewhere, the poem should incorporate screeds of prose by other hands: from one point of view, this is an aspect of the way the poem

---

[25] Hugh MacDiarmid, *Collected Poems: 1920–1976*, 2 vols., ed. Michael Grieve and W. R. Aitken (London: Martin, Brian and O'Keefe, 1978), i. 822. Future references in the main text as *MCP* followed by page number.

[26] Under the pseudonym Daniel Chaucer, 'Stocktaking: Towards a Re-Valuation of English Literature', *Transatlantic Review*, 1/3 (Mar. 1924), 57.

behaves like a textual object by foregrounding the various discourses of which it makes use. From another point of view, the poem's discursive character means that it can easily accommodate argumentative prose. Whatever one may think of the passage from Ford, as a cultural analysis with which MacDiarmid wholeheartedly agreed, it is true that the post-war poetry of the latter can link passion, lucidity, and precision about natural phenomena in an arresting way, as in the poem 'Crystals Like Blood' (1949), where the speaker picks up and describes in engaging detail 'a broken chunk of bedrock', half brown limestone and half 'greenish-grey quartz-like stone', then moves on by association of ideas to the extraction of mercury by means of iron pile-drivers, and concludes with a thought of his dead and buried beloved and her influence, that 'My treadmill memory draws from you yet' (*MCP* 1054).

V

MacDiarmid's style, its lucid connectedness and capacity for organized exposition, constitutes a kind of opposite to the specific evocation of experience found in the modernisms we have explored previously. His style is at one with his theoretical communism: he is not prepared to renounce a structured explanation of society, and not prepared to renounce a poetic method which values organization and the expressive use of syntax. He would not, in other words, fall foul of the strictures imposed by Lukács. With David Jones, we move back towards the other camp, the poetry of experience, but by no means so far as to rule out erudition and allusiveness. As with Eliot or Joyce, the mind's movement is shown to be infused with historical association. *The Anathémata* (1952) was Jones's second long work. (*In Parenthesis,* an interpretation of Jones's experiences in the Great War, had come out in 1937.) In certain respects it easily surpasses MacDiarmid's efforts at making the poem an object. Its appearance on the page is strikingly various, with illustrations, footnotes, a preface, and quotations from various languages. But in other respects—its fragmentariness, allusiveness, and use of juxtaposition—it also behaves like those modernist poems that seek a new language for experience. Indeed, in combining these two aspects—poem as object, and poem as fragmentary evocation of experience—it wears the aspect of a high modernist work such as *The Cantos* or *The Waste Land*. Like these, it seeks continuities with the archaic past in order to point the way to contemporary renewal. And as with these also, it finds those continuities to be most vital where they can reveal the insights to be found in ancient myth and ritual. Jones's prime ritual, as a Catholic convert, is the Mass: but he finds precursors of its narrative in the distant European past, and, being a London Welshman, in Welsh tradition. In its first section, 'Rite and Foretime', he goes back as far as the Stone Age. Despite this, the emphasis is quite as much on continuity as on disjunction. The turpitude of the modern age does not negate, as one feels it can do in Eliot and Pound, a beneficent influence that comes down to us from rituals and behaviour at the dawn of time. Indeed, there is more of a similarity here with H.D. and her idea of the palimpsest. Jones speaks of 'continuings', and these 'continuings' are substantial and essentially connected. Jones's 'deposits', as he calls them, go all the way down through strata at the bottom of which is 'before all time', and in some sense the 'New Light' of Redemption shines with elements already existent in the 'fore-time':

From before all time
> the New Light beams for them
> [...]
Lighting the Cretaceous and the Trias, for Tyrannosaurus must
somehow lie down with herbivores, or, the poet lied,
which is not allowed.[27]

Read in its entirety, this passage suggests that Isaiah's prophecy (Isaiah 11:6) is not only a vision of the future but an insight into the essence of all history: the wolf has always dwelt with the lamb. The benignity of Christ has always existed, and we need to recognize that fact. It is Jones's purpose to induce this recognition, rather than some revelation leading to the renunciation of the past. It is in this sense that for Jones, as Saunders Lewis says, 'The Mass concertinas all history'.[28] It also repeats the creative action of the artist. One of the special interests of Welsh tradition for him is the way in which the Celtic Druids and bards can be seen as echoing the same message. Thus it is that Britain offers a particular connection with all the layers of past time.

Ancient Britain, as much as any other ancient history, is also central to the subject matter of Basil Bunting's great poem, *Briggflatts* (1965). As we have observed, Bunting, like Jones, was interested in Welsh poetry. A connected interest was the Celtic past of northern Britain, when the poet Aneurin sang the rulers of Rheged (a long-forgotten Cymric kingdom comprising much of north Cumbria and south-western Scotland) and Taliesin sang the tribe of the Gododdin (a Cymric people who once ruled the area from Edinburgh to Teesside, until defeated by the Northumbrians). The Norse are also recalled, and the tough, lithe musicality of Bunting's line is meant to mimic the assonance and alliteration of times unsullied by the false smoothness of recent ages. As he says, 'Clear Cymric voices carry well this autumn night | Aneurin and Taliesin, cruel owls [...] || before the rules made poetry a pedant's game' (*Briggflatts* IV).[29] But it is not only their lack of pedantry that motivates him: it is not possible so to exalt the ancient past of a particular region without suggesting the discovery of some essential spirit there. Yet as much as these models from the north of England, it is the work of his friend Pound that Bunting's versification recalls. Its springing, syncopated rhythm and dense texture of sounds are reminiscent, in particular, of the Pound of the Confucius translations, and this can serve at least to remind one that, while Bunting shares Pound's delving into past poetries, unlike Pound he makes a virtue of doing so in a region that might seem marginal to the European tradition. *Briggflatts* takes its name from the village near

---

[27] David Jones, *The Anathémata* (1952; 3rd edn., London: Faber & Faber, 1972), 73–4.
[28] Saunders Lewis, 'Epoch and Artist', *Agenda*, 5/1–3 (1967), 112–15 (115).
[29] Basil Bunting, *The Complete Poems*, ed. Richard Caddel (Oxford: Oxford University Press, 1994), 57.

Sedbergh, in Cumbria (in fact spelt 'Brigflatts') where he often spent summers as a boy. The village is home to an ancient Quaker meeting house, a fact of special significance to Bunting, who was raised as a Quaker: in a sect, that is, whose practice of silent meditation and valuing of honesty might be thought to encourage habits of truthfulness and careful perception such as are enacted in the poem. The opening section harks back to the poet's adolescent love for a local stonemason's daughter some fifty years previously. The poem is unsurprisingly frank about physical desire, which it celebrates, but it is also a kind of muse poem in its sense of haunting recollection: 'She has been with me fifty years. | | Starlight quivers. I had day enough. | For love uninterrupted night'.[30] The actions of the stonemason are beautifully recalled in lines whose rhythm enacts the process of the chisel, and whose spirit is at one with the mason's art of exactitude, rather as it might be in Pound. Yet the paradox of writing—that it evokes what it can never be—is only exacerbated by the stonemason working on tombstones while his daughter and the young poet embrace. This yearning absence stretches from the beginning of life to its end, and a good part of the poem's authority derives from its restrained lyricism and tone of undaunted celebration of life.

VI

No one generalization is adequate to categorize all the modernist poetic survivors post-1945, and many of the following remarks do not work as well for H.D. as for those born locally, which is not surprising. Yet there is a tendency to transfer to the regional and national some of the European themes of high modernism. The Irish Literary Revival provided a model for this endeavour, and the recourse to the Celtic past, albeit in a form bearing no resemblance to the Celtic Twilight, is revealing of this connection. And even Irish poets such as MacGreevy and Devlin, who had no wish to reproduce a Yeatsian idea of ancient Ireland, credit a kind of pan-Celtic mysticism. All of these poets are inimical to 'empire', as David Jones calls it in *The Anathémata*, and it is possible to see in their work the struggle to identify an alternative London, an alternative England, Scotland, Wales, or Ireland. Set free from the dead weight of recent history, the denizens of these places could reconnect with their truer selves by drinking from ancient springs which were only a walk away, and which shared something of one's being. Another way of looking at these facts is to recognize how the valuing of the local and regional is entirely congruent with the 'make it new' imperative of modernism. For it is easier to represent a renewal of the self, its perceptions and poetic, by starting from what lies to hand for that self than it is from some wider concept such as 'the mind of Europe'. Such a wider concept may be discovered and illuminated, but only by entering into its living and particular local embodiment.

---

[30] Bunting, *Complete Poems*, 62.

All of these poets continued to find new readers. In Britain, the modernist revival of the 1960s saw various new modernist poets, such as Roy Fisher, Tom Pickard, Tom Raworth, and Lee Harwood, published by Fulcrum Press, London. But this press also brought out David Jones's *The Tribune's Visitation* (1969), as well as a number of volumes by Bunting, most notably his *Collected Poems* in 1968. Nor can the work of more mainstream poets be kept separate from the modernist survivors: it is generally, and surely rightly, assumed that Geoffrey Hill's *Mercian Hymns* owes something to the method of David Jones, its interweaving of past and present, its interest in what used to be called 'the Dark Ages'. This means that Jones is also a remote influence on Heaney's *North*, which most acknowledge to be indebted to *Mercian Hymns*. Neo-modernist poetry in Britain remains fascinated by the idea of reading a particular place as a palimpsest capable of revealing an alternative history: witness Iain Sinclair, in *Lud Heat*.[31] New British ventures, such as the series of editions and critical studies emerging from Salt Press, offer some evidence that the work of late modernists and neo-modernists is receiving more serious interest from the academy and poetry readers. The course of events in Ireland has been different. When they began writing in the 1930s, the Irish modernist poets were not congenial, as Terence Brown puts it, to the 'populist rural values' of the still young Irish state.[32] A parallel suggestion, and one less demeaning to established Irish writers, might be that poets were able to appeal to rural values even while themselves avoiding populism, for the reason that a frank, realistic, and properly rigorous depiction of life in the Irish countryside would seem more truthful than the fancies of Yeats. Recent years have at last seen a resurgence of interest in the Irish modernists, most clearly signalled by an anthology of critical reappraisals edited in 1995 by Patricia Coughlan and Alex Davis.[33]

Contemporary Irish poetry can no longer be caricatured as limited to bucolic subject matter and the poetics of Thomas Hardy. But this caricature was never much more than that in any case, a fact that has long been evident even in the works of poets from Northern Ireland, often portrayed as wedded to conservatism of matter and manner. This hardly seems a credible summary of the poetry of Medbh McGuckian, its surrealism surely indebted to the work of John Ashbery, or of Ciaran Carson's adaptation of the long line of C. K. Williams to his own semiotic and historical investigations of the streets of Belfast. In the Republic, something of the American long line has also imparted itself to the work of Paul Durcan, with its strange narratives; and some of the best work of Eavan Boland is an adaptation of techniques learnt from Plath to more politically articulate uses. In recent times, Ireland has combined an affirmation of its venerable American connection with an enthusiastic embrace of the European Union, and her poetry offers a correlative of this overlap of international links, with younger poets such as Justin

---

[31] Iain Sinclair, *Lud Heat: A Book of the Dead Hamlets* (London: Albion Village Press, 1975).

[32] Terence Brown, *Ireland: A Social and Cultural History* (Ithaca, NY: Cornell University Press, 1981), 129.

[33] Patricia Coughlan and Alex Davis (eds.), *Modernism and Ireland: The Poetry of the 1930s* (Cork: Cork University Press, 1995).

Quinn looking to East European models. All this is leading to a reappraisal of the Irish modernists who started writing in the 1930s. In Britain, by contrast, a more patient reassessment seems to be in train, with the work of Geoffrey Hill attracting ever-growing attention not only for its moral seriousness, but also for its resistance to easy assimilation. The latter point has indicated a way to the common ground that exists between his poetry and that of modernists and neo-modernists who achieved a similar combination of qualities guided by different poetic lights.

Select Bibliography

Adorno, Theodor, *Aesthetic Theory* (1970), ed. Gretel Adorno and Rolf Tiedemann, ed. and trans. Robert Hullot-Kentor (2nd edn., London: Continuum, 2007).

Beckett, Samuel, *Poèmes [suivi de Mirlitonnades]* (Paris: Éditions de Minuit, 1978).

Belis, Andrew [Samuel Beckett], 'Recent Irish Poetry', *The Bookman*, 86 (Aug. 1934), 235–6.

Brown, Terence, *Ireland: A Social and Cultural History* (Ithaca, NY: Cornell University Press, 1981).

Bunting, Basil, *The Complete Poems*, ed. Richard Caddel (Oxford: Oxford University Press, 1994).

Chaucer, Daniel, 'Stocktaking: Towards a Re-Valuation of English Literature', *Transatlantic Review*, 1/3 (Mar. 1924).

Coffey, Brian, *Poems and Versions 1929–1990* (Dublin: The Dedalus Press, 1991).

Coughlan, Patricia and Davis, Alex (eds.), *Modernism and Ireland: The Poetry of the 1930s* (Cork: Cork University Press, 1995).

Crawford, Robert, *Devolving English Literature* (2nd edn., Edinburgh: Edinburgh University Press, 2000).

Davis, Alex and Jenkins, Lee M. (eds.), *Locations of Literary Modernism: Region and Nation in British and American Modernist Poetry* (Cambridge: Cambridge University Press, 2000).

Devlin, Denis, *Collected Poems of Denis Devlin*, ed. J. C. C. Mays (Dublin: The Dedalus Press, 1989).

H.D. [Hilda Doolittle], *Trilogy: The Walls Do Not Fall; Tribute to the Angels; The Flowering of the Rod* (Manchester: Carcanet, 1973).

du Plessis, Rachel Blau, 'H.D. and Revisionary Myth-Making', in Alex Davis and Lee M. Jenkins (eds.), *The Cambridge Companion to Modernist Poetry* (Cambridge: Cambridge University Press, 2007), 114–25.

Gillis, Alan, *Irish Poetry of the 1930s* (Oxford: Oxford University Press, 2005).

Goodby, John, *Irish Poetry Since 1950: From Stillness Into History* (Manchester: Manchester University Press, 2000).

Hamilton, Ian, 'Four Conversations: Thom Gunn, Philip Larkin, Christopher Middleton and Charles Tomlinson', *London Magazine*, 4/6 [=4/8] (4 Nov. 1964), 64–85.

Jones, David, *The Anathémata* (1952; 3rd edn., London: Faber & Faber, 1972).

Lennon, Joseph, *Irish Orientalism: A Literary and Intellectual History* (Syracuse, NY: Syracuse University Press, 2004).

Lewis, Saunders, 'Epoch and Artist', *Agenda*, 5/1–3 (1967), 112–15.

Lukács, Georg, *The Meaning of Contemporary Realism* (1957), trans. John and Necke Maunder (London: Merlin Press, 1963).

MacDiarmid, Hugh, *Collected Poems: 1920-1976*, 2 vols., ed. Michael Grieve and W. R. Aitken (London: Martin, Brian and O'Keefe, 1978).
MacGreevy, Thomas, *Collected Poems of Thomas MacGreevy: An Annotated Edition* (Dublin: Anna Livia Press; Washington DC: Catholic University of America Press, 1991).
Mahon, Derek, 'Burbles (after Samuel Beckett)', *Hermathena*, 156 (Summer 1994).
Pound, Ezra, *The Classic Anthology Defined by Confucius* (London: Faber & Faber, 1955).
Sinclair, Iain, *Lud Heat: A Book of the Dead Hamlets* (London: Albion Village Press, 1975).
Smith, Stan, *Irish Poetry and the Construction of Modern Identity: Ireland Between Fantasy and History* (Dublin: Irish Academic Press, 2005).
Tomlinson, Charles, 'The Middlebrow Muse', *Essays in Criticism*, 7 (Apr. 1957), 208-17.
Wheatley, David, 'Labours Unfinished: Beckett's *mirlitonnades* and the Poetics of Incompletion', *Fulcrum: An Annual of Poetry and Aesthetics*, 6 (2007), 500-6.

CHAPTER 2

THE THIRTIES BEQUEST

MICHAEL O'NEILL

THIS chapter explores the work and influence of poets who came to prominence in the 1930s, especially W. H. Auden and Louis MacNeice, and also Stephen Spender.[1] All were poets who produced major work both during and after the 1930s, the 'low dishonest decade', as Auden called it in 'September 1, 1939', with which they are most immediately associated.[2] Auden and MacNeice, in particular, exercise influence in apparent and surprising ways, the former as formal mentor and ideological guide, the latter as exuberant yet melancholy lyricist of the urban and individual. MacNeice praises the particular; Auden looks for the general law that underpins a detail. For Auden, 'poetry makes nothing happen', where the phrasing calculates its double suggestions to a nicety: poetry is not a causal agent; poetry does have the capacity to give a local habitation and a name to the 'nothing' of imagination, and is, as the same poem ('In Memory of W. B. Yeats') goes on to remark, 'A way of happening' (89). For MacNeice, in his most representative poem 'Snow', 'World is crazier and more of it than we think, | Incorrigibly plural'.[3] His language, omitting a definite article before 'World', enacts the control-threatening bombardment of stimuli that are 'Incorrigibly plural'. Auden's language, after the arrestingly abrupt challenges posed by his earliest and, for some admirers (such as Seamus Heaney), most impressive poems, is at once propositional and part of a sequential meditation.

Spender, for his part, occupies a place on the poetic spectrum that is very much his own. Mocked by poets such as a brashly hip Thom Gunn for his supposed exhibition of vulnerability (Gunn praises 'the overdogs from Alexander | To those who would not play with

---

[1] There are, of course, many poets from the 1930s who have influenced later writers. They include C. Day Lewis, Bernard Spencer, Rex Warner, John Cornford, and many others. For a superb overview, see Valentine Cunningham, *British Writers of the Thirties* (Oxford: Oxford University Press, 1989).

[2] Unless indicated otherwise, Auden's poetry is quoted from W. H. Auden, *Selected Poems: Expanded Edition*, ed. Edward Mendelson (London: Faber & Faber, 2009), which prints the poems as they were originally published; here 95.

[3] MacNeice's poems are quoted from Louis MacNeice, *Selected Poems*, ed. Michael Longley (London: Faber & Faber, 1988); here 23.

Stephen Spender'), he is remarkable for his conviction that, in an age of political extremes, fidelity to subjective experience has a unique value.[4] Indeed, Gunn himself shows more than a smack of Spender in later work: 'My Sad Captains' reads as a pared-down, syllabic version of 'I think continually of those who were truly great': both poems conclude in mutedly elegiac fashion with comparable images, Spender recalling those who 'left the vivid air signed with their honour', Gunn admiring his heroes as they 'withdraw to an orbit | and turn with disinterested | hard energy, like the stars'.[5] Spender's commitment to humanist uncertainty has been influential: 'he had not been born for dogma' was MacNeice's tight-lipped compliment about his fellow poet's falling out with the British Communist Party over the latter's play *Trial of a Judge*, a compliment repeated with muted satisfaction by Spender himself. In his essay, 'Poetry and Revolution', Spender asserts, near the end, that 'The majority of artists today are forced to remain individualists in the sense of the individualist who expresses nothing except his feeling for his own individuality, his isolation'.[6] In some ways, through his 'feeling for his own individuality, his isolation', Spender is an exemplary figure, who has exercised greater influence than is often conceded.

At the same time, while he wears his regard for uniqueness with a unique difference, Spender's concerns find reflections in Auden and MacNeice. As Edward Mendelson has recently observed, Auden believed that a poet should possess a 'personal voice...unique to the person who spoke it'. Yet this belief is accompanied by the awareness, for Auden, that 'the only way anyone learns to speak is by imitating other people's voices'.[7] MacNeice, for his part, champions the individual self whilst allowing for its continual ambivalence. He is often a poet of the self's near-dissolutions into shadows, reflections, discovering his unnervingly virtual other in a poem such as 'Reflections': 'there I am', he writes, 'standing back to my back' (138), making a discovery of the self's alienated otherness echoed in many other poems.[8]

The essay is organized into two main sections, focusing, in turn, on Auden and then, more briefly, on MacNeice and, much more briefly still, on Spender as poets in their own right and as shapers of the work of others. Throughout, influence is understood to cover a wide range of phenomena: from direct imitation to fostering a climate favourable to the production of particular kinds of poetry.

---

[4] Thom Gunn, 'Lines for a Book', *Collected Poems* (London: Faber & Faber, 1993), 56.

[5] All quotations from Spender's poetry are taken from Stephen Spender, *New Collected Poems*, ed. Michael Brett (London: Faber & Faber, 2004), here 17 (correcting a typographical error in the last line which mistakenly reads 'singed' for 'signed'); Gunn, *Collected Poems*, 129.

[6] Stephen Spender, *The Thirties and After: Poetry, Politics, People 1933–1975* (London: Fontana, 1978), 33; MacNeice's comment, 53.

[7] Edward Mendelson, 'W. H. Auden', in Claude Rawson (ed.), *The Cambridge Companion to English Poets* (Cambridge: Cambridge University Press, 2011), 508.

[8] See Edna Longley, 'The Room Where MacNeice Wrote "Snow"', in *The Living Steam: Literature and Revisionism in Ireland* (Newcastle upon Tyne: Bloodaxe Books, 1994); she notes of 'Reflections' that, in it, 'a solipsistic hall of mirrors...dissolves [the poet's]identity', 269.

I

'We never step twice into the same Auden', joked Randall Jarrell in 1941, and his legacy to later poets includes formal variety and nimbleness of ideological stance.[9] In the 1930s alone, Auden published post-Wordsworthian blank verse, meditations in rhymed stanzas, ballads, sonnets, irregular odes, sestinas, songs. Throughout the thirties, he was the sombre yet zestful analyst of capitalism's woes. The poetry implies, through images of illness or aberration, the presence of sickness in society and the need for 'the destruction of error' (part IV of 'It was Easter as I walked in the public gardens' (13)). Auden can be seen embracing this doom-mongering with a keen enthusiasm in a poem such as 'Consider this and in our time', whose appeal lies in portentous images and a seemingly omniscient perspective, as its opening lines indicate:

Consider this and in our time
As the hawk sees it or the helmeted airman:
The clouds rift suddenly—look there
At cigarette-end smouldering on a border
At the first garden party of the year. (16)

These lines suggest why Auden would exercise such sway over his contemporaries and later poets. 'Consider' adapts quasi-biblical admonition to its own socio-economic vision, a vision equated with that of 'the hawk' or the 'helmeted airman'. Ted Hughes's 'Hawk Roosting' finds a precursor text here, even as Auden looks back to an all-surveying gaze he associated with Thomas Hardy and implies a ratiocinative power of which Hughes is often wary. A phrase such as 'helmeted airman' suggests the coexistence of the ancient and the modern: the modern 'airman' appears as though some 'helmeted' warrior from the *Iliad*. That air of covering in the same panoptic glance the contemporary and the near-mythical owes something to Eliot, but it is less expressive than is sometimes the apparent case in Eliot of a satirical view of the present. Whereas Eliot is suffused with elegiac foreboding in *The Waste Land*, Auden is tonally mobile, poker-faced, and yet capable of a high-spirited verve in the face of economic crashes and forebodings of war. The syntactically taut detail of the 'cigarette-end smouldering on a border | At the first garden party of the year' is typical of his suggestively 'smouldering' effects and tones. The manner is disengaged, superior, knowing (as in those near-swaggering definite articles and the equivocally menacing reference to 'a border').

Above all, this opening adapts its admonitory tone to 'our time', the aftermath of the Wall Street Crash of 1929, and it states emphatically poetry's duty to be relevant to the present. The poem's style synthesizes influences: the alliterative compactness associates

---

[9] Jarrell's remark is the epigraph to an essay of 1941, 'Changes of Attitude and Rhetoric in Auden's Poetry'; quoted from Aidan Wasley, *The Age of Auden: Postwar Poetry and the American Scene* (Princeton: Princeton University Press, 2011), 34.

itself both with Anglo-Saxon poetry and with Hopkins, while the language suggests an analytical intelligence that has assimilated Marx and Freud in its insights into 'England, this country of ours where nobody is well'.[10] Thus, the close of the poem traces 'The convolutions of your simple wish' (itself a phrase that illustrates Auden's air of authority and insight) to their predestined conclusions, as the unwitting 'Seekers after happiness' are condemned 'To disintegrate on an instant in the explosion of mania | Or lapse for ever into a classic fatigue' (17). These lines announce a poet in control of his form, able to lengthen the staple pentameter in a mimesis of 'explosion of mania' or of a yawn associated with 'classic fatigue'.

In his valuable study of Auden's influence on an array of American poets, Aidan Wasley argues that 'Auden advances upon Eliot's formulation of poetic influence by introducing the question of choice, one of his touchstone themes', quoting the poet's remark in *The Dyer's Hand* that 'Originality... means a capacity to find in any work of any date or place a clue to finding one's authentic voice. The burden of choice and selection is put squarely upon the shoulders of each individual poet and it is a heavy one'.[11] In his own practice, Auden suggests such a process of 'choice and selection', and it is among his legacies to poets that he sharpens awareness of this process. He returns, as noted, to Anglo-Saxon poetry, drawing on a line from 'Wulf and Eadwacer' to conclude an unrhymed sonnet that depicts the poet as a 'trained spy': 'Control of the passes was, he saw, the key | To this new district, but who would get it'. The 'he' is both aware and powerless; the 'key' seems to lie in the hands of hostile forces, 'Parting easily who were never joined' (5).[12] The poem might almost ironize the very 'choice' that Auden preaches, and among his own most influential bequests has been the interplay between a poet in apparent formal control and subject matter that suggests absence of control. 'We are lived by powers we pretend to understand', a line from his elegy for Ernst Toller, analyses and enacts this duality; the line's tone and diction are calm and incisive, verging on the epigrammatic; the meaning directs us towards our status as puppets pretending to be agents.[13]

In his 'Letter to Lord Byron' he wittily refuses to use the ottava rima form deployed by the Romantic poet in his most famous poems (such as *Beppo* and *Don Juan*) for fear he 'should come a cropper'. Instead, he writes his admiring yet critical epistle to Byron in rhyme royal, Chaucer's stanza in *Troilus and Criseyde*. Auden gleefully reads Wordsworthian mountaineering as incipiently a form of proto-fascist egotism; he is glad that he has Byron's warrant for finding the poet of the Lake District a 'most bleak old bore', even as the use of 'bleak', a word deployed with force by Wordsworth, pays a backhanded compliment to the Romantic poet. At the same time, he refuses entirely

---

[10] W. H. Auden, *The Orators*, *The English Auden: Poems, Essays, and Dramatic Writings, 1927–1939*, ed. Edward Mendelson (London: Faber & Faber, 1977), 62.

[11] Wasley, *Age of Auden*, 96.

[12] For the allusion, see John Fuller, *A Reader's Guide to W. H. Auden* (London: Thames and Hudson, 1970), 33–4.

[13] W. H. Auden, *Collected Poems*, ed. Edward Mendelson (London: Faber & Faber, 1976), 199; for the discussion of agency and puppetry, see Wasley, *Age of Auden* on James Merrill's response to Auden, esp. 90–2.

to let Byron off the hook of the charge that he might be found 'at the head of his storm-troopers', though the subsequent assertion, 'Injustice you had always hatred for', brings one closer to Auden's view and to his own concern with justice.[14]

Among others, Tom Paulin has been an adept inheritor of the mantle of ideological critique; indeed, his early advocacy in 'A New Society' of 'an order that's unaggressively civilian' has more than a little in common with the later Auden who praises Terminus 'for giving us games and grammar and metres' (304), while Paulin's own subsequent work argues with the Auden who turns away from poetry as political agency.[15] Paulin's dialectical bent is Yeatsian in inspiration, the practice of a poet making poetry out of a quarrel with himself, but he also calls Auden to mind as promoter and antagonist in his 'Where Art is a Midwife'. With humorous effectiveness, Paulin evokes censors learning 'about literature', in order to decode threats against the state. His poem takes issue with the Auden, who in 'New Year Letter' asserts, much as he does in his elegy for Yeats, that 'Art is not life and cannot be | A midwife to society'.[16] Auden's convoluted argument in the following lines does not quite clinch his case; if art builds its 'abstract model of events | Derived from past experiments', it is for readers to 'decide | To what and how it be applied'.

Derek Mahon, too, has learned how to construct poems with what, in *The Double Man*, Auden calls 'an awareness of the dialectic'.[17] His poem on barbarism and art, 'The Snow Party', turns, as John Redmond also notes in 'Auden in Ireland' (Chapter 34), on the same word ('elsewhere') that Auden uses as the conclusion of 'The Fall of Rome': Auden imagines, in an alternative to the civic and the urban, with their corruption and angst, how 'Altogether elsewhere, vast | Herds of reindeer move across | Miles and miles of golden moss, | Silently and very fast' (189). It is among the most ecologically pure imaginings in twentieth-century poetry. Mahon in many poems is addicted, however ironically, to a return to nature and silence after the collapse of capitalism and industry. In 'The Snow Party' he reverses Auden's perspective; 'Elsewhere' in Mahon's poem locates a place where 'they are burning | Witches and heretics | In the boiling squares'. But he returns to Auden's own final vision of silence in his concluding tribute to the 'silence | In the houses of Nagoya | And the hills of Ise'.[18]

At the same time, Auden's refusal to be pinned down in a poem such as 'The Fall of Rome' is characteristic: he may yearn for the pure silence of nature; he knows that human beings are more likely to dwell in cities. This 'awareness of the dialectic' bequeaths its own legacy, one that does much to explain the success of possibly the most plurally contextualized tribute to him, Paul Muldoon's '7, Middagh Street'. Muldoon, in fact, brings

---

[14] *The English Auden*, 172, 183, 180.
[15] Tom Paulin, *A State of Justice* (London: Faber & Faber, 1977), 19.
[16] Qted from Paul Keegan (ed.), *The Penguin Book of English Verse* (London: Penguin, 2004), 1069; 'New Year Letter' from Auden, *Collected Poems*, ed. Mendelson, 162.
[17] Cited in Wasley, *Age of Auden*, 14.
[18] Derek Mahon, *Collected Poems* (Loughcrew: Gallery Press, 1999), 63.

Auden into connection with MacNeice in his poem, which makes capital out of the superabundance of talented, idiosyncratic people dwelling with Auden in 7 Middagh Street in New York; they include Gypsy Rose Lee (the burlesque artist), Chester Kallman (Auden's lover), Salvador Dalí, Benjamin Britten, and Louis MacNeice. The poem begins with 'Wystan', but ends with 'Louis', allowed something that resembles, without having the absolute authority of, the last word in accord with MacNeice's own rejection of Auden's view that 'poetry makes nothing happen':[19] 'It is an historical fact that art *can* make things happen and Auden in his reaction from a rigid Marxism seems... to have been straying towards the Ivory Tower.'[20] MacNeice will be the subject of fuller discussion in the chapter's second half, but Muldoon's collocation of the two voices is attuned to their intimacies and distance: Auden almost dogmatically recommending uncertainty, yet aware, as his Kierkegaardian villanelle has it, 'Look if you like, but you will have to leap' ('Leap before You Look' (123)); MacNeice, with tentative robustness, committed to art as its own kind of moral action, and ventriloquized by Muldoon as asserting: 'For poetry *can* make things happen—| not only can, but *must*.' As interpreted by Muldoon, the work of art for MacNeice is 'in itself a political gesture', Muldoon's rhyme of 'gesture' with 'oyster' highlights the gestural nature of art in a way that brings out the potentially hollow theatricality of 'gesture'.[21] Yet the 'gesture' is 'a way of happening'; thus refuting, as, indeed, Auden's elegy for Yeats itself finally refutes, the belief that, in a negative sense, 'poetry makes nothing happen'.

At the close of Auden's 'Journey to Iceland', a journey undertaken with MacNeice, he depicts the artist turning to art as a hurt person turns to a refuge: 'again the writer | Runs howling to his art' (51). MacNeice, for his part, in 'Postscript to Iceland', sets the trochaic verve of his quatrains in dramatic tension with loneliness and fear, concluding: 'Our prerogatives as men | Will be cancelled who knows when; | Still I drink your health before |The gun-butt raps upon the door' (36). For all its inventive hi-jinks, *Moon Country* by Simon Armitage and Glyn Maxwell, in which the two younger poets revisit Iceland in homage to their forebears, never manages to braid response to politics and revelations of feeling with the same force. If *Moon Country* seems often to be an exuberant exercise, it reminds us, by contrast, that Auden and MacNeice turn their exercises into a full-scale campaign.[22] David Herd, commenting on his sense of the only partial success of *Moon Country*, argues that to read the book is 'to feel the lack of a strong

---

[19] See Edna Longley, 'The Room Where MacNeice Wrote "Snow"', for the view that 'it may not be quite accurate to say that "7, Middagh Street" *has* a last word', given that 'Its form is that of a corona', 265.

[20] Louis MacNeice, *The Poetry of W. B. Yeats* (1941; London: Faber & Faber, 1967); see Edna Longley, *Louis MacNeice: A Study* (London: Faber & Faber, 1988), 41 for insightful discussion.

[21] Paul Muldoon, *Poems, 1968–1998* (London: Faber & Faber, 2001), 192. See Peter Robinson, *Poetry, Poets, Readers: Making Things Happen* (Oxford: Oxford University Press, 2002), esp. ch. 2, for a detailed and nuanced account of the issues at stake in Auden's elegy for Yeats.

[22] Simon Armitage and Glyn Maxwell, *Moon Country: Further Reports from Iceland* (London: Faber, 1996), 104–5.

public voice in mainstream British poetry'.[23] Certainly Auden provides an act that is hard to follow, and yet he has inspired valuable public poetry. His sonnet sequence *In Time of War* reconceives a form associated with love as one suited to the destruction of love which is war. The sonnets set the Sino-Japanese conflict in a long perspective of human imperfection and, indeed, human possibility; the sub-theme of the poet's role runs through them, sometimes prompting historical summary, as in sonnet VII, where the estrangement of the poet is brought out (he 'looked at men and did not like them' (75)), sometimes assuming a Rilkean jubilation: 'Certainly praise: let song mount again and again | For life as it blossoms out' (XIII; 78).

Yet this poem turns from celebratory post-Romanticism to the social responsibility which, whatever Auden's later twistings and turnings, remains among his major bequests to British poets: 'But hear the morning's injured weeping, and know why' (78). In many ways, a distillation of Auden's thirties poetry, the sequence shows how a poet can speak to his time: 'maps can really point to places | Where life is evil now: | Nanking; Dachau' (XVI; 80). Such geopolitical awareness transcends national culture, an intimation of the 'post-nationalist' poet discerned and valued by Wasley.[24] The poem implies that not only can maps point to places 'Where life is evil now', but that it has a duty to point in such a way. Whilst this portentous truth-saying seems to be set aside by Auden's later belittling of poetry's pretensions, it is arguable that his assumption of a wryly Horatian manner can never wholly disguise the impulse to preach he finds discreditable in himself.

In Time of War suggests, too, how the metronomic swing of the iamb can mimic technology's frightening takeover in modern society, even as it marshals a vigilance necessary to fight against it: 'A telephone is speaking to a man' is how the same sonnet's second line reads, but Auden forcefully affirms the centrality of human experience as the poem continues: there may be 'a plan || For living men in terror of their lives' (80), yet 'living' reminds us of their shared and essential humanity. This reminder is curbed, though not abolished, by the poem's swerve into the recognition that 'ideas' have a life and a meaning of their own. When James Fenton writes 'In a Notebook', his elegy for events in South-East Asia, he recalls Auden's thirties political manner. But, much as he reworks Auden's capacity for poignant light verse (in, say, 'Funeral Blues') to create his own affecting versions of song-like pathos (as in 'Nothing'), so here he uses his predecessor's manner to achieve his own 'authentic voice'. Fenton's ottava rima may include a nod towards Yeats, but, as he distinguishes between three stanzas in italics which purport to have been found 'In a Notebook', and two in roman type which bring the uneasy idyll to a bitter end, Auden's creative influence can be felt. It is less a matter of diction than of stance. Even here influence is far from imitation. Auden assumes a near-omniscient tone; Fenton advertises the presence of masked subjectivity. The first person appears as

---

[23] David Herd, 'Two Go Back to Poets' Island', *The Independent*, 10 Nov. 1996; [www.independent.co.uk]; accessed 13 Apr. 2012.

[24] See Wasley for the view that Auden's elegy for Yeats and his 1940s work 'provided a vital example in writing poetry that can best be described as "post-national"', 74.

both innocent and blinkered in the final italicized stanza: '*And I sat drinking bitter coffee wishing | The tide would turn and bring me to my senses | After the pleasant war and the evasive answers.*'²⁵ The 'wish' seems a fatal one, since an unpleasant war will bring him to his senses at the close, where the poetic self reads his notebook entry now that 'The villages are burnt, the cities void':

And I'm afraid, reading this passage now,
That everything I know has been destroyed
By those whom I admired but never knew;
The laughing soldiers fought to their defeat
And I'm afraid most of my friends are dead.

The idiom of English reticence ('I'm afraid' is often used as what might be called hyperbolic understatement) recalls the tight-lipped style employed by early Auden, a poet who is, one feels, 'Always afraid to say more than he meant' ('From the very first coming down' (4)).²⁶ Fenton's sound effects, too, serve semantic purposes in ways typical of Auden. His use of assonance and off-rhyme bring to mind Auden's development of Owenesque techniques of pararhyme. So, here, 'now' passes into 'know' and then 'destroyed', 'knew', 'fought', and 'most': a cunning sequence of interlinked sounds that suggests how what has happened 'now' has meant that everything the poet can be said to 'know' has been 'destroyed | By those whom I admired but never knew'. As a result those whom he did 'know' have 'fought to their defeat', and, close to the bone, 'most of my friends are dead'.

Fenton's narrator hints at his own muffled complicity in the destruction the poem laments.²⁷ 'In a Notebook' senses on its pulses an awareness Fenton ascribes to Auden that 'The symbol has revolted, the daydream has disobeyed. And this, as Auden knew, was something that must always eventually happen'.²⁸ The subject of complicity—of the entwining of the private and the public—is among Auden's central thirties themes, illustrated by the movement of 'Out on the lawn I lie in bed': a seemingly innocuous line that suggests how even at its most private the self is part of a public space. In the poem, Auden gives thanks for his personal good fortune ('Lucky, this point in time and space' (30)), including the experience of idyll-like enchantment that he experiences with friends in the evening; yet, as he looks at the moon, the poem's scope expands. 'She climbs the European sky' (31), he asserts, a line in which the adjective warns unhectoringly of present and coming troubles, and he goes on to incriminate himself and his

---

[25] Quoted from Keegan (ed.), *The Penguin Book of English Verse*, 1060–1.

[26] Gareth Reeves, in the course of a fine reading of the poem, comments that the line in question is 'all the more arresting for its under-spokenness', '"This Is Plenty, This Is More Than Enough": Poetry and the Memory of the Second World War' [oxfordhb-9780199559602-e-31], in Tim Kendall (ed.), *The Oxford Handbook of British and Irish War Poetry* (Oxford: Oxford University Press, 2007), 587.

[27] See Joe Moran, 'Out of the East: James Fenton and Contemporary History', *Literature and History*, 9/2 (2000), 53–69 (esp. 59–61).

[28] James Fenton, 'Auden on Shakespeare's Sonnets', in *The Strength of Poetry* (Oxford: Oxford University Press, 2001), 208.

friends unsparingly of indifference to public crisis; they may be 'gentle' (31), but the word serves more to stigmatize their upper-class status than to indicate their capacity for kindness since they 'do not care to know, | Where Poland draws her Eastern bow, | What violence is done' (31). Moreover, closer to home, they do not 'ask what doubtful act allows | Our freedom in this English house, | Our picnics in the sun' (31–2). The urbane conversational voice, housed within a tight lyrical form, deftly suggests connections and contrasts. Personal good suddenly seems like public wrong; valued, near-epiphanic moments emerge as sneered-at 'picnics in the sun' when seen as the product of unfair social privilege. Auden balances the poem's feelings in a pair of scales whose pans tremble without being overset; he concludes with a metaphor of revolution as a cleansing flood that will sweep away unfairness, yet he pleads that what he values about the present may be permitted to survive into the imagined utopian future, doing so through an image of parental voices heard amidst 'a child's rash happy cries' (33). The image is expertly managed, suffused with longing and hope, aware of its own contrivance.

The resulting 'unlamenting song' (33) sets a standard for many subsequent socially aware poems to try to reach. In 'Modern Love', Douglas Dunn alludes in his title to Meredith's sequence of sonnets about unhappy love, contrasting it with the domestic contentment expressed in the poem. But the setting and the tone are written in the long shadows cast by Auden's poem. 'It is summer, and we are in a house | That is not ours'.[29] What marks it as a poem of the 1970s rather than 1930s is Dunn's tactful caution about any Audenesque panoramic gesture, a caution the more striking because elsewhere Dunn shows himself to be a poet capable of vigorous polemic, able to voice the 'child's rash happy cries'. In 'Gardeners', Dunn imagines with sententious humour overthrowing an unjust status quo, anticipating how 'Townsmen will wonder', come the revolution, 'We did not raze this garden that we made, | Although we hanged you somewhere in its shade'.[30] The couplets, there, have the skilled accomplishment of the light verse which Auden likes to adapt to serious themes. But 'Modern Love' refuses to move beyond its confines, even while knowing that those confines are there to be moved beyond: 'Our lives flap', Dunn observes in laconic style, as though the lives flapped in the desultory breeze of self-concern, and yet he continues by implying the real if modest value of what he calls 'domestic love': 'and we have no hope of better | Happiness than this'. An anti-Utopian note is struck there, by way of Larkin's 'Mr Bleaney' (compare 'having no more to show' in its final stanza), as though rebuking Auden's self-condemnatory impulse.[31] Dunn refuses Auden's class guilt.

Again, Andrew Motion, who in 'Letter to an Exile' addresses an unspecified figure with the half-reproach, 'but you had visible danger—Spain waiting, | Europe waiting', articulates in 'Anne Frank Huis' his own version of Auden's dialectic between private

---

[29] Douglas Dunn, *Selected Poems 1964–1983* (London: Faber & Faber, 1986), 51.
[30] Dunn, *Selected Poems*, 106.
[31] Philip Larkin, *Collected Poems*, ed. Anthony Thwaite (London: Faber & Faber with the Marvell Press, 1988), 102.

and public, and his precursor poet's emphasis on chance.[32] Thus, Motion leaves a house which is haunted by Anne Frank's terrifying, never-mentioned fate 'with one enduring wish for chances | like my own'. The poem is Audenesque yet perfectly new; it employs a diction which blends 'wish' with implicit analysis of the way in which that wish is conditioned and conditional upon 'chances', pointed up by Motion's positioning of the word at the line-ending in the revised version in *Selected Poems 1976–1997*; earlier, the break had occurred after 'like'. Where Motion recalls Spender more than Auden is the way in which he uses 'I' in the poem. When he articulates his lucky chance as the ability 'to leave as simply | as I do, and walk at ease', he both foregrounds the sense of individual self and leaves potently submerged the larger idea behind the poem.[33] Auden will typically use the word 'I' in a context that immediately locates the self in a world where it has social obligations: 'All I have is a voice | To undo the folded lie' ('September 1, 1939' (97)). In 'Alone', he questions the self-sufficient reality of the self, 'Perhaps, in fact, we never are alone'.[34] Spender, too, questions the reality of the self in 'An "I" can never be great man' (6), but his major lesson to later poets is to put into practice one of Auden's own dicta from 'Writing': 'Some writers confuse authenticity, which they ought always to aim at, with originality, which they should never bother about.'[35] Spenderian authenticity often takes the form of accepting the self's limited vantage-point, while suggesting that such limits might possibly be an intense form of focalization.

At the same time, Motion's career involves attempted escapes from the possibly limiting authenticity supplied by the self, and he experiments with secret and overt narratives in which attention is given, in explicit or implicit fashion, to poetry as a mode of representation. 'Bathing at Glymenopoulo', placed directly after 'Anne Frank Huis' in his anthology co-edited with Blake Morrison, uses 'I' differently; here, the gap between poet and 'I' opens in that the latter is evidently not the former, yet it narrows, too, in the way in which composing poet seems at times to impinge on the identity of supposedly fictive narrator, 'Iras, I have you by heart, giggling'. At such moments, one can watch a contemporary poet seek to find his way forwards from a legacy bequeathed by thirties poetry: a way forward through an obstacle-ridden territory that might be mapped as 'History' and 'the Self'.

As they seek to negotiate this territory, poets continually respond to Auden. His influence is evident in many poems of dissent and homage. The most famous of these is Donald Davie's 'Remembering the 'Thirties', which serves as a manifesto of the Movement's recoil from grand gestures and as a rebuke of this recoil. 'A neutral tone is nowadays preferred' uses its passive voice to disavow commitment to neutrality, and prefaces a raising of two cheers at least for the ability 'To find the stance impressive

---

[32] 'Letter to an Exile', *The Pleasure Steamers* (Manchester: Carcanet Press, 1978), 12.
[33] Cited, as is the next Motion poem, from Andrew Motion, *Selected Poems 1976–1997* (London: Faber & Faber, 1998), 16, 25.
[34] Cited from *Collected Poems*, ed. Mendelson, 244.
[35] W. H. Auden, *The Dyer's Hand* (London: Faber & Faber, 1963), 19.

and absurd | Than not to see the hero for the dust'. Debunking 'An idiom too dated, Audenesque' may lead us to 'miss the point'.³⁶ 'Impressive and absurd': Auden, one may feel, is too nimble-footed ever to seem 'absurd', and yet the Movement radar registered supposedly portentous or potentially pretentious effects with hypersensitive alertness. Larkin finds Auden to be a poet 'committed', as few others have been, 'to [his] period', that period being the thirties with its 'dominant and ubiquitous unease'.³⁷ But Auden, one of 'boyhood's heroes' for Larkin, continues to function as a presence in poems by the later poet such as 'Ambulances', where Auden's way of speaking to and for a shared sense of isolation and necessarily 'cut off' perspective finds a fresh incarnation.³⁸

Larkin expressed his disappointment that Auden's *For the Time Being* (1945) seemed to 'be blown up by words & ideas, instead of reduced to mortal perspective by feelings'.³⁹ Those 'mortal' feelings, however, rely for their expression in Larkin, more than he acknowledges, on his reading of a poet whose most famous love-poem concedes both his faithlessness and his feelings for a 'living creature' who is 'Mortal guilty, but to me | The entirely beautiful' ('Lay your sleeping head, my love' (53)).⁴⁰ More generously, Elizabeth Jennings concludes her 'Elegy for W. H. Auden' with the single line, separated from the unrhyming tercets of the rest of the poem, 'The Sea stands still but your landscape moves', acknowledging, by way of an allusion to *The Sea and the Mirror*, how Auden himself changed and changed the poetic landscape for others.⁴¹ The poem 'Lines for W. H. Auden: 21st February, 2007', 'read out' at a Christ Church College 'Celebration of W. H. Auden' and written, one infers, by Peter McDonald, moves between affectionate address and wider generalization; it evokes Auden's gifts to later poets, including the way in which 'with one phrase or a rhythm, you might have evoked in an instant | the day as it was here, deep in a winter routine', and it captures a style of Audenesque reflection on which poets such as Peter Porter have been able to draw: 'The future, doubtless, will make as little sense as the present, | and we should never expect too much of the past.'⁴² If the mocked Eliot of Henry Reed's 'Chard Whitlow' seems briefly to be an inspiration here, the poem also recalls the later Auden for whom, in Heaney's words, 'the line is doctrinaire in its domesticity, wanting to comfort like a thread of wool rather than shock like a bare wire'.⁴³ In Auden, slackening often gives way to tautness, as in 'Under

---

³⁶ Cited from Robert Conquest (ed.), *New Lines: An Anthology* (1956; London: Macmillan, 1967), 72, 71.

³⁷ Cited from Paul Hendon, *The Poetry of W. H. Auden: A Reader's Guide to Essential Criticism* (Cambridge: Icon, 2000), 108.

³⁸ *Selected Letters of Philip Larkin*, ed. Anthony Thwaite (London: Faber & Faber, 1992), 460. For 'cut off', see 'Who stands, the crux left of the watershed', 3.

³⁹ *Selected Letters of Philip Larkin*, 127.

⁴⁰ For further discussion of the two poets, see Nicholas Jenkins, 'The "Truth of Skies": Auden, Larkin and the English Question', in Zachary Leader (ed.), *The Movement Reconsidered: Essays on Larkin, Amis, Gunn, Davie, and Their Contemporaries* (Oxford: Oxford University Press, 2009).

⁴¹ Elizabeth Jennings, *Collected Poems* (Manchester: Carcanet, 1986), 125.

⁴² [http://www.towerpoetry.org.uk]; accessed 9 April 2012.

⁴³ Seamus Heaney, 'Sounding Auden', in *Finders Keepers: Selected Prose 1971–2001* (London: Faber & Faber, 2002), 197.

Which Lyre: A Reactionary Tract for the Times', of which John Fuller writes: 'There are a number of good academic jokes, appropriate to the poem's occasion, but it survives, with a sympathetic insistence, its witty after-dinner tone.'[44]

Auden's way of framing a subject as a topic for thought has been creatively enabling, not merely an occasion for poetic wool-gathering. When Derek Mahon makes a paysage moralisé out of a disused shed in County Wexford, his mode is, initially, Audenesque, even as difference (with at least the Auden of 'In Praise of Limestone') emerges by the end, as John Redmond notes in 'Auden in Ireland' (Chapter 34). Mahon's poem reaches out in a fantastical, saddened metaphor to convert a shed of mushrooms into the 'Lost people of Treblinka and Pompeii'.[45] In his poem, Auden is determined to avoid extremes, noting that 'The best and worst never stayed here long' (190).

In other poems, Mahon has learned something of Auden's capacity for an extended cultural span of vision; 'The Hunt by Night', for example, turns Uccello's painting into a point of departure for a desperate, elegant meditation on the human condition, referring to 'a cave | Where man the maker killed to live'.[46] If the paradox of 'man the maker' killing in order to live duplicates effects in Auden, such as the description in 'Spain' of 'the | Fumbled and unsatisfactory embrace before hurting' (57), the vast scale of reference brings to mind Auden's delight in switching from present to past and back again as though millennia were linked, mere blinks of an eye; so in 'Moon Landing', he shrugs syllabic and half-disdainful shoulders at mankind's (and for Auden it is *man*kind's) latest 'phallic triumph': 'from the moment || the first flint was flaked this landing was merely | a matter of time' (307). 'St Mark's Square', section X of *The Hudson Letter* pays graceful tribute in its loose-limbed couplets to Auden: 'you remind us of what the examined life involves— | for what you teach is the courage to be ourselves, | however ridiculous'. Mahon concedes that Auden may have been 'often silly', much as Auden told Yeats, 'You were silly like us', but he admires his forebear for being to able to

> prescribe a cure
> for our civilization and its discontents
> based upon *agapè*, baroque opera, common sense
> and the abstract energy that brought us here,
> sustaining us now as we face a more boring future.[47]

Mahon sees Auden, in essentials, as Auden saw Freud, that is, as a healer. But he also sees him as an embodiment of entertaining miscellany, a devotee of 'baroque opera' and a champion of 'common sense'. His career bears witness, too, to 'abstract energy', 'abstract' suggesting an energy that is not satisfied by an immediate, 'concrete' 'purpose', but has a role that is 'sustaining', even as we face a 'more boring future'.[48] The let-down in the final

---

[44] Fuller, *A Reader's Guide to W. H. Auden*, 185.
[45] Mahon, *Collected Poems*, 90.
[46] Mahon, *Collected Poems*, 150.
[47] Mahon, *Collected Poems*, 204.
[48] For further discussion of this section of *The Hudson Letter*, see Hugh Haughton, *The Poetry of Derek Mahon* (Oxford: Oxford University Press, 2007), 244–5.

phrase suggests that Auden stands, in Mahon's mind, for those many other writers who won an answerable style from the prospect of despair.

And such a style allows for a wit and verve that not all readers of Auden have wholly appreciated. Geoffrey Hill has sought, as poet and critic, to demonstrate a critical vigilance about his own and others' use of language. In a discussion of Auden's 'In Memory of W. B. Yeats', he objects to the clause 'where executives | Would never want to tamper' (which follows the assertion that poetry 'survives | In the valley of its saying') as 'an error'; it supposedly 'trivializes...the activities of the world of commerce and commodity' and also 'the various ways in which the overreachings and shortcomings of business values might be met in justice'.[49] The clash is a fascinating one. Hill recalls Leavis's worry about Auden's alleged 'combination of seriousness and flippancy'.[50] Auden's lines, for their part, resist Hill's would-be magisterial reproof. Auden is a poet aware of the significance of finance, of how the world is shaped by 'brokers...roaring like beasts on the floor of the Bourse', to borrow a line from the close of the first part of 'In Memory of W. B. Yeats'. His lines do not so much 'trivialize' as suggest that there are those to whom 'the valley of [poetry's] saying' will seem so trivial that they would not wish to 'tamper' with it. Meeting 'in justice' the spheres of poetry and 'commerce and commodity' phrases a desired ideal in an idiom that risks being strained; Auden's modes of justice depend often on grace, urbanity, the discipline of a poetry increasingly suspicious, as he puts it in 'Ode to Terminus', of 'self-proclaimed poets who, to wow an | audience, utter some resonant lie', of 'our colossal immodesty' (304). His varieties of scepticism about poetry form a bracing alternative to, as well as the indirect inspiration for, Hill's investigations into the proprieties of poetic and critical discourse.

Seamus Heaney derives eloquence from his belief in 'what Auden once called "the mass and majesty" of the reality we inhabit and should be measuring up to—"all | That carries weight and always weighs the same" '. 'The Shield of Achilles', from which Heaney quotes, shows for him the fact that 'Cadence with a head of intelligence and strong shoulders of syntax still has a lot of carrying power'. What Heaney is arguing in favour of is a poetry that will not accept a 'reduced power of speech', but can move from ordinary speech into what he credits Mahon with: 'a magniloquence that has high canonical sanction'.[51] And one of those canonical sanctioners is Auden. The process can be seen at work in many of Heaney's poems that seek to combine both the 'rich' and the 'strange' (for him early Auden offers the more valuable latter, later Auden the impressive former).[52] In 'A Stove Lid for W. H. Auden', he takes as his epigraph the lines from 'The Shield of Achilles' that

---

[49] Geoffrey Hill, 'Language, Suffering, and Silence', in *Collected Critical Writings*, ed. Kenneth Haynes (Oxford: Oxford University Press, 2008), 405.

[50] Cited from Hendon, *The Poetry of W. H. Auden: A Reader's Guide to Essential Criticism*, 61.

[51] Dennis O'Driscoll, *Stepping Stones: Interviews with Seamus Heaney* (London: Faber & Faber, 2008), 196, 197.

[52] Heaney, *Finders Keepers*, 199.

he mentions in his interview, 'The mass and majesty of this world, all | That carries weight and always weighs the same', using a 'cast-iron stove lid' as his befitting emblem of such 'mass and majesty'. As he describes the stove-lid, Heaney seems to celebrate his own poetry's wish to pay homage to things, in this case a thing that brings to mind 'The fit and weight and danger as it bore | The red hot solidus to one side of the stove'. Auden's poem describes the danger of militarized dehumanization directly; it also, in the stanzas depicting Hephaestos' work, suggests the artist's amoral commitment to representation of what is, here 'An artificial wilderness | And a sky like lead' (206). Both poets, that is, deal with an artist's commitment to and possible complicity in 'being'. Auden's forger cannot prettify the bald facts; Heaney's poetry serves, if the stove-lid is read as an image of its own activity, as a means of embodying and coping with life's 'fit and weight and danger'. As 'hell-mouth stopper, flat-earth disc', the stove-lid stands for an obdurate trust in the value of poetry, one in accord with the final line's injunction to 'Think of dark matter in the starlit coalhouse'.[53] Heaney's preference for a poetry that conjoins 'dark matter' with what is 'starlit' has much in common with Auden's judicious weighing of opposites and his sense of humane responsibility. Allied with verve, wit, and formal mastery, these qualities promise to generate much that is new and live in present and future poetry.

II

In a reading whose point of departure and return is Auden's 'Homage to Clio', Muldoon notes how 'History is rather provocatively associated with silence' in poems such as Auden's 'The Fall of Rome', a remark whose provocations include wondering where Muldoon himself stands in relation to history.[54] But he is most responsive to the thirties bequest as it is embodied in MacNeice's poetry, and not just his thirties work, as Edna Longley has shown. Her essay on 'Varieties of Parable' in both poets includes among many other insights the notion that 'If MacNeice's thrust in his later work is to pursue the quest but question it, Muldoon's may be the other way round'. MacNeice's quest takes the form of bleak urban nightmare in 'Charon', where a remorseless syntax and grammar lead to the encounter with 'the ferryman just as Virgil and Dante had seen him', who comments: 'If you want to die you will have to pay for it' (153). Longley is perceptive when she observes both that 'The ferry-terminus of "Charon" is another dead end' and that it sustains 'a cosmic awe, a grasp of the infinite'.[55]

MacNeice's 'grasp of the infinite' has an exhilarating existential bravura. In an earlier poem, 'The Sunlight on the Garden', he uses an intricate patterning of internal rhyme to create a stanzaic cage. The poem parades its virtuosity as it concedes that it cannot hold

---

[53] Seamus Heaney, in *District and Circle* (London: Faber, 2006), 71.
[54] Paul Muldoon, *The End of the Poem: Oxford Lectures in Poetry* (London: Faber & Faber, 2006), 352.
[55] Edna Longley, ' "Varieties of Parable": Louis MacNeice and Paul Muldoon', in *Poetry in the Wars* (Newcastle upon Tyne: Bloodaxe Books, 1986), 235, 237.

'the minute | Within its nets of gold'. Still, as 'Our freedom as free lances | Advances towards its end', MacNeice holds his head high, alluding to *Antony and Cleopatra* ('We are dying, Egypt, dying') with resolution and gladness (38). Derek Mahon, with Michael Longley one of MacNeice's major heirs, salutes such courage in his bravura elegy for the dead poet in 'In Carrowdore Churchyard' (subtitled '*at the grave of Louis MacNeice*'). This elegy gracefully and zestfully obeys a traditional convention when it alludes to the dead poet's work, modulating into a reference to 'Snow': 'This, you implied, is how we ought to live— | The ironical, loving crush of roses against snow, | Each fragile, solving ambiguity'.[56] The verb 'implied' pays tribute to the MacNeice who concludes 'Entirely' with the assertion that 'in brute reality there is no | Road that is right entirely' (70); for its part, 'solving' hesitates between 'resolving' and 'dissolving', much as it does in Larkin's 'glimpse' of 'the solving emptiness | That lies just under all we do' ('Ambulances').[57] The 'crush of roses against snow' economically sums up the imagistic contest and alliance in 'Snow', one that issues in MacNeice's gnomic statement that 'There is more than glass between the snow and the huge roses', which in itself illustrates his influential trick of playing with hackneyed phrases. Michael Longley joins in the allusive game set going by MacNeice when he returns to MacNeice the latter's tribute to Yeats: 'there is nearly always a leaping vitality—the vitality of Cleopatra waiting for the asp'.[58]

During his associative riff on MacNeice in *To Ireland, I*, in a section that takes its title ('Alone Tra-la') from the older poet's 'The Taxis', Muldoon finds 'Snow' to be a poem of 'simultaneous abuttal and rebuttal', and his poems abut onto and half-rebut MacNeicean realms.[59] In response to the 'leaping vitality' of his forebear, one with Shakespearean resonances, he develops intertextual links until they expand across the lake of a poem's surface in endless circles, as occurs in this section from 'Yarrow', which mixes trauma with droll, deadly linguistic play:

'Look on her. Look her lips.
Listen to her *râle*
where ovarian cancer takes her in its strangle-hold'.[60]

Death is mediated by the latest in the poem's allusions to *King Lear*, this time to the moment when Lear seeks to persuade himself that Cordelia still breathes. Muldoon uses the allusion with quietly bitter irony since the woman does still breathe, but with difficulty. The reader listens to the '*râle*', the abnormal respiratory croak of the dying, with a circumspect tension, since in Muldoon we look at his words as much as we look beyond them; the virtual world evoked by words is always likely to be a verbal world. When, two sections later, he corrects himself to say, ' "Ovarian," did I write?

---

[56] Mahon, *Collected Poems*, 17.
[57] For discussion of Larkin's debt to MacNeice, see Stephen Regan, ' "Coming up England by a Different Line" ', in Fran Brearton and Edna Longley (eds.), *Incorrigibly Plural: Louis MacNeice and His Legacy* (Manchester: Carcanet Press, 2012).
[58] Cited at the close of Michael Longley's introduction to *Selected Poems*, p. xxiii.
[59] Muldoon, *To Ireland, I*, 93.
[60] Muldoon, *Poems, 1968-1998*, 387.

Utarine',[61] he corrects his poem in mid-flow in a way that is typical of MacNeice, too, as when the older poet debunks national piety in *Autumn Journal* XVI: 'The land of scholars and saints: | Scholars and saints my eye, the land of ambush, | Purblind manifestoes, never-ending complaints' (62). Yet to quote those lines is to realize how Muldoon eschews direct comment on Ireland in his poetry, preferring to spin a poetic yarn, to speak nearly always in quotation marks. He shares with MacNeice an admiration for Robert Frost, as Edna Longley has argued, especially in relation to their shared interest in syntax. Longley quotes MacNeice's comment in an essay on Frost: 'A sentence in prose is struck forward like a golf ball; a sentence in verse can be treated like a ball in a squash court.'[62] MacNeice, to sustain the metaphor, delights in hammering the ball off all the walls, as at the end of 'Soap Suds', where the poem itself 'Skims forward through the hoop and then through the next and then || Through hoops where no hoops were' (145), in a disorientating way that takes us backwards as much as it zooms us forward; Muldoon deploys the drop shot with deadpan effectiveness; just when we expect the expansive, we get the non-committal, the incremental. So he begins the concluding stanza of 'The Frog' with the lines: 'There is, surely, in this story | A moral. A moral for our times.' The irony of 'surely' is at the expense of those who would search for 'A moral for our times', an oblique dig at the Auden who addressed 'our time'.

As in this poem, Muldoon is often deflating about 'story' and its manipulation by the poet, which does not prevent him from being freewheelingly associative in longer poems. Generally, his language is quick in post-MacNeicean fashion to turn its gaze on its existence as language, as here where he finishes by asking whether he should squeeze the moral out of the frog 'like the juice of freshly squeezed limes, | or a lemon sorbet?'[63] The frog has turned into a metaphor of a metaphor, into a sponsor, too, if not a prince, of the quotidian, as morals metamorphose into a delicious, hedonistic drink. MacNeice is more evidently a haunted poet, even if celebrating 'The drunkenness of things being various' ('Snow' (23)). His language is ready to search out the possibility of lyric epiphany that does not ironize itself, though it may concede its existential ephemerality. An example is 'Selva Oscura', where the Dantean title prepares us for a poem of loss and discovery, each uncannily wearing the features of the other. Both 'Lost in the maze | That means yourself' and on the verge of seeing 'Some unknown house—or was it mine?', the poet is the ancestor of many contemporary writers who compute a calculus of loss and recompense (143). Michael Longley, for example, in 'Aschy' swings with MacNeice-like swiftness (for all the poem's stately movement) between recognition of ageing and delight in a 'weird sanctity' that he associates with 'that tonic called *aschy*'.[64] Assured, but not complacent, the poem's

---

[61] Muldoon, *Poems, 1968–1998*, 388.
[62] Edna Longley, ' "Varieties of Parable" ', 224.
[63] Quoted from Keegan (ed.), *The Penguin Book of English Verse*, 1079.
[64] Michael Longley, *Collected Poems* (London: Cape, 2006), 295.

demeanour recalls the increasingly pragmatic and serendipitous way in which MacNeice was prepared to write poems of which it could be said, of which he said, 'that they found their own form'.[65] Tom Paulin's movement towards a poetry that finds its own form, as in his collection *Walking a Line*, takes to a brilliantly lithe extreme the mercurial side of MacNeice that is fascinated by 'faces balanced in the toppling wave' ('Train to Dublin' (22)). Paulin devises fluidly punctuated, rapid syntax, 'all supporting something with no centre' ('Across the Howrah Bridge').[66] In the volume, he is prepared to talk directly, as indeed MacNeice does in 'Neutrality'. In this poem, MacNeice repudiates the Irish Free State's position in the Second World War in his final rejection of the thirties dream of 'The neutral island', even as he understands the insidious longing to believe that innocence and escape from history are still possible; instead, the island-dreams are 'bitterly soft reminders of the beginnings | That ended before the end began' (95). Paulin's tones are less 'bitterly soft' than sternly bitter in poems such as 'Desertmartin', but, as in MacNeice, direct talk goes hand in hand with delight in the unpredictable.

Paulin speaks for many admirers of MacNeice and says much about his own investment in his predecesor's work when he applauds 'the feeling of unease and displacement' in the older poet's work, which means that 'his imagination is essentially fluid, maritime and elusively free'.[67] He illustrates MacNeice's powers through analysis of 'House on a Cliff', which, with its oscillation between 'Indoors' and 'Outdoors', is at once enclosed and open to mystery. Different as they are from MacNeice, Spender's poems also possess a quality of intransigent fidelity to feeling and a readiness to open out to what in 'Thoughts during an Air-Raid', one of his best poems about the Spanish Civil War, he calls 'that incommunicable grief | Which is all mystery or nothing' (110). Spender has had relatively little significant critical attention, but his poems have stubbornly insinuated themselves into the sensibilities of poets who are determined to write of what they feel, not what they ought to say.[68] His tactic is constantly to register the self's capacity for feeling; the error is to suppose that he automatically condones or uncritically endorses the feeling. Indeed, he is often self-critical, laying bare the self's egotism in poems such as 'My parents kept me from children who were rough'. As in a Blake song, we need to empathetically mistrust the teller of such tales of privileged angst: 'I longed to forgive them, yet they never smiled' (9) is a line inviting judgement as well as, or rather than, sympathy. Tony Harrison's investigations of class struggle in his sonnet sequence 'The School of Eloquence' are complexly Spenderian in their dual

---

[65] 'Louis MacNeice Writes…[on *The Burning Perch*]', in *Selected Literary Criticism of Louis MacNeice*, ed. Alan Heuser (Oxford: Clarendon Press, 1987), 248.
[66] Tom Paulin, *Walking a Line* (London: Faber & Faber, 1994), 85.
[67] 'The Man from No Part: Louis MacNeice', *Ireland and the English Crisis* (Newcastle upon Tyne: Bloodaxe Books, 1984), 75, 76.
[68] For an attempt to redress the balance, see Michael O'Neill and Gareth Reeves, *Auden, MacNeice, Spender: The Thirties Poetry* (Basingstoke: Macmillan, 1992).

attitude to the self; the self who experiences and the self who writes are one another's uncanny, complicity-ridden doubles.[69] Spender has supplied in his practice a model for those who wish to negotiate between traditional and modernist forms; rarely slick, his line is often capable of an incantatory music, as in 'The Double Shame' whose conclusion is heavy with conceded fault: 'And you lacked the confidence to choose | And you have only yourself to blame' (156). For many later lyric poets searching for a mode of credible expression, Spender's 'One More New Botched Beginning', like his career as a whole, might serve as a wry but genuine illustration of the ever-fresh potentialities of poetry. Like MacNeice and Auden, Spender exercises an influence that goes beyond direct echo or allusion; all three poets have become their conscious and unconscious admirers, even if admiration can express itself as apparent inclination to do otherwise or would-be rejection.

SELECT BIBLIOGRAPHY

Armitage, Simon, and Maxwell, Glyn, *Moon Country: Further Reports from Iceland* (London: Faber, 1996).
Astley, Neil (ed.), *Bloodaxe Critical Anthologies 1: Tony Harrison* (Newcastle upon Tyne: Bloodaxe, 1991).
Auden, W. H., *The Dyer's Hand* (London: Faber & Faber, 1963).
Auden, W. H., *Collected Poems*, ed. Edward Mendelson (London: Faber & Faber, 1976).
Auden, W. H., *The Orators, The English Auden: Poems, Essays, and Dramatic Writings, 1927-1939*, ed. Edward Mendelson (London: Faber & Faber, 1977).
Auden, W. H., *Selected Poems: Expanded Edition*, ed. Edward Mendelson (London: Faber & Faber, 2009).
Brearton, Fran, and Longley, Edna (eds.), *Incorrigibly Plural: Louis MacNeice and His Legacy* (Manchester: Carcanet Press, 2012).
Cunningham, Valentine, *British Writers of the Thirties* (Oxford: Oxford University Press, 1989).
Dunn, Douglas, *Selected Poems 1964-1983* (London: Faber & Faber, 1986).
Fenton, James, 'Auden on Shakespeare's Sonnets', in *The Strength of Poetry* (Oxford: Oxford University Press, 2001).
Fuller, John, *A Reader's Guide to W. H. Auden* (London: Thames and Hudson, 1970).
Gunn, Thom, *Collected Poems* (London: Faber & Faber, 1993).
Haughton, Hugh, *The Poetry of Derek Mahon* (Oxford: Oxford University Press, 2007).
Heeney, Seamus, *Finders Keepers: Selected Prose 1971-2001* (London: Faber & Faber, 2002).
Hendon, Paul, *The Poetry of W. H. Auden: A Reader's Guide to Essential Criticism* (Cambridge: Icon, 2000).
Herd, David, 'Two Go Back to Poets' Island', *The Independent*, 10 Nov. 1996; [www.independent.

---

[69] Spender's review of Harrison's *Continuous* is alert to Harrison's dealings with class; in a characteristic way, Spender put himself on the other side ('we snobs') whilst admiring Harrison for the ambiguities present in a line such as 'Poetry's the speech of kings. You're one of those' which Spender points out has a double meaning when the punctuation is omitted': see Stephen Spender, 'Changeling', in Neil Astley (ed.), *Bloodaxe Critical Anthologies 1: Tony Harrison* (Newcastle upon Tyne: Bloodaxe, 1991), 222.

co.uk].

Hill, Geoffrey, 'Language, Suffering, and Silence', in *Collected Critical Writings*, ed. Kenneth Haynes (Oxford: Oxford University Press, 2008).

Jenkins, Nicholas, 'The "Truth of Skies": Auden, Larkin and the English Question', in Zachary Leader (ed.), *The Movement Reconsidered: Essays on Larkin, Amis, Gunn, Davie, and Their Contemporaries* (Oxford: Oxford University Press, 2009), 34–61.

Jennings, Elizabeth, *Collected Poems* (Manchester: Carcanet, 1986).

Keegan, Paul (ed.), *The Penguin Book of English Verse* (London: Penguin, 2004).

Larkin, Philip, *Collected Poems*, ed. Anthony Thwaite (London: Faber & Faber with the Marvell Press, 1988).

Longley, Edna, *Poetry in the Wars* (Newcastle upon Tyne: Bloodaxe Books, 1986).

Longley, Edna, *Louis MacNeice: A Study* (London: Faber & Faber, 1988).

Longley, Edna, *The Living Steam: Literature and Revisionism in Ireland* (Newcastle upon Tyne: Bloodaxe Books, 1994).

Longley, Michael, *Collected Poems* (London: Cape, 2006).

MacNeice, Louis, *The Poetry of W. B. Yeats* (1941; London: Faber & Faber, 1967).

MacNeice, Louis, *Selected Poems*, ed. Michael Longley (London: Faber & Faber, 1988).

Mendelson, Edward, 'W. H. Auden', in Claude Rawson (ed.), *The Cambridge Companion to English Poets* (Cambridge: Cambridge University Press, 2011), 508–24.

Moran, Joe, 'Out of the East: James Fenton and Contemporary History', *Literature and History*, 9/2 (2000), 53–69.

Motion, Andrew, *Selected Poems 1976–1997* (London: Faber & Faber, 1998).

Muldoon, Paul, *Poems, 1968–1998* (London: Faber & Faber, 2001).

Muldoon, Paul, *The End of the Poem: Oxford Lectures in Poetry* (London: Faber & Faber, 2006).

O'Driscoll, Dennis, *Stepping Stones: Interviews with Seamus Heaney* (London: Faber & Faber, 2008).

O'Neill, Michael, and Reeves, Gareth, *Auden, MacNeice, Spender: The Thirties Poetry* (Basingstoke: Macmillan, 1992).

Paulin, Tom, *A State of Justice* (London: Faber & Faber, 1977).

Paulin, Tom, *Walking a Line* (London: Faber & Faber, 1994).

Porter, Peter, 'Auden's English: Language and Style', in *The Cambridge Companion to W. H. Auden*, ed. Stan Smith (Cambridge: Cambridge University Press, 2005), 123–36

Reeves, Gareth, '"This Is Plenty, This Is More Than Enough": Poetry and the Memory of the Second World War' [oxfordhb-9780199559602-e-31], in Tim Kendall (ed.), *The Oxford Handbook of British and Irish War Poetry* (Oxford: Oxford University Press, 2007), 579–91.

Robinson, Peter, *Poetry, Poets, Readers: Making Things Happen* (Oxford: Oxford University Press, 2002).

Spender, Stephen, *The Thirties and After: Poetry, Politics, People 1933–1975* (London: Fontana, 1978).

Spender, Stephen, *New Selected Poems*, ed. Michael Brett (London: Faber & Faber, 2004).

Wasley, Aidan, *The Age of Auden: Postwar Poetry and the American Scene* (Princeton: Princeton University Press, 2011).

CHAPTER 3

THE UNBURIED PAST: WALKING WITH GHOSTS OF THE 1940S

LEO MELLOR

In *Dining on Stones* (2004) Iain Sinclair's fierce moral swipes memorably indicted lazy forms of motion as leading to lazy forms of composition: 'sit at your PC as you sit in the car: pod person. Lose yourself in the rhythms of the walk: pedestrian, ped person [...] It went back through literature.'[1] He is right; traditions of foot-slogging perambulation as necessary for literary work—and thought—have a long past and range widely through divergent societies. As Rebecca Solnit has noted in her study of walking and the cultural imagination, the effort of bipedalism has historically been linked to creativity, focus, and the imaginative arrangement of knowledge, in numerous authors from Rousseau to Kierkegaard.[2]

The literary history of the written walk or walker's writing covers many genres, from the nineteenth-century *flâneur* to the situationist *dérive*. There are literatures of the walker as author—or character—from *Ulysses* to the British new nature writing of the 2000s; or of digressive steps creating hybrid forms—from W. H. Hudson to W. G. Sebald. But poetry offers a special and problematically intensive case. For from Romanticism onwards a walk could so often appear to become, in the view of one critic, 'inevitably about the "self"—its coalescence or its liberation'.[3] Here poetry from walking becomes a process of release and individualization: with aesthetic coherence a continual companion. This essay will address the work of five complex contemporary poets who complicate such a pattern, bringing forms of peripatesis that reveal disorienation in the self

---

[1] Iain Sinclair, *Dining on Stones* (London: Picador, 2004), 130.
[2] Rebecca Solnit, *Wanderlust* (London: Verso, 2001).
[3] Jeffrey Robinson, *The Walk: Notes on a Romantic Image* (Norman, Okla.: University of Oklahoma Press, 1989), 17.

and the landscape: Colin Simms, Andrew Crozier, Rod Mengham, John Goodby, and John Wilkinson. All use concepts of motion in their poetry, but all take it a lopingly long way from a simple walk in the woods. Indeed walking and writing do not emerge as a thematic pairing, but rather coexist in very different ways in each poet; for this is poetry where the apprehension of the world, and the placing that world in language, is *produced*—not altered—by movement through a landscape. The passage through the topographical and the scribal passages are thus mapped, intimately, upon each other.

Yet there is nothing new under the sun. Or, at least, there is nothing new in modern, and especially, late modernist, poetry. This might feel counter-intuitive; but in reading works from the five poets chosen then the articulation of interconnections—with past poems and poets—rises slowly at the back of the mind. Making visible the connections between eras may take different forms: it can be eased out of the implicit through lexical echoes or repeated tropes, or it may be illustrated overtly through dedications and lines of homage. It may also show up in anthologies, by for example the practice of choosing a totemic writer from another decade—as in the mode practised by Iain Sinclair, in one of his other roles as an editor, and justified thus: 'I invited a number of the poets to nominate significant figures from previous generations; thus demonstrating that a oujia board wasn't required to establish contact with an intelligent and provocative body of poetry.'[4] Moreover his sensibility for digressive forms of walking-as-composition, popularized in works such as *London Orbital* (2002) and *Lights Out for the Territory* (1997), allow a way of counterpointing the 1940s with the 1990s. Thus this chapter also examines key past poets who have influenced the five contemporary poets chosen. This is not to make a claim that these previous poets are significant for their poems of walking or traversing—if indeed they wrote any; rather it is to show how the contemporary poets considered can only create their own versions of perambulation because of their awareness—and reuse—of literary history. For rendering sensory experience of landscape, of moving through it—especially on foot—with all the accruing of sensation and detail, has proved to be a particularly potent place for poets who are interested in continuities and connections. Tracing such connections is not however simply a project of legitimization—or the unfolding and concomitant unbraiding of influences. Rather it is a case, specifically in this chapter, of showing why and how the most complexly engaging poetry of the 1940s and the present can be traced for interrelation, and how poetry that relies upon movement is a good place to glimpse tracks of a precursor.

Colin Simms

Simms has been working, writing, and publishing as a poet-naturalist since 1960. His recent collections—*Otters and Martens* (2004), *The American Poems* (2005), and

---

[4] Iain Sinclair, 'Introduction', in Sinclair (ed.), *Conductors of Chaos* (London: Picador, 1995), p. xix.

Gyrfalcon Poems (2007)—bring together works from many earlier fugitive volumes, themselves covering many regions. While he has been mainly based in the north-east of England, his works range across the high latitudes of Canada and North America, populated by the mammals and birds of prey he studies. The poems themselves vary from interlocking sequences to discrete observations, and from detailing a single view over a flooded river to the bricolaging of letters, speech, and scientific data.

In *Otters and Martens* the taxonomic classification of two different species of mustelids unify poems that are taken from across time and space, spanning the 1960s–2000s and moving from the Yukon to the becks of Northumberland. Yet the closely held desire to report comes through in the sheer effort recognized overtly or covertly in the works. For example in the poem '(from some Welsh Fieldwork)' the very title shows a tentative partiality—this is only 'some' of the work—with a parenthetical acknowledgement of the aesthetic encounter, one that stems from a naturalist's laborious and cumulative fieldwork. Yet the poem begins with precognitive apprehension, as sharp as hairs pricking on the back of a neck: 'Before I know I'm picking up particular pattern | I'm picking up that pattern of sense and on memory'. From this initial tracking the temporal markers shift, and the expanse of stalking and waiting is calibrated with the steps of the creature herself—'footfall against leaf fall'. The poem ends with an acknowledgement of the stuttering limitations of such an endeavour: 'I mutter as she does, sing under my breath and heart | response no matter how foolish, totter toward its art....'.[5]

In such care for knotted cadences, and the self-aware act of observing-the-observer-writing, Simms is heir to a wide tradition of thoughtful naturalist poets, and belongs to a lineage of those such as Richard Caddel who have written in this particular part of the north-east. But more than any other he is heir to the specific terrain of Basil Bunting (1900–85). Bunting's influence on Simms's writing affects both the physical characterization of the terrain of the Northumbrian landscape, and the expansive range of other far-flung places, but also—vitally—the phonic vista of sound-patterning. Yet the term 'landscapes' for Simms's observed spaces is inadaquate; partly because they do not range as far—and mythologize the space—as Bunting does for the valley around the Brigflatts meeting house. But also because for Simms they are so often aquatic as they are composed of dry land. His poem 'Loch Maree' shuffles together the names of material substances—rocks, earth, water—alongside his own hyphenated coinages for movement. The present participles dart and glide and are—like the otter ducking below the surface—tantilizing in their incompleteness:

lochside silverschistsand disturbed-to-black-below
pattern-padded pewter-grad velvet-hollows grain added otter pattern
wind off water levelling sibilant bevelling gritscreen bankscree
whistle   reminding you of   distant wigeon whee-oo (17)

---

[5] Colin Simms, *Otters and Martens* (Exeter: Shearsman Books, 2007), 110. All further parenthetical references are to this volume.

Later we are back to the body of the observer, with the tenaciousness of language in an inhospitable environment; but the effort in noticing and aligning an essence—while not or translating the scene, is a hard one. In Bunting's *Briggflatts* the patterning does not give such an enveloping totality, though the musicality of the water is present, as the distinct force of the individual words remain separate. Yet the scene here too is built up from the rocks 'sandstone…grit…the becks ring on limestone | whisper to peat'.[6] But here too such materials are not only valuable as a layer of creavity; they are observed by an aware figure *in* the poem who is trying to find the right terms for them: 'Fierce blood throbs in his tongue | lean words'. The patterning of both Bunting and Simms, which in Bunting's case is linked back to an alliterative tradition, is also a way of understanding a landscape that refuses more conventional evocations of pastoral fecundity—or lush welcome. In Simms's poem of an exhaustive trek, 'Otters in the Kirk Field Burn', the method of alliterative overload is also a way of indicating the amount of ground to be covered in the act of walking. The conjunctions offer an uneasy gait through the clotted 'g's' of waterlogged terrain; themselves reminiscent of Bunting's 'bogged orchard' or the 'quaggy past'[7] that has to be traced in *Briggflatts*. The effort is palpable:

This morning's wet and wearying miles before the dawn
The stumble in bramble and off stones in bog and gleg
With thanks to the moon, between squalls, in acknowledgement:
But tracked at respectful distance wandering dog otter (50)

Yet the movement here, as in so many of Simms's other poems, is held in check by that one word on the fourth line—'respectful'. For this is a form of stalking that, while abandoning the kill as ultimate aim, needs to follow and be shaped (as a poem) by a force outside the poet's control—the animal. In Simms's 'Lines' the pine marten has recognizable features that want to be translated or tied into a grid position by analogy: 'the face of mart | a pace a map is like, yet neat | condensed energy and edgy senses' (160). Such a hoped-for translation onto 'lines' created to box and give grid-references on paper will not work, but other—poetic—lines might. For the encounter is unpicked *as* the desire to fix or shape the encounter in these last three stanzas:

for this is a survivor and he listens
'with his heels', his (invisable) sable eyes
which say what we cannot quite see
yet are given, if we are able to receive
radio somehow, the gift of self

of 'isness'; which is *his*, not our business
it is self, or what we see of it
breath, footprints, scats, or nothing even
ever misleading We *know* nothing
which way he went, he went

---

[6] Basil Bunting, *Complete Poems*, ed. Ric Caddel (Newcastle upon Tyne: Bloodaxe Books, 2000), 61–2.
[7] Bunting, *Complete Poems*, 69, 75.

riddles, still the day sudden
we'll never find out if it was...
or why is all illegiable on the edge
of that edginess, expecting everything—
except we windfall, given nothing. (160–1)

This question of 'isness', the unalterable 'otherness' of the creature tracked and engaged with, has recently become one of significant philosophical import, especially within the field of ecocriticism. How far poetry might be able to shape a language of limit, of understanding the gap as *itself* a thing of beauty, might usefully complicate further the waters of this argument.[8] Simms has been placed along with others in the anthology *The Ground Aslant* (2010) as embodying a new form of nature writing that engages with both man in the landscape and such *otherness* of what can be found there.[9] Here again in posing the question through the repeated focus on a particular species, the commitment to the act of observation, Simms is in dialogue with Bunting. For Bunting, especially in *The Spoils* (1951), is concerned not only with the spoilation and loot gained and noted in the aftermath of the Second World War; he is seeking a language for loss at the moment when the natural world renders itself back to a state beyond language, even beyond form:

In watch below
mediative heard elsewhere
surf shout, pound shores seldom silent
from which heart naked swam
out to the dear uninteligible ocean.[10]

Andrew Crozier

While studying English at Cambridge, Andrew Crozier (1943–2008) became interested in expansive forms of modernist and contemporary American poetry, modes that thus offered a decisive alternative to the grip of the Movement on British culture. This led to his work on Charles Olson and a role co-editing the magazine *The English Intelligencer*. Crozier founded the Ferry Press, publishing *Brass* by J. H. Prynne as well as, among others, works by John Rodker and the Objectivist Carl Rakosi—who Crozier was key in rediscovering. He was co-editor (with Tim Longville) of the influential anthology *A Various Art* (1987) that tried to map out the contours of a non-mainstream tradition of

---

[8] For the practice of 'becoming-animal', see Eric Santner, *On Creaturely Life* (Chicago: University of Chicago Press, 2006) and Giorgio Agamben, *The Open: Man And Animal* (Palo Alto, Calif.: Stanford University Press, 2004).

[9] Harriet Tarlo (ed.), *The Ground Aslant: An Anthology of Radical Landscape Poetry* (Exeter: Shearsman Book, 2011), 21–9.

[10] Bunting, *Complete Poems*, 57.

British modernism. Crozier's own poetry circled around finding a demotic but truthful language for the perception of space, and this moved from metaphysical shape-shifting in *The Veil Poem* (1974) to works that had a freewheeling open-field aesthetic that owed much to Charles Olson. But as well as an American tradition, Crozier's own work emerged from a British, historically contingent, post-Second World War inheritance—one that can begin to explain his particular use of the walk as an ordering principle.

Looking back over wartime poetry in 1945 Stephen Spender attempted to give an explanation for what had happened to Surrealism during the Second World War: 'Surrealism has ceased to be fantasy, its "objects" hurtle round our heads, its operations cause the strangest conjunctions of phenomena in the most unexpected places, its pronouncements fill the newspapers. The youngest and newest school of English poets signified this occasion by calling themselves "apocalyptics".'[11] These 'younger poets', the New Apocalyptics, comprised a movement that is pivotal to the understanding of what happened to Surrealism in British culture. Recent scholarship has begun to untangle how they so dominated wartime culture, and also to unpick why post-war literary judgements so marginalized and mocked them.[12] However, the centrality to this movement of the poet-theorist J. F. Hendry, instigator of the initial manifesto and editor of the anthologies, has still to be explored. Hendry was chosen by Crozier in *Conductors of Chaos* as a forgotten but influential figure, and although Crozier did not explicitly justify Hendry's inclusion in personal terms, it is clear there is continuity between the two.

But who was J. F. Hendry (1912–86)? Born in 1912, his nomadic life led him from the University of Glasgow with a degree in modern languages, through travel in the Balkans, to a role as a wartime intelligence officer, before ending as a professor of translation theory in Canada. During the 1940s he published two books of poetry: *The Bombed Happiness* (1942) and *The Orchestral Mountain* (1943), plus three anthologies, co-edited with Henry Treece, which included his theoretical essays as well as his own poems. How writers came to label themselves 'Apocalyptic' is itself complex, and critics have tracked how this loaded term was used in the late 1930s: from the continuing influence of Revelation on D. H Lawrence, to George Barker 'achieving Apocalypse' in 1937 as political awareness. However, the programme produced by Hendry and Henry Treece in early 1938 attempted to define what 'Apocalyptic Writing' should be at that precise historical point. This manifesto brought together a desire for 'greater freedom, economic no less than aesthetic, from machines and mechanistic thinking' with an attack on 'the Machine Age [that] had exerted too strong an influence on art', before concluding with a battle cry: 'Myth, as a personal means of reintegrating the personality, had been neglected and despised'.[13] Marina MacKay's critique of this text—'as Modernist

---

[11] Stephen Spender, 'Some Observations on English Poetry Between Two Wars', in Henry Treece and Stefan Schimanski (eds.), *Transformation*, 3 (n.d., c.1945), 176.

[12] See Andrew Duncan, *Origins of the Underground* (Cambridge: Salt Publishing, 2007) and Keith Tuma, *Fishing by Obstinate Isles: Modern and Postmodern British Poetry and American Readers* (Evanston, Ill.: Northwestern University Press, 1998).

[13] Reprinted in Francis Scarfe's *Auden and After* (London, Routledge & Kegan Paul: 1942),155.

manifestos go theirs was a little impoverished'[14]—shows pointed understatement; but it is located within the problematic double-inheritance of surrealism and technophobic high modernism. But the weight of cultural judgements was, from the 1950s onwards, one of near unanimously virulent antipathy.[15] A barb will suffice to demonstrate; A. T. Tolley felt that 'Hendry's poem "Apocalypse" is representatively dreadful'.[16] So what did Crozier find of value in Hendry's work? Partly it was the interlacing of the critical and poetical, as he wrote himself: these were 'separate activities in their own distinct domains of intelligence within a single project'.[17] But there were also lyric forces at play, offering models for how poetry could incorporate the active urge for searching in the aftermath of violence. In Hendry's bleakly drained lyric 'London before Invasion' the cityscape wishes to become a sign:

Walls and buildings stand here still, like shells,
Hold them to your ear. There are no echoes even
Of the seas that once were. That tide is out
Beyond the valleys and hills.[18]

Yet all it produces is only 'an ebbing beyond laughter and too tense for tears'. The scribal—and even the linguistic—is finally blotted out by the close: 'all time adrift in torrents of blind war'. Such difficulties of converting material experience into poetical interrogations intensifies in Hendry's poems from the later war period, especially those in memory of his wife who was killed in an air raid. In *The Orchestral Mountain: A Symphonic Elegy*, Hendry offers a model for such a despairing kind of search that spreads out across lexical forms and overleaps the bounds of conventional syntax in the pain of its questing:

Spiders of patience, I try to find you in a tangle
Of memories, hidden perhaps like an anemone.
I too conjure you up through the ganglia
Of nerve's fear; and, more than sick money,
Child or science, seek through the brain's storm
Two flowers I dropped, your face and form.[19]

The urgency of a loss and the resultant searching are not just in the physical realm—they also consist of trying to find a language or form of negation that can encompass the enormity of what has gone. Crozier had written versions of the quest poem before, and

---

[14] Marina MacKay, *Modernism and World War II* (Cambridge: Cambridge University Press, 2007), 85.
[15] See James Keery's series of twelve articles in *PN Review* from 2003 to 2005, collectively entitled 'The Burning Baby and the Bathwater', *PN Review*, 29/4 (Mar. –Apr. 2003), 58–62, to 31/6 (July–Aug. 2005), 57–61.
[16] A. T. Tolley, *The Poetry of the Thirties* (London: Victor Gollancz, 1975), 365.
[17] Crozier, introduction to J. F. Hendry, in Sinclair (ed.), *Conductors of Chaos*, 72.
[18] Crozier, introduction to Hendry, in Sinclair (ed.), *Conductors of Chaos*, 74.
[19] J. F. Hendry, *The Orchestral Mountain: A Symphonic Elegy* (London: Routledge & Kegan Paul, 1943), 20.

The Veil Poem can be understood as such in its attempt to hold together semantic units—much influenced by George Oppen—in a form where the very act of reading catalyses the disparate elements. But it is Crozier's 'Free Running Bitch' (1995), his last great work, which shows most visibly the centrality of motion as constitutive to composition—and which is also indebted to Hendry in some notable ways. The poem opens with a mix of the matter-of-fact objects, a fragility of information—and the idea of pursuit:

Believe it. But he won't. He stayed in May
followed by June. Soon, poetry in slow
motion, queues in traffic, like stopping for
time to think, at the same time,
more or less, in the same place (what
did he think?) Would I believe it,
it's in the diary. No, it's on notices.
In the year planner, in several year planners,
its colour coded for a month, and the month
after: knowable frequency equations
for different colours.[20]

Across ten sections of the poem, as the deferrals mount and the lyric voice (however battered) runs through many material sensations, 'all the changes | as good as random' come thick and fast, so too do the disavowals that the language could hold such an endeavour. In the sixth section its tension crackles 'an | illegible map of home. Don't run, don't pass, | don't play, don't follow, don't hang on, don't forget'.[21] The listing of negatives here turns, swerves, and loops round in the very last phrase to an affirmation. The language is still using us in the final (tenth) section as we attempt to keep pace with the sensations as they circle and twist. The breathless pain is now of a real chase played out in woodland:

follow the sound in, criss-cross between the quick
slender growth and fallen trunks, angled branches,
see her head down follow her nose through bracken
and bramble and vanish, broken outline of variegated
fawn and white slip through dappled light,
[…] on the scent of exhaustion after some hours
of this, see, she returns on tentative bloody feet.[22]

Of course the influence of Hendry cannot explain all of Crozier's later work, nor should it. A late poem given here in its entirety, 'Star Ground', takes the materiality that has so tormented 'Free Running Bitch'—with the desperate deferral in perception sprinting along behind—and makes it rather drift, dissolve, and constellate in the 'resistance' of love:

---

[20] In Sinclair (ed.), *Conductors of Chaos*, 61–70, at 61.
[21] Sinclair (ed.), *Conductors of Chaos*, 62, 66.
[22] Sinclair (ed.), *Conductors of Chaos*, 70.

Difference of coarse and fine
The abrasion of the sky
Snow drifts along the hedge
In plumes and spurs
At ground level
Swept clear and bare
Ice chips like glass

Light scatters on dry gusts of air
Shrinks and breaks apart
Frost heaves all night
To rise like waves
Spent on the margin
On the enduring
Particular resistance of our love[23]

John Goodby

An astonishingly overt way of both acknowledging and playing with an inheritance from 1940s poetry comes in the work of John Goodby. As a critic he has lamented how responses to Dylan Thomas seem strangely fixed, a perceptive if depressing observation. Yet while Goodby's academic revisionist project has reawoken an interest in Thomas's complexities as a writer so, too, has his creative work—notably the astounding book *uncaged sea* (2008). This is a performance text, an effort to rework Thomas's entire oeuvre—the *Collected Poems* 1934–1952—through fragmenting and realigning the text along systematic principles. Here, the influence of John Cage is palpable. Goody terms the form 'mesostic', that is a form of an acrostic but with the capitalized letter falling in the midst of every line. Throughout the poem, every part of Thomas's full name—Dylan Marlais Thomas—is spelt out in the stanzas. This playfulness may seem merely game-like; a more single-author-fixated version of the formulations used to compose cut-up works such as Giles Goodland's *Capital* (2006). But what makes it aesthetically powerful, and also understandable as a journey, is in the *mise-en-page*:

>   Dust. And what's
> him flY
>   Love
> should heAr
>   iN the kiss?

---

[23] Andrew Crozier, *Star Ground* (Laughton: Silver Hounds, 2008), n.p.

>   time would takeMe
>   thAn his stiff
>   of gRace
>   wouLd
>   trades, thAt
>   tIckled by the
>   rub through the houSe
>
>   lighT and love
>   My wisHes
>   Of
>   walking warM
>   heArt, whack their
>   In the first, Spinning [24]

The eye of the reader has thus to wander both across the page—and through the entire oeuvre of Thomas, encountering famous lines or phrases now reawakened by being taken out of their well-studied and preserved context. Yet the text of *uncaged sea* is also for performance and Goodby has showcased it with the ensemble 'boiled string' from 2003 onwards. Thus movement is here also rendered through performance as well as by sight, the name resonating and being chased through the fractured parts of Thomas's overfamiliar poems.

But forms of mosaicing influence can come to prominence in other ways too: Goodby's *Illenium* (2010) shows a rather different kind of pedestrian movement, but one—again—that uses Thomas. *Illenium* is a book-length sequence of sonnets; all broken or partial in some way, all recounting the particularities of life, love and language in a corner of South Wets Wales (as this is what his corner of South West Wales swirls into).[25] It is a traumatized sonnet sequences; for they are distressed in their form: oscillating between gap-happy *mise-en-page* lacunae and lines sagging into blankness. Found or reworked texts are here too: Enid Blyton's Famous Five make appearances in several sonnets, becoming part of the repetition-with-variations that both mimics the workings of the mind—especially the workings of a mind with lustful urges—and the desire to weave a sequence from a fevered language that is continually fracturing apart. Absurdity abounds, captured from the start in an epigraph taken from a newspaper report: 'A young girl, who was blown out to sea on a set of inflatable teeth, was rescued by a man on an inflatable lobster. A coastguard spokesman commented: "This sort of thing is all too common these days." 'But dark laughter offers not just the energy of despair. Pleasures in minutiae slam together before another gap looms; and concentrated plosive power ebbs onto a foreshore, if not into linguistic foreplay. The booze-drench of romanticism in the poems, of the kind that can find 'Carmarthen's Latin Quarter' and desire to 'ride out into

---

[24] John Goodby, *Uncaged Sea* (Hove: Waterloo Press, 2008), 25. All further parenthetical references are to this volume.

[25] John Goodby, *Illenium* (Exeter: Shearsman Books: 2010), 11, 8.

the sea-town afternoon to look for you', also owes something—probably a bit more than something—to Thomas's inescapable presence in Swansea.

Yet *Illenium*, like the more obvious scars on *uncaged sea*, is also traumatized in form: it is centripetal, circling obsessively on a linguistic as well as physical terrain as it tries to retell or reframe memories of desire—and of loss—among a group of friends. This occurs through snatches of conversation, a whirl of overheard references, and violently bitten-off epithets. The way to trace senses here is to search for movement, the physical encounters contained and transcribed within a specific locale. *Illenium* seems to owe something, intentionally or not, to Shakespeare's sonnet 129, with its opening: 'The expense of spirit in a waste of shame | Is lust in action'. For lust in Goodby's works seems always held, dialectically or not, against 'waste'—as both a noun and a verb. Nevertheless, they also glimpse beauty in thoughts as well as in views:

Beyond September Port Talbot softened as so often
By wind.   Lie thou, Ted, now.
I am certain of nothing but the hollyness of the herd's inflictions.
To be close is close enough this weather
The wicked little mystery!
Just fyi   'i looked in the mirror just now and didn't recognise myself'.[26]

Beyond the movement through these vistas—whether domestic or coastal—shame hangs over this sequence. The emotion is repeatedly invoked or alluded to as a drive that might explicate behaviours—but also as vital in the dirty process of being alive when 'a screwdriver [is] the key to the *tŷ bach* door'. 'Rahg gywilydd' ('for shame') is a potent piece of controlling language, and it enters these poems sometimes covertly, and sometimes through direct quotation. Cognates and variants on 'sham', 'shame', and 'ashamed' spin together—much as Thomas resoundingly plays through the palate and palette of a biblically charged language. But this shame for Goodby generally, helpfully, precludes self-pity. The voice is demotic, conspiratorial, pleading implausible justifications, and the sonnets are full of moments of confession—but in their restlessness and fleeing from self-indulgence they are never paused enough to become leadenly confessional.

Rod Mengham

Mengham's work over the past two decades has ranged over a terrain he has made his own, a zone of shifting texts that refuse designations or easy identification. This very problem of classification is itself strange; for these multifarious prose-based (but not always continuous-prose) works, which include poems, phenomenlogical travelogues, and meditations on walking to grid-references, are thematically and practically so

---

[26] Goodby, *Illenium*, 20.

often about the complexities of naming, knowing, and the routes taken—as well as the roots (linguistic or biological) that can thus be found. The idea of movement as in itself a way of knowing is key, but threats still loom ominously, albeit with humour, as 'The Boeotarchts Shall Hear of This' instructs: 'Never put a razor inside your thoughts | even as a joke'.[27] The accumulation of disparate sensations as *only* made possible by walking, can be seen most vividly in recent works such as 'Icarus Alight' where the headlong rush pulls debris into mythological significance:

> He is beginning to feel traction on the respiratory zone, gravity unwinding the lungs, shrinking capacity, hurrying past Canary Wharf and onto the Isle of Dogs, searching for a ditch in which to lie down and monitor the tidal volume, remote sensing the energy transfer between glucose and the liabilities market, bonus-mongering behind open doors and poetry's frozen assets, closed tanks, oxygen inertia, the perished mouthpiece, the rusted valve. Between the concrete ramps of the Silvertown road system is a triangle of grass with a broken bale of hay and an old bath to collect water. At a racing trot, a black horse comes flying out of Tidal Basin Road and carries him in its slipstream.[28]

Beyond apocalyptic steeds in a London drosscape, the geographical spread of Mengham's encounters moves worldwide, from Australia through to rural Ireland. 'Batavia' typifies these works as the objects encountered, here a sunken mass of corroding stone—a putative portico brought out by the colonial Dutch for the Sea Gate at Djakarta, are transformed not by an actual run past, but rather by the slow sideways crawl of investigative thought as it moves across the surfaces. As the tactile qualities begin unlocking otherness, this prose poem initially concerns a future dreamt of but which never happened. It sprawls through the visible and invisible spectrums: 'It was a time to sow and a time for the radio signals to break up' as 'Flaws in the stone, areas of more or less hardness and resistance, open up and give way to pockets of memory, crypts for the imagination of architect and mason'. The physical object is unleashed from entropic dissolution into the brine of the Javan sea; the aesthetic filling of fractures and hollows brings possibility. But the gap between narrator and object remains, the repeated movements across the poly-encrusted stonework unleashes thoughts beyond what could be imagined by the narrator: 'The gate did not know this, it would dream of another place, where the sound of bees comes down the chimney and the fields are prepared for dancing.'[29]

With their unsettling range, dream-state fluidity, and imaginative expansiveness these texts are the inheritors of many aspects of late modernism, but especially the prose poems and Surrealist reports of Humphrey Jennings (1907–50). Jennings was central to Surrealism in Britain, as a co-organizer of the International Surrealist Exhibition,

---

[27] Rod Mengham, *Unsung* (Cambridge: Salt Publishing, 2001), 96.
[28] Rod Mengham, *Les Citadelles: Revue de poésie*, 17 (2012), 114–17.
[29] Rod Mengham, *Diving Tower* (Cambridge: Equipage, 2006), n.p.

author of collages and poems, and promoter of the movement via print and radio.[30] Two of the more slow-flowering products of this engagement were his many subsequent years of work on *Pandemonium*,[31] and his contributions to Mass-Observation, which he co-founded early in 1937 with the anthropologist Tom Harrison and the poet Charles Madge. Best known now as a polymathic film-maker, Jennings's prose can still unlock the strangeness in an 'anthropology of ourselves', unleashing the overlooked or quotidian. An example of this transformative vision can be seen in 'Summer 1940' where at the climax the poem offers an epiphanic shift out of (social) realism and into the revelatory:

> For an hour the hard edges of the mill-tied town alter and begin to open like a rose. The deformed become sculpture, and the Gods themselves, whose eyes have so long peered out of letter-boxes, come out into the streets again and reveal themselves to Man.[32]

Jennings's war films and poems share this technique, of isolating a fragment— a sound, or an image—and then juxtaposing it with others. In the text 'War and Childhood' (1943) this juxtaposition attempts to create the memory of the First World War in the midst of the Second World War with details dissolving into uncertain perception: 'Utterly gone—only the wind and broken glass and rough tiles made smooth by the sea. Only still visions of bloodshot eyes brimming over with fear. Nothing. War. Childhood'. This breaking of sentence length and the upswell of fear from beneath is held in check in others of Jennings's works, such as the majestic anaphoric refrain of 'I see London' (1941). What Mengham takes and uses from Jennings is its anthropological aspects, the cold-eyed investigation of how language might render strangeness and lead us to doubt our perception. In 'Five year plan in four years' (2006) this builds threateningly, with layers of artifice peeling back before the gaze is averted from any final horror:

> The narrative begins with expulsion, the shunning of sympathizers, secret informers, a belief in connivance. A single police car in the sun, parked up with open door, the afternoon cigarette, the endless fields, creeping stubble fire. [...]
> Further and further away from the houses along the forest paths as they get smaller and smaller, she finds orchids, ragged robin and death's head mushrooms. The deep, muffled explosions become clearer, the dogs are raging.[33]

Menace can come in other forms too. In his prose poem about Flag Fen, a Cambridgeshire ancient site, Mengham constructs a careful narrative that appears to be showing the reader around an archaeological excavation with courteous deliberation and wonder at destruction:

> Everyday objects in tip-top condition, flint tools and beautifully modelled pots, were dumped in huge quantities. High status ornaments and valuable weapons

---

[30] See Kevin Jackson, *Humphrey Jennings* (London: Picador, 2004).
[31] Finally published as *Pandemonium: The Coming of the Machine as Seen by Contemporary Observers*, ed. Mary-Lou Jennings and Charles Madge (London: André Deutsch, 1985).
[32] *Humphrey Jennings Film Reader*, ed. Kevin Jackson (Manchester: Carcanet Press, 1993), 295.
[33] Rod Mengham, *Bell Book* (Cambridge: Wide Range Chapbooks, 2012), n.p.

were deliberately smashed and decommissioned before being reassigned to another dimension, which is where the dead must live. The ancestors required food in the after-life, and so packed lunches were provided.[34]

The humour here owes something to Jennings but also to a longer history of the British inventive uncanny, notably Edward Upward's 'The Railway Accident' (1929). Yet there are also hints of a suppressed or battened-down lyric intensity amid the wonder at potlatch and destruction. But where or how does a lyric 'I' overtly emerge in these works? It comes through in the edges of observation, in the speech-codes yelping and the anachronism thrown in to fuel a hidden fire—or to gather the ashes from it. Such a tendency—towards suppression and then acknowledgement—is even more pronounced in Mengham's Grimspound poems.

These are a sequence of meditations from the mid-2000s, mainly in unrhymed couplets. Each involves the poet returning to Grimspound—a prehistoric site on Dartmoor—and each poem is titled simply with the date that a particular walk was taken. This is poetry as reportage, noting bird, lichen, wind, and 'moss sump' around the two-thousand-year-old enclosure. But it is also poetry as mediation across vast stretches of time through quotidian objects, objects scoured by wind or buffeted by rain. Hence the intimacy of the second-person pronouns bring a laconic guide or instructive feel:

if you follow Grimlake upstream, it soon
becomes a delta, then a marsh, then a quag
and there is no way to trace it back to source

wherever the flow is faster and deeper
there is a more visual distortion
when the flow of time finds a direction[35]

Eventually this leads to the revelation of authorship—with the body of the poet in the very landscape he writes of. But this 'the flow of time' which rests on a material streambed—while at the same instant putting the scribal body in the same space as the unspeaking dead—is reminiscent of Jennings's mediation on a collective unconscious, in the practice of Mass-Observation; or even, in his prose poems, something akin to a defamiliarization that opens up wormholes in time, letting past processes and individuals re-emerge. It can be as simple as this haptic moment: 'I perceive in the grey picture all the colours that were once there, | not only the simple division of the prism | Brilliant orange iron ore peacock coloured coal | I perceive also the hues of the men who built the city'.[36]

---

[34] Rod Mengham, 'Soluble Culture', *Kenyon Review*, 25/3–4 (2003), 72–7 (72).
[35] In Neil Wenborn and M. E. J. Hughes (eds.), *Contour Lines: New Responses to Landscape in Word and Image* (Cambridge: Salt Publishing, 2010), 78–85 (83).
[36] Humphrey Jennings, 'As I look' (1949), 300.

John Wilkinson

Wilkinson is a subtle yet unrelenting poet, emerging from a Cambridge School interest in the processes of language, and its inadequacies, as it shifts and reforms to capture transient experiences. In his oeuvre the rebarbative and violent surface of the poetry shakes above questions of the political unconscious working through idiom, with these elements being brought to bear on a range of forms. His critical work has been collected in *The Lyric Touch* (2007) and the most recent poetry in *Down to Earth* (2008).

Many of Wilkinson's works—from *Iphigenia* (2004) to the collection *Lake Shore Drive* (2006)—involve processes of transit and discovery, but they always flee or flicker from any literalness: tenses twist, no stable character emerges, no conventionally lyric 'I' gives a vantage point. Thus physical journeys are suborned into linguistic or metaphorical excursions, commodified phrases and slang are pressure-tested or become strangely beautiful. But in reading *Sarn Helen* (1997) the title gives an incontestable physical fact—as Sarn Helen is the name of the Roman road that runs from north to south the length of Wales, immediately giving a landscape to be encountered, a particular nexus of language, and a movement through historical as well as geological strata. The poem starts violently *in medias res*:

bayoneted. If any will hear the truth must cling best
avoid blow dragonflies, cling on by nail-feasance
over a cataract which scours a giant curtain wall,
or was it short-of-time shrunk the unseeming aimless
river to a bank's sediment?[37]

From the start there is a fierce journey with perils brought into focus through syntactical dislocation. The first five pages set out the journey—and it *is* a journey (if only when apprehended in retrospect)—in solid thirty-line blocks which then act, as stepping stones, to both indicate transitory security and the need for onward movement. Even on the first page the passage moves from macro to micro, from the 'giant curtain wall' down to 'filaments' and 'a razor blade's width'. What exactly is being described is perpetually in question as deferral of verbs and the detritus of objects pile up together, but so do the disillusionments: the forest is 'shrink-wrapped', while the seals disport themselves with 'transmitters pinned behind perked-up ears'.

Yet in Wilkinson's continual suspension of a final meaning, diverting the reader from an easy path of interpretation, and in his accretion of material debris whilst traversing a Welsh landscape, he owes much to another poet—a debt made overt in the dedication to *Sarn Helen*, which he dedicates as a 'Homage to Lynette Roberts and for Friends in Swansea'. The past decade has seen the literary recovery of Lynette Roberts (1909–95), a poet who will in future years be seen as central to a variety of fields: to the complexities

---

[37] John Wilkinson, *Sarn Helen* (Equipage: Cambridge, 1997), 5. All further references will be given parenthetically.

of Welsh culture, to interwar British modernism—and to questions about the possibility of poetry as an all-encompassing artform. Taken together, her diaries, stories, and poems, with their fascination with the material world, refractions of gender, and fears of air warfare, offer a way of understanding the growth of her unique aesthetic. Already the renewed availability of her poetry and prose has begun to transform the history of Welsh modernism—and, therefore, twentieth-century culture more generally.[38] Born in Buenos Aires to parents of Welsh descent, Roberts's brief flowering as a writer in the 1940s was cut short by personal and professional events—but even in that short time Roberts impressed such diverse figures as Robert Graves (who dedicated *The White Goddess* to her), Alun Lewis, Edith Sitwell, and T. S. Eliot, with Faber publishing both her *Poems* (1944) and *Gods with Stainless Ears* (1951).

In Roberts's work the environment flashes into vivid visibility, whether in contemplation or in transit, as she attempts to find a language for corporeal apprehension—the placing of perception as a totalizing and physical response. Such sensitivity to a disordered landscape—of war, chemicals, mythology—is linguistically charged and spiky, high-tensile and complete with unsettlingly quotidian objects. For Roberts's work laceratingly renders the experience of wartime fear and horror into forms which would enable her to report on what she had seen through a process of juxtaposition of bodily fragments of experience. These processes of poetical estrangement and renewal offer a model for the apprehension of Wilkinson's work—but the link is not merely formal; the debt to Roberts's subject matter must also be acknowledged. For Wilkinson takes after Roberts when she writes of disparate conjunctions of objects and sensations, from aniline dyes and coracles, anti-aircraft flares and hedgerow birds—but does not order them to produce nostalgia or to laud the new world. Rather they are all seen as poetical properties that can be experienced and denoted most vividly *through* their juxtaposition: many violent—such as in 'Swansea Raid' (1943). This was published as a short story but feels like an explosive prose-poem, here forces become literally illuminating, with the full range of scientific language tearing at the resistantly pastoral analogy:

> From our high village overlooking the Towy we can see straight down the South Wales Coast. Every searchlight goes up. A glade of magnesium waning to a distant hill that we know to be Swansea. Swansea's sure to be bad. Look at those flares like a swarm of orange bees. They fade and others return. A collyrium sky, chemically washed $Cu.DH^2$. A blasting flash impels Swansea to riot.[39]

The bodies here, of the observer and her friend, are defined through both wonder and vulnerability in this new landscape; for as David Jones, another complex Anglo-Welsh

---

[38] Central to the renewed interest in Roberts has been the publication of two volumes: *Diaries, Letters and Recollections*, ed. Patrick McGuinness (Manchester: Carcanet Press, 2008), and *Collected Poems*, ed. Patrick McGuinness (Manchester: Carcanet Press, 2005). All further references to the *Collected Poems* will be given parenthetically.

[39] Roberts, *Diaries, Letters and Recollections*, 103.

modernist and one admired by Roberts,[40] suggested: 'it is not easy in considering a trench-mortar barrage to give praise for the action proper to chemicals—full though it may be of beauty'.[41] *Gods with Stainless Ears*, Roberts's book-length 'heroic poem', takes such a question as an aesthetic and moral challenge. Composed in 1941–3 it is a dream-like war narrative nearly 700 lines long, unfolding in five parts each composed of five line stanzas—each part opening with an epigraph in Welsh and a prose argument. The narrative is epic: expansively full of unsettling detail, but also replete with zooms and close-ups as it swoops in for scenes or pulls back for planet-breadth totality. In her introduction Roberts states how the filmic—or rather the imagination reordered by the cinematic—was inspirational: 'when I wrote this poem, the scenes and visions ran before me like a newsreel' (43). The subtitle 'a heroic poem' attempts to redefine the heroic, offering poetry of endurance where Home Front civilians can encompass—and experience—all in war as worthy of poetry. The poem tracks a soldier and his partner, circling outwards and revealing visions, first the muddy estuary landscape around Llansteffan (where the poem was composed) before vaulting into orbit and viewing the earth itself. The language is sharp, involved, and asks much of the reader—the range of unfamiliar words compete with temporal disjunctions. The first part ends with an austere yet lyrically poised crescendo:

Drowned in water-swills of crossing waves; lifting
Asteroid heads, so alike, so different from
The petroleum sky: striking death too soon,
And nearer and sooner than they should: this dawn
Mauve as iron, whimpers as the biting jest. (51)

But the voyage of the man and woman, the 'soldier and his girl', sweeping and swinging around the world, allows a greater lexical range and a more ominous looming threat as movement unravels:

We by centrifugal force...rose softly...
Faded from bloodsight. Was, he and I ran
On to a steel escalator, the white
Electric sun drilling down on the cubed ice;
Our cyanite flesh chilled on aluminium

Rail. Growing taller, our demon diminishing
With steep incline. Climbed at gradient
42°; on to a trauma stratus
Where a multitude of birds, each wing
A sunset against sheet of ice, dipped (65)

---

[40] See accounts of their meetings and Roberts's visit to Jones's 1947 exhibition, *Diaries, Letters, and Recollections*, 179, 187.

[41] David Jones, Preface to *In Parenthesis* (London: Faber & Faber, 1937), p. xiv.

This final, chilling, section of the poem forces the corporeal into violent conflict with the material debris of a landscape shaped and shattered by war. Despite 'strokes of mapping pens stretching page of | music over vast terrain', this is inhospitable to anaesthetic—and to life. 'The Madonna with a heart of tin' leads only to ravens with 'beaks of bone breaking up the wound of winter' (68) as Roberts's patterning of consonants, her version of the Welsh-language form *cynghanedd*, accentuates the violent ruptures. Wilkinson's own expansive transit through a landscape of violence in *Sarn Helen* now appears more familiar, as does his attempts at 'calibration' of the value:

Throat like sandpaper spasms on the manrope knot
but it was what I have to excess. Granted its width,
its breadth & distance, what calibration serves to fold
edgeless, radiant, erasive, your saved up fervencies (31)

Furthermore, as in Roberts's work, so much rests here on the tricks and flickers of perception—and finding a language for such perception. For Roberts's influence on *Sarn Helen* includes authenticating an involved critique, one that is aware of the lyric moment as a singular event, but one which can be shattered and repeatedly refracted. Wilkinson himself writes when praising Roberts that hers is 'a poetry of intensities... demand[ing] a respect for repetition and persistence' as it exhibits a sustained oscillation between dialects, scientific jargons, linguistic surfaces, and internal worlds.[42] Such a movement thus becomes 'peristaltic, immutably in places while also pressing forwards'.[43] One result is that *Gods with Stainless Ears* is filled with tellingly reflective and cold surfaces, as McGuinness notes: 'glass and prisms, shiny metals and alloys, water, mirrors, ice and polished surfaces'.[44] Even the spectral frosty light at the end presages doom:

Salt spring from frosted sea filters palea light
Raising tangerine and hard line of rind on the
Astringent sky. Catopric on waterice he of deep love
Frees dragon from the glacier glade
Sights death falling into chilblain ears. (69)

In Wilkinson the transit through Sarn Helen does not have such a welcome to *thanatos*, rather it ends in a perceptual, if not perpetual, hall of mirrors: 'So off-beam | in thought's topography [...] | tumbling down in bright shiny parcels' (30)—or just where 'the fused projection nets had left in purgatory | a spectre of flesh & blood' (31). The continual lexical disorientation, and barely suppressed violence beneath the surface, means *Sarn Helen* is a counterblast to the pastoral walking poem by its gyratory inclusions; and—as such—becomes a true homage to Roberts.

---

[42] John Wilkinson, 'The Water-Rail of Tides', in *The Lyric Touch: Essays on the Poetry of Excess* (Cambridge: Salt Publishing, 2007), 189–94 (194).
[43] Wilkinson, 'The Water-Rail of Tides', 194.
[44] Patrick McGuinness, Introduction to Roberts, *Collected Poems*, p. xxii.

Coda

In T. E. Hulme's formulation, poetry is easily discernable from prose on a level of (psychic) topography, for: 'verse is a pedestrian taking you over the ground'.[45] But it is always useful to know who might have walked this way before, and one might be able to find unexpected tracks. Moreover walking as a metaphor for reception might also become useful. For some of the best critical work on rewardingly difficult poets, such as J. H. Prynne, has held the idea of movement—exertion—as a way of visualizing the effort needed in the writing *and* the reading process, the commitment and concomitant endurance that will be necessary for interpretation, and pleasure.[46]

Select Bibliography

Agamben, Giorgio, *The Open: Man And Animal* (Palo Alto, Calif.: Stanford University Press, 2004).
Basu, Jay, 'The Red Shift: Trekking J. H. Prynne's *Red D Gypsum*', *Cambridge Quarterly*, 30/1 (2001), 19–36.
Bunting, Basil, *Complete Poems*, ed. Ric Caddel (Newcastle upon Tyne: Bloodaxe Books, 2000).
Crozier, Andrew, *Star Ground* (Laughton: Silver Hounds, 2008).
Duncan, Andrew, *Origins of the Underground* (Cambridge: Salt Publishing, 2007).
Goodby, John, *Uncaged Sea* (Hove: Waterloo Press, 2008).
Goodby, John, *Illenium* (Exeter: Shearsman Books: 2010).
Hendry, J. F., *The Orchestral Mountain: A Symphonic Elegy* (London: Routledge & Kegan Paul, 1943).
Hulme, T. E., 'Romanticism and Classicism', in Herbert Read (ed.), *Speculations: Essays on Humanism and the Philosophy of Art*, (London: Routledge and Kegan Paul; 2nd edn. 1936; repr. 1987).
Jackson, Kevin, *Humphrey Jennings* (London: Picador, 2004).
Jones, David, Preface to *In Parenthesis* (London: Faber & Faber, 1937).
MacKay, Marina, *Modernism and World War II* (Cambridge: Cambridge University Press, 2007).
Mengham, Rod, *Unsung* (Cambridge: Salt Publishing, 2001).
Mengham, Rod, 'Soluble Culture', *Kenyon Review*, 25/3–4 (2003), 72–7.
Mengham, Rod, *Diving Tower* (Cambridge: Equipage, 2006).

---

[45] T. E. Hulme, 'Romanticism and Classicism', in *Speculations: Essays on Humanism and the Philosophy of Art*, ed. Herbert Read (London: Routledge and Kegan Paul; 2nd edn. 1936; repr. 1987), 135.
[46] Jeremy Noel-Tod, 'Walking the Yellow Brick Road: A Pedestrian Account of J. H. Prynne's Poems', in David Kennedy (ed.), *Necessary Steps* (Exeter: Shearsman Books, 2007), 89–102; and Jay Basu, 'The Red Shift: Trekking J. H. Prynne's *Red D Gypsum*', *Cambridge Quarterly*, 30/1 (2001), 19–36.

Mengham, Rod, *Bell Book* (Cambridge: Wide Range Chapbooks, 2012).
Mengham, Rod, *Les Citadelles: Revue de poésie*, 17 (2012), 114–17.
Noel-Tod, Jeremy, 'Walking the Yellow Brick Road: A Pedestrian Account of J. H. Prynne's Poems', in David Kennedy (ed.), *Necessary Steps* (Exeter: Shearsman Books, 2007), 89–102.
Robinson, Jeffrey, *The Walk: Notes on a Romantic Image* (Norman, Okla.: University of Oklahoma Press, 1989).
Santner, Eric, *On Creaturely Life* (Chicago: University of Chicago Press, 2006).
Simms, Colin, *Otters and Martens* (Exeter: Shearsman Books, 2007).
Sinclair, Iain, *Dining on Stones* (London: Picador, 2004).
Sinclair, Iain, 'Introduction', in Sinclair (ed.), *Conductors of Chaos* (London: Picador, 1995).
Spender, Stephen, 'Some Observations on English Poetry Between Two Wars', in Henry Treece and Stefan Schimanski (eds.), *Transformation*, 3 (n.d., c.1945).
Solnit, Rebecca, *Wanderlust* (London: Verso, 2001).
Tarlo, Harriet (ed.), *The Ground Aslant: An Anthology of Radical Landscape Poetry* (Exeter: Shearsman Book, 2011).
Tolley, A. T., *The Poetry of the Thirties* (London: Victor Gollancz, 1975).
Tuma, Keith, *Fishing by Obstinate Isles: Modern and Postmodern British Poetry and American Readers* (Evanston, Ill.: Northwestern University Press, 1998).
Wenborn, Neil, and Hughes, M. E. J. (eds.), *Contour Lines: New Responses to Landscape in Word and Image* (Cambridge: Salt Publishing, 2010), 78–85.
Wilkinson, John, *Sarn Helen* (Equipage: Cambridge, 1997).
Wilkinson, John, 'The Water-Rail of Tides', in *The Lyric Touch: Essays on the Poetry of Excess* (Cambridge: Salt Publishing, 2007), 189–94.

CHAPTER 4

'OBSCURE AND DOUBTFUL': STEVIE SMITH, F. T. PRINCE, AND LEGACY

WILLIAM MAY

IN 2002, the then Poet Laureate Andrew Motion struggled with an upstairs window sash in the northern suburbs of London. His business that afternoon was to recite two Stevie Smith poems from the first floor of her former house in Palmers Green. A gaggle of onlookers nodded gratefully as he paid tribute to the authority of her verse, suggesting a surprising fondness for a writer who might yet fight him for the title of Hull's third most famous poet.[1] This was a laureate's duty of commemoration, celebrating both Smith's centenary and the installation of a blue plaque outside the house where she had spent most of her 68 years. Its significance seemed ambiguous: this benign civic gesture located Smith on the edge of things, a space which, as Alison Light has noted, woman poets have often inhabited.[2] It is perhaps no surprise that one of the poems he read was Smith's 'Tenuous and Precarious', words which have often been used to describe her posthumous reputation.[3] Yet Motion, who would brand himself *Public Property* (2002) in the poetry collection of the same year, was also keen to divide this public ownership between as many of his deceased colleagues as possible. Here was a living poet's burden that, for a poet long dead, could make a rather wonderful gift. Perhaps Smith offered Motion something that afternoon too: for a short while, this outpost of suburban London might lend him the shelter of marginality.

---

[1] The city has only partial claim on them: Smith moved from Hull at 3, and Motion took up a post at the university in the 1970s.

[2] Alison Light, 'Stevie Smith, Women Poets and the National Voice', *English*, 43/177 (Autumn 1994), 237–59.

[3] See e.g. Christopher Ricks, 'Stevie Smith', in *The Force of Poetry* (Oxford: Oxford University Press, 1984), 255.

Certainly, Motion's most direct allusion to Smith in his corpus, 'Close' from *Love in a Life* (1991), finds the speaker covertly admiring Smith's distance and irrelevance. Here he rewrites her most famous poem, 'Not Waving but Drowning': the speaker in 'Close' drowns at sea while his wife and children, oblivious, look on. Motion's monologue follows a posthumous trail as the dead speaker packs up the picnic things and then finds his ghostly presence unremarked on:

Nobody spoke about me
or how I was no longer there.
It was odd, but I understood why:
when I had drowned I was only
a matter of yards out to sea
(not *too far out*—too close),
still able to hear the talk
and everything safe in view.[4]

The dramatic situation of the poem is both a retread and an inversion of Smith's: the dead swimmer in her poem is solitary, too far away, and falls victim to the indifference of casual acquaintances; the speaker in 'Close' is subject to the suffocating complacency of family life. Motion replaces Smith's anxiety about her voice going unheard ('Nobody heard him, the dead man'[5]), with his terror of going unremarked upon ('Nobody spoke about me'); far better, Motion's poem suggests, to be peripheral and ignored than to be central but of little consequence. The point is made more explicitly in his direct quotation from Smith's poem—'*too far out*'; the phrase is included within his text yet impossible to fully ventriloquize. The three words are only on grudging and temporary loan—everywhere in Motion's poem is comfort, security, and full visibility—all is 'safe in view'. Here is a poet buoyed up by the comforting reference points of John Keats, Edward Thomas, and Philip Larkin, recording the desire to be out of his depth. Yet Motion's dream of the marginal is fleeting, and goes unfulfilled.

His most recent collection, *The Cinder Path* (2009), is instructive here, picking its way carefully through literary tradition. His first post-laureateship volume is preoccupied with legacy, inheritance, and the canon. There are biographical allusions to Keats, Tennyson, Brooke, and Cowper,[6] titles that gesture to Coleridge ('The Ancient Mariner') and Marvell ('The Mower'), and works that take literary conversation as their subject ('Talk about Robert Frost')—the latter, unsurprisingly, more indebted to Frost than the talk-poem. The Spencer Gore painting that adorns the front cover and provides Motion with the title of this collection reaffirms the sense of a sturdy and workable tradition: the cinder path of the painting is unswerving, and without deviation. The collection's

---

[4] Andrew Motion, 'Close', *Love in a Life* (London: Faber & Faber, 1991), 26.

[5] Stevie Smith, 'Not Waving but Drowning', *Collected Poems* (London: Penguin Books, 1978), 256. Future references to this collection will be cited as *CP* and appear in the text.

[6] See 'Bright Star' (24), 'Cecelia Tennyson' (41), 'The Grave of Rupert Brooke' (28), 'The Life of William Cowper' (33), *The Cinder Path* (London: Faber & Faber, 2003).

eponymous poem asserts 'I know what it means | to choose the cinder path';[7] if there is a hint of regret here, there is also the reassurance of progress. Yet, elsewhere, the pathways do not seem so clear: 'The English Line' suggests a frailer and rather more tentative lineage. Its opening image of 'snow-flecked buddleia' is deceptive: here is a scene that stubbornly refuses to transform itself via the poet's imaginative perception—we find only a 'worn-out cable/snake comparison' and the 'ruins of a retaining wall'.[8] If the poem is his laureate swansong, the swan in the poem is tellingly 'Mute'—the plaintive death-hymn of Tennyson's dying swan has been replaced with the image of swan rootling around in a 'wind-hammered plastic bag'. Poet Laureates, like swans, are under the purview of the ruling monarch, but here is a consort that no longer wants to sing. It may be significant that 'the cinder path' is also an allusion to Motion's favourite poem by Smith, 'The Galloping Cat' (*CP* 563). Her fearsome and irreverent cat on its morning rounds 'galloping around' and 'doing good' nevertheless manage to get beneath 'the cinder path of wrath'. An apparently throwaway monologue seems, momentarily, to go deeper and further than the most solemn of lyrics. Rereading Motion's titular poem with Smith's in mind, we find, once more, a desire for alternatives to the English line, or the need for a lineage more uneven and messy than the orderly baton-passing from laureate to laureate might suggest.

Motion's unexpected, and largely unpaid, debt to Smith suggests the lines of contemporary poetry are neither as continuous, nor as starkly drawn, as some accounts might suggest. Peter Middleton has noted that a contemporary volume of poetry can expect to sell 200 to 300 copies 'irrespective of whether published by a leading trade press or a small independent publisher'.[9] It will take more than sales figures to determine who might belong to the mainstream. A line drawn in the sand can be endlessly remade. Andrew Duncan has described the notion of a centre as 'a paranoid fantasy of being controlled by a hostile and malevolent agency',[10] and Motion's appropriation of Smith allows us to speculate on why a 'centre' might be just as far away from where a poet wants to be as the periphery. The way we read tradition in contemporary poetry often follows familiar patterns of uncoupling and rejecting a known canon; to use Lynn Keller's terms, we track 'continuity' and 'divergence' from our modernist inheritance.[11] However, the curious and precarious lives of the poets on the edge of things may offer an alternative way of considering influence. This chapter considers the importance of two marginal poets, Stevie Smith (1902–71) and F. T. Prince (1912–2002), in contemporary poetry, exploring the unusual kinds of co-option and appropriation afforded writers on the edges of British poetic history.

---

[7] Motion, 'The Cinder Path', *The Cinder Path*, 31.
[8] Motion, 'The English Line', *The Cinder Path*, 23.
[9] Peter Middleton, 'Institutions of Poetry in Postwar Britain', in Nigel Alderman and C. D. Blanton (eds.), *A Concise Companion to British and Irish Postwar Poetry* (Oxford: Wiley-Blackwell, 2009), 252.
[10] Andrew Duncan, *Centre and Periphery in Modern British Poetry* (Liverpool: Liverpool University Press, 2005), 52.
[11] See Lynn Keller, *Re-Making It New: Contemporary American Poetry and the Modernist Tradition* (Cambridge: Cambridge University Press, 1987).

The Marginal Poet

Their marginality aside, it is hard to think of two poets more unalike than Stevie Smith and F. T. Prince—even their surnames oppose the regnant and the workmanlike. Popular perceptions of their work and its limitations are equally diametric: Smith's whimsy, agnosticism, and irreverent misquoting seemingly have little in common with Prince's Catholic, academic, and sometimes portentous verse. Between them, their poetry explores a disorientating range of forms: Smith's final collection *Scorpion*, for example, takes on occasional poems ('O Pug!', *CP* 547), monodies ('Grave by a Holm-Oak', *CP* 568), religious verse ('How Do You See?', *CP* 516), myths ('The Forlorn Sea', *CP* 528), dramatic monologues ('The Galloping Cat', *CP* 593), narrative poems ('The House of Over-Dew', *CP* 553), ballads ('The Sallow Bird', *CP* 539), and odes ('The Donkey', *CP* 535). Elsewhere, limericks, epigrams, and concrete poetry complicate the already bewildering mixture. Prince is similarly eclectic, if more orthodox, in his choices: epistle and epithalamium give way to strambotti, narrative poetry, and a series of later dialogue poems ('A Byron-Shelley Conversation', *CP* 231; 'Not a Paris Review Interview', *CP* 245).[12] Occasionally, as in the Hood-like dimeters of Prince's final collection, we might hear a cadence in common. For both poets, too, Robert Browning is an important source. Yet a writer who accused professors of covering poets 'with the vile slime of commentary'[13] is not likely to take her place alongside a poet best known for his Milton scholarship.[14]

The only time they meet in print is in George Stonier's 1938 review for *New Statesman and Nation*. He celebrates Prince's first collection, *Poems*, and backs him as a 'winner', but notes his independence from the likes of Auden and Spender—here is a poet with a 'feminine gift'. Smith's second collection, *Tender Only to One*, is a more startling point of departure: 'how on earth am I to describe Smith to anyone who hasn't read her?', Stonier exclaims.[15] While the review finds much to praise in their work, the seeds are sown here for the bumpy reception of both poets' writings after the war. In this respect, the poets begin to have a little more in common. Their uneven reputations hinge on one over-anthologized work ('Not Waving but Drowning' to Prince's 'Soldiers Bathing'); a period of success in the late 1930s gives way to an extended period in the 1950s when journals and periodicals regularly returned their work. Only towards the end of their lives, via the championing of a younger generation, did their poetry find a new audience.

For Prince, this meant a move from Faber to the Fortune Press, from Fulcrum to Menard, and finally from Anvil to Carcanet; Smith's publishing history was similarly wayward, taking in Jonathan Cape, Chapman and Hall, André Deutsch, and Longman.

---

[12] F. T. Prince, *Collected Poems* (Manchester: Carcanet Press, 2003). Future references to this collection will be cited as *CP* and appear in the text.
[13] Stevie Smith, *Over the Frontier* (London: Virago, 1980), 54.
[14] See F. T. Prince, *The Italian Element in Milton's Poetry* (Oxford: Oxford University Press, 1954).
[15] George Stonier, 'Five Poets, Five Worlds', *New Statesman and Nation* (3 Dec. 1938), 930.

Rupert Hart-Davis, who first published Smith in 1936, was also the long-time Prince fan that produced the lavish *The Doors of Stone* (1962). These rocky receptions make their poetic networks both more tenuous and more faithful: as Smith remarked, 'there isn't an editor in London who hasn't been asked to collaborate with me'.[16] Similarly, the poets who rally around Prince in the 1960s and 1970s show a devotion unlikely were his work still to have been published by Faber. 'i influence the past'[17] asserts Tom Raworth's poem 'Tracking', and he lobbies throughout the 1960s and 1970s for publishers to take on Prince's work. His sense of Prince's poetic significance and the need for his veneration is linked explicitly to his own view of his 'contemporaries'. As he writes to Prince in 1970, 'I almost despair, looking at the acres of boring, whimsical writing that seem to make up "The Poetry Revival".'[18] Buried within this campaign is also a personal frustration with British poetry publishing. Similarly, Smith often becomes the slighted, misrepresented poet who subsequent generations might rescue. In 1990, John Horder and Chris Saunders published *Stevie: A Motley Selection of Her Poems*. Both poets offer fourteen-poem 'cycles' of her verse, appending their selection with a vituperative essay on the way her work has been marginalized and dismissed as eccentric by the academy. Significantly, Horder both begins and ends his selection with a poem entitled 'How far can you press a poet?'.[19]

Publishing history aside, something curiously archaic and anachronistic haunts both their careers: in 1930s Oxford, while Auden and Spender are probing the documentary and the lyric, Prince is writing a dramatic monologue based on Henry James's *The Ivory Tower*. In the 1960s, when the work of the New York School is making its presence felt on the London performance circuit, Prince takes to writing an autobiographical verse memoir about his time in Oxford. Smith, too, is stubbornly out of time: in the year the *New Statesman and Nation* publishes Henry Reed's 'The Naming of Parts', Smith writes a poem insisting 'it is to the poets' merit | To be silent about the war' (*CP* 208). She takes to the 1960s poetry performance circuit in Victorian dress, as if consciously offering herself as a relic, curiously askew. For both poets, anachronism becomes a kind of quiet rebellion.

While Prince and Smith suffered the vicissitudes of post-war publishing, their works also offer mediations on their own marginality, constructing a canon of the peripheral and out-of-step. This is often inextricable from the publishing context of the poems themselves. Prince's first poem to be chosen by T. S. Eliot for publication was 'Epistle to a Patron', its tenor and subject ironic given how Prince's 'patron' would respond to his work after publishing *Poems* in 1938:

For my pride puts all in doubt and at present I have no patience,
I have simply hope, and I submit me
To your judgement which will be just. (*CP* 16)

---

[16] John Gale, 'Death Is a Poem to Stevie Smith', *The Observer* (9 No. 1969), 21.
[17] Tom Raworth, *Tottering State: Selected Poems 1968–1987* (London: Paladin, 1988), 91.
[18] Tom Raworth to F. T. Prince, 30 Sept. 1970, F. T. Prince Archive, Hartley Library, University of Southampton, 4/2/5.
[19] Stevie Smith, *Stevie: A Motley Selection of Her Poems by John Horder and Chris Saunders* (Warwick: Greville Press, 2002).

The shift from this voice to Prince's later works is telling: in 'Finis Coronat Opus', included in the 1993 *Collected Poems,* Prince ruminates on his desire 'to write what nobody peruses' (*CP* 301). In *Memoirs of Oxford* (1970), Prince's poetry is a process of 'cutting, cancelling, rubbing, fingering' (*CP* 143), setting up the poem in direct contrast to the ribald fluency of Auden's 'Letter to Lord Byron' (1937). Smith, too, was acutely conscious of the factors that shape a writer's reputation, and in the poem 'The Choosers' placed the critic squarely between the writer and posterity:

Who shall we send to fetch him away
This young-man Author of the Month of May?
We will send Mr Puff to fetch him away,
We are the Choosers and stand in the way. (*CP* 376)

The Choosers, and the choices they make, are ill-informed; her poem protests that they pick 'inferiorly with grafted eyes'. Elsewhere, as in poems such as 'To School!' (*CP* 269) or 'No Categories' (*CP* 258), Smith sets forth strident positions on the tyranny of poetic groups and cliques.

This concern with their liminal position and the politics of poetic reception is reflected throughout their work and their writing on other poets, helping to build an alternative English line based on difference—on the irregular, or the ungarlanded. Smith is anxious about admitting to influences, confessing conspiratorially to anyone who might listen in the 1960s that she read nobody's poetry but her own, yet her radio broadcast on Thomas Hood suggests a certain affinity with his collected works, 'all too faithfully collected, unpruned, printed and set off on their hundred years of kicking if unlaurelled life'.[20] Yet laurels can come with their own danger too, as both writers make clear: Prince's pamphlet poem *Afterword on Rupert Brooke* (1976) finds pathos in a poet over-praised in their own lifetime, and canonized for the wrong reasons. Prince's afterword asks us to 'pause and look again' (*CP* 171).

Other extra-textual gestures both irreverent and playful offer Prince and Smith as two sides of a significant tradition of marginality. Smith was known to write poems on the pages of magazines that had rejected her work. She copied her poem 'Sappho' onto an empty space in her copy of *Agenda* from 1960, just below Peter Whigham's 'Seven Translations from Sappho'.[21] Her act of defacement might be read as a defiant dialogue with Sappho herself, a poet typified by blank spaces and erasures, and an attempt to mark her own absence from the literary mainstream. Similarly, Prince's extensive journals find him poking fun at the limitations of Movement poetry. In July 1958, a few days after the unexpected publication of one of his poems in *The Sunday Times,* Prince takes the rare step of writing out a contemporary poem in full in his journal: 'Arrival' by Philip Larkin. There is a meta-textual quality to this most metaphysical of Larkin poems. Even

[20] Script for the programme 'Thomas Hood' for *Book of Verse,* 87, produced by John Arlott and broadcast on the BBC Eastern Service on 8 June 1946, held at the BBC Written Archives Centre, Reading.
[21] See her copy of *Agenda* 4 (Autumn 1960), in the Stevie Smith Collection, Special Collections, University of Tulsa.

as the poem muses on the desire to hide from the world and avoid 'wounding it', both the poem and its publication announce Larkin's arrival in, and stranglehold over, post-war poetry; Larkin's arrival marks Prince's departure, or erasure. Prince's comments here are telling: 'I feel this poem by Larkin should have come to something better, and should like to take the first two lines and write it in my own way.'[22] This is a poem that, like many of Larkin's, longs to return to a point of obscurity and anonymity: 'For this ignorance of me | Seems a kind of innocence.'[23] Yet it is penned by a poet who no subsequent writer can ever be in ignorance of—Larkin can never be unknown, or wait to be rediscovered. Here Larkin expresses the same desire to be invisible that would haunt his later biographer, Andrew Motion. Prince's casual project of rewriting Larkin shows us how we might use the marginal to rethink traditions of post-war poetry. To 'recover' an obscure voice from a previous generation allows writers to resituate their work, and to reimagine a poetry scene that 'should have come to something better'. It is a creative act of reimagining literary history, offering its primary appeal to post-war poets determined to put the marginal poet at the centre of things. The remainder of this essay explores how Prince and Smith provided both a cautionary and exemplary model for poets writing in their wake.

Tributes and Revivals

The most obvious trace left by Prince and Smith is the series of poetic tributes or eulogies they inspired. The gesture of a tribute is ambivalent; they can memorialize poets, but keep them at bay. For a writer whose lineage and influence seems difficult to parse, Stevie Smith is not short on poetic elegies. This is perhaps symptomatic—an elegy can be a gift paid with a keen sense of duty, burden, or expediency; here is a way for a poet to wash their hands of anything more knotty and complicated than baffled affection. Patricia Beer's 'In Memory of Stevie Smith' (1971) is typical in this respect, reading less like an elegy than a crossword clue: 'A heroine is someone who does what you cannot do | For yourself and so is this poet'.[24] The awkward syntax seems grudging, euphemistic, as if reluctant to name its subject, admitting their friendship was 'not close'. She goes on to praise Smith for her discovery of 'Marvels'—'a cat that sings', 'a corpse that comes in | Out of the rain'—and her ability to strike compassion in 'strange places'. Smith's work becomes a poetic almanac by degrees whimsical and grotesque; this is carefully balanced alongside Beer's circumspection, which creates a crisp kind of occasional poem far removed from the irreverent and wayward poet it commemorates. It pays homage rather than pledging affiliation. Beer recalls Smith's most famous poetic creations— Mrs Arbuthnot, Mrs Courtley, or Phoebe and Rose—only to conclude they 'must have died | long ago', suggesting a frailty to Smith's posthumous reputation. The image of the

---

[22] F. T. Prince, 8 July 1958, F. T. Prince Archive, University of Southampton, 3/1/5.
[23] Philip Larkin, 'Arrival', *The Less Deceived* (London: Faber & Faber, 1955), 5.
[24] Patricia Beer, 'In Memory of Stevie Smith', *Collected Poems* (Manchester: Carcanet Press, 1988), 114.

corpse brought in from the rain is telling: it appears in no Smith poem, but seems rather a description of Beer's tribute itself, which is more post-mortem than celebration of her work.

Smith's supposed eccentricity often seems a barb for the next generation of woman poets, and a reason to disentangle themselves from her legacy. Fleur Adcock's poetry has often been compared to Smith's, but in interview she is quick to dismiss her influence: 'Well she was such an oddity. She was Stevie Smith, bless her!'[25] Her idiosyncrasy makes hers an implausible and dangerous inheritance. Vicki Feaver is similarly divided, confessing in 2001 that she began by loving her, tried to write a thesis about her and hated her, and then came to love her 'precisely because she is so resistant to academic criticism'.[26] Here, her presence is acknowledged while her distance from the respectable is confirmed. Feaver's own poetry catches some of this admission and demotion—in *A Handless Maiden* (1994), she domesticates 'The River God', rewriting Smith's deranged deity into a benign figure who shuffles about in slippers.[27] The outsider is tamed, and their danger defused. She tries a different and perhaps more telling tactic in 'Lily Pond', which finds its murderous speaker in a perpetual act of drowning and resuscitating its victim: 'Thinking of new ways to kill you | and bring you back from the dead'.[28] This poem offers more general analogies for the way a female tradition of post-war poetry has treated Smith's work, sometimes reluctant to have the marginal at its centre.

By contrast, 'Blake's Purest Daughter', by Brian Patten, offers something much closer to hagiography. The poem is a kind of pagan catechism, as the speaker questions the four elements in turn on the purpose of death. The elegy ends with an envoy and entreaty:

Sweet Stevie elemental
Free now from the personal,
Through sky and soil
Fire and water
Swim on, Blake's purest daughter![29]

Patten's half-rhymes of 'elemental/personal' suggest an ear for Smith's own phonic playfulness, but also transform the speaker of her most famous poem into a hero, swimming on against the tide. She performs a similar role in his poem 'The Critics' Chorus or, What the Poem Lacked': in a defence of newly 'chaotic' poetry, Patten offers Smith's indifference to critics as a model. She, oblivious, is 'fingering a rosary made of starlight' as the literary choosers dismiss her work as doggerel.[30] Patten's canonization of Smith, casting himself as her hierophant, is a useful way of reading 1960s appropriations of her and her work more generally. At the behest of Michael Horovitz, Smith took part in at least

---

[25] Julian Stannard, 'An interview with Fleur Adcock', *Thumbscrew*, 17 (Winter 2000–1), 5–15 (13).
[26] Vicki Feaver, 'Castaway Poems', *Poetry News* (Spring 2001), 8.
[27] Vicki Feaver, 'The River God', *The Handless Maiden* (London: Cape, 1994), 9.
[28] Feaver, 'Lily Pond', *The Handless Maiden*, 38.
[29] Brian Patten, 'Blake's Purest Daughter', *Grinning Jack* (London: Paladin, 1990), 105.
[30] Patten, 'The Critics' Chorus, or What the Poem Lacked', *Grinning Jack*, 117.

fifteen of the 'Live New Departures' art circuses between 1959 and 1968, singing her poems to off-kilter and keening rhythms, each performance bringing her a wider audience than before. Smith's success at these events both puzzled and inspired the younger generation. Al Alvarez noted 'she could scarcely have been more out of place'.[31] She was not always enamoured of her new-found lionization, or the poets that celebrated her—she dismissed McGough as a 'rhymester'.[32] Yet her ability to be both central to the poetry performances of the 1960s and still out of place helped to confirm her eccentric and peripheral presence. It is at this point that she begins to take her place in a British lineage of iconoclasm. Her anachronism offers her a point of entry into the canon. In Randall Stevenson's *The Last of England?* (2004), the twelfth part of the thirteen-volume *Oxford English Literary History*, Smith is co-opted as a proto-postmodernist, writing poems that 'seem to despair of making language function convincingly'. Stevenson's argument hinges on an authorial voice which is at once emblematic, 'unique, historically and socially, to England in the late 1950s and early 1960s', prescient of the postmodern theories that would follow ten years after the author's death, and deeply nostalgic, Smith's poems presenting themselves as 'swansongs for the vacuous gentility whose longevity so riled A. Alvarez in 1962'.[33] In pointed opposition to the 'canon-maker' Alvarez, Smith appears as a warning from the past, a dusty relic whose very anachronistic presence becomes curiously symptomatic of a period unsure of its future.

In both tributes I have discussed, Smith is a lonely heroine, and marginality is the price paid for her veneration. Notions of periphery and obscurity similarly inform the most direct tribute to Prince by a post-war British poet, 'The Late Poem' by Lee Harwood:

Today I got very excited when I read some
poems by Mallarmé and Edwin Denby, and later
in the evening, by F. T. Prince.
I don't get 'very excited' very often,
but today was an exception;
and the fact I got 'excited' was only
increased when I realised two of them—Denby
and Prince—are still alive and are probably
now asleep in their beds in nice apartments.

Ted Berrigan has met Edwin Denby.
I don't know anyone who's met F. T. Prince.
I wish I could meet F. T. Prince;
Maybe I will one day, but it will have to be soon
as he must be getting old.[34]

---

[31] Al Alvarez, 'Deadly Funny', *The Observer* (3 Aug. 1975), 21.
[32] Quoted in Frances Spalding, *Stevie Smith: A Critical Biography* (London: Faber & Faber, 1988), 268.
[33] Randall Stevenson, *The Oxford English Literary History*, xii. *1960–2000: The Last of Engand?* (Oxford: Oxford University Press, 2004), 143.
[34] Lee Harwood, 'The Late Poem', *Collected Poems* (Exeter: Shearsman Books, 2004), 58.

Harwood is writing from, and perhaps to, the New York that was his inspiration for much of the 1960s. Robert Sheppard has noted the irony of Harwood's allusion here—the scholarly poetry of Prince appears in a poem he would barely recognize as such.[35] In keeping with the New York School, the allusion to Prince might as well be to a bar, or a pop song, or a local shop: it is a poetic allusion stripped of portentousness, apparently ingenious enough to tell us nothing but what it is. We might even read Prince's obscurity as the price of admission into Harwood's poetic inventory: he is sufficiently unknown to be allowed a name-check, and to ward off the allusive reader keen to attribute anything more to the poem. There is a delight in his peripheral status—the unmet Prince who belongs to no contemporary network Harwood can puzzle out. Yet the apparently desultory mention is complicated by the urgency and belatedness of this 'late poem'. The direct referent for the title is seemingly the lateness of the hour: the speaker imagines his poets 'now asleep in their beds'. Prince is also the poet Harwood comes to latest in the text. There is also the concern that Prince is 'getting old', and that his obscurity, while making him a fitting allusion for an avant-garde poet, might make him more difficult to track down, that Harwood's poetic entreaty might come too late. But belatedness can be read into this poem in other ways, too. The work details the poetry Harwood has been reading of late; it is also a contemporary poem that seems to have come late to the party. It is Frank O'Hara's 'The Day Lady Died' rewritten for a poet still—to Harwood's surprise—among the living.

This poetic envoy, centring round the desire to meet F. T. Prince, eventually finds its recipient, and they begin corresponding in the late 1960s. Harwood first approaches him to write a blurb for his collection *The White Room* (1968). Prince's refusal to do so is significant, stemming directly from his sense of himself as a poet on the edge of things: 'my position and my reputation are such—so obscure and doubtful—that any remarks of mine would do you no good at all'.[36] Prince's ambiguous epithet suggests not only that his reputation might be uneven, but that he might have left no imprint whatsoever. Yet he is equally doubtful about Harwood's recent work, warning him that 'having mastered your technique, it is now mastering you'. Linking Harwood's recent work with Ashbery and O'Hara, he accuses him of 'a quite unusually secure and cosy kind of Bohemianism, really more American than anything else [...] nothing could be more alien to the European past'. Here, the obscure and doubtful poet seems unsure about the poetry he feels too insignificant to endorse. Yet the importance of his critique is twofold: Harwood shows Prince's letter to Stuart Montgomery, then editor at Fulcrum, who goes on to publish Prince's next volume on the strength of it. Prince's concerns about the direction of Harwood's also prompt a major re-evaluation and rethinking on Harwood's part—he writes no new work for the following five months,[37] eventually reshaping his

---

[35] Robert Sheppard, 'It's a Long Road', in Sheppard (ed.), *The Salt Companion to Lee Harwood* (London: Salt Publishing, 1994), 8–24 (21).

[36] F. T. Prince to Lee Harwood, 30 Aug. 1967, F. T. Prince Archive, Hartley Library, University of Southampton, 4/4/2.

[37] Lee Harwood to F. T. Prince, 17 Oct. 1967, F. T Prince Archive, Hartley Library, University of Southampton, 4/4/2.

poetry to include the European tradition 'missing' from his 1960s verse. 'The Late Poem' writes Prince into a contemporary idiom whilst showing Harwood a way out of it.

Singular Talents

The post-war embrace of the marginal poet does not come without its qualifications, or its puzzlement on either side: Prince confesses to Anthony Rudolf of the avant-garde poets writing to venerate him: 'I really can't make much of them [...] and wonder why they make anything of me. Not that I don't like to be liked, but both my strength and my burden is that I have to make sense—I can't make any of them.'[38] Here, the peripheral poet maintains his place on the edge, even as a new generation of writers cluster around him. Smith, too, seemed happier as an outsider than a patron. Yet the singularity for which both Smith and Prince were admired raised a difficult problem for their devotees. Paying tribute to poets whose reception and output may have been irregular, uneven, or doubtful can lead to seemingly unusual results. Yet acknowledging them as an influence appears still more uncertain. Andrew Motion is mindful that 'golden opinions' will not necessarily have a popularizing effect on a poet's work;[39] the term 'poet's poet' qualifies rather than inviting comment. Nevertheless, it is significant that the two contemporary poets most influenced by Smith and Prince were Sylvia Plath and Geoffrey Hill respectively, their swift canonization perhaps coming at the expense of their forebears. In the final section of this chapter, I will consider how these poetic pairs remade each other's work, and so helped define and confirm their marginal position. A Bloomian model of influence imagines poetic tradition as a series of battles between strong poets; what kinds of contests might take place in the fight for the marginal?

When, in 1962, Sylvia Plath wrote a letter declaring herself a 'desperate Smith addict' she was looking for allies and contemporaries in a country apparently indifferent to her work.[40] Fifty years later, when critics mention this letter, one of the last Plath ever wrote, it is more usually to give Smith a temporary pass into the canon.[41] The inversion, representing the dramatic posthumous reassessment of Plath's work, suggests that the battle for the periphery is as significant for the centre, marking the vital difference between the singular and the marginal. The inference is that singular poets might only displace, rather than sustain, each other's work. While Plath and Smith's work shares a number of features—rhythmic

---

[38] F. T. Prince to Anthony Rudolf, 14 Mar. 1977, quoted in Anthony Rudolf, ' "I have written other poems, you know" ', *PN Review 147*, 29/1 (Sept.–Oct. 2002), 27.

[39] Andrew Motion, 'William Barnes: An Introduction', in *Ways of Life: On Places, Painters, and Poets: Selected Essays and Reviews 1994–2008* (London: Faber & Faber, 2008), 174.

[40] Sylvia Plath to Stevie Smith, 19 Nov. 1962, in Jack Barbera and William McBrien (eds.), *Me Again: The Uncollected Writings of Stevie Smith* (London: Virago, 1982), 6.

[41] See e.g. Linda Anderson, 'Gender, Feminism, Poetry: Stevie Smith, Sylvia Plath, Jo Shapcott', in Neil Corcoran (ed.), *The Cambridge Companion to Twentieth-Century English Poetry* (Cambridge: Cambridge University Press, 2007).

irregularities that deliberately disrupt the lyric line, a concern with the psychic possibilities of landscape, and a preoccupation with female religious iconography—critics have tended to label Plath's idiosyncrasies as genius, and Smith's as eccentricity. Jane Dowson and Alice Entwistle's *A History of Twentieth-Century British and Irish Women's Poetry* (2005) attempts a sort of recompense, devoting a sole chapter to Smith's work, and arguing that the critical preoccupation with Plath has overshadowed other voices from the period.[42] Yet the recalcitrant attitude towards Smith's work comes in response to a poetry that often interrogates the outsider. One of the most popular poems she read during the 1960s performs and parodies the legacy of the marginal poet:

Pearl
To an American lady poet committing suicide because of not being appreciated enough.

Then cried the American poet where she lay supine:
'My name is Purrel; I was caast before swine.' (*CP* 475)

After the poem's publication in 1966, Smith included it in many of the performances she gave before her death five years later. The poet's introductions attempt to mitigate the sense of the poem as having a specific historical referent without opening up the work to biographical interpretation. Her first draft for an introduction to the poem depicts Pearl as a fictional character that the performing Smith is about to bring onto the stage:

> Pearl, the American lady poet who comes next, thought she was not as appreciated as she should be, I have made her American as I want two syllables on Pearl, or something nearer than you get in English.

Here, Smith makes clear that the subject's nationality is a phonic necessity rather than an indication of a real-life referent. Yet the framing device reintroduces the sense that Smith has transformed her original subject, raising questions about the primary source for the work. The second draft for the introduction (and one that Smith used when performing the poem at the Edinburgh Festival and readings throughout 1969 and 1970) simply removes the information that Smith has 'made her American', entirely eliminating the sense that Smith has reworked the poem from a self-portrait into a mask. This puzzling poem is unsure whether to fix itself as a tribute, a parody, or a confession, and seems equally perplexed as to who should be paying tribute to whom. In this way, the territory of the singular affords little room for companions.

The relationship between Geoffrey Hill and F. T. Prince shows similar points of tension. They first meet in 1970, and a letter from Hill to Prince written in the same year confirms the sense of Prince's symbolic 'outsider' status:

> Our work already has a relationship, in being set apart from most of the poetry that holds the place of worldly power in our age—though I confess that I would

---

[42] Jane Dowson and Alice Entwistle, *A History of Twentieth-Century British and Irish Women's Poetry* (Cambridge: Cambridge University Press, 2005), 6.

be incapable of the kind of sustained meditative narrative that you build in your new book.[43]

Here are poets apparently outside the power structures of contemporary poetry; Hill suggests an affinity through a shared commitment to poetry that is isolated and uncompromising. Yet his qualification about Prince's *Memoirs in Oxford* is telling, and suggests the singular Prince is as much a threat as an ally. The letter prefigures a critical manoeuvre Hill will make in his 2002 public tribute to him in *PN Review*. The article praises the 'prudish luxuries' and careful locutions of Prince's 'Epistle to a Patron', but becomes more disavowal than celebration: Hill denounces all his work after 1938's *Poems*, after which Prince is apparently ridden by the hag Sincerity.

> Already, in the communing of 'Soldiers Bathing', it is as if the poet were silently reproaching himself for an earlier violent preciosity. I am saying that the criteria, the creative intuitions, that went into the making of *Poems* (1938) were well-founded. Confessional sincerity is the undoing of *Memoirs in Oxford* (1970).[44]

Hill's use of 'communing' as a pejorative term is revealing about the kinds of public gestures a poem should or should not make—for Hill's version of a singular poet, it is no better than self-reproach. Further accounting for Prince's decline, Hill states of the decade in which the early poems were composed: 'Poets of the 1930s—for evident and good reasons—gave much attention to questions of just and unjust rule, the public good (again one wants to add: in ways totally incomprehensible to the poets of today.)' Once more he compounds a conviction about a poetic 'locution' with a sense of the past's lost possibilities, accompanied by opinion about 'the society of your contemporaries'.[45] Prince's poetic gifts are explained by the decade that shaped him, and so generic; Hill's talents are in contradistinction to the present, and therefore exceptional.

'Prince's is an equivocating oratory',[46] Hill adds, yet his defensive tribute seems similarly equivocal about his own indebtedness to Prince's work. In fact, it extends beyond affinities between Prince's 'An Epistle to a Patron' or 'To a Friend on his Marriage' from *Poems* (1938) and Hill's 'To the (Supposed) Patron' or 'The Bidden Guest' from *For the Unfallen* (1959), a title not only indebted to Lawrence Binyon's 'For the Fallen', but to Prince's 'For the Deserted', 'For Fugitives', and 'For Beggars and Thieves' in the 1938 collection. Prince's influence is felt in 'Strafford' in *Doors of Stone* (1963), echoed in 'Funeral Music' from *King Log* (1968), while the scholarly passions inspiring Prince's later poems, 'Drypoints of the Hasidim' (1975), 'Afterword on Rupert Brooke' (1977), and 'A Last Attachment' (1979) animate Hill's *The Mystery of the Charity of Charles Péguy* (1983).

---

[43] Geoffrey Hill to F. T. Prince, 18 Nov. 1970, F. T. Prince Archive, Hartley Library, University of Southampton, 4/2/5.
[44] Geoffrey Hill, 'Il Cortegiano: F. T. Prince's Poems (1938)', *PN Review 147*, 29/1 (Sept.–Oct. 2002), 30.
[45] Hill, 'Il Cortegiano', 30.
[46] Hill, 'Il Cortegiano', 30.

Yet Hill makes no reference in his essay to work Prince published over two further decades of activity beyond *Memoirs in Oxford* (1970).

A fitting place to observe this displacement is in the poets' 1960s tributes to Tommaso Campanella, the Renaissance poet and philosopher who spent twenty-seven years imprisoned in Naples after being accused of conspiracy. Prince's comes first, published in *The Doors of Stone* (1962); Hill includes the poem 'Men are a Mockery of Angels' in the 'Four Poems Regarding the Endurance of Poets' published in *King Log* (1968). For both Hill and Prince, Campanella becomes a representative figure for the marginalized poet. He writes his most important works incarcerated; Hill and Prince, similarly, must work outside the poetic networks of power. Hill's parenthetic aside in 'September Song'—'(I have made | an elegy for myself it | is true)'[47]—hangs over this poem too. In Campanella, he pays tribute to a poet whose endurance (in both senses) might be compared with his own. While Hill's has a concision more effective than Prince's replication of Campanella's 'unending' torment, the debt to Prince's poem is striking. Prince's dramatic monologue offers us 'Sighs are my sustenance' (*CP* 105); 'the cries' in Hill's poem are 'my bread'.[48] Prince's mention of 'finite angelic sweetness' offers Hill his title. Prince's Campanella looks forward to 'the bread of honest joy'; Hill's recalls 'a joy past all care'. The Prince monologue describes Campanella's transgression as offering 'too much light'—the light in Hill's poem is 'derisive', and derivative might be a word hanging at the edges. Yet Hill reshapes Prince's poem in significant ways—his truncated form offers its own kind of incarceration for Campanella, a limitation that once again puts the poet in charge of the jailor. Whilst Prince's poem finds Campanella wondering if his trenchant positions have been 'in vain', and finds him bleakly awaiting the time when 'I repent', Hill's tribute ends with a call to arms:

But we are commanded
To rise, when, in silence,
I would compose my voice.

Here Campanella becomes a heroic figure of revolution, the writer a latter-day marginal poet might use to 'compose' their own voice.

Yet the scale of Hill's debt is only matched by the impossibility of repaying it. As a self-professedly marginal poet, Hill's subsequent canonization can only come in determined resistance to his contemporaries—a poet saluting the imprisoned Campanella can have no need of an inmate. A singular talent must remain peerless. A. N. Wilson's assessment of his work, coming from a review of *The Orchards of Syon* (2002), is only one of many to find Hill without contemporary precedent:

> Since we have lost the capacity to understand the language of our forebears, each new poet with any serious claim to importance must drag with him the poetic baggage of

---

[47] Geoffrey Hill, 'September Song', *King Log* (London: André Deutsch, 1968), 19.
[48] Hill, 'Men are a Mockery of Angels', *King Log*, 35.

the past and refashion it. Eliot and Pound were the great bearers of the burden in the early to mid 20th century. Lowell continued the task. Other than translators of older poetry, no English-born poet until Hill even understood the nature or meaning of the task. The work of Hill is a phoenix rising from European ashes.[49]

Hill's lionization as the phoenix, the solitary figure rising, like Campanella, to compose his voice, makes Prince's legacy yet more doubtful. The poet incarcerated and unattended-to becomes, by a Houdini-like gesture, not Hill, but Prince. Hill is afforded the gift of singularity; Prince remains marginal.

Legacies

In Alan Hollinghurst's novel *The Stranger's Child* (2011), biographers, editors, and ex-lovers fight out the poetic legacy of Cecil Valance, a fictional war poet whose anthology-favourite 'Soldiers Dreaming' makes his work briefly well known, if not well regarded. Hollinghurst's nudge to F. T. Prince's poem 'Soldiers Bathing' (1942) is surely not accidental: like Valance, Prince's reputation was both sustained and skewed by the popularity of this one poem. In Hollinghurst's novel, the poet's posthumous reputation is an expedient for the 'rodent-like' biographer hoping to make his mark, for family members with ancient scores to settle, or reviewers playing identity politics. Although interest in Valance's poetry grows after his death, it doesn't outlast the prurient interest in his life, which continues long after his poems have been dismissed as second-rate. Yet Hollinghurst's allusion is fitting in other ways, too: Prince's work is preoccupied with poetic legacy, and how poets' lives are remembered and rewritten. He writes *Afterword on Rupert Brooke* in response to the biographical revelations of the 1960s, and reminds us 'We must take all there is, and see and weigh it all | If possible' (*CP* 171). Perhaps there is a call for a wider and more nuanced understanding of influences on contemporary poetic landscape here too: one that finds room for both Smith and Prince.

This chapter began with 'Close', Andrew Motion's allusion to Smith's most famous poem 'Not Waving but Drowning', a work which seems to be perpetually rewritten by poets attempting to track their own distance from the centre of things.[50] Another poem by Motion from the same collection, 'It is an Offence', seems its antithesis, a guilty admission that a tradition shorn of centres and peripheries might become a battle for territory. Its stark title seems to echo Smith's indignant animal poem, 'This Is Disgraceful and Abominable' (*CP* 338). Yet whereas Smith's poem railed against animal cruelty, Motion's

---

[49] A. N. Wilson, 'A phoenix rising from European ashes', *Spectator* (7 Sept. 2002): [http://www.spectator.co.uk/books/20178/a-phoenix-rising-from-european-ashes.thtml]. Accessed 1 May 2012.

[50] See e.g. Elizabeth Bartlett's 1976 poem 'Not Dying but Sleeping', which considers the 'legacy' of an old woman found dead in her home, *Two Women Dancing: New and Selected Poems* (Newcastle upon Tyne: Bloodaxe Books, 1995), 103–4.

seems to argue for microchipping: the poem's speaker begins by railing at an ex-racing dog with a habit of crapping outside his own front door. The daily process of clearing up after him at first prompts anger, before giving way to a curious kind of respect for the animal's persistence and sense of ritual. Finally, he begins to see an analogy between the defecating dog and his own relationship to a poetic tradition, expressed in a tellingly Smithian cadence:

I admit that I also yearn to leave my mark on society,
and not see machines or people trample it foolishly[51]

The poem's strict sonnet form seems already to mark some kind of barrier between Smith's world and his own, even as the bumpy half-rhyme pledges a brief phonic affinity. Yet the two contradictory impulses Motion explores in this poem—policing, ordering, and removing versus that of marking, preserving, retaining—sets out the challenge to us in situating contemporary poetry, and considering how much messiness we allow into its history.

SELECT BIBLIOGRAPHY

Alvarez, Al, 'Deadly Funny', *The Observer* (3 Aug. 1975), 21.
Anderson, Linda, 'Gender, Feminism, Poetry: Stevie Smith, Sylvia Plath, Jo Shapcott', in Neil Corcoran (ed.), *The Cambridge Companion to Twentieth-Century English Poetry* (Cambridge: Cambridge University Press, 2007).
Dowson, Jane and Entwistle, Alice, *A History of Twentieth-Century British and Irish Women's Poetry* (Cambridge: Cambridge University Press, 2005).
Duncan, Andrew, *Centre and Periphery in Modern British Poetry* (Liverpool: Liverpool University Press, 2005).
Feaver, Vicki, 'Castaway Poems', *Poetry News* (Spring 2001), 8.
Gale, John, 'Death Is a Poem to Stevie Smith', *The Observer* (9 No. 1969), 21.
Hill, Geoffrey, 'Il Cortegiano: F. T. Prince's Poems (1938)', *PN Review 147*, 29/1 (Sept.–Oct. 2002), 28–31.
Keller, Lynn, *Re-Making It New: Contemporary American Poetry and the Modernist Tradition* (Cambridge: Cambridge University Press, 1987).
Light, Alison, 'Stevie Smith, Women Poets and the National Voice', *English,* 43/177 (Autumn 1994), 237–59.
Middleton, Peter, 'Institutions of Poetry in Postwar Britain', in Nigel Alderman and C. D. Blanton (eds.), *A Concise Companion to British and Irish Postwar Poetry* (Oxford: Wiley-Blackwell, 2009), 252.
Prince, F. T., *The Italian Element in Milton's Poetry* (Oxford: Oxford University Press, 1954).
Prince, F. T., *Collected Poems* (Manchester: Carcanet Press, 2003).

---

[51] Andrew Motion, 'It is an Offence', *Love in A Life*, 39.

Raworth, Tom, *Tottering State: Selected Poems 1968-1987* (London: Paladin, 1988).
Sheppard, Robert, 'It's a Long Road', in Sheppard (ed.), *The Salt Companion to Lee Harwood* (London: Salt Publishing, 1994), 8-24.
Smith, Stevie, *Over the Frontier* (London: Virago, 1980).
Smith, Stevie, *Stevie: A Motley Selection of Her Poems by John Horder and Chris Saunders* (Warwick: Greville Press, 2002).
Spalding, Frances, *Stevie Smith: A Critical Biography* (London: Faber & Faber, 1988).
Stannard, Julian, 'An interview with Fleur Adcock', *Thumbscrew*, 17 (Winter 2000-1), 5-15.
Stevenson, Randall, *The Oxford English Literary History, xii. 1960-2000: The Last of Engand?* (Oxford: Oxford University Press, 2004).
Stonier, George, 'Five Poets, Five Worlds', *New Statesman and Nation* (3 Dec. 1938), 930.

CHAPTER 5

THE MOVEMENT: NEVER AND ALWAYS

MARTIN DODSWORTH

KINGSLEY Amis, Robert Conquest, Donald Davie, D. J. Enright, Thom Gunn, John Holloway, Elizabeth Jennings, Philip Larkin, and John Wain, the nine poets represented in Conquest's anthology *New Lines* (1956), are conventionally agreed to be the poets of the Movement. The element of convention in this list must be emphasized; these poets never came together with the intention of forming a group, and indeed, most of them denied membership of the Movement at one time or another. The waffling introduction to *New Lines* does not help. Conquest has written:

> The 'Movement' as first met with was a journalistic coinage, a catch-phrase only later peripherally applied—by overspill—to desiccated verses then emerging to counteract what were seen as the excesses of the 1940s. No such overview united those I anthologized in *New Lines,* and my first draft of its introduction...had a paragraph specifically rejecting the Movement appellation.[1]

Following Blake Morrison, whose book *The Movement: English Poetry and Fiction of the 1950s* (1980), is the fullest account to date, scholars see these poets as sharing a 'consensus' about the aims and means of poetry. This position is not without its difficulties. Bernard Bergonzi has set the problem out clearly. If Movement poetry is to be identified by intrinsic factors such as 'formality, compression of sense, wit, and a moral concern', then 'one has to acknowledge that these qualities are to be found in many texts outside the milieu and circumstances of the Movement'. If, on the other hand, it depends on extrinsic factors such as class origin and education (all the *New Lines* poets, with the exception of Conquest, were from middle-class homes and educated outside the grand

---

[1] Robert Conquest, 'New Lines, Movements, and Modernisms', in Zachary Leader (ed.), *The Movement Reconsidered* (Oxford: Oxford University Press, 2009), 307.

and expensive public school system), then 'one has no way of telling, by critical examination, whether or not a text belongs to the Movement'.[2]

In this chapter I shall write about the poets included in *New Lines* as 'Movement poets', but in the consciousness that there is something arbitrary about doing so. The arbitrariness has much to do with the fact that the Movement, often referred to at the time as 'the new movement', was, in Conquest's words 'a journalistic coinage'. There was more to it than that, but its journalistic origins are important, because they account for the vagueness of the whole phenomenon. And it is not just that: they rendered the Movement suspect by contagion, as it were. A young Bernard Bergonzi, for example, writing in 1955 in an Oxford little magazine, observed that there were a number of writers 'who, given a similar publicity machine, might be groomed for stardom in a movement of a very different sort…pursuing a more or less "romantic" line, and all equally removed from the "neo-classical" or "neo-metaphysical" predilections of "the Movement" as now established'.[3] Furthermore, although it now seems uncontroversial to identify the Movement with the nine poets represented in *New Lines*, there were other poets in 1955 who seemed meant to be part of it. Morrison himself names three ' "outsiders" who have a sympathy with the group endeavour equal to, and in some cases greater than, that of the "official" members': Anthony Thwaite, George MacBeth, and Vernon Scannell.[4] Thwaite's first book of poems, *Home Truths* (1957), was published by Larkin's own small-press publisher, the Marvell Press, little more than a year after *The Less Deceived*; and MacBeth's first book was one of the subjects of the *Spectator* review that set the whole 'journalistic' Movement off. Whilst Scannell's credentials are suspect, other poets of the time associated with the Movement were: A. Alvarez; Bergonzi whose *Descartes and the Animals* still gives pleasure; Philip Oakes who, like Amis and Wain, was published by the press of the School of Art at Reading University; Jonathan Price, reviewed alongside MacBeth and Davie in *The Spectator*, and whose posthumous book, *Everything Must Go* (1985), bears Larkin's posthumous commendation; G. J. Warnock, better known as an Oxford philosopher; and Gordon Wharton, published not only at Reading but also by the Fantasy Press, whose pamphlet series was an important platform for the new poetry. These poets make up the penumbra of the Movement, and any consensus to which it was party. Like the ghosts begging for blood from Ulysses' sacrifice, they should not be forgotten—though habitually denied, as, for the most part, they will be here. Their ghostly presence should be felt, both when Movement style is discussed, and when its complex history is traced.

The presence of those ghosts at the feast (some, fortunately, merely metaphorical ghosts in 2011) is a reminder that the times themselves played a part in the formation of the Movement. As for individuals, the line of descent traced by Morrison, from Amis,

---

[2] Bernard Bergonzi, *Wartime and Aftermath: English Literature and Its Background, 1939–1960* (Oxford: Oxford University Press, 1993), 137–8.

[3] Bernard Bergonzi, 'The Literary Situation—I', *Departure* II, 6 (1955), 15.

[4] Blake Morrison, *The Movement: English Poetry and Fiction of the 1950s* (Oxford: Oxford University Press, 1980), 9.

Larkin, and Wain, contemporaries at Oxford, is generally accepted, though contestable. Certainly, Donald Davie has not been given his due. History; Larkin and his friends; Davie—only when these have been considered can we assess the importance of journalists and their concerns to the Movement.

Firstly, then, the history. The Movement came to the fore in the mid-fifties, at a time when Britain was still recovering from the effects of the Second World War. David Kynaston calls his social history of the years 1945–51 *Austerity Britain* and has little difficulty in justifying his title. Britain was steadily losing power and influence in the age of the hydrogen bomb. There was little comfort in the aftermath of the Korean War; the Cold War was well on its way. Conditions at home reflected the loss of imperial glory. In the early fifties the mood was grey and austere. Food rationing did not end until 1953; much war damage in the cities remained to be made good. The post-war Labour governments had striven to create a fairer society, but not a more cheerful one. Detachment and poise were a way of coping with reduced status in a rapidly changing world. The 'cool, scientific and analytical' tone associated with the Movement was part of this way of coping. So was irony, the weapon of the underdog.

The 1950s saw a shift in politics from the left, which had triumphed in the first post-war general election, to the right. The Conservatives regained power in 1951, not so much because the country wanted policies as that it wanted less discipline and more fun. The desire for change was reflected in poetry too. There was a reaction against the poetry of the forties, particularly strong after the death of Dylan Thomas in 1953, but evident before that, for example in attitudes to the New Apocalypse, a term used loosely enough and particularly applied to the poetry of Henry Treece. Since forties poetry was characterized as the product of a visionary rapture thought careless by followers of the charismatic Cambridge critic F. R. Leavis, there was a natural case to be made for the opposite, a poetry that was reasoned and careful—careful of its reader and, above all, of its words. Bergonzi cites the editorial in the January 1950 number of *Poetry London*: 'What is needed is not so much the "inspired" poem as a revival of *style*: first class workmanship rather than the prophetic tone.'[5] Two years later, *Chanticleer*, a little magazine which only ran for four numbers, used its first editorial to discuss 'the *terrible state of chassis* [sic—last words of Sean O'Casey, *Juno and the Paycock*] now existing in the world, and... its sorry plight economically and culturally'.[6] *Chanticleer* resumed the cultural point in its second number: 'there is precious little to laugh at in this hydrogen age... society is such today that we either speak out or perish' (2 (Spring 1953), 2). The editors' call for 'the rediscovery of the *story element*' in poetry was not generally successful, and is indicative of the continuing uncertainty of the time. 'Speaking out', however, was successful. A plain style, the consequence of rejecting forties poetics, is characteristic of Movement poetry. If, as Davie's 'Remembering the Thirties' has it, 'a neutral tone' was preferred, it was in response to a general feeling, one with its roots in 'the *terrible state of chassis*' seen as prevailing in the world at the time.

[5] Bergonzi, *Wartime and Aftermath*, 160.
[6] 'Editorial', *Chanticleer*, 1 (Autumn 1952), 2.

This is to put the emphasis a little differently from Blake Morrison, who says bluntly that 'The origins of the Movement can be traced back to Oxford in the early 1940s, when a number of key friendships were made',[7] notably that of Amis and Larkin, contemporaries at St John's, where Wain arrived after Amis had gone into the Army. Although Wain had much less talent as a poet than the other two, he was to play an important part in promoting both of them (and others) in his 1953 series for radio, *First Reading*. Amis and Larkin both published first books of poetry with the unprestigious Fortune Press, Larkin in 1945 (*The North Ship*) and Amis in 1947 (*Bright November*). Larkin reflected the strong influence of Yeats; Amis was more diffusely Romantic; but neither had much to do with 'speaking out' in a cool scientific and analytical tone or with the irony these poets were later to develop. In so far as they were interested in a 'movement', it was one that would promote themselves and their friends. Larkin is indisputably the most compelling poet associated with *New Lines*, and it is hard not to see Morrison's account of the genesis of the Movement as a belated tribute to this fact. Larkin's work was on the whole respectfully received in the early fifties, but his status as the epitome of Movement values was only acquired later, after the publication of *The Less Deceived* (1955). It was done to such effect that he later seemed, on occasion, to be its only begetter. This is not so.

By starting his account of the Movement with Larkin and Amis at Oxford, and by stressing their acquaintance there with Wain and Jennings, Morrison loads the dice heavily in his own favour. One reason that the Cambridge poets, Enright, Davie, and Gunn, can be represented as of less significance is simply that they did not at the outset know each other. Yet, given the greater emphasis on critical intelligence and the relations between literature and society in Cambridge English throughout the forties and into the fifties, it may be argued that the Cambridge poets, who all studied English there, were driven more urgently to find a way of 'speaking out' in poetry than their Oxford colleagues. Enright and Davie both wrote significantly on what was needed in poetry. The same cannot be said for Amis or Larkin.

Davie published *Purity of Diction in English Verse* in 1952. It was largely written in his in-laws' house in Plymouth, where he was also writing poems: 'essay and poem', he commented later, 'were equivalent and almost interchangeable attempts to grapple with the one same reality' and he continued:

> That reality was post-war... What I and my friends of those days took for granted was that the Second World War had invalidated even those radically diminished principles and sentiments that had survived the war of 1914–18... We had to go back to basics.[8]

For Davie, 'basics' meant renewed attention to the diction and syntax of poetry—the successor to *Purity* was a study of poetic syntax. It is no accident that the account of diction came first—it is evidently closer to the concern with 'speaking out' in poetry voiced

---

[7] Morrison, *The Movement*, 10.
[8] Donald Davie, *Purity of Diction in English Verse and Articulate Energy* (London: Penguin Books, 1992), pp. ix–x.

elsewhere. *Purity of Diction* was a book with clear intentions: 'I should like to think that this study might help some practising poet to a poetry of urbane and momentous statement'.[9] 'Statement' is designed to challenge; back to basics meant that poetry should say things worth saying. The challenge in that thought is respectably disguised as an academic book about Eliot's aphorism that 'to have the virtues of good prose is the first and minimum requirement of great poetry'. Davie demonstrates such prose virtues in poetry from eighteenth-century poets such as Goldsmith, Johnson, and Wesley, but always with an eye to the modern practitioner. A 'chaste' or 'pure' diction is first among these virtues. It is '"central" in Arnold's sense; it expresses the feeling of the capital, not the provinces. And…it is central in another way, central to the language, conversational not colloquial, poetic not poetical. The effect is a valuable urbanity, a civilized moderation and elegance…' (26–7). If 'the poet's choice of diction is determined in part, at any rate, by the structure and the prevailing ideologies of his society' (10), then conversely it is possible that choice of diction could change society for the better. If Davie had been asked why society should need changing, he probably would have pointed to two sites of modern evil, Dachau ('At Dachau Man's maturity began') and Hiroshima.[10] He writes about poetry with the moral strenuousness required by the iniquity he perceived in the world. That is why he admired the 'strength' of seventeenth-century poetry, its 'compression and concentration', qualities that he practises in his own poetry even as he commends them to others:

A poem is less an orange than a grid;
It hoists a charge; it does not ooze a juice.
It has no rind, being entirely hard.

The poem from which these lines come ('Poem as Abstract') was first published in March 1952, well in advance of *Purity of Diction*. Other poems on the nature of poetry were to follow: 'Zip!', 'The Owl Minerva', 'Method: for Ronald Gaskell', and 'Rejoinder to a Critic'. They were much commented on, and may be seen as part of a programme to reform English poetry, or to form a 'movement'. The essay 'Augustans New and Old', in which he associated himself with Larkin, Amis, and other poets whom Conquest would include in *New Lines*, further advanced the programme. They were the 'new Augustans', supporting 'the standards of human decency and enlightened common sense'.[11] The success of Davie's parallel between contemporary poets and those of the eighteenth century may be seen, for example, in F. W. Bateson's 1957 review of Larkin and Davie:

As Pope and Gay derive from Dryden and Rochester without ceasing to be poets who are different in kind from their models, so Larkin and Davie, though derivative in the same way, are clearly writing a new kind of poetry that is only indirectly implicit in Auden's or Empson's.[12]

[9] Donald Davie, *Purity of Diction in English Verse* (London: Routledge & Kegan Paul, 1967), 106. Further references are to this second edition, which includes 'A Postscript, 1966', not found elsewhere.
[10] Donald Davie, '*New Lines* and Mr. Tomlinson', *Essays in Criticism*, 7/3 (July 1957), 344.
[11] Donald Davie, 'Augustans New and Old', *Twentieth Century*, 158/945 (Nov. 1955), 469.
[12] F. W. Bateson, 'Auden's (and Empson's) Heirs', *Essays in Criticism*, 7/1 (Jan. 1957), 77.

Davie thought that *Purity of Diction* might have made a manifesto for the Movement 'if the group of us had ever cohered enough to subscribe to a common manifesto',[13] and was pleased that it had been read with enthusiasm by Amis. If it was never generally so regarded, the fault lay most likely with the journalists of *The Spectator* who announced the coming of the Movement as actuality.

There were two journalists involved. The first was Anthony Hartley, who had been a contemporary of Amis and Larkin at Oxford and was now drama critic for the weekly as well as the person responsible for choosing which poems to print (there were poems every two or three weeks). He started in the job at much the same time that Wain began his *First Reading* broadcasts, and both immediately promoted in a distinctive fashion young poets who were to be part of the Movement or associated with it. Hartley also reviewed poetry from time to time. On 27 August 1954 he reviewed two books (Thom Gunn's *Fighting Terms* and George MacBeth's *A Form of Words*) and two pamphlets of poems (by Donald Davie and Jonathan Price) all published by the small Fantasy Press at Eynsham, just outside Oxford. He used his review to announce the arrival of 'the only considerable movement in English poetry since the Thirties'.

Hartley set the scene for his 'discovery' by representing Auden and his fellows as discredited and superannuated. As for the poets of the forties, 'apart from Dylan Thomas no new poet of stature was produced by this romantic reaction'. The new poetry acquired an air of historical authenticity by this disparaging of its predecessors. It is not presented as simply a matter of a new poetic style, and a tone that was 'cool, scientific and analytical.' Like Davie, Hartley relates the new poetry to a new attitude to society, declaring that it presents: 'A liberalism distrustful of too much richness or too much fanaticism, austere and sceptical. A liberalism egalitarian and anti-aristocratic...'. The austere scepticism may be taken as a gloss on what Hartley meant by 'cool', and the anti-aristocratic posture might be what he meant by 'scientific'; the whole cool-analytical-scientific package clearly relates to the new social order supposed to emerge following the war. 'Modern' authorities supposed to underlie the 'new movement' (the phrase often appears in the journalism of the next two years) are named—F. R. Leavis, who had taught Davie and who was firmly opposed to literary 'fashion', and 'the logical positivist philosophers', because they shared a distrust of rhetoric, as well as Ogden and Richards, the authors of *The Meaning of Meaning*. By this means the new poetry was given a wider intellectual context. Some Movement poets (Davie, Holloway) were to find this more congenial than others.

Hartley did not only provide his new movement with a definition of style and with intellectual respectability; he named poets other than the four under review who were also part of the movement: Amis and Wain, and, as poets who were 'less scared of emotion' than the others, Larkin and the now-almost-forgotten Philip Oakes.

These poets were all distinguished by their 'attempt to introduce meaning—and complex meaning at that—at a time when English poetry [had] been ravaged by the

---

[13] Davie, *Purity of Diction*, 197.

indiscriminate use of evocatory images'. The phrase 'complex meaning' nods in the direction of William Empson, whose poetry Hartley detected at the root of much of the new work. Empson was often cited as an important influence, but the extent of this influence is generally exaggerated. Davie remarked that 'only Mr Wain and Mr Alvarez adopt at all consistently the poetic procedures of Mr Empson'.[14] Empson's importance lay in his availability as a legitimating sponsor for the new poets; Auden, Spender, and friends were still tainted by Auden's flight to the United States at the beginning of the war, as also by the general discrediting of their politics in the light of the Nazi-Soviet pact at the start of the war and of the Russian takeover in Eastern Europe after it. Auden's American books were perceived as a falling-off from the earlier work, and Spender had ceased to write much poetry at all. By contrast, Empson had spent the war in London. In 1952 his return to England from a teaching post in China focused attention on him once again.

Hartley's review was bold in the claims that it made, and was the template for an even bolder account of turmoil and change in the English literary scene. This was an unsigned piece in *The Spectator* for 1 October, called 'In the Movement' and designed as a circulation-booster, written by the literary editor J. D. Scott, though often attributed to Hartley at the time. The challenging definitive in its title and the reaction it secured have given 'In the Movement' more status than it deserves. It clinched *The Spectator*'s claim to be literary top dog among the weeklies and focused attention on the poets published there. But it did not significantly improve on Hartley's account of what the new movement's characteristics were. Where he is not simply derivative, Scott coarsens the terms of the argument:

> [The Movement] is bored by the despair of the forties, not much interested in suffering, and extremely impatient of poetic sensibility...as well as being anti-phoney, [it] is anti-wet, sceptical, robust, ironic, prepared to be as comfortable as possible in a wicked, commercial, threatened world.

Scott complicated things by widening the scope of the Movement to include novels, not only those of Amis and Wain, but also, incongruously, of Iris Murdoch. This merely muddied the waters. *Lucky Jim* and *Hurry on Down* may be able to throw light on the poetry of their authors, but they have not done so yet. They do offer a new kind of hero, but not one that Davie, Gunn, or Holloway would have wished to be identified with, despite the fact that they shared class origins (more or less) and grammar school education with Amis and Wain. Morrison writes of 'the Movement novel' but as a genre it does not exist.

Scott certainly succeeded in provoking controversy. Evelyn Waugh wrote to request 'the courtesy of individual attention' for young writers. Denis Donoghue denied that Davie and Gunn were influenced by the metaphysicals or William Empson; they were in fact striving for 'the virtues of late eighteenth-century poetry, in particular, of

---

[14] Davie, 'Augustans New and Old', 467. See also Deborah Bowman, '"An Instrument of Articulation": Empson and the Movement', in Leader (ed.), *The Movement Reconsidered*, 155–76.

Goldsmith, Denham, Johnson and Cowper'. The young poets Anthony Thwaite and Alan Brownjohn wrote differently sceptical letters (but scepticism was a Movement quality, though not admired by Davie).

The terms on which Hartley and Scott established the Movement were not very specific, though they do clearly have something to do with the general desire for a poetry that 'spoke out' and with Davie's notion of a reformed and urbane style reflecting a new society. Neither Hartley nor Scott was quite clear about who was in the Movement and who was not (which is why, in one sense, the Movement never was), and neither of them was in a position to offer a manifesto. Their purposes were journalistic and the outcome of their work was fairly described by Ian Hamilton as a 'P. R. job'.[15] This was Larkin's point of view; he wrote of Hartley as 'very stupidly crying us all up', and in so far as he recognized a Movement style, he thought it disabling; Jonathan Price was 'handicapped at present by "movement" idiom'.[16] Amis described Hartley's piece as 'a load of bullshit' and told Robert Graves not to take it 'too seriously'.[17] The conclusion seems inescapable that the Movement existed only because people wanted there to *be* a new literary movement. This is the explanation, if explanation be needed, for the easy recruitment to it of MacBeth, Oakes, Price, and Wharton alongside Amis, Davie, Gunn, and Wain. Seen from the second decade of the twenty-first century, the Movement, defined as those who contributed to *New Lines*, looks very different from the way it appeared at the time, and much less nebulous. It must be remembered that our point of view is retrospective.

In the fifties it was not easy for young poets to get their first book published. That is why the Fantasy Press (which published six of the Movement poets in its pamphlet series, three of them also in book form) and the Reading School of Art (who published Wain and Amis) were so important. When Amis and Larkin managed to get their first poems published in the forties they also had gone to a small publisher. Enright, publishing his first poems from a commercial publisher in 1953, was ahead of the game (but also at something of a tangent to the rest of the Movement poets). Conquest and Jennings were published in 1955, the one by Macmillan, the other by André Deutsch. Wain and Amis benefited from the success of their first novels, their poems appearing in 1956—Amis's *A Case of Samples* from Gollancz, who also published his novels, Wain's *A Word Carved on a Sill*, unexpectedly, from Routledge, not Secker. Four of Conquest's nine poets, then, had only just appeared on the scene in 1955 and 1956 as far as the general public was concerned—Enright was the only one who could be said to be, in a modest way, established already. It was a good moment for them all to be brought together in an anthology linked to the current big topic in poetry circles, the 'new movement'. *New Lines* can be thought of as the crest of a wave, with Enright, Jennings, Conquest, Amis, and Wain running before and the others, who soon found mainstream publishers, running after: Davie (Routledge) and Gunn (Faber) in 1957, Holloway (Routledge) in 1960.

---

[15] Ian Hamilton, 'The Making of the Movement', in *A Poetry Chronicle: Essays and Reviews* (London: Faber & Faber, 1973), 129.

[16] *Selected Letters of Philip Larkin*, ed. Anthony Thwaite (London: Faber & Faber, 1992), 230, 236.

[17] *The Letters of Kingsley Amis*, ed. Zachary Leader (London: HarperCollins, 2000), 405, 409.

Larkin's case was special. His earlier lack of success with the big firms had led to *The Less Deceived* appearing, albeit to great acclaim, from George Hartley's tiny Marvell Press in 1955. His next book, *The Whitsun Weddings*, was, however, published in 1964 by Faber, the leading publisher for poetry. The '*Spectator* P. R. job' was completed by Conquest's anthology, and the Movement acquired a sort of substance.

According to Bernard Bergonzi, 'Movement poetry existed as a tenuously coherent entity only from about 1953 to 1956 and was already beginning to fragment when *New Lines* put it on the map'[18]—the Movement was almost gone as soon as it had appeared on the scene. Just three years after *New Lines* came out, Davie was able plausibly to write as if it were all over, blaming 'pusillanimity' as the reason 'which brought the whole thing to a halt and broke it up before it was under way'.[19] This account, coloured by Davie's reaction against his own part in the Movement, as we shall see, was not seriously challenged.

If Conquest had been able to provide a greater rationale for his choice of poets, if he had been able to supply them with a manifesto, things might have gone differently. Instead, reviewers complained mightily about his introduction: 'one cannot help being struck by its hesitating vagueness and extraordinarily negative attitude', wrote David Wright in *Encounter*.[20] The book's success was based on its choice of poems, not on the accompanying prose. Conquest's choice was on the whole sound; he merely added Thom Gunn to those assembled by Enright in his own anthology, *Poets of the 1950's*, published in Japan a few months earlier. It is possibly in tribute to services rendered that Enright's own poems, which sit uncomfortably with the others, were included. Wain, Holloway, and Conquest have not worn well, but the rest still deserve our attention in ways that other contenders of the time (Alvarez, Oakes, and Wharton, for example, interesting as some of their work may be) do not.

One review of *New Lines* deserves special mention. In *Essays in Criticism* Charles Tomlinson, a former student of Davie's, disliked the journalistic background to the anthology and the willing exploitation by contributing poets of further opportunities for publicity: 'the new type of poet has been advertised in the ingratiating image of the average man'; his review was titled 'The Middlebrow Muse'.[21] He remarked a general 'faculty for self-congratulation, afforded by playing a conscious game with your own feelings and those of your reader' (212). His weightiest criticism was that

> They show a singular want of vital awareness of the continuum outside themselves, of the mystery bodied over against them in the created universe, which they fail to experience with any degree of sharpness or to embody with any instress or sensuous depth. (215)

---

[18] Bergonzi, *Wartime and Aftermath*, 164.

[19] Donald Davie, 'Remembering the Movement' (1959), in *The Poet in the Imaginary Museum: Essays of Two Decades*, ed. Barry Alpert (Manchester: Carcanet Press, 1977), 72.

[20] David Wright, 'A Small Green Insect Shelters in the Bowels of my Quivering Typewriter', *Encounter*, 6/4 (Oct. 1956), 75.

[21] *Essays in Criticism*, 7/2 (Apr. 1957), 208.

This was brave criticism; someone, presumably Davie, had shown Tomlinson's own poems to both Enright and Conquest for inclusion in their anthologies, and both editors had rejected them. Enright went so far as to suggest that the experience had affected Tomlinson's view of the book.[22] There is substance to Tomlinson's criticism, irrespective of what had or had not happened. In fact, he had not known what was going on; and either anthology would have been improved by his inclusion. His lucidity and syntactic brio would not have been out of place there, either.

Although Davie wrote in reply to Tomlinson, his defence was not strong. It was based on the poets' supposed negative virtues: 'the poetic tradition is in a healthy state when the poor poetry of a period is not vicious but merely dull.'[23] He was in an awkward position since his own review of Enright's second book of poems had accused Enright of 'Common-Mannerism'—the same vulgarity that Tomlinson found in Conquest's anthology. When, in summer 1959, Davie announced that the Movement was over, thanks to its 'pusillanimity' he was clearing his own bad conscience:

> On 10 May 1952, I confided to my journal: 'In my poetry of the last six months I have made concessions to vulgarity—in the shape of point and glitter, striking similes, rhetorical gawds, memorable lines, anything that emphasizes the detail at the expense of the whole. And I shall continue to do so, in hopes of public favour.'[24]

In 1959 he declared 'an end to attitudinizing'. His preferred task for poetry now is that it should be 'a way of knowing the world we [are] in, apprehending it, learning it'. Poetry will acknowledge that on occasion 'the world...imposes its own conditions'.[25] Davie, in short, had learnt from the example of Charles Tomlinson, the addressee of Davie's poem 'To a Brother in the Mystery',[26] where 'mystery', I think, alludes to the passage from Tomlinson already quoted. It was Tomlinson's example, tempered by that of Pasternak, that Davie was now to follow. His criticism of the Movement as 'conceding too much...to the insularity which has ready its well-documented and conclusive sneer at Colette and Marianne Moore, Cocteau and Gide and Hart Crane'[27] had as much to do with his quarrel with Valéry in *Purity of Diction* and with his own self-reproach as with Amis and Larkin's dislike of 'foreign travel and foreign languages'. By 1974 Davie was ready to agree with Ian Hamilton that the Movement had indeed been 'a take-over bid and it brilliantly succeeded'.[28]

The consequence of Davie's gradual disillusionment with the Movement was that it became possible for Larkin, hitherto a figure slightly on its margin, to become its

---

[22] D. J. Enright, '*New Lines* and Mr. Tomlinson', *Essays in Criticism*, 7/3 (July 1957), 345.
[23] Davie, '*New Lines* and Mr. Tomlinson', 344.
[24] Donald Davie, *These the Companions: Recollections* (Cambridge: Cambridge University Press, 1982), 68.
[25] Davie, 'Remembering the Movement', 74.
[26] Davie, *Collected Poems 1950–1970* (London: Routledge & Kegan Paul, 1972), 106, first published *Encounter*, 15/6 (June 1960), 29–30.
[27] Davie, 'Remembering the Movement', 72–3.
[28] Davie, 'The Varsity Match', *Poetry Nation*, 2 (1974), 77.

representative, the role that he plays, for example, in the introduction to Alvarez's *The New Poetry* (1962). This was partly the result of the great success of *The Less Deceived*, which came on the very heels of *New Lines*. Popularity and publicity were much more concerns of Amis and Larkin than they were of Davie. 'With you as general', Amis wrote to Wain at the end of 1953, 'the boys could move right into control'.[29] But Amis's poetry dried up after *A Case of Samples*, and it was Larkin who was left 'in control'. There is an adolescent tinge to this craving for recognition, but the crudity of language belies, and is perhaps meant to belie, something more serious.

Amis and Larkin today appear unlikely associates for Davie, but at the beginning he had taken them for colleagues in the remaking of English poetry and English society, and he never really gave up on them. Their lucidity seemed to coincide with his own 'urbanity', though Davie was 'conversational' where the other two were colloquial. All three were indeed trying to resituate poetry, trying to bring it closer to the society for which it was written. Davie's 'urbanity' joins pure diction with 'economy of metaphor...achieved by judgment and taste...It purifies the spoken tongue, for it makes the reader alive to nice meanings.'[30] This was the reason he used what he later called 'inert gestures of social adaptiveness—"no doubt", "I suppose", "of course", "almost", "perhaps"...'[31] in his poems. These 'gestures' are like the colloquialisms of Amis and Larkin, except that Davie wants to draw the reader into the discourse of the urbane poet, whereas the others seek to assimilate the poem to the 'real' world inhabited by their reader. Davie came to feel as unhappy with what underlay their colloquialisms as with his own 'inert gestures'. Amis's promotion of popular forms of fiction in the pages of *The Spectator* did not meet with Davie's approval. Reviewing Enright, it seems unlikely he had only Enright in mind when he warned that 'there seems to be a genuine danger that impatience with cultural pretentiousness is turning into impatience with culture'.[32] Whilst 'Get stuffed: books are a load of crap' should not be taken to represent Larkin's settled opinion; it too is designed to call 'culture' in question in a way that Davie would find just as unsympathetic as Larkin's dismissive references to Pound in the introduction to *All What Jazz* (1970). Larkin's declaration in favour of the poems of Hardy obscured the diverse origins of Movement formalism, in particular, Davie's debt to Wesley and the other eighteenth-century poets discussed in *Purity of Diction*, and rejected the moral strenuousness Davie had associated with it: 'When I came to Hardy it was with the sense of relief that I didn't have to try and jack myself up to a concept of poetry that lay outside my own life.'[33]

Larkin's justifiable predominance in English poetry of the sixties and seventies made it difficult to see exactly how the Movement had been remade in his image. This was a major factor in its now-you-see-me-now-you-don't quality. The journalistic aspect,

---

[29] *The Letters of Kingsley Amis*, ed. Leader, 342.
[30] Davie, *Purity of Diction*, 68.
[31] Davie, 'Remembering the Movement', 72.
[32] Donald Davie, 'Common-Mannerism', in *The Poet in the Imaginary Museum*, 43.
[33] Philip Larkin, *Required Writing: Miscellaneous Pieces 1955–1982* (London: Faber & Faber, 1983), 175.

too, attracted polemic and publicity rather than informed criticism. Even Davie, in his 'Remembering the Movement', was essentially taking advantage of its potential for being argued against. That was also the case with Alvarez's *The New Poetry* (1962).

This anthology was an odd performance all round. It had poems by six of the Movement poets (Conquest, Holloway, and Jennings were left out). The twelve other British poets included R. S. Thomas, Charles Tomlinson, Ted Hughes, and Geoffrey Hill. In the original edition two American poets were added to these—Robert Lowell and John Berryman—and two more in the enlarged and revised edition of 1966. In a prefatory note, Alvarez explained that he was 'simply attempting to give my idea of what, that really matters, has happened to poetry in England during the last decade'.[34] Yet his 'fighting introduction',[35] subtitled 'Beyond the Gentility Principle', is largely given over to the idea that his British contributors stand for *nothing* 'that really matters'—and this discrepancy between his choice of poets and commentary upon them was noted by contemporary reviewers.

He writes off the thirties and the forties much in the fashion of Hartley and Scott, and goes on to dismiss the Movement also. The forties are condemned for 'a blockage against intelligence' (19) and the fifties for 'an attempt to show that the poet is not a strange creature inspired; on the contrary, he is just like the man next door' (20–1). This accusation has something in common with Davie's charge of 'Common-Mannerism', but Alvarez associates it with 'gentility': 'a belief that life is always more or less orderly, people always more or less polite...that God, in short, is more or less good'(21). He uses the broad brush of journalism—no room for critical detail. 'I am...suggesting that [modern English poetry] drop the pretence that life, give or take a few social distinctions, is the same as ever, that gentility, decency, and all the other social totems will eventually muddle through' (23). In the cause of a poetry that will face 'dominant public savagery' he invokes the need for poets to address the evil in western society that made the Nazi death-camps possible. He appears ignorant that Davie and Gunn had both written about atrocity.

Because the Movement was without definition, it lent itself conveniently to Alvarez's purpose of promoting a poetry that coped with 'experience sometimes on the edge of disintegration and breakdown' (24–5). The *coup de grâce* comes when he contrasts Larkin's 'At Grass' ('elegant and unpretentious and rather beautiful in its gentle way...nostalgic re-creation of the English scene' (26)) with Hughes's 'A Dream of Horses' (Hughes's poem 'is unquestionably *about* something' and his horses 'reach back, as in a dream into a nexus of fear and sensation' (27)). Even if Alvarez were accurate in his characterization of the two poems, this would be bad criticism, voicing an unreasoned preference for one kind of poetry over another and using rhetoric in the place of argument. But the potential to disturb in the last lines of 'At Grass', which evoke

---

[34] A. Alvarez (ed.), *The New Poetry* (Harmondsworth: Penguin Books, 1962), 15.

[35] Blake Morrison and Andrew Motion (eds.), *The Penguin Book of Contemporary British Poetry* (Harmondsworth: Penguin Books, 1982), 13.

a subjection not confined to retired racehorses ('Only the groom, and the groom's boy, | With bridles in the evening come') is something other than nostalgic. Its creepiness is not 'savage'—nothing so blatant—but it is not well described simply as 'genteel' or nostalgic. As for the savagery, as Alvarez sees it, of Hughes, it is hard to find any bearing on atrocity, and hard not to accuse Alvarez of thoughtless posturing in invoking the Holocaust as he does.

Seven years later a different kind of posturing figures in Ian Hamilton's account of the making of the Movement, which is allotted 'its distinctive niche in the history of publicity'[36] but otherwise exists as something for the writer to triumph over: 'It is difficult...to fathom how such largely tame and awkward verses could ever have been found dazzlingly fresh and skilful.' There is not much specificity. Elizabeth Jennings is written off on account of her 'laborious obsession with "the mind"' (131) and quotations are offered, but the obsession and the laboriousness both have to be taken on trust. He describes the poems of Amis, Davie, and Wain about poetry as 'saturated with a strategic, blow-striking self-awareness, [inhabiting] an imaginative world dominated by trivial exigencies of literary warfare' (133), a striking generalization but difficult to sustain in relation to the eleven very different poems he names. He does not attempt to sustain it.

By this time poetry in Britain was increasingly directed at specialized audiences. Women's poetry, Afro-Caribbean poetry, 'underground' or 'alternative' poetry were all coming into being, and the Movement could serve to vindicate such new kinds by being visibly out of fashion. The back cover of Michael Horovitz's anthology *Children of Albion* (1969) declares that a new generation of poets has 'almost completely dispelled the arid critical climate of the fifties', and in the 'Afterwords' at the end of the volume the Movement is characterized in a quotation from Michael Hamburger as 'full of literary allusions and...of a piddling wit, a trivial ingenuity that cries out for the applause of learned colleagues'. Horovitz puts the boot in with his comment: 'That was the Movement—that *was*!'[37] The Movement had to die in order that other poetries should live.

It was still dying fourteen years later when Andrew Crozier, whose poems had appeared in Horovitz's anthology, published 'Thrills and Frills: Poetry as Figures of Empirical Lyricism'. It is a piece that should be better known; despite an ungainly style, Crozier offers an astute commentary on the Movement's relationship to subsequent poetry in the mainstream, that is, published by any of the large commercial publishing houses. For example, he rejects Alvarez's factitious contrast of Larkin's horse poem with Hughes's, denying that there is any great difference between them: 'neither poet questions the sources or conditions of such feelings as they represent, but takes them

---

[36] Hamilton, 'The Making of the Movement', 130.

[37] Michael Horovitz, *Children of Albion: Poetry of the Underground* (Harmondsworth: Penguin Books, 1969), 317.

for granted'.[38] This supposedly unquestioning quality of both Larkin and Hughes (and, indeed, of Heaney also) is taken to be characteristic:

> In the poetic tradition now dominant the authoritative self, discoursing in a world of banal, empirically derived objects and relations, depends on its employment of metaphor and simile for poetic vitality...Poets are now praised above all else as inventors of figures—as rhetoricians, in fact—with a consequent narrowing of our range of appropriate response. Poetry has been turned into a reserve for small verbal thrills, a daring little frill round the hem of normal discourse...It does not wish to influence the reader's perceptions and feelings in the real world... (229–30)

What Crozier dislikes, and uses the Movement to attack, is the first-person lyric, which he believes to be in itself an impoverishing constraint on poetic expression. Even Davie's use of 'we', he says, 'implies a restricted group, and is far from being generously inclusive'. In Movement poetry, he says, 'we detect in the poet's authority a relentless determination of poetic discourse and foreclosure of its intended audience' (205).

This contrasts strangely with Davie's accusation of an enfeebling irony at work in the Movement, but, then, the Movement is not really what Crozier's essay is about. He questions the Movement's rejection of forties style: 'The mode is lyric, but treats the person as a site in which experience is to be acted out as conflict' (229). He instances W. S. Graham as a poet who has not received his due, and goes on to praise Charles Tomlinson also. His poetry suggests 'that language might be compatible with what it refers to rather than necessarily appropriated to the special register of the poet's sensibilities' (231). Tomlinson is said to be not part of the canon, as, presumably, Graham was not; the scene is set for Crozier's final manoeuvre. There are other people, he says, who were not part of the 'canon':

> In *Thomas Hardy and English* [he means *British*] *Poetry* Donald Davie...writes about other poets, from the sixties, who conduct their writing in ways quite independent of the norms of the canon. It is a comment on the narrowness of our critical culture that such challenges have not been fully recognized and taken up. (231–2)

He is referring with coy obliquity to Davie's chapter on Roy Fisher and his paragraphs on J. H. Prynne. The whole of his negative account of the Movement is in fact directed towards this insinuated praise. In Crozier's essay the Movement's half-life serves the ends of the Cambridge School of poetry, rather as it does in Randall Stevenson's *The Last of England?* (2004).[39] But until critics are prepared to look at what the Movement offers in its own right, rather than using it as the foil for some other idea that must triumph, it will always be with us.

---

[38] Andrew Crozier, 'Thrills and Frills: Poetry as Figures of Empirical Lyricism', in Alan Sinfield (ed.), *Society and Literature 1945–1970* (London: Methuen, 1983), 218.

[39] Randall Stevenson, *The Last of England?* (*The Oxford Literary History*, vol. xii; Oxford: Oxford University Press, 2004).

Morrison's book, informative and well researched, does not exploit the Movement in this way, but is overcommitted to Larkin, Amis, and Wain. This leads him to spend far too much time on the novels of the last two and to exaggerate the role of class origins in these writers' work. His characterization of the Movement as anti-Romantic and anti-modernist needs to be handled with care. Amis and Larkin both have a difficult relationship with what they think of as Romanticism because neither of them wants to give too much of himself away; the vehemence with which they address the topic betrays the extent of their involvement, which is unsurprising, since both want to develop the Romantic themes of love and sympathy.[40] As for anti-modernism (not a criminal offence, by the way), Davie, who grappled with the arch-modernist Pound and his successors all his life, made much of its presence in Larkin and Amis.[41] It must be admitted that they gave him plenty of ammunition. It should be remembered, however, that French symbolism is an important part of the background to Larkin's poems.[42] His anti-modernism is in tune with his populism, as is Amis's, but is not the whole story. We have already seen, too, that their populism is more complicated than at first appears. The simple anti-modernism label did, of course, consolidate Larkin and Amis as national favourites and put Davie at a satisfying distance from 'their' Movement. Yet Davie's early Movement practice may be seen as Modernist; there is an analogy between the way he used Wesley's stanza form in the fifties and the way Pound used Gautier in *Mauberley*. Davie obliquely drew attention to this himself.[43]

The Movement has always been with us as an item of unfinished business in the history of English poetry. There has been extensive discussion of Larkin, and there have been some good accounts of Gunn, but Davie's poems have never recovered from the eclipse brought on by his retreat from the Movement. He was not an easy man, and he was not an easy poet, but there is much worth discovering in his bulky *Collected Poems*. Jennings and Enright, the one quickly going into poetic decline, the other taking some time to mature, are both still waiting for their due. But once this agenda has been accomplished will the Movement be with us still?

We can reasonably expect it to be so, even if the only coherence it has is that of poetic practices and beliefs overlapping here and there among the poets concerned. In its imperfect form, it represents the last-gasp last stand of a poetry that was setting out to be, not British, not Scottish, Welsh, or Irish, but English. The 'Englishness' of

---

[40] On the Romantic characteristics of Larkin, see John Bayley, 'Larkin and the Romantic Tradition', in *The Order of Battle at Trafalgar and Other Essays* (London: Collins Harvill, 1987), 49–56, and 'The Last Romantic: Philip Larkin', in *The Power of Delight: A Lifetime in Literature. Essays 1962–2002* (London: Duckworth, 2005), 208–19.

[41] Donald Davie, *Thomas Hardy and British Poetry* (London: Routledge & Kegan Paul, 1973).

[42] See Barbara Everett, 'Philip Larkin: After Symbolism', *Essays in Criticism*, 30/3 (July 1980), 227–42.

[43] That is, if one puts together Pound's suggestion that he might just as well have used the Bay State Hymn Book as Gautier as a model in *Mauberley* (quoted in Davie, *The Poet in the Imaginary Museum*, 88) with Davie's reference to *The Methodist Hymn-book* in his in-laws' house (Davie, *Purity of Diction*, p. ix).

Conquest, Gunn, Holloway, and Jennings is not obvious, though it is arguable in every case. The idea of England is of great importance for the other Movement poets. The society in which Davie's pure language was to do its work was emphatically English, and England remained a prime concern for him, for example in his poems from *The Shires* (1974). Larkin carefully posed himself by a road-sign reading ENGLAND for a famous photograph and evoked Englishness with varying degrees of success in poems like 'Show Saturday' and 'To the Sea'. The ideal society which hovers behind so many Movement poems is an English society, unselfconsciously, and perhaps unconsciously, self-privileging, the society into which their authors were inducted as poets at Oxford and Cambridge. This historical and cultural aspect of Movement poetry is the reason we may expect it to be always with us, for it is an image, however hazy, of a unified culture, the projected antithesis of the cultural diversity with which we have become familiar over the last half-century.

Select Bibliography

Alvarez, A. (ed.), *The New Poetry* (Harmondsworth: Penguin Books, 1962).
Amis, Kingsley, *The Letters of Kingsley Amis*, ed. Zachary Leader (London: HarperCollins, 2000).
Bateson, F. W., 'Auden's (and Empson's) Heirs', *Essays in Criticism*, 7/1 (Jan. 1957), 77.
Bayley, John, 'Larkin and the Romantic Tradition', *The Order of Battle at Trafalgar and Other Essays* (London: Collins Harvill, 1987), 49–56.
Bayley, John, 'The Last Romantic: Philip Larkin', in *The Power of Delight: A Lifetime in Literature. Essays 1962–2002* (London: Duckworth, 2005), 208–19.
Bergonzi, Bernard, 'The Literary Situation—I', *Departure* II, 6 (1955), 15.
Bergonzi, Bernard, *Wartime and Aftermath: English Literature and Its Background 1936–1960* (Oxford: Oxford University Press, 1993).
Bradley, Jerry, *The Movement: British Poetry of the 1950s* (New York: Twayne, 1993).
Conquest, Robert (ed.), *New Lines: An Anthology* (London: Macmillan, 1956).
Conquest, Robert, '*New Lines*, Movements, and Modernisms', in Leader (ed.), *The Movement Reconsidered* (Oxford: Oxford University Press, 2009).
Crozier, Andrew, 'Thrills and Frills: Poetry as Figures of Empirical Lyricism', in Alan Sinfield (ed.), *Society and Literature 1945–1970* (London: Methuen, 1983), 218.
Davie, Donald, 'Augustans New and Old', *Twentieth Century*, 158/945 (Nov. 1955), 469.
Davie, Donald, '*New Lines* and Mr. Tomlinson', *Essays in Criticism*, 7/3 (July 1957), 344.
Davie, Donald, *Purity of Diction in English Verse* (London: Routledge & Kegan Paul, 1967).
Davie, Donald, *Collected Poems 1950–1970* (London: Routledge & Kegan Paul, 1972).
Davie, Donald, *Thomas Hardy and British Poetry* (London: Routledge & Kegan Paul, 1973).
Davie, Donald, 'The Varsity Match', *Poetry Nation*, 2 (1974), 77.
Davie, Donald, *The Poet in the Imaginary Museum: Essays of Two Decades*, ed. Barry Alpert (Manchester: Carcanet Press, 1977).
Davie, Donald, *These the Companions: Recollections* (Cambridge: Cambridge University Press, 1982).
Davie, Donald, *Purity of Diction in English Verse and Articulate Energy* (London: Penguin Books, 1992).
Enright, D. J. (ed.), *Poets of the 1950's* (Tokyo: Kenkyusha, 1955).

Enright, D. J., '*New Lines* and Mr. Tomlinson', *Essays in Criticism*, 7/3 (July 1957), 345.
Everett, Barbara, 'Philip Larkin: After Symbolism', *Essays in Criticism*, 30/3 (July 1980), 227–42.
Hamilton, Ian, 'The Making of the Movement', in *A Poetry Chronicle: Essays and Reviews* (London: Faber & Faber, 1973).
Holloway, John, 'New Lines in English Poetry', *Hudson Review,* 9/4 (Winter 1956–7), 592–7.
Horovitz, Michael, *Children of Albion: Poetry of the Underground* (Harmondsworth: Penguin Books, 1969).
Larkin, Philip, *Required Writing: Miscellaneous Pieces 1955–1982* (London: Faber & Faber, 1983).
Larkin, Philip, *Selected Letters of Philip Larkin*, ed. Anthony Thwaite (London: Faber & Faber, 1992).
Leader, Zachary (ed.), *The Movement Reconsidered* (Oxford: Oxford University Press, 2009).
Morrison, Blake, *The Movement: English Poetry and Fiction of the 1950s* (Oxford: Oxford University Press, 1980).
Morrison, Blake, and Motion, Andrew (eds.), *The Penguin Book of Contemporary British Poetry* (Harmondsworth: Penguin Books, 1982).
Stevenson, Randall, *The Last of England? (The Oxford Literary History*, vol. xii; Oxford: Oxford University Press, 2004).
Wright, David, 'A Small Green Insect Shelters in the Bowels of my Quivering Typewriter', *Encounter*, 6/4 (Oct. 1956), 75.

CHAPTER 6

'IN DIFFERENT VOICES': MODERNISM SINCE THE 1960S

JEREMY NOEL-TOD

> ...when an inverse brand of professional unhappiness
> taps on its wrist watch "as a realist I..."—then
>
> set this boy free
>
> No this isn't me, it's just my motor running
> Denise Riley, 'When it's time to go'[1]

A recent polemic by Gabriel Josipovici, *Whatever Happened to Modernism?*, concluded that the most prominent British novelists of the post-war period are 'pseudo-Modernists' who have misunderstood modernism's revolutionary legacy as a licence for 'unflinching realism', rather than the self-conscious textual struggle with the representation of reality itself.[2] Josipovici's charge might be broadened to include British poetry of the same period, which has been dominated by realist assumptions about the lyric speaker since Philip Larkin emerged as the most popular of the Movement poets from the 1950s. Central to modernist poetics is the explosion of the idea that the voice of a poem can be read like a character in a novel. As Hugh Kenner wrote fifty years ago, at the birth of modernist studies, the speaker of T. S. Eliot's 'The Love Song of J. Alfred Prufrock' (1915) is only 'the name of a possible zone of consciousness' where the material of the poem 'can maintain a vague congruity'.[3] The publication of the drafts of *The Waste Land* (1922) in 1971 corroborated Kenner's hypothesis. Borrowing a phrase from Charles

---

[1] Denise Riley, *Selected Poems* (London: Reality Street Editions, 2000), 59.
[2] Gabriel Josipovici, *Whatever Happened to Modernism?* (New Haven: Yale University Press, 2010), ch. 14.
[3] Hugh Kenner, *T. S. Eliot: The Invisible Poet* (London: W. H. Allen, 1950), 35.

Dickens about a character reading aloud from a newspaper, Eliot originally intended to call his collage of styles and allusions 'He Do the Police in Different Voices'.

Eliot's editorial collaborator on *The Waste Land*, Ezra Pound, was simultaneously beginning his projected epic of world history, *The Cantos*. Both were Americans living at the heart of the British Empire after the First World War when they conceived the complex multiplicity of their major works, and by the 1930s were recognized as major figures. After the Second World War, however, post-imperial British culture shrank from poetic avant-gardism. The work of J. H. Prynne, for example, whose collected *Poems* (1999) describe their author as 'Britain's leading late Modernist poet', has largely been neglected and even scorned by literary journalists and editors—so much so that Prynne's inclusion alongside Larkin in the most recent edition of *The Oxford History of English Literature* was controversial enough to warrant discussion on BBC Radio 4's current affairs programme, *Today*. During this debate, the critic Iain Sinclair declared that comparing Larkin to Prynne was like comparing 'nougat to electricity'. Another way of hearing the difference is to consider who or what speaks in the poems. The autobiographical persona under which Larkin collected his various lyric voices—many derived from modernism—was, as Al Alvarez wrote, 'the image of the post-war Welfare State Englishman...hopeless, bored, wry'.[4] Prynne's work, meanwhile, has increasingly replaced any form of poetic 'persona' with the 'dialectical philosophical proposition' outlined by Theodor Adorno's 'On Lyric Poetry and Society' (1957), in which the antagonism between individual and society is negotiated through the poem's 'identification with language'.[5]

Modernist poetry is characterized by its pursuit of this dialectic in a world so polyvocal that any single voice is necessarily relative. Eliot's most influential critical essay, 'Tradition and the Individual Talent' (1919), described composition as a 'process of depersonalisation': 'poetry is not a turning loose of emotion, but an escape from emotion; is not the expression of personality, but an escape from personality'. More recently, the poet Denise Riley has defined her work in a tradition of 'continuing modern lyric' with reference to the phenomenology of Maurice Merleau-Ponty: 'we are not wholly enclosed in our separateness but are outside ourselves from the start and open to the world'.[6] The drama of the modernist poem lies in the struggle to escape the limitations of a subjective point of view and so achieve Eliot's 'more valuable' thing: a collective experience of language that transcends the stratification of modern life.[7] This is the drama of 'The Love Song of J. Alfred Prufrock' and *The Waste Land*, which begin in the first-person plural ('Let us go then, you and I') only to break down into a multitude of registers and perceptions, which the first-person voice of the poem periodically attempts to wrest into coherence ('Till human voices wake us and we drown').[8]

---

[4] Al Alvarez (ed.), *The New Poetry* (rev. edn., Harmondsworth: Penguin Books, 1966), 24–5.

[5] Theodor Adorno, 'On Lyric Poetry and Society', trans. Sherry Weber Nicholsen, in *Notes to Literature*, ed. Rolf Tiedemann (Columbia University Press, 1991), 37–54 (44).

[6] Denise Riley, *Infinite Difference: Other Poetries by U.K. Women Poets*, ed. Carrie Etter (Exeter: Shearsman Books, 2010), 4.

[7] T. S. Eliot, *Selected Essays* (3rd edn., London: Faber & Faber, 1951), 17–21.

[8] T. S. Eliot, *The Complete Poems and Plays* (London: Faber & Faber, 1969), 13–17, 61.

Visiting Eliot in 1948, the young poet Lynette Roberts confessed that this struggle had brought her to a 'crossroads'. As Roberts saw it, her future writing faced a choice between two modes:

> That of returning to the elemental words and simple voices—i.e. basic rural cultures, earth rhythms... what we will be forced back to if that atom war arises. A cleansing purity and rebirth of sound, recreation refolding of the world such as we had the refolding of various strata, Icelandic stone and bronze age etc. And... hitting against that view which is one of isolation, severe pruning, the whole discordant universe, the cutting of teeth, one rhythm grating against another, the metallic convergence of words, heavy, colourful rich and unexplored.[9]

The two collections by Roberts that Eliot published as an editor at Faber and Faber, *Poems* (1944) and *Gods with Stainless Ears* (1951), drew on her life in an isolated Welsh village during the war. They succeeded in occupying a position between these voices, evoking rural culture during discordant air war. Her post-war feeling that she had to choose between the two may be one reason why she wrote little more. Roberts's crossroads, however, marks the spot where later voices can still be heard:

> The place-work of
> willed repeat gains a familiar tremor in jointure, we say
> sustainable our mouth assents slave dental unbroken torrid reason
> will commute previous and lie down. None more credible, mirror
> make up flat sat batch pinup gruesome genome. Now get out.
> J. H. Prynne, 'As Mouth Blindness'[10]

Prynne's poetry has been dismissed by Craig Raine as 'emulatively difficult', a 'take on modernism' perversely dedicated to 'the notion that the reader shouldn't expect anything in the way of conventional "meaning" since the poetry was anyway fetched up from the dark womb of the poet's unconscious'.[11] Raine's notion of the 'dark womb' of Prynne's ' "new" poetic' is indebted to C. K. Stead's image of the 'Dark Embryo' of Eliot's verse in his study of modernism, *The New Poetic* (1964). Following 'Tradition and the Individual Talent', Stead described the modernist dialectic around poetic 'meaning' as a negotiation between the rational and the irrational in the process of composition. Comparing Prynne's unfamiliar manner with the annotated difficulties of Eliot, Raine and others have concluded that irrationalism has taken over. But the reader who listens to the echoes in these lines of the 'whole discordant universe' of the early twenty-first century will begin to hear Roberts's two voices continuing their contest.

'The place-work of willed repeat | gains a familiar tremor in jointure' may not itself sound like a 'simple voice', but it offers a commentary on the attractions of such a voice.

---

[9] Lynette Roberts, 'Visit to T. S. Eliot', *Diaries, Letters and Recollections*, ed. Patrick McGuinness (Manchester: Carcanet Press, 2008), 150.

[10] J. H. Prynne, 'As Mouth Blindness', *Sub Songs* (London: Barque Press, 2010), 6.

[11] Craig Raine, 'All jokes aside', *Guardian*, 11 Mar. 2008 [http://www.guardian.co.uk/books/2008/mar/11/poetry.thomasstearnseliot].

Collective speech builds a 'familiar' feeling of community through the repetition of certain words: 'we say', for example, 'sustainable' as a palliative to environmental degradation, with its connotations of a more thoughtful consumerism. Cutting against the propositional opening of the sentence, however, is an agrammatical middle section: 'our mouth assents slave dental unbroken torrid reason'. Here, 'our' seemingly reasonable assent to such language is structurally attacked, in a paratactic torrent that implies that it is rapacious, acquiescent sophistry to substitute a new name for the same arrangement ('will commute previous and lie down'). The last line of the poem accelerates this 'convergence' of contemporary language and thought structures, mixing cosmetics, manufacturing, and science in one 'gruesome' period. The final three words comment again on the enslaving effect of such a mesh of forces, while switching to a voice of unexpected directness: 'Now get out.'

Prynne's poem seems impatiently to dismiss its reader, as if there were nothing more to be said. We might compare the end of *The Waste Land*, where, having surveyed its 'arid plains' and disordered lands, the poem breaks down into anarchic babble ('London bridge is falling down falling down falling down'), with a pathos by turns despairing and aggressive: 'These fragments I have shored against my ruins | Why then Ile fit you'. In an essay written during the composition of his poem, Eliot argued that

> it appears likely that poets in our civilization, as it exists at present, must be *difficult*. Our civilization comprehends great variety and complexity [...] The poet must become more and more comprehensive, more allusive, more indirect, in order to force, to dislocate if necessary, language into his meaning.[12]

The Waste Land represents both the attempt to achieve this ambition and the poet's failure to reconcile indirect expression with directed 'meaning'. As the drafts show, Eliot struggled to make the poem both more comprehensive and more pointed in its social criticism, but Pound cut the more expository parts as the least poetically successful.

The poetic success of *The Waste Land* resulted from the convergence of two different voices with a common ambition to comprehend the modern world in verse: Eliot through complexity and variety, Pound through lucidity and compression. As Pound had written in his 1913 list of 'don'ts' for the would-be 'Imagist' poet, 'use no superfluous word, no adjective which does not reveal something...don't be "viewy"'.[13] A 2010 poem by Prynne's contemporary, R. F. Langley, illustrates how radically pared a contemporary modernist poetic can be. 'To a Nightingale' describes the experience of listening to the song of the bird on an empty country road. It ends

>   I am
> empty, stopped at nothing, as
> I wait for this song to shoot.

---

[12] Eliot, *Selected Essays*, 289.
[13] *Literary Essays of Ezra Pound*, ed. T. S. Eliot (London: Faber & Faber, 1954), 4–6.

The road is rising as it
passes the apple tree and
makes its approach to the bridge.[14]

There are no complex words or constructions in Langley's conclusion, which extends into the immediate landscape without exerting further agency. 'I am | empty', says the poem, inverting the familiar volitional meaning of the phrase '[to] stop at nothing': 'stopped at nothing', the speaker has been taken beyond the self by the song of a bird that cannot be seen.

Like Pound's translations of Chinese poetry in *Cathay* (1915), or the elemental Imagist poems of H.D., Langley's lyric clarity refracts the depersonalized nature of any individual's language. As T. E. Hulme put it a hundred years ago:

> The great aim is accurate, precise and definite description. The first thing is to recognise how extraordinarily difficult this is. It is no mere matter of carefulness; you have to use language, and language is by its very nature a communal thing; that is, it expresses never the exact thing but a compromise—that which is common to you, me and everybody. But each man sees a little differently, and to get out clearly and exactly what he does see, he must have a terrific struggle with language, whether it be with words or the technique of other arts.[15]

Hulme's criticism, which had an important influence on both Pound and Eliot, defined the new spirit of modern art as an exacting 'classicism' in reaction against the vague sentimentalities with which 'Romanticism' was associated by the end of the nineteenth century. The early modernists nevertheless had many questions in common with the early Romantic poets about the identity of the lyric speaker. One of Eliot's voices in *The Waste Land* is onomatopoeiac birdsong, recalling the Romantic trope of the lyric-poet-as-bird, whose song is both beautiful and obscure. Prynne and Langley also invoke this tradition through their titles. A 'sub song' is the muted, jumbled practice music of a bird out of season, while 'To a Nightingale' alludes to John Keat's ode, in which the speaker also experiences the ecstasy of the bird's song as a kind of living death ('I wait for this song to shoot').

Hulme's polemical conception of 'classicism' might be understood as a poetic of analysis, which foregrounds the poet's 'faculty of mind to see things...apart from the conventional ways in which you have been trained to see them' and 'the concentrated state of mind...necessary in the actual expression of what one sees'. As he says in his 'Lecture on Modern Poetry', the 'distinct new art' that resulted from this way of writing also implied a new way of reading, intended to be 'read in the study' rather than 'chanted' like traditional forms.[16] This distinction also implies the frequently irregular and ambivalent quality of modernist prosody. All these characteristics can be observed in the poems

---

[14] R. F. Langley, 'To a Nightingale', *London Review of Books*, 18 Nov. 2010, 25.
[15] T. E. Hulme, *Selected Writings*, ed. Patrick McGuinness (Manchester: Fyfield, 1998), 78.
[16] Hulme, *Selected Writings*, 64.

by Prynne and Langley, whose unexpected constructions and enjambments ask readers to pause over 'conventional ways' of reading. They also imply an art understood most profoundly when read in the study, a careful and repeated act which allows for the appreciation of ambiguity and allusion. The title of Prynne's poem from *Sub Songs*, for example, alludes to the lines from Milton's 'Lycidas' in which the poet criticizes the 'Blind mouths!' of corrupt seventeenth-century priests. 'Mouth blindness', though, is also a modern term for the effect radiation therapy can have on a patient's sense of taste. 'As Mouth Blindness', then, can be read as another of the poem's identifications with the diseased language of its society, as well as a warning about the obscurity of its own speech.

Another implication of modernist poetry's withdrawal into the study was that it would not be a popular art form (Hulme's example of a contemporary poem with a wide circulation was a 6-foot-long piece of doggerel printed on a poster outside a music hall). The desire to reach a wider readership nevertheless continued to animate modernism's dialectic between private and collective voices. In Britain, T. S. Eliot's later poetry and criticism was especially influential in endorsing a retreat from the anarchy of *The Waste Land* in 1922 towards the reassuring presence of an authoritative speaker. In 1942, he commented that 'if the work of the last twenty years is worthy of being classified at all, it is as belonging to a period of search for a proper modern colloquial idiom'.[17] With *Little Gidding*, the last of his *Four Quartets*, published in the same year, Eliot effectively concluded his poetic career with a sequence which spoke reassuringly of 'a condition of complete simplicity' to be attained at 'the end of all our exploring'.[18] The accepted story of British poetry in the post-war period has commonly followed the later Eliot in presenting modernist poetics as an experimental 'search' that ended in the discovery of more reliable forms of speaking voice, rather than an artistic tradition which proceeds in a permanently experimental spirit. On this view, modernism was a movement of mad scientists whose monsters had to be tamed, or a disciplinarian form of literature bent on denying the average reader the pleasure of comprehension. To quote the imaginary 'judge' of Philip Larkin's 1957 manifesto-essay 'The Pleasure Principle': 'It is time some of you playboys realised...that reading a poem is hard work'.[19]

Between these two caricatures of modernism—which ran in parallel with the academic narrative of a 'mature' movement, now worthy of historical study—post-war moderation staked its claim. In 1956, Robert Conquest lamented the 'collapse in public taste' caused by an increasing emphasis on the metaphorical and the irrational in mid-century poetry. His *New Lines* anthology presented the poets of the Movement as the representatives of a new interest in 'the real person or event'. In Conquest's book, W. B. Yeats—whose modernist reinvention of his own voice continued to work with traditional form and first-person argument—was 'the great poet of the century'.[20] A few years later, Al Alvarez used another anthology, *The New Poetry* (1962), to attack the

---

[17] T. S. Eliot, *On Poetry and Poets* (London: Faber & Faber, 1957), 38.
[18] Eliot, *Complete Poems*, 197–8.
[19] Philip Larkin, *Required Writing: Miscellaneous Pieces 1955–1982* (London: Faber & Faber, 1983), 81.
[20] Robert Conquest (ed.), *New Lines: An Anthology* (London: Macmillan, 1956), pp. xiv–xv.

'gentility' of Movement poetics, as embodied by Larkin's 'man next door persona'.[21] But Alvarez's ideal poetics also desired to rein in modernism's depersonalized analyses and verbal excesses. The formula for the new poetry would combine 'the psychological insight and integrity of D. H. Lawrence'—the most personal of the free verse pioneers— with the 'formal intelligence' of Eliot. The tempered Lawrentianism of Ted Hughes was Alvarez's antidote to Conquest and Larkin.

The New Poetry's quarrel with *New Lines* appeared to offer readers a renewed form of modernism's opposition to dominant critical taste. However, the fact that both Hughes and Larkin were considered for the British Poet Laureateship in 1984—when the job still mainly consisted of writing public poems in praise of the Royal Family—confirmed the common ground of conservatism between the two sides. In the same year, Edward Lucie-Smith commented in a revised edition of his anthology, *British Poetry since 1945*, that the 'full reconciliation between the modernist spirit and British poetry which I looked forward to in 1970 has yet to take place'. But 'full reconciliation' was itself always arguably counter to the antagonistic spirit of modernism.[22] When Ezra Pound, writing in Wyndham Lewis's magazine *Blast*, called the typical book reviewer of *The Times*

You slut-bellied obstructionist,
     You sworn foe to free speech and good letters,
You fungus, you continuous gangrene

he was not angling for a truce.[23] And when Larkin later named Pound as the poet who epitomized what he objected to about modernist aesthetics, he acknowledged a deliberately uncompromising position with one of his own.[24]

The real opposition to Larkin and the Movement in the 1960s took the form of what Eric Mottram called the 'British Poetry Revival', whose leading figures included Prynne and Tom Raworth.[25] Like the early modernists, these writers published through small presses and magazines on the margins of a formally and discursively normative literary culture. Many continue to do so. As Raworth wrote in a recent parodic squib, which seeks to offend just as Pound did:

I could go on like this all day

Ti-tum ti-tum and doodly-ay
With every now and then a glance
To see if I've still on my pants
And if I have, if that stain's jism
Or just a trace of modernism[26]

---

[21] *The New Poetry*, 23–32.
[22] Edward Lucie-Smith (ed.), *British Poetry since 1945* (rev. edn., Harmondsworth: Penguin Books, 1985), 24.
[23] 'Salutation the Third', *Blast*, 1 (1914), 45.
[24] Larkin, *Required Writing*, 297.
[25] Eric Mottram, 'The British Poetry Revival 1960–1975', in Robert Hampson and Peter Barry (ed.), *New British Poetries: The Scope of the Possible* (Manchester: Manchester University Press, 1995), 15–50.
[26] Tom Raworth, 'Envoi', *Windmills in Flames: Old and New Poems* (Manchester: Carcanet Press, 2010), 45. The poem parodied is Peter Porter's 'Last Words', *Max is Missing* (London: Picador, 2001), 3.

Modernism is figured here as the literally seminal moment of modern poetry, but one whose original excitement has become a source of embarrassment. Raworth has consistently advocated a poetics of excitement. As he writes at the end of the mock-critical tract 'How to Patronise a Poem': 'i have tasted fire | goodbye, pleasant butter'.[27] In the work championed by Mottram, modernism's experimentation with lyric voice was seen as an extension of the Romantic poets' enquiry into the spontaneous powers of the imagination, 'revived' after the abeyance in the 1940s and 1950s of an avant-garde poetic culture in Britain. The social disruption and contraction of the war (including paper shortages for magazines and presses) played a part in this, as did the moderate views of the later Eliot. The leading figure in England of the post-*Waste Land* generation, W. H. Auden, left for America at the end of the 1930s, and over the war years turned—like Eliot in *Four Quartets*—towards a more centripetal speaking voice. In the same period, Ezra Pound's imprisonment in Pisa at the end of the war for supporting the Italian Fascists was a significant event in the public narrative of modernism's folly. Another was the death—reputedly by drink—of Dylan Thomas in 1953, cutting short a sonorously British surrealism which had emerged as a popular native form of modernist verse (Thomas's influence on the 'New Romantic' poetry of the 1940s was the implicit target of Conquest's *New Lines* introduction).

The controversial publication of Pound's *The Pisan Cantos* (1948) also drew attention to the connection between modernist aesthetics and Fascist politics. As Eric Mottram saw it, Pound's revolutionary example bequeathed a number of principles to the British Poetry Revival, including the reinvention of traditional forms, the expansion of subject matter, and the critical location of the poet to modern politics and economics. But Pound's complicity in the poetics of authoritarianism was also a significant problem for later liberal and left-wing aspirants to early modernism's 'full-blooded articulation of inventive imagination'.[28] Donald Davie put his finger on the difficulty when he described how

> the literary intellectual who in his classroom toys with the anti-democratic opinions of a Pound or Yeats or Wyndham Lewis, Lawrence or Eliot, transforms himself into a social democrat as soon as he attends his university senate, voting there, and perhaps speaking eloquently, in favor of 'freedom of inquiry'—a principle which his authors regarded without enthusiasm, if not indeed with animosity, much as some of them profited by it.[29]

To appreciate the formal innovation of these authors is not necessarily the same thing, of course, as to 'toy' with their political opinions, which were often expressed more dogmatically in prose than verse. But neither is it a simple matter to separate the two in the critical epistemology of university English studies, which emphasizes the continuity of form and content (itself a modernist ideal). Post-war British poets consequently

---

[27] Raworth, 'Envoi', 23.
[28] Mottram, 'British Poetry Revival', 24.
[29] Donald Davie, *Thomas Hardy and British Poetry* (London: Routledge & Kegan Paul, 1973), 5.

looked to the democratic modernism of Pound's American contemporary, William Carlos Williams, in which the poet is less anxiously at odds with the crowd of modern life. As Andrew Crozier wrote in *A Various Art*, an anthology which offered an alternative to Lucie-Smith's mid-eighties view that the American influence had peaked, its modernism was 'not that of Pound and Eliot but that of Pound and Williams'.[30]

The Eliotic narrative of modernism's maturation, however, allowed poets on the conservative wing of modern British poetry to align the early modernist desire for coherence and clarity with a renewed poetics of the authoritative observer. In the 1960s, the poet, editor, and critic Ian Hamilton advocated precisely written poems which had their 'roots in Imagism', albeit with 'far more human content than their models', an aesthetic that influenced a generation of acclaimed domestic-realist poets including Hugo Williams, David Harsent, and Craig Raine.[31] In the 1970s, the lone figure of Geoffrey Hill positioned his own formalism in corrective relation to the politically wayward modernists by arguing that their concentrated language was a mode of 'truthtelling' that combines 'the atonement of aesthetics with rectitude of judgement'.[32] Almost every strand of contemporary British poetry, in other words, has found it desirable to weave itself into some version of modernism, as encouraged by Eliot's argument in 'Tradition and the Individual Talent' that 'the introduction of the new (the really new) work of art' among the monuments of literary history will cause the whole canon to be 'modified': a paradoxical tradition of the new that allows for its own perpetual rewriting.[33]

In a valuably non-partisan contribution to the history of the hundred-year British 'poetry wars', Peter Howarth has observed that the significance of the argument between the Georgians and the Imagists, during which the main principles of modernist poetry were articulated, 'does not make sense without understanding how close the two sides originally were'. In the early 1910s, both groups were arguing for a poetry which communicated more directly than that of the Victorian period through 'a realism premised on removing the filters of custom'. The crucial difference lay in the form of poetic voice each conceived as a vehicle for this ambition. The Georgians turned to unconventional subject matter, while the Imagists foregrounded the unconventional voice of free verse. For one side, realism was the documentary expansion of the representation of reality. For the other, it was the formal reinvention of this representation. As Howarth suggests, the disagreement can be traced back at least another hundred years to the Romantic period. Wordsworth's Preface to *Lyrical Ballads* called for poets to represent the lives of real people in language which 'does not differ from that of good Prose'. But his collaborator, Samuel Taylor Coleridge, later argued the importance of finding a 'correspondent difference of language' for the special complexity of poetic expression.[34]

---

[30] Andrew Crozier and Tim Longville (eds.), *A Various Art* (1987; repr. Paladin, 1990), 12.

[31] Quoted in David Harsent (ed.), *Another Round at the Pillars: Essays, Poems and Reflections on Ian Hamilton* (Manaccan: Cargo Press, 1999), 66.

[32] Geoffrey Hill, 'Poetry as Menace and Atonement' (1978), in *Collected Critical Writings*, ed. Kenneth Haynes (Oxford: Oxford University Press, 2008), 3–20 (12).

[33] Eliot, *Selected Essays*, 15.

[34] Peter Howarth, *British Poetry in the Age of Modernism* (Cambridge: Cambridge University Press, 2005), ch. 1 (pp. 19–21).

Ezra Pound's definition of the Imagist ideal as 'an intellectual and emotional complex' requiring non-prosaic expression implies the same logic (as, indeed, does his view that Wordsworth could be 'unutterably dull').[35] Contemporary neo-Georgians have nevertheless attempted to reclaim the inheritance of modernist poetry from its Coleridgean position. An acute caricature can be found in Don Paterson's 2004 T. S. Eliot Lecture, which argues against 'that peculiar and persistent brand of late romantic expressionism, almost always involving the deliberate or inept foregrounding of form and strategy over content—almost in a demonstration of their anti-naturalism, of the fact they did not evolve together'.[36] Again, a form of realism is at stake. Paterson's representative figure of a contemporary anti-naturalist aesthetic is J. H. Prynne, who has written in defence of 'the matter of difficulty in poetic language', and how it may be 'developed as a method and a structure of discourse':

> When links in text-cohesion are violated or cut off, when extreme ambiguity displaces recognisable topic-focus, when discourse levels and fields of reference are switched abruptly and without sign-posts, these features may begin to comprise a second-order strategy of pattern-making in a new way.[37]

Although Prynne's later work has gone much further in substituting 'extreme ambiguity' for 'topic-focus', 'The Glacial Question, Unsolved', from his early collection, *The White Stones* (1969), exemplifies many of these strategies. Only two printed pages long, its subject is the formation of the British Isles:

In the matter of ice, the invasions
were partial, so that the frost
was a beautiful head
                      the sky cloudy
and the day packed into the crystal
as the thrust slowed and we come to
a stand, along the coast of Norfolk.
That is a relative point, and since
the relation was part to part, the
gliding was cursive; a retreat, followed
by advance, right to north London.[38]

Packing geophysical prehistory into crystalline lyric form, Prynne here performs his own cursive gliding across the conventional boundaries of 'text-cohesion'. Abrupt switches between 'discourse levels and fields of reference' suggest their 'own second-order

---

[35] *Literary Essays of Ezra Pound*, 4–7.
[36] Don Paterson, 'The Dark Art of Poetry' (9 Nov. 2004) [http://www.poetrylibrary.org.uk/news/poetryscene/?id=20].
[37] J. H. Prynne, 'Difficulties in the Translation of "Difficult" Poems', *Cambridge Literary Review*, 1/3 (Easter, 2010), 151–66 (157).
[38] J. H. Prynne, *Poems* (Newcastle upon Tyne: Bloodaxe Books, 1999), 65.

strategy of pattern-making', which—like *The Waste Land* and *The Cantos*—juxtaposes ancient and modern worlds in verse. Like the coast forming 'thrust' that is the poem's subject, Prynne's sharply enjambing argument pushes out towards the 'fringe | of intellectual habit', where the question of 'our' place in the world remains unsettled. It ends:

We know this, we are what it leaves:
the Pleistocene is our current sense, and
what in sentiment we are, we
are, the coast, a line or sequence, the
cut back down, to the shore.

These lines are followed by a list of references, again recalling *The Waste Land* and its Notes, which suggested that the symbolic meaning of the poem could be found in its correspondence to Grail legend. Prynne's 'References', however, come at the end of a poem that strays constantly between 'fields of reference', and point the reader only towards further questions of interpretation. The 'glacial question' that the poem poses is whether we are really as modern as we thought. Geologists have commonly agreed that mankind is in the epoch of the Holocene ('wholly new'), following the Pleistocene glaciations in the Northern Hemisphere two million years ago, during which most modern mammals, including humans, evolved. But 'The Glacial Question, Unsolved' quotes a research paper from 1955 suggesting that the conditions of the Pleistocene may still characterize our experience. The critical vista that the end of the poem opens up turns on the last word. What modern British society considered 'sure' may be more like the shifting 'shore' of the small land-mass it occupies. 'Unsolved' questions of language, and the knowledge it carries, are brought to the reader's attention as a 'matter of ice': unstable and world-changing.

The part of Prynne's text that seems most openly to advertise its affinity to modernist precedent, therefore, is also the point where a modernist ideology is most acutely criticized. 'The Glacial Question, Unsolved' reveals itself to be a poem about the pattern-making habits of modernist poetics as well as one indebted to them. The image of an unfinished process which 'as we | move...adjusts the horizon' resembles the perpetually 'readjusted' world of Eliot's 'tradition', said to go back as far as 'the rock drawing of the Magdalenian draughtsman'.[39] By extending the view of who 'we' are beyond the origins of human civilization itself, Prynne undercuts Eliot's anthropocentric assumptions, in a poem where the lyric voice is displaced by the empiricism of modern science. This is an alternative 'realism' to the naturalistic interpretation of Wordsworth's image of the poet as a 'man speaking to men' in the Preface to *Lyrical Ballads*. But Prynne's emphatic use of the first-person plural makes clear that this poetry has not abandoned the ideal of a collective discourse. Rather, it continues the modernist dialectic between the private and the public voice in the light of new knowledge, moving between Lynette

---

[39] Eliot, *Selected Essays*, 16.

Roberts's 1948 conception of a simple voice born out of the 'refolding of the various strata' of society and the 'whole discordant universe' of modern thought.

Two critical accounts of what happened to the 'high' modernism between the 1920s and the 1950s are helpful in identifying the distinctively British modernism of 'The Glacial Question, Unsolved'. In post-*Waste Land* poetry by W. H. Auden ('Look, stranger, on this island now'), Hugh MacDiarmid ('On a Raised Beach'), and David Jones (*The Anathémata*), the topos of geology becomes a way of reflecting on contemporary questions of national identity for an Englishman, a Scotsman, and a Welshman respectively. Jed Esty has described the 'late modernist' world of such works as the 'shrinking island' of Great Britain in the 1930s, where imperial decline resulted in a new cultural localism or 'anthropological turn' away from internationalism.[40] Another definition of 'late modernism' has been advanced by Tyrus Miller, who detects in the same decade a reopening of 'the modernist enclosure of form onto the work's social and political environs', which explored 'the political regions that high modernism had managed to view from the distance of a closed car' (a 'closed car at four' is to be found in the London of *The Waste Land*).[41]

The focus in both accounts on the decentralized localities of late modernist writing illuminates the centrality of Basil Bunting's long poem, *Briggflatts* (1966), to the reconfiguration of a modernist poetics in post-war Britain. In this late 'autobiography', Bunting, who had been a protégé of Pound, recalled his modernist youth in London, seeking the juxtaposed perceptions and abrupt metric of the Imagist city ('counts beat against beat, bus conductor | against engine against wheels against | the pedal, Tottenham Court Road'). Three decades later, he found the subject matter for a work of meditative accuracy in the pastoral landscape of his native Northumberland ('fell-born men of precise instep | leading demure dogs').[42] In *Briggflatts*, Eliot and Pound's global poles of private and collective voice are mapped onto personal history and local landscape. These are also the co-ordinates of Geoffrey Hill's prose-poem sequence, *Mercian Hymns* (1971), five years later, which explores mythical correspondences between the ancient and modern Midlands of his childhood, complete with Eliotic notes. It might be observed, however, that Hill's autobiographical England preserves a Georgian paradise at the heart of a modernist style. The identity of person and place in *Mercian Hymns* and later meditative works such as *The Triumph of Love* (1999) is essentially stable. So, too, is the Northern Irish farm childhood at the heart of Paul Muldoon's formally extraordinary long poem 'Yarrow', from *The Annals of Chile* (1994), which knowingly imitates *The Waste Land* with its fragmentary quotations and Grail-quest narrative, but subordinates these to the autobiographical mode.

---

[40] Jed Esty, *A Shrinking Island: Modernism and National Culture in England* (Princeton and Oxford: Princeton University Press, 2004), 1–22.

[41] Tyrus Miller, *Late Modernism: Politics, Fiction, and the Arts Between the Wars* (Berkeley: University of California Press, 1999), 3–25.

[42] Basil Bunting, *Complete Poems,* ed. Ric Caddel (Newcastle upon Tyne: Bloodaxe, 2000), 65, 79.

For Hill and Muldoon, the post-war inheritance of modernism has become a personal one, entangled with the poet's own formative experiences. Bunting's late modernist autobiography, though, ends with a choric vision of human history as a 'strong song' of language heading towards open horizons. Poets such as Peter Larkin, Thomas A. Clark, Colin Simms, and Helen MacDonald have brought this more impersonal notion to bear on the contemporary nature poem, a genre recently anthologized as 'radical landscape poetry'.[43] Such writing finds in wilderness and rural life a correlative of modernist poetry's cultural eccentricity. As Peter Riley puts it in a portrait of the modern poet as Shelley's 'unacknowledged legislator' of pastoral values:

> Driving back from
> the wedding between dark fields, the night layers
> carefully hand aeroplanes down to Stansted,
> and somewhere over the fields is a small embanked lake
> with one elm, under which the controller
> of weddings and stars sits crouched, tapping messages.[44]

Conversely, post-war poets whose experimental oeuvres have been associated with particular British cities—Roy Fisher in Birmingham, Allen Fisher in South London, Edwin Morgan in Glasgow—have extended the urban modernism of two epics of American settlement, William Carlos Williams's *Paterson* (1946–58) and Charles Olson's *The Maximus Poems* (1960–75).

The defining quality of late modernist poetry in Britain, however, is not its identification with a bounded locality, but the textual triangulation it seeks between reader, speaker, and the shaping forces of the world. As Prynne commented on his own work in 1985:

> It has mostly been my own aspiration, for example, to establish relations not personally with the reader, but with the world and its layers of shifted but recognisable usage; and thereby with the reader's own position within this world.[45]

The shifting layers of modernist writing can be thought of as their own place or stage, where the relationship between lyric subjectivity and the world becomes a drama of language. Such a theory is implicit in two critiques of the typical speaker of mainstream British poetry by poets associated with Prynne. Andrew Crozier has argued that the Faber-published poetry of Larkin, Hughes, Seamus Heaney, and Craig Raine—despite differences of style and degrees of modernist allegiance—essentially constitutes a static tradition of 'the authoritative self, discoursing in a world of banal, empirically derived objects and relations, [which] depends on its employment of metaphor and simile for

---

[43] Harret Tarlo (ed.), *The Ground Aslant: An Anthology of Radical Landscape Poetry* (Exeter: Shearsman Books, 2011).
[44] Peter Riley, 'Essex Skies', *A Glacial Stairway* (Manchester: Carcanet Press, 2011), 66.
[45] J. H. Prynne, quoted as epigraph to Peter Riley, *Reader* (London: no publisher, 1992).

poetic vitality'. Crozier contrasts the lyricism of Charles Tomlinson as writing that takes up William Carlos Williams's motto 'no ideas but in things' by attempting a 'material' identification with the object of description rather than mediating it through the 'special register of the poet's sensibility'.[46] Similarly, Veronica Forrest-Thomson's anti-naturalistic theory of modern poetry in *Poetic Artifice* (1978) argues that Imagism was in a tradition that encouraged the reader to perform the 'good naturalisation' of finding formal relationships between words, as opposed to the 'bad naturalisation' of referring poetic language directly to a world of common knowledge, as in the classroom-friendly animal poems of Ted Hughes.[47]

Forrest-Thomson quotes one of her own poems, 'Pastoral', in illustration of a well-naturalized nature poem. It ends:

The gentle foal linguistically wounded,
squeals like a car's brakes, like our twisted words.

The importance of the 'gentle foal', she comments, is not as a real creature, but as a phrase whose sounds mutate into 'linguistically wounded' (which in turn becomes 'twisted words')—a verbal relationship that embodies the emotional theme of the poem's car crash: 'pre-occupation with linguistic problems prevents contact with the physical world'.[48] Forrest-Thomson's explicit preoccupation with questions of language looks back to the criticism of William Empson, as well as the modernist meta-lyricism of Laura Riding, in which 'Exactly I and exactly the world | Fail to meet by a moment, and a word' ('The World and I').[49] Forrest-Thomson's theory treats contemporary experimentalism as continuous with the early modernist poetic of the 'disconnected image-complex'. But the explicit slippage between writing and reality in her work creates the kind of effect that has been widely theorized as 'postmodernist'.

In the work of a mid-century British poet such as W. S. Graham, who in the 1960s and 1970s spoke openly from 'the other side of the words', the textual self-consciousness associated with postmodernism can be heard as a development of modernism's fragmentary self rather than a clean break. Yet the term has not found the same place in the critical discourse around post-war British poetry as in America, where it has been broadly employed as 'the most encompassing term for the variety of experimental practice since World War II'.[50] Linguistic resistance again signifies a historical dispute. Anthony Mellors's description of J. H. Prynne's 'late Modernism' as one that 'radically questions [the modernist] tradition of determining the indeterminate and unifying the fragmentary' by 'continually displac[ing] the ground on which sense, reference and

---

[46] Andrew Crozier, 'Thrills and Frills: Poetry as Figures of Empirical Lyricism', in Alan Sinfield (ed.), *Society and Literature 1945–1970* (London: Methuen, 1983), 199–233 (229–31).

[47] Veronica Forrest-Thomson, *Poetic Artifice* (Manchester: Manchester University Press, 1978), 112–63.

[48] Forrest-Thomson, *Poetic Artifice*, 125.

[49] Laura Riding, *Selected Poems: In Five Sets* (London: Faber & Faber, 1970), 56, 189.

[50] Paul Hoover (ed.), 'Introduction', *Postmodern American Poetry: A Norton Anthology* (New York: Norton, 1994), p. xxv.

value are based' may sound like another critic's definition of postmodernist scepticism.[51] The important point, though, is that the ground of modernism has been 'displaced' but not abandoned, as in the established story of post-war British poetry (where 'postmodernist' can be applied to the narrative poetry of Andrew Motion, on the grounds that it left Philip Larkin nonplussed).[52] 'The Glacial Question, Unsolved' may call into doubt the notion that the 'matter' of a poem can be made to cohere by reference to its notes, but it also continues the modernist attempt to find new forms of poetic thought and voice for a new world of philosophical and scientific enquiry.

The term 'late modernism' nevertheless concedes a qualified continuity, which leads Drew Milne to suggest that 'neo-modernism' would be a more positive description of the attempt to renew the ambition of the early modernist response to historical conditions.[53] The continued use of the term 'modernist' also reflects the ongoing recuperation of a British avant-garde over the last half-century, in ways that expand the modernist canon around and beyond the early dominance of Eliot and Pound. Milne has described how the delayed publication of David Jones's posthumous fragments meant the work became 'part of the small-press context of 1980s British poetry'.[54] In 2006, John Wilkinson lamented that Lynette Roberts's recently republished poetry had 'faltered not only for personal reasons, but because in post-war Britain there was no one to hear it. Tradition came to mean a commonsense parochialism, and modernism became academic.' Admiring the 'clenched but mobile stanzas' of Roberts's poem about the Second World War in Wales, *Gods With Stainless Ears* (1951), Wilkinson contradicts the narrative of modernism's mid-century decline by invoking a neglected example from the past as a model for new poetry which might 'pulse with sociolinguistic intensities— that is, language as it occupies subjects and subjects as they occupy language'.[55] *Gods With Stainless Ears* ends with a vision of a post-war world netted by the 'red competitive lines' of the airline industry, the 'skylanes' and 'thin | Strokes of mapping pens', and a '[n]etwork of rails: pylons and steel installations'.[56] The opening lines of Wilkinson's *Iphigenia* (2004) read as a homage to Roberts's vision of industrial entanglement, as well as a manifesto statement for an experimental verse of original 'errancy':

A different line gives & takes & plays,
corded with lines of flight.
At outset
    Out of errancy

---

[51] Anthony Mellors, *Late Modernist Poetics from Pound to Prynne* (Manchester: Manchester University Press, 2005), 11.

[52] Sean O'Brien (ed.), *The Firebox: Poetry in Britain and Ireland after 1945* (London: Picador, 1998), p. xxxvi.

[53] Drew Milne, 'Neo-Modernism and Avant-Garde Orientations', in Nigel Alderman and C. D. Blanton (eds.), *A Concise Companion to Postwar British and Irish Poetry*, (Chichester: Wiley-Blackwell, 2009), 155–75 (165).

[54] In Iain Sinclair (ed.), *Conductors of Chaos* (London: Picador, 1996), 260.

[55] John Wilkinson, 'The Brain's Tent': [http://bostonreview.net/BR31.5/wilkinson.php].

[56] Lynette Roberts, *Collected Poems*, ed. Patrick McGuinness (Manchester: Carcanet Press), 67–8.

lines of flight deviate from loaded flightpaths;
    & down a perplexed line,
some further line off our intended furrow
lags, resumes,
    detours ahead,
jerks & leaves its knots to hang in the air,
stratified cloud-cuckoo-land.[57]

Wilkinson's network of knotting lines ends in the sky, a 'cloud-cuckoo-land' of imaginary possibilities. It is an apt image for the modernist poetic tradition in Britain after a hundred years. Since the 1960s, many of its lines have been drawn through the critical tradition of English studies at Cambridge University, where I. A. Richards, William Empson, and F. R. Leavis were among the first academics to take Eliot and Pound seriously, and Prynne, Langley, Riley, Wilkinson, and Forrest-Thomson later studied. Despite Prynne's provocative observation in 2005 that 'the American literary tradition is a mere teenager...an offshoot of English culture...perhaps in five hundred or a thousand years it might become a mature culture', it is clearly paradoxical to insist on a national tradition for an inherently cosmopolitan poetry, whose British origins embody a meeting of American and European poetics (Prynne has also been a long-standing advocate of Continental modernist writing).[58] In the post-war period, the New York School and later the American Language poets brought new lyric voices to Cambridge and beyond. As Eliot predicted, the effect has been to rewrite literary tradition again, so that the experimentalism of Gertrude Stein has begun to emerge as equally influential as Eliot, Williams, or Pound. The prominence of contemporary American female experimental poets since the 1970s has also begun to diminish the 'cliquishness and vocal dominance of men' in the social and promotional networks of the British Poetry Revival.[59]

The monolithic notion of a 'modernist tradition' has also been put aside in the last two decades by younger poets and critics, who have preferred to use the term 'linguistically innovative'.[60] In 1949, Basil Bunting wrote of Pound's *Cantos*, 'These are the Alps, | fools! Sit down and wait for them to crumble.'[61] The presence of high modernism in the landscape of recent British innovative poetry is perhaps better figured by Trevor Joyce's poem 'The Turlough', which uses the Japanese renga form to evoke a unique kind of

---

[57] John Wilkinson, *Iphigenia* (London: Barque Press, 2004), 3.

[58] J. H. Prynne, 'Keynote Speech at the First Pearl River Poetry Conference, Guangzhou, China, 28th June 2005', *Quid*, 16 (2006), 7–17 (7). See ' "Modernism" in German Poetry', *Cambridge Review*, 9 Mar. 1963, 331–7: 'We have perhaps grown too used to the idea that...it was the Anglo-American revolutionary initiative that consolidated the European importance of "modernism" ' (331).

[59] Emily Critchley, quoted in Carrie Etter (ed.), *Infinite Difference: Other Poetries by U. K. Women Poets* (Exeter: Shearsman Books, 2010), 10.

[60] Robert Sheppard, *The Poetry of Saying: British Poetry and Its Discontents* (Liverpool: Liverpool University Press, 2005), 143–4. See also Jon Clay, 'Introduction', *Sensation, Contemporary Poetry and Deleuze* (London: Continuum, 2010), 1–11.

[61] Bunting, *Complete Poems*, 132.

disappearing and reappearing Irish lake. Its broken refrains recall the closing lines of *The Waste Land* as a form of 'elsewhere': 'It is raining elsewhere'; 'London Bridge is falling down elsewhere'; 'There is thunder now elsewhere'.[62] High modernist poetry has now itself become one of the strata of the collective past which the voice of the present investigates. In the post-Prynne political critique of Keston Sutherland's *Hot White Andy*, Pound's opening cry in *The Pisan Cantos* at the downfall of his political idealism—'The enormous tragedy of the dream in the peasant's bent shoulders'—becomes an aggressive multiple-choice option in the new world of Chinese communist-capitalism: 'WANT HOT ANDY CHENG? | Want the enormous tragedy of the dream?';[63] Vahni Capildeo's second collection, *Undraining Sea* (2009), maps a transnational lyricism onto Williams's *Paterson* and its belief that 'a man is indeed a city'; Jeff Hilson's mock-Renaissance sonnet sequence, *In the Assarts*, 'buy[s] staples' from the 'Smyrna merchant' of *The Waste Land* by anagrammatic mix-up with the British stationery chain Rymans;[64] and in Glasgow, Peter Manson has returned to one of the sources of modernist verse by translating the French Symbolist poetry of Stephane Mallarmé. In 'Between Cup and Lip', Mallarmé's (capitalized) invocation of the 'seamless' impersonality of high art is itself fragmented to form a base for the quotidian bathos of Manson's own poem. The resulting struggle between voices renews the modernist attempt to encompass contemporary reality without simplifying the otherness of lyric expression:

SOLITUDE kills real people, A REEFer is just for now, A STAR

turns on TO ANY TRICK THAT VALIDATES self, my image, cast down on yOUR CANVAS, my motive, SEAMLESSLY OPAQUE.[65]

Select Bibliography

Adorno, Theodor, 'On Lyric Poetry and Society', trans. Sherry Weber Nicholsen, in *Notes to Literature*, ed. Rolf Tiedemann (Columbia University Press, 1991), 37–54.
Alvarez, Al (ed.), *The New Poetry* (rev. edn., Harmondsworth: Penguin Books, 1966).
Bunting, Basil, *Complete Poems*, ed. Ric Caddel (Newcastle upon Tyne: Bloodaxe, 2000).
Clay, Jon, *Sensation, Contemporary Poetry and Deleuze* (London: Continuum, 2010).
Conquest, Robert (ed.), *New Lines: An Anthology* (London: Macmillan, 1956).
Crozier, Andrew, 'Thrills and Frills: Poetry as Figures of Empirical Lyricism', in Alan Sinfield (ed.), *Society and Literature 1945–1970* (London: Methuen, 1983), 199–233.
Crozier, Andrew and Longville, Tim (eds.), *A Various Art* (1987; repr. Paladin, 1990).
Davie, Donald, *Thomas Hardy and British Poetry* (London: Routledge & Kegan Paul, 1973).
Eliot, T. S., *Selected Essays* (3rd edn., London: Faber & Faber, 1951).
Eliot, T. S. (ed.), *Literary Essays of Ezra Pound* (London: Faber & Faber, 1954).

---

[62] Trevor Joyce, *Stone Floods* (Dublin: New Writers' Press, 1995), 10–11.
[63] Keston Sutherland, *Hot White Andy* (London: Barque Press, 2007), n.p.
[64] Jeff Hilson, *In the Assarts* (London: Veer, 2010), 43.
[65] In Jeff Hilson (ed.), *The Reality Street Book of Sonnets* (Hastings: Reality Street Editions, 2008), 323.

Eliot, T. S., *On Poetry and Poets* (London: Faber & Faber, 1957).
Eliot, T. S., *The Complete Poems and Plays* (London: Faber & Faber, 1969).
Esty, Jed, *A Shrinking Island: Modernism and National Culture in England* (Princeton and Oxford: Princeton University Press, 2004).
Etter, Carrie (ed.), *Infinite Difference: Other Poetries by U.K. Women Poets* (Exeter: Shearsman Books, 2010).
Hill, Geoffrey, 'Poetry as Menace and Atonement' (1978), in *Collected Critical Writings*, ed. Kenneth Haynes (Oxford: Oxford University Press, 2008), 3–20.
Hilson, Jeff (ed.), *The Reality Street Book of Sonnets* (Hastings: Reality Street Editions, 2008).
Hilson, Jeff, *In the Assarts* (London: Veer, 2010).
Howarth, Peter, *British Poetry in the Age of Modernism* (Cambridge: Cambridge University Press, 2005).
Hulme, T. E., *Selected Writings*, ed. Patrick McGuinness, (Manchester: Fyfield, 1998).
Josipovici, Gabriel, *Whatever Happened to Modernism?* (New Haven: Yale University Press, 2010).
Joyce, Trevor, *Stone Floods* (Dublin: New Writers' Press, 1995).
Kenner, Hugh, *T. S. Eliot: The Invisible Poet* (London: W. H. Allen, 1950).
Langley, R. F., 'To a Nightingale', *London Review of Books*, 18 Nov. 2010, 25.
Larkin, Philip, *Required Writing: Miscellaneous Pieces 1955–1982* (London: Faber & Faber, 1983).
Lucie-Smith, Edward (ed.), *British Poetry since 1945* (rev. edn., Harmondsworth: Penguin Books, 1985).
Mellors, Anthony, *Late Modernist Poetics from Pound to Prynne* (Manchester: Manchester University Press, 2005).
Miller, Tyrus, *Late Modernism: Politics, Fiction, and the Arts Between the Wars* (Berkeley: University of California Press, 1999).
Milne, Drew, 'Neo-Modernism and Avant-Garde Orientations', in Nigel Alderman and C. D. Blanton (eds.), *A Concise Companion to Postwar British and Irish Poetry* (Chichester: Wiley-Blackwell, 2009), 155–175.
Mottram, Eric, 'The British Poetry Revival 1960–1975', in Robert Hampson and Peter Barry (eds.), *New British Poetries: The Scope of the Possible* (Manchester: Manchester University Press, 1995), 15–50.
O'Brien, Sean (ed.), *The Firebox: Poetry in Britain and Ireland after 1945* (London: Picador, 1998).
Paterson, Don, 'The Dark Art of Poetry' (9 Nov. 2004) [http://www.poetrylibrary.org.uk/news/poetryscene/?id=20].
Prynne, J. H., 'Keynote Speech at the First Pearl River Poetry Conference, Guangzhou, China, 28th June 2005', *Quid*, 16 (2006), 7–17.
Prynne, J.H., *Poems* (Newcastle upon Tyne: Bloodaxe Books, 1999).
Prynne, J. H., *Sub Songs* (London: Barque Press, 2010).
Prynne, J. H., 'Difficulties in the Translation of "Difficult" Poems', *Cambridge Literary Review*, 1/3 (Easter, 2010), 151–66.
Raine, Craig, 'All jokes aside', *Guardian*, 11 Mar. 2008 [http://www.guardian.co.uk/books/2008/mar/11/poetry.thomasstearnseliot].
Raworth, Tom, 'Envoi', *Windmills in Flames: Old and New Poems* (Manchester: Carcanet Press, 2010).
Riding, Laura, *Selected Poems: In Five Sets* (London: Faber & Faber, 1970).
Riley, Denise, *Selected Poems* (London: Reality Street Editions, 2000).

Roberts, Lynette, *Diaries, Letters and Recollections,* ed. Patrick McGuinness (Manchester: Carcanet Press, 2008), 150.
Roberts, Lynette, *Collected Poems,* ed. Patrick McGuinness (Manchester: Carcanet Press).
Sheppard, Robert, *The Poetry of Saying: British Poetry and Its Discontents* (Liverpool: Liverpool University Press, 2005).
Sinclair, Iain (ed.), *Conductors of Chaos* (London: Picador, 1996).
Sutherland, Keston, *Hot White Andy* (London: Barque Press, 2007).
Tarlo, Harret (ed.), *The Ground Aslant: An Anthology of Radical Landscape Poetry* (Exeter: Shearsman Books, 2011).
Veronica, Forrest-Thomson, *Poetic Artifice* (Manchester: Manchester University Press, 1978).
Wilkinson, John, *Iphigenia* (London: Barque Press, 2004).

CHAPTER 7

TWO POETRIES?: A RE-EXAMINATION OF THE 'POETRY DIVIDE' IN 1970S BRITAIN

HELEN BAILEY

AN INSTITUTIONAL GATEWAY

WRITTEN between 11 September 1973 and 5 January 1974, Roy Fisher's poem 'Sets' captures a sense of unease about the future of British poetry. This anxiety, prevalent among many poets in the decade, stemmed from an acute awareness of conflicted literary movements and their impacts on the overarching historical narrative of poetry. Fisher's poem illustrates this process of grouping, whilst also pointing towards the conflicts that inevitably occur as poets disagree over who should or should not have a legacy within the growing poetic 'civilization':

If you take a poem
you must take another
and another
till you have a poet.

And if you take a poet
you'll take another, and so on,
till finally you get
a civilization: or just
the dirtiest brawl you ever saw—
the choice isn't yours.[1]

---

[1] Roy Fisher, 'Sets', *The Long and the Short of It: Poems 1955–2005* (Tarset: Bloodaxe Books, 2005), 146.

It is often assumed that this 'dirtiest brawl' was played out by two principal groups of British poets in the 1970s: the 'avant-garde' and the 'mainstream'. However, this is a somewhat crude view that fails to take into account the individuality of poets and the unique nature of their poems as modes of expression at particular moments in history.

This essay will re-examine the perception of a binary split by exploring the participation of poets in the review section of the BBC's now-defunct magazine, *The Listener*. Drawing on the Institutional Theory of Art, a concept inspired by Arthur C. Danto's essay, 'The Artworld' (1964), it considers the extent to which widely circulated magazines like *The Listener* acted as 'cultural brokerages' that determined a poet's success or failure in mainstream culture. As a respected institution *The Listener* could choose to employ and drop writers at any time in accordance with its own cultural stance. This meant that it conferred a degree of authority on its reviewers, who in turn had the power to 'make' or 'break' the poets they reviewed, regardless of their status in the smaller, more partisan sphere of the little magazines.

But *The Listener*'s institutional hegemony was not completely autocratic, because its power, in turn, was dependent on the acquisition of money and prestige. In order to circulate widely, it needed financial investment and a means of establishing itself as an 'authority' in contemporary culture. This intellectual kudos was secured through the collaboration of well-known academics, poets, and other writers who had already gained prestige in the public domain, and who therefore had significant influence over the 'cultural stance' of the magazine. However, the 'stance' became increasingly unclear as inevitable divisions emerged between reviewers, poets, and readers about who should and should not be allowed into mainstream culture through such an 'institutional gateway'. By exploring the review sections of *The Listener* in the early 1970s, this chapter seeks to reconsider the idea of a simple split between 'mainstream' and 'avant-garde' poets, revealing a number of complexities both between and within each of the supposed 'camps'.

In an article published in the magazine on 5 April 1973, Anthony Thwaite described a dream in which a painting had been constantly 'changing, undergoing a metamorphosis to suit the [...] interpretation' of the television personality who was analysing it. 'Everything was in a state of flux', he explained, 'nothing would stay still. I woke up bewildered, afraid and unsure of my bearings'. Thwaite attributed this dream to his own sense of unease about 'the state of poetry and its future prospects' but he was by no means alone in his anxiety.[2] As Randall Stevenson observes, it is impossible to 'overlook how far sureties failed' in the latter half of the twentieth century.[3] During the 1960s and 1970s, poets and critics were regularly voicing their concerns about 'a variety of contemporary pressures' which they felt were 'eroding the range, resources, and poetic potential of the English language'.[4] Not least among these pressures was the economic downturn that

---

[2] Anthony Thwaite, 'The Two Poetries', *The Listener*, 89/2297 (5 Apr. 1973), 452. Subsequent citations from *The Listener* will not include the journal title or issue numbers.

[3] Randall Stevenson, *The Oxford English Literary History*, xii. *1960–2000: The Last of England?* (Oxford: Oxford University Press, 2004), 1.

[4] Stevenson, *The Last of England?*, 258.

hit the UK in the early 1970s. In such difficult financial conditions, not unlike those of today, it was inevitable that the arts—and poetry in particular—were forced to retrench and justify their value. As Andrew Duncan writes, 'the resulting struggle for legitimacy has never ended'.[5]

The 'anxiety symptoms' of Thwaite's dream could be seen as indicative of this uneasy atmosphere in a post-war culture that was experiencing rapid change whilst simultaneously coming to terms with memories of war. Adorno famously pinpointed the cultural memory of the Holocaust as the end of traditional poetic forms, denouncing as barbaric all attempts to write lyric poetry after Auschwitz and claiming that the state of society is directly proportional to the state of the collective intellect. The regression of society, evidenced by the atrocities of the Holocaust, he argued, was simultaneously the result and cause of an 'intellectual regression' that no longer had the capacity to conceive beauty in its pre-Holocaustic form. However, he was also aware that the cultural 'consciousness of adversity' still paradoxically required the continued existence of art, since it was 'now virtually in art alone that suffering [could] still find its own voice, consolation, without immediately being betrayed by it'.[6] The subsequent critical reception of Adorno's self-consciously contradictory argument is particularly significant, as writers and critics have tended to focus on his 'apparent despair of poetry', rather than on 'his assertion of its continuing potential'.[7] The search for an end point to art, or at least for an end point to each artistic movement, appears to be hampered by a sense of failure and incompletion. As Arthur C. Danto has observed, 'it began to seem as though the whole main point of art in our century was to pursue the question of its own identity while rejecting all available answers as insufficiently general'. Danto took this negative, almost apocalyptic idea further, arguing that art had become so intertwined with theory, philosophy, and the 'movements' that encompass them, that 'virtually all there is at the end *is* theory, art having finally become vaporized in a dazzle of pure thought about itself, and remaining, as it were, solely as the object of its own theoretical consciousness'.[8]

For poetry, this preoccupation with theory and philosophy meant a growing self-consciousness about the linear, historical progression of poetic movements and reputations, and thus a tendency to be always already in search of the next 'big thing'. This was exacerbated by the 1973–5 recession, which meant that poetry found itself sidelined

---

[5] Andrew Duncan, *The Failure of Conservatism in Modern British Poetry* (Cambridge: Salt Publishing, 2003), 138.

[6] Theodor W. Adorno, 'Commitment', in *Aesthetics and Politics: The Key Texts of the Classic Debate with German Marxism*, trans. and ed. Ronald Taylor (London: New Left Books, 1977), 177–95 (188).

[7] Stevenson, *The Last of England?*, 252.

[8] Arthur Coleman Danto, *The Philosophical Disenfranchisement of Art* (New York: Columbia University Press, 1986), 110 and 111. Danto later qualified this position, arguing that 'it was never part of my thesis that art would stop being made—I had not proclaimed the *death* of art! "The End of Art" had rather to do with the way the history of art had been conceived, as a sequence of stages in an unfolding narrative. I felt that the narrative had come to an end, and in this regard, whatever art was now to be made would be posthistorical'. See Arthur Coleman Danto, 'Introduction: Art Criticism After the End of Art', in *Unnatural Wonders: Essays from the Gap Between Art and Life* (New York: Columbia University Press, 2005), 3.

by some of the large publishing companies in favour of novels that had comparatively higher sales figures. The result was a heightened sense of anxiety over the suitability of the poets getting published and the impact that this would have on the 'historical narrative'. Such narratives, George Dickie argued in a discussion of his Institutional Theory of Art, are determined by 'some person or persons acting on behalf of a certain social institution (the artworld) [who] has conferred the status of candidate for appreciation' on a work of art.[9] This meant that reviewers in magazines such as *The Listener* could have a significant influence on the direction of poetry. However, their inheritance of this power also meant that the views they put forward were more fiercely questioned and opposed than in the smaller arenas of little magazines.

Movements and Counter-Movements

In his book, *The Deregulated Muse*, Sean O'Brien writes that 'arguments about literature have as much to do with cultural power as with the words on the page that excited us in the first place'.[10] Indeed, since the Movement positioned itself as a conservative reaction to both high modernism and the New Apocalyptics, poetry of the 1960s and 1970s had become increasingly caught in a rapid, eddying current of movements and counter-movements. Each would raise the age-old question: 'What is Art?' on its own terms and then '[offer] itself as a possible final answer'.[11] Little magazines were instrumental to the establishment of these movements. According to the definitions set out by David Miller and Richard Price, these were largely non-commercial enterprises that published 'the work of a group of artists or writers who assert[ed] themselves as a group'.[12] In a similar vein, the British Library defines them as publications that 'champion work by a very small number of authors, or a particular style, or attempt to provide a cross-section of what its editor sees as the contemporary scene'.[13] Inevitably, each editor and each group of poets had their own ideas about the 'contemporary scene' (and they were usually at the centre of it). By grouping together in this way to create what Roy Fisher termed a 'civilization' (strength in numbers) they could try to influence the poetry scene. The problem was that few single movements were ever quite big or universal enough to monopolize the art world and dictate its direction.

Some poets felt that verse should be using the 'traditional' forms of the past, but with freer, more colloquial language, just as composers such as Stravinsky, earlier in the

---

[9] George Dickie, *Aesthetics: An Introduction* (Indianapolis: Pegasus, 1971), 101.
[10] Sean O'Brien, *The Deregulated Muse: Essays on Contemporary British & Irish Poetry* (Newcastle upon Tyne: Bloodaxe Books, 1998), 18.
[11] Danto, *Philosophical Disenfranchisement*, 110.
[12] David Miller and Richard Price (eds.), *British Poetry Magazines 1914–2000: A History and Bibliography of 'Little Magazines'* (London: British Library and Oak Knoll Press, 2006), p. x.
[13] See [http://www.bl.uk/reshelp/findhelprestype/journals/littlemagazines/littlemagazines.html], accessed 22 Jan. 2011.

century, had used neoclassical devices in the *Pulcinella Suite* and elsewhere. A version of this approach can be seen in Donald Davie's 1974 publication, *The Shires*, a nostalgic response to the 1972 Local Government Act which abolished the traditional county structure. His poem 'Westmorland' opens with:

Kendal… Shap Fell! Is that in Westmorland?
For one who espouses the North,
I am hazy about it, frankly. It's a chosen
North of the mind I take my bearings by,
A stripped style and a wintry.[14]

Here, Davie's opening exclamation brings to mind the area near Ullswater that was Wordsworth's 'chosen | North', inspiring much of his poetry, such as the famous 'Daffodils'. As one of the counties that were disestablished in 1972, the uncertainty about whether or not Shap Fell is part of Westmorland communicates Davie's anxiety about the change in the area. The mention of Kendal also recalls Wordsworth's fierce objection to the proposal of a Kendal-Windermere railway line in 1844, perhaps inspiring us to consider what his reaction might have been to the disappearance of his favourite county.[15] The Romantic poet is evoked as 'the mind' against which the 'I' of the poem measures himself in his own time: 'It's a chosen | North of the mind I take my bearings by'. However, instead of emulating the style of the Romantics, Davie uses colloquial language, creating 'a stripped style and a wintry' landscape that contrasts with the flamboyant style, sun-infused imagery, and 'unconsidered spontaneity (or apparent spontaneity)'[16] of Wordsworth's idyllic 'host of golden daffodils'. Antony Easthope suggests that Davie's *The Shires* 'draws on picture postcard clichés to protract a fantasy of England as "country" […] in a poetic discourse that might well be called "Neo-Georgian" '. Comparing this with Davie's earlier poem, 'A Winter Talent', which takes an anti-Romantic stance, rejecting what René Wellek has called the Romantic attempt to 'reconcile man [sic] and nature',[17] Easthope goes on to claim that by the seventies, the poet had been 'sucked back into the orbit of […] a poetic Englishness that [could] keep open its lifeline back to Hardy and beyond only by constantly warding off the "invasion" […] of modernism'.[18]

---

[14] Donald Davie, 'Westmorland', *The Shires* (London: Routledge&Kegan Paul, 1974), n.p.
[15] William Wordsworth, 'Suggested by the Proposed Kendal and Windermere Railway' (12 Oct. 1844). See William Wordsworth's Lake District Collection in the Literary Landscape section of the British Library Online Exhibition, MS 44361 f. 278, [http://www.bl.uk/onlinegallery/onlineex/literland/wordsworth/windermere/027add000044361u00278000.html], accessed 22 Jan. 2011.
[16] Antony Easthope, 'Donald Davie and the Failure of Englishness', in James Acheson and Romana Huk (eds.), *Contemporary British Poetry: Essays in Theory and Criticism* (Albany, NY: State University of New York Press, 1996), 17–33 (18).
[17] René Wellek, 'Romanticism Re-examined', in Northrop Frye (ed.), *Romanticism Reconsidered* (New York: Columbia University Press, 1963), 107–33 (133).
[18] Easthope, 'Donald Davie and the Failure of Englishness', 31.

In his review of Davie's book, John Fuller described the collection as being 'not so much a pulling up of anchors as an establishing of roots, of context, of love of a kind'. It is clear from his review that Fuller was sympathetic to the restrained and disciplined approach of so-called 'mainstream' poets like Davie to language and form, using adjectives and phrases such as 'tight-lipped', 'meticulous', 'controlled', 'scrupulous decorum', and 'razor-edge' to describe what he deemed to be the praiseworthy attributes of his style. Nevertheless, he went on to give a somewhat lukewarm opinion of Davie's place in the 'historical narrative' of poetry, concluding that 'Major poets, alas, are always counted on the thumbs of one hand, but I think Davie is good enough to be numbered among the fingers'.[19] Here, Fuller's choice of words ('major poets', 'good enough') reflects the predominant canon-focused critical preoccupation of the time. Compared to the current tendency to judge and rank poets on their celebrity and literary prominence, the discussion between reviewers in *The Listener* in the early seventies placed more emphasis on trying to enforce quantifiable value judgements, fitting poets and their works into an overarching canonical narrative.

According to Stevenson's somewhat polemical book, however, this direction led to 'the lingering languor [of] the Movement',[20] exemplified by the formalistic, somewhat underwhelming rustic works of a poet such as Molly Holden. Her poem, 'The Fields For Miles', attempts to reinstate a past appreciation of the countryside in the 'hard | and cruel after war', but her descriptions of pastoral England are so constrained and understated that they become disappointingly bland and watery, insipid even:

[…] what I most remember about
that winter is not that it was hard
and cruel after war but that, one morning,
from a shabby train, and cold, I saw
along the line and in unseen, remembered counties,
the trees all over England blossoming with frost.[21]

Here, Holden's use of frail words like 'shabby', and her final image of the universality of 'trees all over England blossoming with frost' makes the poem seem trite in its pointedness. This is not helped by the unvaried rhythm of the lines, which gives them a monotonous, lacklustre quality. But even Davie's more critically acclaimed *The Shires* has a tendency towards the lacklustre, as Fuller suggests when noting that 'here and there [it] wears something of the air of a sketch-book'.[22]

Whilst some poets felt that poetry's new direction should involve the rearticulation of traditional forms, others wanted an almost complete rejection of the past, championing those who went against the grain of the Movement by embracing new forms and new ways of using language. But this direction, too, had its drawbacks. In 'The Invisible

---

[19] John Fuller, 'Touch of Frost' (24 Oct. 1974), 545–6. My italics.
[20] Stevenson, *The Last of England?*, 270.
[21] Molly Holden, *Air and Chill Earth* (London: Chatto and Windus, 1971), 11.
[22] Fuller, 'Touch of Frost' (24 Oct. 1974), 546.

Avant-Garde', John Ashbery asserts that 'recklessness is what makes experimental art beautiful' because of the very real possibility of its failure.[23] He goes on to suggest that in order for the avant-garde to grow naturally to a point where it can burst out of the underground to become the next 'big thing', it needs to develop out of sight, away from mainstream culture. As Peter Barry points out, this principle (in theory) should be fairly easy to achieve, since 'by definition, almost, the quality of something new will not easily be recognized by major publishers, who must cater for an existing set of public tastes'. Underground poets, he continues, tend to embrace this neglect because they distrust and disagree with 'public tastes'. This means that an attitude develops where 'not being known, not being published, even, becomes a badge of honour, a mark of quality', as exemplified by Eric Mottram's advice to the Malaysian writer T. Wignesan in the mid-1960s: 'Don't write anything you can get published!'[24] In the introduction to their anthology *Other*, Richard Caddel and Peter Quartermain suggest that 'by avoiding—or being avoided by—the mainstream of literary culture, many [...] writers retain a freedom to develop as they wish'.[25] In *Liquid City*, Iain Sinclair, too, argues that this neglect is an ideal climate for creative development. 'Poetry is back where it belongs', he writes: 'in exile'.[26]

One problem for poetry in the 1960s and early 1970s was that few underground poets were, ironically, lucky enough to be neglected. The avant-garde was being exposed to the scrutiny of a consumer culture that was hungry for anything claiming to be breaking the mould. In 1969, for instance, Penguin published Michael Horovitz's anthology, *Children of Albion: Poetry of the Underground in Britain*, which included works by, among others, Roy Fisher, Adrian Mitchell, Edwin Morgan, and Tom Raworth.[27] Buying into such 'anti-establishment' poetry, Penguin Books, an important and wholly mainstream publishing company, showed its awareness of a growing market for self-confessed alternative art. With the cultural desire to buy into anything pertaining to the avant-garde, the possibility of failure was severely diminished. This meant that the beauty of the avant-garde could no longer be derived from its recklessness, since there was now a much greater chance of its success. As such, the 'risk factor' became both artificially created and artificially appreciated. In other words, it was an avant-garde movement that was wished into being by a portion of society where alternative culture had (ironically) become fashionable. The chance of an avant-garde poet's failure was therefore slim, because he or she could expect people to buy into their avant-garde *label* rather than necessarily their poetic attributes.

[23] John Ashbery, 'The Invisible Avant-Garde', in *Reported Sightings: Art Chronicles 1957–1987*, ed. David Bergman (Manchester: Carcanet Press, 1989), 391.

[24] Peter Barry, *Poetry Wars: British Poetry of the 1970s and the Battle of Earls Court* (Cambridge: Salt Publications, 2006), 184–5.

[25] Richard Caddel and Peter Quartermain (eds.), *Other: British and Irish Poetry Since 1970* (Hanover, NH: Wesleyan University Press, 1999), p. xvi.

[26] Marc Atkins and Iain Sinclair, *Liquid City* (London: Reaktion Books, 1999), 38.

[27] Michael Horovitz (ed.), *Children of Albion: Poetry of the 'Underground' in Britain* (Harmondsworth: Penguin, 1969).

Some poets tired of this superficial success. For instance, following the publication of his first book *The Relation Ship*, for which he received the Alice Hunt Bartlett prize in 1969, Tom Raworth began to grow disdainful of his own achievement. He dismissed his previous writing as 'an adolescent's game, like the bright feathers some male birds grow during the mating season. I look at the poems and they make a museum of fragments of truth. And they smell of vanity, like the hunter's trophies on the wall'.[28] Rather than being anxious to be included in a mainstream narrative of poetry, Raworth seemed more concerned by his failure to be understood by those who knew him best. In 'Letters from Yaddo', he transcribed a letter from his father, who admitted that he struggled to grasp his son's work. 'There seems to have been a poetry explosion', his father wrote, 'and the resulting poeticised particles are too small for me to handle mentally with any satisfaction. Sometimes I seem to hover on the edge of a meaning to these minutiae of sensibility, but finally it eludes me. Perhaps it is a private world that I am not supposed to enter. A pity, because beauty does not lose by being shared'.[29] Raworth's father had in fact lived through the high modernist moment and had enjoyed the writing of James Joyce, so he was not averse to new, innovative approaches to literature. However, the 'risk factor' of Raworth's avant-gardism seems in this case to have alienated someone who not only recognized the value of new forms, but who was also personally invested in the poems, wanting to be able to understand and appreciate them. Instead of 'flabbergasting' the masses, Raworth's avant-garde approach bewildered one of his closest relatives.[30]

The letter also suggests that this new, supposedly 'avant-garde' branch of poetry was in many ways an imitative or recycled version of previous counter-cultural movements. Peter Robinson observes that the idea 'that we have been here before is not lost on Raworth senior, for he adds apologetically: "I hope you will not think of us as James Joyce thought of his aunt"'.[31] Tom Raworth recognizes this sense of imitation in his poem 'Gaslight', with the lines: 'someone else's song is always behind us' and 'what we write is ever the past'.[32] Regardless of his contemporary public acclaim, to cause someone so close to feel both excluded and inadequate may have also left Raworth questioning his success. However, it is equally possible to see the misunderstanding between father and son as a simple clash of expectations about what poetry should set out to achieve. Whilst Raworth senior saw it as a private world made public, expecting to understand and share in it, his son expected (and perhaps desired) to be misunderstood, to be peripheral to the main narrative of poetry. He was not interested in being a key propeller in the avant-garde counter-movement, out of which it was hoped a new singular mainstream poetry would emerge, phoenix-like, from the chaotic poetry scene. Instead, it

---

[28] See Peter Robinson, *Twentieth Century Poetry: Selves and Situations* (Oxford: Oxford University Press, 2005), 218, citing Tom Raworth, 'Letters from Yaddo', *Visible Shivers* (Oakland and Novato, Calif.: O Books with Trike, 1988) n.p.
[29] Raworth, 'Letters from Yaddo', *Visible Shivers*, n.p.
[30] Robinson, *Twentieth Century Poetry*, 226.
[31] Robinson, *Twentieth Century Poetry*, 225, citing Raworth, 'Letters from Yaddo'.
[32] See Robinson, *Twentieth Century Poetry*, 227, citing Tom Raworth, 'Gaslight', *Act; Collected Poems* (Manchester: Carcanet, 2003), 102.

seems that he wanted to occupy a permanent position outside of the masses, to be a truly alternative voice, a sidelined 'Other' that could resist the values dictated by all forms of popular culture.

Standing on One Side of the Gulf

Based on the simple idea of counter-directional forces in poetry, Thwaite's article expressed his concerns over what he perceived to be a binary split between two 'warring [camps]' that now found themselves in 'a state of deadlock or separatism'.[33] On one side of what he described as an expanding 'gulf' were the 'pop' or 'underground' poets who believed in 'the transparent virtues of spontaneity, immediacy, [and] energy released by both poet and audience in an instant flash of communion'. Raworth's 'That More Simple Natural Time Tone Distortion' displays many of these characteristics. With each line comprising just one or two (and rarely more than three) words, the poem is fast-paced, eruptive, and seemingly spontaneous. Its lack of punctuation and capital letters makes each word, regardless of its grammatical function, as significant as any other. Not even the personal pronoun is given a capital letter. As such, each word conveys an immediate energy that lasts only as long as it takes the next word to be uttered:

[...]
that i will bear
two face
and allegiance
mister cheap justice
bubbles
in
the silent
night
no control
over
extremities
[...][34]

Here, the words spill out one after another like the involuntary utterances of a stream of consciousness, which more formalistic, mainstream poets might call at best 'incoherent', at worst 'mindless doggerel'.[35] By dismissing the avant-garde in this way and using their influence over 'the major organs of culture' (such as large publishing houses, literary journals, and the media), Caddel and Quartermain argue that the mainstream has

---

[33] Thwaite, 'The Two Poetries' (5 Apr. 1973), 453.
[34] Tom Raworth, 'That More Simple Natural Time Tone Distortion' (1974), in Caddel and Quartermain (eds.), *Other*, 199–200.
[35] John Fuller, 'The Gulf' (24 Feb. 1972), 251.

'[driven] the Other underground by virtue of simply defining them as Other'.[36] So, as Thwaite saw it, underground poets stood on one side of the divide, firm in their conviction that poetry is most effective when it is hard-hitting and conveys a sense of urgency; and mainstream poets stood on the other side, equally firm in their belief that 'art has a great deal to do with shape, form, control, and that a good poem shouldn't reveal all its facets and depths and resonances at a single hearing or reading'.[37] As we will see, however, the split was not as simple as this. There were as many sides to the argument as there were poets to express them.

Thwaite was not the only one to observe an apparent poetic dichotomy. Just a year earlier, John Fuller had written a controversial review in *The Listener*, entitled 'The Gulf', in which he asked, 'How can one turn from the encompassable decencies of Molly Holden to the ramblings of Michael Horovitz without at least tipping one's hat to the gulf that separates them? After all', he continued, 'every reader is likely to find himself on one side or the other, fairly stranded'.[38] As reflected in recently published, overtly polemic anthologies, it is clear that this apparently fundamental division is still thought to have some currency in studies of British poetry during the period. Sean O'Brien's *The Firebox*, for instance, largely represents poets that Thwaite would have placed in the mainstream camp, with a few anomalous inclusions from 'undergrounders' like Roger McGough and Roy Fisher, who were both included in Horovitz's *Children of Albion*, and who have since become too widely known to be easily omitted from such a volume.[39] A notable absence from the anthology, however, is Jeremy Prynne. This is a surprising omission, given how influential Stevenson considers him to be both on the 'Cambridge School' of poets, and on poetry of the period in general: 'his strategies and their difficulties were paradigmatic of postmodernist poetry generally, and of the work included in *A Various Art* [...] in particular'.[40] Conversely, *Other* sets itself up as an alternative spread of poetry, mostly including lesser-known underground poets. Interestingly it, too, excludes Prynne. In line with Stevenson's claim, it might be tempting to argue that these omissions reflect a more general oversight that has in fact allowed him to develop undetected, thus making him one of the most important and influential of postmodernist poets. However, the exclusion is more likely to have been self-imposed through Prynne's own reluctance to be anthologized.[41]

---

[36] Caddel and Quartermain (eds.), *Other*, p. xxii.
[37] Thwaite, 'The Two Poetries' (5 Apr. 1973), 453.
[38] Fuller, 'The Gulf' (24 Feb. 1972), 251.
[39] See Sean O'Brien (ed.), *The Firebox: Poetry in Britain After 1945* (London: Picador, 1998) and Horovitz (ed.), *Children of Albion*.
[40] Stevenson, *The Last of England?*, 234.
[41] 'The difference, perhaps, between the general obscurity of British poets and the obscurity of Prynne is that he has made few efforts to publicise himself: he doesn't give interviews, is not willingly photographed, produces his barely publicised work through small presses in (rather beautiful) limited edition chapbooks, and rarely features in mainstream publications except as an idle shorthand for a wide variety of avant-garde writing'. Robert Potts, '"Through the Oval Window': Robert Potts on why the famously obscure poet Jeremy Prynne deserves wider acclaim in the UK', *The Guardian* (10 Apr. 2004), 36. The few anthologies that Prynne has featured in are those compiled by his friends, such as Andrew Crozier and Tim Longville, *A Various Art* (Manchester: Carcanet Press, 1987).

Both Thwaite and Fuller tended to position themselves outside the 'dirt[y] brawl' of the poetry scene and its divisions, distancing themselves by commenting on it, and perhaps attempting to influence it from an observational perspective. In a list poem from his 1977 collection, *A Portion for Foxes*, Thwaite fills over two pages with the names of poets who were included in Rosalie Murphy's 1970 anthology, *Contemporary Poets of the English Language*.[42] His concluding lines suggest his concern about the ever-increasing number of contemporary poets:

What is it, you may ask, that Thwaite's
Up to in this epic? Yeats'
Remark in the Cheshire Cheese one night
With poets so thick they blocked the light:
'No one can tell who has talent, if any.
Only one thing is certain. We are too many'.[43]

Although the final couplet suggests that Yeats was concerned about the crowded poetry scene, he was writing at a time when there were considerably fewer published poets than in the 1970s. Until the 1960s, successful poets tended to be highly educated (often holding Oxbridge degrees), but by the 1970s, they were coming from a variety of social, educational, and financial backgrounds. With greater access to education, many people from poorer families were joining the 'meritocracy': Donald Davie, for instance, came from a lower middle-class family and was educated in Cambridge. But even more than improvements in access to education, poetry was beginning to be opened up to the population more generally through workshops and other practical writing courses. A new philosophy was emerging: that *anyone* could write poetry, regardless of class and regardless, even, of education. This liberal 'open-to-all' attitude worried many poets, such as Thwaite, Fuller, and even the meritocratic Davie. Thwaite feared that the plethora of poets, separated into what he perceived to be two camps (liberal vs. conservative), would ultimately become so divided that they would have neither the ability nor the inclination to communicate with one another, thus causing 'a serious split in our literary culture'. He ends the article on the somewhat dismal prediction of a future with 'two poetries':

> one the preserve of school-teachers and dons who go on talking in a lecture-room vacuum about form and standards and interpretation, and who manipulate people through exams, and the other a blurred area dominated solely by sensation and fashion, and having the popular and fluent transience of the record charts.[44]

---

[42] Rosalie Murphy, *Contemporary Poets of the English Language* (Chicago: St James Press, 1970).
[43] Anthony Thwaite, 'On Consulting "Contemporary Poets of the English Language"', in *A Portion for Foxes* (Oxford: Oxford University Press, 1977), 30–2 (32).
[44] Thwaite, 'The Two Poetries' (5 Apr. 1973), 454.

Of course, we have only to look at the current GCSE poetry syllabus to see the inaccuracy of Thwaite's prophecy. Poems by Brian Patten and Carol Ann Duffy feature alongside those of Seamus Heaney, Ted Hughes, Philip Larkin, and Vernon Scannell.

But far more problematic than an incorrect prediction about poetry in the education system is the idea of the binary split itself. Indeed, it seems a somewhat crude characterization of the complex divisions that were occurring in this period. These intricate rifts were apparent not only in terms of what Al Alvarez called the 'shabby gang warfare that makes the literary life peculiarly unspeakable',[45] but also in terms of the very different styles, views, and aims of individual poets. As Michael Horovitz pointed out in his response to Thwaite's article, 'a basic rationale for [...] art is, after all, that each practitioner is an exception'.[46] Despite dismissing this pluralistically schismatic situation as the mere 'surface dust' of a more fundamental dichotomy, it seems to me that by doing so, and by moulding it into a singularly black / white structure, Thwaite was attempting to create some kind of order out of the 'unspeakable' chaos of the poetry scene. This oversimplification was felt at the time by both Horovitz, who criticized Thwaite for 'exaggerat[ing] the "gulf" between the putatively rival camps', and Malcolm Warner, who wrote that Thwaite had 'failed to appreciate [...] the sociological complexity linking "the two"—and pray why not more?—"poetries"'.[47]

THE LARKIN–DAVIE CONTROVERSY

The year 1973 was important for debates in *The Listener* involving the so-called 'poetic binary'. Not only did Thwaite's article appear in April, but it was also the year that Philip Larkin's controversial anthology, *The Oxford Book of Twentieth Century English Verse*, was published. This book sparked a heated debate in *The Listener* when Donald Davie gave it a particularly scathing review, labelling it an irresponsible 'calamity'. His complaints were mainly directed at Larkin's inclusion of poets from the other side of the 'divide', such as Brian Patten, Adrian Henri, Adrian Mitchell, and Roger McGough. More specifically, he objected to the inclusion of Patten's 'Portrait of a Young Girl Raped at a Suburban Party'. The first two stanzas of this poem read:

And after this quick bash in the dark
You will rise and go
Thinking of how empty you have grown
And of whether all the evening's care in front of mirrors
And the younger boys disowned
Led simply to this.

---

[45] Al Alvarez, *Risky Business: People, Pastimes, Poker and Books* (London: Bloomsbury, 2007), 207.
[46] Michael Horovitz, 'No need to feel choked', Letters (3 May 1973), 586–7.
[47] Malcolm Warner, 'No need to feel choked', Letters (19 Apr. 1973), 517.

Confined to what you are expected to be
By what you are
Out in this frozen garden
You shiver and vomit—
Frightened, drunk among trees,
You wonder at how those acts that called for tenderness
Were far from tender.

Davie dismissed Patten's work as 'implausible and ineffective' in the imagination's failure to 'enter', 'penetrate', '[open] up', and 'transform' the poem.[48] This triggered a string of conflicting responses from a large number of poets, critics, and other readers, which continued over three months and only ceased, with great reluctance and one or two further postscripts, when the editor of *The Listener* stepped in to close the correspondence on 14 June. Certainly, Patten's poem is explicit in its subject matter. Before we even start reading, the title reveals most of its content: the scene ('a Suburban Party'), the subject ('a Young Girl'), the event ('Raped'), and the intent of the poem ('Portrait'). By setting up the poem in this way, Patten exposed himself to criticism from the likes of Davie, who argued that 'By the end of the fourth dishevelled stanza we are precisely where we were after we had read the title', and from Peter Dunn, who claimed that the poem is 'nowhere near a *portrait*, which is a thing specific, not to say individual. [...] This girl is far too generalised to bear the weight of such a promising title'.[49]

Although the poem in my opinion is not the complete failure that Davie labelled it, nor even as bad as Dunn made it out to be, there is perhaps some justification in the latter's opinion that it has both weak and strong elements that struggle to blend into a cohesive whole. 'Like most bad poems', Dunn wrote, 'this one is "good in parts" [...] But the parts do not add up to an artistic whole. Maybe they were not intended to, but if so, that is both our loss, as readers, and Brian Patten's'. Phrases such as 'And after this [...]', 'Thinking of how [...]', 'And of whether [...]', and 'You wonder at how [...]' are syntactically clumsy, causing areas of the poem to lack impact and direction. The awkwardness of the syntax, as well as the pockets of stark language, like 'spew up among flowers' in the third stanza, contrast against the more elevated (in Dunn's words, 'pretentious') imagery of the final two lines of the poem: 'When planets rolled out of your eyes | And splashed down in suburban grasses'.[50] Here, Patten evokes powerful imagery by combining the cosmic idea of 'planets' with the intimate, sensual effect of texture-rich, alliterative language like 'rolled out of your eyes' and 'splashed down in suburban grasses'. Dunn referred to these lines as 'striking but ineffective, bearing no relation to the rest of the imagery'. Likening syntax to 'the connective tissue of the body of the poem', he also argued that it 'suffers from a kind of horrifying grammatical dystrophy. It goes flabbier the more one reads it'. However, this lack of cohesion could in fact be viewed as a

---

[48] Donald Davie, 'Larkin's Choice' (29 Mar. 1973), 421 and 420.
[49] Peter Dunn, Letters (7 June 1973), 758.
[50] Brian Patten, 'Portrait of a Young Girl Raped at a Suburban Party', in Philip Larkin (ed.), *The Oxford Book of Twentieth-Century English Verse* (Oxford: Oxford University Press, 1973), 624.

linguistic reflection of the sexual act 'that called for tenderness' being distorted and corrupted by the rough, soullessness of the rape: a 'quick bash in the dark'.

Some contributors suggested that there was a sociological relevance to the piece that made its inclusion justifiable in an anthology of poems 'carry[ing] with them something of the century in which they were written' (one of the three categories which Larkin had used to rationalize his selection in the preface to his anthology).[51] Martin Bell responded to Davie's comment about the irrelevance of the suburban element of the poem, claiming that this 'is more shocking [...] because it has become respectable and the sort of thing one expects at parties', whilst the phrase 'A quick bash in the dark' reflects the 'trivial attitude of the average suburban saloon-bar predatory male'.[52] Peter Dunn criticized Bell's method of defending Patten's poem, arguing that he had 'substitut[ed] sociology for literary criticism' and that 'the sociological accuracy of the poem neither adds to nor detracts from its literary value'.[53]

Other participants in the debate commented on the poem's simplicity and communicativeness. Jock Mackenzie compared it to Davie's own 'Robinson Jeffers at Point Sur', claiming that Patten's 'Portrait' engages the reader much more readily than Davie's 'esoteric rambling' where the reader is left 'know[ing] nothing at all'. He went on to express his opinion that by including 'some of the more readily communicative verse of this century', the anthology was 'far from [an] irresponsible selection'.[54] Richard Ball entered the debate, accusing Davie of being unable to appreciate the 'simplicity and effectiveness' of Patten's poem, which, he argued, would have been spoiled by 'too much indulgent imagination or sophistication about language'.[55] Similarly, Zahir Jamal remarked that 'prodding glumly at Patten's inert lines won't tell Donald Davie [...] what they're supposed to be'. Instead, he suggested, the simplicity of the poem illustrates 'what happens when a young man addresses the academy with one wary eye on the discotheque'.[56] The tension between 'academy' and 'pop' poetry was also highlighted by Peter Leek, the publishing director of Allen and Unwin (Patten's publisher), who wrote in to criticize Davie's inability to see any poignancy in the poem and to argue that Patten's appeal to young people and his sales figures (over 35,000 copies of his three collections of poetry had been sold by 1973) were evidence that 'he touche[d] some poetic spring'.[57] Indeed, whatever his reasons for including the piece in the anthology, it is clear that it appealed in some way to Larkin: perhaps, Robinson suggests, as 'an echo' of his own poem, 'Deceptions'.[58]

Despite supposedly belonging to the same mainstream 'camp', the Larkin–Davie controversy reveals a serious and fundamental divergence in the creative and critical

---

[51] Larkin (ed.), *The Oxford Book of Twentieth-Century English Verse*, p. vi.
[52] Martin Bell, Letters (31 May 1973), 724.
[53] Dunn, Letters (7 June 1973), 758.
[54] Jock Mackenzie, Letters (12 Apr. 1973), 483.
[55] Richard Ball, Letters (12 Apr. 1973), 483.
[56] Zahir Jamal, Letters (5 Apr. 1973), 449.
[57] Peter Leek, Letters (19 Apr. 1973), 516.
[58] Peter Robinson, ' "Readings will grow erratic" in Philip Larkin's "Deceptions" ', *Cambridge Quarterly*, 38/3 (2009), 277–305 (294). See esp. 292–4 for a comparison of the two poems.

visions of the two poets. Whilst Larkin admitted that he had 'no real desire to lay down the law about anything',[59] Thwaite suggested that Davie wanted 'a prescriptive, exclusivist anthology [...] which at the same time would allow him his own debatable candidates: in goes Elaine Feinstein, out goes May Wedderburn Cannan'.[60] With no agreed pattern for progression, even from within the camps, a raft of complexities can be seen exfoliating from the initial, crudely simplistic binary of mainstream versus underground poetry.

The responses to the review illustrate that it was not simply a case of choosing one side or the other of the 'gulf'. Richard Ball wrote in to express his doubts over 'Davie's sense of what makes a good poem',[61] whilst others agreed with Davie's criticism of both Patten and Larkin. Evidently not a fan of Larkin, Tom Scott, for instance, called the book a 'disgraceful anthology', remarking that his 'only quarrel with [Davie's] review [...] is that he pays lip-service to the current fashion for grossly overrating Mr Larkin's own minor, rather drab poetry'. 'English poetry has reached an all-time low in the past decade or two', he continued, 'but it's not as bad as this anthology paints it'.[62] Others leaped to Larkin's defence over his inclusion of poets like Patten. Jamal, for instance, wrote that 'posterity will be grateful to Philip Larkin for catching that moment in our time when the Muse left her seat to become a performing artist'.[63] Of course it remains open to question, nearly four decades later, whether this has turned out to be true. Despite still being in print, the anthology has not become the landmark publication that he predicted.

Whilst many contributors honed in on the individuals involved in the controversy, there were some who were more concerned by the broader implications of the debate. Frederick Grubb, for instance, commented that 'in the wrangle over whether or not Brian Patten is a poet, an aspect of Mr Larkin's ideology of selection, or lack of ideology of selection, is being ignored'. Grubb's criticism of the anthology was centred on Larkin's privileging of 'the Liverpool boys' over 'the Newcastle boys [...], the Manchester boys, the Leeds boys, the Hull boys, the Glasgow boys, the Belfast boys, even the London boys [...] and many true poets in other towns and in the country, such as Norman Nicholson, George Mackay Brown [...] and Roy Fisher for a start'.[64] In a similar vein, John Montague highlighted further geographical divisions, calling attention to the 'unaware and amateurish' representation of Irish poets in Larkin's anthology. He also noted the absence of David Jones, claiming him to be 'the greatest living British poet' because he 'blends all our traditions'.[65]

---

[59] Philip Larkin, '"A great parade of single poems"—Philip Larkin, poet, librarian and anthologist discusses his *Oxford Book of 20th-Century English Verse* with Anthony Thwaite' (12 Apr. 1973), 474.

[60] Anthony Thwaite, Letters (17 May 1973), 552.

[61] Ball, Letters (12 Apr. 1973), 483.

[62] Tom Scott, Letters (19 Apr. 1973), 516.

[63] Jamal, Letters (5 Apr. 1973), 451.

[64] Frederick Grubb, Letters (3 May 1973), 587.

[65] John Montague, Letters (28 June 1973), 837.

Another area of division that was commented on in the protracted debate was that of academic and class-based snobbery. Gerald Butt accused Davie of 'refus[ing] to recognise that such poetry [as Patten's] has been part of the scene for some years and that it would be dishonest of any anthology not to recognise this'. Making reference to Thwaite's article, he went on to suggest that it was 'this kind of academic snobbery which [was] causing the gap between "the two poetries" to widen'.[66] As a poet-scholar, teaching at that time in Stanford University, there does seem to be a hint of academic snobbery in Davie's remark that it was a 'grievous misfortune' that Larkin should have such a 'mocking scepticism about the possibility of critical discrimination among poems'.[67] Indeed, Ursula Temple dismissed Davie's review as a simple case of his becoming 'excitable over the riff-raff getting into his Royal Enclosure of Poetry'.[68]

The inclusions and exclusions of any anthology will always be debatable, but this anthology was made more contentious by Larkin's selection and exclusion of poets who had not yet completed their oeuvre, as well as by the title of the book itself, which offered a dubious promise of authority. The Oxford label conferred a kind of 'definitive' institutional status upon the anthology, which gave Larkin an immense amount of power to filter poets into (and out of) the seeming 'Oxford canon'. These were inevitably based on his own preferences, because regardless of the extent to which anyone attempts 'to put [their] own taste reasonably in the background',[69] it is impossible to evaluate poetry without personally engaging with it on some level. At the same time, the anthology fails to give a full picture of the *twentieth-century* English verse promised in its title, because the century was far from being over when Larkin compiled it. This incomplete perspective meant that some poets who have since become prominent figures in twentieth-century British poetry, such as (among many others) Carol Ann Duffy, Andrew Motion, Norman Nicholson, David Jones, George Mackay Brown, and Roy Fisher, were not included in this supposedly representative 'twentieth-century' anthology.

In an interview with Anthony Thwaite, Larkin acknowledged that his anthology was intrinsically flawed, admitting that it could not accurately represent contemporary poetry. Despite being adamant that he could not think of 'anybody substantial that [wasn't] represented', he was aware that some poets may not have been fully represented and that he had left out poems that he subsequently regretted, such as a representative entry from the 1970 book, *Crow*, which has since become one of Ted Hughes's most discussed works.[70] Nevertheless, Larkin explained that his strategy for dealing with his contemporaries and with more up-and-coming poets was to say 'right ho, five or six of each and let time do the sorting out', since those who were 'going to be good [were] not yet fully good'. He was reluctant to over- or under-represent any of his contemporaries

---

[66] Gerald Butt, Letters (19 Apr. 1973), 516.
[67] Davie, 'Larkin's Choice' (29 Mar. 1973), 420.
[68] Ursula Temple, Letters (12 Apr. 1973), 483.
[69] Larkin, '"A great parade of single poems"' (12 Apr. 1973), 474.
[70] Larkin, 'A great parade of single poems' (12 Apr. 1973), 474.

because only time would tell how important they would become to twentieth-century English verse. 'For all we know', he told Thwaite, 'the poets of the Fifties and Sixties may not be Larkin and Hughes at all: they may be Davie and Brian Patten'. Although this was a throwaway comment, perhaps containing a small jibe in Davie's direction after his scathing review of both Larkin and Patten, it is interesting how Larkin frames his predictions in sets of two: 'Larkin and Hughes' and 'Davie and Brian Patten'. This either / or proposition enforces the prevalent view of the time that poetic divisions occurred in pairs and overlooks the more complex debate that was actually taking place.

Despite speaking of his uncertainty about the legacy of contemporary poets, Larkin seemed sure that he had comprehensively included all those who were at least in the running. He would not acknowledge the possibility that he had completely excluded poets who might turn out to be highly influential. A group who became extremely significant to the historical narrative of poetry in the twentieth century, but who were seriously under-represented in this anthology (and many others like it) were women. Not only are they scarce in the Larkin anthology, they are also conspicuously silent in the subsequent debate in *The Listener*. The male-dominated correspondence comes closest to a discussion of women only in relation to Davie's objection to Patten's 'Portrait of a Young Girl Raped at a Suburban Party'. Interestingly, no female perspectives were offered on this poem. Instead, it was concluded by Martin Bell that the young girl 'was asking for what she got, but deserved at least more tenderness'.[71] This discussion about whether or not the girl deserved the rape reveals a masculine discourse that shifts the blame onto her: according to Bell, she is 'obviously a teaser'. Bell claimed that despite the girl 'obviously' asking for what she got, the man who raped her really ought to have known better and been more chivalrous. This enforces a patriarchal hegemony that denies the girl any control over her own situation. By labelling her a 'poor girl' in the same breath as 'obviously a teaser', Bell casts her as a victim of her own supposedly weak and provocative nature, whilst Patten's own use of language in the lines: 'Confined to what you are expected to be | By what you are', reinforces this masculine perception of her Eve-like weakness. Bell wrote that Patten was attempting to restore to the young girl some of the tenderness that she had deserved, and yet this apparent restoration is still very much external to the girl herself. Regardless of the way she is treated, the poem and the subsequent discussion of it still leaves her the subject / victim of masculine voices. She is not given her own voice, nor is she even viewed or commented on from a female perspective. The lack of female participation may suggest that women were not reading or engaging with it because they were not interested or felt that it was unprofitable to contribute.

The editor finally closed correspondence about the anthology after Martin Bell's irrelevant and patronizingly 'sober note' that 'girls should not be treated trivially and callously, however foolish they may be'.[72] Perhaps this comment, as well as the notable absence of female voices in the general debate (with the singular exception of

---

[71] Martin Bell, *Letters* (10 May 1973), 724.
[72] Martin Bell, *Letters* (14 June 1973), 805.

Ursula Temple) reveals more about the gendered nature of the poetry scene up until the mid-1970s than any vocalization could. Indeed, poetry publication was something of a 'boys club'. Taking Thwaite's suggestion that Davie would have replaced May Wedderburn Cannan with his own 'debateable candidate', Elaine Feinstein, it would seem that even the few women poets who were included in the anthology were always on the borderlines of exclusion. A notable example of this was the exclusion of Elizabeth Daryush. Both Davie[73] and Michael Schmidt remarked on her absence from the anthology. Schmidt referred to the poet Yvor Winters, who had described her as 'one of the few distinguished poets of our century', and to Roy Fuller, who had given a lecture on her at Oxford as 'a formal innovator and an important neglected figure'.[74] He went on to conjecture whether Larkin 'rejected her work after mature deliberation, or whether he passed over it in ignorance or because the age that had selected Brian Patten's poem had failed to respond to [her] more subtle, honest and durable work'. It is only in the second half of the 1970s that female voices were beginning to be heard in *The Listener*, both as poets and reviewers. Patricia Beer and Anne Stevenson, for instance, took on more prominent roles, reviewing publications by women poets such as Freda Downie's *A Stranger Here* (1977), Elizabeth Jennings's *Consequently I Rejoice* (1977), Kathleen Raine's *The Oval Portrait* (1977), and A. A. Cleary's *Men Homeward* (1977).[75] This advocacy helped pave the way for a new wave of poets who emerged in the 1980s, including Carol Ann Duffy, Wendy Cope, and Helen Dunmore.

Conclusion

With so much disagreement over the way forward, poetry appeared to have reached an impasse in the 1970s—at least as far as its linear direction was concerned. As Danto put it, this was an 'age of [artistic] pluralism', where 'you [could] be an abstractionalist in the morning, a photorealist in the afternoon, a minimalist in the evening. Or you [could] cut out paper dolls or do what you damned please', because 'when one direction is as good as another direction, there is no concept of direction any longer to apply'.[76] Perhaps this is the inherent disadvantage of attempting to comment on one's own culture from within. Indeed, the poetry world became so preoccupied over what it thought it *ought* to be, attempting to map out a course for itself through theories and reviews, that it failed to recognize what it *actually* was. Even with the benefit of some degree of hindsight, it

---

[73] See Donald Davie, Views (10 May 1973), 611.
[74] Michael Schmidt, Letters (10 May 1973), 620.
[75] Anne Stevenson, 'Poems of Isolation' (11 Aug. 1977), 189–90. A. A. Cleary was reviewed by Anne Stevenson, 'Night-time tongue' (13 July 1978), 62–3. Of these, incidentally, Patricia Beer, Elizabeth Jennings, and Kathleen Raine were among the 30 women (out of 207 poets overall) included in the Larkin anthology.
[76] Arthur Coleman Danto, 'The End of Art', *Philosophical Disenfranchisement*, 115.

is difficult to pinpoint exactly what was happening to poetry during this period underneath the chaotic, self-conscious wrangling over where it should be going.

It is useful, nonetheless, to be aware of the tendency to oversimplify these divisions because it gives us some insight into the cultural and artistic anxieties that were felt during this decade of social, political, and economic upheaval. In an introduction to *The Deregulated Muse*, aptly entitled 'Who's in Charge Here?', Sean O'Brien suggests that for some, the need for order is symptomatic of the continued 'legacy of discredited attitudes', such as 'Anglocentricity, centralisation, the imposition of minority tastes [and] possessive academic obfuscation'. Nevertheless, he notes, there are others who would argue that the need to make sense continues because the very nature and existence of poetry is dependent on language, one of the most fundamental sense-making tools. It therefore 'risks losing its essential nature if it does not maintain a vigilant regard for its own interests as an art made of language'.[77] The reduction of complex poetic divisions into a simple mainstream/avant-garde split may well then illustrate the reactive need in critics and poets to comprehend and control the apparently directionless poetry scene.

With the rise in paper prices causing many publishers to make cuts, these were increasingly uncertain times for poets. Generally sidelined by 'mainstream' publishing houses such as Faber & Faber, Gollancz, and Routledge, they found themselves trying to carve out a new direction through a number of emerging, smaller houses that specialized in poetry, including Anvil, Carcanet, Ceolfrith, Peterloo Poets, and Enitharmon.[78] The reduction of the debate into a mainstream/avant-garde binarism was one of the principle ways that the attainment of a new 'direction' was attempted. But this need to make clear-cut divisions was not unique to 1970s poetry. The tendency to seek order through binary oppositions is an instinctive sense-making method frequently employed by critics and theorists (although resisted by post-structuralists) in order to present complex ideas, debates, and literary approaches as manageable components. Nevertheless, it is important to be aware of this tendency to simplify, since there is a real danger of overlooking poets, poems, or aspects of poetry, both in the past and the present, that have been (or are being) sifted out of literary debates and 'canons' because they do not fit comfortably within such parameters.

Despite the critical tendency to examine the poetry of this period in terms of a fundamental binarism (we have only to look at *The Firebox* and *Other* to see the continuation of this perception) the Larkin–Davie controversy shows us that more complex divisions

---

[77] O'Brien, *The Deregulated Muse*, 20.
[78] See Anne Stevenson, 'Putting out the Poets' (17 Feb. 1977), 220–1 (220). 'It may seem an odd reversal of procedure to review publishers before poets, but there are several publishers of poetry in Britain who deserve accolades. [...] Among [the] "small" publishers of poetry, Harry Chamber's Peterloo Poets must rank with the most enterprising. Anvil, Aquila, Enitharmon and the Menard Press also deserve a share of the laurels, though there is not space here to do them justice. [...] Gollancz now has an impressive poetry list. Turning over these (in many cases) beautifully got up and tastefully printed volumes, it is easy to speculate that there are more attractive presses these days than poets deserving publication. Nevertheless, it is good that so many new gates are open [...] [to] poets passed over by the London establishment'.

were at work in the poetry of the 1970s. It encourages us to view with caution, and even to re-examine the polemic divisions which are frequently taken for granted in debates over contemporary poetry. We might even reiterate the questions posed by Malcolm Warner in 1973:

> Was there ever *one* poetry? Will catastrophe strike if there are any number of 'camps'? Is there 'a public', a single one, which alone recognises the merit of good poems today? As society becomes increasingly complex, why should we resist a plurality of critical schools?[79]

What we see during the 1970s among poets and critics in *The Listener* is a 'struggle for legitimacy',[80] for a place in the perceived 'civilization' of poetry. The idea of a binary split was one of the symptoms of this struggle; it was a need to legitimize the chaos by superimposing order onto it. However, in reality, this was far from an orderly tug-of-war. It was, as Roy Fisher's 'Sets' aptly puts it, a messy 'brawl', with each individual feeling called upon to justify and defend his or her own right to a place in the poetry scene. It is a struggle, indeed, that has not ended, as poets are obliged to come to terms with their own positions in the broader publishing arena, attempting to resist exclusion from a poetry world which itself is sidelined by a prose-dominated literary culture.

Select Bibliography

Adorno, Theodor W., 'Commitment', in Ronald Taylor (trans. and ed.), *Aesthetics and Politics: The Key Texts of the Classic Debate with German Marxism* (London: New Left Books, 1977).
Alvarez, Al, *Risky Business: People, Pastimes, Poker and Books* (London: Bloomsbury, 2007).
Atkins, Marc and Sinclair, Iain, *Liquid City* (London: Reaktion Books, 1999).
Barry, Peter, *Poetry Wars: British Poetry of the 1970s and the Battle of Earls Court* (Cambridge: Salt Publications, 2006).
Caddel, Richard and Quartermain, Peter (eds.), *Other: British and Irish Poetry Since 1970* (Hanover, NH: Wesleyan University Press, 1999).
Danto, Arthur Coleman, *The Philosophical Disenfranchisement of Art* (New York: Columbia University Press, 1986).
Dickie, George, *Aesthetics: An Introduction* (Indianapolis: Pegasus, 1971).
Duncan, Andrew, *The Failure of Conservatism in Modern British Poetry* (Cambridge: Salt Publishing, 2003).
Easthope, Antony, 'Donald Davie and the Failure of Englishness', in James Acheson and Romana Huk (eds.), *Contemporary British Poetry: Essays in Theory and Criticism* (Albany, NY: State University of New York Press, 1996), 17–33.
Fisher, Roy, *The Long and the Short of It: Poems 1955–2005* (Tarset: Bloodaxe Books, 2005).

---

[79] Warner, Letters (19 Apr. 1973), 517.
[80] Duncan, *The Failure of Conservatism in Modern British Poetry*, 138.

Holden, Molly, *Air and Chill Earth* (London: Chatto and Windus, 1971).
Horovitz, Michael (ed.), *Children of Albion: Poetry of the 'Underground' in Britain* (Harmondsworth: Penguin, 1969).
Miller, David and Price, Richard (eds.), *British Poetry Magazines 1914–2000: A History and Bibliography of 'Little Magazines'* (London: British Library and Oak Knoll Press, 2006).
Murphy, Rosalie, *Contemporary Poets of the English Language* (Chicago: St James Press, 1970).
O'Brien, Sean, *The Deregulated Muse: Essays on Contemporary British & Irish Poetry* (Newcastle upon Tyne: Bloodaxe Books, 1998).
O'Brien, Sean (ed.), *The Firebox: Poetry in Britain After 1945* (London: Picador, 1998).
Patten, Brian, 'Portrait of a Young Girl Raped at a Suburban Party', in Philip Larkin (ed.), *The Oxford Book of Twentieth-Century English Verse* (Oxford: Oxford University Press, 1973), 624.
Robinson, Peter, *Twentieth Century Poetry: Selves and Situations* (Oxford: Oxford University Press, 2005).
Stevenson, Randall, *The Oxford English Literary History*, xii. *1960–2000: The Last of England?* (Oxford: Oxford University Press, 2004).
Thwaite, Anthony, 'The Two Poetries', *The Listener*, 89/2297 (5 Apr. 1973), 452.
Wellek, René, 'Romanticism Re-examined', in Northrop Frye (ed.), *Romanticism Reconsidered* (New York: Columbia University Press, 1963), 107–33.

CHAPTER 8

A DOG'S CHANCE: THE EVOLUTION OF CONTEMPORARY WOMEN'S POETRY?[1]

DERYN REES-JONES

> Intellectual freedom depends upon material things. Poetry depends upon intellectual freedom. And women have always been poor, not for two hundred years merely, but from the beginning of time. Women have had less intellectual freedom than the sons of Athenian slaves. Women, then, have not had a dog's chance of writing poetry.
>
> Virginia Woolf, *A Room of One's Own*[2]

---

[1] I am exceptionally grateful to Lavinia Greenlaw, Clare Pollard, and Kate Potts for the generous and stimulating responses to my questionnaire, and all ensuing email conversations.

[2] First published 1929. I am using the reissued Penguin edition, from 2002 here, 106.

1. **But, you may say, the debates around the validity of women's poetry are over. Intellectual freedom has been achieved; the material condition of women in the past fifty years has altered in profound ways. Questions of gender in relation to poetry have become 'old hat'. I will try to explain...**

Virginia Woolf's wonderfully moving, but nevertheless enigmatic description of the coming-into-being of the woman poet in *A Room of One's Own* was published nearly a hundred years ago. Yet there is much in the questions Woolf asks about women, writing, and the literary tradition to which we might return, not least as we approach the centenary of its publication in 2029, a year that Woolf suggests will be when the woman poet is 'born'. With the appointment, for the first time in its history, of a woman to the British Poet Laureateship, the appointment of two Welsh women to the position of National Poet of Wales, and, at the date of writing, a Scottish woman Makar, and with prominent women poets recently at the helm of prestigious, Arts Council-funded poetry publications, it would be easy to conclude that the time for highlighting the sex of poets was well and truly over.[3] And yet it would also be fair to say that the puzzle about women's complicated relationship to poetry simply won't go away. For despite these recent landmark successes for women, one of the many and lingering problems for women poets has been the absence of a critical tradition which interrogates and absorbs their work. As several recent commentators have pointed out, women poets are reviewed less than men poets, and in different ways; they win fewer prizes; fewer women send to magazines; fewer appear in prestigious literary publications.[4] And though in many ways we might feel secure about the presence of women's poetry in our tradition, historically there have been popular women poets whose reputation has faded to anonymity with the passing

---

[3] Carol Ann Duffy (b. 1953), British Poet Laureate (2009–); Gwyneth Lewis (b. 1959), National Poet of Wales (2005–6); Gillian Clarke, (b. 1937), National Poet of Wales (2008–); Liz Lochhead (b. 1947), Scottish Makar (2011–); Colette Bryce, (b. 1970), editor *Poetry London* (2009–); Kathryn Gray (b. 1973), editor, *New Welsh Review* (2008–11); Fiona Sampson (b. 1968) editor, *Poetry Review* (2005–12); Zoë Skoulding (b. 1967), editor, *Poetry Wales* (2008–).

[4] See Eva Salzman and Amy Wack, (eds.), *Women's Work* (Bridgend: Seren, 2008).

of time.[5] The recent resurgence of discussion concerning the value of continuing to think about 'women's poetry' as a critical category is symptomatic of the pervasive sense of unease that still resides in the relationship between women and poetry. Perhaps it is more accurate to say that the puzzle which it is hard to name, isn't just one that won't go away, but one that won't go away simply.[6]

In *Consorting with Angels*[7] I examined the way in which the difficulty of creating a poetic self in poetry was negotiated by a range of strategies by women poets. In this essay, following on from there, I explore the synergy that is created in the intersection of a self represented and rooted in the materiality of the female body, and an idea of the self that reflects postmodern and feminist concerns about the human subject that are less dependent on the body as a framing metaphor for the self. In charting a series of snapshots across the three generations of women who wrote after Woolf, and who have benefited from a stronger awareness of the women poets writing earlier in the century than their predecessors might, it will become evident that this problematizing of the representation of the lyric 'I' in relation to the body is one which has been, and continues to be negotiated as women poets have written, and write, themselves into a literary tradition; and that, despite the radical differences in women's material conditions when compared to women a century ago, anxieties about the body are pervasive, and still sit at the centre of the difficulties our culture has with poetry written by women.

'Great poets do not die', writes Woolf:

> they are continuing presences; they need only the opportunity to walk among us in the flesh. This opportunity, as I think, it is now coming within your power to give her. For my belief is that if we live another century or so—I am talking of the common life which is the real life and not of the little separate lives which we live as individuals—and have five hundred a year each of us and rooms of our own; if we have the habit of freedom and the courage to write exactly what we think; if we escape a little from the common sitting-room and see human beings not always in their relation to each other but in relation to reality; and the sky too, and the trees or whatever it may be in themselves; if we look past Milton's bogey, for no human being should shut out the view; if we face the fact, for it is a fact, that there is no arm to cling to, but that we go alone and that our relation is to the world of reality and not only to the world of men and women, then the opportunity will come and the dead poet who was Shakespeare's sister will put on the body which she has so often laid down. Drawing her life from the lives of the unknown who were her forerunners, as her brother did before her, she will be born.

---

[5] A prime example is that of Adelaide Proctor (1825–64) who was, after Tennyson, considered one of the most popular poets of the nineteenth century, the favourite poet of Queen Victoria, championed by Charles Dickens and Coventry Patmore. Her poems were widely set to music and sung as hymns. She is remembered now primarily for her poem 'The Lost Chord'. See Gill Gregory, *The Life and Work of Adelaide Procter: Poetry, Feminism and Fathers* (Aldershot: Ashgate, 1998).

[6] See e.g. 'Jo Shapcott asks if there is such a thing as female poetry', *The Guardian*, 9 Nov. 2009: [http://www.guardian.co.uk/books/booksblog/2009/nov/09/do-women-write-female-poetry]. Accessed 11 May 2012. Zoë Brigley, 'Celebrating Not Complaining', *Poetry Wales*, 46/4 (Spring, 2011), 24–5. Letter from Kate Clanchy et al. to *Poetry Review*, 99/2 (Summer, 2009), 122–4.

[7] Deryn Rees-Jones, *Consorting with Angels: Modern Women Poets* (Tarset: Bloodaxe Books, 2005).

This dense paragraph, with its clear evocation of Eliot's earlier essay 'Tradition and the Individual Talent' (1919), has triggered a range of feminist responses, not least Gilbert and Gubar's when, discussing Judith Shakespeare's suicide at the end of *A Room*, they quote Woolf's urgent demand: 'who shall measure the heat and violence of the poet's heart when caught and tangled in a woman's body?'[8] Here, though, Woolf sets gender and the woman poet's relationship to her body at a stranger angle, and the paragraph elicits as many questions as it answers. What's interesting returning to it as a touchstone for thinking about the future of poetry written by women in this evolutionary narrative, is the nature of the relationship Woolf sets up between the material body and the floating consciousness of the woman poet as she attempts to find a narrative of female poetic succession.

Many questions remain to be asked of Woolf's prognostication. Within her schema, can a woman assume a male poet's body in order to become herself as a woman poet? Does the body that the contemporary poet assumes always have to be the body of a *woman* poet from the past? Are we to see what Woolf calls reality as a gender-free world? And not least, how are we to understand Woolf's use of the word 'body'? Surely not simply in terms of its materiality, but perhaps rather as the signifier for a more metaphorical sense of being present in the world? In *Orlando*, for example, Woolf's pseudo-biographical fiction of the coming into being of a woman poet, written a year before *A Room of One's Own*, the woman poet evolves over the centuries from an androgynous man to a woman, who by the end of the novel, has buried her poems in the earth, and returns to her bodily self to give birth. As I have shown elsewhere, *Orlando* is connected, through multiple allusions, to a novel written by the birth control reformer Marie Stopes,[9] and the models of creativity and evolution that *Orlando* appears to propose prompt some further pause for thought here in the context of a developing poetic tradition. One question that must immediately be asked is whether this idea of evolution in poetry is teleological, and whether it assumes, in a divergence from Darwin, a model for women of progress or 'improvement' (around which, anyway, hang many questions: improvement of poetry? improvement of ways of reading poetry? improvement of the hospitality of the tradition?).[10]

Woolf herself wrote little poetry, choosing instead a kind of poetic prose that drew specifically on the framed subjectivity of the dramatic monologue. Her interest in women's poetry, however, saw her commissioning a series of women's poetry under the editorship of Dorothy Wellesley at the Hogarth Press. A desire for a lyric 'I' to remove herself from a body which limits her sense of her own presence is notable in the work of two of the most significant women poets Woolf published, and whose work has only

---

[8] See Sandra Gilbert and Susan Gubar (eds.), *Shakespeare's Sisters* (Bloomington: Indiana University Press, 1979), p. xv.

[9] See Marie Stopes, *Love's Creation*, ed. and introd. Deryn Rees-Jones (Sussex: Academic Press, 2012).

[10] See e.g. Laura Marcus, who argues that Woolf's writings in fact look towards a feminism of the 'provisional' and 'incomplete' which subverts contemporary representations of 'The New Woman' and 'The Modern Girl' in Sue Roe and Susan Sellers (eds.), *The Cambridge Companion to Virginia Woolf* (Cambridge: Cambridge University Press, 2000), 214.

recently been put back properly into print. Hope Mirrlees's long poem *Paris*, published in 1920, begins with the lines 'I want a holophrase', a holophrase being, as Sandeep Parmar writes in her excellent introduction to Mirrlees's *Collected Poems*: 'a primitive linguistic structure that expresses a complex concept in a single word or short phrase'.[11] The poem continues: 'NORD-SUD || ZIG-ZAG | LION NOIR | CACOA BLOOKER' as the self at the centre of its narrative travels and switches in the compacted references to the underground station and the posters which line its walls in a series of binaries. Parmar goes on to quote Jane Harrison, Mirrlees's partner and one of the dedicatees of *A Room*, when she defines a holophrase as 'utterances of a relation in which the subject and object have not yet got their heads above water, but are submerged in a situation'.[12] Mirrlees's 'I' wanders through Paris; her demand for a self which is both compact and complex are echoed by her refusal to locate herself in any fixed place, creating a ghostly presence that wanders across the city and which 'scorn[s]the laws of solid geometry'. There she can transcend the material body as she '[S]tep[s] boldly into the wall off the Salle Caillebotte | And on and on...' (*CP*, 4).

The work of poet Joan Easdale, who Woolf nurtured from when Easdale was only 14, also captures in essence some of the anxieties of the woman poet's relationship to her body. At the very beginning of her last, long, and astonishing poem, *Amber Innocent* (1939) Easdale describes a scene in which her heroine hides in a room in which her brother-in-law sits:

The warmth of her breath on the velvet
Made in the shadow a momentary bliss.
Deeper she buried her face and her face
Seemed all of her. Her lashes brushing the pile were part
Of some sequestered woodland dark.
She lived in her face. Her body might be
A negative pillar alone.

She knew that her brother-in-law sat
In a chair behind in the world.
Most likely his eyes were sizing her shape
From her neck's dun curve down to her still shoes.
But Amber was all in her forest's shade,
It was only her face that held herself.[13]

Woolf's encouragement and editorial support of poets who were clearly exploring ideas that chimed with her own thinking (and in the case of Mirrless perhaps even helped to form her thinking) is not surprising. Those two ways of engaging with the body: turning

---

[11] Hope Mirrlees, *Collected Poems*, ed. and introd. Sandeep Parmar (Manchester: Carcanet Press, 2011), p. xl.
[12] Mirrlees, *Collected Poems*, p. xl. Hereafter *CP*.
[13] Joan Easdale, *Amber Innocent* (London: Hogarth Press, 1939). Repr. in original format in Celia Robertson, *Who Was Sophie? My Grandmother, Poet and Stranger* (London: Virago, 2008).

it into a ghostly presence, or wishing to hide or problematize its materiality, are a striking and, still resonant way of talking about the woman poet's anxieties about her presence and coming-into-being in the twenty-first century. But before we look forward to the women writing today, I want for a little while longer, to continue looking at the idea of a poetic tradition, and what it might mean to women.

2. The scene, if I may ask you to follow me, was now changed

In her reading of the relationship between two of the most influential of North American women poets, Elizabeth Bishop and Marianne Moore, Joanne Feit Diehl sees the object relations theory of Melanie Klein and Christopher Bollas as offering

> an alternate paradigm to male, modernist tradition, a paradigm based upon a female-centred model for literary influence that traces the processes of influence relations in terms of the pre-Oedipal stage, thereby acknowledging the primary importance of the mother and hence the literary foremother [...] the possibility of a heuristic theory that finds its origins in the mother–infant relationship and locates the psychodynamics that inform every future artistic production in the initial scene of the infant at the mother's breast.[14]

Object-relations theory offers a reconfiguration of the relations between gender in terms of its emphasis on the relationship between mother and child. But it is one that, in producing an alternative to an Oedipal model, may also reinscribe essentialist notions of both masculinity and femininity. While Bishop and Moore's relationship must be read as a very particular case (Bishop's own loss of her mother at an early age being so acute a factor in the personal and literary dynamic between these women), what seems crucial here is the emphasis on the pre-Oedipal connection as a way of understanding a distinct strategy in women's poetry which takes into account the potential for relations of influence and identification between men and women in a way which fails to maintain the phallocentrism of the Oedipal triangle. If object-relations theory per se places the mother–daughter relationship at its centre, risking a reinscription of a maternal line over a paternal one, it is here that I find the work of Jessica Benjamin particularly useful as a way of developing Feit Deil's dynamic of creative production.

In *The Bonds of Love: Psychoanalysis, Feminism and the Problems of Domination* (1988), Benjamin writes that in order to avoid an Oedipal model that repudiates femininity, we must look to 'the boy's early dis-identification with the mother and his

[14] Joanne Feit Diehl, *Marianne Moore and Elizabeth Bishop: The Psychodynamics of Creativity* (Princeton: Princeton University Press, 1993), 110.

oedipal separation from her in a neglected phase of playful, secondary identification with femininity'.[15] For Benjamin the erasure of femininity, what she refers to as 'the dangerous apparition of women', becomes part of the 'symbolic unconscious' 'when domination is institutionalised':

> the lack of opportunity to encounter women's subjectivity makes it impossible to break the magic spell of the omnipotent mother. The effort to destroy or reduce the other is an inevitable part of the childhood struggle for recognition, as well as a way of protecting independence. But it is another matter when—as in the domination of women by men—the other's independent subjectivity really is destroyed, and with it the possibility of mutual recognition. (*BofLove*, 176)

Benjamin calls for the 'social abolition of gender domination', and what she calls 'a dissolution of gender polarity, a reconstruction of the vital tension between recognition and assertion, dependency and freedom' (*BofLove*, 176). This social call might also be seen in terms of literary influence and the establishment of our relationships between poetic peers and predecessors of both genders. It might, as well, be read in terms of institutional domination, specifically in terms of the literary canon and its ownership of poetic space as well as its inscriptions of femininity. Benjamin's model offers a way of rereading the importance of the Oedipal complex that Harold Bloom places at the centre of the struggle for supremacy within the male literary tradition, rethinking the Oedipal complex as a psychic model of gender identification; it opens up the possibility of a new model of poetic lineage which means that women 'must claim their subjectivity and so be able to survive destruction' at the same time as then being able to 'offer men a new possibility of colliding with the outside and becoming alive in the presence of an equal other' (*BofLove*, 221).

Before I move on to look at the work of some more recent poets, however, I want finally to turn to the work of Terry Castle whose reading of the ghostly nature of the lesbian presence in literature is also of use here in reading the work of contemporary poets who I would argue are attempting to sidestep the body as a site of fixed identity, and to think about desire and subjectivity, and the kind of 'mutual recognition' Benjamin envisages.

In *The Apparitional Lesbian* (1993) Castle draws on the work of the prolific poet and novelist Sylvia Townsend Warner to set up an aesthetics of lesbian fiction. At the end of her chapter Castle suggests that archetypal lesbian fiction 'decanonizes, so to speak, the canonical structure of desire itself', continuing:

> It dismantles the real, as it were, in a search for the not-yet-real, something unpredicated and unpredictable. It is an assault on the banal: a retriangulation of triangles. As a consequence, it often looks odd, fantastical, implausible, 'not there'— utopian in aspiration if not design. It is, in a word, imaginative.[16]

---

[15] Jessica Benjamin, *The Bonds of Love: Psychoanalysis, Feminism and the Problems of Domination* (New York: Pantheon Books, 1988). Henceforth *BofLove*.

[16] Terry Castle, *The Apparitional Lesbian: Female Homosexuality and Modern Culture* (New York: Columbia University Press, 1993), 90–1.

Castle in thus analysing the essence of lesbian fiction also sees it as symptomatic of a refusal of the Oedipal model, a refusal that Benjamin sees as necessary for the establishment of female subjectivity. It's interesting, too, that Castle chooses in her discussion to write about Warner who was, of course, also a poet, and whose poems are recently—and quite rightly—being reassessed. The ghostly nature and disembodied quality of the woman who stands outside the heterosexual triangle, can also be seen within her poetry in poems such as 'The Traveller Benighted' where Warner writes: 'As though I'd shed it like a husk, | My body casts no shade; | I walk suspended in the dusk | Just as a spirit might'.[17] While Castle's argument is specific to a lesbian aesthetic, identifying a strategic negotiation of a heterosexual world, that renegotiation is not solely pertinent to a lesbian poetics, but works both as 'symptom' and strategy in its repositioning of a female subject in contemporary poetics.

3. That one would find any woman in that state of mind in the twentieth century was obviously impossible

I am necessarily being highly selective in this essay, but I want to continue thinking about the relationship between an embodied self and the world, and way in which women poets have attempted to work around the negotiation of self and other in relation to gender by looking at the work of Anne Stevenson (b. 1933). Stevenson, though strongly interested in connections between women, as her critical work on Bishop and her extraordinary poems to Sylvia Plath clearly testify, is much less enamoured of a connection to a specifically feminist politics: 'Politics', she writes, 'simplifies human issues by reducing them to blocks of black and white, right and wrong: poetry seeks to express humanity's complex contradictory nature.'[18] In her poem 'The Figure in the Carpet' a body is constructed by the speaker of the poem, which '[m]ight be human', but the carpet speaks back: 'Usually | I am man or woman | I do not ask. I feel happiest | when I melt into the plan | without description'.[19] This isn't androgyny, but a kind of sexlessness and there is a point where Stevenson's humanism, and individualism, can frequently move to a position that sits in parallel with a feminist politics' desire to resist a crude positioning of the gendered self. Stevenson's small poem 'Vertigo' neatly encompasses the mind-body dialogue as it places the self standing on an abyss: 'If you love me, said mind | take that step into silence. | If you love me, said body | turn and exist' (*Poems*,

---

[17] Sylvia Townsend Warner, *New Collected Poems*, ed. Claire Harman (Manchester: Carcanet Press, 2008), 40.

[18] Anne Stevenson, 'Rights and Responsibilities', *Poetry Wales*, 46/4 (Spring, 2011), 25.

[19] Anne Stevenson, *Poems 1995–2005* (Tarset: Bloodaxe Books, 2004), 290–1. Henceforth *Poems* in the text.

28). Vertigo suggests wobble, and a failure to be able properly to align the relationship between self and world; a world that might easily be turned upside down. By positioning herself on this 'wobble' Stevenson adopts a position of movement and between-ness that offers both mind and body a place from which to anticipate each other's presence. Though the clear peril of vertigo is that balance is lost, the poem remains poised, and on the edge of the binary, and, in fact by its very existence illustrates the very place from which, for Stevenson, the poem is born.

In an excellent discussion of Stevenson, the poet Emma Jones describes her work as 'characterised as the playful collaboration of plural writing selves',[20] capturing brilliantly the ambivalence in Stevenson's work towards a gendered self:

> The self at odds with the self: the writing self who is compelled to work, but is at odds with a self suspicious of language; the self who desires identity and community, who is pitted against the self for whom identity and community are a kind of stultification: the feminine self who celebrates feminine experience, but is resisted by the self who desires freedom from definition by gender and is suspicious of feminist claims to power.[21]

Stevenson has spoken of the relationship in her work between the 'I' who writes and the 'I' in the poem describing that 'I' as 'more a reflection in a mirror'.[22] While many poets might recognize the process of identifying with the 'I' who is nevertheless a transformative 'other' when writing a poem, Stevenson's particular image of herself in her poems is explored elsewhere by Sara Johnson who picks up on the 'there and not there-ness' of Stevenson's writing, focusing on Stevenson's rather extraordinary description of herself as someone who 'can see through the glass to the trees or buildings outside; at the same time you also see your face, or really, through your face'.[23] Johnson reads this use of 'I' as 'you' as having the 'capacity to represent a presence that is both opaque and transparent, there and not there'.[24] In other words, Stevenson creates a self who is both identifying self and other, creating what Johnson describes as 'a lively dialogue between the originating, controlling "I" of the poet herself and a more enquiring and delicate pronoun, which slips in and out of its own skins and ghosts'.[25]

It seems important to set Stevenson here as a poet of a generation who was in close correspondence with an admired poetic predecessor, Elizabeth Bishop, and who also numbered among her immediate generation Sylvia Plath and Anne Sexton; if her work

---

[20] Emma Jones, ' "To serve a girl on terrible terms": Anne Stevenson's Writing Selves', in Angela Leighton (ed.), *Voyage Over Voices: Critical Essays on Anne Stevenson* (Liverpool: Liverpool University Press, 2010), 173.

[21] Jones, ' "To serve a girl on terrible terms" ', 174.

[22] 'An Interview with Anne Stevenson', *Oxford Poetry*, 1/2 (1983), 43–9 (49). Cited by Sara Johnson, ' "Not exactly a *persona*": Pronouns in Anne Stevenson's Poetry', in Leighton (ed.), *Voyages Over Voices*, 164.

[23] 'An Interview with Anne Stevenson', in Susan Blake (ed.), *Common Ground: Poets in Welsh Landscape* (Bridgend: Poetry Wales Press, 1985), 202–16 (214). Cited by Sara Johnson in Leighton (ed.), *Voyages Over Voices*, 164.

[24] Leighton (ed.), *Voyages Over Voices*, 174.

[25] Leighton (ed.), *Voyages Over Voices*, 171.

has been touched in various ways by these women predecessors, then it is vital also to see her as the poet who managed to negotiate 'the life more terrible' (*Poems*, 386), resisting material annihilation, silence, or disregard. Having Bishop, Plath, and Sexton as key poetic predecessors has in many ways, as I have elsewhere argued, been central to British women's negotiations of their poetic selves. In this attempt to map out the variety of responses to bodily representation, I contrast now two poets, Lavinia Greenlaw (b. 1962) and Colette Bryce (b. 1970), who continue to work through this negotiation of dialogue between subject and object, self and other in their work.

Greenlaw's first collection *Night Photograph* (1993) saw her using narratives about science as a way of developing an authoritative, and ostensibly neutral and objective, poetic voice. Her interest (as with Stevenson) in the work of Bishop, as well as in the discourse of science, suggests a move towards a kind of poetic androgyny where there is a desire to move away from gendered poetic models. She writes:

> I have never been conscious of my work being associated with a new wave of women poets. I was aware, from the mid-Eighties, when I began to go to workshops and readings, of a new wave forming, but not of it being specifically female, nor of there being a discrete female part to it; that was partly its point.[26]

Having been originally driven by a strong narrative impulse, Greenlaw has, in her maturity, become a poet who, using fragment and suggestion, is increasingly preoccupied by an exploration of a disembodied poetics of perspective. Greenlaw has written, for example, how if she writes 'about anything in particular' it is 'about how we see and how we try to see': 'Like Elizabeth Bishop, I'm as interested in the idea of a place as the place itself and think the actual and the imagined versions are equally valid, even after I have arrived.'[27] In her clear reference to Bishop's poem 'Santarém' in this statement, Greenlaw points to the imaginative reach of place as geographical as well as psychological location, suggesting a preoccupation with knowledge 'occupied, not with objects, but with the way that we can possibly know objects even before we experience them'.[28]

Greenlaw returns to Bishop's 'Santarém' on several occasions in her collection, *Minsk* (2003),[29] a volume that repeatedly questions the reliability of vision. In 'Blackwater' we are presented with a landscape 'Where the coastline doubles up on itself | as if punched in the gut by the god Meander', and we are asked to imagine

an estuary where the eye can't tell
sea from river, hill from valley,
near from far, first from last, in from out
any one thing, in fact, from any other. (*Minsk*, 12)

---

[26] Unpublished interview with the author, 2008.
[27] Lavinia Greenlaw, 'A Note on the Text', in *Questions of Travel: William Morris in Iceland* (London: Notting Hill Editions, 2011), p. xxiv.
[28] Greenlaw, 'A Note on the Text', p. xxiv.
[29] Lavinia Greenlaw, *Minsk* (London: Faber & Faber, 2003). Henceforth *Minsk*.

The capital of Belarus, situated on the Svislach and Nemiga rivers, becomes the geographical focus for the title poem: a poem that, through 'questions' of travel, interrogates family origins. Minsk becomes the place to which it is impossible to return:

in settlement, change into exchange,
where history runs to meet itself

as here, where the headwaters of two rivers
are met by the confluence of two rivers. (*Minsk*, 48)

The self has become a way of looking, disembodied but totally implicated in the otherness of all that it sees, and which in seeing it creates. Greenlaw's most recent collection of poems, *The Casual Perfect* (2011)[30] takes its title from Robert Lowell's poem 'To Elizabeth Bishop'. There Greenlaw's recall of Lowell's 'unerring muse' sees her in dialogue with male and female poetic predecessors Bishop and Lowell, as much as she is with an idea of muse and inspiration.

Invariably in the volume, Greenlaw's poetic 'I' is disembodied as words become a poetic body with the self located in the world of the text and the imagination. In 'A Dutch Landscape for Isla McGuire' (*CasP*, 35) it is Vermeer who becomes a trace for an elegy to a female relative in the poem that begins by summoning an art-historical account of the experience of engagement with a landscape in art. Here is an experience or a thought at a remove: an account of a painter's own account, mediated again through the telling of it to Isla McGuire, and then through its retelling in the poem. This hall of mirrors retranslates when the person being addressed looks back out at the addressee with the altered up-close perspective of the telescope. Distance here is irrelevant precisely because, for the subject of the poem, Isla McGuire, with her failing eyesight, what should be too close has become refocused in its perspective. That surreally-oriented gaze finds the landscape within the self through its looking. Isla McGuire was an anaesthetist, although this information is buried within the poem to become the more elusive and dreamlike statement 'You saw your patients through their sleep'. This anaesthetized sleep sees (and the word, as with so many of Greenlaw's seemingly casually introduced words, is heavily weighted) the body 'unframed' folding in on itself as we as reader are invited into the 'unfolding' body. It is perhaps fair to say that Greenlaw here follows Bishop's mobility of thought, but rather than like Bishop setting the landscape as a mediator for a back and forth reflection, Greenlaw actually drives us to the interior body as it is here juxtaposed with the dead relative whose sleep is of a more permanent—and perhaps even less interior—kind. Throughout *The Casual Perfect*, Greenlaw engages with the idea of form, whether poetic or bodily form, and their separations and elisions. In 'Kata' (a Japanese word meaning 'form') the poem emerges as 'A dance between movement and space, | between image and imperative'. In 'The Literal Body', perhaps her most definitive engagement with the relationship between the body and the mind, Greenlaw reinvents the literal as 'what her

---

[30] Lavinia Greenlaw, *The Casual Perfect* (London: Faber & Faber, 2011). Hereafter *CasP*.

body remembers most clearly | is being held by breaking glass' (*CasP*, 10) so that the body, in fact metaphorized ('her skin is feathers | and her teeth are eggshell'), becomes reconfigured, and in this state of anxious extremes where pain and loss of sensation are attributed to the 'feminine side' her hand still seeks the basic comfort of human touch.

By contrast, Bryce continues to situate the body as both site of political inscription and potential coherence of the self, while also problematizing it. The absence of the body becomes a symptom of damage and displacement. In 'The Negatives',[31] the idea of an inherited female tradition is explored via an oblique narrative that uses the trope of holiday snaps. In the poem Bryce uses the absent physical presence of a woman in photographs as an extended metaphor for the absence of women in a poetic tradition. The female presence and her body is rendered unpreserved: the speaker of the poem has 'trusted the camera to the men'. Here the female body, immersed, naked in water, literally dissolves. The poem begins with the absenting from the scenario of two women, Lottie and Sylvie, whose names perhaps ask us to think of Charlotte Mew and Sylvia Plath, two poets who famously committed suicide. The speaker of the poem refuses this exit, and instead strips off to bathe in the company of the men. The men who are named in the poem recall and suggest canonical poets: Coleridge, a William who is both Wordsworth and Yeats, a louche, cheroot-smoking Lowell or Frost, a fastidious Tom Eliot seem to be set up to characterize male poets' difficulties with women, in particular their bodies. The use of first names in the poem neatly sidesteps allegory as well as patriarchy, while still alerting us to the fact that this scenario is peopled by allusively present poets.

In the case of Coleridge and Yeats the objects with which they are associated also recall key moments in their poetics or imaginative writings which more specifically problematize male relationships with the feminine, both the maternal and the virginal. Coleridge holding a stone which looks like a skull called Yorick makes us think of his essay on Hamlet, himself the hero of a famous Oedipal triangle which has also at its centre the image of a ghost. (We cannot forget Hamlet's 'too, too solid flesh'.) Nor of course can we forget that it is through Hamlet that Eliot develops his idea of the objective correlative, offering his own criticism of Coleridge's overly subjective reading of *Hamlet* and his suggestion that the female figure at the centre of the play represents the failure of the ability to represent the maternal in the Oedipal triangle. Such glances towards male literary history and myth in the poem remain elusive and dreamlike. Yeats's 'Leda and the Swan' is a poem about a rape of male and divine mythic violation and domination of the female body: in Bryce's poem the cottage perhaps references Wordsworth's ruined cottage, or Leda and the swan's broken tower. The woman who speaks this poem's deep anxiety about her own presence sees her dissolving into the material of the photograph, sinking into the scenario of nature as she becomes almost indistinguishable from the water which she describes as 'slipping the silk from my skin | the soft water, clinging like silk'.

The body here becomes the site from which to hold onto the self: 'I grip my wrist. Yes, it is real | with its ghost pulse, its pale blue rivers' but actually the presence of the women

---

[31] Colette Bryce, *The Heel of Bernadette* (London: Picador, 2000), 28–9.

has been lost to celluloid; there seems to be no record on the negatives, but there is also a sense that somewhere there is a lost film on which the women might appear. This pervasive sense of ontological anxiety is one which is played through in Bryce's work, and the speaker of the poem describes her 'image fading like frost, my face | a pattern vanishing on glass. | You begin, of course, to doubt yourself. | And now, there is only my word for it'. Photographically the negative is the reverse colour of the photograph: where black is white and white is black. The women don't exist in these negatives, but here is a sense that the word negative stands not just for a binary opposite, a lacuna, a no place.

There are many subtleties to Bryce's poem, the desire not to simply locate blame with men but in what I referred to earlier via Benjamin, to point up the institutionalization of domination. The chemist in the poem, who has lost the photographs, is, we are told, 'an honest man', a line that recalls Brutus in Julius Caesar—so that even while the poem works to illustrate the difficulty of women's presence and representation it recalls Shakespeare in an internal performance of active engagement with the canon. The final lines of the poem see the woman poet fading from tradition, from poetic images of femininity which allow her no subjectivity, warning us, perhaps against our disbelief, in the inherent dangers of representing the female body: 'My image fading like frost, my face | A pattern vanishing on glass'.

One of my intentions here is to show the diversity and prevalence of engagement with anxieties around the female body and in the final part of this section I set alongside each other two further poets, both slightly older than Greenlaw and Bryce, and arguably two of the most influential women poets of their generation: Jo Shapcott (b. 1953) and Denise Riley (b. 1948). Throughout her work, Shapcott has set up the binary of male and female in poetry in order to deconstruct it, moving in her most recent work towards what Luce Irigaray might term a 'sensible transcendental'.[32] In her early sequence of poems about a pair of characters, Robert and Elizabeth, Shapcott sets up two versions of narratives which enact a dialogue between male and female writers in the nineteenth and twentieth centuries: Robert and Elizabeth Browning, and Robert Lowell and Elizabeth Hardwick. She also flanks the poems with quotes from letters Swift sent to Esther Vanhomrigh so that a complex historical network of relations between men and women in the context of desire and creativity are set up. The sequence of eight poems begins with 'Having Fun with Robert and Elizabeth', and starts, as it ends, with them sitting down to write 'each listening to interpret the faint sounds | of the other's scourings on the paper'.[33] Moving between first person and third person the poems experiment with perspective: of telling and seeing in different voices and from different points of view. In the penultimate poem of the sequence knitting becomes a metaphor for the act of creation:

The meaning is all in the gaps:
a pattern of holes marked out by woolly colour,
a jumper made of space, division and relations. (*HB*, 32)

---

[32] See Luce Irigaray, *An Ethics of Sexual Difference* (Ithaca, NY: Cornell University Press, 1993).
[33] Jo Shapcott, *Her Book: Poems 1988–1998* (London: Faber & Faber 2000), 25. Hereafter *HB*.

For Shapcott, like Stevenson, it is precisely this space between the material and the invisible which offers for her a place of transformation. In her versions of the French poems of Rilke we see Shapcott working in dialogue with a male voice to create a space between her readings of the feminine and Rilke's. More latterly this place of dialogue has been with the artist Helen Chadwick, whose own artistic practice was marked by a shift from depiction of her own female body in her art, to more abstract work which she described as being more 'deft'.[34]

Until included in a Penguin selection with Douglas Oliver and Iain Sinclair, Denise Riley's work had been published by small independent presses. She has avoided the mainstream poetry world's preoccupation with prizes, while at the same time becoming one of the most respected voices that cross the mainstream/avant-garde divide. As Frances Presley has pointed out in a discussion of Riley's early poem 'A Note on Sex and the Reclaiming of the Language':

> Riley's feminism derives originally from Simone de Beauvoir, and from existentialist philosophy. The woman has to be the subject-for-itself, a consciousness, and not a thing-in-itself, the other, the Savage.[35]

Rather than think in Shapcott's deconstructive way, Riley problematizes the nature of the divide between self and other, body and imagination, often preoccupied with the boundary between inner and outer self, or selves, so that cutting or holes becomes a metaphor for a kind of transgression between worlds. In 'Wherever You Are, Be Somewhere Else'[36] she sets up the external body and the interior body in a way which shows the complexity of the relationship between them:

A body shot through, perforated, a tin sheet
beaten out then peppered with thin holes,
silvery, leaf-curled as their edges; light flies

right through this tracery, voices leap, slip side-
long, all faces split to angled facets: whichever
piece is glimpsed, that bit is what I am, held

in a look until dropped like an egg on the floor
let slop, crashed to slide and run, yolk yellow
for the live, the dead who worked through me. (*SP*, 47)

---

[34] For a detailed discussion of 'Deft' see my ' "Wanderer, incomer, borderer | liar, mother of everything I see": Jo Shapcott's Engagement with Landscape, Art and Poetry', in Neal Alexander and David Cooper (eds.), *Poetry & Geography*, (Liverpool: Liverpool University Press, 2013).

[35] Frances Presley, 'The Grace of Being Common', *how2* Sept. 1999 at [http://www.asu.edu/pipercwcenter/how2journal/archive/online_archive/v1_2_1999/current/readings/presley.html]

[36] Denise Riley, *Selected Poems* (London: Reality Street Editions, 2000), 47–9 (47). Henceforth *SP*.

In making reference to the egg here, Riley is directly referencing Lacan's 'hommelette', his punning term used to describe the pre-Oedipal child (the little girl-boy made from broken eggs), who as yet can make no distinction between self and other: 'whose characteristic is not to exist, but which is nevertheless an organ'.[37] Riley slips this allusion into a complex and fluid web of descriptions of subjectivity. As Carol Watts has pointed out, however, Riley is most likely in her poems to reference Merleau-Ponty, and it is Merleau-Ponty's positioning of the body which is also helpful in understanding Riley's work.[38] Stéphanie Ménasé characterizes Merleau-Ponty's philosophy as suggesting that 'embodiment brings to our perceptual experience an *a priori* structure whereby it presents itself to us in consciousness as an experience of a world of things in space and time whose nature is independent of us'.[39] Riley's poems offer a process of continuous working through of thoughts and feelings; her whole impulse is one that suggests hesitation, self-questioning, and movement. The material body is there, but only to be questioned as a vehicle for knowing the self. In a poem like the often quoted 'Dark Looks' Riley interrogates the relationship between the poem and the poet head-on:

Who anyone is or I am is nothing to the work. The writer
properly should be the last person that the reader or the listener need think about
 yet the poet with her signature stands up trembling, grateful, mortally embarrassed
and especially embarrassing to herself, patting her hair and twittering If, if only
I need not have a physical appearance! To be sheer air, and mousseline! (*SP*, 74)

As Watts points out what is at stake for Riley is 'not the perils of transcendence but the externality of the lyric self in the world, the acknowledgement of its embodiedness' (*CWP*, 164). Watts continues:

> [T]he lyric 'I' becomes an assemblage of bodily sensations, a place of synaesthetic interchange. Mouth, ear, eye, touch. The effect of this is to site consciousness in bodily terms, to see the passions as a means of speculation [...] This is not, however, to realign the embodied self with a traditional lyric expressivity. (*CWP*,164)

Instead, in fact, in her strategy of drawing extensively on pop songs in her poems, Riley sets alongside her shifting endlessly modulating 'I' the lyrics of what Richard Hoggart calls the 'forced intimacy'[40] of pop's emotions, so that in a surprising way Riley can juxtapose versions of ideologized collective sentiment alongside an 'I' who both enjoys

---

[37] Jacques Lacan, *The Four Fundamental Concepts of Psychoanalysis*, ed. Jacques-Alain Miller, trans. Alan Sheridan (London: Penguin Books, 1991), 197–8.
[38] Carol Watts, 'Beyond Interpellation? Affect, Embodiment and the Poetics of Denise Riley', in Alison Mark and Deryn Rees-Jones (eds.), *Contemporary Women's Poetry: Reading/Writing/Practice*, with a Preface by Isobel Armstrong (Basingstoke: Macmillan, 2000), 157–72. Henceforth *CWP*.
[39] M. Merleau-Ponty, *The World of Perception*, with a foreword by Stéphanie Ménasé (Abingdon: Routledge, 2004), 9.
[40] See Simon Frith, 'Why do Songs Have Words', in *Taking Popular Music Seriously: Selected Essays* (Aldershot: Ashgate, 2007), 209–38 (214).

and ironises them. As she writes in 'A Misremembered Lyric' (*SP*, 51), for example, she splices and disturbs lines from Gene Pitney's song into her own line of thoughts:

> A misremembered lyric: a soft catch of its song
> whirrs in my throat. 'Something's gotta hold of my heart
> tearing my' soul and my conscience apart, long after
> presence is clean gone and leaves unfurnished no
> shadow.

In Pitney's version it is the soul and the senses that are kept apart. By placing the quotation marks where she does Riley extricates and owns part of the song. As the underlying melody of the song carries through the rhythms of her own lyric, it leaves the material body, the heart, so to speak, in another person's voice. As Riley's poem progresses, lines from the song continue to infiltrate her own lines, as well as lines from *The Cascades*' song 'Rhythm of the Rain'. If language in this poem works by a series of sound associations and autosuggestions, the gender of the disembodied 'I' also remains ambiguous, an ambiguity no doubt heightened by Marc Almond's 1989 camped-up cover version of the song, sung in duet with Pitney, which cleverly sets heterosexual and homosexual desire in lively dialogue. Riley's interest in these songs suggests not only an engagement with destabilizing the reception of the lyric, but of the exchange between cultural constructs of masculinity and femininity in adopting and integrating a voice into her own lyric.

4. The smooth gliding of sentence after sentence was interrupted. Something tore, something scratched

By way of contrast to these poets I turn now to the writing of two younger poets, Clare Pollard (b. 1978) and Kate Potts (b. 1978). Pollard who has to date four full-length collections, has been publishing with a mainstream press since her debut collection, *The Heavy-Petting Zoo* (1998), appeared when she was 19. Selima Hill, describing Pollard's work, has said that it is 'raw, reckless, and more bloody-minded than an older, so-called wiser poet would dare to be' and Pollard represents an interesting and contrasting case study, not least because she now works as a mentor for young poets. Throughout her publishing history Pollard has been conscious of the relationship between her poems and the representation of herself as a woman poet. When questioned about this she has reflected on her interest

> through confessionalism and also my dramatic monologues...the idea of performance of self. Trying on different possible selves. What to reveal/expose. Creating an image. On all my books I've used photos of myself that I suppose play with ideas about who 'Clare Pollard' is. *Bedtime* is a book that in many ways is about

sex and toys with self-exposure, so the shot is supposed to refer to this. I guess I was playing with the sexuality of youth, but it's supposed to be jokey too. (I'm wearing a T-Shirt, after all). On the back of *Look, Clare! Look!*—about travelling—I've a photo of me in China. On the back of *Changeling*, which is folky, I'm out in the snow in a sheepskin coat. The photos are supposed to make people feel the content of the book is the 'real' me, that I'm living it, as well as writing it, although this is, of course, an illusion. I don't think this is an expressly female thing necessarily—you can see this kind of performance of self in Lowell, O'Hara, Seidel... Frost was a great self-mythologiser. Although the idea of femininity as masquerade is interesting—perhaps with makeup and fashion women have more opportunity to play 'fancy dress' as it were. I enjoy blurring art and life.[41]

It is tempting to see Pollard's earlier work as expressing the anxieties and naïveties, as well as the energies and excitement of many young women in their early twenties, symptomatic and representative of a developmentally inevitable and rather joyful self-regard.[42] Pollard's work is certainly still maturing, but her deep awareness of the politics of her playfulness, and her thoughtfulness about her own representation of herself in her poems, are revealed in part and by proxy, in her discussion of the work of Anne Sexton:

Melodrama is interesting as a site where female and camp tastes intersect—and so, I would argue, is Sexton's work. As she constantly references popular culture—from movies, to cartoons, to ads—there is something very 'campy' detectable in her vulgar, slangy, OTT style, and perhaps, finally, it is worth taking note of this if our reading of her work is not to be too serious. Camp is an 'excuse note' for Sexton, allowing her to smuggle supposedly trivial female concerns and influences into the predominantly male, 'high art' world of poetry. [...] When Sexton stresses that she is 'an actress in my own autobiographical play', we can begin to see her self-proclaimed pose as 'housewife-poet' as containing an element of drag—especially as we know that after her breakdown, Sexton basically ceased to do most domestic duties. (Her husband Kayo was affectionately known as 'mother').[43]

Playing with the idea of a self who is to be looked at Pollard risks placing herself at her most vulnerable, something she freely acknowledges. So in her poem 'My Bed',[44] which is framed through images of herself and Marilyn Monroe on the back and front covers, she plays with the stereotypes of female sexuality in a manner that makes us acutely aware of her ability to represent images that might in the past have been seen to manipulate her. The poem itself, with its reference to Tracey Emin's *Bed*, a staged autobiographical

---

[41] Email to the author, Aug. 2011.

[42] I am grateful to the participants of the conference at the 'Saying the World' festival, University of Newcastle, Nov. 2010 for feedback on my responses to this poem.

[43] Clare Pollard, 'Her Kind: Anne Sexton, the Cold War and the Idea of the Housewife' in *Critical Quarterly*, 48/3 (2006), 1–24 (24).

[44] Clare Pollard, *Bedtime* (Tarset: Bloodaxe Books, 2002), 35–7. Hereafter *BT*.

drama of a self in disarray, instead satirizes self-publicity, and asserts control of its own experiences, even down to the regularity of its rhyme scheme: 'As poetry's | in need of press, I thought I'd do the same—show you the place I slept and dreamt and came' (*BT*, 35). In speaking the ordinariness of her experiences Pollard flirts with ideas of female propriety in her imagery of 'cum-rags' and rashes, wet-patches, vomit, and drunkenness, steering a difficult line between satirical brio and the presentation of the self in a way which suggests an uncomplicated relationship between expression, experience and identity: 'It hasn't been the craziest of beds, | you'd find as interesting all about— | just as I've not the most exciting head | only some massive need to write things out'. Pollard writes:

> In terms of reception... I've certainly come across a lot of stereotyping. Even recently, I saw someone online call me a 'chick-lit poet' which I found pretty annoying. My last two books have mainly been about globalisation, good and evil, responsibility and mortality, not liking shoes and looking for Mr Right!! But because I'm young and female people make assumptions about the content of my work. In terms of how I've been marketed, perhaps—being a young woman got me both good and bad attention. I was lucky in how much press I got for my debut, but also encountered an awful lot of bitchiness. There was a sense, perhaps, that my success came too easily, and for the wrong reasons. To be fair, I used my youth and gender to a certain extent—my titles and cover-images are quite flirtatious. But I was always entirely serious about my poetry. The hope was that the arresting imagery would lure readers in, not that they would dismiss the work as fluff without even reading it! I was probably fairly naïve in this. I should add that the most vicious criticism of my work has always been from female reviewers.[45]

In her most recent collection, *Changeling* (2011),[46] Pollard's anxieties about how to represent a female self are worked through in a Gothic tale of errant femininity, 'In the Wood', which recalls Dante's *Inferno* as well at Rossetti's 'Goblin Market'. Whereas in Dante the male poet loses his way in the dark wood where he encounters the ghost of Virgil, who has been sent by his beloved Beatrice to rescue him, in Pollard's poem the female narrator returns to her children, and motherhood, having spent a tempestuous night of sex with a hermaphrodite centaur:

We drank from waters warped, then, drunk,
I broke a rabbit's neck. I ate.
I carved my name on every tree, and hers,
and let her teach to me
that love deserves the dark house and the whip;
that sex and sweat and flesh and drink and power
are all this body wants (*C*, 60)

---

[45] Email to the author, July 2011.
[46] Clare Pollard, *Changeling* (Tarset: Bloodaxe Books, 2011). Hereafter *C*.

Although this image of the sexualized female recalls in some sense the 'moral pornography' of Angela Carter, what complicates this poem for me is the return to the maternal as a retreat from sexuality, and it compares interestingly with the first poem in Carol Ann Duffy's *The World's Wife* (1999). In Duffy's poem, 'Little Red Cap', an ingénue in a wood gains poetic experience, again through sexual experiences, and at some psychic cost, but walks free, having slain the wolf, to sing in the forest alone. The singing that goes on at the end of Pollard's poem is however a lullaby to her children as the poem seems to suggest that there must always be a choice between the sexual and the maternal, rejecting the possibility of wild maternity, or at the very least being anxious about it as a possibility.

By contrast Kate Potts, in her debut collection *Pure Hustle* (2011),[47] appears to be less interested in narrative than the observational detailed regard of Bishop, Shapcott, and Greenlaw. Potts is one of a new generation of poets who are more willing to cross the divide between the mainstream and linguistically innovative poetics that might be seen to connect directly with the work of Riley, and she has named Plath, Duffy, Jackie Kay, Kate Clanchy, and Anne Carson as having been, along with Shapcott and Greenlaw, important to her. For Potts, thinking about how to position herself as a woman and a poet are, as in Pollard's case, very much a component in her approach to her work. She writes:

> I probably began by writing about more 'traditionally female' subjects (love, sex, relationships, the body). I'm not sure how much of this was down to subtle pressures and expectations and how much was due to using poetry as a means to express the difficult or otherwise inexpressible, or just a lack of bravery—a fear of anything else somehow not quite being 'my place'. On the other hand, I think there are ways in which I initially avoided being 'stereotypically feminine' in terms of style and content (I was a little afraid of being 'over the top' or writing anything too 'pretty'), and my writing is far freer and better since I stopped worrying about this. I don't avoid subjects that are seen as stereotypically female—that seems to me counterproductive. I do try to be brave enough to write about whatever I want to write about in whatever way I want. This is an ongoing issue, but it's a far, far smaller one than it used to be.[48]

Read alongside Pollard's heightened awareness of the effect of gender on her work, it is difficult to imagine that other women interviewed might not share such experiences, albeit in varying degrees and with varying results in terms of their own poetics.[49] In contrast to Pollard's foregrounding of the body as a site of masquerade and play that draws on a tradition of American confessionalism, there is a distinct absence of the body in *Pure Hustle*; and if the body does appear, it is ungendered. There are ghosts too: 'You contemplate chaos, prostration, | beginning again in a new place' ('Ghost no 1', *PH*,

---

[47] Kate Potts, *Pure Hustle* (Tarset: Bloodaxe Books, 2011). Hereafter *PH*.
[48] Email to the author, 11 Sept. 2011.
[49] This essay is part of an ongoing project, and the questionnaire sent to Pollard and Potts will be circulated to a broad range of women poets.

21) or, walking the city at night as 'You tightrope walk the cracks' ('Ghost no 2', *PH*, 36). In 'Your Second Skin' (*PH*, 42), interestingly co-written with another young poet, Sarah Howe, Potts writes of a skin which 'Lies still in its shellacked case, folded in rice papers, oiled | To an almost purple sheen—|| With porous muzzle, with self-lubricating silicon plumes for ease | And comfort all day long'. In this poem, in particular, the influence of Shapcott's early scientific tone can be heard, as the creation of femininity is located in the skin, the self being something far removed from the 'compromise' of an external self the poem ironically denies it is:

To begin, simply score your self from nape to sternum, separate
your peel from pith

and shuck off that standard-issue rind. Fresh from the box,
the fabric's even heft will seal your seams.

5. Naturally creative, incandescent, undivided... It is fatal for anyone to think of her sex...

With only eighteen years to go until that somewhat arbitrary date of 2029, an adult life away, when the woman poet, according to Woolf, will be born, it has never seemed more apposite to reflect on the anxieties and workings-through of representations of the gendered bodily self that a generation of women have undertaken. The 'mutual recognition' that Benjamin espouses, the 'emotional attunement, mutual influence, affective mutuality, sharing states of mind' (*BofLove*, 16) which might serve as a model for dialogue between male and female poets, as well as her aspirations for the future of the relationships between men and women which she sees as both 'modest and utopian' (*BofLove*, 223) offer an important place of destination. Jane Dowson has written of the dialogic nature of women's poetry that 'every poem is arguably in dialogue with the literary tradition and implicitly with the reader'.[50] Negotiating the other in such a dialogue might involve a conscious as well as an unconscious engagement with the body and I would argue in fact, contra Woolf, that women and men writing today need more than ever to think of their sex, and the way in which they position the body in relation to the lyric 'I'. If, in the light of my readings of Benjamin and Castle, the poetic tradition can be rethought in terms not of lineage, with all the baggage that carries, but as a coalescence and connection between women and men, as imagination, retriangulation, and the mutual recognition between the sexes that derives from a 'dissolution of gender polarity',

---

[50] Jane Dowson, Introduction to *The Cambridge Companion to Twentieth-Century British and Irish Women's Poetry* (Cambridge: Cambridge University Press, 2011), 7.

we might look forward to a blossoming of poetic writing that we have never seen before. Fatal, then, for poets not to think of their sex, but vital, too, that they do it in a way that negotiates difference in a different way.

Select Bibliography

Benjamin, Jessica, *The Bonds of Love: Psychoanalysis, Feminism and the Problems of Domination* (New York: Pantheon Books, 1988).
Brigley, Zoë, 'Celebrating Not Complaining', *Poetry Wales*, 46/4 (Spring, 2011), 24–5.
Bryce, Colette, *The Heel of Bernadette* (London: Picador, 2000).
Castle, Terry, *The Apparitional Lesbian: Female Homosexuality and Modern Culture* (New York: Columbia University Press, 1993).
Dowson, Jane, Introduction to *The Cambridge Companion to Twentieth-Century British and Irish Women's Poetry* (Cambridge: Cambridge University Press, 2011).
Easdale, Joan, *Amber Innocent* (London: Hogarth Press, 1939).
Feit Diehl, Joanne, *Marianne Moore and Elizabeth Bishop: The Psychodynamics of Creativity* (Princeton: Princeton University Press, 1993).
Frith, Simon, 'Why do Songs Have Words', in *Taking Popular Music Seriously: Selected Essays* (Aldershot: Ashgate, 2007), 209–38.
Gilbert, Sandra and Gubar, Susan (eds.), *Shakespeare's Sisters* (Bloomington: Indiana University Press, 1979).
Greenlaw, Lavinia, *Minsk* (London: Faber & Faber, 2003).
Greenlaw, Lavinia, 'A Note on the Text', in *Questions of Travel: William Morris in Iceland* (London: Notting Hill Editions, 2011).
Greenlaw, Lavinia, *The Casual Perfect* (London: Faber & Faber, 2011).
Gregory, Gill, *The Life and Work of Adelaide Procter: Poetry, Feminism and Fathers* (Aldershot: Ashgate, 1998).
Irigaray, Luce, *An Ethics of Sexual Difference* (Ithaca, NY: Cornell University Press, 1993).
Jones, Emma, '"To serve a girl on terrible terms": Anne Stevenson's Writing Selves', in Angela Leighton (ed.), *Voyage Over Voices: Critical Essays on Anne Stevenson* (Liverpool: Liverpool University Press, 2010).
Lacan, Jacques, *The Four Fundamental Concepts of Psychoanalysis*, ed. Jacques-Alain Miller, trans. Alan Sheridan (London: Penguin Books, 1991).
Merleau-Ponty, M., *The World of Perception*, with a foreword by Stéphanie Ménasé (Abingdon: Routledge, 2004).
Mirrlees, Hope, *Collected Poems*, ed. and introd. Sandeep Parmar (Manchester: Carcanet Press, 2011).
Pollard, Clare, *Bedtime* (Tarset: Bloodaxe Books, 2002).
Pollard, Clare, *Changeling* (Tarset: Bloodaxe Books, 2011).
Potts, Kate, *Pure Hustle* (Tarset: Bloodaxe Books, 2011).
Rees-Jones, Deryn, *Consorting with Angels: Modern Women Poets* (Tarset: Bloodaxe Books, 2005).
Riley, Denise, *Selected Poems* (London: Reality Street Editions, 2000).
Shapcott, Jo, *Her Book: Poems 1988–1998* (London: Faber & Faber 2000).
Stevenson, Anne, 'Rights and Responsibilities', *Poetry Wales*, 46/4 (Spring, 2011), 25.
Stevenson, Anne, *Poems 1995–2005* (Tarset: Bloodaxe Books, 2004).

Stopes, Marie, *Love's Creation*, ed. and introd. Deryn Rees-Jones (Sussex: Academic Press, 2012).
Townsend Warner, Sylvia, *New Collected Poems*, ed. Claire Harman (Manchester: Carcanet Press, 2008).
Watts, Carol, 'Beyond Interpellation? Affect, Embodiment and the Poetics of Denise Riley', in Alison Mark and Deryn Rees-Jones (eds.), *Contemporary Women's Poetry: Reading/Writing/Practice*, with a Preface by Isobel Armstrong (Basingstoke: Macmillan, 2000), 157–72.

CHAPTER 9

CAT-SCANNING THE LITTLE MAGAZINE

RICHARD PRICE

The Beatles and a Brontosaurus

COMPUTED axial tomography, 'CT-' or 'CAT-scanning', is a procedure in which multiple X-ray photographs are taken from different positions along a single axis. A composite three-dimensional image is rendered from the results. In medicine it is a particularly powerful diagnostic tool because it allows radiologists to see soft tissues, normally beyond the scope of ordinary X-ray machines. Other branches of sciences use the invention, too: for example it can be used in the non-destructive investigation of the fossilized embryos in dinosaur eggs.

The first CAT-scanning equipment was invented in the late 1960s when experiments by Godfrey Hounsfield, who was based at the EMI Central Research Laboratories in Hayes, Middlesex, enabled the development of a commercially available scanner.[1] A working prototype was used in a hospital as early as October 1971. It is said that EMI were able to fund Hounsfield's research on the back of the Beatles' enormous commercial success.[2] Fittingly, it would appear that this famously idealistic pop group, a product of a complex fifties and sixties counter-culture of which poetry magazines were such a part, had inadvertently funded this remarkable instrument of public health, spreading the message of 'Love, Love, Love' in the most practical of ways.

---

[1] E. C. Beckmann, 'CT Scanning the Early Days', *British Journal of Radiology*, 79 (2006), 5–8.
[2] 'The Beatles greatest gift...is to science', [Anonymous article], Whittington Health [The Whittington Hospital NHS Trust] News Archive, Jan.–Mar. 2005, [www.whittington.nhs.uk|default.asp?c=2804&t=1].

In tribute to that relationship perhaps the metaphor of CAT-scanning might be applied to the study and appreciation of little magazines? This would certainly involve looking in multiple ways at a single magazine in order to render its complexity in a concentrated, composite form. It would allow readers to see more in retrospect than the basic bone structure represented by a magazine's celebrity authors: all a magazine's authors and all its other contributors, be it illustrator or correspondent on the letters page, all its advertisements, its graphic design, its economics and marketing; the CAT-scan would detect the soft tissue, the living organs, of the magazine.

More than this, in the same way that the data underlying individual CAT-scans can be aggregated to identify material patterns across the particular category under study—be it patients with a particular medical condition or the eggs of a particular species of dinosaur—so the CAT-scanning project would go further than commentary on individual magazines. The project would press on to look across many examples—in the reasonable expectation that this would identify common characteristics, building indeed to a kind of aesthetics, perhaps even demonstrating the little magazine, like the novel, like the artist's book, to be an art form in its own right. Such a project would eschew anecdotal approaches to literary history, which so often perpetuate the folklore surrounding this or that author, this or that movement. Rather, it would take a data approach rooted in indexing, pattern recognition and number; it would observe and aggregate 'behavioural traits' rather than amplify myth.

The Fortnightly, That Monthly

One behavioural trait any little magazine must have is what can be termed 'periodicity', the expectation that it will reappear, that it is indeed a 'periodical'. After all, a magazine is not a magazine if not intended to go beyond the first issue (there are one or two interesting exceptions to this, but more about that later).

Periodicity is a key aesthetic cue—indeed for all serial literature not just little magazines. Importantly, little magazines as a population exhibit a particularly large range of responses to periodicity, sometimes slavishly observing rules of frequency, sometimes rebelliously flouting them. This is an indicator of the meta-magazine role that little magazines can have: they are not always simply conveyors of text but can be highly reflexive commentators on the otherwise unacknowledged set of signs that serial publications of all kinds emit.

Periodicity is also one of the aspects of a magazine that can be 'flattened' by traditional forms of literary study and by trends in republication. Following the work of a particular author through the paper trail of first publication it is easy to isolate his or her texts from the environment of their publication. In the 1910s and 1920s misplaced devotion to a single author might miss that one 'magazine' was in fact a newspaper (the *New Age* for instance), another was a monthly (the *English Review*), another was issued only in term-time (many student magazines), and yet another was the erratic creation of an ad-hoc collective (the Vorticists' *Blast*), yet in each of these cases the circumstances of publication, the expectation of audience as a function of publishing frequency, is likely to be different and to have a bearing on either the intention of the author and (more certainly) on the nature of that text's reception. Context may not be *entirely* everything but if audience behaviour counts for anything there is a difference between a poem published in a weekly and an annual, even if the poem is the same poem.

Attuning to this is made more difficult by the reprinting of excerpted materials without proper signalling of the nature of their original publication, and even by the levelling of the library catalogue where all kinds of materials are gathered together, creating the distracting conditions in which frequency, which may be faithfully recorded, is not understood as the para-aesthetic data it in fact is.

Analogous to the 'punctum' described by Roland Barthes as the moment encapsulated in a still photograph as it is taken in by its reader, and so a fundamental building block in an aesthetic theory for photography,[3] precisely when and how a magazine is received is a fundamental aspect of its meaning. Indeed the means of delivery—whether postal or bookshop, whether issued at readings, whether in galleries, pubs, bookshops, seminar rooms, or more imaginative venues—all are part of the richer meaning of the magazine. A magazine is not just a work but a work that is issued in a particular way on a particular occasion and in the expectation of a particular sequence.

Mark Morrisson details one example of this in his discussion of Ford Madox Ford's the *English Review*.[4] As Morrisson explains, this magazine, launched in 1908, adopted a monthly frequency which in so doing asserted genre similarity to the *Mercure de France* and to the confusingly titled *The Fortnightly* which was, apart from a short time at the beginning of its life, also a monthly. For the *English Review* this monthly regularity was integrated with certain format considerations mimicking those of *Mercure de France* and *The Fortnightly*, such as a monthly round-up feature, attuning itself to a particular audience that was not looking for news breaking. (Such structural deployment may actually help to create or at least maintain such an audience.) News, it was felt, could be handled by daily and weekly serial publication of one kind or another, a principle which is essentially in force today even if 'twenty-four hour' news has increased the frequency—so the *English Review* could devote itself to longer pieces that reflected on broader issues. It also published greater literary content that might take a month to absorb in the round.

Sometimes the 'event' of a magazine is synchronized with an external event that is so important it becomes a time marker itself. The self-designation of *Blast*'s second issue, its last, the 'War Number', aligned the magazine to the First World War almost as if subject and time had coalesced. This gave the magazine an importance, perhaps a self-importance that appeared to shadow the appalling rhythm of world events. As Mark

---

[3] Roland Barthes, *Camera Lucida: Reflections on Photography*, trans. Richard Howard (London: Jonathan Cape, 1982), 40–60.

[4] Mark Morrisson, 'The Myth of the Whole and Ford's *English Review*', in *The Public Face of Modernism: Little Magazines, Audiences, and Reception* (Madison: University of Wisconsin Press, 2001), 17–53.

Morrisson also demonstrates, the magazine was privately trying to cover the ineptitude of its irregular publication schedule and was arguably taking advantage of the war as a marketing opportunity.[5]

This meeting between an external event and 'magazine event' is related more broadly to special issues—a translation issue, a green issue, etc.—which similarly assert a coherence and importance to their topic and while appearing to try to move a particular subject up a news agenda may as likely be attaching the magazine to a topic which has more marketing force than the magazine itself.

As the *Blast* instance shows, the reason for this may not be as obvious as it seems. Like shareholders as much as actual consumers being the target of advertising (since advertising alone may bolster confidence in the brand), sometimes the funder of a magazine may be the most significant target for a themed issue, for example when a State-sponsored magazine demonstrates through a themed issue that it is publishing work of a kind fostered by that State. Ian Hamilton Finlay gently mocked such a practice perhaps in his special issue of the 1960s magazine *Poor. Old. Tired. Horse.* (ie P.O.T.H. or POTH) when for its twenty-third outing he ran a whole number devoted to the humble, lisping 'Teapoth'.

The posthumous life of a magazine attracts journalistic interpretations of frequency, especially focused on the ending of a magazine, the final note in the sequence of publication. Here the CAT-scanner needs the literary historian to compensate for distortion from the electromagnetic excitements they may have brought into the lab with them: in the lab it's best to switch the gossipy mobile phone off, or at least switch it to flight-safe.

Wyndham Lewis's *Blast*, like Ford Madox Ford's the *English Review*, may be an example where posthumous fame is built on rather Romantic ideas of the nobleness of failure, and failure is another aspect of periodicity. How a magazine comes to grief can, of course, say a lot about its nature, including its lack of adaptability, but can easily become too significant a part of its history when read back by later commentators with an aggrieved accusation of the vulgar wider public not being ready for the art of the future. Peter Barry's account of the wrestling for power of the Poetry Society during the 1970s, a conflict in which the editorial role of the *Poetry Review* was a key issue, demonstrates how differing models of accessibility and innovation may well be issues at the heart of a magazine's demise, or at least at the heart of radical editorial change.[6] But these models are not straightforward: the simplistic Romantic narrative of positive anarchist collectivists pitted against, say, State control and middlebrow taste is inadequate to the complexity of the world of publishing.

Censorship, too, is a much more complicated affair than at first may appear. When censorship brings a magazine to an untimely close, as with *Klaxon* in Ireland in 1923 (following a favourable review of Joyce's *Ulysses*),[7] libertarian impulses are naturally

---

[5] See Mark Morrisson, 'Marketing British Modernism', in *Public Face of Modernism*, 117–18.

[6] Peter Barry, *The Poetry Wars: British Poetry of the 1970s and the Battle of Earls Court* (Cambridge: Salt Publishing, 2006).

[7] David Miller and Richard Price, *British Poetry Magazines 1914–2000: A History and Bibliography of 'Little Magazines'* (London: British Library, 2006), 27–8.

offended and 'the State' identified as the villain. But the State is far from a unitary body, and just because public taste is short-circuited and second-guessed by the usual forces involved—printer, police, funder, and advertiser—it doesn't mean that a majority of the public wouldn't indeed have acted in the same way given the chance.

Looking across the whole life of a magazine, one tone encoded by erratic periodicity might be a bumbling amateurism hybridized with connoisseurship. For example, the sound and visual poetry magazine *And*, edited by Bob Cobbing and others from 1954, achieved only eleven irregularly spaced issues in its first five decades of life. Was that a testament to do-it-yourself poetics outside commercial considerations, eschewing the building and maintaining of an audience by regular publication, or evidence of a high quality threshold, that Cobbing published only when the work was good enough?

Certainly Cobbing's remarkable achievement with the small press Writers Forum, running parallel with *And* (if *And* could ever have been said to 'run'), gives the lie to inactivity or bumble. Energy, openness, 'driven-ness', would be better nouns for a publishing programme of hundreds of books, amounting to one of the most significant artistic interventions in contemporary poetry in England in the last century. If the CAT-scanner's variables are fixed in a certain way then the role of Writers Forum might be identified as para-periodical in operation so prolific it was and so responsive to topical events—and so keen, too, on periodical-like distribution methods (dating publications by month, and tying publication into regular public workshop schedule).

Across the century there are fascinating examples where periodicity is deliberately activated aesthetically. Under normal bibliographic conventions the books produced by the Imagists shouldn't fall into the magazine category but after the first volume, *Des Imagistes* (1914), the next two asserted that they were 'an annual anthology' (the 1915 and 1916 volumes). This simple apparently utilitarian phrase suggested at least two things—that this was a winnowed collection taking the best from the last year, and there would now be a reasonable expectation for successive annual volumes (as indeed there were, for a short time): this was a discerning movement that was here for the long term. Additionally this attuned the reader to the Imagists as a group operating within a recently established market of serial publication: anthologies of modern poetry. The annual Georgian poetry volumes, despite their mixed posthumous reputation for lukewarm innovation, had demonstrably trail-blazed for the Imagists in genre terms; unlikely as it may seem, they were in one sense the avant-garde's avant-garde.

Activated periodicity could have charm. The last issue of William Nicholson and Robert Graves's *The Owl*, vol. 2 no. 3 issued in November 1923, is marked by a knowing and elegiac change of title, *The Winter Owl*—the time of issue, and the knowledge that it is the last issue, has bubbled over and transformed the magazine's name. This is followed through in artistic direction: gone are the warm soft blush-red colours Nicholson had adopted for previous issues and instead here is something bluer, greyer. Reference to the seasonal captures a traditionalist perhaps pastoral aesthetic. It is a dignified, bittersweet farewell.

One much later magazine provides a final example of self-consciousness in periodicity. Strictly speaking Tom Clark's *Once* only had one issue. *Once* had the subtitle *a one-shot magazine*, and though it was probably issued in 1965 it was undated. After all, why would you date what you knew would be a one-off magazine? But the magazine was in fact resurrected—its next reincarnation was called *Twice*. That only appeared once, and that set the pattern for succeeding issues, though various creative flourishes added some teasing permutations: *Thrice, Thrice and a 1|2, Frice, Vice, Spice, Slice, Ice, Nice, Dice*, and, finally, *Lice*.

SUCCESS!

Little magazines are traditionally associated with ideas of marginality: political radicalism, support for one minority or another, support for the art form of poetry itself (conceived as a Cinderella art), and for various kinds of aesthetic extremes. This is conventionally cross-referenced to other-worldly economics, an idea that little magazines are necessarily non-commercial. The CAT-scan needs to be careful with this approach, indeed needs to put it to the test.

In assessing 'commercial success' it is of course possible to measure longevity and, though more difficult to evidence, circulation. Little magazine accounts, including subscriber lists (whose addresses can be mapped onto class structure maps of the period, if available) are valuable but rare finds in archives and editors are generally reluctant to disclose figures while the magazine is still being published. I suppose that if there is the data then a magazine that lasts for a long time, has a large circulation, and makes a profit, could then be assigned high-scoring values and 'commercial success' confirmed, but the words 'commercial' and 'success' are both fraught. To place this in the relief of a negative example, so-called 'failed' magazines may have a kind of impact not measured by these criteria (Wyndham Lewis's *Blast* is still the subject of wonder, exploration, and debate) and this may include long-term *economic* success for some of the participants.

While there are classic examples of 'successful' magazines that have consistently failed to make artistic impact—the best-selling long-lasting *Poetry Review* (successfully artistically failing for most of its 100 years)—there are others that are not the commercial enterprises they seem. The most notorious example is probably *Encounter*: this ran from 1953 to 1990 with a circulation of what appears to be tens of thousands of readers per issue. So far so good news story: but *Encounter* was secretly part-funded by the Central Intelligence Agency (the CIA) as a means of soft propaganda in the Cold War. This only came to light in 1967. Several authors withdrew their involvement in disgust (W. H. Auden, John Betjeman, Robert Creeley, Ted Hughes, Robert Lowell, and Christopher Middleton). It would appear that *Encounter* was not, after all, a commercial publication; rather, it was practically a product of a planned economy, a sleight-of-hand planned economy, in this respect not so unlike the one its backers were trying to destroy.

Even so, the State/private dichotomy seems inadequate to the fascinating complexity of literary artefacts, perhaps little magazines especially. As far as *Encounter* is concerned, commerce was arguably still at play whether or not it was State-funded because the Cold War was, among many other harder, angrier, deadlier things, in part a commercial conflict about literary and art products, all of which are not just caught in a mercantile mesh but, I would argue, are part of its fabric. Is 'commercial' a helpful word in a suffusedly material world? The material nature of a magazine CAT-scan does not produce the reductive results a 'follow the money' approach might suggest it would: rather it reveals layers of association between aesthetics, individual participants, and institutions of various kinds.

Poor. Old. Tired. Horse., Ian Hamilton Finlay's magazine of the 1960s, was commercial enough to survive five years of regular publication until Finlay decided to end its run. For most of its life it didn't send out the conventional cues of 'success': for example, although Finlay's sister operation, the Wild Hawthorn Press, produced beautifully realized books with high production values, *Poor. Old. Tired. Horse.* has a quaint, typewritten quality to many of its issues; many were produced on mimeo stencil. Mercantile ambition doesn't seem to be the right framework through which to view the magazine. However, as a means by which Finlay began to position himself (on paper) alongside the American avant-garde poetry milieu he published and then as a means, gradually, to position himself within the visual arts economy, it can indeed be seen as a commercial success. It is a classic example of how a little magazine, however well it does outwardly, can operate very effectively as a networking node, establishing a nub of contact between the editor and his or her contributors, a considerable measure of success which would not be obvious by looking at the magazine through the single dimensions of longevity or circulation (interesting though these elements also are).

Rather, the CAT-scan needs to refocus, to see more clearly, what the nature of funding for a particular magazine was—even photocopied, stapled, magazines—and how this may have contributed to the identity of the magazine itself—and, importantly, to the measurable success of its editors and contributors after the demise of the magazine or of their involvement in it: the little magazine is probably not just a node in a network but the creator of networks that have a much longer life beyond the magazine itself.

If the theoretical CAT-scan will be lucky to detect magazine archives with accounts it might glean useful references to costs and funding from editor and contributor correspondence held in various collections here and abroad; memoirs are risky because of hindsight but need to be looked at; oral history is another way of getting closer to the money trail. Contextual information can be gathered from any advertisements in the magazine—if the magazine doesn't have any advertisements or fliers then of course someone or something else was funding it, and that is part of what the magazine is: the optimum CAT-scan will detect that funder.

From the 1960s, a magazine of any longevity was often funded by an Arts Council or regional arts association and their broadly regional or culturally nationalist agenda is usually reflected in content: *Chapman* (1970–), for example, funded by the Scottish Arts Council, or *South West Review* (1977–85) published by South West Arts. However, it would be a mistake to see the productions as always social realist regional equivalents of tractor music—the CAT-scan would be able to collect content data and begin to say more about that hypothesis. Educational institutions (a university or university department or university society) appear to be significant funders too. *Poetry & Audience* was funded by the University of Leeds's Student Union from its first issue in 1954. The CAT-scan would see if various kinds of funding association with the university (central official funding, student union, English department, informal student group, for example) influenced, say, the level of didacticism in their texts, the number of translations, adherence to or deviance from curriculum, and other aspects which might reasonably be associated with university life. Once measures were established comparative studies could begin their work to see pattern and pattern difference.

Looking at the wider picture, one hypothesis might be that university-based magazines compete with State-funded territory magazines by asserting either depoliticized texts (they think), or gendered and internationalist political concerns which lack self-consciousness about home regionality and home nationality, and vice versa. An empirical model might test such a research question.

The CAT-scan would triangulate more detailed measures of patronage by seeing allegiances between editors and contributors built up in and expressed through magazines continued in the later careers of these participants, be it within the world of newspaper and broadcast literary journalism, the prize-judging circuit, the prestige anthology, the university department, and so on. Little magazines that 'failed' to the casual eye may have been very successful in creating other kinds of value for their participants with that value continuing to be realized many years after the demise of the magazine. Because a series of artistic alliances that are maintained through the years is a major part of what an intellectual culture is, little magazines are worth testing as an early expression of this culture or set of interlocking cultures and how friendship is expressed and mobilized within literary networks. Where the university is involved, it may also be a way of seeing patterns of behaviour beneath aesthetic differences which exist between and within 'mainstream' and 'avant-garde' forms of poetry, differences which the data already suggest are a playing-out of the consequences of the massive over-representation of Oxford and Cambridge agency: in the geographical index of *British Poetry Magazines 1914–2000*, apart from the special case of London, which far exceeds all locations, no other cities beat the productivity of Oxford (83 different titles) and Cambridge (71) in this period; the few that come close are university cities (Dublin, 61; Edinburgh, 53).[8] Poetry 'differences' in this light come over more as a series of high-end turf wars whose rarefied environment may look like intellectual and aesthetic debates—and of course are, too—but whose result is the perpetuation of widespread adherence to whatever rules are articulated, distributed, and controlled—metaphorically speaking, of course—by a tiny number of eminent gangster 'families' whose apparent differences give the false appearance of functional diversity in the poetry system.

---

[8] Miller and Price, *British Poetry Magazines 1914–2000*, 356–63.

Controls

The CAT-scan needs to look at other kinds of magazine to understand the nature of its subject. In the language of the laboratory, it needs a 'control'.

The *Poetry Review* is ideal for this because it has many of the attributes little magazines would be shy to claim, but which are key to *Poetry Review*'s self-image: popularity, longevity, and the ability (or desire) to represent the whole of the UK. World significance and intellectual authority are also fundamental, though admittedly some little magazines might claim these!

Encapsulating its establishment credentials in recent years *Poetry Review* has begun to call itself the poetry magazine 'of record', a phrase which seems to have jumped the species barrier since it is normally reserved for newspapers—*The Times* was for many years regarded as the newspaper of record, probably because of its then serious tone, its apparently broad coverage, its relatively large and widespread circulation, its London location, and even its reporting of the royal calendar.

Poetry Review uses some of these attributes for a similar claim but it also mobilizes the apparent authority of others—through the woven web of citation—to do so. In the words of recent former editor Fiona Sampson: '*Poetry Review* is a world-class publication and Britain's longest-running and most prestigious poetry magazine. Started in 1911, it continues to be "the magazine of record" (Michael Schmidt in *The Guardian*) and as well as being the UK's bestselling poetry magazine, is hailed by Andrew Motion as "required reading".'[9]

In fact, although the act of citation can seem, as it were, to guarantee the guarantee, Sampson is mistaken in seeing Michael Schmidt as endorsing *Poetry Review* in the quoted article. He says exactly the opposite: '*Poetry Review* [...] as the organ of the Poetry Society might be thought (erroneously, it seems to me) to have a duty to be a magazine of record.'[10] It is also clear that Schmidt's indefinite article, '*a* magazine'—which allows plurality even while entertaining authority—has become a definite article in Sampson's retelling. *Poetry Review* might have been one among many by Schmidt but in Sampson's telling it is now self-special, the One and Only.

A CAT-scan would go further than face value, however. A study of the authors *Poetry Review* has featured and reviewed in the last ten years, say, cross-checked against a range of other magazines operating in the same period would test the face-value veracity of its claim. A survey of book publication, say, publisher by publisher, would map particular authors that appear in *Poetry Review* to particular presses and their editors, which in turn could be analysed for company size, geographical location, and column-inch coverage in the general print media (there is a dilemma about the direction of cause

---

[9] Fiona Sampson, 'Press Release: *Poetry Review* Editor Fiona Sampson encourages us to explore poetries we don't yet know in Britain' [Autumn 2007].

[10] *The Guardian*, Saturday, 15 July 2006; electronic version at [http://www.guardian.co.uk/books/2006/jul/15/featuresreviews.guardianreview1].

and effect here, so such a survey would have to be handled carefully). Because poetry is, of course, a formal art, you could also map formal analytics of poems that appear in the different magazines, and you could do the same using subject descriptors: is there a correlation between certain presses, print media coverage, and the frequency of their authors' publication in *Poetry Review*, as opposed to the broader set of other poetry magazines, and, if so, how does that affect the meaning of that authoritative-sounding word 'record'? (There is an innate contradiction in the claim, between representation or witness and quality, which a CAT-scan would theoretically tease out.) Such an empirical account would not prevent more detailed, nuanced work; it would inform the parameters of later qualitative discussion. Without an empirical underpinning, commentary in this area should find it hard to escape the claim of bias, unconscious or otherwise.

There are wider-ranging comparisons to be made quantitatively. If the posthumous reputation of a single magazine can affect true understanding of it, this can also be the case when particular 'golden ages' (arguably, the British Poetry Revival of the 1960s and 1970s) and apparent 'low points' (conventionally, the 1940s) are discussed, or else when concepts of nationality are brought up, for instance the alleged insularity of the English. Devising empirical ways of testing legends and their varied lives (since legends do wax and wane), can help to understand not only the literary infrastructure of the day but also the extent to which anecdotal observations later become so-called accepted fact. The CAT-scan would be a means of testing today's assumptions, of testing today's claim to authority.

In the case of the British Poetry Revival, the phrase used to describe an apparent surge in poetry experimentation and a concomitant increase in poetry magazines in the 1960s and 1970s, it is worth stating that there is quantifiable evidence for the scale of this: from 1963 to 1970 tens of new magazines were beginning each year (not hundreds, not thousands, as you might have thought, but certainly a sizeable shift from previous decades).[11] However, productivity was not limited to the long 1960s. Poetry publication again revived in the late 1970s and 1980s—at least thirty new titles appeared in most of the years in the period 1976–2000.[12] The CAT-scan doesn't worry that no romantic phrase for this period has appeared to give it the status of the British Poetry Revival; it just notes the facts.

Other myths can be exposed. Did UK post-war interest in American contemporary poetry really begin as late as the 1960s? (*The Poet*, edited by W. Price Turner from 1952 to 1956, and publishing Cid Corman, Robert Creeley, and William Carlos Williams, suggests not). Is the UK really insular? In the period 1914–2000 the presence of nearly one hundred poetry magazines with a significant translation mission suggests the case is far from proven.[13] The CAT-scan project should also be an international one, if only to reality-check national assumptions.

---

[11] Miller and Price, *British Poetry Magazines 1914–2000*, 122.
[12] Miller and Price, *British Poetry Magazines 1914–2000*, 216.
[13] Miller and Price, *British Poetry Magazines 1914–2000*, 367.

Literary criticism tends to deal with individuals—either famous individuals or those the critic argues should be famous. Book history tends to deal with presses, distribution, and marketing which work on impressive but conventional business models, or—for publishing in the literary arena—are associated with the famous individuals beloved of literary academics. This is a form of biography-led storytelling which has its place but sometimes confuses narrative with wider understanding. Today, however, there is no reason why the fantastic aggregating energies released by the inspired use of modern technology should not be applied to the history of literature. The vibrant long tail of little magazine (and small press) publication would be a very good place to start: an overarching project is yet to be made that links book history and literary criticism via such empirical analysis, interrogating at survey level what is known about these publications and the literary infrastructure in which they exist. The first steps towards a theory for computed axial tomography for little magazines have been made in the last twenty years or so within little magazine research, with some crucial isolated examples going back much further (examples of which are given in the Select Bibliography), but the next task is to begin to build some CAT-scan prototypes.

To Shake the Torpid Pool[14]

In the meantime, here is a basic range-finding exercise, an attempt to look at the relationship between little magazines and small press pamphlets, scanning down the century in the hope that patterns might emerge that could be tested in more detail at a later time. Here are ten pamphlets from across the last century: Edward Thomas, *Six Poems* [1916]; W. H. Auden, *Poems* (1928); Dylan Thomas, *18 Poems* (1934); Philip Larkin, *The North Ship* (1945); Roy Fisher, *City* (1961); Ian Hamilton Finlay, *Glasgow Beasts...* (1961); Bob Cobbing, *Six Sound Poems* (1968); J. H. Prynne, *Fire Lizard* (1970); Denise Riley, *Marxism for Infants* (1977); and Kathleen Jamie, *Black Spiders* (1982). I have chosen them to represent different kinds of poetry, different kinds of poets, and different communities of publication. Being only ten they can hardly be truly representative, but reflecting on them can form the basis of further more empirical investigation.

Friends

Almost all of these publications are either self-publication or publication by a friend. The two that appear to be published by someone else—Finlay's *Glasgow Beasts* (The Wild Hawthorn Press) and Bob Cobbing's *Six Sound Poems* (Writers Forum)—were in

---

[14] The title is taken from W. H. Auden's 'II' ('I chose this lean country'), *Poems* ([London:] SHS, 1928), 11.

fact self-published, since the presses concerned were owned by the authors and co-run with friends. Friends of the poet in question published five of the pamphlets. In Edward Thomas's case, the artist-publisher James Guthrie; Auden is published by Stephen Spender; Roy Fisher by Michael Shayer and Gael Turnbull (as Migrant Press); Prynne by friends Barry MacSweeney and Elaine Randell (as Blacksuede Boot Press); and Denise Riley by her friend Wendy Mulford (as Street Editions).

Two authors appear neither to be self-published nor published by friends—Philip Larkin and Kathleen Jamie. It is interesting that Larkin and Jamie, characterized today as more mainstream poets, appear to have begun their publication history without an obvious help from any old boy or new girl network. In a romantic history of the avant-garde this is counter-intuitive—perhaps there is an expectation of the little press world bravely operating outside the philosophy of 'it's not what you know but who you know'. That may be a serious misunderstanding of the poetry infrastructure, little press or mainstream. *Who you know* in the little magazine world is likely to be very significant for initial and later publication, and for whether your work is reviewed or undergoes critical study.

The more empirical survey work to test and quantify this would take in measures of association that went beyond the printed page, including, as it were, body presence solidarity: for example, the hosting of events to promote friends, those attending those such events, and so on. Class, gender, and educational affiliation might also help to understand better the history of little magazines. It's not a surprise that the female poets on this list of pamphlets emerge only later on in the century, but the role women had as editors in little magazines within modernism—Dora Marsden, Harriet Monroe—and as poets themselves—H.D., Mina Loy—is not reflected in such a selection: does this mean that men in this period simply did not reciprocate publishing favours as they clearly did man to man?

A key set of questions revolves around the issue of acts of friendship. How does little magazine publication, and little press publication, itself constitute an initiating act of friendship, that then has active power later on in the participants' lives?

The spectrum of friendship relationships is a key and under-researched concept in little press publishing even though it comes up incidentally again and again in critical studies. The circles of friendship around, say, Ezra Pound or Ford Madox Ford; the friendship within the modern Scottish renaissance—Catherine Carswell, Lewis Grassic Gibbon, Edwin Muir, Hugh MacDiarmid, and Neil Gunn; the Bloomsbury group, MacSpaunday, and so on. All work through complex friendship processes that have to varying degrees been studied case by case but not, I think, tested empirically or properly theorized.

I'd suggest that little magazines and little presses initiate, develop, and continue lasting or critical acts of friendship. However, did such friendships work within existing power structures, with the aim of advancement and incorporation, or offer a counter to them, with the aim of offering aesthetic and even political alternatives? Did they augment and maintain the pre-eminent cultural capital of high-brand institutions like Oxford or Cambridge, the geographical location of London and the South East as 'the centre', and the status of the male as the arbiter of taste? Or could magazines and presses offer opportunities to those outside those zones of power?

One aspect of such a social sciences approach is to go beyond the life of a press or magazine, to track the lives of a magazine's contributors after the publication has seemed to 'fail'. Such tracking would follow authors and editors into other publishing realms—review journalism, the broadcast media, more capitalized presses, and so on. Furthermore, scrutiny would extend to the judges and the judged in literary competitions, grants, and to appointments at universities and the arts, and a network of behaviour mapped.

The controls spoken of earlier would be needed here: in mainstream publishing, 'the old boy network' is friendship plus the power to appoint, to deploy a marketing budget. Both little press and mainstream publishing can quietly infer an objectivity of standards neither can truthfully meet because microscoping down to a concept of standards in so much moot poetry is a category error. Nor, within certain limits, should any press feel the need to be objective. Friendship in little or large presses is an enabler of publication which, to the outside world at the time, may be unnoticed and so appear, outside a circle of friends, to be more disinterested than it is. Friendship is privately inscribed in the public act of publication: 'between you and me, you are my friend because-and-*as-demonstrated by* the fact that I am willing to make you and your works better known by publishing them'. Perhaps only when friendship itself can be mobilized as a positive—'a collaboration', 'a school', 'a movement'—does it announce itself more publicly.

It's important to avoid a view of friendship as a negative force in the arts. The public good of private friendship underwrites artistic and intellectual community. Finding a neutral vocabulary that avoids both positive and negative terms might be helpful, perhaps using the concept of an index of association. In the little magazine world analysing a data set containing, for example, editor, publisher, advertiser, and contributor information to establish the relationship between these variables would be one way of understanding its nature, with particular rewards when extended to wider access media.

Since the poet as editor is such a common element in both the little press and the little magazine world it is already safe, if not quite redundant, to say that this is a key node of reciprocation.

The Campus Magazine

Another pattern that is obvious in the ten pamphlets, and which, as we've seen, correlates with little magazines too, is the massive over-representation of Oxford and Cambridge in publication. Of the ten poets, at least half are well known as having an Oxbridge education. At least four of the ten publishers are Oxbridge-educated. Some of the functions that little magazines serve come into play earlier for these exclusive university attenders, with networks being kick-started through the school magazine. It is safe to say that the schools concerned would be overwhelmingly private schools. There is also the anomalous position of the student magazine or newspaper, for example Oxford's *The Cherwell* and *Isis*. These types of publication are not generally classified as little magazines but they are probably significant within the poetry infrastructure—it's no surprise that one of Larkin's poems in *The North Ship*, 'This was your place of birth', was published in *The Cherwell*.

This is an opportune moment to revisit the issue of university publication in more detail, using, as before, the place of publication logged by the *British Poetry Magazines 1914-2000* survey.[15] In the period 1914-39, the megalopolis of London dominates with about half the new titles in our survey (117 of 236). Next Dublin is, if anything, slightly more productive than either Oxford or Cambridge, accounting for just over 7 per cent of new titles in our survey, while Oxford and Cambridge account for just less than 6 per cent (since we are now looking at very small numbers the difference is probably not significant). The period 1914-39 is of course a huge swathe of history and more needs to be done to break this down to clarify better publication patterns. In terms of new titles the 1940s were proportionally quiet for Oxbridge, but the 1950s are more active.

That decade saw the average rate of new titles per year increase in these university towns at a time when little magazines overall were being produced less across the country. Quite a few other university towns—Belfast, Hull, Newcastle upon Tyne, Manchester, Liverpool, and Edinburgh—produced more new titles per year than they had in the previous decade. This seems to confirm that the 1950s was a time of cultural rebuilding in poetry, setting the literary foundations that underwrite the 1960s. It's no great shock that the universities were part of this, but it is interesting to see circumstantial evidence of it at least in the pattern of little magazine publication. The overall *decline* in the 1950s of the little magazine in terms of *number* (from 152 in the 1940s to 125 in the 1950s) might be better considered as the unsustainability of so many magazines outside a war context (the fraught but substantial leisure time for the military and for those on the home front was particularly suited to the lo-fi form of print). The fifties can be seen as a time when the UK saw a clarifying and founding of poetry networks by those who had been children or young adults during the war, and who were now taking advantage of wider access to university education in an environment of cultural as well as physical rebuilding.

As it happens, at least three little magazines from the 1950s relate in this way to the pamphlets in the list. Bob Cobbing's magazine *And* began in the 1950s. Although it started as the magazine of a north London group called Arts Together it soon became a Writers Forum title, so there is a direct link between the magazine, the press, and the pamphlet portfolio *Six Sound Poems* published in 1968. Cobbing's background however was not university education: he was grammar school taught, then went on to teacher-training college; there is also his Dissenting and Quaker background to think of as models of support and artistic procedure: the workshop, say, as a secular

---

[15] Miller and Price, *British Poetry Magazines 1914-2000*, 356-63.

Quaker meeting.[16] With this in mind—and thinking of similar non-establishment backgrounds in writers associated with London groupings—some of the apparent animosity between London and Cambridge 'schools' of poetry can perhaps be put down to differences in learnt formal approaches to the making, workshopping, and means of dissemination of poetry but also to rivalry between modes of education, at times, as with genteel-seeming Oxford versus Cambridge debates, even a turf war over educational hegemony. From the outside, however, the differentiation has a good cop/bad cop effect: both groups of poets benefit from the interest their apparent conflict generates and a UK perspective is concentrated within the London-Cambridge nexus to the exclusion of the overwhelming majority of the country.

Roy Fisher's *City* emerged from Migrant Press, the imprint of two men who had known each other since they were schoolchild boarders at a Cambridge private school in the 1940s.[17] Michael Shayer and Gael Turnbull set up the magazine *Migrant* in the 1950s, moving into relatively regular pamphlet publication once they closed the magazine in September 1960. Finlay's Wild Hawthorn Press was also directly influenced by Migrant, magazine and press, and may have been brought into being directly because of it. For Finlay, the conventional publishing model of progression from little magazine to small press was reversed: only after Wild Hawthorn Press had been established did he set up, in 1962, the classic little magazine *Poor. Old. Tired. Horse*. This may have been because Wild Hawthorn was largely a means of self-publication, whereas *Poor. Old. Tired. Horse.* (with a little help from Gael Turnbull's address book) was a way of continuing and radically widening the poetry network Turnbull and Shayer had built around and through *Migrant*. Unlike the Migrant publishers, Finlay did not have a university education, never mind a Cambridge one. Fisher's education, at Birmingham University, may also mark a post-war difference in relative accessibility.

Finally there is J. H. Prynne's *Fire Lizard,* published by Barry MacSweeney and Elaine Randell under their Blacksuede Boot Press imprint. Again this can be seen, admittedly very broadly, as a consequence of a chain of events set up in the 1950s by the emergent little magazine and little press infrastructure: Prynne was the final editor of the Cambridge magazine *Prospect*, set up in 1959 by Elaine Feinstein and concluding in 1964. Roger Banister and Peter Redgrove's *Delta* was also a force in Cambridge in the 1950s and 1960s. Later Prynne went on to co-edit series 3 of the magazine *English Intelligencer* in 1968. Randell, while she was co-running the Blacksuede Boot Press, was also editing the magazine *Amazing Grace*. It's evident, too, that Cambridge University is, if not a protagonist in these publications, an enabling, or provoking, environment. There appears to be a slight quantitative difference, too—in the 1950s Cambridge produced more new little magazines per year than any other location except London—on average, one new little magazine per year. This rate was sustained in the period 1960–75 (though Oxford

---

[16] I am grateful to Steve Willey, Queen Mary University Collaborative PhD student at the British Library, for this information about Cobbing's background.

[17] Information in this paragraph concerning Migrant is taken from Richard Price, 'Migrant the Magnificent', 2009, [www.hydrohotel.net\EssaysMigrant1.htm].

began to publish more) and in arguably the key period 1966–72 was higher. When that is mapped on to the appearance of presses that publish Cambridge-associated poets—Andrew Crozier's Ferry Press and John Riley's Grosseteste Review—the suggestion is that there is something like a critical mass both being represented and stoked. More quantitative information—a survey of little presses, for example—would help build up a better data set to put the correlation in perspective.

Generators

In the meantime here is a simple comparison of the association between little magazines and presses between two fascinating periods: the classic modernist period of 1914 to 1939, and modernism refigured in the period 1960–75. These time periods are of a different duration, which make comparisons difficult—they are, after all, constructed using post-hoc notions of modernism and its rebirth—so analysis needs to proceed with caution.

In the first period there were some 236 new magazines, on average about 9 new titles per year. Of the 236 new magazines approximately 23 had an associated book imprint: publishing single author collections, anthologies, or in some cases local history: a book press to new magazine ratio of just under 1:10. For every ten new magazines there was a book imprint associated with one of them.

In the second period, 1960–75, there were 539 new magazines in our survey (on average about 34 new titles per year). Of these 539 new magazines 141 had an associated book imprint, so a book press to new magazines ratio of about 1:4. For every four magazines there was a book press associated with one of them. In other words, not only were there quite simply many more little magazines per year in the 1960s and first half of the 1970s, a little magazine was much more likely to have a little press associated with it as well.

This may go to the heart of a problem of communication in the 1960s and 1970s. Such poetry fecundity would have posed difficulties within a centralized and near-unitary media that had not necessarily moved in the same direction as the little press infrastructure. Even if sympathetic, the established reviewing and publishing organs would have found it physically impossible to accommodate such prodigious diversity. The classic modernist period in the UK, often seen as a model and inspiration for the British Poetry Revival, worked in a quite different way. Comparatively few magazines, comparatively few presses, meant, arguably, a comparative ease of transmission into the reviewing press and beyond. The name of Eliot's journal, *The Criterion*, is a clue to the assumption of authority in the earlier period, a hierarchy-accepting mantle that would be much more problematic for later Revival magazines (even if, among the 'Cambridge' poets, they would passively or actively take advantage of the immense educational authority of their 'brand', there would be no imaginative leap in naming, of the kind enacted by the Imagists or Objectivists, only a conservative sheltering beneath the long-established and perhaps rather threadbare university colours of the Cambridge umbrella, a bedraggglement of poetic ambition).

The electric power industry furnishes, hopefully, a useful analogy here. At the moment a very small number of very large power generators produce power distributed through the National Grid. It is possible now for a small number of small power generators to localize energy production by solar power and wind-generation on domestic properties and even to feed that into the National Grid. However, even hundreds of thousands or millions of such small-scale producers would fail to make their *political* presence felt on the National Grid as a large community of small-scale producers, unless they organized collectively. At least the product, electricity, is already in a communicable form that the National Grid immediately 'understands'. The same could not be said for the different varieties of little press poetry, especially with that community's paucity of reviewing and contextual articles, as demonstrated in Peter Barry's account of the period in the 1970s when the *Poetry Review* was in the control of experimental poets and was particularly uncommunicative about the work it was publishing.[18] The history of twentieth-century little presses points to the widespread benefits of constructive anarchy at numerous local levels, and the limits of the influence such constructive anarchy may achieve. Indeed the establishment in the late 1960s of the Association of Little Presses, by Bob Cobbing among others, was a recognition of this though the CAT-scan would establish if ALP was a way into a more powerful transmitting infrastructure or simply the construction of a parallel but less effective network instead.

Cross-Under

Finally, some of the pamphlets suggest format crossover with little magazines. *Fire Lizard*, *Six Sound Poems*, and *City*, all make a similar statement about the potential of a small press book to be a time-bound event closer to periodical than book publication. Prynne's *Fire Lizard* declares the occasion of its publication, the colophon stating that it is 'written in Cambridge, New Year's Day 1970'. Perhaps the presentation copy dedicated to Charles Olson, lodged now in the Ed Dorn archive at the University of Connecticut, was an alternative Christmas card: 'For Charles, across the water, with love, New Year's Day 1970, Jeremy'.

Both Fisher's and Cobbing's work are dated not just with a particular day but with a month: May 1961 says the title page of *City*, September 1968 says the colophon of *Six Sound Poems*. This indicates that Migrant Press and Writers Forum, even when they didn't specifically mention a periodical-like date on their publications (they often did), were functioning as somewhere between a little magazine and a book publisher; they were probably issuing books regularly to a list of subscribers. Their slim lightweight

---

[18] Barry, *The Poetry Wars*, 172.

nature also made them more postable and again this is a characteristic of magazine culture. Writers Forum's frequently meeting workshop was a further means by which its little press books were sold as the occasion for launches of new work; such regularity strengthened the sense of each Writers Forum publication being an instalment in an open-ended series of booklets.

In short this simple, range-finding CAT-scan, suggests that little presses and little magazines in the British Poetry Revival period didn't just have a symbiosis but, in some special cases, they were practically the same thing.

Select Bibliography

Barry, Peter, *The Poetry Wars: British Poetry of the 1970s and the Battle of Earls Court* (Cambridge: Salt Publishing, 2006).

Barthes, Roland, *Camera Lucida: Reflections on Photograph*, trans. Richard Howard (London: Jonathan Cape, 1982).

Beckmann, E. C., 'CT Scanning the Early Days', *British Journal of Radiology*, 79 (2006), 5–8.

Brooker, Peter, and Thacker, Andrew (eds.), *The Oxford Critical and Cultural History of Modernist Magazines*, i. *Britain and Ireland 1880–1955* (Oxford: Oxford University Press, 2009).

Clyde, Tom, *Irish Literary Magazines: An Outline and Descriptive Bibliography* (Dublin: Irish Academic Press, 2003).

Görtschacher, Wolfgang, *Little Magazine Profiles: The Little Magazines in Great Britain, 1939–1993* (Salzburg: University of Salzburg, 1993).

Hoffman, Frederick J., Allen, Charles, and Ulrich, Carolun F., *The Little Magazine: A History and Bibliography* (2nd edn., Princeton: Princeton University Press, 1947).

Miller, David, and Price, Richard, *British Poetry Magazines 1914–2000* (London: British Library, 2006).

Morrisson, Mark, *The Public Face of Modernism: Little Magazines, Audiences, and Reception* (Madison: University of Wisconsin Press, 2001).

Sullivan, Alvin (ed.), *British Literary Magazines: The Modern Age, 1914–1984* (London: Greenwood, 1986).

CHAPTER 10

BOOKS AND THE MARKET: TRADE PUBLISHERS, STATE SUBSIDIES, AND SMALL PRESSES

MATTHEW SPERLING

I

ACCORDING to poet, book-dealer, and publisher Peter Riley, the distinction between small presses and others 'becomes illusory' when it comes to poetry, since 'so-called big publishers produce poetry books in very small editions, sometimes below 1000', and 'the only really commercial poetry publishing in this country concerns poets laureate, Nobel prize winners, and some popular entertainers'.[1] Since the 1970s, the pressures of conglomeration and its required economies of scale have made most poetry uneconomical for large publishing houses, except as a nearly loss-leading 'prestige indicator'. In the last four decades, the poetry lists cut by large houses include those of Secker and Warburg, Routledge and Kegan Paul, Hutchinson, Chatto and Windus, and the publisher of this essay, Oxford University Press. All contemporary poetry is self-evidently marginal in culture and society, and all poetry publishing is relatively small-scale: 'a matter', as Blake

---

[1] Peter Riley, 'Small Press Poetry Catalogue 1', cited in Ken Edwards, 'UK Small Press Publishing since 1960: The Transatlantic Axis' (1996), archived online at [http://epc.buffalo.edu/authors/edwards/edwards_press.html] (para 2).

Morrison says, 'of the small-time entrepreneurs, minuscule sales, and (at best) miniature profit margins of published verse'.[2] From the readers' point of view, contemporary poetry is the interest of a minority: an Arts Council report into 'the poetry market' at the end of the twentieth century found that of the nearly two million poetry books bought in a calendar year—itself a small fraction of total book sales—contemporary poetry made up only 3 per cent of them, with 90 per cent of that coming from one imprint, and 67 per cent from one author.[3]

Except for Seamus Heaney, then, all are small in the Lilliput of contemporary poetry publishing. But there are still distinctive features of the 'small press' which differentiate it from either a trade publisher's imprint with a poetry list, such as Picador, Jonathan Cape, or Faber and Faber, or a mid-size independent publisher of poetry established on a business footing, often with the support of State subsidy, such as Anvil, Bloodaxe, Carcanet, or Salt. Nigel Wheale, the poet and scholar behind the small press Infernal Methods, named some of these features in 1992:

> A small press is one, or rarely more than two individuals who, usually in their spare time and at their own expense, write or edit poetry, print and bind it more or less competently, and circulate it, almost invariably at a loss, or at best only barely covering their costs. [...] Print-runs for small-press editions are generally from two hundred to five hundred copies, and these are usually distributed by the publisher direct to readers, with often a fair proportion of the edition or magazine remaining behind in the attic/cellar.[4]

For many small presses, these conditions remain largely unchanged today, but behind Wheale's plain-dealing description there lies a hinterland of personal and cultural histories, political and aesthetic commitments, which motivate and shape small-press activities.

The story of Andrea Brady and Keston Sutherland's Barque Press is typical of many of the conditions of recent small-press activity. Barque is now a strongly established part of the UK network of small presses publishing avant-garde writing, though Brady and Sutherland started the press in 1995 while undergraduates at Cambridge (Brady as a junior-year-abroad student from Columbia University). Using borrowed resources, they embarked on the press with 'no plan other than poetic excitement', as Brady recalls:[5]

> Our first publication, embarrassingly enough, was called *20 Poems*, and it was a selection of Keston's and my poetry, the title a reference (roughly) to our ages. Jeremy

---

[2] Blake Morrison, 'Poetry and the Poetry Business', *Granta* 4: Beyond the Crisis (Spring 1981), archived online at [http://www.granta.com/Magazine/4/Poetry-and-The-Poetry-Business] (para. 5).

[3] Ann Bridgwood and John Hampson, *Rhyme and Reason: Developing Contemporary Poetry* (London: Arts Council of England, 2000).

[4] Nigel Wheale, 'Uttering Poetry: Small-Press Publication', in Denise Riley (ed.), *Poets on Writing: Britain, 1970–1991* (London: Macmillan, 1992), 9–20 (9).

[5] Andrea Brady, email to the author, 5 May 2011; all subsequent unattributed words of Brady's come from the same source.

Prynne photocopied the inside pages for us, as he did for all our first books, late at night in the Caius College library. He was extremely fastidious about aligning the pages and cleaning the duplicator screen. We then collated by hand and stapled the book using a long-armed stapler borrowed from Robinson College library. The name was my idea—I suggested it in the computer room when we were laying out *20 Poems*. It was meant to be a temporary measure and Keston has never really liked it, I think, but it's too late to change it. It was supposed to play on the bark being worse than the bite, but also the sense of a small and imperilled craft and yet a childish exploratory device—like Rimbaud's drunken boat. Setting out onto a stormy sea without much sense of being seaworthy.

While Brady and Sutherland's circumstances changed—finishing their degrees in Britain and the US, returning to Cambridge for graduate study, relocating for academic posts in London and Sussex respectively—Barque's commitment to publishing new work continued at a steady rate. The press has now issued more than sixty books, ranging from writers younger than Brady and Sutherland, to new work by writers long associated with 'Cambridge poetry' such as Andrew Duncan, John Wilkinson, and J. H. Prynne, including *Triodes* (1999), *To Pollen* (2006), and *Sub Songs* (2010), the last in a remarkable oversize format, the size of an AA Road Atlas, with 17-pt text designed by Prynne's daughter, who is a typesetter.

In publishing Prynne and having him help produce its first books, Barque connects to a continuous history of small-press operations going back to the 1960s. Before that, poetry had a much greater presence within commercial publishing houses—in 1935 poetry was the sixth largest category in total book sales[6] —but publishing was then still largely a 'gentleman's profession', and poetry books were often not expected to make a profit. Small-press publishing was largely a matter of 'private presses' and luxury editions, in the tradition of William Morris's Kelmscott Press, or the Cuala Press run by W. B. Yeats's sisters Elizabeth and Lily. The emphasis was on high-grade materials, craft values, and limited editions, often with a distinctly fetishistic attitude towards the artisanal qualities of the artefact, wickedly caught in Flann O'Brien's parody:

> You know the limited edition ramp. If you write very obscure verse (and why shouldn't you, pray?) for which there is little or no market, you pretend that there is an enormous demand, and that the stuff has to be rationed. Only 300 copies will ever be printed, you say, and then the type will be broken up for ever. Let the connoisseurs and the bibliophiles savage each other for the honour and glory of snatching a copy. Positively no reprint. Reproduction in whole or in part forbidden. Three hundred copies of which this is Number 4312. Hand-monkeyed oklamon paper, indigo boards in interpulped squirrel-toe, not to mention twelve-point Campile Perpetua cast specially for the occasion.[7]

---

[6] Cited in Morrison, 'Poetry and the Poetry Business', para. 9.
[7] Flann O'Brien (Myles na Gopaleen), *The Best of Myles*, ed. Kevin O'Nolan (London: MacGibbon and Kee, 1968), 228.

This 'limited edition ramp', in the spirit of Morris's medievalizing socialism, effectively mimics a pre-capitalistic economy, producing luxury goods in limited quantities for elite consumption. It continues in the present day in many forms, with a poetry publisher such as Enitharmon, for instance, offering signed limited editions alongside their regular hardback and paperback range. As well as buying Paul Muldoon's *Plan B* in a £15 hardback, the 2011 Enitharmon catalogue offers the chance to buy it in a £125 signed limited edition of 150, 'bound in Dubletta rust-coloured cloth and housed in a cloth-bound slipcase'. The trade in limited editions also continues in the genre of the artist's book, of which the works produced by Ronald King's Circle Press are the foremost British examples to feature poetry—collaborating authors have included Roy Fisher, Penelope Shuttle, Richard Price, and George Szirtes.[8]

From the 1960s things were transformed by what Ken Edwards of Reality Street Editions calls 'the burgeoning of a self-help publishing movement'[9] which meant that an avant-garde writer such as Prynne could avoid the commercial publishing houses to issue works quickly and cheaply from poet-run imprints such as Andrew Crozier's Ferry Press, which published *Aristeas* (1968) in an edition of 526, or Iain Sinclair's Albion Village Press, which published *A Night Square* (1973) in an edition of 200. The revolution in small-press publishing is commonly attributed to the expansion of higher education provided for by the post-war settlement, and the technological advances, such as the mimeograph machine and offset lithography, that enabled cheap and easy modes of reproduction—what Wheale calls 'the complex history of changing relations between educational provision and attainment, technological possibilities, and poetic enthusiasm'.[10] In a US context, the advent of small-press publishing has been called the 'mimeograph revolution'.[11] For Edwards, this is the history of how 'poets in the British Isles since 1960 have seized the means of production'.[12] It might be argued that the dominant classes have never been very strongly committed to subsuming the work of poets for capitalist exploitation, so that the means of production was given away as much as 'seized'. Much small-press activity is only enabled by the relative material comfort and leisure time afforded to people who have sold their labour to some other employer (typically, a higher education institution).[13] But nonetheless, the symbolic social and political significance of the DIY publishing movement has been a strong source of inspiration for small-press poets.

---

[8] On the Circle Press, see Andrew Lambirth, *Cooking the Books: Ron King and Circle Press* (New Haven and London: Yale Center for British Art/Circle Press, 2002); Matthew Sperling, '"The Making of the Book": Roy Fisher, the Circle Press and the Poetics of Book Art', *Literature Compass*, 4/5 (July 2007), 1444–59; and Richard Price, '"Ear-jewels catch a glint": *The Half-Year Letters*', in Peter Robinson (ed.), *An Unofficial Roy Fisher* (Exeter: Shearsman Books, 2010), 132–41.

[9] Edwards, 'UK Small Press Publishing', para. 8.

[10] Wheale, 'Uttering Poetry', 13.

[11] See Steven Clay and Rodney Phillips (eds.), *A Secret Location on the Lower East Side: Adventures in Writing, 1960–1980* (New York: Granary Books, 1998).

[12] Edwards, 'UK Small Press Publishing', para. 1.

[13] See Robert Crawford, *The Modern Poet: Poetry, Academia, and Knowledge since the 1750s* (Oxford: Oxford University Press, 2001), esp. 'Coda: The Poet's Work', 267–85.

The material conditions in which poetry is reproduced, distributed, and read, often have a direct bearing upon the nature of the poetic work. Brady and Sutherland's Barque Press, for instance, publishes poetry with a clear sense of how small-press ventures, in Nigel Wheale's words, can enable reader-writer-publishers to 'constitute a knowable community for their activity, developing a context of writing and response which becomes intrinsic to the writing process',[14] as Brady explains:

> Barque has been a means of providing material and symbolic support to a community of writers who are also friends. We've always made it a priority to support younger or 'emerging' poets, taking risks on publishing work which might seem in some cases inexpert or not-yet-fully-fledged, because we recognise (given the history of the press) the importance for a poet's development of getting work into a capsule which can be circulated and responded to. We've also been able to publish senior writers who have influenced us. The work we publish is work we are reading and admiring, and inevitably some of its traces can be found in our own writing.

The communitarian aspect of small-press activity, as 'a means of providing material and symbolic support', is inextricable from the literary and aesthetic decisions of the poetry.[15] The lines of influence are apt to run both ways between younger and more senior writers; some of Prynne's sequences of the later 1990s and 2000s, with their grid-like stanzaic blocks of dense syntactic variance, arguably seem influenced by Barque Press writers four decades younger than him.

All publications from Reality Street Editions, the small press run by poet Ken Edwards, have part of their means of material support marked into the back of the book, in the form of a list of subscribers to the 'Reality Street Supporter' scheme:

> Currently, about 80 people belong to this. For an annual subscription, supporters get one copy of every book the press publishes, and their names printed in the back of the books if they wish. This support, and the interest it creates, is absolutely vital to the press.[16]

Edwards names '[t]he construction of writers' and readers' communities, for mutual benefit'[17] as the chief role of the small press, and his press bears this out in several ways. It was founded in 1993, as an amalgamation of Edwards's Reality Studios imprint

---

[14] Wheale, 'Uttering Poetry', 9–10.

[15] See also Andrea Brady's article 'For Immediate Delivery', in Maria Fusco and Ian Hunt (eds.), *Put About: A Critical Anthology on Independent Publishing* (London: Book Works, 2004), 139–47, which considers the ambiguous potential of the blogosphere as a site for radical collective dissent: 'Do blogs offer models of participation, plurality, interactivity and community which value the virtual but deny the material?' (146).

[16] Rob McLennan, '12 or 20 (Small Press) Questions: Ken Edwards on Reality Street', rob mclennan's blog (12 Feb. 2011), archived online at [http://robmclennan.blogspot.com/2011/02/12-or-20-small-press-questions-ken.html].

[17] McLennan, '12 or 20 (Small Press) Questions'.

and Wendy Mulford's Cambridge-based Street Editions, and has published important collections of British and North American innovative poetry including Denise Riley's *Selected Poems* (2000) and the 1996 anthology *Out of Everywhere: Linguistically Innovative Poetry by Women in North America and the UK*, edited by Maggie O'Sullivan.

An alternative form of community spirit is represented by the long-running Writers Forum, founded by visual and sound artist Bob Cobbing, and run after Cobbing's death by Lawrence Upton and (until recently) Adrian Clarke. Writers Forum has published more than 1,000 titles over the last five decades, using low-tech printing tools, first the Gestetner ink duplicator and then an office photocopier and stapler, to reproduce work as inventively and cheaply as possible. It operates outside of the economics of scarcity—as Upton says, in response 'primarily to needs felt by artists and poets rather than to a series of business plans', with types of publication which include 'records, tapes, items in boxes, and items in plastic bags', all under the sign of Cobbing's manifesto: 'I publish the unpublishable'.[18]

II

Publishing directed at shaping and supporting specific communities suffers from the ever-present danger of seeming insular. Nigel Wheale acknowledges that it would be idealistic to describe small-press endeavours as a form of egalitarian 'mass writing', since 'networks of informal publishing [...] are themselves regulated by acquaintance and education'.[19] Iain Sinclair's caricature of the small-press world, in his introduction to *Conductors of Chaos*, the anthology of avant-garde poetry he edited for Picador in 1996, pictures the challenge of tracking down small-press publications as a sort of quest adventure: the curious reader needs to be either 'well enough connected (Cambridge/Brighton/London) to be part of the samizdat circuit, or unfortunate enough to drink at one of the pubs where they still have readings in a back room', and '[t]he plethora of pamphlets and chapbooks cannot be located without a team of private detectives and a hefty bank balance'.[20]

Many small-press ventures of the last fifteen years have made marked efforts to expand the constituency for experimental poetry online. In contrast to Sinclair's portrayal of hard-to-track-down, fugitive publications, most new small-press volumes are now only a Paypal transaction away. Poetry readings are no longer the preserve of the

---

[18] Lawrence Upton, 'Writers Forum: Life by 1000 Books', in Jerome Rothenberg and Steven Clay (eds.), *A Book of the Book: Some Works and Projections about the Book and Writing* (New York: Granary Books, 1999), 431–9 (431, 436, 438). See also Upton's article, 'Bob Cobbing and the Book as Medium: Designs for Poetry', *Readings: Responses and Reactions to Poetries*, 4 (2009), archived online at [http://www.bbk.ac.uk/readings/issues/issue4/upton_on_cobbing].

[19] Wheale, 'Uttering Poetry', 16.

[20] Iain Sinclair (ed.), *Conductors of Chaos: A Poetry Anthology* (London: Picador, 1996), p. xiv.

locals and regulars in obscure pub back rooms, but are advertised, digested, and sometimes broadcast on blogs, newsfeeds, and other social networking technologies.

Small-press publishing, with its responsiveness to material conditions and its emphasis on community building, is by no means exclusively the domain of avant-gardists and Left intellectuals at odds with the perceived mainstream. Recent histories of John Fuller's work with his Sycamore Press and Peter Riley's pamphlet series Poetical Histories point to more similarities than differences between the endeavours, even though Riley is commonly associated with the radical ambitions of 'Cambridge poetry' and Fuller commonly regarded as father figure to a number of more conservative poets emerging from Oxford to work close to the commercial mainstreams of metropolitan literary culture.[21]

Fuller's Sycamore Press published more than fifty pamphlets and broadsheets between 1968 and 1992, while Riley's Poetical Histories issued sixty-two pamphlets between 1985 and 2004. Both ventures represent substantial achievements sustained over several decades, and yet both editors stress their contingency upon chance beginnings and material conditions. Riley was walking past an abandoned building in Wirksworth, Derbyshire, when he saw 'a room full of old machines' that turned out to be 'the abandoned workshop of an old printer who had died some years previously'. From the printer's widow Riley bought 'a quantity of mould-made paper probably dating from before the 1940s', and from this basis conceived the series, which featured most of the writer-publishers so far mentioned in this article, and many others, including Nicholas Moore, Helen MacDonald, Barry MacSweeney, and Grace Lake (the pseudonym of Anna Mendelssohn, imprisoned from 1971 to 1976 for her associations with the Angry Brigade). In 2004 we reach the last, unnumbered but sixty-second entry in the series, Riley's own poem *Only the Song*, published, in Riley's words, 'as a gift to the subscribers who have supported the series through its history'—whereupon '[t]he series ended because there was no paper left'.

John Fuller similarly puts the initiative to start Sycamore Press down to a chance material find, this time via his wife: 'After the birth of our third daughter, Prue was given by an imaginative friend not a bowl of grapes but a book of type', and having acquired the type, Fuller bought 'an old Arab clamshell press for £20' in 1968 (equal to roughly £500 in 2009), which 'had formerly produced cricket scores for distribution in the University Parks'.[22] The other material condition that sponsored the Sycamore Press is related by the author of its first publication, James Fenton:

> John [...] had bought a new house in Oxford near Lady Margaret Hall, in a handsome modernist development where each home had two lock-up spaces. The possession of an extra garage [...] had set them thinking. The space was enough for a press.[23]

---

[21] See Ryan Roberts, *John Fuller and the Sycamore Press: A Bibliographic History* (Oxford: Bodleian Library and Oak Knoll Press, 2010), and Peter Riley, 'Poetical Histories: The Whole Story', *April Eye* (2007), archived online at [http://www.aprileye.co.uk/histories.html]. Subsequent quotations from Riley are from this source.

[22] Roberts, *John Fuller and the Sycamore Press*, p. vii.

[23] Roberts, *John Fuller and the Sycamore Press*, 12.

There is a comical aspect to the contrast between Riley finding his paper in a depressed former mining town, among the dispossession of British heavy industry, and Fuller's possession of an extra garage in North Oxford—but both ventures share an awareness of how poetry publishing is responsive to its social and material conditions. Publishing happens not just with, but also *because of*, paper, type-blocks, and workshop space.

Both imprints sought to shape a poetic community. Riley describes the 'highly traditional, balanced and symmetrical' design values of the Poetical Histories as bibliographically signifying forms, in terms which combine the aesthetic with the literary-historical and with a sense of writerly community: they were an attempt 'to embody a statement about the nature of the modernity I was promoting [...] a modernity entirely in line with the history of English poetry from the 16th Century'. Fuller's enterprise is no less community-forming: through his Sycamore activities, he became the 'presiding genius' of Oxford poetry, according to Andrew Motion, while Bernard O'Donoghue describes Fuller's Sycamore work as 'the most remarkable instance of writerly generosity and solidarity'.[24]

The same writing can have several lives in a range of small-press and commercial formats. When Roy Fisher published his *Collected Poems 1968*, the book also bore the phantom title *The Ghost of a Paper Bag*, for reasons Fisher explains:

> that is part of the history of the book: what the book is, is a collection of poems I'd published or really a collection of pamphlets or other works. [...] Typographically, I wanted the title *The Ghost of a Paper Bag*, which was still how I thought of the book, ghosted in in grey, inside the book, but it got ghosted in in black on a page of its own, and it is still sort of drifting around there in the book. [...] You get remarks on some books that say 'This book is made from recycled paper.' My books maybe ought to have a warning saying 'This book is made from recycled books'.[25]

Fisher has published his 'recycled books' in a range of formats, from artist's books and micro-press pamphlets, to book publication with Fulcrum Press, Oxford University Press and latterly Bloodaxe. As a poet unusually alert to the material conditions in which his work is presented, Fisher allows bibliographic forms to exert a shaping pressure on the literary work itself: when 'people write and say would I write a pamphlet, and they have a format which is so many pages and so many copies', he has found himself 'perfectly likely to think it would have been nice to have filled one of those pamphlets', and so 'would write a work that shape'.[26]

Another writer who has taken the small-press book as a factor in composition in recent years is Geoffrey Hill. Hill's collection *A Treatise of Civil Power* (2005/2007) exists in two forms: a pamphlet from Andrew McNeillie's Clutag Press, in a limited edition of 200 copies, and a trade paperback from Penguin Books (and Yale University

---

[24] Roberts, *John Fuller and the Sycamore Press*, 31, 33.
[25] Roy Fisher, *Interviews Through Time and Selected Prose* (Kentisbere: Shearsman Books, 2000), 46, 92.
[26] Fisher, *Interviews Through Time and Selected Prose*, 67.

Press)—but the texts in each are radically different. In a public conversation with his publisher McNeillie, Hill has described how he used the Clutag pamphlet as the occasion for an experiment: he wanted to write in a 'loosened' style of 'dramatic loquaciousness' in the spirit of John Berryman—'to sound not always biting back on my words'.[27] He subsequently came to judge the experiment a failure, and so rewrote the book for the Penguin version, revising a number of poems, and discarding most of the pamphlet's long title poem, retaining only eight of its forty-two stanzas, now transformed into the components of six separate lyrics. The Penguin publication allowed him to improve the contents of the book, but in other ways it fell short: as Sophie Ratcliffe wrote, its cover 'offers a photographic reproduction of the original's embossed paper', with 'something naff' about the 'comically ersatz feel' of the result, 'akin to wood-effect vinyl'.[28] Hill also gave a lower-case *p* to the word '*power*' on the title page of the Clutag pamphlet, in homage to the typography of Milton's 1659 pamphlet from which he took his title, but this was regularized into upper-case '*Power*' by Penguin, against his wishes.[29] For Hill, the trade publisher's refusal of his lower-case *p* represented 'a loss of a sense of historical depth'—just as Penguin had been reluctant, in 1998, to allow him to publish a book with a title as obscure as the one he wanted, *Tempus Aedificandi, Tempus Destruendi*, which he renamed *The Triumph of Love*. For Hill, 'publishing is an exercise every author ought to confront', for in doing so, and bringing poetic design up sharp against the designs of the marketplace, he or she 'confronts the recalcitrance of the world itself'.

III

The small-press community, Andrea Brady says, is 'largely structured around admiration and antipathy, cooperation and competition, just as the mainstream is, but without the cash'. Yet State subsidy from arm's-length bodies such as, primarily, Arts Council England (ACE) has sometimes made cash available to both of these communities, and has substantially underwritten mid-size poetry independents such as Anvil, Bloodaxe, and Carcanet. In 2005 Barque Press received funding from the literature department of ACE, on a one-off basis, which brought the press onto a viable and independent financial footing, meaning that, as Brady says, 'we don't have much money, but we at least have some in a dedicated bank account, and don't have to reach into our own funds very often'. The grant enabled them to publish several books, some of them perfect-bound

---

[27] 'A Literary Manuscript Masterclass: Geoffrey Hill in Conversation with Andrew McNeillie', St Anne's College, Oxford, 27 Feb. 2009, for all words from Hill.

[28] Sophie Ratcliffe, 'Awkward Beauty', *New Statesman* (11 Oct. 2011), archived online at [http://www.newstatesman.com/poetry/2007/10/civil-power-hill-love-treatise].

[29] See Charles Lock, 'Beside the Point: A Diligence of Accidentals', in Piers Pennington and Matthew Sperling (eds.), *Geoffrey Hill and His Contexts* (Oxford: Peter Lang, 2011), 43–60, on the typography of the two books.

rather than stapled, and to produce a DVD documenting the readings of Che Qianzi, J. H. Prynne, and others at the 2005 Pearl River poetry conference in Guangzhou, China.[30]

Although glad of ACE's support, Brady found the process of applying for funding 'long, detailed, mind-boggling and very labour-intensive'. This is a common theme in small-press publishers' dealings with the vast bureaucratic machinery of ACE, as Charles Boyle of CB Editions says:

> Once upon a time the Arts Council literature department was widely viewed as an exclusive gentlemen's club; now everyone can get in but the extreme bureaucracy is baffling. Take the lift to the second floor, the doorman will say, go through the double doors on your left, take the second right, the first left and knock on the door marked 'Excellence'.[31]

The Arts Council's development was well documented in competing histories published around its fiftieth anniversary.[32] The organization has its origins in wartime, when the Committee for Encouragement of Music and the Arts was established with John Maynard Keynes named as chair in 1941. As Boyle suggests, the Arts Council's origins were indeed something resembling 'an exclusive gentlemen's club', as it took up the slack caused by the decline of private patronage to subvent the high-cultural interests of the leisure-class fraction who made up the audience of the Royal Opera House, in the hope that these interests would spread to the broader populace. The Arts Council's sponsorship of an epic verse competition for the Festival of Britain in 1951, with Robert Conquest and Jack Clemo among the prizewinners, was said by judge John Hayward (T. S. Eliot's confidant and protector) to represent 'the first public support for the art since the post of Poet Laureate had been created', coinciding with 'the nadir of the publication of poetry by commercial firms'.[33] The Council's annual report for 1970–1 gave a rationale for subsidizing poetry which was more or less unchanged from the philosophy behind the quango's origin: in 'an economic world where it is a simple untruth that worthwhile activities must necessarily succeed', it argued, 'recognition by a single perceptive mind can amply justify support to maintain an activity which can rarely find an adequate public'.[34] The paternalistic tone echoes Keynes's view that the cultural responsibility of welfare-capitalism was 'to furnish those few, who are capable of "passionate perception", with the ingredients of what modern civilisation can provide by way of a "good life"'.[35] The description of a 'single perceptive mind' sounds close to the idea

---

[30] *River Pearls: The First Pearl River Poetry Conference, Guangzhou, China, 2005* (London: Barque Press, 2008).

[31] Charles Boyle, 'Short Cuts', *White Review*, 3 (2011), archived online at [http://www.thewhitereview.org/features/short-cuts/] (para. 3).

[32] See Andrew Sinclair, *Arts and Cultures: The History of the 50 Years of the Arts Council of Great Britain* (London: Sinclair-Stevenson, 1995), and Richard Witts, *Artist Unknown: The Alternative History of the Arts Council* (London: Warner 1998).

[33] Sinclair, *Arts and Cultures*, 81.

[34] Cited in Randall Stevenson, *Oxford English Literary History, xii. 1960–2000: The Last of England?*, (Oxford: Oxford University Press, 2004), 153.

[35] Cited in Alan Sinfield, *Literature, Politics and Culture in Postwar Britain* (3rd edn., London: Continuum, 2004), 57.

of art-lovers as a self-infatuated class of individuals of superior refinement, whose private pleasures should be stumped up for by everybody's taxes. It depends whose perception of perceptiveness gets to be authorized.

On the other hand, in 2013 such unembarrassed resistance to the claims of the 'economic world' can't help but seem stirring. By our time, several decades of relentlessly pursued neo-liberal policy have seen the takeover of such a socially withdrawn, top-down perspective by an ostensible agenda of egalitarianism and 'accountability' underpinned by the logic and vocabulary of market values. The 2011 document *Achieving Great Art for Everyone: A Strategic Framework for the Arts* lays out ACE's plans for the next decade to deal with the 29.6 per-cent cut in State funding ordered by the Coalition Government's Comprehensive Spending Review. In contrast to the 1970–1 confidence in the 'simple untruth' of the economic bottom line, the 2011 version cautiously hedges its bets between different forms of argument in justification of spending public money: it may be that 'art is intrinsically valuable', and it may be that 'it is necessary for a successful economy, to our national prestige, to our mental health, to our social cohesion, to our sense of identity, to our happiness and to our well-being'— which is to say that '[i]ntrinsic and instrumental arguments all have their place'.[36] Poetry is mentioned twice in the document. First, the Chief Executive of ACE notes that 'poetry goes from strength to strength', on the basis that Faber have published some pamphlets by new poets, and some books by ACE-funded presses have been shortlisted for major prizes; then Seamus Heaney is quoted approvingly by Marina Warner, to the effect that 'We go to poetry, we go to literature in general, to be forwarded within ourselves'.[37] ACE documents are fond of this juxtaposition of mundane committee-speak with guru-like sound bites of a pious self-help humanism: in his foreword to a 2010 report on 'Poetry and Young People', Andrew Motion explains that 'the members of the Review Group [...] agreed to work together because we know that poetry allows people to discover what it means to be more completely and intensely a human being'.[38]

Unfortunately, to be completely and intensely a human being tends to require a fair bit of cash, and following George Osborne's Comprehensive Spending Review, 2011 was not a good year for poetry subsidies from ACE. On the one hand, Faber and Faber received ACE funds for the first time, awarded £40,000 annually until 2015 for their New Poets programme of pamphlets, readings, and mentorship, while Carcanet's grant went up from £113,888 for 2011–12 to £120,000 for 2012–13, and Bloodaxe's grant of £92,638 was maintained at the same level. But Anvil's grant went down from £87,768 to £60,000, while the Poetry Book Society (PBS) (£111,299), Arc Publications (£34,196), and Enitharmon (£46,401) had their grants cut altogether, calling the future viability of all three operations into question. The cutting of the PBS grant had been hinted in the 2009 Strategic Development Report on the 'poetry sector' produced by BOP Consulting,

---

[36] *Achieving Great Art for Everyone: A Strategic Framework for the Arts* (London: Arts Council England, 2011), 4.
[37] *Achieving Great Art for Everyone*, 7, 38.
[38] *The Motion Report: Poetry and Young People* (London: Booktrust/Arts Council England, 2010), 4.

which recorded the view, common among consultees, that the people and organizations making up the perceived 'establishment' were not at present 'the most effective leaders for the sector—with particular concerns that the Poetry Society and Poetry Book Society are no longer clear about their roles, with gaps and overlaps', and with 'frustration [...] over Arts Council England's support for this "establishment".'[39] But the rationale behind the cutting of Arc and Enitharmon is difficult to discern, since, as Charles Boyle says, their work 'is completely in accord with ACE stated priorities'.[40] The fact that these two presses and the PBS were cut while Faber and Faber were awarded substantial funds was a source of some dismay, since Faber is a profitable company which could comfortably fund a not-for-profit programme developing young poets itself, if it wished to keep the place as the premier publisher of new poetry in the UK it has traditionally occupied since T. S. Eliot joined the firm, then known as Faber and Gwyer, in 1925.

IV

The economics of poetry publishing have been predominantly small-scale for as long as poetry has been sold for money at all. In his life of Milton, Dr Johnson gives a detailed account of the deal Milton struck with his printer for *Paradise Lost*:

> he sold his copy, April 27, 1667, to Samuel Simmons, for an immediate payment of five pounds, with a stipulation to receive five pounds more when thirteen hundred should be sold of the first edition: and again, five pounds after the sale of the same number of the second edition: and another five pounds after the same sale of the third. None of the three editions were to be extended beyond fifteen hundred copies.[41]

Sales were fairly slow; the second payment of £5 took two years to arrive. Calculated against average earnings, £5 in 1667 is equivalent to around £7,000 at 2009 rates, so Milton's initial fee would place him high up the echelons of poetic earners today.[42] It still fails to amount to a living wage on its own, but today Milton could capitalize on his success by going 'On the Circuit', as Auden calls it in a late poem, with his 'gospel of the Muse'.[43] He could give readings and make media appearances; teach workshops or

---

[39] *Thrive! Poetry Project: Strategic Development Report* (London: Arts Council England, 2009), 4.

[40] Boyle, 'Short Cuts', para. 1.

[41] Samuel Johnson, *The Lives of the Poets: A Selection*, ed. Roger Lonsdale and John Mullan (Oxford: Oxford University Press, 2009), 85. I am grateful to Jamie Baxendine for allowing me to read his unpublished work on poetry and political economy, which suggested several of the examples in this section.

[42] Calculated using Lawrence H. Officer (ed.), 'Purchasing Power of British Pounds from 1264 to Present', *Measuring Worth* (2011), [www.measuringworth.com]. A calculation against the retail price index gives the much lower figure of £660, but average earnings seems the best indicator in this context. All subsequent historical currency conversions come from the same source.

[43] W. H. Auden, 'On the Circuit' (1963), *Collected Poems*, ed. Edward Mendelson (rev. edn., London: Faber & Faber, 2007), 728–30.

Arvon courses; seek roles as poet in residence, mentor, or competition judge; become a creative writing teacher in a university. He might even win the T. S. Eliot or Forward Prize, or the Costa Book of the Year. When Dr Johnson pondered the relative smallness of Milton's advance and the slowness of the sale, he decided that they were not, as has sometimes been thought, signs of 'neglected merit'. On the contrary, the sales figures were a success in the circumstances:

> The sale of thirteen hundred copies in two years, in opposition to so much recent enmity, and to a style of versification new to all and disgusting to many, was an uncommon example of the prevalence of genius. The demand did not immediately increase; for many more readers than were supplied at first the nation did not afford.[44]

Milton's success was more remarkable, then, given that *Paradise Lost* was a work of radical politics and formal innovation—its mode of articulation 'new to all and disgusting to many', in a phrase that would well describe the reception of much experimental poetry today. Johnson pictures Milton's reputation growing among the small community of poetry readers by word of mouth—'stealing its way in a kind of subterraneous current through fear and silence'—while the poet remains 'calm and confident, little disappointed, not at all dejected, relying on his own merit with steady consciousness, and waiting without impatience the vicissitudes of opinion'.[45]

Johnson's word 'merit' is carefully chosen. The claim of *merit* is that it exists outside of the social context in which its *worth* to other people may be determined; the *OED*'s oldest sense of the word is 'The quality [...] of being entitled to reward from God'. The merit of a work of poetry, in this traditional view, is therefore separate from and discontinuous with its social worth or economic value; Milton would have been truly entitled to no more or less esteem if *Paradise Lost* had sold 10,000 copies or 10 copies in the first two years.

Poetic merit resists being equated with economic value. And yet they repeatedly collide when a poem enters the world in which it is to be reproduced, distributed, and read. For Karl Marx, the story of Milton's fiver was representative of the ambivalent socio-economic conditions of poetic work. In his account of productive and unproductive labour in the discarded part 7 to volume i of *Capital* (written 1863–6), Marx takes poetry as the first instance of how, in certain circumstances, 'labour with *the same content* can be either productive or unproductive':

> For instance, Milton, who wrote *Paradise Lost*, was an unproductive worker. On the other hand, a writer who turns out work for his publisher in factory style is a productive worker. Milton produced *Paradise Lost* as a silkworm produces silk, as the activation of *his own* nature. He later sold the product for £5 and thus became a merchant. [...] A singer who sings like a bird is an unproductive worker. If she sells

---

[44] Johnson, *Lives of the Poets*, 86.
[45] Johnson, *Lives of the Poets*, 86.

her song for money, she is to that extent a wage-labourer or merchant. But if the same singer is engaged by an entrepreneur who makes her sing to make money, then she becomes a productive worker, since she *produces* capital directly.[46]

Writing and singing seem paradoxical: they both are and aren't commodities, and the performance of them can be either 'productive' or 'unproductive' labour, and somehow these questions can be determined either by discovering the motivation with which they were originally carried out, or retrospectively, by examining the exchange relations they entered into after their creation. Marx ends his account by acknowledging the unresolved status of poetic work: 'for the most part, work of this sort has scarcely reached the stage of being subsumed even formally under capital, and belongs essentially to a transitional stage'.[47]

But, as Blake Morrison writes, 'poets have generally been more used to hard-nosed business negotiation [...] than all this would suggest': for instance,

> Pope made over £5000 through subscriptions to the *Iliad*, Byron earned nearly £3000 for the copyright of *Childe Harold*, then asked for and got from John Murray £3000 for one Canto of *Don Juan*; Tennyson's reaction on being offered what was then the largest fee for a poetry book was to say: 'My dear! We are much richer than we thought we were. Mr Smith has just offered me 5000 guineas for a book the size of the Idylls. And if Mr Smith offers 5000, of course the book is worth ten.'[48]

Coming into the twentieth century, the hard-nosed poetic negotiator with an eye for a modernist publicity coup could command almost equally impressive returns. Lawrence Rainey's study of *The Waste Land*'s publication has shown that Eliot earned the staggering sum of $2,800, or £612, for the poem's transatlantic appearances in 1922–3, in the journals *The Criterion* and *The Dial* and in book format from Boni and Liveright and the Hogarth Press—a figure equivalent to almost £120,000 in 2009, calculated against average income.[49] Wheale suggests that the rediscovery of the 'marketing strategies' used by Eliot and Pound renders the avant-garde achievement 'less heroic, and much more calculating'.[50] But this seems romantic in the face of Rainey's subtle analysis of how the invention of modernism is 'inseparable, finally, from the contradictory network of uses in which it had been historically constituted', all of them driven by 'conflicting imperatives'.[51] One of these imperatives was Eliot's own grasp of how poetic merit trumps

---

[46] Karl Marx, *Capital: A Critique of Political Economy*, trans. Ben Fowkes, introd. Ernest Mandel (London: Pelican Books, 1976; repr. Penguin Books, 1990), i. 1044 (appendix).

[47] Marx, *Capital*, i. 1044 (appendix).

[48] Morrison, 'Poetry and the Poetry Business', para. 6. At 2009 rates calculated against average income, Pope's £5,000 (1713) = almost £9,000,000; Byron's £3,000 (1819) = £2,000,000; and Tennyson's '5000 guineas', i.e. £,5250 (1860) = £3,000,000.

[49] Lawrence Rainey, 'The Price of Modernism: Publishing *The Waste Land*', in *Revisiting 'The Waste Land* (New Haven: Yale University Press, 2005), 71–101 (100), previously in Rainey's *Institutions of Modernism: Literary Elites and Public Culture* (New Haven: Yale University Press, 1999).

[50] Wheale, 'Uttering Poetry', 15.

[51] Rainey, 'The Price of Modernism', 100.

economic value, ironically turned into a negotiating tool to make him more money: to the editor of *The Dial*, Eliot argues that he should be paid more for his poem than George Moore was paid for a short story because 'people should learn to recognize Merit instead of Senility'.[52] —echoing Johnson's description of Milton's 'steady consciousness' of his own merit in the face of small sales.

The financial rewards possible for the likes of Byron, Tennyson, or Eliot remained exceptional for their day, with Milton's modest returns more like the best a poet could expect. In 1950, on the eve of State subsidy for poetry, Cecil Day Lewis remarked that 'for the last 150 years the publishers themselves have been the chief patrons of poetry', since they 'have been willing to lose money on a writer they believed in'.[53] This is still borne out some decades later by Blake Morrison's 1981 analysis of the Secker and Warburg poetry list, then edited by Anthony Thwaite, which issued eight books a year:

> The current printing and sales figures at Secker make fairly chastening reading. The average print run for a poetry book is 500 (it used to be 800); these are in hardback only, an earlier experiment in simultaneously issuing hard and paperback copies having failed; and the bulk of sales are to libraries. Efforts to get bookshops to stock poetry are particularly unrewarding. [...] Not surprisingly Secker falls well short of recouping the £25,000 a year it spends on poetry—the return is about £15,000.[54]

An annual loss of £10,000 in 1981 is equal to almost £45,000 in 2009 (calculated against average income), and must seem a substantial amount for a commercial firm to commit to the charitable patronage of contemporary poetry—especially when we look back at the Secker volumes that resulted, with their drably uniform '"striped toothpaste" covers'[55] and their often less than thrilling contents, from the likes of George MacBeth, D. J. Enright, and Alan Brownjohn, writers of integrity and invention but perhaps not originality, all now rapidly receding from literary memory.

When Eliot became a publisher in 1925, joining Faber, he remembered the lessons learnt from his own negotiations with the marketplace. In his 1952 article 'The Publishing of Poetry', based on a talk given to the Society of Young Publishers, he gives a picture of the intricacies of poetry publishing based on a quarter-century's experience:

> the most important difference between poetry and any other department of publishing is, that whereas with most categories of books you are aiming to make as much money as possible, with poetry you are aiming to lose as little as possible. And I maintain that it takes as much canniness to achieve this result with your poetry as it does to make comfortable profits from some other kinds.[56]

---

[52] Rainey, 'The Price of Modernism', 79.
[53] Cited in Morrison, 'Poetry and the Poetry Business', para. 11.
[54] Morrison, 'Poetry and the Poetry Business', para. 10.
[55] Morrison, 'Poetry and the Poetry Business', para. 14.
[56] T. S. Eliot, 'The Publishing of Poetry', *The Bookseller*, 2450 (6 Dec. 1952), 1568–70 (1568).

Eliot's 'canniness' emerges in his account of how to negotiate the various forces acting upon the poetry publisher. First there is the sense of 'responsibility towards society' which makes a firm feel it 'should do something for English poetry, by publishing the best poetry, written in our time, that it can get hold of'; but this needs to be balanced against the demands of managing your 'prestige':

> You won't get prestige—not the right kind—merely by taking over poets who have already established their reputation: the firm itself must have had something to do with building that reputation. You must be known to have backed the right authors long before they became famous.[57]

Finally, a firm's poetry list needs to have the right combination of the 'three classes' into which Eliot divides poets in terms of sales. There are 'the poets who actually make some money', who might sell 3,000 copies of a new book within a year, and maintain steady sales on a back list; then there are the poets who 'have proved their worth' in consistent critical acclaim, and 'ought not to show more than a small deficit on a book at the end of twelve months'; and then 'the poets on whom you are losing money', the young ones who may join the second class if they have 'staying power', or may not, and with whom the editor should nonetheless be prepared to stick 'through thick and thin' if convinced of their 'exceptional merit'.[58]

V

Don Paterson, the Poetry Editor of Picador since 1997, has described Eliot's article as 'the Bible for surviving as a trade publisher of poetry'.[59] Picador is an imprint of Pan Macmillan, a subsidiary of the Stuttgart-based Georg von Holtzbrinck holding company, which had a consolidated revenue of €2,358 million in the fiscal year 2009. Within Macmillan, Picador is a relatively small 'prestige' imprint, with the main focus on high-grade literary fiction. Within Picador, the poetry list is smaller still, publishing only a handful of new books a year. As a commercial publisher with no grant, Picador is bound by a 'different set of rules', Paterson explains, from a publisher such as Bloodaxe or Carcanet, since Picador must operate within the 'strict economic constraint' of the 'in-house account'. A Picador book needs to sell on average 1,500 copies in order to be commercially viable, and if this sale is unlikely to be reached, then the editor is 'obliged to find ways of cross-subsidizing' within the poetry list in order to publish

---

[57] Eliot, 'The Publishing of Poetry', 1568.
[58] Eliot, 'The Publishing of Poetry', 1569.
[59] 'Plenary Panel of Poet-Publishers: Peter Fallon (Gallery Press), Don Paterson (Picador), Michael Schmidt (Carcanet Press)' at the conference 'British and Irish Poetry 1960–2010', Queen's University, Belfast, 16 Sept. 2010. All subsequent words of Paterson's are from this source.

the work. Publication of a high-selling volume will underwrite publication of work less likely to find a broad commercial market. So, in October 2011 Picador published *The Bees*, the new collection from Poet Laureate Carol Ann Duffy, in an ornate hardback marked up at £14.99 (and heavily discounted by major sellers such as Amazon), with a concerted media campaign leading to warm reviews in every national broadsheet—and, as Paterson says, 'that's what allows me to publish John Kinsella', whose book *Armour* came out quietly in paperback the following month with nothing like the same marketing drive.

For a poetry imprint to survive in the devouring maw of a large trade publisher is very difficult. For a short period in the late 1980s, under the editorship of John Muckle then Iain Sinclair, the Paladin imprint of Grafton Books, shortly to be swallowed by Harper Collins, was allowed to publish in glossy commercial format books by writers more often found in tiny samizdat editions, such as the contributors to *Future Exiles: Three London Poets* (1992)—Allen Fisher, Bill Griffiths, and Brian Catling. Paladin also published two landmark anthologies of small-press writers, *The New British Poetry 1968–1988* (1988) and *A Various Art* (1990; first published by Carcanet in 1987). But the commercial pressure of surviving within Harper Collins, a subsidiary of News Corporation from 1989, was too great, and the entire series was pulped in 1992 when, in Sinclair's words, 'Rupert Murdoch's accountants saw no reason to tolerate low-turnover cultural loss leaders'.[60]

Another cut that caused much grief came in 1998, when Oxford University Press announced that it was cancelling its poetry list, which had been built up over three decades, and included major figures such as Basil Bunting, Roy Fisher, Charles Tomlinson, and Peter Porter, as well as younger writers such as Jamie McKendrick, Alice Oswald, and Jo Shapcott. The decision received much negative media attention.[61] It even entered political debate: an early day motion in the House of Commons, proposed by Labour MP Derek Wyatt and signed by sixty-seven members, said that

> this House deplores the decision by Oxford University Press to abandon publishing contemporary poetry; notes the remarkable quality of OUP's poetry list, built up by Jon Stallworthy and Jacqueline Simms; understands that OUP has not lost money through publishing modern poetry, which in any case represents a minute proportion of OUP's turnover of £282 million; further notes that OUP subvented the University of Oxford over the last five years to the tune of £53 million; is astonished that the Delegacy (the academic board) have countenanced such a policy by the Press; and considers this an act of philistinism, with no plausible justification.[62]

---

[60] Cited in Ian Brinton, *Contemporary Poetry: Poets and Poetry since 1990* (Cambridge: Cambridge University Press, 2009), 36.

[61] See e.g. Robert Potts, 'Neither Rhyme Nor Reason', *The Guardian* (24 Nov. 1998); James Fenton, 'Beware the Philistines of Publishing', *The Times* (25 Nov. 1998); and Valentine Cunningham, 'Mammon's Imprint', *Times Higher Education Supplement* (12 Feb. 1999).

[62] 'Early Day Motion 107: Oxford University Press Poetry List' (9 Dec. 1998), archived online at *The UK Parliament Website*: [http://www.parliament.uk/business/publications/business-papers/commons/early-day-motions/].

Justification was eventually offered by Sir Keith Thomas, who cited the 'difficult trading conditions' caused by currency devaluations in the Far East and Latin America, and the conglomeration of its major rivals and of booksellers, as reasons why OUP's need 'to make a reasonable financial return to its owner' (which is to say, the University) made it uneconomical to continue publishing a poetry list which 'has never even faintly threatened Faber's primacy in this area'.[63] Since 'most commercial publishers have given up publishing new poetry', Thomas argued, to ask OUP to carry on publishing new poetry 'is to invite it to subsidize creative writing, to behave as if it were an outlying department of the Arts Council'.[64]

If even a large publisher with the benefits of a university's tax-exempt charitable status cannot justify the limited financial returns available from poetry, the situation is near impossible for an independent poetry publisher attempting to grow into a self-supporting and profitable business. The difficulties faced by Salt Publishing in recent years illustrate this well. Founded in 2000 and run with great energy and expertise by Chris and Jen Hamilton-Emery, Salt dramatically expanded its poetry list, keeping large numbers of titles available using print-on-demand technology, and rivalling presses such as Bloodaxe and Carcanet as one of the major independent poetry publishers. But this entailed a considerable financial risk for a small family business, and after the credit crunch of 2008 Salt had to launch yearly campaigns asking readers to buy 'Just One Book' in order to save the company. Salt's fortunes only revived when it became a fiction publisher and had Alison Moore's *The Lighthouse* shortlisted for the 2012 Man Booker Prize, making it Salt's best-selling title many times over.

The personal nature of the 'Save Salt' campaign, appealing to its readers on an individual basis, bore out the truth of Don Paterson's assertion that even in the relatively market-pressurized situation of a trade publisher, it is a 'readership' and not a 'market' that poetry publishers are dealing with. However, it can be difficult to reach that readership; the relationship between writer and publisher, publisher and reader can seem more distant at commercial trade presses. Ken Edwards records his experience of publishing *New British Poetry* with Paladin, but finding the marketing department unable to connect with readership:

> I found one of the most frustrating aspects of being involved with the editing of *The New British Poetry* at Paladin in 1988 was the lack of connection with a readership: the HarperCollins sales force, one felt, had little idea of the specific market the book was addressing, let alone any notion of a community of readers. They had the means to get books into any bookshop in Britain, something most small press operators would envy, but they didn't know who any of their readers were.[65]

---

[63] Keith Thomas, 'The Purpose and the Cost: Why the Oxford University Press Must Concentrate on the Things It Does Best', *Times Literary Supplement* (5 Feb. 1999).
[64] Thomas, 'The Purpose and the Cost'.
[65] Edwards, 'UK Small Press Publishing', para. 5.

This lack of connection to a known readership can apply to the most successful of trade-published poets. Paul Farley, author of several collections published by Picador, winner of several prizes, and one of the poets included in the Poetry Book Society's 'Next Generation' campaign in 2004, has remarked that '[m]y generation haven't had criticism; they've had marketing'.[66] And even one of Faber's best-selling poets can find cause to be unhappy with the remoteness of her relations with publisher and marketplace, in her 'Reflections on a Royalty Statement':

They've given me a number
So they will know it's me
And not some other Wendy Cope
(They publish two or three),
When I go to see them
I wear a number-plate
Or sometimes I salute and say,
'032838.'[67]

Wendy Cope extended her concern with her rights as author in an article protesting against the breach of her copyright by enthusiasts of her poetry who reproduce it on the Internet without paying her a fee—joking that her gravestone epitaph should read 'Wendy Cope. All Rights Reserved'.[68] (Academics often contribute to this breaching of copyright in a fairly major way when preparing course packs and handouts; the excerpt reprinted earlier, however, has been trimmed to fall within the definition of 'fair use' for purposes of criticism or review, meaning that Cope was not paid for this either.)

So even successful Faber and Faber authors can feel short-changed by poetry publishing—and even Faber in its own way has to cross-subsidize publication of new poetry. Very few new poetry books are published by Faber each year, in small print-runs which nonetheless frequently end up in remainder bookshops; the majority of the new poetry output is dwarfed by a tiny number of star names (notably Seamus Heaney), by Faber's formidable back catalogue (Eliot, Larkin, Hughes, Plath), and by Faber's highly successful fiction and non-fiction publishing. Since the musical opened in 1981, Faber has also been the beneficiary of the monstrous commercial success of Andrew Lloyd Webber's *Cats*, loosely based on Eliot's work in *Old Possum's Book of Practical Cats* (1939); former poetry editor Craig Raine describes the company as 'swimming in *Cats* money'.[69]

Two years later a second Cameron Mackintosh production became another unlikely revenue source for poetry. James Fenton was commissioned in 1983 to write a libretto for the English adaptation of *Les Misérables*, but had his efforts dismissed for being '*too*

---

[66] 'The poets speak', *The Guardian* (9 Apr. 2005), archived online at [http://www.guardian.co.uk/books/2005/apr/09/featuresreviews.guardianreview5].

[67] Wendy Cope, *Serious Concerns* (London: Faber & Faber, 1992), 42.

[68] Wendy Cope, 'You like my poems? So pay for them', *The Guardian* (8 Dec. 2007), archived online at [http://www.guardian.co.uk/books/2007/dec/08/featuresreviews.guardianreview14].

[69] Tom Tivnan, 'Raine o'er me', *The Bookseller* (11 Feb. 2010), archived online at [http://www.thebookseller.com/profile/raine-oer-me.html].

poetic, too intellectual, and in parts just not singable'[70] —leaving him nothing to show for more than a year's work but around 1 per-cent annual royalties on a musical that has now grossed nearly $2 billion dollars worldwide. By a savagely ironic accident of late capitalism, the mass products of the culture industry return the publishing house and the poet to a pre-capitalistic economic status, underwriting Faber's publication of new slim volumes so that their loss-making potential poses no real risk, and transplanting Fenton to a reconstituted leisure class, freed by his private income to pursue arts journalism, gardening, antique collecting, lyric poetry, and service on the boards of charitable trusts.[71]

The boundaries between small-press operations and the trade market are occasionally permeable. Canadian experimental poet Christian Bök's *Eunoia* is in some ways a challenging work, with its rigid formalism of design, described by the author as 'a univocal lipogram, in which each chapter restricts itself to the use of a single vowel' (as in, 'Dutch smut churns up blushful succubus lusts; thus buff hunks plus hung studs must fuck lustful sluts').[72] It was first published by Ontario's Coach House Press in 2001, before being published in the UK seven years later by the large Edinburgh-based independent Canongate, part of the 'Faber Independent Alliance' of ten publishers who share administrative, marketing, and distribution resources, and in 2009 had a 3.9 per-cent market share of UK book sales.[73] The Canongate edition was a masterstroke of commercial opportunism: released in November 2008, it was marketed less as a work of poetry than as a stocking filler for wordgame lovers and puzzle enthusiasts. With a tie-in feature on BBC Radio Four's *Today* programme, inviting listeners to join in the Oulipean fun ('Can you write using only one vowel? Email us your attempts'),[74] a Santa-red cover strewn with tinselly silver and white letters, and a blurb from broadcaster and former Conservative MP Gyles Brandreth ('a must for verbivores'), the book became the eighth best-selling title in the UK in Christmas week.

Similarly, Christopher Reid published two small-press collections in 2009 which both crossed over into a wider market. *A Scattering*, the first book published by Craig Raine's Areté Books, was chosen as the Costa Book of the Year, carrying off a prize purse of £30,000. *The Song of Lunch* was first issued by Charles Boyle's CB Editions, before reappearing in 2010 in a Faber and Faber edition which, as the back cover says, was '[p]ublished to tie-in with a major BBC Two dramatization for National Poetry Day, starring Alan Rickman and Emma Thompson'. Where the first edition of *The Song of Lunch* had a plain cover of manila boards bearing only the author and title in green

---

[70] Edward Behr, *The Complete Book of Les Misérables* (New York: Little, Brown, 1989), 79.

[71] David Jenkins, 'James Fenton: 21st Century Renaissance Man', *The Telegraph* (18 Nov. 2007), archived online at [http://www.telegraph.co.uk/culture/3669373/James-Fenton-21st-century-renaissance-man.html].

[72] Christian Bök, *Eunoia* (Edinburgh: Canongate, 2008), 103, 79.

[73] See Andrew Franklin, 'Declaration of independents', *The Guardian* (Saturday, 8 July 2006), archived online at [http://www.guardian.co.uk/books/2006/jul/08/featuresreviews.guardianreview7].

[74] 'Beautiful Vowels', *Today*, BBC Radio 4 (30 Oct. 2008), feature archived online at [http://news.bbc.co.uk/today/hi/today/newsid_7697000/7697762.stm].

lettering, the Faber edition kept the CB typesetting of the inside of the book, with its ornate ligatured initials, but gave the cover to a full-page colour photograph of Rickman and Thompson, with the BBC logo prominently stamped in the bottom right. As former editors at Faber and Faber, Reid and Raine have long experience within London trade publishing, and therefore less far to travel to the land of prizes and broadcast adaptations than most small-press poets and publishers; but nonetheless the attempts of the mainstream media and high-street booksellers to turn Reid's low-key, delicate, determinedly modest poetry into a unit-shifter were strikingly incongruous.

VI

The success of CB Editions suggests good reasons not to be downcast about the future of poetry publishing—which, as Charles Boyle reminds us, will go about its work inventively and stubbornly for as long as poetry is being written:

> *Writing*, of course, is not being cut. [...] Some of it at least will find its way into publication. A little (someone's idea of 'the new big thing') directly into the mainstream. Some by self-publishing, which digital printing has made far more affordable than it used to be. Some on the net, dispensing with the whole idea of the book. And some, still, through the medium of small presses.Because small presses are flexible. They are not accountable to shareholders or owners demanding instant high returns. Their overheads are minimal. They are run, most of them, by people who are mad—which may be a weakness commercially but is in fact their strength, because their madness is a form of obsession with good writing, which is where it all starts. Everything else—the design, the marketing stuff (and the blurbs and the bleeds and the AIs and the lead times and all the other jargon that makes publishing seem a thing of mystery: it isn't)—is an extra and can be added on.[75]

Select Bibliography

Auden, W. H., 'On the Circuit' (1963), *Collected Poems*, ed. Edward Mendelson (rev. edn., London: Faber & Faber, 2007), 728–30.
Behr, Edward, *The Complete Book of Les Misérables* (New York: Little, Brown, 1989).
Bridgwood, Ann and Hampson, John, *Rhyme and Reason: Developing Contemporary Poetry* (London: Arts Council of England, 2000).
Brinton, Ian, *Contemporary Poetry: Poets and Poetry since 1990* (Cambridge: Cambridge University Press, 2009).
Clay, Steven and Phillips, Rodney (eds.), *A Secret Location on the Lower East Side: Adventures in Writing, 1960–1980* (New York: Granary Books, 1998).

---

[75] Boyle, 'Short Cuts', paras. 15–16.

Cope, Wendy, *Serious Concerns* (London: Faber & Faber, 1992).
Crawford, Robert, *The Modern Poet: Poetry, Academia, and Knowledge since the 1750s* (Oxford: Oxford University Press, 2001).
Cunningham, Valentine, 'Mammon's Imprint', *Times Higher Education Supplement* (12 Feb. 1999).
Eliot, T. S., 'The Publishing of Poetry', *The Bookseller*, 2450 (6 Dec. 1952), 1568–70.
Fenton, James, 'Beware the Philistines of Publishing', *The Times* (25 Nov. 1998).
Fisher, Roy, *Interviews Through Time and Selected Prose* (Kentisbere: Shearsman Books, 2000).
Lambirth, Andrew, *Cooking the Books: Ron King and Circle Press* (New Haven and London: Yale Center for British Art/Circle Press, 2002).
Lock, Charles, 'Beside the Point: A Diligence of Accidentals', in Piers Pennington and Matthew Sperling (eds.), *Geoffrey Hill and His Contexts* (Oxford: Peter Lang, 2011), 43–60.
O'Brien, Flann (Myles na Gopaleen), *The Best of Myles*, ed. Kevin O'Nolan (London: MacGibbon and Kee, 1968).
Potts, Robert, 'Neither Rhyme Nor Reason', *The Guardian* (24 Nov. 1998).
Price, Richard, '"Ear-jewels catch a glint": *The Half-Year Letters*', in Peter Robinson (ed.), *An Unofficial Roy Fisher* (Exeter: Shearsman Books, 2010), 132–41.
Rainey, Lawrence, 'The Price of Modernism: Publishing *The Waste Land*', in *Revisiting 'The Waste Land*' (New Haven: Yale University Press, 2005), 71–101.
Roberts, Ryan, *John Fuller and the Sycamore Press: A Bibliographic History* (Oxford: Bodleian Library and Oak Knoll Press, 2010).
Sinclair, Andrew, *Arts and Cultures: The History of the 50 Years of the Arts Council of Great Britain* (London: Sinclair-Stevenson, 1995).
Sinclair, Iain (ed.), *Conductors of Chaos: A Poetry Anthology* (London: Picador, 1996).
Sinfield, Alan, *Literature, Politics and Culture in Postwar Britain* (3rd edn., London: Continuum, 2004).
Sperling, Matthew, '"The Making of the Book": Roy Fisher, the Circle Press and the Poetics of Book Art', *Literature Compass*, 4/5 (July 2007), 1444–59.
Stevenson, Randall, *Oxford English Literary History*, xii. *1960–2000: The Last of England?*, (Oxford: Oxford University Press, 2004).
Thomas, Keith, 'The Purpose and the Cost: Why the Oxford University Press Must Concentrate on the Things It Does Best', *Times Literary Supplement* (5 Feb. 1999).
Upton, Lawrence, 'Writers Forum: Life by 1000 Books', in Jerome Rothenberg and Steven Clay (eds.), *A Book of the Book: Some Works and Projections about the Book and Writing* (New York: Granary Books, 1999), 431–9.
Wheale, Nigel, 'Uttering Poetry: Small-Press Publication', in Denise Riley (ed.), *Poets on Writing: Britain, 1970–1991* (London: Macmillan, 1992), 9–20.
Witts, Richard, *Artist Unknown: The Alternative History of the Arts Council* (London: Warner 1998).

PART II

SENSES OF FORM AND TECHNIQUE

CHAPTER 11

'SPACE AVAILABLE': A POET'S DECISIONS

JEFFREY WAINWRIGHT

> Space available.   Multi-use.   Flexible.
> Clean.   All facilities.   Could suit poem.
> Restrictions: must not use words
> in any way intended to destroy meanings.
> (It will prove impossible.)

IT would be easy to object to the injunction contained in this squib of mine. A perennial debate in modern poetics centres upon 'meanings', and the lines of the objection would be that the particular language use that announces itself as 'poetry' is not concerned to offer semantically coherent propositions, indeed its project is to destroy them. The modern history of the debate can be dated from the *l'art pour l'art* opposition to the utilitarianism of the nineteenth century, as in the magnificent disdain of Gautier's pronouncement that a work of art 'is not a jellied soup', to the intense language scepticism of post-structuralists which holds that all propositions are semantically compromised (except their own). But because *form* matters—by which I mean an organization of verbal utterance in excess of the needs of 'simple' discursive communication—some shadow of this argument is going to fall across the consciousness of any poet who reflects upon his or her practice. (I place the word 'simple' in inverted commas there since, as Wittgenstein showed, no verbal communication is absolutely straightforward. The wonder is that we achieve 'anything at all' with the language we have.[1]) But even the most callow of beginning poets will have been smitten by the sensuous qualities of words and their combinations, and drawn to take notice of the shapes that the codes of 'poetry' have evolved. They will have been captured by form.

---

[1] Ludwig Wittgenstein, *Philosophical Investigations,* no. 120 (3rd edn.), trans. G. E. M. Anscombe (Oxford: Blackwell, 2001), 42ᵉ.

For some this is a defining captivation. In the 1960s I became aware of 'concrete poetry' as practised by artists such as Dom Sylvester Houédard and Ian Hamilton Finlay. At the time I found their indifference to semantics in what they insisted on calling 'poetry' incomprehensible and outrageous. But for them the semiotic character of letters possessed a valency far more compelling as art than their appearance in mere semantic items. What temperamental elements draw individuals towards one or another aesthetic preference is too intricate a question to be addressed here, but my own contemporaneous formation was taking place in response to quite other imperatives.

In the poetic milieu of Leeds University in the 1960s 'meaning' was all but all. To sketch the 'scene', or my inflection of it: Leeds was unusually hospitable to an enthusiasm to write poetry at that time. Crucially the existence of Eric Gregory Fellowships in Poetry, Art, and Music—the first institution of artists-in-residence at a British university—provided a respected but extracurricular focus for student creativity. In Poetry the Fellow's wide brief to foster student writing centred upon *Poetry and Audience*, a weekly magazine sold every Friday for 1*d.*, whose otherwise student Editorial Board included the Fellow. Parallel to this, and a small host of other literary, cultural, and political student magazines, was the national literary quarterly *Stand*, at that time edited in Leeds by a former Gregory Fellow and recent graduate, the poet Jon Silkin. In the academic department was Geoffrey Hill, then at the slow, private labour towards *King Log* (1968) and really only known to students through his exacting tutorial standards and the dour theatrical wit of his equally demanding lectures. More informally visible was the Marxist critic Arnold Kettle, author of *An Introduction to the English Novel*.

Kettle had little to do with poetry, but was a signal presence in the political character of this Leeds literary environment. In large measure the contrarian stance of student life was a response to national and international discontents. Through the dire winter of 1962–3 unemployment was mounting towards three million, an exhausted and etiolated Tory government was crawling through the risible embarrassments of the Profumo scandal, and, dominating everything, was the threat of nuclear war culminating in the Cuba crisis. The Campaign of Nuclear Disarmament (CND) was the principal vector of oppositional activity, especially among students. On the other hand, things were also getting better: feminism was still virtually unheard of but contraception was readily available from Student Health.

'Leeds poetry' was dyed in these waters. Our vision of the art was set by the notion of 'engagement'. (The later theoretical idea that we hapless poets were part of the problem rather than part of the solution was still a few years away.) The figure of Jon Silkin was central here. A dropout from a substantial and cultured family who had done National Service and a series of manual jobs through his twenties and had founded his magazine *Stand* in the early 1950s before coming to Leeds as Gregory Fellow and staying on to take a degree, he was an enormously charismatic and authoritative figure. He saw his magazine and all his work as agency for social change. The *work* of the magazine included not only its editing and publication but its personal face-to-face selling as four times a year Silkin would set off on a national tour, principally of university towns, to sell the current issue in person. This was not just a commercial imperative but a vital part of what he saw as the process of the magazine, proselytizing for the principles the magazine stood for and engaging in an endless series of dialogues.

So what did *Stand* stand for? An issue from 1963 contained a vigorous taped conversation between Silkin and Anthony Thwaite. Silkin to Thwaite:

> You would tend to say that the important thing is whether the poem is good or not; and I would tend to ask the poet to grow by relating himself to an actuality shared by many people. I'd be willing to have bad poetry for the time being, if I thought the area of preoccupation for the poet might expand; whereas all I can see for the future, with the direction that you are looking in, is an increasingly diminishing area and an increasingly private one.[2]

Thwaite professes himself bewildered by this and counters by asking Silkin whether he chooses poems for *Stand* by saying ' "this is a bad poem saying the right sort of thing about what ought to be done to society, therefore I am going to print it". At some level you make some sort of aesthetic judgment about it.' Predictably Silkin sidesteps this by challenging the terms of 'aesthetic judgement' and insists that the question to be asked of a poem is ' "does it succeed in communicating something that is important to human beings" ', to which Thwaite's response is 'No, does it succeed in saying what it has to say? And it may in fact be something of minimal importance to human beings.' But Silkin sees this kind of 'importance' as non-negotiable, for him the stance of the poem is inextricable from its aesthetic success:

> What I'm trying to say is that if the poet could concern himself with an area of human suffering that is outside his own class or group experience he might write better poetry. A better aesthetic can only be the result of a higher consciousness of the interacting of more and more human beings.[3]

To a beginning, undergraduate poet like myself whose sympathies lay on Silkin's side of what is essentially a political argument, the problem was how to achieve this 'better aesthetic'. For me the readiest solution lay in choice of subject matter. I looked to topics outside myself, often with documentary sources. 'Three Poems on the Battle of Jutland 1916' was an early example in that the impetus for the poem and most of its material came from a newspaper article commemorating the fiftieth anniversary of the naval battle, one that crucially included recollections of ordinary seamen, the 'scalded stokers | Suddenly washed of their dust.' '1815', which sought to juxtapose the triumphalism of Waterloo with the deprivation and callousness of the burgeoning Industrial Revolution, was similarly motivated and, sensing a lode to be mined, more extensively researched. To me these poems were exploring, with no little indignation, a great subject: the submerged history of working people as they lived and died at work and at war. What Silkin derided as the 'personal and private' had no part in these poems, nor did the first-person

---

[2] *Stand*, 6/2 (1963), 21.
[3] *Stand*, 6/2 (1963), 22.

singular which I felt as no sacrifice as it accorded with my temperamental disposition. I thought of them as having the objective cast of History.

One thing I never thought about at this time was the implications of my title for the Jutland poem: 'Three Poems on ...'. My hope for the poems was that they played their part in a wider movement towards a 'higher consciousness'. I did agonize about the purpose and usefulness of poetry in playing any part in effecting social change, and increasingly defensive before the charge that debates such as that between Silkin and Thwaite as to which kind of poetry would assist liberation were beside the point as poetry was in any case an elitist and increasingly irrelevant form. But my commitment, or addiction, to the *form* of poetry, to its particularity went unexamined. But I was writing *poems* on these subjects and what did that imply?

At the same time as I was writing 'Jutland' and '1815' in the late sixties I was absorbing other influences, although I did not at the time think of them as 'other'. In 1965–6 I took Geoffrey Hill's postgraduate course in Modern American Poetry. I was already well disposed to American literature simply because it was not English, or rather 'English'. But Hill's course, which went from Whitman to Lowell via Dickinson, Pound, Stevens, Crane, and Tate introduced me to a sustained study of modernist poetry, most particularly Pound, and more generally to an intense consciousness of the poem as a made thing, an artefact whose detail and complexity was the way that it engaged the world outside itself. I consciously discovered here the Poundian definition of the image, as in Imagism, 'that which presents an intellectual and emotional complex in an instant of time'[4] and the idea of the poem's method to 'juxtapose with science' one image against another and allow the meaning to form itself across the distance between them, like an electrical charge. Also there was the idea of the persona as the voice in the poem and the notion of 'impersonality' as a way of avoiding that dreaded first-person singular. Moreover Pound's dictum in 'How to Read' that 'great literature is simply language charged with meaning to the utmost possible degree'[5] to be posed against 'the fogged language of the swindling classes' lent his poetics a satisfyingly political slant, despite Pound's Fascism. Why, temperamentally, these ideas made such an impression is largely a mystery. In part certainly it had to do with the bracing masculine vigour of Pound's denunciations of 'a lot of wish-wash that passes for classic or "standard" poetry', of 'emotional slither', 'sincere self-expression', and his countervailing advocacy of 'perfect control', the 'objective', 'clarity', 'hardness'. For a boy such as myself from a working-class background and still defensive about the effete and effeminate image of poetry, Pound provided a necessary reassurance just as the closer example of Ted Hughes did. I'm not judging this, merely reporting upon it.

The 'Three Poems... Jutland' and '1815'[6] were both written under the sway of these ideas. They aimed for terseness and clarity, striving to have the images make the point without the intervention of a discursive, authorial voice. '1815' begins:

Above her face
Dead roach stare vertically

---

[4] 'A Retrospect', in *Literary Essays of Ezra Pound*, ed. T. S. Eliot (London: Faber & Faber, 1954), 4.
[5] 'A Retrospect', 23.
[6] Jeffrey Wainwright, *Heart's Desire* (Manchester: Carcanet Press, 1978), 24, 11; *Selected Poems* (Manchester: Carcanet Press, 1985), 30, 40.

Out of the canal.
Water fills her ears,
Her nose, her open mouth.
Surfacing, her bloodless fingers
Nudge the drying gills.

The succeeding sections depend on their images: 'deep-chested rosy ploughboys | Swell out of their uniforms'; Wellington's 'spruce wit sits straight | In the saddle'; 'The lock-keeper bends and pulls her out | With his bare hands'; the dying mill-owner's 'fat body clenches— | Mortified'. The method is to juxtapose these images and to 'charge the words with meaning to the utmost degree' as in the punning use of 'mortified'. The use of short lines too is meant to cut any tendency to eloquence.

In retrospect it is perhaps surprising—or a tribute to his open-mindedness—that Jon Silkin published these poems in *Stand* and reprinted '1815' in his *Stand* anthology of 1971, *Poetry of the Committed Individual*, for in his introduction to the latter he developed his antipathy to 'Imagism' and its influence on contemporary poetry. The problem as Silkin saw it was how to marry the clarity and sensuousness of the image with discursiveness:

> It is problematic because the nature of Imagism is that it rejects discursiveness; it wants enactment rather than description. And it wants enactment of a kind that also I think tends to reject narrative. So that the question for us has been whether a poem could use the hard, clear and sensuous image in such a way as to share its nature with the explicitly addressed issues without losing its essentiality.[7]

His suspicion is that absence of discursiveness and narrative fosters aestheticism and he elaborates his misgivings in a discussion of Geoffrey Hill, whose work is in fact generously represented in the anthology. Hill's sonnet sequence 'Funeral Music' he criticizes as lacking the structure through either a narrative sequence or in the discursiveness that 'an extended work' requires:

> Hill meets this problem (at least in 'Funeral Music') partly by placing outside the poem [in the accompanying 'essay'] those explanations, scene-settings and minimal narrative gestures which would in his own mind apparently, reduce his concentration of intensity, rhetoric and imagistic impulse. There is no discursiveness, no explanatory matter, no narrative, inside the poetry. The purity of the poetry must remain unimpaired.[8]

In 1971 I had not taken in the substance or importance of the issue Silkin raises. I did have a half-theorized notion of the need to create poetic artefacts successful in themselves according to the criteria and taste I had absorbed from my reading and literary education. This might be characterized as concern for 'the purity of the poetry'. On the other hand I was continually beset by an anxiety as to the usefulness of such poetry, or its point at all. Was I wasting the space available, not only the page before me, but my life?

---

[7] Jon Silkin (ed.), *Poetry of the Committed Individual: A Stand Anthology of Poetry* (Harmondsworth: Penguin Books, 1973), 29.
[8] Silkin (ed.), *Poetry of the Committed Individual*, 33.

I want to continue by looking at a poem I wrote in 1977–8, 'Thomas Müntzer', published first in *Stand* and then in my first collection *Heart's Desire*.[9] 'Thomas Müntzer was a Protestant reformer in the early years of the German Reformation. He was a radical and visionary both in theology and politics…'. A note beginning with these words stood in front of the poem by way of orienting readers and giving them some essential 'background'. Although I did not think of it in these terms I suppose what I thought I was doing here was to clear up the 'prose matter' before the start of the poem proper. As the headnote makes clear I had at my disposal a discursive account of Müntzer's life, times, and significance as I saw it. If this was not to be part of the poem what was the distinctive matter that would be?

An early and vital decision in the poem's composition was to make the poem a dramatic monologue. Here the example of the Poundian persona stood before me. Inventing an inner life for Müntzer gave me all sorts of possibilities. I found I could be free in such things as settings. For instance, the poem begins:

Just above where my house sits on the slope
Is a pond, a lodge when the mine was here,

Now motionless, secretive, hung in weeds.

This scene was in fact based upon a place of old mine-workings in the Welsh mountains that had long had a fascination for me. I had no interest in trying to write a 'place' poem about it and my response to it, but I could use it as part of Müntzer's life, and the image of the rowan tree in section III comes from the same place. Similarly in section IX my wakeful son is transmogrified into Müntzer's son by eliding his nightly wanderings with a documentary scrap: 'At his baptism we dressed him in white | And gave him salt as a symbol of this wisdom.' Thus I found I could make a collage of material I had read, not all of it about my protagonist, seen and experienced. In this respect the poem could be called 'personal' in that each detail seized my sensibility in a way that was urgent and unmistakable but it was material to be used otherwise, not in self-expression. The poem relied a good deal on historical research and thus might have seemed to be open to systematizing, but in fact nothing found its way into the poem that did not possess this passport to my imagination, this sensuous palpability. I 'know' that I am writing a poem about Thomas Müntzer 'protestant reformer in the early years of the German Reformation…', and through him elegizing the perpetual victims of history and weighing the idealisms and tragedies of revolutionary political action and the forces of 'History', but at another level who knows what I am writing about? In some sense one is writing an unknown poem in following the impulses of words and images, and images in words:

I lie out all summer spread like a coat
Over the earth one night after another

Waiting to catch her. And then

---

[9] Wainwright, *Heart's Desire*, 31-7.

She is mine and the rowan blooms—
His black roots swim out and dive to subdue her—
His red blood cracks in the air and saves me.

The poem is structured in twelve parts, each composed of three unrhymed triplets of irregular and strongly accented lines. By the time I wrote 'Müntzer' I had written a thesis on William Carlos Williams and studied the models of American free verse quite extensively and enthusiastically. But whilst I had never tried to practise verse forms, or even to write in deliberate metre or to write in rhyme, I derived a shape for 'Müntzer' with a high degree of symmetry. This was the most extensive poem I had written to date and it just came to require as the composition proceeded a mould to contain the material. Dodecal systems had been impressed upon me in childhood through the times table and £.s.d. and seemed the most comprehensible. To divide the poem into numbered sections enabled me to retain the elements of fragmentation and juxtaposition that I had already learnt and to suggest the erratic movement of Müntzer's consciousness and his movement between registers as well as incorporate other voices. Narrative sequencing I felt to be both beyond me, and I felt it to be a distraction from the intensities of Müntzer's mind as I imagined it.

As for the line itself I had no preconception as to its metric. I knew I wanted a line around ten syllables in length but this line was governed by the overall *shape* I had in mind. I usually find that it is the visual shape and the aural pitch of a poem that occurs first along with very few actual words, rather as Mandelstam writes of hearing 'a tune in his head' before he has the words of a poem. This is another of the urgent mysteries of poetry as a verbal act: the tune and shape that must be followed. Given the structure of stanza and section, and the symmetry of the whole, it would not be accurate to call the verse 'free'. But there is considerable variation in the prosody as the rhythm adjusts to the tone and subject. For example:

My **son** will not **sleep**. The **noise**
And **eve**ry **mov**ing **part** of the **world**
Shuttles **round** him, **mak**ing him **regard** it,

Giving him—**only four years old**!—no **peace**.

The tendency—I note now—is towards four stresses [in bold] per line but their disposition is various according to what I am hearing. The reason free verse lines appeal to me is because of the variety of rhythmical movement they enable, not only within lines but through them too. I am not doctrinaire about this and do not feel committed to either the 'strictly free' nor the devotees of 'craft'.

In much of my writing—though not latterly—'form' has been most conspicuous in the shape of stanza and sections, as for instance in the long sequence 'The Red-Headed Pupil'[10] which consists of two parts, each of twenty-four sections, each of twelve lines in the consistent pattern of stanzas containing three, four, and five lines. Again this

---

[10] Jeffrey Wainwright, *The Red-Headed Pupil* (Manchester: Carcanet Press, 1994).

predilection for dodecapartite structures is evident although in this case an accidental element was that the shape of the stanza series—three, four, and five lines—was suggested by the pattern of the bell strokes in an Italian village where I was staying as the sequence began to take shape. Accidental or not, the common element in these structures is a felt need to organize my material in a symmetrical fashion. Having begun the work, soon after its likely scale has become apparent I sought for a satisfying pattern in which to pour and so discipline the slip of my thought and imagination. I shall return to this issue in relation to later work.

There are then formal aspects of 'Thomas Müntzer' that suggest its drive towards an independent 'poetic' goal. It is hard to deny that first and foremost a poet wants to write a poem in accordance with his or her notion of what the word 'poem' means. The idea that one is engaged in selfless 'truth-telling' is a vanity and a delusion. Nonetheless one tries it. As I remember the compositional process of 'Müntzer' the problem of its ending sat abysmally before me. The essential problem was to find the right words when I did not know what I wanted to say. The Müntzer I had created could be made forlornly tragic, vitiated, or heroically tragic, confident of the ultimate triumph of the people. An orthodox Marxist analysis would point to the latter and see Müntzer as resigned to the insignificance of his own death: 'To have any love for my own fingered | Body and brain is a luxury.' But I could not find the positive and defiant fanfare that should follow this. He tries to rise to find the necessary certainty: 'History, which is Eternal Life, is what | We need to celebrate', but the rhythm is meant to falter as 'History' is elided into the 'Eternal Life' of his religious belief. He must then spell out what this means and he cannot get past a halting formulation: 'Stately tearful | Progress...' with its contradictory epithets to 'Progress', whose position at the start of a line rallies briefly before the concluding phrase '...you've seen how I have wept for it.' 'Wept' is a crucial word, for unqualified defiance could have been carried by 'fought', or complete disintegration by concluding with the run of dots after 'Progress'. Yet how the word 'wept' is to be interpreted remains ambiguous. *How* the 'you' will in fact have seen this cannot be certain.

In the last three or four years I have found that I have revisited the thoughts explicit and implicit in the last section of 'Thomas Müntzer' in three other poems. The meaning of 'History', how far its processes can be understood, whether it has any 'processes' at all, whether it might include concepts like 'Progress' or is 'one damned thing after another' is an irrepressible question for me. Moreover I must be aware that the leisure to ponder these questions is a privilege of happenstance, of generation and geography. A child born only ten years earlier than myself, starved to death in the Ukraine, had no opportunity to consider the 'paths' of history. These thoughts also become part of the problem.

The tone of 'What Must Happen'[11] is the poem that most affects to stand aside from its topic. It began with the arrival—I can't recollect, if I ever knew, from where—of the phrase 'Now all the Sciences of History are at the door'. This immediately suggested itself as a

---

[11] *Times Literary Supplement*, 5659 (16 Sept. 2011), 25.

refrain and it becomes so through the four sections of the poem. It makes a long line, fourteen syllables and seven iambic stresses, but it presented itself as too much of a piece to break. I liked the iambic beat, and the portentousness of these 'knowers' impatient enough to impart their wisdom to present themselves 'at the door' like salesmen or census-takers. For seven or eight typescript versions of the poem the phrase was its title. But for quite a long time before that I could not figure out what to do with it and it wandered in and out of several possible drafts of poems quite different from its eventual home, a not unusual instance for me. I find I often know a germane form of words before I can fill out the appropriate material around it. In this instance the case became a comparatively formal structure of four sections, each containing three quatrains. Internal rhyme and metre are fugitively present so that there is a recurrent tension between the imposed order of 'the Sciences' and the disarray that confronts them. This is most evident in the fourth and final section where 'the Sciences', by now weary and discomposed, still cling to their expectation of orderly explanation in lines whose metric becomes increasingly distracted:

Now all the Sciences of History are at the door
Or tent-flap, fly-screen, wire-entanglement
And peer in. Still on their jotters there's little spilt
Or spattered, and still they will reiterate:

'Time must be History, and History an Idea
Patient of its uncoiling
To an End [...]'

In particular any regularity of metric folds in the reiteration of the last three lines here and the whole section features several sentence breaks in mid-line that have not featured in the imputed self-confidence of the first three sections. Those sections feature three historical periods and 'scientific' ideas. The first evokes the imperial clash of France and Russia in the Napoleonic period, where the Hegelian 'World's Reason and his suite' stumble. The second 'science' belongs to the revolutionary moments, of right and left, of the twentieth century and the fine disregard for the individual as History passes through their corpses:

Their willing corporals stun and storm,
Their strapped-up martyrs charge and call:
'Fools, did we think we should live forever?
Look how historical the future is!'

The third section satirizes the neo-conservative making of the world without any concern for History or even precedent, couched in the emollient terms of a globalized salesman:

'There is no past, all things are new, we act: we are.'

So just sign where it says: 'In none we trust',
....
[']How historical you were, and now how free!'

By that fourth section 'the Sciences' are sensing their dismay but cannot abandon their commitment to meaning. History is an Idea or 'Otherwise we fall through, | Like light through glass, nothing now and nothing then.' Again the ending was hugely problematical. I don't know if I am committed to the idea of a 'Science', still less which one. The poem has meant to present each candidate as risible and yet the alternative is nihilistic, a falling through life 'like light through glass, nothing now and nothing then.' The whole poem aims to be a bitter comedy, signalled at the outset by the epigraph from Emily Dickinson: 'Funny—to be a Century— | And see the People—going by—', and this is maintained at the very end by the soldier-boys eager to need to shave. I end again though with a question, and as simple and as discursive a one as I could muster: 'What must happen, what need not?'

A nice justification of the poetic mode when it finds itself entangled in such topics is that such uncertainty is wholly appropriate to the genre, and that the poetic sensibility is too refined to accede to the kinds of certainty that the politician must aspire to. Tempting as this is I can't see that it stands much scrutiny. As Wordsworth said, a poet is 'a man speaking to men' and it is hard to see why this act should be characterized by fastidiousness in excess of the facts. If I ask: 'What must happen, what need not?' it is because I can't begin to answer in whatever discourse the question is posed. If there is a fastidiousness that does accrue to the poet here it might reside in the presentation of the depths of the words 'must' and 'need'. There is a realism about 'must' that admonishes idealism but whose insistence draws it towards the callous. The auxiliary verb 'need' is not simply functional but carries something of the weight of the substantive word 'need' which gives an urgency but also a plangency. 'Happen' is also a word poised above the imponderable, at once a common, functional item with the connotations of 'happenstance' and random occurrence, but also carrying the import of 'what befalls'. For me poetry has always involved an engagement with the several dimensions of individual words, especially familiar ones. The rhythmic structure of the sentence—'**What must happen, what need not?**'—with its series of stressed syllables carries I hope not just a concluding emphasis but a kind of stolidity, a resigned but dogged plod towards a closure. Poetry is the unhurried space that enables this kind of contemplation.

In an interview with Marius Kociejowski, published in the volume *Palavers & A Nocturnal Journal* Christopher Middleton makes an obvious but too seldom appreciated point:

> It's a funny thing about language, you see, it is very difficult to create. You can create in paint, dance and music because they give themselves to this but language has this literal attachment to the world of what they call reference, to *things*, to *concepts*, to discourse about the real world, so its levitation into the realm of creation is that much more difficult.[12]

---

[12] Christopher Middleton, *Palavers & A Nocturnal Journal* (Exeter: Shearsman Books, 2004), 30.

Improbable as it often seems, language does have referents and its 'use' cannot avoid them. But what then does Middleton mean by 'creation' as opposed, presumably, to representation? In 'A Nocturnal Journal 1997–1998' he describes two 'niches' for poetry, first the poem 'that invites its referents, supposedly mute, to speak for themselves...phenomena revealed' (he includes W. C. Williams in this type), and second the poem 'which invites *words* to unsay or gainsay their usual speech and show their latent innermosts: the word itself as a secret *phenomenon*'.[13] Undoubtedly too one's experience of words is that they are themselves 'phenomena' which possess an independent palpability and a variegated history of contexts and associations which can, at least in part, 'unsay or gainsay their usual speech'. For me the form of the poem is the space where words as referents and words as phenomena fuse. In one sense then language becomes both the medium and the subject of the poem, sometimes, as in my sequence 'Is our language complete?' referentially.[14] The title phrase is from Wittgenstein's *Philosophical Investigations*, no. 18: '...ask yourself whether our language is complete'[15] and the sequence provides a partly comic argument back-and-forth on the proposition. The first section concludes with a reference to Esperanto, the artificial language whose universal currency had utopian ambitions:

In Stoke-on-Trent post-war we were keen on Esperanto.
Here, where breathing could be difficult,
was an inspiration to get out the door,
to world peace, nation same-speaking peace unto nation,
so charas could criss-cross from Dresden to Dresden,
Burslem to Bialystok,
happy wanderers, buying pots of tea effortlessly,
and explaining the laws of cricket faultlessly
to Russians Germans Poles and Jews,
without an itch and nary a crux word.

Hopefully there is some exuberance in the nine-line sentence here and in the satire of the quixotic ambition guyed as naïve and provincial. Yet the hope may be naïve but it is still hope, and very much 'post-war', and the poem's performance is breezily insensitive. All five poems are voluble whether they are pretending to argue the case for the 'completion' of language or of its unsatisfactory fumbling or mendacity. It is not meant to have any of the restraint of philosophical discourse but rather to relish elaboration of image and verbal sound. Within the inflation there is a proposition that is an affirmation that our language is what we have, whether or not it is perfectible. The sequence ends:

As the nightingale *with her sweet self she wrangles*
we must just strive with our creature tongue.

---

[13] Middleton, *Palavers*, 121.
[14] Jeffrey Wainwright, *The Reasoner* (Manchester: Carcanet Press, 2012).
[15] Wittgenstein, *Philosophical Investigations*, 7^e.

The interpolation of the quotation from Crashaw must, strictly regarded, appear rococo. But the wonderful tension in Crashaw's phrase between the 'sweet self' of the nightingale and the combative word 'wrangles' itself demonstrates the indelibility of the baroque in language use, and the insistence with which some wordings can force themselves irresistibly into seemingly foreign territory. It is meant to contrast too with the succeeding phrase with its blunt, phonic repetition 'must just strive...'. Alongside its propositional tendency I hope the poem offers interest and some fascination of its own in the athleticism of words.

So I am saying that 'we must just strive' to say what we sense wants to be said with words, even though we know that the words can seem to be animated by quite other impulses, an animation that they have acquired through their long history and ever-changing styles of use, and that this is part of their fascination and quality. One thing that we persist in thinking we can say will describe our ontological position in the universe. The territory I am thinking of lies in such usually joking questions as 'why are we all here?' or 'what does it all mean?' or 'why is there something rather than nothing?' (The last two indeed have provided the titles for two substantial books of philosophical synthesis in the past twenty-five years, Thomas Nagel's *What Does It All Mean?* (1987) and Leszek Kolakowski's *Why Is There Something Rather than Nothing?* (2007)). I am as interested as the next person in answering these questions, I am also interested in the language and habits of such inquiry, and not just as it is systematically conducted by philosophers and theologians, but in the more fugitive moments of realization, wonder, or comic puzzlement that visit us all from time to time. Thus, several years ago, I was struck by the following words from a review by the philosopher Jerry Fodor:

> ...sometimes, out of the corner of an eye, 'at the moment which is not action or inaction', one can glimpse the true scientific vision: austere, tragic, alienated and supremely beautiful. A world that isn't for anything, a world that is just there.[16]

I am not inclined, still less equipped, to debate the implications of Fodor's statement, but I became very interested in the intimations of his experience of this thought, 'sometimes...one can glimpse', at the words used to describe 'the true scientific vision: austere, tragic, alienated and supremely beautiful', and by the bold formulation of 'A world that isn't for anything, a world that is just there.' Eventually a sequence of poems, 'Mere Bagatelle'[17] grew out of my pondering Fodor's words alongside a series of sights, occurrences, and observations in my daily life and memories.

The thirty-nine numbered poems are comparatively minimalist in style, mostly brief, using short lines and lower case. Their manner alludes to note-form jottings in accord with the diffidence with which, chancing to look up at the night sky or out on to the lawn, the thought of how the universe actually is regarded. The 'truth', Fodor's 'true scientific vision'—or 'it'—plays hide-and-seek through the sequence, 'there, there, there it is!', in stars or soil, in sun blazing on a distant window, in a shadow-trick of light 'a little

---

[16] Jerry Fodor, 'Peacocking', *London Review of Books*, 18/8 (18 Apr. 1996), 20.

[17] Jeffrey Wainwright, *Clarity or Death!* (Manchester: Carcanet Press, 2008), 39–82.

sashay | on the kitchen floor'. Certain words also recur through the poems, three from the Fodor epigraph, 'glimpse', 'austere', and 'beautiful', as well as others, 'real', 'imperturbable', 'bless'd'. The experience of any of these words tells us they go in various ways:

this fact can be called 'austere'
as in 'an austere regime'
or 'that was an austere look
she gave me' (3)

'Bless'd' is a word that can be used for 'anything that can get | into a robble' (12) as well as in 'talking to those | who cannot hear or cannot reply | or are truly busy' and 'of course it's not stupid | to talk to no effect' (13). The 'austerity' of fact and the counterfactual assertion that 'it's not stupid | to talk to no effect', returns in a poem late in the sequence which is about my mother's death:

what is not austere,
and what is not true,
and what is not stupid
to say,
is folded in your note,
to be found in the event,
in your special box,
which—paraphrased—says:
when you read this
I shall have gone
to be with your father again,
that is where I really
want to be

this is the kind of way
we look at death,
it is not—especially when
elaborated—austere,
and it is not true,
and it is not a stupid thing
to say   (30)

Perhaps whatever we say about 'the true scientific vision'—'*it*'—is paraphrase. Moreover, whatever we say is a paraphrase of whatever some intimation within our being tells us we want to say. The *forms* of poetry, with their precious distractions, are the recognition of paraphrase in this sense, and besides the 'beautiful' natural universe that 'is just there', their human beauties—like that of all art—hold their place: 'words, and other | of our imaginings— | lines, sounds— | are the confounding | of Nature—' (23). 'Mere Bagatelle' are scratches of 'meaning' in a universe I cannot presently describe as other than 'meaningless'. But they are scratches which I believe are not stupid things to say, even when the problems of poetics interfere:

to be so imperturbable
would be to be
something soughing—
alliteration again,
it stole up on me
again

but I am not
to be laughed at,
this is my little rage
for order,
balance,
I do not want
to fall off

a poem should be
a paean
to law and order—
what else is there?
justice?
a 'land of'?

'soughing' is always
as of the wind,
was when *swōgan*,
do not be perturbed,
there is always the wind,
button up your overcoat (27)

This poem is a mood rather than a summation—I think I have shown how the experience of writing poems has taught me the difficulties of summary. But 'my little rage | for order, | balance' will work for how I currently think about poetics. The 'space available' to poetry in the sense of 'media share' may be small, but what might currently be done within that space in terms of the variety of style and discourse has wider possibilities and fewer stipulations than any other of the verbal forms. It is extensive enough to tread the limen of reference, and can seem most exciting when it does so. Perhaps my early struggles with the issues of political proposition were the result of choosing poetry as my chosen medium in the first place. My sense now when thinking about poetry as a 'form' is that it both belongs and does not belong among the varieties of discursive utterance. It belongs because words cannot escape all vestige of reference, but it does not adhere to the expected manners of their deployment. It is easy to construct this defensively and see poetry as a tiny resistance, a recalcitrant nook where the babble is muffled—'what else is there? | justice? | a land of?' More than this however I feel grateful for the moral luck that has enabled me to live with the *form* that is poetry, and I button up my overcoat.

Select Bibliography

Pound, Ezra, 'A Retrospect', in T. S. Eliot (ed.), *Literary Essays of Ezra Pound* (London: Faber & Faber, 1954).

Fodor, Jerry, 'Peacocking', *London Review of Books*, 18/8 (18 Apr. 1996).

Middleton, Christopher, *Palavers & A Nocturnal Journal* (Exeter: Shearsman Books, 2004).

Silkin, Jon (ed.), *Poetry of the Committed Individual: A Stand Anthology of Poetry* (Harmondsworth: Penguin Books, 1973).

Wainwright, Jeffrey, *Heart's Desire* (Manchester: Carcanet Press, 1978).

Wainwright, Jeffrey, *Selected Poems* (Manchester: Carcanet Press, 1985).

Wainwright, Jeffrey, *The Red-Headed Pupil* (Manchester: Carcanet Press, 1994).

Wainwright, Jeffrey, *Clarity or Death!* (Manchester: Carcanet Press, 2008).

Wainwright, Jeffrey, *The Reasoner* (Manchester: Carcanet Press, 2012).

Wittgenstein, Ludwig, *Philosophical Investigations* (3rd edn.), trans. G. E. M. Anscombe (Oxford: Blackwell, 2001).

CHAPTER 12

CONTEMPORARY POETRY AND CLOSE READING

ADAM PIETTE

A new form of close reading, practical criticism as taught by I. A. Richards, was inaugurated in 1920s Cambridge. This is where close reading officially begins—but we can see Richards working with forms of the biblical, rhetorical, and textual editing versions of close reading that had accompanied the establishment of English Studies. Richards asked students studying the English Tripos to read poems 'blind'—without benefit of any knowledge of their historical provenance or author. The texts were short lyrics in the main, and Richards recorded the student readings in terms of their prejudices or 'protocols'. For Richards the exercise enabled one to judge how far reading is an act of over-reading or fanciful illusion as much as demonstrating the power of certain poems to establish currents of feeling in reader responses. For the first time, poets could see how their poems were being read by young amateurs; they could register both the power of habit in ordinary interpretation, but also the care and attention of readers if invited to attend to poems with sufficient time and in sufficient detail. Richards's account of the experiment led to the establishment of practical criticism as a practice at Cambridge, eventually leading to the assumption in most university courses of English Literature of the importance of close reading of short lyrical poems as a valuable pedagogical tool.

What students undergoing practical criticism were supposed to learn was the unpacking of metaphors in the texts, the acquisition of the conventions governing poetry from a poet's point of view, and sensitivity to the poetic techniques coded into any given poem—as forms of knowledge, not empty ornaments. I. A. Richards's student William Empson took practical criticism a step further with his brilliant book, *Seven Types of Ambiguity* (1930). There, Empson analysed specific quibbles in the canon with the attention of the textual editor, but also with the scientific eye of Richards for intelligible and classifiable relations. He defined seven kinds of ambiguity, permutations on conflicts and double meanings implicit when metaphor becomes scrambled or close-packed in various ways. Richards had concentrated on metaphor as the key sign of poetry, and broken it into its two terms: the tenor (the term to be comparatively defined) and the vehicle (what the tenor is compared to). Empson had revealed what happens when tenor and vehicle are mutually complex, thus generating more than one meaning. Close reading in Cambridge was dominated by Empsonian attention to the subtle plural significances of patches of difficult text.

The genesis of close reading at Cambridge owes a great deal too to the influence of T. S. Eliot, whose meticulous gift for quotation and intriguing interpretation of those quotations became a model for the things one ought to be able to say about a poem if it were to be deemed worthy of attention. In other words, Eliotic close reading became a matter of fine judgement—a poem was worth considering if it could be shown that it contained lines that could 'take' close attention, and give up valuable matter. Eliot's prestige in the history of close reading was magnified by his modernist masterpiece, *The Waste Land*: its difficulty, learning, its host of subtle and barbed notes, and the haunting nature of every line made it the ideal poem for the ideal close reader with an ideal insomnia. To read closely, in this Eliotic context, meant also being able to discriminate historically, to be able to 'place' a text, however blind, in its correct period, to identify its allusions, to sense and demonstrate its play with tradition.

Cambridge close reading was taken up by American poet-critics in the 1930s and 1940s on the strength of Eliot's prestige. Close reading became the principal tool of analysis and critical interpretation for the New Critics, a collection of poets and scholars that grew out of the Southern Agrarians and became identified with such journals as the *Kenyon Review*. Cleanth Brooks, René Wellek, W. K. Wimsatt, John Crowe Ransom, Allen Tate, R. P. Blackmur, Robert Penn Warren, and Yvor Winters collaborated in disseminating New Criticism throughout Anglo-American literary culture, and had a substantial effect during the Cold War in consolidating a certain form of cerebral, quasi-metaphysical lyric poetry as the norm in the academy. New Criticism took from Richards the idea that poems are verbal artefacts that transcend their compositional occasions and context, and need not have anything to do, even, with the poets who wrote them. They turned away from the chatty biographical criticism that had dominated journals till then, and demanded that readers of poetry be technically expert interpreters of poems, capable of detailed line-by-line metrical analysis, and parsers of the conflictual meanings as Empsonian ambiguities. The net effect was to divorce the poem from history, to turn it into a fabulously artificial icon which readers could slowly meditate upon, weighing meanings against meanings, sounding out the interplay of metrical beat and voice accent, hunting for intellectual irony, the specific tropes characterizing a poem's particularity. Within New Criticism there were disputes, especially between those who thought of poems principally as vehicles for delicate balancing of complex emotions and neo-Christian moral codes, and those who favoured a much more rigorously cognitive, logical, and cerebral idea of poetry, as with Ransom. But all of the American New Critics did an enormous disservice to close reading by the quixotic and politically motivated decision to turn their backs on history, compositional context, and the poet as maker. The Cold War turn against 1930s radical commitment would massively consolidate the elevation of poem to verbal icon and well-wrought urn, an empty abstracting-out of devices, structures, and textures. By disinvesting poems of contexts and concentrating on formal features as control mechanisms for dangerous indeterminacies and impulses, the New Critics not only bowdlerized the material, but actively sought to restrict the canon to Eliot's choice of metaphysical poets (Donne and Marvell in particular), twentieth-century poets to contemporaries like Stevens and Berryman, poets who, in Ransom's words, are 'technically experienced' and therefore 'have command of their own imagination'[1] but who do not write poems obscure with history and literary tradition like the modernists.

The disservice to close reading is most evident when we remember Empson, hailed by the New Critics as their hero, whose own practice was resolutely historicizing. Ransom made sure this tendency was scripted out of sight in *The New Criticism* in his critique of Empson's over-elaborate readings of the line 'Bare ruin'd choirs, where late the sweet birds sang' from Shakespeare's Sonnet 73 in *Seven Types*. Empson's reading of the line is a justly famous *locus classicus* of close reading as unpacking of connotations. Empson argues that the comparison between the forest boughs and the church choir in Shakespeare's line works

> because ruined monastery choirs are places in which to sing, because they involve sitting in a row, because they are made of wood, are carved into knots and so forth, because they used to be surrounded by a sheltering building crystallized out of the likeness of a forest, and coloured with stained glass and painting like flowers and leaves, because they are now abandoned by all but the grey walls coloured like the skies of winter, because the cold and Narcissistic charm suggested by the choir-boys suits well with Shakespeare's feeling for the object of the Sonnets, and for various sociological and historical reasons ('for oh, the hobbyhorse is forgot', and the Puritans cut down the Maypoles), which it would be hard to trace out in their proportions; these reasons, and many more relating the simile to its place in the Sonnet, must all combine to give the line its beauty, and there is a sort of ambiguity in not knowing which of them to hold most clearly in mind. Clearly this is involved in all such richness and heightening of effect, and the machinations of ambiguity are among the very roots of poetry.[2]

What looks like over-reading becomes less so if one reflects on the comparison of tenor (the boughs) and vehicle (the choir). Shakespeare's metaphor works because churches themselves are metaphors, churches being built to resemble stone forests. It also works because of the specific erotic situation that the sonnets develop, Shakespeare's love for a self-absorbed and haughty aristocrat. And most importantly it is keen to imagine itself back to the sociocultural situation of the compositional context. Empson is open-minded about what might constitute a useful catalogue of implicit resemblances, ranging from Shakespeare the poet ('Shakespeare's feeling') through immediate contextual cultural information (Puritan drives against old churches and customs) to broader

---

[1] John Crowe Ransom, *The New Criticism* (Norfolk, Conn.: New Directions, 1941), 334.
[2] William Empson, *Seven Types of Ambiguity* (London: Chatto & Windus, 1953), 2–3.

historical material (medieval church architecture and the Reformation). Such historical material compacted into the line constitutes its beauty for Empson: and his own long sentence is beautiful simply for having untangled the historical threads out for us. This historical and cultural form of close reading is what is explicitly censored by Ransom: '[Resemblances] that introduce the history of the poet and the history of the period are of a kind that [Empson] always fancies highly and has the greatest skill in managing; they are the learned ones, involving the "literary" allusions, and the hardest ones for the ambitious reader to forego' (*New Criticism*, 122–3). Ransom uses underhand rhetoric to boost his point, a fake populist sarcasm marshalled against Empson's learning, backed up by an anti-literary sneer. To be ambitious, Ransom is saying, means doing without fanciful and elitist historical information. Nowhere does he actually argue clearly why the histories of poet and period are irrelevant. The New Critical close reader must forgo Empson's historical readings of the choir-forest metaphor, according to Ransom (those which concentrate on 'Shakespeare's narcissistic interest in the choir-boys' and 'the Puritans' bad treatment of the songs and beauties of the churches'), because 'these are meanings within the vehicle that do not have any correspondents within the tenor' (128). Ransom effectively uses a purely literary argument to de-historicize the poem. Metaphors cannot admit information from their historical period or from the author because that breaks the rules Richards developed for making sure tenor and vehicle correspond. Again, nothing is said to show how or why historical and cultural contextual information is illicit, except in the mechanical sense that it is difficult to imagine who the Puritans and choirboys might be on the bird-bough side of the comparative equation—but not impossible: the choirboys are the birds, the Puritans the forces that have made it so 'late' in the day for such music. A metaphor must have its limits in order to act as a metaphor (where both like and unlike are at play).

Why, for instance, is the extraordinarily moving line about the bare ruined choirs so affecting? Partly, surely, because it conjures up the lost world of Catholic culture that the Reformation in England destroyed; and because it goes to the heart of early modern feeling for ruins and their meanings. The Renaissance was concerned with trying to work some new humanist energy from the reinterpreted ruins of classical culture, and the line resonates with that too. What a line, though, what a magnificent, sounding line: 'Bare rn'wd [ruin'd] quiers, where late the sweet birds sang'. The line takes us to secretive Catholic nostalgia for England's lost monasteries; to Renaissance mystique about ruins and dead voices. But it must fit the subject too: it must be about the poet, and as such, it speaks of Shakespeare's own fears about losing his power to sing, through deadening old age, when knowing himself to be the best poet ever to have written in English.

The censoring of Empson's historical intelligence in the New Critical adoption of Cambridge close reading is therefore worse than a simple difference of emphasis. It robbed the technique of its most vital source of energy, the historical imagination. New Critical formalism also turned its back on Eliot: for he had always argued that poetry was an intervention into the traditions and histories of the language. 'Historical sense as Eliot talks about it', Ransom argues, 'seems to be what makes you see your own little effort of poetry, if you are a poet, as the moment when you had the happiness of being the mouthpiece of 'The Great Tradition' (146). This is witty but crude. It may have bite, especially targeting Eliot's 'excess of reverent feeling' for tradition; but it cannot justify a disdain for historical sense as such—nevertheless, the joke is the only thing offered up as argument by Ransom. Anti-historicism was so taken for granted by all the New Critics that they failed to have a theory which made clear why such forgetting should always be the poet's unconscious ablution before composing. R. P. Blackmur's influential essay on Wallace Stevens, for instance, praised poems like 'The Snow Man' and 'Sunday Morning' because 'you only need the dictionary and familiarity with the poem in question to clear up a good part of Mr. Stevens's obscurities', whereas with Eliot 'the reader must be familiar with the ideas and the beliefs and systems of feeling to which Eliot alludes', and with Pound 'combinations of classical and historical references' are likely to leave readers confused.[3]

American close reading became institutionalized as the primary mode of interpretation of poems in the 1940s, 1950s, and 1960s universities, creative writing programmes, and mainstream poetry scene. Schools devoted to the pursuit of it, like The Movement and Philip Hobsbaum's The Group in the UK, the academic poet-critics in the US (Lowell, Snodgrass, Roethke, Jarrell), educated a generation in the virtues of the technique, soldering the relationship between New Critical shibboleths and sustained attention to the lyric. And as a pedagogical tool, close reading of the New Critical kind—slow, technical reading of free-standing short poems—is still invaluable. As Douglas Mao has argued, it might even be demonstrated that New Critical close reading was always principally and essentially a pedagogical instrument for the training of a new broader student population in an era of democratic mass education. With the expansion of the academy, no common ground of knowledge could be assumed with first year undergraduates: close reading of poems without prior knowledge of context could therefore act as both a reflection of, and a germination from, the uncertainty about a democratic student body's knowledge base.[4] But even here, as David Daiches argued in 1950, the New Critics' demand 'that all works should be treated as though they were contemporary and anonymous' requires students 'to do without the tools which [the New Critics] themselves are continuously using, though often not consciously'. For their power to make judgements about a poem's complexity, structure, and internal consistency is reliant on 'historical discrimination'.[5]

The determination to restrict poems to an unreal and anonymous contemporaneity became overtly political in the 1950s. Close reading poetics as an ahistorical affective-logical construct was seduced by the dynamics of the Cold War. The work Allen Tate undertook for the Cold War liberal propaganda institution, the CIA-funded Congress for Cultural Freedom (CCF), is indication of the tight fit between New Criticism in the 1950s and the cultural front of the Cold War national security state.

---

[3] R. P. Blackmur, 'Examples of Wallace Stevens', in Frank Lentricchia and Andrew DuBois (eds.), *Close Reading: The Reader* (Durham, NC: Duke University Press, 2003), 111–35 (126).

[4] Douglas Mao, 'The New Critics and the Text-Object', *ELH* 63/1 (1996), 227–54.

[5] David Daiches, 'The New Criticism: Some Qualifications', in *Literary Essays* (New York: Philosophical Library, 1957), 167–79 (175).

The Cold War *Kulturkampf* of the CCF encouraged hard liberal existential humanism, an embattled, 'tragic', and alienated individualism, and an apolitical psychologism. Robert Lowell, whose poetry is forcefully engaged with history, might be seen as an exception to the New Critical drive. And yet the historical material in the poems was consistently identified by the host of Lowell critics (Helen Vendler in particular), as 'inextricably bound up' in Michael Thurston's words, 'with Lowell's prominent New England family and therefore with Lowell's personal psychology'. It was New Criticism shaped by the Cold War turn against political history that led to this 'overemphasis on the personal, the familial, and occasionally the medical in Lowell's life and verse [obscuring] the dedication to poetry as public and empowered utterance that runs throughout Lowell's career'. Lowell's resistance to the Cold War in the 1960s anti-Vietnam demonstrations came too late: close reading was now identified not only with the academy, with an apolitical fetishizing of the lyric as art object: it was also understood to be the technique of choice of the Cold Warriors of poetry. Readings that emphasized historical and political considerations were semi-consciously equated with Marxist materialism. Close reading preserved the aesthetic freedoms of the individual democratic reader, each poem a playground of affects and psychological (at times psychoanalytic) struggles controlled by a host of neutralizing mimetic devices.

The culture wars of the late 1950s, 1960s, and 1970s were fought over the function of poetry in most universities. In Cambridge, F. R. Leavis waged a long war with left-wing literary historians such as Basil Willey. The ideological struggle was reproduced in different forms till the McCabe affair in the early 1980s, when students struck for the Marxist criticism and critical theory of Raymond Williams, Colin McCabe, and Stephen Heath as ranged against the close reading taught by Christopher Ricks. In the States, Donald Allen's anthology, *The New American Poetry*, offered the public a new radical process-defined poetry as a direct alternative to the close-reading academic poets and critics. The rise of critical theory, in particular the deconstructionist critique of structuralism in all its forms, including the structures dear to the New Critics, challenged the dominance of New Critical and Leavisite close reading practices in English Literature programmes.

There are, however, important continuities between some of the key interpretative strategies of critical theory and New Critical analysis. As Andrew DuBois has shown, there was an acknowledgement that, despite the questionable emphasis on organic context, structures of irony, paradox, and ambiguity, and a set of protocols discouraging biographical, political, or historical material, New Criticism's key tool of close reading need not be considered a purely formalist procedure. Praising Cleanth Brook's brilliant reading of Keats's 'Ode on a Grecian Urn' in his essay 'Keats' Sylvan Historian: History without Footnotes' from the 1947 *The Well Wrought Urn*, DuBois notes 'that there's nothing inherent in Brooks' method that makes it politically dubious. On the contrary, it seems that the *literary* critic must necessarily first establish the intrinsic context of the literary object; otherwise, all extrinsic moves (which are also "contextual" moves) are themselves suspicious'.[6] Lentricchia and DuBois, with their *Close Reading* reader,

---

[6] Lentricchia and DuBois, 'Introduction', in Lentricchia and DuBois (eds.), *Close Reading*, 8.

contrast Brooks's close reading of the ode with Kenneth Burke's essay, 'Symbolic Action in a Poem by Keats' from his *A Grammar of Motives*, however, to show how close reading need not work within Brooks's narrow circumspection (implied by his subtitle, 'history without footnotes'). Burke is unafraid of Marxist and psychoanalytic readings, uses biographical material from Keats's letters, contextualizes the poem within the specific moment of Romanticism and Romantic philosophy, and makes much sensitive play with the fact of Keats's illness in the construction of his reading. Yet the reading is nevertheless as close and painstaking in its attention to the detail of the ode as Brooks's. This is an Empsonian admixture, I would argue, a fusion of New Critical close reading with engagement with wide-ranging forms of external evidence prompted by the detail of the poem. For DuBois, Burke's example is 'as a methodological conciliator. In our peaceable post-Burkean critical kingdom, the lion may henceforth lie down with the lamb, the formalist and cultural critic be one' ('Introduction', p. 11).

Indeed, close reading is a feature of many of the key critical methodologies that grew out of the turn to theory. Semiotics as theorized and practised by Roland Barthes made an amalgam between the intense attention to grammar and codes of post-Saussurean linguistics, New Critical close reading, and French *analyse de texte*. Balzac's short story *Sarrasine* is subjected to elaborate decoding in *S/Z*, each sentence analysed for its charge of semantic, cultural, linguistic, and factual signs. Deconstruction is based on a wily and playful form of close reading of philosophical and literary texts using linguistic analysis to display the contradictions governing signification. Paul de Man acknowledged a debt to New Criticism in deconstructionist procedures in his defence of the importance of reading in culture. For de Man, New Criticism was proto-deconstructionist since it could not fail to attend to the structures of language in its readings. Its insistence on the need to read first without prejudice allied it to the philosophical and linguistic basis of deconstruction: one must first read 'prior to any theory' and attend to language before teaching literature 'as a substitute for the teaching of theology, ethics, psychology, or intellectual history'.[7] The phenomenological grounds of deconstruction, encouraging a Heideggerian attention to raw language and its compacted energies, as it were *before* dialectical movement starts its engine up, made sense to de Man as analogous to New Critical attention to the bizarre particularities of a text before the urge to rationalize is allowed its sway over texts. With Derrida, the plural and differentiating play of signifier, signified, and sign in all texts meant that one could very profitably contaminate philosophy's abstract rigours with art's play, audacity, and contradictory variousness, just as art's elaborate rhetoric and hide-and-seek with its readers could be liberated by philosophy's stern command to keep the reading mind focused on the abstract relations of language. With *Glas*, Derrida split his book into two columns, one column exploring the radical fissures and *différance* within Hegel's philosophical rhetoric, and the other close-reading a novella by Genet: the art was in the eye's invitation to cross-pollinate the discourses, thus helping actively to deconstruct the stabilities and determinations of the language of

---

[7] Paul de Man, *The Resistance to Theory* (Minneapolis: University of Minnesota Press, 1986), 24.

philosophy and art.[8] The close reading being practised in both columns become invitations to read closely against any set ideological procedures implicit in the conventions of criticism and logic.

It is often assumed that the turn to theory meant a thoroughgoing refutation of New Critical close reading, replacing its aesthetic and formalist concerns with political readings focused on sexuality, race, class, gender, post-colonial, and identity politics. Yet the major proponents of each of these fields would rarely go so far as to reject close reading as such. The attention to the detail of text, in other words, is more than a scholarly tradition, but an ethical necessity. 'Between the mysterious history of a textual production', Umberto Eco once wrote, 'and the uncontrollable drift of its future readings, the text qua text still represents a comfortable presence, the point to which we can stick.'[9]

This brief conspectus of the history of close reading should, one would hope, convince the opponents of complexity and formalism in poetry that reading with the intimacy first promulgated by Empson and Richards is more than a mere technique. Close reading is another term for the attention all literary writing hopes and expects from its readers. The pace of the engagement with language, the care and the speculation, the imaginative work, and the historical questions which close reading involves constitute the meditative and loving time and effort all artworks need and request their publics to give. The desire and the request are often written into the language of poems in the tactful and coded forms their modes of address assume.

A more specific matter remains to be explored, namely the relations between close reading and contemporary poetry. As we have seen, Richards, Empson, and the New Critics concentrated almost exclusively on poems in their advocacy. Theory tended to use close reading to analyse textual manoeuvres in philosophical and experimental prose, extending those techniques out of literary zones into popular culture, film, and the semiotics of cultural expression. The equation of close reading with poetry remained, however, especially in the pedagogical uses of the technique in universities. And it was not just poetry, but the particular genre of the short lyric that became the identified field for the practice of close reading. This has had unfortunate consequences. It is lazily assumed that since close reading works so well with short lyrics, then it *only* works well with short lyrics. It is then even more tendentiously presumed that the technique must shore up that old enemy the single, unified subject, the I-voice. With creative writing programmes in the States generating hundreds of graduates writing thousands of brief ten- to fifteen-line free verse lyrics of emotional angst, there has been a further assumption: that close reading as pedagogical tool tends to manufacture, at an industrial rate, poets (and poetry readers) who are self-absorbed, technically narcissistic, and slaves both to the fiction of their own expressive selves, and the monitors of tradition in the academy and literary history.

Poetry is the arena for the textual voice as compact of affect, history, and culture, a zone where private languages of feeling, where contact with the other, or solitary engagement

---

[8] Jacques Derrida, *Glas* (Paris: Galilée, 1974).
[9] Umberto Eco, 'An Author and His Interpreters', in *Reading Eco: An Anthology*, ed. Rocco Capozzi (Bloomington, Ind.: Indiana University Press, 1997), 59–72 (70).

with an object of desire, can be performed within a semi-public realm, thus creating lines of communication between the subject and cultural history, historical culture. Nothing is off bounds in a poem, which can touch the nerves of the unconscious as well as the lineaments of international history. The key here is that what poetry does *happens* in compacted form within lines, or as distributed across the page. As a genre, therefore, its only appropriate reading style *is* close reading. Close reading is a habit of attention to the ways the different kinds of material come together in the formal design. The close reading analysis simply separates out the elements so they become plainer to see. The analysis does what the intense and intimate reading of poetry can do in a flash.

There has been a further assumption damaging to the continued idea of close reading, which is that it only works with *lyric* poetry, and therefore is limited to what is defined as the reactionary libidinal economy of the post-Romantic sonnet and other intimate short forms. Advocates of lyrics in the contemporary era risk being shot down as close reading traditionalists, but there again so many doors are unnecessarily slammed shut with this exclusionary attitude. Lyrics are political, radical, compacted, cultural, and treacherous little texts that are aimed both to seduce and convert, but also to dramatize the forces of language within the mind of power (and powerlessness). The argument is less that history matters, than that close reading is the only valid way into history as story, the (hi)stories of voice in language as addressed to the loved one, to power, or the reader, from the liminal zone of poetry. Close reading is the key to the poem's staging of its ways of inhabiting history. It is also the only way to read the long poem, the experimental text, or the modernist and postmodern epic. Any poem that is also a serious artwork challenges its readers with invitations to engage closely with its surfaces, textures, and vocal complexities.

As an example of the ways close reading can be used fruitfully with difficult contemporary texts, I would like briefly to close-read Denise Riley's 'Song', which demonstrates many of the perplexities of the association of close reading to short lyric. Poems can preserve their mystery even after many attempts at inhabiting their small worlds. Readers sometimes assume they have a right to rifle a poem's surface meanings, like opening a fridge expecting a full meal. Denise Riley's poem 'Song' is partly about the poem's resistance to such expectations:

Some very dark blue hyacinths on the table
A confession or two before dusk
flings open the fridge with loud relief
Listen honey I

A warm disturbing wind cruises the high road

where in curtained rooms children
are being beaten then so am I again but no-one's
asking for it, I'm asking for something different now[10]

---

[10] Denise Riley, *Selected Poems* (London: Reality Street, 2000), 58. In interview, Riley has remarked on this poem that it is 'very swift but in terms of content unambiguous and anything but conventionally "lyrical". In some of these darkly lyrical pieces, what I think in retrospect I've done is to put a shadowy or painful content into a short, musical form', Romana Huk in conversation with Denise Riley, *PN Review* 103, 21/5. [http://www.pnreview.co.uk/cgi-bin/scribe?item_id=1912] [Accessed: 21 Oct. 2011].

It is a great shock when we hit and begin to take in the implications of 'being beaten'. We expected 'sleeping' but now, suddenly, the domestic environment of kitchen and bedroom is a site of menace, violence, assault. A reader must retrack, reread the first five lines, and register the tremor of that violence in phrases which at first sight had simply been about a couple in a kitchen. The disturbing wind enacts the deep disturbance cruising through the poem once we know this is a poem about domestic abuse.

Rereading is rehearing, going over the sounds again, becoming newly alert to the darker patterns of subversive significance cruising through the lines. One aspect of the poem's hiddenness lies in its internal sounds, curtained by our primary inattentiveness, but which we are invited to attend to by the broken urgency of 'Listen'. Internal rhymes, or more strictly sound effects, are the most fragile of poetry's qualities. In free verse such as Riley's, the ordinary voice and its ordinary sounds seem to dominate, and, accordingly, readers might be tempted to rush through the sound textures as though merely listening to neighbourly chat. Riley shocks us into something different by revealing the poem's violence, and relates this revelation to alertness to internal sounds, as in sounds internal to the house of the poem, not only with 'Listen', but also with the title which asks us to sing this, to sound the words, and with the figure for sound there in the disturbing wind.

If one listens to the honeyed sweetness of the sounds, certain strange patterns emerge, patterns and questions. Why the f-alliteration in the third line? Do we take the internal sound-repetitions patterned in 'very dark blue'—'confession or two' seriously? Why is it sweet and disturbing to hear how the phonemes of 'hyacinths' are rearranged in the fragmentary 'Listen honey I', and reinforced by the 'high' of line five and the repetition of 'I' in the last section? More importantly, with a poem so powerfully voicing a victim's resistance to abuse, is it not impertinent, tactless, in disturbing bad taste to dwell on such formalist detail?

Answers can begin to take on form if a semantic mystery is cleared up first. Riley puts heavy accentual stress on those hyacinths—'sóme véry dárk blúe hýacinths'—inviting readers to find out why. The *OED* entry tells the story: 'In ancient mythology the flower is said to have sprung up from the blood of the slain youth Hyacinthus, and the ancients thought they could decipher on the petals the letters AI, or AIAI, exclamation of grief.' In Ovid's version, Hyacinthus is slain by accident by his lover Apollo, his death inaugurating not only the birth of the flower and the scripting of the pain of death in nature, but also the birth of poetry as lament for violence done: 'on my tongue thou shalt for ever dwell; | Thy name my lyre shall sound, my verse shall tell; | And to a flow'r transform'd, unheard-of yet, | Stamp'd on thy leaves my cries thou shalt repeat' (1717, Dryden-Garth version). The flowers on the table are not only an emblem for domestic violence, but also a figure for poetry's relation to violence as such, how poetry is thought to repeat the cries of pain and grief. And the grief is there in the internal rhymes on 'I', in phonetic script written 'ai'. Such poetry does not give voice to the victim, but empowers, again, the abusive force. It is the abuser's broken apology in 'Listen honey I' which rearranges the sounds of 'hyacinths'—the apology and its fake grief (masking real relief) is stamped on the leaves of poetry, fashioning its 'AI' as repetition of the tyrannical 'I': 'my cries thou shalt repeat'.

Riley is asking for something different now, a poetry that does not passively accept the violence of the world by display of the AIAI of bodily pain, as in the confessional tradition of Plath and Sexton: 'A confession or two before dusk' is sarcastic and angry about that tradition, sarcasm reinforced by the sing-song repetition of 'very dark blue'. Lowell is remembered too: 'A warm disturbing wind cruises the high road' recalls ' "To speak of the Woe that is in Marriage" ', the sonnet written in the abused wife's voice, fearful for her life: 'My hopped up husband drops his home disputes | and hits the streets to cruise for prostitutes | … | My only thought is how to keep alive'. Lowell reprises the third line of the Wife of Bath's Prologue ('To speke of the wo that is in mariage'), thus alluding to the Wife's account of her relationship with her fifth husband, Jankin, who beats her and subjects her to the verbal assault of traditional misogynistic texts (Jankin's beating makes her deaf in one ear for daring to tear a page out of one of those texts). Confessional poetry is locked into the domestic cycle of power relations implicit in modern marriage, at worst collapsing the female poet's subjectivity into repetition of the 'monotonous meanness' of the Jankin male's lustful voice.

Riley refuses to accept the curtained subjectivity of the I-voice, which, for her, helps to disguise domestic violence through fear and traumatic withdrawal into the self. The I-voice of lyric is Hyacinthus to Apollo's casual power, forced at a deep level to repeat the abuser's grief as pattern for its cries, as though, in the vicious words of the abuser's exculpation, the voice were 'asking for it'. The withdrawal into traumatic self is written into the poetic tradition in the self-enclosing 'house' of the poem's internal sounds. The abuser's post-violating release, mimed in the alliterative 'flings open the fridge with loud relief', is answered by the angry 'different', opening the poem's door onto other sounds, modes of lyric outside the closed internal system fabricated by victimized repetition (AIAI) of power's fake grief.

If Riley's 'Song' invites close reading of its intimate effects in order to perform its act of dissent to the confessional tradition of close reading and lyric production that grew up under the influence of New Criticism, then it must be acknowledged that close reading is simply the manner of language-savouring and language-inhabiting which all poetic texts invite readers to perform. And that savouring need never be apolitical or ahistorical, as 'Song' also demonstrates in its summoning of classical, 1950s, and feminist occasions. As a further proof of this, and also of the ways in which long poems also invite such inhabiting and surmise, I would like to ponder on the act of allusion in contemporary poetry, for it is through allusion that poetry constructs its lines of engagement with history and culture. As example of an extract from a long poem too, it is appropriate to explore specifically Roy Fisher's elaborate allusion to the *Gawain*-poet in the 'Gradbach Hill' section of his 1986 sequence *A Furnace*:

Gradbach Hill, long hog's back
stretching down west among taller hills
to the meeting of Dane river
with the Black Brook skirting its steeper side,
the waters joining
by Castor's Bridge, where the bloomery

used to smoke up into the woods
under the green chapel;
the hill,
stretching down west from Goldsitch
a mile from my side yard, shale measures
on its back and the low black spoilheaps
still in the fields,
darkens to an October sunset
as if it were a coal,
the sun sinking into Cheshire, the light
welling up slow along the hillside,
leaving the Black Brook woods
chill, but striking for a while
fire meadows out of red-brown soft-rush,
the dark base, the hollows, the rim swiftly
blackening and crusting over.[11]

This long sentence stretches down the page like the hill it describes, putting into words what seems at first reading a simple though eloquent description of the view from the 'side yard' of Fisher's Derbyshire hillside home. The sunset ignites the landscape very much in the here and now: the poem stretches round the present tense 'darkens', preceded by present participles describing the hill's geography and then by present participles tracking the sun's effects. Yet one tiny verbal detail contradicts this, 'used to', small-scale trace of the ghost presence of past practices in the same landscape. The detail is backed up by a note to the poem at the end of *A Furnace*:

> *Gradbach Hill.* In North-West Staffordshire close to Three Shires Head, where Derbyshire, Cheshire, and Staffordshire meet. Facing it across the Black Brook is the rocky cleft called Lud's Church, a place whose supposed connection with the composition of *Gawain and the Green Knight* I am willing to believe in.[12]

Fisher is at once making sure his allusion to *Gawain* is noticed ('the green chapel' refers to the 'grene chapelle' where Gawain must meet the Green Knight for the beheading game) as well as ensuring we understand that the allusion is based on cultural-geographical fact.

It was in the late 1950s that Professor Ralph Elliott of Keele University identified the Roaches area of the Staffordshire Peaks as the most likely candidate for the encounter, scrupulously following up the signs in the text. Lud's Church is an astonishing cathedral-like gorge cut through gritstone, 50 feet deep, 300 feet long, rising from a cave-like entrance up to moorland made freakish by strangely eroded gritstone tors. It lies concealed above woods which lead down to the whitewater-rushing rivers Fisher

---

[11] Roy Fisher, *A Furnace* (1986) in *The Dow Low Drop: New and Selected Poems* (Newcastle upon Tyne: Bloodaxe Books, 1996), 158.
[12] Fisher, *Dow Low Drop*, 188.

names, where there are remains of a very ancient smithy, or 'bloomery'. All these details are mentioned in the *Gawain*-poet's account of the area: the gritstone outcrops ('rughe knokled knarrez with knorned stonez'), the rivers meeting in whitewater ('Bi a forgh of a flode that ferked thare; | The borne blubred therinne as hit boyled hade'), the concealed cave-like entrance ('a hole on the ende'), the high walls of the gorge green with moss ('ouergrowen with gresse in glodes aywhere, | ...a creuisse of an olde cragge'), its sinister resemblance to a cathedral nave: 'This oritore is vgly, with erbez ouergrowen | ...Hit is the corsedest kyrk that euer I com inne!' cries poor terrified Gawain.[13]

What clinched it for Elliott is the fact that Gawain hears the Green Knight before he sees him, hears him grinding his axe 'as one vpon a gryndelston hade grounden a sythe' with such a din that it recalls the boiling waters of the Dane and Black Brook below: 'hit wharred and whette, as water at a mulne'. The presence of the remains of the bloomery at the site and its connection to the rivers below Lud's Church mean that this is a place where, from very ancient times, perhaps dating as far back as the Iron Age, iron was worked for the making of scythes, swords, and axes (a later poem in *A Furnace* refers to Axe Edge just to the north above Three Shire Heads, where three rivers rise, the name summoning 'anvil-cloud' and 'hoof-strike flashes' to Fisher's cast of mind). This industry is linked to the pagan savagery and power of the Green Knight, like some wild Hephaestus nature god, reminding us that metalworking was once thought a dangerous, blasphemous transformation of the dark gifts of the mountains, a ripping from the hill leaving great gashes like Lud's Church, a dark troll-like underground activity, a mining of sinister stolen energies. King Ludd was a mythical figure which the Green Knight is partly calqued from, trace element of a Celtic sun god powerful enough to demand the gift of iron from the forces of the earth. It is this subversive power which enables the knight to compel recognition from the modish latecomers at Camelot.

Upon this mythical landscape transformed by the *Gawain*-poet is superimposed, in Fisher's late twentieth-century mind, the other lost landscape of the North, the dead mining industry visible in the 'spoilheaps | still in the fields'. And it is the dark seam connecting the Green Knight's bloomery to that industry which forms the real force of this allusion. For this is no guidebook poem or mawkish antiquarianism pointing out the sights, but a vision of the northern landscape that sees the old industry lost amongst the traces. The sun god Ludd is now the poet seeing with the illumination of the setting sun the hidden crevices of history, the smoking of the old iron-smelting sites as well as the old collieries and drift mines that stretched from here up to Oldham in the North, an ancient history that once linked the country to the industrial towns which form the principal subject of Fisher's testimonial project.

If the allusion has power it is because it has ramifications, like a geological fault linking collieries underground, beyond the mere chance connection of bloomery and spoilheaps. The *Gawain*-poet's alliterative verse is recalled in the elaborate sound system of Fisher's poem: note the h, l, g, and o repetitions in the first line, t and l in the second, b

---

[13] *Sir Gawain and the Green Knight*, ed. William R. J. Barron (Manchester: Manchester University Press, 1993).

and s in the fourth, 'bridge'-'bloomery' in the sixth, etc., the internal rhymes ('down'-'Dane'), pararhymes ('chapel'-'hill''shale'-'fields'), the long riff on 'bach', 'back', 'black', the delicate assonantal strings hinting at end rhyme towards the close ('light', 'side', 'while'). Old forms of English are remembered in the compounds, with 'shale measures', 'spoilheaps', 'fire meadows', 'red-brown soft-rush'. The diction too is predominantly Anglo-Saxon, tapping at that ancient seam. There is a *Gawain* kind of wit at work too. If *Gawain and the Green Knight* is a comic poem, satirizing the erotic dilemmas of a fashionable court with raw material from the harsh hinterland, then so too is Fisher's poem witty in its stretching out of the conventions of post-industrial pastoral, challenging the reader to take stock of the sunset image as merely linguistic waste product of the cliché 'gone west'. These industries *have* gone west, just as Gradbach Hill 'stretches down west' following the sun's course towards Cheshire.

Yet none of this would work, the allusion would fail, Fisher argues, if the mind's eye could not register the old history as potent presence even in the vision of its passing away. The sun may mock the landscape by making it resemble a dying coal fire, like the cruel theatrical illusion of an industrial heritage museum. But Fisher's imagination, his cast of mind, is keen to do justice to the smelters and miners of the region, forcing Gradbach Hill to yield the lost fires of their technology. There in the last four lines of his poem, Fisher recreates in remarkable detail the ways the old bloomeries and furnaces worked. The bloomery was an early form of furnace made of clay for the smelting of ironstone, creating a 'bloom' of iron and steel (as the furnace could not reach the melting point of iron). The ore would be poured down the top onto a fire fanned by air, and a liquid slag tapped from the base. The technology is there in the poem with the fire meadows of the hot blooming metal forming above the dark base of the slag. And it is through this tight metaphorical fit of sunset shadow and blaze and the bloomery process that Fisher grounds the techniques 'borrowed' from the *Gawain*-poet: for the heart of the alliterative rhyming, the beats and repeats on 'black', are all about coal, the dead mining industry which is the poem's secret secondary subject. The energy a poet draws upon in his or her own region is at once the local textual and cultural history and the ordinary energies being worked by the generations who have made the landscape what it is. If we pay close attention to the metaphor, however, we begin to understand that Fisher has closed the bloomery down, its 'rim' blackening and crusting over, the bloom of fiery metal darkened because the industry itself is 'over'.

The allusion to the *Gawain*-poet works because it is about work done in the body of the country. Indeed, the poem manages to say something about *Gawain and the Green Knight*, hinting that its true theme may have been the relationship of court to the secret iron industry hidden in the hills. At the same time, the medieval poem illuminates Fisher's poem by making us wonder at the analogues to the ancient powers medieval superstition saw running their legendary world. What are the fabulous forces that have beheaded the dark industrial base? Are we to enjoy its passing by happy visits to the industrial museums, watching history from our side yards as though it were as natural as a sunset on a hill? What is the role of the individual's cast of mind in a landscape littered with the spoilheaps of history? Answers might be had by following Roy Fisher's mind as he recreates the old measures and soft rush of history, acknowledging all the while the harsh politics that saw it all go west.

His allusion at once marks out the territory of true poetry, the real country we live in and its long past, a country of deep feeling for the afterlives of past communities. It signals too the kindred companionability of *Gawain*-poet and Fisher, notating continuities of subject and treatment, acknowledging the dark historical differences. It helps Fisher in his exploration of very complex changes in social and cultural history, the loss of the industrial base and the identification of the new gods of this world. It is also light and playful, a comic salute to past good writing about the same region, yet used elegiacally to salute a dead way of life. And finally, it signals a more obsessive, difficult struggle with a voice from the past, forcing the *Gawain*-poet to attend to the endgame of his story, the blackening, crusting processes of history that have killed off forms of life and work that used to stretch back to the Iron Age.

The long poem in contemporary practice is none the less a challenging invitation to engage closely with its various forms of allusive engagement with environments textual, cultural, and geographical, and Fisher's example demonstrates that the training in close reading that most contemporary poets will have received at school and university and poetry forum need not be abandoned as old-fashioned and politically suspect. On the contrary, that training was always a complement to the reading practices and compositional practices of all poets at work in the environments of language.

As Douglas Oliver has written, in the prose sections accompanying his poem sequence (of lyrics), *The Island that is All the World*, to read a poem is to agree to accept, provisionally, and within the time-scheme of the reading experience, that a unifying language event on the page can take place:

> a whole poem takes its place in the larger web of language and literature but always as itself; so all the islands of ourselves expand out to the larger self and the larger self takes its place in the great, unconscious universe, but always as itself, and is a shining in that blackness. [...] Unity of form disappears into ambiguous dark whenever we examine it analytically, but its heart is always the beating heart of a poem: it is the precious origin of our lives' form, or of a true politics.[14]

Close reading helps readers to construct a poem out of the distracted elements of their own lives and the lives of others; and it is through such loving attention, or heartbeat sensitivity to the elemental story in poetry's forms of language, that poems begin to act upon the world.

---

[14] Douglas Oliver, *The Island that is All the World*, in *Three Variations on the Theme of Harm* (London: Paladin, 1990), 37–109 (107).

Select Bibliography

Blackmur, R. P., 'Examples of Wallace Stevens', in Frank Lentricchia and Andrew DuBois (eds.), *Close Reading: The Reader* (Durham, NC: Duke University Press, 2003), 111–35.
de Mann, Paul, *The Resistance to Theory* (Minneapolis: University of Minnesota Press, 1986).
Empson, William, *Seven Types of Ambiguity* (London: Chatto & Windus, 1953).
Mao, Douglas, 'The New Critics and the Text-Object', *ELH* 63/1 (1996), 227–54.
Oliver, Douglas, *The Island that is All the World, in Three Variations on the Theme of Harm* (London: Paladin, 1990).
Ransom, John Crowe, *The New Criticism* (Norfolk, Conn.: New Directions, 1941).
Riley, Denise, *Selected Poems* (London: Reality Street, 2000).

CHAPTER 13

'ALL LIVIN LANGUAGE IS SACRED': POETRY AND VARIETIES OF ENGLISH IN THESE ISLANDS

SIMON DENTITH

I start with a short poem, 'Landfall', by Robin Robertson:

The fishboxes
of Fraserburgh, Aberdeen,
Peterhead, the wood that broke
on your beach, crates that once held herring,
freshly dead, now hold distance, nothing but the names
of the places I came from, years ago;
and you pull me from the waves,
drawing me out like a skelf,
as I would say:
a splinter.[1]

The poem turns on the use of the word 'skelf'; while the poem is written in English, the Scots word is held, as it were, in quotation marks, and it carries with it a weight of affect, not only of the personal act of rescue that the poem records, but of a whole social and

---

[1] Robin Robertson, 'Landfall', *The Wrecking Light* (London: Picador, 2010), 71. The word 'skelf' also occurs as a marker of linguistic difference in 'Originally' by Carol Ann Duffy, *Selected Poems* (London: Penguin Books, 1994), 65–6; while Peter Robinson has used the English dialect word 'spelk', another of these pervasive splinters, to provoke the particularity of childhood memory, 'The Spelk', *The Look of Goodbye: Poems 2001–2006* (Exeter: Shearsman Books, 2008), 115.

cultural history of loss and displacement. The use of the word 'skelf' stands in, briefly, for a whole way of life now lost as the fishing industry of North East Scotland, from where Robin Robertson comes, has disappeared. 'Skelf' is a fragment, a splinter, of a residual social and linguistic world.

'Landfall' indicates one use at least of non-standard English in contemporary poetry: to provide a resource or specific linguistic flavour or pungency unavailable in standard forms. But this is to cast the matter in altogether too restricted a way, and presumes, as another reading of Robertson's poem might suggest, the primacy of Standard English. Non-standard forms, in such a view, can only appear in poetry as residual traces or colours surrounded by the regionally or socially unmarked discourse of 'normal' English. This chapter will propose something rather different. It suggests instead that for the speakers of non-standard English (that is, for the majority of the inhabitants of these islands), the passage into poetry is always going to be marked by difficult linguistic and therefore social negotiations; that pressing on such negotiations are diverse class, regional, national, and ethnic histories; and that the apparently aesthetic and formal choices made by contemporary poets about such matters as diction, vocabulary, and language reveal differing strategies in relation to the inescapably socially-marked linguistic actualities of diversely speaking people. But it will also propose something more positive, something less simply a matter of explication and analysis: that these complex layerings of language have locked into them a powerful popular energy, and that poetry, as it approaches the characteristics of vernacular speech, can release these energies in linguistically and culturally revivifying ways. Such energies are not only a product of the rediscovered histories awaiting release by acts of poetic recovery, as in the example of 'Landfall' (and of numerous other poems, as we shall see); they are also let loose when poetry connects with and draws on the actual and diverse spoken vernaculars of these islands.

In fact, a characteristic kind of contemporary poem dramatizes the situation of simultaneous claim on, and repudiation of, the language in which the English poetic canon is spoken; there is a small group of poems that tell of the first experience of poetry as it is encountered in school, and of the problematic nature of this encounter. The pithiest of this small genre of 'fraught-initiation-into-poetry poems' is perhaps Tom Leonard's poem 'Poetry':

> the pee as in pulchritude,
> oh pronounced ough
> as in bough
>
> the ee rather poised
> (pronounced ih as in wit)
> then a languid high tea...
>
> pause: then the coda—
> ray pronounced rih
> with the left eyebrow raised
> —what a gracious bouquet!

Poetry.
Poughit. Rih.

That was my education
—and nothing to do with me.[2]

The poem could hardly be clearer in repudiating a certain class-marked inflection of the meaning of poetry. These paradoxical poems of claim-and-repudiation unerringly locate the initial encounter with poetry in the education system, the condition for the understanding of poetry but also the site in which vernacular speakers are taught to lose the characteristics of their speech. The repudiation in Leonard's poem is evident enough; the claim is in the simple act of writing poetry at all. As Tony Harrison puts it, referring to his father's dismissal of poetry, 'I've come round to your position on "the Arts" | but put it down in poems, that's the bind'.[3]

Harrison himself provides another poem of the same kind in 'Them and [uz]', which similarly dramatizes the disjunction between the Received Pronunciation (RP) accents of the teacher and the local speech which 'Poetry' requires each child to overcome. Here is the voice of that teacher:

'Poetry's the speech of kings. You're one of those
Shakespeare gives the comic bits to: prose!
All poetry (even Cockney Keats?) you see
's been dubbed by [Λs] into RP,
Received Pronunciation, please believe [Λs]
your speech is in the hands of the Receivers.'[4]

These words are produced under the sign of irony, of course, and the poet's resistance to them is indicated by the presumably subsequent bracketed interjection 'even Cockney Keats?'. The lines nevertheless lay out a certain notion of poetry which aligns it with fine speaking understood in class-marked terms: the poem after all comes in a collection originally called *The School of Eloquence*. Harrison's use of the phonetic alphabet for the dialectal variant [uz] | [Λs] has the interesting consequence of making the poem impossible to speak without, for the RP speaker, imitating a Leeds voice, and for the Leeds speaker, imitating RP. The poem thus makes the dilemma it dramatizes inescapable in its own performance.

The doubleness of the negotiation with the poetic tradition is explicated more fully in 'Them and [uz]' than in Leonard's 'Poetry': the movement into poetry for Harrison is at once a repudiation and a gain, as he makes clear in the second sonnet of the pair when he promises to 'occupy | your lousy leasehold Poetry'. The most evident aspect of this ambivalent movement is around the language that he speaks. Poetry, it seems, is spoken

---

[2] Tom Leonard, 'Poetry', *Outside the Narrative* (Exbourne: Etruscan Books, 2009), 37.
[3] Tony Harrison, 'A Good Read', *Selected Poems* (2nd edn., London: Penguin Books, 1987), 141.
[4] Harrison, 'Them and [uz]', *Selected Poems*, 122.

in Received Pronunciation. Schooling is the condition of entry into the poetic tradition, but for someone who speaks a working-class variety of English that entry into the tradition can never be a painless assumption of an inheritance, but, in the class-marked circumstances of Harrison's education, is inevitably marked by loss and alienation. However, this is ultimately a productive situation; it is the condition out of which this poetry is produced.

Harrison's striking phrase for this whole process, 'Poetry...'s been dubbed by [Λs] into RP', captures what is not an incidental process; the meaning of poetry is indelibly marked by this transition through the linguistic standardization which characterizes education. Both the poems by Harrison and Leonard are dominated by the matter of class; they remind us, if we need reminding, that a primary axis of linguistic differentiation in these islands remains that of class. Harrison's formulation however points to the longevity of this process; in relation to a poem which refers to Wordsworth as well as Keats, it is worth remembering that the diction of poetry has been a matter of dispute along class lines at least for the last two hundred years—Hazlitt after all hailed Wordsworth's 'levelling Muse'.[5] Nevertheless both Harrison (b. 1935) and Leonard (b. 1944) are of a generation whose experience of the educational system was especially marked by class-inflected linguistic hierarchies of the kind to which they object. In addition, their experiences led them to write poetry of very different kinds, where the vernaculars in which they speak appear in different ways. Harrison's 'Them and [uz]' is a strange linguistic object when spoken, one which requires the reader to mimic both Leeds and RP accents. But this poem is untypical of Harrison's poetry at least in the attempt to reproduce phonetically the sound of Leeds speech; most of Harrison's poetry, with the signal exception of *V*, is written in Standard English, and even *V* sets out to include, if not exactly to reclaim, an aggressive urban demotic characterized more by differences of vocabulary and register than phonetic or grammatical differences. Leonard's poetry, by contrast, though not 'Poetry' itself, attempts to reproduce Glasgow demotic speech orthographically; this is not 'eye-dialect', but it is not phonetic reproduction either. The national differences are doubtless important here; while Leonard does not exactly write in Scots, the national differentiation from Standard English reinforces the class dynamic which principally impels his decisions about writing in the vernacular. The closeness of Leonard's linguistic politics to, for example, James Kelman's practice in his novels is also evident; closely associated Glasgow writers of the same generation, both polemically insist on the distinctiveness of local speech, seek to reproduce it orthographically (though to different degrees), and repudiate the hierarchy implied by the use of Standard English.

Seamus Heaney's 'Ministry of Fear' (1975) is another of these poems which locates the coming-into-poetry in a process of schooling which is at once exclusionary and productive:

I tried to write about the sycamores
And innovated a South Derry rhyme
With *hushed* and *lulled* full chimes for *pushed* and *pulled*.

---

[5] William Hazlitt, 'Mr. Wordsworth', *The Spirit of the Age* (1825; London: Collins Publishers, 1969), 139.

Those hobnailed boots from beyond the mountain
Were walking, by God, all over the fine
Lawns of elocution.[6]

Heaney (b. 1939) records an experience of schooling contemporaneous with those of Harrison and Leonard, and, like them, his claim on the tradition of poetry is complicated, and its complications are most salient in relation to the actual sounds he speaks. In this phase of the poem this is in part a question of class, though the 'hobnailed boots from beyond the mountain' are peasant boots rather than proletarian ones. But it is also clear from the rest of the poem that the fault-lines in Heaney's education are also sectarian and national: a School Inspector is quoted as saying that 'Catholics, in general, don't speak | As well as students from the Protestant schools', while the poem famously ends with the assertion that 'Ulster was British, but with no rights on | The English lyric'. Poetry is born out of this interlocking set of prohibitions and deformations, with the result that the diction of Heaney's poetry will be a matter of contestation and discovery throughout his career, permanently marked by the particular historic national-linguistic situation in which he was born, raised, and educated.

We can draw from this generation of writers the thought that the linguistic politics of class are crucial to their formation and practice as poets; a younger generation is equally marked by the politics of immigration and ethnicity, which have their own diverse linguistic histories. In another of these poetic manifestos, Daljit Nagra (b. 1966) similarly takes his distance from the poetic idioms made available in the classroom. In 'Kabba Questions the Ontology of Representation, the Catch 22 for "Black" Writers...', Nagra attempts to reproduce the heavily accented English of a first-generation immigrant from the Indian subcontinent, though Nagra was born in Britain and this is therefore an act of mimicry. The substance of the poem is the speaker's repudiation of the poetry offered to his son at GCSE.

The paradoxes in this instance are at least as great as those we encountered with the comparable poems by Harrison, Leonard, and Heaney, though the gesture that the poem makes is a similar one, repudiating the 'otherness' offered his son by the categories of the GCSE anthology, and equally repudiating the tokenistic tour of the nationalities in these islands via Seamus Heaney, William Blake, and Gillian Clarke, who are alluded to in the poem as representative of the cultures of Northern Ireland, England, and Wales. The poem also repudiates the poems by Indian writers that the anthology provides, which, although they are not named, are easily recognized as 'Sacrifice' by Taufiq Rafat and 'Night of the Scorpion' by Nissim Ezekiel. What it offers instead is its own performance of Indian English, since all the alternatives appear equally self-defeating; this is the voice of the man who now appears to be the poet's father, referring to his own son's serio-comic mimicry of the latter's Indian voice:

so hee is used in British antologies—
   he hide in dis whitey 'fantum' English, blacked,
      to make me sound 'poreign'![7]

---

[6] Seamus Heaney, 'The Ministry of Fear', *North* (London: Faber & Faber, 1975), 57–9.

[7] Daljit Nagra, 'Kabba Questions the Ontology of Representation, the Catch 22 for "Black" Writers...', *Look We Have Coming to Dover* (London: Faber & Faber, 2007), 43.

The poem has thus become very overtly self-referential, acknowledging its own performance of potentially comic Indianness, and even anticipating its inclusion in future anthologies. But there is a serious point here, from which the language of the poem issues: that the poet of Indian descent is in effect caught in an aporia, since both the English-language poems of subcontinental writers like Rafat or Ezekiel, and Punjabi-language poetic forms, position him as foreign to himself. Hence Nagra is forced to adopt this 'whitey "fantum" English, blacked'.

Daljit Nagra provides here a serio-comic staging of his own predicament as a poet. It cannot of course be assimilated to the practice of other first- and second-generation poets from elsewhere than the Indian subcontinent, who draw on different linguistic inheritances—poets from the Caribbean, for example, some of whom speak Creole as their mother tongue, though in widely varying inflections. But, along with these other poems by poets of an earlier generation, it does permit us to begin to map out the various linguistic histories which provide the conditions in which contemporary poets must operate. It can be described as a set of cross-cutting determinations, in which the deformities of class as they act upon language are cut across with complex national and regional affiliations (the 'three parts of Briten' referred to by Nagra, though we should say that the national-linguistic formations in all parts of Britain and Ireland are riven and complex, and regional England adds further complications); the presence of immigrant communities of greater or lesser antiquity, with their own linguistic inheritance, provides a further limitation and possibility. In this group of powerful poems focused on the experience of coming-into-poetry via schooling, these complex determinations are made visible and in all cases allude to the actual spoken English, the diction, accent, register, and modulation, which is at issue in the assumption of the tradition of the English lyric.

Tony Harrison is the poet in English who most consistently inhabits the linguistic contradictions created by class. In fact his most controversial poem, *V* (1985), is precisely about language, the poem being sparked by the defacing of his parents' gravestone by obscene graffiti. The poem consists in part of an imaginary dialogue or slanging-match between Harrison himself, and a skinhead whose linguistic violence the poem at once repudiates and reclaims:

What is it that these crude words are revealing?
What is it that this aggro act implies?
Giving the dead their xenophobic feeling
Or just a *cri-de-coeur* because man dies?

So what's a cri-de-coeur, *cunt? Can't you speak*
the language that yer mam spoke. Think of 'er!
Can yer only get your tongue round fucking Greek?
Go and fuck yerself with cri-de-coeur*![8]*

---

[8] Tony Harrison, *V* (Newcastle upon Tyne: Bloodaxe Books, 1989), 17.

In these two stanzas, the first, in Standard English, is the voice of the poet; the second, whose linguistic difference is indicated by italics and some changed orthography, is the imagined voice of the poet's interlocutor, who later turns out to be the poet's alter ego, what he himself would have become were it not for the education which has taken him out from his class and estranged him from the language spoken by his parents. There is therefore a linguistic hierarchy in the text: Harrison-the-poet's words contain and outflank Harrison-the-skin's. But as with all such hierarchies, the language that is 'placed' has the capacity to explode the categories into which it has been put, and certainly in the case of *V* the shock value of the skinhead's words resonate powerfully outside the poet's efforts to contain them. Indeed the poem exactly dramatizes this tension, seeking to comprehend both the educated poet whose education and life experience has taken him way beyond Leeds or the district of Beeston, and the skinhead whose life experience, especially in the light of deindustrialization and the deskilling of the working class, leaves him nothing but aggression and linguistic violence towards the past, and towards the current beneficiaries of the class hierarchies of the country. The poem enacts, in its formal and linguistic dispositions, the separations and degradations imposed upon people and the language that they speak by a system in which class transition is simultaneously a linguistic and educational transition.

V is not therefore a dialect poem, nor even a poem about dialect; the language spoken by Harrison's skinhead alter ego retains traces of dialect but is more like ordinary Leeds vernacular shifted sharply into aggressive mode by the repeated swear words. Its force in part derives from the contrast with the Standard English which surrounds it. English in England is a language without dialects, meaning those varieties which are marked by lexical and grammatical differences as well as differences of accent. But this does not mean that it is a language without variety; such regional and class variety is obviously heard in Harrison's poetry. Nevertheless the distance between his poetry and the dialect poetry of the nineteenth century indicates the massive linguistic transition over the previous century, which has seen the effective elimination of dialect from the indigenous Englishes spoken in England. The vernacular linguistic energy that feeds Harrison's poetry is clearly that of class, and while it is regionally located comparable negotiations could have been made in all regions of England.

By contrast, another Yorkshire poet, Simon Armitage (b. 1963), does not characteristically seek to reproduce Northern speech orthographically in his poetry, though he does claim that part of his project as a poet is to find ways of making his poems reflect the way he actually speaks.[9] He has however written some dialect poems, which demonstrate some of the possibilities of the mode, as in 'The Phoenix':

Tvillage cuckoo wer caught one spring
To trap tgood weather, an kept in a tower baht roof.
Tnext morning tbird'd sprung; tMarsdeners reckoned
Ttower wernt builded igh enuff. A ladder wer fetched

---

[9] See his comments on this at: [http://www.poetryarchive.org/poetryarchive/singleInterview.do?interviewId=1419]

To bring tbird dahn, but nubdy'd clahm.
Trust, tha sees. Tladder maht walk. Chap maht be stuck
In clahdcuckooland till Kingdomcumsdy, Godknowswensdy.
Meanwahl, tbird wer nested in Crahther's chimney.[10]

There is a danger here of the poem confining itself to a damaging localism: an association of dialect with comedy that perhaps reinforces the linguistic hierarchy against which Tony Harrison complained. Where the poem escapes that danger is in its interplay between the comic and deflating localism of the anecdote which it records, and the possibilities suggested by 'Kingdomscumdy, Godknowswensdy': this local episode suddenly suggests a mythical time realized in these serio-comic puns which depend on vernacular expressions and use them to take the anecdote beyond the comically folkloric—or better, which use the comically folkloric to suggest mythical possibilities unreachable otherwise.

In general, then, while it is true that the various impulses which created nineteenth-century dialect poetry in England have died out along with the dialects they celebrated, it is also true that the strongly class-marked varieties of English can still be heard in some poetry, and that they provide a kind of limit case for the poetry dubbed into RP in which most poets in English write.

The situation in Scotland is therefore radically different, since the linguistic situation is so different, and since there is an unbroken tradition of poetry in Scots which goes back to the Middle Ages—leaving to one side, as I must, the persistence of poetry in Gaelic. That tradition of poetry in Scots, controversially renewed by Hugh MacDiarmid and others in the early twentieth century, has persisted throughout the subsequent ninety years, and has been renewed again in significant ways by poets writing now. The controversy about MacDiarmid's 'Lallans' can be deduced from one of the names given to the language he used: Synthetic Scots. Most relevantly to this essay, the attempt at synthesis that MacDiarmid made—both a synthesis of several dialects, and of spoken language with dictionary words—can be seen as an attempt at establishing an alternative Standard variety of the language from that provided by Standard English.

Poetry in Scots thus differs markedly from dialect poetry in English, since Scots has its own tradition as a literary language and because Scots as a distinct vernacular language, with its own varieties, has survived much more strongly than the traditional dialects in England. Thus Robert Garioch (1909–81), for example, who writes predominantly in Scots, is able to draw on traditions that are not present for Simon Armitage when he seeks to use his own speech, and those of the people he comes from, in his poetry. A poem like 'Scunner 1', for example, has a particular expressiveness because it can use vernacular Scots to address the specific situation of the Scottish Sabbath:

---

[10] Simon Armitage, 'The Phoenix', *Selected Poems* (London: Faber & Faber, 2001), 135.

Sinday nicht, and I'm scunner wi ocht
I hae ever socht, or wished, or bocht;
My bit of life crined aa ti nocht
But a sour taste, and a dour thocht.

Bells yammer: the kirks are bricht
Wi thousand-watt electric licht.
My sawl blinters in the fricht
Of its ain mirk, on Sinday nicht.[11]

Scunner: 'disgust' perhaps most appropriate here; *crined*: shrunk or shrivelled; *blinters*: flickers or glimmers. The poem starts and ends with 'Sinday nicht'; the first use suggests a particular occasion, while the concluding phrase suggests that this is a general condition on Sunday night. There's no problem here for Garioch in writing about Scottish Sundays: he is simply using a vernacular that is available to him.

Though perhaps this is not so simple, as the controversies about Lallans in the early years of the twentieth century sufficiently attest. Garioch himself was explicit in insisting that the language he used was a literary language that required more than a transcription of spoken Scots:

> Naethin cud be mair artificial than to gaun ti a fairmhouse wi a wee notebuik, notin doon the words iz thi tumble frae the lips o the fermer an his guid wife: subsequently connin them weel at hame, an manufacturing a poem accordin ti the limitations o the speech o siclike country buddies. A poem o this kind is mibby pure eneuch: bit like mony anither pure article, it's no muckle the better for 't.[12]

Garioch thus abjures purity in favour of the variety of a language with a long and complex history, so that the strength of his poetry is precisely its capacity to draw on multiple registers which include differing registers within Scots itself.

One continuing possibility for poetry in Scots is therefore a poem like the following:

Binna feart, hinny,
yin day we'll gang thegither
tae thae stourie
blaebillwids,
and loss wirsels—

see, I'd raither
whummel a single oor
intae the blae of thae wee flo'ers
thun live fur a' eternity
in some cauld hivvin.

Wheest, now, till I spier o ye
Will ye haud wi me?[13]

---

[11] Robert Garioch, 'Scunner 1', *Collected Poems* (Edinburgh, Polygon, 2004), 153.
[12] Quoted in Robin Fulton, 'Introduction' to Garioch, *Collected Poems*, p. xiii.
[13] Kathleen Jamie, 'Speirin', *The Tree House* (London: Picador, 2004), 14.

This poem appears in a collection of poems in which the majority are written in Standard English; in its original context therefore it takes on some force by the mere fact of linguistic difference. There is undoubtedly, despite this, a connection between the topic of the poem and the choice that Kathleen Jamie (b. 1962) has made in writing this poem in Scots; the poem is precisely about the intensity of the local and particular as against the coldness of the universal. The linguistic quiddity of Scots here, the delight in such words as *stourie* (dusty) and *whummel* (tumble or perhaps drown, be overwhelmed), provides an especially rich idiom for the expression of this density of affect directed to the intense but transient here and now.

Kathleen Jamie's Scots-language poetry represents one possibility for contemporary poets in Scotland. Another is represented by writing more self-consciously modernist in spirit. Andrew Greig (b.1951), for example, whose lyrical poetry is not characteristically written in Scots, has written two large ambitious poems in the modernist idiom which include Scots as part of a deliberate attempt to represent the linguistic diversity of Scotland. *Western Swing* (1994) has the following note: 'this text may suggest not so much a kleptomaniac with a bad memory as an attempt to acknowledge, respect and harness the plurality (literary, linguistic, artistic and social) of a culture and a generation'.[14] This involves the inclusion of Scots sections, duly ironized by being prefaced by the assertion that the language has been arrived at after having been put through a 'MacDiarmidtron' ('an early synthesiser...that shifts linguistic register to a dense Scots from many parts and periods. Best decoded (and sometimes created) by a *Jamieson's Dictionary of the Scottish Language*. Prime cuts are MacD's early short lyrics and *The Drunk Man*. See also Sydney Goodsir Smith'). This is fighting talk, but it nevertheless produces poetry like the following, which is far from ironic:

Can onybody see us? I hae ma doots.
Gin there be a God,
    yon great een canna keek through
    sae sma a crack in time as oors
tae spy whit's gaun doon here!

Yon Absolute is tae long sichtit,
and oor world's tae nearby
    for his kenning—believe me,
    we graipple here wi dreids and fairlies
he canna even see.[15]

There is no reason, of course, why theology should not be written in Scots. As with the poem by Kathleen Jamie, this extract too uses Scots to particular effect: part of the point of the poem is the effect of bathos created by the image of God being unable to focus

---

[14] Andrew Greig, *Western Swing: Adventures with the Heretical Buddha* (Newcastle upon Tyne: Bloodaxe Books, 1994), 112.

[15] Greig, *Western Swing*, 73.

on the doings of human beings as he tries to 'keek' into our homely lives, dominated by the locally significant fears of 'dreids' and 'fairlies'. But the point of the whole long poem *Western Swing* is precisely that this idiom, though an entirely legitimate one, is only one of many available in contemporary Scotland, and the poem, just as much as *The Waste Land*, weaves together differing idioms to mutually ironic and contrasting effect.

Also consciously in the modernist tradition, Robert Crawford (b. 1959) and W. N. Herbert (b. 1961) use Scots to address a contemporary Scotland. As is the case with Greig's poetry, the effects often depend on the disjunction between the historic idiom of Sots and the emphatic contemporaneity of the subject matter, as in Crawford's poem 'Ghetto-Blastir':

Ghetto-makars, tae the knackirs'
Wi aw yir schemes, yir smug dour dreams
O yir ain feet. Yi're beat
By yon new Scoatland loupin tae yir street

Wi a Jarre-lik puissance, ghetto-blastin
Auld sangs crooned doon
Yir reedy beeks, wastin and tastin
O deid pus. See us? We're foon

Wi whit's new...[16]

The 'ghetto-makars' here are both the makers of ghettos (the 'schemes' of line 2), and also the ghettoized 'makars' or poets stuck in a traditional past. The lift and aggression of these lines, reminiscent perhaps of MacDiarmid, seeks to crash Scots into contemporaneity, as the speaker of the poem says later: 'We're grabbing | What's left of the leid [language] tae mak anither sang | O semiconductors...'. The poetry that emerges draws its energy in part from the striking disjunctions between the registers of traditional Scots and the ghetto-blasting modernity that it seeks to address. Something similar could be said about the rambunctious Scots-language poetry of W. N. Herbert, who also rejects any notion of language purity and draws on the linguistic energies of multiple dialects and registers.

These poets using Scots are to be distinguished therefore from Tom Leonard (b. 1944), and the poetry that follows from him, which as we have seen emerges from elsewhere on the linguistic spectrum. Leonard seeks to speak in the urban vernacular of the Glasgow working class, which bears relation to Scots of course but is not identical to it. His poetry in fact is more like an attempt to reproduce phonetically a class vernacular: it is driven as much by the dynamic of class as by any national agenda. As he writes in 'Ghostie Men',

right enuff
ma language is disgraceful

---

[16] Robert Crawford, 'Ghetto-Blastir', in Donny O'Rourke (ed.), *Dream State: The New Scottish Poets* (2nd edn., Edinburgh: Polygon, 2002), 105.

ma maw tellt mi
ma teacher tellt mi
thi doacter tellt mi
thi priest tellt mi.[17]

The poem then lists many more disapproving voices (including the introduction to the *Scottish National Dictionary*), before concluding

ach well
all livin language is sacred
fuck thi lohta thim.

This is a very different linguistic and poetic manifesto from that proposed by Robert Crawford, 'We're grabbing | What's left of the leid [language] tae mak anither sang'. Leonard is reclaiming an urban demotic not on the grounds of its antiquity but because it is 'livin language'; the poem draws its energy from the speech of the Glasgow working class that is perhaps more speculatively imagined in Crawford's poetry.

Leonard's attempt at an orthographic reproduction of urban demotic has had a number of imitators, using not only Glaswegian speech but the vernaculars of other Scottish cities too.[18] As I suggested earlier, the appropriate comparison for this is best found in the novels of James Kelman and Irvine Welsh, and their project is premised on a class more than a national politics, though doubtless it would be hard to draw a watertight distinction between the linguistic politics of class and nation, just as it is difficult to draw a neat line between traditional Scots and the various urban demotics that have succeeded it. Certainly the ways that class, region, and nation intersect in language are especially productive in Scotland and have produced a variety of differing poetic strategies in ways that are not matched elsewhere in these islands.

The range and depth of poetry written in Scots undoubtedly surpasses anything written in the other traditional English-related languages, including the poetry from Northern Ireland, which, despite the extraordinary pantheon of famous names, has not produced a comparable poetry in a language other than that of Standard English. This is not to say that questions of diction are unproblematic for writers from Northern Ireland, as we have already seen from the earlier discussion of Heaney's 'Ministry of Fear'. Indeed, to take the case of Heaney: his poetry has been constantly interested in matters of language, detecting traces of its own distinctiveness both in the occasional survival of Gaelic (as in the early poem 'Broagh', for example), and in the 'Northern', Viking, or Anglo-Saxon roots of the English spoken by the Irish farming people from whom he comes. The advice he hears from the Viking 'longship's swimming tongue' in 'North' (1975) was powerful if rather enigmatic:

---

[17] Tom Leonard, from 'Ghostie Men', in Douglas Dunn (ed.), *The Faber Book of Twentieth-Century Scottish Poetry* (London: Faber & Faber, 1992), 339.

[18] See O'Rourke (ed.), *Dream State* for several examples.

It said, 'Lie down
In the word-hoard, burrow
The coil and gleam
Of your furrowed brain.

Compose in darkness.
Expect aurora borealis
in the long foray
but no cascade of light.

Keep your eye clear
as the bleb of the icicle,
trust the feel of what nubbed treasure
your hands have known'.[19]

The injunction to 'lie down in the word-hoard' here appears to mean advice to draw upon the varied riches that are dormant but possible in the language that Heaney already speaks, bearing with it as it does traces of the Viking past that so marked the ancient history of these islands and specifically the history of English. The immediate fruits of this advice include such oddly connoting words as 'bleb' and 'nubbed'. Later in his career Heaney would be tempted by another foray into the historic riches of the English that he had always spoken, when making his translation of *Beowulf*; in the 'Introduction' to his translation he writes of the release he achieved when he discovered the word 'þolian' (to suffer) in *Beowulf*, and could connect it with a saying of his aunt's, 'They'll just have to learn to thole'.[20] This discovery enabled a kind of reconciliation for Heaney, in that he could now cease to see the Gaelic which his ancestors had spoken, and from which they had been displaced, as in competition with the English and its roots which he actually spoke—even while acknowledging that 'thole' had made its way over to Ulster with the Scots planters who had brought it, whence it had made its way across to 'the locals who had originally spoken Irish'(p.xxv). Heaney's 'word-hoard' was always-already cut through with historic conflicts, but this discovery for Heaney made these conflicts less fraught.

Michael Longley is another poet from Northern Ireland whose diction draws frequently on the vernacular (I relish a 'duncher', or old hat, in 'Laertes', a translation from the *Odyssey* where Cowper has 'casque'). But he has only occasionally used Ulster Sots in a more extensive way, as in another translation from the *Odyssey*, the poem 'Phemios and Medon':

Still looking for a scoot-hole, Phemios the poet
In swithers, fiddling with his harp, jukes to the hatch,
Lays the bruckle yoke between porringer and armchair,
Makes a ram-stam for Odysseus, grammels his knees,
Then bannies and bams wi this highfalutin blether: . . .[21]

---

[19] Heaney, 'North', *North*, 10–11.
[20] Seamus Heaney, 'Introduction', *Beowulf* (London: Faber & Faber, 1999), p. xxv.
[21] Michael Longley, 'Phemios and Medon', *Collected Poems* (London: Jonathan Cape, 2006), 229.

There is undoubtedly some comedy in this, since Longley uses Ulster Scots to describe the comic figures of the poet and the herald who have escaped the massacre of the suitors by hiding ignominiously. However, this is not the only story here, for the poem allots this language to the narration of the poem, and assigns a parody of highfalutin Standard English to the comic figures. The poem thus overturns the expected linguistic hierarchy. The situation is further complicated by the fact that this is a translation, or at least an imitation: the cultural authority of Homer has been readily assimilated to that of the vernacular. In fact, the poem might best be understood in terms of a long tradition of translation into vernacular non-standard languages, where equivalents to the popular or demotic qualities of the originals cannot be found in traditional poetic diction (Garioch's extended translations of Belli's sonnets are a case in point, where the vernacular energies of Scots provide a powerful equivalent for Belli's poems in Roman dialect).

At all events, Longley's poem captures something of these energies also, providing a valuable contrasting note in the characteristically grave idiom of his poetry. Another poet from Northern Ireland, Tom Paulin, has written of the 'wild dash and wit and loving playfulness of Northern Irish speech'; the poetic example he provides, however, is from a Belfast street-song.[22] As is always the way with vernacular poetry, the poetry is enlivened not only by the aural qualities of the sounds themselves, though this is important, but also by the poem's capacity to participate in or exploit the immediacies of spoken language. In that respect poetry in non-standard English is always a carnivalized language, releasing the locked linguistic energies held in place by the habitual alignments of poetry with Standard English.

These various poets use differing strategies for the use of non-standard English in poetry, which could be broadly distinguished in these ways: the presence of skelfs or traces of an often historic diction which provides a particular intensity to moments in a poetry predominantly written in Standard English; the use of what is in effect another language, be it Scots or Ulster Scots (remembering always that the best distinction between a dialect and a language is that a language is a dialect with an army and a navy, so that what appear to be linguistic distinctions are in fact social and historical ones); the attempt to reproduce orthographically the various demotics of contemporary Britain; and various modernist or postmodernist strategies which combine or play off against each other the different linguistic registers available in the contemporary world. In my last set of examples, drawn from poets of Caribbean descent, comparable strategies are visible, though the historic language which provides one range of possibilities for poetry is of course the Creole or Nation language bought by immigrants from the Caribbean.

An early poem by Linton Kwesi Johnson (b. 1952), 'Reggae Sounds', is a reflection on the meaning of reggae cast predominantly in Standard English, but using also some

---

[22] Tom Paulin, 'Introduction', *The Faber Book of Vernacular Verse* (London: Faber & Faber, 1990), p. xxi.

suggestion of spoken Caribbean English, and certainly drawing on the rhythms of reggae itself:

Rhythm of a tropical electrical storm
(cooled doun to the pace of the struggle),
flame-rhythm of historically yearning
flame-rhythm of the time of turning,
measuring the time for bombs and for burning.

Slow drop. make stop. move forward.
dig doun to the root of the pain;
shape it into violence for the people,
they will know what to do, they will do it.

Shock-black bubble-doun-beat bouncing
rock-wise tumble-doun sound music;
foot-drop find drum, blood story,
bass history is a moving
              is a hurting black story.[23]

This is a poem which seeks to combine the rhythms of spoken Anglo-Caribbean vernacular with the rhythms of reggae music itself and make them speak revolutionary politics; or rather, the enunciation of these rhythms becomes in itself an act of searching for and articulating such a politics. Especially in the last stanza of the poem with its emphatic trochaic and dactylic rhythms Johnson's language enacts the synthesis that the poem thematically announces.

Which leads immediately to one of the most striking aspects of Linton Kwesi Johnson's poetry, and of the dub poetry that he helped to initiate in England (though it also began simultaneously in the Caribbean itself): its status as an emphatically oral form, and its closeness to and reliance on the rhythms of Caribbean popular music, initially reggae but increasingly all the varieties of rap. So a more characteristic reggae poem would be, for example, 'Reggae fi Dada', which uses Nation language and which is driven by a strong beat:

galang dada
galang gwaan yaw sah
yu nevah ad noh life fi live
jus di wan life fi give
yu did yu time pan ert
yu nevah get yu jus dizert
galang goh smile inna di sun
galang goh satta inna di palace af peace

---

[23] Linton Kwesi Johnson, 'Reggae Sounds', *Selected Poems* (London: Penguin Books, 2006), 17.

o di waatah
it soh dep
di watah
it soh daak
an it full a hawbah shaak [24]

Perhaps even this is not a characteristic Johnson poem if by that one expects the megaphone politics of some of his poetry, for this is a tender and personal poem, drawing on some scarcely submerged religious vocabulary to wish something like peace or consolation on the 'dada' that the poem addresses. Johnson's sense of his own aesthetic is powerfully expressed in a later poem, 'If I Woz a Tap-Natch Poet', which acknowledges his own pantheon of 'tap-natch' poets, but which nevertheless asserts the value and distinctiveness of his own dub rhythms:

still
inna di meantime
wid mi riddim
wid mi rime
wid mi ruff base line
wid mi own sense a time

goon poet haffi step in line
caw Bootahlazy mite a gat couple touzan
but Mandela fi him
touzans a touzans a touzans a touzans [25]

This may be an aesthetic for 'the meantime', but it is provisionally sufficient, and its sense of itself includes not only that finely realized transition into its own insistent rhythm, but also its inevitable connection to a politics necessary for the moment—in this particular meantime, the successful defeat of apartheid. In Johnson's hands at least dub poetry insists on its own spoken urgencies in a language that itself needs to be spoken or performed to realize its full power.

Something similar can be said about another dub poet, Jean 'Binta' Breeze (b. 1956) whose poetry in performance is likewise close to reggae—so much so that in reading her long poem, 'Tongue Your Funky Rhythms in My Ear', on the importance of reggae, she breaks into sung quotations from Desmond Dekker and Bob Marley.[26] Like Johnson also, Breeze's poetry draws on many registers, and uses the resources of Standard English as much as Jamaican English, and indeed all the way-stations in between:

---

[24] Kwesi Johnson, 'Reggae fi Dada', *Selected Poems*, 50.
[25] Kwesi Johnson, 'If I Woz a Tap-Natch Poet', *Selected Poems*, 94–7.
[26] Jean 'Binta' Breeze, 'Tongue Your Funky Rhythms in My Ear', *Third World Girl: Selected Poems* (Tarset: Bloodaxe Books, 2011), 148–56.

why yuh looking so down an out, chile
like dem bruk up yuh spirit
an sen yuh out wile
wat happen to dat brilliant smile
dat could push de grey out de sky
dat could mek a man waan lef im woman and chile...[27]

Here the poetry is scarcely 'dub', but uses Nation language in a different way, to capture the rhythms of an older woman speaker, so that the solicitude and tenderness of the older speaker is caught in this vernacular; the simple care that passes down the generations of women is most appropriately caught in the demotic tones that the poem uses, non-standard language being an appropriate medium for the transmission of personal affect. But Breeze's poetry slips in and out of Nation language and draws on different registers and accents to fit the different occasions of her poem.

Breeze was brought up in Jamaica, and lives both in England and the Caribbean, so she is only arguably a 'British' poet, and discussion of her poetry and its linguistic resources tempts one too far, perhaps, towards the large subject of Caribbean poetry with all its great richness in the twentieth century. But these divisions are arbitrary and porous. The wider point is that poetry written by poets of Caribbean descent draws on a distinctive linguistic inheritance which makes available to them very directly the energies of the spoken language, and which can align their poetry also with the rhythms of reggae and rap. This inheritance allows them to write in very different idioms, as the Liverpool poet Levi Tafari (b. 1960) indicates:

> I sometimes write poetry in the Jamaican nation language, sometimes it might have a kind of West African rhythm and a reggae beat, or even hip hop rap style, which I know is American, but also part of the African-American experience.[28]

These are not simply equivalents, of course; Benjamin Zephaniah (b. 1958) has written about the incommensurability of some kinds of linguistic experience in his poem 'Translate':

Who will translate
Dis stuff.
Who can decipher
De dread chant
Dat cum fram
De body
An soul
Dubwise?

---

[27] Breeze, 'hole mi han', *Third World Girl*, 160–1.
[28] See the profile of Tafari at [http://www.contemporarywriters.com/authors/?p=auth02d2m455312627214]

Wot poet in
Resident,
Wot translator
Wid wot
Embassy,
Wot brilliant
Linguistic mind
Can kick dis,
Dig dis
Bad mudder luvin rap?

Sometimes I wanda
Why I and I
A try so hard fe get
Overstood,
Mek we juss get
Afrocentric,
Dark,
Who in space
Who on eart
Who de hell we writing fa?

Sometimes I wanda
Who will translate
Dis
Fe de inglish?[29]

This is an appropriate place to conclude discussion of the poetic energies created by vernacular Caribbean English; it asserts the uniqueness of a certain synthesis of music, language, race, and religion, its incommensurability, as I say—but it does so paradoxically in a poem that, despite its use of Nation language, scarcely needs translation. This is the opposite of Tony Harrison's despairing paradox that 'I've come round to your position on "the Arts" | but put it down in poems, that's the bind'; where for Harrison the choice that had been forced on him was to adopt an idiom permanently removed from his parents and the people he comes from, Zephaniah, in this poem at least, seems to offer the opposite solution of a poem at one with his audience but restricted to them.

At stake in all these discussions is the relationship of poetry to the speech that surrounds it. The group of poems of educational induction into 'poetry' indicates the fraught relation of the poetic canon to the standardizing or centripetal forces at work in English as a national language, but indicates also the potentially productive character of this tension. Other recent and contemporary poets have used the resources of both historic and

---

[29] Benjamin Zephaniah, 'Translate', *Too Black, Too Strong* (Tarset: Bloodaxe Books, 2001), 83.

evolving Englishes in ways that are freer from the paradoxes and dilemmas that afflict Harrison and to some extent Heaney and Daljit Nagra. Certainly the temptations and rewards for a poetry that speaks directly and in the idiom of its immediate community are great. But so also are the resources of a language after fifteen hundred years of creolization, adaptation, and assimilation, and this history can offer surprising possibilities for contemporary poets. Heaney's own rediscovery of the Anglo-Saxon roots of the language his community already spoke, inseparable from a history of colonization and dispossession, should remind us however that the remarkable resources of the differing Englishes available come laden with particular social histories, so that the choices poets make about matters of diction and register are never only aesthetic ones. Roy Fisher once wrote, in a poem for Michael Hamburger, that 'He knows good Englishes'.[30] So they are. But the complex social, national, and ethnic history of these islands means that they are not all good for all people on all occasions. A pluralism both of language and of poetic inclusiveness of language—Andrew Greig's honouring 'the plurality...of a culture and a generation'—is surely itself to be honoured, but it needs also to recognize the limits suggested by Benjamin Zephaniah's question:

Who will translate
Dis
Fe de inglish?

Select Bibliography

Armitage, Simon, *Selected Poems* (London: Faber & Faber, 2001).
Breeze, Jean 'Binta', *Third World Girl: Selected Poems* (Tarset: Bloodaxe Books, 2011).
Crawford, Robert, 'Ghetto-Blastir', in Donny O'Rourke (ed.), *Dream State: The New Scottish Poets* (2nd edn., Edinburgh: Polygon, 2002), 105.
Fisher, Roy, *The Thing about Joe Sullivan* (Manchester: Carcanet Press, 1978).
Greig, Andrew, *Western Swing: Adventures with the Heretical Buddha* (Newcastle upon Tyne: Bloodaxe Books, 1994).
Harrison, Tony, *Selected Poems* (2nd edn., London: Penguin Books, 1987).
Harrison, Tony, *V* (Newcastle upon Tyne: Bloodaxe Books, 1989).
Hazlitt, William, *The Spirit of the Age* (1825; London: Collins Publishers, 1969).
Heaney, Seamus, *North* (London: Faber & Faber, 1975).
Jamie, Kathleen, *The Tree House* (London: Picador, 2004).
Johnson, Linton Kwesi, 'Reggae Sounds', in *Selected Poems* (London: Penguin Books, 2006).
Leonard, Tom, 'Ghostie Men', in Douglas Dunn (ed.), *The Faber Book of Twentieth-Century Scottish Poetry* (London: Faber & Faber, 1992), 339.

[30] Roy Fisher, 'Style', *The Thing about Joe Sullivan* (Manchester: Carcanet Press, 1978), 64.

Leonard, Tom, *Outside the Narrative* (Exbourne: Etruscan Books, 2009).
Longley, Michael, 'Phemios and Medon', in *Collected Poems* (London: Jonathan Cape, 2006).
Nagra, Daljit, *Look We Have Coming to Dover* (London: Faber & Faber, 2007).
Paulin, Tom, *The Faber Book of Vernacular Verse* (London: Faber & Faber, 1990).
Robertson, Robin, *The Wrecking Light* (London: Picador, 2010), 71.
Robinson, Peter, *The Look of Goodbye: Poems 2001–2006* (Exeter: Shearsman Books, 2008).
Heaney, Seamus, *Beowulf* (London: Faber & Faber, 1999).
Zephaniah, Benjamin, *Too Black, Too Strong* (Tarset: Bloodaxe Books, 2001).

CHAPTER 14

MISREMEMBERED LYRIC AND ORPHANED MUSIC

ZOË SKOULDING

The word 'lyric' ties Western contemporary poetry to its memory of music even now that it is read, heard, and appreciated in a largely separate context. As the French poet Jacques Roubaud insists, having traced the origin of Western poetry back to the troubadours, 'A song is not a poem and a poem is not a song... It's an insult to poetry to call it song. It's an insult to song to call it poetry'.[1] However, contemporary poetry has registered the changing experience of song since the advent of recording technology through particular understandings of relationships between environment, context, memory, and lyric voice. The musicality of poetry is often seen as relating to musical notation, for example in terms of rhythm, but here I will look instead at how the use of recording rather than notation as a compositional tool in certain areas of contemporary music has parallels with memory and quotation of song lyrics in poetry. The four poets in this chapter are all variously situated within the diverse context of experimental poetry from the UK, and while any broad definition of such work is inadequate, especially within the increasingly fragmented groupings of recent poetry, a helpful distinction noted by Richard Caddel and Peter Quartermain is that in contrast to the 'closed, monolineal utterance' that typified much mainstream poetry of the late twentieth century,[2] oppositional writers tended to adopt 'an open poetry of exploration and even interrogation characterized by a play of possible meanings, rather than by the enunciation of a meaning forwarded by thesis',[3] in which emphasis has been shifted from the writer's

---

[1] Jacques Roubaud, 'Prelude: Poetry and Orality', trans. Jean-Jacques Poucel, in Marjorie Perloff and Craig Douglas Dworkin (eds.), *The Sound of Poetry, the Poetry of Sound* (Chicago: University of Chicago Press, 2009), 18.

[2] Richard Caddel and Peter Quartermain, *Other: British and Irish Poetry since 1970* (Hanover, Conn.: Wesleyan University Press, 1999), p. xv.

[3] Caddel and Quartermain, *Other*, xxvii.

expression to the reader's construction of meaning. The possibility of the expressive lyric self as a source of meaning is therefore made problematic by a shift towards 'language itself as a source of experience within the poem'.[4] All such definitions are questionable, and the work of these writers from different generations reveals contrasting approaches both to lyrics and to the question of lyric itself. Denise Riley (born 1948) has lived in Cambridge and the Welsh poet John James (born 1939) still does; Sean Bonney (born 1969) lives in London, as does Caroline Bergvall (born 1962), though her background is French-Norwegian. While these details may have relevance, what is more central to this discussion is that all have, on occasion, responded to the lyrics of recorded songs that have formed soundtracks to their cultural environments.

The use of popular lyrics and musical references in poetry can offer a critique of authorial authority, since while writing has historically occupied a culturally privileged position, response to shared sound is part of everyday life in social spaces. Sound is owned by those who hear it. Song has traditionally circulated in a group setting, just as poetry in its oral form would have done; but writing and reading have become more solitary acts. Recorded song maintains its social aspect because until the widespread use of headphones it had to exist in a physical space—on the radio, in the supermarket, or leaking through the floorboards of the room upstairs. Popular song lyrics, therefore, tend to be socially experienced, defining generations and groupings within shared cultural memories. When poets quote song lyrics, as in the examples I will discuss, the different contexts of poem and song are brought into a productive clash, since quotation is, as Walter Benjamin has noted, always an interruption of context.[5] This enables new understandings of lyric subjectivity and its relation to the collective, and therefore political, domain. Furthermore, song lyrics are more than just language, as they emerge from the sound mesh of a musical context. Recalling lyrics involves the memory of sound, a replay of melody and sonic texture that cannot be dissociated from the words themselves.

The means by which modern music has absorbed and been shaped by the impact of recorded sound provides some insights into parallel processes in poetry; a twentieth-century interest in the materiality of sound, which through recording can be isolated from its source, has an equivalent in understandings of poetry that emphasize the materiality of language. The American poet Nathaniel Mackey has commented on the shared etymology of 'orphic' and 'orphan'; drawing upon writings on music by Steven Feld and Victor Zuckerkandl respectively, he explores music and poetic language on the one hand in relation to social rupture, as 'a music that turns on abandonment, absence, loss', suggesting that 'Music is wounded kinship's last resort', and on the other in terms of the materiality of sound, since poetic or musical meaning cannot be separated from the physical existence of the signifier.[6] Noting Octavio Paz's 'characterization of

---

[4] Caddel and Quartermain, *Other*, xxvii.
[5] Walter Benjamin, *Illuminations*, trans. Harry Zorn (London: Pimlico, 1999), 148.
[6] Nathaniel Mackey, 'Sound and Sentiment, Sound and Symbol', in Charles Bernstein (ed.), *The Politics of Poetic Form: Poetry and Public Policy* (New York: Roof, 1990), 90.

language as an orphan severed from the presence to which it refers and which presumably gave it birth', Mackey points out that 'Music encourages us to see that the symbolic is the orphic, that the symbolic realm is the realm of the orphan... Poetic language is language owning up to being an orphan, to its tenuous kinship with the things it ostensibly refers to.'[7] Poetry's point of connection with music undermines the referential character of language; while this intensifies lyric affect, it also breaks the link between language and the subject as its originating source.

A similar set of conclusions in music has been enabled by sound recording, notably through Pierre Schaeffer's major contribution to contemporary music, his notion of the *objét sonore* or 'sound object'.[8] For example, Schaeffer's libretto for the 1953 opera *Orphée 53*, written with Pierre Henry, refers to the image of the beheaded Orpheus, the severed head that goes on singing. He describes a moment in the performance:

> Orphée chantait : *On raconte—Que décapité—Orphée—L'appelait—L'appelait encore...Eurydice, Eurydice...* Rien ne se passait plus sur scène. Pierre Henry déchaînait les haut-parleurs à coups de clavecin préparé, de tam-tam, de détonations, tandis que passait sur une bande pré-enregistrée une voix qui parlait grec, mais désarticulée, arrachée, criée, râlée.

> Orpheus was singing: *It's said—that decapitated—Orpheus—called her—called her still...Eurydice, Eurydice...* Nothing more was happening on the stage. Pierre Henry was unleashing blasts of prepared harpsichord, tom-toms, explosions from the loudspeakers, while on a pre-recorded tape there was a voice speaking Greek, but dislocated, torn, shouting, and groaning.[9]

Memory is central to the image of Orpheus looking back, and to his repeated calling, but at the same time recorded sound is cut from its source to become the basis of new compositional possibilities. This is the starting point of electro-acoustic music; rather than proceeding from a written score, such music begins with sound phenomena that are manipulated into a composition. The notion of the orphan/orphic is, however, closely tied to the question of affect, and an attention to phenomena in an environment insists on a public and shared dimension of both language and sound. As Trevor Wishart points out, 'there is no such thing as an *unmusical* sound object':[10] with the advent of recorded sound, all sounds are equal, and equally capable of being regarded as music, so music is what is discovered through listening. There are productive contradictions in this area, since work such as Schaeffer's can tend towards the entirely non-referential, to a pure music. At the same time, sounds are often haunted by their sources as their recontextualization results in a proliferation of new meanings.

---

[7] Mackey, 'Sound and Sentiment, Sound and Symbol', 90.
[8] Thom Holmes, *Electronic and Experimental Music: Technology, Music, and Culture* (London: Taylor and Francis, 2008), 45.
[9] Marc Pierret, *Entretiens avec Pierre Schaeffer* (Paris: Éditions Pierre Belfond, 1969), 103, my translation.
[10] Trevor Wishart, *On Sonic Art* (York: Imagineering Press, 1985), 6.

The poems I discuss here suggest an analogous compositional technique based on sound phenomena within a given environment, though the musical references made in the poems, and hence my reference points, are not the works of avant-garde composers like Schaeffer but from the popular culture that saturates everyday life. Pop music has been faster to adapt to the impact of recording technology because the very notion of 'popular' has come to depend on such technologies, while sampling is well established as a technique that recontextualizes song fragments, creating new music while relying on a degree of hauntedness in the memory of its source recordings. Furthermore, recording levels out differences not only between different sounds but between different types of music, since, as Chris Cutler explains, 'a record makes all musics equally accessible';[11] he goes on to describe the 'sound intoxication' of the 1960s in which the work of high art composers such as Varèse, Schaeffer, and Stockhausen influenced the cross-play of high and low art for a new generation of musicians experimenting with recorded sound borrowed from existing sources.[12] Yet it was more difficult for classical composers to adapt to such possibilities because of 'the non-negotiable concern with originality and peer status—and also with the craft aspect of creating from scratch'. The mainstream of classical composition proved resistant to such techniques, but as Cutler writes: 'To the extent that sound recording as a medium negates that of notation and echoes in a transformed form that of biological memory, this should not be so surprising. In ritual and folk musics, for instance, originality as we understand it would be a misunderstanding—or a transgression—since proper performance is repetition.'[13] In low art or popular music, folk-derived practices such as the cover version, or making variations on a traditional form, meant that such concerns with originality were far less problematic. Recording can therefore be said in some senses to return modern music to social meaning and memory-based patterns of transmission that are as old as music itself.

The use of quotation from song lyrics in poems points to a relationship between memory and lyric expression that is related to these changing possibilities in music. In particular, the song encountered as recorded sound, itself a repetition, is repeated and manipulated as source material in the poem. Quotation of song lyrics is a form of remembering, yet it inevitably involves change when the mass-produced song, as Walter Benjamin puts it, meets 'the beholder or listener in his own particular situation',[14] instead of retaining an aura of uniqueness. If poetry has often been read as the unique expression of the lyric self, pop lyrics produce temporarily inhabited identifications where the emphasis is more on the listener than the writer. In Denise Riley's poem 'A Misremembered Lyric', which quotes both the Cascades' 'Rhythm of the Rain', written

---

[11] Chris Cutler, 'Plunderphonia', in Christoph Cox and Daniel Warner (eds.), *Audio Culture: Readings in Modern Music* (London and New York: Continuum, 2008), 147.
[12] Cutler, 'Plunderphonia', 147.
[13] Cutler, 'Plunderphonia', 141.
[14] Benjamin, *Illuminations*, 215.

by John Claude Gummoe, and Roger Cook and Roger Greenaway's 'Something's Gotten Hold of My Heart' as sung by Gene Pitney, the poet is that listener:

> A misremembered lyric: a soft catch of its song
> whirrs in my throat. 'Something's gotta hold of my heart
> tearing my' soul and my conscience apart, long after
> presence is clean gone and leaves unfurnished no
> shadow. Rain lyrics. Yes, then the rain lyrics fall.
> I don't want absence to be this beautiful.
> It shouldn't be; in fact I know it wasn't, while
> 'everything that consoles is false' is off the point—
> you get no consolation anyway until your memory's
> dead; or something never had gotten hold of
> your heart in the first place, and that's the fear thought.[15]

The mourning of absence echoes the melancholy of the Cascades song, which is in turn invoked as an absence within the poem. Yet Riley's quotation of song lyrics does not imply mourning of a lost connection with the lyrical directness of song but an exploration of the process of misremembering. The substitution of 'gotta' for 'gotten' suggests a mishearing that subtly anglicizes the phrase, giving the song a physical and social context as language that has lodged in the ear, via a 1960s radio in Britain, rather than the eye. The more obvious alterations here, 'tearing' for 'dragging', and 'soul and conscience' for 'soul and senses', emphasize the dislocation that takes place in the original song. The action of the 'something' that gets hold of the heart is mirrored by the song itself, which is also an external entity that acts on the body, its whirring suggesting a machine. That machine is cadence, the onward propulsion of a phrase that drives it towards resolution, even if that resolution is kept in doubt and suspense. 'Something' is both language and affect. The interruption of the quotation signals the point at which the communally recognized text and melody of the song is appropriated by an individual memory and subject to its distortions, the dactylic rhythm of the song giving way to the hesitations and repetitions of inner speech.

In her prose writings, Riley posits an understanding of language that starts from the collective, and in which private consciousness is the internalization of public linguistic intercourse, rather than the reverse. Much of Riley's argument in this and other works concerns the internalizing of negative speech, but she points out here:

> It's true enough, though, that not only imperious accusation is apt to indwell. So can lyric, gorgeous fragments, psalms and hymns; beautiful speech also comes to settle in its listeners. There is an unholy coincidence between beauty and cruelty in their verbal mannerisms; citation, reiteration, echo, quotation may work benignly, or as a poetics of abusive diction... perhaps the happily resonant indwelling of lyric may be explained in ways also fitting the unhappy experience of being mastered by hard words far better forgotten.[16]

---

[15] Denise Riley, *Selected Poems* (London: Reality Street Editions, 2000), 51.
[16] Denise Riley, *Impersonal Passion: Language as Affect* (Durham, NC and London: Duke University Press, 2005), 13.

Language operates as a force, fused with affect that runs unwilled through the body and through memory. Remembering is the process by which 'speech comes to settle in its listeners', through repetition and reiteration. Sound, equally, in a process that is intensified by the repetition and memory of recording, comes to inhabit its listeners. It is true that verbal abuse, being 'hooked' by a hook line, or absorbing a line of poetry involve different degrees of force and different degrees of consent and collaboration on the part of the listener. Yet the parallels between violent and beautiful language might be seen, for example, in hymns or religious liturgy, in which a powerful ecclesiastical patriarchy is sustained through the interpellation of worshippers as guilty sinners. Popular song, perhaps more invitingly, may situate the listener within a discourse of romantic love, which might at certain times be willingly inhabited, yet precisely because it cannot fully embody the speaker's presence its promises and intensities are ultimately experienced as a form of linguistic wounding. As Riley writes:

> If we compare the aftermath of hearing 'I love you' with the aftermath of hearing 'I hate you', in both instances the speaker may fight to sever the utterance from its vanished utterer. With the former declaration, the struggle is to find compensation in the teeth of impermanence (those words were definitely said to me, so at least I can be sure that once I was loved even though their speaker has gone). And with the latter, to find protection from the risk of permanence (those words were directed at me, but it wasn't especially me who was hated, I just accidentally got in that speaker's way).[17]

This is inconsistent, however, and Riley suggests that a saner response is to acknowledge 'my own sheer contingency as a linguistic subject' and to acknowledge 'language's powerful impersonality'. In 'A Misremembered Lyric' the speaker distances herself from guilt via a line from a 1920s music hall song: 'Do shrimps make good mothers? Yes they do'.[18] Similarly, Riley sees a means of distancing the self from the painful absences of romantic language by becoming 'a walker in language' who recognizes her own contingency and impersonality as 'someone who is herself accidentally spoken'.[19]

This sense of contingency is crucial to Riley's use of lyrics, which may be considered in relation to adoption (Riley is herself adopted), though there are differences between adopting a child who takes one's own name, and 'adopting' a line from another text, which emphasizes the fact that it was written by someone else. Clarifying this point, Susan Schultz writes:

> Riley's use of quotation, in 'Lure, 1963' and other poems, enacts an adoptive use of texts. If her text has a 'nature', a point she would no doubt argue against, then the pop song lyric has a very different 'nature'. And yet they are related, as in an adoptive family. Unlike many poets, including John Ashbery, with whom Riley has a poetic

---

[17] Riley, *Impersonal Passion*, 27.
[18] The Two Gilberts, 'Do Shrimps Make Good Mothers?' (Regal, 1924).
[19] Riley, *Impersonal Passion*, 27.

relation, Riley does not mock the pop song or simply incorporate its form into her own lyric. Instead, the pop song is an integral part of the texture of her own poem, revealing naked emotions that she cannot, while being restrained within the highly controlled syntax of her own sentences, lines... Further, through her use of citation at the back of the book, she not only covers her copyright duties, but also makes it clear that these quotations come from particular places and moments in history. Her adoption, in the lingo of this day, is 'open', even as the frequent lack of quotation marks diminishes the differences between Riley's language and that of the pop lyricists from whom she borrows.[20]

To consider quotation not simply as interruption of context but as adoption entails an outward-looking and social aspect to lyric, and to language itself, yet importantly, as Schultz notes, this does not diminish the importance of emotion to Riley's work. What emerges is an articulation of emotion within a series of social and historical frames. The recorded song lyric is a form of public language, often heard in public spaces, which is internalized to become part of the 'inner speech' that constitutes the familiar terrain of lyric poetry. As Riley suggests, the topography of 'inner' and 'outer' is unsettled by the notion of a linguistic unconscious[21] and 'it's conceivable that the unconscious is better imagined not as a deep pouch of self, but as something outside of it, and hanging between people'.[22] This understanding of the exterior self places the poem in the realm of the social more explicitly than confessional lyric, while also accommodating affect. It's also how we might imagine the music that pours out of radios and loudspeakers, becoming both a physical presence and a shared pool of expression in countless pubs, supermarkets, and cars.

The question of environment is further explored in 'The Castalian Spring'; Riley draws on the Greek myth of Castaly, the fountain that is the source of song.[23] Her treatment is full of ironic comedy: the speaker, having drunk from the spring, turns into a toad and wonders 'What should I sing out on this gratuitous new instrument?'[24] Her new voice remains stubbornly external, a music that is heard as part of the physical environment around her rather than an expressive emanation from the self. The voice is, above all, a sounding-out:

The voice hears itself as it sings to its fellows—must
Thrum in its own ears, like any noise thumping down
Anywhere airwaves must equally fall.[25]

---

[20] Susan M. Schultz, '"Unlock a Marvell karaoke": Quotation as Adoption in the Work of Denise Riley', *How2* [http://www.asu.edu/pipercwcenter/how2journal/vol_3_no_1/cambridge/schultz.html], accessed 29 July 2011.

[21] Denise Riley, *The Words of Selves: Identification, Solidarity, Irony* (Stanford, Calif.: Stanford University Press, 2000), 15–16.

[22] Denise Riley and Jean-Jacques Lecercle, *The Force of Language* (Basingstoke: Palgrave, 2004), 36.

[23] Riley, *Selected Poems*, 87–91.

[24] Riley, *Selected Poems*, 88.

[25] Riley, *Selected Poems*, 90.

As soon as a voice sounds it is meshed into other sounds with the potential for interference in transmission. It is exactly this interference that places music in the realm of the social. As the toad sings, there is a fusion of voice and instrument, body and environment that deconstructs the notion of poetic source: 'Into the cooling air I gave tongue, my ears blurred with the lyre | Of my larynx, its vibrato reverberant into the struck dumb dusk'. The sonorous density of the lines accentuates the way in which words fall through the ear into memory, the repeated sounds echoing to the point that they sound familiar despite the unexpected inversion of 'struck dumb dusk'.[26]

The poem is a sounding-out of poetic possibilities, as the toad weighs up the respective merits of 'girlish hellenics' and the 'responsibility to | Speak to society'. Written in the context of a bitterly oppositional UK poetry scene, the poem playfully considers alternative approaches to poetic community, yet its concerns have a wider reach in terms of cultural memory:

I fished for my German, broke out into lieder, rhymed
Sieg with *Krieg*, so explaining our century; I was hooked
On my theory of militarism as stemming from lyricism.[27]

Quotation of German lyrics relates, as Riley suggests to 'the language of early nineteenth-century song cycles, in which words and notes hang intimately together', but this evocation is simultaneously troubling, with its pun on hook lines, because 'it's not yet possible to use the German language to talk about group emotion and identity without recalling, in Reich's contentious phrase, a mass psychology of fascism'.[28] Of course the role of lyrics in ideological coercion is far more widespread; the poem's reference to the Bob Marley song 'One Love' evokes not only 1960s communal optimism but also the way in which advertising has co-opted such sentiments, for example, as Riley notes, Coca-Cola's 'one world' television adverts.[29] The song lyrics both evoke and question linguistic affect. Cutting the lyrics from their musical source and resituating them in a poem reveals the machinery at work in collective memory, and demonstrates how ideas adhere to remembered sound.

The recorded song is a single performance, evoking a social and historical context; it is not abstracted and timeless. As a result, we can see the interruption of different periods: Riley's evocation of 1960s music in a poem written many years later draws attention to the social formation of the lyric voice and an awareness of the poet's own role as performer in it. In her influential work *'Am I That Name?' Feminism and the Category of 'Women' in History*, Riley playfully adapts Sojourner Truth's famous rhetorical question 'Ain't I a woman' to 'ain't I a fluctuating identity';[30] exactly how this identity fluctuates over time is charted in her poems' reflexive response to verbal-musical environments.

---

[26] Riley, *Selected Poems*, 88.
[27] Riley, *Selected Poems*, 88.
[28] Riley, *Words of Selves*, 104–5.
[29] Riley, *Words of Selves*, 104.
[30] Denise Riley, *'Am I that Name?' Feminism and the Category of 'Women' in History* (Minneapolis: University of Minnesota Press, 1988), 1.

The introduction of a visual element in 'Lure, 1963' adds a further dimension, as the orphaning of lyric from its expressive source is placed in the context of painting.[31] The poem enacts a double ekphrasis, describing a painting by Gillian Ayres while simultaneously rechannelling 1960s song lyrics. The line 'I roam around around around around' adapted from the song by Ernest Maresca encapsulates the wandering of the lyric 'I', dislodged here from an anchoring selfhood.[32] The lack of figurative reference in the painting becomes a means of exploring the poem's proximity to music, the question being not about whether a poem, painting, or song can 'express feelings' but a severing of the subject from fixed reference points that allows meaning to proliferate. The simultaneous affect and materiality of the painting's surface evoked by a phrase such as 'Flood, drag to papery long brushes | of deep violet' is paralleled by the quotations from lyrics where apparent emotional directness ('When will I be loved?'; 'it's in his kiss') sings without direction through the fractured surface of the line. Reference to other art forms than poetry makes possible the intensity of affect in Riley's poetics, which proceed from Merleau-Ponty's assertion that 'I am from the start outside myself and open to the world'.[33] Rather than becoming a lament for the lost lyric source, the poem allows a circulation of fragmented references that were outside to begin with.

Riley's use of quoted lyrics in her poems both denies and recuperates the possibility of the poem as song, a tension that is evident in her recent work, 'A Part Song', written after the death of her son in his young adulthood.[34] The title, along with its more general implications of loss and incompleteness, suggests not only that it is a song in parts—either simultaneous as vocal harmony or linear as in a poem sequence—but also that it is 'partly' song. The sequence begins by asking 'You principle of song, what are you *for* now', and moves through a range of voices that circle this question in rage, despair, comic irony, passionately focused memory, and calm reflection, including adapted quotation from other texts: 'She do the bereaved in different voices'. The lost son is figured as Orpheus 'Airily flirting with Persephone', yet the poem cannot retrieve the dead, and must, in that sense, fail:

It's all a resurrection song.
Would it ever be got right
The dead could rush home
Keen to press their chinos.[35]

At the same time, the poem reverberates with 'the thought | Of me being sung in by you', since it is through lyric's exteriority and its absences that the possibility of music is created.

---

[31] Riley, *Selected Poems*, 50.
[32] Ernest Maresca, 'The Wanderer' (Warner-Tamerlane, 1960).
[33] M. Merleau-Ponty, *The Phenomenology of Perception* (London: Routledge, 2002), 530.
[34] Denise Riley, 'A Part Song', *London Review of Books* (9 Feb. 2012), 14.
[35] Riley, 'A Part Song'.

Absence is explored differently in the following poem by John James from *Berlin Return*, 1983, quoted here in its entirety, though he shares with Riley an interest in how sense perceptions can be recontextualized to cut across the boundaries of art forms:

SONG

after Richard Long & Johnny Cash

for an hour I walk a line to you
then mark the distance on a map

each of the following days
I walk the line & the sculpture becomes

slower & slower from day to day,
day to night, day night day,

till Wednesday moving slow the train rolls in
& you come walking out[36]

Richard Long's development of the walk as a gestural trace in the landscape, the line of a walk apparently going nowhere, is superimposed with the Johnny Cash song 'I walk the line'.[37] The line of the poem is also suggested here, connecting the visual line and the line of the song, which makes the distance seem to be one of duration, rather than spatial, in an auditory rather than visual space. Although there is a map, what is marked on it is a period of time, an unfolding process of response to the sculpture that is becoming 'slower and slower'. Cash's lyrics are echoed throughout the poem, for example in the transposition of his lines 'As sure as night is dark and day is light | I keep you on my mind both day and night', which are evoked and then subtly adjusted to emphasize temporal movement. There is a sense of the poem inhabiting the same kind of temporal space as the artwork, which is itself the recording of a movement, and the process of writing itself is suggested in its repetitions.

James's improvisation on Cash highlights another aspect of recorded music that is relevant here, which is that recording removes the emphasis from the notation that has dominated Western classical music, and replaces it with performance. Whereas notation reveals the structure of a piece of music at a glance, previous pre-notation approaches to music relied on listening and responding over time. As Wishart notes:

> Music…cannot be divorced from the medium of sound and enters into our experience as part of an immediate concrete reality; it impinges on us and in doing so it affects our state. Furthermore, as Susanne Langer remarks in *Feeling and Form*, in its articulation of the time-continuum of concrete experience, it corresponds directly with the continuum of our experiencing, the continuous flux of our response-state (Langer 1953: chapter 7).[38]

---

[36] John James, *Collected Poems* (Cambridge: Salt Publishing, 2002), 210.
[37] Johnny Cash, *I Walk the Line* (Sun Records, 1956).
[38] Wishart, *On Sonic Art*, 17.

Just as Richard Long's works explore the role of time and the body in experiencing landscape as against the abstraction of pictorial representation, so James's use of lyrics presents a continuous flux of perception in relation to both the artwork and the country song. This resonates with Gilles Deleuze's notion of difference and repetition, in which the past and future are drawn into the perception of the present, so that 'The past and the future do not designate instants distinct from a supposed present instant, but rather the dimensions of the present itself in so far as it is contraction of instants'.[39] The perceiving self is not a static 'I' who speaks but a changing and responsive entity composed and recomposed throughout the poem.

As in Riley's 'Lure, 1963', the use of song lyrics in the poem offers a positioning of the subject in response to a contemporary artwork, yet because it is recalled quotation it does not settle into a stable position that might fix a definitive meaning to Long's work. The 'you' of the poem creates a sense of purpose and direction in 'the line' that is present in the song but less obviously in Long's sculptures. However, the 'you' of the song is simply that, the subject position of a freely circulating lyric recalled and repeated in a new context. Through quotation, the poem can both evoke lyric affect and keep a distance from it. The 'you' is a 'you' remembered and repeated from a surrounding cultural environment, yet is potentially a different 'you' at each reading. This recursive repetition suggests not only the transmission from one particular song to one particular poem, but also the relationship with every 'you' in a long line of lyric expression that appears to have neither beginning nor end. The 'I' of the poem is equally dislodged from originatory authorship by its relationship with the song while retaining the kind of authenticity that derives from the repetition of cultural materials. It would nevertheless be misleading to suggest that James's musical references indicate any interest in egoless anonymity, since his poetics takes its lead from Frank O'Hara's 'personism', with a focus on the poem's conversational engagement. This is developed through his adoption of a number of personae, a series of performances that evoke not only the lyrics of songs but also the cultural worlds from which they emerge. 'Song' brings together the rarefied, silent air of the art gallery with the airwaves carrying American music across the UK, which, though far removed from its geographical source, is inhabited with a familiarity that makes it ever-present. The resulting cultural clash is the poem, caught between the abstractions of contemporary art and the lyric directness of popular song. It is also a means of defining clashes of generation and class, and for James a clash with 'Cambridge' itself. John Wilkinson describes a 1970s reading in Kettle's Yard, Cambridge, a museum of modernist works exhibited in the collector's house alongside collections of pebbles and other natural objects, its aesthetic broadly in line with Long's:

> John James lurched into the withdrawing-room sanctum in a black bondage suit of synthetic material, some petroleum by-product, improbably strapped to make every movement unpredictable, stocky, hair brushed up black and spiky with Corimist no doubt, and he delivered lines like a flame-thrower: *War/A Former Boiling*.[40]

---

[39] Gilles Deleuze, *Difference and Repetition* (London: Continuum, 2004), 91.
[40] John Wilkinson, *The Lyric Touch: Essays on the Poetry of Excess* (Cambridge: Salt Publishing, 2007), 39.

Wilkinson describes James's relationship with his surroundings as an 'exquisite antagonism', on the one hand resonating with the modernist aesthetic of the museum, but on the other fiercely resisting its genteel atmosphere and the class relations implied by it.

James's musical references are often a form of cultural mapping, so that rather than invoking an anonymous tradition he draws on the associations of particular iconic figures. 'The Ghost of Jimi Hendrix at Stokesay Castle' begins from a nostalgic perspective: 'it's 1983 & purple shoes are dancing | on a whiff of fading sandalwood', yet it looks back both at the 1960s and the longer history suggested by the building. It incorporates misheard or misremembered lyrics from 'Purple Haze', bringing psychedelic American youth culture into collision with a notion of English heritage that is questionable because 'The Experience was an English act | but the English house is not one building'[41]—a historical national identity cannot be sealed off from the cultural influences of the media-saturated present. For Pete Smith, the title 'suggests a form of palimpsest at work, with James building textually on Hendrix lyrics and culturally on the posturing that was a part of the Hendrix persona'.[42] The ghostliness of the poem consists of the songs that haunt it:

What is this haze all round
don't know if I'm going up or going down
lately things just do not seem the same

Haunting provides a more unsettling image than adoption for the process of remembering and incorporating lyrics. The psychedelic haze of perception implied in the source of the lyrics is *détourné*, that is, placed in a new context to produce a subversive critique; its effect is to defamiliarize the English country house because the haze is not, as for Hendrix, in the brain, but external. Music is not purely a matter of personal experience but part of broader social and cultural concerns. The poem also quotes from the documentary of the Woodstock film, and from Frank O'Hara, 'we fight for what we love not are', but the 'we' of this statement is contested by the cultural interpenetrations explored in the poem.[43] The poem becomes a cover version, a set of references that allows the memory of particular cultural moments to be re-enacted—not in nostalgia but as a disruption of context.

Song lyrics may be experienced as 'sound objects', and as Wishart comments, all sound objects are musical; however, lyrics are not only sound objects, since even the most banal lyrics are often charged with intensity and linguistic affect. To turn now to a more recent text, Sean Bonney's sonnet sequence *The Commons* makes extensive use of quoted lyrics from folk, blues, and punk, often violently juxtaposed in a way that registers both the sonic textures and the lyrical qualities of wide-ranging sources, as

---

[41] James, *Collected Poems*, 281–7.
[42] Pete Smith, 'The English Experience', in Simon Perril (ed.), *The Salt Companion to John James* (London: Salt Publishing, 2010), 238.
[43] Frank O'Hara, *Collected Poems* (Berkeley and Los Angeles: University of California Press, 1995), 305.

it searches for viable forms of public language against a background of economic and social collapse. His jittery post-punk performance style is insistently disruptive, resisting synthesis and pitching language against itself, as can be heard in the opening lines of *The Commons*: 'The cuckoo is a |—BANG—| he was a big freak'.[44] The folk song's interruption by the explosive interjection of Betty Davis suggests the gleeful cartoon shooting of the cuckoo and a shattering of the respectful frame within which folk music can often be placed by the elevation of tradition.[45]

Bonney states that his approach is to work improvisationally with folk and blues music's performance mode of transmission rather than acknowledging the textual authority of recorded versions; in this, his work responds to the dynamic of these traditions and their political possibilities. He notes how 'the singer would incorporate shreds of the already existing tradition, thus forging an individual voice from fragments of a collective culture extending physically and temporally through history'.[46] The single voice, therefore, contains a strongly social element that emerges through a process of listening to other versions; the voice is not a unique source but the product of plural feedback. In traditional music, songs have historically developed through lines of transmission that can be traced geographically, as an embellishment here or a different ending there has been added in various communities or regions; but Bonney's sources do not suggest a musical community as much as they do an extensive record collection and an idiosyncratic navigation of it. This is not to diminish the ways in which the poem articulates a social poetics, but it is worth noting that it does so in ways that are both related to and distinct from the oral transmission of traditional song. The question of ownership of music is raised ironically:

my record collection
all these colonised notes
kill little birds like me[47]

This last line, from the ballad 'Henry Lee', can be read as a comment on the violence of recontextualization as songs are ordered in recorded form; they are preserved, but also therefore in some sense trapped and dead outside a lived social performance. The experience of listening to music from disparate periods out of context is increasingly commonplace in the twenty-first century as the MP3 player, even more so than records, tends to flatten out distinctions between different genres and contexts, yet the impression of reading Bonney's poem is of sharp clashes, stops and starts, rather than seamless continuity:

---

[44] Sean Bonney, *The Commons* (London: Openned Press, 2011), 1.

[45] For a more detailed discussion of the cuckoo's significance in this poem see Ian Davidson, *Radical Spaces of Poetry* (Basingstoke: Palgrave, 2010), 34–5.

[46] Sean Bonney, [http://resources.voiceworks.org.uk/constellations/sean_bonney.html], accessed 31 July 2011.

[47] Bonney, *The Commons*, 18.

black is the colour of my
gestural forthrightness
gently drops the rain
cold blows the wind
in May 1968, most
young people were working in
Woolworth's, the cosmetics counter
was so adventurous, a
cloister of learning &
trust, all was represental-
cold / blows the future
ballads of the
—blank—
my true love[48]

In juxtaposing lyrics from 'Black is the colour of my true love's hair' and 'The Unquiet Grave' with reference to an anglicized (and de-romanticized) May 1968, the poem places the past in the context of political unrest, following Benjamin's concept of historical materialism in which memory is appropriated 'as it flashes up in a moment of danger', from the perspective of the present. The process here is not precisely one of mis-remembering, but of violently reordering memory to create new and potentially revolutionary connections with the past. The cutting of lyrics from their sources, which are multiple and anonymous to begin with, thus has a double function in the poem; it creates continuities between communities by drawing on collective memory, but it also ruptures familiar connections to create new meanings in the present.

There are risks in this approach, particularly in the case of blues music, which emerges from a particular history of racial oppression. Rey Chow has suggested that Benjamin's violent recontextualization is 'as much a precise description of imperialism's relentless destruction of local cultures as it is a "politically correct" metaphor for redeeming the history of the repressed', while Lisa Robertson, commenting on this quotation in relation to a poetics of the fragment, notes that 'the material fragment of language is an anthropological souvenir which represents the successful colonization and administration of a differential symbolic'.[49] The orphaning of the lyric from its collective social context might be seen as potentially undermining the voicing of social protest with which *The Commons* is explicitly concerned. However, this would be to overlook the ways in which the poem resists completeness, and resists the absorption of quotation into a new structure. Furthermore, it tends to mobilize the linguistic affect of sources that are often lost, forgotten, or in the process of becoming so. If adoption is associated with birth, this process is more connected with death, with bringing dead voices to life and thereby releasing their subversive power. The repressed supernatural is a recurrent motif in the poem, and zombies are deployed in the poem as 'gratuitous cartoon violence' that cuts

[48] Bonney, *The Commons*, 7.
[49] Romana Huk (ed.), *Assembling Alternatives: Reading Postmodern Poetries Transnationally* (Middletown, Conn.: Wesleyan University Press, 2003), 391.

across the mournful cadences of folk songs with abrupt humour ('fingers & | eyes, you can't have 'em'). Yet the dismembered lyric, like the head of Orpheus, carries on singing, so that phrases like 'my own true love', 'my lily-white hands', or 'she got him up upon her back | and carried him to the earthen lake' carry resonances in both image and sound (for example in the imported ballad metre) from their previous contexts that are accentuated through sharp interruption. The songs are disembodied in their loss of context but they retain their potential to disrupt. Ian Davidson has noted that Bonney's work is

> a form of cultural history that draws on folk memory, particularly of post-Thatcherite Britain, and the folk memory memorialized in the Child Ballads, yet the fragmented nature of the form of the poem, its unconventional use of syntax and its moments of ellipsis, defeat memory as it develops. [...] [T]he poem must [...] be read as a non-representational cultural form, and as a material interjection into everyday life. Its irreducibility impossible to absorb as a meaning; it always awkwardly sticks its wings out halfway down this reader's throat.[50]

The sources, because of their insistent relationship to the materiality of sound, cannot be fully absorbed into memory or the 'body' of the poem, but this is what creates the poem's potential to disturb collective structures of meaning. The use of quotation may in this respect be elucidated by Mackey's description of 'musics that haunt us like a phantom limb'; he suggests that

> ...the phantom limb is a felt recovery, a felt advance beyond severance and limitation which contends with and questions conventional reality...a feeling for what's not there which reaches beyond as it calls into question what is. Music as phantom limb arises from a capacity for feeling which holds itself apart from numb contingency. The phantom limb haunts or critiques a condition in which feeling, consciousness itself, would seem to have been cut off...The phantom limb reveals the illusory rule of the world it haunts.[51]

The idea of music as the phantom limb of the poem suggests possibilities that are always broken, are already lost, but which may be partially inhabited as a means of challenging the apparent wholeness or completeness of the poem, and thereby the completeness of the social structures within which it is written.

Such ghostliness is not comforting or redemptive, as the image of adoption may be; it insists on disturbance. The different rhythms and cadences of the lyrics in the poem draw attention to the voice as multiply composed; the voice is plural and performative, actively carrying the trace of other voices. It is in the sound of the sung or spoken words as they are heard,

as a spore left inside the language,
not a code made of letters,
but social utterance flaming

---

[50] Davidson, *Radical Spaces*, 40.
[51] Mackey, 'Sound and Sentiment, Sound and Symbol'.

Such plurality of context, which is increasingly a part of media-inflected and globalized linguistic experience, creates a situation in which the quoted lyrics disrupt each other to create what the information theorists would classify as 'noise', that is, 'any undesirable signal in the transmission of a message'.[52] This definition presupposes an agreement on the centrality of a singular 'message' and also on what is 'desirable' in terms of how that message is received. If one person's noise is another person's signal, living with each other's noise might be considered a central issue for any form of collective understanding. In its investigation of what can be transmitted through a common code, *The Commons* activates shared musical memory but at the same time it disputes the possibility of 'the common' through the use of juxtaposition to create verbal interference. Lyric expression is therefore transformed into a collective mode that negotiates the anger and pain of repressed voices from the past without incorporating them or neutralizing their power within a falsely reassuring vision of community.

The experience of song as embodied utterance is paradoxically emphasized by recording, and throughout the past century traditional songs that might previously have circulated anonymously have become identified with the versions of individual singers. The memory of a song is not just the memory of a lyric and its tune, but of the voice itself and the absent body that produced it. Ian Penman has described the impact of particular recordings, quoting James Baldwin:

> 'It was Bessie Smith, through her tone and cadence, who helped...reconcile me to being a "nigger"'. Tone and cadence, mark you—not any incendiary or explicit lyric.
>
> Lyrical 'authenticity' has been consistently over-valued in the dominant (white) discourse, so much so you'd think it was virtually immaterial whether there was a microphone there or not, and a mouth to sing into it. Such phallogocentric criticism cannot bring itself to imagine that, say, the 'softest' song in the world might equally bear the harshest truth. [...] The microphonic song insinuates encoded, bodily truths in a code often so subtle (with such infinite gradation of tone) as to be almost inaudible...We can see here that Song is a 'survival' in at least two or three senses, a living on, an echo of something unsaid.[53]

The aesthetics of sampling that marks Bonney's technique evokes memories not only of songs, but of particular voices. The distinctive characters of voices, are not, of course, represented in the poem, but readers or listeners are likely to supply a ghost soundtrack, filling in fragments of remembered vocal textures where they know them.

If, as I have suggested in this chapter, the orphaning of lyric expression from an originating subject is paralleled in developments in sound-based music, the listener, and specifically the listener's body, becomes the site of adoption or haunting. In Caroline Bergvall's work, which is primarily poetry but exceeds the boundaries of any single

---

[52] Abraham Moles, *Information Theory and Esthetic Perception*, trans. Joel E. Cohen (Urbana: University of Illinois Press, 1968), 78.

[53] Ian Penman, 'On the Mic: How Amplification Changed the Voice for Good', in Rob Young (ed.), *Undercurrents: The Hidden Wiring of Modern Music* (London: Continuum, 2002), 28–9.

art form, this possibility is central. Resident in the UK since 1989, Bergvall draws on her bilingual French-Norwegian background to explore aspects of linguistic identity in a poetics that spans the page as well as visual art, sound, and performance. Her '1DJ2MANY (wired Madeleine)' brings the quoted lyric into a different relationship with language and embodiment through her use of a gallery context.[54] In this piece made for a gallery installation in 2010, Bergvall recites collaged lyrics from love songs in various genres including pop, disco, jazz, indie, and rap, which form what she describes, with reference to Proust's exploration of involuntary, embodied memory, as 'a sonic Madeleine'. Her collaborator, Adam Parkinson, has made a composition from the recorded voice by treating it, interrupting it with flashes of white noise, and directing the sound through different channels to spatialize and disorientate the listening experience. The lyrics (also published as a poem in the catalogue) are clear in some places, lost or distorted in others. There is a stop-start quality to the recording that is reminiscent of switching a radio between stations. As Vincent Broqua comments:

> Something in this juxtaposition of so many different voices and rhythms both creates a singular voice and yet, as with sampling, allows the listener to hear the disjunction of different textual materials [...] The familiarity of it all is therefore defamiliarized, or in fact it is the process of remembering the lines as familiar lines, which defamiliarizes the apparent unity and coherence of the voice uttering the song.[55]

When Bergvall reads the poem live, as she did in the Hay Jamboree 2010, there is a stronger and more continuous movement towards the poem's climax (the lengthening stanzas also encourage a sense of continuity on the page, despite the forward slashes that mark off each quotation). Bergvall breaks into song in places, both in the live reading and the recording, physically inhabiting pop's discourse of desire. The ironic humour of her remix is a strong element throughout, enhanced by her deadpan French-Norwegian delivery of Anglo-American colloquial excitement. It is a reminder that the words are not hers and that her body shaped by its different languages can only partially inhabit them—but equally it demonstrates to listeners the extent to which we have all inhabited such discourses that are not, originally, our own.

Ooh ahh, sock it to me like you want to oh
my hormones are jumping like a disco /
I love to love you baby /
you can ring my bell, ring my bell /
Can you feel this beat, it's an obsessive heartbeat /
just can't get you out of my head /
Fever, in the morning
fever all through the night

---

[54] Caroline Bergvall, *Middling English* (Southampton: John Hansard Gallery, 2010), 2–7.
[55] Vincent Broqua, 'Caroline Bergvall's Language-siting', in Bergvall, *Middling English*, 55.

The body is central to much of this piece, not only in the physical references of the lyrics themselves but in the structural movement towards a Serge Gainsbourg-inflected climax. Yet for all this corporeal insistence, the body remains stubbornly absent, constantly deferred as the text exploits the gap between urgent expression of desire and the circulation of such expressions as commodified cultural artefacts that construct bodies and their desires. This gap creates a level of irony that is manifested as humour in Bergvall's performance as well as developing an understanding of language's existence outside the body. As Bergvall writes:

> In the installations, in relation to using language in audio-spatial ways—it works on this idea of ghosting, and of the doubling; the inscriptive and the disembodied—calling on the audience's own responses; guiding or forcing understandings.[56]

However, just as orphaned lyrics are adopted in Riley's work, the ghostly, disembodied lyrics of Bergvall's sampling find temporary embodiments through performance. The body is important here not just as the source of a voice but also in the audience's response to lyrics as they are perceived through involuntary memory in a particular physical context. The listener hears the sound differently at different points in the room, so an active participation is invited in the form of the audience's movement. The title suggests not only an excess of DJs, but also the way in which one DJ might be addressing many people; if the songs are orphaned from their embodied source, and even from the recordings by which they have become known, they rely on the audience to fill in a context from a pool of collective memory. This sense of interconnectedness is indicated by a large structure of taut wires running across the gallery space, and by Bergvall's introductory comment:

> I want to create active circuits, a circulation between historical elements and contemporary narratives [...] I will create a space that is both sparse and satirical, messy and structural, which addresses processes of interconnection, intercalculation, distribution, interception—what it means, positively, to be tied to everything else.[57]

In this context, the wires situate the lyrics within the dynamics of transmission, and the list of titles and artists of the songs running down one wall is likely to be noticed at different points by different viewers, depending on the personal trajectories they bring to the piece. Riley's description of the unconscious as 'hanging between people' is here given a visual equivalent, though if 'hanging' suggests passivity the emphasis here is on active processes. This understanding of the lyric self and memory as 'wired', that is, socially and technologically mediated, always interconnected, is heightened by the fusion of artistic forms in which the experience of listening to music is passed through

---

[56] Bergvall, *Middling English*, 58.
[57] Bergvall, *Middling English*, 9.

a process of textual composition and then returned to as altered context, that of the gallery, as recorded sound.

Each of the poets I have discussed is concerned with song lyrics as a shared, public language from which the expressive qualities of lyric may be derived. If the language of lyric is always already orphaned, cut from the personal originatory source that has shaped traditional ideas of lyric expression, the poems discussed here suggest possibilities for its adoption within a wider social and cultural context, where the notion of authorship is expanded to acknowledge multiple voices, particularly from recordings that have become part of a collective lyric consciousness. The quotation of lyrics develops and critiques a long historical relationship between poetry and song in the light of changes in musical technology, reconnecting poetry with its history of emotive urgency but also investigating and challenging the implications of lyric affect. If poetry has been severed from music, music activated through the quoted lyrics in these examples remains as a haunting and disruptive presence within the poem. It is in the reader or listener, finally, that the process of adoption takes place, and the reader whose misremembering (since all remembering is misremembering) supplies the poem's absent music. This is neither a restoration of completeness nor a melancholic yearning for it, but an exploration of the social possibilities of poetic language that is both orphaned and orphic.

Select Bibliography

Benjamin, Walter, *Illuminations*, trans. Harry Zorn (London: Pimlico, 1999).
Bergvall, Caroline, *Middling English* (Southampton: John Hansard Gallery, 2010).
Bernstein, Charles (ed.), *The Politics of Poetic Form: Poetry and Public Policy* (New York: Roof, 1990).
Bonney, Sean, *The Commons* (London: Openned Press, 2011).
Caddel, Richard, and Quartermain, Peter, *Other: British and Irish Poetry since 1970* (Hanover, Conn.: Wesleyan University Press, 1999).
Cox, Christoph, and Warner, Daniel (eds.), *Audio Culture: Readings in Modern Music* (London and New York: Continuum, 2008).
Davidson, Ian, *Radical Spaces of Poetry* (Basingstoke: Palgrave, 2010).
Holmes, Thom, *Electronic and Experimental Music: Technology, Music, and Culture* (London: Taylor and Francis, 2008).
Huk, Romana (ed.), *Assembling Alternatives: Reading Postmodern Poetries Transnationally* (Middletown, Conn.: Wesleyan University Press, 2003).
James, John, *Collected Poems* (Cambridge: Salt Publishing, 2002).
Merleau-Ponty, M., *The Phenomenology of Perception* (London: Routledge, 2002).
Moles, Abraham, *Information Theory and Esthetic Perception*, trans. Joel E. Cohen (Urbana: University of Illinois Press, 1968).
Perril, Simon (ed.), *The Salt Companion to John James* (London: Salt Publishing, 2010).
Pierret, Marc, *Entretiens avec Pierre Schaeffer* (Paris: Éditions Pierre Belfond, 1969).
Riley, Denise, *'Am I that Name?' Feminism and the Category of 'Women' in History* (Minneapolis: University of Minnesota Press, 1988).
Riley, Denise, *Selected Poems* (London: Reality Street Editions, 2000).

Riley, Denise, *The Words of Selves: Identification, Solidarity, Irony* (Stanford, Calif.: Stanford University Press, 2000).

Riley, Denise, *Impersonal Passion: Language as Affect* (Durham, NC and London: Duke University Press, 2005).

Riley, Denise, and Lecercle, Jean-Jacques, *The Force of Language* (Basingstoke: Palgrave Macmillan, 2004).

Roubaud, Jacques, 'Prelude: Poetry and Orality', trans. Jean-Jacques Poucel, in Marjorie Perloff and Craig Douglas Dworkin (eds.), *The Sound of Poetry, the Poetry of Sound* (Chicago: University of Chicago Press, 2009).

Schultz, Susan M., ' "Unlock a Marvell karaoke": Quotation as Adoption in the Work of Denise Riley', *How2* [www.asu.edu/pipercwcenter/how2journal/vol_3_no_1/cambridge/schultz.html].

Wishart, Trevor, *On Sonic Art* (York: Imagineering Press, 1985).

Young, Rob (ed.), *Undercurrents: The Hidden Wiring of Modern Music* (London: Continuum, 2002).

Wilkinson, John, *The Lyric Touch: Essays on the Poetry of Excess* (Cambridge: Salt Publishing, 2007).

CHAPTER 15

'THE DEGREE OF POWER EXERCISED': RECENT EKPHRASIS

CONOR CARVILLE

In the boom years of the end of the twentieth century when every country was obliged to have its biennale or international art fair and the summer blockbuster exhibition became a staple tourist attraction, visual art began to command audiences of an unprecedented scale. As the attendance figures at London's Tate, the Guggenheim in Bilbao, and the Mori Museum in Tokyo proved, there had emerged an appetite for contemporary art that seemed at odds with its often transgressive, obscure, or otherwise challenging subject matter. It is worth speculating on the historical conditions for this emergence, and the possible price paid for it. That British culture, alongside that of most of the world, has become immensely visually sophisticated in the years since 1950 is beyond contention. The speed and depth of social penetration of mass culture and media technologies marks out a change that is in many ways unparalleled. In the process, as has often been remarked, aesthetic strategies first explored by modernist artists were rehearsed in the context of mass culture and advertising. At the same time, however, the commerce between modernism and the new visual culture had never been one way. As Marshall McLuhan wrote to Ezra Pound in June 1948: 'Your *Cantos*, I now judge to be the first and only serious use of the great technical possibilities of the cinematograph. Am I right in thinking of them as a montage of personae and sculptured images? Flash-backs providing perceptions of simultaneities?'[1]

That McLuhan, one of the earliest theorists of the media age should have written in such terms to Pound, founder of Imagism and advocate of a strongly visual poetics couched in a rhetoric of energy and power, raises questions central to this essay. What

---

[1] McLuhan to Pound, 16 June 1948, in *Letters of Marshall McLuhan*, ed. Matie Molinaro, Corinne McLuhan, and William Toye (Oxford: Oxford University Press, 1987), 193.

exactly is the relationship between Pound's aesthetics and the condition that McLuhan's great rival as analyst of the image economy, Guy Debord, dubbed the society of the spectacle? More specifically, if, as some have argued, a continuum can be asserted between Pound's stress on the immediacy of the visual image and his authoritarian politics, what can his work offer to a radical poetry that sets itself in strict opposition to what Hal Foster has called 'the stunned subjectivity and arrested sociality supported by the spectacle'?[2]

The practice of ekphrastic poetry provides an arena where such questions can be tested, and there has been a much-discussed expansion in such poetry over the last twenty years. And yet it may be that this expansion is not primarily an attempt to examine or come to terms with the changed relationships between word and image, but rather an index of the pervasiveness of the latter. For it is remarkable how little attention this poetry has paid to the way in which the rapid transformations in post-war visual culture have impacted on ways of seeing, thinking, being, and therefore writing. Having said that, what follows concentrates on one strain of ekphrasis that, rather than simply exploiting the pictorial as an aid to lyric effusion or idiosyncratic narrative, deploys the specific resources of poetry in order to attend to the sheer power of the image in our time. That all three of the poets concerned take their bearings from a tradition which is to some extent Poundian adds an extra charge to their use of ekphrasis, for reasons already adverted to. Indeed it may well be that a special sensitivity to Pound's aesthetic politics and its implications for the present determines the astringently critical, self-reflexive approach to ekphrasis that these poets exhibit.

R. F. Langley's *Journals* record an August 1994 visit to a church at Westhall, near his home in Suffolk, where he finds himself admiring the poppy-heads on the sixteen carved bench-ends in the southern aisle. He decides to play a game with them:

> I put my panama hat on the third one from the back. It punches the folded crown half out, and the hat tilts as if it were facing along the bench towards the head at the inner end, against the wall. As if it were pushed back off a forehead... It stands out. It makes the head into a head... The hat becomes stuff, because it is on a thing. The poppy-head becomes human because it has a hat on it. The exchange rocks to and fro interestingly, and a little worryingly.[3]

In this short vignette Langley catches at a subject that crops up often in the *Journals* and forms a central concern of his poetry: the extent to which an object—often a painting or sculpture—can be attended to in all its sensuous specificity without having a human subjectivity foisted upon it: the cultivation of what Langley calls elsewhere 'non-egocentric attention to the particular'.[4] This is of course a variation on a long-standing issue for philosophical aesthetics; however, the way in which Langley's description eventually

---

[2] Hal Foster, *The Art-Architecture Complex* (London: Verso, 2011), 250.
[3] R. F. Langley, *Journals* (Exeter: Shearsman Books, 2006), 62.
[4] Langley, *Journals*, 117.

settles on an ambiguous exchange between attraction and dismay locates his account closer to psychoanalysis. It is Freud's uncanny rather than Kant's purposefulness without purpose that informs the movement he writes of. Or more likely, it is the psychoanalytical aesthetics of Adrian Stokes that lies somewhere behind the musings.

Stokes, a critic and essayist sometimes regarded as the successor to Ruskin and Pater, drew on Kleinian theory to fashion a subtle and suggestive account of the relationship between the psyche, the object, and artistic form. It was Stokes that introduced Ezra Pound to the Tempio Malatestiano in 1926, thereby preparing the ground, Donald Davie argues, for Cantos 17, 20, and 47. It was Davie meanwhile who was the main advocate of Stokes's work for younger poets that he taught in Cambridge—including Charles Tomlinson, J. H. Prynne, Langley himself, and, indirectly, Peter Robinson. Prynne has described the attraction of Stokes's work in a letter to Tomlinson:

> The tensile equilibrium between the projection of our inner needs and the resistance to our awareness of the palpable external world (the recurring theme of 'inner' and 'outer') forms the context of a full range of appetencies and satisfactions which thus articulate the experience and render it luminous, without separating it from the perceptual immediacy that Stokes values so highly.[5]

In what follows I want to pursue this tensile equilibrium through a reading of four ekphrastic poems which exhibit, to greater or lesser degrees, that relationship between 'a finely articulated objectivity', 'a complex emotional relevance', and 'the formal resources of art' that Prynne finds in Stokes's work. In doing so I will be suggesting that these poems also deploy ekphrasis to question the connections between Stokes's way of looking at art and Pound's aesthetically based politics, by taking the act of looking at art as a paradigm for relations—in particular the formation of subjectivity—which are also social and political. As we shall see, what Prynne calls the resistance of the palpable external world is central to this questioning.

Peter Riley, another poet associated with Cambridge, has a more distant relationship with Stokes than some of those already mentioned. In his obituary for Langley he emphasizes Langley and Prynne's admiration for the critic in a manner that implicitly excludes his own work: 'encouraged by Donald Davie, they forged a new aesthetic out of the study of Ezra Pound and others, including the art historian Adrian Stokes'. Shortly after this he notes that Langley and Prynne 'undertook a study of Italian Renaissance art using Stokes's books, going on an extended tour of northern Italy'.[6] And yet Riley's *The Glacial Stair* (2011) includes an account of a similar, much more recent journey: 'Bits and Pieces Picked up in April 2007' is alternatively titled 'Six Days in Tuscany with Roger Langley'. Its opening stanza evokes the first of those six days

---

[5] J. H. Prynne, 'Letter to Charles Tomlinson' (May 1961), Ian Brinton, 'Prynne in *Prospect*', *Salt Magazine*, 3, [www.saltpublishing.com/saltmagazine/issues/03/text/Brinton_Ian, accessed 27 Mar. 2012].

[6] Peter Riley, 'R. F. Langley Obituary', [http://www.guardian.co.uk/books/2011/mar/07/rf-langley-obituary, accessed 27 Mar. 2012].

by at once alluding to Stokes's criticism in terms which echo Prynne's description, and yet also implicates it within a much broader horizon of conflict and ideological control:

Sunday

The depth of incision into the stone: the degree of power exercised.
The balance and turn of the perceiving body, in attendance,
carved, light or deep, by the nervous system.[7]

Stokes's investment in the virtues of carving over modelling closely informs these lines, and his profoundly corporeal account of the act of attending to art is also present. Further than this, the references to the exercise of power and the carving of the body also suggest that the same terms can be used to describe contemporary forces, physical and discursive, of violence and coercion. A continuum is asserted between the act of making and responding to art and the way in which perceiving bodies are inscribed by the ideological and the social. Hence, for Riley, as for the other poets we will look at, ekphrasis is the occasion for an examination of material practices of making and looking which are also disciplinary practices of subject-formation. As we shall see, however, the ekphrastic poems considered also offer their own specific practices of looking, thinking, and being.

Riley embarks on a more extensive ekphrastic exercise in 'Poems to Paintings by Jack B. Yeats', also known as 'Time Sets All Things Right'. The sequence numbers ten poems in all, published in two separate books, six of them in *Passing Measures* (2000), a selection of poems from thirty years of small press work, and the rest in *The Day's Final Balance: Uncollected Writings 1965–2006* (2007). Riley has also posted a series of notes to the poems on his website, where he specifies the images they are based on. Three of the paintings that Riley writes about depict people singing, and, as he points out in his notes to *Music in the Train* (1922), this is a common subject for the painter: 'Yeats several times depicted people listening to music in an absent, mesmerised, slightly saddened or solemnised way, as if acceding to a common fate.' Slightly later he describes the same painting as representing a 'trance of belonging' with the train 'bound for glory' (presumably this refers to the establishment of the Irish Free State—a polity to which Yeats, as a Republican, was implacably opposed).[8] Leaving aside the idealization implicit in these phrases, Riley's reading seems to be based on a notion of the spontaneity and immediacy of live performance as inculcating or reflecting forms of community that have since been superseded. This is of a piece with his interest in improvised and folk music more generally. Importantly, it also reflects his investment in lyric poetry itself as song: 'Song is a thing which enhances our belonging by singing away from our immediate mundanity', as he has put it in interview.[9]

---

[7] Peter Riley, *The Glacial Stair* (Manchester: Carcanet Press, 2011), 48.
[8] Peter Riley, 'Notes to Poems and Pictures by Jack B. Yeats', [www.aprileye.co.uk/yeatsnotes.html, accessed 27 Feb. 2012].
[9] Peter Riley and Todd Nathan Thorpe, 'Peter Riley in conversation with Todd Nathan Thorpe', [jacketmagazine.com/35/iv-peter-riley-ivb-thorpe.hstml, accessed 27 Feb. 2012].

More immediately relevant to our interests here is the way in which these poems consider the self-identity of oral culture not through direct reflection on song itself, but through its materialization as a visual object. For Riley, as for Keats, ekphrasis involves reflection on festive practices of music and song but also, in its conversion of sound to silent image-object, marks the definitive loss of those practices. The poem that results is of course itself a form of song, but it is one reliant on the printed word and consumed, for the most part, in solitary reading. In this sense the poem participates in the pathos of the silent painting or funeral urn. At the same time, as we shall see, the poem reflects on the painting's status as an object, as well as its own material status as text in order to assert the continuing possibility of lyric communication.

'The Little Watercolour at Sligo' is composed of five unrhymed tercets. Riley's notes tell us: 'I have only a memory of this. It was hung in the little gallery at Sligo, and it showed, as described, a small man standing in a village street at night singing, with his mouth wide open.'[10] The poem remembers an absent painting, one that represents an attractive form of communicating presence. And yet, in Riley's ekphrasis the efficacy of that representation resides partly in its ability to capture a moment of indeterminacy, the risky moment when it is unclear whether a singer is going to succeed in holding the given note or not. This is directly set out in the first stanza:

The point of pain
At which the voice
Cracks or cruises.[11]

The evocation of pain lends immediacy to the opening of the poem. At the same time the phrasing of the initial line moves undecidably between a description of an instant in time, a description of pain, and a moral justification for suffering: pain as instant, affliction, and test. In any case the test is passed, the pain recedes and the moment is surmounted for, as the poem has it, 'The little fat man | Makes it' and the singer

Cruises, out across time

Nameless and small, he
Sails a stranger's psyche, saying
Cast your (care) crown. This

Is success, this is being, this
Is where love fastens us to the earth...[12]

On first reading no major difficulties of interpretation are presented. Riley's poem celebrates the achievement of Yeats's painting: communication has been achieved between

---

[10] Peter Riley, 'Notes to Poems and Pictures by Jack B. Yeats', [www.aprileye.co.uk/yeatsnotes.html, accessed 27 Feb. 2012].

[11] Peter Riley, *Passing Measures* (Manchester: Carcanet Press, 2000), 120.

[12] Riley, *Passing Measures*.

painter and 'stranger' 'across time'. The pathos of 'the little fat man', 'nameless and small' in 'village night', is redeemed in an ending which, through its constellation of terms like care, being, earth, and song also registers Riley's enduring interests in Heideggerian phenomenology. And yet there are several small shifts that must be given their proper weight here. Although the first stanza describes a voice which 'Cracks or cruises', when the word 'cruise' reappears in line 9 it refers not to a voice but to 'he', to the little fat man himself, or more precisely to his representation in the painting. It is not the voice that carries here in other words, but the image of the singer. Secondly we are told that 'his | Mouth' is 'like a typographical O'. Riley's poem thus adverts to its own status as print, but more importantly registers that status in a violent image of standardization radically at odds with the poem's ostensible concern with the man's singular presence and voice. Yeats's fluid, expressionistic painting style is wrenched into textual terms in a way that dramatizes the active, interventionist quality of the ekphrastic imagination. And yet the simile also acknowledges that this wrenching, while certainly violent, does manage to provide a voice for the figure, a voice that is inevitably missing from the painting. We should note in this respect that the letter O, printed in the upper case, as it is in Riley's poem, is of course the conventional indicator of apostrophe. By substituting the letter for the character's mouth Riley may be forcibly accommodating the oral to the textual, but he is simultaneously allowing the subject of the painting to address us.

The simile of the 'typographical O' also clearly insists on the visual qualities of the poem we are reading. Such an attention to the materiality of the text establishes an affinity between painting and poem as objects in the world, an affinity that accords with a more general insistence throughout the poem on the roots of both art and love in finitude, the body, and culture. That is to say, from the poem's opening, where pain is seen as the inevitable corollary of any attempt at aesthetic production, to the penultimate line where love 'nails us to the earth', art's potential for transcendence and transformation is balanced by an insistence on its constitutive entanglement in the actual. The body of the poem is merely the most immediately available instance of this resistant yet indispensable materiality. By drawing attention to this fact in a self-reflexive image that simultaneously regrets and yet refuses to relinquish its status as text, Riley suggests that transcendence is not only inevitably imbricated with materiality but that the latter is indispensable to the very possibility of the former. A further consequence of this, one that we saw examined in 'Bits and Pieces Picked Up in April 2007', is that art is also necessarily implicated in earthly powers of domination and exploitation.

As mentioned earlier, line 12 of the poem—'saying | Cast your (care) crown'—is attributed to the painting's central figure. If we exclude the word 'care', as we are invited to do by the parenthesis, then the phrase can be read as a request to throw a coin, an interpretation that sits well with the image of the singer performing in the street. The central figure's song thus contains an implicit request for recognition, for care in the sense of empathy, although this is couched in terms of a commercial transaction rather than an ethical one. This is perhaps why the request is described as a 'saying' rather than a singing, the former understood as the prosaic, material substrate that underpins the aesthetic performance. It is this material 'saying' that the poem can and does directly communicate, rather than the song. At the same time the request remains an injunction to care, and the complete line signals to ideas of release or transcendence as much as to materiality. The verb 'cast', for example, suggests, together with the idea of throwing a coin, the process of making a thing (a sense to which we will be returning) and the action of freeing oneself from something. Drawing on the latter meaning we might now gloss the line as 'free yourself of your crown of cares', with care now understood as worry or ordeal. Unlike the previous passive request for alms, such an interpretation grants the painting an active power, one that can absolve the viewer from their trials and deliver them from the world.

In the context of the poem as a whole the dominant reading of the line might be paraphrased as 'bestow your empathy', a reading which includes aspects of both interpretations. The viewer of the picture is addressed or summoned by the image of the man, and by the artwork that represents him, to enter into an ethical relation of care. However it is important to insist on the poem's reservations when it comes to its account of this address. If, as mentioned earlier, the verb 'cast' is understood primarily as the act of making, modelling, or forging, then to 'cast a (care) crown' might also be to congratulate oneself for the act of giving. In such a reading the act of charity works to buttress the giver's complacent sovereignty rather than set up an ethical relation of equals. Indeed we can see the viewer's disposition towards the painting in similar terms. The relationship between the viewer of the painting and the figure within it, like that between donor and recipient, can be self-serving as much as it can be self-sacrificing. One can expose oneself to the painting's call in all one's vulnerability, willing to be transformed by it, or one can rely on it to confirm an already existing sense of the self. Likewise the ekphrastic poet runs the risk of simply appropriating the artwork, instrumentalizing it as the occasion for a poem that floats free of it. To obviate this 'The Little Watercolour at Sligo' grants the ethical call its due weight but also, and perhaps more importantly, explores the material contexts of that address to the viewer, its complicity with less exalted forces of material need and the body in pain. In doing so the poem maps this conflict onto its own relationship with materiality, including the materiality of its own form. Riley's description of Yeats's painting in terms of an ambivalent call is thus more than matched by the ambivalent call of his own poem.

Charles Tomlinson's relationship with Stokes is stronger than Riley's, indeed he has included quotations from Stokes's criticism as part of his own visual compositions.[13] More conventionally he has given the following account of the significance of Stokes's work for his appreciation of Cézanne:

> His Faber *Cézanne* appeared [in 1947] and I read it one year later ... His image for the division of Cézanne's volumes and their interaction was 'trees reflected by slightly undulating water'. This, almost a metaphor for the nature of human perception itself, brings to mind the passage in Wordsworth's *The Prelude* Book IV[14]

---

[13] See Charles Tomlinson, 'Cloudhead' (1970), *Eden: Graphics and Other Poems* (Bristol: Redcliffe Poetry, 1985), 64.

[14] Charles Tomlinson, *Modern Painters*, 2/1 (Spring 1989), 109–10 (110).

Tomlinson then goes on to quote the section where Wordsworth describes 'one who hangs down-bending' over the side of a boat to peer through still water:

Yet often is perplexed and cannot part
The shadow from the substance, rocks and sky,
Mountains and clouds, from that which is indeed
The region, and the things which there abide[15]

Wordsworth's celebrated description asserts the confusion of shadow and substance when reflected images commingle with the sight of the 'grots, pebbles, roots of trees' on the bed of a lake. Yet the syntax, together with the way rocks are paired with sky and mountains with clouds, also suggests that a similar epistemological 'perplexity' holds more generally. There is at once an investment in the apprehension of the real or material, and the concession that it can never be grasped separately from the images that shroud it. As we shall see, the way in which Tomlinson reads Stokes through Wordsworth here throws considerable light on his own aesthetic.

A good example of the way in which Tomlinson's ekphrastic poetry tackles questions of materiality, corporeality, and the politics of aesthetic experience with which we have been dealing is 'A Meditation on John Constable'.[16] This poem begins with an epigraph from Constable himself: 'Painting is a science, and should be pursued as an enquiry into the laws of nature. Why, then, may not landscape painting be considered as a branch of natural philosophy, of which pictures are but the experiments?' Here Constable clearly sees his work as exploring what we might now think of as the laws of physics. For Tomlinson this entails an investigation of the bodily processes of perception: Constable's painting of a landscape is pre-eminently a notation of the process of his looking, what Tomlinson calls in the poem 'the labour of observation'. To look at a painting, indeed to experience any art, is thus to participate in such an experiment in the lived procedures of bodily perception and cognition. Towards the end of the poem Tomlinson describes a reciprocation between body and object which suggests the kind of 'tense equilibrium' we saw Prynne write of:

       ...what he saw
Discovered what he was and the hand—unswayed
By the dictation of a single sense—
   Bodied the accurate and total knowledge
In a calligraphy of present pleasure.

If the reference to an accurate and total knowledge seems at odds with Wordsworth's perplexity, we shall see that it is the act of painting itself that sublates these opposites.

The poem begins with a description of clouds moving across the face of the sun. Its opening moments, spilling down as they do through tiers of enjambed verb phrases, are

---

[15] William Wordsworth, *The Prelude*, iv. 263–6 (London: Penguin Books, 1988), 153.
[16] Charles Tomlinson, *Collected Poems* (Oxford: Oxford University Press, 1985), 33–4.

notable for their dynamic sense of movement, their graphic description of the way in which the relationship between the sun and the clouds is a fluid, mobile, ever-changing one:

>   Clouds
> Followed by others, temper the sun in passing
>   Over and off it. Massed darks
> Blotting it back, scattered and mellowed shafts
>   Break damply out of them, until the source
> Unmasks, floods its retreating bank
>   With raw fire. One perceives (though scarcely)
> The remnant clouds trailing across it
>   In rags, and thinned to a gauze.
> But the next will dam it. They loom past
>   And narrow its blaze. It shrinks to a crescent
> Crushed out, a still lengthening ooze
>   As the mass thickens, though cannot exclude
> Its silvered-yellow. The eclipse is sudden…

Using a series of terms that recall the sensuous qualities of paint, Tomlinson carefully tracks the way the sun is 'tempered' and 'blotted back' by the 'massed darks' of the clouds, until it breaks through in damp shafts and 'unmasks', only to be 'crushed out' and finally to 'lengthen' into an 'ooze' 'as the mass [i.e. the cloud] thickens'. The manner in which the clouds are described as riverbanks through which the sun pours emphasizes the way the poem sees them as material forces which physically channel the light of the sun, light understood in equally tangible terms as both 'raw fire' and 'flood'. So framed, the account takes what is a relation of surface and depth (i.e. distant sun and closer clouds filtering it) and figures it instead as the immediate physical interaction and concatenation of material forces across a single plane. One has the strong sense that what is being described here is more the rough impasto texture of Constable's canvas than what it represents. Like the rocks and sky of *The Prelude*, these clouds and sun are engaged in a drama of substance and shadow where one cannot be detached from the other. This is one of the ways in which Tomlinson sees Constable as abandoning what he calls illusion (specifically the illusion of conventional perspective that might hold depth apart from surface) in favour of a more expressive aesthetic that records the subjective 'feelings' of the painter as much as the 'law' of what is viewed:

> He admired accidents, because governed by laws,
>   representing them (since the illusion was not his end)
> as governed by feeling. The end is our approval
>   Freely accorded, the illusion persuading us
> That it exists as a human image.

It is at this point in the poem that Tomlinson clearly translates Constable's aesthetic into an ethical disposition. The acknowledgement of subjective feeling by the painter fosters a 'freely accorded' approval by the viewer, rather than one that is enforced through an astringent objectivity. It is in this way, I suggest, that the poem seeks to distinguish itself from the Poundian heritage of an aesthetically founded politics. The implication is that the self-reflexivity involved in overtly imbuing objective description with the painter's subjective 'feeling' renders the direct and coercive manipulation of affect in the viewer all the more difficult. If it is clear that what we are being confronted with is one person's record of their emotional reaction, then it is easier to recognize it as a human image and thus assent to it as a universal. In a further step, Tomlinson goes on to associate this process with what he calls 'constancy':

> ... it must grow constant;
> Though there, ruffling and parted, the disturbed
>   Trees let through the distance like white fog
> Into their broken ranks. It must persuade
>   And with a constancy, not to be swept back
> To reveal what it half conceals.

The reference to the way the painting must grow 'constant', is repeated, after a digression to which I will return, as the necessity for a 'constancy' that is 'not to be swept back | to reveal what it half conceals'. Again there is an argument here for the priority of an aesthetic that privileges nuance and interaction rather than an impossible and ultimately nihilistic passion for the real, for the direct representation of the thing itself. In these terms constancy can be taken to refer once again to the way the heavily worked surfaces of Constable's paintings emphasize their own materiality and in doing so assert their status as artificial 'human images'. This is reinforced by the interpolated reference to the tree and the white fog (the latter image reworking the previous account of the clouds). To say that a pale distance glimpsed behind trees is 'like' fog is apt on a purely visual level: the reader imagines a whitish sky apparent in wisps and fragments. The simile also has a strongly retroactive effect on the phrase 'the trees let through the distance'. It is no longer a matter of the gaps in the trees allowing the distance to be glimpsed, rather the logic of the simile means that the distance is figured as moving towards us, percolating through the foliage like fog, closing up the gaps, and rising to the surface of the painting. The original opposition between trees and distance, surface and depth is thus pressed into a continuum between foliage and fog, and the integrity of the picture plane asserted once again.

This notion of the uniform surface is one to which we will return in a moment, but before doing so it is worth noting the following from Stokes's Cézanne essay, read by Tomlinson in 1948:

> Cézanne's organization has nothing to do with the trompe-l'oeil, with the holes of distance in a picture that seem to penetrate into the wall on which a picture hangs... No one will deny his realization of an immense volume. But he was at pains to achieve this volume without sacrificing... the two-dimensional character of the picture-space. As a consequence his texture and brush-stroke, unconcerned with the effect of trompe-l'oeil, could be employed with far greater effect to induce volume and the affinities between volumes.[17]

---

[17] Adrian Stokes, *Cézanne* (London: Faber & Faber, 1947), 2.

In 'Meditation on John Constable' Tomlinson too is concerned to dispute the relevance of *trompe-l'œil* or, as he terms it 'illusionism', and as with Stokes it is around the questions of distance that he defends his position. Hence although he is arguing for the constancy of the 'human image' he does so using a simile that recalls the rhetoric of inconstant clouds and mist with which we saw him begin the poem. Rather than the Romantic rhetoric of the poem's opening however, Tomlinson's image of a Whistlerian fog prepares the way for a much more modernist space of a single mottled or tessellated surface, a constancy that hangs like a fog rather than moves like cloud, that cannot be swept back and as a result insists on its own artifice, a space that has more in common with Cézanne than it does with Constable. The upshot is a poem that on the one hand asserts the possibility of a subjective 'human image' that records sense perception and on the other attests to the materiality of the art object. It is in the tense equilibrium, in Prynne's phrase, between these two points that Tomlinson's poem locates an aesthetic that allows the viewer to freely accord their approval, rather than have it extorted from them.

R. F. Langley's *Journals* recount a visit to see Bellini's *Saints Christopher, Jerome and Louis of Toulouse* in the church of San Giovanni Crisostomo in Venice. We know from the same source that the church was dark, that visitors used a coin-operated light source to view the altarpiece, and that when he returned the next day Langley was content to look at it in natural light, to the surprise of a local priest. In the poem he based on this visit the onset of night and the corresponding withdrawal of the image from sight are imagined as a curfew and the voice of the poem seems to be positioned, initially at least, as an authority enforcing this curfew, speaking of his 'turn | around the valley', and of outposts and castles.[18] This terminology suggests a defensive tone, as do the series of clipped, capitalized phrases which follow: 'And "Check," I say, and "Split," and | "Cover up my fire."'

It's curfew, and I do my turn
around the valley, settling down
outposts of mine, the little, farflung
castles, Roche this and Rocca
that. And 'Check,' I say, and 'Split,' and
'Cover up my fire.' I rouse my
sentinels under relict clouds,
happy with some altostratus
and a roll of rosy billows
processing off the peaks. I start
the spleenwort by the door, argue
small slips and petals which still snap
with love or hate although it is
so dark and late. I stipulate
which bits matter. White chips go in
grey spaces.

---

[18] R. F. Langley, *The Face of It* (Manchester: Carcanet Press, 2007), 44.

We can draw on two authorities to help us here. Given Langley's interest in etymology, one recourse is the *OED* ('Take hold of a word and | turn it on' as he puts it in 'Cook Ting').[19] Looking up 'curfew', we find the following: 'OF. *cuevre-fu, quevre-feu, covre-feu* (13th c.), f. *couvre*, imper. of *couvrir* to cover + *feu* fire'. And so here we have a source for the last of the three phrases quoted. With this clear, the line as a whole now suggests a mind stopping, backtracking, and examining a word by 'splitting' it into its constituent parts and rendering the result as a sentence. And yet it does more than this. The *OED* definition of 'curfew' itself is given as '1.a. A regulation in force in medieval Europe by which at a fixed hour in the evening, indicated by the ringing of a bell, fires were to be covered over or extinguished; also, the hour of evening when the signal was given, and the bell rung for this purpose'. By including this etymological exercise the poem thus relates the idea of curfew not to what the *OED* calls the word's 'extended use', i.e. 'a restriction imposed upon the movements of the inhabitants of an area for a specified period', but rather to the end of the brief period of electric light paid for in order to examine the painting. The rest of the poem takes place in darkness.

Our second source comes again from the *Journals*. After informing us that Richard Wollheim considers this Bellini 'one of the greatest paintings in the world', Langley goes on to 'take a clue from earlier than Wolheim, from Adrian Stokes',

> who talked about how, in paintings, foreground figures seem to be convex and backgrounds concave. He suggested that we seek part-object relationships as we enter and search about in the concavity, but stand back and are confronted by the convex foreground figure, accepting it as itself, not defending ourselves by *splitting*, accepting it as complex and self-sufficient. And sometimes the whole picture can step up to us like that, asserting itself.[20]

Here we have a second source for the term 'Split', which supplies another dimension to what is actually happening in the opening moments of the poem. For this section does indeed involve a 'searching about' in the background of the picture: 'settling down | outposts of mine, the little far- | flung castles, Roche this and Rocca | that'. On this reading the subsequent 'covering up'—i.e. the moment when the artificial coin-operated light goes out—may suggest the beginning of an alternative relationship with the picture, one that, as the picture is allowed to recede into darkness, is less defensive and cedes a greater autonomy to the picture itself. This emphasis on the material and temporal contexts for viewing the picture is figured strongly throughout the poem.

As the poem proceeds there is an increasing sense of the encroaching dark, now that the fire has been covered up: it is 'late and dark', 'white chips go in grey spaces', summer pastures are visible only in the 'gloaming at his [Jerome's] back'. This dynamic is counterpointed by the way in which, as the picture withdraws or recedes from the narrator, the

---

[19] Langley, *The Face of It*, 9.
[20] Langley, *Journals*, 128 (my emphasis).

figures within it, in particular that of St Jerome, seem to begin to assume an agency that challenges and eventually surpasses that of the narrator:

But gradually,
the old man's face becomes more than
it was. His profile is on the
sky above the mountains. Nor does
he look at me, but only at
his book. He veils his eye and sucks
his lip, as he considers what
is read.

In Stokes's terms these lines describe the picture 'stepping up' to us, and there is a clear relationship asserted between this process and the poem's increasing references to darkness and withdrawal. The more the picture sinks into the gloom, the more it is allowed to assert its presence. In his *Journals* Langley notes the formal qualities of the painting: Bellini's use of the arch and the way in which the interior space of the painting is represented as continuous with the space of the church itself, so that the saint seems 'to move forward to be beneath the arch that is well in front of him'. However this movement is described as part of or alongside another kind of movement, a flattening of the picture plane itself. In a manner very similar to the role of the fog in Tomlinson's poem, an insistence on the material surface of the painting is related to a collapse in perspective:

> The whole picture closes up forwards, steps to meet you...Jerome's simple profile and silhouette do not suck at or swallow the rest of the picture and you can, most fantastically...assume that all the scenery behind him in the mountains is spread inside his mind, and is proffered to us by his thought, fetched from there, where it is, in the distance, to be more a part of the whole thing, the whole picture as one equal thing, far and edge to edge, brought forward against this actual space in San Giovanni.[21]

Langley's description, here, by his own admission, is 'fantastical'. We can perhaps more readily grasp it if we consider it in terms of Michael Fried's notion of absorption. For Fried this term describes painted figures immersed in their own worlds, never acknowledging the gaze of the viewer. He has argued over several books that this kind of absorption has consequences for the relationship between the viewer and the painting as a whole.[22] Specifically, such absorption promotes a similar concentration on the part of the viewer, allowing them to devote attention equally to all parts of the image, to the canvas as a whole.

One paradigmatic image of absorption is the act of reading, and Langley makes Jerome's intense involvement with his text a key aspect of the poem in terms which

---

[21] Langley, *Journals*, 128–9.
[22] See e.g. Michael Fried, *Absorption and Theatricality: Painting and the Beholder in the Age of Diderot* (Berkeley: University of California Press, 1980).

accord exactly with Fried's descriptions of such figures: 'Nor does | he look at me, but only at | his book. He veils his eye and sucks | his lip, as he considers what | is read'.[23] The way in which the representation of such intense, oblivious concentration on a task can promote the viewer's even attention to the picture plane is accurately captured by Langley's notion of the face failing to 'suck or swallow' the rest of the painting. But Langley goes further than this. In both the *Journals* and the poem the viewer's gaze is described as slipping along a kind of Möbius strip, a single surface that leads uninterruptedly from the external landscape to the saint's inner life and out again.

This process is linked on the one hand to the way small details of lighting shepherd the viewer's gaze, and on the other to a more general spatial economy where, as Langley puts it 'the open opens in insideness'.[24] Hence the poem describes Jerome reading as follows:

And so it starts to move.
The castles and the clouds and the
asplenium which I still make
out, splayed on the rock, are taking
their places in his head. He has
a mind for them.

Langley remarks at one stage in the *Journals* that the brightest point in the picture is the small fragment of the page visible beside the spine of Jerome's book, and reminds us that the page as a whole must be equally bright from the saint's point of view, as though its text were 'written on snow'. This point of light calls to another point on a tower in the background: 'the distant tower and the near page…fixing the journey in to the look across' according to Langley's prose account.[25] In his opposition between a perpendicular and a horizontal axis here, between 'the journey in' and 'the look across', Langley again emphasizes the way in which the picture deflects depth into surface, 'closes up forwards, steps to meet you'. As we shall see, the choice of this fragmentary glint as the point of entry for the gaze's 'journey in' is significant in other ways too. For the moment it is enough to note that the *Journals* speculate as to the source of this light, without making their conclusion specific. In Langley's poem by contrast this brightness elicits the phrase 'the moon picks | at a corner of the page', a phrase which leads directly to the final sentence of the poem:

The moon picks
at the corner of the page. I
turn myself around to thank him,
the old man, the moon, Bellini,
hoping the next words he reads will
mention me, as someone waiting

---

[23] R. F. Langley, *Collected Poems* (Manchester: Carcanet Press, 2000), 44.
[24] Langley, *Journals*, 128–9.
[25] Langley, *Journals*, 130.

in the nave, at twilight, here in
line fifty-seven, arrested
by green and rose. By rose and brown.

The word 'picks' is working fairly hard here, suggesting first a fastidious delicacy, secondly an attempt (by the moon) to turn the page, and finally, in what I suggest is the most immediate sense, the fragment of light that Langley dwells on in the *Journals*. The phrase that follows—'I turn myself around to thank him'—echoes the opening lines of the poem: 'I do my turn | around the valley'. Yet where the former attempted to establish a sense of authority, the latter evinces gratitude, humility even, in keeping with the narrative arc of a poem which moves from confident assertion to transported reception. A reader pausing at this point in the poem might justifiably assume that it is the moon that is the recipient of this gratitude. However as the line continues over the break it appears that it is the old man that is being thanked. This hesitation between moon and old man, not to mention the introduction of Bellini himself, sets up a complex and shifting set of relations between viewer, painter, subject of painting, context of viewing, and eventually the material space of the poem itself that it is nigh on impossible to exhaust. I want to track just one pathway through these transactions here, as we move towards a conclusion.

If one holds on to the initial sense that the speaker's gratitude is addressed to the moon, it follows that the gaze turns away from the picture plane and towards the source of the light that 'picks at the corner of the page'. This suggests that the light source illuminating the page is actually behind the viewer, outside the diegesis, an effect which the *Journals* note also of Bellini's *The Agony in the Garden:* 'a scene lit from the front, so that the walls of Jerusalem glow, though there is a sunset beyond them'. In a sense then this turning away at the end of the poem is also a turning deeper into the imaginary space of the picture, now conceived as extending past the viewer and into the depths of the church. The viewer is in effect hailed or interpellated by the glimmer of the page and in turning around to acknowledge the source of the light participates fully in the painting's construction of an illusory space.

Yet this is to ignore a series of subtle qualifications that insist that the agency of the viewer must also be recognized, that his is a presence resistant to being wholly captivated by the painting's spectacle. Thus it is specifically 'as someone waiting | in the nave, at twilight' that the viewer or voice of the poem must be 'mentioned' by Jerome's text and thereby included in the painting. This is a powerful counterweight to the sense of the painting as an aesthetic object so compelling that it transforms its viewers into incidental characters in its own narrative. The implication is that the viewer's particularity, his angle of vision, his subjective and material experience of seeing the painting must be registered and preserved as a constitutive condition of the painting's disclosure.

Such an acknowledgement extends also to the form of the poem itself when we find the viewer described as not only 'waiting |in the nave' but also 'here in | line fifty-seven'. In a self-consciously modernist moment, the materiality of text and embodiment of the reader coincide, the situatedness of the subject finding a correlate in the worked surface of the object. The implication here is similar to that which we found in Tomlinson's 'Meditation': overt acknowledgement of the artwork's constructed nature allows the audience to critically examine its own relationship to the object. Where Langley's position goes beyond Tomlinson's, striking thereby a stronger chord with Riley's work, is in the way that it acknowledges the co-implication of the potentially coercive qualities of the aesthetic image with its ability to provoke thought and emotion.

In a recent letter to the *Chicago Review* John Wilkinson notes that 'even the (politically) perilous aesthetic of Imagism could take a dialectical turn in the poetry of Zukofsky and Oppen'.[26] Peter Robinson has staged a similar argument, suggesting that the commodified, mass cultural images that play across the glassy surfaces of Tom Raworth's poems are counterpointed by his investment in the messy dynamics of human relationships, whether of family or community.[27] It is a cognate dialectical turn that the current chapter has been pursuing in the work of three poets who have, like Raworth, drawn deeply on Pound's Imagism and the Objectivist poetics that succeeded it. Each of the poems considered here moves between, on the one hand, familiar modernist epistemological insights concerning the status of the image as object and, on the other, phenomenological issues to do with the embodied perceptions of the viewer. Where Robinson sees Raworth as pitching a sense of lived community against manufactured group identities based on consumption, I have argued that Tomlinson, Riley, and Langley contest the power of the image by attending to its palpable designs on us with the utmost patience and sensuous delight. As a consequence these poems record what we saw Prynne call, after Stokes, a 'tensile equilibrium' between the 'palpable external world' of the aesthetic object and the 'inner needs' of the situated observer. In doing so they demonstrate how art can open a space of reflection that unfolds in time and estranges us rather than, as with much contemporary visual practice—and spectacle culture more broadly—simply pinioning us to the moment and to what we have been taught to think of as the self.

Select Bibliography

Foster, Hal, *The Art-Architecture Complex* (London: Verso, 2011).
Fried, Michael, *Absorption and Theatricality: Painting and the Beholder in the Age of Diderot* (Berkeley: University of California Press, 1980).
Langley, R. F., *Collected Poems* (Manchester: Carcanet Press, 2000).
Langley, R. F., *Journals* (Exeter: Shearsman Books, 2006).
Langley, R. F., *The Face of It* (Manchester: Carcanet Press, 2007).
Riley, Peter, *Passing Measures* (Manchester: Carcanet Press, 2000).

---

[26] John Wilkinson, 'Review of Simon Jarvis' *The Unconditional*', *Chicago Review*, 52/ 2–4 (Autumn 2006), 369–75 (374). Peter Riley responds to precisely this statement in a letter in the following issue.

[27] Peter Robinson, 'Tom Raworth and the Pop Art Explosion', in *Twentieth Century Poetry: Selves and Situations* (Oxford: Oxford University Press, 2005), 206–29.

Riley, Peter, *The Glacial Stair* (Manchester: Carcanet Press, 2011).
Robinson, Peter, 'Tom Raworth and the Pop Art Explosion', in *Twentieth Century Poetry: Selves and Situations* (Oxford: Oxford University Press, 2005), 206–29.
Stokes, Adrian, *Cézanne* (London: Faber & Faber, 1947).
Tomlinson, Charles, *Collected Poems* (Oxford: Oxford University Press, 1985).
Wilkinson, John, 'Review of Simon Jarvis' *The Unconditional*', *Chicago Review*, 52/ 2–4 (Autumn 2006), 369–75.

CHAPTER 16

CINEMA MON AMOUR: HOW BRITISH POETRY FELL IN LOVE WITH FILM

SOPHIE MAYER

TONY HARRISON, writer and director of the 1998 feature film *Prometheus*, his achievements celebrated in a monumental *Collected Film Poems*, has a strong claim to be considered British and Irish poetry's foremost cinephile and even cineaste. Only two other British artists have achieved the double of published volume of poetry and feature film: celebrated film-maker Derek Jarman (whose early poetry I discuss later) and Margaret Tait, almost unknown within both the cinematic and poetic communities. Her body of work, spanning the 1950s to 1990s, includes three volumes of poetry, thirty-two short films, and one feature, and marks her as the only British artist truly making film poems. Fil Ieropolous notes that the cinematic film-poem flared briefly in Britain in the 1990s, with seasons programmed by the British Film Institute and the magazine *Film Poem Poem Film*, both curated by Peter Todd, but notes little relation to, or impact on, the contemporary poetry scene.[1] Tait, a regular contributor to the magazine, is an exception, but her absence from both poetry anthologies and the very recent attention that has developed, posthumously, to her work, speak to the difficulties she faced.

Her cinematic career began in Italy, where she studied at the home of Italian neo-realism, the Centro Sperimentale di Cinematografia, after National Service as an army medic. Upon her return to Britain, Gavin Lambert organized a screening of her short films at the London Film Society.[2] Rather than stay in London, then (as now) the film-making and distribution centre of the UK, Tait returned to Edinburgh and started

---

[1] 'Poetry-Film & The Film Poem: Some Clarifications', [www.studycollection.co.uk/poetry.html].
[2] Sarah Neely, ' "Ploughing a lonely furrow": Margaret Tait and "Professional" Filmmaking Practices in 1950s Scotland', in Ian Craven (ed.), *Movies on Home Ground: Explorations in Amateur Cinema* (Newcastle upon Tyne: Cambridge Scholars Press, 2009), 303.

Rose Street Films, before moving to the Orkneys in the 1960s. Her early work included the short film *The Leaden Echo and the Golden Echo* (1955), rooted in Gerard Manley Hopkins's poem, and *Hugh McDiarmid—A Portrait* (1964), but her poetic practice also informed a film that has, on the surface, little to do with poetry, *Land Makar* (1981). In using the Scots word *makar* to refer to the female farmer who is the subject of the film, Tait advocates for the artisanal sense of *makar* (which poetry, from *poiesis*, making, shares): to make, to have an effect on the material world. The film shows the farmer inscribing her knowledge of the land in the furrows she makes; it shows, simultaneously, how she is made *by* the land. Through her observation, in which her innovation of the camera mirrors the farmer's innovation of the tractor—two women gleefully and practically bringing technology to their work—Tait sets up a mirroring, investigating how *her* making in cinema might be related to, or descended from, the land *makar*'s.

She suggests as much in the poem 'Pavement Artist', where the artist's work moves from the textual to the photographic:

Spilling of the ink-pot,
Tearing of the page,
Intruding with blundering fingers
Into the micro-picture gauge.

Those 'blundering fingers' suggest film-making as a haptic and embodied artisanal practice, which she analogizes as lighting a heathfire and/or a

light-house for you
To guide you in the mirk.
You'll see the regular flashing,
You'll count,
And by the known timing,
By recognition of the formula once learned,
You'll know it's me.[3]

The rhythmic signature of light-writing (photo-graphy) vividly marks out Tait's unique career with its balance of technical skill, aesthetic acumen, and location in folk tradition.

Despite being championed by both Edwin Morgan and MacDiarmid, with whom she made one of her most tender and poetic films, Tait's poetry, which she self-published, had never been anthologized and is hard to access. Yet her poems, 'roughly shattering things, too, to see what's there', are *sui generis*.[4] They are closest to the work of her near-contemporary W. S. Graham, demonstrating a similar attention to detail and horizontal movement between precise natural observation and vivid fantasy.

---

[3] Margaret Tait, *Subjects and Sequences* (Edinburgh: Interim Editions, 1960), 30–2.
[4] 'Seeing's Believing and Believing's Seeing', quoted in Ali Smith, 'The Margaret Tait Years', in Peter Todd and Benjamin Cook (eds.), *Subjects and Sequences: A Margaret Tait Reader* (London: LUX, 2004), 8.

What music is for Graham, film is for Tait: a framework for perception. As she writes in 'Now':

I used to lie in wait to see the clover open
Or close,
But never saw it.
I was too impatient
Or the movement is too subtle,
Imperceptible
And more than momentary
[…]
Cinematographically
I have registered the opening of escholtzia
On an early summer morning.
It gave me a sharp awareness of time passing,
Of exact qualities and values in the light,
But I didn't see the movement
As movement.
I didn't with my own direct perception see the petals moving.
Later, on the film, they seem to open swiftly
[…]
But I didn't see them moving open.
My timing and my rhythm could not observe the rhythm of their opening.[5]

The conversational syntax and rhythms of the poem give it the transparency and simplicity of William Blake's 'Auguries of Innocence'. There is a sense of a child's perception recalled by an adult, wherein the 'exact qualities and values' of that remembered perception are at once layered under and filtered through the technical exactitudes echoed in the polysyllabic single word line 'cinematographically'. Yet the cinematographic does not represent a fall into experience, creating a nostalgia for an Edenic unmediated perception. Rather than bemoaning the denaturalization of perception, the speaker says that the camera 'gave [her] a sharp awareness' not obtainable with the naked eye; even though she is a poet, her 'timing and [her] rhythm' are not objectively or scientifically adequate to the rhythm of a flower. Tait teases apart the lyric cliché of the poet's heightened perception, and at the same time makes perceptual exactitude, accomplished through the tool of film, central to her poetic practice.

Apart from the *Aspects of Kirkwall* (1977–81) series, made for the Orkney Tourist Board, Tait worked outside the funding, post-production, and distribution structures of British cinema; similarly, her elegantly self-published poetry remains unanthologized: her work in each media mutually reinforces her location outside the market. This stands in sharp contrast to the strategic use of cinematic references in contemporary poetry, to reach the movies' wide market, and with the use of poetry in contemporary mainstream cinema, as with W. H. Auden's 'Stop all the clocks' in Mike Newell's *Four*

---

[5] In Todd and Cook (eds.), *Subjects and Sequences*, 118–20.

Weddings and a Funeral (1994, written by Richard Curtis), positioning Auden as the premier and paradigmatic British film poet, whereby poetry stands and serves for a nostalgic mourning. Such quotation—marking high culture and high emotion—includes poetry within 'heritage' drama, a reference to past social and cultural forms. Auden's most famous contribution to cinema, a celebration of new forms of motion and documentation in his rhymed voice-over for the General Post Office's landmark documentary *Night Mail* (Harry Watt, 1936), has become subject to similar recuperative nostalgia value.

Harrison paid tribute to Auden in his 2002 film for ITV's South Bank Show, a contemporary poetic documentary of savage political wit called *Crossings*. His film poems' use of television and film as an extension of the public role of the poet has been ably analysed by Peter Robinson.[6] In the introduction to his *Collected Film Poetry*, Harrison points to the influence on his work of European post-war art-house and pre-war avant-garde cinema seen at the Leeds University Film Society, including Auden's *Night Mail* and Soviet cinema.[7] Jefferson Hunter comments, quoting the poet's own description, that 'For Harrison, the "combined prosodies of film and poetry," the "flickering momentum of the flicks" and the "metrical beat of poetry" together depict, perhaps constitute the only way of truly depicting... the need to grasp the significant details of life'. Harrison's film poems, for all their audacious intellectual and verbal scope, resonate with the British tradition of cinematic social realism, in their use of archival footage, kitchen sink drama, and assertions of documentary authenticity. For Harrison, the camera's eye is the poet's eye, seeking and presenting truth in strong beats, and the film form his work mandates is as transparent as possible in order to make the work accessible to television viewers; as Hunter notes, both verse and film forms are 'generally straightforward... often carefully managed pastiche or homage'.[8]

Television, rather than cinema, has been central to the audio-visual representation and dissemination of poetry in the British Isles, although there is decreasing space for it in the schedules. Bloodaxe co-produced Tyne Tees Television's *Wordworks* series (Rob Cowley, May–June 1992), featuring several major names in current British mainstream poetry such as Carol Ann Duffy, Jo Shapcott, and Benjamin Zephaniah, who has matched Harrison in the breadth and invention of his use of televisual media to engage readers and listeners, not least in *Dread Poets' Society* (Andy Wilson, 1991), which inverts its mainstream cinematic reference to blow away heritage resonances of poetry. Yet British television has still to find a competent idiom for screening poetry. As *The Guardian*'s TV Matters columnist Mark Lawson notes, 'programmes containing poetry routinely try to find pictorial equivalents for every image. A mention of a

---

[6] Peter Robinson, 'Shared Intimacy: A Study of Tony Harrison's Public Poetry, with Specific Reference to His Poetics, the Political Status of His Work, and His Development of the Genre of the Film/Poem' (PhD, University of Hull, 1998).

[7] Tony Harrison, *Collected Film Poetry* (London: Faber & Faber, 2007), p. x.

[8] Jefferson Hunter, *English Filming* (Bloomington: University of Indiana Press, 2010), 285.

blackbird draws on the archives of the ornithological unit.'[9] Televisual poetry in Britain rarely questions the nature of the medium, actively seeking both the mass audience and documentary authenticity it appears to confer.

By contrast, Andrea Brady's recent collection *Wildfire*, a merciless study of incendiary devices, creates a shatter pattern that connects Greek fire to CNN's shock and awe. For Brady, the cinematic extends from the photographic (as developed to document the American Civil War) to the televisual and digital: film is part of a continuum of technological shocks to memory and materiality. The book is illuminated by a series of photographs and engravings—one in which a figure holds up his own skin, one of an alchemist's alembic. The 'wildfire' of the title is both visual media and what they depict:

On the home
front a pen of sparklers writes apocrypha
and recipes on the body of the state-
sponsored torture artist.[10]

This recounting of embedded media, in which the body of the artist or writer documenting war not only belongs to but (in the interval of the hyphen and enjambment) *is* the state, recalls Harun Farocki's searing collage-film *Bilder der Welt und Inschrift des Krieges*, in which the film-maker refilms photographs and footage in order to ask us to look again, ethically—to strike a balance between looking respectfully and looking away.

In Simon Perril's *Nitrate*, published in Spring 2010 like *Wildfire*, film in(tro)duces a new physical sensation that, rather than suggesting or foreclosing an ethical way of being in the world, may offer a cure. Nitrate, as Perril notes in his 'Afterward', arose from the American Civil War's collision of nitrocellulose (guncotton) and collodion, which was originally intended as a liquid bandage. Like the *pharmakon* analysed by Jacques Derrida, at once the word for paint or dye, poison and medicine, cinema as art both wounds and heals.[11] Perril titles one poem 'The First Audiences Reported Feelings of Sea-Sickness,' although this enduring myth has been comprehensively countered by Tom Gunning.[12] A homage to Méliès ends by describing the cinematic era as 'the nauseous pill | a century of thrill and illusion' ('Melomania'); and Blake's worm turns up in Jekyll and Hyde ('Ovid on Nitrate'). Motion sickness is the result, in Perril's analysis, of film's perilous speeding up of photography's 'dead time' ('Stations across Shape'), a deadness that continues to haunt film (Hyde to its Jekyll). *Nausée* is induced by cinema's synchronic arrival with the standardization of time, a topic that Perril treats in the middle section of the book, 'The Intermission', in which the speaker finds occasion to

---

[9] Lawson, 'TV Matters: *The Life of Muhammad*', *The Guardian*, G2, 6 July 2011, 27.
[10] Andrea Brady, *Wildfire* (San Francisco: Krupskaya, 2010).
[11] Jacques Derrida, 'Plato's Pharmacy', in *Dissemination*, trans. Barbara Johnson (London: Athlone, 1981), 61–172.
[12] Gunning, 'An Aesthetic of Astonishment: Early Film and the (In)credulous Spectator', in Linda Williams (ed.), *Viewing Positions* (New Brunswick, NJ: Rutgers University Press, 1995), 114–33.

intermit from the interminable grind of regulated dailiness, only to find himself 'cursing the interval'.[13]

Poetry's apprehension of film, whether ekphrastic, ecstatic, or experimental, is haunted by the temporal lag between film/filming and the viewer, and cinematic time's impact on perceptual memory and attention, demanding a poetics that repeats filmic optics, wherein the movement of the image is an illusion created by the 'flicker effect' caused by the gaps of black leader between the stills, and the speed at which the film strip moves through the projector. Dziga Vertov argued that film occurs in the gaps of leader, which he called 'the interval', a theoretical formation taken up by Gilles Deleuze and Trinh T. Minh-Ha, particularly with regard to experimental cinema.[14] Formally, cinema has altered both the temporality (rhythmical, referential, denotative, and narrative) and address of all post-photographic poetry, as its camera movements, cutting, and apostrophic inversion have permeated the perceptions of writers and readers; yet few contemporary British and Irish poets acknowledge this, and fewer still work confidently and explicitly with filmic form.

Of those who do, Simon Barraclough has been the most visible and energized, as poet-in-residence for the Film Programme on Radio 4 in 2008–9. With poet Isobel Dixon and the British Film Institute's Mark Fisher, Barraclough co-curated two poetry events that engaged poets to generate new poems in response to film: one relating to Alfred Hitchcock's *Psycho* (1960), and one to the BFI's Mediathèque public archives. A selection from *PsychoPoetica* appears in *Manhattan Review*, 14/2, and various of the poems engendered are distributed across recent collections by individual poets such as Dixon, creating the sense of an emergent media and cinema literacy absent in earlier generations.[15] Other recent signs of poetic cine-literacy include Malgorzata Kitkowski's PoetryFilm nights, based at the Renoir in London, the Film issue of *Staple*, and Salt's publication of collections such as Perril's *Nitrate*, David McCooey's *Outside*, and Barraclough's *Los Alamos Mon Amour*.[16] Poems in Andy Jackson's *Split Screen* anthology engage with cinema in the ekphrastic or mythopoeic modes. The submission guidelines, which ask poets to pair/set in competition two cult figures or texts, demand a kind of slash poetry, a poetry in which film and television are pick 'n' mix, not intertexts but a patchwork of textures, indices of subjective memory and affect that are usefully popular: a reference to a particular actor, television moment, or film scene can serve to interpellate the reader into the poem via a resonance that is at once a temporal locator (often nostalgic) and part of a larger cultural mythology.

---

[13] Simon Perril, *Nitrate* (Cambridge: Salt Publishing, 2010), 73, 17, 19, 23, 11, 39.

[14] Dziga Vertov, *Kino-Eye* (Berkeley: University of California Press, 1984); Gilles Deleuze, *Cinema 2: The Time-Image* (New York: Continuum, 2005); Trinh T. Minh-Ha, *Cinema Interval* (New York: Routledge, 1999).

[15] Isobel Dixon, *The Tempest Prognosticator* (Cromer: Salt Publishing, 2011).

[16] David McCooey, *Outside* (Cromer: Salt Publishing, 2011); Barraclough, *Los Alamos* (Cambridge: Salt Publishing, 2008).

While cinema as an industry—and an aspect of the culture industry—has affected the related socio-economic practices of literature and publishing, few are the poets who critique, or even acknowledge, the construction of what Garrett Stewart usefully labels 'the cinematic', that concatenation of star power, industrial technology, global economics, and narrative propaganda that characterizes the external operations of cinema.[17] By contrast, he proposes 'the filmic' as a referent for formal and aesthetic operations in their medium-specificity; all films partake of both aspects to different degrees. When British poets come to address cinema, which they do so belatedly due to English high modernism's fiat against the commercialism of the cinematic (and consequent refusal to acknowledge the evident impact of the filmic on its poetics), the majority (of that minority) do so in thrall to, and embroiled in, the cinematic, and with little strategic grasp of the filmic. For the most part, British poets write as, and from the position of, the film viewer of apparatus theory, sutured into the film without protest, drawing on the desiring infantile sensation of mastery of vision to reconfigure the physical world as (a shadow of the) cinema.

This is perhaps most apparent in Barraclough's 'Los Alamos Mon Amour'; the title, of course, a riff on one of the most poetic of French art-house films, Alain Resnais's *Hiroshima Mon Amour* (1959), with its allusive, fragmentary, and imagistic screenplay, addressing the visual affect of 'seeing' Hiroshima, by novelist and playwright Marguerite Duras, although the poem makes no direct reference to the film. There is, however, a powerful stanza that engages the themes of visuality and witness in relation to atrocities that are central to Duras's screenplay.

Eyelids are gone, along with memories
of times when the without could be withheld
from the within: when atoms kept their sanctity
and matter meant. Should I have ducked and covered?

Barraclough wants the boundary to hold firm, and 'the without [to] be withheld | from the within', a very English response to the impact of cinema that is first seen in T. S. Eliot's *The Waste Land*, as will be discussed. The atom bomb, and implicitly cinema, which shares its drastic illumination and dissolution of borders, erases our ability to look away ('Eyelids are gone'), but also our memories: they figure each other as a loss of innocence, sanctity, and meaning. How can poetry be written after cinema has opened our eyes?

The final sentence of the stanza ducks the question, followed by a strange clause 'Instead of watching' balanced by the opening of the fourth stanza, 'I might have painted myself white': the implication being that the speaker *did* watch the destructive effects of the Los Alamos detonation (from a safe, that is historical, distance), but frames this witnessing as a counterfactual subjunctive scenario in which the speaker is in a fallout cellar, a subliminal reference to Elle's incarceration in her family's cellar in *Hiroshima*

---

[17] Garrett Stewart, *Between Film and Screen: Modernism's Photo Synthesis* (Chicago: University of Chicago Press, 1999), 266–88.

Mon Amour after her family discovers her affair with a German soldier. Whereas the film refuses nostalgia and the possibility of witness, in 'Los Alamos Mon Amour', a lost wholeness of vision and selfhood is mourned: the dispersed radioactivity has 'been flung through' the speakers' cells.[18] The screen that should separate inside and outside does not hold, and the influential film conjured by the title has been unreferenced, overwritten, 'blown out' by the poem. A subsequent poem in the collection, 'The Open Road', rewrites the history of photography, cinema, and chemistry to ask 'What if colour film came first', suggesting it would create a nostalgic longing for monochrome, in which memory both has and is a 'silver screen'.[19] In a counterfactual mode similar to the twist in 'Los Alamos', this counter-historical quandary at once buys into the narrative of progress put forth by the American film industry, whereby each technological development such as colour improves film (i.e. makes it more commercially successful) and nostalgizes the palette of early film as that of desire and memory.

Barraclough is the paradigmatic writer of an increasingly cine-literate poetic community, one wherein Hollywood and American independent cinema of the last five decades (and, to a lesser extent, the canon of European art house as admired by Harrison) has replaced, to some extent, biblical and classical mythology as a shared referent for writers and readers, finally overcoming the veto issued by T. S. Eliot, the cardinal high modern whose pronouncements dictated the alienation between poetry and cinema in Britain, at a time when James Joyce was embracing the filmic in his prose, and European poets were collaborating with film-makers under the banner of Surrealism and beyond. A poetic cinema was not confined to pre-war cross-medium experimentation, but proved formative for the development of a filmic alternative to the increasing hegemony of American cinema after the war. Several of the premier post-war Italian art-house film-makers—Pier Paolo Pasolini, Bernardo Bertolucci, and Federico Fellini—were published and prizewinning poets before they picked up a camera; Pasolini continued to write poetry throughout his career and, like Jean Cocteau, poet and director of the quintessential poetic film *Orphée* (1950), his films draw on poetic texts from the Euro-Western classical tradition such as *Decameron* (1971), *The Canterbury Tales* (1972), and Greek tragedies.

Auden's commission for the GPO notwithstanding, only David Gascoyne, who translated poems by Salvador Dalí and Federico García Lorca (author of an unproduced screenplay, 'Viaje a la luna'), explicitly explored the possibilities of cinema, writing a film script 'Procession to the Private Sector', which remains similarly unproduced.[20] Eliot's fiat was one of omission: in his essay 'The Metaphysical Poets', he praised French poet and film theorist Jean Epstein's 'brilliant and extreme' *La Poésie d'aujourd'hui* but told his readers that it 'is not requisite to associate oneself' with Epstein's theory on the alignment of modern poetry with cinema, which has yet to be translated into English.[21]

---

[18] Barraclough, *Los Alamos*, 1.
[19] Barraclough, *Los Alamos*, 7.
[20] David Gascoyne, 'Procession to the Private Sector: Surrealist Film Scenario, 1936–1982', in Michel Rémy, *David Gascoyne, ou l'urgence de l'inexprimé* (Nancy: Presses universitaires de Nancy, 1984), 157–74.
[21] T. S. Eliot, 'The Metaphysical Poets', in *Selected Prose* (London: Faber & Faber, 1975), 65.

Yet David Trotter, who points out Eliot's dismissal of Epstein, locates a particular trace of the filmic in *The Waste Land*, worth examining in depth because it prefigures contemporary attempts at writing cinema.[22]

It is impossible to say just what I mean!
But as if a magic lantern threw the nerves in patterns on a screen.[23]

The speaker's/spectator's nerves are made visible, *as if* the camera/projector were an MRI machine capable of literalizing the work of the new psychoanalytic science that was beginning to filter into England in the early 1920s.

It is this vulnerability that Eliot fears about cinema: that, through the excitations that Perril's collection diagnoses as symptomatic of the filmic, cinema will both intensify neurosis and reveal him as a hysteric. Ed Madden suggests that Eliot therefore mobilizes apotropaic tropes whereby 'male meaning supplants female materiality'.[24] Like the novel before it, the feature film was initially seen as a female entertainment, one fashioned by men to sell the image of femininity and the representation of affect specifically to female consumers, which persists in current film reception in the figuration of 'the feminine as cinematic specularity', the association between the female and the cinematic: surface, technology, consumption, affect.[25] 'Representations of cinema rarely appear in Eliot's work, but when they do they are often linked to the female image.'[26] Fresca, a figure deleted from *The Waste Land* on Ezra Pound's advice, is a decadent poet—at once Belinda and Celia. In the first version of 'The Fire Sermon', Fresca is compared, as 'Venus Anadyomene', to Aeneas' recognition of mother Venus, who is represented as a screen goddess:

So the close rabble in the cinema
Identify a goddess or a star.
In silent rapture worships from afar.[27]

There is an elision between the seductions of the cinematic and its female star; not only that, but the female star comes to stand for the cinematic as commercial, industrial distraction.

As apparatus theory asserts, the interval is also a property of the psychoanalytic, and is thus a sexual formation: the set-up of standard cinema, with the projector located behind the viewer and the screen in front, 'suturing' the viewer into the camera's position and point of view, acts on infantile processes of identity and language acquisition.

---

[22] David Trotter, *Cinema and Modernism* (Oxford: Blackwell, 2007), 29.
[23] T. S. Eliot, 'The Waste Land', *Collected Poems 1909–1962* (London: Faber & Faber, 1974), 16.
[24] Ed Madden, *Tiresian Poetics: Modernism, Sexuality, Voice, 1888–2001* (Cranbury, NJ: Associated University Presses, 2008), 62.
[25] Madden, *Tiresian*, 134.
[26] Madden, *Tiresian*, 133.
[27] T. S. Eliot, *The Waste Land: A Facsimile and Transcript of the Original Drafts including the Annotations of Ezra Pound* (London: Faber & Faber, 1971), 28–9.

In its psychoanalytic anchoring, apparatus theory connects its interval to the desiring operations of memory and perception. It is for these operations that the cinematic stands in contemporary British poetry: as a figure of desire bound up with memory, and vice versa. Jeremy Reed's work does this artfully, as in 'Far Out', where the poem meditates ruefully on a flamboyant, desired figure captured in

a blank frame punctuating every three
as a phased, abstract possibility
...a fiction born
around the many faces of a star[28]

wherein the 'star' is both a sexual and an economic formation, subject at once to Reed's queer and Marxist interrogation.

As the cinematic, in Britain, is imbricated with the cultural hegemony of America (Reed's star is, of course, lost in the US), where its myths, technologies, narratives, and economic model (its cinematic) originate, the star is thus also a Statue of Liberty whom Eliot the reactionary has left behind. In turning away from cinema, British poetry turned away from America (and vice versa), while, from Vachel Lindsay onwards, American poets absorbed, entered, and were entered by cinema. Daniel Kane's *We Saw the Light* makes clear the complexities and extent of the involvement of post-war American poets with film. Avant-garde centres such as Canyon Cinema in San Francisco and Anthology Films in New York attracted both poets and film-makers, and a small number of poet/film-makers such as Abigail Child and Theresa Hak Kyung Cha, who also anthologized film theory in *Apparatus*. Key figures such as Frank O'Hara, Robert Duncan, and Allen Ginsberg were all cinephiles and, in the case of Ginsberg, involved in film-making, appearing in Robert Frank and Alfred Leslie's infamous *Pull My Daisy* (1959).[29] It's hard to imagine a comparable record of any post-war poetry scene on the other side of the Atlantic: Philip Larkin larking around, or J. H. Prynne posing for the camera. That movies are now showing in British poetry is perhaps attributable as much to the influence of the vernacular, spontaneous, contemporaneous address of O'Hara and Ginsberg on poets such as Barraclough, as it is to increasing cine-literacy as a result of the availability of films beyond the art-house circuit, on television, video, and DVD.

That influence, and its cinematicity, is first visible in the work of Derek Jarman who, like Ginsberg, was deeply influenced by William Blake. Blake's significance for experimental American cinema and Beat poetics cannot be overstated: his hand-made illuminated manuscripts offer the earliest, and most comprehensive, example of a truly filmic poetics, yet his influence is far more palpable in American, than in British, contemporary poetry. Jarman's films include *Angelic Conversation* (1985), a visionary realization of William Shakespeare's sonnets, and *War Requiem* (1988), which dramatizes

---

[28] Jeremy Reed, 'Far Out', in Iain Sinclair (ed.), *Conductors of Chaos* (London: Picador, 1996), 400.
[29] Daniel Kane, *We Saw the Light: Conversations between the New American Cinema and Poetry* (Iowa City: University of Iowa Press, 2009).

Benjamin Britten's setting of Wilfred Owen's poems. His published writing is highly poetic—allusive, allegorical, and figural—and often contains fragments of lyric, but it is little known that he published a pamphlet, *a finger in the fishes mouth*, with a chapbook press in 1972.[30]

'Poem for Coleridge July 64' appears therein opposite a postcard showing Santa Claus Toyland, with a large inflatable Santa on top of a Date Shop.

Sitting watching the fire
one's mind turns outwards
not to a mythical childhood
nor to a village idyll
nor to hope for any foreseeable future[31]

But rather, it turns (in both senses) to cinema, which offers 'consolation | as well as shine', the possibilities of alternative desire, as well as consumer gloss; the 'city composed of promises' must be Los Angeles, the dream factory, another version of the pleasure dome hinted at in the postcard, as well as (via *Citizen Kane* (Orson Welles, 1941), the *sine qua non* of US cinema) a reference to Xanadu (whose model, William Randolf Hearst's house, is on the cliffs between San Francisco and LA). Cinema has replaced both temporal and local nostalgia, as well as shamanic speculation. The speaker, 'watching the fire', sees the endless darkness that surrounds it, the cinematic frame, the black interval. Samuel Taylor Coleridge is in that interval, as the poet-natural philosopher interested in *vision* in both its natural and supernatural senses, which cinema—technological and occulted—appears to combine and magnify. Yet the poem's line of descent is Jarman pastiching Ginsberg pastiching O'Hara pastiching Langston Hughes pastiching Whitman pastiching Blake, a line strongly marked in American film poetry, and which marks cinema as America(n), but also as Blake's *America*.

Like Jarman, Isaac Julien—who would later make the documentary *Derek* (2008) in the archives of Jarman's life and work—also turned to and travelled through America when seeking inspiration for a poetic filmic praxis, and specifically for a praxis emerging from African post-colonial identity: his film *Looking for Langston* (1989) is an unmatched poetic documentary, its form suffused with poetic graphic matches, repetitions, cuts, and shifting relations between language and image. Its tone is not elegiac or nostalgic but investigative, even imperative. The interval between poetry and film becomes a space for exploring dislocation and relocation, cultural interconnection and mistranslation. John Akomfrah uses poetry similarly in *Nine Muses* (2010), a feature film that, in line with his work with the Black Audio Film Collective, layers samples from Naxos recordings of classic poetry over found footage of Windrush generation migration and (dis)integration from BBC regional archives. Poems by Shakespeare, Eliot, and John Milton are appropriated as the internal narration of the immigrant's alienation, a

---

[30] See Steven Dillon, *Derek Jarman and Lyric Film: The Mirror and The Sea* (Austin: University of Texas Press, 2004).

[31] Derek Jarman, *A Finger in the Fishes Mouth* (Bettiscombe: Bettiscombe Press, 1972), n.p.

colonial heritage turned on its head as Derek Walcott does in *Omeros*. Loosely structured, like Walcott's epic poem, around *The Odyssey* (using Anton Lesser's reading of Ian Johnston's translation), *Nine Muses* draws on the lyric tradition that emerges from al-Andalus, wherein the lover, God, and the lost homeland are fused into a figure of beauty and longing.[32]

That lyric tradition figures also in Sally Potter's *YES* (2004), where the characters speak in rhymed couplets of iambic pentameter, but the protagonists' romantic exchanges are informed not by the English sonnet tradition, but by Arabic love poetry.[33] Potter, like Jarman and Julien a graduate of the British Film Institute's Production Board, had previously had characters reciting poems by Shakespeare, Percy Bysshe Shelley, Edward Thomas, and others, at moments of romantic and erotic drama, in *Orlando* (1993), her adaptation of Virginia Woolf's playful history of British poetry. In Potter's film, the critical history merges into the cinematic form, which makes vivid reference to the lyrical, anti-realist strand of British cinema from Michael Powell and Emeric Pressburger (who made *A Canterbury Tale*) to Peter Greenaway. It is this small group of film-makers, emerging in the late 1970s and early 1980s from a politically active milieu, and at a unique moment when artisanal/punk cinema was challenging industrial hegemonies American *and* British, who come closest to the filmic alchemy Epstein envisioned and Eliot pooh-poohed.

This magical, visionary cinema is even more absent in British poetry than it is in British cinema. In the contemporary era, it has appeared mainly in the specialist magazines *Vertigo* and *Artesian*, edited by poet and curator Gareth Evans, who has been the driving force behind the forthcoming film *Patience* (Grant Gee, 2011), an innovative mobilization of the work of W. G. Sebald that, through its unusual treatment of *mise en page* as *mise en scène*, develops a new poetics of verbal language in cinema.[34] Theoretically and philosophically engaged with questioning mimesis and representation, this filmic work is part of a scattered, pathless page and screen anti-tradition, not least because British cinema is resolutely realist rather than imagist. It is salutary to imagine what might have occurred had British poetry kept alive the Imagist moment, and its metaphysical and filmic expansion in the work of H.D.: the anti-Eliot, a poet who not only knew, loved, and wrote about cinema in *Close Up*, the first English-language film-theory magazine that she co-founded, but who developed an exquisite filmic poetics in *Helen in Egypt*, a poem deeply concerned with the occult mysteries (from *muein*, to close the eye) as they stretch from ancient Egypt to modernist cinema.

Helen in Egypt suggestively models Helen as a starlet, taking up the Euripidean myth of Helen's presence in Troy as an *eidolon*, a dream-projection and exploring the crystallization of the female object, projection, and the two-dimensional screen image. Helen

---

[32] See María Rosa Menocal, *Shards of Love: Exile and the Origins of the Lyric* (Durham, NC: Duke University Press, 1993).

[33] See Sophie Mayer, 'Yes', in *The Cinema of Sally Potter: A Politics of Love* (London: Wallflower, 2009), 190–201.

[34] Presentation by Chris Darke, 'Film Criticism Now', University of Kent, 11 Nov. 2011.

never went to Troy: she remained behind in Egypt where she has become a priestess in the mysteries of Apollo, god of light, who projects scenes from Troy and its aftermath for her on a variety of surfaces: walls, the sails of boats, her own dress and veil, paralleling hieroglyphs with the projected image. The poem's double syntax—prose headers, like old-fashioned intertitles; and stanzaic verse—constantly reconfigures the reader's perceptions of Helen (as cinema). Through filmic figurations such as moving writing on the wall, the appearance of a black sign on a white sail, and Helen's merging with and emergence from her torn veil, H.D. attempts to find a voice *for* cinema, for the female icon as cinema, for the female muse of lyric poetry who has become cinema. The projection and the scene often merge, engaging with that troubling affective melding that Eliot's 'as if' is so—literally—unnerved by. Influenced by H.D.'s psychoanalytic training with Freud, Helen's thoughts and feelings are 'thrown in patterns upon the screen'; often described as black marks on a white background, this projection suggestively elides poetic writing and the film image.

This occult poetics of the female star appears in Gavin Selerie's cine-magnum opus *Roxy*, which is both a nostalgic elegy for fleapits past, and an invocation of the Helen-as-goddess/strumpet whom H.D. so thoroughly dismantles. In this 1996 book-length sequence in which cinema itself appears embodied as a B-movie expressionist femme fatale, the seductive, vanishing spirit of cinema Selerie calls 'paramount flesh' who is all surface and always for sale, because '[g]irls get used to chopped-up images'.[35] This reverie for a form at once seductive and/because repellent also appears in Andrew Duncan's poem 'Cinema', which concludes Eliotically that, in the cinema, 'our nerves quiver like aspens and are as still as cherries in chocolate | ... Coma! Luxury! Sensation! Vice!'[36] While Selerie and Duncan both play wittily and erotically with the cinematic, there is an insistence on that collusive triangulation of affect, populism, and capitalism in the flattened curves of the starlet, whose surface of beauty gives the speaker the fantasy of mastery of vision, even as she eludes him: he is at once viewer, critic, protagonist, director, and editor. 'She was hugely present | on a strip porous to light', says Selerie, noting later that 'Roxy, your absence is Egyptian darkness'.[37]

Roxy's argument for a return to the 1930s star—a return that is also, etymologically and mythologically, a return to an Orientalized and hierarchized master/slave dynamic—is coupled with a psychogeographical nostalgia for old cinemas and film studios, as in Selerie's poem 'Up from the Vault'.[38] Cinema, specifically the abandoned Stoll Studios in Cricklewood, here becomes part of the derelict industrial landscape of Britain, a parallel to closed mines and shipworks, a former national industry whose viewers were, argues the poem, part of its workforce. This is a striking poem, one that reveals the technical and formal operations of both film-making and film viewing without the mystic eroticism of *Roxy*, but also participates in the insistent nostalgizing of cinema that marks the

---

[35] Gavin Selerie, *Roxy* (Hay-on-Wye: West House Books, 1996), 16, 28.
[36] In Sinclair (ed.), *Conductors of Chaos*, 97.
[37] Selerie, *Roxy*, 17.
[38] Gavin Selerie, *Music's Duel* (Exeter: Shearsman, 2009), 310–16.

work of Barraclough: the dream of a vanished golden age that, like the gilded starlet, is part of Hollywood cinema's own mythology. Selerie repositions film, and its star, as the new lyric muse (dead and nostalgized on a pedestal), a speechless focal point around which the poet remakes language: the prompt might be her, but the intervention is all his. The book ends with a three-page-long multiple redefinition of the word 'roxy' (as slave and sex worker) that argues for returning the film star to her, in a quotation taken from Molly Haskell's *From Reverence to Rape*, 'mystical, quasi-religious' status. Selerie ignores what Laura Mulvey famously demonstrates in 'Visual Pleasure and Narrative Cinema', that such reifying specularisation is a precursor to sadistic punishment.[39]

It is therefore no surprise that those who become self-aware of their place in the apparatus and question it are those necessarily informed, specifically, by the development of apparatus theory instigated by feminism. Potter's film *The Gold Diggers* (1981) figures this most thoroughly through Ruby, played by Julie Christie. Ruby is the female star as alchemical principle, the transformative stone that makes gold: she appears in the guise of the kohl-eyed silent film star, as a beret-wearing spy, as the fairytale heroine, belle of the ball, and—in reference to her role in *Dr Zhivago* (David Lean, 1965)—as a daughter struggling to remember her mother, prompted by her rescuer, a financial worker named Celeste (Colette Lafont). After the credits, a female voice—Ruby's, we will discover—intones a poem, which is repeated (with prepositions reversed) by Celeste:

I am born[e] in a beam of light.
I move continuously yet I am still.
I am larger than life, yet do not breathe.
Only in the darkness am I visible.
You can see me but never touch me
I can speak to you but never hear you
You can know me intimately, and I know you not at all
We are strangers and yet you take me inside of you.
What am I?
We have ninety minutes to find each other.

This reversal of the reverential/rapist desire (and the fear of exposure and penetration evinced by Eliot) projected by the subject of the apparatus onto the screen is expressed through a delicate and inventive translation of theoretical issues into film poetics, a strategy I employ in the 'star poems'.[40] In 'Star Power', a reflection on *The Gold Diggers*, Celeste responds to Ruby's challenge, not with references to images or events in the film, but by interrogating the astral eidolon: 'what | does a star wish on? || How does a star | turn itself on?', concluding, 'we are ghosts of it || fragments and pale | imitators, as stars are'.[41] As in *Helen in Egypt*, the impossible subject position of the female star as narrator of her own life

---

[39] Laura Mulvey, 'Visual Pleasure and Narrative Cinema', *Screen*, 16/3 (1975), 6–18.
[40] Sophie Mayer, *Her Various Scalpels* (Exeter: Shearsman, 2009), 13–26.
[41] Mayer, *Her Various Scalpels*, 21–2.

extends and inverts metaphors of stardom, marks an imitation into something that suggests the glittering frisson of filmic possibility for the feminist viewer, writer, and film-maker.

Kona MacPhee's 'My Life as a B Movie' mediates, through a mainstreamed and ironised version of feminist theory, between the filmic and cinematic, as well as between theoretical and affective responses.[42] References to 'heavily-foreshadowed, third-act fallings-out' use ironic reflexivity to shatter the ekphrastic account of a generic romantic comedy, and suggest the ways in which viewers, as identified by bell hooks, deploy a 'resistant' look, a sophisticated self-knowledge and cultural awareness while (not) enjoying a film.[43] Suspension of disbelief and negative capability, the tools employed by poets and film-makers to engage their audiences, are challenged by this self-awareness: the experience of cinematic viewing informs our reading experience, and vice versa. MacPhee's poem suggests a viewer who can deconstruct both poetic and film form but is still fighting her oppression by them, as it ends:

the spooling lines of credits rolling over me
like ripples on a pond in which I've drowned already
somewhere in another town, another movie.

This is a speaker who knows she is subject to projection, but/and therefore who *can* say what she means when her nerves are thrown on the screen.

So there is a possible mediation (or medium), and it appears primarily in the work of female poets, some of whom—such as Sascha Aurora Akhtar, Carolyn Jess-Cooke, Sharon Morris (whose poems frequently refer to films by her partner, Jayne Parker), and Cherry Smyth—also work as film-makers, curators, or critics. Caroline Bergvall interpolates cinema through a framework of performativity and embodiment in poems such as 'Hands on, Catullus', where Catullus' poem 101, about travel and grief, is reconfigured as a series of 'short files'. The second, 'On Distention', translates the mourning poet's aporia into a specific filmic evocation:

> A great many times I lose my hair from sheer déjà-vu, trying to escape the
> stairs are gigantic, shot in wide angle, sounds familiar only until it happens
> to you. (Lost a finger on the way out, found two as I was shutting the door.[44]

The referent, signalled as filmic by 'wide angle', is Maya Deren's *Meshes of the Afternoon* (1939), and the suggestion that this silent film 'sounds familiar' in its invocation shapes a particular audience for the poem, one versed in avant-garde American and/or feminist cinema. The poem suggests that the filmic déjà-vu is a distension of both loss and displacement, as well as a form of Catullus' funerary gift; in the film, Deren finds not a finger, but a key as she opens the door. The poem reads the film reading the poem.

---

[42] In Roddy Lumsden, *Best of British Poetry 2011* (Cromer: Salt, 2011), 67.
[43] bell hooks, *Black Looks: Race and Representation* (Boston: South End Press, 1999).
[44] Sinclair (ed.), *Conductors of Chaos*, 3.

Denise Riley, premier experimental poet of the visual field, imagines becoming film itself, yet mediates the ethereal implications of such signification for the female poet. In 'Lyrical', her 'vein | nets tracked as patted' echo Eliot's patterned nerves:

To be air or a black streak on air, or be silt.
Be any watery sheen threading brackish, or vein
nets tracked as patted under their skin glaze, running all ways.

The opening infinitive 'To be air or a black streak on air' is forcefully filmic, not only in the figuration of being an image projected through the air, but in its use of the infinitive as a phantasmatic imperative. The resolution of solid flesh into air is marked with dis-ease when

quartz needles shower from the cut mouth of the speaker
though the voice opens to fall:

If you can see me, look away
but swallow me into you.[45]

The second two lines are set as a separate stanza and italicized, an unsourced quotation reminiscent of Ruby's voice-over in *The Gold Diggers*, poured from a 'speaker', human or mechanical, or—in the era of cinema—the former always-already being the latter.

In the shower of needles, there is a needling echo of the shower scene in *Psycho*, paradigmatic instance of the undermining of the female voice. The 'cut mouth' applies both to the stab wounds on Marion Crane's body (echoed by her open, screaming mouth) and to the silencing of her voice by death, and by the soundtrack's elision of her screams into Bernard Herrmann's famous 'stabbing' violins. A quartz needle is used as a sensor in microscopy, turning sound vibrations into images. Sound and image collapse into each other in these lines in such a way as the reader has to pause the film rolling in her imagination. The voice opens not to *full* but to *fall*, the double 'll' repeated in 'swallow'. Eyes and mouth are again confused in what appear to be quoted lyrics: '*look away / but swallow me into you*'. This is highly suggestive of the process of film viewing, the 'dream of translucence' that Riley cites two lines later.

As Redell Olsen illuminates, Riley frequently addresses herself through both visual art and technology to both the modern and modernist.[46] Riley makes frequent reference to art-house cinema, citing Akira Kurosawa in 'The Castalian Spring'—a poem about the Muse—and quotes Jeanne Moreau's lines from *Les Valseuses* (aka *Going Places*, Bertrand Blier, 1974) in 'Dark Looks', whose title suggests the black market economy of the gaze enforced by cinema, and in which the lyric image now necessarily circulates.[47] Olsen herself has emerged as a film-maker as well as a poet, organizing the first UK

---

[45] Sinclair (ed.), *Conductors of Chaos*, 401.
[46] Redell Olsen, 'Postmodern Poetry in Britain', in Neil Corcoran (ed.), *The Cambridge Companion to Twentieth-Century English Poetry* (Cambridge: Cambridge University Press, 2008), 50.
[47] Denise Riley, *Selected Poems* (London: Reality Street Editions, 2000), 87, 74.

neo-benshi film-telling night for POLYply in September 2011, at which she performed a multimedia 'telling' of documentary footage of women industrial textile workers, a frequent referent for feminist cinema, including Potter's *Thriller* (1979), which located Mimi from *La bohème* as a textile homeworker living among artists.

Olsen's collection *secure portable space* includes the sequence 'corrupted by showgirls', its title corresponding to the poems' critical approach to the seductions of cinema both hymned and castigated by modernist male poets. The subject is the (often fatal) violent containment of the body (particularly and paradigmatically the female or feminized body) within the photographic or cinematic frame. As the final poem in the sequence shows, the body—even as it is framed in and by death—is resistant:

XVI

Dishonoured Marlene Dietrich (1931)

A spy clad in feathers, she goes to her death before a firing squad, after stopping
to reapply her make-up in the reflection of the sword of one
of her gaolers.[48]

The poem distorts and is distorted by the temporality of the film, flashing back from the final shot with a (sword) cut to the penultimate exchange. The lag induced and not quite covered up by the apparatus resides in the double meaning of 'before', implying that the anterior temporality of the character's life leading up to her final scene overrides her death.

It suggests that we, as spectators, are 'before' the screen in the same way: the violence of Barraclough's cinematic explosion is here arrested, deflected, and transfigured *by* the temporal play that the filmic enables. In reapplying her make-up, Dietrich draws attention to the status of cinema and the cinematic star as made-up: fictional, constructed, and exaggerated for effect. As Emily Critchley remarks in her poem 'Past Filmic Tense', 'the rules (of film noir) dictate that the female is predator even when | she is incidentally nature'.[49] The poem accords to her gesture the performative nature described by Judith Butler: this is a reflexive interval, taken up by the poem as it re-evaluates the filmic frame as a 'secure portable space' in which the star can 'make-up', that is compose or create the film, as the title accords radically authorship of *Dishonoured* to Dietrich rather than the film's director, Josef von Sternberg. Here, the cinematic and filmic are inverted, as Dietrich's star power becomes a formal and aesthetic practice within the frame. Rather than inviting nostalgia via a cinematic referent or for a pre-photographic innocence, 'corrupted by showgirls' connects cinema and its star to the museum (the star is '[b]orn a glass case for exhibiting valuable or delicate goods', much as Ruby in *The Gold Diggers* is born ethereally in a beam of light[50]), and suggests that cinema is as valuable and as critical a space for cultural self-reflection and intervention as the museum or gallery, and one that can be critiqued much as the museum has been by critical ethnographers,

---

[48] Redell Olsen, *secure portable space* (London: Reality Street Editions, 2004), 34.
[49] Emily Critchley, *Love / All That / & OK* (London: Penned in the Margins, 2010), 53.
[50] Olsen, *secure*, 32.

to draw attention to issues of framing, authenticity, authorship, and ownership. It also suggests that the intervention will arise not from the passively desiring spectator, but from the object of desire as she reclaims, however pyrrhically, her agency.

'At other times, in order to put myself across the footlights I have to imagine that I am a man who sews'.[51] 'corrupted' opens with a meditation on spectatorship that names the action of suture whereby the spectator is brought into the present of the film, and specifically its reliance on identification with the male protagonist, but also ironizes the feminizing association of masculinity and the domestic work of sewing. The sequence then goes on to undermine this claim through its bold re-vision of female bodies, and the feminization of the body, on screen, reflecting Dietrich in the blade of a sword. Olsen offers a way out of the male gaze and its mastery of vision—and beyond the radical feminist refusal of cinematic pleasure—through fragmentation, contradictory renarration that shifts point of view, and playful *mise en page* that disrupts expectations of the frame. By claiming an affinity with the object of desire as she is subject to the threat of violence (and as she repudiates it), Olsen suggests, as Riley does, that the power of filmic poetry is that (the ability to articulate) meaning arises in the pattern our nerves make on the screen.

Select Bibliography

Brady, Andrea, *Wildfire* (San Francisco: Krupskaya, 2010).
Critchley, Emily, *Love / All That / & OK* (London: Penned in the Margins, 2010).
Deleuze, Gilles, *Cinema 2: The Time-Image* (New York: Continuum, 2005).
Dillon, Steven, *Derek Jarman and Lyric Film: The Mirror and the Sea* (Austin: University of Texas Press, 2004).
Dixon, Isobel, *The Tempest Prognosticator* (Cromer: Salt Publishing, 2011).
Eliot, T. S., *The Waste Land: A Facsimile and Transcript of the Original Drafts including the Annotations of Ezra Pound* (London: Faber & Faber, 1971).
Gascoyne, David, 'Procession to the Private Sector: Surrealist Film Scenario, 1936–1982', in Michel Rémy (ed.), *David Gascoyne, ou l'urgence de l'inexprimé* (Nancy: Presses universitaires de Nancy, 1984), 157–74.
Harrison, Tony, *Collected Film Poetry* (London: Faber & Faber, 2007).
Hunter, Jefferson, *English Filming* (Bloomington: University of Indiana Press, 2010).
Jarman, Derek, *A Finger in the Fishes Mouth* (Bettiscombe: Bettiscombe Press, 1972).
Kane, Daniel, *We Saw the Light: Conversations between the New American Cinema and Poetry* (Iowa City: University of Iowa Press, 2009).
Lumsden, Roddy, *Best of British Poetry 2011* (Cromer: Salt, 2011).
Madden, Ed, *Tiresian Poetics: Modernism, Sexuality, Voice, 1888–2001* (Cranbury, NJ: Associated University Presses, 2008).
Mayer, Sophie, *Her Various Scalpels* (Exeter: Shearsman, 2009).
McCooey, David, *Outside* (Cromer: Salt Publishing, 2011).

---

[51] Olsen, *secure*, 9.

Menocal, María Rosa, *Shards of Love: Exile and the Origins of the Lyric* (Durham, NC: Duke University Press, 1993).
Minh-Ha, Trinh T., *Cinema Interval* (New York: Routledge, 1999).
Mulvey, Laura, 'Visual Pleasure and Narrative Cinema', *Screen*, 16/3 (1975), 6–18.
Neely, Sarah, ' "Ploughing a lonely furrow": Margaret Tait and "Professional" Filmmaking Practices in 1950s Scotland', in Ian Craven (ed.), *Movies on Home Ground: Explorations in Amateur Cinema* (Newcastle upon Tyne: Cambridge Scholars Press, 2009).
Olsen, Redell, *Secure portable space* (London: Reality Street Editions, 2004).
Olsen, Redell, 'Postmodern Poetry in Britain', in Neil Corcoran (ed.), *The Cambridge Companion to Twentieth-Century English Poetry* (Cambridge: Cambridge University Press, 2008).
Perril, Simon, *Nitrate* (Cambridge: Salt Publishing, 2010).
Reed, Jeremy, 'Far Out,' in Iain Sinclair (ed.), *Conductors of Chaos* (London: Picador, 1996), 400.
Riley, Denise, *Selected Poems* (London: Reality Street Editions, 2000).
Selerie, Gavin, *Roxy* (Hay-on-Wye: West House Books, 1996).
Selerie, Gavin, *Music's Duel* (Exeter: Shearsman, 2009).
Smith, Ali, 'The Margaret Tait Years', in Peter Todd and Benjamin Cook (eds.), *Subjects and Sequences: A Margaret Tait Reader* (London: LUX, 2004).
Stewart, Garrett, *Between Film and Screen: Modernism's Photo Synthesis* (Chicago: University of Chicago Press, 1999).
Tait, Margaret, *Subjects and Sequences* (Edinburgh: Interim Editions, 1960).
Trotter, David, *Cinema and Modernism* (Oxford: Blackwell, 2007).
Vertov, Dziga, *Kino-Eye* (Berkeley: University of California Press, 1984).

CHAPTER 17

SINGING SCHOOLS AND BEYOND: THE ROLES OF CREATIVE WRITING

PETER CARPENTER

THE year 1994 was one of some moment for 'creative writing': *Writing Poems* by Peter Sansom was published by Bloodaxe Books. A 'handbook' of lasting influence, it is an accessible and wise survey of creative writing and the age, a source of ideas for 'workshop techniques and writing games', and above all a spur to reading poetry 'from the inside'. In his introduction, Peter Sansom cites Keats to make a careful distinction in a debate central to this essay. He sets out his position by way of an assent ('In fact, I agree with those who think that no one can teach you how to write') followed by a qualification ('Keats's amazingly rapid development as a writer, though, is itself proof that people *can learn* to become better writers').[1] I will take his supporting quotation from a Keats letter a little further than Sansom does:

> I have written independently without Judgment. I may write independently, and with Judgment, hereafter. The Genius of Poetry must work out its own salvation in a man: It cannot be matured by law and precept, but by sensation and watchfulness in itself—That which is creative must create itself—In Endymion, I leaped headlong into the sea, and thereby have become better acquainted with the Soundings, the quicksands, and the rocks, than if I had stayed upon the green shore, and piped a silly pipe, and took tea and comfortable advice. I was never afraid of failure; for I would sooner fail than not be among the greatest.[2]

---

[1] Peter Sansom, *Writing Poems* (Newcastle upon Tyne: Bloodaxe Books, 1994), 7.
[2] John Keats to James Hessey, 9 Oct. 1818, *Letters of John Keats*, ed. Robert Gittings (Oxford: Oxford University Press, 1975), 156.

First, Keats stresses the subtlety and delicacy in the creative process ('sensation and watchfulness' rather than some rigid plan or set of universally applicable laws or rules) and, second, the daring involved ('the Soundings, the quicksands, and the rocks'), the need to risk and accept failure rather than staying safe and taking 'tea and comfortable advice'. Writing, the sort that proceeds beyond 'craft', the sort that costs not less than everything as Eliot puts it, for one's personal and professional life, does not necessarily blossom from 'comfortable advice'. It is uncomfortable if you attempt what Sansom puts at the heart of the business: '*saying genuinely what you genuinely need to say*'.

Another learning experience came to mind, as narrated by Ted Hughes:

> At quite close quarters I had watched Robert Lowell's writing classes transform Anne Sexton from a housewife who had written a few undistinguished lines but who wanted to learn how to write better, into a remarkable author able to express, overwhelmingly, all that she was... almost every young writer I met had worked—in just that 'apprentice' role—with some chosen 'master'.[3]

I remember reading Sansom's book avidly; its most important lessons to me were how vital the reading of contemporary poetry (informed and living reading) was to anyone who hoped to write meaningfully, to say genuinely what there was genuinely there to say. Many of the arguments concerning the institutional flourishing, the roles and potential worth of creative writing over the past fifty years or so in the UK and Ireland establish a false or simplistic fault-line between writing as something that can or cannot be taught (along a 'nature' versus 'nurture' dichotomy). These forget or do not want to recognize the intricacy and fragility of the learning experience for adults and children alike, the risks involved, the need to accept failure, for any learning. Further to this, there is an easy pigeonholing of 'creative writing' as something rather flimsily 'non-academic'; this does not want to remember the precepts that Sansom sees as vital: learning arising from the fruitful and needful reading of other poets. The writing exercises in Sansom's book, still 'alive', should be taken in the cast of his advice that a good workshop should have more discussion of 'published poets'. Again, qualifications: 'I don't mean as students to pass exams, and still less in the spirit of those old "poetry appreciation" classes. I want them to look at these poets as fellow practitioners, going to poems to further their own writing through developing new enthusiasms and exploring new procedures and perspectives.'[4] Nothing new here. T. S. Eliot, among others, was fond of Ben Jonson's distinctions concerning 'imitation':

> the third requisite in our poet or maker is imitation: to be able to convert the substance or riches of another poet to his own use... not as a creature that swallows what it takes in crude, raw or indigested, but that which feeds with an appetite, and hath a stomach to concoct, divide, and turn all into nourishment.[5]

[3] John Fairfax and John Moat, *The Way to Write* (London: Hamish Hamilton, 1981), p. xii.
[4] Sansom, *Writing Poems*, 66–7.
[5] T. S. Eliot, 'The Age of Dryden', in *The Use of Poetry and the Use of Criticism* (London: Faber & Faber, 1975), 53–5.

Michael Donaghy puts a new spin on Jonson's 'concoct, divide, and turn all into nourishment':

> Students sometimes enrol in poetry classes in order to learn what they take to be a series of formal rules for writing verse, so in my workshops I'm at pains to emphasise that there are no rules for writing poetry. Or rather there are innumerable sets of unforeseeable rules; imagine a game of chess incorporating all the known manoeuvres with their infinite permutations but add as legitimate moves licking the chess pieces one by one on the chessboard or slapping your opponent with a rubber chicken.[6]

Donaghy stresses the serious play involved; he has five rules (beyond his wonderfully acute advice to geniuses—'please stay at home and write your opus' if you don't want advice), the first of which is: 'READ IT...Literature is a conversation. You have to know what and how poets are writing before you enter that dialogue.' The greatest teachers of creative writing have in my experience been the wealthiest and most avid readers, not parading their knowledge, but allowing others into a dialogue with poems and poets, often flipped into a conversation, or as part of a 'you'd enjoy that' extra.

This chapter is intended neither as another 'guide' nor as a further essay in the chronicling of creative writing over the last fifty years or so in the UK. There are many excellent and comprehensive versions of both. Its focus is on poetry specifically, but sometimes it embraces broader notions of creativity (when examining the nature of 'workshops', for example, and the role of key organizations, such as the Arvon Foundation). It does, though, seek to address some of the central and attendant questions that often arise when the roles of creative writing are debated. I have approached these via a series of questions put in an interview with the poet and educator Anthony Wilson.[7]

First, some of the arguments put against the growth and importance of creative writing. In an article to mark the publication of Andrew Cowan's book *The Art of Writing Fiction* (London: Longman, 2011) we have, for example, Will Self's 'I'm still not convinced creative writing can be taught...I say, go and get a job, a fairly menial one instead. Otherwise what are you going to write about?...you need to autodidact.'[8] To have the experience so as not to miss the meaning. John Lucas plays brilliant devil's advocate in an article that ruefully considers the current 'propitious conditions' for creative writing:

> Adam Czerniawski once remarked 'we cannot at will increase the number of poets by organizing favourable conditions'. Such conditions are nowadays often taken to be a *sine qua non*, for the production of worthwhile poetry. Well, up to a point, Lord Copper. But it does make you wonder how they managed in earlier times. No Poetry School, no Arvon Foundation. Would Clare have been a better poet if he'd spent a week or so at Totleigh Barton? Which favourable conditions would have helped him? Of course, he shouldn't have been an impoverished farm labourer. But that's because

---

[6] Michael Donaghy, 'May I Make a Suggestion?', *Poetry London Newsletter*, 31 (Autumn 1998), 33.
[7] Interview conducted between 3 and 9 Oct. 2011.
[8] Will Self, 'Fantasy Fiction', *The Guardian* (10 May 2011, Education), 2.

nobody should be an impoverished farm labourer...Of course, he shouldn't have been locked up in a lunatic asylum...Of course, Clare deserved better than anything his editors were able or willing to do for him...Of course, of course. But for all that, he wrote those wonderful poems, poems, we had better remind ourselves, that were for a long while reckoned lower in the scale than those, for example, of Chauncy Hare Townshend or Martin Tupper or Eliza Cooke or P. J. Bailey or...[9]

Lucas's first point, as he reviews a recent anthology of verse, seems straightforward: do the right conditions (advice, online and otherwise, designated spaces conducive to writing, ease of access) actually promote 'worthwhile' poetry. (He then turns Czerniawski's questioning of the increase of 'the number of poets' to accommodate 'worthwhile'.) So, it is a question of 'value' (which 'gangs', to use Roy Fisher's terminology, promote and extoll the virtues, the worth of one poem or poet over another) and thereby an examination of the 'canon' in the light of such opportunities out there to help poets thrive. His 'up to a point' does not though take into account either enhancement for experience or art for an increased number, and puts posterity as a judge of worth via the (extreme) analogy of Clare. We might note any number of accomplished and 'worthwhile' poets (Simon Armitage, Carol Ann Duffy, Moniza Alvi, Alan Brownjohn, Wendy Cope, for example) who have acknowledged their debt to an Arvon experience. Lucas makes further qualifications, but then goes on to consider the publication and reception of poets who have marked out a career:

> it isn't difficult to bring together work by a vast number of people who claim to be poets. But then in any one year there are probably ten times that number staking such a claim as they enrol for or come to the end of creative writing courses throughout the UK. I have lost count of the number of submissions Shoestring Press has received from tyros who in their covering letters tell me that they have emerged from their MA in Creative Writing with good degrees, a sheaf of poems, and that their tutors think they are now ready for their first book.[10]

Lucas here highlights a problem in expectation, then a problem for editors and publishers: where do all these poets, or those 'staking such a claim', actually end up. He concludes thus: 'We are in a time when very different traditions don't so much compete for our attention as permit tolerant disregard of each other. I'm not sure that this is a good thing. As some poets are surely better than others, so some traditions are richer, even, I want to say, truer.'[11] The 'tolerant disregard' Lucas points to is a benign model of allowance; the editors and contributors of *Tears in the Fence* or *Fire* might not be too bothered about the output of *Poetry London*, for example, but their coexistence is a matter of importance in the spectrum, given the growth of the smallest presses into some of the largest and most influential arbiters of 'taste' or 'worth', as with Bloodaxe and Carcanet, for example. John Lucas's derision of the 'poet as careerist' path, and other well-aimed

[9] John Lucas, 'The Anthology Business', *The Dark Horse*, 25 (Summer–Autumn 2010), 22.
[10] Lucas, 'The Anthology Business', 22–3.
[11] Lucas, 'The Anthology Business', 27.

bricks should nevertheless make us ponder the end products of the democratic impulses behind courses.

Roy Fisher distinguishes between a misapprehension concerning Peter Robinson's poetry taken to be at the 'formalist end of the field' and what he terms an 'Official Verse Culture' out there.[12] Fisher is distinguishing between Robinson's verse and a perceived trend or mode in writing spawned by the courses that Lucas puts the skids under:

> This is a manner widely practised and published over several recent decades, in which the poems, hung from their titles, propose their occasions, anecdotes, locations or general topics in a disguised version of the way a lecturer will open a subject. There can be a wide range of personal tones in this poetry, from lyricism to near-bombast, but always the tell-tale defining signs are present. The work's mode of operation is to display, explain and, however subtly, to judge what it addresses itself to. The mode has the characteristics of an essay, even a paraphrase. 'Life' is written up, elevated a little way, into 'art' in a way that in the most popular instances gives the reader a sense of value received in return for the labour of reading. There will be decoration, a packaging of figures from what Stuart Mills called 'the bottomless school satchels of the metaphor-mongers'; but the Official Verse Culture depends mostly on an easy conversational style that has absorbed the relaxations, though not the excitements and constraints, of modernism. It is quite difficult to write badly in this idiom, and it's much used, prophylactically or curatively, in Creative Writing courses.

This is a terrible reminder of what is out there when people write in bad faith, when they 'write to order', when they forget the Peter Sansom maxim (*'saying genuinely what you genuinely need to say'*) and when tutors and editors and publishers do not spot the signs and tell the writers concerned, but it is a model that seems to apply to adult rather than school courses. An alternative model for the writing of poetry (writing honestly and trying to find the technical means to meet that honesty, leading readers towards a furtherance in self-knowledge and enjoyment of language) might be applied at any age level. Roy Fisher's healthy anarchic resistance to the shams of what can happen is also evident in his verse (for example in 'The Making of the Book' or 'A Modern Story') and it reminds us that the greatest and most lasting poetry is often a reaction against sterile or ill-conceived or outworn dictums, the mistakes of a previous generation. (With this in mind, note Fisher's aside on the 'excitements and constraints' of modernism being sidestepped.) And in his most recent collection *Standard Midland* even Basil Bunting's memorable and oft-reheated advice to young poets is turned on its head in *'Adjectives': the Novel; the Movie* in reaction to the opening of Bunting's fourth rule ('Fear adjectives; they drain nouns'). It opens thus: 'Defending more than defensive. Ill-equipped, formal, luxurious. Defending'.[13]

---

[12] Adam Piette and Katy Price (eds.), *The Salt Companion to Peter Robinson* (Cambridge: Salt Publishing, 2007), 23.

[13] Roy Fisher, *Standard Midland* (Tarset: Bloodaxe Books, 2010), 35.

The impulse and the reality behind the majority of writing courses are often very different and in itself a form of counter to the doubts and examples of bad faith and practice held up for derision by John Lucas and Roy Fisher. Put next to this an account of what Allison McVety experienced at her first Arvon, an 'Open' course, 'Starting to Write':

> In August 2004 and just three weeks after booking a place on an Arvon Residential course, I was on a bus and heading for a pre-Doomsday manor house in Devon.... As much as an Arvon poetry course is about the writing and reading of poems, it is also about finding a writing practice, about the suddenly real concept of having a life in writing. That first Arvon was the moment when I realised that this might be possible. It wasn't that I was suddenly writing any better, more that I had the map for how to write better poems. My first book, *The Night Trotsky Came to Stay*, began in 2004; not with the poems, but off the back of the poems I drafted and re-drafted at Arvon (although 'Helsinki' began in response to an exercise given by my tutors that week at Totleigh Barton and made the cut).
>
> And while the exercises were brilliant for stimulating ideas, it was the one-to-one sessions, those 30 minute gems with a tutor, looking at a poem, considering its merit and how to make it fly. I learned about line endings: to consider the effect of balance, whether to weight the end of a line, or weight the start, to turn a sentence on its head, to cut out the irrelevant, to let go sometimes, of the literal truth for the poem's own truth to come through, to discover that sometimes a poem begins or ends someplace else—maybe even three stanzas in from the current start. I heard poems much more acutely, learned when to step out and observe, and when to be in the thick of them.
>
> I became interested in recording the lives of my parents and lives of their parents as people rather at a distance to me, seeing them in their own right, giving them their teenage years back and the three Arvon courses I went on enabled me, to realise that ambition... Sometimes there is a tremendous joy in discovering just how irrelevant you are to the poem being written.
>
> Coming home exhausted, after the week, I was buzzing with poems and thoughts about writing better poems. And over the months and years after being on one of these courses, I'm still learning and putting into practice what I got from my tutors and fellow students.[14]

The significance of the experience ('about the suddenly real concept of having a life in writing') is matched by the leaps in learning ('there is a tremendous joy in discovering just how irrelevant you are to the poem being written') that render 'ego' redundant, allowing for a true voice of feeling. Here's the poem that McVety mentions; she comments on its genesis: 'This poem comes from my time as a technical trainer for an IT company. I went to Helsinki for most of December one year, when there was only three hours daylight and shortly after a report had been issued linking Finland's high suicide rates to the light deficiency and alcohol'. See what you think:

---

[14] Interview with Allison McVety, Oct. 2011; *The Night Trotsky Came to Stay* was shortlisted for the Forward Prize for Best First Collection.

Helsinki

It's four o'clock—someone's painted the sky
with bitumen. Snow pummels
the windscreen, we drive at 80 Km an hour,
wipers skating over thin ice: my driver
places too much faith in snow chains.

The dashboard says it's minus 20, I think
it's lying—breath can be sliced, even in cars.
When we stop I see lunatics gathering
in shirt-sleeves, huddled under the canopy
of a long moon, smoking roll-ups.

If I survive the journey I'll eat the herring
the waiter offers me in his ice-white coat
in the dining room; I'll drink water,
retire, listen to the sound
of people climbing walls.[15]

McVety's early poem reveals a control of craft; she subtly puts the reader in the back seat of the car with the private terrors. In the voiced trepidation and imagined near-misses, the diction astutely nudges towards, then moves away from, the safe recourses of cliché (the wipers 'skating over thin ice'; the sliced bread turned to 'breath' that 'can be sliced') and the poet avoids full rhymes and easy resolutions in sound patterns. Half-rhyme, consonance, and internal rhyme are used in a simultaneously playful and elusive way ('painted' and 'chains', 'huddled' and 'roll-ups', 'waiter' and 'water', for example) and the line endings are used to exploit surprises just around the corner ('painted the sky | with bitumen' and 'the canopy | of a long moon'). The vowel sound of 'ice' is echoed and played upon throughout ('drive...wipers...ice...minus...sliced' via the three heavy stresses on 'ice-white coat' through to 'retire' and 'climbing'). Clipped diction (as in the haunting and compacted last lines, with the hints of madness, of people 'going up the wall') and control of line length add to the mystery of the whole business and there are echoes, conscious or otherwise, of extras straight out of Prufrock 'in shirt sleeves', no longer lonely pipe-smokers leaning out of windows, but moon-canopied 'lunatics' huddled around their roll-ups. For this reader, McVety learns from the 'excitement and constraints of modernism' and the resultant poem is an example of apprentice work that is authentic and memorable, distinct from the mannered self-indulgences delineated in Fisher's model of 'Official Verse Culture'.

I asked Anthony Wilson how he would counter sceptics who doubted the importance or validity of creative writing courses in higher or adult education:

> I have a hunch that the liberal-humanist position, which says that through engaging with the creative writing of others learners come to understand, explore and

[15] Allison McVety, *The Night Trotsky Came to Stay* (Huddersfield: Smith/Doorstop, 2007), 42.

question the world and their place in it, and thus understand others better, could be under threat. This is not because CW is 'weaker' than other subjects, but because the territory it requires learners to explore is so deeply contested. I do believe young people want meaning and direction in their lives. In an age of secular relativism will courses which necessarily explore that very relativism be seen to be equipping learners for a world in which people fly planes into buildings? We are more secular than ever before, but also more extreme, or fundamentalist, as we have got used to saying. What does CW have to offer learners from non-traditional backgrounds or first generation university entrants? In an increasingly competitive HE marketplace all courses are going to have to think about their 'widening participation' practices—how does CW engage with this, and will this mean a shift in ethos, in pedagogic approaches and content?

The endangered 'liberal-humanist' position that Anthony Wilson cites, underpins many of the experiences that we might have to quantify in the future to guarantee their very existence. For example, the term 'singing schools' in the title arose on the first school Arvon trip I took in 1994 during a conversation with the teacher and writer Michael Baldwin. (Maybe we had in our minds Heaney's 'Singing School' and behind that, Yeats's injunction to Irish poets in 'Under Ben Bulben' to 'sing what is well made'). We were trying, without much success, to think of historical equivalents for the process, the formula that Arvon had come up with, that prompted the 'magic' of the experience for our students. One of the major problems for those who advocate the teaching of creative writing is this elusive nature of the creative process. Talking to a well-known figure in the field of 'well-being', the argument eventually centred upon how creative writing could be 'measured' as an experience and in its effects, to convince governments of its value. The answers come over in individual accounts and lifelong memories and learning adaptations. Those controlling budgets and ideologies, those keen on targets, those who want to be convinced by measures of 'achievement' in learning that need 'assessment objectives' to be drummed into systems of teaching and judgement are not likely to be convinced by statements such as this one from Ted Hughes: 'the slightly mesmerised and quite involuntary concentration with which you make out the stirrings of a new poem in your mind'.[16]

The week back in 1994 was revelatory and its impact lasting. The guest reader was Hughes himself, whose *Poetry in the Making* (Faber 1967), based around talks broadcast by the BBC from 1961 to 1965, was an early landmark in the evolving story of how creative writing is taught and perceived in the UK. Arvon courses themselves began as a reaction to a perceived problem in the teaching of poetry; the very first courses were aimed at children and specifically to counter a dry-as-dust and potentially murderous dissection of poems in schools. Also, to find a 'space' that was not in a school. The impact on those concerned was often life-changing. Nick Stimson, now a poet, educator, theatre administrator, was on the first course:

---

[16] Ted Hughes, *Poetry in the Making* (London: Faber & Faber, 1967), 17.

> When we got back to Crediton total shell-shock set in for all three of us, we wandered about the streets not wanting to go home...I think it had been a rather shattering experience. What would we now do back home since we weren't the same people. We had been called on to write as if writing mattered—and for the first time someone hadn't just put a tick or a mark at the bottom of one's writing. I think what was shattering was that suddenly *everything* mattered.[17]

The key lies in this: 'we had been called on to write *as if writing mattered*'. So, a living line was established between the person tutoring and reading the work beyond the functionary 'tick or a mark at the bottom of one's writing'. And yet teachers at GCSE, for example, are still called upon to do just the latter, to reduce something that 'matters' to a mark out of 20 with a series of gradations from a 'starred A' down.

Looking to the future, a second related question I asked Anthony Wilson was what he saw as the biggest challenges facing those teaching creative writing (poetry) over the next decade:

> Creative Writing (CW), like everything else in education, faces questions of 'usefulness'. These are only going to intensify over the next decade. This is not because CW is inherently weak, it is a sign of increasing instrumentalisation of education in all sectors. The people teaching CW (and poetry within that) are therefore faced with the challenge of making strong rationales with which to defend their subject and their practice. The liberal-humanist defence has long been made use of; I wonder if this will continue to be enough. One area I see potential conflict is in that of assessment. With student fees rising we are going to see a more litigious culture in HE than ever before. Students will consciously and actively demand better teaching and good grades. How CW fares in this new context will be interesting to watch.

The growth of influence and changes in direction for Arvon from its founding in 1968 up to the present day, especially the steer towards 'Open' courses for adults, is worth reference. As a further counter to Lucas's polemic, Alan Brownjohn offers the value of the course in the consequent release that they allowed to 'people of all ages and classes from workplaces and families and the general routines of their other, perhaps, less creative, lives'.[18] The movement from creative writing out of the margins, viewed with ill-disguised suspicion by some academic institutions, is another strand to be monitored as it moves into primary, secondary, and higher education, with a particular boom in universities after pioneering courses at the University of East Anglia (UEA) and the University of Warwick. By 2007 David Morley's *The Cambridge Introduction to Creative Writing* had comprehensively charted his journey 'from a position of scepticism' to the confident statement that 'Creative writing can be taught'. He goes on: 'Once upon a time it was taught through the writing and speaking exercises embedded in rhetoric and the dramatic arts. We lost this, but have created a second chance.'[19] From such a viewpoint 'The Questioner

---

[17] John Moat, *The Founding of Arvon* (London: Frances Lincoln, 2005), 34.
[18] Alan Brownjohn, 'Early Arvon: The Formative Years', *Poetry Review*, 100/2 (Summer 2010), 58.
[19] David Morley, *The Cambridge Introduction to Creative Writing* (Cambridge: Cambridge University Press, 2007), 252.

who sits so sly,'[20] who doubts the whole business (of that 'hit or miss chance of starting somebody off on a new feeling about themselves, which might be illusory... which might even—horror!—fix them in a determination to become writers') might be accommodated or countered in argument and practice. A democratic theory ('a space given to people of all ages and classes', as Brownjohn puts it) has still to rub shoulders with vestiges of hierarchical expectations and structures in assessment. These were built into the history of creative writing university courses of 'master and apprentice' or experience meeting raw enthusiasm. Writing about the genesis of workshops, reflecting on the UEA model, Jon Cook puts it like this:

> the workshop was essentially a place where an experienced writer might help others less experienced. The analogy was with a masterclass. Dedicated writers learnt from other equally dedicated but more experienced writers about their limits and potentials. The focus of the writing workshop was not the writing exercise, but the exposure of an individual writer's work to detailed scrutiny...[21]

This is not a new idea: one only has to think of that living interrelation between one writer and another that Eliot admired in Jonson's model of imitation, of Pound editing Eliot, Frost advising Thomas, the collaborating poets of The Group, or the flourishing of both writing and reading groups in the UK and Ireland today. Cook goes on to discuss 'the ideal of democratic participation... against the ideal of a master class, a place where a new generation of significant writers finds its voice'.[22] The Questioner, akin to John Lucas, then asks: 'Do we want or need more poets?' A response might have to be political in its implications. I agree with David Morley: 'Creativity is partly a birthright in that it rests in everyone as a potential, as a version of human freedom, of our possibility.'[23] In his preface to an anthology of a decade of writing at the University of Warwick, featuring over sixty writers who have gone through 'The Practice of Poetry' course, Morley stresses the importance of created spaces for writers of poetry. He also rebuffs the world/book dichotomy and turns the autodidact argument on its head. He looks to the future, a commitment to the importance of interdisciplinary communities. The play of science and poetry provides a pivotal example:

> The natural world makes the poetry of this planet. For me, the study of natural history is one way of looking at the earth's poems. In negotiation with young poets, the poetry workshop evolved over years to reflect the ways we engage with the world. I have always thought of an empty page as open space. Poets sometimes need to find open spaces in which to write, in which to ignite language and listen to the world. Writing is an act of community. Writing on your own is lonely but effective, but writing in a group has advantages too, not least the *esprit de corps* that comes from being in a creative community. It's not just a question of company. Where we write

[20] Ted Hughes, 'Preface', *The Way to Write*, p. xiv.
[21] Jon Cook, *The Creative Writing Coursebook* (London: Macmillan, 2001), 298.
[22] Cook, *The Creative Writing Coursebook*, 299.
[23] Morley, *The Cambridge Introduction to Creative Writing*, 258.

affects how we write. A stanza is a room. Seminar rooms are fine, but you can't play many games in them or listen to birds calling through birches.[24]

David Morley's *The Cambridge Introduction to Creative Writing* is dedicated 'to teachers' and he, with many other educators and writers, has worked hard to set up a 'legacy', a word already hijacked by the promotional industry. Bearing in mind, Morley's statement ('Writing is an act of community'), I asked Anthony Wilson what kind of an impact he thought new technologies for writing and reading are having/will have, for better or worse:

> The advent of eBooks is going to make it easier for some people to publish a book and reach an audience and even sell than ever before. Whether this is a good thing (more democratic, etc), I don't know. Writers are going to become more responsible for selling their 'product', like mini-businesses. There will be more of everything, and the already small 'mainstream' space for attention to poetry in the shape of reviews and discussion will shrink. In the less regulated space (i.e. blogs, slams, community events) it will expand. Writers and poets are going to have to get used to being hybrid—living and moving between these two spaces and audiences.

Wilson's almost term 'hybrid-living' is fascinating when one considers recent advocacies for ingrained and prevalent social networking methods (Facebook and Twitter, for example) as potential models for writing.

In another of the more valuable, well-judged, and enduring guides to secondary school teaching (enduring, because it is not knotted into a series of bureaucratic assessment objectives from a short-lived curricular initiative), Cliff Yates interviews Peter and Ann Sansom; Peter Sansom gets to the heart of 'why I want people to write':

> because they'll understand something which is very simple and very fundamental but which is very difficult to believe if you haven't experienced it. The difference is not looking at the poem from the outside, like a finished artefact, but from the inside. It's a living thing, not part of the canon of English literature. The advantage of having a writer in the classroom is that the writer has got time to read poems, has been changed by the reading of poems and understands them from a practitioner's point of view, rather than as a critic or examiner.[25]

Both Peter and Ann have talked with me about affinities between their writing workshops and other gatherings that aim at spiritual enlightenment (such as Quaker meetings, for example). Anthony Wilson had this to say on the subject:

> There are affinities, of course. As Don Paterson said once, anyone that denies the spiritual dimension of writing poems is just not facing up to the truth. The affinities are varied and multi-layered. There is ritual involved (you pass round poems, you

---

[24] David Morley, *Dove Release: New Flights and Voices* (Tonbridge: Worple Press, 2010), 8.
[25] Cliff Yates, *Jumpstart: Poetry in the Secondary School* (London: The Poetry Society, 2004), 105.

talk, you discuss, you write, you feedback, an 'expert' in the room gives blessing—or not); people enter silence together, and emerge from it slightly different from how they went in; people have the opportunity for discussing and presenting material that really matters to them; plus there is a kind of contract involved: I would baulk at the idea of a priestly function, but nevertheless as a workshop leader you are implicitly inculcating participants into a new way of thinking and seeing and behaving. That is very similar to more explicitly religious practice. I see services/gatherings and workshops as parallel to each other in terms of practice, even though their function and purpose is different. This is not fanciful. It is intensely social, which is why participants make such rapid progress at workshops in my experience.

So from Wilson's response, there are a number of further considerations: the notions of texts as 'living things'; Wilson's emphasis on the 'intensely social ... spiritual' dimensions to workshops; and the inculcation of those at workshops 'into a new way of thinking and seeing and behaving', given the rituals of such events. And an attendant issue is how far future government policies will allow such arguments to affect assessment policy; when 'product' rather than the educational value of process comes first, the concern for poems to be experienced as 'living things' is imperilled.

I come at this chapter from the position of a teacher of creative writing in secondary and higher education, publisher and editor, and poet; someone who has had the good fortune to work closely with and learn from good practice, as well as highly skilled practitioners (David Morley, Peter and Ann Sansom, Anthony Wilson, Michael Donaghy, for example) and I have thus allowed myself to be a pupil or 'apprentice'. I have also had the chance to witness the impact of creative writing courses on young people and adults in a variety of contexts. In 1993 I went on an Arvon Foundation Writing Course at Totleigh Barton, Devon. I had written, mostly poetry, from an early age and through university, but had then lost confidence in it and had sidelined it, however much it nagged. I had been a teacher for thirteen years, but nothing prepared me for the initial terror and excitement of reading out in front of the group, of showing work to the two tutors (Kathleen Jamie and Sean O'Brien) or the rush of being liberated by a week (a whole week) of writing workshops and reading and talk. The fear factor that Allison McVety talks of needs to be experienced by teachers if they are going to be able to provide 'living' reading and writing experiences in poetry for their students.

Arvon represents a 'community of feeling': this was what I wanted to do and where I belonged. I had to know one thing: to continue, or forget it. The tutors allowed me to continue, gave me a well-managed 'yes, but...'. Thus followed years of shaping work, immersing myself in reading, allowing material to gestate, rejecting most of it, then sending it out to publish. It was, though, that initial jump which kicked it off. Going back to Arvon to teach was a privilege. In 1994 I took the first of our annual trips to Devon with a fellow teacher (Richard Evans, a Poetry Society 'Poetry Teacher Trailblazer') and a group of apprentice writers: the work they produced astonished us. Our Arvon anthology last year had an editorial written by one of the students that stresses the sanctity of this new-found environment and reinforces David Morley's observations on the nature of the 'space': 'Arvon is unique. It sounds clichéd, doesn't it? However, it is far removed from any cynicism. It is fair to say that getting over a dozen teenage boys to happily inhabit a place with no TV, no internet or even mobile phone signal is no mean feat.'[26] Here then is a view that resists the 'more of everything' media influx.

Also, very often, the writing journeys started by such funded and fostered 'spaces', such equations between the world and the poem, start educational journeys for those concerned as they themselves allow others such experiences. Such journeys of mentoring proceed backwards and forwards from reading itself towards a search for new perspectives, different ways in and out of reading. As Ted Hughes puts it, 'far-reaching inner changes, creative revelations of our inner self, the only part of us with any value, are usually triggered in the smallest fraction of time. The operations of the inner life are more analogous to microbiology than to the building of a motorway.'[27] Such triggers, the intensities of workshops, time limits, found spaces, new communities, also inform the restraints of workshops themselves. Form is meaning: what might be seen as initial restraints (in form or time) very often liberate. A time limit provides pressure but removes anxiety: no one is expected to produce a great work in a matter of minutes, but often, for this reason, the germ of something special emerges. And to write poems, students of any age need to read them. Workshops are sustained by models of 'good practice' that range from Anglo-Saxon kennings to 'The Rime of the Ancient Mariner' to Benjamin Zephaniah's 'Body Talk'. Creative writing is creative reading: imitation and influence are allies. Seamus Heaney puts it thus:

> In practice...you hear something in another writer's sounds that flows in through your ear and enters the echo-chamber of your head...in such a way that your reaction will be—'Ah, I wish I had said that, in that particular way'. This other writer, in fact, has spoken something to you, something you recognize instinctively as a true sounding of aspects of yourself and your experience. And your first steps as a writer will be to imitate, consciously or unconsciously, those sounds that flowed in, that in-fluence.[28]

On the subject of reading, a secondary and major impact of changes in thinking about how poetry could be taught came in the evolution of poetry textbooks from the late 1960s and early 1970s. Many still stand up to the best of those being produced today, and certainly eclipse those tied to forms of assessment. The marvellous Touchstones series, *Poetry Workshop*, *Starting-Points*, *Words*, for example, were encouraged by editors, academics, and teachers (David Holbrook, B. A. Pythian, Michael and Peter Benton, Geoffrey Summerfield, for example) who encouraged 'experimentation' among English teachers, and a move away from dulling methodology and examination-driven analysis and assessment. One of the many exceptional features of these books was the new learning in contemporary poetry that challenged and informed both students and teachers.

---

[26] Paul Merchant, *Dreams of the Blue Whale* (Tonbridge: Tonbridge School, 2010), 2.
[27] Fairfax and Moat, *The Way to Write*, p. xv.
[28] Seamus Heaney, 'Feeling into Words', in *Preoccupations: Selected Prose 1968–1978* (London: Faber & Faber, 1980), 44.

Teachers could come across good poems by Tony Connor, Brian Jones, Miroslav Holub, Ferlinghetti, Peter Porter, Edwin Morgan, Alan Ross, and Edwin Brock, for example, alongside Shakespeare, Frost, or Keats. There was a democratic and thought-provoking rubbing of shoulders between old and new that provided models for an increasing number of opportunities for other anthologies (*The Rattle Bag* edited by Hughes and Heaney in 1982; *The School Bag*, 1997; *Staying Alive*, 2002, *Being Alive*, 2004; *Emergency Kit*, ed. Shapcott and Sweeney, 2004; *Being Human*, 2011). From the introduction to one of these texts we have a warning to teachers: 'A final word: poems cannot be written on demand and we would emphasise that in using the Creative writing sections teachers should encourage discussion of our suggestions and not present them to the class as "exercises" which must be completed.'[29]

This echoes a much older cry concerning our freedoms and poetry, freedoms that are possible by a guardianship of language, rather than a mainstream state-funded coerciveness. Here are some of Shelley's words from his *Defence of Poetry* (1821): 'Poetry is not like reasoning, a power to be exerted according to the determination of the will. A man cannot say, "I will compose poetry." The greatest poet even cannot say it; for the mind in creation is as a fading coal, which some invisible influence, like an inconstant wind, awakens to transitory brightness.' We need to balance new-found freedoms, writing spaces, and communities, with the imposition of methods or structures 'according to the determination of the will'. We can look back to 1940 with the University of Iowa's Writer's Workshop, working from the initial premise of 1896 to 'teach Verse Making', to George Baker's 47 workshop at Harvard from 1906 to 1925, or indeed to Aristotle's Poetics in Athens from 384–322 BC, but we should beware the state demanding poetry at will, the poem to praise the tyrant for any future Mandelstam. Equally there is the 'whole web of attitudes' that lead to easy dismissal of creative writing as a subject, a prompt, a discipline. Ted Hughes puts it thus:

> the usual English response to the idea of the American Creative Writing class. I had met it too often to doubt it...almost inevitably, dismissive, and usually derisive as well...a whole web of attitudes—commonly secreted but rarely interrogated—which all seem to share one decisive accent, and it is a negative accent: negative towards any deliberate cultivation of excellence, negative towards the methodical release of creative energy, negative towards enthusiasm, negative towards the future.[30]

With such a perilous balancing act in mind, I put two final questions to Anthony Wilson. First, how important was it that current and future governments backed the teaching of creative writing via policy and grants:

> I'm not so sure about this one. I think if a university/institution knows what it is doing, and the CW staff there are confident in the rationales they use to teach it, CW in HE will survive very well. I'm more anxious about small magazines, presses, arts

---

[29] *Touchstones 1* (London: Hodder and Stoughton, 1968), p. x.
[30] Fairfax and Moat, *The Way to Write*, p. xii.

organisations and festivals (NAWE, The Poetry Trust) who need government money. They need active support, there is no question of that. We are not a civilised society without them.

And last, whether there was a danger of creative writing becoming too mainstream and losing its 'alternative' appeal:

> Possibly, yes. But in the end the power and scope of poetry is determined by individual poets and how far they are prepared to make it happen in their lives, as Heaney says. Auden tells us poetry is a 'way happening, a mouth'—this is in no one's control but the poets. This won't change, whatever the economic situation, whatever the policy of the government of the day. Continuing to make it happen is up to us. Being a poet, or rather, committing to the art-form of poetry, like religion, should be something that sets you free. But you need to commit to it daily. Everything else is noise.

This seems the right place to end. The threats to 'a civilised society', a state where everything 'is noise' set against a liberating commitment to poetry as an art form, the way of happening: it is in 'no one's control but the poets'—and their readers.

Select Bibliography

Bell, Julia, and Magrs, Paul (eds.), *The Creative Writing Coursebook* (London: Macmillan, 2001).
Brownjohn, Alan, 'Early Arvon: The Formative Years', *Poetry Review*, 100/2 (Summer 2010).
Casterton, Julia, *Creative Writing: A Practical Guide* (3rd edn., London: Palgrave Macmillan, 2005).
Eliot, T. S., 'The Age of Dryden', in *The Use of Poetry and the Use of Criticism* (London: Faber & Faber, 1975).
Fairfax, John, and Moat, John, *The Way to Write* (London: Hamish Hamilton, 1981).
Heaney, Seamus, *Preoccupations: Selected Prose 1968–1978* (London: Faber & Faber, 1980).
Hughes, Ted, *Poetry in the Making* (London: Faber & Faber, 1967).
Koch, Kenneth, *Wishes, Lies and Dreams: Teaching Children to Write Poetry* (New York: Chelsea House, 1970).
Lamotte, Anne, *Bird by Bird: Instructions on Writing and Life* (New York: Barnes and Noble, 1994).
McVety, Allison, *The Night Trotsky Came to Stay* (Huddersfield: Smith/Doorstop, 2007).
Merchant, Paul, *Dreams of the Blue Whale* (Tonbridge: Tonbridge School, 2010).
Moat, John, *The Founding of Arvon* (London: Frances Lincoln, 2005).
Morley, David, *The Cambridge Introduction to Creative Writing* (Cambridge: Cambridge University Press, 2007).
Morley, David (ed.), *Dove Release: New Flights and Voices* (Tonbridge: Worple Press, 2010).
Roffey, Monique (ed.), *Young Writers' Apprenticeships 2004/5* (Tonbridge: Worple Press, 2005).
Sansom, Peter, *Writing Poems* (Newcastle upon Tyne: Bloodaxe, 1994).
Wilson, Anthony, 'Finding a Voice? Do Literary Forms Work Creatively in Teaching Poetry Writing?', *Cambridge Journal of Education*, 37/3 (2007), 441–57.
Wilson, Anthony, 'Teachers' Conceptualisations of the Intuitive and the Intentional in Poetry Composition', *English Teaching: Practice and Critique*, 9/3 (2010), 53–74.

Wilson, Anthony (ed.), *Creativity in Primary Education* (2nd edn., Exeter: Learning Matters, 2009).

Wilson, Anthony, and Hughes, Sian (eds.), *The Poetry Book for Primary Schools* (London: The Poetry Society, 1998).

Yates, Cliff, *Jumpstart: Poetry in the Secondary School* (London: The Poetry Society, 2004).

PART III
POETRY IN PLACES

CHAPTER 18

HISTORICAL AND ARCHAEOLOGICAL: THE POETRY OF RECOVERY AND MEMORY

HEATHER O'DONOGHUE

A surprising number of British and Irish poets in the twentieth and twenty-first centuries have looked back to the medieval past in a 'Northern' British or Irish setting. I shall argue that this specific intersection of time and place—what Bakhtin has called a chronotope—forms the basis of a distinct tradition of difficult, allusive, and essentially nationalist poetry.

The medieval past cannot of course be actually remembered by contemporary poets, but can be recovered or memorialized by a poet's learned knowledge of Anglo-Saxon history or Old Norse myth, though allusions to them may be perceived as somewhat arcane, or highbrow. An extension of such textual engagement is the technique of imitating, and sometimes debunking, past literary traditions. And voices given to bog bodies, or mythical beings, or historical figures of the Middle Ages, may simply 'bring the past to life', as the cliché has it, but may also function as a highly irreverent expression of continuity, with the implicit assumption that human nature is not susceptible to historical change—especially if the speakers are given an aggressively contemporary idiom. More directly, poets may evoke the past, and its relationship with the present, through descriptions of the archaeology of landscape; of material remains, or assemblages of grave goods; and, of course, of bodies buried in the earth. Place names, and etymologies—words themselves as historical, quasi-material objects—and even the physical textuality of actual vellum manuscripts, provide evidence for, and therefore routes back into, an imagined past which may then be re-created and repeopled.

One can trace this tradition from its most recent practitioners, which this essay will be primarily concerned with, back through the twentieth century. Ted Hughes and Seamus

Heaney have of course been highly influential, most particularly in their (very different) takes on the part played by the Vikings in the histories of 'Northern' England and Ireland. Heaney's volume *North* (1975) is a celebrated, and much-discussed, instance, in which he relates Viking violence to the Troubles in the North of Ireland. In *Wodwo* (1967) and *Remains of Elmet* (1979) Hughes repeatedly alludes to Viking ferocity, finding its modern counterpart in contemporary vandals. Basil Bunting in *Briggflatts* (1966) and Geoffrey Hill in *Mercian Hymns* (1971) interweave characters from the Anglo-Saxon kingdoms of Northumbria and Mercia with semi-autobiographical scenes from their own childhoods. In less personal terms, Hugh MacDiarmid and David Jones both turned to Old Norse myth in their pursuit of the ineffable. MacDiarmid deploys the two great cosmic symbols of Old Norse myth—the World Tree, Yggdrasill, and the World Serpent, the Miðgarðsormr—to represent the idea, or metaphysical concept, which can never be fully grasped. In 'A Drunk Man Looks at the Thistle' (1926), the tree, ironically figured as a thistle, is the mysterious link between real and ideal worlds; elsewhere—in 'To Circumjack Cencrastus' (1930), for instance—the serpent is the big fish which it would be catastrophic actually to land.[1] Throughout his work, David Jones uses the Cross upon which Christ was crucified as a sign parallel to and encompassing Yggdrasill, transcending historical and cultural difference.

Hugh MacDiarmid's concern with the competing claims of Scandinavian and Celtic ethnicities for the national origins of Scotland is insistently played out in his poetry, and David Jones saw, at least in the early part of the First World War, what he calls 'the genuine tradition of the Island of Britain'[2] being borne by the working-class soldiers he stood with; this 'genuine tradition'—with its admixture of Old Norse elements—informs both *In Parenthesis* (1937) and *The Anathémata* (1952). In fact, the tradition of recovering or re-creating a united past for the British Isles stretches even further back to poets like Thomas Gray, whose great unfinished magnum opus was an anthology of poetry encompassing Anglo-Saxon, Norse, and Celtic verse, or William Blake, who used Old Norse myth and literature extensively in his elaborate creation of a mythic prehistory of Albion. Such intersections of history, myth, and nationalist politics remain a recurrent theme in contemporary poetry.

The tradition of recovering the past through written text, that is, through literature, history, and myth, is most obviously exemplified in W. H. Auden's work. Auden came to Old English and Old Norse at university, and even earlier, the books in his father's library formed his literary tastes.[3] In spite of his celebrated trip to Iceland, Auden's poetry is not dominated by a specific chronotope. Rather, he refuses direct engagement with an actual time and space. His allusions are literary and philological. Humphrey Carpenter has claimed that the *Oxford English Dictionary* came to be 'the chief ideological work on which he based his poems', and he chose it as his one essential 'Desert

---

[1] See Heather O'Donoghue, '*Miðgarðsormr*', *Archipelago*, 3 (Spring 2009), 20–31.

[2] David Jones, *In Parenthesis* (London: Faber & Faber, 1937), p. x.

[3] See Sveinn Haraldsson, '"The North begins inside"': Auden, Ancestry and Iceland', in Andrew Wawn (ed.), *Northern Antiquity* (Enfield Lock: Hisarlik Press, 1994), 255–84.

Island' book, as if his engagement with language itself were mediated through texts.[4] His long poem, *The Age of Anxiety* (1947), though set in a New York bar near closing time, is actually a reworking of the Old Norse myth of Ragnarök,[5] and his many translations of Old Norse poetry, and imitations of Old English and Old Norse metres and poetic diction, may be best seen as part of the same academic, or literary, engagement with a textual past. Amongst others, Paul Muldoon has continued a tradition—now sometimes termed postmodernist—of a purposefully ahistorical, freewheeling textual playfulness; it is perhaps significant that two poems of Muldoon's, 'Yggdrasill' (*Quoof*, 1983) and 'Rune' (*Hay*, 1998), both play on the obscurity and arcane nature of Norse myth, and its capacity to destabilize or even erase meaning: the message at the top of Yggdrasill, the mythical tree of wisdom, is empty, and the runic stave resists explanation.

There is a distinct line of descent from all these poets to a group of poets writing today in what is recognizably the same tradition, whether textual or ostensibly observational. Poets do not appear and publish in neat succession, but I intend to consider in turn, in roughly chronological order, the work of Pauline Stainer, Kathleen Jamie, Andrew Waterhouse, Ian Duhig, Don Paterson, and Robin Robertson. Not all of the work of these poets—and in some cases, in fact, rather little of it—can be classed as poetry of recovery and memory. But for some of them it is a dominant concern, and in others, sporadic or even isolated recourse to particularly memorable or central facets of it will be enough to justify their inclusion in the group. I will conclude with a brief consideration of the work of Lavinia Greenlaw and Peter Reading, as striking counter-examples.

The recollection of the past in the present is a constant theme in the poetry of Pauline Stainer. Her debt to David Jones is evident throughout, not only in the dense allusiveness of her work (more than one reviewer has agreed with Kevan Johnson that 'one could ask for more clues',[6] and David Morley has explicitly compared her to David Jones and Geoffrey Hill in precisely this respect[7]) but also in the insistently religious themes and lexis she uses. In her first collection, *The Honeycomb* (1989), 'Flora in Calix-light' references the title of a watercolour by David Jones, with the religious symbol of the chalice—the flowery 'calix' of the title—as its central focus. Stainer sees the chalice as radiant with religious significance, and makes a characteristic link with the past: after all, she asks,

did not the Saxon king
in the ship-burial
suffer ten silver bowls
chased with crosses
at his shoulder?[8]

---

[4] Humphrey Carpenter, *W. H. Auden: A Biography* (Boston: Houghton Mifflin, 1981), 419.
[5] See Heather O'Donoghue, 'Owed to Both Sides: W. H. Auden's Double Debt to the Literature of the North', in David Clark and Nicholas Perkins (eds.), *Anglo-Saxon Culture and the Modern Imagination* (Woodbridge: D. S. Brewer, 2010), 51–69.
[6] *Times Literary Supplement* (23 June 1995), 30.
[7] *The Guardian* (22 Nov. 2003).
[8] Pauline Stainer, *The Honeycomb* (Newcastle upon Tyne: Bloodaxe Books, 1989), 44.

The religious symbol transcends any one particular faith: the unnamed Saxon king in the Sutton Hoo ship burial (the focus of a sequence, 'Little Egypt', in *Parable Island*, a later collection by Stainer) may well have been a pagan ruler who recognized the power of Christianity. In 'The Blood-spoor' a bright trail of blood across the landscape leads the speaker again to a Saxon past, to a ploughed field which looks 'As if the Saxon princes | Had cast their clay-quilt', even though ironically the action of the plough has almost obliterated the burial mound on the hillside.[9] 'Figures in a Landscape' also uses the image of a patchwork, fabric landscape: Stainer's eponymous figures, a mysterious 'king and queen', focalize the world for the reader—'You can see the landscape through their eyes'—and from their dreamy perspective it is 'wide, green-folded', the work of human hands.[10] But who are these strange figures? It is never made clear. They are witnesses to the past in both senses, and have stood the test of time; stubble burning has not diminished them, and 'an assayer's fire' will only enhance them. They are themselves part of the landscape—her 'silver-torque' is a snail's trail; their crowns are 'field-garlic'. They have 'bronze cheek-bones'—are they monumental brasses?—but their limbs are 'lichened', like ancient stone statues or megaliths. Perhaps they are idols erected and worshipped in past ages, and what endures is not their physical entities, but their mythic significance.

Stainer's ultimately mythic world is more a timeless spatial *imaginaire* than any actual chronotope. As John Greening has said of *The Lady and the Hare*, Stainer's 2003 collection of new and selected poems, 'we never really leave the mind and imagination of Pauline Stainer'.[11] The title sequence from *The Ice-Pilot Speaks* (1994) opens with deceptively specific indications of time and place: 'It is Ascension Week' (but the religious calendar is cyclic rather than chronologically linear) in *'ultima thule'*—the very far North, somewhere beyond the actuality of the map.[12] The graphic realization of an icy world dominates this sequence, countering the vagueness of mythic time. The sequence is a tissue of allusions to various journals of Arctic and indeed Antarctic discovery. Its overriding theme is the ultimate human constant—death—tempered to some extent by what is arguably the other: sex. Some sections of the poem are framed as memories of the warmth of human sexual contact, but these memories seem infinitely distant, even hallucinatory. More urgent is the repeated questioning in the poem, an attempt to express the bleakness and purity of the sights and sounds of this strange half-imaginary landscape. Stainer invokes the mysterious music of Satie and Varèse, the dreadful and unimaginable noise of the Piper Alpha oil rig fire in the North Sea, and then asks about sounds which can never be articulated:

What is song
when the shroud
is left unlaced at the mouth?[13]

---

[9] Stainer, *The Honeycomb*, 38.
[10] Stainer, *The Honeycomb*, 15.
[11] *Times Literary Supplement* (30 Apr. 2004), 32.
[12] Pauline Stainer, *The Ice-Pilot Speaks* (Newcastle upon Tyne: Bloodaxe Books, 1994), 9.
[13] Stainer, *The Ice-Pilot Speaks*, 12.

Such inexpressibility inevitably ushers in the idiom of religious myth. In a sudden startling allusion to Christian and Norse myth,

Christ turns
on Yggdrasill
under the strobe lights.[14]

Yggdrasill, the great World Tree, was also the tree on which the god Óðinn, the High One, hanged himself for nine nights in pursuit of wisdom—specifically, the knowledge of runes, that is, mastery of written language. Stainer also alludes to Óðinn and the runes in *Parable Island* (1999); in 'Sourin' (a place on the island of Rousay, where Stainer was living at the time) the pitiful sight of a swan hanging from power lines evokes Óðinn hanging from Yggdrasill. Stainer's connection is perhaps the folk belief in the swansong—the mystical singing of the dying bird, as if death brought it, like Óðinn, a means of articulation.

That Christ should 'turn' on Yggdrasill echoes David Jones's repeated conflations of Christian symbol and Norse myth; for both divinities, sacrifice involved hanging and resurrection. At the climax of *The Anathémata*, Christ's crucifixion is figured as his 'riding' (the word always used of Óðinn's sacrifice in Old Norse sources) of 'the Axile Tree'—the tree which forms the axis between heaven and earth, that is, Yggdrasill, in Norse cosmology, or the Rood, in Christian sources, around which the earth itself turns.[15] Yggdrasill as a cosmic symbol may even have originated as an ancient Lappish conception of a great central axis culminating in the Pole Star, around which the heavens seem to turn. Stainer's constant concern with the quality of light—evident in all her work—finds here its most evocative site: the Northern Lights whose eerie flickering illuminates a distinctively Northern crucifixion, the reference to strobe lighting bringing what is distant into sudden contact with the here and now.

From this point in the sequence, explicit allusions to Old Norse myth begin to build up. A ship, sunk with its heavy cargo of southern sugar, rises to the surface as the sugar dissolves, like ice melting; this physical evanescence is compared to the yet more ephemeral imprint of the hooves of Óðinn's eight-legged horse, Sleipnir, on a glacier. Óðinn's son, Baldr, was killed by his blind brother Höðr, who shot at him with an apparently harmless missile: an arrow made of mistletoe. But its soft stem was mysteriously transformed into a rigid javelin. Stainer describes the mistletoe, which is perhaps, in ancient myth, a symbol of resurrection, as well as the instrument of Baldr's death, as 'shafting' Baldr—a graphic rendering of the plant's transformation, but also playing on the word as a term for a beam of light, which Stainer often represents as a lethal weapon especially a blade.[16] There is another veiled reference to the death of Baldr in the classic 'bog body' poem, 'Lindow Man': archaeologists 'found mistletoe in [his] gut' and he suffered a 'triple death'—a ritual execution like Baldr. But Lindow Man is not given voice: again,

---

[14] Stainer, *The Ice-Pilot Speaks*, 14.
[15] David Jones, 'Sherthursday and Venus Day', *The Anathémata* (London: Faber & Faber, 1952), 243.
[16] Stainer, *The Ice-Pilot Speaks*, 15.

the topos of inexpressibility dominates the poem, and the significance of his death is labelled 'unspeakable'.[17]

Stainer cites various transformations which visual and poetic art can bring about, culminating with the ultimate creative transformation:

>   as on the evening
> of the first day
> a man's hair
> comes out of the ice.[18]

This is a reference to one account of the creation of gods and giants in Old Norse myth, as described by the thirteenth-century Icelandic mythographer Snorri Sturluson: the mythic cow Auðumbla licked blocks of ice, and on the first day, a man's hair appears as Auðumbla licks him into shape. Here, man is created not from earth, or dust, but from ice.[19]

The final allusion to Old Norse myth in 'The Ice-Pilot Speaks' is to the elegiac and oddly archaeological motif of the chessboard of the gods. In *Völuspá*, the Eddaic poem of pagan Creation and Apocalypse, the golden age of innocence enjoyed by the gods in Ásgarðr is characterized by their carefree game of chess in the meadow, but this idyll is disrupted by the arrival of three mysterious giantesses, and all manner of violent and faithless events ensue, culminating in Ragnarök, the doom of the gods.[20] But as in Christian tradition, there is life after apocalypse; after cataclysm and conflagration a new earth will arise, and

>   There will once more
> the miraculous
> golden chequers
> be found, in the grass,
> those that in the old days
> they had owned. (stanza 58)

These chess pieces are like archaeological finds, material evidence of an antediluvian world that is otherwise no more than the memory of stories. But Stainer's take on the gods' game of chess is more pessimistic. Quite at odds with the renewal and recovery in the Norse poem, Stainer sees their play as 'the game that must be lost'.[21] *Völuspá* had represented the chess pieces as a material evidence of a past age, but for Stainer the old gods and their world have gone, and their only recovery is through poetry.

---

[17] Pauline Stainer, *The Wound-dresser's Dream* (Newcastle upon Tyne: Bloodaxe Books, 1996), 48.
[18] Stainer, *The Ice-Pilot Speaks*, 16.
[19] *Snorri Sturluson: Edda*, trans. Anthony Faulkes (London: J. M. Dent & Sons, 1987), 11.
[20] *Völuspá*, in *The Poetic Edda*, ii. *Mythological Poems*, ed. and trans. Ursula Dronke (Oxford: Oxford University Press, 1997), 7–24.
[21] Stainer, *The Ice-Pilot Speaks*, 17.

Stainer's latest volume, *Crossing the Snowline* (2008), contains poems written after a long fallow period following the death of her daughter. The title is ambiguous: is Stainer coming back out of the cold—like Le Carré's spy, Smiley—or is she at last returning to a familiar spatial *imaginaire*, that polar wasteland which proved so productive? Whichever it is, we see in these poems the same topoi which dominated her earlier work: allusions to Old Norse myth in 'The Raven Master', the landscape giving up its medieval secrets in 'The Sifting', and the emergence of ghosts of the people buried in it in 'The Whitening'. Frances Leviston has described Pauline Stainer as 'guarding the power of our occult and mythological heritage'.[22] This concern, in tandem with her fascination for Northernness, means that Old Norse myth is an inevitable element in her poetry. Myth is not only a means of recovering the past, but also an instrument for expressing the continuity of sign and symbol—as David Jones did. The transformative power of art in general, and poetry in particular, is quintessentially mythic.

The Scottish poet Kathleen Jamie, in marked contrast to Pauline Stainer, has been called 'strikingly unbookish',[23] and much of her work consists in the immaculate depiction of directly observed scenes or images, most often from the landscape. In her collection *The Queen of Sheba* (1994) the bitterly comic poem 'Arraheids' characterizes Scottish tradition as sourly disapproving of precisely the sort of poetry of recovery and memory I am concerned with. Jamie gives voice to eponymous arrowheads in an Edinburgh museum—such artefacts from the past as might trigger in a poet some reverie about their context. However, these 'sherp | chert tongues, that lee | fur generations in the land' seem (ironically) to resist exploitation by a poet. They are voices from the past—not 'arraheids | but a show o grannies' tongues', stridently censorious about the poetic imagination, castigating poetic types who 'fancy | the vanished hunter, the wise deer runnin on'. Their culminating question—'whae dae ye think ye ur?'—is not, however, successful in its attempt to humble the poet, for the answer is the joyous and triumphant title poem of the collection: 'The Queen of Sheba!'[24]

Jamie defiantly gives voice to imagined figures from the past in *The Queen of Sheba*. In 'Sky-Burial', for example, the speaking voice is the corpse on the bier, on its way to be exposed to excarnation by carrion birds. The setting is characteristically Northern (indeed even Heaney-esque)—'bog weeds', 'peat-lips', 'forests', 'old wolves', 'deer-spoor'. And there is one startling verbal echo of a medieval text: a child is imagined shyly asking the question no one else dare: '*where do they go, the dead?*' The corpse has a necessarily solipsistic answer:

here,   here,
                        here,

dramatically echoing the voice of martyred St Edmund of East Anglia, whose head, severed by marauding Vikings, lost in a wood, and miraculously guarded by a wolf, is said

---

[22] *The Guardian* (20 Dec. 2008).
[23] Gerald Mangan, *Times Literary Supplement* (16 Aug. 2002), 22.
[24] Kathleen Jamie, *The Queen of Sheba* (Newcastle upon Tyne: Bloodaxe Books, 1994), 40.

by the Anglo-Saxon cleric Ælfric of Eynsham to call to his loyal subjects in exactly these words in order that they can reunite it with his body for a reverent burial.[25] The corpse in 'Sky-Burial' cannot hope for such restoration: 'The wind unravels me | winter birds will arrive'.

More typical of Jamie's work, however, is her insistence on the supremacy of the actual natural world over the textual one. In 'Skeins o geese', she sees how 'Skeins o geese | write a word across the sky', or, with uncanny visual accuracy,

Wire twists lik archaic script
roon a gate. The barbs
sign tae the wind as though
it was deef.

In this poem, the past 'lies | strewn around', like archaeology, but the mystical, natural language of landscape is untranslatable: 'Whit dae birds write on the dusk? | A word niver spoken or read'.[26] Jamie's use of myth is not confined to explicit allusion, but transforms mythic motifs and patterns into wholly new narratives. In 'One of us' the plural speaking voice announces: 'We are come in a stone boat, | a miracle ship'.[27] 'The stone boat' is the title of an Icelandic fairy tale, though it occurs too as an element in folk tales of other traditions.[28] The travellers in the stone boat are also associated with Celtic motifs: they wear 'sealskin cloaks', 'penannular brooches', and their slippers are made from 'feathery | guga's necks'—*guga* being the Gaelic word for a young gannet. What we see here is the intermingling of Celtic and Norse elements which is—as Hugh MacDiarmid insisted—characteristic of Scotland (and as Heaney even more controversially suggested, of Ireland[29]). The medieval ethos is suddenly shattered as the mysterious travellers pick their way past 'rusty tractors' and see 'No-one | nothing but a distant | Telecom van'. They are clearly time travellers, arrived from an unknown past into a desolate present; like the Telecom van, they are involved with messages across big distances. Jamie presents their arrival into this world—a classic collision of past and present—as richly comic: they describe their solemn sacred symbols ('the | golden horn of righteousness, | the justice harp') as 'our tat'—'what folks expect' of them, and their shape-shifting abilities as 'silly magic'. But they can still cause a stir. Transformed into swans, they literally stop the traffic: 'a dormobile | slewed into a passing place; cameras flashed'.

So who are these enigmatic visitants? As swan maidens, their arrival recalls the Old Norse mythic poem *Völundarkviða*, in which three swan maidens take three brothers as

---

[25] Jamie, *The Queen of Sheba*, 44–5. See *Ælfric's Life of St. Edmund* in *A Guide to Old English*, ed. Bruce Mitchell and Fred C. Robinson (5th edn., Oxford: Blackwell, 1992), 195–203.

[26] Jamie, *The Queen of Sheba*, 64.

[27] Jamie, *The Queen of Sheba*, 43.

[28] Andrew Lang, *The Yellow Fairy Book* (London: Longmans, Green, 1894).

[29] See Heather O'Donoghue, 'Heaney, *Beowulf* and the Medieval Literature of the North', in Bernard O'Donoghue (ed.), *The Cambridge Companion to Seamus Heaney* (Cambridge: Cambridge University Press, 2009), 192–205.

lovers, but seven years later depart as mysteriously as they arrived, impelled by a force as ineluctable as that which drives the migration of actual birds.[30] But the end of Jamie's poem moves beyond the recollection of old myths. The visitants seem to be carrying out an undercover assignment. They make use of safe houses; they 'hold | minor government jobs, lay plans, and bide [their] time'. They have infiltrated our society. This project taps into a series of related contemporary myths. Are they fifth columnists, 'the enemy within', as Thatcherite rhetoric would have it? Or simply the bearers of a yet-to-flourish ideology, whose day will come? The sinister power of this modern myth needs no specificity to do its work; the poem's title, 'One of us', with its negative implication '*not* one of us', exploits our anxieties about hidden threats to our security.

In 'The horse-drawn sun' Jamie invests another ancient mythic idea with modern relevance. At first, the poem's speaker seems to be the ubiquitous bog body: 'We may lie forsaken in the earth's black gut'. But the speaker who experiences a thrilling exhumation—a 'struggle to surface | after thousands of years', and then 'the plough-share | tearing the earth overhead'—is not a human body but 'a horse of the light'—a beast of burden drawing the sun behind it.[31] The figure of the sun being moved across the sky by a horse-drawn chariot is familiar from a number of mythologies, including Old Norse, and, insofar as it has survived, perhaps Anglo-Saxon too. Jamie's horses—rather like the mythic animals in Edwin Muir's 'The Horses'—are similarly not only sentient, but also wiser than the human world, and comprehend the inadequacies of a decayed modern age. As revenants from a long-gone past, their curiosity about contemporary humanity is terrifyingly condescending: 'Let's see what they've lost. What they've become'. Jamie's myths are renewed, not simply recycled.

Andrew Waterhouse, in his last collection, *2nd* (2002; published posthumously, and unfinished) also resurrects Northern voices from the past, but the chronotope of his sequence 'Good News from a Small Island' is minutely specific: his voices speak from the vellum pages of the Lindisfarne Gospels, as he re-creates in fine detail the methods of its scribe and illustrator Eadfrith, its binder Æthelwald and cover decorator Billfrith, and finally, its tenth-century Anglo-Saxon glossator Aldred. Waterhouse imagines the physical genesis of the volume, the concerns and the attitudes of those who worked on it, and in the process he produces a vivid depiction of time and place, again, the Northern medieval.

'Attempted Ballad for the Man Trapped on the Letter "C"' playfully voices the resentment of a human head depicted on the initial page of St John's Gospel, the archetypal 'new beginning' (the Word) that ironically marks the beginning of the head's incarceration on the page:

'I hate whoever drew me like this,
with only a head and a sneer,
my single eye staring out
at my thirteen hundredth year'.[32]

---

[30] *Völundarkviða*, in *The Poetic Edda*, ii. *Mythological Poems*, ed. and trans. Dronke, 243–54.
[31] Jamie, *The Queen of Sheba*, 52 (wrongly paginated in the table of contents).
[32] Andrew Waterhouse, *2nd* (Norwich: The Rialto, 2002), 30.

This comic treatment of the past voice is extended in 'Hairstyles of the Evangelists'; Waterhouse irreverently compares the portraits of Matthew, Mark, Luke, and John in the Lindisfarne Gospels with modern figures. Matthew, for instance, is 'an old hippy', but 'Mark has gone | a perm too far, like Kevin Keegan'.[33] There is perhaps a serious point here about the unchanging face (almost literally!) of humanity across time, somewhat comparable with Heaney's shock at the familiar-looking faces of the bog bodies in a Danish museum case. But to later readers, Waterhouse's allusions are no more familiar than the medieval portraits with which they are compared, a point which Waterhouse himself wryly anticipates:

Sad Luke's mullet
Is a bastard child of the '80's.
Best forgotten.

Several of the poems in *2nd* are drafts, the same poems sometimes appearing in different versions. But one fully finished poem, 'The Illustrated Calf', goes much further than the 'Good News from a Small Island' sequence in bringing the past to life. With the epigraph that 'the vellum pages of old manuscripts will take on the curves of their original shape over time', from a handbook on book restoration, Waterhouse imagines the Gospel volume not merely reverting to the original shape of the vellum from which its pages have been cut, but actually coming back to life as a calf, the text still visible on the living creature:

Now, Luke's healing hand
settles over the calf's heart and it shivers
in the rain, takes a second first breath,
kicks out, begins to gallop across the grass.[34]

In Anglo-Saxon riddles, an inanimate object is typically given a voice with which it enigmatically describes itself, and in one riddle, a voice given to a Bible or Gospel book begins by describing its original existence as an animal slaughtered for its vellum.[35] The author of the riddle, like Waterhouse, recounts in loving detail the processes of book production, but there is none of the joyous sense of release we find in 'The Illustrated Calf', nor the potential for the resurrection of the calf to stand for both Christ's resurrection, or, more pertinently, the bringing to life of the book with each reading. All these senses were evidently recognized by Ian Duhig since in his collection *The Lammas Hireling* (2003), the poem 'Rosary', subtitled 'i.m.', is for Andrew Waterhouse, and builds on the conceit of Waterhouse's poem.[36]

In both *The Lammas Hireling* and *Nominies* (1998), Duhig's attitude towards history is split between a blokeish jokiness and a serious exploration of how poetry can recover

---

[33] Waterhouse, *2nd*, 17.
[34] Waterhouse, *2nd*, 41.
[35] *A Choice of Anglo-Saxon Verse*, parallel trans. Richard Hamer (London: Faber & Faber, 1970), 103–5.
[36] Ian Duhig, *The Lammas Hireling* (Basingstoke: Picador, 2003), 66.

the past. Stephen Burt has observed that 'Duhig wants above all to reveal a continuity between archaic...and contemporary...experience'.[37] This aim is often expressed through satire, a debunking of the past. David Kennedy maintains that 'we romanticize history into something grand to counteract the absurdities of the human predicament. Duhig wants us to know that history just isn't worth it'.[38] *Nominies* presents ample evidence of this latter approach. 'A Line from Snorri Sturluson', for instance, purports to quote the thirteenth-century Icelandic mythographer and literary theorist, who in his treatise on Norse poetic diction, lists the many synonyms for sea.[39] Duhig, while acknowledging that as a poet this is his job too, goes on to describe a squalid contemporary seascape, with used condoms, discarded ice-cream cornets, and piles of dogshit. In burlesque spirit, Duhig, calling his own dog 'Fenris, wolf to Loki!', alludes to the malevolent half-god of Old Norse myth, Loki, who sired monsters, including the apocalyptic wolf Fenrir (not 'Fenris').[40] Duhig's dog, in its unattractive snuffling around in the shallows, knows 'more depths than Thor's lip', a witty reference to the Old Norse story of how the god Thor unwittingly tried to drink dry a horn whose far end dipped into the ocean; his prodigious draughts are said to have caused the tides.[41] But with his fake quotation and his misspelt name, Duhig otherwise plays fast and loose with the tradition he invokes. Similarly, in *The Lammas Hireling*, Duhig debunks the celebrated story of the great Icelandic saga hero Njáll, whose peaceable instincts and legal skills are not enough to avert tragedy, or halt the course of a violent feud; he and his wife and grandson are burnt to death in their house. The speaker in 'Wise, Brave Old Njal' attributes to Njáll a series of tedious, invented aphorisms and then provocatively claims that if he'd been there, he'd have 'lent a match'.[42] Irreverence is a favourite mode; a comedy scribe in Duhig's first collection, *The Bradford Count* (1991) is sick of his work; he longs for a racier text to copy than '*The Grey Psalter of Antrim*' and dreams of gifting it to 'Halfdane the Sacker | that he might use it to wipe his wide Danish arse'.[43]

The object of Duhig's satire can be the crude transformation of Norse myth in contemporary culture. In 'Ken's Videos, Seahouses'—Seahouses being a small fishing village on the ever-resonant Northumbrian coast—Duhig represents himself as pondering whether to rent a Hollywood film, *The Vikings*. Ken presses the attractions of 'a recent *Beowulf*' ('the hero an exiled Arab poet played by Antonio Banderas') and Duhig wittily picks up on the most notorious misrepresentation of Viking culture to represent his indecision: 'On the horns of a helmet, I hesitate, lost.'[44] Duhig's references to history and

---

[37] *Times Literary Supplement* (26 Sept. 2003), 25.
[38] *Times Literary Supplement* (18 Oct. 1991), 23.
[39] *Snorri Sturluson*, 139ff.
[40] Ian Duhig, *Nominies* (Newcastle upon Tyne: Bloodaxe Books, 1998), 20. For parentage of Fenrir, see *Snorri Sturluson*, 26.
[41] *Snorri Sturluson*, 42–3.
[42] Duhig, *The Lammas Hireling*, 36.
[43] Ian Duhig, 'Margin prayer from an Ancient Psalter', *The Bradford Count* (Newcastle upon Tyne: Bloodaxe Books, 1991), 62–3.
[44] Duhig, *The Lammas Hireling*, 30.

myth are chiefly bookish ones, playing with textual traditions. Even the quartet 'Four More Sides to the Franks Casket', a poem ostensibly inspired by a material object—the delicate eighth-century ivory reliquary of that name—tells us less about the object itself than about Duhig's own esoteric medieval learning, and there is a characteristically jokey riff on an imagined medieval revisionism responsible, amongst other things, for traducing 'gentle St Grendel' and his mother 'Our Lady of Danes' as the notorious monsters of *Beowulf*.[45]

When Duhig won a Northern Arts fellowship, commissioned to produce 'something commending the literature and landscape of the region',[46] the resulting poems in *The Lammas Hireling* were still overwhelmingly 'bookish', several of them adopting the familiar technique of ventriloquizing voices from the past, though not for comic effect. Not all of them found favour with critics: Alan Brownjohn described 'Brother Robert's Double Vision', in which a medieval monk speaks of being troubled by ominous dreams, as 'dutiful',[47] and Stephen Burt feared that the jaunty tone of 'DXCVII' (the year in which Pope Gregory initiated his evangelizing mission to the English) leaves us with 'a Pope less serious than the occasion demands'[48]—this is the downside of what Jules Smith has termed Duhig's 'medievalist modernism'.[49] The title poem, however, has won universal acclaim, though many critics found it mysterious. 'The Lammas Hireling' returns to a familiar chronotope, the Northern past, the title and the first line suggesting a Northern Irish setting. However, the mythic quality of the poem's narrative transcends time and place, and there are no proper names. The poem's speaker has hired a farmhand, and, like the sacral kings of old tradition, the new help, though silent and unsociable, seems to have caused the farm to prosper: the cattle 'only dropped heifers, fat as cream'.[50] But apparently haunted by the voice of his dead wife, the farmer kills the hireling, whose corpse undergoes a strange transformation into the shape of a hare—a sinister animal in many folk traditions. The farmer's cattle no longer prosper (they are 'elf-shot', a term from Anglo-Saxon charms) and he is wracked by irrational guilt.

I do not know of any Germanic myth or narrative that matches these events, although as we have seen Duhig does not always slavishly reproduce his sources or influences. And yet aspects of this elliptical tale are strongly reminiscent of the Old Icelandic saga of Grettir—a saga perhaps best known for its striking analogues to the action of the Old English poem *Beowulf*.[51] Grettir pits himself against a series of humanoid creatures: trolls, berserks, the zombie-like ghost of a Swedish farmhand. One of his adversaries is the silent and unsociable Glámr, who is first killed by some unknown force and then returns as an *aptrganga*—one of the walking dead. The moment Grettir, himself a

---

[45] Duhig, *The Lammas Hireling*, 34–5.
[46] See Alan Brownjohn in *The Independent* (23 Jan. 2004).
[47] Brownjohn in *The Independent* (23 Jan. 2004).
[48] See n. 16.
[49] [http://www.contemporarywriters.com/authors/?p=auth5689224102ee61D662iUrY377ECF].
[50] Duhig, *The Lammas Hireling*, 4–5.
[51] Trans. as *Grettir's Saga* by Jesse Byock (Oxford: Oxford University Press, 2009).

hired hand, is about to kill this creature, the moon comes out from behind the clouds—just as it does in Duhig's poem as the farmer kills the hireling. The killing has a permanent effect on Grettir, as it does on Duhig's farmer: Grettir was ever afterwards afraid of the dark. The weird hired hand, the farming context, the murder, the moon, and the continued psychological reverberation of the killing, combined with a similar atmosphere of menace and the uncanny, all suggest some influence from the saga on Duhig's poem. But he has transformed the narrative into a tale of guilt, just as Kathleen Jamie created her new myth about insecurity in 'One of us'.

Deliberately arcane references characterize 'Behoof', in which Duhig muses on the many kinds of horse in Western (and indeed Eastern) culture, as a comic riposte to Dickens's reductive Gradgrind. Early definitions are medieval: 'Siege engine. Saxon land art. | Ritual bride for Celtic kings'.[52] But as the poem progresses, references are piled up in an ahistorical jumble, and include two specific allusions to horses of Old Norse myth, Skinfaxi ('Shining mane'—according to Snorri Sturluson, the horse which pulls Day's chariot, thus lighting up the world)—and Hrimfaxi (Soot, or Frost-mane, pulling Night's chariot, its bit-spittle spraying the earth with dew).[53] However, these allusions seem to function simply as arcane additions, useful for a bit of light-hearted morphological wordplay: 'Hack for taxi, tack for Faxi, | Brass facts. That's that'.

Like Duhig, Don Paterson is another distinctively 'bookish' poet who has been compared with Muldoon in this respect. In his tricksy collection *God's Gift to Women* (1997), a walled-up railway tunnel is seen as the depository for cultural and historical odds and ends. The casual reference to 'Fenrir, Pol Pot, | Captain Oates' suggests that Paterson is simply heaping up the names of larger than life figures from the past.[54] Paterson has described himself as 'not really a poet of place'[55] and in his most celebrated poem about recovering the past, 'The Alexandrian Library' in *Nil Nil* (1993), history is wholly textual—it is represented by a nightmarish journey through a post-industrial wasteland to a shop selling a vast and various array of unwanted and outdated books. This postmodernist depiction of the past naturally contains a medieval component (interpolated with a quick joke about forgetting):

> ...a grimoire in horrible waxpaper,
> a lost Eddic cycle of febrile monotony,
> *Leechdom and Wortcunning; Living with Alzheimer's*
> and Tatwine's gigantic *Aenigmae Perarduae*.[56]

The further back into the past one reaches, the more primitive and inexpressive literature and language are seen to become, the poet's voice reduced to no more than an 'ur-bark'.[57] In *Landing Light* (2003), the poem 'Incunabula' describes the work of

---

[52] Ian Duhig, *The Speed of Dark* (London: Picador, 2007), 18–19.
[53] *Snorri Sturluson*, 14.
[54] Don Paterson, '00:00: Law Tunnel', *God's Gift to Women* (London: Faber & Faber, 1997), 6.
[55] [http://www.donpaterson.com/interviews.htm#].
[56] Don Paterson, *Nil Nil* (London: Faber & Faber, 1993), 30.
[57] Paterson, *Nil Nil*, 31.

scribes—'Sunk in their slow proofreading'—with a sympathetic engagement reminiscent of Waterhouse's Lindisfarne poems.[58] But perhaps there is a sting in the title: incunabula are the earliest *printed* books, and Paterson's point may be that this painstaking and even nerve-wracking craft—'a single letter lost or doubled ruins | not just the manuscript but the whole school'—is about to be outdated.

In *Rain* (2009) there is, with one extraordinary exception, no explicit reference to a Northern medieval past, but the problem with identifying allusions which have been creatively transformed is that the deeper the poet's engagement, and the greater the transformation, the more uncertain identification of the possible source becomes. Writing of one of his twin sons, in 'Correctives', Paterson observes how the child stills a slight shudder in his left hand 'with one touch from his right'. He represents this as a sort of small but hugely significant epiphany, a demonstration of 'the one hand's kindness to the other' not granted to everyone to have either experienced or seen.[59] There is a striking parallel with the Eddaic poem *Hamðismál*, in which two brothers, setting out on a doomed revenge mission, are offered help by their half-brother, who promises to support them 'as one foot another'.[60] His offer, implying that he is as integral a part of their brotherhood as two feet are part of one body, is not understood by the two full brothers, who mock his metaphor in revealing terms: 'How can a foot | help a foot, | or a hand grown from the body's flesh | help a hand?' Paterson's short poem seems to explore precisely this idea; his son 'understands | that the whole man must be his own brother'. If this is indeed inspired by the Old Norse legend of Hamðir and his brother Sörli, it is very far indeed from the casually explicit incorporation of proper names from a myth-kitty.

Rain is dominated by the long sequence 'Phantom', in memory of the poet Michael Donaghy. In section V, Paterson imagines a cosmic other world which overturns long-held conceptions of the relationship between life and death:

> We come from nothing and return to it.
> it lends us out to time, and when we lie
> in silent contemplation of the void
> they say we feel it contemplating us.
> This is wrong...[61]

Paterson's contention is that earth itself is the void, brought to life and meaning by the paradoxical (and oddly Platonic) play of 'bright shadows' on it from a 'something vast and distant and enthroned'. But what happens when 'the dark light stills', and this vast mind rests? It is at this point that Paterson reaches for the great image of the Old Norse World Tree to express a cosmic regression from enlightenment:

---

[58] Don Paterson, *Landing Light* (London: Faber & Faber, 2003), 7.
[59] Don Paterson, *Rain* (London: Faber & Faber, 2009), 16.
[60] *Hamðismál*, in *The Poetic Edda*, i. *Heroic Poems*, ed. and trans. Ursula Dronke (Oxford: Oxford University Press, 1969), 161–7.
[61] Paterson, *Rain*, 55.

       the tree will rise untethered to its station
between earth and heaven, the open book
turn runic and unreadable again.

This is a precisely measured and considered deployment of mythic allusion appropriate to the lofty solemnity of Paterson's elegy. Old Norse cosmology is not funny, or arcane, or symbolic of a shared past which poets in English can recover: it is testimony to an unwelcome, unwanted, and dark prehistory.

In Robin Robertson's second collection, *Slow Air* (2002), one wonders if the speakers in the poem 'Apart', who are evidently sailors, 'drawn to the edges', returning home laden with 'unimaginable gifts' which have still not satisfied their greed, and pointedly not wearing pilgrims' badges, are Viking raiders.[62] In Robertson's next collection, *Swithering* (2006) we have a classic chronotopic poem, 'Sea-Fret' (the north-eastern term for a sea mist, linked by wordplay (sea-fretted) to the idea of erosion and decay). The subject of 'Sea-Fret' is the medieval priory at Tynemouth, on the Northumbrian coast that was built on the site of an Anglican monastery, later fortified, and still used as a defensive structure after the Dissolution of the Monasteries. Here, the collision of past and present is dramatically represented in the juxtaposition of the sacred and the military: 'The chantry's rose-window | sights east along the barrel |of the rusted 6-inch gun'; warfare is described in terms of monastic discipline, with its uniforms, its bells, and its rituals.[63] But the coastal battery is now disused, and has become, like the priory, archaeology in itself.

A long poem in Robertson's most recent collection, *The Wrecking Light* (2010), proceeds by constructing landscape through the recitation of place names: a technique perhaps inherited from the Irish *dinnshenchas* tradition, as practised by, for instance, Seamus Heaney. Robertson's journey in 'Leaving St Kilda' is a circumnavigation of the now uninhabited island, consisting of a rich list of the place names as the traveller passes them. As Adam Newey has put it, 'this incantation of placenames becomes a motif of the bridgeless gulf between those man-named clefts and stacks and the sea-birds that have replaced humanity there'.[64] Some of the names are Gaelic, but others are Norse—place names demonstrate the historical intermingling of the Norse and Celtic element in Scottish ethnicity.

The Wrecking Light also contains a buried body poem. 'Grave Goods' describes an elaborate assemblage of clearly Northern and perhaps medieval or prehistoric artefacts: 'carved figurines of elk, snakes and humans | a wild boar's leg-bone whittled and whetted | into a dagger'.[65] The poem's speaking voice is the body itself, disappointed by an afterlife of an inanimate collection of material objects and the ritually deposited bodies of what might be family members. Robertson also gives a voice to the dead in 'The Great Midwinter Sacrifice, Uppsala'; his speaker is Adam of Bremen, whose actual

[62] Robin Robertson, *Slow Air* (Basingstoke: Picador, 2002), 3.
[63] Robin Robertson, *Swithering* (Basingstoke: Picador, 2006), 36.
[64] *The Guardian*, 20 Feb. 2010.
[65] Robin Robertson, *The Wrecking Light* (Basingstoke: Picador, 2010), 56.

eleventh-century account of sacrificial rituals there is one of the most basic—if also the most sensational—sources for Scandinavian paganism.[66]

Lavinia Greenlaw recovers the past through landscapes—the River Thames, for instance, in 'River History' from *Night Photograph* (1993)—or with a voice speaking from history, like Galileo's wife, in the same collection. In her third volume, *Minsk*, (2003) Greenlaw adopts a medieval or early modern idiom in 'Lord Yarborough's Defence' to mimic the language of a charter describing the infinitely slow accretion of the estate being laid claim to. The long poem 'Blackwater' describes the course—both topographical and temporal—of the Essex river, 'stumps of Saxon fishtraps' exposed at low tide, medieval traders imagined populating its banks. The Blackwater is presided over not by ancient deities, but by invented gods: Meander, Inertia, Stasis, and Moribund.[67] Time and place have almost come to a standstill.

But it is with the final set of poems in *Minsk* that Greenlaw most concentratedly explores the effacement of time and, paradoxically, place: 'The Land of Giving In' is a series inspired by Greenlaw's visit to the Arctic. Greenlaw's subject is the emptiness of the North, the monochrome 'black of Arctic winter and the blank white of Arctic midsummer', as she has put it.[68] The Land of Giving In is a place where the sun never sets in summer, and the familiar diurnal cycle is transformed into a sort of cosmic palindrome in 'Heliotropical': 'At midnight, the sun glides into reverse, | Like Anna backwards, a god having second thoughts.'[69] Time here is neither idling, nor even standing still, but has a reverse gear.

The passage of time is an enduring theme in the poetry of Peter Reading, but his project is far from an attempt to recover the past; his theme is its very unrecoverability. The title of *Evagatory* (1992) alludes to the celebrated Old English elegy 'The Wanderer', which, together with its Old English companion piece, 'The Seafarer', Reading repeatedly reworks both here and in '*[untitled]*' (2001).[70] In *Evagatory*, at 'Edge of black Baltic', we hear the 'Germanic drone of a drunk salt's slurred dirge'—and what follows is a free but vividly evocative translation of part of 'The Seafarer'.[71] The repeated phrase 'province of hyperborean bleakness' (in *Evagatory* there are no page numbers and no titles) recalls the Arctic setting exploited by Stainer and Greenlaw, but the dominant image in Reading's work is of textuality becoming unreadable.

The Old English elegies, like much Old English verse, survive in more-or-less fragmentary forms, and the idea of the fragility of a textual tradition is accentuated by Reading's characteristically experimental forms, with poems half finished, or reworked, sometimes appearing as already fading away on the page, or in tantalizing fragments. The title page (if we can call it that) of '*[untitled]*' is a picture of a short runic inscription: in

---

[66] For a translated quotation of the relevant passages, see E. O. G. Turville-Petre, *Myth and Religion of the North* (London: Weidenfeld & Nicolson, 1964), 244–6.
[67] Lavinia Greenlaw, *Minsk* (London: Faber & Faber, 2003), 11–13.
[68] [http://www.telegraph.co.uk/culture/books/3607141/A-writers-life-Lavinia-Greenlaw.html].
[69] Greenlaw, *Minsk*, 68.
[70] For the Old English originals, see *A Guide to Old English*, 271–5 and 277–82 respectively.
[71] Peter Reading, *Evagatory* (London: Chatto & Windus, 1992), no page numbers.

its opacity it stands as a lesson to anyone who believes that poetry may endure through time, let alone be used to recover a past, as the epigraph makes clear: 'Our runes, like theirs, will be undecipherable; impartial Time will wipe the slate clean, wordless.'[72] The poem 'Dog's Tomb' begins with a visual representation of a worn, only barely readable gravestone inscription in Latin: 'Who blindness and senility prepared for darkness and insensibility.'[73] Material objects specifically designed to speak to posterity are unreliable as witnesses to the past; the inscription is only 'just legible', and becomes fainter and more corrupt as it is repeated throughout the volume. One might make a surprising connection here—with the visual art of the poet David Jones, whose representations of inscriptions, with their 'rubbed and worn texture that tells as a metaphor for the fret and passage of time', are nevertheless understood by art critics to give 'the visual effect of the endurance of the word'.[74] Nothing could be further from Reading's hopeless nihilism.

Greenlaw's Arctic is a landscape wiped clean of visual stimuli and cultural symbols, and time there is scarcely linear, let alone a steadily moving vehicle for history. It is almost as if she means to cleanse her North from its possibly suspect political and ideological associations. For Peter Reading, all kinds of texts—even those purposefully designed to endure, and commemorate—will become physically fainter, more fragmentary, and ultimately be forgotten; they are far from being fit instruments for recovery or memory. One might claim that Reading is consciously—and pessimistically—defining himself against the poetry of recovery and memory, contesting poetry's claim to be more enduring than brass. What then, of those working *within* the tradition I have claimed to define? In an essay published almost half a century ago, 'Myth and History in Recent Poetry', Terry Eagleton argued that 'myth provides a measure of freedom, transcendence, representativeness, a sense of totality; and it seems no accident that it is serving those purposes in a society where those qualities are largely lacking'.[75] It may be that contemporary poetry of recovery and memory serves the same purposes today.

Select Bibliography

Carpenter, Humphrey, *W. H. Auden: A Biography* (Boston: Houghton Mifflin, 1981).
Duhig, Ian, *Nominies* (Newcastle upon Tyne: Bloodaxe Books, 1998).
Duhig, Ian, *The Lammas Hireling* (Basingstoke: Picador, 2003).
Duhig, Ian, *The Speed of Dark* (London: Picador, 2007).
Greenlaw, Lavinia, *Minsk* (London: Faber & Faber, 2003).
Haraldsson, Sveinn, '"The North begins inside"': Auden, Ancestry and Iceland', in Andrew Wawn (ed.), *Northern Antiquity* (Enfield Lock: Hisarlik Press, 1994), 255–84.
Jamie, Kathleen, *The Queen of Sheba* (Newcastle upon Tyne: Bloodaxe Books, 1994).

---

[72] Peter Reading, *[untitled]* (Tarset: Bloodaxe Books, 2001), 9.
[73] Reading, *[untitled]*, 42 *et passim*.
[74] *David Jones*, ed. Paul Hills (London: Tate Gallery, 1981), 68.
[75] In Michael Schmidt and Grevel Lindop (eds.), *British Poetry Since 1960: A Critical Survey* (Oxford: Carcanet Press, 1972), 233–9 (239).

Jones, David, *In Parenthesis* (London: Faber & Faber, 1937).
Lang, Andrew, *The Yellow Fairy Book* (London: Longmans, Green, 1894).
O'Donoghue, Heather, '*Miðgarðsormr*', *Archipelago*, 3 (Spring 2009), 20–31.
O'Donoghue, Heather, 'Owed to Both Sides: W. H. Auden's Double Debt to the Literature of the North', in David Clark and Nicholas Perkins (eds.), *Anglo-Saxon Culture and the Modern Imagination* (Woodbridge: D. S. Brewer, 2010), 51–69.
Paterson, Don, *Nil Nil* (London: Faber & Faber, 1993).
Paterson, Don, *Landing Light* (London: Faber & Faber, 2003).
Paterson, Don, *Rain* (London: Faber & Faber, 2009).
Reading, Peter, *Evagatory* (London: Chatto & Windus, 1992).
Robertson, Robin, *Slow Air* (Basingstoke: Picador, 2002).
Robertson, Robin, *Swithering* (Basingstoke: Picador, 2006).
Robertson, Robin, *The Wrecking Light* (Basingstoke: Picador, 2010).
Stainer, Pauline, *The Honeycomb* (Newcastle upon Tyne: Bloodaxe Books, 1989).
Stainer, Pauline, *The Ice-Pilot Speaks* (Newcastle upon Tyne: Bloodaxe Books, 1994).
Stainer, Pauline, *The Wound-dresser's Dream* (Newcastle upon Tyne: Bloodaxe Books, 1996).
Turville-Petre, E. O. G., *Myth and Religion of the North* (London: Weidenfeld & Nicolson, 1964).

CHAPTER 19

LONDON, ALBION

JOHN KERRIGAN

As the second chapter of Blake's *Jerusalem* approaches its dreadful climax, the builder, artist, and shaman Los sets out with 'his globe of fire to search the interiors of Albions | Bosom'. It is a quest to find the tempters and criminals who have destroyed human particularity, and it leads Los into East London:

He came down from Highgate thro Hackney & Holloway towards London
Till he came to old Stratford & thence to Stepney & the Isle
Of Leuthas Dogs, thence thro the narrows of the Rivers side,
And saw every minute particular, the jewels of Albion, running down
The kennels of the streets & lanes as if they were abhorrd.[1]

This vision of moral petrifaction is dependent on geography. Los beats the bounds of the city before probing its poorer districts. In the 'winding places' of the river-front, in the district now known as Docklands, he finds the rationalism of Urizen precipitating an inhumanly 'intricate' street plan, and his search for the root of this system leads 'To where the Tower of London' (in the East) 'frownd dreadful'. This site, and this direction, carried a special intensity for Blake, because he associated the East with Luvah, Jesus, and (in his logic) their contrary, Hate. It also anticipates a Victorian and later tendency to view the East End as a site of limits, extremes, and obscurities, to regard its poverty and wealth of human potential as representative not just of the metropolis but of the state of Albion itself.

It is a tendency that persists. To think of modern Britain's last great moral triumph is to think of the Blitz in Poplar, of East Enders sleeping in the Underground and the docks going up in smoke. The older, and more recent, trauma of immigration and racial violence also has a place in the East End. Many of the waves of immigrants that have changed the

---

[1] *Jerusalem: The Emanation of The Giant Albion* (1804), pl. 45 (or pl. 31), in *The Poetry and Prose of William Blake*, ed. David V. Erdman, commentary by Harold Bloom (New York: Doubleday, 1965). 'Kennels' are 'channels, gutters'.

complexion of the country have passed through Whitechapel and lived along Brick Lane, from Huguenot weavers in the seventeenth century to Irish labourers in the 1840s, Jews in the 1880s, and Bangladeshis at the moment. Stark juxtapositions of wealth and poverty have long been familiar in London. During the three decades from the mid-1960s that are the focus of this chapter, especially the years of Tory government under Mrs Thatcher and John Major (1979–97), anxiety about the emergence of 'two nations' found much to worry about East of Aldgate. The contrast between yuppies with Filofaxes and the unemployed in high-rise blocks was at its sharpest along Los's route from Stepney to the Isle of Dogs. Spitalfields was patchily gentrified, and the City itself—the financial institutions, not the people—built a new Tower of London at Canary Wharf, where the 'intricate' streets of the poor were dwarfed by the gleaming fortress of high finance.[2]

The mythopoeic potential of all this was not lost on the heirs of Blake. An impressive array of poets turned their attention to the chartered streets that run between the Guildhall and Canning Town, and mapped out, with prophetic ardour, truths about the condition of England. In what follows, I shall look at four of them: Iain Sinclair, Allen Fisher, Peter Reading, and Geoffrey Hill. In choosing to start from Blake, and from Sinclair's contention that 'Myth is what place says',[3] I do not mean to slight such poets as Michael Hofmann, who wrote loco-descriptive pieces about the London that Fleur Adcock calls 'Thatcherland'.[4] Nor do I plan to argue that maintaining a Romantic, visionary outlook—as Aidan Dun did, in his recycling of Blake, Shelley, and Chatterton into a long poem about King's Cross, *Vale Royal* (1995)—is a reliable formula for success. Some of the best verse written in and about London came from Ken Smith, who brought a documentary, politicized eye to bear on unemployment, social division, and the overburdened prison system:[5] 'From Canning Town to Woolwich | the tall cranes rust.'[6] Bill Griffiths, Old English modernist and Hell's Angel, wrote a densely questioning poetry ('Can cities have health? | and, are they surer places?'). He had a nose for London in decay ('By Post Office and Sidney Square drains | in the May heat, that complete stench, | is dark, strong'), and he knew how to refashion Blake: 'Gog, Marylebone, Bees, Ironbridge, | Albion, Amyl Nitrate, Devil's Island, Wembley.'[7] All this remarkable work I must set aside, for reasons of space and clarity, along with the *A to Z* of the London, avant-garde scene that flourished during the seventies and eighties: Actual Size Press, Gilbert Adair, Clive Bush, cris cheek, Bob Cobbing, Ken Edwards, the International

---

[2] On Docklands as emblematic, see Doreen Massey, *Docklands: A Microcosm of Broader Social and Economic Trends* (London: Docklands Forum, 1991), 7.

[3] Iain Sinclair, *Suicide Bridge: A Book of the Furies. A Mythology of the South & East* (London: Albion Village Press, 1979), n.p.

[4] e.g. 'Albion Market' and 'From Kensal Rise to Heaven', Michael Hofmann, *Acrimony* (London: Faber & Faber, 1986), 32–5; Fleur Adcock, *The Incident Book* (Oxford: Oxford University Press, 1986), 47–53.

[5] e.g. 'Three Docklands Fragments', *The Heart, The Border* (1990); Ken Smith, *Shed: Poems 1980–2001* (Tarset: Bloodaxe Books, 2002), 144–5; 'As it Happens', *Wormwood* (1987), in *Shed*, 110–17.

[6] Ken Smith, "Movies after Midnight", in 'The London Poems', *Terra* (1986), in *Shed*, 63.

[7] 'The Hawksmoor Mausoleum', 'Paracycle', 'On Insurance', in Allen Fisher, Bill Griffiths, and Brian Catling, *Future Exiles: 3 London Poets* (London: Paladin, 1992), 247–51, 287, 257–8.

Sound Poetry Festival, Barry MacSweeney, Eric Mottram, the New River Project, Reality Street, Robert Sheppard, and Sub Voicive.[8]

There are also exclusions by gender. In *Contemporary British Poetry and the City* (2000), Peter Barry asks why women poets are almost entirely absent from his book. His answer is that he has favoured work that represents 'an external, denoted reality', whereas 'more common with women poets is an appropriation and internalisation of geography so that it represents and embodies such things as states of mind, and structures of feeling. [...] for many women poets geography is "always already" psychic geography, place is already space'.[9] To judge from such collections as Jo Shapcott's *Of Mutability* (2010), London is still an inwardly contingent, somatic space for women poets, not a mapped-out place. 'Place and language are less certain', as Shapcott says, of herself and others, 'and...shifting territories are the norm.'[10] Certainly, during the decades in question, the Blakean, prophetic mantle was most often draped around male shoulders. There is no shortage of radical ambition in the London poetry of Maggie O'Sullivan.[11] Nor lack of political edge in the Cambridge/London verse of Wendy Mulford and Denise Riley. When Mulford quotes Blake, however, in 'Changed Priorities Ahead', her feminism turns away from the public sphere and makes the political personal:

Good Morning May Day.
So we spent it talking.
Isn't that a kind of loving too?
action is not necessarily fast as
'a tear is an intellectual thing'[12]

For Denise Riley, a modernist-prophetic belief that poetry could tear down the structures of Thatcherism and bring about a socialist revolution by the sheer power of parataxis deserves a mocking rebuke

Not your landscapes stiffened with figurines of an ageing woman politician, it is
    harder than that
Not your happy here-we-go-down-together dream of a roseate catastrophe
Nor your reassuring conviction that whole governments

---

[8] See Robert Sheppard, *The Poetry of Saying: British Poetry and Its Discontents 1950–2000* (Liverpool: Liverpool University Press, 2005), chs. 4–10 and his 'The Colony at the Heart of the Empire: Bob Cobbing and the Mid-1980s London Creative Environment', *When Bad Times Made for Good Poetry* (Exeter: Shearsman Books, 2011), 108–33.

[9] Peter Barry, *Contemporary British Poetry and the City* (Manchester: Manchester University Press, 2000), 16.

[10] Jo Shapcott, 'Confounding Geography', in Alison Mark and Deryn Rees-Jones (eds.), *Contemporary Women's Poetry: Reading/Writing/Practice* (Basingstoke: Macmillan, 2000), 40–6 (42).

[11] Maggie O'Sullivan, *Alto: London Poems 1975–1984* (London: Veer Books, 2009) and *Body of Work* (Hastings: Reality Street Editions, 2006).

[12] Wendy Mulford, *Late Spring Next Year: Poems 1979–1985* (Bristol: Loxwood Stoneleigh, 1987), 32. The quotation is from 'I saw a Monk of Charlemaine', *Jerusalem*, pl. 52.

Will pale and stagger under the jawbones of your dismembered syntax
Vain boy! it keeps you busy, though you know
That Belgrade and Zagreb still shelter many post-surrealists, as does
    East Central One.[13]

This now sounds enjoyably correct. But it took some courage to write at a time when deprivation and confrontation (the Miners' Strike, the Poll Tax riots) could make poetry seem an indulgence if not addressed to public questions. The darkening of the cultural and social climate that followed the optimism of the sixties—Sinclair dates a change to 1975[14]—intensified the demand for relevance and vision. The alternative vitality of the counter-culture began to dissolve. Unemployment went up, and spending on public services down. The effects across Albion, but especially in London, were dire. In its submission to the laws of Benthamite political economy, laws that took on the lineaments of an occult form of money worship,[15] Thatcherism seemed to be producing a London reminiscent of Blake's: a city dominated by forces so much more powerful than individual agency that it could be more justly represented in the visionary mode of *Jerusalem*, where Leutha's dogs howl in the prostitute-streets of the East, than by means of so-called realism.

Los did not return to British poetry from nowhere. Blake had been a hero of the sixties counter-culture. In Michael Horovitz's celebrated anthology, *Children of Albion* (1969), Los is enlisted as an anti-Vietnam War activist, an agent of poetic radicalism opposed to British timidity. For Horovitz and others, the modern equivalent was Allen Ginsberg, whose prophetic, Beat-style inspirations frequently echo Blake. His readings at Better Books and the International Poetry Incarnation (Royal Albert Hall), in the summer of 1965, were credited with bringing to life the Poetry Underground.[16] His second major visit to London, in 1967, was documented by Iain Sinclair in a short film and in *The Kodak Mantra Diaries* (1971), first steps into the hyper-productivity that Sinclair has maintained for more than four decades. Ginsberg claimed to have begun his career when, in a moment of 'auditory hallucination', he heard Blake's 'deep earthen grave voice' reciting 'Ah Sun-flower' and 'The Sick Rose', and he later informed an interviewer that 'the voice of Blake [...] is the voice I have'.[17] Almost as important for Sinclair and his contemporaries was Ginsberg's advocacy of other American modernists, William

---

[13] Denise Riley, 'Seven Strangely Exciting Lies' (pub. 1993), sect. v, 'Rep', *Selected Poems* (London: Reality Street Editions, 2000), 80. In Riley's *Mop Mop Georgette: New and Selected Poems 1986–1993* (London: Reality Street, 1993), the same passage had read 'West Central One'; the truths of place will out.

[14] Iain Sinclair in conversation with Kevin Jackson, *The Verbals* (Tonbridge: Worple Press, 2003), 86.

[15] Cf. Sinclair, *Verbals*, 135.

[16] For a live and direct account, see Jeff Nuttall, *Bomb Culture* (London: MacGibbon and Kee, 1968), 238–40.

[17] 'Allen Ginsberg: An Interview', with Thomas Clark, *Paris Review*, 37 (1966), 13–55 (36); *Allen Verbatim*, ed. Gordon Ball (New York: McGraw-Hill, 1974), 21.

Carlos Williams, Charles Olson, and Louis Zukofsky.[18] That is the creative chemistry that informs Sinclair's first major collection, the darkly rhapsodic *Lud Heat* (1975).

Its darkness is defining. In Sinclair the democratic openness of Olson's and Williams's free verse is impacted with superstitious matter, while the vatic sublimities of Ginsberg are modulated into a prose that is high on thanatopic irrationalism. *Lud Heat* is partly a record of a period of employment in the Tower Hamlets Parks Department, and its fractured, 'vorticist' verse adumbrates rather vividly how the hard pastoral of gardening ('cutting & bruising the dull grass carpet') is meshed into an economic system: 'we return to base | zoned to the time arm || worksheet filled.'[19] But there is a larger charting ambition: to divine the mystic geometry that connects the Hawksmoor churches with the Tower of London, Blake's Lambeth with the tumuli on Parliament Hill. Here the inspiration is neither Williams's *Paterson* nor Olson's *Maximus*, but old, rediscovered books on the pre-Roman building of London by King Lud and on ley-lines.[20] The results are displayed in a map (drawings, photos, and diagrams witness to the film-maker in Sinclair), a cat's cradle of triangles, squares, pentangles, and hexagons binding the City and the East End. It is a structure of ominous energies, which Sinclair animates by invoking the urban myths that link the 1811 Ratcliffe Highway murders with Jack the Ripper, the Kray twins (post-war London gangsters), and 'the battering to death of Mr Abraham Cohen, summer 1974, on Cannon Street Road, ... three ritualistic coins laid at his feet, as they were in 1888 at the feet of ... the first Ripper victim' (11).

The Blake of *Lud Heat* is not a visionary builder, but an initiate of Egyptian tyranny, an annalist of human sacrifice. When Sinclair first quotes *Jerusalem*, he characteristically reminds us that, while the poem was being written, the Ratcliffe highway murders were committed, and he adds that 'Swedenborg, the feeder & source for Blake was buried in Wellclose Square, alongside the Ratcliffe Highway' (15). These essentially arbitrary relations are forged with such prolific intensity that the result is narrative paranoia, a growing belief in the reader that, in a territory so thick with homicide, occult energies must be at work. The later prose book *Lights Out for the Territory* (1997), that brought Sinclair to general attention, patched together from journalism that is street-wise as well as exalted, is self-mocking about its author being 'congenitally incapable of accepting the notion of "accident".'[21] In *Lud Heat*, the humour is less urbane, the commitment to coincidence more morbid. Death is always imminent; the gardeners of Tower Hamlets can hardly keep order in their dog-patches without graves yawning open at

---

[18] Iain Sinclair, *The Kodak Mantra Diaries: October 1966 to June 1971* (London: Albion Village Press, 1971), 41.

[19] Iain Sinclair, *Lud Heat: A Book of the Dead Hamlets. May 1974 to April 1975* (1975; 3rd edn., Uppingham: Goldmark, 1987), 35.

[20] E. O. Gordon, *Prehistoric London: Its Mounds and Circles* (London: Covenant, 1914); Alfred Watkins, *Early British Trackways* (Hereford: Watkins, 1922) and *The Old Straight Track* (London: Methuen, 1925).

[21] Iain Sinclair, *Lights Out for the Territory: 9 Excursions in the Secret History of London* (London: Granta Books, 1997), 104.

their feet. London is built on plague pits, on Roman cemeteries. Dense quotations from De Quincey, J. G. Frazer, and others rework the city as a palimpsest, a riddle of blood and brick into which the reader is led.

Sinclair's death obsessions, and his urge towards revelatory obscurity, are apparent in the two parts of *Lud Heat* that quote Los's journey through the East End. The first citation comes in 'The Vortex of the Dead!', a ghoulishly cheerful chapter which focuses on St Dunstan's, Stepney, and which is jolted into Gothic word-spurts, signature verb-less clauses, when the Tower Hamlet gardeners attempt to save the site for civic modernity by clearing away old sepulchres (79). Again, at the end of the book, five pages of continuous, obsessive prose are broken only by the quotation from Blake which indicates that the culminating quest of the work follows 'the route of Los again' (108). The hero of this chapter 'turns out of Albion Drive' (the street in which Sinclair happens to live) 'into Queensbridge Road, south, over Suicide Bridge' only to reach an abandoned machine-gun bunker, the shape of which, self-parodically, links the original Spitle Field, the fence around the Cerne Abbas giant, and the London stock-exchange booths. Here, library work later establishes, a stone coffin was once exhumed. Death marks the spot.

It is a commonplace of psychogeography, the mode of urban critique and subversive creativity that was encouraged by Situationism, that to cut across the official routes of policed and redeveloped cities is politically vital work. In Michel de Certeau's terms, the 'pedestrian rhetoric' of walking can have 'a mythical structure', countering the rationalism of the centre.[22] By retracing the steps of 'Blake the psychogeographer',[23] the opium-fuelled walks of De Quincey, and the darker passages of Dickens and Sherlock Holmes, early Sinclair follows paths that may be bloody, Gothic, or absurd but are unassimilable by Urizen. (It is also, one is tempted to insert, a very male undertaking. The idea that individuals can assert their freedom by traversing urban back-channels was being subjected, during just these years, to withering feminist analysis.) As Sinclair has put it himself, a stronger term than psychogeography—'a *psychotic* geography—stalking the city'—is needed for his manic detailing. 'I wanted it to include *everything*. Patterns and lines and ways of moving.'[24] Only this degree of attention to minute particulars, and to the energy that they store up from discarded forms of life, can hope to resist the obliteration of Lud's town by liberal economics that was taking hold at the time through demolition, gentrification, and the slapping of blue plaques on walls to mark up place as heritage.

To an extent that, by conventional political measures, is almost paradoxical, and that drew Sinclair's most attentive reader, Peter Ackroyd, into an occult, regressive celebration of squalor, murder, and church architecture in *Hawksmoor* (1985), *Lud Heat* and the books that follow react against the enlightened, civic rationalism of the Left as much

---

[22] *The Practice of Everyday Life*, trans. Steven Rendall (1984; Berkeley: University of California Press, 1988), 102.
[23] Sinclair on 'William Blake of Soho', in Neil Spencer, 'Into the Mystic', *The Observer*, 22 Oct. 2000.
[24] Sinclair, *Verbals*, 75.

as the deregulated economics of the Right.[25] Sinclair's work is driven by mistrust and disappointment at the failure of the welfare state and the effect of its redevelopments—from the destruction of the close-packed, Victorian terraces and factories that provide the *mise en scène* of the Ripper plots in the novel *White Chappell, Scarlet Tracings* (1987), through the Jewish, cabbalistic East End that has shrunk to *Rodinsky's Room* (1999), to Sinclair's attacks on the sterility of the Dome and the Olympic Village (both, Labour initiatives) in *London Orbital* (2002), *Hackney, That Rose-Red Empire* (2009), and *Ghost Milk* (2011). If there is a risk in the later books of Sinclair turning into the Betjeman of what remains of the New Left, the striking thing about his earlier work is that so much of its energy is caught like an infection from the Urizenic system he opposed. As Robert Bond astutely says of *Lud Heat*'s successor: 'Sinclair's 1979 *Suicide Bridge*... caught the tone and the meaning of the newly-emergent Thatcherite, rabid, uncontrolled, quasi-inevitable greed: ... Gradgrind Britain, speeding.'[26]

This book extends *Lud Heat* by matching Blake's attention in his late, prophetic works to the larger fallen state of Albion. Individuals named in *Jerusalem*, such as Hand, Slade, and Skofield return in updated form, commanding the principalities. Particular attention is given to the lands of the East, up the railway line to Cambridge ('the city of death'), because Sinclair finds compelling the arcane creativity (and hepatitis) of J. H. Prynne, and of Newton's descendant, Stephen Hawking, who, in line with Blake, reconfigures *The Large Scale Structure of Space-Time*.[27] A long time in the writing, and full of deeply worked-out matter, *Suicide Bridge* is still far from being Sinclair's finest work; it issues an early warning that, as with his West Country novel, *Landor's Tower* (2001), he would weaken if he moved away from the force field of London. The abrupt idiom of the *Lud Heat* prose, hypnotically effective when continuous, falls loose when cut up as verse. The big, Blakean catalogues feel inert. Less would mean more in Sinclair's poems of the eighties. Yet the writing can find its objects—as in the fear of a mobster-style businessman, another character from *Jerusalem*:

Kotope, in fear, plunges through ancient systems,
his Rolls Royce Corniche cruises the eastern city, [...]
Penton Mound, Merlin's Cave,
                            Percival Street,
St John Street, Old Bailey, .The Temple
[...]
Kotope stares at the lowlife,
a jugular twitch, something dirty
is under his nails:
he arranges for a small assassination

---

[25] Cf. Patrick Wright, *A Journey through the Ruins: The Last Days of London* (London: Radius, 1991), 164–5.
[26] Robert Bond, 'Babylon Afterburn: Adventures in Iain Sinclair's *The Firewall*', *Jacket* 35 ([http://jacketmagazine.com/35]).
[27] In section 2 of *Suicide Bridge*, quotations drawn from this 1973 book by S. W. Hawking and G. F. R. Ellis.

Sinclair would later denounce the market-appeal of Ulster poetry: 'Bog and bomb and blarney: a heap of glittering similes burnished for westward transit'.[28] From one angle, though, *Suicide Bridge* is a British *North*. The bog corpses that, in Heaney's book (1975), sanctify the ground through atrocity, and mark out the territory of the tribe, resembling paramilitary victims 'slashed and dumped',[29] find an uneasy, period parallel in the gangland assassinations and animal-for-human sacrifices that hype-up Sinclair's book. His photos of animal corpses are like nothing so much as the plates in P. V. Glob's *The Bog People* that stimulated Heaney's better-known poems. The sub-anthropology of human sacrifice that runs from *Lud Heat* into *Hawksmoor* hangs over the entire enterprise. 'Place is fed by sacrifice of the unwary [...] Place, finally, can be only one thing: where you die.' Equally unexpected from an urban laureate is Sinclair's shamanistic, totemic descant on animals and topography. 'The track is the heated spoor of our own ancestral animal-host: hare, raven, salmon, wolf, or boar.' We could invoke Beuys, Castaneda, and the whole sixties interest in Archaeology and Anthropology that reaches us more orthodoxly through Ted Hughes. In Sinclair, though, the ethos is nomadic and invasive, place a travesty. He turns Deleuze and Guattari sinister. After declaring 'Myth is what place says,' he adds, 'And it does lie.'[30]

Thinking about London after Blake did not have to lead to homicide. In Allen Fisher's *Place*—a long, discontinuous work written through the same years as *Lud Heat* and *Suicide Bridge*—similar ingredients recur: Olsonian technique, an interest in the origins of Lud's town, sheafs of found material, patterns of historical recurrence, ley-lines. The book even includes an epistolary analysis of *Lud Heat*, which brings out the influence of Blake. Fisher, however, graphs the times and topologies of South London (especially Blake's Lambeth) through a rational democratizing idiom, in which creativity is collective, enlightenment not a dirty word, and the aim is emancipation. As he writes to Sinclair,

> To give sense of emotional attachment to locality, to the knowable and unrepeatable, does not mean to do so as an individual. The territorial ties are not made alone. There are subtle mechanisms at work subjugating our psyches, trying to keep and often succeeding to keep, our senses['] awarenesses at a lower level than they need be in view of the social and economical potential of our situation. Kant held that enlightenment meant the liberation of people from the bondage for which they were themselves to blame.[31]

---

[28] 'Introduction' to Iain Sinclair (ed.), *Conductors of Chaos* (London: Picador, 1996), pp. xiii–xx (xiii).
[29] Seamus Heaney, 'The Grauballe Man', *North* (London: Faber & Faber, 1975), 35–6.
[30] These quotations are from 'Intimate Associations: Myth and Place', the opening section of *Suicide Bridge*.
[31] 'To Iain Sinclair, on the publication of his book "Lud Heat" in 1975', Stane, *Place Book III* (1975), repr. in *Place* (London: Reality Street Editions, 2005), 152–3 (152).

Fisher's account of *Lud Heat* plays down the Gothic and the creatively wayward. 'Your concern is energetic and about energy', he declares, in a Blakean register: 'It is in inter-relationships of situational fields, lapping, overlapping. Where area, the town, becomes radius for action and where action takes place. Throughout "LUD HEAT" evidence of this action is given' (153).

All this is true, yet cumulatively not. The description is closer to *Place*, with its open-ended appetite for information, the poem as active process, creating a sense of community. *Place* is not a sacred book, like the privately printed, handsome first edition of *Lud Heat*, but a set of activities, a civic production that was published over a decade in different media (mimeographed booklets, live and taped performances, poster, microfiche), along with booklists ('resources') to make the project collaborative. It only appeared as a big paperback, with a map of the City, the East End out to Whitechapel, and Southwark/Lambeth on the cover, as late as 2005. To revisit *Place* in this form is to be impressed by the animation of so much matter, by the constantly active intelligence that cuts and juxtaposes, and works the space of pages. We find geology and underground rivers, workhouses, Celtic archaeology (like Sinclair, Fisher has lapped up David Jones), snooker, spiral trajectories, and radiation out to the north (to Dove Cottage and the Grampians).

There was, however, a change. Fisher's theoretical programme, advanced by the 'new pertinence' that he found in J. H. Prynne's *Down Where Changed* and similarly intractable, engaged collections by cris cheek and Eric Mottram[32] was overtaken by an enthusiasm for quantum mechanics. Topography became topology. Mathematics was mixed up with reader response theory, all fields in flux, while the verse became more abstract, leaving the reader too little history in the language to work with. Take *Unpolished Mirrors* (1979–81), the final book of *Place*, which responds to the full-scale onset of Thatcherism in step with *Suicide Bridge* by 'adopt[ing] the oracular style of Blakean monologue':[33]

I stand exposed to such a field of established types
    determining any morphology inside planned zones
a method general enough to allow my break it
    flexibility precise enough
to   spatial continuity
[…]
    to mobile consumer chromiums
obliterating memory and place

held down by labyrinthine clarity
    the stench
under the continuous dome   the heat of London
    imposing memory
where spaces no longer read the locality
make space by clearing the place[34]

---

[32] See Allen Fisher, 'Necessary Business' (1980–5, rev. 1990), *The Topological Shovel* (Willowdale, Ont.: The Gig Editions, 1999), 22–52.

[33] Robert Sheppard, 'The Necessary Business of Allen Fisher', in Fisher, Griffiths, and Catling, *Future Exiles*, 11–17 (14).

[34] Fisher, *Place*, 405–6.

You can see what Fisher means, and what he shares with Sinclair. But the idiom is too easily convinced of its sufficiency to the subject ('general enough...precise enough'). Is this what the Olson of *Maximus* meant by a 'high energy-construct'?[35] Contrast one moment among many in *Lud Heat*, where Sinclair points to the loss of old London: 'These facts fade. The big traffics slam by. A work ethic buries ancient descriptions' (16). This gives us the core of Thatcherism out of Weberian sociology and a recognition that the past is always already reduced from live entity to description, all in fourteen words—about the size of a haiku. No doubt 'slam by' overdoes it (most traffic in London crawls), but Allen Fisher's 'stench | under the continuous dome' does not get up your nose.

As Thatcherism took hold, Fisher began another long project, *Gravity as a Consequence of Shape*,[36] with a sequence called *Brixton Fractals*. The 'evidence' of place went into abeyance, but Blake looms even larger as an influence and participant. Fisher tells us that 'The poems were made directly or indirectly relative to the first fifteen pages in William Blake's notebook'.[37] Those pages are notoriously disordered; but that was, if anything, a spur to a poet with an appetite for chaos theory. Blake is relocated to Brixton, where he is caught up as a process poet and visual artist (like Fisher himself), writing and engraving an unfinished artefact against the background of the riots of 1981:

Blake leans back from his window
down onto the page
eyes partially blind from flowing
writes vigorously across the faces
drawn there, saying
the tear is an intellectual thing,
crossing it out,[38]

This is the staple mode. The move from a raw to a cooked style, from information-assemblage to discursive lucidity, has won Fisher admirers, but there are too many points where the verse lacks what his letter to Sinclair called 'energy' and 'action'. J. H. Prynne is on to this when he objects that 'The...more tonally uniform sentence strings seem to lose traction precisely at the prosodic and syntactic junctions'.[39]

Later in the *Gravity* project, we do return to raw 'evidence' as the questions about human value and how it differs from market price, emergent in *Brixton Fractals*, are engaged with directly. In the books from the early nineties reprinted in *Entanglement* (2004), economics is processed through the pseudoscientific argot that Fisher picked up

---

[35] Charles Olson, 'Projective Verse', *Collected Prose*, ed. Donald Hall and Benjamin Friedlander (Berkeley: University of California Press, 1997), 239–49 (240).

[36] Now collected as a trilogy: *Gravity* (2004), *Entanglement* (2004), and *Leans* (2007).

[37] Allen Fisher, *Gravity* (Great Wilbraham: Salt Publishing, 2004), 271.

[38] Fisher, 'Banda', *Gravity*, 3–14 (10). This is the first of about a dozen named appearances of Blake in *Gravity*. 'For the tear is an intellectual thing' (cf. the Wendy Mulford poem earlier) is crossed out on the eighth page of Blake's Notebook.

[39] J. H. Prynne, 'A Letter to Allen Fisher', *Parataxis*, 8–9 (1996), 153–8 (154).

from semi-popular books about fractals. The dominant spirits are the ghosts of Marx, Marcuse, and Althusser: '*Consciousness creates itself as it produces the world. What it lacks is control of this production. Work becomes a means and consciousness dissolves into substructures of capital or money*.'[40] The quest is on to establish 'how the law of value is constructed' (122). Fortunately, an explanation can be located, if only in the language world of Theory: 'The determination of value by spatial use of time gets hidden beneath the apparatus as it varies in the relative values of its production. What mystifies the Scientist rolls the social character of labours, where production controls the producers instead of producers['] control of production' (123). This, as we shall see, was only one, rather abstract response to the crisis in the meaning of 'value' that was created by the resurgence of liberal economics.

I began by describing Los as a 'builder, artist, and shaman'. The last part of that definition cannot be found in the usual scholarship, but Alicia Ostriker seems to me correct, in her essay on Blake, Ginsberg, and shamanism, that when Los, 'Frightened with cold infectious madness' in *The Four Zoas*, 'became what he beheld', and 'Infected Mad [...] dancd on his mountains', he should not be thought of as a rabies victim.[41] With a sixties Blake in mind, we can see another side of Los: the tribal priest gripped by what Mircea Eliade, in *Shamanism* (1964), calls a 'sickness-vocation'; a sacred figure who takes on the sufferings of his people and, in a state of autointoxication, purges them. Sinclair identifies a similar pattern of creative ardour when, in *The Shamanism of Intent* (1991), he writes about such artists as Gavin Jones, Steve Dilworth, and Brian Catling, who were committed to 'a "sickness-vocation", as Eliade has it' and 'twinned with all the other avatars of unwisdom: scavengers, antiquarians, bagpeople, outpatients, muggers, victims, millenial babblers'.[42]

In *The Shamanism of Intent*, Sinclair develops the links made in *Suicide Bridge* between place and totemic animal, between art and located burial. Another abandoned, wartime bunker—dug out as a studio by Gavin Jones—is reclaimed:

> Jones scratched his way beneath the coarse thatch of wire-grass and rubble. Something was down there that he *had* to reach [...]
> Joyful derangement spun out in a vortex from this site, this recaptured nowhere. The shaman without a tribe is still a nib of energy. His hurt is perceived as wisdom. The entropy of the ravished villages of East London was being challenged by the sculptor's frantic acts, his predatory laughter. If the skyline was to be dominated by a crop of alien verticals, self-reflecting exclamation marks, steel shouts, then we must burrow like moles. [...]

---

[40] Allen Fisher, 'Pulling Up and Quasi Queen' (1996), here quoted from *Entanglement* (Willowdale, Ont.: The Gig, 2004), 99–124 (119).

[41] 'Blake, Ginsberg, Madness, and the Prophet as Shaman', in Robert J. Bertholf and Annette S. Levitt (eds.), *William Blake and the Moderns* (Albany, NY: State University of New York Press, 1982), 111–31 (115). See *Four Zoas* (pp. 52, 57), *Poetry and Prose of Blake*, ed. Erdman, 329, 332. Ostriker is rejecting the unlikely rabies theory of W. H. Stevenson.

[42] Iain Sinclair, *The Shamanism of Intent: Some Flights of Redemption* (Uppingham: Goldmark, 1991), 7.

> Place spoke: by keeping its silence, letting argument force its way through cracks and fissures like a blind spring. (9–11)

After a decade under the shadow of Eliade's 'Bird-of-Prey Mother', i.e. Mrs Thatcher,[43] labour has become solitary, broken, homeless. Artists and writers were leaving London (as Allen Fisher did, at this time), and the fugitive, small presses were being crushed by the economics of printing. Go the way of *Jerusalem*, then. Publish privately, in handfuls of copies. 'Anti-commodities', in Ken Edwards' phrase, 'insofar as the labour which made them retains its visibility'.[44] Print-runs of twenty-one, down to twelve, then ten, like Sinclair's books of verse in the early 1980s.[45] Given away, not sold. Against the arrogance of Canary Wharf—that 'crop of alien verticals', trapped in the futile narcissism of 'self-reflecting exclamation marks'—the artist must, in the spirit of Blake's contraries, dig in among the outcast.

The introduction to Sinclair's *The Firewall: Selected Poems: 1979–2000* describes the election of Mrs Thatcher in 1979 as a 'fault line', indeed 'a chasm. The *Nosferatu* shadow of the She-Devil lay across the land. There would be no more poetry, no free dinners.'[46] If there were no poetry there would be no *Selected*. Hyperbole is Sinclair's muse. But there was clearly a change in conditions. The attempt to write Part Two of *Suicide Bridge* stalled.[47] With his left hand Sinclair wrote an overblown, successful novel about eighties London and its art scene, *Downriver* (1991), dominated by a Thatcher figurine called 'the Widow', but as a poet he had 'to start again, from zero.' 'Throwaway poems, the looser the better, are quietly prophetic' is how Sinclair justifies their immediacy,[48] their affinity with 8mm film.

Consider the title poem of *Autistic Poses* (1989), which describes a dole queue. 'her heels worn raw', it abruptly starts, 'two bacon-coloured patches | dollar-sized'. This is a zoomed-in image of run-down aggravation, the cost of unemployment counted in a currency that (without gross didacticism) puts London into the sphere of Reaganomics. Next in the queue is no better off:

> black crombie,
> collar turned up &
> covered in white doghair
>
> 'I haven't been well'
>
> damp snuffling ahead,
> dry rasping cough behind

---

[43] Quoted from Eliade, *Shamanism of Intent*, 5, the bird's Thatcherism is elaborated on 17–18.
[44] Ken Edwards, 'Writing and Commodities' (1985), quoted in Sheppard, *Poetry of Saying*, 39.
[45] Sinclair, *Fluxions* (1983), *Flesh Eggs & Scalp Metal* (1983), and *Autistic Poses* (1985) respectively.
[46] Iain Sinclair, *The Firewall: Selected Poems 1979–2000* (Buckfastleigh: Etruscan Books, 2008), 9.
[47] Sinclair, *Verbals*, 100–1.
[48] Sinclair, *Firewall*, 11.

There is autism right through the system, not just in the disconnected postures of the run-down unemployed, but in the officialdom that shovels out subsistence, dividing London in order to rule it:

our official, no brahmin,
low caste as an umpire,
shovels out reluctant benefits

on his wall a map of London
cut off at the Thames

the South is not simply *terra incognita*
it doesn't exist[49]

Sinclair's still under-the-radar books from the early Thatcher years are full of such quick-cut frames of deprivation and dysfunction. Rejects with 'twitchy | parrot moods' in Old Holborn, 'sheepheaded beaten | men [...] dole-scratching'.[50] Walking along the Thames 'well over the limit' after lunch, with a clattering, scrap-metal view of 'the morbid stalk of Canary Wharf', we get a swiftly detailed account of deregulated appetite: 'want it enough & you can, have it all'.[51] It is not that Sinclair gives up on vision ('14 Die in Tree Feud' is compounded of Blakean 'contraries', and ends with a phrase from *A Vision of the Last Judgement*: 'that love, call'd Friendship').[52] It is rather that, in these quick, stunted poems he leaves behind him the grandeur of *Jerusalem*, compelled by the 'Marks of weakness, marks of woe' that Blake saw around him in 'London'.[53]

Solitary, broken, homeless. In London, during the eighties, homelessness rose from about 16,000 households to a monstrous 38,000, plus 65,000 single people.[54] Some, like Ackroyd in *Hawksmoor*, romanticized the subculture of vagrants. Others, including Peter Reading, foregrounded the squalor. Not too much should be made of locality, yet it has to be significant that, though Reading lived longest in Liverpool, Shropshire, and more recently Australia, his work on the condition of England gravitated to London in the 1980s. His book about the homeless, *Perduta Gente* (1989), makes much of St Botolph's, EC3, a church in Sinclair territory which is marked in the atlas of social work as one of the sites of charity: a place where winos get handouts.

His dystopian vision of London got going in *Ukulele Music* (1985). This calculatedly ramshackle compilation of lyric and narrative fragments, punctuated by fictional letters, tabloid drivel, a journal of naval misadventures, and extracts from a ukulele instruction manual, deals, inter alia, with the experiences of a cleaning-lady called Viv, a caricature Cockney

---

[49] Sinclair, *Firewall*, 74.
[50] Sinclair, 'Serpent to Zymurgy', *Autistic Poses*, in *Firewall*, 75.
[51] Sinclair, 'Scraps and Green Heaps', *Jack Elam's Other Eye* (1991), in *Firewall*, 104.
[52] Sinclair, *Autistic Poses*, in *Firewall*, 78; *Poetry and Prose of Blake*, ed. Erdman, 549.
[53] *Songs of Experience* (1794), in *Poetry and Prose of Blake*, ed. Erdman, 18–32 (26–7).
[54] Roy Porter, *London: A Social History* (London: Hamish Hamilton, 1994), 372.

whose very name (from *vivere*) is a tribute to the Blitz spirit. Spouting cheery banalities, she holds her life together in a vandalized and violent city, plagued by foul-mouthed youngsters and kiddy-ravaging dogs, even when it becomes apparent that her own son, Trev, is a mugger. In the face of this, poetry seems futile, a strumming on Homer's lyre no less fatuous than the ukulele's 'plinkplinka plonk'.[55] In *Going On*, doubled up in this collection, Reading wrestles or shadow-boxes with the question of what his distichs add to the world by mocking the squeamishness of his reviewers, but he also, less evasively, trashes his own verbal surface by cultivating mimicry, vagueness, and pedantry, or he strips words—which can only be verbiage—from his stanzas, to leave the inane/sophisticated dactylics of 'Tum-tee-tee | tum-tum' exposed (98). The broken disorder displays the wilful carelessness of a formalist who wants us to believe in the cruel arbitrariness of structure.

That becomes evident, with local force, when Reading interrupts his account of a particularly nasty mugging in order to glance, in square brackets (with a despair which cannot escape self-revolting self-regard), at the ironical poetic geography of the post-sixties Waste Land:

Muse! Sing the Rasta. who stabbed out a
baby's eye with a Biro
      thereby persuading its mum
      that she should give him her purse

[Halve the hexameter after three
dactyls, making it 2 lines;
      halve the pentameter thus—
      this way it fits on the page.]

down in the crazed uriniferous
subway underneath Blake St.
      (leading to Wordsworth Estate)
      spattered with drooled viscid spawl. (57)

The alarming crash of gears, as the epic slips into the brutal, the horribly logical into the pedantic, unsteadies the reader ahead of the lexically indulgent exactness of 'drooled viscid spawl'. For the Rasta and his victims, the names of the great Romantic poets are nothing more than street signs. For the ineffectually educated reader, 'Blake St.' and 'Wordsworth Estate' are ironic reminders of the optimism that put up housing projects in a spirit of democratic progress (to build Jerusalem in England's green and pleasant land), only to create hellish subways in which violence assaults the innocent.

This bleak vision is elaborated in *Perduta Gente*. Reading's title alludes, of course, to those who must abandon all hope when they enter Dante's underworld—an inferno figured, here, by the cardboard city '*Under* the Festival Hall' and the crypt of St Botolph's church.[56] *Perduta Gente* is not moralistic about those who find themselves living in hell. If anything, it has instructive designs in quite the other direction. The reader cannot miss how, among the usual mix of found and fabricated materials—this time reproduced

---

[55] Peter Reading, *Ukulele Music* (London: Secker & Warburg, 1985), 50.
[56] Peter Reading, *Perduta Gente* (London: Secker & Warburg, 1989), n.p.

as facsimile, in different typefaces, cut up into collage—there is a biblical strain, one which clashes with the scanned-in ads for property-boom apartments overlooking the Thames. 'How doeth the citie sit solitarie that | *was* full of people?' the poet asks, out of Lamentations. The procedure is Blakean—to use one ailing city as a metaphor for the failures of the nation—just as Jeremiah's Jerusalem stands for the spiritual condition of Israel; and the writing becomes the more so because, in the Protestant-millenarian pastiche that follows, Reading strikes a visionary note:

Woe vnto them that decree
vnrighteous decrees and that turn
the needy from iustice and robbe
the rights from the poore of my people.

What will ye doe with yr wealth
in the day of the storme which shall come
from afarre, when all that remaines
is to crouch with those ye haue oppressed?

This nuclear-apocalyptic passage resonates with the story of 'Boris the Swine'. When his mishaps are pieced together, it looks as though he was irradiated during an accident at his workplace, a Nuclear Power Station, told the newspapers and lost his job, but not before he had stolen a number of secret documents about the effects of radiation (extracts are printed in *Perduta Gente*). When Boris's wife died of cancer—perhaps a victim of the radioactivity—he took to drink and drugs, slept in a pigsty, and ended up on the streets. 'Don't think it couldn't be you—| bankrupted, batty, bereft', the poem keeps warning us. The holes in the welfare safety net, which put 'more and more nutters, | alcos and dossers' on the streets, prompt this. Boris's ailment is not a sickness vocation but it is heroic in the resilience with which he protests (scattering secret papers from his squat) and, for a time, survives.

The book was indeed prophetic, not yet in predicting nuclear disaster in London, but in the sense that the poet, written out and blocked, became, as he put it later, 'something of a "lost person" myself'[57] after its publication. He also managed to get himself sacked from the animal feed factory where he had worked for many years. When the output resumed, with *Evagatory* (1992), the sarcastic-engulfing gloom was both more universal and more political. There is an impression—almost Larkinian, though conveyed, as often, through parody—that things are going from bad to worse because old English values are being lost:

53 bus approaching the terminus;
    dapper sartorial English elder
suited in Manx tweed, close-clipped grey tash:

Too much is wrong, Gibbonian undertones,
    schooling and bread and dress and manners,
era's decline, Elgarian sadnesses;[58]

---

[57] 'Lannan Report' (1992), cited in Isabel Martin, *Reading Peter Reading* (Newcastle upon Tyne: Bloodaxe Books, 2000), 17.
[58] Peter Reading, *Evagatory* (London: Chatto & Windus, 1992), n.p.

Predictably, by now, decline is tracked to London. A recurrent feature of *Evagatory* is a skull, a cranium in profile, filled with map-work and increasingly blurred text, a motif that (to put our pessimism into perspective) eventually metamorphoses into a map of the flight paths of Voyagers 1 and 2 beyond Pluto.

The depiction of subjectivity starts with the image of a head and spinal column packed with EC1. Here, apparently, is our centre, already inside the observer (the skull-city that Blake called Golgonooza), and perception, the pointing eye, is given an arrow from the margin of a page of the *A to Z*, indicating a turnover to Spitalfields and beyond, while the mouth vainly chunters its classical, metrical schemes. What is the burden of this song? Over the page-turn, another vision from the number 53 (the year of Elizabeth II's coronation) approaching its terminus:

Only a troubled idyll now possible,
pastoral picnic under an ozone hole,
England, *The Times* screwed up in a trash-bucket,
   gliding astern, the Thames, the old prides,
     end of an era, nation, notion,
         Albion urban, devenustated

Riled or despairing, Reading invokes the bogeywoman who detested yet was blamed for England's feculent decline. In line with his obsession with translation, his Mrs T figurine is represented in two columns, one in Euro mockery, a kind of obscene Esperanto ('Gobschighte damapetty, | gobby Fer-dama'), the other awkwardly literal:

Wonderful little Madam,
self-mocking Iron Lady,
who some said was a windbag,
some said talked
like an arsehole, like
a termagent

Yet this turns out to be a sideshow. The Elgarian sadnesses are measured against unimaginable distances (out beyond the solar system) and an interstellar timescale that makes the despair bred by London's, and so Albion's, decline perversely empty, as though nihilism might anaesthetize loss. The poet once raised the topic of cultural nostalgia in order to hedge his position: 'I may feel nostalgia, as everybody does, about certain things, but I'd hope that my stuff isn't nostalgic'.[59] That would be simply true were it not so often the case that he offers *nothing* as the alternative to nostalgia.

---

[59] Interviewed by Alan Jenkins, 'Making Nothing Matter', *Poetry Review*, 75/1 (Apr. 1985), 5–15 (11). For a warmer embrace of nostalgia and Elgarian, end-of-empire sadnesses, see Reading's 'Going, Going', *Island* (Australia), 42 (Autumn 1990), 33–7.

Peter Reading described Geoffrey Hill as his idea of what a real poet is[60]—an interesting tribute given that an equally familiar line was set by Tom Paulin when he contrasted the 'reactionary preciosity of England's leading conservative poet' with Reading's laudable radicalism.[61] Hill has long been accused of cultural nostalgia, but he has protested that he seeks to analyse, rather than to amplify, a sentiment that has been in the air of the country since the Great War.[62] Whether *The Mystery of the Charity of Charles Péguy* (1983), a poem about the death of old France, and of old Englands closer to home, in the trenches of the First World War, escapes nostalgia is doubtful. But the poems that I want to end with, from *Canaan* (1996), have no illusions about the voracity of a conservatism that conserves nothing.[63] 'Aspiring Grantham | rises above itself', one squib begins.[64] With a little too much disdain, Hill sees Mrs Thatcher—born and bred in Grantham—as all about selfish aspiration, an apologist for greed on the back of wartime sacrifices. Grantham is not, however, at the centre of his attention. The text that engages most fully with Elgarian sadnesses—a lyric sequence called 'Churchill's Funeral' (43–50)—reverts to London. It is about the condition of England seen through EC1, and it remembers not just the Great War but the Blitz, before concluding with a poem about the City which grapples with Reading's theme: 'Woe vnto them that...turn | the needy from iustice'.

The Elgarian influence goes deep, but it is also strikingly up-front. Section I of 'Churchill's Funeral' is headed by a quotation from the composer:

> ...one dark day in the Guildhall: looking at the memorials of the city's great past & knowing well the history of its unending charity, I seemed to hear far away in the dim roof a theme, an echo of some noble melody...

Endless London
mourns for that knowledge
under the dim roofs
of smoke-stained glass,

the men hefting
their accoutrements
of webbed tin, many
in bandages,

with cigarettes,
with scuffed hands aflare,
as though exhaustion
drew them to life;

---

[60] 'Making Nothing Matter', 6.
[61] Tom Paulin, *Minotaur* (London: Faber & Faber, 1992), 290; cf. 'A Visionary Nationalist: Geoffrey Hill', *Minotaur*, 276–84.
[62] John Haffenden, *Viewpoints: Poets in Conversation* (London: Faber & Faber, 1981), 93.
[63] Haffenden, *Viewpoints*, 86.
[64] Geoffrey Hill, 'Dark-Land', *Canaan* (Harmondsworth: Penguin Books, 1996), 13.

In writing this elegy for the Great War dead, and for living men back from the front, arriving at a London station, Hill was no doubt attracted to the epigraph from Elgar, describing the inception of his London overture, *Cockaigne*, by that Péguy-sounding phrase, '*the history of its unending charity*'. To consult the biography of Elgar cited in Hill's notes,[65] however, is to find an extensive network of associations and implications. Elgar, for instance, like Hill, was a Worcestershire man whose loyalty to the West Midlands was such that to image Englishness through London meant establishing a new reach, or polarity.

It is notable, in terms of that geography, that the history of *Cockaigne* went back to a rereading of *Piers Plowman*. Elgar was steeped in the poem around 1900, ensuring that it was quoted in relation to *The Dream of Gerontius*, and calling it 'my Bible'.[66] As his biographer reminds us, though Langland's poem is a dream-vision, it is not escapist. It moves from a 'faire felde ful of folke' in the Severn Valley to a London occupied by the seven deadly sins. Langland is stirred by wealth and poverty, including the unrewarded state of the poet. This attention to socio-economic injustice made *Piers*, for centuries, esteemed by Protestant radicals, and it continues to attract for those reasons. Peter Reading, for instance, recalls reading *Piers Plowman* as an art student: 'I loved the topography of the beginning—by then I knew the area: "On a May Morwening on Malverne Hills". [...] I was attracted to the vigour [...], to what isn't messing about.'[67] In Elgar's correspondence, at the time, there is much anxiety about earning money, and the commission to write *Cockaigne* served the double purpose of generating income[68] and allowing the composer to revel in the medieval fantasy of the 'land of Cockaigne', a place without financial cares which by tradition was associated with 'The land of Cockneys: London & its suburbs'.[69]

A preoccupation with art and ease and business, with *otium* and *negotium*, similarly runs through the lectures that Hill was revising during the composition of 'Churchill's Funeral', published as *The Enemy's Country* (1991). Hill asks how far the philosopher and poet can stand aloof from 'the proper business of discourse and communication'[70]—the poet, he concludes, must be creatively implicated—and how far Dryden was compromised, how far enabled, by the poverty which required him to write for money (and to be paid with clipped coin and brass).[71] Can poetry, as he would put it later, set over against market value the 'intrinsic value' of an art object? It is an issue that remains latent in the first part of 'Churchill's Funeral', but it comes out strongly in later

---

[65] Hill, *Canaan*, 75, citing Jerrold Northrop Moore, *Edward Elgar: A Creative Life* (Oxford: Oxford University Press, 1984).

[66] Moore, *Elgar*, 323–49; also Moore's note on the Chandos (CHAN 8429) recording of the Cockaigne Overture, 1985.

[67] 'Making Nothing Matter', 5.

[68] On the final page of the score, Elgar quoted *Piers Plowman*, 'Meteless & monelees on Malverne hulles'; Moore, *Elgar*, 346.

[69] From Elgar's definitions of Cockaigne, pointed to by Hill's note; Moore, *Elgar*, 342.

[70] Geoffrey Hill, *Collected Critical Writings* (Oxford: Oxford University Press, 2008), 176.

[71] Hill, *Collected Critical Writings*, 180.

sections, including III, which is headed by lines from Blake's *Milton*: '*Los listens to the Cry of the Poor Man*'.[72]

Before returning to London's wealth and poverty, however, I want to finish quoting Section I, since, in summoning the ghosts of those who gave their lives, in mysterious charity or confusion, for Britain and the Empire, in 1914–18, it remains grounded in Hill's reading of Elgar's biography, and his response to the famous marching song, mainstay of Conservative Party conferences, 'Land of Hope and Glory', headed '*Nobilmente*' in the score:

with scuffed hands aflare,
as though exhaustion
drew them to life;

as if by some
miraculous draft
of enforced journeys
their peace were made

strange homecoming
into sleep, blighties,
and untouched people
among the maimed:

nobilmente it
rises from silence,
the grand tune, and goes
something like this.

It does violence to Hill's poem, which is composed as a single sentence, to quote it in two pieces. Even with its back broken, however, the poignancy of the ending is apparent. The lyric seems to loop back into the endlessness of London's charity, or into Elgar's and Hill's noble cadences, as though finishing on a colon: yet the full stop is there, ending a period (both grammatical and historical) which goes 'something like this', as 'this' itself goes.

Churchill retains a remarkable ability to make Left and Right agree about the calibre of his leadership during the early months of the war. Hill, who is clear-eyed about the dated, melodramatic allure of Churchill's wartime speeches,[73] re-creates but probes the mythology of 1940 in those parts of his sequence that deal with the Blitz. Take Section III, headed by that epigraph from Blake's *Milton*:

Los listens to the Cry of the Poor Man; his Cloud
Over London in volume terrific low bended in anger.

The copper clouds
are not of this light;

---

[72] See *Milton*, pl. 42, in *Poetry and Prose of Blake*, ed. Erdman.
[73] *Poetry and Prose of Blake*, ed. Erdman, 537.

Lambeth is no more
the house of the lamb.

The meek shall die rich
would you believe:
with such poverty
lavished upon them,

with their obsequies
the Heinkels' lourd drone
and Fame darkening
her theatres

German bombers make literal the visionary frowns of Los, sending angry billows of smoke over the London docks, and the poet does not raise against them the stereotype of Viv. He can imagine what human price was paid to make 'Spartan cryptograms like "Go To It" and "London Can Take It"...so invested and enriched'.[74] The Luftwaffe, he wryly notes, lavished upon the poor a great deal of what they already had: that homelessness and poverty which the New Testament ('would you believe') promises will bring the meek heavenly riches.[75]

Demos the god of democracy does not earn this poet's adoration. But neither do the sleaze merchants who 'slither-frisk | to lordship of a kind' (1), the 'grandees risen from scavenge' denounced in the three poems called 'To the High Court of Parliament' which introduce, punctuate, and conclude *Canaan*. Addressing Barry's and Pugin's Houses of Parliament beside the Thames, Hill asks

Who can now speak for despoiled merit,
            the fouled catchments of Demos,
as 'thy' high lamp presides with sovereign
equity, over against us, across this
densely reflective, long-drawn, procession of waters? (72)

The bitterness of this account of a society become so radically corrupt that 'equity' is the same as 'indifference' and 'densely reflective' can mean 'stupidly opaque' is provoked by many resentments. But one of them can be isolated in that reference to 'fouled catchments': the sprawling hutches and warrens in which the people are disposed, while grandees pick at carrion. This is Hill's lofty way, in fact, of describing bad housing and broken industry, lorded over by fat cats.

It may be that emigrating to Boston in 1988 freed Hill into commenting more directly on the state of Albion than he had managed while in England—that, combined with a loosening of his verse line which owes much to American examples. Whatever the sources of the energy that pour through his later books, in *Canaan*, writing to the moment, he takes on an immediacy disconcertingly like Peter Reading.

---

[74] *Poetry and Prose of Blake*, ed. Erdman, 537.
[75] Matthew 5.

His sometimes stilted archaizing feeds the sense of futility, excoriating itself with irrelevance. If Hill is to be described as 'Britain's leading conservative poet', the tag can only pass muster if one concedes that, for him, the Tories are now laissez-faire liberals. Ruskin and Blake are guiding spirits at 'Churchill's Funeral'—not the spirits one would associate with Mrs Thatcher when casting herself, during the Falklands War, as Churchill's political daughter. Hill's account of the City, the press, and the judiciary, during the poverty-stricken boom of the eighties, in the final section of his sequence, is not likely to endear him to readers of the Murdoch press ('*The Times*, screwed up in a trash-bucket').

It is a strong poem, which measures up well beside the texts we have looked at so far. In its sociopolitical outlook, and slightly stagey prophetic rage, it shares more than might be expected with Reading, but it lacks the self-rubbishing technique which, in *Ukulele Music* or *Evagatory* can seem an easy gesture of despair. It also, patently, shows the limitations of Allen Fisher's assemblages and Sinclair's protean automatism, because its historical claims are more answerable than the archival deposits of *Place* or the occult riffs in *Lud Heat* or *Suicide Bridge*, and, compared with *Autistic Poses*, its folding syntax makes multiple, often subtle, implications available to the active reader who is called into judgement. The aim, in Hill's own terms, the terms he developed in his lectures on value in the late 1990s, is to achieve what Hopkins called *pitch*, to create specific, verbal felicities which may be born of the poet's 'conceptual discursive intelligence' but which attest to the perplexed, layered, and morally articulate history of the language being used.[76] When poetry is worked at and through in this way, it may not escape (as Ruskin hoped art would) from exchange value—the only sort of value that neo-Victorian England was coming to believe in—but it can, Hill wants to believe, manifest an '*Intrinsic value*' which is 'implicate with active virtue' and 'Partaking of both | fact and recognition, [...] be therefore, | in effect, at once agent and predicate.'[77] In other words, the 'purchase'[78] of language, when it is poetically active, should provide a responsible counter-value to the financial recklessness of the City.

The poem begins with the passage from *Jerusalem* from which this chapter started:

... *every minute particular, the jewels of Albion, running down*
The kennels of the streets & lanes as if they were abhorr'd.

The brazed city
reorders its own
destruction, admits
the strutting lords

to the temple,
vandals of sprayed blood

---

[76] Hill, *Collected Critical Writings*, 391.
[77] Geofrey Hill, *The Triumph of Love* (Harmondsworth: Penguin Books, 1998), 37. Cf. 'Pindarics' sect. 8, *Without Title* (London: Penguin Books, 2006), 52.
[78] Hill, *Collected Critical Writings*, 392.

obliterations
to make their mark.

The spouting head
spiked as prophetic
is ancient news.
Once more the keeper

of the dung-gate
tells his own story;
so too the harlot
of many tears.

Speak now regardless
judges of the hour:
what verdict, what people?
Hem of whose garment?

Whose Jerusalem—
at usance for its bones'
redemption and last
salvo of poppies?

The City is 'brazed' because it has been through the fire of war, but also because it is 'brazen'. While the jewels of Albion—its people—are thrown out of work and into the gutter, it shamelessly commands its refurbishment. The new Blitz is one of rebuilding, a luxurious elevation of the City into skyscraping splendour. Into this temple of Britishness, or Mammon, the moneylenders strut: lords of the new dispensation, clutching their cellular phones: bankers, yuppies, usurers who make their Deutschmark. Doing violence, as capitalism does, they spray blood and destruction around them—which is instantly forgotten. But then, as redevelopment proceeds, the bloody history of Lud's town is vandalized over with concrete. And the agents of misinformation, the media with its talking heads, are subdued to the new economy: concerned to manufacture opinion, to market novelty itself, they turn out stories so instantly obsolete that they are spiked by the editor as redundant. False prophets making profits. Would that these traitors to Albion had their heads chopped off and impaled on London Bridge, as of old, Hill's ambiguities mutter through clenched teeth.

Let the poet, then, become a prophet,[79] and mobilize the idiom of Jeremiah also favoured by Peter Reading. To tell the truth about lies, in stanza 4, is elliptically to allude to the repetitive news of the tabloids, to 'the keeper || of the dung-gate' (the editor, as it were, of *The Sun*, imagined as a figure in Nehemiah), and to the harlot who may be fallen Jerusalem but whose hypocritical-sounding 'many tears' have the ring of best-selling repentance. The City is the city of Fleet Street—the press, now moved to Wapping—as well as Lloyds and the Baltic Exchange, and it deals in the largest sense with waste

---

[79] On a degree of detachment, see Marcus Waithe, ' "Whose Jerusalem?":Prophecy and the Problem of Destination in Geoffrey Hill's "Caanan" and "Churchill's Funeral" ', *English*, 51 (2002), 26176.

and prostitution. The Isle of Leutha's Dogs, spreading across the square mile. Land of Hope and Glory. Green and pleasant land. Hence the final challenge, bracing but undermined by despair. 'Speak now regardless'—speak without favour, but also, across the line-break, speak now *heedless* 'judges of the hour'. What is your verdict upon Albion? Who and where are the people, and whose garment can now be touched, like Christ's in Matthew (9, 14), for a cure to our chronic ills? Who now, in Tokyo or Frankfurt, perhaps, owns the London traversed by Los, that the endless charities of the past should be unredeemable for even a final day of remembrance (the poppies of Remembrance Sunday)[80] without our having to borrow at interest what is needed to buy back pawned bones? In these cumulatively dense stanzas, where each line recoils with doubts that resolve into growing pessimism, Blakean vision finds a grim conclusion. Everything in Thatcher's London—including, notoriously, the cemeteries[81]—is up for sale, or already sold, and the only wealth that flows freely is the potential of Albion's people, going down the drain.

Geoffrey Hill never subscribed to the hippie version of Blake. In the lecture 'Poetry and Value' (2001), he accuses 'Ginsberg and his British counterparts' of claiming Blake for irrationalism and of reducing 'Without Contraries is no progression' into a 'marketable slogan' (a sharp thrust, given their advocacy of Blake as an enemy of the market).[82] More recently, in 'After Reading *Children of Albion* (1969)', he questions the durability of the values subscribed to by the counter-culture: 'Children of Albion now old men and women | compromised by the deeds they signed in Eden | forsaking dearth.'[83] Unsympathetic in every sense, the poem uses old age as a riposte to youthful optimism, turning against the Albert Hall internationalists a line from John James found in the Horowitz anthology: '*The dancers, faces oblivious & grave,*— | testing testing | the dancers face oblivion and the grave.' It seems right to endorse the rebuke in Peter Robinson's 'Clear as Daylight', which prints Hill's three last lines as an epigraph, but respects the ageing children's share in the common lot: 'outliving children of Albion | who face death now, as best they can, | while the first birds sing.'[84] Given Hill's tone in 'After Reading', and the history of antagonism behind it, it would be foolish to claim that Blake somehow united the very different poets discussed in this chapter. It is not excessive to conclude, however, that the unleashing of liberal economics led to some astonishing, high-voltage convergences in the poetry of prophecy and vision written about London, Albion.

---

[80] The poem was first published, under the title 'Carnival', in the *Sunday Correspondent*, on Remembrance Sunday, 1990.

[81] In 1987 three cemeteries were sold to developers by the Conservative-led Westminster City Council for 15p.

[82] Hill, *Collected Critical Writings*, 481.

[83] Geoffrey Hill, *A Treatise of Civil Power* (London: Penguin Books, 2007), 23.

[84] Peter Robinson, *English Nettles and Other Poems* (Reading: Two Rivers Press, 2010), 33.

Select Bibliography

Adcock, Fleur, *The Incident Book* (Oxford: Oxford University Press, 1986).
Barry, Peter, *Contemporary British Poetry and the City* (Manchester: Manchester University Press, 2000).
Bond, Robert, 'Babylon Afterburn: Adventures in Iain Sinclair's *The Firewall*', *Jacket*, 35 ([http://jacketmagazine.com/35]).
Fisher, Allen, *Place* (London: Reality Street Editions, 2005).
Fisher, Allen, *Gravity* (Great Wilbraham: Salt Publishing, 2004).
Fisher, Allen, Griffiths, Bill, and Catling, Brian, *Future Exiles: 3 London Poets* (London: Paladin, 1992).
Gordon, E. O., *Prehistoric London: Its Mounds and Circles* (London: Covenant, 1914).
Haffenden, John, *Viewpoints: Poets in Conversation* (London: Faber & Faber, 1981).
Heaney, Seamus, *North* (London: Faber & Faber, 1975).
Hill, Geoffrey, *Canaan* (Harmondsworth: Penguin Books, 1996).
Hill, Geoffrey, *A Treatise of Civil Power* (London: Penguin Books, 2007).
Hill, Geoffrey, *Collected Critical Writings* (Oxford: Oxford University Press, 2008).
Hofmann, Michael, *Acrimony* (London: Faber & Faber, 1986).
Jenkins, Alan, interview 'Making Nothing Matter', *Poetry Review*, 75/1 (Apr. 1985), 5–15.
Martin, Isabel, *Reading Peter Reading* (Newcastle upon Tyne: Bloodaxe Books, 2000).
Massey, Doreen, *Docklands: A Microcosm of Broader Social and Economic Trends* (London: Docklands Forum, 1991).
Mulford, Wendy, *Late Spring Next Year: Poems 1979–1985* (Bristol: Loxwood Stoneleigh, 1987).
Nuttall, Jeff, *Bomb Culture* (London: MacGibbon and Kee, 1968).
Olson, Charles, *Collected Prose*, ed. Donald Hall and Benjamin Friedlander (Berkeley: University of California Press, 1997).
O'Sullivan, Maggie, *Body of Work* (Hastings: Reality Street Editions, 2006).
O'Sullivan, Maggie, *Alto: London Poems 1975–1984* (London: Veer Books, 2009).
Prynne, J. H., 'A Letter to Allen Fisher', *Parataxis*, 8–9 (1996), 153–8.
Reading, Peter, *Ukulele Music* (London: Secker & Warburg, 1985).
Reading, Peter, *Perduta Gente* (London: Secker & Warburg, 1989).
Reading, Peter, *Evagatory* (London: Chatto & Windus, 1992).
Riley, Denise, *Selected Poems* (London: Reality Street Editions, 2000).
Robinson, Peter, *English Nettles and Other Poems* (Reading: Two Rivers Press, 2010).
Shapcott, Jo, 'Confounding Geography', in Alison Mark and Deryn Rees-Jones (eds.), *Contemporary Women's Poetry: Reading/Writing/Practice* (Basingstoke: Macmillan, 2000), 40–6.
Sheppard, Robert, *The Poetry of Saying: British Poetry and Its Discontents 1950–2000* (Liverpool: Liverpool University Press, 2005).
Sinclair, Iain, *The Kodak Mantra Diaries: October 1966 to June 1971* (London: Albion Village Press, 1971).
Sinclair, Iain, *Suicide Bridge: A Book of the Furies. A Mythology of the South & East* (London: Albion Village Press, 1979).
Sinclair, Iain, *Lud Heat: A Book of the Dead Hamlets. May 1974 to April 1975* (1975; 3rd edn. Uppingham: Goldmark, 1987).

Sinclair, Iain, *The Shamanism of Intent: Some Flights of Redemption* (Uppingham: Goldmark, 1991).
Sinclair, *Lights Out for the Territory: 9 Excursions in the Secret History of London* (London: Granta Books, 1997).
Sinclair, Iain, *The Verbals* (Tonbridge: Worple Press, 2003).
Sinclair, Iain, *The Firewall: Selected Poems 1979–2000* (Buckfastleigh: Etruscan Books, 2008).
Smith, Ken, *Shed: Poems 1980–2001* (Tarset: Bloodaxe Books, 2002).
Watkins, Alfred, *Early British Trackways* (Hereford: Watkins, 1922).
Watkins, Alfred, *The Old Straight Track* (London: Methuen, 1925).

CHAPTER 20

THE 'LONDON CUT': POETRY AND SCIENCE

PETER MIDDLETON

READING THE CUT

TWENTIETH-CENTURY metropolitan London has not only been the centre of new developments in British art, film, and music, as well as the political, economic, administrative, and fashion centre of British culture, it has also been the site of several literary avant-gardes whose poets have produced much of the leading modernist British poetry. Poetry movements that began in the 1960s with concrete poetry and flourished in the short-lived but quality poetry presses Fulcrum, Cape Goliard, and Trigram, have now produced a substantial body of major poetry. Yet while other cities have given their name to similar poetic movements, London remains unidentified with this achievement. An informal nexus of poetry publishers, bookshops, and venues have sustained a radical poetic culture, with a strong international flavour, that has persisted in the face of considerable institutional neglect. This history has not however led to an acknowledged London style (compare the poetry of the New York School), although many of these poets have shared a conviction that poetry can and ought to do political work, and after the demise of the well-capitalized poetry presses in the mid-1970s also shared a belief in the importance of a low-cost system of poetry publication and circulation. These poets have formed well-defined networks, but not attempted to define a singular London identity to distinguish themselves. The network that emerged in the late 1970s, in which poets such as Bill Griffiths, Allen Fisher, Maggie O'Sullivan, Ken Edwards, and Lawrence Upton played central roles, was tied together not only by shared attachment to London, but by a passion to defend the civic life its culture represented, against all sorts of ideologically driven damage. They looked to older poets, notably Tom Raworth,

Eric Mottram, and Bob Cobbing, as mentors and for inspiration. The result was a poetry with a strong consciousness of its roots in a radical tradition reaching back through high modernism to William Blake, a poetry of intense affect that challenges the forms of life embedded in the dominant discourses of government, consumerism, science, and industrial modernity.

Although this group of poets may lack a well-established public identity, they have developed a formal practice that I shall argue is distinctive enough to call the 'London Cut', alluding both to London's long dominance of demotic cultural trends in clothes and hair, as well as to a specific style of poetic splicing. I don't intend to demean the poetics by associating it with London fashion, but rather to use this allusion to indicate that just as hairstyles were an important part of the way working-class and lower-middle-class youth defined themselves, so too this poetics has its roots in cultures outside the middle-class elites shaped by private education, dominant universities, and access to power, cultures that still struggle to find expression as other than the confirmation of stereotypes. The 'London Cut' I shall be exploring here is a widely employed poetic strategy of fast transitions between registers that is supported by an accompanying stability of emotional tone, a type of collage that acts structurally as an affirmative warrant in the place of the proposition, or polished sentence that is made subject to the disintegrative effect of splicing.

The poets I concentrate on—Raworth, O'Sullivan, and Fisher—have been among its most accomplished exponents. Raworth's fine-grained poetic collage of found texts creates a tessellation of the sometimes incommensurable cultures (class, epistemic, geographical, and historical) that coexist in London, and has proved enormously influential on later generations of London poets because it enables them to enact the cacophony of demands articulated by these jarring cultures. O'Sullivan is a verbal experimenter who is willing to admit both science and the sacred into her practice of modern divination, open to both the energies identified by the sciences and intuitions suppressed by a materialist modernity. Fisher's project uses the splice to capture the fractal dimensions of contemporary knowledge, particularly as ideas radiate from the natural sciences and mutate across different fields of experience. This concern with science is, I argue, a driving force behind the London Cut. In the latter part of the essay I shall show in detail how and why this force operates by looking in greater detail at the poetry of Fisher. First I discuss three short poems by Raworth, O'Sullivan, and Fisher to explore how the Cut works, how it constructs an epistemological tension between different registers of discourse, phenomena, and cultural politics, and how an interest in science is latent in the Cut.

Tom Raworth works with phrases cut from their context. This is the 88th of the 111 stanzas of 'Eternal Sections':[1]

forces that operate
in such an electrically shielded place

---

[1] Tom Raworth, *Collected Poems* (Manchester: Carcanet Press, 2003), 429.

the needle turned on its axis
a charge on amber or glass
are regarded as side effects
strange and implausible
stronger the closer you get
in the period before hypnosis
this simply re-orientation
presents an intricate, complex
picture of matter
bound tightly to its constituent
electron currents
with the brain in a region

Like most of the sections, this appears to belong to a specific domain of discourse, which in this case might be the history of science, of early experiments with electricity mixed with writing about research into the role of electrical currents in neurophysiology. Raworth is silent about his sources. Although we have the feeling that some or all of this is found language, the text deflects attention from any interest in its allusions and intertexts back onto its internal workings, to the extent that much of the text becomes meta-textual. We are likely to regard the possible image of troops leading a charge on amber as an implausible semantic side effect of this process, and want to replace 'simply' with the syntactically correct 'simple'. By the absence of punctuation, by parataxis, and above all by the decontextualizing of phrases, Raworth draws out the latent figures and intimations within familiar discourses making them turn strange and sometimes implausible. How can the brain be 'in a region'? Was the period before hypnosis a historical time, like the time before television, or is it a moment in a subject's life before they submit their will to another's? The text leaves us wondering about the significance of the many epistemological discourses that appear momentarily only to fade at the cut, their large claims pinned down to just a few disjunct and faltering phrases. This is experimentation that leaves us deeply uncertain about the text's commitments. It has no propositions to offer and their absence is felt. In this poetic world there is no power to affirm knowledge, only the measurement of its effects against the regular cut.

Experiment is also central to the poetics of both O'Sullivan and Fisher, the latter of whom repeatedly enacts sites of experimentation in his flickering poetic narratives. His depiction of experiment in the poem 'After George Bataille's "Landscape"' provides a helpful measure of what O'Sullivan achieves in her poetry. He describes a laboratory experiment in which an electrode in a test tube containing a known substance is placed in a mysterious substance, so that 'the free electrode | interprets the unknown by summating | that which is moving and surrounding it | with that which is already known and connected to it'. Summing up, he writes that these 'electrodes | constitute the nerval body of | my thought' (266) suggesting that the instruments of science can help the poet distinguish between the known and the unknown character of everything from matter to mind. O'Sullivan also imagines experimental tools for studying resemblances and what she calls below 'disresemblances' between known and unknown, although her tools are different. She experiments directly with the catalysis of words, bringing readers to one limit of poetry, the liminal word that is not quite a word and not quite a meaningless string of letters, finding phonemes and phoneme clusters that oscillate between lexical and non-lexical identities.

As we can see in the following section of the poem 'Another Weather System', her words are often not quite signifiers, sometimes words as we don't know them, words in throes, words kettled or falling away from the page, words as stutters, moans, murmurs, and pulses. There are even words that do momentarily blague themselves as signifiers, claiming to be 'a spell rolling backwards':

```
a mist on tongue
            (a spell
     rolling backwards)
                  the Day lies
             half
                  w|starts
       the Daily life of held—
Vaga Shized         SURT HURLS
       tiara luna
                       trupled—
                     wounds
last infra rooting
            fraction-headlights
            —held words—
disresemblances

     the year, drawn
            white, its
     NORTH BLACK WINTERING
                  drapes pitch
Blades Teeter
Bones Break
Ursas looted
Salt Owns
Halts it[2]
```

The poetry can feel very small or terrifyingly large, imminently integrable or a rubble dump where horrors lurk, so that words seem familiar, grow old, are revived or damaged, keeping the element of surprise on their side. We ask of each word, where has it come from, what does it do, in what world could it even exist? These words take us in to their thinking, and if that sounds as if they might deceive us, that too is possible amongst their ghostlier demarcations. She writes a poetry that brings to light strange intracellular

---

[2] Maggie O'Sullivan, *In the House of the Shaman* (London: Reality Street Editions, 1993), 15. Reproducing the exact spacing of the published text in a different edition is almost impossible—the layout here is an approximation.

phonetic structures and the wreckage of bibliographic codes that might form a new ecology of poetic thinking, a proto-science of language that treats it as homologous with the organism.

Allen Fisher's *Ring Shout* (2000) is a cycle of twenty-three short poems on many traditional poetic themes: the sentiments ('When so much you have loved torn from you | and you expect to remain the same' (128)); the sense of place ('On a moderately hilly lowland | marked either side by hills and in the south | by a river' (129)); nature ('Oak birds storm at each other' (138)); and art ('the body of Delacroix dated against | blue-grey lead on the surface of Anselm Kiefer's | wood' (137)). Moments of harmony ('Listening carefully perception misses | insect feet but combines flies and | oak birds with distant aircraft' (138)), and quasi-pastoral rituals ('The antlered men stamp into a | field of tulips to gather material' (137)) evoke however faintly the poetry of Thomas Gray, William Collins, William Wordsworth, Thomas Hardy, and Edward Thomas, to name only a few. But this continuity with the poetic tradition is sharply interrupted by two distinctive features: disjunctive collage and esoteric scientific jargon. Both features are evident in section 7:

Sounds on the tape record
the recorder's action beyond
alternating bands of dark magnetite
and light silicates propose complex
microlife 3,500 million years ago.
Lee Morgan lives with
Freddie Hubbard in the night
of the cookers and Graham
Mancur's Evolution
quarrel with sense perceptions

Resolution in excess to system
a hyperacuity reserved for angels and machines
Honour and justice based on pleasant
distinctions of product and production (130)

A sharp intra-syntactical cut occurs between lines 2 and 3 for instance, though we can construct a continuing semantically meaningful sentence in which the tape recorder somehow notices the sounds created by the magnetic ore. This cut is followed by other sharp transitions between sentences: from palaeology to jazz (a reference to Morgan and Hubbard's album *Night of the Cookers* and Moncur's *Evolution*) to abstract reflections on the limits of measurement in real systems and finally to the distinction between labour and commodity. Fisher is interested in just how the geologists come to believe in the existence of very ancient micro-organisms, as well as in the poetic richness of some of the terminology like micro-life and 'alternating bands' (a phrase which leads him to think of the jazz performers).

Reading *Ring Shout* in this way could be deceptive, like making judgements on the Pompidou Centre by concentrating solely on the aesthetics of a single girder. The extracts from 'Eternal Sections' and 'Another Weather System' are themselves only modest components in a larger system, but in both cases the passage discussed is paradigmatic of the structural and thematic patterns that constitute the entire poem. *Ring Shout* is somewhat different. It is just a small part of a very large and unfinished structure—a poem sequence entitled *Gravity as a Consequence of Shape*, which is probably the most self-reflexive, self-analytical (at least at the formal level) British poem of the twentieth century. Characters, images, concepts, and phrases are constantly folded back into the mix, changing their shape and significance. The poem's roots reach deep into a visionary British literary culture of the post-war period that traces its lineage back to Blake, a radical, epistemologically sophisticated culture that constantly submits itself to agonized self-questioning about the possibility of human betterment.

In an article on his poetics for *boundary 2*, Fisher makes this remarkable claim: 'A poet's attitude to and understanding of quantum field theory will affect that poet's experience of gravity, drawing, and reading.'[3] Despite many affiliations to the mainstream English poetic tradition, this poetic cutting and explicit allusion to recent sciences together also mark a discontinuity. I shall now go on to argue that this discontinuity derives not only from aesthetic radicalism, but also from a critical interest in the cultural impact of the hard sciences widely shared by post-war British writers, who combine a critical reserve towards the many failings of science, with a buoyant willingness to treat new scientific discoveries as tools for progressive thought and aesthetic practice.

SCIENCE IN POST-WAR BRITISH WRITING

Science has been a notable preoccupation of a number of British writers with an interest in social critique. In her autobiography, Doris Lessing laments her lack of knowledge, and the skills to acquire it, required for understanding modernity: 'My trouble was that I didn't have mathematics, physics—couldn't speak their language. Because of my ignorance, I know I have been cut off from the developments going on in science—and science is where our frontiers are, in this time. It is not to the latest literary novel that people now look for news about humanity, as they did in the nineteenth century.'[4] Like many of her later novels, the second volume of her autobiography from which this comment is drawn, explores the aspirations and risks entailed by 'the great dream of mankind', and it is scientists who she believes are most actively concerned with such developments of human society.[5] 'News about humanity' is now more likely to be found in an article in *Nature* than in a new cultural text, and the 'news that stays news' is more likely to be written by a physicist than a poet.

Lessing's conviction that the sciences are, in the words of Allen Fisher, deeply engaged with 'ideas of the culture dreamed of', has been shared by a number of British writers in

---

[3] Allen Fisher, 'The Poetics of the Complexity Manifold', *boundary 2*, 26/1 (Spring, 1999), 115–18 (115).
[4] Doris Lessing, *Walking in the Shade: Volume Two of My Autobiography, 1949–1962* (London: Harper Collins, 1998), 31.
[5] Doris Lessing, *The Sweetest Dream* (London: Harper Collins, 2004), 111.

the past half-century, in the work of novelists such as J. G. Ballard, Ian McEwan, Kazuo Ishiguro, and of poets such as J. H. Prynne, Lavinia Greenlaw, Andrea Brady, and Ken Edwards. Edwards entitled one of his books of poetry, *Good Science*, a title that is not merely ironically alluding to that most pejorative of judgements that an experiment or method is 'bad science' because, perhaps like poetry, it is too inventive or subjective, but also suggesting that poetry can be a type of 'good science'. He hints at what this might entail in a witty concussion of oxymorons in his Preface:

> See clearly with clear eyes. Be strong, harmonic and geological. Shun high-tech special effects. As a constant reminder of the possibilities, hold up a kaleidoscope to 'our expanding universe'. Do not always trust machines... Take scientific notes. 'Gulp down the tawny herds.' Hope for 'an explosion of verbal glass.' Differentiate. Invent the language everybody already speaks. Make a contract with language; then break the contract. Imitate everybody; originate nothing. Tell lies rather than half-truths.[6]

The flip-flopping between extremes, between originality and imitation, and between precise observation and dazzling reorganization of what the universe offers, is a tactic for both endorsing the sciences and insisting on poetic autonomy. Edwards, like the other British writers, tends to be critical of the ethical dangers posed by supposedly value-neutral sciences and the technologies they have created, as well as committed to overcoming his own and others' ignorance of the potential value of the technicalities of the new sciences. On the whole, this writing does not pursue exact knowledge of changing scientific theories; scientific developments are treated as paradigms of history, power, and desire.

Two poets have, however, gone further than writing about the cultural and rhetorical resonances of these paradigms: Allen Fisher and J. H. Prynne. I discuss Fisher's scientific poetics in more detail in a moment. Prynne is a poet of immense learning and subtlety, who has been based in Cambridge throughout his career where he has befriended and sometimes taught several generations of poets. Since his break with Movement poetics after his first book, *Force of Circumstance and Other Poems* (1962), he has shown a persistent, detailed, and scrupulous attention to both the disciplinary and the ontological implications of specific scientific research, as well as reflecting on its epistemological, rhetorical, and metaphorical generativity.

Two questions raise themselves. Why might poets consider the vast increase of scientific knowledge so relevant to poetry, and its corollary, is poetry capable of any sort of worthwhile response to the sciences beyond that of cheerleader or critic of the social impact of scientific discoveries and ideas? Isn't Edwards right to hint that poetry is more kaleidoscope than microscope? A partial answer has already been proposed by reference to Lessing: a poet concerned to understand how contemporary society might become less violent, exploitative, more just, more educated, more integrated into shared social purposes, will be aware that scientific research offers everything from medical improvements and better communications, to models of cooperative understanding

---

[6] Ken Edwards, *Good Science: Poems 1983–1991* (New York: Roof Books, 1992), 1, 3.

embedded in its own research protocols. Science aspires to be progressive. The limitations of this progressivism are obvious in many areas too: the close association between scientific funding and military investment, the unintended side effects of many scientifically designed processes, notably pollution and climate change, and the exclusion of many aspects of human achievement from scientific models of matter and minds. Poets interested in the historical forces at work today will therefore be in a somewhat similar position to their predecessors faced with utopian political projects, trying to distinguish valid ideals from coercive and destructive practices.

Prynne and Fisher share a conviction that new knowledge matters because it presents a demand for assessment. New knowledge is not like a book and inert until it is read; new knowledge is an active political force and requires engagement. This demand is not the same as that which motivates the engagement of other similar specialists in the precise domain of, say, a scientific paper on algae in Antarctic ice; this is an engagement with the claims being made on the wider community, for attention, action, and reconceptualization. What distinguishes the writings of Prynne and Fisher is their recognition that this work of the concerned citizen requires an understanding of the new science on its own terms. They ask what is being claimed, and what are the implications for its own domain and for other areas of knowledge outside that domain. They both know that one person, one poet, can only do so much. They don't see themselves as publicists for a particular new idea, whether the chemical basis of memory or the quantum physics of entanglement. There is too much to learn, understand, and humanize, so they incorporate into their projects a recurrent emphasis on the exemplarity of their undertaking, and they select scientific sources in which wider claims of significance are particularly evident.

Prynne's poem 'Thanks for the Memory', from *Wound Response*, reads like a slab of pure scientific discourse:

An increase in the average quantity
of transmitter (or other activating substance
released from the VRS) arriving
at the postsynaptic side over an extended
period of time (minutes to days) should lead
to an augmentation in the number of receptor sites
and an expansion of the postsynaptic
receptor region, through conversion of receptor
monomers into receptor
polymers and perhaps some increase in
the synthesis of monomers. [None
of these ideas bears upon the
chemical basis of depolarization
induced by acquisition
     of transmitter
     by receptor.
     There is evidence[7]

---

[7] J.H. Prynne, *Poems* (Tarset: Bloodaxe Books, 2005), 220.

The scientific intensity of this admittedly extreme example of his poetry, is not surprising, because it reprints unaltered except for the free verse lineation, a passage from a 1972 scientific paper, 'A Molecular Basis for Learning and Memory'.[8] The choice of this article lies in its latent neuroscientific claim to be able to locate mind in the brain, claims that are briefly on show in its opening paragraph: 'In spite of considerable effort (1–4), our understanding of learning and memory is still rather limited.'[9] Prynne in effect wants his readers to ask who is included in the pronoun 'our', and just what 'considerable effort' is being referred to. Religious teachers, humanist scholars, artists, and poets have devoted an enormous amount of effort to the understanding of how people learn, and how they remember: this effort is almost synonymous with the history of thought. But the following sentences of the paper make explicit that the authors have in mind a different collective of thinkers and efforts: 'Knowledge about neuronal activity (5, 6) and numerous behavioral experiments (1, 2) have provided the base for a scheme involving at least three stages of information storage.' Knowledge is what counts, and knowledge belongs to the neuroscientists. Whatever we call the outcome of the efforts of the non-scientists who studied learning and memory, its non-molecular character excludes it from modern knowledge. In relation to this narrow definition of knowledge, Prynne's title contains several interlaced meanings: the poem is thanking the neuroscientist for this knowledge of memory, the author is thanking the article for giving him the memory of this new scientific knowledge, and finally an allusion to the vernacular idiom, 'thanks for the memory', which in common British usage enacts a sarcastic inversion when addressed to an interlocutor with the force of something approximating to 'I wish that you had not done that because I will have to remember it'. The title intimates dismay at the aggrandizement of these concepts, learning, memory, and knowledge, by a narrow, reductionist model of human action. Prynne's poem does not however dismiss the validity of the underlying science within its own domain. Implicit in the working of the poem, and pervasively elsewhere in his work, is the assumption that the science deserves close attention because of the rigour of its observation, analysis, and reasoning, while it also requires a civic, ethical questioning about its claims on us for wider significance.

In my interpretation of the poem, I have to say that the text '*intimates* dismay' because after his fourth volume of poetry, *Brass* (1971), Prynne's poems rarely offer extractable propositions that can be ascribed as endorsed positions of the author. Statements like this from 'Questions for the Time Being'—'What goes on in a | language is the corporate & prolonged action | of worked self-transcendence'—largely disappear. The poems brilliantly retain the syntactical music of argument, but they emulsify statements that might be read as authorial commitments to propositions and all the inferences and entailments that accompany them. What survives is a conviction that poetic language can be meaningful,

---

[8] Edward M. Kosower, 'A Molecular Basis for Learning and Memory', *Proceedings of the National Academy of Sciences of the United States of America*, 69/11 (Nov. 1972), 3292–6. I owe this reference to Timothy Thornton: [http://thecadfaelforecast.wordpress.com/2011/06]

[9] Kosower, 'Molecular Basis', 3292. The numbers in brackets refer to the bibliography of the paper—I have retained them to convey the texture of the article and its style of allusion to existing knowledge.

that reference remains active, and reasoning vital, while publicizable sound-bites recede. The poet Alan Halsey usefully contrasts the American situation with the British, comparing an 'enthusiasm of many "language" poets for theoretical writing and the merging of theory and practice in cross-genre "interdisciplinary" texts which can ostensibly be placed in the framework of a (broadly speaking) post-structuralist critique', with a British awareness of theory that has not been translated 'into similarly intergeneric writing'.[10] Such comparisons risk caricature, but I would suggest that a British poetic resistance to theoretical dogmas about language has a counterpart in an emergent understanding of language as a site of knowledge, epistemic and ethical, as a normative social practice. This is a pre-theoretical understanding, still on the way to more systematic articulation.

ALLEN FISHER'S SCIENTIFIC RESOURCES

Allen Fisher, like other leading London poets Tom Raworth and Maggie O'Sullivan, did not go to university after leaving school, and worked in the building trade until he took a degree in mid-career. His self-education meant that he was not inculcated with the sense that the boundaries between disciplines and knowledge were natural divisions, and he developed a keen interest in aesthetics, music, visual art, and specific areas of physics and biology. As part of his education, he ran several small presses, joined the British Fluxus movement, and worked for a decade on several extended poetry projects, including the major predecessor to *Gravity*, the project *Place*. *Place* sent beams of Situationist and Fluxus practice into an Olsonian open field: a thematic interest in thick description of the local history and geography of London is folded back into a politics in which the text is part of an ensemble of practices. Olson himself thought of his work as in an important sense 'scientific' and throughout his career referenced science journals and current research especially in the science of archaeology (regularly published in *Scientific American* and other science journals aimed at the lay reader), even calling his collected poems, *Archaeologist of Morning*. Olson's exhortation to his Black Mountain students—'there is no limit to what you can know'—and his lifelong insistence that poetry ought to be a scene of inquiry, are beliefs that Fisher shares.[11] Poetry should aspire to knowledge of all possible fields and it can and should investigate their relevance to social transformation to what he calls the 'culture dreamed of'.[12]

Place was published in several editions; the first appeared in 1974 subtitled 'typescript'. A 'Foreword' to this edition tells us that 'as publication of *Place* is not expected before 1980 that is after its abandonment, this book serves as a preview of Book I'.

---

[10] Alan Halsey, 'An Open Letter to Will Rowe', PORES 4 (2006). [http://www.pores.bbk.ac.uk/4/halsey.html Accessed 22.09.2011].

[11] Charles Olson, *The Special View of History* (Berkeley: Oyez, 1970), 29.

[12] Allen Fisher, *Ideas on the Culture Dreamed Of* (London: Spanner, 1982). This small self-published book is at once a dictionary of key terms for Fisher's poetics, and a preliminary mapping of the Gravity project.

Abandonment? Aren't all books the memorials to finished acts of writing? But note the word 'abandonment' as well as the timescale: *Place* is as much a project as a book, and a project whose future in 1974 can be plotted, just as a building or science project can be projected forward. The use of cuts and complex discourse has had consequences for the reception of his poetry, not least by apparently rendering it largely unassimilable by the main institutions of publishing and reviewing. Only one book by Fisher (strictly speaking as part of a trio of poets) has appeared from a mainstream press, *Future Exiles: Three London Poets*, from Harper Collins in 1992 (the three poets are Fisher, Bill Griffiths, and the artist Brian Catling). *Place* was published, like many of his books, by Fisher's own press, in this case Aloes Books; this was self-published poetry and therefore Fisher retained control over its production, a control which even allowed for the use of coloured inks. Books were produced by using stencils on a Gestetner machine, and though *Place* is perfect bound, the stapler was the usual method of codexing. A later book, *Brixton Fractals* (1985) was assembled by copying the pages from magazine and pamphlet production and so retained the different fonts and layout of its first appearance. Indeed many of the books and magazines printed between the mid-1970s and the early 1990s looked handmade, and many of the poets were their own publishers: Allen Fisher, J. H. Prynne, Lee Harwood, Tom Raworth, Maggie O'Sullivan, and Alan Halsey, amongst many others. One step up from manuscript circulation, they were producing their work for small coteries of readers mostly known to them.

Another strong influence on Fisher's work is visual art. Like Raworth and O'Sullivan, Fisher is not only interested in the history and contemporary practice of art, he also has his own art practice. Indeed, unlike his contemporaries he actually undertook professional art training (while working on the *Gravity* project), studying first at Goldsmiths College and then Essex University. This background has given him both an independence from dominant literary ideology and a first-hand knowledge of what he calls 'facture', the material production of art, that informs both his poetics and his actual publications (a drily witty example of this occurs at the end of *Ideas on the Culture Dreamed Of*, whose final page gives a detailed breakdown of the costs of producing the book ('Spine glue 5.40'), and then the calculations that were used to arrive at the wholesale and retail price—a way of saying that facture cannot elude commodification). His interest in science, and in collaged cutting between discourses, narratives, images, and prosodies, emerges from this strong sense of belonging to a radical art culture. Other influences, notably from the work of more radical scientific thinkers such as C. H. Waddington, René Thom, and David Bohm can be discerned too. Fisher heeds Bohm's argument that although in modern institutions 'art, science, technology, and human work in general, are divided up into specialities, each considered to be separate in essence from the others' this hinders cultural development: 'the notion that all these fragments are separately existent is evidently an illusion, and this illusion cannot do other than lead to endless conflict and confusion'.[13] *Ring Shout* might have been written to demonstrate this.

---

[13] David Bohm, *Wholeness and the Implicate Order* (London: Routledge, 2002), 1–2.

The poems in *Ring Shout* allude to new discoveries in genetics, astronomy, physics, and palaeontology, and are accompanied by a list of 'Resources', that includes detailed references to scientific papers in the science journal *Nature*, and a number of books on subjects such as neuroscience, toxicity, and cellular periodicity. This is followed by endnotes giving further details on the Sonic Hedgehog and Hox genes, on botany, and on the ethologist Konrad Lorenz. These references are not offered with the Dadaist irony that permeates T. S. Eliot's endnotes to *The Waste Land*. Fisher is crediting authority to the knowledge in these sources while insisting on both the relevance to poetry of this knowledge and the right of the poet to have a say about it. In an exchange of letters with Karen Mac Cormack, Fisher affirms just how much his scientific sources matter:

> My research [into] crowd-out, decoherence, traps and damage, continues became delayed by British Library's loss of Physics papers (they never did find them). In any case I had to jump back to review my torn comprehension of quantum mechanics and revisit the methods and practices in calculus and field theory, two areas of practice I have never used enough to be entirely familiar with. I'm very struck by recent work on the subject reflecting on John Bell's work after his death in 1996. Anyway, back at the farm I was shocked into waking when I noticed new work in decoherence this year which looks like it's going to sort the whole matter that engages me, that of perception, phenomena and truth, and as you note, focus.[14]

'Crowd-out' is a neologism of Fisher's, which he elsewhere glosses as 'a proposal for inventive perception, which permits a multidisciplinary approach to everyday life and a set of practical approaches and constructions that encourage and permit complexity facilitated by deliberate shifts of limits'.[15] Crowd-out entails an active, experimental approach to experience. In his letter to Mac Cormack, strong verbs similarly emphasize the importance of understanding the new science; he is as concerned about his own limited grasp as well as the possibility that new research has altered the state of knowledge. This is not knowledge for its own sake. He is not just curious about quantum physics and its theory of decoherence the way one might be curious about the lives of celebrities or the customs of people in another part of the world; he believes that this knowledge can help with ('sort') pressing issues for his writing and reading of poetry, aesthetic issues of perception, focus, and truth.

As he makes clear in the same exchange with Mac Cormack, Fisher thinks of the sharp cut as a means of indicating the many-sidedness of everyday life. The resulting collage 'can be defined as more than one plane of reality presented in one plane of reality, a kind of simultaneity or a kind of cubist enterprise', and he endorses the practice of 'a syntactic or paratactic continuity that provides a ground for demonstration of sudden

---

[13] Allen Fisher to Karen Mac Cormack, 28 June 2001, *Philly Talks: Fisher/Mac Cormack*, 19 (17 Oct. 2001), 2–3.

[14] Allen Fisher, 'Traps or Tools and Damage', in Louis Armand (ed.), *Contemporary Poetics* (Evanston, Ill.: Northwestern University Press, 2007), 348.

change'—characterized in the vocabulary of 'quantum leap'. And 'this requires research and experiment', even 'pasting the geneticist's enterprise onto the capitalist method, shifting the burglar's ingenuity into the realm of both, where the singular purpose of the latter crowd-outs any difference with the other'. In support of this counterpointing of different domains of knowledge and action he slightly misquotes Fernand Braudel: 'Each set we have singled out for the purpose of exposition is in real life inexplicably mingled with the others' (the translation of Braudel says that these sets are 'inextricably mingled').[16] The understandable mistake in an informal exchange of letters points to Fisher's preoccupation with the inexplicable and our attempts to explain it, as well as reminding us that it is the inextricability of science and technology with the sentiments, the landscape, and art, that is one of the great challenges to our understanding.

Observing Science in *Brixton Fractals* and *Ring Shout*

Poets working with science have to negotiate some fundamental challenges. Truth belongs to the sciences. Discourses of physics and molecular biology carry with them truth claims of a highly precise kind, and normally only trained practitioners can write or utter these discourses reliably because everything that is said also carries with it a degree of warrant for its truthfulness. This is why peer review is central to the sciences. Anyone else using the language does so in citational mode, and this brings further difficulties because today's scientific truth is tomorrow's error. Most scientific articles have the citation lifetime of a mayfly. Although it is a tendentious exaggeration to say that poets deal in timeless truths, when even the language of the emotions changes over the centuries, this formulation does point to a feature of poetry that can easily be taken for granted. Its ordinary field of reference is extremely stable. What we call poetic themes are usually those topics, objects, and moods that are least affected by changes in knowledge and politics. In addition to the challenges of epistemic priority, and the fleeting nature of scientific facts, actual scientific practice in the laboratories and in the field is far removed from the everyday life of most non-scientists, and the scientific communications though often widely available are so specialized that only someone who knows both the language and has experience of the experimental practice and theoretical debates can properly understand them. Popular images of scientific practice are quite far removed from the actuality, so poets are often at a disadvantage in even understanding what new discoveries mean in terms of the habitus that produces them.

Fisher treats the discoveries of the sciences with conceptual tact, part of the basis of civic life, and so has no difficulty accepting that sometimes the sciences provide us with

---

[16] Fernand Braudel, *The Perspective of the World: Civilization and Capitalism 15th–18th Century*, vol. iii, trans. Sian Reynold (Berkeley: University of California Press, 1992), 45.

our best knowledge of aspects of the world. At the same time he believes strongly that a poet can wield similar authority over the production of knowledge, both as a practitioner with his own projects of inquiry, and by creating his own poetic form of laboratory space where all sorts of materials from the contemporary world including the sciences can be tested, combined, exploded, and synthesized. Even when he was writing the *Place* project Fisher was beginning to find scientific practice could provide both instructive metaphors and knowledge relevant to this poetic history because it could incorporate many relevant kinds of knowledge of the city and its history. Fisher has continued to extend a body of poetry that is probably the most sustained contemporary attempt to understand the changed scientific landscape in which poetry operates. He does it in several ways. He realizes that science, however complex its laboratories and institutions, depends utterly on its system of peer-reviewed communications, and so he reads, cites, and submits to Oulipian indignities the texts of working scientists as they talk to one another. Fisher also presents a series of archetypal figures amongst whom are scientists that he sets down in the landscapes of Brixton, Hereford, and England. Most remarkably of all he finds ways to *détourne* recent scientific theories and put them to work on pressing issues of perception, reception, and cognition that affect the arts and poetry. Maybe *détourne* is not quite the right term here because this is not a 'pataphysical game. Fisher remains respectful for instance of the theory of decoherence even as he is stretching its application to another domain than that for which it was developed. He cleverly retains some epistemological connection between the concept's justifiable domain and that which he wants to investigate so that it is at least possible that the principle at work, in this case in the subatomic realm, scales up to the field in which he is interested.

We can see what this commitment to conceptual tact and civic life entails by looking closely at one of the early poems from Fisher's major project, 'Boogie Break' (the title is taken from a long list of dances that Fisher arbitrarily uses to title his poem sequences in *Gravity as a Consequence of Shape*; the title having no direct connection with the content of the poem). This four-section free verse poem of more than 160 lines is part of the sequence *Brixton Fractals*, the first section of *Gravity* to be published. It presents readers with a familiar urban landscape viewed through a 'technical language' that probably 'exhausts and pinches' readers unfamiliar with contemporary physics. The scene is the icy High Road in Brixton, a multicultural inner London area marked by poverty, and we observe the actions of a character who has already been introduced earlier in the sequence, the Mathematician, as he mysteriously interacts with a female character called the Busker, while he measures ice flow. The tone is icy too. Past tense narrative, interrupted by frequently enigmatic explanatory comments, uses a technical lexis in a free verse line that eschews most prosodic effects:

Took the walkover at the park to change transport
in a squeezed State.
The noise first expressed as random in phase
fluctuated and obscured gravity. It
shifted the discourse into a gap where

measurement relied on quantum non-demolition.
The Mathematician took notes on a microchip blackboard
obscured from a saxophone Busker by a bend
in the wall. Out of a desire to minimise uncertainty,
enhanced by the squeeze,
a massive irruption of bright colour
in soft, contrasted hues
gave a volume, tore the Busker from the wall
and suspended her,
cut her image surfaces into prism clashed edges into
the non-trivial significance of her libidinal investment.
Her energy glowed.
In this phase-sensitive, nonlinear interaction
the Mathematician was provided with heightened
signal-to-noise rations. It presented the discourse
with data bus technology to reach an escalator
with many user sites, but no repeaters.
As the mathematician noted,
No classical analogue exists
for this State without ideologemes.

Such technical language exhaust-fumed
reflection, left my pinched head in
a juxtaposition of buzzes and roars.
I biked back to the High Road to witness
where they reread the ice. (G 74)

A scientific lexis makes strange what starts out as an ordinary journey in the city because a different mode of conceptualization, one derived from contemporary physics, is allowed to provide the narrative. The State, the government, perhaps metonymically the nation, is squeezed by unequal distribution of resources that makes many people feel an economic squeeze, and the policing of their activities and desires that squeezes and constrains them. Noise, whether of the city or the mixed information and discourses of the poem itself, obscures the seriousness or gravity of the situation or the tone of the text. This juxtaposition of elements that don't absorb or demolish one another creates a distinctive measure. Even the Mathematician's notes transform into the sounds of the brass instrument. The entire passage moves from an external landscape of park and footbridge to the making of some sort of picture, and the archetypal figures of the Busker and the Mathematician become the shorthand for psychological processes of perception and creativity. About all that gives them distinguishing features besides their actions and indirect discourse, is gender: the Mathematician is male, the Busker female. But for most readers it will be the unfamiliar language of 'random in phase', 'quantum non-demolition', 'heightened signal-to-noise' that predominates.

As *Gravity* proceeds this language will become more and more salient. 'Philly Dog' refers to 'each human timespace' (E 87) rather than experience, memory, or history, and includes such lines as this:

I am a homeorhetic system
of attractor surfaces of chreods, necessary pathways,
located in multi-dimensional spacetimes
in which crossovers correspond to catastrophes
Folds on the surface that suspend descriptive
referential functions and any temporal character
of my experience and lead into a world unfolded
by every narrative (E 87)

This and similar passages are organized around the attempt to represent moments of transformation. The indistinct narrator of 'Boogie Break' 'changes transport', the noise changes phase, colour 'irrupts', and the Busker is turned into an image and releases energy. Even the thought processes of the narrator are transformed into noise. In the passage from Philly Dog, the narrator represents himself as a system that can undergo sudden transformations or 'catastrophes', alluding in part to the theories of René Thom about morphogenesis. In the introduction to his study of what he called catastrophes, Thom begins by observing that 'the universe we see is a ceaseless creation, evolution, and destruction of forms and that the purpose of science is to foresee this change of form and, if possible, explain it'.[17] Thom is one of the most referenced of scientists in Fisher's work. Fisher describes his own principles, in terms that echo Thom, as a 'transformational poetics' and the central principle could be called metamorphosis.[18]

With this concept of transformation in mind we can now return to 'Boogie Break' and the Mathematician, to explore in further detail how Fisher is employing the scientific discourse. The narrative varies from the surreal—

a massive irruption of bright colour
in soft, contrasted hues
gave a volume, tore the Busker from the wall
and suspended her,
cut her image surfaces into prism clashed edges into
the non-trivial significance of her libidinal investment.

—to the prosaic: 'The Mathematician leaned over the ice | measured the displacement of markers | to compute its creep, | as a function of stress, the ice's and his'. As the poem proceeds, this dual focus on the stress in the ice and the stress experienced by the Mathematician, serves as a counterpoint between the experimental analysis of crystal lattices and the construction of poetic narrative:

The limits of this analysis relied on recurrences.
Periodicity in lattices determined his seeing, allowed
arrangements to discern production and segmentation in

---

[17] René Thom, *Structural Stability and Morphogenesis: An Outline of a General Theory of Models* (Reading, Mass.: W. A. Benjamin, 1975), 1.
[18] Fisher, 'The Poetics of the Complexity Manifold', 116.

how he described it. He determined how
such might be organised and thus controlled
through the inscriptions of his shape in gravity.
This resulted in the construction of a simple anachronic model,
a paradigmatic reading of a mythic discourse
which correlated coupled contradictions.

What is the Mathematician actually doing? The apparent precision of the language only serves to obscure what is happening, but this is not a parody of scientific reporting with the aim of mocking the seriousness and the jargon; this is an attempt to translocate the scientific discourse to the domain of writing, and in doing so to identify the axiomatics of the Mathematician's perspective on the world, his 'attempt to avoid what his unknowing would invent'. This is a form of poetic epistemology that disavows indiscriminate imaginative metamorphoses that tear objects and people from their contexts, their walls.

At the start of section 4 of 'Boogie Break', we are told that the Mathematician 'started again, this time to specify | what might be discussed from what he perceived directly'. Earlier the Mathematician had been measuring ice, and now he concentrates on finding tiny plants growing in ice:

He searched for algae
trapped in water columns.
He looked for pale ochre
as a sign of brash or pancake ice.
He found frazil ice to indicate ice growth.
It was a search for the interface
where congelation ice would form as an established sheet
and thicken the floes, where
dreams are ghostly shapes discernible only through
the gravity of waking.

This language is taken from an account by three American scientists (David Garrison et. al.) of the causes of algal concentration in the Weddell Sea. Biologists have a liking for the history of their science, and these are no exception: 'Dense algal populations in young sea ice may have been recognized as early as the mid-nineteenth century, since Hooker (cited by Alexander) described discoloured brash and pancake ice ("…a pale ochreous colour").'[19] Fisher's poem does not treat this as found language and cite whole clauses unchanged; he picks up individual words and occasionally a short phrase, then alters tenses and paraphrases concepts, as in the case of this sentence: 'Frazil ice generally characterizes the initial stages of sea ice growth; most floes then thicken because congelation ice forms under an established ice sheet at the ice-water interface.'

---

[19] David L. Garrison, Stephen F. Ackley, & Kurt Buck, 'A Physical Mechanism for Establishing Algal Populations in Frazil Ice', *Nature* 306 (24 November, 1983): 363–5, 363.

Fisher makes no secret of his source. It is listed in the eleven pages of 'Resources' for *Gravity*, along with an impressively wide range of other literary, philosophical, political, and scientific texts. What are we to make of the relatively direct connection between the article in *Nature* and 'Boogie Break'? We can begin to answer this question by considering the research paper on ice-dwelling algae a little more closely. Scientific papers are usually explicit about the potential impact of their discoveries, and this article is no different: it announces in its very first sentence that knowing how algae can grow abundantly in ice is important for understanding the nutritional resources available to 'pelagic communities' in cold regions. Ice, a material usually thought of as sterile, turns out to be a vital source of life for the creatures in these Antarctic seas. Fisher's Mathematician is a composite of both generic and specific scientific researchers, with a little of these American biologists in him, and even a little of the famous British botanist Joseph Hooker. By keying his poem into this scientific paper, Fisher is tacitly asserting that poetry should take account of the new knowledge that emerges in the scientific journals.

How then can we sum up the use of scientific language in 'Boogie Break'? This discourse has entered the atmosphere of the metropolis that represents modernity and is presented by the poem as quite ordinary, a sort of discursive pollution perhaps, or in a much more positive metaphor, as the transport system of this contemporary society. Without it you won't get very far. This ordinariness leads to another striking feature of the poetic text, the way that almost all the scientific language becomes ambiguous in its contexts. The narrator mentions a 'squeezed state', which might be the crowding on a bus or a tube, or it might be, given the interest in politics, the squeeze exerted by the State (especially given the capitalization of the noun), but a 'squeezed state' has special meaning in quantum mechanics too. Under certain conditions or squeezed states the effect of the uncertainty principle can be minimized so that both the momentum and the position of a particle can be calculated to a high degree of accuracy. Most important of all is Fisher's exemplary demonstration of a pragmatist belief that scientific ideas like those that surface in the poetry can be of use outside their specialist domain. His working assumptions have some similarity to those of the philosopher of science, Nancy Cartwright, as she outlines them in *The Dappled World*, her critique of attempts to create a unified science, or even a single all-embracing physical theory of the universe. She argues that 'our most wide-ranging scientific knowledge is not knowledge of laws but knowledge of the natures of things, knowledge that allows us to build nomological machines never before seen giving rise to new laws never before dreamt of'.[20] And she contrasts her approach with that of the philosopher of science Bas van Fraassen, who asks the question 'If science offers a representation of nature, what precisely does it represent?',[21] whereas her question is 'how can the world be changed by science to make it

---

[20] Nancy Cartwright, *The Dappled World: A Study of the Boundaries of Science* (Cambridge: Cambridge University Press, 1999), 4.

[21] Bas C. van Frassen, *Scientific Representation: Paradoxes of Perspective* (Oxford: Oxford University Press, 2008), 269.

the way it should be'.[22] This simultaneously ethical and political question is the one that Fisher pursues.

POETRY AS PROJECT

Gravity is Fisher's most ambitious project. Instead of an incrementally additive sequence based on narrative, ideas, autobiography, or any of the other logics of linear structure, this immense poem continually folds back on itself. This is a process manifest in the reappearance of phrases, figures, images, and ideas from earlier in the poem, that are then reconfigured, examined from new perspectives. Although this folding has precedents in much modernist writing, including Ezra Pound's *Cantos*, Louis Zukofsky's 'A', and George Oppen's 'Of Being Numerous', the process is different in some ways too. Its main purpose is to create a poem that is not a linear structure, despite its sequential appearance on the pages of the books. Each poem in the long sequence has multiple connections to other sections, connections that extend beyond self-citation, or a dialectical re-examination of arguments, to a reassemblage of materials that can take some parts of the text to the edge of intelligibility. The aim is to create a three-dimensional structure in the reader's mind, to break free latent and as yet unrevealed potentials for meaning. This folding reveals 'processes courting the edges of unrecognisability' by employing not only a range of visual forms but a considerable range of compositional methods too. Narrative is interrupted by paratactic statements, by collaged found materials from art, history, and the sciences, by homonymic rewritings, and by the demands of intricate numerologically driven structures (such as those in *Fish Jet*). Occasionally passages obtrude into the reader's consciousness that seem to summarize much of the text. In the final section of 'Waddle' we read:

Presentations of surprise generate
positive prediction errors
encoded neuronal messages modify
synaptic connection in snares
of reason, absoluteness and knowledge
the decision to be
in misery
made by someone else. (238)

We can read this reflexively as a description of the intended effect of the rapid paratactic cutting from line to line and one subject matter to another. Yet even here the swerve in the final three lines partially erases the force of the confident statement about the cognitive effects of the technique. Who is this 'someone else', and why are we now directed towards the problem of whether unhappiness is a choice or a fate?

---

[22] Cartwright, *The Dappled World*, 5.

'Pulling Up & Quasi Queen' comes closest to providing an extended meditation on the themes of the book:

> In the poem I am never myself, but speak beyond myself, the poem is that transportation of the self evident before the invention of wheels, perhaps evident in the ecstatic. This serial composition offers an initial dismissal of the dialectical universe. This in no way shifts away from the potential of constraints in combinatorial serial form or physical jouissance of perception. (124)

Does the deictic refer to the entire poem, or book, as 'this serial composition', or is this a sentence whose referent is suspended by the aesthetic act of its placement in an italicized paragraph set apart by a white space from those before and after, and not to be connected to preceding and successive sentences by any dialectic or syntactically driven logic? *Entanglement* is a work in which no phrase or sentence can be treated as a reliable synecdoche of the whole. There is no meta-poetic language here if by that is meant a metalanguage for representing the operations of the poem that is itself unaffected by the poem.

Fisher thinks of this meta-poetics in terms of project: 'The idea of project is that its conception precedes its facture, and sometimes that conception is instantaneous and sometimes it takes many months to plan.'[23] One way to understand just how much is entailed by thinking of the poetry as a project is to think of this as an enactment of the commitment necessary for a fulfilled life so elegantly described by Kwame Anthony Appiah in *The Ethics of Identity*: 'the ethical dimensions of the life include *both* the extent to which a person has created and experienced things—such as relationships, works of art, and institutions—that are objectively significant *and* the degree to which she has lived up to the projects she has set for herself'.[24] Living up to the projects requires more than willpower, it also requires extensive reflection on the resources available for such living. Appiah cites a pertinent comment on this requirement by another philosopher, James Griffin: 'Sometimes desires are defective because we have not got enough, or the right, concepts. Theories need building which will supply new or better concepts, including value concepts'.[25] Much of Fisher's work can be read as the creation of imaginative concepts that might assist the development of a better society out of all sorts of building materials from the contemporary world, including the sciences.

Take Fisher's recurrent interest in decoherence and spontaneous symmetry breaking, both esoteric theories in recent quantum physics apparently far removed from the exigencies of both art and everyday life. Why does he think these theories matter? We can glimpse an answer by looking at one of the best accounts of the vicissitudes of physics during this period in which Fisher has been working as a poet and when physics began

---

[23] Fisher, 'The Poetics of the Complexity Manifold', 116.
[24] Kwame Anthony Appiah, *The Ethics of Identity* (Princeton: Princeton University Press, 2005), 162.
[25] James Griffin, *Well-Being: Its Meaning, Measurement, and Moral Importance* (Oxford: Oxford University Press, 1986), 12–13. Cited in Appiah, *Ethics of Identity*, 178.

to lose its cultural kingship of the castle, *The Trouble with Physics* Lee Smolin's critique of string theory.

Smolin argues that the achievement in the early 1970s of what is generally known as the Standard Model, or more esoterically as quantum chromodynamics—the unification of particle theory under the gauge principle—was the last major discovery of nuclear physics. This achievement depended on the concept that has greatly interested Fisher, the concept of spontaneous symmetry breaking, whose significance Smolin explains:

> Before this, it was thought that the properties of the elementary particles are determined directly by eternally given laws of nature. But in a theory with spontaneous symmetry breaking, a new element enters, which is that the properties of the elementary particles depend in part on history and environment...not just on the equations of the theory but on which solution to those equations applies to our universe.[26]

The problem is that the orderly wave behaviour of a particle sometimes breaks down, and the orderly superposition of a multitude of wave-forms is lost. John Polkinghorne explains that the theory of how quantum phenomena can behave in this manner is part of the attempt to understand the larger puzzle of how it is that the tiny subatomic particles and the forces that drive them can generate the macroscopic world where we live. A theory of decoherence has been one proposed solution to this question, because it envisages a way in which quantum level phenomena might be affected by their environment, the 'enveloping sea of photons'.[27] Light in other words may be the link between the small and the large.

Why then is Fisher interested enough in these models of symmetry breaking, of decoherence, and quantum phenomena not to treat them merely as obscure abstract mathematics? He believes that they are attempts to make explicit the assumptions about causality, matter, space, and time that we all share because they are so deeply embedded in our cultural knowledge. Smolin, for instance, believes that 'quantum theory and general relativity are both deeply wrong about the nature of time...We have to find a way to *unfreeze* time—to represent time without turning it into space. I have no idea how to do this'.[28] The possibly mistaken idea of time as a spatial dimension is not an invention of scientists; it is an abstract simplification of a common-sense belief. Mathematical models are often like this. They are both precipitations of the doxa and attempts to try then to remould these draft concepts into new ways of thinking about simple features of our world such as causality or stability. Fisher's poetry repeatedly asks its readers to ponder on the implications of such ideas for our aesthetics and our lives.

---

[26] Lee Smolin, *The Trouble with Physics: The Rise of String Theory, the Fall of a Science, and What Comes Next* (London: Penguin Books, 2006), 61.

[27] John Polkinghorne, *Quantum Theory: A Very Short Introduction* (Oxford: Oxford University Press, 2002), 43.

[28] Smolin, *The Trouble with Physics*, 256–7.

As a poet, Fisher approaches these questions through language. In his essay *Necessary Business* Fisher describes a poetic practice that was widely shared in the 1980s and early 1990s:

> engagements with scientific vocabulary, historical memory, colloquial speech and perceptive description, encourage readers to find words mean as much as they can. It is to cultivate a plurivocity and thus ensure for the language its meaningfulness, its avoidance of co-optation by the State. Distinct from the intentional analysis of a possible future, their poetry approaches evocations of vision. It dissuades from the competence of eidetics and empirics by bringing towards production a relativistic phenomenology of vision. Theirs are the dimensions of promise and hope: the former is present as distress and joy, the latter as latent and potentially can be made possible, by the participating reader.[29]

It ought to strike one at first as odd that he talks about ensuring the meaningfulness of language. Isn't language what we mean by meaning? Isn't language always full of meaning, too full, of literal, metaphorical, ironic, coercive, wheedling, intimating, allusive, and inferential meanings? However rebarbative, words, as opposed to neologisms, non-phonetic sounds, or non-chirographic squiggles, are meanings. Or is the problem something to do with the making of meaning, the meaning of what is said? What does the State have to do with it? And how is poetry to apply this corrective to semantic pathologies? Through the mixing of scientific vocabulary, history, speech, and observation that Fisher discerns in poetic practice? These are versions of questions that continue to be asked today, and are the nearest thing to a comprehensive description of the state of British poetry: a state of questioning about the possibility of making meaningful statements, statements capable of promise and hope. For Fisher, as for Raworth, O'Sullivan, and many of his contemporaries, language is a potential site of inquiry, and in poetic form it enables thinking to take place through sound, sight, and intellection. Language is social action, reference is always striving to happen, and knowledge is not representation but intervention. Research, knowledge, dialectic, and cognitive poetic forms: these are what the London Cut makes possible in its collage poetics.

Select Bibliography

Appiah, Kwame Anthony, *The Ethics of Identity* (Princeton: Princeton University Press, 2005).
Bohm, David, *Wholeness and the Implicate Order* (London: Routledge, 2002).
Braudel, Fernand, *The Perspective of the World: Civilization and Capitalism 15th–18th Century*, vol. iii, trans. Sian Reynold (Berkeley: University of California Press, 1992).
Cartwright, Nancy, *The Dappled World: A Study of the Boundaries of Science* (Cambridge: Cambridge University Press, 1999).
Edwards, Ken, *Good Science: Poems 1983–1991* (New York: Roof Books, 1992).

---

[29] Allen Fisher, *Spanner: Necessary Business*, 25 (1985), 237.

Fisher, Allen, *Ideas on the Culture Dreamed Of* (London: Spanner, 1982).
Fisher, Allen, 'The Poetics of the Complexity Manifold', *Boundary 2*, 26/1 (Spring, 1999), 115–18.
Fisher, Allen, 'Traps or Tools and Damage', in Louis Armand (ed.), *Contemporary Poetics* (Evanston, Ill.: Northwestern University Press, 2007).
Garrison, David L., Stephen F. Ackley, & Kurt Buck, 'A Physical Mechanism for Establishing Algal Populations in Frazil Ice', *Nature* 306 (24 November, 1983): 363–5
Griffin, James, *Well-Being: Its Meaning, Measurement, and Moral Importance* (Oxford: Oxford University Press, 1986).
Halsey, Alan, 'An Open Letter to Will Rowe', *PORES* 4 (2006). [http://www.pores.bbk.ac.uk/4/halsey.html Accessed 22.09.2011].
Kosower, Edward M., 'A Molecular Basis for Learning and Memory', *Proceedings of the National Academy of Sciences of the United States of America*, 69/11 (Nov. 1972), 3292–6.
Lessing, Doris, *The Sweetest Dream* (London: Harper Collins, 2004).
Lessing, Doris, *Walking in the Shade: Volume Two of My Autobiography, 1949–1962* (London: Harper Collins, 1998).
O'Sullivan, Maggie, *In the House of the Shaman* (London: Reality Street Editions, 1993).
Olson, Charles, *The Special View of History* (Berkeley: Oyez, 1970).
Polkinghorne, John, *Quantum Theory: A Very Short Introduction* (Oxford: Oxford University Press, 2002).
Raworth, Tom, *Collected Poems* (Manchester: Carcanet Press, 2003).
Smolin, Lee, *The Trouble with Physics: The Rise of String Theory, the Fall of a Science, and What Comes Next* (London: Penguin Books, 2006).
van Frassen, Bas C., *Scientific Representation: Paradoxes of Perspective* (Oxford: Oxford University Press, 2008).

CHAPTER 21

'DAFTER THAN WE CARE TO OWN': SOME POETS OF THE NORTH OF ENGLAND

DAVID WHEATLEY

HULL, more grandiosely Kingston upon Hull, sits on the Humber estuary on the far eastern edge of the M62. As a city, it is post-industrial, underdeveloped, and much ridiculed for its unregenerate qualities (designated the UK's no. 1 'crap town' in 2003), but not without pockets of striking and unsung beauty. The 'Kingston' of its name was conferred by Charles I, who would later be refused entry to the city in an incident credited with triggering the Civil War. Andrew Marvell and William Wilberforce were its MPs, and Stevie Smith was born there in 1903, paying it homage in poems such as 'The River Humber', despite leaving for London at the age of 3. In 1955 Philip Larkin was appointed to the university's Brynmor Jones Library, publishing *The Less Deceived* in the same year and going on to a certain degree of literary fame before his death there in 1985.

In later life William Empson was much exercised by the question of whether Andrew Marvell contracted malaria in the swamps of seventeenth-century Hull, and down the centuries the city and its hinterland have remained an uncertain, in-between territory. Islands form and disappear, over decades, in the shifting sands of the Humber estuary. East Yorkshire has one of the fastest-eroding coasts in Europe, its many lost settlements (memorialized in Christopher Reid's 'Charms of Lost Villages') now giving their names to natural gas fields. When the narrator of Will Self's *Walking to Hollywood* (2010) takes a walk along the East Yorkshire coast, he takes care to remain always within a few feet of the edge, allowing him to take a journey that quite possibly no one else will ever complete. Further inland, the Hull floods of 2007 did much damage, and form a backdrop to Sean O'Brien's *The Drowned Book*. Urban change also leaves its trace. Larkin's 'pastoral of ships up streets'[1] alludes to the presence of docks in the city centre before the

---

[1] Philip Larkin, *Collected Poems*, ed. Anthony Thwaite (London: Faber & Faber, 1988), 136.

laying-out of what are now Queen's Gardens in 1935. The slums of Dunn's Terry Street have long since been demolished, though just across the road from it today can be found one of the last remaining undeveloped Second World War bomb sites in Britain, on the site of the Swan pub. Peter Didsbury's work is much haunted by abolished pasts and their uncanny residue, such as the 'bargeist' or 'bear-ghost' of 'A Fire Shared', which evokes nineteenth-century Irish cholera victims, and Henry Mayhew's pure-finder, otherwise a 'dog-shit collector', still seen 'about these streets | till as late as 1950s' (the dog dirt was used in tanneries).[2]

The twentieth century has seen a variety of regionalist movements come and go. John Hewitt, doughtiest of Ulster regionalists, insisted the poet 'must be a *rooted* man'.[3] Liverpool, Leeds, Newcastle, and Belfast have all had their 1960s poetry revivals, but Larkin was too unclubbable a soul for the concept of a Hull 'scene' to seem plausible, or at any rate not until the arrival in Hull of Douglas Dunn and the publication of his *Terry Street* in 1969. With the emergence through the 1970s of a younger generation that included Peter Didsbury, Sean O'Brien, and Douglas Houston, Hull poets became a recognizable (and saleable) enough breed for Bloodaxe to devote a 1982 anthology to them, *A Rumoured City*. Crucial too was John Osborne's journal, *Bête Noire* (1986–96), whose disgruntlement with London-centric literary culture (comparable to that of James Simmons's *Honest Ulsterman* in Belfast) sometimes spilled over into *Blast*-style manifestoes, rendered in appropriately explosive typography; no less important was the magazine's associated reading series. But while the Liverpool poets formed an aesthetic collective in their anthology, *The Mersey Sound* (1967), the Hull poets, despite close personal ties, were from the outset a happenstance of individual talents.[4] In a much-cited distinction, Patrick Kavanagh finds a world of difference between the parochial and the provincial, the one celebratory and self-assertive, the other consumed with insecurity and secondariness.[5] Applied to the aura-free environments in which much contemporary life takes place, however—its supermarkets, call centres, or traffic jams—Kavanagh's distinction has less to tell us. Hull is in many ways a classically provincial city, combining local distinctiveness with an ingrained awareness of the indifference and contempt with which it is viewed from a metropolitan distance. Lacking parochial individuation, provincial cities are (in the imaginations of those who do not live there, at least) interchangeable, feeding the pathos of Douglas Dunn's 'Backwaters' ('silent places,

---

[2] Peter Didsbury, 'Far from the Habitations of Men', *Scenes from a Long Sleep: New & Collected Poems* (Tarset: Bloodaxe Books, 2003), 21.

[3] John Hewitt, 'The Bitter Gourd: Some Problems of the Ulster Writer', in *Ancestral Voices: The Selected Prose of John Hewitt*, ed. Tom Clyde (Belfast: Blackstaff Press, 1987), 115.

[4] See Peter Robinson, *Liverpool Accent: Seven Poets and a City* (Liverpool: Liverpool University Press, 1996), and Edna Longley's account of some other 1960s collectives in 'Back in the 1960s: Belfast Poets, Liverpool Poets', in Nicholas Allen and Eve Patten (eds.), *That Island Never Found: Essays and Poems for Terence Brown* (Dublin: Four Courts Press, 2008), 139–67.

[5] 'Parochialism and provincialism are direct opposites... A provincial is always trying to live by other people's loves, but a parochial is self-sufficient', *November Haggard: Uncollected Prose and Verse of Patrick Kavanagh*, ed. Peter Kavanagh (New York: The Peter Kavanagh Hand Press, 1971), 69.

dilapidated cities | Obscure to the nation, their names spoken of | In the capital with distinct pejorative overtones').[6]

One distinction between Hull and a metropolis such as Dublin or London is the extent to which the writer tackling it encounters a blank slate, or if not a blank slate exactly then a more adaptable palimpsest. Any attempt to uphold the 'parochial' side of Kavanagh's distinction is further complicated by the fact that none of the aforementioned writers was born in Hull. As befits a port, connections with other regional scenes have been vital and reciprocally formative: Larkin had fond memories of Belfast, Roger McGough studied at Hull, Dunn was friendly with Derek Mahon and Michael Longley, and Tom Paulin too studied at Hull (its influence is apparent in his first book, *The Strange Museum*). Larkin's foreword to *A Rumoured City* is a model of graceful and unemotional praise for his adoptive city, its diffident tone belying a serious truth: Hull is a 'working city, yet one neither clenched in the blackened grip of the industrial revolution nor hiding behind a cathedral to pretend it is York or Canterbury'; it is a 'town that lets you write'.[7] A sequel to *A Rumoured City*, *Old City, New Rumours*, edited by Carol Rumens and Ian Gregson, appeared in 2010, featuring the original writers alongside a rich but defiantly various second seam, including Sam Gardiner, Angela Leighton, Andrew Motion (a lecturer at Hull between 1976 and 1980 but not in *A Rumoured City*), Caitríona O'Reilly, and Christopher Reid.

Chief among the risks in a regional heave against the decadence of the metropolitan centre is a descent into parish-pump boosterism: Dunn's introduction to *A Rumoured City*, one notes, is at pains to resist the label 'provincial'. *Bête Noire*'s celebration of the 'Hull poets' stresses the non-local origins of its writers, and how many have passed through and not returned. None the less, with its lovingly detailed maps of the city, signposting the poets' addresses, drinking holes, and sites of inspiration, the project has something of the readymade tourist trail about it, conferring instant heritage status on its erstwhile roustabouts. If there is a context of regional identity to recent writing from Hull, I do not propose to explore it. In any case, the studied vagueness of Larkin's topography (to take Larkin as our starting point) was from the outset a distinguishing feature of his writing in and about Hull and the surrounding countryside. Examined in closer detail, this turns out to have as much to do with Larkin's peculiar place in accounts of contemporary British poetry, somewhere between the margin (Hull) and the metropolitan centre (Faber & Faber), as it does with his treatment of place per se. His relationship to his physical environment also lays down important and influential markers for future Hull poets, as we shall see.

Larkin's posthumous travails are by now a well-rehearsed story, but a brief recap may be in order. The publication of his *Selected Letters* in 1992 and, a year later, Andrew Motion's *Philip Larkin: A Writer's Life*, triggered a series of shocks among Larkin's admirers. As blows rained down from Tom Paulin ('the sewer under the national monument'),

---

[6] Douglas Dunn, 'Backwaters', *Selected Poems 1964–1983* (London: Faber & Faber, 1986), 41.

[7] Philip Larkin, 'Foreword', to Douglas Dunn (ed.), *A Rumoured City: New Poets from Hull* (Newcastle upon Tyne: Bloodaxe Books, 1982), 9.

Lisa Jardine, and others, Larkin's work threatened to shrivel to a footnote in the life and times of Larkin the notorious reprobate.[8] The intervening years have seen a concerted campaign to restore his good name, a revisionist turn that depends heavily on reinstating the division between his public and private selves. Larkin cultivated a crabby-jocular persona, which allowed him to play to the philistine gallery ('*Foreign* poetry? *No!*' he told Ian Hamilton in 1964[9]), on the understanding, among his admirers at least, that this was not serious behaviour (Barbara Everett's essay 'Philip Larkin: After Symbolism' unanswerably states the case for his debt to French poetry). Applying this syndrome to Larkin's treatment of place, familiar patterns—first of opposition, then of complicating ambivalence—begin to emerge. Despite his thirty years of residence there, Larkin never names Hull in his work. The 1981 poem 'Bridge for the Living' is a sing-song piece of Betjemanese ('Tall church-towers parley, airily audible'),[10] but this was a commissioned poem, written to mark the opening of the Humber Bridge. More indicative of his feeling for place is the mysterious 'Here', which opens *The Whitsun Weddings*. Its elliptic qualities can be gauged from the outset by the difficulty in identifying who or what the subject is of the opening sentence ('Swerving east, from rich industrial shadows, | And traffic all night north...').[11] The subject can only be 'swerving' itself, the narrative tracking shot that zeroes in on the city, intimately in but not of its surroundings.

The locals are not an impressive sight, the 'residents from raw estates' who descend rapaciously on 'cheap suits' in the department store, 'A cut-price crowd, urban yet simple'. Is this class-baiting on Larkin's part? To accuse him so baldly is already to beg several questions, given the poem's reluctance to drop its veneer of impersonality. The pleasures of trading the city for the empty landscape beyond it, which we may wish to identify with the plain of Holderness and Spurn Point, go beyond any return to nature, here where 'loneliness clarifies' and 'silence stands | like heat'.[12] There is no observing 'I' to immerse in the landscape; there are no personal pronouns at all. If we insist on projecting a poet into the landscape, his preferred territory is an empty and featureless marginal zone; when in the city he tunes in like a radio to its energies and attitudes, but refuses to stake a claim to any of these attitudes himself. How did so elusive, uncooperative a poet ever manage to be mistaken for a representative everyman, the kind of writer whose Englishness it is obligatory to preface with the epithet 'quintessential'? In his *Larkin, Ideology and Critical Violence*, John Osborne has engaged with the identitarian basis of much existing Larkin criticism, both positive and negative, arguing that his critics respond to a normative white, heterosexual, masculine Englishness which they themselves have first projected onto the work. But, once these layers of misrepresentation are stripped away, what remains? Seamus Heaney has used the phrase 'Placeless

---

[8] For a summary of these controversies, see John Osborne, *Larkin, Ideology, and Critical Violence: A Case of Wrongful Conviction* (Basingstoke: Palgrave, 2008).

[9] 'A Conversation with Ian Hamilton', in Anthony Thwaite (ed.), *Further Requirements: Interviews, Broadcasts, Statements and Book Reviews* (London: Faber & Faber, 2001), 19–26 (25).

[10] Larkin, *Collected Poems*, 203.

[11] Larkin, *Collected Poems*, 136.

[12] Larkin, *Collected Poems*, 136.

Heaven' of Patrick Kavanagh, but the closing epiphany of 'Here' presents us with a heavenly placelessness, a placeless place that is nonetheless 'here', shifting, unstable, and Protean.

Another element in this mix is politics. 'The Large Cool Store', written immediately before 'Here' in June 1961, stays in an urban setting but succeeds in emptying this social space of all that would normally make it familiar and reassuring. The laid-out women's underwear suggests a different world from that in which the customers spend their working days, and sparks a reverie on the contrast between the mundane and the romantic, the workaday and the privileged, concentrated on the grammatically ambivalent but tantalizing lines beginning 'To suppose | They share that world, to think their sort is | Matched by something in it'.[13] My previous insistence on the vagueness of the speaker's identity in 'Here' bears repeating, but as we arbitrate the class politics of 'The Large Cool Store' the question of who is speaking is only one among several factors. Were the poem spoken by a defined male narrator, 'their sort' could be recuperated as satire at his expense, but satire does not quite capture the tone. The alternative is that 'their sort' is indeed meant pejoratively, before shading into the anaphoric idealizations of the final stanza. These last lines allow 'their sort' to find a correlative in the world of romance, showing:

How separate and unearthly love is,
Or women are, or what they do,
Or in our young unreal wishes
Seem to be: synthetic, new
And natureless in ecstasies.

Once again the temptation to round out the poem with our own attitudinizing is strong: surely, for all his indulgence of their romantic daydreams, the narrator looks down on this nascent consumer class as it threatens to get above itself. The ecstasies are 'natureless' because of the cheapening commodification of desire, in the workaday theatres of consumer capitalism, but also because of the abject, empty joys to which the poem's depersonalizing world view has condemned itself. Osborne allows that the use of 'their sort' appears to situate the narrative in the 'male domain', but uses the 'natureless'-ness of the shoppers' ecstasies to infer a critique of consumerism ('capitalism reinvented the sexuality of working women [...] while leaving the same patriarchal business interests in charge').[14] This is to push the poem towards an unambiguous stance, but an alternative strategy might be to see Larkin as exploring a zone of complicity in which the final 'ecstasies' are no less reduced and alienated than the snobbery of the previous verse, and in the absence of an identifiable speaker it is the large cool store itself that bodies forth this zone of complicity. (This is to read the poem more sceptically than James Booth, who hails its 'yearning for an impossible world'.[15]) Larkin allows his 'ecstasies'

---

[13] Larkin, *Collected Poems*, 135.
[14] Osborne, *Larkin, Ideology and Critical Violence*, 210.
[15] James Booth, *Philip Larkin: Writer* (London: Harvester Wheatsheaf, 1992), 125.

to stand, finally, but at the cost of a certain shop-soiling. Our romantic daydreams and our disabused cynicism may not be opposites after all, but uncomfortably symbiotic on each other.

'Like any reality', Henri Lefebvre has written, 'social space is related methodologically and theoretically to three general concepts: form, structure, function.'[16] Larkin's framing of social space in poems such as 'Here', 'The Large Cool Store', 'The Importance of Elsewhere', or 'Friday Night at the Royal Station Hotel' encourages us to think afresh on all three of these levels. Why is the English home of 'The Importance of Elsewhere' so much more uncomfortable than the 'elsewhere' of Ireland? In Ireland, the 'insisting so on difference' forces an accommodation with his surroundings, based on a recognition of self and other, whereas back in the home place there is no longer a dyadic experience, not just of the other, but of the self too. Why does it take a large empty hotel to get the idea of home properly in focus, in the letters of exile written in 'Friday Night at the Royal Station Hotel'—whose exile and from where? These considerations are reflected in the critical discourse surrounding Larkin, most notably that of the Movement, which installed Larkin as the outstanding lyric poet of his generation. In what quickly became a cliché, discussions as to whether the Movement did or did not exist (even its members seemed unsure) quickly became one of the defining characteristics of the Movement.[17] Where Larkin is concerned the pattern among revisionist critics, stung by the philistine outrage that followed the biography and *Selected Letters*, has been to highlight the symbolist or modernist dimension of Larkin's work and downplay the image of commonsensical empiricism, and as Osborne's work demonstrates, these issues remain very much live and contested.

Nevertheless, a paradox remains. If 'the Movement' is one form of shorthand for the parochial philistinism that bedevils debates about Larkin, it is puzzling that non-Movement-aligned contemporaries of Larkin are in such short supply in Osborne's study, whether Basil Bunting, W. S. Graham, Roy Fisher, or J. H. Prynne, to list but four. The critical tradition surrounding these writers is impeccably cosmopolitan, but the path would appear blocked on both sides: first, by Larkin's lifelong Eeyorish pronouncements on modernism, and, second, by Charles Tomlinson's attack on Larkin in his 1961 essay 'Poetry Today', and Donald Davie's repeated acts of auto-defenestration from the Movement, in 'Remembering the Movement' (1959). Davie returned to the fray in *Thomas Hardy and British Poetry* (1973), placing Larkin squarely in the frame as the *echt*-English Movement stooge ('the effective unofficial laureate of post-1945 England')[18] who would not be joining him on his Black Mountain adventures. What would a reading of Larkin look like that placed him in the above-listed company rather

---

[16] Henri Lefebvre, *The Production of Space*, trans. Donald Nicholson-Smith (Oxford: Blackwell, 1991), 147.

[17] For a recent reconsideration of the Movement and its legacy, see Zachary Leader (ed.), *The Movement Reconsidered: Essays on Larkin, Amis, Gunn, Davie and Their Contemporaries* (Oxford: Oxford University Press, 2009).

[18] Donald Davie, *Thomas Hardy and British Poetry* (London: Routledge & Kegan Paul, 1973), 64.

than that of D. J. Enright, Robert Conquest, and John Wain? Osborne's argument confirms his anomalousness in the Movement ranks without transplanting him into the implied more fitting and congenial contexts in which he might flourish at last.[19] But perhaps 'congenial' is the wrong word here. The social spaces of 'Here' and 'Friday Night at the Royal Station Hotel', though thrilling on the page, remain edgy and uncomfortable locations, and it is as such that they most effectively resonate through the work of the Hull poets who would follow.

Douglas Dunn (b. 1942) came from Scotland to study at Hull, staying on and off for eighteen years. His début collection, *Terry Street* (1969), is a classic of post-war social realism in its depiction of English working-class life, comparable to Alan Sillitoe's *Saturday Night and Sunday Morning* (1958) or the cultural anthropology of (former Hull University lecturer) Richard Hoggart's *The Uses of Literacy* (1957). Dunn was a colleague and friend of Larkin's at the Brynmor Jones Library, and, throughout, *Terry Street* shows a Larkinesque oscillation between detachment, disapproval, and eulogy. The author has only recently arrived in Hull, but its condition of urban deprivation seems age-old and immutable: 'Yet there is no unrest. The dust is so fine. | You hardly notice you have grown too old to cry out for change.'[20]

Where the question of class is at issue, as it frequently is in these poems, the reader cannot help but overlay their neutral tone with inferred value judgements (though it may be stretching the concept of neutrality to describe drunken revellers, as 'After Closing Time' does, as 'the agents of rot, | The street tarts'[21]). Dunn's outsider perspective as a Scot provides a framework for supplying these judgements, though to draw on it is perhaps to project the more outspoken and political Dunn of *Barbarians* (1979) back onto his younger self. In 1981 he told John Haffenden of his 'active dislike of Terry Street' and 'the kind of society which allowed such streets to exist', but when he praises the 'remote communities' of Scotland to Robert Crawford in 1985 for their 'valuable' ethics, Dunn grants them virtues from which Hull, a remote city if ever there was one, has been debarred.[22]

'Incident in the Shop' exemplifies the authorial tension between empathy and detachment, but as in Larkin's 'Deceptions', the portrait of a female victim of male brutality is uncomfortably inflected by an apparent stinting of fellow feeling. Her good looks are 'unstylized', 'She wears no stockings', but does wear 'cheap detergent' and a

---

[19] A striking exception, and one of the few serious attempts to bridge the critical gap between Prynne and Larkin, is Steve Clark's 'Prynne and the Movement' (*Jacket*, 24 (Nov. 2003), [http://jacketmagazine.com/24/clark-s.html]), which makes a *tu quoque* case for the presence of unpleasantly right-wing trace-elements in the Cambridge poet's work. Andrew Duncan's 'Response to Steve Clark's "Prynne and the Movement"' (*Jacket*, 24 (Nov. 2003), [http://www.jacketmagazine.com/24/duncan.html]) is sarcastically unconvinced. On 9 Jan. 1975 Larkin reported to Robert Conquest that Peter Ackroyd was 'pissing against the wind with his Prynne and co', *Selected Letters*, ed. Anthony Thwaite (London: Faber & Faber, 1992), 519.

[20] Douglas Dunn, *Terry Street* (London: Faber & Faber, 1969), 14.

[21] Dunn, *Terry Street*, 26.

[22] John Haffenden (ed.), *Poets in Conversation* (London: Faber & Faber, 1981), 11–34 (19); Robert Crawford, 'Douglas Dunn Talking with Robert Crawford', *Verse*, 4 (1985), 26–35 (26).

'plastic belt'.[23] Why such an abundance of deprecation in such a short (twelve-line) poem? Are we wrong to sense an undertow of voyeurism and exploitation? Dunn's use of pronouns throughout *Terry Street* is highly revealing in this regard. The locals are 'they' rather than 'we'. 'Window Affairs' begins with a 'we' ('We were looking at the same things'),[24] but turns its shared experience with a neighbouring woman into a heightened experience of apartness, marked (as in 'Young Women in Rollers') by a pane of glass. There is (Larkinesque touch) 'nothing to say' and the woman remains 'Untouchable | [...] in a world of foul language', though only two poems before he had aspired to break the glass and connect ('I want to be touched by them, know their lives').[25] When 'New Light on Terry Street' shifts from the third-person plural to 'you' in its final line the poet may be inching one step closer to his neighbours or, just as plausibly, addressing himself in the second person in disapproval at his bogging down in such dispiriting company.

'The Silences' strikes an anthropological note, pitched somewhere between the archaeological excavations of Didsbury's work and the more distancing strategies of the (as yet unborn) Martians:

They are a part of the silence of places,
The people who live here, working, falling asleep,
In a place removed one style in time outwith
The trend of places. They are like a lost tribe.[26]

'Lost' is a loaded term here, and recalls Barthes's excoriation in *Mythologies* of the term 'lost continent' for Africa: who has lost the tribe of Terry Street and how might it be found? When Derek Mahon speaks of a 'lost tribe', in 'Nostalgias', singing 'Abide with me' on a 'desolate headland', there is an implied critique of the Northern Irish Protestant tribe from within, but Dunn repudiates any such intimacy with his neighbours.[27] Writing twenty-five years after the book's publication, Dunn remembered his embarrassment at being filmed walking at a student's request along Terry Street in 1975, lest anyone he knew saw him: 'Why?—I suppose it was because I didn't "belong" there, while others did, and I knew it.'[28] It is peculiar, for all Larkin's jibes in his letters about the working class, that it should be the left-leaning, working-class Dunn who felt the need so strongly to dissociate himself from the English proletariat, and to make of this dissociation not just a personal, but an artistic, point of principle.

[23] Dunn, *Terry Street*, 18.
[24] Dunn, *Terry Street*, 33.
[25] Dunn, *Terry Street*, 33–4 (30).
[26] Dunn, *Terry Street*, 32.
[27] Derek Mahon, 'Nostalgias', *Collected Poems* (Loughcrew: Gallery Press, 1999), 75. Mahon's own contribution to Hull poetry, 'Going Home' (dedicated to Douglas Dunn), is easily overlooked, given its non-appearance in *Collected Poems*, but voices a 'poetry of | Leavetaking and homecoming' combined at the Hullish 'end | Of the rainbow' in *The Snow Party* (Oxford: Oxford University Press, 1975), 6–7.
[28] Douglas Dunn, 'Memories of 26 Flixbro Terrace, Terry Street, Hull, 1966–1968', *Terry Street: A Bête Noire Special Edition* (1994), 14.

When David Kennedy (paraphrasing Ian Gregson) comments on the 'ruined' nature of Dunn's lyricism,[29] he places the link between lyric and community in a relationship of dynamic negativity. One symptom of this is the on-off switch Dunn reserves for his 'particular community' in *Terry Street*, dividing the book into two halves (Terry Street poems and other), with even an expedition to the south bank of the Humber in part two counting as parole from the confines of Flixbro Terrace. Also in part two is 'A Poem in Praise of the British', which steps back from particularity to explore broader notions of community and belonging. The chain of associations awoken in Dunn is insistently post-imperial, not to mention military. 'What a time this would be for true decadence!',[30] he announces exultantly, but, as in Larkin before him, indulgence in the carnivalesque is strictly rationed, sinking into more modest pleasures and a nostalgic look at the 'archives of light, where greatness has gone'. 'Greatness' here is tinged with large amounts of irony, but constricting though British horizons may be, the pleasures of disillusionment, satire, and attack still outweigh the attractions of elsewhere, for now at least. Scotland is marginally present in *Terry Street* (in 'Ships' and 'Landscape with One Figure') but his British rather than merely English or Scottish viewpoint affords Dunn a vitally dyadic understanding of 'The Importance of Elsewhere', since 'elsewhere', it turns out, is also home, and home is elsewhere.

It is one of the peculiarities of contemporary poetry criticism that Larkin and his near-contemporary Roy Fisher's work should so seldom have been compared, but Fisher's ambivalent relationship to his native Birmingham is rich in affinities with the roots-disowning stance of Larkin's 'I Remember, I Remember'. On the one hand Fisher announces that 'Birmingham's what I think with', at the start of his 'Texts for a Film', while on the other he casually plays down the question of topography: 'The "place" tag is not very meaningful to me.'[31] If this convergence is under-attended to in Larkin studies, it is fruitfully in evidence in the work of Peter Didsbury (b. 1946). Like a trawlerman swearing in ancient Greek, Didsbury's poems combine the wistfully highbrow with a harder edge, an intimacy with historic Hull with the obligatory get-out clause for a Hull poet of birth elsewhere (Didsbury's first six years were spent in Fleetwood, Lancashire). Though a late starter and increasingly Larkinesque in his gaps between collections, Didsbury is one of the significant post-war English poets. His books are *The Butchers of Hull* (1982), *The Classical Farm* (1987), *That Old-Time Religion* (1994), and *A Natural History* (incorporated in *Scenes from a Long Sleep: New & Collected Poems* (2003)); a list of Didsbury poems that will keep their place in future anthologies would include 'The Hailstone', 'The Drainage', 'The Flowers of Finland', 'Three Lakes by Humber', 'Eikon Basilike', 'Glimpsed Among Trees', 'The Rain', 'A Bee', 'A Malediction', 'An Expedition', 'Cemetery Clearance', and 'Tailor in a Landscape'. A measure of the difficulty that has attached to

---

[29] David Kennedy, *Douglas Dunn* (Tavistock: Northcote House, 2008), 16.
[30] Dunn, *Terry Street*, 61.
[31] Roy Fisher, *The Long and the Short of It: Poems 1955–2005* (Tarset: Bloodaxe Books, 2005), 285; interview with Robert Sheppard, *Interviews Through Time & Selected Prose* (Exeter: Shearsman Books, 2000), 86.

placing Didsbury can be seen in Andrew Duncan's attribution of his late development to Didsbury's reading of only 'mainstream' poets in his youth, a career narrative which Didsbury himself has described in interview as 'false. False spelt "bollocks" '.[32]

More so than either Larkin or Dunn, Didsbury's has been a whole career spent writing in, of, or against Hull. At their most direct, his loco-descriptive poems can be entirely straightforward, or straightforward-seeming. If 'Three Lakes by Humber' shows Didsbury at his closest to the spirit of William Carlos Williams, what ideas are there in the nothing-but-thinginess of a description such as: 'Bright green: | silent stock-car 33 | lies rotting in its acid'?[33] The key word may be 'rotting', and the baggage of nostalgia for post-war decline it entails. Railways abound in Didsbury's work, as they also do in Larkin and O'Brien, and the use of nitric acid in early photography adds a sepia glow to this vignette. The acid, in this case, would be an agent of revelation as well as corrosion. The description turns out to be not so direct, after all. In a chapter on Hull in his *Contemporary British Poetry and the City*, Peter Barry is moved to generalize on the shared compulsion of Hull poets to approach but crucially overshoot the realist style-sheet. Hull poets 'like to use an "urban-symbolic" mode, and some degree of "urban-generic" setting, but they tend not to employ loco-specific cartographic material'.[34] History, it seems, is partly to blame. Didsbury's poetry, Barry argues, posits a dichotomy between imagination and material, 'material' covering both history and politics. Of the poem 'Building the *Titanic*', from *The Butchers of Hull*, he comments that the writer appears to stress the 'helplessness and powerlessness of his subject matter'. Workers pour through the gates of the Harland and Wolff shipyard oblivious of the looming catastrophes of the *Titanic*'s sinking and the First World War, in which many of them will lose their lives; they are described with ironic authorial omnipotence, without a twinge of knowing regret for their coming ordeals. Pointing out several factual inaccuracies in the poem when compared with its nominal inspiration (a 1911 photograph of the shipyard workers from the Ulster Folk and Transport Museum), Barry diagnoses a '(mis)conceive[d]' relationship to the ' "real" ', adding ominously that this may be of a piece with the 'decline of general interest in it'.[35] Is Didsbury an irresponsible hierophant of the imagination? It is true his tone may strike the casual reader as arch—

We work a black change on you.
Resolved into coats and moustaches
You are free, now, to consort like wolves on the snow.
We turn you into a thousand German orchestras.[36]

---

[32] Andrew Duncan, 'Didsbury', on Andrew Duncan, personal website: [http://www.pinko.org/20.html, accessed 18 Aug. 2010], David Wheatley, 'Interview with Peter Didsbury', *Metre*, 16 (Autumn 2004), 41–55 (41).

[33] Didsbury, *Scenes from a Long Sleep*, 176.

[34] Peter Barry, *Contemporary British Poetry and the City* (Manchester: Manchester University Press, 2000), 111.

[35] Barry, *Contemporary British Poetry and the City*, 116.

[36] Didsbury, *Scenes from a Long Sleep*, 174.

—but I see no grounds for Barry's questions as to 'Why [...] the poet is doing this, other than because he can?' (why else would any writer?), and 'why the poet is imposing yet another layer of victimhood on those who are depicted in the photograph'. To Barry, the gap between historical pain and poetic privilege remains unbridged, recklessly so. Didsbury's prestidigitatory ways with his subject matter are somehow an affront, a moral shortcoming that becomes an aesthetic one too. But Didsbury is not the only modern poet to have grappled with the question of how to elegize history's nameless victims, or failed to conjure a universal panacea for their pain. 'I would not dare | Console you if I could', Larkin suggests of the rape victim in 'Deceptions';[37] Heaney's speaker can only 'almost' love the victim of 'Punishment'; and 'History to the defeated | May say Alas but cannot help nor pardon', as Auden wrote in 'Spain', an ethical judgement complicated by his subsequent rejection of the poem and writing 'This is a lie' in the margin beside this most emotive line. If Auden could not solve this problem, Didsbury may reasonably be excused condemnation for failing to do so too. The task of the poet is to imagine, not imagine he can make personally amends for, the tragedies of history.

Barry's moralizing way with Didsbury's work invites a challenge as to why linguistic playfulness and social history should seem incompatible, and which if any style can claim an ethical monopoly on the past. Stephen Dedalus thought God 'a shout in the street', and in the early Didsbury poem 'A Daft Place' the proverbial daftness (northern flat 'a', please) becomes an isograph of localness, half-quaint, half-minatory, with its 'daft new names', 'daft front doors', and 'sweet daft secrets', but punningly detached from formal possession when the place is finally 'dafter than we care to own'.[38] With its bumptious peasants, offal-eating, and 'stories thwacked like bladders', the Brueghelesque 'In Britain' devotes twenty-eight lines to rollocking vulgarity before earthing the poem in violent territoriality ('The stories, reasons for killing each other'), if one in which, again, it is impossible to situate the speaker with any degree of certainty (who *is* speaking?). Whose Britain is this anyway? Just as Didsbury effortlessly summons Finland, Turkey, or the classical world, his Hull might be the poetic daydream of a Chinese or Sumerian poet, in the huge, oneiric hall of mirrors that is his work.

Didsbury's first two books were printed with specially wider pages to accommodate his longer lines, and the journal most closely associated with Hull poetry in the 1980s and 1990s, *Bête Noire*, also rejoiced in a generous girth and other design eccentricities, such as its outsized sans serif majuscules and telephone directory-sized page count. Its editor, John Osborne, has published the most comprehensive account of Didsbury's work in *Bête Noire*, stressing its anti-realist qualities and amenability to postmodernism and theories of the death of the author. Yet once again for a Hull poet, the suggestion of postmodernity means anything but a break with the past. In interview Larkin vigorously rebutted any taint of lingering Christian belief (though Geoffrey Hill has demurred, placing him among the 'residual beneficiaries' of the Anglican 'torpor' he finds in Eliot's *Four Quartets*[39]). Didsbury's

---

[37] Larkin, 'Deceptions', *Collected Poems*, 32.
[38] Didsbury, 'A Daft Place', *Scenes from a Long Sleep*, 199.
[39] Geoffrey Hill, 'Dividing Legacies', in *Collected Critical Writings*, ed. Kenneth Haynes (Oxford: Oxford University Press, 2008), 379.

engagement with the Anglican tradition, by contrast, though complex, is subject to no such disavowals. Nowhere is this more majestically on show than in the luxuriant and mysterious poem 'Eikon Basilike', which takes the form of a walk through 'the empty heart of the city'. Mention has been made of Hull's links to the Civil War and refusal of admission to King Charles: *Eikon Basilike* was the title given to the king's supposed autobiography, published shortly after his execution, and subtitled (as Didsbury's last line reminds us) 'The Portraicture of His Sacred Majestie in His Solitudes and Sufferings'. Despite this Catholic framework, Osborne also finds multiple allusions to Cromwell in the poem.[40]

As in 'The Rain', there is recourse to deep linguistic structures but a sense of playful arbitrariness about them too, as hinted at by references to Esperanto and 'horrible Volapük'. 'The Hailstone' speaks of 'a usable language getting used', and here Didsbury suggests a narrative propelling itself forward as though by ghostly inertia: 'It was a case of etcetera etcetera'. The reader might wonder why the cityscape of 'Eikon Basilike' is so unpeopled, and whether Didsbury is not anticipating the melancholy absence of its subjects from the scene of history so familiar from the work of W. G. Sebald. But as solitudes go, this is anything but self-indulgent. The convergence of Anglo-Catholic spirituality and a heavy-industrial backdrop recalls the beautiful conclusion of Tarkovsky's *Stalker*, which juxtaposes a monstrous power plant and the tender image of the Stalker carrying his daughter on his shoulders—a daughter with psychokinetic powers, as we learn in the film's last scene. Where the end of Didsbury's poem is concerned, revelation comes at the cost of a severe self-rebuke. The narrator attempts to articulate the name of the absent God hovering over all his cityscape ('Something—Something—G—B. | Like a name of God. But the letters were all wrong').[41] The fact that he has 'no problem' supplying from his 'sad and emotional erudition' the subtext of the name *Eikon Basilike* is small comfort. Rather, it hints at the real pain involved in the failure Barry has described to connect 'material' and 'imagination'. The speaker is left with the image of the king but not the king himself, the pageantry of the sovereign imagination but no real kingdom in which to exercise it. The poem is both a critique of the Romantic imagination, written at its late, postmodernist fag end, and of the recourse to theology as a vain and desperate attempt to regain this disappeared majesty. If this suggests Didsbury learns his style from a despair, to borrow Empson's phrase, the eirenic surfaces of his work could not be less melodramatic about their plight. The name of God alone may be divinity enough to be going on with, after all.

Sean O'Brien (b. 1952) follows Dunn more closely than Didsbury in the savage indignation of his politics, but in the course of seven volumes from *The Indoor Park* (1983) to *November* (2011) has worked a vein of psychogeographical engagement with the North, and more specifically Hull and Newcastle, that transcends narrow conceptions of political verse. The bare biographical file reads: born in London but raised in Hull, educated at Cambridge then again at Hull, before a move to Newcastle by way of Brighton and Scotland. His slippery way with the loco-descriptive has not escaped the attentions of

---

[40] John Osborne, 'Peter Didsbury', *Bête Noire*, 6 (Winter 1988), 7–41.
[41] Didsbury, *Scenes from a Long Sleep*, 127.

Peter Barry, but has enabled him to return to Hull across the three decades of his work, as the mood takes him. While Didsbury alternates between Hull and a range of exotic alternatives, O'Brien typically concentrates his fugues on the temporal axis. 'History' is an overdetermined word in O'Brien, its legacy of toxic politics all too live, and its occurrence will often trigger a foregrounded disjunction between lives of privilege and those led elsewhere, in marginal zones of poverty and obsolescence. Hull is stereotypically an underdeveloped region, which is to say out of step with perceived metropolitan wisdom and progress, and there can be something out-of-synch about O'Brien's political poems too, as when he includes an anti-Thatcher rant in *The Drowned Book* almost two decades after she left office (though the rehabilitation of the Thatcherite legacy under David Cameron wrong-foots any premature verdict on the datedness of such a poem). But as the social polarization of the Thatcher years showed, different parts of Britain can seem to work to radically different clocks, or calendars.

The settings of O'Brien's poems are sometimes named and sometimes not. If the former, O'Brien is tempted by a bolshie regionalism unknown in Larkin or Didsbury, and which tends to coincide with his more industrially formalist moods, as in 'Song of the South' ('We change our casts and eat our meat. |There are no negroes on our street')[42] and 'A Northern Assembly'. The latter unabashedly maps out its territory, from the Humber to the Tweed, before announcing that 'the North is poetry'.[43] O'Brien's friendship with Dunn in Hull, followed by a period in Dundee (where Dunn had moved on leaving Hull) between 1989 and 1991, offers a compelling map of politico-poetic influence, but for all the sloganeering self-confidence of these poems they are less artistically assured than those he writes in his more quizzical, less cantankerous moods (not that these do not have their politics too). Many of these latter poems are pitched as mini-allegories. The sea in 'Interior' is 'muttering *history, history* as if | That should explain these haunted roads, | Ancestral nowheres';[44] 'Do we live in small murderous towns | Where history has ended up?', O'Brien asks in 'The Genres: A Travesty of Justice'.[45] A ruling class silences the voices of the exploited, yet O'Brien's allegorizing style is repeatedly drawn to epiphanies of marginalization, freezing his nameless figures in postures of abjection and defeat 'On the wrong side of England, forever | [. . .] And if we should wonder what for, we must hope | That as usual it does not concern us'.[46] In line with my contrast between a metropolitan 'here' and an impoverished 'elsewhere', the provincial 'here' becomes an elsewhere even to its own inhabitants (the provincial/parochial divide again), who seem pushed 'to the side of their own lives', as Larkin puts it in 'Afternoons'.[47] This disjunction often takes the form of narrative self-denial: 'There need be no regret |For we do not exist'; another poem invokes 'futures | That nobody lived' (O'Brien is fond of

---

[42] Sean O'Brien, *The Frighteners* (Newcastle upon Tyne: Bloodaxe Books, 1987), 22.
[43] Sean O'Brien, *Downriver* (London: Picador, 2001), 22.
[44] Sean O'Brien, *Ghost Train* (Oxford: Oxford University Press, 1995), 5.
[45] O'Brien, *Downriver*, 78.
[46] O'Brien, *Ghost Train*, 7.
[47] Larkin, *Collected Poems*, 121.

his redundant future anteriors); trying to describe the nameless men in 'Cities', a third poem concludes that 'Whoever it is must already be dead'.[48]

Peter Barry found Peter Didsbury wanting as a witness to history, and O'Brien's poems in their different way take considerable care not to allow 'imagination' to give raw historical 'material' the slip. But while Barry reads Didsbury's transformations of a crowd of Belfast dockyard workers as culpably flippant, O'Brien insists on the transformations he works on his subjects the better to testify on their behalf at the tribunal of historical justice. 'The Ideology' is an important statement of O'Brien's political aesthetics, its self-reflexive style impossible to mistake for experimental tricksiness (O'Brien has long been a critical scourge of the avant-garde). 'I mistrust the poem in the hour of its success', Roy Fisher wrote in 'It is Writing',[49] and O'Brien too sets a bracing tone. An empty, inauthentic 'they' (the Heideggerian *das Mann*) rubs uneasily against the remains of Keats's 'beauty and truth'. A group of girls is standing outside a pub:

The poem ages them. They go indoors.
They marry or not and bear children
And die, and are found in mid-shriek
In a different poem, still there in the cold

Wearing hardly a stitch, being happy
The way those who live with industrial parks and asbestos
Are happy, because if they weren't they would die,
On the need-to-know basis of beauty and truth.[50]

Barry comments astringently on O'Brien's tendency to extrapolate from local detail to muffled apocalypse, a line about listening with the dead as 'the end of the world | Comes six months late by pigeon post', eliciting the response that 'I cannot see what difference it would make to the poem if the end of the world had come (say) a year late and on a tractor, or by second-class mail and with a 40p surcharge'.[51] His point is that O'Brien's material appears to put up insufficient resistance to the overlaid transparencies of entropy and doom. But this is to miss, first of all, the desperate irony of O'Brien's defeatism in lines like those quoted and, second, the way in which the poem's forking paths of actuality and might-have-been, past and future anterior, establish a template of resistance to the brutal one-way narratives of progress and obsolescence, prosperity and poverty. The victimization of the girls outside the pub is mimetically reproduced ('The poem ages them'), while the various futures in store for them mount up in 'a different poem', which something or someone will write on their behalf (Larkin's 'something hidden from us'). There is a terrible compassion in these poems, their kindness camouflaged under their sternly neo-Brechtian demeanour. The canals, compost heaps, and tenfoots (Hullish for laneway) of O'Brien's poems recall the mouldy suburban landscapes of Raymond

---

[48] Sean O'Brien, *HMS Glasshouse* (Oxford: Oxford University Press, 1991), 4, 50; *Downriver*, 34.
[49] Fisher, *The Long and the Short of It*, 221.
[50] O'Brien, *Downriver*, 9.
[51] Barry, *Contemporary British Poetry and the City*, 120.

Briggs's *Fungus the Bogeyman*, and no less than in Briggs something strange and apocalyptic is lurking in the drains and ditches, as in 'Postcards to the Rain God', a poem written for Peter Didsbury's fiftieth birthday:

Sad, very sad, intones the locality, watching,
You can't see him but he's there:
The after-downpour smell of shit and dockleaves
From the blindside of the fence.[52]

The poetic weather of Larkin, Dunn, Didsbury, and O'Brien can seem unremittingly Anglo-Saxon, but Carol Rumens's refraction of the spirit of Larkin through the work of Eugenio Montale in her 2008 collection *Blind Spots* contributes an unexpectedly Mediterranean chapter to the annals of Hull poetry. Hull is a city of two rivers and despite the Humber's broader dimensions and Marvellian pedigree, it is the river Hull to which she gravitates.[53] The mud banks of the Hull present a Protean, in-between poetic terrain, mixing elements indiscriminately, much as 'The Whitsun Weddings' summoned horizons 'where sky and Lincolnshire and water meet'. In a footnote Rumens glosses the word 'Ambhas' as both the Sanskrit for water and a possible origin for the name Humber, into which the river Hull flows. The sense of the sequence as a cento of text upon text is heightened by Rumens's quoting her two epigraphs from Montale in rival translations, those of William Arrowsmith and Jonathan Galassi. The Projectivist unruliness of some of these poems on the page is a useful reminder that the Hull mud is not a place for bogging down in, formally at least. In 'The Whitsun Awayday' Rumens updates Larkin's 'The Whitsun Weddings' (as another Hull poet, Maurice Rutherford has done in a poem, 'The Autumn Outings', anthologized by Rumens and Gregson in *Old City, New Rumours*). Elizabeth Bishop too has summoned the spirit of rivers, in 'The Riverman', and her poetic animism is no less strong in Rumens's work. When the river spirit speaks at the end of the poem it is in a spirit of mythic authority, or *genius loci*, but in a vernacular, cliché-conscious way ('*I'm history. So are you*.')[54] Myth is domesticated and, simultaneously, the familiar mythologized.

In its improbability, Rumens's reassignment of Montale's sun-drenched Ligurian poems to the river Hull may smack of Borges's fantasies, in his story 'Pierre Menard, Author of The Quixote', of the *Imitatio Christi* as written by Céline or James Joyce, but the transplant takes surprisingly well.[55] Just as the sea breaks down barriers in 'Spurn Head', the poems crash over boundaries, muddy the waters between the original and the translated ('Sunflower Chorus', 'Word Flashes: A Montale Lexicon'), and erode the ground

---

[52] O'Brien, *Downriver*, 62.
[53] For more on the literary qualities of the river Hull, see Shane Rhodes, *Heartlands: Words and Images from the River Hull Corridor* (Hull: City Arts Unit, 1998); David Wheatley, 'Postcard from Hull', *Poetry Review*, v97/3 (Autumn 2007), 119–20; and David Wheatley, 'River Worship', in Joan McBreen (ed.), *The Watchful Heart: A New Generation of Irish Poets* (Cliffs of Moher: Salmon Poetry, 2009), 204–6.
[54] Carol Rumens, 'The Whitsun Away Day', *Blind Spots* (Bridgend: Seren, 2008), 15.
[55] Montale was 'an Eyetie bugger' for Larkin, as quoted in Kingsley Amis, *Memoirs* (London: Hutchinson, 1991), 57.

under our feet the better to watch it fetch up in strange and unexpected new formations. One of the highlights of the book is 'The Cinque Terre', with an unmistakable watery pun in the 'Cinque' of its title. *Stretto*, in the poem's last line, is a term in fugue describing the piling-up on itself of the fugue subject, so that it becomes its own answer, and provides a metaphor for the overwriting and tessellated allusiveness in which Rumens is engaged. The artist's vocation, Rumens avers, is:

to be the storm that sets things flowing, to pour
as the rusting waste-pipes finally
      open their mouths and
        open their
rusting barbarous mouths   and roar
    and lather
      the rain-fugue over
the staves   dislodge or vivify
some shuddering root   and pour

his corrosive, solving *stretto* back to the pounding salt-wash[56]

'In a pig's arse, friend', the speaker of Larkin's 'Vers de Société' might riposte, but its fluent pluviophilia make this a recognizably Hull poem, in the sense of being a poem about Hull, or Italy, or nowhere, but one which has passed through the intestine of one or all those literary places before rewarding us with its rich and varied music. Hull, Larkin noted in his foreword to *A Rumoured City*, keeps its face 'half-turned towards distance and silence, and what lies beyond them'.[57] The Hull poem too, for all Larkin's fabled stay-at-home qualities, has been peculiarly adept at looking beyond its confines and striking out for unfamiliar territories, with always the promise of encountering at last 'unfenced existence | Facing the sun, untalkative, out of reach'.[58]

Select Bibliography

Amis, Kingsley, *Memoirs* (London: Hutchinson, 1991).
Barry, Peter, *Contemporary British Poetry and the City* (Manchester: Manchester University Press, 2000).
Booth, James, *Philip Larkin: Writer* (London: Harvester Wheatsheaf, 1992).
Davie, Donald, *Thomas Hardy and British Poetry* (London: Routledge & Kegan Paul, 1973).
Dunn, Douglas, *Terry Street* (London: Faber & Faber, 1969).
Fisher, Roy, *The Long and the Short of It: Poems 1955–2005* (Tarset: Bloodaxe Books, 2005).
Haffenden, John (ed.), *Poets in Conversation* (London: Faber & Faber, 1981).
Hewitt, John, 'The Bitter Gourd: Some Problems of the Ulster Writer', in *Ancestral Voices: The Selected Prose of John Hewitt*, ed. Tom Clyde (Belfast: Blackstaff Press, 1987).

---

[56] Carol Rumens, 'The Cinque Terre', *Blind Spots*, 18.
[57] Larkin, 'Foreword' to Dunn (ed.), *A Rumoured City*, 9.
[58] Larkin, 'Here', *Collected Poems*, 137.

Hill, Geoffrey, 'Dividing Legacies', in Kenneth Haynes (ed.), *Collected Critical Writings* (Oxford: Oxford University Press, 2008).
Kennedy, David, *Douglas Dunn* (Tavistock: Northcote House, 2008).
Larkin, Philip, *Collected Poems,* ed. Anthony Thwaite (London: Faber & Faber, 1988).
Leader, Zachary (ed.), *The Movement Reconsidered: Essays on Larkin, Amis, Gunn, Davie and Their Contemporaries* (Oxford: Oxford University Press, 2009).
Lefebvre, Henri, *The Production of Space,* trans. Donald Nicholson-Smith (Oxford: Blackwell, 1991).
O'Brien, Sean, *The Frighteners* (Newcastle upon Tyne: Bloodaxe Books, 1987).
O'Brien, Sean, *HMS Glasshouse* (Oxford: Oxford University Press, 1991).
O'Brien, Sean, *Ghost Train* (Oxford: Oxford University Press, 1995).
O'Brien, Sean, *Downriver* (London: Picador, 2001).
Osborne, John, 'Peter Didsbury', *Bête Noire,* 6 (Winter 1988), 7–41.
Osborne, John, *Larkin, Ideology, and Critical Violence: A Case of Wrongful Conviction* (Basingstoke: Palgrave, 2008).
Rhodes, Shane, *Heartlands: Words and Images from the River Hull Corridor* (Hull: City Arts Unit, 1998).
Robinson, Peter, *Liverpool Accent: Seven Poets and a City* (Liverpool: Liverpool University Press, 1996).
Wheatley, David, 'Postcard from Hull', *Poetry Review,* 97/3 (Autumn 2007), 119–20.
Wheatley, David, 'River Worship', in Joan McBreen (ed.), *The Watchful Heart: A New Generation of Irish Poets* (Cliffs of Moher: Salmon Poetry, 2009), 204–6.

CHAPTER 22

AUDEN IN IRELAND

JOHN REDMOND

CONSIDERING the impact of his writing on poets such as John Ashbery, Robert Lowell, Frank O'Hara, James Merrill, John Berryman, Ted Hughes, Sylvia Plath, Geoffrey Hill, and Philip Larkin, the claim that Auden is the most influential poet of the twentieth century seems a reasonable one. Even without mentioning what Samuel Hynes called 'the Auden generation', it is hard to think of a major cluster of poets anywhere in the English-speaking world untouched by his influence. At the same time, his impact has many sides. Like a twentieth-century Emerson it is possible to fashion a model of Auden for every occasion, one to suit (almost) every taste. We speak readily enough—perhaps too much—about the division between the 'English' Auden and the American one, but there are many versions of the poet to admire and follow: the Italian Auden, the Austrian Auden, the 'Norse' Auden, the Horatian, Rilkean, and Goethean Audens, the pedagogical, paranoid, journalistic, engaged, disengaged, partial, neutral, utopian, anarchistic, Christian, high modernist, neo-Augustan, operatic, dramatic, 'Ariel', and 'Prospero' versions of the poet. To struggle with Auden's influence is, in part, to be influenced by Auden's struggles—especially the way he struggled with himself.

From the 1930s onwards, he has been a powerful influence on more than one generation of Irish poets: those from the North including John Hewitt, Derek Mahon, Tom Paulin, Paul Muldoon, Michael Longley, and John Montague, and those from the Republic including Patrick Kavanagh, Paul Durcan, Anthony Cronin, Eavan Boland, and Thomas Kinsella. This relationship is not, however, as widely advertised as it might be. Because Auden's writing is identified neither with the struggles of literary nationalism, nor with the reaction to it embodied by critical revisionism, his impact on Irish poetry tends to be downplayed. A further complicating factor is that Irish poetry, since the 1960s, has been dominated by poets from Ulster, who are happier to salute one of Auden's peers: Louis MacNeice.

Auden's influence is at once deflationary and permissive. At the same time as proposing a less exalted role for poetry, he offers a much wider sense of what poems can be. One way of thinking about the Irish poets considered in this essay—Patrick Kavanagh,

Derek Mahon, and Paul Muldoon—is to mark their varying degrees of contentment with the deflationary freedom of Auden's example. Typically, those who follow in his footsteps accept the force of his anti-Romanticism. They disavow the vatic model of the poet. Nevertheless, they are not immune to the seductive force of the Romantic model— and this is not surprising given that Auden's own response to Romanticism was less of a clean break and more a turbulent, drawn-out exit.

Purely on the level of form, Auden's influence has been vast, although this should not merely be equated with the somewhat conservative formalism we associate with British poets such as John Fuller and James Fenton, or with American poets such as Richard Wilbur and Anthony Hecht. Auden's influence can be identified with the employment of specific poetic forms e.g. ballad, sonnet-sequence, French fixed-forms, or (as we shall consider here) the verse-letter, as well as the adoption of approaches including the use of a casual, mixed idiom and a science-inflected vocabulary. More interestingly perhaps, Auden's poetry asks questions at the very point where the formal shades into the existential. What is the poem for? Towards whom is it directed? In a world of proliferating discourses, how should the poem get along with other forms of expression?

Apart from the range of his technical experiments, Auden also provided a powerful example of how a poet might live. His various allegiances—social, moral, political, even geographical—were inflected with significance for later writers. Particularly in the grandiose wake of Yeats and the Revival writers, the energetically sceptical Auden of the 1930s was decisive for the career of Patrick Kavanagh. Instead of identifying the poet with nation, community, or literary movement, Auden created an image of the poet as a cosmopolitan *Wandervögel*, a picture of contemporary self-reliance. While this alluringly rootless figure is an implicit presence in the work of Derek Mahon, he is explicitly portrayed in Paul Muldoon's mid-career long poem '7, Middagh Street', albeit with a greater emphasis on the poet's bourgeois proclivities. This poem, like many others by Muldoon, deploys one of the significant motifs of later Auden: the association of the poem with the consumption of food, and the association of the poet with workaday figures such as the waiter and the chef.

While it is not inaccurate to read Patrick Kavanagh's career as a reaction to the Celtic Revival, such a reading may be reductive in that he is thus too much remembered for what he wrote against. That Kavanagh was in favour of many things, including Auden's poetry, tends to be forgotten. It is unfortunate that Irish criticism has preferred to see him as somehow beyond influence, as a plain-spoken ephebe. Seamus Deane's description of the poetic persona we encounter in Kavanagh's first book of poems is a good illustration of the usual view: 'The poem is translucent. Kavanagh emerges as he entered, still persistently himself. He is a bare-faced poet. No masks. In this he is revolutionary.'[1] The desire to read Kavanagh as a radical innocent is curiously ahistorical and has led to some strange critical emphases. Despite the evidently modernist procedures of 'The

---

[1] Seamus Deane, 'Irish Poetry and Nationalism', in Douglas Dunn (ed.), *Two Decades of Irish Writing* (Cheadle: Carcanet Press, 1975),10.

Great Hunger', for example, the collection of essays *Modernism and Ireland: The Poetry of the 1930s* explicitly excludes Kavanagh. The poet's most important long poem—it is among the most important Irish poems written between Yeats's death and Heaney's first books—was composed in 1941, but the editors do not cite this as a reason to exclude him.[2] The opportunity to read him beside true-blue modernists like Brian Coffey, Denis Devlin, and Thomas McGreevey is therefore missed.

Kavanagh did not disguise his admiration for Auden's work. In the essay, 'Pietism and Poetry', for example, he placed Auden in the company of Yeats and Eliot.[3] Not so daring a move, but in 'Literature and the Universities', he went further and put Auden in the company of Milton and Shakespeare.[4] In his most considered treatment of the English poet, the essay 'Auden and the Creative Mind', a comparison with Shakespeare was repeatedly made:

> Shakespeare and Auden in common give the impression that they have found a formula and that they could employ ghosts to turn out their particular line till there would be no need for another poet for a long time.[5]

Not only did the essay stirringly endorse the value of Auden's work, it held his poetry out as a corrective to the influence of Yeats. Amusingly enough, such an alignment led Kavanagh in a separate essay to co-opt Auden into the pantheon of Irish writers:

> Those 'Ireland' writers, who are still writing…could not see that the writers of Ireland were no longer Corkery and O'Connor and the others but Auden and George Barker—anyone anywhere who at least appreciated, if he could not cure, their misfortune.[6]

Despite these proclamations, Auden's influence on his work has been little remarked and less analysed. The major critical account of Kavanagh, by Antoinette Quinn, glances at the English poet a few times, but does not address his impact in detail. While she recognizes that, by 1941, Auden was an influence on Kavanagh's poetry she observes that, with respect to '*The Great Hunger* this new literary influence is unrecognisable'. Consequently, Quinn struggles to explain the enormous leap in style represented by Kavanagh's long poem, proposing merely that we see it as 'a rural sequel' to Joyce's *Dubliners*.[7] Yet how fundamentally different are the styles of *Dubliners* and 'The Great

---

[2] Patricia Coughlan and Alex Davis, 'Introduction', in Coughlan and Davis (eds.), *Modernism and Ireland: The Poetry of the 1930s* (Cork: Cork University Press, 1995) 1–23 (12).
[3] Patrick Kavanagh, 'Pietism and Poetry', in *Collected Pruse* (London: MacGibbon & Kee), 244–6 (244).
[4] Kavanagh, 'Literature and the Universities', in *Collected Pruse*, 236–40 (238).
[5] Kavanagh, 'Auden and the Creative Mind', in *Collected Pruse*, 247–53 (250–1).
[6] Kavanagh, 'Waiting for Godot', in *Collected Pruse*, 266–7 (266).
[7] Antoinette Quinn, *Patrick Kavanagh: Born-Again Romantic* (Dublin: Gill and Macmillan, 1991), 139.

Hunger'. Joyce's collection radiates coolness and subtlety. Kavanagh's long poem, by contrast, is a blast of lyricism, bile, and distress.

One of the few extended efforts to address the question of Auden's influence was made by Douglas Houston, who observed: 'To focus on relations between the poetries of Patrick Kavanagh and W. H. Auden is less to trade in stylistic influence than to discern imaginative and spiritual affinities.'[8] Like other commentators, Houston is reluctant to identify Auden's poetry with a decisive transformation in Kavanagh's writing. Nevertheless, I think that the huge stylistic leap from *Ploughman and Other Poems* (1936) to *The Great Hunger* (1942) can only be explained by Kavanagh's exposure to Auden's poetry. In the long poem 'The Great Hunger', the I-persona of Kavanagh's early work is largely replaced by that Audenesque standby: a 'we-persona'. Instead of a subject whose concerns are, for the most part, private, we find a subject that is deeply absorbed with the public and with history. From the first section of this poem, we are drawn into the spiritual predicament of the farmer Patrick Maguire, and offered a guided tour of his life by an indeterminate third party. The 'we-persona' is introduced in the fourth line: 'If we watch them an hour is there anything we can prove | Of life... '.[9] Maguire might be an exemplary rural figure, but that does not mean that the speaker, in the manner of Yeats's 'Fisherman', experiences any spiritual uplift. Instead, he marks out his apparent distaste for, and his emotional distance from, his subject. This clinical stance, with its undercurrents of emotional repression, is one closely associated with the analytical chill of Auden's early style (e.g. 'Consider if you will how lovers stand | In brief adherence...'[10]).

Through much of 'The Great Hunger', the speaker appears strangely uninvolved. A diagnostic finality runs through his comments: 'We will wait and watch the tragedy to the last curtain.'[11] The speaker's tone is assured and decided, superior to both audience and subject. In the context of Auden's influence, the reference to a theatre curtain might remind us of the didactic approach of the Englishman's verse-plays, where a superior instruction is aimed at the audience: (e.g. 'We show you man caught in the trap of his terror, destroying himself', 'We will show you what he has done', 'We would show you at first an English village: you shall choose its location'[12]). That the tone and manner of Auden's verse-plays were a critical influence on Kavanagh's work might be explained by their way of foregrounding the question of audience. Worried about how to project himself, Kavanagh's speaker imagines an audience as present, even though the unlikely and

---

[8] Douglas Houston, 'Landscapes of the Heart: Parallels in the Poetries of Kavanagh and Auden', *Studies*, 77 (Winter 1988), 445–59 (445).

[9] Patrick Kavanagh, 'The Great Hunger', *The Complete Poems* ed. Peter Kavanagh (New York: The Peter Kavanagh Hand Press, 1972), 80.

[10] W. H. Auden, *The English Auden: Poems, Essays and Dramatic Writings 1927–1939*, ed. Edward Mendelson (London: Faber & Faber, 1977), 438.

[11] Kavanagh, 'The Great Hunger', 80.

[12] Auden, 'So, under the local images your blood has conjured', *English Auden*, 280. W. H. Auden and Christopher Isherwood, *Plays and Other Dramatic Writings by W. H. Auden, 1928–1938*, ed. Edward Mendelson (Princeton: Princeton University Press, 1988), 241. Auden, 'The Summer holds', *English Auden*, 282.

mysterious nature of this entity is itself a reason for us to ponder the poet's sincerity and balance. In the final section we are told: 'The curtain falls— | Applause applause'.[13]

From his beginnings as a dramatist, Auden favoured the reduction of characters to caricatures and scapegoats. This was sharply evident in 'Paid on Both Sides', his early mumming drama. In that play, Katherine Worth remarks: 'one is reminded of "Sweeney Agonistes" in the violence of its break with realism, its feelings for spontaneous, popular forms of English drama, especially pantomime and the most primitive form of all, the Mummer's Play'.[14] Two characters from the mumming tradition appear in 'Paid on Both Sides', the 'Man-Woman' and the 'Doctor'. Auden liked to use such figures because, as he put it, 'drama is not suited to the analysis of character, which is the province of the novel. Dramatic characters are simplified, easily recognised and over life-size'. Dramatic speech, as he conceived of it, should have, 'the same compressed, significant and undocumentary character as dramatic movement'.[15]

This combination of ritual and caricature must have appealed to Kavanagh—in section 12 of 'The Great Hunger', for instance, the mother and her children are described as puppets: 'she held the strings of her children's Punch and Judy'.[16] Kavanagh would explicitly portray mumming in later works like 'The Christmas Mummers' and 'The Wake of the Books'. According to Halpert, in some mumming plays 'the act of ploughing or of making a plough is connected with mimicry of the sexual act'.[17] Often a man dressed as a 'female' was wooed by a Ploughboy whom she would reject in favour of a fool. The use of the plough and of the Man-Woman ('it cut him up in the middle, till he became more woman than man') converge with some aspects of 'The Great Hunger'.[18]

Often in Auden's work, the use of a collective pronoun ('We have brought you they said a map of the country') as a vehicle for questioning others eventually puts itself in question. Implicitly the 'we-persona' asks, 'Who are we?', 'Why are we not the subject of the poem?', 'How do we differ from the subject?' These questions bear sharply on 'The Great Hunger'. Occasionally Kavanagh's 'we-persona' becomes suddenly agitated: 'Watch him, watch him, that man on a hill whose spirit | Is a wet sack flapping about the knees of time'.[19] While not abandoning his knowingness, the speaker's imperative repetition here is that of the warder watching the dangerous prisoner. Again, it is a tone powerfully present in Auden's work:

Watch him asleep and waking
Dreaming of continuous sexual enjoyment or perpetual applause.[20]

---

[13] Kavanagh, 'The Great Hunger', *Complete Poems*, 103.
[14] Katherine Worth, *Revolutions in Modern English Drama* (London: Bell, 1972), 106–7.
[15] Auden, *English Auden*, 273.
[16] Kavanagh, 'The Great Hunger', *Complete Poems*, 99.
[17] H. Halpert, 'A Typology of Mumming', in H. Halpert and G. M. Story (eds.), *Christmas Mumming in Newfoundland* (Toronto: University of Toronto Press, 1969), 57.
[18] Kavanagh, 'The Great Hunger', 94.
[19] Kavanagh, 'The Great Hunger', 81.
[20] Auden, 'So, under the local images your blood has conjured', 281.

In section 13, the speaker again puts his detachment aside, in order to upbraid some patronizing tourists who are observing Maguire from their cars. Then, as suddenly as the knowing tone had vanished, it returns:

That was how his life happened.
No mad hooves galloping in the sky,
But the weak, washy way of true tragedy—
A sick horse nosing around the meadow for a clean place to die.[21]

As Basil Payne has indicated, these lines are reminiscent of the idea of tragedy (and the way in which it is expressed) in Auden's 'Musée des Beaux Arts'.[22] They are especially reminiscent of the point where the 'dreadful martydom' occurs: 'Where the dogs go on with their doggy life and the torturer's horse |scratches its innocent behind on a tree'.[23] In both cases, the long line imitates the casual motions of a horse and the place, 'some untidy spot', is of no particular importance. As so often in 'The Great Hunger', the we-persona appears to be an amalgam of unresolved relations between Kavanagh, his audience, and Auden.

In his later career Kavanagh struggled to overcome the strains of Auden's voice in his poetry and this proved far from easy. How was a poet so fixated on poetic worthiness to deal with a precursor far worthier than himself? That Kavanagh had a Darwinian conception of 'the great poet' is not in doubt: 'I scarcely believe in the theory of the "mute inglorious Milton". There might well be mute Bowens or Priestleys or Blundens, but hardly a Milton, a Shakespeare, an Auden.'[24] But was *he* a Blunden or an Auden? On what scale was *he* built? As the matter of influence increasingly preoccupied his poems so too did the legacy of Auden:

Auden knows all the answers, and the question
Is where we can find a question to ask.
We ring all the changes on the emotions
Re-weave and re-weave the shoddy...[25]

In this poem 'Grey Liffey', the speaker is explicitly anxious about influence; uncertainty about the self is reflected in a tense mixture of singular and plural pronouns. As Spenser is the acknowledged master of a medieval, romance world, so is Auden of a modern, Freudean one. Wondering how to prosper in the shadow of such precursors, a shift occurs in the poet's vision away from the message and towards the medium. As soon as Kavanagh realized that, in philosophical, psychological, and social terms, he had nothing profound to say, he was in a position to 'give back' the measured knowing terms that

---

[21] Kavanagh, 'The Great Hunger', 101.
[22] Basil Payne, 'The Poetry of Patrick Kavanagh', *Studies*, 49 (1960), 282.
[23] Auden, 'Musée des Beaux Arts', *English Auden*, 237.
[24] Kavanagh, *Collected Pruse*, 266.
[25] Kavanagh, 'Grey Liffey', *Complete Poems*, 271.

he had borrowed from Auden. Once they were relinquished he could write, casually and fruitfully, about the absence of a subject. The poem 'Is' provides a good example:

The important thing is not
To imagine one ought
Have something to say,
A raison d'être, a plot for the play.[26]

In such poems, Kavanagh's eye begins to look through living nature. We are reminded of Heaney's judgement in 'The Placeless Heaven: Another Look at Kavanagh': 'In the poetry of Kavanagh's later period, embodied first in "Epic" and then, in the late 1950s, in the Canal Bank Sonnets, a definite change is perceptible. We might say that now the world is more pervious to his vision than he is pervious to the world.'[27] In the absence of a definite poetic subject, water becomes his preferred metaphor, providing occasions for purification, reduction, and emptiness. Gradually, Kavanagh loses his anxiety about his audience and about Auden. We might characterize this as the state of deflationary freedom, so common in poets following in the footsteps of the Englishman. In Kavanagh's various Canal Bank poems, the poetic self is emptied out to return to its original 'I am'. The trope of panorama is now inverted—the speaker remains passive and the light is brought *to* him, as in 'Lines Written on a Seat on the Grand Canal':

Fanatastic light looks through the eyes of bridges—
And look! A barge comes bringing from Athy
And other far-flung towns mythologies...[28]

Rather than presenting himself as an agitated seer, here Kavanagh uses the force of Auden's bird's-eye view by becoming what is seen. The poet empties himself out, aspiring to the condition of a humble object: 'just a canal-bank seat for the passer-by'. Paradoxically, Kavanagh's poems were most successful when they appeared to be least ambitious.

Especially in Auden's early poetry, his anti-vatic stance coexists with plenty of vatic moments. As he acknowledged after writing '1 September 1939', the transition to a new way of writing was punctuated by frequent relapses. Similarly, in the work of Derek Mahon, we find a poet who has been convinced of the need to lay Romantic impulses to one side, but who nonetheless struggles to do so. This engenders, as it does in Kavanagh, a constant self-scrutiny, where the poet monitors 'unchaste' impulses with a view to their suppression. Both Mahon and Kavanagh, in following Auden, have canons substantially marked by the suspicions they hold towards their younger selves. For Mahon, one of the formal consequences of this has been the eventual dominance of this later career by one particular form: the verse-letter.

[26] Kavanagh, 'Is', *Complete Poems*, 287.
[27] Seamus Heaney, 'The Placeless Heaven: Another Look at Kavanagh', in *The Government of the Tongue: The T. S. Eliot Memorial Lectures and Other Critical Writings* (London: Faber, 1988), 5.
[28] Kavanagh, 'Lines Written on a Seat on the Grand Canal, Dublin, "Erected to the Memory of Mrs. Dermot O'Brien"', *Complete Poems*, 295.

In his early verse-letters, 'Beyond Howth Head' and 'The Sea in Winter', as in his late ones, *The Yaddo Letter* and *The Hudson Letter*, Mahon dwells on large themes in a loose manner. 'Beyond Howth Head', the concluding poem of *Lives* (1972), is a satirical reflection on Irish society of the time, with particular attention paid to matters of sex and religion:

What can the elders say to this
For girls must kiss and then must kiss
and so by this declension fall
to write the writing on the wall.[29]

The tone of the poem does not change much even when the writer is addressing matters which might be seen as more serious. As Seamus Deane has written:

> The only freedom [in 'Beyond Howth Head'] is that of writing even though the audience is that of the inner group, the chosen few. Because the audience is fit, the poem can be humorous, sophisticated and knowing. Because the audience is few and freedom so intangible, the poem is elegiac, saddened in its recognition of the loss and strife which had been so freely endowed by the past.[30]

For these modern verse-letters, the genial and imposing models are Auden's 'Letter to Lord Byron' (1936) and 'New Year Letter' (1940). Mahon's verse-letters are generally true to those principles which Auden fleshed out in his first experiment with the form:

I want a form that's large enough to swim in,
   And talk on any subject that I choose,
From natural scenery to men and women,
   Myself, the arts, the European news...[31]

Auden hoped that writing with other people explicitly in mind (as one must in a verse-letter) would be a stay against the writer's natural solipsism. This is one of the reasons why the form appeals to Mahon. The popularizing tendency, the knowledge that the poet is relaxed and taking short cuts, leads in these verse-letters to a peculiarly self-conscious kind of informality. Auden, for instance, makes jokes about the difficulty of rhyming in 'Letter to Lord Byron' ('There is no other rhyme except anoint'), while Mahon occasionally abandons rhyme in 'The Sea in Winter' and 'Beyond Howth Head'. It is revealing that even Kavanagh had a go at the form. His 'A Letter in Verse' gives up its rhyme scheme in mock-desperation:

...By the Lord Harry
George Barker is superior at this carry-
On in rhymed letter.[32]

---

[29] Derek Mahon, 'Beyond Howth Head', *Lives* (London: Oxford University Press, 1972), 34.
[30] Seamus Deane, 'Derek Mahon: Freedom from History', in *Celtic Revivals* (London: Faber, 1985), 156–65 (158).
[31] W. H. Auden, 'Letter to Lord Byron', *The English Auden*, 172.
[32] Kavanagh, 'A Letter in Verse', *Complete Poems*, 282.

As exercises in social observation, Mahon's verse-letters depend on another Audenesque trope: the panorama. Typically, his speakers tend to be uninvolved in the scenes which they describe, and yet the descriptive 'eye' of the poem is often very mobile, like a camera on a bus or a helicopter. The poems often create an active and dynamic impression, demonstrating the narrator's descriptive power and moving quickly from one point to the next:

Spring lights the country: from a thous-
and dusty corners, house by house,
from under beds and vacuum cleaners,
empty Kosangas containers,
bread bins, car seats, crates of stout,
the first flies cry to be let out...[33]

In the 1930s the Marxist world of feeling gave many poets a sense of historical omniscience, which duly transferred itself into their rhetoric and their imagery. One memorable example is Auden's 'The Summer holds...' with its sun-kissed vision of 'Europe and the islands' (which Mahon echoes with 'Spring lights the country...').[34] Such long perspectives, as disclosed by the panoramic trope, and the related device of the list, tend to universalize whatever they include and enable the poet to range from one moment in space or history to another at high speed. When Mahon uses them in his verse-letters it is as a means to putting himself beyond the illusions of society, facing the simple reality of the elements: 'morning scatters down the strand | relics of last night's gale force wind; | far out, the Atlantic faintly breaks'.[35] These lines are of the sort, which Dillon Johnston had in mind, when he wrote: 'Mahon establishes a "theoptic" view in which human endeavour dwindles before the vastness of history and of the heavens.'[36]

Both 'The Sea in Winter' and 'Beyond Howth Head' compare the value of a communal experience with the value of a hermit's life. In 'Beyond Howth Head', the option of eremeticism—a kind of surrogate for vatic self-sufficiency—is presented and, after brief consideration, withdrawn:

I too, uncycled, might exchange,
(since 'we are changed by what we change')
my forkful of the general mess
for hazel-nuts and water-cress
like one of those old hermits who,
less virtuous than some, withdrew
from the world-circles women make
to a small island in a lake.[37]

[33] Mahon, 'Beyond Howth Head', *Lives*, 37.
[34] Auden, 'The Summer holds', *English Auden*, 281.
[35] Derek Mahon, 'The Sea in Winter', *Poems 1962–1978*, 110.
[36] Dillon Johnston, *Irish Poetry after Joyce* (Notre Dame, Ill.: University of Notre Dame Press, 1985), 241.
[37] Derek Mahon, 'Beyond Howth Head', 37.

The second line here, is a quote (acknowledged) from Auden's 'New Year Letter'. To see ethics through the prism of geography—a change of location may be a change of life—is reminiscent of poems like 'Islands', 'Mountains', and 'In Praise of Limestone'. Since Mahon, in his poetry, usually presents his immediate surroundings in a negative light (a symptom of his early dislike for Northern Ireland), the idea of elsewhere often promotes a *superior* alternative world:

Elsewhere the olive grove,
Le déjeuner sur l'herbe,
Poppies and parasols,
Blue skies and mythic love.
Here only the stricken souls
No spring can unperturb.[38]

Mahon also uses the idea of 'elsewhere' in one of his best-known poems, 'The Snow Party'. Although the poem is not a direct comment on the Northern Irish situation it contrasts two scenes—one refined, one brutal—In a manner which suggests the coexistence of the artist's dream-kingdom with a grittier reality ('Elsewhere they are burning | Witches and heretics | In the boiling squares.')[39] In 'The Fall of Rome', we find a similarly phrased juxtaposition of different worlds. After piling up surreal details about Rome in its most decadent phase, Auden abruptly glances away, 'Altogether elsewhere', to the contrasting motion of 'vast | Herds of reindeer'.[40]

As we might expect from a poet whose sensibility divides between the vatic and the anti-vatic, Mahon's poetry is tonally various and accommodates frequent changes of diction. Accompanying the dilations and contractions of his vision, his tone tends to fluctuate between extremes. Mahon's poems tend to fret about their own worldly competence and so, by way of compensation, adopt a briskly superior tone, even as they disparage worldliness. Whereas some of Mahon's poems offer a positive vision of what poetry can do ('Rinsing the choked mud, keeping the colours new'[41]), other poems, and particularly those which consider the value of his own work, emphasize its trivial nature. 'Heraclitus on Rivers', in which Auden's suspicion that 'poetry makes nothing happen' is a ghostly presence, is a good example:

Your best poem, you know the one I mean,
The very language in which the poem
Was written, and the idea of language,
All these things will pass away in time.[42]

---

[38] Derek Mahon, 'North Wind: Portrush', *The Hunt by Night* (London: Oxford University Press, 1982), 13.

[39] Derek Mahon, 'The Snow Party', *The Snow Party* (London: Oxford University Press, 1975), 8.

[40] W. H. Auden, 'The Fall of Rome', *Collected Poems,* ed. Edward Mendelson (1976; rev. edn. London: Faber & Faber, 1991), 333.

[41] Derek Mahon, 'In Carrowdore Churchyard', *Night-Crossing* (London: Oxford University Press, 1968), 3.

[42] Derek Mahon, 'Heraclitus on Rivers', *Poems 1962–1978* (Oxford: Oxford University Press, 1979), 107.

While this poem disparages human effort in general, it is written with such an air of assumed authority that one is inclined to wonder how the speaker can affect such certainty. A comparison with the unconvincing authority of Kavanagh's speaker in 'The Great Hunger' suggests itself. Also one wonders why the negation of human endeavour is so extreme, unless the speaker has some stake in the unqualified nature of his statement? Rather as a student will assume an air of worldliness to pre-empt the challenge of the fully adult world, the tone which is used here is at once beguiling and unpersuasive. 'After Nerval' provides another example of Mahon's dramatic-sounding negations:

> Your great mistake is to disregard the satire
> Bandied among the mute phenomena.
> Be strong if you must, your brusque hegemony
> Means fuck-all to the somnolent sun-flower
> Or the extinct volcano.[43]

In a typically paradoxical manner, the poem criticizes the 'brusque hegemony' of the powerful in a tone of voice which is itself brusquely hegemonic. The speaker's dismissiveness is enjoyable and energetic, but it is most usefully read as the performance of a divided self. Hence the diction of the poem divides between the grandiose and the throwaway, between the sonorously poetic 'somnolent sunflower' and the anti-poetic 'fuck-all'.

Mahon has learnt the Audenesque habit—perhaps it might be called a 'tactic'—of self-reproof and self-revision. Like the English poet he has enthusiastically shorn away much-loved parts of his canon. Even his most popular poems, like 'A Disused Shed in Co. Wexford', are apt to be altered:

> Even now there are places where a thought might grow—
> Peruvian mines, worked out and abandoned
> To a slow clock of condensation,
> An echo trapped forever, and a flutter of
> Wildflowers in the lift-shaft,
> Indian compounds where the wind dances
> And a door bangs with diminished confidence,
> Lime crevices behind rippling rainbarrels,
> Dog corners for shit-burials... [44]

Reading through the original version of the poem in *The Snow Party*, one would surely have been caught up by that compound 'shit-burials'. It was, for Mahon, a typical juxtaposition of high style and low style, rather like Auden's use of 'dildo' in the early version of 'In Praise of Limestone'. But, as typically and correctly as Auden altered 'dildo', Mahon, in *Poems 1962–1978*, revised 'A Disused Shed' so that 'shit-burials' became 'bone-burials'.[45] Mahon's change was no doubt prompted by a desire to observe biological accuracy

---

[43] Derek Mahon, 'After Nerval', *The Snow Party* (London: Oxford University Press, 1975), 23.
[44] Mahon, 'A Disused Shed in Co. Wexford', *The Snow Party*, 36.
[45] Mahon, 'A Disused Shed in Co. Wexford', *Poems 1962–1978*, 79.

in respect of actual canine habits (dogs don't bury their waste), but the secondary poetic effect of the change was that the compound was no longer as conspicuously colloquial as before.

One danger of being an Auden-influenced poet is that one can easily decline—as many writers of the 1930s did—into the Audenesque. Mahon's later poetry, mostly limited to the form and tone of the verse-letter, represents such a decline. But 'A Disused Shed in Co. Wexford' was written at a time when he still sought to *overcome* Auden's influence.

As Kavanagh in his kenotic phase found, one way to ease your influences is to overturn them, deflect them. Something like this movement, which in most poems takes place at a micro-level from moment to moment, occurs with a drastic level of intensity in 'A Disused Shed', at the point where stanza 1 shifts to stanza 2. Mahon's poem opens with a kind of panorama of panoramas, an ecstatic dilation which vibrates with distant voices. Most prominent amongst these is the voice of Auden whose panoramic method the poem appropriates only to terminate. We sense we are in Auden-territory right away with the reference to abandoned mines—indeed the first stanza of the poem occupies territory much like Auden's 'Who stands, the crux left of the watershed' with its 'long abandoned levels', its 'damaged shaft', and 'dismantled washing-floors'.[46] Other well-known Audenic panoramas can be distantly discerned, from 'The Fall of Rome' ('In a lonely field the rain | lashes an abandoned train'), to the self-advertising exoticism of 'Spain' ('Yesterday all the past. The language of size | Spreading to China along the trade-routes'), to the serenely maternal 'In Praise of Limestone', a poem which 'the lime-crevices' of 'A Disused Shed' brings to mind, ('beneath | a secret system of caves and conduits; hear these springs | That spurt out everywhere with a chuckle.')[47]

As though afraid of becoming 'An echo trapped forever' the poem swerves away from this composite dilation with an abrupt contraction of its vision. An opening that had promised an Audenesque continuation is decisively interrupted. The quest for poetic originality is prosecuted, here, by a kind of deliberate blindness, whereby one secondary world is shut down in favour of another. So against the sound of Auden, the poem inside the shed begins to overhear Theodore Roethke, Plath, Heaney, Samuel Beckett, and J. G. Farrell. The poem stops being one kind of echo, empties itself out in order to the voices of others.

If Auden is a primary influence for Mahon and Kavanagh, this is not the case for Paul Muldoon. His major influence is Robert Frost. But Auden is an important secondary presence in Muldoon's work and is explicitly the subject of one of his major long poems, '7, Middagh Street'. Of all the poets considered in this chapter, Muldoon is the one most comfortable with the deflationary freedom of Auden's late style. The principal example

---

[46] Auden, 'Who stands, the crux left of the watershed', *English Auden*, 22.

[47] Auden, 'The Fall of Rome', 332; Auden, 'Spain 1937', *English Auden*, 210; Auden, 'In Praise of Limestone', *Collected Poems*, 540.

of this is 'the dinner-party poem', a type which recurs in Muldoon's canon, and of which '7, Middagh Street' is the prime example.

After his more prophetic and political phase, Auden's poetry from the 1940s onwards celebrated an ordinary citizen with ordinary appetites. His work became more bourgeois than bohemian. 'To-night at Seven-Thirty', a dinner-party poem written in 1963, where he celebrates 'men | and women who enjoy the cloop of corks' gives one the flavour of this later style.[48] While in that poem Auden considers the ideal arrangement of dinner-party guests, Paul Muldoon, in his early poem 'Paris', engages in a similar operation. In this case, however, there are principally two people depicted ('A table for two will scarcely seat | The pair of us!') and the table arrangement under consideration envisages their potential selves 'strategically deployed'.[49] The poem worries about how the loss of one's origins may appear, after a time, to those one has left behind. While it is uneasily in favour of cosmopolitanism—preferring 'Chicken Marengo' to chicken and chips— the poem also wants to mark and remember its origins. It is uncertain about what the couple have become. The title, 'Paris', is, on one level, a shorthand for cosmopolitanism, and it sets the poem in the same city as a later Muldoon long poem, 'The Bangle (Slight Return)' where the poet is found in 'a restaurant off the Champs Elysées'. Paris, though, has wider issues in mind. As it concludes, it gestures towards the Peace Conference of 1919, thinking of 'men sitting down to talk of peace | Who began with the shape of the table'.[50] It is a characteristically ambiguous conclusion. Talks about the shape of the table may be the equivalent of 'talks about talks', an indication of differences so intense that the participants cannot even agree who should be present.

Auden's influence on this kind of poem in his canon is acknowledged in Muldoon's '7, Middagh Street', a portrait of a Thanksgiving dinner at Auden's New York house where the guests include Carson McCullers, Salvador Dalí, and Louis MacNeice. Images of consumption dominate. Like 'The Age of Anxiety' the poem is organized as a series of monologues and, through these, the guests recall several impromptu feasts. Auden remembers one such occasion in a New Hampshire hospital where he is visited by Eleanor Clark who smuggles in 'a pail of oysters and clams'.[51] Carson McCullers, in her monologue, recalls Auden's unusual injunction at a Thanksgiving Dinner ('We'll have crawfish, turkey, | salad and savoury, | and no political discussion').[52] This indicates the hostility of Auden towards politics as a crude, self-contained subject and his preference for the humanized nuances of dinner-table speech. MacNeice, in his monologue, similarly brings to mind a previous dinner with Auden, where the pair were confronted by different sorts of kipper: 'one tasted of toe-nails, one of the thick | skin on the soles of the feet'.[53] In line with Muldoon's trope of culinary antagonism, this part of the poem is

---

[48] Auden, 'To-night at Seven-Thirty', *Collected Poems*, 710.
[49] Paul Muldoon, 'Paris', *Poems 1968–1998* (London: Faber & Faber, 2001), 59.
[50] Muldoon, 'Paris', 59.
[51] Paul Muldoon, '7, Middagh Street', *Poems 1968–1998*, 179.
[52] Muldoon, '7, Middagh Street', *Poems 1968–1998*, 179.
[53] Muldoon, '7, Middagh Street', *Meeting the British* (London: Faber & Faber, 1987), 55.

a kind of hallucination of cannibalism. It is echoed by McCullers's reference to the 'Last Supper' and Dalí's painting *Autumn Cannibalism*. The latter was a second formulation of the painter's views on the Spanish Civil War—replacing the first one, *Soft Construction with Boiled Beans: Premonition of Civil War* (which is twice mentioned in '7, Middagh Street'). 'Autumn Cannibalism' features a nightmarish dining experience where, amidst gestures of refined pleasure, the two rubbery participants eat each other in a manner somewhat reminiscent of Auden's Spanish Civil War lines in 'The Capital' ('Dim-lighted restaurant where lovers eat each other').[54]

Although scarcely a Lawrentian, Muldoon does not forget that we are animals too, and likes to remind us how dead men are consumed in the guts of the living. Quite apart from the various dining occasions it recalls, '7, Middagh Street', rather like Muldoon's canon as a whole, is a bizarrely extended menu. A formidable range of food and drink is paraded before the reader—from a wedding cake to bathtub gin, from a raw beefsteak to smoked quail, from grits and greens to a crumpled baguette. The almost inexhaustible menu of his canon is a metaphor for poetry's excessive function. It leaves the reader with the feeling that Robert Harbison once associated with literary lists: that there are more things in the world than you had remembered.

As Mikhail Bakhtin likes to remind us, from a political, or class, point of view, the dinner-party poem emphasizes bourgeois values at the expense of others:

> Let us again stress...that the banquet images in the popular-festive tradition (and in Rabelais) differ sharply from the images of private eating and private gluttony and drunkenness in early bourgeois literature. The latter express the contentment and satiety of the selfish individual, his personal enjoyment, and not the triumph of the people as a whole....[55]

One is more inclined to notice the importance of the dinner party, when one's perspective opens from a marginalized position—as some feminist criticism reminds us. In Helena Michie's study of food in nineteenth-century French novels, *The Flesh Made Word*, we find that women are generally excluded from participation in eating at table while the consumption by males is closely described. Michie makes the point that social hierarchies are implicit in the dinner-party scheme:

> If food is both a moral and a class question, dining rituals take on the serious purpose of defining moral good and upholding class structure. The language of etiquette books leaps from notions of what is polite to pronouncements on what is moral.[56]

The preparation of food necessarily involves the break-up of once-living things and so dinner-party poems are frequently metonymical, invoking portions of larger entities. In Northern Irish poetry, metonymy is often an oblique commentary on the fragmentary

---

[54] W. H. Auden, 'The Capital', *Collected Poems*, 1.
[55] Bakhtin, *Rabelais and His World*, (Bloomington: Indiana University Press, 1984), 301.
[56] Helena R. Michie, *The Flesh Made Word* (New York: Oxford University Press, 1987), 8.

nature of the body politic break-up, and Muldoon's dinner-party poems often have the edge of ritualized violence. Certainly this is true of his early poem 'The Marriage of Strongbow and Aoife', where the speaker watches his companion struggle with 'a spider-crab's | crossbow and cuirass'.[57] In that poem the process of consumption is implicitly antagonistic. As Ronald Marken has pointed out:

> The prevailing images are those of invasion and fatal piercings; the speaker identifies with the doomed spider-crab. This feast is no genteel affair, but an event of rowdy, even epic, proportions.[58]

As in 'Paris', conflict is ambiguously present at the dinner table. The author's proxy in these poems seems himself to be incapable of violent activity, but he never loses sight of the world of action. Nor does he lose sight of the world of labour.

Muldoon's most considered early treatment of violence through the medium of the dinner party is 'Lunch with Pancho Villa', where his dining companion is a thinly disguised IRA man. As the speaker's leading question in that poem reminds us ('Is it really a revolution though?') Muldoon's dinner parties are never fully harmonious.[59] There is always an edge of some kind. To eat with someone else, even the waiter, is often an antagonistic act.

At the heart of *Hay*, his most overtly agrarian collection, we find 'The Plot'. It is a type of concrete poem which multiplies the word 'alfalfa' around a typographical window in which the single word 'alpha' appears. While an accompanying quotation suggests that we interpret what follows in a sexual light, the agrarian sense of 'plot' gives a plot to the volume: in the beginning there was grass. Like many of Muldoon's collections, *Hay* ends with a long poem, 'The Bangle (Slight Return)'. The poem itself is a more-than-slight return to an earlier short poem called 'The Bangle' itself partly set in a restaurant, 'Le Petit Zinc'. 'The Bangle (Slight Return)' has three main levels: a series of references to 'The Aeneid', an imagined voyage of Muldoon's father to Australia, and a fancy dinner in a restaurant on the Champs Elysées. With his accustomed smoothness, Muldoon moves between these not-obviously-related three levels. The long poem meditates on the large consequences of single decisions—Aeneas choosing to turn back to Troy, Muldoon's father choosing (or not choosing) to head for Australia, and Muldoon in the restaurant choosing or not choosing to connect with an old flame that he spots there. These three foregrounds become each other's distant backgrounds. It is instructive to see how the unheroic, contemporary act of eating in an upscale restaurant is complicated by distant scenes from mythology and counterfactual history.

As a good Frostean, Muldoon likes to remind us always of the world of labour and his dinner-party poems frequently make reference to 'the help'—a waiter, a waitress, a chef. In 'The Bangle (Slight Return)', our hero is confronted by a sniffy waiter who, through

---

[57] Muldoon, 'The Marriage of Strongbow and Aoife', *Poems 1968–1998*, 157.
[58] Ronald Marken, 'Review of *The Wishbone*', *Canadian Journal of Irish Studies*, 12/1 (June 1986), 111.
[59] Muldoon, 'Lunch with Pancho Villa', *Poems 1968–1998*, 41.

his 'tuts and twitters and whistle-whines' provides a kind of culinary 'Remember You Are Mortal'.[60] Again, the table is an agon, theatrically disharmonious. In the poem, Muldoon's old flame sits down 'at the next table but one', a phrase which sends us back to a much earlier poem 'Holy Thursday'. There, as a couple contemplate their failing relationship, a waiter also sits down at the next table but one. The narrator, in a slightly alienated state, directs his attention towards the staff member who, in pretending to serve himself, 'smiles, and bows to his own absence'.[61]

Sticklers for technique, both Auden and Muldoon set much store by technical mastery, the exquisite act, the recipe exactly followed. In the poem 'Sext', part of the sequence 'Horae Canonicae'—perhaps Auden's most important political poem—the actions of a chef are set forth as one example of the kind of specialized expertise which holds up civilization. Auden sees a Heidegerrian magic in the process of careful making ('you have only to watch his eyes: a cook mixing a sauce').[62] A similar emphasis on expertise is exhibited in Muldoon's dinner-party poem 'Sushi', where the couple watch 'the Master chef | fastidiously shave | salmon, tuna and yellowtail'.[63] In 'Sushi', typical elements of the dinner-party poem combine: the languorous evocation of detail, the faint self-indulgence of the speaker's tone, and the homage paid to a master. It is, too, an apt metaphor for the poetic process: concentration, self-absorption, and the awe felt before a great influence.

It is revealing to see how Muldoon ends *Plan B*, one of his most recent books, with a dining ritual. The last word of the book is 'tormentil', a herb, which may remind us how his long poem 'Yarrow', a poem named after a herb, concludes with reference to 'ravensara', a spice. In 'A Hare at Aldergrove', the tormentil, a common yellow-petalled flower, along with 'a salad of blaeberry and heather', is consumed by a hare with which the poet hazily identifies.[64] Tormentil is apparently known for its healing properties, although the word obviously makes us think of 'torment' (torture is an abiding concern in the book.) While the dining ritual is ambiguously caught up with violent subject-matter, Muldoon also has the more pacific nature of eating in mind. As the poem meditates on post-conflict Northern Ireland, the hare, chewing things over, links the eating act to a relaxed form of thinking. Speaking of the photographs interspersed through *Plan B*, Muldoon writes warmly about how they offer an 'invitation to meditate', and how 'the very idea of a "subject" soon begins to seem crudely inappropriate'.[65] Muldoon's late practice of thinking about everything is a version of Kavanagh's late practice of thinking about nothing. The problem of a subject dissolves and with it the related traps of sermons, tracts, and prophecies. If '7, Middagh Street' explicitly embraced the Audenic dinner-party, *Plan B* embraces the deflationary freedom of Irish poetry after Auden.

---

[60] Muldoon, 'The Bangle (Slight Return)', *Poems 1968–1998*, 462.
[61] Muldoon, 'Holy Thursday', *Poems 1968–1998*, 89.
[62] Auden, 'Sext', *Collected Poems*, 629–30.
[63] Muldoon, 'Sushi', *Poems 1968–1998*, 174.
[64] Paul Muldoon, 'A Hare at Aldergrove', *Plan B* (London: Enitharmon Press, 2009), 63. The poems in *Plan B* have now been collected in *Maggot* (London: Faber & Faber, 2010).
[65] Muldoon, 'Introduction to Plan B', *Plan B*, 7.

Select Bibliography

Alcobia-Murphy, Shane, *Sympathetic Ink: Intertextual Relations in Northern Irish Poetry* (Liverpool: Liverpool University Press, 2006).
Auden, W. H., *The English Auden: Poems, Essays and Dramatic Writings 1927–1939*, ed. Edward Mendelson (London: Faber & Faber, 1977).
Auden, W. H., *Collected Poems*, ed. Edward Mendelson (1976; rev. edn. London: Faber & Faber, 1991).
Auden, W. H., and Isherwood, Christopher, *Plays and Other Dramatic Writings by W. H. Auden, 1928–1938*, ed. Edward Mendelson (Princeton: Princeton University Press, 1988).
Campbell, Matthew (ed.), *The Cambridge Companion to Contemporary Irish Poetry* (Cambridge: Cambridge University Press, 2003).
Clark, Heather, *The Ulster Renaissance: Poetry in Belfast, 1962–1972* (Oxford: Oxford University Press, 2006).
Corcoran, Neil, *After Yeats and Joyce: Reading Modern Irish Literature* (Oxford: Oxford University Press, 1997).
Corcoran, Neil (ed.), *The Chosen Ground: Essays on the Contemporary Poetry of Northern Ireland* (Bridgend: Seren, 1992).
Coughlan, Patricia, and Davis, Alex (eds.), *Modernism and Ireland: The Poetry of the 1930s* (Cork: Cork University Press, 1995).
Deane, Seamus, *Celtic Revivals: Essays in Modern Irish Literature 1880–1980* (London: Faber & Faber, 1985).
Halpert, H., and Story, G. M. (eds.), *Christmas Mumming in Newfoundland* (Toronto: University of Toronto Press, 1969).
Haughton, Hugh, *The Poetry of Derek Mahon* (Oxford: Oxford University Press, 2007).
Heaney, Seamus, *The Government of the Tongue: The T. S. Eliot Memorial Lectures and Other Critical Writings* (London: Faber, 1988).
Houston, Douglas, 'Landscapes of the Heart: Parallels in the Poetries of Kavanagh and Auden', *Studies*, 77 (Winter 1988), 445–59.
Johnston, Dillon, *Irish Poetry after Joyce* (Notre Dame, Ill.: University of Notre Dame Press, 1985).
Kavanagh, Patrick, *Collected Pruse* (London: MacGibbon & Kee, 1967).
Kavanagh, Patrick, *The Complete Poems*, ed. Peter Kavanagh (New York: The Peter Kavanagh Hand Press, 1972).
Kendall, Tim, *Paul Muldoon* (Bridgend: Seren, 1996).
Kendall, Tim, and McDonald, Peter (eds.), *Paul Muldoon: Critical Essays* (Liverpool: Liverpool University Press, 2004).
Longley, Edna, *Poetry in the Wars* (Newcastle upon Tyne: Bloodaxe Books, 1986).
Longley, Edna, *The Living Stream: Literature and Revisionism in Ireland* (Newcastle upon Tyne: Bloodaxe Books, 1994).
McDonald, Peter, *Mistaken Identities: Poetry and Northern Ireland* (Oxford: Oxford University Press, 1997).
Mahon, Derek, *Night-Crossing* (London: Oxford University Press, 1968).
Mahon, Derek, *Lives* (London: Oxford University Press, 1972).
Mahon, Derek, *The Snow Party* (London: Oxford University Press, 1975).
Mahon, Derek, *Poems 1962–1978* (Oxford: Oxford University Press, 1979).
Mahon, Derek, *The Hunt by Night* (London: Oxford University Press, 1982).

Marken, Ronald, 'Review of *The Wishbone*', *Canadian Journal of Irish Studies*, 12/1 (June 1986), 111.
Michie, Helena R., *The Flesh Made Word* (New York: Oxford University Press, 1987).
Muldoon, Paul, *Poems 1968–1998* (London: Faber & Faber, 2001).
Muldoon, Paul, *Plan B* (London: Enitharmon Press, 2009).
Paulin, Tom, *Ireland and the English Crisis* (Newcastle upon Tyne: Bloodaxe Books, 1984).
Payne, Basil, 'The Poetry of Patrick Kavanagh', *Studies*, 49 (1960), 282.
Quinn, Antoinette, *Patrick Kavanagh: Born-Again Romantic* (Dublin: Gill and Macmillan, 1991).
Quinn, Antoinette, *Patrick Kavanagh: A Biography* (Dublin: Gill and Macmillan, 2001).
Smith, Stan (ed.), *Patrick Kavanagh* (Dublin: Irish Academic Press, 2009).
Wills, Clair, *Improprieties: Politics and Sexuality in Northern Irish Poetry* (Oxford: Clarendon Press, 1993).
Wills, Clair, *Reading Paul Muldoon* (Newcastle upon Tyne: Bloodaxe Books, 1998).
Worth, Katherine, *Revolutions in Modern English Drama* (London: Bell, 1972).

CHAPTER 23

'OTHER MODES OF BEING': NUALA NÍ DHOMHNAILL, PAUL MULDOON, AND TRANSLATION

MARIA JOHNSTON

> Translation is not mechanical reproduction. It is transformation [...] Translation implies in both a geometrical and linguistic sense, movement, a resistance to fixity. Its momentum is dialogical.
>
> Michael Cronin[1]

IN her most recent bilingual collection *The Fifty Minute Mermaid* (2007) we find Nuala Ní Dhomhnaill putting her personae into 'extreme situations, on the linguistic edge'[2] as they are forcibly transferred from one world to another, a movement that effectively signals this most shape-shifting of poet's career-long interest in traversing boundaries of space, time, nation, language, genre, and selfhood; that is to say, her profound investment in the activity of translation itself. An English-born Irish-language poet of transit and linguistic transactions Ní Dhomhnaill occupies and troubles the fluid frontiers between linguistic, cultural, historical, and ontological realities. 'I'm all for transgression—for breaking boundaries', she has professed, her avowed mission to be 'severely disruptive'[3] within the Irish context. This is a poet whose reading and cultural life admits

---

[1] Michael Cronin, *Translating Ireland: Translating, Languages, Cultures* (Cork: Cork University Press, 1996), 5–6.
[2] Nuala Ní Dhomhnaill, 'Mermaids Out of Water: Nuala Ní Dhomhnaill agus an Mhuruch', RTÉ Radio 1, 26 Mar. 2003.
[3] Ní Dhomhnaill, 'Adaptations and Transformations: An Interview with Deborah McWilliams Consalvo', *Studies: An Irish Quarterly Review*, 83/331 (Autumn 1994), 313–20 (315, 320).

of no boundaries, who is influenced as much by Japanese aesthetics, Eastern philosophies, Turkish literature, classical literature, American models—she learnt about the use of personae or masks and the necessarily 'ambiguous relation'[4] of these to the writer or narrator from poets such as John Berryman—as she is by Seán Ó Ríordáin, Máire Mhac an tSaoi, and Irish myth and folklore: 'I will use classical or Turkish or even Northern, Chinese, Japanese or any kind of mythology that serves my purpose.'[5] Her poetry and poetics reduce all of the usual critically sacrosanct, simplifying categories and polarities to a state of redundancy, if not utter meaninglessness. Ní Dhomhnaill has always been, in Frank Sewell's words, a 'truly post-modern *bricoleuse*,'[6] from her beginnings as a poet in Cork with the *Innti* group of poets—'the authentic indigenous beats' as Declan Kiberd has recognized and a truly 'counter-cultural force'[7] —right up to this moment in the new twenty-first century. She is, as Dillon Johnston has perceptively noted, 'a poet who brings an unusual international perspective into the often parochial Irish-language enterprise.'[8] Nothing is off limits for this most outward-looking of poets as she travels and translates, forging a poetry of endless movement, of metaphor and metamorphosis.

Given the scope of Ní Dhomhnaill's poetry, its technical and thematic range, it is unsurprising that such a diversity of contemporary Irish poet-translators have looked to, and continue to look to, her poetry for inspiration and provocation. The bilingual collections of her work to date—these include *Selected Poems/Rogha Dánta* (1986; with translations into English by Michael Hartnett as well as Ní Dhomhnaill herself); *Pharaoh's Daughter* (1990; translated by a selection of poets including Medbh McGuckian, Ciaran Carson, Michael Hartnett, Seamus Heaney, Michael Longley, Derek Mahon, and John Montague); *The Astrakhan Cloak* (1992; with translations by Paul Muldoon); *The Water Horse* (1999; with translations by Medbh McGuckian and Eiléan Ní Chuilleanáin), and, most recently, *The Fifty Minute Mermaid* (with translations again by Muldoon)—have established Ní Dhomhnaill as one of the most prominent contemporary Irish poets writing in any language. More than that, this roll call of translators effectively defies the segregating, polarizing terms of gender, class, tradition, school, and language that are used to delineate maps of the Irish poetic terrain. Yet for some commentators this large number of translators has been problematic; reviewing *Pharaoh's Daughter*, Douglas Sealy criticized the cacophonous 'bewildering variety of tones'[9] produced by its thirteen translators, missing how the book might perhaps more accurately be read as thirteen ways of looking at Ní Dhomhnaill. Alert instead to how the rich variety of the translational activity enabled by Ní Dhomhnaill's poetry should be viewed rather as a mark of the poet's achievement, Alan Titley, reviewing the same collection, celebrates these

---

[4] Ní Dhomhnaill, 'Mermaids Out of Water'.
[5] Ní Dhomhnaill, 'Poetry and Identity: An Interview with Nuala Ní Dhomhnaill', *Nordic Irish Studies*, 6 (2007), 127–32 (129).
[6] Frank Sewell, *Modern Irish Poetry: A New Alhambra* (New York: Oxford University Press, 2000), 192.
[7] Declan Kiberd, *The Irish Writer and the World* (Cambridge: Cambridge University Press, 2005), 14.
[8] Dillon Johnston, *Irish Poetry After Joyce* (2nd edn. New York: Syracuse University Press, 1997), 288.
[9] Douglas Sealy, 'A New Voice for the Seanachie', *Irish Times* (8 Dec. 1990), 9.

as poems in which 'folklore/tradition shack up with modernism/feminism': 'she has been well and truly heanied, muldooned, mahonied, carsonised and hartnettified by her translators so that we never step into the same Nuala twice'.[10] Thus, far from producing a Babel-like 'heterophony of voices', as Caoimhin Mac Giolla Léith astutely observes: 'it is one of the protean Ní Dhomhnaill's many virtues that so many poets can find in her work something that either responds to or anticipates their own concerns'.[11] More than this, Ní Dhomhnaill's work, as a vigorous, ongoing dialogue with her contemporaries (as well as with her predecessors), makes possible vital interlingual, intertextual, and international conversations that testify to the expansive and ever-expanding bilingual space that is 'Irish' poetry.

The practice of translating poetry in Irish into English has never been without its difficulties, dogged as it has been by particular political and cultural concerns. Another Irish-language poet Biddy Jenkinson famously defined her refusal to be translated into English as 'a small rude gesture to those who think that everything can be harvested and stored without loss in an English-speaking Ireland'[12] and Ní Dhomhnaill has not escaped charges of too permissively allowing her work to be appropriated by others into versions or loose imitations. Ní Dhomhnaill's most succinct response to this contentious topic comes in the form of her clear-sighted 1993 essay 'Traductio ad Absurdum' wherein she argues perceptively for translation as the best alternative to stagnation and stultification, to what she terms the 'status quo of the fifties and sixties' throughout which poems in the Irish language were mere 'token pieces of exotica' in service to the 'shibbolethic language policy of the Irish Republic'.[13] Critical of the Irish revivalist mindset, she has stated that what keeps her going is 'the desire to take Irish back from that grey-faced Irish-revivalist male preserve'.[14] Irish is for this poet a living language, not a moribund 'cultural artifact' and Ní Dhomhnaill continues to fight against the identity politics that would typecast her as an 'Irish poet' and therefore little more than a 'bit of cultural furniture' or 'something out of Tutankhamen's tomb'.[15] 'Where I find I belong is in the cultural politics which insists on the importance of Irish as well as English', she has asserted.[16] Part of her mission then is to 'disabuse people' of entrenched 'certainties', particularly with regard to the Irish language and culture, and instead 'encourage the possibilities beyond the claustrophobic and self-satisfying attitudes of the mainstream Irish establishment' through writing in a language that is 'contrary to the literary monoglot', thus exemplifying how the Irish language 'offers us the possibilities of other modes of being'.[17]

---

[10] Alan Titley, 'Blooming Bigamy', *Books Ireland* (May 1991), 89–90 (90).
[11] Caoimhin Mac Giolla Léith, 'More Canon Fodder', *Irish Review*, 11 (Winter 1991/2), 127–33 (132).
[12] Biddy Jenkinson, 'Letter to an Editor', *Irish University Review*, 21/1 (Spring–Summer 1991), 34.
[13] Ní Dhomhnaill, 'Traductio ad Absurdum', *Krino*, 14 (Winter 1993), 49–50.
[14] Ní Dhomhnaill, in Ní Dhomhnaill and Medbh McGuckian, 'Comhrá, with a Foreword and Afterword by Laura O'Connor', *Southern Review*, 31/3 (Summer 1995), 581–614 (589).
[15] Ní Dhomhnaill, 'Adaptations and Transformations', 314.
[16] Ní Dhomhnaill, 'Poetry and Identity', 128.
[17] Ní Dhomhnaill, 'Adaptations and Transformations', 318–19.

It is rather the living poetic quality of the language itself—'the euphony of Irish prosody', with its capacity for 'elegance' and 'beautifully cadenced' articulation[18]—that this most linguistically attuned of poets strives to bring out, challenging easy binaries, staid ideologies, and received narratives in order to create works of art that engender change and renewal. The Irish language is for Ní Dhomhnaill one 'of enormous elasticity and emotional sensitivity; of quick and hilarious banter and a welter of references both historical and mythological; it is an instrument of imaginative depth and scope'.[19] As the many poets that are drawn to translate her work implicitly understand, far from being a monolinguist or essentialist in her deployment of the Irish language, its history and lore, Ní Dhomhnaill is a poet of the world, mindful of the dangers of a monoglot or monocultural existence, and, moreover, as a skilled verbal technician is more than usually sensitive to the vibrancies and vibrations of different languages. Indeed, what awakened in her the impulse to write poetry in Irish was her life-altering immersion in the Turkish language and culture, and so her poetics in Irish comes out of an expansive world view that is enriched by other cultural and linguistic realities beyond the narrow precepts of Irish cultural nationalism. Ní Dhomhnaill's remembered instance of being sleepless in Turkey, listening, 'in the middle of the Anatolian night' to recordings of Máirtín Ó Direáin 'intoning "faoiseamh a gheobhadsa, seal beag gairid" ' neatly encapsulates her transnational poetics.[20] Translation, as transgression, transmission, transformation, goes to the heart of this restless poetics that resists fixity and closure to embrace openness, vitality, and variety. Each of the poets that embark on the translation process with her are alive to the boundlessness of her poetic resource, to the richness of her unique imagination, and ultimately, to the full meaning of that verb or action word, 'to translate'—to carry over, to transfer—which Ní Dhomhnaill's lively, dynamic work enacts.

Ní Dhomhnaill herself defines the 'work of the writer' as 'one of adaptation and transformation, if not only transposition'.[21] Translational activity is therefore central to the enterprise. For Ní Dhomhnaill, the success of a poetic translation lies in the translator's ability to 'get the voltage that is behind the words'[22] and, crucially, depends upon the interaction between poet and reader-translator. In Ní Dhomhnaill's view, herself and her 'translators' form a 'camaraderie of equals' within which there is a clear reciprocity of influence and a sense of ongoing conversation: 'We really do influence each other', she has revealed.[23] In this way, the Irish poets she 'can learn from and appreciate' are McGuckian, Carson, Ní Chuilleanáin, and Muldoon.[24] Indeed, very much in the spirit

---

[18] Ní Dhomhnaill, 'Comhrá', 602.
[19] Ní Dhomhnaill, 'Why I Choose to Write in Irish: The Corpse that Sits Up and Talks Back', *New York Times Book Review* (8 Jan. 1995), 27–8.
[20] Ní Dhomhnaill, in Liam Carson, 'Dark but Funny and Transformative', *Fortnight* (Sept. 2004), 20–1 (21).
[21] Ní Dhomhnaill, 'Adaptations and Transformations', 313.
[22] Ní Dhomhnaill, 'Comhrá', 601.
[23] In Scott R. Greenberg, 'Poetry in Emotion', interview with Scott R. Greenberg, *The Pitch*, 15 Mar. 2001, [www.pitch.com/2001-03-15/calendar/poetry-in-emotion].
[24] Ní Dhomhnaill, 'Comhrá', 605.

of this conversational mode, the bilingual collection *The Water Horse* was billed on its publication in 1999 as a three-way 'conversation' between 'three of Ireland's leading poets' (Ní Dhomhnaill, McGuckian, and Ní Chuilleanáin). Again, what was so striking about this collaboration was how each voice in the trio was able to sound together while still retaining its own distinctive timbre, thanks to the wide-ranging harmonics of Ní Dhomhnaill's poetics; as one reviewer of *The Water Horse* noted, we get 'three distinct, assured, well cultivated voices'.[25] This conversational method was effectively illuminated in the aptly titled 'Comhrá' (conversation) that took place in 1995 between Ní Dhomhnaill and McGuckian, her translator. At one revealing moment during this conversation, the occasion of McGuckian apologizing for 'taking liberties' in translating Ní Dhomhnaill's 'Toircheas 1' prompted Ní Dhomhnaill to reflect on her own sense of what translation may be: 'I think those liberties were fine. That is what translation is. It doesn't really matter if the words mean different things. The most important thing is to get the voltage that is behind the words.'[26]

As came to light through this penetrating poetic exchange McGuckian, rather than simply responding to a Ní Dhomhnaill poem with a gloss or word-for-word paraphrase in English, produces translations that are ambiguous, open-ended texts, and which have her engaged as an active, creative reader, interpreting the layers of meaning, the symbolism and metaphorical charge beneath the surface meaning of the words and carrying these over into her own distinctive cast of English. Thus, the description 'Ar an tslí | a sheolann gaileoin néalta tríd an aer' (literally 'the way a cloudy galleon sails through the air') becomes in McGuckian's conveying, 'as the sleepwalk of treasure-laden clouds'—making for, what Ní Dhomhnaill terms, 'an exact voltage translation'. The cloud galleons symbolize 'the pregnant us', Ní Dhomhnaill as poet-reader interprets it in the course of this probing dialogue. In this way then, the metaphor itself may be seen to become laden, pregnant with possibility, as it travels from Irish into English and back. 'Is there a word for sex in Irish?', Ní Dhomhnaill was once teasingly asked by a fellow countryman,[27] ignorant of what Ní Dhomhnaill understands as the powerful 'erotic tradition of pre-modern Ireland'.[28] It may be said that for her the poetic act is akin to the sexual act; life-giving, stimulating, forceful, and unrepressed, it is also driven by oppositions and darker energies. The activity of translation affords many such 'treasure-laden' instances as the translation process, itself a fertile, meaning-making process, gives birth to new possibilities, engendering and extending metaphors through movement across the frontiers of language and of the creative mind. Indeed, that suggestive, polysemous term 'crib' points to how the original poem may be seen as analogous to the crib of a newborn into which burgeoning life is placed and from which it goes forth into the world—one thinks of the Moses-basket of Ní Dhomhnaill's famous statement on poetry as translation, 'Ceist na Teangan'. That the poem is ultimately concerned most of all with the

---

[25] Siobhán Ní Fhoghlú, 'How Was It for You?', *Poetry Ireland Review*, 66 (Autumn 2000), 116–18.
[26] Ní Dhomhnaill, 'Comhrá', 600–1.
[27] Ní Dhomhnaill, 'Why I Choose to Write in Irish', 27–8.
[28] Ní Dhomhnaill, 'Adaptations and Transformations', 315.

poetic process itself becomes clear as McGuckian goes on to explain how the 'quiet' of the opening line relates to the intervals of creative silence that are also part of her ongoing poetic conversation with Ní Dhomhnaill: 'how can I explain to you why I have not translated you for the last five years or so', McGuckian translates her own translation. Central then to the act of translation is the thrust of ongoing conversation, of two creative beings in dialogue across languages, across inseminating semantic frontiers, and across, finally, the 'quiet', the empty space.

As stated, Ní Dhomhnaill deems those translations that get the 'voltage' of the original as the most successful and her own critical terminology emphasizes how the dominant move in this process of transmission hinges on the action of 'getting across'. John Montague's 'The Broken Doll' ('I saw it as a very pre-Raphaelite poem and that is the quality that he gets across marvellously in English'); McGuckian's translation of 'Geasa'; Derek Mahon's 'The Race' ('it gets the hurried breathlessness of the original dead on'); and Montague's version of 'Blodewedd' ('he gets the sound across very well') are all examples provided by the poet of how her translators capture the spirit of the original, the charge behind the words and their ostensible meanings.[29] In the same analysis, Ní Dhomhnaill's attentive reading of 'Blodewedd' is instructive in the way that it uncovers audible linguistic disturbances in the translation—one specific line sounds 'more bathetic than it does in Irish'—and this serves to remind us of 'how very differently the two languages operate'. Such moments of tension and frisson must be seen to be a vital, stimulating part of the process. In the same way, as a result of the 'prosodic registers of English' Michael Longley's 'Aubade' turns Ní Dhomhnaill's 'Aubade' into a 'much more Edwardian, dainty Miss Tippy Toes poem'. Longley thought he had 'improved on the original; tidied it up a bit', Ní Dhomhnaill somewhat indignantly recounts, thereby indicating the stylistic differences and even combative tensions that can drive such activities. The process of translation is ultimately enlivened and sustained by such tensions, conflicts, conversations, and crossovers. Ní Dhomhnaill, herself a shrewd reader and self-critic, can see how the differences between the two languages of Irish and English can, through the translational process, be, if not overcome, then certainly made to enrich each other and bring out qualities and interpretative possibilities in the other. It is a process of mutual reciprocity in which both poems converse with each other across the borders of the page, the borders of language.

For Ní Dhomhnaill reading her own poems in translation, most successful of all in the way that it relays that 'voltage' is Muldoon's 'My Dark Master' (his rendering of 'Mo Mháistir Dorcha') as it overcomes seemingly insurmountable difficulties in moving between Irish and English poetic forms. As Ní Dhomhnaill elucidates, Muldoon circuitously 'got around the problem' posed by the four-line stanza in Irish with its characteristic end-falling cadence by employing repetition and parallelism akin to that used in 'The Psalm of Psalms' or 'The Song of Inanna', thus coming 'as near as you can get, I think, to a modern Irish/Gáidhlig classical metre. [...] I thought it was a marvellous way of

---

[29] Ní Dhomhnaill, in Kaarina Hollo, 'Acts of Translation: An Interview with Nuala Ní Dhomhnaill', *Edinburgh Review*, 99 (Spring 1998), 99–107 (103–4).

getting the right "voltage" '.³⁰ The clearly compatible relationship of Muldoon and Ní Dhomhnaill as 'poet' and 'translator' (though as we'll see these terms are not as clear-cut as we'd like to think) was inaugurated in the early 1980s when Ní Dhomhnaill received in the post an unsolicited translation by Muldoon of her 'An Crann', and it has only strengthened over the decades since *Pharaoh's Daughter* (1990) through *The Astrakhan Cloak* (1992) and into the present century with *The Fifty-Minute Mermaid* collaboration. It is important to emphasize the word 'collaboration' at this point. Not only have reviewers remarked on this aspect—Bernard O'Donoghue welcomed *The Astrakhan Cloak* as 'a more extensive venture in a proven collaboration between two of the very best modern Irish poets'[31]—but both Ní Dhomhnaill and Muldoon have spoken of their partnership in terms of mutual respect and cooperation. For Ní Dhomhnaill, within the 'camaraderie of equals' that is the poet and her translators, it is her interactive correspondence with Muldoon (he is, along with Eiléan Ní Chuilleanáin, Ní Dhomhnaill's 'favourite' among her translators) that stands out above all others:

> Some poets [...] lack that humility and think that they have much better Irish than they have. Paul on the other hand—probably because he really has very good Irish—is most undefensive. When I faxed him the poem that was to be in *Poetry Chicago*, he rang back and asked questions like 'Who are those cows with the long horns?' [...]—that kind of give and take, which I love, and which is genuine and loving. But he's the only one I've ever had that level of undefensive interaction with.[32]

'[G]enuine and loving', this is a unique poetic relationship of 'give and take', the dialogic momentum evident in Ní Dhomhnaill's representation of their working practices. Muldoon's equal admiration is no less evident: 'the act of translation forces me to try to come to terms with one of the most interesting bodies of work in contemporary poetry', he has declared.[33] Moreover both Muldoon and Ní Dhomhnaill have influenced each other's original poetry: Muldoon dedicated *Kerry Slides* (1996) to her and famously stated that the 'only image worth a fuck' in his *The Prince of the Quotidian* (1994) is the 'eelgrass and bladderwrack' of Ní Dhomhnaill.[34] He has also pointed to how 'the form of "Bhí an seisear againn" ' ('There were six of us') is influenced metrically by Ní Dhomhnaill's 'An Bád Sí' (translated by Muldoon as 'The Fairy Boat') but the line of influence does not stop here for, as Laura O'Connor reminds us in her recent examination of Muldoon's work in the Irish language: 'Ní Dhomhnaill composed the Immram sequence with Muldoon's oeuvre in mind, and hence their intertextual debt to each other cuts both ways.'[35] On the critical front, Ní Dhomhnaill has also aligned herself with

---

[30] Ní Dhomhnaill, 'Acts of Translation', 103–4.
[31] Bernard O'Donoghue, 'Meeting Half-Way', *Times Literary Supplement* (14 Apr. 1995), 23.
[32] Ní Dhomhnaill, 'Acts of Translation', 99–100.
[33] Muldoon, 'Translator's Note: "The Mermaid in the Hospital" ', *Poetry Magazine*, 190/1 (Apr. 2007), 56.
[34] Paul Muldoon, *The Prince of the Quotidian* (Oldcastle: Gallery Press, 1994), 38–40.
[35] Laura O'Connor, 'The Bilingual Routes of Paul Muldoon / Pól Ó Maoldúin', *Irish Studies Review*, 19/2 (May 2011), 135–55 (148).

Muldoon, coming to his defence when, in a discussion of Eavan Boland's essay 'Outside History', she pulls up the author for 'unfairly overlook[ing] Paul Muldoon's constant attempts to deconstruct the literary "spéirbhean" ' in his collection *Quoof*.[36] In this way she shows not only how acute a reader she is of Muldoon's work but how appreciative she is of his subversive strategies and, moreover, of the necessity of such strategies in unsettling received ideas to do with Irish cultural and literary traditions.

Yet critics have commented on theirs as an unlikely, even unequal, pairing. Reviewing *The Astrakhan Cloak* Barra O'Seaghdha begins by stressing the 'strangeness of this encounter' pitting the enigmatic, quintessentially postmodern Muldoon (all 'allusiveness', 'elusiveness', 'shifting ground', 'deliberate banality and parody') against a Ní Dhomhnaill who is, in O'Seaghdha's simplistic formulation, rooted in 'love, longing, lore', the selfsame qualities that, in O'Seaghdha's view, serve only to damagingly perpetuate enduring images of the Irish language as 'elemental and anti-modern'.[37] 'Sometimes the translation is more effective than the original', O'Seaghdha asserts with reference to Muldoon's 'The View from Cabinteely' which, unlike Ní Dhomhnaill's original, manages to be 'sinister right from the start' and is therefore more effective. Critics often miss nuances in Ní Dhomhnaill's poems that Muldoon brings out. In a similar way, Dillon Johnston in his reading of Muldoon's translation of 'Titim i nGrá' from the same collection offers it as an example of Muldoon's 'tendency to draw towards the surface of the translation mythic references more submerged in the Irish poem' with Muldoon specifically 'extend[ing] the possibility of a demon lover' that Johnston feels is only hinted at in Ní Dhomhnaill's poem.[38] However, Johnston's take is strangely inaccurate as the 'mythic references' he unearths are clearly visible in Ní Dhomhnaill's original poem—and indeed across the whole collection *Feis*—to the point where it would be impossible to read the poem without thinking of the myth of Persephone and, by extension, the demon lover that has haunted the whole of Ní Dhomhnaill's oeuvre. Johnston, in thrall to the postmodern trickster, hails Muldoon as inveterate punster for the way that he plays on the double meaning of 'fall' but what Johnston misses again is that this pun first surfaces in Ní Dhomhnaill's crib and so the playfulness works both ways. As well as exposing the limitations of such cursory critical approaches, Johnston's oversight inadvertently throws light on how the crib may function as an interesting middle ground between poem and translation, poet and translator. Ultimately, Muldoon may be seen to be the only one reading Ní Dhomhnaill with due attentiveness: the translator is therefore uncovered as the ideal discerning reader and, by extension, the ideal critic.

The failure of critics to read across languages and avoid the pitfalls of the narrow critical lens is even more pronounced throughout Kaarina Hollo's assessment of *The Astrakhan Cloak*. Again Muldoon's translation of 'Titim i nGrá' is called into question. For this critic, Muldoon 'completely abandons the imagery of the original' in what is, in

---

[36] Ní Dhomhnaill, 'What Foremothers?', *Poetry Ireland Review*, 36 (Autumn 1992), 18–31 (31).
[37] Barra O'Seaghdha, 'The Tasks of the Translator', *Irish Review*, 14 (Autumn 1993), 143–7.
[38] Dillon Johnston, *The Poetical Economies of England and Ireland, 1912–2000* (Basingstoke: Palgrave, 2001), 174–5.

Hollo's strongly worded indictment, a 'drastic and unwarranted emendation'.[39] Lacking close engagement with the language and technique of the poems of both Muldoon and Ní Dhomhnaill, Hollo's critique of Muldoon's translational practices is instead largely given over to enumerating Muldoon's crimes against the original, concluding that, of the thirty-one translations in the book, at least fourteen have 'serious problems'. This is attributed to the reckless Muldoon's wayward tendency to 'smooth rough edges, to make things more lyrical, to alter and "improve", to make things more whimsical'. As a result of Muldoon's 'lack of empathy for the original' Ní Dhomhnaill's poems are thus, in Hollo's damning moral judgement, 'denied a fair representation' with Muldoon's mere 'versions' comprising a book that 'does not do justice' to the 'wide scope, openness and eclecticism' of Ní Dhomhnaill's work. This charge is not substantiated by Hollo's close readings of the poems under examination and her criteria—the privileging of vague ethical terms such as 'empathy' and 'fidelity' in her prosecutorial, courtroom-style legalese—cannot be sustained in the face of both poets' studied meditations on translation as a process. Muldoon's own sense of poetic translation centres on Philip Lewis's theoretical term 'abusive fidelity': 'honouring the flaw, honouring the bubble, honouring the infelicity'.[40] In fact, what Muldoon and Ní Dhomhnaill's collaboration achieves is the troubling of not just language itself as they expose the slipperiness of words through pun, paradox, and play, but also, as we shall see, the complication of narratives of reading that position poet and translator in separate categories, with one subordinate to the other in this severely debilitating victim-appropriator paradigm. The open-ended dialogue between poet and translator complicates any notions of language as transparent or of translational activity as straightforwardly fluent. As with the trauma of Ní Dhomhnaill's displaced merfolk, translation is marked by dislocation, radical instability, and contingency, but its risks are undertaken out of a sense of love, of 'give and take', to repeat Ní Dhomhnaill's own sense of her exhilarating translational interplay with Muldoon.

A crucial part of their translational relationship—indeed, the success of this interlingual collaboration—seems to centre on the fact that both Ní Dhomhnaill and Muldoon share fundamental ideas about the writing process itself and make use of similar formal strategies. The poetics of both turn on the dynamics of metaphor and metamorphosis, musicality and multiplicity. Both share ultimately a translational, boundary-crossing poetics as each is drawn inexorably to the unknown, the other-worldly.[41] Muldoon and Ní Dhomhnaill are kindred poetic spirits and true collaborators in the larger creative enterprise, invested in the process of bringing poems into the world, carrying them over from some unfathomable beyond onto the page as borders are traversed, crossed, and double-crossed. Moreover, both understand the creative process as one of translation.

[39] Kaarina Hollo, 'From the Irish: On *The Astrakhan Cloak*', *New Hibernia Review*, 3/2 (Summer 1999), 129–41.

[40] Muldoon, 'Amores: A Public Conversation About Translation', Slought Foundation, 5 Feb. 2009, [http://slought.org/content/11416].

[41] Indeed, Ní Dhomhnaill has noted that Muldoon, when selecting from poems by Ní Dhomhnaill to translate for *The Astrakhan Cloak*, was drawn to those that 'had an "otherwordly" dimension or intrusion'. 'Acts of Translation', 102.

In the preface to his pamphlet of translations *When the Pie was Opened* (2008) Muldoon revealed how he has been 'fascinated by the art of translation' since his formative years. More particularly, it was through a routine schoolroom translation assignment that Muldoon was himself 'translated into writerdom'; the movement of translating from Irish into English setting him off on the process of discovery that is for him the very definition of poetic making. Yet even the most studious Muldoon devotee will be somewhat surprised by this account of the birth of his poetic consciousness. For, as Rui Carvalho Homem has remarked, 'many readers of contemporary poetry would not think of Muldoon as a poet-translator'.[42] More particularly, in my view, they may not think to locate the source of his poetic journeying in his negotiations with the Irish language.[43] In a way that draws him even closer to Ní Dhomhnaill Muldoon is himself a poet who not only translates from, but writes original poems in, the Irish language, under the name of Pól Ó Maoldúin. As a poet who is self-consciously 'becoming more and more interested in [...] the style one would associate more often with song, the ballad tradition, the anonymity of the poet, the sense that there are many more hands, mouths, heads, involved in the poem' he looks back to the Irish scribes, valuing their ability to compose in the dark (metaphorically as well as literally) while inventing complex poetic techniques: 'learning these very complex forms with these terrific internal rhymes—*ceangal* as it's known in Irish'.[44]

Poetry in Irish is thereby crucial to Muldoon's poetics and he is increasingly keen to correct critical narratives that would overlook this fact: 'Irish played, still plays, a much larger role in my poems than most people would imagine...I see that a huge amount of formal aspects of Gaelic poetry are carried over into my own poems.' Here again, as with Ní Dhomhnaill previously, the action of 'carrying over' best expresses the workings of the creative, composing mind. Indeed, as David Wheatley was among the first to observe, it was through working on translating Ní Dhomhnaill's poetry that Muldoon's interest in the Irish language increased.[45] In a more recent interview with Laura O'Connor, Muldoon's continuing debts as a poet in English to the Irish tradition are clear as he professes how his 'interest in the sonnet [...] comes paradoxically not from the sonnet tradition in English but from trí rainn agus amhrán'.[46] A New Age Gaelic sonneteer, Muldoon approaches the traditional form from unexpected angles that shed light on the extent to which the Irish, British, and European poetic traditions

---

[42] Rui Carvalho Homem, *Poetry and Translation in Northern Ireland: Dislocations in Contemporary Writing* (Basingstoke: Palgrave, 2009), 133.

[43] In the same study, Homem almost completely overlooks Muldoon's all-important translations of the poetry of Nuala Ní Dhomhnaill, the poet whose work he has translated most often. Referring to these as mere 'versions' Homem judges Muldoon's translations from Irish as inferior, even sidelining them as 'ancillary'. Homem, *Poetry and Translation in Northern Ireland*, 156–7.

[44] Muldoon, in Patrick McGuinness, 'Speculating: Patrick McGuinness Interviews Paul Muldoon', *Irish Studies Review*, 17/1 (Feb. 2009), 103–10.

[45] See David Wheatley, 'The Aistriúchán Cloak: Paul Muldoon and the Irish Language', *New Hibernia Review*, 5/4 (Winter 2001), 123–34.

[46] Muldoon, quoted in Laura O'Connor, 'The Bilingual Routes of Paul Muldoon', 141.

are vitally intertwined. This deep interest in Irish-language poetry and its long tradition binds him ever closer to Ní Dhomhnaill; they even share a common landscape in the Kerry Gaeltacht—Ní Dhomhnaill's 'psychic stomping ground'[47]—where Muldoon lived before departing for the United States and dual Irish-American citizenship in 1987. In her astute discussion of Muldoon's work in the Irish language, O'Connor remarks on how 'Muldoon and Ní Dhomhnaill's shared susceptibility to the "literary charge" [to use Muldoon's phrase] of Corca Dhuibhne enhances the chemistry of their collaboration through translation'.[48] Indeed, another defining image supplied by Ní Dhomhnaill describes herself and Muldoon walking together across the landscape of Ventry in Corca Dhuibhne with Muldoon characteristically delivering an 'impromptu peroration' on the Irish mythological race the Fir Bolg over the course of their ambulatory dialogue.[49] These same Fomorians provide Muldoon with his analogy for the petrifying artistic gaze in his poem 'The Outlier' which locates the poetic persona as a detached outsider 'between two stones' in what has been read as a portrait of Muldoon as artist.[50]

'Every poem is a leap into the sea of unknowingness',[51] Ní Dhomhnaill has declared and for both herself and Muldoon the writing process itself entails journeying through indeterminacy. Poetic composition is therefore a translational process of tentative searching, directed by the sound of words themselves through which sense or 'meaning' is discovered in the act itself. As Ní Dhomhnaill has explained elsewhere: 'When it's something that's beyond my comprehension that's trying to break into meaning, then poetry is the form it takes for me.'[52] Thus, 'the sound pattern emerges first, then the words, then the meaning, in that order [...] The meaning can change quite arbitrarily, depending on whether the sound is right or not'.[53] Muldoon's experience of composing poems is exactly the same as he searches for 'chimes that are intrinsic or inherent rather than imposed'[54] and meaning emerges from there:

> They begin with an image, or maybe a couple of images, a phrase or two [...] it's really only in the process of the poem getting written that one discovers what the idea of the poem is [...] Generally as I'm starting a poem I've no idea what the pattern is going to be, I've no idea what the poem is about, and it is only through the course of its being written that I discover what it is.[55]

---

[47] Ní Dhomhnaill, 'Comhrá', 588.
[48] O'Connor, 'The Bilingual Routes of Paul Muldoon', 148.
[49] Ní Dhomhnaill, 'Acts of Translation', 99.
[50] Muldoon, *Horse Latitudes* (London: Faber and Faber, 2006), 47–8. Helen Vendler reads the poem as a 'minimalist autobiography'. Vendler, 'Fanciness and Fatality', *New Republic* 235/19 (6 Nov. 2006).
[51] Ní Dhomhnaill, 'Comhrá', 604.
[52] Ní Dhomhnaill, in Greenberg, 'Poetry in Emotion'.
[53] Ní Dhomhnaill, in Carson, 'Dark but Funny and Transformative', 20.
[54] Allie Lee, 'Paul Muldoon Reads and Discusses his Poetry', *Daily Gazette*, 26 Mar. 2009, [http://daily.swarthmore.edu/2009/3/26/muldoon].
[55] Muldoon, Interview with Jack Klaff, *Intelligence Squared* (Dec. 2009), [www.intelligencesquared.com/talks/paul-muldoon-on-poetry-and-childhood].

'It has to represent, *be* a revelation of some description, some kind of revelation, however modest, however minor [...] Some modest shift in how we see the world,' Muldoon concludes. The poem is therefore 'mimetic of some process of discovery' as Muldoon has stated, in terms that are exactly similar to Ní Dhomhnaill's. In both there is the sense of starting out with no idea of the destination, hovering between the known and the unknown,[56] the conscious and the unconscious. It is truly a transformative trajectory, as Muldoon has said elsewhere: 'Almost certainly some little change [...] takes place, in the process of the poem getting written.'[57] It is moreover for Ní Dhomhnaill a process of 'transaction' in which something is created rather than defined: 'A good poem in itself is the most alive form of language that you can imagine. It does change your life. It often expresses something that you have refused to admit before.'[58] The poem must embody discovery, surprise, revelation, shifting perceptions, and slippages, with the act of writing in the dark—to return to Muldoon's Irish scribes—finally breaking on some moment of revelation, on what Muldoon has called, recalling Robert Frost, a 'momentary clarification'. For Ní Dhomhnaill 'all poetry is translation' as she is alive to, 'plagued' indeed, by the 'seeming arbitrariness of so much that finally finds its way into the page and the compromises and accommodations necessary in even getting it that far.'[59] Once again, Muldoon echoes this in his assertion that 'One might say indeed that the "original" that we first read is itself...a translation of something and that it has a relationship to some version of an *ur*-poem...some version of a poem against which it is testing itself as it's coming into being.'[60] For both poets, all poetry is translation, transaction, and their individual pronouncements on poetic composition, as given voice to here, combine to create an illuminating commentary on poetry and translation and poetry as process.

Unsurprisingly, the views of both poets on the act of interlingual translation itself are often identical. Muldoon's sense of translation as transmutation is evident: 'My own sense is that the poem, if we focus on the poem, is inevitably becoming a different thing as it goes from one language into the other.'[61] Once again, Ní Dhomhnaill agrees that the poem necessarily becomes a different thing, finds its own way in the world: 'If a really good translation has occurred then an appropriation of the original has also occurred and then it belongs to the translator.' In this way, although the originals remain hers, the energies of translation require that 'the poems are almost another generation, they say bye-bye mummy and off they go.'[62] Indeed, translation's importance lies in bridging

---

[56] Muldoon, 'How to Compose Poetry', *Big Think*, [www.5min.com/Video/How-to-Compose-Poetry-27544354]. Muldoon elucidates: 'So the focus of knowing upon unknowing and the negotiation back and forth, to and fro, between not knowing and knowing, not knowing and knowing, that's where it gets done.'

[57] Muldoon, in Dillon Johnston, 'Interview with Paul Muldoon', *Arch Literary Journal*, 1 (Feb. 2008), [http://archjournal.wustl.edu/node/100].

[58] Ní Dhomhnaill, in Greenberg, 'Poetry in Emotion'.

[59] Ní Dhomhnaill, 'Acts of Translation', 106–7.

[60] Muldoon, 'Amores: A Public Conversation About Translation'.

[61] Muldoon, 'Amores: A Public Conversation About Translation'.

[62] Ní Dhomhnaill, in Loretta Qwarnstrom, 'Travelling Through Liminal Spaces: An Interview with Nuala Ní Dhomhnaill', *Nordic Irish Studies*, 3 (2004), 65–73 (66).

the gap between what Ní Dhomhnaill views as a 'disenfranchised audience' of non-Irish readers or speakers and thus making possible access to a larger linguistic landscape both of the mind and of reality.[63] Ní Dhomhnaill has described her 'laissez-faire' attitude to translation yet she is equally quick to draw the line ('put her foot down') whenever the 'question of mistranslation' arises. For both poets, translation is ultimately not only an important act of reading in Ní Dhomhnaill's words but the closest form of reading: 'Every act of translation is first of all an enormously careful act of reading' for a poet who is 'inclined to look on a poem as a bit like non-representational art; somehow a wide enough generalization from the specific that everyone can come along and hang their own personal hang-ups on it'.[64] 'I translate Nuala Ní Dhomhnaill's poems for one very simple reason: I want to read them, and translation is the very closest form of reading of which we may avail ourselves'[65] Muldoon has asserted, confirming the fact that to read is to translate.

With these vital, revitalizing formulations from both poets regarding the invigorating processes of poetry and translation in mind, we can now undertake a close reading of the poem 'Gan do Chuid Éadaigh' from *Pharaoh's Daughter* and Muldoon's translation of it into his own brand of Hiberno-American-English as 'Nude'. For a critic such as Alan Titley this is an example of a 'quirky' translation and decidedly not of the 'true and accurate' variety, as he explains: ' "Gan do Chuid Éadaigh" is made into "Nude" by Paul Muldoon and "do bhróga ar a mbíonn | I gcónaí snas" is muldooned as "your snazzy loafers", and so it goes'. Thus, 'in the hands of a master we can get a new poem that bears a relationship to the original, but that relationship is opaque'.[66] Titley clearly feels that something has been lost in this translation and his misgivings about truth and accuracy warrant closer attention as the intricacies of poetic translation must concern us now. In trying to determine just how 'opaque' the relationship is between original poem and translation it is helpful to present first off Ní Dhomhnaill's launch-pad or 'crib'. Here are the opening lines in her functional translation:

> Though I much prefer you | minus your clothes |—your silk shirt | and your tie | your umbrella tucked under the oxter | and your three-piece suit | tailored in sartorial elegance. [in the height of fashion]
>   your shoes which always sport | a high shine | your doe-skin gloves | on your hands | your crombie hat | tipped elegantly over the ear—| none of them add | a single whit to your presence.[67]

---

[63] 'It's not their fault they haven't Irish, not even here in Ireland. And that's where a translation comes in.' Ní Dhomhnaill, 'Adaptations and Transformations', 316.
[64] Ní Dhomhnaill, 'Acts of Translation', 107.
[65] Muldoon, 'Translator's Note: The Mermaid in the Hospital', 56.
[66] Alan Titley, 'Turning Inside and Out: Translating and Irish 1950–2000', *Yearbook of English Studies*, 35 (2005) 312–22 (321).
[67] Ní Dhomhnaill, Typescript with Holograph Emendations of the Crib of 'Gan do Chuid Éadaigh', Paul Muldoon Papers, Box 28 Folder 5, Emory University.

Ní Dhomhnaill's 'Gan do Chuid Éadaigh' is a subversive, sexually- and sonically-charged love poem which has the female poet address, dress, and undress her male love-object in what is a knowing, playful reversal of literary tradition as the male is mischievously objectified. The addressee is of course the ubiquitous demon lover of Ní Dhomhnaill's poetry, here being courted and titillated through the skilful workings of a most assured and adept poetic technique. In what is a bravado display of her own poetic prowess the poet has her way with her bad-boy beloved as the poem unfolds, emphasizing the fact that she, crucially, is in control of both poem and subject. Deliberately playing on the sound of the signifier 'fear' ('man' in Irish) as she goes (we get in the opening lines alone 'fearr', 'fearthainne', 'fhaobhar', 'fairsing'), she turns his very identity on its head with a sly twist of her tongue. The challenge then for Muldoon is to match Ní Dhomhnaill in her immaculately turned-out, exquisitely embellished, clean lines:

Is fearr liom tú	The long and the short
gan do chuid éadaigh ort—	of it is I'd far rather see you nude—
do léine shíoda	your silk shirt
is do charabhat,	and natty
do scáth fearthainne faoi t'ascaill	
is do chulaith	tie, the brolly under your oxter
trí phíosa faiseanta	in case of a rainy day,
le barr fheabhais táilliúrachta,	the three-piece seersucker
	suit that's so incredibly trendy,
do bhróga ar a mbíonn	
i gcónaí snas,	your snazzy loafers
do lámhainní craiceann eilite	and, la-di-da,
ar do bhois,	a pair of gloves
do hata *crombie*	made from the skin of a doe,
feircthe ar fhaobhar na cluaise–	
ní chuireann siad aon ruainne	then, to top it all, a crombie hat
le do thuairisc,	set at a rak-
	ish angle—none of these add
	up to more than the icing on the cake.

What first strikes one about Muldoon's fashioning is the division of Ní Dhomhnaill's eight-line stanzas into stanzas of four lines that intensifies the musical momentum over the line and stanza breaks. Also striking is his choice of the title 'Nude' (instead of the more long-winded 'without your clothes on' or even 'naked') which, with its saucy-sounding 'ooh' vowel, strikes the tone of insistent, sensuous mouth-music that will be sustained through the words 'you', 'suit', 'smooth', 'sinewy', 'root', and 'nude' again (repeated at poem's end). Muldoon picks up on Ní Dhomhnaill's 'snas' and turns it into 'snazzy'; Irish thus generating English through a consonance of sound across the makeshift language barrier. This is effected in the opening line too where Muldoon's 'short' not only half-rhymes with 'shirt' but looks across to the 'ort' of Ní Dhomhnaill's second line just as 'shirt' will sing across to half-harmonize with her 'carabhat'. Sound is paramount for both poets. Chains of 's' sounds mingle with harder consonant sounds throughout both the Irish and English enunciations. In true macaronic fashion, Muldoon's opting for the word 'seersucker', a Hindustani word, comprises a tribute to Ní Dhomhnaill's cosmopolitan imagination and multilingual cast of mind and ear, and the punchy alliteration of 'seersucker | suit' contributes perfectly to the overall mouthiness of the whole sensuous, ear-delighting enterprise.

Here too, the edges of rhyme are toyed with in disruptive fashion as Muldoon manipulates 'rak- | ish' to rhyme with 'cake' (which in turn leaps across languages to chime with the 'thuairisc' of the Irish), the severing of the word 'rakish' across the line break amplifying the threat inherent in Ní Dhomhnaill's bad-boy muse as Muldoon exploits the polysemous possibilities of the English language to create tremors in both meaning and form. Indeed, at this point Muldoon's own comments on his procedures in translating the last line of the song 'An Spailpín Fánach' may be instructive: for although the 'meaning of the last line [...] is somewhat distorted in my English rendering [...] it's a distortion that, like a funhouse mirror, is meant to include some clarification—in this case, on the use of the scythe as weapon'.[68] Slight distortions, ripples of dissonance and disarray are themselves part of the process and only add to the charge, in this case the at-times-violent charge, of the activity. Not only then does the male muse's naked body have the destructive ability to 'drive men and women mad' and 'send | half the women of Ireland totally round the bend' (in Ní Dhomhnaill's crib 'have half the women of Ireland | totally undone') but this danger is intimated from the start with Ní Dhomhnaill's description of his 'hata *crombie*' ('crombie hat') as 'feircthe ar fhaobhar na cluaise': 'feircthe' means the 'hilt of a dagger' as well as the 'peak' of a hat. In the same way, later in the poem we get Ní Dhomhnaill's deliberate word-choice of 'bhásta' (instead of 'coim') for 'waist': as 'bhásta' also means the bellyband of a harness the threat of entrapment is bound up in its signification, but, more than that, undertones of mortality itself are audible when we consider that the 'bás' in 'bhásta' is the Irish word for 'death'. A smooth, sinister mover, the beloved is captured in Ní Dhomhnaill's lithe, sinuous language of protracted vowels and propulsive alliteration as an 'ainmhí allta [...] amuigh | san oíche | is a fhágann scimhle ina mharbhshruth'. This deliberate movement and its shadowy resonances are picked up by Muldoon's scintillating enjambments—that are themselves mimetic of physical agility—as well as through darkly intensifying chains of assonance and alliteration, as disconcerting half-rhymes wilfully wrong-foot the innocent uninitiated:

The br*ill*-
iant s*l*i*nk* of a wild animal, a dream-
*c*at, *say*, on the prowl,
leaving *m*urder and *may*hem

in its *wake*.

[68] Muldoon, *When the Pie Was Opened* (London: Sylph Editions, 2012), 9.

That the poet can handle and put order on such a man through the manoeuvres of language and line breaks is living proof of her own poetic proficiency and linguistic flair.

Rhymes, chimes, and chains of alliteration continue to flow copiously across the two languages, so, for example, the internal rhyme and alliteration in Irish—'tá corp gan mhaisle, mhácail | nó míbhua' (in the crib, 'a peerless body | without blemish or fault')—becomes in equally soft, sensual-sounding English,

...a body unsurpassed
for beauty, without so much as a wart

or blemish, but the brill-

as Muldoon reinforces Ní Dhomhnaill's patterns of alliteration and assonance to perpetuate the linkages of *ceangal* in Muldoon's beloved Irish poetic tradition. In Ní Dhomhnaill's original the repeated 's' sound suggests sensuality as the body is controlled and aroused. These are ear-tickling, sense-stirring lines of sonic liquidity and heightened sensuous appeal:

Do ghuailne leathan fair*s*ing
i*s* do thaobh
chomh *s*lim le *s*neachta *s*éidte
ar an *s*liabh;

and their effects are again answered by Muldoon: 'your broad *s*inewy | *s*houlders and your flank | *s*mooth as *s*now on a *s*now-bank' (the crib version lacks the chimes of rhyme, the softness of the liquid harmonies as it translates: 'Your broad strong shoulders | and your skin | as smooth as windblown snow | on the mountainside'). Long vowels emphasize orality, the mouth itself as the other 'seat of pleasure', and thus the tactile, physical qualities of both languages. Generating harmonies, modulations, and suspensions across dissolving linguistic borders, Muldoon and Ní Dhomhnaill enact a heady music as one language ricochets off the other, the Irish energizing and opening up possibilities of sound for the English and vice versa.

In this way, beneath the technical display of the poet's carefully composed strategies, 'behind the outward | show' as Muldoon puts it in English, we get to the heart of the poem's concerns, that is, to the subject of poetic composition and the artistic life itself. Ní Dhomhnaill's artful poem is, above all else, a love poem to the art of poetry that is then extended and underscored by Muldoon to form a combined large-scale orchestration; one that performs the possibilities of translation, as two poets, male and female, come together and a coupling, a linguistic duet composed of unending call and response over the language barriers, ensues. Muldoon's pithy 'la-di-da' in the third stanza is pivotal. As a reference to the signature catchphrase of the eponymous, cross-dressing heroine of Woody Allen's 1977 film *Annie Hall* (which concerns the relationship between Alvy Singer and Hall who is herself in the process of becoming a singer), it encapsulates the poem's dominant theme, and technique, of performance. Modes of musical, linguistic performance as well as the performance of gender are all key—not for nothing has Ní Dhomhnaill been held up as a 'mistress of the song of the wandering line with its subtle and wavering rhythms'[69]—enforcing the fact that this sexually charged, linguistically sophisticated performance piece may be read not only as a dual-language duet but even, at times, as a healthy, vivifying duel, between poet and translator. Ní Dhomhnaill's original poem is at once a love poem and a statement of artistic authority. Bound up in the poem's sexual power play are the elements of risk and danger that both love and the activity of translation itself entail.

Love is the impulse behind creativity and behind linguistic adventuring: as Ní Dhomhnaill herself has pointed out, 'The word for "lover" and the word for "folk-poet" are the same in Turkish, *ashik*. And I understand the connection.'[70] Muldoon too, ever-alert to the 'voltage', the multiple frequencies across languages, understands how the impetus of translation releases meanings that the reader in either language—including the poet-as-reader—might not have been aware of as they composed their original. In this way, this translation by Ní Dhomhnaill's favourite of her many linguistic suitors, far from being 'opaque' or 'inaccurate' (to rehearse Titley's objections), is exemplary in its attentions to her own strategies, seductions, and sleights of hand, and is thereby completely given over to getting 'the voltage that is behind the words' in Ní Dhomhnaill's electrifying phrase. Not only this, but his translation pays homage to her deeply embedded sense of the 'euphony of Irish prosody'. Audible to the reader as both poems dialogue with each other—across the page break as across the sound barriers of language—are kinky chimes of internal and near rhymes and meaningful chains of assonance and alliteration whose sonic weave and weft matches that of the beloved's dark skin. This poem, as an interactive, interlinguistic dialogue, is not only as sophisticated, intricately-crafted, and expertly turned out as its stylish subject but is as alive, promiscuous, head-turning, mind-altering, and physically stimulating. Thus, the poet's rakish beloved becomes an embodiment of the poem itself and 'Gan Do Chuild Éadaigh' can fruitfully be read as a commentary on poetic translation and, more particularly, on how poetry itself, as a vital, regenerative activity, multiform and multilayered, is ultimately brought to life through the death-defying force of translational intercourse.

In his *The Cambridge Introduction to Modern Irish Poetry* (2008), Justin Quinn concludes his short discussion of Muldoon and Ní Dhomhnaill as translator and poet with the following throwaway dismissal: 'Muldoon is a far superior poet, and ultimately his translations amount to a criticism of [Ní Dhomhnaill's] limitations.'[71] By close-reading a single poem by Ní Dhomhnaill alongside its translation by Muldoon, such unsubstantiated critical judgements are themselves exposed as limited as the full force of the Irish-language poet's talents are revealed. We see instead how crucial the dialogical process of translation is and how the poetic exchange between both poets is of the first importance in understanding how not only the translational process works, but the compositional process of poetry itself in any language. Unlike original composition,

---

[69] Titley, 'Blooming Bigamy', 90.

[70] Ní Dhomhnaill, *Gaelcast Interview with Nuala Ní Dhomhnaill*, [www.gaelcast.com/?page_id=58].

[71] Justin Quinn, *The Cambridge Introduction to Modern Irish Poetry, 1800–2000* (Cambridge University Press, 2008), 150.

readers tend to think of translation as a stable process that involves working within the safe confines of an existing text. However, as Muldoon has remarked, translation is itself an act of discovery, truly an act of original composition as it has the poet-as-translator venturing into the unknown. This truth goes to the very heart of Muldoon and Ní Dhomhnaill's poetic practice; for both, as we have seen, the writing of a successful poem is a process marked by profound humility in the face of uncertainty as the poet starts out with no idea of where the poem will lead him or what shape it will take. Not only this but reader and writer, word and world, are all changed, and shifted in their positions, by the process which Muldoon has likened to 'alchemy': that 'little change that takes place, in the process of the poem getting written'. For both poets translation is a constantly moving, open-ended act, a labour of love, and as such it is vital, dynamic, unstable, charged with exhilarating tensions and energies, and itself an unending process of infinite permutations and possibility.

'In the old tradition of Irish there is no such thing as a fixed text', Ní Dhomhnaill reminds us.[72] The engagement of a range of poets with Ní Dhomhnaill's work may be seen as a tribute to the unending possibilities that her work opens up, through which translation becomes an active, vivifying, and enabling process. Indeed, the diverse strategies of translation that are on display across the oeuvre testify to Ní Dhomhnaill's limitless, multilingual, multicultural imagination and to her own profound understanding of how the very act of putting thoughts into words in any language is itself an act of translation. As Ní Dhomhnaill's playful poetry is profoundly aware, meaning in any one language is inherently variable and slippery, never fixed or without ambiguity, and so these pressures and energies exert themselves all the more when multiple languages come into contact; a reality that Ní Dhomhnaill and her translators in their collaborative project have continued to expose. By examining closely the step-by-step, line-by-line process that translation is for Muldoon, and attending to 'Gan do Chuid Éadaigh' with the consideration that it demands, much is illuminated about, not only Muldoon's poetics and that of Ní Dhomhnaill, but about the act and art of translation itself and, by extension, the indeterminate, limitless processes of reading and writing which must continue to sustain and challenge us all.

Select Bibliography

Cronin, Michael, *Translating Ireland: Translating, Languages, Cultures* (Cork: Cork University Press, 1996).
Dhomhnaill, Ní, 'What Foremothers?', *Poetry Ireland Review*, 36 (Autumn 1992), 18–31.
Dhomhnaill, Ní, 'Traductio ad Absurdum', *Krino*, 14 (Winter 1993), 49–50.
Dhomhnaill, Ní, 'Adaptations and Transformations: An Interview with Deborah McWilliams Consalvo', *Studies: An Irish Quarterly Review*, 83/331 (Autumn 1994), 313–20.

---

[72] Ní Dhomhnaill, 'Adaptations and Transformations', 320.

Dhomhnaill, Ní, 'Why I Choose to Write in Irish: The Corpse that Sits Up and Talks Back', *New York Times Book Review* (8 Jan. 1995), 27–8.
Dhomhnaill, Ní, 'Poetry and Identity: An Interview with Nuala Ní Dhomhnaill', *Nordic Irish Studies*, 6 (2007), 127–32.
Dhomhnaill, Ní and Medbh McGuckian, 'Comhrá, with a Foreword and Afterword by Laura O'Connor', *Southern Review*, 31/3 (Summer 1995), 581–614.
Hollo, Kaarina, 'Acts of Translation: An Interview with Nuala Ní Dhomhnaill', *Edinburgh Review*, 99 (Spring 1998), 99–107.
Hollo, Kaarina, 'From the Irish: On *The Astrakhan Cloak*', *New Hibernia Review*, 3/2 (Summer 1999), 129–41.
Homem, Rui Carvalho, *Poetry and Translation in Northern Ireland: Dislocations in Contemporary Writing* (Basingstoke: Palgrave, 2009).
Jenkinson, Biddy, 'Letter to an Editor', *Irish University Review*, 21/1 (Spring–Summer 1991), 34.
Johnston, Dillon, *Irish Poetry After Joyce* (2nd edn. New York: Syracuse University Press 1997).
Johnston, Dillon, *The Poetical Economies of England and Ireland, 1912–2000* (Basingstoke: Palgrave, 2001).
Kiberd, Declan, *The Irish Writer and the World* (Cambridge: Cambridge University Press, 2005).
Mac Giolla Léith, Caoimhín, 'More Canon Fodder', *Irish Review*, 11 (Winter 1991/2), 127–33 (132).
McGuinness, Patrick, 'Speculating: Patrick McGuinness Interviews Paul Muldoon', *Irish Studies Review*, 17/1 (Feb. 2009), 103–10.
Muldoon, Paul, *The Prince of the Quotidian* (Oldcastle: Gallery Press, 1994).
Ní Fhoghlú, Siobhán, 'How Was It for You?', *Poetry Ireland Review*, 66 (Autumn 2000), 116–18.
O'Connor, Laura, 'The Bilingual Routes of Paul Muldoon / Pól Ó Maoldúin', *Irish Studies Review*, 19/2 (May 2011), 135–55.
O'Donoghue, Bernard, 'Meeting Half-Way', *Times Literary Supplement* (14 Apr. 1995), 23.
O'Seaghdha, Barra, 'The Tasks of the Translator', *Irish Review*, 14 (Autumn 1993), 143–7.
Quinn, Justin, *The Cambridge Introduction to Modern Irish Poetry, 1800–2000* (Cambridge University Press, 2008).
Qwarnstrom, Loretta, 'Travelling Through Liminal Spaces: An Interview with Nuala Ní Dhomhnaill', *Nordic Irish Studies*, 3 (2004), 65–73.
Sealy, Douglas, 'A New Voice for the Seanachie', *Irish Times* (8 Dec. 1990), 9.
Sewell, Frank, *Modern Irish Poetry: A New Alhambra* (New York: Oxford University Press, 2000).
Titley, Alan, 'Blooming Bigamy', *Books Ireland* (May 1991), 89–90.
Titley, Alan, 'Turning Inside and Out: Translating and Irish 1950–2000', *Yearbook of English Studies*, 35 (2005) 312–22.
Wheatley, David, 'The Aistriúchán Cloak: Paul Muldoon and the Irish Language', *New Hibernia Review*, 5/4 (Winter 2001), 123–34.

CHAPTER 24

WRITING [W]HERE: GENDER AND CULTURAL POSITIONING IN IRELAND AND WALES[1]

ALICE ENTWISTLE

> Our epoch is one in which space takes for us the form of relations among sites.[2]

PERHAPS the best-known voice of our contemporary poetic moment, Seamus Heaney, has never stopped inspecting the relationship between poet and place. Famously, this popular figure declares of the problematic cultural terrain in which his oeuvre is rooted:

> irrespective of what culture or subculture may have coloured our individual sensibilities, [when] our imaginations assent to the stimulus of the names, our sense of the place is enhanced […] We are dwellers, we are namers, we are lovers, we make homes and search for our histories [and] it is to […] the stable element, the land itself, that we must look for continuity.[3]

The conviction echoes the tradition of poetry which reaches back to William Langland, and knits Heaney into the topical strain of such progenitors as A. E. Housman, Thomas Hardy, David Jones, Patrick Kavanagh, Hugh MacDiarmid, Dylan Thomas, or more latterly R. S.

---

[1] A version of this chapter was first delivered at the Symposium 'Ireland and Wales: Correspondences', convened by the Ireland-Wales Research Network at Cardiff University in Sept. 2009; another can be heard as 'Neither Here Nor There', Scholarcast 18, in the UCD [University College Dublin] Scholarcast Series 4 'Reconceiving the British Isle: The Literature of the British Isles' [http://www.ucd.ie/scholarcast/scholarcast18.html].

[2] Michel Foucault, 'Of Other Spaces' (1967), *Heterotopias* [http://www.foucault.info/doc/documents/heterotopia/foucault.heterotopia.en.html].

[3] Seamus Heaney, 'The Sense of Place', in *Preoccupations: Selected Prose 1968–1978* (London: Faber & Faber, 1980), 131–49 (132, 148–9).

Thomas. And then there's Philip Larkin, applauded by Heaney himself for his 'obstinate insistence that the poet is [...] a real man in a real place'.[4]

Seeded in this ancestry, Heaney's work has informed much late twentieth-century critical thinking about the relationship between poet, poetic, and place, not least the part played in it by time. Thus Thomas Docherty finds 'The Grauballe Man' constructing itself 'as a writing which occurs as an event', its temporal 'movement of emancipation' countering the '"punctuality" of the Modern, which is concerned to map [...] points in time as if they were [...] stable points in space'.[5] Docherty's reading of Heaney's 'spatial present as a moment bifurcated, divided, [...] historical' anticipates David Kennedy's more recent examination of the cultural political resonances of the preposition—technically, *temporal deictic*—'now' in poems about the Troubles in Northern Ireland.[6] Deixis, for linguists, marks the capacity of language to point and position through specifiers like 'this' and 'that', Kennedy's 'now' and its obverse 'then', and the pairing I am most interested in: 'here' and 'there'. Like me, Kennedy centralizes a linguistic mechanism which critical readers of poetry mostly overlook, in order to examine how and why a text's deictic markers might seem to signify in ways that reach beyond their function. As he rightly notices, textual deixis can hardly but register the cultural-political contexts on which any utterance, literary or not, might give. Keith Green confirms that while deictics are considered to be 'as a rule, egocentric [...] they are also referential. Reference always takes place within a subjective frame. Deictic reference is thus [...] partly tied to context and partly creates that context'.[7] More simply, Gisa Rauh calls deixis a 'mechanism of relating', which is precisely why a poem's deictic markers, read back into their historical, geographical, or cultural contexts, can powerfully influence its signifying life.[8] Like Docherty, Kennedy is chiefly concerned with the temporal complexities of his primary texts. I am more interested in his presumption, with Heaney, that it is *possible* to locate the poet, in and through the poem, in any given place. Lothar Fietz has described how the notion of 'place' (in classical pedagogy a word for a rhetorically useful point of reference in an argument) came to serve the now-truistic division of a regional or 'peripheral' cultural consciousness from its more 'universal' centre.[9] As Fietz's co-editor reveals, the intrinsically hierarchical resonances of the centre–periphery paradigm have echoed through critical interest in British and Irish 'poetries of place' from at least the time of Matthew Arnold,

---

[4] Heaney, 'Englands of the Mind', in *Preoccupations*, 150–69 (164).

[5] Thomas Docherty, 'Ana-; or Postmodernism, Landscape, Seamus Heaney', in Antony Easthope and John O. Thompson (eds.), *Contemporary Poetry Meets Modern Theory* (Toronto: University of Toronto Press, 1991), 8–80 (68).

[6] Thomas Docherty, 'Ana-; or', 70; David Kennedy, '"Now", "now", "even now": Temporal Deixis and the Crisis of the Present in Some Northern Irish Poems of the Troubles', *Irish Studies Review*, 18/1 (2010), 1–16.

[7] Keith Green (ed.), *New Essays on Deixis: Discourse, Narrative, Literature* (Amsterdam: Rodopi, 1995), 17.

[8] Gisa Rauh, 'Aspects of Deixis', in Rauh (ed.), *Essays on Deixis* (Tübingen: Gunter Neu Verlag, 1983), 47.

[9] Lothar Fietz, 'Topos/Locus/Place: The Rhetoric, Poetics and Politics of Place 1500–1800', in Hans-Werner Ludwig and Lothar Fietz (eds.), *Poetry in the British Isles: Non-Metropolitan Perspectives* (Cardiff: University of Wales Press, 1995), 15–30 (15).

and perhaps especially towards the end of the twentieth century.[10] Heaney himself insists that if 'a literary scene in which the provinces revolve around the centre is demonstrably a Copernican one, the task of talent is to reverse things to a Ptolemaic condition. The writer must re-envisage the region as the original point.'[11] The 'region' is a sufficiently problematic term, especially in the context of the complex cultural landscapes of the United Kingdom, for Heaney's use of it to be worth querying. Are regions best understood in geographical terms, as signifying the geopolitical terrain between various species of border? Or as looser sociocultural constructs eliding the bounds of parish, district, county, or province, and/or other demarcation zones? How are they best distinguished and/or characterized for those who might identify with them? Bernard O'Donoghue's 'Westering Home' circles this conundrum:

Though you'd be pressed to say exactly where
It first sets in, driving west through Wales
Things start to feel like Ireland. It can't be
The chapels with their clear grey windows,
Or the buzzards menacing the scooped valleys.
In April, have the blurred blackthorn hedges
Something to do with it? Or possibly
The motorway, which seems to lose its nerve
Mile by mile. The houses, up to a point,
With their masoned gables, each upper window
A raised eyebrow. More, though, than all of this,
It's the architecture of the spirit;
The old thin ache you thought that you'd forgotten—
More smoke, admittedly, than flame;
Less tears than rain. And the whole business
Neither here nor there, and therefore home.[12]

This shrewd text discerns a kind of cultural commonality between the notionally peripheral geographies of Wales and Ireland which it sets centre-stage. Yet the commonalities are laid bare not so much in the features of the increasingly remote rural landscape through which the text 'westers'—the manifestly Welsh chapels and buzzards—as in the uncertainties ('possibly') ascribed to the faltering motorway; the sceptically 'raised eyebrow[s]' (punningly 'up to a point') of the houses, and the mildly political-seeming gesture at some kind of scant shared 'spirit': that 'old thin ache'. The nuances combine in those cryptic last lines: 'And the whole business | Neither here nor there, and therefore home.'

O'Donoghue's phrasing profoundly destabilizes the deictic function which we might ordinarily expect to ascribe to 'here' and 'there'. Firstly we cannot be sure to what those

---

[10] Hans-Werner Ludwig, 'Province and Metropolis, Centre and Periphery: Some Critical Terms Re-examined', in Ludwig and Fietz (eds.), *Poetry in the British Isles*, 47–69.

[11] Seamus Heaney, 'The Regional Forecast', in R. P. Draper (ed.), *The Literature of Region and Nation* (London: Macmillan, 1989), 10–23 (13).

[12] Bernard O'Donoghue, 'Westering Home', *Here Nor There* (London: Chatto & Windus, 1999), 51.

locating markers refer, let alone in which direction or where they might point us: the very nature of the 'business' which is 'neither here nor there' is never in fact made clear. The parallels between Wales and Ireland? The attention we have been asked to pay them? Or the very nature of the places themselves? The poem's shrugging-off of itself—'neither here nor there'—only compounds its disingenuous slippage from the unclear space between its deictics into the tension-filled site of 'home'. Crawford identifies 'the theme of home [as] perhaps the major theme of twentieth-century poetry in the English-speaking world'.[13] In O'Donoghue's carelessly equivocal, deliberately anti-deictic, construction the conventionally comforting idea of 'home' is paradoxically both marked and refused.

William Howarth links deixis—in which 'meaning develops from what is said or signed relative to physical space'—with efforts to represent that space: 'The landscape contains many names and stories [...] writing them becomes a way of mapping cultural terrain.'[14] To some extent, 'mapping' any such terrain necessarily inscribes the mapper's sense of relation to (or place in) it. Pertinently, Susan Stanford Friedman figures identity as 'a positionality, a location, a standpoint, a terrain, an intersection, a network, a crossroads of multiply situated knowledges'. However, she also admits that since identity depends on 'a point of reference; as that point moves [...], so do the contours of identity'.[15] The remark points up the issue of cultural affiliation in the now devolved but still conflicted nation-states embedded in the United Kingdom. At the close of the twentieth century amid the realities of devolution, Wales and the two Irelands together and separately inscribe a condition of not simply topographical but *political* in-betweenness. O'Donoghue leaves us questioning how far anyone might orient themselves in this uncertain, duplicitous, landscape.

What happens to a sense of identity when its founding point of reference—what cognitive linguists might call its 'deictic *origo*'—is refused or deferred as O'Donoghue contrives? And what part might gender play in such a process? This essay links the 'identifying poets' Ciaran Carson and John James with a generation of female successors, the complexities of whose own post-millennial cultural contexts play out in poems which often self-consciously unsettle and sometimes deny altogether the orienting specificities which place deictics like 'here' and 'there' supply. They echo Michel Foucault:

> We are in the epoch of simultaneity [...] the epoch of the near and far, of the side-by-side, of the dispersed [...], when our experience of the world is less that of a long life developing through time than that of a network that connects points and intersects with its own skein.[16]

---

[13] Robert Crawford, *Identifying Poets: Self and Territory in Twentieth Century Poetry* (Edinburgh: Edinburgh University Press, 1993), 14.

[14] William Howarth, 'Some Principles of Ecocriticism', in Cheryl Glotfelty and Harold Fromm (eds.), *The Eco-Criticism Reader: Landmarks in Literary Ecology* (Athens, Ga.: University of Georgia Press, 1996), 69–91 (80).

[15] Susan Stanford Friedman, *Mappings: Feminism and the Cultural Geographies of Encounter* (Princeton: Princeton University Press, 1998), 19, 22.

[16] Foucault, 'Heterotopias'.

I

As Paul Werth has noted, the markers of deixis work at least partly through their capacity to 'call up an entity and keep it in mind'.[17] This capacity has been shrewdly exploited by Ciaran Carson, writing out of the entrenched cultural divisions of his native Belfast. The award-winning *Belfast Confetti* (1989) tirelessly searches the risks and exigencies of self-positioning amid the city's notoriously freighted streetplan. Published a decade before O'Donoghue's poem, whenever and wherever Carson's buoyantly mobile text points it is with astute, if casual-seeming, imprecision. Take the moment when, having been ambushed on a bike-ride through the city, the speaker of 'Question Time' is interrogated by a group of unidentified captors. The incident is recollected by the victim in the deictically confusing present historic tense: 'I am this map which they examine [...] a map which no longer refers to the present world, but to a history, these vanished streets; a map which is this moment, this interrogation, my replies.'[18] Note how the implied 'here' of 'this map...this moment' and the implied 'there' of 'history, [the] vanished streets' merge self-protectively in 'I', both rooted and defying placement in present and vanished worlds alike. The fragment not only projects but mediates what Eavan Boland has described as the 'duality to place [...] the place that happened and the place that happens to you', while testifying to the cultural-political significance of that duality.[19] The text's subtle cognitive shifts point us relentlessly back into the tensions of Belfast's cultural fabric, what the poet has himself wryly described as the city's 'patchwork of sectarian enclaves'; if nothing else, those shifts help to make sense of, and are made sense of *by*, the inescapable context of the Troubles.[20]

Against that difficult historical but also geographical backdrop, Carson's map works both to yoke *and* separate self and world (the city), each trapped in yet eluding the cultural-political tensions set in motion by the encounter. As Christian Jacob notes in his magisterial study *The Sovereign Map*, 'The map results from a double construction, that of its author and that of its readers—a symmetrical process, a twofold construction [...] of encoding and decoding.'[21] Jacob's pertinent observation is further compounded by the link Carson himself makes between the cultural valence of the fabric-backed street-map, in a Belfast whose industrial heritage was partly founded on the linen industry, and the crucial presence of the reader in the process of textual signification. In a resonant moment, the poet pauses to construct reading as an act of collaborative authorship, enabling the reader to recognize his or her own co-creation of a textuality which

---

[17] Paul Werth, 'How to build a world (in a lot less than six days, using only what's in your head)', in Green (ed.), *New Essays on Deixis*, 49–80 (64).

[18] Ciaran Carson, *Belfast Confetti* (Oldcastle: Gallery Press, 1991), 63.

[19] Eavan Boland, *Object Lessons: The Life of the Woman and the Poet in Our Time* (London, New York: Vintage, 1996), 154.

[20] Ciaran Carson, email to the author, 23 Feb. 2010.

[21] Christian Jacob, *The Sovereign Map: Theoretical Approaches in Cartography throughout History* (Chicago: University of Chicago Press, 2006), 185.

Carson, like Derrida, thinks of as 'tissue', a literal fabric: 'It is a textile thing, a weave. And I, as reader, weave myself through space and time; I am both here and there.'[22] Hence, in reading as well as being read, the ambushed apparently vulnerable 'I' of 'Question Time' proves—crucially—able to *map* as well as be mapped; to *position* in being positioned. It is the manifestly deictic, and in that powerfully metaphoric, function of cartography which permits him to dismantle and critique the political divisions fissuring Belfast's cultural history from inside and outside the city at the same time.

As John Goodby reports, despite being recognized as a 'young poet of Wales' in 1978, Cardiffian John James's cultural roots are only now beginning to be more widely acknowledged.[23] Yet this determinedly non-mainstream poet has no straightforward relationship with the country, let alone the city, he left in 1957. A seam of self-conscious historicity runs through James's repeated poetic encounters with Wales. As Wendy Mulford—another Wales-born expatriate—puts it, 'the Cardiff that fuels the poetry is the Cardiff of [James's] childhood and adolescence'.[24] Perhaps unsurprisingly, therefore, when James points, whether into or out of Wales, it is rarely with the kind of forensically self-conscious particularity with which Carson guides us across Belfast. Even in 'Last Days of the Vulcan', one of relatively few poems to address James's home city directly, the pointing is indirect—ventilating and extending rather than situating the perspective—from the start, by 'seeking anchorage in marshland at the margin of the city | pace beneath the railway bridge space opens out the gate | to Adamstown'.[25]

To Mulford's sympathetic mind, the 'anchorage' James seeks here is 'complicated': 'this is heimat, where he belongs—and where he cannot live. That homeland is the source of his imaginative power; in "exile" it feeds him. All his poems arguably are derived from, and communicate, a sense of *not quite being at home.*'[26] Certainly stance and position are repeatedly problematized in an oeuvre which takes the complexities of writing and reading place(s) very seriously ('Hengrove', 'Local', and 'The Conversation'). 'Inventory' goes so far as to ascribe a familiar journey 'its own self-consciousness [...]: we hold on hard | to the being able for it [...] || Having known it; or about to'.[27] The equipoise—or irresolution—is lent a more explicitly aesthetic cast in the trans-regional gallery-space of 'Toastings', in which painters and paintings drawn from all kinds of places are simultaneously represented and appraised. Balanced between numerous implicit oppositions including the two art forms (linguistic/poetic and visual), between painted and painting, interior and exterior environments, and between graphic and meditative modes, this richly detailed work comes suggestively to rest in the deferred perspectival spaces which seem to be its chief interest. The poem closes on the signpost-like sculpture of an

---

[22] Carson, 'This is what Libraries are for', *Dublin Review,* 10: [www.thedublinreview.com].

[23] John Goodby, ' "Deflected Forces of Currents": Mapping Welsh Modernist Poetry', *Poetry Wales,* 46/1 (2010), 52–8; Meic Stephens and Peter Finch (eds.), *Green Horse: An Anthology by Young Poets of Wales* (Swansea: Christopher Davies, 1978), 102–6.

[24] Wendy Mulford, ' "A city boy at heart": John James and the Industrial South Welsh Heartland', *Poetry Wales,* 44/1 (2008), 20–4 (21).

[25] John James, 'Last Days of the Vulcan', *Poetry Wales,* 44/1 (2008), 20.

[26] 'A City Boy', 21.

[27] John James, *Collected Poems* (Cambridge: Salt Publishing, 2002), 49–50.

aboriginal walker which both subverts and aestheticizes the deictic processes he seems to figure, 'eyes wide open on the line of sight | suggestion of the path to be trod | the means by which it will be | made & by which that trace will be perceived'. It seems to be as a result of the sculptor's seamless imbrication of the near (or here) and far (there), actual and imminent in the piece—'bringing it right back home' while 'pointing into the sky | you can look up there'—that it finally promises, again anti-deictically, 'quiet entry | into the prior & continuing existence of place some time'.[28]

Between them, Carson and James—arguably alongside such more-or-less explicitly 'identifying' writers as Medbh McGuckian, Paul Muldoon, Lee Harwood, Peter Riley, Chris Torrance, and indeed Mulford herself—might be taken to anticipate the scepticism with which a younger generation of poets, in this account all women, view the question of cultural place from a post-millennial situation complicated for them in ways that their (male) forerunners and counterparts arguably escape.

II

Friedman notes the paradox that identity is 'unthinkable without some sort of imagined or literal boundary. But borders also specify the liminal space between, the interstitial site of interaction, interconnection, and exchange'. Hence, she speculates, late twentieth-century feminism's interest in the exposure and exploration of 'the structures interlocking home and elsewhere'.[29] And as many argue, the gendering of the domestic 'home' can render it profoundly conflictual.[30] For Harriet Davidson, Adrienne Rich's 1983 poem 'In the Wake of Home' and her key essay 'Notes Toward a Politics of Location' together confirm the home as 'the site of a complicated struggle between the desire to return to a place of sheltered belonging and the desire to leave oppressive social structures'.[31] For women especially, that struggle may deepen when the domestic 'home' is mapped onto the similarly ambivalent cultural space of 'homeland':

> Men are incorporated into the nation metonymically. [Whereas] the nation is embodied within each man, and each man comes to embody the nation [...] women are scripted into the national imaginary [as] not equal to the nation but symbolic of it.[32]

---

[28] James, *Collected Poems*, 179.

[29] Friedman, *Mappings*, 3, 6.

[30] See e.g. Alice Entwistle, '"At Home Everywhere and Nowhere": Denise Levertov's "Domestic Muse"', in Jane Dowson (ed.), *Women's Writing 1945–1960: After the Deluge* (London: Palgrave, 2003), 98–114; and Jane Dowson and Alice Entwistle, *A History of Twentieth-Century British Women's Poetry* (Cambridge: Cambridge University Press, 2005).

[31] Harriet Davidson, 'In The Wake Of Home: Adrienne Rich's Politics and Poetics of Location', in Easthope and Thompson (eds.), *Contemporary Poetry Meets Modern Theory*, 166–76 (168).

[32] Joanne P. Sharp, 'Gendering Nationhood: A Feminist Engagement with National Identity', in Nancy Duncan (ed.), *Bodyspace: Destabilizing Geographies of Gender and Sexuality* (London: Routledge, 1996), 97–108 (99).

Carson and James have their own reasons for calling attention to, or seeking to trouble, the kinds of referential certainty traditionally ascribed to deictic markers. O'Donoghue's poem is more explicitly determined to frustrate efforts to position 'home' in any fixed way. Writing out of their different national, or 'regional', contexts Belfast-born Sinéad Morrissey, Dubliner Catherine Walsh, and Bangor-based Zoë Skoulding arguably have better reason to ventilate by unsettling the defining function of the spatial deictics 'here' and 'there'. Amid the gender power-relations haunting the cultural-political problematic of home/land for women, all three urge a more *relational* construction of cultural positioning in the 'Atlantic Archipelago' than the now-debased opposing of centre and periphery through which such relationships are mostly understood.[33] In doing so, all three summon Rich's effort 'to indicate the sense [of] belonging to a certain culture and also to disrupt the sense of that culture or that self as unitary, all the while maintaining her sense of political and ethical purpose'.[34] In this manoeuvring each confirms Lee M. Jenkins, noting how 'In the lived experience, as in the poetics, of many women, "home" is a condition of "dwelling-in-displacement"'.[35] In their differing negotiations with various kinds of cultural, political, and aesthetic displacement Morrissey, Walsh, and Skoulding endorse Bonnie Honig's sympathetic insistence that the 'dilemmatic' space of the home 'be recast in coalitional terms as the site of necessary, nurturing, but also strategic, conflicted, and temporary alliances'.[36]

The youngest and most conventionally lyric poet of my examples, Sinéad Morrissey has a perhaps predictably tense relationship with the Belfast in which she grew up in the seventies, against the lurid backdrop of the Troubles, and left more or less as soon as she could, on the point of publishing her first collection: 'I'd always had a horror of ending up back in the Northern Ireland where I grew up.'[37] In even Morrissey's first collection, *There was Fire in Vancouver* (1996), a fastidious interest in the city's awkward cultural status and legacy is scored through by a fugitive-seeming poetic sensibility. The central poem of the short early sequence 'Mercury' is called, aptly, 'Nomad'. This vagrant ('It's this leaving of villages'), evasively self-interrupting text resolutely refuses to allow itself, or us, any locating pause:

The repeated conclusion
It's not here either—
Beauty, home, whatever—
That leaves you where you are,

---

[33] See John Kerrigan, *Archipelagic English: Literature, History, and Politics, 1603–1707* (Oxford: Oxford University Press, 2008).

[34] Davidson, 'In the Wake of Home', 169.

[35] Lee M. Jenkins, 'Interculturalism', in Jane Dowson (ed.), *The Cambridge Companion to Twentieth-Century British and Irish Women's Poetry* (Cambridge: Cambridge University Press, 2010), 119–35 (119).

[36] Bonnie Honig, 'Difference, Dilemmas, and the Politics of Home', in Seyla Benhabib (ed.), *Democracy and Difference: Contesting the Boundaries of the Political* (Princeton: Princeton University Press, 1996), 257–77 (269).

[37] Sinéad Morrissey, 'Interview with Declan Meade', Sept. 2002 [http://www.stingingfly.org/sample/sinéad-morrissey-interview].

Where you always are—
Side-stepping yourself[38]

Morrissey herself acknowledges the part played by 'travel' in her writing ('it opened me up to things I wouldn't have been exposed to otherwise'), yet hers often seems the imaginary less of tourist than migrant: 'I try to write not so much about these other places, but about my experience of being there.'[39] Jenkins defines interculturalism as 'a discursive space which accommodates differences *and* commonalities' (author's emphasis).[40] Mobilizing and negotiating between the divergent yet often contiguous-seeming cultural experiences of 'here' and 'there', Morrissey's often gendered poetics acquires an 'intercultural' cast which makes a particular impact in *Between Here and There* (2002).

This volume, poised between the fixities of its deictic title, is arranged in two clearly defined halves. The divided textual space which the collection signposts is therefore self-doubling: either of its two constituent sections, and/or the places each represents, might constitute a 'here' or 'there' depending on which we are reading: as a consequence all kinds of (a)symmetries of cultural and experiential otherness come to compete with each other in and across the different texts and sections in a confused loop of recognition and alienation. As it turns out the second part ('Japan') was written first, while the poet was living and working in East Asia; the same interview reveals that the poems of the unnamed first section were written after her return to Belfast: 'there was a big gap between writing the last part and the first part'. The 'tension of being somewhere which wasn't where you were from' colours much of the volume; it also explains why 'I needed to come home and settle in one place. I'd missed the crucial years of the Peace process and I was fascinated to come back and see Belfast under the peace [...]. Even though it was where I was born, it was still a new space for me.'[41]

Belfast remains a lodestone through the four collections Morrissey has published to date, her itinerance always moderating the city's never wholly reassuring presence in her idiom. The renewing, defamiliarized perspective which the revenant brings 'home' from the 'there' of other places imbues the opening poem of *Between Here and There*, emphatically located 'In Belfast': 'Here the seagulls stay in off the Lough all day'. The deictically marked near and familiar 'here' of the city's streets and everyday business are viewed with a mixture of suspicion and admiration confirming both the speaker's knowledge of and yet sense of remoteness from it: 'I [...] tell myself it is as real to sleep here | as the twenty other corners I have slept in'. The ambiguities qualify the blurred vision of the final stanza:

This city weaves itself so intimately
it is hard to see, despite the tenacity of the river
and the iron sky; and in its downpour and its vapour I am
as much at home here as I will ever be.[42]

---

[38] Sinéad Morrissey, 'Nomad', *There was Fire in Vancouver* (Manchester: Carcanet Press, 1996), 34.
[39] Morrissey, 'Interview with Declan Meade'.
[40] Jenkins, 'Interculturalism', 119.
[41] Morrissey, 'Interview with Declan Meade'.
[42] Sinéad Morrissey, *Between Here and There* (Manchester: Carcanet Press, 2002), 13.

So equivocal a sense of relation to the city tempers the kind of home it can offer a speaker so quick to discern in it the dislocating otherness of 'there'. As Irene De Angelis has pointed out, Morrissey's ambivalence about her home city may reflect a sense of 'cultural dislocation' the poet herself retraces to her parents' membership of the Irish Communist Party: she thinks of herself as inhabiting a peculiarly unaffiliated space in the complex political-ideological map of Belfast:

> To be neither Catholic nor Protestant was too far removed from the dominant frame of reference. However [...] Morrissey's family background also left her with an enormous sense of freedom. Asked what lies 'Between Here and There' Morrissey answered 'nothing. It's being inbetween [sic] that counts. It's tolerance of transitions'.[43]

In this restless poetics, whether the transitions figure or depend on the kind of considerable dislocation which is examined in 'Japan'—is resolved in 'In Belfast'—the tolerance they inscribe, or necessitate, is what interests me. *Between Here and There*'s title poem investigates the 'inbetween', of both tolerance and transitions, signified in and by a foreign culture's belief system. In this subtle text, difference is framed in the implicit gap between the visitor-speaker and those whose efforts to interpret the mysteries of their temples fall so far short of explanation. The poem's several topoi—including 'a graveyard for miscarriages'—come to seem almost literally suspended between the worlds of the living and the dead, between actual and represented ('a basin of stone bodies in two parts: square body, round head', with all the poignancy those fragments enshrine), and finally, with courteous discretion, between spiritual conviction (given voice by Japan's greatest Buddha) and visiting scepticism. And then there is the decidedly unpriestly Nagasawa, 'his champion karaoke voice his miracle foot massage | [...] his rockhard atheism', piously self-transforming into 'the man who can chant any you-name-it soul | between here and Ogaki to paradise' (46).

Read back into the sociopolitical problematics of Belfast and of Northern Ireland, Morrissey's 'tolerance of transitions' conceives the deictic markers 'here' and 'there' as two-way portals into a political-cultural and poetic sensibility valuably charged by 'displacement, relocation, cultural translation and untranslatability'.[44] She summons Edna Longley, demanding that Northern Ireland reunderstand itself as 'a frontier-region, a cultural corridor, a zone where Ireland and Britain permeate one another [...and] relax into a less dualistic sense of its own identity'.[45]

Like Morrissey's, Zoë Skoulding's poetry has invariably sought to unsettle and interrogate rather than fix the idea of cultural and ideological positionality. Like Carson she uses the compacted cultural symbol of the map to do so. As Jacob says, '[any] map invites

---

[43] Irene De Angelis, 'Sinead Morrissey: Between Northern Ireland and Japan', *Journal of Irish Studies*, 20 (2005): [www.carcanet.co.uk]

[44] Jenkins, 'Interculturalism', 121.

[45] Edna Longley, *From Cathleen to Anorexia: The Breakdown of Irelands* (Dublin: Attic Press, 1990), 23, 24.

reflection on the relationship of the place with the image, the place of the map and the place of real space'.[46] Shifting between place and text/image, 'Preselis With Brussels Street Map' locates us simultaneously in the immediately sensual 'here' of upland west Wales and the more remote, more exotic, and more textualized 'there' of Europe's bilingual cosmopolitan civic centre:

Up Europalaan under blue
        reach of sky   bare feet in spongy moss
I need a map to tell me where I'm
not   along the avenue de Stalingrad
                squeal of a meadow pipit

skimming
        over rue de l'Empereur
tread softly on the streets   the sheep trails
        between bird call and bleat echo
a street folds across two languages here and there[47]

In a text as preoccupied with dichotomy and relation as any of those I read here, and in a double and divided landscape(s) reminiscent of Morrissey's, the reader is persistently and provocatively situated both 'here *and* there'. We are partly condemned to this paradox by the very activity of [map] reading; as Jacob notes: 'The viewer is at the same time outside the representation and enveloped by it. This is the place I occupy, whence I see, but also the space in which I see myself and where I am not.'[48] The ambiguities are further compounded by the poem's refracting of the relationship between cultural and linguistic complexity in the twinned, similarly bilingual environments of Wales and Belgium: for Skoulding, as for Irish poet-critic Eamon Grennan, 'The simple fact of dual language [...] becomes itself an image of possibility, the possibility of accommodation and the richness that is its consequence.'[49]

Bradford-born and raised in Ipswich, Skoulding came to Wales (where she went on to settle, near Bangor) as a young adult. Her writing has always been preoccupied with the linguistic and by extension cultural richness and possibility which charges Welsh, as much as Irish, aesthetic life. Now firmly embedded in, and identifying—albeit cautiously—with, her country of domicile, the politically sensitive tendencies of Skoulding's construction of place and/or locatedness resound in the meshing perspectives of 'Preselis with Brussels Street Map'. In interview, some years before her appointment to her current role as editor of *Poetry Wales*, Skoulding remarked, 'Even while you're in one location, you're simultaneously linked to many others.'[50] The comment summons

---

[46] Jacob, *The Sovereign Map*, 165.
[47] Zoë Skoulding, *Remains of a Future City* (Bridgend: Seren, 2008), 50.
[48] Jacob, *The Sovereign Map*, 99.
[49] Eamon Grennan, *Facing the Music: Irish Poetry in the Twentieth Century* (Omaha, Nebr.: Creighton University Press, 1999), 375.
[50] Zoë Skoulding and Fiona Owen, 'A City of Words': Zoë Skoulding interviewed', *Planet*, 166 (2004), 57–62 (61).

cultural/political geographer Doreen Massey, declaring that 'The global is in the local in the very process of the formation of the local'.[51] In the next breath, Skoulding reveals that her own anti-essentialist attitude to the idea of location, or perhaps to the possibility of locatedness, licenses, fuels, and justifies the creative and professional claims she makes, as both writer and editor, upon her own cultural context: 'For me, this [sense of global inter-connectedness...] gets beyond there being an essential Wales and who it belongs to and who's allowed to write about it.'[52]

As she has explained elsewhere, Skoulding's creative maturation has been nurtured by her sense of the aesthetic possibilities that Wales affords her:

> I write in English in a bilingual country, and I know that this context makes me see English as a provisional circumstance rather than something to be taken for granted: my national identity as a writer is therefore a set of negotiations rather than a fixed point within clearly defined national boundaries. Complex relationships between languages and cultures define Wales as much as *Cymraeg* itself does, and they define Europe too.[53]

Given these views, it perhaps shouldn't surprise that Skoulding has described the process of writing itself in suggestively (anti-deictically) *dynamic* terms: as 'a way of being deliberately in between, of moving through the contradictory space between here and there (or global and local, Welsh and English, human and nonhuman)'.[54] Shifting us between text and context, from the aesthetic to the political, the analogy she draws between writing and mobility is not original. However, it merits attention for reminding us that spatial deixis can be unsettled for reasons which resonate beyond the geopolitical limits of place, having to do with the cultural politics of the aesthetic. In poetry, this takes us to the question of poetic form, gender politics, and the restive, scrupulous idiom of Catherine Walsh.

Born in Dublin in 1964, Walsh has been publishing her uncompromising, spatially self-conscious poetry since the mid-eighties, mostly with radical 'little' presses like her own hardPressed Poetry, co-founded with Billy Mills (although her two latest collections are with Shearsman). Walsh has never earned much critical attention, even from enthusiasts of non-mainstream poetries, perhaps because her work discourages readers from taking any of it for granted. The Gaelic title of *Idir Eatortha* (1996) loosely translates as *Between Worlds*. Its sometimes reproachfully, often cryptically, paratactic habit is more often than not very funny, and invariably suggests Walsh's unswerving belief in the cultural eloquence of the aesthetic:

'where is it?' 'well where is it?'
[scraping of shovel on concrete]

---

[51] Doreen Massey, *Space, Place and Gender* (Cambridge and Oxford: Polity and Blackwell, 1994), 120.
[52] Skoulding and Owen, 'A City of Words', 61.
[53] Zoë Skoulding, 'Border Lines', *Poetry Wales*, 42/4 (2007), 40.
[54] Zoë Skoulding, 'Wandering Where I Am', *Poetry Wales*, 42/3 (2007), 23–7 (24).

[short rapid brushstrokes—hard bristle on concrete]
'grainy, grainy green, greyey green, just green'
'a just green leaf on a'

...

'OK then, a green leaf on a grainy grey pavement'
'pavement's wrong'
'what's it?'
'footpath, a grainy grey footpath.'
[clattering of spade, brush on wooden cart]
      [humphing]
[heavy breathing]
        [trundling cart]
'sound of wheels'
     /quietly
'what, is the sound of wheels'
'on a grey footpath?'
'what is the sound of a green leaf on a grainy'
'no, not grainy, then'
'start again'
'Here we are. There's where it is.'[55]

Arguably conversing with both Beckett and Joyce, this perhaps mercilessly indeterminate-seeming fragment, flaunting its conversationality, may well (though it needn't) appear dialogic. But whether we understand it as interior monologue, or as dialogue between two possibly more voices, we are left asking *who*, precisely, is talking? What about? Why? Into what contexts are these lines—each in its separate, at times comically minute, adjustments—pointing (us) or being pointed?

One of Walsh's finest critics, Alex Davis, rightly warns that her 'disjunctive, disorienting poetry acknowledges language as a medium which constructs our relation to others, to objects, to ourselves. Her poetic subjects are always *Idir Eatortha*, caught between two worlds.'[56] Thus the multiple 'worlds' mediated by a sharply intelligent poetics orbit the central problematic of language, the 'meaning' of its constituent parts always dependent on the negotiations that the assignation of 'meaning' requires. Poised between voice and/or voices (and sounding at times very like a group writing-exercise), between singular and plural, between writing and talk, text and intertext, between partiality and completed-ness, my self-editing excerpt insistently demands that we consider how we might read (or 'position') it. On one hand, it conjures Grennan, arguing that 'Talk is "Irish" and is community, and wherever any of us is writing we are all trying to talk—trying in our various ways, our personal dialects, to talk ourselves and our world into

---

[55] Catheine Walsh, *Idir Eatortha* ([n.p.]: Invisible Books, 1994), 37–8.
[56] Alex Davis, *A Broken Line: Denis Devlin's Irish Poetic Modernism* (Dublin: University College Dublin Press, 2000), 170.

existence, into coexistence.'[57] Yet the text's dualities just as convincingly recall Goodby, alerting us to 'Ireland's interstitial geographical position between the two most powerful Anglophone cultures' and their common 'history of colonisation, plantation, settlement and emigration.'[58]

Goodby's topographic reading of Walsh's multidimensional work ventilates Davis's centralizing of her sense of the relational potentiality of language. What gets lost in Davis's remarks is this poetics' determination to articulate itself in and through its airily cryptic forms: those spatial arrangements into which the text organizes itself, and demands that we read—or perhaps map—it. The final line leaves us somewhere equally, productively, unclear: between the 'here' of the 'we' (who might and might not include us) and the 'there' of an all-too ambiguous 'it'. In her terrific work *On Form*, Angela Leighton argues that we come closest to understanding form—and specifically poetic form—when we construct it as function:

> To be a 'capacity for' knowing, rather than an object of knowledge, shifts attention to a kind of knowing which is an imaginative attitude rather than an accumulation of known things [...] it does not close down into an achieved interpretation but remains open to endless permutations of meaning.[59]

Walsh herself declares: 'I don't see why there should be any one definitive interpretation of anything anybody has written. Or any two or three definitive explanations or interpretations.'[60] Her prizing of the potential of language-as-text implicitly argues the cultural-political import of the aesthetic; I like to read it, with Goodby, as dramatizing 'the refusal of contemporary Irish poets to be contained by the boundaries of the island, the confines of explicitly "Irish" subject matter'.[61] Walsh's testing idiom insistently inscribes, and is nuanced by, its author's self-conscious resisting of the oppressive effects of the kind of aesthetic positioning which menaces her: that instinct for me makes most satisfying sense of the complex, mobile spatial/formal possibilities of the fragment quoted, not to say this wilfully anti-deictic rejoinder:

>   stop right there.
> here. here, there, any place. space. stop right there, that's
> here, was there, was here there any where—what a load of[62]

---

[57] Grennan, *Facing the Music*, 375.

[58] John Goodby, *Irish Poetry Since 1950: From Stillness into History* (Manchester: Manchester University Press, 2000), 10.

[59] Angela Leighton, *On Form: Poetry Aestheticism and the Legacy of a Word* (Oxford: Oxford University Press, 2007), 27.

[60] Catherine Walsh, *Prospect Into Breath: Interviews with North and South Writers,* ed. Peterjøn Skelt (Twickenham and Wakefield: North and South, 1991), 181.

[61] Goodby, *Irish Poetry*, 371–2.

[62] Walsh, *Idir Eatortha*, 39.

These words suggest Walsh's inclination to understand her relationship with her own cultural context in terms of a predicament extending beyond questions of place and theme. Of her particular literary heritage, she contends, 'You are only supported if you are a part of that tradition, that same tradition which must celebrate above all else your sense of Irishness and your sense of being part of an ongoing linear tradition of Irish writers, writing out of a sense of bondage almost.'[63] Katie Conboy's sympathetic account of Eavan Boland's strained sense of relationship with her own native literature points to the influence of gender, as well as literary, politics on the sense of compromise which Walsh describes. Ireland's patriarchal literature, she explains, has ensured that 'Women have [...] been put in their place and kept there, and theirs has not been the "place of writing" but rather the place of the written—the defined, the fixed, and the permanent'.[64] Walsh's ruthlessly anti-referential dismantling of the gendered and literary fixities inflecting the aesthetic expectations of the conventional poetry-reader repudiates the kind of literary-cultural positioning to which the critical community and the academy at large also inclines:

> The work [...] is deliberately written to have a certain kind of ambiguity. It is not meant to be opaque [...] I am simply trying [...] to [make] a person aware of context or idea and after that to have them question it. I don't have any answers for any of the things I write about. But if I can make people question these things and approach them from different angles, even *if by the way I write, I necessitate their approaching it in several different ways, one after the other, or simultaneously or on different occasions in different ways*, well that's wonderful.[65]

I want to conclude by returning to Skoulding, whose disingenuously entitled pamphlet *From Here* (2008) replays the cultural-political power of the aesthetic from another perspective again.[66] This slender pamphlet, juxtaposing 12 nine-line lyrics by Skoulding with visual images by New York artist Simonetta Moro, develops on Walsh's challenging poetic and political example in both its deliberate testing of generic and formal limits, and its interrogation of the too-easily occluded cultural politics of authorship. A note at the end of the pamphlet explains:

> 'From Here' was an email collaboration during the summer of 2008 that began with a chance meeting one rainy afternoon during [...] a conference and festival of psychogeography at Manchester Metropolitan University. Over the following weeks Simonetta sent drawings from New York, I sent poems back from Bangor in north Wales and the sequence developed as a conversation.

---

[63] *Prospect Into Breath*, 188.
[64] Katie Conboy, 'Revisionist Cartography: The Politics of Place in Boland and Heaney', in Kathryn Kirkpatrick (ed.), *Border Crossings: Irish Women Writers and National Identity* (Dublin: Wolfhound Press, 2000), 190–203 (193).
[65] *Prospect into Breath*, 184–5 (my emphases).
[66] Zoë Skoulding and Simonetta Moro, *From Here* ([n.p.]: Ypolita Press, 2008).

Generated in the shared intercontinental, intercultural *virtual* space of email and the Internet, disturbing the aesthetic divide between text and image, *From Here* rings the changes in a neglected tradition of female poetic collaboration, in the logic of its generic and authorial dynamism. To what and/or whom do we look for the contexts by which we might interpret this text? In both cases, in both ways at once. Not only do the spare, elegant, lens-like texts and images contrast, converse, yet combine with each other in the space of the printed construct—the artefact—they inhabit. Thematically and visually, images and texts alike also invite us to imagine ourselves into the notionally antithetical positions of both observer/reader and participant/interlocutor, while simultaneously denying any such controlling perspective. The transatlantic 'conversation' out of which the work grew, meanwhile, self-evidently compounds these hermeneutic instabilities: the professional and cultural differences between Skoulding and Moro, as well as their geographical separation from each other, are somehow paradoxically both heightened and collapsed by their creative cooperation.

A cooperative or collaborative approach to creative expression has been widely recognized as radically disturbing the cultural and aesthetic status of the normally singular author, let alone his or her language, imaginative energy, and artistic practice: 'As a liminal space of encounter, collaboration emphasises the dissemblance of self and reveals the contradictions of an identity grounded on categories or enclosure. Collaboration explores the space [and] interdependency between self and Other.'[67] In the essay framing 'Neither the One nor the Other' (co-written with Elizabeth James), Presley recovers the collaborative female partnership of Carey Caplan and Ellen Rose, relishing how '"We" emerges from the space between our individual, different voices, its meanings elusive, dispersed, always deferred, never unitary'.[68] However in both senses their mutual estrangement is significant to the success of their collaboration; as Lucy Lippard says, 'the "stranger" unites "here" and "there"'.[69]

An experienced collaborator, Skoulding has considered the practice in depth, as is revealed in an essay co-written with her colleague and friend the poet Ian Davidson. The account, describing and examining how their jointly-authored poetic compositions come into being, constructs literary collaboration as 'as much an act of reading as it is an act of writing. On receiving a section of the poem, we each have to read it before responding. It is an act of interpretation and an act of discovery'.[70] This shared, step-by-step writing practice emerges as 'negotiation of an unmapped space [...] involv[ing] a

---

[67] Ann Vickery, *Leaving Lines of Gender: A Feminist Genealogy of Language Writing* (Hanover, NH: Wesleyan University Press, 2000), 249.

[68] Frances Presley, 'Working Notes', 'Neither the One Nor the Other', *How 2*, 1/6 (2001), 4: [www.asu.edu/pipercwcenter/how2journal/archive].

[69] Lucy R. Lippard. *The Lure of the Local: Sense of Place in a Multi-Centered Society* (New York: the New Press, 1997), 42.

[70] Ian Davidson and Zoë Skoulding, 'Disobedience: Collaborative Writing and the Walk Poem', in David Kennedy (ed.), *Necessary Steps: Poetry, Elegy, Walking, Spirit* (Exeter: Shearsman Books, 2007), 28–36 (32).

continuous response to a moving and unpredictable textual landscape'.[71] In this aspect of its argument, this bi-vocal, bifocal essay's understanding of its ambulatory co-reader(s) / collaborator(s) comes empoweringly to embody, as Michel de Certeau promises, 'both a near and a far, a *here* and a *there* [which] also has the function of introducing an other in relation to this "I" and of thus establishing a conjunctive and disjunctive articulation of places'.[72] In *From Here*, the complexities of collaboration are sharpened and compounded in a technological format that firmly resists any conventionally singular or static perspective or deictic frame. As Davidson himself notes, the Internet 'redefines relationships between space and place, changes relationships between people and places, breaks down relationships between space and time'.[73]

Staging the creative possibilities enshrined in the proliferating spatiality of the internet, *From Here* endorses Massey's description of a 'simultaneous multiplicity of spaces: cross-cutting, intersecting, aligning with one another, or existing in relationships of paradox or antagonism'.[74] The complexities Massey adumbrates are, at least in part, what prompt geographer Nigel Thrift to declare that 'place in this new "in-between" world [is, by definition] compromised: permanently in a state of enunciation, between addresses, always deferred'.[75] 'Disobedience' affirms, 'In a culture of simultaneous existences here and elsewhere one is just as likely to connect one place with another as to dig down through the depths of associations in a single location'.[76]

In *From Here*, as in *Idir Eatortha*, the usually separate, separable distinctions between author and reader, between text and exegesis (between, if you like, various aesthetically reified versions of 'here' and 'there') are collapsed, implicitly in order to refuse or frustrate by dynamizing the kinds of entrenched, often gendered, cultural hierarchies perpetuated in aesthetic convention. Like Carson and, in his less politically assertive way, O'Donoghue, in refusing to point—spatially or aesthetically—such works 'point' us towards a different, or changing, kind of cultural future, by skirting, dissolving, and/ or literally displacing the hierarchical logic of the centre–periphery dialectic described here. Their authors offer a more open-ended understanding of place—or perhaps emplacement—through the more responsive, more relativistic, always potentially dynamic, terms of 'positioning', in the historical, political, and aesthetic (as well as geographical) connections they mine. Amid their many differences, Morrissey, Walsh, and Skoulding all deliberately problematize what Eavan Boland once called 'the cartography of the poem' in response to the increasingly complex demands of our contemporary

---

[71] Davidson and Skoulding, 'Disobedience', 33, 34.

[72] Michel de Certeau, *The Practice of Everyday Life* (Berkeley: University of California Press, 1984), 98–9.

[73] Ian Davidson, *Ideas of Space in Contemporary Poetry* (London: Palgrave, 2007), 163.

[74] Massey, *Space Place and Gender*, 3.

[75] Nigel Thrift, 'Inhuman Geographies: Landscapes of Speed, Light and Power', in Paul Cloke, Marcus Doel, David Matless, Martin Phillips and Nigel Thrift (eds.), *Writing the Rural: Five Cultural Geographies*, (London: Paul Chapman, 1994), 191–248 (222).

[76] Davidson and Skoulding, 'Disobedience', 30.

cultural moment.[77] In some ways Heaney himself seems to come close to anticipating their often unsettling searching of the difficulties of self-orientation amid the sociocultural dynamisms of their historical moment: 'My regional forecast is that in the new awareness created by translations and communications, all of us can find co-ordinates to establish (if necessary) a second literary home-from-home.'[78] Perhaps more appositely, Davidson retrieves Chantal Mouffe, warning that 'we are in fact always multiple and contradictory subjects, inhabitants of a diversity of communities [...] constructed by a variety of discourses and precariously and temporarily sutured at the intersection of those subject positions'.[79] Honig's model seems to offer an endorsingly undecideable glossing of these three poets' apparently collective desire 'to found a home where we are, or to make a home out of the "I" that each of us is(n't)'.[80]

Select Bibliography

Boland, Eavan, *Object Lessons: The Life of the Woman and the Poet in Our Time* (London, New York: Vintage, 1996).
Carson, Ciaran, *Belfast Confetti* (Oldcastle: Gallery Press, 1991).
Conboy, Katie, 'Revisionist Cartography: The Politics of Place in Boland and Heaney', in Kathryn Kirkpatrick (ed.), *Border Crossings: Irish Women Writers and National Identity* (Dublin: Wolfhound Press, 2000), 190–203.
Crawford, Robert, *Identifying Poets: Self and Territory in Twentieth Century Poetry* (Edinburgh: Edinburgh University Press, 1993).
Davidson, Harriet, 'In The Wake Of Home: Adrienne Rich's Politics and Poetics of Location', in Easthope and Thompson (eds.), *Contemporary Poetry Meets Modern Theory*, 166–76.
Davidson, Ian, *Ideas of Space in Contemporary Poetry* (London: Palgrave, 2007).
Davidson, Ian and Skoulding, Zoë, 'Disobedience: Collaborative Writing and the Walk Poem', in David Kennedy (ed.), *Necessary Steps: Poetry, Elegy, Walking, Spirit* (Exeter: Shearsman Books, 2007), 28–36.
Davis, Alex, *A Broken Line: Denis Devlin's Irish Poetic Modernism* (Dublin: University College Dublin Press, 2000).
De Angelis, Irene, 'Sinead Morrissey: Between Northern Ireland and Japan', *Journal of Irish Studies*, 20 (2005), 16–34.
de Certeau, Michel, *The Practice of Everyday Life* (Berkeley: University of California Press, 1984).
Docherty, Thomas, 'Ana-; or Postmodernism, Landscape, Seamus Heaney', in Antony Easthope and John O. Thompson (eds.), *Contemporary Poetry Meets Modern Theory* (Toronto: University of Toronto Press, 1991), 8–80.
Dowson, Jane and Entwistle, Alice, *A History of Twentieth-Century British Women's Poetry* (Cambridge: Cambridge University Press, 2005).

---

[77] 'An Interview with Eavan Boland', in *Eavan Boland: A Sourcebook*, ed. Jody Allen Randolph (Manchester: Carcanet Press, 2007), 112.
[78] Heaney, 'The Regional Forecast', 22.
[79] Chantal Mouffe, 'Radical Democracy, Modern or Postmodern', in Davidson, 'In the Wake of Home', 167.
[80] Honig, 'Difference', 271.

Entwistle, Alice, '"At Home Everywhere and Nowhere": Denise Levertov's "Domestic Muse"', in Jane Dowson (ed.), *Women's Writing 1945-1960: After the Deluge* (London: Palgrave, 2003), 98-114.

Fietz, Lothar, 'Topos/Locus/Place: The Rhetoric, Poetics and Politics of Place 1500-1800', in Hans-Werner Ludwig and Lothar Fietz (eds.), *Poetry in the British Isles: Non-Metropolitan Perspectives* (Cardiff: University of Wales Press, 1995), 15-30.

Friedman, Susan Stanford, *Mappings: Feminism and the Cultural Geographies of Encounter* (Princeton: Princeton University Press, 1998).

Goodby, John, *Irish Poetry Since 1950: From Stillness into History* (Manchester: Manchester University Press, 2000).

Goodby, John, '"Deflected Forces of Currents": Mapping Welsh Modernist Poetry', *Poetry Wales*, 46/1 (2010), 52-8.

Green, Keith (ed.), *New Essays on Deixis: Discourse, Narrative, Literature* (Amsterdam: Rodopi, 1995).

Grennan, Eamon, *Facing the Music: Irish Poetry in the Twentieth Century* (Omaha, Nebr.: Creighton University Press, 1999).

Heaney, Seamus, 'The Regional Forecast', in R. P. Draper (ed.), *The Literature of Region and Nation* (London: Macmillan, 1989), 10-23.

Honig, Bonnie, 'Difference, Dilemmas, and the Politics of Home', in Seyla Benhabib (ed.), *Democracy and Difference: Contesting the Boundaries of the Political* (Princeton: Princeton University Press, 1996), 257-77.

Howarth, William, 'Some Principles of Ecocriticism', in Cheryl Glotfelty and Harold Fromm (eds.), *The Eco-Criticism Reader: Landmarks in Literary Ecology* (Athens, Ga.: University of Georgia Press, 1996), 69-91.

Jacob, Christian, *The Sovereign Map: Theoretical Approaches in Cartography throughout History* (Chicago: University of Chicago Press, 2006).

James, John, *Collected Poems* (Cambridge: Salt Publishing, 2002).

James, John, 'Last Days of the Vulcan', *Poetry Wales*, 44/1 (2008), 20.

Jenkins, Lee M., 'Interculturalism', in Jane Dowson (ed.), *The Cambridge Companion to Twentieth-Century British and Irish Women's Poetry* (Cambridge: Cambridge University Press, 2010), 119-35.

Kennedy, David '"Now", "now", "even now": Temporal Deixis and the Crisis of the Present in Some Northern Irish Poems of the Troubles', *Irish Studies Review*, 18/1 (2010), 1-16.

Kerrigan, John, *Archipelagic English: Literature, History, and Politics, 1603-1707* (Oxford: Oxford University Press, 2008).

Leighton, Angela, *On Form: Poetry Aestheticism and the Legacy of a Word* (Oxford: Oxford University Press, 2007).

Lippard, Lucy R., *The Lure of the Local: Sense of Place in a Multi-Centered Society* (New York: the New Press, 1997).

Longley, Edna, *From Cathleen to Anorexia: The Breakdown of Irelands* (Dublin: Attic Press, 1990).

Massey, Doreen, *Space, Place and Gender* (Cambridge and Oxford: Polity and Blackwell, 1994).

Morrissey, Sinéad, *Between Here and There* (Manchester: Carcanet Press, 2002).

Mulford, Wendy, '"A city boy at heart": John James and the Industrial South Welsh Heartland', *Poetry Wales*, 44/1 (2008), 20-4.

Presley, Frances, 'Working Notes', 'Neither the One Nor the Other', *How 2*, 1/6 (2001), 4.

Sharp, Joanne P., 'Gendering Nationhood: A Feminist Engagement with National Identity', in Nancy Duncan (ed.), *Bodyspace: Destabilizing Geographies of Gender and Sexuality* (London: Routledge, 1996), 97-108.

Skoulding, Zoë and Owen, Fiona, 'A City of Words: Zoë Skoulding interviewed', *Planet*, 166 (2004), 57–62.
Skoulding, Zoë, 'Border Lines', *Poetry Wales*, 42/4 (2007), 40.
Skoulding, Zoë, 'Wandering Where I Am', *Poetry Wales*, 42/3 (2007), 23–7.
Skoulding, Zoë, *Remains of a Future City* (Bridgend: Seren, 2008).
Skoulding, Zoë and Moro, Simonetta, *From Here* ([n.p.]: Ypolita Press, 2008).
Stephens, Meic and Finch, Peter (eds.), *Green Horse: An Anthology by Young Poets of Wales* (Swansea: Christopher Davies, 1978).
Thrift, Nigel, 'Inhuman Geographies: Landscapes of Speed, Light and Power', in Paul Cloke, Marcus Doel, David Matless, Martin Phillips and Nigel Thrift (eds.), *Writing the Rural: Five Cultural Geographies* (London: Paul Chapman, 1994), 191–248.
Vickery, Ann, *Leaving Lines of Gender: A Feminist Genealogy of Language Writing* (Hanover, NH: Wesleyan University Press, 2000).
Walsh, Catherine, *Idir Eatortha* ([n.p.]: Invisible Books, 1994).

CHAPTER 25

THE ALTERED SUBLIME: RAWORTH, CROZIER, PRYNNE

ROD MENGHAM

THIS essay considers a reconfiguring of the sublime in British poetry of the 1970s and 1980s that coincides with theoretical activity around the ways in which the concept of the sublime is being renewed and diversified in relation to shifts in the experience and understanding of geographical and historical relations. It borrows the phrasing of Christopher Dewdney's text *Alter Sublime* (Toronto: Coach House Press, 1980), whose title seems to take the form of a cryptic injunction: alter the sublime; do something new with it; change your idea of it. It is as if in response to an injunction of this kind that Fredric Jameson's recommendations in the closing remarks of his seminal essay 'Postmodernism' (1984), as well as Jean-François Lyotard's insistence in *The Postmodern Condition* (1979; English translation, 1984) on new forms of 'being together', both involve an updating of the notion of the sublime. During the early 1980s, the aesthetics of postmodernism seemed to become increasingly congruent with just such a revaluing of the aesthetics of the sublime.

In the conclusion of his essay 'Postmodernism, or the Cultural Logic of Late Capitalism', Jameson observes that former sources of the effects of the sublime, such as nature and the unconscious, have become incorporated progressively into the processes of commodity production; so that even the Brazilian rainforests no longer seem intact, are no longer protected by the invulnerability of size or seemingly infinite capacities for regeneration, while the unconscious has become saturated by the languages of the media and advertising industries. The new context for the sublime is provided by the global extension of contemporary communications networks that stretch the capacity of the individual mind to an extent where it cannot grasp imaginatively the scale of the operations engaged in its own formation. The subject of postmodernism is understood as being formed in a social process in which the familiar coordinates of gender, class, nation, race are no longer sufficient even though they retain a powerful residual importance in the transition to a global system of de-territorialized constraints and manufactured needs and desires. Jameson's response to this position is to argue the case for what he calls 'cognitive mapping', a form of activity that would require the 'coordination of existential data (the empirical position of the subject) with unlived, abstract conceptions of the geographic totality'.[1] Jameson presumes that in the early 1980s there is no cultural practice available that could be defined by its need to induce in the reader a sense of her or his place in what is nothing less than a global system, but which at the same time is ready to confront the fact of unrelatedness in the postmodern world. He takes it for granted that the kind of doubleness he wants to promote is as yet 'unimaginable', but there was in fact a form of 'cognitive mapping' available in the 1970s and 1980s in the texts of a number of poets, variously tracing the social and political transformations of the subject that are available to consciousness while at the same time working out the speculative history of a mutation in the species that is necessarily closed to the perceptual apparatus of the individual human being. The kind of mapping that occurs in the work of these poets is perhaps more adequate than the brand of 'cognitive mapping' Jameson outlines the need for. It is his introduction of a cognitive element into the procedure which raises problems, particularly with regard to the conditions of reception of the work of art and the kind of aesthetic judgement it calls forth in respect of the discourse that Jameson considers most appropriate in this context: the discourse of the sublime.

It is in the work of Jean-François Lyotard during the 1980s that a counter-argument to Jameson's emphasis on the cognitive can be found. Lyotard's *Peregrinations: Law, Form, Event* (1988) reviews Kant's schema in the Third Critique of the three kinds of synthesis needed in order for objects to be present to knowledge: the synthesis of apprehension in intuition; the synthesis of reproduction in the imagination; and the synthesis of recognition in the concept. In the first of these, the manifold and discontinuous data of place and time presenting themselves to consciousness are gathered together in a unique intuition, an apprehension. In a sense, the only evidence that apprehension has occurred is found in the mind's ability to retain the effects of apprehension and re-present them at a later moment, a moment when they are no longer present. This is the synthesis of reproduction carried out by the imagination. The role of the imagination at this level is to work as a form of remembrance, reproducing something that has already been given. In the third stage of synthesis, recognition provides a means of organizing the data, of submitting them to different categories of understanding such as causality and purposefulness. Arching over all three separate stages of the process is a general principle of synthesis which Kant names the 'transcendental apperception', a form of pure and original consciousness which could be attached either to the faculty of the understanding or to that of the imagination.

---

[1] Fredric Jameson, *Postmodernism, or, The Cultural Logic of Late Capitalism* (London: Verso, 1991), 52.

If the transcendental apperception is operating through the understanding, then what it chiefly enables is a self-conscious knowledge of data, but if it is operating through the imagination, then what it chiefly enables has only a slender relationship to cognition—it is rather a feeling, or sensing, of other possible forms in which the data could be synthesized. When the object of perception is a work of art, the synthesizing that goes on will identify a form of purposefulness in the data but will prevent the recognition of concepts that would identify a specific purpose. At this level, the imagination is not subordinate to understanding, is not carrying out the task of reproduction, but is capable of a productive activity enabling it to present new forms to the mind as it apprehends data; enabling it to enlarge the scope of the synthesizing activity. In other words, the aesthetic experience is one in which the activity of the imagination necessarily exceeds that of the understanding; and the 'mapping' which occurs extends the territory of the mind beyond that of individual cognition.

In Lyotard's account of Kant, the peculiar form of pleasure that arises from the apprehension of a work of art is the outcome of a mutual transaction between the operations of imagination and understanding. It is a mutuality that is never finally grasped in cognitive terms, that never becomes an object of knowledge; it can only be felt, sensed, approached, intimated, remaining always just out of reach. The understanding can only be present as an implication of its partner the imagination, as a horizon that is never finally touched but which is capable of stimulating the imagination to behave as if the transfer of its material into conceptual form were inevitable and imminent, thus underlining both the powerful pressure of determination and the level of creativity needed to subvert the dominance of preconceptions. It is worth noting that Jameson's formulations tend not to privilege the imagination over the understanding. For Jameson, it is not the centrality of the productive imagination overriding the syntheses of recognition that is needed, but a form of 'cognitive mapping' (whose scope is 'unimaginable') that can be planned for, determined, preconceived, but not seized by the imagination. For Jameson, preconceptions, programmes, 'grand narratives' must, in the final analysis, be maintained, despite being nuanced by a sophisticated awareness of the facility with which critical distance can be lost under postmodernism, and the extent to which social space for a language of communicative rationality has been all but abolished.

The topicality of the discourse of the sublime for Jameson consists in the opportunity it gives him of adapting its terms in the construction of a utopian dialectic of form and un-form. For Lyotard, the engagement with Kant represents a much more sustained, intricate, and comprehensive exploration of the scope of this discourse. (In *Peregrinations*, Lyotard claims to have spent the previous five years reading the *Critique of Judgement*.) Lyotard's attraction towards Kant's aesthetics of the sublime is towards what he sees as its emphasis on experimentalism, on that pressure within the work of art towards the presentation of what finally remains unpresentable; a situation he identifies with a distinctly positive direction within postmodernism that opposes it to the practice of modernism, that can be aligned with an aesthetics of fragmentation as opposed to an aesthetics of totalization. He outlines the implications for artistic practice in these terms in a passage in *The Postmodern Condition* that is worth quoting at length; in the first place, because it is a forceful exposition of his justification of a contemporary discourse of the sublime, and in second place, because it also reveals a remarkable paradox in his thinking:

> The postmodern would be that which, in the modern, puts forward the unpresentable in presentation itself; that which denies itself the solace of good forms, the consensus of a taste which would make it possible to share collectively the nostalgia for the unattainable; that which searches for new presentations, not in order to enjoy them but in order to impart a stronger sense of the unpresentable. A postmodern artist or writer is in the position of a philosopher: the text he writes, the work he produces are not in principle governed by pre-established rules, and they cannot be judged according to a determining judgement, by applying familiar categories to the text or to the work. Those rules and categories are what the work of art itself is looking for. The artist and the writer, then, are working without rules in order to formulate the rules of what *will have been done*. Hence the fact that work and text have the character of an *event*; hence also, they always come too late, for their author, or what amounts to the same thing, their *mise en oeuvre* always begins too soon.[2]

The remarkable paradox at work in this passage inheres in the proposition that 'the postmodern artist or writer is in the position of a philosopher', as if the criteria that govern one field of enquiry—art—could be transferred for use in another field of enquiry—philosophy. What is remarkable about this is that it goes against the grain of Lyotard's otherwise stubborn insistence in *The Postmodern Condition* on the autonomy of separate spheres; on untranslatability, incommensurability; on the lack of adequate metalanguages, grand narratives, plans, programmes, preconceptions. In *Peregrinations*, however, this paradoxical tendency is reaffirmed, in the transference of artistic experimentation into another field, this time the field of politics itself—the sphere of grand narratives par excellence. The twist in all this, of course, is that the criteria art and politics are supposed to share consist of a lack of any criteria whatsoever; the only thing they have in common consists of an abhorrence of consensus. The advantage Lyotard reaps from Kant is the authority he derives from the earlier philosopher for his own refusal to give 'meaning to an event or imagine a meaning for an event by anticipating what that event will be in reference to a pre-text'.[3] In politics, as in art, the requirement is to respond to every case *without criteria*, to deploy a reflective, as opposed to determinant, judgement; and thus to establish what Lyotard claims is 'the principle for all probity in politics as in art'. The attempt to dissolve the conditions of narrative that bind together the autonomous spheres turns into a form of recurrence in one sphere after another. In other words, it is found to be creating another grand narrative all of its own. The attempt to dispense with organizing strategies becomes an organizing strategy

---

[2] Jean-François Lyotard, *The Postmodern Condition: A Report on Knowledge*, trans. Geoff Bennington and Brian Massumi (Manchester: Manchester University Press, 1984), 81.

[3] Jean-François Lyotard, *Peregrinations: Law, Form Event* (New York: Columbia University Press, 1988), 27.

itself. As Andreas Huyssen puts it in *After the Great Divide*, 'perhaps Lyotard's sublime can be read as an attempt to totalize the aesthetic realm by fusing it with all other spheres of life'.[4] With characteristic acuity, Huyssen points to Lyotard's misapplication of Kant which suppresses the historical evidence that 'the 18th century fascination with the sublime of the universe, the cosmos, expresses precisely that very desire of totality and representation which Lyotard so abhors and persistently criticizes in Habermas's work'.[5] Huyssen, the professional Germanist, has no trouble in recalling that 'the first moderns in Germany, the Jena romantics, built their aesthetic strategies of the fragment precisely on a rejection of the sublime which to them had become a sign of the falseness of bourgeois accommodation to absolutist culture'.[6]

Historically, then, the sublime can be seen as bound up with the development of precisely the kind of grand narrative leading to terror that Lyotard's whole project is designed to subvert. Moreover, there are reasons to believe, continues Huyssen, that a resumption of the discourse of the sublime during the 1980s might very well lead to a repetition of the same sort of mistake: 'Even today the sublime has not lost its link to terror which, in Lyotard's reading, it opposes. For what could be more sublime and unrepresentable than the nuclear holocaust, the bomb being the signifier of an ultimate sublime.'[7]

However, the bomb, although it is a terrible enough version of the sublime, is not necessarily the ultimate sublime. On the one hand, one could argue that both the bomb of Huyssen's example, and the global communications networks that Jameson cites as the contemporary equivalent of the sublime, are alike inventions of humanity and that this in some degree locates them within the outer limit of representability, in a way that did not apply for earlier apprehensions of the sublime in nature and the unconscious, which were not man-made, or at least not produced as objects within the same economy of meaning. On the other hand, it could be argued that both the bomb and telecommunications are inflections of a purpose that is not limited by the agency of humanity and for which the attribution of an ultimate sublime might be reserved. I put things this way not because this is a direction taken at any point in the contemporaneous theorizations of the sublime but because it is a possibility investigated in certain poems of the 1970s and 1980s, and the crucial theoretical warrant for it is to be found in Heidegger's notion of the *Gestell*, the challenging claim upon humanity which Heidegger sees as the essence of technological development.

There is an essay by Jay M. Bernstein in the aptly titled volume *Life After Postmodernism*, edited by John Fekete, which includes a delineation of the challenge of technology according to Heidegger.[8] The commonly perceived role of technology is

---

[4] Andreas Huyssen, *After the Great Divide: Modernism, Mass Culture and Postmodernism* (London: Macmillan, 1986), 215.
[5] Huyssen, *After the Great Divide*, 215.
[6] Huyssen, *After the Great Divide*, 215.
[7] Huyssen, *After the Great Divide*, 215.
[8] See Jay M. Bernstein, 'Aesthetic Alienation: Heidegger, Adorno, and Truth at the End of Art', in John Fekete (ed.) *Life after Postmodernism* (London: Macmillan, 1988), 86–119.

to 'challenge' everything in the world, to transform it, prepare it, store it, and put it at the disposal of humanity. But the universality of this challenge does not need to imply that humanity is the agency originating it and setting it in hand. It is an anthropological humanism that supposes humanity capable of deciding what comprises reality and what does not. As far as Heidegger is concerned, the notion that humanity creates the challenge is an illusion that reveals human obliviousness to the true nature of being; it is a limitation based on the supposition that there is only humanity and not a larger category of being in which humanity is merely included. Anthropological humanism is only a historical effect of technological development that puts everything at the disposal of humanity and so creates in the human species a sense of authorship.

Interestingly, Heidegger's essay 'Poetically Man Dwells', which concerns Hölderlin, employs the metaphor of mapping or map-making as an illustration of what poetry should not be limited to or by. The space of poetry should properly be the dimension that links together earth and sky, the known and the unknown, while poetry itself should be the means of 'taking a measure for all measuring':

> This measure-taking is itself an authentic measure-taking, no mere gauging with ready-made measuring rods for the making of maps. Nor is poetry building in the sense of raising and fitting buildings. But poetry, as the authentic gauging of the dimension of dwelling, is the primal form of building. Poetry first of all admits man's dwelling into its very nature, its presencing being. Poetry is the original admission of dwelling.[9]

The distinction between different ways of 'taking a measure' is what animates Tom Raworth's poem 'West Wind'. Curiously, Raworth takes as his reference points those two pejorative instances of the sublime provided by Jameson and Huyssen—global communications networks and the threat of the nuclear bomb—but links these to a mentality capable only of producing a concept of the imagination while remaining incapable of activating and exercising the imagination. Computer networks represent the primacy of translatability, of the reduction of knowledge to commensurable terms:

the computer operates
on limited knowledge
anaesthetised
by not knowing
more
it is
what it knows
we cannot
but conclusions
despatch us[10]

---

[9] Martin Heidegger, *Poetry, Language, Thought*, trans. Albert Hofstadter (New York: Harper and Row, 1971), 227.

[10] Tom Raworth, *Collected Poems* (Manchester: Carcanet Press, 2003), 356.

Raworth tries to preserve the importance of the gap between ontology and epistemology; he takes the measure of whatever it is that allows being to exceed the reach of cognitive knowledge, even though this challenge to the 'closed system' is expressed in negative terms—'we cannot'—along with a recognition of the importance of the social context in which human beings are as if 'despatched', object-wise, by 'conclusions' mechanically reached. The nuclear bomb is presented not as inconceivable but in terms of preconceptions, in terms of a latent militarism made manifest at the time of the Falklands War during which the poem seems to have been written. The power of cultural determinism is further enforced through a number of allusions that treat the Falklands campaign as in some sense an after-image of the Crimean War.

The bomb and the computer network, then, do not figure in Raworth's poem as contemporary equivalents of the sublime but are rather the targets of a radical, and quite savage, de-sublimation:

as war
advertises arms
we are pieces
of percentages
through that eye
for credit
is as far
as machines
can trust
what you own
and what you'll earn
while the homeless stare
at nightlong lights
in empty offices[11]

The constant meshing together of militarism, vested interests, and information technology strongly implies the need for a different kind of measure—the measure of poetry—in a situation where 'credit' is given numerical scope, translated into a form of 'trust' whose agent is a machine. Commensurability is thereby disavowed at the same time as it is announced as governing the terms of present social reality. The wordplay is typical of Raworth's persistent adroitness and a demonstration of what his Shelleyan title appears to promise, which is the important role given to the language of poetry as a perhaps uniquely subtle and at least potentially revolutionary means of imagining an alternative social pragmatics. The writing often proceeds apparently without criteria: the syntactically incomplete line 'we cannot' in the first passage quoted, sandwiched between the phrases 'what it knows' and 'but conclusions | despatch us' in such a way that what appears at first an auxiliary verb finds nothing to be auxiliary to, is typical of the way the writing frequently swerves away from grammatical preconceptions, requiring the

---

[11] Raworth, *Collected Poems*, 361.

reader to exercise a reflective rather than a determinant judgement. The cost of unimaginative measure is counted chiefly in general social terms, and conveyed graphically, but the poem is also deeply personal; its tone is set by a meditation on the death of the poet's mother in an embattled national health ward. However, the private selves of an elegiac contract hold smaller promise of a revaluation of values than multiple instances of a being whose conditions escape effective translation; there are numerous little intimations of purpose entirely incommensurate with that of the subject of 'anthropological humanism': 'the candles | want to go out | aram remarks',[12] Aram being a child with a pedigree in Romantic poetry as much as in the family history of the poet himself. These glimpses of an altered sublime often seem like resuscitations of earlier traditions of thought; there are many reprises of literary history, particularly in the last few pages of the text, which make the intimations of a category of being larger than the merely human seem often primarily readerly.

Raworth's negotiation with the tropes of English Romantic poetry is anticipated in some degree by Andrew Crozier's 'The Veil Poem' (1972–4), a highly concentrated sequence of ten poems with a coda that patiently and scrupulously examines and re-examines the elusive threshold between a daily experience of local, contingent realities and the hidden meanings that religious art and vitalist thought attribute to them. Crozier meditates on the plausibility of this 'radiant source' with reference to Islamic art and architecture and, in one poem specifically, with reference to the idealities of Romantic poetry:

Wisdom and Spirit of the Universe!
Thou Soul that art the Eternity of thought!
And giv'st to forms and images a breath
And everlasting motion! There is never
a last thing while we hold others
to us, this page, this carpet, this
green. You may walk in it until
you know each braided inch or let your eye
dwell on it till it reads itself, it is
as the green still springs up under
foot that you realise how the
illusions and transformations of magic
are different from birth and death.
There is always a page or carpet beyond
the arch, not hidden, green to the touch.[13]

Crozier's counterpointing of Wordsworth's 'everlasting' with 'never a lasting thing' evokes both the end of human history ('Last Things') and the prospect of termination in

---

[12] Raworth, *Collected Poems*, 361.
[13] Andrew Crozier, 'The Veil Poem', in *An Andrew Crozier Reader*, ed. Ian Brinton (Manchester: Carcanet Press, 2012), 101.

the world of things.[14] His paradoxical response to Wordsworth is to embrace the material existence of objects, human relationships, and natural cycles, despite their mutability. There is a lastingness to the varied experiences of the sensual world—a world that is quite precisely 'not hidden'—conditional on ceaseless change and transformation. This represents the very opposite of the temporal and spatial boundlessness and changelessness of the Eternal Spirit; it posits a countervailing form of endless renewal that is reflected in the formal possibilities of the poetic sequence, and in the publication history of 'The Veil Poem'. The sequence first appeared as the ten poems numbered 0–9 in *Sesheta* magazine (1972) and was subsequently reissued as a chapbook (Burning Deck, 1974) with the addition of the 'Coda for the Time Being', a title that raised the possibility of further supplements and alterations.

The ending of the first version of the text seems deceptively conclusive:

> The dust beneath my
> fingernails is all the wisdom I have
> to take with me upstairs to my wife.[15]

This has the feel of a definitive statement, expressing commitment to a relationship that will not outlive the human lifespan; everything returns to dust. But it is also a celebration of the daily ritual of reattachment. It ends by endorsing a rhythm that is bound to be renewed.

Throughout the poem, Crozier embeds a domestic setting within a series of references to the arches, corridors, walls, doors, gates, screens, colonnades, roofs, and windows of mosque architecture. The architectural elements are encountered through the visual arrangements of a series of postcards sent to Crozier by the poet Jeff Morsman. The perspectival emphases of the photographs printed on the postcards draw the imagination beyond the architectural thresholds maintained between what is visible to the eye and what is invisible. Crozier's writing hovers constantly around these thresholds, weighing up their implications of sublimation and de-sublimation. The focus on architectural terminology, and on the conditions of 'dwelling' that articulate its spatial and temporal dimensions, moves towards an exploration of the altered sublime that is carried further in the work of J. H. Prynne, specifically with regard to his major poem of the 1980s, 'The Oval Window' (1983).

In much of his work, Prynne has framed human discourse by attention to the stars, rocks, and plants whose rhythms do not answer to the over-humanized version of space and time. Stressing the presence of these rhythms within humanity is to render almost insignificant what is distinctly human. On the other hand, to contemplate the moral dimension in human history is to understand the unique importance of being human. The compound irony in this connection as Prynne's work sees it is that humanity's extension into the universe has been governed by the terms of a self-projection that

---

[14] William Wordsworth, *The Prelude*, book 1, ll. 428–31.
[15] *An Andrew Crozier Reader*, 102.

often corresponds directly to its moral failures. Theoretically, language enables morality and hence we explore the function and scope of discourse, but if language itself is enabled, is brought into being, by something like a pre-existing morality, something which creates language as part of its purpose, then it is important to try to discover the level at which discourse comes into being, the level at which it forms and can be perceived. Writing which is produced within that kind of framework is going to be difficult; not through being fashionably vague, but to the extent that it has to be precise in researching the mutual formations of consciousness, script, and speech.

A reading of Prynne's oeuvre suggests that he would regard the evolution of the mind and brain as a process of interaction with language, that the creation of language was the creation of the selection pressure which allowed the cerebral cortex and consciousness of self to develop. The nature and terms of his research into the workings of language keep on broaching this possibility. Douglas Oliver has suggested that Prynne's employment of neurobiology in his texts was part of an attempt to make them supersede the condition of metaphor for mental process and become something like examples of the process itself: a textuality of consciousness.[16] This makes it sound as if Prynne's poems are trying to be something like transcripts of the 'transcendental apperception' itself. Certainly, in 'The Oval Window', there is a powerful tension being maintained between the synthesis of reproduction and the synthesis of production. There is an investigation into and a questioning of the action of memory. If we want to dissolve the present unity of experience, because, for example, we think it represents the ideological effect of a 'grand narrative'; if we want to dissolve the present unity of experience and reconstruct its elements, the first step we take is likely to depend on the expectation that unity of experience is man-made—it derives from consciousness of self and is not already in some way coded into the pre-conscious arrangements of the nervous system. In other words, if we agree with Jameson, we proceed to the business of 'cognitive mapping', because we assume that unity of experience derives from consciousness of self and not the neural machinery of the brain. However, the kind of research that Prynne's poetry is open to shows that the information acquired by the central nervous system is already selected by something, is filtered by something acting like a form of memory, remembering some things and not others, synthesizing by reproduction the data presented to the nervous system before they are admitted to consciousness. So it is not enough to take a decision, at the cognitive level, to forget the unity of experience that we self-consciously remember, because unity of experience is organized at the deepest of levels.

When we read poetic texts, they are crammed with pre-semantic elements that are only retrospectively organized into complicity with semantic patterns, patterns we discover after reading has begun, when we put memory to work on what, in the process of reading, we have already absorbed. And the semantic patterns we select will accord with our memory of how to read, which derives from our previous experience of other texts. With 'The Oval Window',[17] Prynne has composed an order of texts in the reading of which what

---

[16] Douglas Oliver, 'J. H. Prynne's "Of Movement Towards a Natural Place"', *Grosseteste Review*, 12 (1979), 93–102.

[17] J. H. Prynne, *Poems* (Tarset: Bloodaxe Books, 2005), 311–39.

we ordinarily call memory does not exist. And it is the processes both of remembering and of forgetting that the poem enacts. Its writing considers the 'onset of the single life' (328), in relation to language and the role of the 'oval window', which is part of the ear:

Her wrists shine white like the frosted snow;
they call each other to the south stream.
The oval window is closed in life,
by the foot-piece of the stapes. Chill shadows
fall from the topmost eaves, clear waters
run beside the blossoming peach. Inside
this window is the perilymph of the vestibule.
    Now O now I needs must part,
      parting though I absent mourne.
It is a child's toy, shaken back in
myopic eddies by the slanting bridge:
toxic; dangerous fire risk; bright moonlight
floods the steps like a cascade of water.[18]

The repertoire of description is anchored by reference to mechanisms of the ear: 'window', 'vestibule', 'perilymph', 'stapes', and others elsewhere To employ many of these terms is to use metaphors in a systematic fashion to describe what the words do not originally mean. The reader presented with these words is bound to 'image into image-space' (333) the literal meanings—a window in a house, a vestibule in a building—and so create what is actually the metaphorical space of this particular poem. The architecture of human habitation becomes the metaphorical context for an exploration of the way that language gets processed instrumentally by the ear. The poet takes care to guide the reader's construction of this space so that the window maintains its role as putative threshold, 'fold line' (339), site of dilemma, where information is processed according to either necessity or choice. In as much as the writing takes place, this place is a sill, a point of ingress or egress or, it depends, an obstructive screen. Every page aligns itself with this conceit, and incorporates an 'inlet' (313), 'point of entry', or 'aperture' (315), 'under the lintel' (318) or 'within the frame', sometimes appropriately subliminally: the focus of one page is a figure 'sublimed in white flakes' (334). Every page seems to engage with a thematics of the sublime.

The most obvious and dramatic subversion of textual memory, which is being encouraged to accumulate all this evidence, comes when the relationship of metaphorical and literal description is turned inside out. Because about halfway through, the metaphorical space of the poem (windows in buildings) becomes the literal space of an aperture in a rough stone-wall, rather like that supplied on the cover of the first publication of the poem:[19]

It is not quite a cabin, but (in local speech)
a *shield*, in the elbow of upland water,

---

[18] Prynne, *Poems*, 331.
[19] J. H. Prynne, *The Oval Window* (Cambridge: privately printed, 1983).

the sod roof almost gone but just under
its scar a rough opening: it is, in first
sight, the oval window. Last light foams
at this crest. The air lock goes cold
    in hot sun, blue streak under
lines swarming there, dung on all fours.
The blur spot on both sides gives out a
low, intense hum, sharp-folded as
if to a feral rafter;
                   the field is determined
by the *exit window*, the lens rim or stop
which, imaged into image space, subtends
the smallest angle at the centre.[20]

This 'upland' window is part of a dilapidated structure, a 'dissolving' building remote from human habitation, so that, although a window, it no longer bears reference to human seeing. The structure seems to be in the process of accommodating itself to the landscape—its sod roof almost merges with it—and we are told that its rafter might have turned 'feral'. What it suggests is the adjustment of human priorities to nature; a window that reveals the abstraction or removal of human vision, the downgrading of the challenge presented by a merely human mode of perception.

The removal of 'vantage' (312, 318), of the viewpoint of anthropological humanism, is what the writing desires, even while noting that its presence 'can't be helped' (312). A project that tries to lose the self—the kind of self that humanity is used to—runs the risk of inducing a fear of freedom that will make it perhaps even a matter of urgency 'to be controlled' (315). Failure in the endeavour results only in 'wounded vantage' (315) from the point of view of 'talk of the town' (315), a source of misapprehension that will see in the text a mere displacement of voice, as grotesque as trying to speak through the throat. Yet what is thought of as threatening to a position of vantage encourages an attempt to start 'lifelong transfusion' (316), a perpetual reconstitution of the self, which is unthinkable from the over-humanized point of view. Under the conditions of 'lifelong transfusion', the world might be 'given over' (319) in an untrammelled transaction, although the transitivity of that giving over is subdued by a recognition of the historical power of 'vantage', and the text's own priorities are set in the context of a venal history of other texts in which the 'values' of writing are those of thematic recall, memorial tokens which serve as rewards and ends in themselves. In the poems of anthropological humanism, what we call a 'reading' can be abstracted from the process and experience of reading, by a kind of 'romantic salvaging operation', in which the term 'romantic' is already a transform that bears witness to the history of such operations. A pure transitivity is invoked in terms of both passion and conscious anachronism: 'spring up, O well; sing unto it', but history's answer to this is 'a pool of values in prime | hock to a pump and

---

[20] Prynne, *Poems*, 333.

its trade-offs' (321). The social history of value is the history of humanity's disengagement from the creativity of the world beyond itself. In fact, humanity is so blind to this greater creativity that its attitude towards fellow beings is almost entirely controlled by the terms of self-projection, with the effect that in the text of the world as a whole, 'The two main shadows over the future tense | are pity and the lack of it' (316). Most of the terms by means of which men understand each other are not derived from the source that created them. Accordingly, the 'cost'—in a discourse of values—of human separateness is rated as a very high one in 'The Oval Window'.

In the era of its story, which is to say, of its susceptibility to being narrated by humankind, the world is seen as an accumulation of loss of choice, of moments that were 'fluffed and spilled' (322)—botched moments—effects of a man-made cause distinct from a memory much larger than human memory; the kind of memory evident in the movements of migrating birds: 'The arctic tern | stays put wakefully, each following suit | by check according to rote' (323). From the human angle, at what point could there be a choice to act in anything like this fashion? Yet, the poem insists, there is a choice, of a kind that humanity either learns it is part of, or it sees as running counter to its own will. To accede to a larger memory that forgets most of our own is the constant risk of this writing. The attempt to follow this new, or newly disclosed, course is flawed by habit, and diverted to emotional lucre: 'You must choose the order | of choice, on the nail from which shadows hang' (325). The shadows we have been told about already are 'pity and the lack of it'. The choice to be chosen by writing like this means an extraordinary sustainment, not of alternatives, but of activities that are not in outright competition because one is in rebellion from the other which know itself as both. The writing forgets and remembers; and there is an extreme tension in the language whose constant mutual framing of 'contract' and 'fancy' (336) is, like the oval window, 'closed in life' (331, 336). 'Contract' and 'fancy' are the terms used by the poem, but it might be possible to substitute for them 'understanding' and 'imagination', or 'criteria' and 'lack of criteria'. The tension between 'contract' and 'fancy' creates a host of small local ironies graduating to large-scale cultural ironies; tension in phrases like 'the gift-shop' (312)—where what is to be given has to be bought first—or the 'pay-bed' (322) of the 1980s National Health ward, 'as if there are | two distinct and mutually exclusive actions | depending on one test' (322). The most poignant tension is perhaps present in the meditation on the 'egg-timer' (329), at one and the same time the kitchen rudiment of clock-time and its total opposite, the time of the egg, the temporality of a birth process.

'The Oval Window', then, is a text in which the imparting of a sense of what is unpresentable in the presentation has an extraordinary force and goes far beyond what is sketched in contemporaneous theorizations of the sublime. What the text demonstrates is that the action of human memory involves a form of obliviousness to the challenge that is directed against humanity itself as well as against the rest of the world of which humanity is only a part. The process of forgetting that the text enacts is thus a means of bringing out of concealment the action of a memory that extends far beyond the consciousness of humanity. This is something that cannot be 'cognitively mapped', but it is at the centre of a shared programme of poetic research that allows it to be constantly felt as a possibility.

Select Bibliography

Bernstein, Jay M., 'Aesthetic Alienation: Heidegger, Adorno, and Truth at the End of Art', in John Fekete (ed.) *Life after Postmodernism* (London: Macmillan, 1988), 86-119.
Brinton, Ian (ed.), *A Manner of Utterance: The Poetry of J. H. Prynne* (Exeter: Shearsman Books, 2009).
Crozier, Andrew, *An Andrew Crozier Reader*, ed. Ian Brinton (Manchester: Carcanet Press, 2012).
Dewdney, Christopher, *Alter Sublime* (Toronto: Coach House Press, 1980).
Heidegger, Martin, *Poetry, Language, Thought*, trans. Albert Hofstadter (New York: Harper and Row, 1971).
Huyssen, Andreas, *After the Great Divide: Modernism, Mass Culture and Postmodernism* (London: Macmillan, 1986).
Jameson, Fredric, *Postmodernism, or, the Cultural Logic of Late Capitalism* (London: Verso, 1991).
Johansson, Birgitta, *The Engineering of Being: An Ontological Approach to J. H. Prynne* (Uppsala: Swedish Science Press, 1997).
Kant, Immanuel, *Critique of Judgement*, trans. J. H. Bernard (New York: Hafner Press, 1951).
Lyotard, Jean-François, *The Postmodern Condition: A Report on Knowledge*, trans. Geoff Bennington and Brian Massumi (Manchester: Manchester University Press, 1984).
Lyotard, Jean-François, *Peregrinations: Law, Form, Event* (New York: Columbia University Press, 1988).
Oliver, Douglas, 'J. H. Prynne's "Of Movement Towards a Natural Place"', *Grosseteste Review*, 12 (1979), 93-102.
Prynne, J. H., *The Oval Window* (Cambridge: privately printed, 1983).
Prynne, J. H., *Poems* (Tarset: Bloodaxe Books, 2005).
Purves, Robin, 'What Veils in Andrew Crozier's "The Veil Poem"', *Blackbox Manifold*, 2, ed. Alex Houen and Adam Piette: [http://www.manifold.group.shef.ac.uk/issue%202/Robin%20Purves%202.html]
Raworth, Tom, *Collected Poems* (Manchester: Carcanet Press, 2003).
Reeve, Neil, and Kerridge, Richard, *Nearly Too Much: The Poetry of J. H. Prynne* (Liverpool: Liverpool University Press, 1995).
Wordsworth, William, *The Prelude* (a parallel text), ed. J. C. Maxwell (Harmondsworth: Penguin Books, 1971).

PART IV
BORDER CROSSINGS

CHAPTER 26

DISLOCATING COUNTRY: POST-WAR ENGLISH POETRY AND THE POLITICS OF MOVEMENT

DAVID HERD

1. THE CLAIM

THIS chapter is about the relation between poetry and country. The country in question is England, a geopolitical formation that does not have the status of a nation, but which can sometimes function in discourse as if it does; a country, in other words, which is not identical with a nation state but which has, nonetheless, attracted national sentiment. The literary historical claim the essay makes is that since the Second World War, poetry written in England has learned to live without reference to such rhetoric. In that period, the essay argues, the category of English poetry (as opposed, say, to American poetry, or to poetry written in English) has gradually fallen into disuse. There is nothing about the dissolution of the relation between poetry and England that the essay regrets. Equally, the significance of such a break-up should not be underestimated. In the post-Romantic period poetry has been woven through nation and country in all manner of ways; so much so that, of late, national identity has become a default position for the presentation of poems, in anthologies, say, or in collections of essays. This might seem an innocent gesture. If one thinks, either, that the categories of country and nation are unproblematic, or, that though the categories themselves are problematic, poetry's relation to them is harmless, then there would be no need to scrutinize the connection between the two. The double premise of this essay, however, is that since the Second World War nationhood has become an increasingly troubling political idea, and that, where and when national identity is promoted, poetry can and does become important to that claim.

There are complex reasons, to do with the history of empire, for the fact that poetry written in England should have proved relatively quick to uncouple itself from the rhetoric of a national identity. For those same reasons, to speak of the dislocation of poetry from Englishness is not the same thing as to speak of a dislocation of poetry from, for example, Irishness. Viewed in that way, from the point of view of colonization, the ideas of nation and country do not have a single application. There are circumstances, however, as the chapter considers, in which the application of the rhetoric of belonging is singular, in which from one setting to the next it does mean the same thing. The intention here, then, is to trace the intellectual history through which, in the particular case of English poetry, there has been a gradual dislocation of poetry from the categories of country and nation, and to consider what might be learned from the writing that has emerged.

2. 'Dover Beach'

One point of entry into this history is 'Dover Beach'. These days, Dover is not somewhere one is likely to visit, but is a place, instead, people tend to pass through (unless, that is, and we'll come on to this later, a person finds him- or herself stopped there). Like the harbour at Gloucester, Massachusetts, Dover Beach is one of those locations that the reader of poetry is more likely to encounter as poem than as place. There is a world of difference, of course, between the manner of Charles Olson's rendering of Gloucester and Matthew Arnold's image of Dover, but in both cases the poet clearly establishes his location as his point of view. The value of Arnold's poem in this context lies in the clarity with which it formulated a modern sense of the relation between poetry and geopolitical space; framed it such that, for all the transformations of modernism, it was Arnold's idea of poetry and place that post-war English critics inherited.

Arnold's poem is a record of crisis, his rhetoric twisting between four poles: faith, time, love, and country. With religious faith no longer tenable after the revelations of Darwin, the poem's question is how might the modern sensibility secure itself. One option for Arnold, with Darwin's discoveries in mind, is that the poem might frame itself according to the implications of geological time, the way later J. H. Prynne would, after the example of Olson. It is, however, precisely the prospect of the geological expanse, that Arnold's poem seeks to avoid:

But now I only hear
Its melancholy, long, withdrawing roar,
Retreating, to the breath
Of the night-wind, down the vast edges drear
And naked shingles of the world.[1]

---

[1] Matthew Arnold, *The Poems of Matthew Arnold 1840 to 1867*, introd. A. T. Quiller Couch (Whitefish, Mont.: Kessinger Publishing, 2004), 401.

The thought here is that after faith, what we are left with is geology, hence 'the naked shingles of the world'. Presented in that way, the beach in question could be anywhere, a prospect that, for Arnold, induces melancholy. And so the poem's question is reframed: if the geological narrative that has taken religion's place gives rise to an unbearable lack of specificity, in what might a person seek solidarity? One option is mutual trust. Thus where, in the face of a different crisis, Auden would later propose, in '1 September 1939', that we should love one another or die, Arnold's more taut proposition is that we must establish true relations; where the proposition is placed at the beginning of a syntactically complicated sentence, the multiple clauses of which sketch the contemporary circumstances according to which true human relations are both vital and fraught.[2] Truth, then, in the sense of faithful human relations is one means by which the modern sensibility, and the modern poem, might secure itself.

There is, however, another rhetoric, more specific than that of human truth, by which the poem looks to secure itself intellectually:

>   on the French coast the light
> Gleams and is gone; the cliffs of England stand,
> Glimmering and vast, out in the tranquil bay.[3]

This is Arnold's logic: in the absence of faith, unwilling to contemplate the scale of a geological account of the world, and in the knowledge that true relations are a fragile basis on which to build human solidarity, the poem asserts the claims of political geography. Unable, in the modern moment, confidently to found itself on anything else, the poem comes to recognize itself in the contours of its country.

It is important not to miss the significance of this act of recognition. It is commonplace, of course, for poems and poets to recognize themselves in countries. Thus, as modern and intellectually sceptical a poet as Charles Bernstein, for instance, can unproblematically identify himself—in the introduction to his collection of essays *A Poetics*—through his address to 'American poetry'.[4] The value of Arnold's poem lies in the self-consciousness with which such a gesture of identification is made. 'Dover Beach' does not presuppose an identity with country. Nor, even, does it disguise that identity in the language of organicism. (It is organicism, in the guise of geology, that the poem looks to stave off.) It is a link, rather, that Arnold constructs, in the absence of other links, the poem consciously arriving at a sense of its identity with country in the way an opportunistic politician might assert national identity at a moment of crisis. What the poem also knows, however, is that such a gesture comes at a cost, hence the glimpse, from its geopolitical setting, of 'ignorant armies' as they 'clash by night'. What Arnold formulated, in other words, in 'Dover Beach', was an entirely modern sense of the relation between poetry and country, where that relation is understood as a default position, and where it is known to carry an implicit cost.

---

[2] W. H. Auden, *Another Time* (New York: Random House), 112.
[3] Arnold, *Poems of Matthew Arnold*, 401.
[4] Charles Bernstein, *A Poetics* (Cambridge, Mass.: Harvard University Press, 1992), 1.

I will come back to the cost of poeticizing the national project. It is worth taking a moment, though, before tracking the evolution of Arnold's narrative through the period following the Second World War, to consider what he didn't notice in the writing of 'Dover Beach'. Looking out, as the poem's speaker does, from Dover towards France, he is aware of the 'cliffs of England' as they cast a shadow over the sea from behind him. What the speaker doesn't observe, because he isn't looking that way, is the fort that would have dominated, and still dominates, Dover's Western Heights. Constructed during the Napoleonic Wars in anticipation of an invasion that never came, and not completed until after the wars were over, the Fort has had a series of after lives. During the 1970s and 1980s it was a Young Offenders Prison. Since the late 1990s it has functioned as the Dover Immigration Removal Centre: a place where people who cannot be returned to their so-called country of origin are held indefinitely, and for periods of up to five years. Such centres are emblematic. What they bear witness to is the cost of the compulsion to formulate identity in terms of country and nation. Having felt compelled, or been forced, to leave the place with which they were originally identified, and having been denied a new identity in the place to which they travelled, the detention of such people testifies to what one might call the contradictions of country. Or rather, it bears witness to the contradictions that underpin the term: the English word country deriving from the Latin *contra*, meaning that which is against, or opposed to. It is these contradictions with which this chapter is concerned. The essay's working premise is that in the period since the Second World War, the idea that one can or should identify with country or nation has come under significant pressure, the cost of such identification being the kind of political abandonment the people in a removal centre are obliged to endure. The question that arises is whether, in any meaningful sense, such abandonment is a matter for poetry. My contention is that it is; that precisely because poetry is so readily identified with and through the discourses of nation and country, then poetry has a responsibility to reflect on its relation to the geopolitical state.

Dover is a point of departure: its fortified removal centre presents a contemporary political reality that places pressure on a story of poetry in which poetry and country mutually identify. To understand how that pressure has given rise to new poetic expression, it is necessary first to register the contradictions of a poetic predicated on an idea of country, contradictions to which Donald Davie gave critical voice.

3. Purity of Diction in English Verse

Donald Davie was the most important poetry critic of his generation. His criticism had the great virtue that, as he conducted it, discussion of poetry was always a social act. To write poetry, but also to write about it, was, for Davie, to engage with the defining social questions of one's moment. To cite the title of a collection of essays gathered in his honour, such an engagement was one of the responsibilities of literature.[5] A further virtue of Davie's

---

[5] George Dekker, *Donald Davie and the Responsibilities of Literature* (Manchester: Carcanet Press, 1983).

criticism was its ongoing commitment to literary exchange. As translator and critic, he was instrumental in introducing Pasternak and Mandelstam to UK readers, just as, as critic, he was among the first to consider such New American Poets as Olson, Oppen, and Dorn. He was also, however, deeply committed to the identity of poetry with country. The strength of individual books and essays notwithstanding, therefore, the overarching value of Davie's criticism now, in retrospect, is the narrative it offers, from the point of view of poetry, of the post-war condition. It is not a narrative we should hear in isolation and so I will contrast it later with the account given by Hannah Arendt of human migration in the years following the war. For the moment, though, what needs to be observed is that from its origin in the 1950s, Davie's criticism is a record of the effort to contain poetic language within the contours of country and nation.

For Davie, what that link first amounted to was diction. As he put it, with reference to Arnold:

> A chaste diction is 'central', in Arnold's sense; it expresses the feeling of the capital not the provinces. And it can do this because it is central in another way, central to the language, conversational not colloquial, poetic not poetical. The effect is a valuable urbanity, a civilized moderation and elegance; and this is the effect attainable, as I think, by Goldsmith, and not by Shakespeare.[6]

Not least among Davie's virtues was his willingness to risk polemic. In a passage such as this any number of terms issue a provocation, 'chaste', 'central', 'civilized', 'elegance'. The real provocation, however, and the real measure of his idea of diction, lies in the metaphor by which he initiates his account. Contrasting the poets he means to address with Hopkins, Davie offers an image of the kind of work he has in mind, where 'a selection has been made and is continually being made' and 'words are thrusting at the poem and being fended off from it'.[7] Diction, then, according to Davie's account of English verse is a 'fending off', where such 'fending' is in the interest of an idea of culture, and where that culture is perceived to be under threat.

Here, the threat in question is carried by the colloquial; forms of language that carry forms of culture to which the civilized centre is opposed. In this respect, Davie's critical position would shift somewhat as eventually it came to emphasize the specificity of Thomas Hardy. Another sense of threat, however, remained a constant in his writing, the sense that the contours of nationhood were becoming insecure. To establish the point, Davie refers to André Malraux's image of

> the world of the modern artist as 'le musée imaginaire', upon the walls of which hang examples of all the styles of the past. These styles the modern artist has learnt to appreciate independent of the different cultures of which they were the flowers; and he can choose among them at will, seeking the one he shall use as model.[8]

---

[6] Donald Davie, *The Purity of Diction in English Verse* (London: Routledge & Kegan Paul, 1967), 26–7.
[7] Davie, *Purity of Diction*, 5.
[8] Davie, *Purity of Diction*, 10.

Malraux's artist is a figure Davie recognizes and can talk about; it was a great strength of his criticism that he could characterize as well (and as honestly) the aesthetic options he did not prefer as those he chose to take up. It is highly instructive, for instance, to observe as Davie does (in light of Malraux's formulation), that 'the best modern poems often read as if they were good translations from another language'.[9] There is an important truth in this, and by negation Davie points to the kind of poetry this essay will arrive at: a poetry that establishes linguistic dislocation as a necessary condition of modern expression. It is not this kind of poet, however, that Davie is interested in; the kind of poet, as he asserts, who pays for his freedom with an 'isolated position in his civilization'.[10]

Against such 'freedom', Davie posed the idea of poetic responsibility:

> We are saying that the poet who undertakes to preserve or refine a diction is writing in a web of responsibilities... He is responsible to the community in which he writes, for purifying and correcting the spoken language.[11]

It is integral to Davie's value as a critic that he emphasized the responsibilities of the poet. It is also because of the way he draws the network of those responsibilities that one cannot read his post-war narrative in isolation. As he presents it here, the responsibility of the poet extends to 'the community in which he writes'; in this way, to use a term from *Thomas Hardy and British Poetry*, such responsibility is curtailed. Such curtailment was fundamental to Davie: a sense of limit, as he understood it, was necessary to poetic utterance and his object, in emphasizing diction, was precisely to establish the 'poet's place in the national community, or, under modern conditions... his place in the state'. Diction, as a poetic fending off, was thereby expressly aligned to an idea of nation, both ideas being predicated on an attitude to human movement. Thus:

> As England transformed itself into an industrial state, people were uprooted from native localities and from the social and cultural disciplines of settled communities. Hence the importance, for this literature, of the uprooted, nomadic and classless type of the governess and paid companion.[12]

A wrong view to take of Davie's post-war commentary on poetry and nation is that he was in any simple sense parochial. He read generously across languages and travelled professionally and in both ways ensured an open-ness in English readers to other traditions. Even so, in his theory of diction he found it constantly difficult to reconcile his thinking to the fact of human movement. As he put it, 'With the stay of "common use" thus taken away, the notions of chastity and purity in diction could have no meaning.'[13]

---

[9] Davie, *Purity of Diction*, 10–11.
[10] Davie, *Purity of Diction*, 10.
[11] Davie, *Purity of Diction*, 16.
[12] Davie, *Purity of Diction*, 24.
[13] Davie, *Purity of Diction*, 25.

It seems rather remarkable now, I think, to read a critic of Davie's acumen using the terms 'chastity' and 'purity' in connection with culture only a few years after the Second World War. This is not a point to make lightly: Davie served in the war, and then afterwards was emphatic in his refusal of forms of cultural gesture that, as he saw it, affirmed Fascism. Thus in *Purity of Diction*, as he addresses Pound, he finds the 'development from imagism in poetry to fascism in politics' to be 'clear and unbroken'.[14] Nonetheless, what the post-war moment appears to have called for, for Davie, was a consolidation of national cultural identity, a version of curtailment understood, one can suppose, as a limitation on political expansion. More interesting, though, than either the term 'chastity' or the term 'purity', is the term 'stay', where 'stay' has both the sense of remaining and the meaning of support. Thus the 'stay of common use', to which Davie aligns poetic diction, is related through his wariness of the nomadic, to the desirability of remaining in one place. As Davie theorizes it, poetry works when people stay: when they move, or when they are moved, things start to break down. Which again is not to make a simplistic point; Davie himself had moved throughout the war, and would move later, in his academic career. He would also write movingly about refugees in 'Huntingdonshire', catching a quality of their experience with Poundian precision in registering how they 'lived…in a jacked, abandoned bus'.[15] The claim here is not in any simple sense to do with what Davie as a citizen, or even as a poet, thought. The argument rather is to do with the language in which poetry is described and identified, a language which, in Davie, as in Arnold, all too quickly arrived at the idea of nation. Davie, that is, notwithstanding his own experience and sympathies and for all his critical agility, could hardly think about poetry otherwise than in relation to 'nation' and 'state'. The result was a critical project that veered frequently towards contradiction, the visibility of the contradictions (and the honesty with which he expressed them) being not the least significant aspect of his critical legacy.

Davie himself migrated in 1968, when he left Essex for Stanford. It was from Stanford, and so from the vantage point of dislocation that he wrote the belated follow-up to *Purity of Diction in English Verse*, *Thomas Hardy and British Poetry* (1973). The shift of adjective would suggest that Davie's focus had altered, but as the Foreword made clear, England was still the country he had in mind, *Thomas Hardy and British Poetry* being 'an attempt to define the political temper of the educated classes in England on the basis of the literature which they have produced and responded to in the last fifty years'.[16] The slippage between title and Foreword is explained by the fact that Davie was writing for an American audience, with the express intention of enabling that audience to hear a poetry to which it was no longer listening. Arguably, by the time of the book's writing, the adjectival phrase 'English poetry' had already ceased to make sufficient sense to figure in a title. Precisely because of this, perhaps, *Thomas Hardy and British Poetry* constitutes an even more concerted attempt to tie poetry to country.

---

[14] Davie, *Purity of Diction*, 99.
[15] Donald Davie, *Collected Poems 1970–1983* (Manchester: Carcanet Press, 1983), 27.
[16] Donald Davie, *Thomas Hardy and British Poetry* (London: Routledge & Kegan Paul, 1973), 2.

The substantive difference between the two commentaries is that the basis for the claim to poetic identity is no longer language but place, Davie substituting a theory of poetic diction with a theory of poetic topography. In this respect we are back to 'Dover Beach', Davie's claim being that poetic utterance takes its temper from its topographical situation. As in Arnold, this does not prove an easy proposition to manage within an argument about nation; at various points in Davie's commentary on post-war English poetry topography slides into geology. It is against this slide, the slippage, as Arnold put it, from the specificity of 'Dover Beach' to the 'naked shingles of the world', that Davie positions Hardy. 'Hardy', as he puts it, 'has the effect of locking any poet whom he influences into the world of historical contingency, a world of specific places at specific times.'[17] Again it is important to notice Davie's presiding metaphor. Where his sense of 'diction' constituted a 'fending off', his Hardyesque sense of topography has the effect of a 'locking into'. In both metaphors what is at issue is an act of what Davie repeatedly called curtailment: 'Are not Hardy and his successors right', he asked by way of his leading critical question, 'in severely curtailing for themselves the liberties that other poets continue to take?'[18]

The critical costs of such a curtailment are readily established. Thus a reading of Auden through Hardy entails an explicit topographical restriction:

> 'In Praise of Limestone' contrives, by what is really sleight of hand, to superimpose landscapes of Ischia and even perhaps of Greece on the limestone landscapes which, as we have seen, were the natural habitation for Auden's imagination from his earliest youth.[19]

The critical task is to bring the poet back, to restore him to 'the natural habitation' of his 'imagination', to recover the ground that has been obscured by the introduction of other landscapes, which is to say by poetic 'sleight of hand'. J. H. Prynne, on the other hand, is twice curtailed. Focusing on *The White Stones*, Davie restricts his discussion of that book to those poems which dwell on geology, as opposed, for instance, to poems which deal in abstractions, in questions of quality or of value. An interest in geology, however, does not render the poetry Hardyesque, and so although Prynne's topographies tend (precisely) to evade a national claim the language itself is imagined not to. As Davie has it, with reference to 'The Holy City':

> The structuring principle of this poetry, which makes it difficult (sometimes too difficult), is the unemphasized but radical demands it makes upon English etymologies, so that to follow the logic we have to remember 'trade' as meaning traffic.[20]

---

[17] Davie, *Thomas Hardy and British Poetry*, 3.
[18] Davie, *Thomas Hardy and British Poetry*, 12.
[19] Davie, *Thomas Hardy and British Poetry*, 126–7.
[20] Davie, *Thomas Hardy and British Poetry*, 115.

It is not wrong to find a preoccupation with etymology in early Prynne. It is, however, curious to render that preoccupation in national terms: etymology, after all, like geology tends to exceed national frameworks; the word 'trade' for instance, has its origin in the low German word 'track'.

This is a point worth dwelling on. For Davie, seduced by the language of etymology itself, what the history of words implies is rootedness. A glance at the dictionary, however, indicates otherwise; tells one that language precisely breaches curtailments, word histories flowing through one another in the same way that geologies breach singularities of place. Significant as it was, then, that Davie should have recognized Prynne at such an early point in the poet's career, there is perhaps nowhere in his writing where his critical lexicon seems so ill at ease. *The White Stones* is a book of shifting plates across which cultures and populations migrate, the deep mobility of the language catching the profound sense of movement and circulation that for Prynne, at this moment, constituted human history.

The critical cost of Davie's identification of post-war English poetry with Hardy is that major figures such as Auden and Prynne must be read through a topographical poetic that distorts the work. More significant, however, than such local misreadings, are the implied politics of a commitment to Hardy. One gets a sense of that politics in Davie's conclusion when he partially aligns himself with the correspondents to the local newspapers:

> For such people the present is a very hard time to live in; and the correspondence columns of any local newspaper show them protesting, crying out in pain, seeking ever more hysterical and irrational ways to break out from the impasse in which they find themselves.[21]

In some way that is not made clear, Davie wants his national critical project to answer to this correspondence, the local newspaper constituting for him the basis of a polis as it did, more substantively, for Olson. Which reference takes us to the heart of the question of poetry and place, and in turn takes us back into the issue of poetic Englishness. Thus, one reading of *Maximus* would find there an exportable insistence on locality, Olson's attention to the archive and to the history of his fishing town lending itself to just the kind of emphasis on specificity that Davie found in Hardy and which he made the defining quality of poetic Englishness. Another reading of Olson, however, would find in his account of Gloucester a history of place as intersection; place as a development of forces originating long before and far beyond itself. Already, then, in the first two volumes of *Maximus*, there is a reading of history that held within itself the image of slow, uncurtailed change that Prynne made fundamental to *The White Stones*. Really what *Thomas Hardy and British Poetry* articulated was a moment of division in English poetry, one in which the adjective itself was entirely at stake. There *was* a reading of Olson's Gloucester

---

[21] Davie, *Thomas Hardy and British Poetry*, 174.

that could get one back to Wessex, or even, if one wanted, to a reinforcement of Arnold's Dover. There was also, however, a reading that propelled one out, into a recognition that, in fact, 'the Pleistocene is our current sense'.[22]

One further political claim is to be found in Davie's expression of Hardyesque specificity itself:

> Hardy's feeling for topography and locality, as somehow conditioning the human lives under their influence more powerfully than any theory available to him or us can allow for, is something that can and does persist, as a tradition.[23]

This statement makes a crucial distinction. By its phrasing, what Davie might be heard to address is the 'human condition'. To be clear, though, what the statement is talking about is the topographical 'conditioning' of 'human lives'. It is there, in that shift from 'condition' to 'conditioning' that the cost of a narrative that ties poetry to nation is most acutely felt. Again, it is a distinction one can register through Prynne, the term 'condition' being one of the words on which his early poetry turns: concerned with human-ness, not some national version of it, it is a person's 'condition', not their 'conditioning' that the poems of *The White Stones* look to disclose. Really to register the cost of a language of 'conditioning', however, and in turn to appreciate the value of the obsolescence of 'Englishness', we need briefly to glimpse the arguments of another tradition.

4. Europe

So thoroughly is Davie locked into the specificity of his situation in *Thomas Hardy and British Poetry*, that it is not possible from within the argument itself to grasp the implications of his identification of poetry with country, nation, and state. To understand what is being said, it is necessary to place him in dialogue with what is called the Continental tradition. As regards diction, his analogue in that tradition is Heidegger. Thus in 1951, the year before Davie published *Purity of Diction in English Verse*, Heidegger gave the lecture 'Building Dwelling Thinking', the first of a series of three lectures that would later be published in *Poetry Language Thought*. Their manifest differences of manner notwithstanding, Heidegger and Davie arrived at a strikingly similar account of poetry in the immediate post-war moment, with Heidegger, like Davie, making the case for a purity of diction. Here's Heidegger, then, listening to the language, at the beginning of 'Building Dwelling Thinking', where the issue is how words can be thought to locate a person in a specific place:

---

[22] J. H. Prynne, *Poems* (Fremantle, WA and Tarset: Fremantle Arts Centre Press and Bloodaxe Books, 2005), 66.

[23] Davie, *Thomas Hardy and British Poetry*, 112.

Now, what does *bauen*, to build, mean? The Old High German word for building, *buan*, means to dwell. This signifies to remain, to stay in a place. The proper meaning of the verb *bauen*, namely to dwell, has been lost to us. But a covert trace of it has been preserved in the German word *Nachbar*, neighbour. The *Nachbar* is the *Nachgebur*, the *Nachgebauer*, the near-dweller, he who dwells nearby.[24]

Taking its departure from post-war crises in housing, and taking issue with modernity, the point of Heidegger's lecture is to develop an aesthetic of nearness. He alights on the etymological fact that in building and thinking one has a trace of the word *dwelling*. A 'dwelling', in both senses, is that which remains in a place, a meaning we begin to hear fully, as Heidegger sees it, as we dwell on language itself.

The point of the comparison is to observe that Davie, in his account of language and place, was part of a larger narrative of the post-war condition, a narrative that proposed an image of locality as a counter to the intrusions of modernity. As in Davie, what matters in Heidegger is the 'stay', his chosen word *bauen* signifying 'to stay, or remain', the fact of staying being central to both writers' idea of culture. The stay, to say it in a way that both would have understood, was *the stay*. The question is, what of human movement? How, that is, can a poetic which emphasizes rootedness acknowledge the fact that in the period following the war people often couldn't stay. Again, the point is not in any simple sense to ascribe a view to Davie, but to observe a limitation in the way poetry after the war was, and has been, thought. To put this another way, and to quote Charles Bernstein quoting Jack Spicer's dying words: 'My vocabulary did this to me'.[25] What both Davie and Heidegger present, in other words, is a rhetoric of poetry's relation to place and nation that struggles to register the fact of human movement, such movement being, according to an alternative narrative of the period, the defining element of the post-war condition.

For that alternative narrative, one needs to glance at Hannah Arendt, and in particular at her discussion of 'The Decline of the Nation State and the End of the Rights of Man', which appeared in 1958 as a supplementary chapter in the revised edition of *The Origins of Totalitarianism*. Recently revived by Giorgio Agamben as the basis for his discussion of sovereignty in *State of Exception*, Arendt's chapter observed a post-war reality in which 'the nation-state was no longer capable of facing the major political issues of the time'.[26] This, as she set it out, was the consequence of the series of complex historical interactions that had made mainstream conceptions of racial and national difference possible, and which, following totalitarianism's terrible reinforcement, was the real consequence of the Second World War. The name for that consequence was 'statelessness': 'the newest mass phenomenon in contemporary history, and the existence of an ever-growing new people comprised of stateless persons, the most symptomatic group in contemporary politics'.[27] Dismayed by the reality she found herself describing in the

---

[24] Martin Heidegger, *Basic Writings: Martin Heidegger*, ed. David Farrell Krell (London: Routledge, 1992), 348–9.
[25] Bernstein, *A Poetics*, 196.
[26] Hannah Arendt, *The Origins of Totalitarianism* (new edn., London: George Allen and Unwin, 1960), 261.
[27] Arendt, *Origins of Totalitarianism*, 277.

1950s, a reality in which 'the number of stateless people—twelve years after the end of the war—[was] larger than ever', Arendt pressed deep into the contradictions of the nation state. Only in the modern environment, with its 'completely organized humanity', which is to say, a humanity organized according to the principle of national identity, 'could the loss of home and political status become identical with an expulsion from humanity altogether'.[28] 'Before this', as she put it, 'what we must call a "human right" today would have been thought of as general characteristic of the human condition…Only the loss of a polity itself expels him from humanity.'[29]

Where Davie intersects with Arendt is in their concentration on responsibility. Where they differ is in the reach they ascribe to that term, the measure of that difference being the way they construe the term condition. For Arendt, arguing in ways Agamben would reprise, human movement, especially forced human movement, was the defining feature of the post-war period, a feature that intellectual procedures of all kinds had to come to terms with. What that meant was precisely an insistence on the discourse of the human condition, as opposed to a discourse of human conditioning. To emphasize the latter, as Arendt sets out, is to allow humanity to get tangled up in its specific representations, with the result that if at any point a person is excluded from any one such specific representation, then in fact they are excluded from all such.[30] Which takes us back to Dover, not to the beach, but to the cliffs, and not to Arnold's poem but to the site of detention that now marks the end point of geopolitical space. It takes us back also to 1973, to the year Davie published *Thomas Hardy and British Poetry*, with its slippy handling of the sovereign adjective. Davie, one could reasonably claim, was the last person to write in earnest about English poetry, to move the term 'England' around a critical argument with the intention of restoring its sense. By that moment in the post-war period, the categories of country and of nation had long since come under serious ethical pressure, and some of the poets about whom he was writing were learning how to do without them.

5. A Various Art

Surprisingly, one can put a date on the moment poetry that happened to be written in England publicly dislocated itself from the concerns of nation. In 1987, writing in the introduction to *A Various Art*, the anthology he edited with Tim Longville, Andrew Crozier opened with the following proposition:

---

[28] Arendt, *Origins of Totalitarianism*, 297.
[29] Arendt, *Origins of Totalitarianism*, 297.
[30] To adjust the terms, what the loss of a polity entails, as Agamben makes clear, is the state of exception; that state in which a person falls outside of all national jurisdictions, into a territory of exclusion in which human rights should, in theory, operate, but in which, in practice, a person's vulnerability is re-exposed.

This anthology represents our joint view of what is most interesting, valuable, and distinguished in the work of a generation of English poets now entering its maturity, but it is not an anthology of English, let alone British poetry... Why, then, make such a distinction, as though the work of English or British poets did not belong to the general category of their national poetry?[31]

Complicated as it is by its various caveats and paradoxes, Crozier's statement requires some contextualization. As an anthology, for all that it represents advanced poetic work, *A Various Art* was compromised by a narrowness of selection: there was only one woman poet included, Veronica Forrest-Thomson; there were no poets from black or minority ethnic groups. This needs saying. It needs saying also that, as an introduction to a body of poetic work, Crozier's statement is remarkable for its reticence. The point of comparison, in this regard, is Donald Allen's groundbreaking anthology *The New American Poetry*, published in 1960.

If there was a single common reference for the different poetries of *A Various Art*, it was Allen's anthology, with its own socially singular but aesthetically radical body of work. As Allen put it,

> These poets... are our avant-garde, the true continuers of the modern movement in American poetry. Through their work many are closely allied to modern jazz and abstract expressionist painting, today recognized throughout the world to be America's greatest achievements in contemporary culture. This anthology makes the same claim for the new American poetry, now becoming the dominant movement in the second phase of our twentieth-century literature and already exerting strong influence abroad.[32]

There are many reasons one can give for the success of *The New American Poetry*, as compared to the limited reach achieved by *A Various Art*. In their ambition of circulating experimental bodies of writing, however, they were comparable projects, and one reason for the greater impact of Allen's book was his willingness to pitch his project in the rhetoric of nation. This is hardly to say that the use of national signifiers would have guaranteed Crozier and Longville a comparable effect; Allen had cultural capital, born of economic capital, on his side.[33] It is to say that, in uncoupling poetry written in England from the national frame, Crozier fully appreciated the implications of his decision.

Crozier's refusal to engage with 'the constructed totalities that represent national culture' had both poetic and political motivation. As he saw it,

---

[31] Andrew Crozier and Tim Longville (eds.), *A Various Art* (Manchester: Carcanet, 1987), 1.

[32] Donald Allen (ed.) *The New American Poetry 1945–1960* (Berkeley and Los Angeles: University of California Press, 1999), pp. xi–xii.

[33] The relation of US cultural capital to economic capital is well documented. In trading on the relation between the New American Poetry and Abstract Expressionism, Allen implicitly drew on the benefits of US government funding for international touring exhibitions of Abstract Expressionist work. See Serge Guilbaut, *How New York Stole the Idea of Modern Art* (Chicago, University of Chicago Press, 1985).

> [T]he frame of reference of national culture and the notion of quality have been brought into uncomplicated mutual alignment, as though the prestige of national origin constituted a claim on the world's attention... The longer this show runs on the less it exhibits the organicism implicit in the notion of a national poetry (however complex and dividedly other the nation has become) and the more it bespeaks new Imperial suitings.[34]

As it gestured towards the recent history of poetry, Crozier's reference here was to *The Penguin Book of Contemporary British Poetry*, the title of which didn't register the fact that some of the poets represented came from elsewhere.[35] The larger and more pressing background, however, was political, Margaret Thatcher's Conservative government of the time having laid claim to the flag. In the face of such a claim, with its belated imperial implications, it would have been difficult to imagine a less viable poetic construction than the one proposed by *Thomas Hardy and British Poetry*, except perhaps the project that one masked, which is to say 'Thomas Hardy and English Poetry'. The real question was, where did the refusal of any such project leave poetry? Crozier put it this way:

> What we claim is both the possibility and presence of such variety, a poetry deployed towards the complex and multiple experience in language of all of us. This is by no means, of course, ever one and the same thing, and the poets collected here will be seen to set their writing towards a range of languages... but their variety and mixture equally point to the important common characteristic of these poets, commitment to the discovery of meaning and form in language itself.[36]

This isn't a rallying cry, but Crozier wasn't at a rally. He was contemplating the difficult question of what it meant to uncouple poetry from the category of nation. Complicated as his statement is, what it speaks to is Arendt's intellectual framework rather than Davie's, where for Arendt it was no longer possible to map responsibility (as Davie had) in terms of state or nation. Thus whereas Davie proposed an account of language and responsibility in which both were made meaningful by the contours and conditioning of a specific geopolitical space, Arendt called for a language of responsibility that recognized the human condition as such. Nor was it just, as she saw it, that a geopolitically curtailed sense of responsibility did not extend readily to the situation of the stateless, but that such a curtailment of responsibility reinforced an image of the polis in which the stateless person could find no place. What mattered for Arendt, as it mattered for Crozier, was that the category of nation should cease to be the default position, that thought and language should not settle so readily on circumscribed geopolitical ground. The question here, as it was for Crozier, is what might such a dislocated poetry look like

---

[34] In Crozier and Longville (eds.), *A Various Art*, 11.

[35] Seamus Heaney famously responded to his inclusion in Morrison and Motion's anthology of British poetry with 'An Open Letter' published by the Field Theatre Company, the letter containing the memorable rebuke: 'Be advised my passport's green. | No glass of ours was ever raised | to toast the Queen.'

[36] In Crozier and Longville (eds.), *A Various Art*, 13–14.

in practice? What does it mean, in other words—in Davie's words—for a poem to read like a good translation from another language?

6. False Memory

Poetry that does not belong to the general category of nation is work in various states of progress. The difficulty of the project can be measured by the caveats and complications of Crozier's statement. In the absence of a claim to national identity it is not immediately apparent how or to whom the poetic utterance makes its appeal. It is a corollary, then, of the breaking of the link between poetry and nation that new readerships have to be constructed. Davie predicted this when he spoke of the isolation of the poet in the imaginary museum, an isolation consequential on the fact of not belonging. What Crozier helps one to understand is what is at stake in the notion of not belonging. Or rather, the question Crozier poses is: what might it mean to construe poetry and affiliation in some other sense? It is a question to which any number of recent and contemporary poets have addressed their work. Among the writers Crozier gathers, one could consider the poetry of Anthony Barnett, Jeremy Prynne, or Veronica Forrest-Thomson in this regard. From the same generation one could also contemplate Michael Grant's recent work, with its response to the demands of translation, or the poetry of Denise Riley with its insistence on the solidarities of intense affective states.[37] Like Grant's work, Simon Smith's writing forges English language poetry out of the translated utterance, his most recent volume, *London Bridge*, fixing itself not to place but to the questions of crossing.[38] The work I want to consider by way of conclusion, though, is Tony Lopez's long poem *False Memory*. In doing so the intention is not to make Lopez representative, nor to freight *False Memory* with all the arguments of this essay. It is to suggest that in that sequence (composed over the course of a decade from the early 1990s till 2003) one finds work deeply engaged with the question of poetry's non-national space.

False Memory is a series of eleven sequences of unrhymed sonnets, the principal though not unvarying unit of composition being the alexandrine. Tonally the work is characterized by what one might call continuousness, where what that implies is a continuity of sound. There is not a voice at work in the poetry but rather a relation to language, the writing having arrived at a mode of composition in which all things, or at least all kinds of language, are allowed through. To make the obvious point, this is not a poetry characterized by a fending-off but is, rather, a structured sequence through which language can be thought to pass. The writing is by no means without its emphases, but those emphases are not the sound of an act of expression and the governing tone is, as it were, the sound of the syntax by which Lopez makes a range of idioms visible. It

---

[37] See Michael Grant, *The First Dream* (London: Perdika Press, 2008) and Denise Riley, *Mop Mop Georgette: New and Selected Poems 1986–1993* (London: Reality Street Editions, 1993).

[38] Simon Smith, *London Bridge* (Cambridge: Salt Publishing, 2010).

is a mode of composition that bears directly on the reading experience. Unlike Anthony Barnett's poetry, say, with its clear requirement that one give pause, Lopez's sequence produces a reading experience characterized by speed. To read *False Memory*, in other words, in its formal consistency and fluency of utterance, is to find oneself somewhat abstracted.

One must be wary, always, of reading too confidently from a formal gesture. Even so, and as with John Ashbery's most uniform long poem 'Fragment', the readerly sense of being somewhat abstracted carries one into the meaning of Lopez's work. What one finds at the level of theme and content in *False Memory* is a reluctance to draw observation to the point of specificity. Thus, though the poetry does make use of place names, and though sometimes (though just as often not) the places named will be English, it is not a sense of place that matters to the poem, just a generalized sense that there is a topography. The second sequence of the poem, 'Studies in Classic American Literature', starts this way:

Walking on the crusty surface, coming back
I heard a voice from way inside saying
'Start as you mean to go on' with calm authority.[39]

In part, the achievement of *False Memory* lies precisely in its handling of what Davie termed diction. Always in the poem, then, the situations we pass through have a particularity. One recognizes them as sites and states one has encountered. Often such situations are in some way militarized, and not infrequently the writing is approaching, or crossing, some kind of border. Topographically, in other words, the poem is sufficiently detailed for us to know that the situations the language presents are real. What the poem declines, even so, is that degree of rhetorical specificity that insists on the uniqueness of any given location. What the language fosters is the impression that a person can come and go.

From the second sequence again, consider the poem at sea:

It's cold, dark, you see lights along the water's edge.
The ship leaves its wake on water and steams on:
It is impossible to explain the meaning of art.
Mist gathers, as if we're already far out to sea
Long after the quotas have gone, fish all fished out.
That is when a man is capable of being in uncertainties
Eliminating large areas of the original image.[40]

It's possible we are approaching Dover, or leaving Dover to approach Calais, or crossing some other stretch of water altogether. What matters here is not naming the coast in question, but *not* naming it. The state of understanding to which the poetry aspires is the capability of being in uncertainties, Keats's great phrase perhaps quoted here by

[39] Tony Lopez, *False Memory* (Cambridge: Salt Publishing, 2003), 11.
[40] Lopez, *False Memory*, 13.

way of Charles Olson, who used it to explain Melville. To be capable of being in uncertainties entails, as the poem does not need to say, a refusal of any irritable reaching after fact. Lopez is categorically not in the tradition of Hardy if, as Davie wanted to argue, Hardy locks poetry into a world of specific times and specific places. The world of *False Memory*, by contrast and in opposition, is only ever a semi-specific environment.

In orienting itself this way towards environment, in its semi-specificity, one of the poets Lopez's poem thinks itself through is Wordsworth. Numerous poets figure in *False Memory*—Keats, Pound, Olson—but the way in which the poem refers to Wordsworth is particularly telling. Thus:

A nuclear reprocessing company
Makes a virtual shepherd working dogs
On a Lakeland hillside. Old head and staff
[Track in and zoom.] Over his shoulder we look down
Where a dog runs on lower ground. Green slopes
Fade to the everlasting universe of things
And the flat plane of the water. The blankness
Makes Patrick Caulfield look prophetic
Because the very blue resists absorption
As in the Luton airport flight simulator.
A passage to the limit in lurid carmine.
Then we go with divers and wavy deep stuff
The issues are remote handling and core values
Right out of Wordsworth's *Guide to the Lakes*.[41]

In the context of this argument about poetry and country, it is significant that the poet Lopez arrives at here is Wordsworth, significant in ways that take us back to Davie; Wordsworth being, as it were, the poet on whom Davie opted not to ground a topographical theory of English poetics. In his own account of Wordsworth, in *Articulate Energy: An Inquiry into the Syntax of English Poetry* (1955), Davie set out clearly why he did not belong to a narrative of poetic place, Wordsworth being, as he put it, a poet of 'fiduciary symbols'. The term is derived from a remark by St John Perse, in which Perse identifies language that tries 'to signify rather than represent the meaning'.[42] Such language, abstract in character, 'uses words...like coins as values of monetary exchange', the word as 'fiduciary symbol' being contrasted in Davie's appropriation of the term, to the ideographic tendency in modern poetry.[43] The distinction itself is dubious, not least as Perse tries to make it the point of difference between French and English. What matters rather is the readerly experience of Wordsworth that Davie uses the term to describe. Thus as Davie sees it:

---

[41] Lopez, *False Memory*, 35.
[42] Donald Davie, *Articulate Energy: An Inquiry into the Syntax of English Poetry* (London: Routledge & Kegan Paul, 1955), 97.
[43] Davie, *Articulate Energy*, 97.

> In those passages in *The Prelude* where Wordsworth is trying to convey most exactly the effect of the natural world upon himself, his words ('ties' and 'bonds' and 'influences' and 'powers') will carry the reader only...so long as he does not loiter, so long as they are taken, as coins are taken, 'as values of monetary exchange'. Wordsworth's words have meanings so long as we trust them.[44]

It follows that Wordsworth's is a poetry in which 'syntax counts for nearly...everything'. Semi-abstracted as it is, *The Prelude* secures itself not by the specificity of its reference to its location, but by the agreement it constructs between poem and reader. It is in the movement of the poetry itself, in other words, that a basis of agreement is established. The point is not to stop and check where we are, but to appreciate that we are in communication, that the poem as an act of a language, not as reference to a specific topography, nor to any circumscribed community, is the starting point for exchange. To which it might be objected that poetry always makes an address, that as an act of language it always implies some kind of reader. To which it might be replied that this is a question of degree: that it is possible to approach the reader, as Lopez does, and as Davie thinks Wordsworth does, as if the poet does not already know them.

None of which is to say that we should read Lopez through Davie, but to suggest a context through which we can read Lopez's engagement with Wordsworth; an engagement that through the colour fields of Patrick Caulfield arrives at an abstracted relation to the land. Hence the end of the sonnet in question: 'The issues are remote handling and core values | Right out of Wordsworth's *Guide to the Lakes*.' The language of the first line here is out of some unspecified document, perhaps a corporate manual of some description; a kind of document that in another poetry might appear degraded. As it appears in Lopez's poetry however—a poetry that feeds relentlessly on such documentary trash—the decontextualized idiom is enabled to speak an important truth. The issues *are* remote handling and core values because in the state of semi-abstraction at which the poem arrives, a different kind of perspective can be conceived. The reading experience is not governed by a relation to place, but is formed by a relation that emerges through the language, where that relation is framed by a series of utterances with which we are only ever partially familiar. What holds the experience of the poem together, in other words, is not a restriction on diction nor a reference back to a specific situation, but the fact that as one reads—in one's reading—a linguistic agreement emerges. *False Memory* is not a poetry that calls on one to settle, nor, certainly, does it ever presume that one is already at home. As the poem is experienced so its various registers, syntactically bound, become a common condition.

---

[44] Davie, *Articulate Energy*, 107.

7. From Dover out

The consequence for the poet of not belonging to the category of nation, as Davie saw it, was that he or she would inevitably become isolated 'from civilization', free, as he put it, of the web of responsibilities that bear on the poet who is tied to a specific place. What Hannah Arendt's commentary on the post-war condition allows one to see is that the question of responsibility can be differently construed. Responding to the consequences of the politics of nation, Arendt insisted on the language of the human condition, as opposed to a language of conditioning, on a language that dealt with the specifics not of place but of being human. What such a language must necessarily seek to articulate is the meaning of not belonging to the category of nation. Tony Lopez offers such an articulation in *False Memory*:

Frantic scenes were witnessed in Utopia
And important news was left out or 'twisted.'
Gazing over the visionary landscape, Joan sees
A brighter cloud from which emerges freedom:
The happy cry is taken up by the crowd—
With slimy shapes and miscreated life. It seems
A racist policeman planted the bloody rag
Giving the precise emotional push off. My eye
Turned westward, shaping in the steady clouds
Thy yellow sands and high white cliffs. O England
Ere from the zephyr-haunted brink I turn...
On the cover was a blonde with a revolver
Falling from a window. When I asked him
The boy replied: 'You just can't believe it.'[45]

We are back, momentarily, at the cliffs at Dover, but only to register the cost of their metonymic relation to England. As in Arnold's poem the scene is fringed by violence, except that here such violence is explicitly connected to the poetic construction of a country, a category to which Lopez's writing has no desire to belong. It is not an easy position to maintain, the rhetoric of country coming so readily to hand in the production of poetry. But as the boy says, when pressed, 'You just can't believe it.' The alternative is a language that does not presuppose that people can or must stay. In its progressive syntax Lopez's writing registers poetry's human responsibilities.

Select Bibliography

Allen, Donald (ed.), *The New American Poetry 1945–1960* (Berkeley and Los Angeles: University of California Press, 1999).
Arendt, Hannah, *The Origins of Totalitarianism* (new edn., London: George Allen and Unwin, 1960).

---

[45] Lopez, *False Memory*, 33.

Arnold, Matthew, *The Poems of Matthew Arnold 1840 to 1867*, introd. A. T. Quiller Couch (Whitefish, Mont.: Kessinger Publishing, 2004).
Auden, W. H., *Another Time* (New York: Random House, 1940).
Bernstein, Charles, *A Poetics* (Cambridge, Mass.: Harvard University Press, 1992).
Crozier, Andrew and Longville, Tim (eds.), *A Various Art* (Manchester: Carcanet, 1987).
Davie, Donald, *Articulate Energy: An Inquiry into the Syntax of English Poetry* (London: Routledge & Kegan Paul, 1955).
Davie, Donald, *The Purity of Diction in English Verse* (London: Routledge & Kegan Paul, 1967).
Davie, Donald, *Thomas Hardy and British Poetry* (London: Routledge & Kegan Paul, 1973).
Davie, Donald, *Collected Poems 1970–1983* (Manchester: Carcanet Press, 1983).
Dekker, George, *Donald Davie and the Responsibilities of Literature* (Manchester: Carcanet Press, 1983).
Grant, Michael, *The First Dream* (London: Perdika Press, 2008).
Guilbaut, Serge, *How New York Stole the Idea of Modern Art* (Chicago, University of Chicago Press, 1985).
Heidegger, Martin, *Basic Writings: Martin Heidegger*, ed. David Farrell Krell (London: Routledge, 1992).
Lopez, Tony, *False Memory* (Cambridge: Salt Publishing, 2003).
Prynne, J. H., *Poems* (Fremantle, WA and Tarset: Fremantle Arts Centre Press and Bloodaxe Books, 2005).
Riley, Denise, *Mop Mop Georgette: New and Selected Poems 1986–1983* (London: Reality Street Editions, 1993).
Smith, Simon, *London Bridge* (Cambridge: Salt Publishing, 2010).

CHAPTER 27

MULTI-ETHNIC BRITISH POETRIES[1]

OMAAR HENA

I. Introduction

'WE are multi-national; cosmopolitan—some of us multi-lingual in ways that encompass and extend beyond the standard-English nation-language debate and have residences on earth which defy the makers of treaties and laws of immigration.'[2] Such are the words of E. A. Markham (1939–2008) in his introduction to *Hinterland: Caribbean Poetry from the West Indies and Britain* (1989). Markham's declaration constitutes just one instance of cosmopolitanism in multi-ethnic poetry: how poets, by mixing and overlaying languages, histories, and geographies in their work, illuminate the tensions and ambiguities of representing their positions as minority subjects with overlapping allegiances within and beyond Britain. Markham, like many of his contemporaries, champions what I am calling a 'minor cosmopolitan poetics' to script what it means to be both 'British' and 'worldly' in the era of cultural globalization.

While black peoples have lived in Britain since the Renaissance, the period of decolonization and mass migration has contributed significantly to the flowering of multi-ethnic poetries, particularly since 1948.[3] The racial transformation of Britain

---

[1] I would like to thank David Sigler for his valuable feedback on this chapter.
[2] E. A. Markham (ed.), *Hinterland: Caribbean Poetry from the West Indies and Britain* (Newcastle upon Tyne: Bloodaxe Books, 1989), 18.
[3] For a long view of the history of black British peoples in literature, see C. L. Innes, *A History of Black Asian Writing in Britain* (Cambridge: Cambridge University Press, 2008). Seminal work on ethnic migration, citizenship, and post-1948 black British culture includes Paul Gilroy, *Whitewashing Britain* (Ithaca, NY and London: Cornell University Press, 1997) and Kathleen Paul, *Whitewashing Britain: Race and Citizenship in the Postwar Era* (Ithaca, NY: Cornell University Press, 1997).

would not be without conflict. With the passage of the British Nationality Act of 1948, any person pledging sovereignty to the Crown and residing beyond the geographic borders of England (Scotland, Wales, Northern Ireland, and Ireland, as well as former British colonies) could enjoy the privileges of British citizenship, including movement to and settlement within Britain. On 21 June of that same year, the MV *Windrush* carried 492 passengers from the Caribbean to Tilbury docks. Fleeing unemployment and poverty at home, the *Windrush* generation aspired to start a new life in the 'motherland' through labour in the industry and public services sector. In the 1950s, Britain would become both economically dependent upon the labour that immigrants provided in jobs not desired (or taken) by whites and socially averse to the presence of racial others within Britain's borders.[4] These tensions would erupt in a series of race riots in Notting Hill and Nottingham in 1958 and the tightening of immigration laws and rights. For instance, the Commonwealth Immigrant Act (1962) restricted immigration to those with employment vouchers. Over the course of the following three decades, Parliament took steps to curb immigration and consolidate the meaning of Britishness amidst its inevitable transformation. After Enoch Powell warned that increased immigration would culminate in 'Rivers of Blood' (1968), Parliament passed the Immigration Act of 1971. The Act asked applicants 'where were you born?' and 'who were your ancestors?' so as to grant privilege of movement and residency to white Britons abroad and born within the UK, over darker, post-colonial others who were deemed less than 'British'. On the ground, the boundary between 'black' and 'British' became sharper during the volatile 1970s through police raids on predominantly black communities and the use of 'sus' (suspect) laws. In the run-up to the 1979 election, the Tory candidate Margaret Thatcher worried that the nation would be 'swamped' by peoples of colour. Under Thatcher, Parliament passed the British Nationality Act (1981) which redefined British citizenship not through the shifting borders of allegiance and place (the *ius soli*) but through the stricter boundaries of parentage and race. In effect, the 1981 Nationality Act draws a sharp distinction between people who are born from extant British citizens or residents living in the UK and those who are born elsewhere, and hence other-than-British. Currently, in order for a person to count as a British citizen, at least one parent must already hold citizenship or permanent residence in the UK. In theory, according to Ian Baucom, the 1981 Nationality Act 'sought to defend the "native" inhabitants of the island against the claims of their former subjects by defining Britishness as an inheritance of race', making Britain above all 'a genealogical community'.[5]

Genealogical communities are, as with almost everything, imagined. This essay examines how multi-ethnic poets have dispersed Britain, producing poetic and cultural

---

[4] Bruce King, *The Oxford English Literary History*, xiii. 1948–2000: *The Internationalization of English Literature* (Oxford: Oxford University Press, 2004), 17. King's work provides an excellent overview of black British writing.

[5] Ian Baucom, *Out of Place* (Princeton: Princeton University Press, 1999), 8. See also Simon Gikandi, *Maps of Englishness* (New York: Columbia University Press, 1996) on the debate over post-colonial Englishness.

genealogies that speak to their hybrid experiences of belonging.[6] Black British poets, as Jahan Ramazani eloquently argues, exploit 'the musical, tonal, and imagistic richness of poetry [...] to reimagine themselves as both "rooted and routed" in and through London to Africa and the Caribbean—living and writing, like other transnational poets, between styles, between histories, between hemispheres'.[7] Their far-reaching poetic creations defiantly 'expose, for all Britons', in the words of John McLeod, 'the criss-crossings, the comings and goings, the transnational influences, which arguably inform the construction of all texts and canons that bear the signature "British" '.[8] Mine here is similarly an argument for reading multi-ethnic British writing attuned to its cosmopolitan poetics, debating the linkages between cosmopolitanism and Britishness. Following in the wake of Rebecca Walkowitz's claim for a 'critical cosmopolitanism' informing British literature from the modern to the contemporary era, I also posit that cosmopolitanism and Britishness need not be seen as opposed but, as heuristic concepts, can be understood to be deeply interwoven and co-constitutive.[9]

Three guiding questions frame my discussion: first, how might a reconsideration of E. A. Markham illuminate the complex interplay of aesthetics and politics in multi-ethnic British poetries generally? Secondly, through what strategies of poetic representation have later multi-ethnic poets (here, I consider Lemn Sissay, Patience Agbabi, and Daljit Nagra) contributed to the making and remaking of Britishness? And third, how does this group of poets reveal the exclusivity of the discourses tethered to race and nation, and, meanwhile, invent new models of British belonging through a cosmopolitan poetics that includes the perspectives of ethnic minorities? While this chapter is by no means exhaustive, my hope is that the insights gleaned from the poets under consideration here will bear upon other first-generation, migrant poets including Una Marson, Louise Bennett, James Berry, Mikey Smith, and Valerie Bloom up through second-generation, British-born poets such as Benjamin Zephaniah, Jackie Kay, Moniza Alvi, and Bernardine Evaristo. Throughout, I contend that, within a British context, the question of geographic emplacement is inseparable from the problem of British literary, poetic emplacement. Many multi-ethnic poets show how the political contradictions and social ambivalences of Britishness are inherent in the uneven tradition of English-language poetry itself, from the colonial to the global era. What's more, though, by moulding and adapting the canon, infusing it with hybrid languages, hyphenated experiences, and multiple geographic attachments, contemporary multi-ethnic British poetries make manifest the cosmopolitan constitution of British literature more broadly.

---

[6] On the contemporary literature and post-colonial Britain, see John McLeod, *Postcolonial London: Rewriting the Metropolis* (London: Routledge, 2004); Kadija Sisay (ed.), *Write Black, Write British* (London: Hansib, 2005); Paul Gilroy, *Postcolonial Melancholia* (New York: Columbia University Press, 2005); and Ashley Dawson, *Mongrel Nation* (Ann Arbor: University of Michigan Press, 2007).

[7] Jahan Ramazani, *A Transnational Poetics* (Chicago: University of Chicago Press, 2009), 180.

[8] John McLeod, 'Fantasy Relationships: Black British Canons in a Transnational World', in Gail Low and Marion Wynne Davies (eds.), *A Black British Canon?* (London and New York: Palgrave, 2006), 102.

[9] Rebecca Walkowitz, *Cosmopolitan Style: Modernism Beyond the Nation* (New York: Columbia University Press, 2006), 2–5, 17–19.

II. Minor Cosmopolitanism in E. A. Markham and His Contemporaries

Cosmopolitanism is, of course, a hotly contested term in post-colonial studies.[10] In his essay, 'Comparative Cosmopolitanisms', Bruce Robbins returns the reader to the etymological root of the word 'cosmopolitanism': '*Cosmos* (world) in *cosmopolitan* originally meant simply "order" or "adornment"—as in cosmetics—and was only later extended metaphorically to refer to "the world". Cosmetics preceded totality. Worlding, then, might be seen as "making up" the face of the planet—something that can be done in diverse ways.'[11] The inventiveness and adornments of poetry and poetic language are instances of cosmopolitanism. Poetry too foregrounds how descriptions of the world are fundamentally mediated through language—and with it figuration, metaphor, comparison, substitution, association, synecdoche, and the commingling and juxtaposition of signs that may not at first belong together but share the same discursive space or field. Interpreting cosmopolitanism from a specifically poetic perspective shifts the reader's attention to the properties of textuality: seen in this way, cosmopolitanism is not an ideal state of being but a discursive construct that is made and remade, and hence open to multiple and competing iterations.

The paradox of 'minor cosmopolitanism' functions as follows: multi-ethnic British poetries appeal to cosmopolitan ideals of political freedom, an ethics of human worth and dignity, and the invention of identities through cross-cultural affiliations within and beyond the nation. At the same time, however, multi-ethnic poets, by virtue of their being perceived as foreigners in what is often represented as an unwelcome host country, also emphasize continuing forms of inequality, discrimination, and injustice. This double bind gives rise to heterogeneous symbologies that serve to enunciate cosmopolitan belonging in Britain. The 'minor' of minor cosmopolitanism, as is evident, highlights how minority poets refashion Britishness. But it is also meant to contrast with major cosmopolitan thought and its conventional associations with its white, European, imperial, and largely masculine philosophical derivations. Minor cosmopolitanism—smaller scale in its focus, marginal and peripheral in its orientation, and at times dissonant and estranging in its aesthetic—retains an abiding commitment to democratic worldliness

---

[10] Critical discourse on post-colonial cosmopolitanism is vast. See Homi Bhabha, 'Unsatisfied: Notes on Vernacular Cosmopolitanism', in Laura Garcia-Moreno and Peter C. Pfeiffer (eds.), *Text and Nation: Cross-Disciplinary Essays on Cultural and National Identities* (Columbia, SC: Camden House, 1996), 191–207; James Clifford, *Routes: Travel and Translation in the Late Twentieth Century* (Cambridge, Mass.: Harvard University Press, 1997); Kwame Anthony Appiah, *Cosmopolitanism: Ethics in a World of Strangers* (New York: Norton, 2006); Pheng Cheah, *Inhuman Conditions: On Cosmopolitanism and Human Rights* (Cambridge, Mass.: Harvard University Press, 2007).

[11] Bruce Robbins, 'Comparative Cosmopolitanisms', in Bruce Robbins and Pheng Cheah (eds.), *Cosmopolitics: Thinking and Feeling Beyond the Nation* (Minneapolis: University of Minnesota Press, 1998), 253.

while simultaneously expressing anxious discontent over continuing forms of inequality that inhibit human flourishing in levels that could be national, sub-national, or post-national.

Consider for instance Linton Kwesi Johnson's (LKJ) 'It Dread Inna Inglan':

rite now,
African
Asian
West Indian
an Black British
stan firma inna Inglan
inna disya time yah
far noh mattah wat dey say,
come wat may,
we are here to stay
inna Ingan,
inna disya time yah...[12]

The poem's staccato rhythms, sonic repetitions, and experimental orthography combine with a catalogue of multi-ethnic groupings to inscribe a politics of solidarity (a 'rite' that is paronomastically immediate, political, and ritualized) against assumptions that people from elsewhere are un-English. Many multi-ethnic poets, including LKJ, moreover self-consciously perform (and capitalize upon) cultural difference, whether on the page or on the stage, to contest models of Britishness premised upon ethnic purity and Standard English. Consider also John Agard's now widely anthologized and performed 'Listen Mr. Oxford Don' whose speaker 'making de Queen's English accessory | to my offense'.[13] In other instances, multi-ethnic poets formally symbolize migration and settlement by appropriating the canon, as when Jean Binta Breeze exuberantly rewrites Chaucer in 'The Wife of Bath Speaks in Brixton Market', or when Patience Agbabi grafts the same tale onto a Nigerian woman's social experiences in 'The Wife of Bafa'.[14] Multi-ethnic poets repeatedly question who and what 'counts' as British in the social and poetic spheres. Yet they do so through the ineluctable performance of identity, thus evading national or multicultural imperatives to represent a pure or stable ethnic self. The performative aspect of identity categories makes legible how such categories (whether national, minoritarian, or otherwise) are, at root, imagined fictions that are repeatedly 'put on', thereby disputing the notion that any one person or group solely owns or inhabits a culture. Performances of identity, in short, disrupt the presumed coherence of Britishness, reshaping it into the malleable construct that it already is and thus making it capable of taking on new cultural and political significations.[15]

---

[12] Linton Kwesi Johnson, *Selected Poems* (London: Penguin Books, 2006), 25.
[13] John Agard, *Alternative Anthem: Selected Poems* (Northumberland: Bloodaxe Books, 2009), 16.
[14] Jean Binta Breeze, *The Arrival of Brighteye and Other Poems* (Newcastle upon Tyne: Bloodaxe Books, 2000), 62–4; Patience Agbabi, *Transformatrix* (Edinburgh: Payback Press, 2000), 28–9.
[15] On the genre of performance poetry in Britain, see Carolyn Cooper, 'Words Unbroken by the Beat: The Performance Poetry of Mikey Smith and Jean Binta Breeze', *Wasafiri*, 11 (Spring 1990), 7–13; and Nicky Marsh, ' "Peddlin Noh Puerile Parchment of Etnicity": Questioning Performance in New Black British Poetry', *Wasafiri*, 45 (Summer 2005), 46–51.

Cross-cultural identifications, linguistic contaminations, masked personae, and ceaseless reimaginings of the canon: these comprise some of the central aesthetic features of multi-ethnic British poetries and its minor cosmopolitanism. All of these features can be located within the life and work of E. A. Markham. While the foundational figures of Marson, Bennett, Berry, and John La Rose have received considerable critical attention, E. A. Markham has been largely overlooked in scholarship.[16] This may be due to his more indirect handling of race and post-coloniality. His formalism and clear indebtedness to the tradition of Anglo-European letters also distinguish him from poets writing more squarely in vernacular, performance, or dub styles. Moreover, he tends to subordinate the mainstay political and social themes of British multi-ethnic writing (diaspora, racial exclusion, belonging, and so forth) to a scrupulous attention to poetics. Markham, though, provides a rich case study for reading the cross-cultural energies animating multi-ethnic poetry more broadly.

Like other minority British writers but perhaps even more so, Markham's life is punctuated by a series of migrations. His travels have spanned the Caribbean, England, Wales, France, Papua New Guinea, and Northern Ireland. He was writer in residence at Sheffield Hallam University (1991–2005) before spending his final years in Paris, where he died suddenly in 2008. Born in Montserrat in 1939, Markham arrived in England in 1958 where he worked in the 'rag trade' by sewing ladies' belts and accessories for two years in London's West End.[17] Humorously looking back to this period in his life in his essay 'Taking the Drawing Room Through Customs', he says that he had briefly imagined himself 'as head of a leather and suede empire, belting women—average waist twenty-two inches—from Canada to Nigeria'.[18] I mention this sartorial anecdote because of the prevalence of role-playing across Markham's poetry. In fact, his first collections were authored under the noms de plume 'Paul St Vincent' (who himself took on the persona of 'Lambchops', a traveling Caribbean everyman who often speaks in dialect) and 'Sally Goodman', a white, middle-class English housewife and feminist. Many of these poems are collected in *Living in Disguise* (1986) and *Lambchops with Sally Goodman* (2004).[19] Markham frequently switches racial and gender identities, using masks to show the constitutive fluidity and hybridity of all identity formations. But his

---

[16] Overviews of black British poetry include Fred D'Aguiar, 'Have You Been Here Long? Black Poetry in Britain', in Robert Hampson and Peter Barry (eds.), *New British Poetries: The Scope of the Possible* (Manchester and New York: Manchester University Press, 1993), 51–71; Alastair Niven, 'Bass History is A-Moving: Black Men's Poetry in England', in James Acheson and Romana Huk (eds.), *Contemporary British Poetry* (Albany, NY: SUNY Press, 1996), 293–314; C. L. Innes, 'Accent and Identity: Women Poets of Many Parts', in Acheson and Huk (eds.), *Contemporary British Poetry*, 315–41; Romana Huk, 'In AnOther's Pocket: The Address of the "Pocket Epic" in Postmodern Black British Poetry', *Yale Journal of Criticism*, 13/1 (2000), 23–47; Lauri Ramey, 'Contemporary Black British Poetry', in R. Victoria Arana and Ramey (eds.), *Black British Writing* (New York: Palgrave, 2004), 109–36; John McLeod, 'Fantasy Relationships'; and Ramazani, *Transnational Poetics*, 163–80.

[17] E. A. Markham, *A Rough Climate* (London: Anvil Press, 2002), 91.

[18] Markham, *A Rough Climate*, 103.

[19] See E. A. Markham, *Living in Disguise* (London: Anvil Press, 1986) and *Lambchops with Sally Goodman* (Cambridge: Salt Publishing, 2004).

use of ironic personae that occasionally speak in dialect also ground him in the enduring context of African and Afro-Caribbean oral folklore such as Anancy (or Anansi), which travelled across the Atlantic at the time of the African slave trade. Anancy, the West African spider god and trickster figure known for his verbal ingenuity and linguistic deceit and cunning, has been popularized across a range of genres from children's stories to the poetry of Bennett and Grace Nichols. Anancy also appears in an early poem, 'To My Mother, the Art Critic' and provides yet another layer of disguise through which Markham encodes the slipperiness of racial politics for someone living between worlds.[20]

The dramatic qualities of Markham's work derive, though, not from poetry but theatre. His earliest writings began in plays, including his audaciously titled *The Masterpiece* (1964) performed at St David's University College in Lampeter, Wales, where Markham read English and philosophy. During the 1960s, Markham wrote tirelessly and attempted, unsuccessfully, to have his plays produced while continuing to take courses in East Anglia and the University of London. At this same time, he became more involved in the London art world. He befriended and lived with theatre critic John Elsom. He frequented poetry readings at Avatar in Kensington, and came to know John La Rose and Sarah White, whose New Beacon Bookshop became the most important publisher of Caribbean, African, and Latin American writing in Britain. La Rose and the New Beacon introduced Markham to many of the key texts of Caribbean literature and culture by Jean Rhys, Derek Walcott, Earl Lovelace, Wilson Harris, and George Lamming.

Significantly, Markham encountered Caribbean literature belatedly and, for him, it marked both a homecoming and a departure. Even while acutely aware of imperial stereotypes about Caribbean identity and history, Markham does not relate to his former home as a space of loss, explaining that 'there was no particular trauma in leaving [Montserrat] behind'.[21] Nevertheless, Markham did find himself caught between worlds and forced to negotiate the meaning of 'black' and 'British'. Against the pressures of racial stereotypes in the 1960s, 1970s, and 1980s, he identifies with the necessity to represent and retrieve Caribbean cultures and histories, finding his reflection in the words of John La Rose: 'They [the British] lie about you. They pretend to speak for you and they lie about you.'[22] Hence he was a strong promoter of Caribbean literature and art across a range of institutions and venues. Collaborating with La Rose, Kamau Brathwaite, and Andrew Salkey in the Caribbean Arts Movement (1966–72), he also spent 1970–1 in the West Indies acting as the director of the Caribbean Theatre Workshop.[23] In the 1980s and 1990s, Markham was also a patron saint for promoting Caribbean poetry and short fiction through his various editorial projects, including the journals *Ambit* and *ArtRage*

---

[20] E. A. Markham, *Looking Out, Looking In: New and Selected Poems* (London: Anvil Press, 2009), 28.
[21] Markham, *Looking Out, Looking In*, 91.
[22] Markham, *Looking Out, Looking In*, 94.
[23] On the Caribbean Arts Movement, see Anne Walmsley, *The Caribbean Artists Movement 1966–1972: A Literary and Cultural History* (London: New Beacon Books, 1992).

as well as anthologies of poetry and short fiction, such as *Hinterland* (1989) and *The Penguin Book of Caribbean Short Stories* (1995). Multi-ethnic British poetry has enjoyed increasing visibility thanks to numerous anthologies, publishing houses, and the Arts Council England, about which I will have a brief word in the conclusion of this chapter. As an editor, Markham is also to be credited for making black and Asian British artists visible and audible in the 1980s and 1990s.

And yet Markham's relationship to Caribbean experience significantly differs from those modelled upon nation language or resistant 'writing back'. From his perspective in the 1970s and 1980s, 'West Indians and West Indianness were defined in terms of lack or absence, or being on the periphery. That was OK, that was fine; true in a sense, though all these things together might not be accurate. The problem was what this was being defined against. Against England. Britain. Against an outdated idea of Englishness, preserved by us [West Indians]'.[24] Markham's early education and reading was steeped in the Western tradition. His grandmother's drawing room in Montserrat contained the classics, from the Bible and John Bunyan to Jonathan Swift and a history of Sinn Fein. Later in his life, Markham lived in Northern Ireland working as writer in residence at the University of Ulster in Coleraine (1988–91), thus deepening his affinity with Irish culture and literature in his work. At university, Markham scored top marks in ancient history, Latin, English, and Italian. As an adult in London, he was as enamoured of kitchen-sink drama as he was of avant-garde experimentation in the works of Beckett and Ionesco. This is to emphasize that Markham's upbringing led him to relate to the canon and to the many places he lived with generosity and flexibility. And it is an attitude that becomes accentuated among the younger generation of multi-ethnic British poets, as I will later show.

Across his career, Markham plays with and seeks a way out of totalizing notions of Britishness and Caribeanness that, to him, perpetuate division and that do not match up to the complexity of multi-ethnic belonging. Consider for instance an early poem, 'Roots, Roots' (1984):

My grandmother's donkey had a name
I can't recall. It's not important
for the donkey, a beast of burden
like my grandmother, is dead.
And I am in a different place.

Perhaps the donkey was a horse, a status symbol
or a man, married to my grandmother;
and he lives on with my name.
But then, suppose there was no donkey,
no grandmother, no other place?[25]

---

[24] Markham, *A Rough Climate*, 99.
[25] Markham, *Looking Out, Looking In*, 76.

'Roots, Roots' incites the reader's expectations that the speaker will claim his Caribbean cultural origins after migration to 'a different place'. There are several features of this poem that make it characteristic of Markham's work as a whole. First, the poem exhibits a profound awareness of the demands of a multi-ethnic poet to perform roots, especially at its historical moment in the early 1980s amidst the prominence of Brathwaite's epic trilogy of Caribbean roots and LKJ's dub performances. And yet, despite these demands from within both black British and white British audiences, Markham shrouds himself in disguise. Whatever roots may feed into the poem's creation are withheld, both from the speaking subject ('I can't recall') and the reader who must suspect that they are being led on, if not duped by, Markham's persona. Secondly, the poem's apparent send-up of the demand to perform ethnic identity (as registered through ironic detachment, evasiveness, understatement) belies a muted acknowledgement of the centrality of making and claiming roots precisely *because* of their loss. The supposed non-importance of forgetting of the donkey's name, which is associated with the personal loss of his grandmother, accrues acute significance here through the fact of death and the loss of cultural origins by virtue of dislocation: 'And I am in a different place.' In other words, the poem displays a contradictory relationship to roots, representing them as both confining and necessary to poetic creation. Thirdly, and most importantly, the singularity of the poetic creates new personae, new 'roots' in order to forestall discourses that would seek to fix identity to one geographic location, ethnic make-up, or temporality. Consider the formal symmetry, for instance, between the stanzas. Whereas the first stanza makes declarative statements about roots and their loss, the second shifts into the domain of hypothesis, culminating in a rhetorical question that ironically contradicts the poem's entire project of retrieving origins. And yet, both stanzas mirror one another through the recurrent words 'grandmother', 'donkey', 'name', and crucially 'place'. Markham here displays how declarative statements of roots occur retroactively and, hence, are prone to qualification ('Perhaps'), conjecture ('But then, suppose...'), and undercutting ('no donkey, | no grandmother, no other place'). Markham's controlled experimentation with enjambment, lineation, syntax, and simile all contribute to the poem's abiding tension: that even as the speaker creates the illusion of excavating familial-cultural origins, such excavations are bound to fail. But this failure succeeds in confronting the textual processes of composing identities that occupy multiple 'places' within the discursive space of poetry. Multi-ethnic poetry reveals and conceals the fictive presence of 'roots' that are never single or singular but can only be asserted through repetition and figuration: 'Roots, Roots'.

With his writing, Markham wishes 'to penetrate [his] layers of protective skin. I write simply—and it's not simple—to make myself more human'.[26] His disguises constitute his way of 'making up' (to borrow from Robbins once more) a cosmopolitan identity that is not transcendent from but embedded in and splayed across disparate places. As Markham puts it: 'It seemed short sighted to use England as the only, or main, frame of

---

[26] Markham, *A Rough Climate*, 103.

reference when trying to bring the West Indies into focus. So I vary the frame of reference.'[27] The frames of reference multiply as his career matures and, importantly, as his passport accumulates visas. Consider a later poem entitled 'Hinterland' (1993) composed during his time in Ulster.[28] Living in rainy Portrush, the speaker draws an unlikely, even possibly taboo, comparison between his transnational travels and a wet dream. The poem catalogues a series of migrations, which begins with his early childhood 'fear | Of stretching out a foot from Montserrat | and falling into the sea', to his travels to France, Germany, 'spray-white Sweden', then to Papua New Guinea ('its gift too close to dreams | for waking comfort'), and finally London which he compares to 'a parents' | home from which to rebel'. The poem concludes, though, not in London but back in Portrush, which he describes as 'here, on the edge | Of the edge', a line whose enjambment points self-referentially to the hinterland of the poetic text. The 'hinterland' of Portrush (which seems peripheral in comparison to the European centres listed) folds into the hinterland of the poem and of poetry. The final lines read:

> I pray to the familiar
> In my suitcase, in my head: I have
> Explored the world, tasted its strangeness,
> Resisted and colluded out of strength,
> Out of weakness, failed to colonize it
> With family tongue or name. Are you pleased
> Secretly, with a frown pulling down on relief?
> The treasures I carry in my head fail
> To match the refuse in my case.
> But it will do, and the dreams tonight
> To douse a fear, will perhaps be wet.

What are the symbolic resonances of the conceit of the wet dream when seen as a figure for cosmopolitan attachment? It might signify the uncontrollable anxieties and desires of living between worlds, of realizing in some corporeal way that the fecundity of human experience (let's call it 'cosmopolitanism') cannot be contained in suitcases, memories, nations, bodies, or words.

Poetry, as Markham expresses, can render 'the hinterland of an experience | Still to be reclaimed'.[29] Elsewhere in *Misapprehensions* (1995), Markham makes implicit comparisons between Caribbean migrants and the more recent influx of peoples from Eastern Europe and sub-Saharan Africa, as in the poems titled 'Turkey', 'Yugoslavia', and 'Bosnia, Rwanda'.[30] The range of topographic signifiers alone testifies to the capaciousness of Markham's imaginative identifications with others whose experiences, however necessarily different from his own, find corollaries in his poetic universe. In short, Markham's cosmopolitanism is not a withdrawal from politics into aesthetics. Nor is it

---

[27] Markham, *A Rough Climate*, 102.
[28] E. A. Markham, *Letter from Ulster & the Hugo Poems* (Lancashire: Littlewood Arc, 1993), 11–12.
[29] Markham, *Letter from Ulster & the Hugo Poems*, 11.
[30] E. A. Markham, *Misapprehensions* (London: Anvil Press, 1995).

transcendence from the particular histories and places that have shaped his poetry. Nor is it reducible to a symptom of privilege and learnedness. It is instead a tactic for circumventing exclusionary discourses (whether of empire, nation, race, class, or gender) that attempt to render static what are, in truth, hybrid identities and subjects whose cultural affiliations span multiple languages, geographies, and histories.

III. Globalizing Britishness: Lemn Sissay, Patience Agbabi, Daljit Nagra

The minor cosmopolitanism that distinguishes Markham and his contemporaries accelerates and intensifies among the younger generation of multi-ethnic poets, including Bernardine Evaristo, Moniza Alvi, Lemn Sissay, Patience Agbabi, and Daljit Nagra. Continuing to highlight the racial exclusions underpinning the imperial legacy of Britishness, these poets route Britishness through other spaces, transnationally and globally. What's more, by reinventing the canon, they often raise questions of race, ethnic migration, diaspora, and belonging, marking literary history as a conflictual and open space in which one can locate more heterogeneous conceptions of Britishness.

The act of reimagining Britain as an unbound genealogical community cuts across all multi-ethnic poetry. But it is particularly urgent, and personal, for Ethiopian-British poet Lemn Sissay. Sissay was born in Billange in 1967 to Yemarshat Sissay, who left Addis Ababa to study in Oxfordshire. Yemarshat Sissay would, however, be raped by Sissay's father, Gides Stephanos, who worked as a pilot for Ethiopian Airlines and later died in a crash. Soon after his birth, Sissay was adopted by a Baptist family who renamed him Norman Mark Greenwood, and scorned him as a child of the Devil. During his adolescent years, Sissay moved from one foster care institution to another in Lancashire and suffered recurrent racism. It was not until he was 18 that the government—'no longer my parent, my legal guardian' as he says—released to Sissay his birth certificate and a letter from his mother written in 1968.[31] The birth certificate revealed his given birth-name. The letter from his mother pleaded, in what must have felt like a painfully ironic twist: 'How can I get Lemn back? [...] I want him to be with his own people, in his own country. I don't want him to face discrimination.'[32]

For Sissay, writing poetry has been a therapeutic process to make sense to himself of what it means to both 'British' and 'black', to create for himself the familial roots in art that had been severed in his early life. To date, Sissay has published four collections of poetry: *Tender Fingers in a Clenched Fist* (1988), *Rebel Without Applause* (1992),

---

[31] Lemn Sissay, *Listener* (Edinburgh: Canongate, 2008), 99.
[32] Sissay, *Listener*, 99. Sissay's television documentary, *Internal Flight* (BBC: 1995), and his play, *Something Dark* (published in Deirdre Osborne, *Hidden Gems* (London: Oberon Books, 2009)), movingly recount his search for familial roots.

Morning Breaks in the Elevator (1999), and *Listener* (2008). Sissay's creative output, his promotion of other black artists, and his involvement in publishing across a range of venues and media certainly align him with Markham. What's more, since the 1990s his project of 'Poems as Landmarks' has brought his verse off the page to public spaces in Manchester and London. At present, Sissay is associate artist at the Southbank Centre. In 2010 he became a Member of the Order of the British Empire; he was the first to be named a 'Commissioned Poet' for the 2012 Olympics in London.

Sissay's oeuvre is doubly marked by deep-seated rage over the contradictions of inclusion and exclusion in global Britain and by an exuberant celebration of poetic invention. For instance, in *Rebel Without Applause* his poems on racial violence formally range from rap in 'Gunshot' to prose poems in 'Can You Locate Planet Ethnic?', and concrete poetry in 'Flushed';[33] *Listener* contains riddles and word games in 'Erratic Equipoise' whose series of first letters spell 'P-O-L-I-C-E'.[34] The melding of poetic form and political critique is perhaps best emblematized in Sissay's poetic manifesto 'Bearing Witness':

Bearing witness to the hour
where maladjusted power
realigns its crimes in token signs
then perversely repents with self-punishment.

Bearing witness to the times
where black people define
the debt yet to be paid, you bet
I'll be rhyming the fact when I witness that.[35]

Through intricate internal and end rhyme, 'Bearing Witness' offers poetic discourse as recompense for the 'token signs' of political programmes of development or multicultural assimilation. But despite its romantic belief in the poetic, 'Bearing Witness' also imbricates itself in economic metaphors of transaction and debt collecting. That is, the poem bears witness to itself, as if to say that while poetry may amount to little more than 'token signs' and 'self-punishment' the work of bearing witness to historical injustice remains incomplete and hence belongs to the sovereign domain of poetic *technē*. In 'A Black Man on the Isle of Wight', Sissay mutes his anger through Imagistic techniques of sharp language, metaphoric defamiliarization, and direct treatment of the thing: here, the objectified black body that is compared to ecological elements:

Faces cold as the stones stuck
to the sea's belly
with seaweed for hair
sculpted expressions of fear.[36]

---

[33] Sissay, *Rebel Without Applause* (Newcastle upon Tyne: Bloodaxe Books, 1992), 52, 59, 40.
[34] Sissay, *Listener*, 27.
[35] Sissay, *Rebel*, 11.
[36] Sissay, *Rebel*, 42.

Even as Sissay sculpts the fear of non-belonging, his radio play in verse, 'The Queen's Speech' (commissioned by BBC Radio 4), enunciates a radiant vision of British inclusion, one which would reverse the patterns of colonization by opening itself up to all:

Let them throw down their seeds and let freedom flower.
Let them speak their own language as we speak ours,
So that we might learn the language of tone and trust,
The blessed language of body and the face—the language of us.
The language of listening. [...]

Let the knots of history come undone.
Let your people finish what you begun.
Let us open our arms as they did—Let them come.[37]

Here in the play's concluding speech, Sissay takes on the persona of 'Rabbi Hattenstone', an immigrant born in 1926, the same year as Queen Elizabeth II. The refrain, 'Let them come', performatively espouses an ethics of unconditional hospitality to migrant others. Such a vision of global Britishness is admittedly utopian. But the poetics of the play—its incantatory anaphora and jussive mood 'let us'—hold out a yet-to-be-fulfilled promise of what Britain could become, not to rectify past wrongs but to reimagine a usable past for the sake of building a more equal future.

The transformation of identities that cross races, classes, genders, and spaces comes to relief in the work of Nigerian-British poet Patience Agbabi. Born in 1965, she grew up during the difficult Thatcher years. Like Sissay, Agbabi was raised by white, English foster-parents in Sussex and mid-Wales while intermittently seeing her Nigerian parents. Also like Sissay, she works in both written and performance poetic media. She has published three collections to date: *R. A. W.* (1995), an acronym for 'rhythm and word' and winner of the Excelle Literary Award (1997), *Transformatrix* (2000), and *Bloodshot Monochrome* (2008). She has toured worldwide both individually and with performance groups including Atomic Lip (1995–8) and the spoken-word ensemble Modern Love (2002). In addition to numerous lectureships, most recently at University of Kent, Canterbury (2004–5), she has also held several residencies including one at a London tattoo parlour, Flamin' Eight (1999), where her poems were inscribed on human skin, and another at Eton College (2005) where she organized the institution's first poetry slam. In 2010 Agbabi was distinguished as Canterbury Poet Laureate.

Poetry, for Agbabi, gives expression to her multiple selves and worlds. In many poems, her speakers express the angst of non-belonging, of slipping between the cracks of black and British categories. In 'Serious Pepper' she describes her self-divisions as 'Too Black Too White | in limbo on the edge', and goes on to split her lyric 'I' through phonemic alterations, homonymic substitutions, and punning portmanteau:

I was disperate
    disparate
        diasporate[38]

---

[37] Sissay, *Rebel*, 97–8.
[38] Patience Agbabi, *R.A.W.* (London: Gecko Press, 1995), 15.

Besides being Nigerian-black-British and female Agbabi's 'diasporate' identity also extends to her bisexuality. She uses formal experimentations to pattern the prohibitive discourses of racism, sexism, and homophobia and to write her way out of them through wit and irony. In the sonnet 'Transformatrix', the dark female speaker addresses her muse, a dominatrix, all the while reversing and replaying Shakespeare's 'Dark Lady' sequence:

A pen poised over a blank page, I wait
for madam's orders, her strict consonants
and the spaces between words, the silence.
She's given me a safe word, a red light
but I'm breaking the law, on a death wish,
ink throbbing my temples, each vertebra
straining for her fingers. She trusses up
words, lines, as a corset disciplines flesh.[39]

For Agbabi, bodily and formal constraints are generative of desire and poetic invention, alike. Indeed, if there is anywhere Agbabi 'belongs' it may well be in the vexed and divided terrain of the canon, a bequest of her undergraduate education in English literature and language at Pembroke College, Oxford, and her MA in creative writing at Sussex (2002). Her recent collection, *Bloodshot Monochrome*, contains two sonnet sequences ('Problem Pages' and 'Vicious Circle'), a sestina ('Skin'), and rewritings of Wordsworth ('The London Eye') and Milton ('Coming Down').[40] Even rap-inflected poems that may appear antagonistic towards the history of British letters belie their praise. Consider 'Rappin It Up':

Because I'm rappin it up in a real tight squeeze
I don't cross my i's   I don't dot my t's
Shakespeare   Milton   Pope and Dryden
Wordsworth Eliot Great Tradition
all you poets I don't give a fuck
coz you're dead   I am PA an I am RAPPIN IT UP[41]

Evocative of Public Enemy's Chuck D and Queen Latifah (two of her key influences), Agbabi shreds up the texts of dead white males but only to affirm that same tradition. Placing her initials at the end of a long line of proper names (metonymies for British poetry), she punningly 'wraps up' the canon and, in doing so, extends it. The speaker's 'real tight squeeze' self-reflectively refers to the constraints of the sestet itself. Agbabi's reinvention of the poetic tradition is the signature of her individual talent.

In other poems, though, Agbabi adopts a planetary subject-position to elude territorial belonging. In her widely popular 'Ufo Woman', Agbabi playfully takes on the voice of a

---

[39] Agbabi, *Transformatrix*, 78.
[40] Patience Agbabi, *Bloodshot Monochrome* (Edinburgh: Canongate, 2008).
[41] Agbabi, *R.A.W.*, 63.

Nigerian whose transnational movements between Lagos and London transform her into an alien to both cultures:

They call me Ufo woman, oyinbo
from the old days which translates as weirdo,
white, outsider, other, and I withdraw

into myself, no psychedelic shield,
no chameleonic façade, just raw.
Then I process Ufo and U F O,
realise the former is a blessing:
the latter a curse. I rename myself
Ufo Woman and touch base at Heath Row.

[...]

Call me, I'll be surfing the galaxy
searching for that perfect destination.[42]

Despite the 'curse' of being labelled alien, Agbabi translates herself into a time-travelling planetary subject capable of renaming the scripts of globalization to her own needs and desires. But if 'Ufo Woman' celebrates an intergalactic mobile identity against the static territories of nation states, this is a distinctly ironic self-fashioning: the unbounded speaker is, after all, branded by global commodities, mass media, and digital technology which together produce the de-territorialized subject's state of constant restlessness. Ufo Woman's search for 'that perfect destination' remains incomplete and necessarily so: the fluid movements and local cadences of poetic language in the text mirror the ongoing processes of multi-ethnic self-creation in Britain's global now.

To bring my discussion of minor cosmopolitanism and global Britishness to conclusion, I will dwell with a single poem on ethnic migration by the London-born, Punjabi-Indian poet Daljit Nagra. In his award-winning debut collection's title poem 'Look We Have Coming to Dover!', Nagra reimagines Matthew Arnold's 'Dover Beach' from the perspective of Indian stowaways, all 'huddled' in the bottom of a British cruiser while, above deck, 'cushy come-and-go | tourists' stand at the head of the prow 'lording the ministered waves'.[43] Winner of the Forward Prize for Best Individual Poem 2004, 'Look We Have Coming to Dover!' goes on to describe the tumultuous process by which ethnic migrants, after disembarking from the boat, 'escape hutched in a Bedford van' before working illegally for 'seasons or years', all the while 'unclocked by the national eye'.[44] In its final two stanzas, Nagra commands the reader to 'imagine' himself and his brethren living the dream of economic

---

[42] Agbabi, *Transformatrix*, 16–7.
[43] Daljit Nagra, *Look We Have Coming to Dover!* (London: Faber & Faber, 2007), 31.
[44] *Look We Have Coming to Dover!* was also awarded Best First Collection in 2007 by the Forward Arts Foundation, which since 1991 has sought to expand the UK's reading audience for contemporary poetry through lucrative awards, a national poetry day (usually in early October), and the publication *The Forward Book of Poetry*, which each year collects short-listed and awarded poems from established and new poets.

prosperity and self-sufficiency. The increasingly longer lines in the poem seem to mimic both the rolling sea-waves and the infiltration of ethnic migrants into English social and cultural life:

Swarms of us, grafting in
the black within shot of the moon's
spotlight, banking on the miracle of sun—
span its rainbow, passport us to life. Only then
can it be human to hoick ourselves, bare-faced for the clear.

Imagine my love and I,
our sundry others, Blair'd in the cash
of our beeswax'd cars, our crash clothes, free,
we raise our charged glasses over unparasol'd tables
East, babbling our lingoes, flecked by the chalk of Britannia![45]

Sarcastically imagining multitudes invading England's economy and cashing in on the modern welfare state, thanks to Tony 'Blair', Nagra takes no small pleasure in engaging in the fantasy of Arnold's England as a 'land of dreams, | So various, so beautiful, so new'. (In fact, the latter line serves as the epigraph to Nagra's poem.) Whereas Arnold melancholically yearns for a lost realm of beauty while 'ignorant armies clash by night', Nagra, by contrast, relishes the clashing and mixing of cultures and languages, as he, his lover, and 'sundry others' reorient themselves 'East' to toast their imagined homelands. All the while, he fills his poem with the polyglot sound of 'babbling lingoes' that are even more 'flecked' with the white 'chalk' of the former empire and Standard English. 'Look We Have Coming to Dover!' unabashedly celebrates the advent of the post-imperial moment, of new global migrations and ethnic mixtures spurring Nagra's poetics of global Britishness. Opposing his revelry in cultural hybridity is, however, Nagra's painful awareness of the conjunction of the economic and the political registers, which makes multi-ethnic texts available in the first place. Indeed, the currency of economic language throughout these lines underwrites the process by which diasporic subjects become citizens, affording new modes of belonging and new dwellings in an unwelcoming host country. This strain of the poem counteracts the exuberance of arrival, with England's former colonial others having 'come home' as it were to Dover. In one sense, the text delights in the idea of ethnic minorities contaminating the purity of English culture and poetry. Besides nodding to Arnold's 'Dover Beach', Nagra invokes D. H. Lawrence's *Look! We Have Come Through!* (1917), as well as W. H. Auden's *Look, Stranger!* (1936), and 'Dover 1937'. In another, however, Nagra tallies the human costs migrant subjects must pay before they are recognized as citizens with full belonging in the national community. For instance, the deployment of the pathetic fallacy, a device which Arnold notably uses throughout 'Dover Beach', functions ironically here: Nagra's moneyed moon and sun would seem to naturalize the link between economic solvency

---

[45] Nagra, *Look We Have Coming to Dover!*, 32.

('in | the black', 'banking on the miracle') and political citizenship ('passport us to life'). Following the logic of the poem's syntax, the conjunction of the economic with the political here serves as the necessary precondition ('only then') for diaspora communities to 'hoick' (slang for 'lift') themselves up to the status of the 'human'. Surprisingly perhaps, Nagra shares some of Arnold's melancholia, which lurks behind the poem's concluding exclamation: for as much as England may appear like 'a land of dreams' to newly arrived minorities, it 'Hath really neither joy, nor love, nor light, | Nor certitude, nor peace, nor help from pain' (in Arnold's memorable words) for many of Nagra's figures, implicitly here and far more so in other poems.

Nagra responds to the predicament of melancholic exclusion by demanding recognition, but not in the ways that we might expect. With tongue in cheek, he calls himself a brown-skinned 'native'—which, ironically, he is, having grown up in Sheffield, where his parents managed a corner shop. But he appropriates negative terms of Englishness in order to relocate them within the discursive field of the nation.[46] Throughout, Nagra makes direct and frequent recourse to the 'tradition' of British literature, a tradition freighted with orientalist baggage. In addition to Arnold, he also alludes to Christopher Marlowe in 'For the Wealth of India' (8–9), to Rudyard Kipling in 'The Man Who Would Be English!' (15), and to George Orwell in the collection's epigraph, which reads: 'The people have brown faces—besides, there are so many of them! Are they really the same flesh as yourself? Do they even have names? Or are they merely a kind of undifferentiated brown stuff?' The quotation comes from Orwell's 1939 essay 'Marrakech', which describes his six-month visit to Morocco after he was wounded fighting in the Spanish Civil War. Like other black and Asian British poets, Nagra selectively appropriates the canon to parody the orientalist assumptions within literary texts and to mount political and social questions of citizenship and diasporic belonging. Like Markham, Nagra links up with Irish writers, including Heaney in a rewriting of 'Digging', and Paul Muldoon in 'Yobbos!'. Nagra furthermore blends multiple modes of English—a Punjabi-English dialect that he brands as 'Punglish'—so as to hybridize and pluralize the language, making new dwelling spaces and literary connections within the canon. Like Agbabi and many younger poets, then, the canon for Nagra is less a static, burdensome monument, whether to be revered or shattered, than an open-ended collocation of texts that can be appropriated, adapted, revised, recycled, and extended.

The minor cosmopolitan poetics among multi-ethnic British poets does not merely supplant the shame of racial alienation with a facile celebration of cultural assimilation. Like Markham, the poets studied here do not wax nostalgic for any imagined unity or origin before their dislocation and transplantation. Rather, their poems figure a politico-aesthetic model of hybrid British belonging that speaks directly to the particularity of minority experiences of discrimination and alienation: they unmoor the term 'Britishness' from its racial-ethnic anchoring to let it wander into cross-cultural, cross-racial territory. The cosmopolitan constitution of recent multi-ethnic British

---

[46] Nagra, *Look We Have Coming to Dover!*, 11, 6.

poetries thus opens itself up to include potentially anyone within its sphere of belonging, while remaining highly attuned to those exempt from poetic and political inclusion.

IV. Hybrid Traditions: British Poetry for the New Century

The increasing prominence of black, Asian, and minority poets would seem to indicate a step forward in publication and institutional support. The wider availability of individual collections has become possible through mainstream publishing houses—especially Bloodaxe, Anvil, Carcanet, Jonathan Cape, and to a far lesser degree Faber (which has only published two multi-ethnic poets, Walcott and Nagra)—and to smaller presses, including Peepal Tree Press, Arc, Canongate, and Payback Press. Multi-ethnic poets have been incorporated into the sovereign domain of a multicultural British body politic through government programmes and subsidies (such as the Arts Council England and the Literature Development Agency), national prizes, and public recognition (as in the Poetry Book Society's initiative of 'Next Generation Poets'), and the adoption of minority poets into the Order of the British Empire and the Royal Society of Literature. The anthologies appearing over the years deserve an article-length study unto themselves. To name a few, one might examine the early pioneering work of John Figueroa in *Caribbean Voices* (1966), James Berry's *Bluefoot Traveler* (1976) and subsequent *News for Babylon* (1984), through anthologies of women's poetry such as *A Dangerous Knowing* (1985), Rhondha Cobham's *Watchers and Seekers* (1987), and Jackie Kay's *Charting the Journey* (1988), to the promotion of a younger generation of multi-ethnic writers, as in Sissay's *The Fire People* (1999) and Kwame Dawes's *Red: Contemporary Black British Poetry* (2010).

And yet, the most recent news on the state of multi-ethnic British poetries is not altogether optimistic. The Arts Council England sponsored a report titled *Free Verse*, which concludes that, despite widespread success on the performance circuit, black and Asian poets face considerable difficulties reaching the printed page. Of all of the poetry published in Britain, black and Asian poets comprise 0.64 per cent of listed poets published by mainstream presses and 1.8 per cent among smaller specialist presses. The majority of respondents did not cite discrimination on the part of presses as a significant barrier to publication. Rather, the report suggests a need to make more transparent the criteria of aesthetic value for publication on the part of presses as a step towards closing the gap between the expectations of editors and of poets. The other barrier stems from a need for greater institutional support of poets through mentoring and funding of workshops, conferences, and seminars. *Free Verse* led the Literature Development Agency to initiate The Complete Works Project (TCWP) in 2008–10. TCWP sought out and mentored ten up-and-coming poets and culminated in the anthology *Ten: New Poets from Spread the*

Word (2010), edited by Evaristo and Nagra. This brief sketch points both to significant progress and to work that remains to be done for multi-ethnic poetry to thrive.[47]

The sheer diversity and fractiousness of multi-ethnic British poetry would seem to render it 'beyond definition' (in the titular words of *Wasarifi*'s December 2010 issue). And yet, accepting that all identity categories and poetic groupings (whether 'black British', 'black and minority ethnic', 'multi-ethnic', 'white', or otherwise) are provisional constructs for porous processes of attachment cannot but lead me to the conclusion that 'multi-ethnic poetries' are constitutively British. I here use the word 'British' as synonymous with its hybridity through other spaces, histories, languages, and cultures that are sedimented in poetic texts. In some instances, the hybridity of British poetry has been denied to assert the fiction of an unbroken English literary tradition that bolsters the illusion of racial purity, the myth of a common national history stretching back to 1066, and the dialect of Standard English. Far from a tradition apart, multi-ethnic British poetries disperse the tradition of British poetry, from Chaucer and Milton to Plath and Duffy, into dynamic sites of transnational literary exchange crossing East and West, North and South. Whether in print, on MP3, in performance, in museum installations, or on public transport and human skin, multi-ethnic poetries also contribute to the making and remaking of national identities suited to an increasingly diverse Britain, now and in the coming century.

Select Bibliography

Agard, John, *Alternative Anthem: Selected Poems* (Northumberland: Bloodaxe Books, 2009), 16.
Agbabi, Patience, *Transformatrix* (Edinburgh: Payback Press, 2000), 28–9.
Agbabi, Patience, *Bloodshot Monochrome* (Edinburgh: Canongate, 2008).
Appiah, Kwame Anthony, *Cosmopolitanism: Ethics in a World of Strangers* (New York: Norton, 2006).
Baucom, Ian, *Out of Place* (Princeton: Princeton University Press, 1999).
Bhabha, Homi, 'Unsatisfied: Notes on Vernacular Cosmopolitanism', in Laura Garcia-Moreno and Peter C. Pfeiffer (eds.), *Text and Nation: Cross-Disciplinary Essays on Cultural and National Identities* (Columbia, SC: Camden House, 1996), 191–207.
Breeze, Jean Binta, *The Arrival of Brighteye and Other Poems* (Newcastle upon Tyne: Bloodaxe Books, 2000).
Clifford, James, *Routes: Travel and Translation in the Late Twentieth Century* (Cambridge, Mass.: Harvard University Press, 1997).
Cooper, Carolyn, 'Words Unbroken by the Beat: The Performance Poetry of Mikey Smith and Jean Binta Breeze', *Wasafiri*, 11 (Spring 1990), 7–13

---

[47] See Danuta Kean (ed.), *Free Verse* (Spread the Word, 2006), [www.spreadtheword.org.uk/freeverse/files/free_verse.pdf]. Also see Bernardine Evaristo, 'The Illusion of Inclusion', *Wasafiri* 64 (Winter 2010), 1–6; and Nathalie Teitler, 'The Complete Works: Developing New Poetries in Contemporary Britain', *Wasafiri*, 64 (Winter 2010), 76–80.

D'Aguiar, Fred, 'Have You Been Here Long? Black Poetry in Britain', in Robert Hampson and Peter Barry (eds.), *New British Poetries: The Scope of the Possible* (Manchester and New York: Manchester University Press, 1993), 51–71.
Dawson, Ashley, *Mongrel Nation* (Ann Arbor: University of Michigan Press, 2007).
Evaristo, Bernardine, 'The Illusion of Inclusion', *Wasafiri* 64 (Winter 2010), 1–6.
Gikandi, Simon, *Maps of Englishness* (New York: Columbia University Press, 1996).
Gilroy, Paul, *Whitewashing Britain* (Ithaca, NY and London: Cornell University Press, 1997).
Gilroy, Paul, *Postcolonial Melancholia* (New York: Columbia University Press, 2005).
Huk, Romana, 'In AnOther's Pocket: The Address of the "Pocket Epic" in Postmodern Black British Poetry', *Yale Journal of Criticism*, 13/1 (2000), 23–47.
Innes, C. L., *A History of Black Asian Writing in Britain* (Cambridge: Cambridge University Press, 2008).
Johnson, Linton Kwesi, *Selected Poems* (London: Penguin Books, 2006).
Kean, Danuta (ed.), *Free Verse* (Spread the Word, 2006), [www.spreadtheword.org.uk/freeverse/files/free_verse.pdf].
King, Bruce, *The Oxford English Literary History*, xiii. *1948-2000: The Internationalization of English Literature* (Oxford: Oxford University Press, 2004).
Markham, E. A., *Living in Disguise* (London: Anvil Press, 1986).
Markham, E. A. (ed.), *Hinterland: Caribbean Poetry from the West Indies and Britain* (Newcastle upon Tyne: Bloodaxe Books, 1989).
Markham, E. A., *Letter from Ulster & the Hugo Poems* (Lancashire: Littlewood Arc, 1993), 11–12.
Markham, E. A., *Misapprehensions* (London: Anvil Press, 1995).
Markham, E. A., *A Rough Climate* (London: Anvil Press, 2002).
Markham, E. A., *Lambchops with Sally Goodman* (Cambridge: Salt Publishing, 2004).
Markham, E. A., *Looking Out, Looking In: New and Selected Poems* (London: Anvil Press, 2009).
Marsh, Nicky, '"Peddlin Noh Puerile Parchment of Etnicity": Questioning Performance in New Black British Poetry', *Wasafiri*, 45 (Summer 2005), 46–51.
McLeod, John, *Postcolonial London: Rewriting the Metropolis* (London: Routledge, 2004).
McLeod, John, 'Fantasy Relationships: Black British Canons in a Transnational World', in Gail Low and Marion Wynne Davies (eds.), *A Black British Canon?* (London and New York: Palgrave, 2006).
Nagra, Daljit, *Look We Have Coming to Dover!* (London: Faber & Faber, 2007).
Niven, Alastair, 'Bass History is A-Moving: Black Men's Poetry in England', in James Acheson and Romana Huk (eds.), *Contemporary British Poetry* (Albany, NY: SUNY Press, 1996), 293–314.
Paul, Kathleen, *Whitewashing Britain: Race and Citizenship in the Postwar Era* (Ithaca, NY: Cornell University Press, 1997).
Pheng, Cheah, *Inhuman Conditions: On Cosmopolitanism and Human Rights* (Cambridge, Mass.: Harvard University Press, 2007).
Ramazani, Jahan, *A Transnational Poetics* (Chicago: University of Chicago Press, 2009), 180.
Ramey, Lauri, 'Contemporary Black British Poetry', in R. Victoria Arana and Ramey (eds.), *Black British Writing* (New York: Palgrave, 2004), 109–36.
Robbins, Bruce, 'Comparative Cosmopolitanisms', in Bruce Robbins and Pheng Cheah (eds.), *Cosmopolitics: Thinking and Feeling Beyond the Nation* (Minneapolis: University of Minnesota Press, 1998).
Sisay, Kadija (ed.), *Write Black, Write British* (London: Hansib, 2005).
Sissay, Lemn, *Listener* (Edinburgh: Canongate, 2008).

Teitler, Nathalie, 'The Complete Works: Developing New Poetries in Contemporary Britain', *Wasafiri*, 64 (Winter 2010), 76–80.
Walkowitz, Rebecca, *Cosmopolitan Style: Modernism Beyond the Nation* (New York: Columbia University Press, 2006), 2–5, 17–19.
Walmsley, Anne, *The Caribbean Artists Movement 1966–1972: A Literary and Cultural History* (London: New Beacon Books, 1992).

CHAPTER 28

EUROPEAN AFFINITIES

STEPHEN ROMER

NEARLY a century ago, T. S. Eliot spoke serenely, or with an assumed serenity, of the 'mind of Europe' with its 'ideal order' of literary and cultural monuments; it is a mind, he says, 'which changes' and 'which abandons nothing *en route*'.[1] By 1919, however, in 'La Crise de l'esprit' Paul Valéry, surveying the ravaged and desolate scene after the Great War, wrote his famous sentence: 'Nous, autres, civilisations, nous savons maintenant que nous sommes mortelles'—a sentence that first appeared in Middleton Murry's *Athenaeum*, if less memorably, as 'We civilizations now know that we are mortal.'[2] Both Eliot and Valéry spent time in the interwar years attempting to envisage a future for the 'mind of Europe', Eliot by founding the *Criterion*, a journal that endeavoured to gather in the best that was being thought and written by its poets and intellectuals, and Valéry by presiding over the International Commission for Intellectual Co-operation, an organizational offshoot of the fledgling League of Nations. In his relative exile in Rapallo, meanwhile, Ezra Pound was also in his idiosyncratic way pinpointing a cultural high point in European civilization, namely the Tempio Malatestiano in Rimini. This was a point in the Italian Renaissance in which political determination and artistic patronage came together to create, in the image of Sigismundo, 'a state of mind, of sensibility, of all-roundedness and awareness' which extended down to the smallest details, down to 'the little wafer of wax between the sheets of letter paper'.[3] By analogy, and for all three, what must, what could the mind of Europe, do to advance then, seemed the underlying theme. Fast-forward to 2011, and I find on the website of Literature Across Frontiers, which calls itself a 'European platform for literary exchange, translation and policy debate', a call for nominations for an award 'for the promotion of intercultural dialogue' to be given by the Anna Lindh Euro-Mediterranean Foundation for the Dialogue Between Cultures. Valéry,

---

[1] T. S. Eliot, *Selected Essays* (London: Faber & Faber, 1972), 16.
[2] Paul Valéry, 'La Crise de l'esprit', in *Œuvres*, ed. Jean Hytier (Paris: Gallimard, Bibliothèque de la Pléiade, 1965), i. 988.
[3] See Ezra Pound, *Guide to Kulchur* (New York: New Directions, 1970), 159–62.

who never forgot that European civilization started around the luminous area of the Mediterranean basin, would have been pleased, if perhaps sceptical. The dream of intercultural exchange at a pan-European level is nothing new, then, though it has reached an unparalleled level of outreach and organization.[4]

The subject of the present chapter, as suggested in the deliberately wide sweep of my opening paragraph, is vast. No single account of the reception and resonance of contemporary British and Irish poetry in the 'New Europe', under the general rubric 'European Affinities', can hope to cover the subject. From the evidence of the many gathered sources, I can suggest patterns and tendencies, though even these must remain open to polemic and debate. Certainly the 'European platform for literary exchange, translation and policy debate' is a formidable title, one falling strangely on the ear to a poet-translator, whose experience of such a 'platform' is in a friend's flat or a smoke-filled European café (as they were in those heady days) when individual poems were read and reread, discussed, and painfully or delightedly translated, often over a lengthy period of time. It must sound even stranger to those pioneering spirits in the not-so-distant past for whom translating the poets of the former Soviet bloc had something of the excitement of a samizdat act. It leads one to measure the distance we have come since 1989–90. In this light, the 'platform' seems a logical cultural development or even 'result' of political and technological change. But genuine cultural *affinity, sympathy, and understanding* is another thing, and one that preceded and will most likely outlast, in the hands and minds of 'individuals in odd corners', the merely political will that there should be greater cultural dialogue and exchange.

Recently established European Union-funded bodies like Literature Across Frontiers, with its long list of partners throughout Europe and the world, and government-funded organizations like the Welsh Literary Exchange, the Irish Literary Exchange, or the Scottish Poetry Library, go beyond the traditional remit of the British Council or, in France, the Centre National des Lettres and their equivalents. The last of these traditionally award grants to translations of works from the national language. The newer organizations, often serving smaller, and under-represented linguistic communities, are more 'hands-on' in that they convene actual translation workshops throughout Europe and the world; English is often (and of necessity) used as a bridge language in these endeavours. Anglophone poets are frequently invited to participate in their workshops, and this in turn has resulted in a good deal of translation of their poetry into the different European tongues, the topic most relevant to the present essay.[5] In essence, these literary bodies are a continuation in official form of the more freelance pioneering work of the post-war period with its greater reliance on geographical proximity, happenstance, and individual affinity.

---

[4] See the LAF website: [http://www.lit-across-frontiers.org]
[5] See e.g. Poetry International, Rotterdam, at: [http://www.poetryinternational.org/piw_cms/cms/cms_module/index.php?obj_name=international]

Pioneers and Festivals

Introducing Ted Hughes's programme note to *Poetry International* 1967, Daniel Weissbort observes that Hughes 'believed in the permeability of linguistic, cultural and political borders, and in the ability, in any case, of poetry to transcend these'.[6] The excitement and gravity of the time is clear from Hughes's explanatory note:

> We now give more serious weight to the words of a country's poets than to the words of its politicians—though we know the latter may interfere more drastically with our lives. Religions, ideologies, mercantile competition divide us. The essential solidarity of the very diverse poets of the world, besides being a mysterious fact, is one we can be thankful for, since its terms are exclusively those of love, understanding and patience. [...] If the various nations are ever to make a working synthesis of their ferocious contradictions, the plan of it and the temper of it will be created in spirit before it can be formulated or accepted in political fact.[7]

Hughes co-founded *Modern Poetry in Translation* with Weissbort in 1965, and, reading the backlist of the famous journal (until recently under the editorship of David and Helen Constantine, and now of Sasha Dugdale), we find the names of the major poets from the Eastern bloc and elsewhere, names the next generation grew up with because of this initiative—among them János Pilinszky, Vasko Popa, Ivan V. Lalić, Zbigniew Herbert, Miroslav Holub, Marin Sorescu, Andrei Voznesensky. Translation had become something of a craze, and as Anthony Rudolf recalls, in those days every poet-translator had his or her 'poet'.[8] Undoubtedly, there was reciprocity in the process, although due to publishing circumstances this was delayed. By now, Ted Hughes has major collections in most languages of the European Union.

In retrospect, and in the memories of the participants I have questioned, there is no doubting the seminal effect on translation, and on cross-pollination, of these early international poetry festivals. Take, for example, the Cambridge Poetry Festival, founded by Richard Berengarten (formerly Burns). The first festival, resolutely international in character, took place in 1975, the last in 1985. The index of participants reads like an international Who's Who of poets, many of them also distinguished translators. Tutelary figures like Michael Hamburger attended, alongside Hans Magnus Enzensberger (whom he translated), and David Gascoyne, 'resurrected' after a long period in obscurity, who read, as I recall, with Allen Ginsberg sitting in homage at his feet. Gascoyne who translated so many of the French Surrealists, and later Pierre Jean Jouve, was himself translated into French in the 1980's.[9] This asynchrony is frequent: there is no rule as

---

[6] Ted Hughes, *Selected Translations*, ed. Daniel Weissbort (London: Faber & Faber, 2006), 199.
[7] Hughes, *Selected Translations*, 199–200.
[8] Anthony Rudolf: private communication.
[9] David Gascoyne, *Miserere: Poèmes 1937–1942*, trans. F.-X. Jaujard et al. (Paris: Granit, 1989).

to when (or if) a poet-translator will be translated 'in return', unless in the context of the 'reciprocal'-style workshop.

Also present was the Italian poet and translator Roberto Sanesi, who read alongside Hughes, Charles Tomlinson, and Miroslav Holub. The Milanese poet Sanesi (1930–2001) was one of those gigantic figures that appear from time to time in the firmament of poetry translation: single-handedly he ferried across into Italian Shakespeare's *Sonnets*, plays by Marlowe, Milton's *Paradise Lost*, Shelley's *Adonais*, volumes by Dylan Thomas, Vernon Watkins, and Nathaniel Tarn. In particular, he translated the complete poems of T. S. Eliot, with Eliot's approval—Eliot who had already proved such a major influence on Eugenio Montale. This is a classic example of the affinity and influence I attempt to trace: Sanesi translated Eliot out of love for the work, just as—another example of individual curiosity and pioneering—the Russian lyric poet Aleksandr Kushner translated the work of Philip Larkin in the 1970s. Elaine Feinstein recalls: 'On my first visit to Leningrad, in the seventies, Aleksandr Kushner gave me a copy of four British poets in Russian translation... Dylan Thomas, W. H. Auden, Philip Larkin and Ted Hughes. Brilliantly chosen (and Kushner an excellent translator of Larkin). A presence indeed.' She adds: 'Nothing like that going on now. These days the pattern seems to depend a bit too much on reciprocity.'[10] The influence of Larkin on Kushner is visible, deeply assimilated, in the domestic setting, the quiet utterance leading into a great elegiac sweep of many poems in *Apollo in the Snow*.[11]

Ted Hughes once noted what he called the 'Universal Language behind language' in poems by Vasko Popa, which can resemble surreally tinged fables.[12] One result of this stripped, fabular or allegorical style (also to be found in the Czech poet Holub, and in the *Mr Cogito* sequences of Poland's Zbigniew Herbert) is the relative ease with which it can be translated. This is a crucial consideration, especially when we consider the reverse process, the wide recognition and reception of Hughes's work in Central Europe. The similarly fabular style of *Crow* was written, as Hughes himself explains, in a deliberately devised 'super-simple and super-ugly language which would in a way shed everything except just what he wanted to say'.[13] This primitive 'song-legend' appealed in turn to poets like Pilinszky, who at one time considered translating the sequence into Hungarian. Al Alvarez's prophetic words in the *Observer* about Hughes, repeated in every blurb, and which have ever since surrounded the poet like a nimbus of distinguished damnation—'with *Crow* Hughes joins the select band of survivor-poets whose work is adequate to the destructive reality we inhabit'— undoubtedly served him well on the wider stage of Europe.

---

[10] Elaine Feinstein: private communication.

[11] Aleksandr Kushner, *Apollo in the Snow: Selected Poems 1960–1987*, trans. Paul Graves and Carol Ueland, introd. Joseph Brodsky (London: Harvill, 1991).

[12] Ted Hughes, 'Vasko Popa', *Winter Pollen*, ed. William Scammell (New York: Picador USA, 1994), 220–8.

[13] Quoted in Ann Skea, 'Ted Hughes and Crow' (1998): [http://ann.skea.com./trickstr.htm]

The Case of France

Turning from recent, pioneering history to attempt now a 'snapshot' of the current situation, the only feasible way of filling in some detail is by taking a geographical survey. France, our nearest neighbour, and also the situation which the present writer knows best, is a logical place to start. As so often, in the traditional war embrace that locks the two cultures, the picture is mixed and in some ways anomalous. It could seem as though, since Pound and Eliot turned for new models to Baudelaire, Gautier, Laforgue, and Corbière, the anglophone yearning towards French poetry has been an unrequited love affair. In the 1930s, David Gascoyne single-handedly smuggled a choice of Surrealists across the channel, and helped organize the Surrealist Exhibition in London in 1935. This caused a ripple that was soon dispersed. Surrealism (in its linguistic form at least) has always had a mixed reception amongst our empirical peoples. And after the war, in the 1950s and 1960s, it was America that took the French to their heart, the New York School in particular. From Frank O'Hara who translated Genet, and kept Reverdy's poems in his pocket, through to John Ashbery (Max Jacob, Reverdy, and recently Rimbaud).[14] Nowadays, the Franco-American poetry affair steams ahead, largely carried forward by avant-garde or experimental schools in both countries. In the 1970s and 1980s the anthologizing work of such poets as Michel Deguy, Jacques Roubaud, and Jacques Darras (who co-translated Pound's *Cantos*), and the small publishing house run by Emmanuel Hocquard, Orange Export Ltd—were important *lieux d'échange*. The presence of experimentally leaning American poets in France is now fed and watered by the influential and impressively long-running organization Double Change.[15] Founded by Olivier Brossard and Vincent Brocqua in 2000, and now aided by Omar Berrada, this is a monthly reading series, with an online journal, that has on occasion featured British experimentalists like Mark Ford and Rod Mengham.

On the other hand, *malentendus* have typically arisen when an experimentally minded 'essentialist' or orthodoxly 'non-referential' French poet encounters, say, a poem like 'Mr Bleaney', and the inventory of contextualized 'objects' to be found in his room. French poets of 'presence', notably, like Char, Bonnefoy, Du Bouchet, or Dupin, all of them keen students of Heidegger, were writing of apocalyptic, Presocratic landscape and phenomena; and the inheritors of Barthes and Derrida, juggled the Mallarméan 'signe' only with the greatest mistrust. Nevertheless, there has been the occasional foray, often in poetry journals and anthologies. In the early 1980s the little bilingual magazine *Twofold* was founded by a group of expatriates recently settled in Paris, and a French poet, Paul Le Jéloux. After three issues, the magazine was taken up and distributed by the more established French magazine *Obsidiane*—operating just around the corner in Montmartre. Two larger issues followed (*Twofold* 4 & 5). British and Irish poets including Michael

---

[14] See Arthur Rimbaud, *Illuminations*, trans. John Ashbery (Manchester: Carcanet Press, 2011).
[15] See 'Double Change', [http://doublechange.org/]

Hofmann, James Lasdun, Thomas McCarthy, Jeremy Reed, Peter Robinson, and Stephen Romer were translated into French. A group of contemporary French poets, who were generally in reaction, or out of sympathy with the 'linguistic turn' of their colleagues or immediate seniors, Jean-Claude Caër, Paul Le Jéloux, Jean-Pierre Lemaire, and Jean-Michel Maulpoix, appeared in English. Among more senior poets, David Gascoyne and Jean Follain were featured. *Twofold* went the way of many a little magazine, but *Obsidiane*, under the general editorship of François Boddaert, has become a serious presence in French poetry. That said, the 'dialogue' initiated by *Twofold* with poetry from Britain, has been carried on only sporadically in *Obsidiane* and its subsequent incarnation in 1993 as *Le Mâche-Laurier* which concentrated on poetry written in French. Geoffrey Hill was represented in *Obsidiane*, 18 (March 1982), in a translation of 'The Pentecost Castle' by René Gallet.[16]

Hill's reputation in France is worth dwelling on. The case is atypical in that he has benefited in particular from one pioneering individual, the late critic and *angliciste* René Gallet, who championed his work steadily from the early 1980s. Gallet published not only translations of the poems, but also Hill's critical essay on Hopkins, 'Redeeming the Time', and the crucial interview with John Haffenden. Other translators, notably Jacques Darras and Patrick Hersant, have contributed further texts. As in Britain, his approval rating in the University is high, where he has been supported by Gallet and by Jennifer Kilgore-Caradec, along with a growing number of younger academics. Michael Edwards, who holds the *chaire d'étude de la création littéraire en langue anglaise* at the Collège de France, has also contributed advice and introduction. He also presided over what may be considered Geoffrey Hill's formal *consécration* in France, a lecture and reading at the Collège in March 2008. This is only justice: both in his poetry and his critical work Hill has been deeply attentive to French poetry, philosophy, and theology—all of which culminated in his *The Mystery of the Charity of Charles Péguy* (1983).[17]

In this aleatory business of a national poetry taking notice of another national poetry, even if it is written in the same language (viz. the comparative ignorance in Britain of most poetry being written in the US and Canada, and vice versa), one solution that supplements the work of individuals with specific passions is the hold-all anthology—a kind of showcase that attempts to take a sampling of current work. This was the case in the influential *Modern Poetry in Translation*, 16 (1973), an issue guest-edited by Anthony Rudolf, which show-cased forty-four modern French poets, of very different 'tendencies'. Michel Deguy, with guest-editor Robert Davreu, returned the favour much later in issue 98 of the distinguished review *Po&sie*, and here again representatives of the

---

[16] *Twofold*: revue bi-lingue de la poésie, was edited from Paris,1980–3. For information on *Éditions Obsidiane* see online:[http://perso.numericable.com/editions-obsidiane/index.htm]

[17] For a full bibliography of translations into French, as well as a collection of critical essays in French, see Jennifer Kilgore-Caradec and René Gallet (eds.), *La Poésie de Geoffrey Hill et la modernité* (Paris: L'Harmattan, 2007). The volume includes a rich and polemical discussion of the English and French traditions more generally, by Michael Edwards and Michel Deguy, who supply the 'Préface' and the 'Postface' respectively. For a video recording of Hill's lecture at the Collège de France see online: [http://geoffreyhillzinger.blogspot.com/2008/08/hills-conference-at-college-de-france.html]

'Cambridge School', loosely grouped under the sign of J. H. Prynne, rubbed shoulders with poets such as Geoffrey Hill.[18] In the 'Postface' by Deguy alluded to earlier, he comments on the notion of a subliminal *rivalité* between the two poetries, the English tradition tending to 'scoop' more inclusively, the French tending to 'distill' more exclusively. To correct such an oversimplified view, he rightly alludes to Apollinaire's celebrated poem of moments as they happen, in all their 'impure' dailiness or 'quotidienneté', 'Lundi rue Christine'. That said, the capacity of contemporary British poetry to encompass domesticity alongside metaphysics, to allude to mass culture without sacrificing 'seriousness', is I think considered an enviable one by those poets in Europe who have taken notice of it.

Throughout its long career (the magazine was founded in 1977) *Po&sie* has remained regularly attentive to different tendencies in British and Irish poetry, many issues containing at least one item. Early on we find Prynne in Bernard Dubourg's translation of *Brass* ('Oripeau clinquaille') (issue 3), a selection of Pound's texts on music, translated by Claude Minière and Margaret Tunstil (4), translations of John Montague by Deguy (6), Bunting's *Briggflatts*, translated by Jacques Darras (7), Pound's *Canto LXXXV*, translated by Ghislain Sartoris (22), Eliot's *The Waste Land* translated by Michel Vinaver (31), Hill's *Mercian Hymns* translated by Jacques Darras (36) … We find in later issues, among contemporary figures, Raworth, Middleton, Tarn, Wainwright, Burnside, Heaney, Greenlaw, Davies … Pierre Pachet and Chantal Bizzini translate Auden in two successive numbers (90 & 91). Auden is a good example of a major poet strangely neglected or *méconnu* in France until recently. One possible reason for this may be due to Auden himself, who turned instinctively to the Germanic and Nordic traditions, rather than to the Romance languages. An early selection of his poems, translated by Jean Lambert, was published by Gallimard in 1976, and largely forgotten until Guy Goffette, using his influence at the publishers, reprinted the volume in the prestigious paperback Collection Poésie/Gallimard in 2005 with a preface by himself. He followed it up with an informal biographical essay.[19] Since then, Auden's star has risen in France. In 2009, *The Sea and The Mirror* was published in a bilingual edition by the new and distinctly Anglophile publishing house, Le Bruit du Temps, founded by Antoine Jaccottet.[20]

Of a younger generation than Goffette, the poet-translator Valérie Rouzeau is a rising star in both disciplines. She has recently published major translations of Ted Hughes and Sylvia Plath. To speak personally a moment, I met Rouzeau when she was a student at Tours University, undertaking a translation of Plath's *Crossing the Water* for a Masters degree. Over several years she undertook translations of my own work, aided by Gilles Ortlieb. This was an intense, if sporadic business, an example of what I believe to be the best conditions for poetry translation—close collaboration and interaction

---

[18] See *Modern Poetry in Translation* 16 ed. Anthony Rudolf; *Po&sie* 98, ed. Michel Deguy and Robert Davreu (2001).

[19] Guy Goffette, *Auden ou l'œil de la baleine* (Paris: Gallimard, 2005).

[20] W. H. Auden, *La Mer et le Miroir*, trans. from English and presented by Bruno Bayen and Pierre Pachet (Paris: Le Bruit du Temps, 2009).

between author and translator, affection and a mutual sympathy with each other's work. Ideal conditions, not always easy to come by.[21] Rouzeau's own work gained international prominence recently, in the brilliant translation by Susan Wicks, winner of the Scott Moncrieff translation prize, and shortlisted for the International category of the Griffin Prize.

Rouzeau met Wicks at the annual Festival anglo-français de poésie in Paris, which has been running since the late 1970s.[22] Organized by the French-Canadian poet Jacques Rancourt, for years this festival has been instrumental in bringing poets together, and it was one of the first festivals to pioneer the now standard procedure of providing texts for translation in advance. A serious approach to reciprocal translation was instituted after the first few festivals: the number of invited poets being reduced to twelve, so the daily workshops could make real progress. Rancourt has published the results of this interaction in his annual 'post-festival' magazine *La Traductière*. Hence we find in the archive a host of British and Irish poets descending on the French capital, welcomed in person and in poetry (translated into the language of the host nation).[23] There have been, according to Rancourt, 'encounters' between poets that have proved especially fruitful, and which have led to individual collections.[24]

Traditional Franco-Irish links, fostered by such university associations as the group of *Irlandistes* (SOFEIR), have ensured that Irish poetry has been represented, by Seamus Heaney principally (his poetry is published by Gallimard) but also by John Montague, who has enjoyed a long association with Paris, and held academic posts at the Sorbonne, and by Derek Mahon. Both have a selected poems in French. As far as I can establish, Paul Muldoon has had only one book in French, a translation of *Quoof*, nicely metamorphosed into *Couffe*.[25] As part of their programme of residences, the prestigious Centre Culturel Irlandais in Paris has welcomed Vona Groarke, Leanne O'Sullivan, Paul Durcan, Greg Delanty, and Maurice Riordan in recent years. Again, the presence of an expatriate on the ground has counted for a lot, in this case the academic and translator Cliona Ni Riordain, who frequently invites Irish poets to her regular translation seminar at the Sorbonne.

---

[21] For the result of this collaboration, see Stephen Romer, *Tribut: Poèmes choisis*, trans. Paul de Roux, Gilles Ortlieb, Valérie Rouzeau (Cognac: Le Temps qu'il fait, 2007).

[22] See Ted Hughes, *Poèmes 1957–1994*, trans. Valérie Rouzeau and Jacques Darras (Paris: Gallimard, 2009) and Valérie Rouzeau, *Cold Spring in Winter,* trans. Susan Wicks (Visible Poets, 26; Todmorden: Arc Publications, 2009).

[23] For an archive and index of participants at the Anglo-French Poetry Festival as recorded in *La Traductière*, see [http://www.festrad.com]

[24] See e.g. Jacques Rancourt and Susan Wicks, *Les Pièces du paysage and Portrait of a Leaf as Bird* (Paris: Édition les Céphéides, 2006 and 2007) and Fiona Sampson, *Attitudes de prière,* trans. Jacques Rancourt (Paris: Éditions Transignum, 2009). For Transignum art edition catalogue, containing British and Irish poets in translation, see [http://mapage.noos.fr/secrieriu/transignum/catalogue_Transignum.pdf]

[25] John Montague, *La Langue greffée*, trans. divers hands (Paris: Belin, 1988). Derek Mahon, *La Veille de nuit*, trans. Denis Rigal and J. Chuto (Paris: Éditions la folle avoine, 1996). Paul Muldoon, *Couffe*, trans. Elisabeth Gaudin and Jacques Jouet (Paris: Éditions Circé, 2009).

We cannot leave the French scene without mentioning the mighty bilingual Pléiade *Anthologie bilingue de la poésie anglaise* published in 2005, which stretches from *Beowulf* to Simon Armitage. Whatever neglect or tardiness in terms of reception there can seem to be, this is often made up with interest in France by the appearance of the 'definitive' Pléiade. This is the fruit of years of work on the part of the four editors, and a host of accomplished translators, coordinated by Paul Bensimon. In addition to frequently generous selections of poems, each poet is the subject of a small, concise critical notice—up to date, acute, well-informed—and the whole presentation stands comparison with any anthology published at home. The original project was to have contained a larger number of contemporary poets, but for reasons of space and funding, unfortunately a tumbril of them had to be guillotined. Even so the project seems unequalled anywhere in Europe, in terms of its scope, seriousness, erudition, and devoted attention to the English and the Irish traditions.[26]

In what follows, I propose to highlight variants—examples of dynamism or states of relative torpor—in certain countries of the New Europe. I am entirely indebted to a number of 'expert witnesses' whose views I report.[27] The gaps, including several individual countries, will be all too evident. It is one thing to have lists of which poets have been published where, of who is on the international 'festival circuit', and quite another to gauge any actual *influence* that a foreign poetry may exert on native practice. In many cases, it is simply too early to say, though, as we shall see, there are some 'attested cases' of such influence.

Italy and Spain

More even than France, possibly, Italy has been and remains an object, a body or receptacle of desire. In some cases (notably Ezra Pound's) the desire gets overlaid with fantasy. Pound was perpetually haunted by the loss of that 'radiant world where one thought cuts through another with clean edge, a world of moving energies', as he puts it in his 'Cavalcanti'.[28] 'A world of moving energies' might be an idealized description of poetries

---

[26] *Anthologie bilingue de la poésie anglaise,* edition established by Paul Bensimon, Bernard Brugière, François Piquet, and Michel Rémy (Paris: Gallimard/Éditions de la Pléiade, 2005). The contemporaries who escaped the tumbril were (from Philip Larkin onwards): Patricia Beer, Charles Tomlinson, Thomas Kinsella, John Montague, Thom Gunn, Peter Porter, Jon Silkin, Ted Hughes, Geoffrey Hill, Peter Redgrove, Adrian Henri, Anne Stevenson, Fleur Adcock, Roger McGough, Tony Harrison, Michael Edwards, Seamus Heaney, Derek Mahon, Hugo Williams, Douglas Dunn, Eavan Boland, Jeffrey Wainwright, Craig Raine, Brian Patten, Peter Reading, Ciaran Carson, Tom Paulin, James Fenton, Medbh McGuckian, Paul Muldoon, Carol Ann Duffy, Stephen Romer, Kathleen Jamie, Simon Armitage. A more generous representation, of poets publishing since 1975, was made in the anthology *Quarante et un poètes de la Grande Bretagne*, ed. Patrick Williamson (Quebec: Écrits des Forges, 2003).

[27] My thanks go also to Anthony Rudolf, Michael Schmidt, and Stephen Watts for their valuable help.

[28] Ezra Pound, *Literary Essays,* ed. T. S. Eliot (London: Faber & Faber, 1974), 154.

in reciprocal translation; but, as Jamie McKendrick notes, Italy's modern history is turbulent and sombre: 'the fragility of this state, with acts of murder both "red" and "black", has laid an unavoidable burden of conscience on the language of its poets and writers', and the reception of foreign poetry (to the small minority exercised by such a matter) has been irregular.[29] The massive mid-century presence of Montale is still dominant, and it was this poet who did so much to reciprocate Eliot's passion for Dante (and to some extent Pound's for Cavalcanti) by assimilating this major Anglo-American presence into modern Italian poetry (Montale translated two of Eliot's 'Ariel' poems). Listening recently to Geoffrey Hill reading his own version of Montale's 'La Bufera' in Paris brought home how rich these cumulative strands or textures of 'influence' can become. Massimo Bacigalupo, a distinguished Pound scholar, poet, and translator, and an indispensable figure in all matters relating to Anglo-American poetry in Italy, has commented on Montale's bewilderment at Pound's denigration of all things Anglo-Saxon, and his enthusiasm for Fascist Italy.[30] Creative 'misprision' (to call it that) is also a part of the assimilation of the foreign, or the 'challenge of the foreign' (*l'épreuve de l'étranger*) in Antoine Berman's formulation, relating to translation. The question of mutual influences is a fascinating and often an undecidable one. Poems can create in the reader 'a shock of recognition', in Eliot's phrase, or a drama of identification. And that will have consequences, especially if the reader is also a poet. Jamie McKendrick's fine rendering of Valerio Magrelli's poem 'The Embrace' contains a subliminal metaphor of influence:

As you lie beside me I edge closer
taking sleep from your lips
as one wick draws flame from another.

But the poem's curious exploration, triggered by the shudder of the boiler in the basement, takes a thoroughly McKendrick-like turn in its ingenious exploration through the origins and evolutions of the heating system, 'log pyres, leaf mash, seething resins...', to the triumphant final image which loops us back to the start: 'And we are the wicks, the two tongues | flickering on that single Palaeozoic torch.' McKendrick (b. 1955) has worked closely with Valerio Magrelli (b. 1957 in Rome) and acknowledges the influence the Italian poet may have had on his own work.[31] McKendrick, who taught for some years at the University of Salerno, has a 'selected poems' in Italian (*Chiodi di Cielo*, trans. Luca Guerneri (Roma: Donzelli, 2003)). Guerneri is also the translator (for the famous 'Lo Specchio' collection with Mondadori) of Seamus Heaney, Simon Armitage, and

---

[29] See Jamie McKendrick (ed.), *The Faber Book of 20th Century Italian Poems* (London: Faber & Faber, 2004), p. xiv.

[30] See Massimo Bacigalupo, 'Pound and Montale—Nature, History & Myth', *Journal of Modern Literature*, 23/1 (Fall 1999), 45–58. Consulted online: [http://muse.jhu.edu/journals/journal_of_modern_literature/summary/v023/23.1bacigalupo.html]

[31] Valerio Magrelli, 'The Embrace', in Jamie McKendrick's *Faber Book of 20th Century Italian Poems* (London: Faber & Faber, 2004), 160–1; McKendrick has also published a full collection of Magrelli's poems in translation: Valerio Magrelli, *The Embrace*, trans. Jamie McKendrick (London: Faber & Faber, 2009).

Paul Muldoon. In Mondadori's premier series I Meridiani (the equivalent in Italy of the French Pléiade) Ted Hughes has been published in a major annotated edition (2008);[32] a distinction Hughes shares with only three other English language poets of the twentieth century, Pound (1970, 1985), Yeats (2005), and Plath (2002). The influence of Plath has been strong on Italian women poets such as Antonella Anedda (a selection of her work is currently being translated by McKendrick).

Peter Robinson, who translated several major Italian poets of the modern period (among them Antonia Pozzi, Vittorio Sereni, Franco Fortini, and Luciano Erba), stresses the continuing cultural 'diaspora' of Italy, its existence still as an agglomeration of city states, 'with Milan and Turin almost as important, if not more so, than Rome'. Robinson also has a 'selected poems' in Italian, describing himself as 'a respected guest-poet of Parma at best', thereby reiterating the truth that between 'publication' and 'reception' there is a great gulf.[33] Translation of British and Irish poets goes on steadily. The archive of the venerable international review *Poesia*, published in Milan, reveals cover photographs of Wendy Cope (261), John Montague (242), Seamus Heaney at seventy (240), Ted Hughes (235); other poets presented and translated in recent issues of *Poesia* include Greg Delanty, Thomas Kinsella, Brian Patten, Don Paterson, Derek Walcott, Carol Ann Duffy, Patrick McGuinness, Vicki Feaver, and Tony Harrison. The important contemporary poet and translation theorist Franco Buffoni has a particular interest in Anglo-American poetry. Alongside his translation review *Testo a Fronte*, a series of translation *Quaderni* have been published, including a *Primo Quaderno Inglese* which includes Harrison, Heaney, Hill, and Tomlinson. Buffoni has also tried his hand at translating J. H. Prynne.[34] He has translated Heaney, and shows his influence (according to Bacigalupo): Buffoni has written a poem about the mummified figure, 'Ötzi', found in the Tirol mountains and preserved in Bolzano, in a vein that recalls Heaney's 'Tollund Man'.[35] Bacigalupo, a poet himself, whose ironies have been honed by close reading of Pound's more epigrammatic pieces, has translated (in addition to Wordsworth, Dickinson, Pound, Eliot, Lowell, Stevens, Heaney, and others) two volumes of Tony Harrison, and more recently two volumes of Robin Robertson. Carol Ann Duffy, George Szirtes, and Patrick McGuinness have also had collections in Italian recently.

In Spain, a major shift occurred when English was introduced as the first foreign language taught in school, thereby replacing French. In the 1960s and 1970s, the influences were largely French, but since the mid-1980s there has been something of a seismic shift, with a flurry of translation activity in which British and Irish poetry has been

---

[32] Ted Hughes, *Poesie*, ed. Anna Ravano e Nicola Gardini (Milan: Mondadori, 2008).

[33] Peter Robinson, private communication. For his selected poems in Italian, see Peter Robinson, *L'Attaccapanni e altre poesie*, trans. the author with Ornella Trevisan (Bergamo: Moretti & Vitali, 2004).

[34] For the *Poesia* archive see: [http://www.poesia.it/index.htm]

For Franco Buffoni and the review *Testo a Fronte* see: [http://www.francobuffoni.it/rivista_testo_a_fronte.aspx]

[35] Massimo Bacigalupo, private communication.

taken up in the slipstream of America. According to Jordi Doce (translator of Blake, Eliot, Auden, Tomlinson, Heaney, and Burnside, and the American Charles Simic), the traditions form the same continuum which swept in to the young democracy along with other forms of cultural influence in music, media, and the arts from anglophone culture.[36] Alongside Heaney, John Ashbery has been the most influential poet stylistically in Spain, and there was even a wave of enthusiasm for the poetry of Raymond Carver. Ashbery and Carver both employ a style of free verse that poses no great difficulty for the translator once the register is right. Ashbery is the big 'alternative' figure, with his poetry of unstable subject, wry humour, and non-closure—and a totem of the young avant-garde (as he is, along with Frank O'Hara, in Poland). Philip Larkin, whose poetry was translated in the 1990s and travels less well into Spanish, had the misfortune also of being used as a weapon by the devotees of a 'realist-narrative' school, against the avant-garde tendency (not the first time he has been so misused…). As in Italy, but arriving later, the European-leaning Charles Tomlinson has gained a foothold in Spain, largely thanks to his friendship with Octavio Paz who has translated him.

When the French tradition held sway, the only poets who were known at all widely were Eliot, Yeats, and Dylan Thomas. During the last generation, there has been a positive influx by comparison: Heaney and Muldoon from Ireland, and Larkin, Hughes, Hill, Tomlinson, but also Douglas Dunn, Peter Reading, and John Burnside from England and Scotland. In addition to this the bookshops display a kind of 'anachrony' which adds to the confusion, since not only are contemporaries being published, but they jostle on the stacks with fresh translations of Shakespeare, Donne, Blake, the Romantics, and Yeats (his *Collected* appeared in 2010); and then poets like MacNeice, and Bunting, from the mid-century appear to complicate the picture. As Doce remarks 'the sense of history and tradition is weakened because they all appear simultaneously'. Nor is there any systematic approach to chronology or *series*; even in the case of Heaney, when his stock rose exponentially after the award of his Nobel, this meant that his poetry after *The Haw Lantern* appeared in Spanish, while the earlier work had never been satisfactorily represented. In Spain, and I suspect this is true of all Europe, when it comes to unknown foreign poetry, translators propose—a band that would not survive without curiosity, disinterestedness, and a certain bloody-mindedness—and publishers dispose. In the case of trying to find funding, the withdrawal in the last decade or so of the British Council as an ally has been felt acutely—Jordi Doce joins Jacques Rancourt in France by describing this withdrawal—graphically illustrated by the destruction of the British Council poetry library, in Madrid as in Paris, to make way for a kind of techno-centre—as 'bewildering'.[37] But the *appetite* for foreign poetries is indubitably and hearteningly

---

[36] Jordi Doce (b. 1967), here my 'expert witness', is currently head of the Publishing Department at Madrid's Circulo de Bellas Artes. He wrote an MPhil on Peter Redgrove, and taught in Britain, first at Sheffield, then Oxford throughout the 1990s. He has published four volumes of original poetry, and published several translations, notably a pioneering version of Hughes's *Crow* (*Cuervo*, Madrid: Ediciones Hiperion, 1999) and collections by Hill, Redgrove, and Burnside.

[37] Jordi Doce, private communication.

there in modern Spain, as it is in the important linguistic communities of Catalonia, the Basque country, and Galicia.

The Balkans, the Czech Republic, Slovakia

Emerging from what the writer from the former Yugolslavia Dubravka Ugrešić has called 'a threefold trauma (the stigma of communism, the collapse of Yugoslavia and war, and the newly composed nationalist culture)' the reception of anglophone poetry is hardly top of the agenda in the Balkans.[38] Nevertheless, the emergence of English, over the past three or four decades, as the preferred foreign language taught in schools, and the principal language for international communication (thereby replacing Russian and French) at literary meetings and festivals throughout the Balkans may have advantaged the reception of anglophone poetry in the region. During a time fraught with anxiety and hostilities, created by the break-up of Yugoslavia, and the painful birth of new nation states, it is understandable that in the 1990s politics and propaganda tended to poison a good deal of the discussions on all sides, and indeed the *language* question was as divisive as any. Richard Berengarten has remarked that 'what was known as Serbo-Croat suddenly became three languages'.[39]

And yet even in this conflicted and complex atmosphere, some poets have established reputations, and gained something of a following in the region. Sometimes in one place—David Harsent, for example, is a regular guest of the Sarajevo Literary Encounters series—and sometimes over a wider geographical area. Since his pioneering work in the Cambridge Poetry Festival, described earlier, a major part of Richard Berengarten's career as a poet has been shaped by his sojourn in the Balkans from 1987 to 1990. This stemmed from an invitation from Popa to attend the Belgrade International Writers' meeting in the early 1980s. To consult his bibliography, and the list of festivals he has attended, is to take the measure of what 'European' affinities can extend to, in terms of languages and reciprocal translation work. He has always been concerned by what unites and dissolves national frontiers in poetry, and by projects involving multiple polyglot translation. To take just one example of many, Berengarten's poem 'The Blue Butterfly' was co-translated twice into Serbian, by Ivan Gadjanski and Moma Dimić, and then by Danilo Kiš and Ivan V. Lalić. Berengarten then translated Gadjanski's *Balkan Destiny* (1990) and co-edited the anthology *Out of Yugoslavia* (1993). Meanwhile, he has had a book translated into Greek, five books into Serbian, one into Slovenian, and (forthcoming) books in Romanian and Macedonian. As for literary festivals, he has

---

[38] See Dubravka Ugrešić, 'House Spirits' in *Orient Express,* ed. Fiona Sampson, 3 (Easter 2003), 135.
[39] Richard Berengarten, private communication.

attended many in Serbia, as well as Vilenica and Ljubljiana (Slovenia), Budva and Bielo Plije (Montenegro), and Struga and Tetova (Macedonia). As he notes, 'the best of these events enable cultural threads to be taken up, repaired, and interwoven between the new nations, as they renegotiate the art of good neighbourliness'.[40]

Before she took over as editor of *Poetry Review* (London), Fiona Sampson was a frequent visitor to the Balkans. Her remarkably wide-ranging association with poets and writers from the nations of what has been called the 'European Union Enlargement Region' found expression in the magazine she edited from Oxford, *Orient Express*. Using English as the bridge language, the magazine provided a unique outlet for novelists, essayists, poets, and photographers from the Baltics to the Balkans and the former satellite nations of the USSR. Thus, the essay by the Croatian Dubravka Ugrešić quoted earlier is part of an impassioned debate on Balkan history and identity, that includes contributions by two Slovenians (Primoz Repar and Iztok Osojnic). These appear alongside stories and poems from Estonia, Moldova, the Ukraine, Poland, Romania, Turkey, Bulgaria, Cyprus...Through friendships often developed out of meetings with poets at festivals and workshops, Sampson has been involved in a variety of translation projects, notably of the Estonian Jaan Kaplinski, and has collections of her own poetry published in Macedonia, Romania, and Serbia. Sampson has provided a veritable platform for writerly exchange in a complex region, but she remains adamant that genuine sympathy and imaginative affinity is essential if the translation is to work, and *quality* is everything if the foreign poet is to have any chance of—to repeat this important distinction—*reception* (as opposed merely to publication) in the foreign tongue.[41]

This is a point echoed by the Irish poet Justin Quinn, who has taught for many years in the Czech Republic. It is rare for a translated poet to make a real impact, unless the translation is of care and quality. If not we have bland translatorese. For Quinn, the grant-aided workshop, where Irish poetry is translated into Estonian, say, through a bridge language, can give results that are far from satisfactory, despite the possible value in themselves of such encounters between traditions. In the Czech Republic, interest in translated poetry has actually declined after the emergence of the new Europe. In Slovakia, home to the long-term expatriate poet James Sutherland-Smith, there is a similar pattern. Sutherland-Smith (with his wife Viera) has translated some ninety Slovak poets into English (including seven book-length selections) and his own work has been published; but, aside from Matthew Sweeney, whom Sutherland-Smith invited out, and whose anecdotal, surreally tinged work appealed (the same might be said of Pascale Petit's work, also widely translated in Central Europe), there has been little by way of reciprocal 'uptake'. The Beats, and to a lesser extent the Liverpool poets, had a prolonged

---

[40] For a bibliography, list of festivals, and information on projects embodying 'universals' see Richard Berengarten's website: [http://www.berengarten.com/site/Biography.html]

[41] Fiona Sampson, private communication. For a bio-bibliography of Sampson see the British Council Contemporary Writers online site: [http://www.contemporarywriters.com/authors/?p=auth5691937D 07d081E5C3vui42B641F] For information on *Orient Express* magazine: [http://www.writersartists.net/oexpress/orientex.htm]

influence on younger Slovak poets in the 1980s and 1990s (Sampson reports the same phenomenon in the Balkans).[42] In Hungary, according to experts like George Gömöri and George Szirtes, the appetite for foreign poetry has largely died away since 1989. The same is true of the Russian Federation. Poetry suffers at the expense of the imported fiction best-seller. As for festivals, Quinn is clear-sighted: 'the writers breeze in and breeze out with no follow-through'. And yet, there remains felicitous happenstance: one of Quinn's Czech students, Stepan Nosek, on an exchange programme to Trinity, Dublin, met the poets Vona Groarke and Conor O'Callaghan at their home in Dundalk. On the wall was a painting by a Czech painter, who just happened to be a friend of Nosek's. The latter then translated O'Callaghan's work into Czech, 'which gave him access to registers he couldn't get at previously. Some of his (Nosek's) poems read like O'Callaghan in Czech.'[43]

The Russian Federation

It is this last example, surely, that enables us to say whether a poet has had a verifiable *impact* on the poets of the host country. Translation is an act of accomodation; it is an act of hospitality, of *hospitalité langagière* to borrow a phrase of Paul Ricoeur's.[44] But the result can ramify beyond this, and the translated work can provide access to subject matter and to registers unimagined in the host language; it can add, in a word, to the stock of available reality. On the other hand, of course, the 'ordeal of the unfamiliar' can prove too much, and set up major resistance in the target language. Such is the case of Russian with its strong tradition of rhyme and regular metre. According to Sasha Dugdale, who has worked with major Russian translators, 'the trend is still to look back to the 18/19th centuries',[45] even among the younger practitioners. This is in part due to rights issues, but more to natural imaginative affinity, to a sense of what a poem should look and sound like. It is chastening to recall the mnemonic passion with which classics of English poetry in translation have been committed to heart by Russians—most famously Shakespeare's Sonnet 66 in Pasternak's version. Marina Boroditskaia says that when young she 'loved Shakespeare's *Sonnets*, and Burns and Byron, and Kipling and Stevenson, but dreamed of writing like Tsvetaeva'. Boroditskaia, with Grigory Kruzhkov and a group of younger translators, in association with Sasha Dugdale and the British Council, has translated an anthology of contemporary British poetry, a diverse list of thirty-six poets, from Robert Graves to Simon Armitage, Don Paterson, and Alice Oswald.[46] Despite this initiative, both Boroditskaia and Kruzhkov note that since

[42] James Sutherland-Smith, private communication.
[43] Justin Quinn, private communication.
[44] See essays on translation theory in Paul Ricoeur, *Sur la traduction* (Paris: Bayard, 2004).
[45] Sasha Dugdale, private communication.
[46] See *In Two Dimensions: Contemporary British Poetry in Russian Translations*, trans. Marina Boroditskaia, Grigory Kruzhkov, et al. (Moscow: NLO, 2009).

perestroika the demand for foreign poetry in translation (once a staple of the celebrated Soviet Foreign Literature magazine *Inostranka*) has declined. Kruzhkov sees three reasons for this: poetry translation is no longer subsidized; England 'is not interested in promoting English literature abroad, as distinct from France and other countries which have special programmes and grants for publishing French literature in Russia (the Irish Literature Exchange is a good example too)'; complicated and expensive foreign rights and copyright law.[47]

A THRIVING SCENE: GERMANY AND POLAND

In marked contrast to the situation in countries like Hungary, the Czech Republic, or the Russian Federation, since the 1990s the presence of British and Irish poetry in translation in Germany, and especially in Poland, is a real one in the sense I described earlier: poets have enjoyed not only publication, but *reception*, i.e. a few of them have measurably altered and influenced Polish practice in ways both exciting and unpredictable. Referring to the American tradition, which engages these countries equally, Justin Quinn states the contrast pithily: 'in Poland they want to know what has happened since the New York School, in the Czech Republic they want to know what the New York School is'.[48] Experts on the ground, Iain Galbraith in Germany and Jerzy Jarniewicz in Poland both speak of the exponential increase in the volume of poetry in translation over the last ten years or so. As usual, the reasons are complex, and contingent: but what is certain is that the long-term graft, determination, and investment of a few informed individuals, who are both poet-translators, *and* scholars—or at least with relations in the Academy—has made all the difference. In Germany, what Iain Galbraith calls the 'municipal largesse' of the active *Literaturhäuser* in cities like Hamburg, Bremen, Berlin, Cologne, Munich, Frankfurt, Vienna, clearly creates a climate favourable to the reception of foreign poetry, as do the big international *Literaturfests* in Germany, Austria, and German-speaking Switzerland. Particular to the case of Germany also, is the number of distinguished poet-translators in the field, starting with Michael Hamburger (whose own selected poems are translated into German by a roll-call of the finest poets of the age—fitting testimony to his standing and achievement). Among his successors we might name Christopher Middleton, David Constantine, Michael Hofmann, Richard Dove, Iain Galbraith, Kevin Perryman, Peter Waterhouse, Michael Hulse. There is no question that a 'strong' translator, in the Lowell tradition, like the German-born English poet Michael Hofmann, has given anglophone readers striking new access to writers like Brecht, Benn, Eich, and the pre-eminent contemporary from the former GDR, Durs Grünbein.[49]

---

[47] Grigory Kruzhkov, private communication.
[48] Justin Quinn, private communication.
[49] For Hofmann's translations of these and other poets see *The Faber Book of 20th-Century German Poems*, ed. Michael Hofmann (London: Faber & Faber, 2005).

With poet-translators of this calibre at work, in touch with their German homologues, there has been no shortage of reciprocity, mostly in the shape of sizeable anthologies, notably Galbraith's own *Britische Lyrik der Gegenwart* (1984) and his newly published magnum opus, *Beredter Norden. Schottische Lyrik seit 1900*, a major volume containing sixty-six Scottish poets translated by practising poets in German—the kind of ideal ingathering of all the talents only possible when an editor has lived in the host country for many years and has dealings with so many of its writers. As Galbraith explains: 'The strategy I have developed around this book is to get the translated poetry noticed by procuring a commitment to it from those who incorporate the poetry scene. In so doing I shamelessly—and, I hope, to everyone's advantage—exploit the contacts I have built up through the years by translating German-language poetry into English.'[50] The book is groundbreaking, and not just in Germany, for Galbraith set himself the task of translating from all of Scotland's languages—including Gaelic, different types of Scots, English, and Shetlandic. Translation from the under-represented indigenous languages of Scots, Gaelic, Welsh, Shetlandic is very much the current business of Literature Across Frontiers, the Scottish Poetry Library, Irish Literary Exchange, and related bodies.

Amongst a host of venues and festivals in the German-speaking world, one might serve as an exemplary instance—the privately run Lyrik Kabinett in Munich. The Kabinett, under the direction of Pia Elisabeth Leuschner, has invited several British and Irish poets to read, but also the Israeli poet Gabriel Levin, who publishes in the UK. The bilingual readings are carefully prepared in advance, with verse translations made, mostly by young German poets associated with the centre. On occasion these events have led to further translations and individual volumes by Hamburger, Middleton, Constantine, Hofmann, Paterson, and others. Amongst those who were invited but could not come, Carol Ann Duffy, Lavinia Greenlaw, and John Burnside all have their own volumes, with Burnside most recently translated by Galbraith.[51] Burnside's is a name that recurs in many languages—his delicate lyric style, hauntingly evocative but inlaid with natural detail, and not too 'context-specific'—is clearly 'translatable', and has European-wide appeal.

The vigorous activity of the last ten years in Germany, is matched and even outdone by Poland. In terms of curiosity, hospitality, and in-depth knowledge of British, Irish, and American poetry the new Poland is second to none. Many reasons conspire to make this so. The events of 1989–90 in a sense 'officialized' the turn to Western models—as true of poetry as of market reform. Syllabi changed almost overnight, English replaced Russian as the first foreign language taught in schools. As with Germany, the presence of an active group of poet-translator-scholars (Piotr Sommer, Bohdan Zadura, Jerzy Jarniewicz, Jacek Gutorow, and Tadeusz Pióro) ensured that poetry was included in the heady Western 'mix'. Sommers and Jarniewicz are both editors of the influential journal

---

[50] Iain Galbraith: private communication. For a select bio-bibliography and some examples of Galbraith's translations see his profile in [http://www.mptmagazine.com/author/iain-galbraith-4027/]

[51] John Burnside, *Versuch über das Licht und andere Gedichte,* trans. Iain Galbraith (Munich: Carl Hanser Verlag, 2011).

Literatura na Swiecie, and have produced numbers devoted to British, but also to Welsh, Scottish, and Irish poets. As Jerzy Jarniewicz explains:

> Post-1989 poets felt free to write in their own names, not as spokesmen for the community; they could address private and everyday matters, not great historical processes; they could concentrate on language itself, on the poem's diction, not on its moral gravity; they could experiment with new styles, postmodern, but also formal, rather than follow the parabolic and sometimes more discursive tradition of the great masters (Herbert, Szymborska, Milosz)...[52]

In terms of *reception*, which includes influence, it is clear that Piotr Sommer's translations of Frank O'Hara (1987) broke like a revelation upon Polish practitioners, and even divided them into rival clans, for and against. His translations led to the Polish coinage *oharyzm* or *sommeryzm*.[53] Experts like Jarniewicz and Tadeusz Pióro agree that the New York School—O'Hara and Ashbery especially—has been more influential than any individual British or Irish poets: in this, the situation is reminiscent of France. But Larkin's mordant ironies, and his focus on the quotidian, Tony Harrison's uniquely mixed registers, and the blending of personal and political subject-matter, and Douglas Dunn's *Terry Street*, are frequently cited as having opened up new possibilities to Polish poets.

More recently, the activities of the British poet Rod Mengham, associated with the Cambridge School of poetry, has widened things still further, exposing young Polish poets to Oulipian processes, and to an avant-garde formalism reminiscent of the work of Mark Ford, another bridge-figure known in Poland, his own work deeply influenced by the New York School. And Mengham has done much to anthologize the work of younger Polish poets in English translation, including the new avant-garde Silesian School. Jerzy Jarniewicz, again, usefully sums up further qualities which, in his view, have made British and Irish poetry valuable to Polish writers:

> It shows them that poetry can be humorous; that it can embrace popular and mass culture without compromising itself; that you can be in touch with colloquial language and still care about form, metre, rhyme etc; that it is not the ambitious philosophical or metaphysical contents that makes great poems but credible language, and particularly syntax; British poetry meant beautiful sentences and strong lines.[54]

---

[52] Jerzy Jarniewicz, private communication.

[53] The pioneering role of Sommer in 'spreading the word' about Anglo-American poetry in Poland cannot be overstated. His collection in English, *Things to Translate* (Newcastle upon Tyne: Bloodaxe Books, 1991), was co-translated by John Ashbery, Douglas Dunn, and D. J. Enright, which gives a sense of his close association with the Anglo-American scene. The translator of O'Hara, Lowell, and Reznikoff, and of the Irish poets, Heaney, Mahon, and Carson, he has also published a volume of long interviews with British poets, recently reissued by Sommer: Piotr Sommer, *Zapisy rozmow: Wywiady z poetami brytyjskimii*, ed. Renata Senktas (Wroclaw: Biuro Literackie, 2011). For a profile of Sommer see online: [http://www.poetryinternational.org/piw_cms/cms/cms_module/index.php?obj_id=1453]

[54] Jerzy Jarniewicz, private communication.

This ringing endorsement by an eminent Polish poet-translator of what British and Irish poetry has meant, and may mean, in one country of the New Europe is a tempting place to conclude. It is indeed impressive that no less than forty individual titles have appeared in Poland since 1989, not including appearances in anthologies and literary journals. But once again, and the point was brought home frequently by the many experts I consulted, publication does not entail reception. And the history of reception, in terms of effective distribution, and reviews forthcoming, is at best a chequered one. Another background noise, voiced politely (and less so) by many, concerns the relative withdrawal of British Council support.[55] The unignorable result is that Scottish, Welsh, and Irish poets now receive more attention (thanks to the government-funded bodies mentioned earlier) than English poets. Which leads to a final observation: the best hope for our poetry in Europe lies in translation of quality, most often the fruit of a genuine meeting of minds and sympathies. With the best will in the world, this can be funded, but not faked or engineered. For this reason British and Irish poets should reserve their longest round of applause for those individual long-term grafters, whether expatriates or native-speakers throughout the countries of Europe, who have had the patience to build up the networks of trust and friendship indispensable to true excellence in translation.

Select Bibliography

Auden, W. H., *La Mer et le Miroir*, trans. from English and presented by Bruno Bayen and Pierre Pachet (Paris: Le Bruit du Temps, 2009).

Bacigalupo, Massimo, 'Pound and Montale—Nature, History & Myth', *Journal of Modern Literature*, 23/1 (Fall 1999), 45–58.

Burnside, John, *Versuch über das Licht und andere Gedichte*, trans. Iain Galbraith (Munich: Carl Hanser Verlag, 2011).

Eliot, T. S., *Selected Essays* (London: Faber & Faber, 1972).

Gascoyne, David, *Miserere: Poèmes 1937–1942*, trans. F.-X. Jaujard et al. (Paris: Granit, 1989).

Goffette, Guy, *Auden ou l'œil de la baleine* (Paris: Gallimard, 2005).

Hughes, Ted, 'Vasko Popa', *Winter Pollen*, ed. William Scammell (New York: Picador USA, 1994).

Hughes, Ted, *Selected Translations*, ed. Daniel Weissbort (London: Faber & Faber, 2006).

Hughes, Ted, *Poesie*, ed. Anna Ravano e Nicola Gardini (Milan: Mondadori, 2008).

---

[55] Given this chorus of dismay, I consulted the British Council directly. Paul Howson, former Head of Arts Group, now adviser to the Council, agreed to give me his view of what has happened over the past decade or so, of which I give here a slightly edited version: 'There was a planned and discernible shift in budget, away from Europe (EU and "wider" Europe alike) towards the Middle East, the Indian sub-continent and the emerging economies of Asia Pacific. At the same time, in many countries during the same period there was a gradual change in the nature of the Council's overseas staffing: comparatively expensive London-based posts were replaced where possible by local recruits, individual specialists replaced (often on retirement) by generic project managers. And thirdly, a strategy was introduced which focused on the development of large-scale, multi-country projects.' Howson maintains that the Council has not ceased to consider poetry or translation as important; but the changes outlined have squeezed resources in Europe, and projects concerning poetry, regrettably, can get elbowed out by such events as major exhibitions of visual arts, collaborative theatre productions, and the like.

Hughes, Ted, *Poèmes 1957–1994,* trans. Valérie Rouzeau and Jacques Darras (Paris: Gallimard, 2009).
Kilgore-Caradec, Jennifer and Gallet, René (eds.), *La Poésie de Geoffrey Hill et la modernité* (Paris: L'Harmattan, 2007).
Kushner, Aleksandr, *Apollo in the Snow: Selected Poems 1960–1987,* trans. Paul Graves and Carol Ueland, introd. Joseph Brodsky (London: Harvill, 1991).
Magrelli, Valerio, 'The Embrace', in Jamie McKendrick's *Faber Book of 20th Century Italian Poems* (London: Faber & Faber, 2004).
Mahon, Derek, *La Veille de nuit,* trans. Denis Rigal and J. Chuto (Paris: Éditions la folle avoine, 1996).
McKendrick, Jamie (ed.), *The Faber Book of 20th Century Italian Poems* (London: Faber & Faber, 2004).
Montague, John, *La Langue greffée,* trans. divers hands (Paris: Belin, 1988).
Muldoon, Paul, *Couffe,* trans. Elisabeth Gaudin and Jacques Jouet (Paris: Éditions Circé, 2009).
Pound, Ezra, *Guide to Kulchur* (New York: New Directions, 1970).
Pound, Ezra, *Literary Essays,* ed. T. S. Eliot (London: Faber & Faber, 1974).
Rancourt, Jacques and Wicks, Susan, *Les Pièces du paysage* and *Portrait of a Leaf as Bird* (Paris: Édition les Céphéides, 2006 and 2007).
Ricoeur, Paul, *Sur la traduction* (Paris: Bayard, 2004).
Rimbaud, Arthur, *Illuminations,* trans. John Ashbery (Manchester: Carcanet Press, 2011).
Robinson, Peter, *L'Attaccapanni e altre poesie,* trans. the author with Ornella Trevisan (Bergamo: Moretti & Vitali, 2004).
Romer, Stephen, *Tribut: Poèmes choisis,* trans. Paul de Roux, Gilles Ortlieb, Valérie Rouzeau (Cognac: Le Temps qu'il fait, 2007).
Rouzeau, Valérie, *Cold Spring in Winter,* trans. Susan Wicks (Visible Poets, 26; Todmorden: Arc Publications, 2009).
Sampson, Fiona, *Attitudes de prière,* trans. Jacques Rancourt (Paris: Éditions Transignum, 2009).
Ugrešić, Dubravka, 'House Spirits' in *Orient Express,* ed. Fiona Sampson, 3 (Easter 2003).
Valéry, Paul, 'La Crise de l'esprit', in *Œuvres,* ed. Jean Hytier (Paris: Gallimard, Bibliothèque de la Pléiade, 1965).

CHAPTER 29

SCOTTISH POETRY IN THE WIDER WORLD

IAIN GALBRAITH

Shortly before the turn of the millennium, and over a period of only two years, Scotland lost four of its greatest twentieth-century poets. This essay will focus largely on work published since, or shortly before, the passing of Norman MacCaig (1910–96), Sorley MacLean (1911–96), George Mackay Brown (1921–96), and Iain Crichton Smith (1928–98). Poetry since 1990 has been described, too, as 'Poetry in the Age of Morgan',[1] an appellation convening writers born in the 1950s and early 1960s, for whom Edwin Morgan (1920–2010)—the gifted translator of Montale, Mayakovsky, Brecht, Quasimodo, and many others, whose own work encompassed almost every poetic form—has undoubtedly been a presiding spirit. By contrast, the present survey will feel free to address, however fleetingly, poetry published in the past twenty years by writers of several generations. In passing, we shall consider topics that have been debated by literary critics and scholars between an era in which Scottish culture was 'understandably preoccupied' with its 'own struggles for autonomy',[2] and a present in which 'poetry is as often characterized by a desire to distance itself from any explicit politics of nationalism and to explore and chart a host of alternative agendas'.[3] Eschewing the impossible task of reviewing contemporary Scottish poetry in its entirety, this study will survey a selection of work written in several of Scotland's languages, revealing a variety of ways in which—as far as contemporary poetry is concerned, and increasingly so

---

[1] Donny O'Rourke, 'Poetry in the Age of Morgan', in Ian Brown and Alan Riach (eds.), *The Edinburgh Companion to Twentieth-Century Scottish Literature* (Edinburgh: Edinburgh University Press, 2009), 204–13.

[2] Robert Crawford, *Devolving English Literature* (2nd edn., Edinburgh: Edinburgh University Press, 2000), 329.

[3] Matt McGuire and Colin Nicholson (eds.), *The Edinburgh Companion to Contemporary Scottish Poetry* (Edinburgh: Edinburgh University Press, 2009), 2.

for criticism and theory, too—post-devolutionary Scotland is 'effectively a place to begin thinking about something else',[4] an interrogative base for transaction with the wider world.

In recent years a broad college of critical perspectives has acknowledged the role of Scottish writers and artists in articulating the pressures for political change that issued, in 1999, in the establishment of a Scottish Parliament. For example, the influential *Dream State* poetry anthologies of 1994 and 2002, edited by the poet Donny O'Rourke (b. 1959) and straddling the referendum of 1997 and the events of 1999, could be seen, not least by their editor, to demonstrate that 'Scotland's artists did more than its politicians to dream up a new Scotland'.[5] In the same period, however, and now that national devolution has come to seem irreversible, many poets have emerged from the debates intrinsic to 'home rule' to explore a more open field of dialogical options, one that 'makes connections [...], be they with England or Europe or North America or Afghanistan, or be they with realms which are non-human'.[6] In the past decade, too, critics have begun to analyse the self-conscious transformation of the devolutionary consensus away from topics of national autonomy and the promotion of 'Scottishness' towards a more exploratory, outward-searching period of cultural production. The theorist Eleanor Bell, for example, has written of the changing mood of the 1990s and thereafter as indicating a shift away from 'introversion', providing 'a long-awaited and much-needed potential for Scottish literature to look beyond the often overly fixed boundaries of "home"'.[7] The scholar and poet Robert Crawford (b. 1959) has described a 'cultural maturity that is impatient of being boxed in by the formulaically "Scottish"', while observing that the development of a sense of autonomy in the post-devolutionary era 'requires more than ever an alert and inclusive looking out'. He hopes that poets will now feel 'fine to fly free of local contours', and that critics will 'adopt wider international angles which might align, say, recent Scottish and Australian poetry, or examine more closely Scottish and French cultural links'.[8] In a symposium entitled 'Poets' Parliament', the poet John Burnside (b. 1955), while declaring himself 'strongly pro self-determination', has written of a need to 'define ourselves' as 'what we are open to', not by 'what we are closed against'.[9] And in other statements, pleading for the emancipation of literature in the post-devolutionary era, questions have been raised as to whether, in the words of the Gaelic poet Christopher Whyte (b. 1952), 'the setting up of a Scottish parliament [would] at last allow Scottish literature to be literature first and foremost, rather than the expression of a nationalist movement',[10] or, as the critic Berthold Schoene has put

---

[4] Matthew Jarvis, 'Repositioning Wales: Poetry after the Second Flowering', in Daniel G. Williams (ed.), *Slanderous Tongues: Essays on Welsh Poetry in English 1970–2005* (Bridgend: Seren, 2010), 49.

[5] Donny O'Rourke, *Dream State: The New Scottish Poets* (2nd edn., Edinburgh: Polygon, 2002), 2.

[6] Kathleen Jamie, 'More than Human', in Attila Dósa, *Beyond Identity: New Horizons in Modern Scottish Poetry* (Amsterdam, New York: Rodopi, 2009), 141.

[7] Eleanor Bell, *Questioning Scotland: Literature, Nationalism, Postnationalism* (Basingstoke: Palgrave, 2004), 41.

[8] Crawford, *Devolving English Literature*, 329, 338–9.

[9] *Edinburgh Review*, 100 (1999), 71.

[10] Christopher Whyte, 'Masculinities in Contemporary Scottish Fiction', *Forum for Modern Language Studies*, 34/2 (1998), 284.

it, whether Scottish literature would now be 'allowed to go cosmopolitan rather than native'.[11]

Any concept of cosmopolitanism that is offered as a paradigm for the critical appraisal of literary texts must clearly be nuanced. It is possible, for example, that certain forms of so-called 'micro-cosmopolitanism', encouraging 'bottom-up localization' and 'appropriately deep forms of intercultural engagement', may indeed offer a democratized antidote both to the centralist national state on the one hand and 'macro-cosmopolitan'[12] hegemonies on the other, encouraging instead the kinds of culturally and ecologically sensitive contexts for global citizenship that are, as we shall see, also sought by some Scottish poets. Berthold Schoene understands the necessity of such differentiation, demanding a Scottish cosmopolitanism in which neither an introverted separatism nor a transcendent elite dominate the emerging polis, because society is 'never closed or whole, never fearful or tired of evolving, never conclusively devolved or assembled'.[13] For better or worse, however, a denationalized, cosmopolitan space has indeed become a feature of the contemporary international literary scene. Reviewing Pascale Casanova's work *La République mondiale des lettres* (2008), the Italian-based English novelist Tim Parks has referred to an 'international space' created, on the one hand, through a 'rivalry between the growing number of nations eager to establish a literary prestige, promoting their poets and novelists internationally with the help of government institutions', and, on the other hand, 'by writers seeking to escape from the strictures of more established literary traditions into an emancipated trans-national culture where the text can be "pure" again'.[14] However, Christopher Whyte's demand for 'literature first and foremost' does not attempt to lead Scottish poetry criticism into this transcendent space. His suggestion, formulated in a chapter entitled 'Alternative Approaches' in the critical monograph *Modern Scottish Poetry* (2004), is not that we should ignore the historical or national dimensions of Scottish poetry, but that these aspects should no longer be privileged by Scottish literary critics. Repudiating an observed bias towards 'the question of Scottishness' in poetry criticism, he wishes to reclaim a degree of centrality for poetics and hermeneutics, and to ask what makes poetry different from other genres—to interrogate, in other words, not *Scottish* poetry, but Scottish *poetry*.[15] Whyte's aim is to ask his readers to think anew about the intrinsic values of poetry. In this, he finds an ally in the poet Don Paterson (b. 1963), who has complained that it has been 'the insistence on poetry's auxiliary usefulness—for example in raising issues of cultural identity, as a form of therapy, or generating academic papers—that has encouraged it to think far less of itself, and so eroded its real power to actually inspire readers to think or live differently'.[16]

---

[11] Berthold Schoene, 'Going Cosmopolitan', in Schoene (ed.), *The Edinburgh Companion to Contemporary Scottish Literature* (Edinburgh: Edinburgh University Press, 2007), 8.

[12] Michael Cronin, *Translation and Identity* (Abingdon: Routledge, 2006), 30.

[13] Schoene, 'Going Cosmopolitan', 10.

[14] Tim Parks, 'The Nobel individual', *Times Literary Supplement* (22 Apr. 2011), 14.

[15] Christopher Whyte, *Modern Scottish Poetry* (Edinburgh: Edinburgh University Press, 2004), 23–4.

[16] Don Paterson, 'The Dark Art of Poetry', South Bank Centre T. S. Eliot Lecture, 30 Oct. 2004, [www.donpaterson.com/files/arspoetica/1.html]

'Every poem is an island': Robert Crawford's dictum, in apparent reversal of John Donne's 'No man is an Iland, intire of it selfe',[17] seems at first glance to be making a case for withdrawal from the world. Far from a plea for isolation, however, Crawford is describing a quality of poetic diction. 'To get to a poem', he continues, 'means sailing out from the mainland of routine language'. Robert Crawford's earlier work, under the programmatic title of his collection *A Scottish Assembly* (1990), self-consciously drew on what he termed 'Scottish resources'. In poems of wit and imagination like 'Henry Bell Introduces Scotland's First Commercial Steamship', 'John Logie Baird', 'Scotland' ('Semi-conductor country…'), or 'Alba Einstein', such linguistic and cultural resources were deployed to explore the 'boundless' possibilities for a new political and cultural confidence that would carry his 'chip of a nation' ('Scotland') to national self-determination. While Crawford's most recent work, published as tension mounts in the run-up to Scotland's 'Independence Referendum', appears to revisit an overtly nationalist territory—'Wake up, little country, | Stretch yourself. It's time | To fling the covers back, and sing' ('Reveille')[18]—his poetry, like his scholarly work, has frequently moved much beyond the local grain, with settings ranging from Wyoming to East Westphalia, and subjects from the Bronze Age to communications technology, taking in concrete poetry and translations of Latin verse along the way. A characteristic that runs through much of his work is the desire not to flee the local, but to link the local and the distant, the familiar and the exotic. 'When you spoke about poems in Vietnamese | I heard behind the pride in your voice | Like a ceilidh in an unexpected place | The burning violins of small peoples', he writes in 'Nec Tamen Consumebatur', from *A Scottish Assembly* (1990),[19] and in 'Arbuthnott', from *The Tip of My Tongue* (2003): 'On the swings, one minute | Feet on the ground, the next all up in the air, | | I catch how Kincardineshire's sky's | Transvaalish, Budapesty, Santa Barbaran, | | Zurich on a perfect day'.[20] The poet has even invented a tongue-in-cheek *terminus technicus* for such bonding of centrality and marginality, for poetic transactions between the vernacular local and the wider world: 'Cosmopoliback ofbeyondism'. According to Crawford, 'just as any poem-island has the tang of the back of beyond', it has, too, 'aspects, shared speech-forms, political shapes, faiths, which link it to other places. All poems are connected, most simply through the shared cosmopolis of verse.'[21]

To portray the environment of Scottish poetry as if its reach could be reduced to a dilemma between nationalism and cosmopolitanism, however, would be to traduce the work of poets, whether writing in Scotland or elsewhere, who, in the course of the past decade or earlier, have sought a wide diversity of forms, idioms, aesthetics, poetics, and politics. This is true not only of English-language poets, including Robin Robertson

---

[17] John Donne, 'Meditation XVII', in Donne, *Devotions upon Emergent Occasions*, ed. Anthony Raspa (Oxford: Oxford University Press, 1987), 87.
[18] *Edinburgh Review*, 132 (2011), 104.
[19] Robert Crawford, *A Scottish Assembly* (London: Jonathan Chatto, 1990), 34.
[20] Robert Crawford, *The Tip of My Tongue* (London: Jonathan Cape, 2003), 6.
[21] 'Cosmopolibackofbeyondism', in W. N. Herbert and Matthew Hollis (eds.), *Strong Words: Modern Poets on Modern Poetry* (Tarset: Bloodaxe Books, 2000), 262.

(b. 1955), Jackie Kay (b. 1961), Thomas A. Clark (b. 1944), Frank Kuppner (b. 1951), Kate Clanchy (b. 1965), Iain Bamforth (b. 1959), Angela McSeveney (b. 1964), Peter McCarey (b. 1956), Robin Fulton (b. 1937), Richard Price (b. 1966), Liz Lochhead (b. 1947), or Kenneth White (b. 1936), but also for poets writing in Scots, like William Hershaw (b. 1957), Rab Wilson (b. 1960), and Liz Niven (b. 1952), or in Gaelic, such as Aonghas MacNeacail (b. 1942), Meg Bateman (b. 1959), or Martin MacIntyre (b. 1965). Such writers include Shetlandic poets, too, like Robert Alan Jamieson (b. 1958), the author of *Shoormal* (1986) and *Nord Atlantik Drift* (1999), and Christine De Luca (b. 1947), whose work, displaying an acute awareness of the 'inter-animation' (Mikhail Bakhtin) of languages, uses local concerns and settings to reach out to a wide range of cultures, at the same time importing ideas and images, and indeed whole poems from the Welsh, English, Norwegian, and Swedish, to enrich her own localities and speech. In De Luca's volume *Parallel Worlds* (2005), we find concrete poems in Shetlandic that witness the way a hill overlooking the Sound of Bressay can be transformed by 'A | scud | o snaa' to become 'Mt Fuji abön da Soond' ('Glinderin'), or which track the zigzagging of a 'dolmus' (a Turkish taxi) as it snakes across the page and 'roond da | ruckly bends | on da gaet | ta Gemiler | beach' ('Da rodd ta Gemiler beach'). De Luca feels open to a variety of overlapping identities that she has come to accept as her own over a period of time, such as European and Scots, while writing poems in English and Shetlandic (the language that she describes as holding the most emotional reality for her). Sometimes her poems adventure a heady synthesis of both languages, with neologisms and Latinate inclusions sitting alongside local sounds: 'Wir peerie pilgrimage | on da boat ta Shetland | isna plain sailin' ('Plain Sailin').[22]

Meanwhile, the poems in *Almanacs* (2005) and *Nigh-No-Place* (2008) in which the younger poet Jen Hadfield (b. 1978 in Cheshire) gives voice to the weather and vowels of her adopted Shetland home are pervious to heterogeneous localities and idioms, bird-calls, rain, and sparkling northern light:

The spinner fluchters,
but falters not
in its bee-line for the shore,

twinkling like space-trash;
beyond, the Djub,
green as ten green bottles, galactic roar
('Fishing at Spiggie')[23]

This perfectly measured poem, thirteen lines in all, enacts, in diction and imagery, a breathtaking spatial and temporal arc from local landscape, via the planetary, to a galactic rush; from the biblical ('falters not') and archaic (*djub* is an old Shetlandic 'noa', a

---

[22] Christina De Luca, *Parallel Lines: Poems in Shetlandic and English* (Edinburgh: Luath Press, 2005), 22, 42, 50.

[23] Jen Hadfield, *Nigh-No-Place* (Tarset: Bloodaxe Books, 2008), 41.

fisherman's taboo word for the sea) to the age of space travel. In tensely cast fields, concrete shapes, and traditional stanzas, too, Hadfield's poems draw together the lexis, landscapes, and emotional dimensions of her sojourns in a sensuous salmagundi of localities and soundscapes.

Thematic and idiomatic variety is also to be found in the work of Gaelic poets, such as Rody Gorman (b. 1960) or Kevin MacNeil (b. 1972), whose innovative work, at least in as far as the present author can perceive, has continued to push beyond conventional frontiers, and to reach out to topics, forms, and traditions that have not always been thought to belong to the authentic domain of Gaelic poetry. Innovative vitality, moreover, against the background of a language whose survival has not felt secure in recent decades, and whose speakers and literary arbiters have therefore shown naturally defensive tendencies, has sometimes been viewed as something of a double-edged sword. The work of younger Gaelic poets, 'appearing to have little interest in capturing the traditional soul of Gaelic',[24] could not always count on the unconditional sympathy of senior Gaelic critics. It is not long since Myles Campbell (b. 1944), Fearghas MacFhionnlaigh (b. 1948), Christopher Whyte (b. 1952), and Anne Frater (b. 1967), open to as many new impressions and ideas as any poets of their time, were criticized for losing 'the flavor of tradition', for lacking 'Gaelic convention', and for allowing a gulf to open between the codes of their own work and the basic codes of traditional Gaelic verse. And yet the very estrangement felt by the influential poet and scholar Donald MacAulay (b. 1930) helps mellow his detraction, seeing it as only 'natural', in times of change, that Gaelic poetry 'is being drawn out into the current of the world as a whole by its users, both native speakers and learners'.[25]

Contemporary Gaelic poetry frequently chooses subjects that place it beyond what might be described as conventional Highland settings. Christopher Whyte, who is not only also a scholar and novelist, but also a prolific translator of Russian, Italian, Catalan, and Spanish poetry, has set his poems against Chinese, Italian, or French backgrounds. His writing has been described as exhibiting 'a borderland poetics'. According to this view Whyte's '(in)voluntary liminal status (as gay, as ex-Catholic in a predominantly Protestant country, as a non-native Gaelic writer in English, as a self-uprooted scholar who lived in Italy for twelve years and has now settled in Hungary) is the privileged standpoint from which he can perceive both the value and the elusiveness of borders'.[26] One poem in his volume *Bho Leabhar-Latha Maria Malibran* (*From the Diary of Maria Malibran*, 2009) deals with problems of creativity and sexuality in the life of Pier Paolo Pasolini, and although the poem apostrophizes Pasolini throughout (another poem is addressed to the Russian poet Marina Tsvetaeva, much of whose poetry Whyte has

---

[24] Ronald Black (ed.), *An Tuil: Anthology of 20th-Century Scottish Gaelic Verse* (Edinburgh: Polygon, 1999), p. xxi.

[25] Donald MacAulay, review of Christopher Whyte, *An Aghaidh na Sìorraigheachd / In the Face of Eternity: Eight Gaelic Poets, Gairm*, 157 (Winter 1991–2). Translation by Black (ed.), *An Tuil*, p. lxiii.

[26] Carla Sassi, 'The (B)order in Modern Scottish Literature', in Brown and Riach (eds.), *The Edinburgh Companion to Twentieth-Century Scottish Literature*, 150.

translated into English), it is clear that the conflicts treated so sympathetically in the poem have been felt by its own author. On occasion, the poet's awareness that something in his work has violated conventional Gaelic boundaries erupts ironically into the poem's address: '(tha mi gan cluinntinn a-cheana: | "Dàn mu AIDS! Sa Ghàidhlig!")'—'(already I hear them: | "A poem about AIDS? In Gaelic!")' ('Elegy for Alasdair Cameron', trans. Michel Bryne); or 'An-dràsta ruigidh mi uair eile guth | boireannaich àraidh, 'g ràdh gu h-aimhreiteach | gur rosg, "s nach bàrdachd idir, tha mi sgrìobhadh" '—'I'm interrupted by a voice I know, | a certain woman saying crabbitly, | "This isn't verse you're writing, it's prose" ' ('To Pier Paolo Pasolini', trans. Niall O'Gallagher). The longer title poem, set in and around Paris and adopting the narrative standpoint of the mezzo-soprano Maria Malibran, one of the most celebrated opera singers of the nineteenth century, ends with an ironic envoi, again in the form of the poet's defence. To paraphrase: if the poet's intention had been to keep his reader happy, his poem might have named the various implements in the barn of his dead grandfather, and complained that they were rusty now and of how Tradition dies, or, he might have delivered a soul-searching account of his homesickness for the lost language of his kin, the language our (implicating the Gaelic-speaking reader) children cannot be brought to learn:

An àite sin, sgrìobh mi mu bhoireannach
nach robh facal Gàidhlig aice, nach robh
fhios aice, 's dòcha, gu robh cànan ann
den t-seòrsa.

(Instead, I chose a woman for my subject,
someone who didn't have a single word
of Gaelic—very likely never heard
of such a language.)[27]

Whyte has written of what he has called 'the difficulties and obstacles involved in finding and maintaining a voice in Gaelic', a tongue whose future survival may be in doubt. But he has also written of the joys of finding that voice. In describing the specific task of giving a Gaelic voice to Maria Malibran, and to a life whose Spanish or Neapolitan ambience seemed so very far from the conventions and lexis of Gaelic, he writes: 'I was doing something which often leads poets using stigmatized languages, reified in terms of tonality and subject-matter, to resort to translation. Yet I was not translating, I had found a way of freeing the language of my poetry from the restrictions it labors under in everyday use.' And yet the sense of liberation Whyte describes is not without ambivalence. Writing in Gaelic—as someone who has learned the language rather than having been born into it—is the fruit of a 'determination not to forget', and yet the matter of forgetting or remembering is not all up to him. 'I have a sense', he writes, 'of deriving from, if I do not actually belong to, a disappeared or disappearing people, one of which

---

[27] Christopher Whyte, *Bho Leabhar-Latha Maria Malibran* (Stornaway: Acair, 2009), 16–17, 88–9, 128–9. Translation by Sally Evans.

all traces are being successfully cancelled from both history and literature. I continue to see Glasgow, the city where I was born and grew up, as a place of exile, deportation and amnesia.'[28] Such words have been used unbearably often and in many languages during the sorry history of twentieth-century ethnic displacement. They recall, too, the poignancy of the final stanza of a poem by John Burnside, describing the last moments of a language before extinction, when its last speaker remembers a word 'they had, when he was young, | a word they rarely spoke, though it was there | for all they knew that nobody remembered' ('The Last Man Who Spoke Ubykh').[29]

Burnside's politics and poetics go hand in glove. In terms of the former, he might be described as a 'micro-cosmopolitan' ecologist, aspiring to global rather than national citizenship: 'I'd like terrains in Scotland to be managed by people living there and by people who have a genuine interest in their landscape. [...] I'd like to see no countries but regions, and people who form allegiances together for certain purposes.'[30] Burnside has stated that his earliest poetry was encouraged by reading translations from other languages, and that he started learning Spanish as a way into the work of Lorca, Machado, Guillén, and Paz. He is also a tireless advocate of contemporary American poetry, championing Allison Funk, Brigit Pegeen Kelly, Robert Wrigley, and others. In an essay proposing 'poetry as ecology', Burnside has described the kind of poetry he wants to read and write as being akin to a scientific discipline: a form of *scientia*, by which he means a tentative, questing process that can lead us to 'an understanding of—and *with*—the world, and of our place in it'. Unexpectedly, perhaps, Burnside's elaboration of this kind of knowledge places it within a context of recovery, or retrieval, rather than evoking that paradigm of projective improvement with which science is more commonly linked. His *scientia* is a technique for 'reclaiming the authentic' and 'reinstating the real', and a means of renewing human 'membership of a wider, more-than-human world'.[31] At the same time, the human figures in his poems are less *Homo sapiens* than *Homo quaerens*, seekers of a reality that eludes our practical or historical gaze, summoned to 'the purer urgency | of elsewhere',[32] and 'homesick for the other animals'.[33] Humans, in Burnside's work, have frequently lost their way, forfeited any 'natural' dwelling place in the world, and one message seems to be that poetry can help us to find a way out of the narrow, calamitous place to which ecological neglect has brought us.

An epistemology of recovery might suggest a wistfully utopian outlook, the mournful longing for a 'lost world' in which the currently alienated perspective was preceded by a meaningful sense of belonging. Perhaps it is true that the poet's advocacy of recovery begins with an awareness of our having squandered—through surrender to the reckless

---

[28] Christopher Whyte, 'Translation as Predicament', *Translation and Literature*, 9/2 (2000), 185–7.
[29] John Burnside, *The Good Neighbour* (London: Jonathan Cape, 2005), 59.
[30] 'Poets and Other Animals', in Attila Dósa, *Beyond Identity* (Amsterdam and New York: Rodopi, 2009), 125.
[31] John Burnside, 'Poetry as Ecology', in Robert Crawford (ed.), *Contemporary Poetry and Contemporary Science* (Oxford: Oxford University Press, 2006), 94–5.
[32] John Burnside, *The Asylum Dance* (London: Jonathan Cape, 2000), 11.
[33] John Burnside, *The Light Trap* (London: Jonathan Cape, 2002), 20.

exploitation of natural resources—a more responsible incorporation in the actual. But his science of reclamation does not seek redemption in the past. Burnside's seventh collection, *The Asylum Dance*, opens with an epigraph from Martin Heidegger's 1951 talk 'Building Dwelling Thinking'. The epigraph begins: 'The proper dwelling plight lies in this, that mortals ever search anew for the essence of dwelling, that they *must ever learn to dwell*.' If Burnside's poetry investigates a condition of nostalgia, it does so without sentimentality. *Nostos*, the homecoming, means in this context not going back to the home one has left behind, but a constant process of re-inhabitation. By dwelling in a place, according to Heidegger, we care for it. Dwelling is 'saving the earth': releasing what one cares for to an existence that is beyond, or immune to, pragmatic design. Essentially, however, this relationship with the 'home ground' is not innate or instinctive, not, in other words, constituted by birthright or the rights of nation or ownership. According to this logic, to paraphrase Heraclitus, we do not return to the same home twice. Instead, truly humane work must be that of 'homing' (a word favoured by Burnside since his earliest poetry): repeatedly returning to care anew.

To Burnside, lyric poetry is the heuristic medium that enables us—poet and reader—to 'navigate the world'. Paradoxically, it enriches us with knowledge of reality and of ourselves even as we discover that the goal of our quest, by its very nature, lies beyond the poet's craft. However, if the world 'in itself' withdraws from our descriptive gaze, the poem, Burnside suggests, need not return from such a voyage empty-handed. 'Looking outward', as Mark Doty puts it, 'we experience the one who does the seeing.'[34] What is gained by the poem, one might add, paraphrasing Heidegger, is an understanding of the earth's 'saving': things as they are may indeed elude the directness of our gaze, and yet our attempts to draw closer to them tell us *that* they are there, helping us to understand and assess the relations between ourselves and others. In the intimacy of the relational, according to Burnside, we find the coordinates for any ecology of the real, and a basis for studying a 'meaningful way of dwelling in this extraordinary world'.[35]

Burnside's poem 'Taxonomy' demonstrates one such approximation to the actual—the attempt to calibrate certain multiplicities or differences in natural colour and texture. The poem records the aesthetic exchange that takes place between a questing subject and the objects he is drawn to investigate, an exchange that exemplifies lyric poetry's contribution to mapping the boundaries of experience, knowledge, and language. Dedicated to the American poet Linda Gregerson—who herself has written of the 'resistance' of the factual to language, of how the 'world so rarely || lets us in'[36]—'Taxonomy' speaks of the way poetic language can form around a silent reciprocity (remember that it was understanding not only *of*—but *with*—the world that defined Burnside's concept of *scientia*) between sensuous perception and reflection, with 'looking always worked towards a

---

[34] Mark Doty, *Still Life with Oysters and Lemon* (Boston: Beacon Press, 2001), 67.

[35] Burnside, 'Poetry as Ecology', 95.

[36] John Burnside and Maurice Riordan (eds.), *Wild Reckoning* (London: Calouste Gulbenkian Foundation, 2004), 91.

word: | trading the limits of speech | for the unsaid presence'.[37] Here, Burnside's poetic researches a glimpsed 'otherlife of things' that are 'gifted with absence | speaking a different tongue' ('Fields'). On the one hand, this 'trading' recoups, in John Macmurray's words, the heterocentric dimension of the 'personal other'. Burnside writes: 'For an ecologically *mindful* poet, the task is one of reconnecting, of rediscovering, as it were, one's own nature through connection with a wider reality, with the more-than-human.'[38] On the other hand, the 'unsaid presence' is something that has been 'set free' (Heidegger) by the terms of the same transaction, ensuring that one experiences 'the place in which one lives, tarries, or strays as unknown or strange':[39]

>   like the bird
> I saw one evening on my journey home—
> a migrant foreigner that must have strayed
> to what I knew of sky and open fields:
> some northern bird perhaps
>   its feathers red
> around the throat and chest
>   its hollow song
> so much a question to the self I was
> I came through
>   on the far side of the day
> uncertain
>   plundered
>   given up for lost.
> ('De Anima')[40]

Burnside's poetry, at its best, bodies forth the dynamics of this dialectic, so that the poem's interrogation of our relation to the home-place is invariably also a retrieval of the latency and wildness that human settlement threatens to destroy.

'Trading the limits of speech | for the unsaid presence', Burnside's writing—with its receptivity towards images and ideas across cultural and linguistic borders, its pursuit of European philosophies, and its ear for American sensibilities—also exhibits many of the characteristics that are held to exemplify the broader conception of translation as a function of exchange between cultures, media, disciplines, and periods. Problems of translation and cultural exchange have preoccupied several Scottish writers in recent decades, such questions tending to arise in regions in which the interaction of different languages and histories necessitates mediation in a variety of forms. It is in this context, too, with an awareness of 'the languages and cultures and tradition which surround' her, that Kathleen Jamie (b. 1962) has described writing as 'the scene of our constant

---

[37] Burnside, *The Light Trap*, 7.
[38] Burnside, 'Poetry as Ecology', 99.
[39] Kate Rigby, *Topographies of the Sacred: The Poetics of Place in European Romanticism* (Charlottesville and London: University of Virginia Press, 2004), 89.
[40] Burnside, *The Good Neighbour*, 38.

negotiation'.[41] For some poets, the desire to negotiate with the 'wider world around us' (Jamie) has forged a link between the writing and translation of poetry. Poets of several generations—Ken Cockburn (b. 1960), Robin Fulton (b. 1937), Anna Crowe (b. 1945), Edwin Morgan (b. 1920), Alastair Reid (b. 1926), Robin Robertson (b. 1955), Richard Price (b. 1966), Tessa Ransford (b. 1938), Liz Lochhead (b. 1947) amongst them—have translated work from a broad range of languages and—in text or workshop—reflected on the task of the translator. Historically, the strategies adopted by translator-poets have varied, with some choosing a more scholarly approach, attempting to remain as close as possible to their source, while others, perhaps following a personal affinity with the spirit of the original poem, or resolutely true to their own poetics, have felt the need for starker liberties.

Don Paterson (b. 1963), for example, despite having produced empathic versions of work by Rainer Maria Rilke and Antonio Machado, has expressed a profound scepticism towards the entire project of translation. 'Those things of which poets are most proud', he states, 'depend wholly on idiomatic circumstances, tiny acoustic resonances and tiny shades of meaning and association that can have no direct equivalent in the host language.'[42] In an appendix to his volume *Orpheus: A Version of Rilke* (2006) Paterson has explained what he sees as the difference between a translation and a version.[43] Translation, he writes, 'tries to remain true to the original words and their relations, and its primary aim is one of stylistic elegance', by which he means a tendency to eliminate the very 'idiomatic' irregularities of which he considers poets to be 'most proud'. A translation 'glosses the original, but does not try to replace it'. Versions, by contrast, 'are trying to be poems in their own right'. In other words, they have 'their own course, their own process, and have to make a virtue of their own human mistakes'. However, many readers of poetry would probably seek these qualities in the best translations, too, whose aim, rebuilding the original in a different language, can only be that of creating a new poem, and yet whose distinctive challenge, as Paterson avers, is framed by the translator's knowledge of and commitment to 'the original words and their relations'. If, as Paterson posits, a version intends to fully cast off from the original, its relation to the source text, however pronounced, might not be the primary criterion by which we should judge it. Instead, the compositional strategy of the 'version', borrowing whatever it needs of the original's 'detailed ground-plan and elevation',[44] is no different from that of the poem, which, in Paterson's own terms, is not, in the first instance, to approximate to another poem, but to make readers 'complicit in the creative business of their self-transformation'. As a means to achieving this, Paterson proposes exploring the realm of metaphoricity, and smuggling into language the 'new unity' that results from 'the love affair between two hitherto unconnected terms: two words, two ideas, two phrases, two

---

[41] Jamie, 'More than Human', 144.
[42] 'The Music of Consciousness', in Dósa, *Beyond Identity,* 150.
[43] For further discussion of Paterson's 'Fourteen Notes on the Version' see Peter Robinson, *Poetry & Translation: The Art of the Impossible* (Liverpool: Liverpool University Press, 2010), 30–2, 153–4.
[44] Don Paterson, *Orpheus: A Version of Rilke* (London: Faber & Faber, 2006, 2007), 73.

images, a word and an image, a phrase and a new context for it'.[45] In 'The Wreck', for example, from Paterson's collection *The Landing Light* (2003), the narrator's memory of a past love threads metaphor and simile, line by line, to configure an eerie intimacy as the lovers 'stripped off in the timbered dark, || gently hooked each other on | like aqualungs, and thundered down || to mine our lovely secret wreck. | We surfaced later, breathless, back || to back, then made our way alone | up the mined beach of the dawn'. The transactions of metaphor, germane to translation as to the version and the poem, generate the transformative energy that reaches out to engage with and stimulate change in the world of its readers.

Paterson writes in his 'Fourteen Notes on the Version' that the best-qualified, the bilingual, '[p]aradoxically [...] have no need nor selfish urge to translate at all', unless for pecuniary reasons. What, then, is the 'selfish urge' of the translator? Carol Ann Duffy (b. 1955) may not be a translator in the narrower, inter-lingual sense, but her poems frequently explore boundaries, whether sexual, social, or linguistic. The narrator of her poem 'River', from the collection *The Other Country* (1990), describes the pleasurable disorientation experienced by a woman moving through an almost dreamlike landscape, a boundary zone, who comes to the place along a river where 'the language changes' and where water 'crosses the border, | translates itself, but words stumble, fall back'. Here, she encounters flora and fauna that are arrayed in foreign names. The narrator reflects on the problem of rendering her intense sensation of difference in language, the conundrum of translatability in an environment where the relations between signifier and signified appear unstable, and 'blue and silver fish dart away over stone, | stoon, stein, like the meanings of things, vanish'. The poem asks of the reader what he or she could write on a postcard home (to the mother-tongue) to communicate the feeling of being 'somewhere else'.[46] If an aporia is implied, it is this: if a fragment of the elsewhere is transmitted in all its authentic strangeness, the folk back home won't understand a word; but if I translate it into our own language, its difference will disappear, so that what had inspired me to write home in the first place will remain undisclosed. According to this outlook, there can be no mediation between the foreign and familiar; their respective truths must instead remain unconnected: fragmentary. As Hans Blumenberg has shown,[47] however, the Romantic trope of the fragment, or of the 'incomplete' world, can be traced back not only to the pre-Enlightenment epistemological metaphor of the terra incognita, but also to its modern manifestation in a Kantian context of world-making, and, more directly, to Friedrich Schlegel's positing of the 'still unfinished' world whose completion demands our active participation. In this paradigm, translation, too, is a motor of the continuing creation of the world, a response to the latent futurity in things, the urge to create a whole. Only in a world of absolute values, then, a frozen world lacking past or future, would the aporia phrased above preclude the writing of Duffy's postcard home. The vitality, indeed the very existence, of metaphor, poiesis, and translation, on the other hand, *depend* on the absence of such a world. They are devices by which we keep open our aesthetic and epistemological

---

[45] 'The Dark Art of Poetry', [www.donpaterson.com/files/arspoetica/1.html] [accessed 28 Oct. 2011]
[46] Carol Ann Duffy, *Selected Poems* (Harmondsworth: Penguin Books, 1994), 87.
[47] Hans Blumenberg, *Paradigms for a Metaphorology* (Ithaca, NY: Cornell University Press, 2010), 52–61.

horizons—their inferential, generative, and mediative properties allowing us to contextualize emergent (and vanishing) meaning. Like poetry, and like the woman in Duffy's poem, translation inhabits the border zone, the threshold, the domain of 'langage à l'état naissant'.[48]

Poetry in Scots—in anthologies, journals, and books—is frequently accompanied by a glossary, suggesting that the attention of non-Scots readers must always commute between Scots words and their English definitions, or else be denied access. For similar reasons, little Gaelic poetry has appeared in recent decades without English translations, which have generally been the poet's self-translations. This is often explained by the fear that Gaelic readerships are too small to sustain the costs of publication, or by the hope that translation into the hegemonic language English will give Gaelic writing access to the wider world. However, Corinna Krause, Christopher Whyte, Peter Mackay, and other scholars have shown that dependency on translation into a dominant language is not always a boon. One effect of this hierarchy has been that Gaelic poetry, by Sorley MacLean (b. 1911), for example, has become better known in English than Gaelic, lending to a translation prominence that the source text will never know. Moreover, Corinna Krause's research has pointed to a tendency even among Gaelic native speakers to rely on comparison of the Gaelic with the English translation.[49] Self-translations can be especially insidious, paradoxically appearing to submit the intended 'meaning' of the poet's Gaelic text. An effect of translations can be that the reading experience is ' "decentered" away from the Gaelic text, without coming to rest in the English text'. Instead 'the "poem" that is read by a Gaelic speaker *is*, in effect, the interlingual dialogue between the two languages—it is a text that is part Gaelic and part English, and which, strictly speaking, is centered in the white space between the two columns of print'.[50]

A particularly inventive reversal of this predicament is enacted in recent work by the Dublin-born poet Rody Gorman, who writes in Irish and Scots Gaelic, a prolific translator (of Cavafy, Milosz, Neruda, Holub amongst others) into Gaelic, and of Gaelic writing into English. By contrast with conventional translations, the English versions of the Gaelic poems in *Beartan Briste* (2011) do not undermine the authority of the Gaelic. As Robert Dunbar writes in his introduction to Gorman's volume, 'only those readers with sufficient Gaelic to understand how the context of the original informs meaning will be able to fully appreciate the meaning and the quite distinct artistry of the English'. The second stanza of 'Tìde' (English title: 'tideweathertime'), for example, reads:

Tha mi 'g iarraidh
Gum bi mo chuid dhathan
Ri bualadh air an tìde
Mar a bhios an anail air an fhalaid
Air aghaidh na creige.

---

[48] 'L'Enseignement de la poétique au College de France', in Paul Valéry, *Œuvres*, ed. Jean Hytier, i (Paris: Gallimard, 1957), 1440.

[49] Corinna Krause, 'Translating Gaelic Scotland: The Culture of Translation in the Context of Scottish Gaelic Literature', [www.aber.ac.uk/mercator/images/CorinnaKrause.pdf] [accessed 28 Oct. 2011], *passim*.

[50] Peter Mackay, 'An Guth and the Leabhar Mòr: Dialogues between Scottish Gaelic and Irish Poetry', *Journal of Irish and Scottish Studies*, 1/2 (Mar. 2008), 179–80.

The English 'translation' is given as follows: 'I want my dyecolours to strike the tideweathertime like restbreath on the varnish of the quarrycliffrockface'.[51] According to Aonghas MacNeacail, cited in an appendix in the book, Gorman has presented 'literally every English definition given, for every word, in Edward Dwelly's masterly Dictionary of the Gaelic language'. In fact, while Gorman has selected many of Dwelly's definitions, he has also left others aside. Reading requires similar acts of discrimination on the part of the bilingual Gaelic reader, who, coming across conglomerates like 'quarrycliffrockface' must go back to 'aghaidh na creige' to understand the Gaelic origin of the composite and construct his or her own image from the available options. Here, the English does not displace or dominate the Gaelic but introduces a poetic estrangement, supporting the Gaelic text by making it the key to the English, rather than vice versa, and letting the reader see the Gaelic in a fresh light.

Gorman's reversal of the role of the translation is reminiscent of a different experiment, two decades earlier, in which W. N. Herbert (b. 1961) and Robert Crawford, in their co-authored volume *Sharawaggi* (1990), plundered the Scots word-hoard, often to hilarious effect. The reader turning to the glossary or facing translation for clarification of recondite Scots words is, in turn, confronted by the semantic challenge of the English translation. For the lines, 'Oor boadies mell lik thi raise-net fishin, | Lik a kindlie tae Adam's wine', we read on the facing page: 'Our bodies grow intimate like that kind of fishing where part of the net rises and flows and subsides with the tide, like an ancestral claim to water'.[52] The effect, like that of Gorman's use of English, is to create an estranged English 'translation' experience that is disconcerting enough to point the reader back to the Scots text. Kathleen McPhilemy has described the dynamic thus:

> The presentation of the poems as dual texts is a constant temptation to abandon the Scots for the apparently more accessible English. But after being dragged headlong through Crawford's minimally punctuated rush of imagery, the reader returns to the Scots, where the line-breaks and movement of the verse serve to steady the poem. The reader who perseveres will apprehend neither the Scots or English version in isolation, but his or her own amalgam of both.[53]

Just as we sense the spirit of Edward Dwelly as the ghost in the machine of Gorman's 'translations', Herbert and Crawford commune in *Sharawaggi* with what the poet David Kinloch (b. 1959) has called 'your grandfather's grandfather, the dictionary's ghost'.[54]

---

[51] Rody Gorman, *Beartan Briste agus dàin Ghàidhlig eile / Burstbroken Judgementshroudloomdeeds and Other Gaelic Poems* (Sydney, NS: Cape Breton University Press, 2011), 109.

[52] Robert Crawford and W. N. Herbert, *Sharawaggi* (Edinburgh: Polygon, 1990), 53.

[53] Kathleen McPhilemy, 'Poetry in Scots: A View from the Outside', in W. N. Herbert and Richard Price (eds.), *Gairfish: The McAvantgarde* (Dundee: Gairfish, 1992), 127. For further discussion of *Sharawaggi* see Iain Galbraith, 'Scottish Poetry in German: Paradox, Context, Transaction, Superstition', *Scottish Studies Review*, 9/1 (2008), 90–1.

[54] David Kinloch, 'The Apology of a Dictionary Trawler', in Herbert and Price (eds.), *Gairfish: The McAvantgarde*, 100.

The threshold poem in Kinloch's fourth volume, *In My Father's House* (2005), begins by introducing the central concern of the book: 'Well, Davy-lad, it is lychgate time: | Dad's coffin pausing between two worlds' ('I Set Off upon my Journey to the House of Shaws'). 'Davy' is, of course, David Balfour in *Kidnapped*, who, at the beginning of Stevenson's novel, must leave the secure precinct of his childhood village after his father's death. However, the 'Davy' of the collection as a whole, David Kinloch, writes the world from the 'lychgate' (a gate or porch at the entrance, or exit, to a churchyard; *lic*, in Old English, *Leiche* in modern German, meaning a corpse), a *limen* between life and death, reflecting, in one of the last poems in the book, that the moment of letting go 'which is far the hardest pain | remains' ('A Walk'). This threshold, a place of release and return, is reconfigured in a variety of contexts throughout the volume. Gaston Bachelard's study of the poetics of the threshold in *La Poétique de l'espace* (1958) cites some lines by the poet Michel Barrault: 'Je me surprends à definer le seuil | Comme étant le lieu géométrique | Des arrives et des départs | Dans la Maison du Père' (I find myself defining threshold | As being the geometrical place | Of the comings and goings | In my Father's House).[55] Kinloch's 'Father's House' is full of comings and goings, one feature of which is translation. Since his first volumes *Dustie-fute* (1992) and *Paris-Forfar* (1994), the poet's work—with titles that include *Un tour d'Écosse* (2001) and *Finger of a Frenchman* (2011)—has remained in intermittent dialogue with French literature, people, and places, and translations from several languages, enjoying 'the feeling of simultaneous nearness and distance',[56] have had a prominent place in these collections. At least fourteen of the thirty-seven poems in *In My Father's House* are translations, ten of which are subtitled 'eftir thi German o Paul Celan'. Fittingly, in this view from the lychgate, 'Todesfuge', the most widely known poem by Paul Celan (b. 1920), is here too. 'Todesfuge' is also one of Celan's most well-worn works, and yet we read it in Kinloch's faithful Scots as if for the first time: 'A maun bydes i the hous he flytes wi his snakes he scrieves | he scrieves when it's gloamin tae Deutschland yer gowden herr Margarete | he scrieves it an staps ower the door an the sterns are aw bleezin he wheeps his hunds ower' ('Daithfugue'). Like Alexander Gray's 1930s Scots versions of German ballads and folk songs, which are notoriously difficult to translate into conventional English, Kinloch's Scots invests the 'Todesfuge' with a strangely fresh authenticity. It is perhaps not only the frequent proximity of Scots words to German (nicht: Nacht; lyft: Luft; ligg: liegt; scrieves: schreibt; sterns: Sterne; hunds: Hunde; maister: Meister) that lends it what the German Romantic theologian Friedrich Schleiermacher (1768–1834) called a 'foreign likeness', but rather the capacity of Kinloch's Scots to inhabit the ambiguous world of the threshold, and to give voice to what Paul Celan, echoing Paul Valéry (see above), called 'Sprache *in statu nascendi*:' the emanant language of the poem. 'Thresholds', the poem that follows 'Daithfugue' in the same volume, an elegy for the poet's grandparents, explores liminality 'in the lychgate's shade' as a train marks time on the platform of the

---

[55] Gaston Bachelard, *The Poetics of Space* (Boston: Beacon, 1964, 1994), 223.
[56] 'David Kinloch in Conversation with Richard Price', *PN Review*, 27/3 (Jan.–Feb 2001), 24.

small village of Arrochar, a village that is also a kind of gateway: to the Highlands, to the Kintyre peninsula, and, historically, to Argyll, the march-land of the Gaels. Here it features as a 'space between' in which memory is swept into language, as into 'the pure, thin | air of Translation'.

One of the most colourful translations in Scottish poetry of the past two decades has undoubtedly been the portage of the Queen of Sheba on a camel to a gala in Currie (Midlothian): 'See her lead those great soft camels | widdershins round the kirk-yaird, | smiling | as she eats | avocados with apostle spoons | she'll show us how'. The eponymous queen of Kathleen Jamie's collection captured the imagination of pre-devolutionary Scotland as an upbeat cipher for social liberation: 'The Queen of Sheba', which was 'for so long a Scottish put-down of any claims to ambition or difference (as in: "Who do you think you are? The Queen of Sheba?"), returns personified as a triumphant affirmation of unfettered sexuality, knowledge, difference and escape'.[57] *The Queen of Sheba* (1994) was published by Jamie after returning from travels in Tibet, which had been the setting of her volume *The Autonomous Region* (1993). A previous cycle of poems, 'Karakoram Highway' (1987), had been set in northern Pakistan, and her travel book *The Golden Peak* (1992), too, had been distilled from the experience of travelling in Baltistan. Jamie has set a number of her poems in settings that many readers would consider exotic, and yet, paradoxically, her poetry's transformative skill can both bring its subject closer to home and simultaneously leave it in its foreign element. Scots, albeit comprehensible to many English-language readers, can seem to speak from across a border, a foreignizing idiom which, at the same time, lends a familiar directness and sensuality to its diction and imagery: 'Sits a lassie in red scarf, | wi her heid in her hauns, her heid | achin wi the weicht o so much saun | the weicht o the desert that waits every morn | an blackly dogs her back' ('The Autonomous Region'). And yet Jamie's poetry needs neither foreign parts, nor Scots, nor a camel to reach beyond even the ultimate human boundary. Contemplating the scan of her son's sixteen-week foetus, the narrator of 'Ultrasound' looks to a world beyond our present: 'this new heart must outlive my own'.

Select Bibliography

Bell, Eleanor, *Questioning Scotland: Literature, Nationalism, Postnationalism* (Basingstoke: Palgrave, 2004).

Bell, Eleanor, 'Old Country, New Dreams: Scottish Poetry since the 1970s', in Ian Brown, Thomas Owen Clancy, Susan Manning, and Murray Pittock (eds.), *The Edinburgh History of Scottish Literature*, iii (Edinburgh: Edinburgh University Press, 2007), 185–97.

Black, Ronald (ed.), *An Tuil: Anthology of 20th-Century Scottish Gaelic Verse* (Edinburgh: Polygon, 1999).

Blumenberg, Hans, *Paradigms for a Metaphorology* (Ithaca, NY: Cornell University Press, 2010).

Burnside, John, *The Asylum Dance* (London: Jonathan Cape, 2000).

---

[57] Roderick Watson, *The Literature of Scotland: The Twentieth Century* (Basingstoke and New York: Palgrave, 2007), 328.

Burnside, John, *The Light Trap* (London: Jonathan Cape, 2002).
Burnside, John, *The Good Neighbour* (London: Jonathan Cape, 2005).
Burnside, John, 'Poetry as Ecology', in Robert Crawford (ed.), *Contemporary Poetry and Contemporary Science* (Oxford: Oxford University Press, 2006), 94–5.
Burnside, John, and Riordan, Mark (eds.), *Wild Reckoning* (London: Calouste Gulbenkian Foundation, 2004).
Crawford, Robert, *A Scottish Assembly* (London: Jonathan Chatto, 1990).
Crawford, Robert, *Identifying Poets: Self and Territory in Twentieth-Century Poetry* (Edinburgh: Edinburgh University Press, 1993), 1–15.
Crawford, Robert, *Devolving English Literature* (2nd edn., Edinburgh: Edinburgh University Press, 2000).
Crawford, Robert, *The Tip of My Tongue* (London: Jonathan Cape, 2003).
Crawford, Robert, and Herbert, W. N., *Sharawaggi* (Edinburgh: Polygon, 1990).
Cronin, Michael, *Translation and Identity* (Abingdon: Routledge, 2006).
De Luca, Christina, *Parallel Lines: Poems in Shetlandic and English* (Edinburgh: Luath Press, 2005).
Donne, John, *Devotions upon Emergent Occasions*, ed. Anthony Raspa (Oxford: Oxford University Press, 1987).
Dósa, Attila, *Beyond Identity: New Horizons in Modern Scottish Poetry* (Amsterdam and New York: Rodopi, 2009).
Doty, Mark, *Still Life with Oysters and Lemon* (Boston: Beacon Press, 2001).
Duffy, Carol Ann, *Selected Poems* (Harmondsworth: Penguin Books, 1994).
Gairn, Louisa, *Ecology and Modern Scottish Literature* (Edinburgh: Edinburgh University Press, 2008), 156–91.
Gorman, Rody, *Beartan Briste agus dàin Ghàidhlig eile / Burstbroken Judgementshroudloomdeeds and Other Gaelic Poems* (Sydney, NS: Cape Breton University Press, 2011).
Hadfield, Jen, *Nigh-No-Place* (Tarset: Bloodaxe Books, 2008).
Herbert, W. N., and Hollis, Matthew (eds.), *Strong Words: Modern Poets on Modern Poetry* (Tarset: Bloodaxe Books, 2000).
Jarvis, Matthew, 'Repositioning Wales: Poetry after the Second Flowering', in Daniel G. Williams (ed.), *Slanderous Tongues: Essays on Welsh Poetry in English 1970–2005* (Bridgend: Seren, 2010).
McClure, Derrick J., *Language, Poetry and Nationhood: Scots as a Poetic Language from 1878 to the Present* (East Linton: Tuckwell Press, 2000).
McGuire, Matt, and Nicholson, Colin, *The Edinburgh Companion to Contemporary Scottish Poetry* (Edinburgh: Edinburgh University Press, 2009).
Mackay, Peter, 'An Guth and the Leabhar Mòr: Dialogues between Scottish Gaelic and Irish Poetry', *Journal of Irish and Scottish Studies*, 1/2 (Mar. 2008), 179–80.
O'Rourke, Donny, *Dream State: The New Scottish Poets* (2nd edn., Edinburgh: Polygon, 2002).
O'Rourke, Donny, 'Poetry in the Age of Morgan', in Ian Brown and Alan Riach (eds.), *The Edinburgh Companion to Twentieth-Century Scottish Literature* (Edinburgh: Edinburgh University Press, 2009), 204–13.
Paterson, Don, *Orpheus: A Version of Rilke* (London: Faber & Faber, 2006, 2007).
Price, Richard, '*La Grille*: Contemporary Scottish Poetry and France', in Gerard Carruthers, David Goldie, and Alastair Renfrew (eds.), *Beyond Scotland: New Contexts for Twentieth-Century Scottish Literature* (Amsterdam and New York: Rodopi, 2004), 185–208.

Rigby, Kate, *Topographies of the Sacred: The Poetics of Place in European Romanticism* (Charlottesville and London: University of Virginia Press, 2004).
Robinson, Peter, *Poetry & Translation: The Art of the Impossible* (Liverpool: Liverpool University Press, 2010).
Robinson, Richard, *Narratives of the European Border: A History of Nowhere* (Basingstoke: Palgrave, 2007), 16–39.
Watson, Roderick, *The Literature of Scotland*, ii. *The Twentieth Century* (Basingstoke and New York: Palgrave Macmillan, 1984, 2007), 277–343.
Whyte, Christopher, 'Masculinities in Contemporary Scottish Fiction', *Forum for Modern Language Studies*, 34/2 (1998).
Whyte, Christopher, 'Translation as Predicament', *Translation and Literature*, 9/2 (2000), 185–7.
Whyte, Christopher, *Modern Scottish Poetry* (Edinburgh: Edinburgh University Press, 2004).
Whyte, Christopher, *Bho Leabhar-Latha Maria Malibran* (Stornaway: Acair, 2009).

CHAPTER 30

THE VIEW FROM THE USA

ROMANA HUK

SOME might quip that accounting for a view 'from the USA' of contemporary British poetry needn't take long—given the well-worn story (often referred to *as* a story) that there's been little interest in viewing it at all since the 1950s, when poetic modernism accelerated stateside and died in the UK. (Irish poetry is 'a different story'; more on that anon.) Indeed, so many in the US of varying aesthetic persuasions have rehearsed it even as they've attempted, in major books, anthologies, articles, edited journals, blogs, and flights of reviews to redress the balance—from the long-resident Donald Davie to Donald Hall, Calvin Bedient, M. L. Rosenthal, Merle Brown, Hugh Kenner, John Matthias, Vincent Sherry, Helen Vendler, William Logan, Charles Bernstein, Marjorie Perloff, Linda Kinnahan, Keith Tuma, myself, and others before the end of the last century to Dana Gioia, Robert Archambeau, Charles Blanton, Nigel Alderman, Laura Severin, Charles Simic, Stephen Burt, and others after it—that one might well wonder if the story implodes under its own weight. In any case, I will in this chapter dutifully recount it and simultaneously complicate it, as well as contemplate the undeniable resurgence of US interest in British and Irish poetry over the last two decades. I write in a globalizing moment; this no doubt plays some role in this renewal. But in sync with earlier decades of neglect, recent attention often remains inflected by nationalist-cum-aesthetic agendas, whatever the very welcome 'transnational' critics among us might think. Yet despite these agendas, and their indication of long-running differences between American sensibilities and those they survey abroad, US readings of the scene overseas have played a crucial role in revealing it to be what it is, and has been all along: the diverse, richly developing, and in numerous cases 'modern' (as well as 'postmodern', or 'late modern'; the terms are shifting) field of work that our own story denied it to be. This chapter will make an attempt to explain these ironies and developments while doing two things at once: first, offering readers a sampling of trends in criticism looking east over the last sixty years; second (and no doubt inadvertently at times), offering *up* for critique my own American view of poetry overseas—particularly in the UK, given the limits of my expertise.

I

I'll start preposterously, with the most recent US anthology of *New British Poetry* to appear (Graywolf Press, 2004), because it not only illustrates the old story I've referred to, demonstrating aspects of its legitimacy and longevity, but it also dramatizes some of the newest transatlantic tensions on the rise. I'll use it as a frame, therefore, returning to it in conclusion as well.

Though its book-jacket claim to be 'the only definitive anthology of contemporary British poetry available in the United States' is arguable at best, and at worst surprisingly aggressive towards other recent anthologies, much of what its Preface by co-editor (and former US Poet Laureate) Charles Simic states anecdotally is true. He recalls that 'when [he] was in college in the 1950s, Modernism was regarded with suspicion', and 'one could still find ample selections of British poetry in North American schoolbooks'.[1] In other words, looking overseas seemed the only stay against the third wave of modernist American writing then gathering in the wake of Pound and Williams because British poetry, so the story goes, had never been spoilt by 'Modernism'. Americans *might* have been forgiven for this sweeping vision of UK work, since the story was promoted by the British themselves—those associated, at any rate, with the 'Movement', whose powerful poet-critics and anthologizers (among them Davie, D. J. Enright, Robert Conquest) had the major presses by the horns. But Simic's characteristically smart, tongue-in-cheek, and therefore half-disavowed recollection of such reductive thinking nevertheless confirms it:

> My professors didn't approve of a revolution in taste. For them, there was nothing wrong with Victorian-sounding poems and traditional meters. What they liked about the British was their reluctance to innovate. For us, who were then beginning to write poetry, their enthusiasm made as much sense as being told to ignore the movies and jazz since they are too American.
>
> Reacting to such views, the poets of my generation, and I imagine other readers of poetry, began to ignore what went on in Britain. Philip Larkin's magnificent poetry was not widely read; Geoffrey Hill's even less so...

And this last bit surprises. Movement poet Larkin loomed larger than any other from overseas for decades after the war, championed by leading British critic Christopher Ricks and leading American poets, such as Elizabeth Bishop and Robert Lowell. Why retrieve *his* work now as what was culpably ignored, instead of all the 'Modernist' work occluded by his elevation as the typical British poet who disliked jazz (of the post-1945 variety, anyway) and wrote in 'traditional meters'? It's true that such readings overlook aspects of Larkin's 'innovativeness', as American critics from Bedient to Tuma have duly and respectfully noted over the years. And it's true that US readers in

---

[1] Don Paterson and Charles Simic (eds.), *New British Poetry* (Saint Paul, Minn.: Graywolf Press, 2004), p. xix.

particular—Matthias, Sherry, R. K. Meiners, Brown, and myself, among others—have tended to read Hill as anything but reactionary, despite his virtuosic use of meter and troubled attraction to English/European pasts and religious architectures (especially linguistic ones); still, others couple him with Larkin for writing nothing more modern than 'stylized anglophilia'.[2] One expects acknowledgement here of what we know 'went on' that was *truly* innovative and ignored: work by, for example, Roy Fisher, Basil Bunting, Tom Raworth, and Ian Hamilton Finlay, whom poet-critic Matthias, Simic's contemporary, would finally anthologize with some impatience for American readers in *23 Modern British Poets* (1971).

What Simic suggests instead is that his professors were right: British poetry *has* been all about preservation of the past, while to be 'American' is to embrace the new, like 'movies and jazz'. Indeed, his co-editor, well-known British poet Don Paterson, claims outright that 'poetry actually *read* in the UK demonstrate[s] an allegiance to traditional ideas of form'.[3] Therefore what we find in this anthology, as American writer Sandra Gilbert perceives it, is 'the "newish" poetry':[4] fine writing of the sort Paterson describes, certainly, but not exactly 'new poetry'. In fact, this anthology includes many of the *same* poems and poets that appeared in the 1993 UK anthology called, similarly, *The New Poetry*. And though *that* took the name of A. Alvarez's anti-Movement anthology of 1960, it produced an essentially Movement-descended book, collecting poets who came into view in the 1980s and named as mentors those in the anthology that had extended the dominance of Movement aesthetics: *The Penguin Book of Contemporary British Poetry* (1982). All three could easily and seamlessly be read alongside one another.

This seamlessness was achieved by excluding many 'new' poets along the way. For example, the 1993 group was marketed as the 'New Generation' in 1994—but minus, as its main architect, *Poetry Review* editor Peter Forbes, put it (without explanation), all the 'Afro-Caribbean' and 'performance poets', and all the Northern Irish.[5] Similar things happen between *The New Poetry* and *New British Poetry*. Paterson does explain why the Northern Irish are not represented here: most define themselves as Irish, not British (though a simple title change would have fixed that), and they 'tend to enjoy a far stronger US profile than many of their counterparts on the larger island'[6] (true, if telling—more on this later). Yet why the black British field remains stunted is unclear; award-winning poets in the 1993 anthology have gone missing, leaving only three (two of them long-resident abroad) in this collection of thirty-six poets.[7] Those who know the field must question Paterson's rubric for inclusion, as a number enjoy at least as

---

[2] Richard Caddel and Peter Quartermain (eds.), *Other: British and Irish Poetry since 1970* (Hanover, NH: Wesleyan University Press, 1998), p. xviii.

[3] Paterson and Simic (eds.), *New British Poetry*, p. xxiii.

[4] Sandra M. Gilbert, 'Common Wealth', *Poetry*, 184/3 (June–July 2004), 227–34 (227).

[5] Peter Forbes, 'Talking About the New Generation', *A Poetry Review Special Issue: The New Generation Poets, Poetry Review*, 84/1 (Spring 1994), 4–6 (4).

[6] Paterson and Simic (eds.), *New British Poetry*, p. xxxiv.

[7] Sujata Bhatt, a poet of Indian origins, has spent little time in the UK (currently she lives in Germany). Fred D'Aguiar, of Guyanese parentage, has taught in America since 1992.

much attention as many in this volume. And if it involves 'sell[ing] books' to a 'general audience',[8] the additions made should include J. H. Prynne, for example—whose *Poems* made him, in the late 1990s, one of the best-selling of living poets writing in English, alongside Tom Paulin, Wole Soyinka, Les Murray, and British poets Carol Ann Duffy and Paterson himself (the latter of whom are both included). But then also lost from the 1993 anthology are two poets whose work, like Prynne's, can't be read as formally traditional: Pauline Stainer and Tom Leonard. Among the added are long-established poets James Fenton and Andrew Motion, both of whom appeared in the 1982 post-Movement anthology (co-edited by Motion). Of course, none of those whom Paterson calls the 'Postmoderns'—identifying them with their 'North American equivalent'—appeared in the 1993 anthology, either; and given Paterson's virulent opposition to what he perceives as 'the threat currently presented by [those] Postmoderns and their general ubiquity', *they* go 'unrepresented here'.[9]

Reader, there you have it—the old story, retold yet again as what's ostensibly *New*. The only moral to this twenty-first-century rendition is what Americans long-attuned to writing overseas have come to see for themselves: that we *haven't been able to see* very easily what doesn't fit the tale, even when such 'unrepresented' poetry is 'ubiquitous' in the UK. Although many US critics (myself included) have valued and written about what Paterson pointedly renames 'mainstream' writing, most have also come to resent our restricted view—often, as in this case, perpetuated by our own presses. Usually, in the US (for better or worse), the innovative rules; *Postmodern American Poetry* swiftly became *A Norton Anthology* (1994), for example. However, Norton—that recognized 'authority' in American classrooms—has never published anything (even in its more than 1,400 page anthology devoted exclusively to 'Modern Poetry', or its 2003 update) to disprove this picture of poetry *overseas*.

There's another story to be told here. We know that poetry not contributing to what *The Oxford English Literary History* describes as an era during which 'English literature was never more static'[10] had to be relegated to small press publication, which for decades had no transatlantic visibility. Once upon a time, US readers who wished to learn *more* about poetry overseas had to travel there for extended periods and find it for ourselves. But the Internet has changed all that, as the next sections of this chapter will make clear. And still what Americans find is that the resistance in the UK, Ireland, and some quarters of our own country to 'Modernist' British and Irish poetry and recoveries of their roles in the story of contemporary writing remains many times stronger than any analogous resistance in the US to our *own* innovations. But that resistance has itself been productive of new transatlantic readerships, as we'll see. And it's been fraying for longer than the old story can tell.

---

[8] Paterson and Simic (eds.), *New British Poetry*, p. xxv.
[9] Paterson and Simic (eds.), *New British Poetry*, pp. xxiii, xxviii.
[10] Randall Stevenson, *The Oxford English Literary History*, xii. 1960–2000: *The Last of England?* (Oxford: Oxford University Press, 2004), 270.

II

I'll pick up its earlier threads by quoting Matthias's 1985 recollections of what was being read and not read in the US at mid-century and why:

> When my generation of American poets was growing up in the Fifties we all, I think, quite naturally read the Brits along with the natives. We all cut our teeth on the anthologies then available—those old Oscar Williams and Louis Untermeyer books where you found Hardy toward the beginning and maybe Hughes or Larkin or Tomlinson at the very end, after some Hecht and Snodgrass.
>
> ...Donald Hall—a wonderful advocate of the best British poetry for many years—kept the Atlantic route open in both directions with his two *New Poets of England and America* anthologies edited in 1957 and 1962...It was here, I suppose, that most of us first read Donald Davie, Thom Gunn, Michael Hamburger, Geoffrey Hill, Jon Silkin, Christopher Middleton, George MacBeth, and a range of other poets just too young for, or excluded from the final pages of, the Williams and Untermeyer books. But Hall's first anthology was countered by that defiantly and exclusively American book edited by Donald Allen, *The New American Poetry* [1960]. After that, it was all but over for the British in America. Never mind that certain of the most innovative British and Irish poets might actually have been themselves included in Allen's book had he admitted any un-American activities.[11]

Matthias refigures the end of 'transatlantic unity' as a divorce augured by the growing tendency to separate British from American poetry in anthologies like Untermeyer's, after which '[t]he British half retired to her island feeling insufficiently desirable in America and, as a result of that, made herself unavailable as well, stamped on the back beneath her prices in Australia, New Zealand, South Africa, and Canada: *Not for sale in the USA*'. Gendered in a send-up of tendencies to picture US poets as 'youthful, muscular, jazzily innovative',[12] as Gilbert also wryly recalls them, his dramatized end to American views of anything but Britain's backside highlights the new power relations undermining any other kind in post-war nationalist literary projects.

But Matthias admits he 'exaggerate[s]'; the actual story is much more complicated. There was, for example, the continued interest on the part of key magazines—like *Kenyon Review* and the *Southern Review*, founded in the mid-to-late 1930s by New Critical thinkers John Crowe Ransom and Robert Penn Warren, respectively; or *Sewanee Review*, edited at mid-century by 'Southern Agrarian' Allen Tate—to evidence that one kind of readership remained stable stateside precisely *because* Movement aesthetics enforced formal continuities our 'third wave' modernism had eschewed. More recently, inheritors of New Critical aesthetics—like the celebrated neo-formalist poet, polemicist, and National Endowment for the Arts chairman (2003–9), Dana Gioia, and

---

[11] John Matthias, *Reading Old Friends: Essays, Reviews, and Poems on Poetics 1975–1990* (Albany, NY: State University of New York Press, 1992), 207–8.
[12] Gilbert, 'Common Wealth', 228.

the nation's most loved 'mainstream' critic, Helen Vendler—keep US eyes focused on the Movement poets and their descendants out of fear that, as Vendler put it in 1995, 'our young writers are ignorant of notable British models of poetry in English—models useful because culturally different'.[13] (The subtext here: 'useful' to steer us from our own more errant ways.) Both would let Simic off my hook above; they remind us that 'during the sixties most American poets went further afield for lyric models—to South America, Germany, Russia, Eastern Europe' (where Simic's reading certainly tended), and thus many American readers 'may literally not know of the existence of a Philip Larkin or a Donald Davie'.

Therefore, unlike US critics who have striven to complicate Movement-centred histories of British poetry, Vendler vigorously reinstates them, pursuing as she has lyric models on both sides of the Atlantic at precisely the moment that literary philosophy and her nation's 'postmodernist' poets were rethinking the lyric subject. Her popularity with readers has much to do with not only her own lyrical style, its enviable clarity and punch, but also its wholesale avoidance of that troubling conversation. Vendler tends to read poems as spiritual self-portraits—*Soul Says*, as one book title has it; poetry remains, for her (its sales description tells us), 'the voice of the soul rather than the socially marked self'. Thus, in her reading, Davie's dually drawn work is freed of both 'Poundians (a sect unto themselves)' *and* 'neo-formalists...saving the world from the depravity of free verse'.[14] It becomes, in other words, the work of an American-style individual, whose 'soul' cannot be captured by what she caricatures, in religious terms ('sect', 'saving'), as the stumpings of these critical schools. However, her own aims are the kettle to their opposed critical pots, and she achieves them equally narrowly if always acutely by locating any work's address (in both senses of that word) internally, in projects of self-interrogation, self-invention, and self-styling.

Gioia's views of British poetry strike me as broader, more informed and attuned to his subject's differing discursive landscape and concerns. He sees what Simic, too, sees: that conceptions of lyric in relation to language and society shift like continental plates somewhere in the mid-Atlantic:

> Emerson's limitless faith in the power of the individual to make a new beginning, reinventing everything from his identity to the art of poetry, has had few takers in Britain. Consequently, their poets are less egocentric than ours, who love the first-person pronoun more than anything else in the world. American poems may probe psychological, philosophical, religious and aesthetic issues, but they rarely show much awareness of history, economics, politics.[15]

This is a caricature, of course, as Simic no doubt knows—but there's something to it. Gioia (as his blockbuster of a critical intervention, 'Can Poetry Matter?' (*Atlantic*

---

[13] Helen Vendler, *Soul Says: On Recent Poetry* (Cambridge, Mass. and London: Harvard University Press, 1995), 92.
[14] Vendler, *Soul Says*, 101.
[15] Paterson and Simic (eds.), *New British Poetry*, p. xxi.

Monthly, 1991) made clear) laments in a related way US poetry's 'subculture' of creative writing programmes, with its 'readings [that] are celebrations less of poetry than of the author's ego'; his motives for looking east also involve importing something of the sociality of British work. His view that British poetry 'is intended as public speech'[16] derives from Davie's notoriously black-and-white comparisons of transatlantic poetics—like the latter's pronouncement that 'for the English poet the writing of poems is a public and social activity, as for his American peer it isn't'; seen from this angle, Vendler's approach to Davie appears to disrupt what might indeed be 'other cultural' in her chosen model from abroad. And since the differences that Gioia detects cross mainstream/experimental lines, he's able not only to read without Americanizing his subjects quite as much, but also read further than Vendler into alternative territory. For all his inability (like Davie's) to appreciate the revisionary epic of a David Jones, or even the less radical lyric obscurities of a Medbh McGuckian, Gioia nonetheless places Bunting and Larkin, for example, back-to-back in his lists of essential reading, becoming one of the many Americans who have helpfully ignored lines drawn between them abroad. But both Vendler and Gioia, in their attempts to resecure transatlantic unity through such retrievals—effected while ignoring their own nation's globally-ascendant postmodern poetries—appear to be not only recovering Movement writers but *becoming like them*: i.e., by disavowing, inversely, that *post*modernism ever happened in the US, and arguing that poetry before the transatlantic split provided the best track for our true line all along.

Yet the other storyline tells of things happening at mid-century and since then to regenerate connections to *other* kinds of UK poetry—therefore the title of one recent US anthology attempting to alter accounts.[17] Yet our records of such things have been poor. As Tuma suggested a decade ago, '[i]n the United States, and probably in Britain too, we do not know enough about the transatlantic dialogues that took place among poets of the 1960s and the 1970s'[18] to read writing from that transitional era properly—British *or* American—and in some respects, therefore, to read relations between poetries to this day. Quite frustratingly, this was the moment that British critic and poet Eric Mottram named 'the British Poetry Revival', arising just when the old story tells us modernism died in the UK. But we do know, for instance, of American poets Robert Creeley and Edward Dorn becoming fellow travellers, during this period, of Finlay and Roy Fisher, and US admirers of Bunting enabling his masterpiece, *Briggflatts*, to find first publication in the States. European movements like Fluxus attracted American poets overseas—so that Jackson Mac Low, for example, exhibited at one event alongside British experimentalist Allen Fisher. And there were reading tours of America by British poets (even the semi-reclusive Prynne); many stayed on in teaching positions, keeping Auden company as resident British influences. Beat poets involved in the *New American Poetry* were certainly aware of the live arts ventures of the 1960s in the UK—stewarded and

---

[16] Dana Gioia, *Barrier of a Common Language: An American Looks at Contemporary British Poetry* (Ann Arbor: University of Michigan Press, 2003), 100.

[17] See n. 2.

[18] Keith Tuma, 'Ed Dorn and England', *The Gig*, 6 (July 2000), 41–54 (41).

anthologized by poets such as Michael Horowitz in the south and the Liverpool poets in the north—which were, like them, inspired by jazz and cultural revolution; several even took part in the legendary Royal Albert Hall Poetry Incarnation in 1965 (performed to an audience of seven thousand; it was no doubt here that 'performance poetry' began to earn its bad name overseas). But interesting details languish unremarked—like the fact that Horowitz's quintessentially 'sixties' anthology, *Children of Albion: Poetry of the Underground in Britain* (1969), included both London and Cambridge experimentalists, and that live arts ventures came to involve black British poets and other post-colonial as well as new international citizens—all of which made the British 'underground' look more richly unified in diversity than it would later in the century, and in numerous respects very different from our own.[19]

Yet we also know—thanks to Mottram and later tellers of it[20]—the extraordinary story of the Poetry Society's takeover by the country's most radical edge. They suddenly appeared in 1971 as both the Society's voted-in leadership and in *Poetry Review*, its main organ, which reopened channels between US and UK poets and readers for almost the length of the decade. But while for those years a 'new British poetry' must have seemed on the rise (even Ted Hughes remarked, upon reading *Children of Albion*, that it seemed a 'real departure, a new beginning'), and while too, as Matthias recalls, presses run by these poets 'briefly flourished', and 'multicultural, multiethnic, and feminist influences began to make themselves felt as part of the alternative poetry scene', 'the establishment regrouped', he writes, and the Arts Council 'purged' not only Bunting from the Society's leadership but Mottram, too, from his role as *Review* editor.[21] The whole editorial board was sacked, in part because, as Mottram writes, 'they were incensed by our inclusion of "foreign poets", particularly Americans. This was seen as a treacherous assault on British poetry'.[22] Mottram's edited section of what many consider the first anthology to represent this occluded tradition—*the new british poetry* (1988)—was entitled 'A Treacherous Assault on British Poetry', in jokey recollection of such protectionist behaviour. But at his back he might have heard Paterson's humourless reiteration of that 'threat' nearly twenty years on. Some things don't change; but from stateside, where this coup/crush story has become the stuff of legend, and the poets involved—as well as their descendants—more and more familiar, it's the *resistance* to change and not British poetry itself that doesn't seem to.

---

[19] This would continue through the 1980s, as a look at the contents of one retrospective volume, *Apples and Snakes: The Popular Front of Contemporary Poetry* (1992), makes clear: Cobbing, Leonard, Geraldine Monk, Aaron Williamson, Peter Finch, and others appear alongside black writers Linton Kwesi Johnson, Grace Nichols, John Agard, Valerie Bloom, Benjamin Zephaniah, Merle Collins, Jean 'Binta' Breeze, and others. Though such unities dissolved, the centrality of poetry's performance as a profoundly public art remains clear in the UK tradition—from Johnson and Bob Cobbing to Caroline Bergvall, cris cheek, Fiona Templeton, Patience Agbabe, Sean Bonney, and many more.

[20] See the full account in Peter Barry, *Poetry Wars: British Poetry of the 1970s and the Battle of Earls Court* (Cambridge: Salt Publishing, 2006).

[21] John Matthias, *Who Was Cousin Alice? And Other Questions* (Exeter: Shearsman Books, 2011), 226.

[22] Eric Mottram, 'Introduction: A Treacherous Assault on British Poetry', in Gillian Allnutt, Fred D'Aguiar, Ken Edwards and Eric Mottram (eds.), *The New British Poetry* (London: Paladin, 1988), 133.

Because despite the odds, dear Reader, many of us *have* been reading—and often the British and Irish poetry less read overseas. This may in part be due to its dialogue with our poetries, but not because it's 'like' our work. The idea that these alternative writers form, as Paterson claims, a 'North American equivalent' is untenable to us; they've rarely looked to American readers like our own work. As British critic Drew Milne argues, in America 'radical' poetry exhibits 'more explicitly liberal models of formal radicalism', as opposed to 'the political radicalism of the European avant-garde'.[23] Bewaring generalizations, it may be that what Simic noted about the mainstream extends to the UK avant-garde: 'history, economics, politics' play a larger role there than formal departure, and what Milne calls connections to 'the history of poetry in English' are—like and *very* unlike the Movement—stronger. Indeed, debates about whether British and Irish innovations have met US definitions of terms like 'modernist' and 'postmodernist' have helped shift the meanings of such words. As Milne argues, '[a]lternative models need to be found through which to read the peculiarities of modernism in the British isles'. Some have already been proposed by American readers. I'm telling a little more of that story now.

III

By the time US critic Hugh Kenner was making transatlantic waves with his version of the old story in *A Sinking Island* (1988), retrieving only Bunting and Tomlinson from what he saw as the UK's general literary demise, and Frank Kermode was retorting with *The Uses of Error* (1991), published by Harvard, which included his protective 1980 review of Enright's *Oxford Book of Contemporary Verse* wherein he argued that the Movement's supposed 'Gentility' should be read as 'Civility', though '[a]nyone who turns on to less civil American, or indeed British, stimuli will of course avoid it' (360), much had already been done to make both seem sallies from an old battle lost on both sides.

In the UK, Matthias recalls, for example, the importance of Manchester-based *Poetry Nation Review* (1973–) as one vehicle for transatlantic dialogue that continued beyond *Poetry Review*'s retrenchment given that, like Davie before him, its editor Michael Schmidt (editor too of Carcanet Press, which has published both British and American experimentalists) 'manifests a fruitful tension between his commitment to British poetry where it is least influenced by American or continental modernism...and a wary fondness (which he often tries to stifle) both for some American writing in the Pound-Williams (or even Stevens-Ashbery) tradition and for British poets...who have produced a body of interestingly related work'.[24] Yet Schmidt was also arguing, alongside

---

[23] Drew Milne, 'Neo-Modernism and Avant-Garde Orientations', in Nigel Alderman and C. D. Blanton (eds.), *A Concise Companion to Postwar British and Irish Poetry* (Oxford and Chichester: Wiley-Blackwell, 2009), 155–75 (160).

[24] Matthias, *Reading Old Friends*, 210.

co-editor Peter Jones in their 1980 collection of essays on *British Poetry since 1970*, that the 1970s witnessed '[n]o major movements, no dominant new poets, no serious literary debate in the public arena'[25]—as though the debacle at the Poetry Society and all the new work in *Poetry Review* before Mottram's sacking simply hadn't happened. Such discrepancies were provocative, and critical response stateside began to ignite.

But it wasn't only the most inflammatory stuff that fired the imagination then— like Perloff's editing, in 1977, a special issue of *Contemporary Literature* on 'The Two Poetries: The Postwar Lyric in Britain and America', and later being invited into debates about the state of 1970s British poetry in *PN Review 19* (7/5, 1981). Both were certainly generative, even if, due to the visibility problem, Perloff like Kenner formed her arguments about 'new' British work from reading of a range of poets more like Schmidt's than Mottram's. Thus her verdict that the British write under a 'persistent and burdensome sense of tradition'[26] led to her surprising confirmation of Davie's allegation—the most quoted fragment of transatlantic criticism in the last sixty years—that American readers are simply unable to 'hear the British poet, neither his rhythms nor his tone of voice'.[27] She also produced what sound to us now like 'old story' views: American poets are 'energetic', and 'believe they can do something new and exciting', while British poets are 'modest', given the 'cautious, pragmatic and empirical milieu' within which they'll be judged. Comparing specifically lyric forms she finds that Americans use increasingly 'natural' and 'colloquial language', whereas the British preserve a 'consciously "literary" idiom', which depends on 'convoluted syntactic patterns' we'll need to translate like a foreign language one day.[28] Yet there are, as with Simic's and Gioia's generalizations, truths of a kind here. For example, delivering the 'natural voice' has rarely been a goal in British poetry—whether Davie's, Hill's, Fisher's, Prynne's, or, say, Veronica Forrest-Thomson's— focused as it is on language as social artifice rather than 'natural' footprint. As Lawrence Kramer (a contributor to the issue) concludes, Americans 'capture the phenomenology of perception itself'[29] in their post-Objectivist lyric modes that commute self into something Heideggerian—or later, Derridean. As Perloff explains, ours became a 'highly theoretical climate', one that 'turn[ed] away from England toward France, oddly repeating the pattern of T. S. Eliot's career some sixty years ago'.[30] Therefore, she finds that by the late 1970s a gap was opening, too, between critical worlds: whereas 'postmodernism' was being debated theoretically by poets and critics stateside, the British scene appeared to her to be lingeringly Leavisite in its distrust of philosophy in such matters, and to be

---

[25] Quoted in Marjorie Perloff, 'One of the Two Poetries', *PN Review 19*, 7/5 (May–June 1981), 47–51 (47).

[26] Marjorie Perloff, Introduction: 'The Two Poetries: the Postwar Lyric in Britain and America', a special issue of *Contemporary Literature*, 18/3 (Summer 1977), 263–78 (264).

[27] Donald Davie, *With the Grain: Essays on Thomas Hardy and Modern British Poetry*, ed. Clive Wilmer (Manchester: Carcanet Press, 1998), 166.

[28] Perloff, 'The Two Poetries', 265, 264, 269.

[29] Quoted in Perloff, 'The Two Poetries', 274.

[30] Perloff, 'The Two Poetries', 265.

producing 'short, practical and somewhat impressionistic critical essays on a given poet or poets' rather than a *poetics* with which we could enter into debate.

But a number of US journals and serials were starting the conversation nonetheless, in part by broadening the range of British and Irish poets we could see. Alongside *Contemporary Literature* was *boundary 2*, which coupled theoretical discussions with readings of poetry—including a special issue in the 1970s on Nathaniel Tarn; the acclaimed *Tri-Quarterly*, after 1964 an international magazine with Anania as a contributing editor; *Agni* in Boston, which published much writing from overseas—including two mini-anthologies of younger British and Irish poets edited by Logan in 1983; *Chicago Review*, which has often looked eastward, and is now a key player in twenty-first-century transatlantic relations; even *Sewanee Review*, given its attempts, after 1974, to expand pictures of British Commonwealth and Irish work. Significant, too, was Gale's production of two volumes, edited by Sherry, of *Poets of Great Britain and Ireland* in its *Dictionary of Literary Biography* series, as we used these substantial essays on individual poets as reference points, particularly with students. And Sherry's were filled with not only then-fringe figures such as Elaine Feinstein, John Riley, and Ken Smith, but also writers using 'traditional forms renewed by the shifts in attitude in the 1960s'.[31] Such balanced revisions of the old story allowed for new readings of, for example, the work of Tony Harrison, who had appeared in the post-Movement Penguin anthology of 1982 but was from the start interested in 'occupying' traditional forms with a difference. Sherry—a Poundian scholar not confined to any 'sect unto themselves', and a reader of British work quite capable, as his book on Hill made clear, of hearing British rhythms and tones—did much to disturb such binary thinking and reading.

Other books by Americans that sparked my own interest were about poets largely forgotten overseas—like Arthur Salmon's obscure and uneven but groundbreaking little book on *Poets of the Apocalypse* (1983): poets of interest to American writer Kenneth Rexroth, who anthologized some of them (alongside Denise Levertov) as 'New Romantics' at mid-century. Salmon's recovery of this post-surrealist anarchic impulse in British poetry helped me later understand its continuing relevance for the British avant-garde. For though David Gascoyne, the lonely British surrealist of the 1930s, complained in 1989 about the continuing lack of philosophical engagement in British poetry, snarling that 'the poets most frequently acclaimed... are probably inclined to regard the very word "ontology" with mistrust or distaste',[32] the unacclaimed J. F. Hendry, for example, synthesized many philosophical strands from the thirties to probe ontology in a distinctly British way, in my view, by inquiring after what he termed its generative 'Social Pathology' rather than its existential angst. Even more illuminating books included *Double Lyric* (1980) by Merle Brown, critic and founding editor of *The Iowa Review*. It too explored ontology as inextricable from the social impulse, and as challenged by post-war understandings of 'self' as not opposed to, but composed *by*, 'the other'. Jon

---

[31] Vincent Sherry (ed.), *Poets of Great Britain and Ireland since 1960* (Detroit: Gale Research, 1985), p. xvii.

[32] David Gascoyne, contribution to 'The State of Poetry' issue, *Agenda*, 27/3 (1989), 30–5 (31).

Silkin embraced its reading of his poetry and recommended it to me—*pace* the scathing reviewer in *PN Review 26* (8/6) who claimed that Brown's 'neo-idealist theory' could not but 'bend' any poem's meaning. At times what Perloff called a Leavisite mistrust of philosophy *has* perhaps narrowed British readings of their own poetry—or of their own literary philosophy, as Brown illustrates by rereading Leavis himself. He finds Leavis always thinking 'collaboratively', 'sensing how the poet, as distinct from [him]self, is [in turn] listening critically to the expressive language'[33] continuous with the world beyond self—a model Brown argues Leavis developed in his debates with Ludwig Wittgenstein in Cambridge (and recorded in his wonderful prose piece, 'Memories of Wittgenstein'). Just as US poetry was beginning to explode old notions of subjectivity, and dispense with lyric as a relic, Brown demonstrated that the UK's 'continuities' with past lyric practice allowed for *revisions* of it instead, issuing out of post-war imperatives to rethink selfhood alongside ethics.

And certainly, as my references to his work have already made clear, Matthias must be named one of the most important American readers of British and Irish poetry after the war. He trained a number of those mentioned in this essay, like Sherry, Archambeau, Kinnahan, and myself; his work informed and inspired Tuma as well, perhaps his greatest successor. A frequent reviewer in the seventies of British poetry for the central US magazine (based in Chicago), *Poetry*, Matthias also began in the eighties to author a review column on British and Irish poetry called 'Not for Sale in the USA' in *Another Chicago Magazine* (yet 'another' of the city's Anglo-friendly journals). In the course of such reviewing and exhorting, he brought into US consciousness not only those poets he'd anthologized in 1971, but also younger figures like Harrison and Ash alongside those not normally read with them: Prynne, John Riley, Tom Lowenstein, and others. He remains the best American reader of poets whose work isn't easily categorized as radical *or* mainstream, and of long poems that resist anthologizing and require patient attention, like those of Roy Fisher or Peter Reading. If anyone dampens Davie's dismissal of American readers for not being able to 'hear the British poet', it's Matthias; indeed, reading him read the great Anglo-Welsh late-modernist David Jones (whose work he single-handedly anthologized and explained for American readers), it's impossible not to recall how much better his ear proved than Davie's when the latter turned to *The Anathémata* and heard only 'monotony'.[34] What this might prove is that at times, it's precisely *British* readers who can't hear British poets, at least when they're doing something perhaps more 'Modernist' than preservationists would allow (however well Davie read certain *American* ultra-modernists).

Equally importantly, Matthias introduced Americans to poets from Wales and Scotland as well as Ireland, foregrounding contextualizing issues; he thereby became one of the first stateside to problematize the catch-all use of 'England' in titles like Hall, Simpson and Pack's anthology, and to point up the cultural disunity and productive

---

[33] Merle E. Brown, *Double Lyric: Divisiveness and Communal Creativity in Recent English Poetry* (London: Routledge & Kegan Paul, 1980), 220.
[34] Davie, *With the Grain*, 233.

cacophony the 'United Kingdom' represents. As even highly attuned and prolific reviewer (and poet) Logan remembers: when he travelled to the UK in 1981—just before compiling the two *Agni* mini-anthologies of younger British and Irish poets I mentioned above—'[he] was naïve enough not to know the difference between "English" and "British", and was unsure how "Irish" fitted either'.[35] As it happened, Irish poetry came to enjoy far more visibility in the States, as Paterson notes—perhaps because about 40 million here self-identify as part Irish; perhaps because even more identify with poetries defining themselves, as we have, against our former colonizer's models. And perhaps American readers—always interested in revolution—began to appreciate Irish poetry after the 1970s because it was 'forged anew in the crucible of a decade's troubles in the north'.[36] *And* we could actually see some of its more adventurous work—anthologized as it was by presses like Faber & Faber who, without compunction, took on as editors 'modernist' and 'postmodernist' Irish writers such as John Montague and Paul Muldoon. Everyone welcomed this shot in the arm for otherwise 'static' 'British' poetry; indeed, it became *so* visible that the marketing of 'New Generation' writing could by a certain point no longer afford to be eclipsed by the not so comple(i)mentary Irish, perhaps. Whatever the reason, Irish poetry has for years toured the US—while poets from devolving Wales and Scotland haven't seemed able to avail themselves of that option. Gioia writes, symptomatically, that 'the development of regional poetic movements in the United Kingdom, especially among distinct national groups like the Scottish or Welsh, has too often resulted in a parochial kind of poetry unlikely to interest overseas readers'.[37] I couldn't disagree more—but the fact is that fewer Americans understand their histories and therefore what's at stake in *their* continuing attempts to push back against 'English' overdetermination.

Matthias had help in returning American eyes to, say, that giant of Scottish modernism, Hugh MacDiarmid, from the work done on his daunting oeuvre by Nancy Gish. British scholar David Norbrook notes that while English readers of MacDiarmid have 'seldom progressed beyond such sallies' as Ian Hamilton's dwelling on the obscene potential in Scots phrases like 'mither fochin' scones', 'American writers like Gish have been more willing to recognize that dialect words are not necessarily funny'.[38] But of course even this bit of praise is comic, whereas Americans, not brought up on that often invidious intra-national comedy are, as Norbrook suggests, more respectful of non-English British and Irish work. Matthias, with less knowledge of their languages and dialects than Gish—who has written helpfully about other Scottish writers too, such as Liz Lochhead and Jackie Kay—nonetheless listens differently to, for example, the work of that great liminal figure, Sorley MacLean. Encountering it in the original Gaelic

---

[35] Michael Hofmann and William Logan, 'A Conversation on British and American Poetry', *Poetry*, 84/3 (June–July 2004), 212–20 (213).

[36] Matthias, *Reading Old Friends*, 210.

[37] Gioia, *Barrier of a Common Language*, 3.

[38] David Norbrook, 'What Happened to MacDiarmid?', *London Review of Books*, 8/18 (23 Oct. 1986), 24–6 (26).

'to gain a feeling, after a while, for MacLean's language and forms as he engages subjects', he then considers the aptness of John Herdman's translation of MacLean into Scots, given MacDiarmid's powerful influence. But ultimately he leaves us with the problem highlighted, rather than lightened or diluted, quoting as he does poet Iain Crichton Smith (sounding like Wittgenstein): 'a different language is a world | we find our way about in with a stick'.[39] 'In Scots it sounds like MacDiarmid', Matthias muses. 'In Gaelic it sounds like nothing else at all'.

And not least, during a dismal time for women's poetry overseas—when even the revised, 1985 version of Edward Lucie-Smith's groundbreaking Penguin anthology, *British Poetry Since 1945*, could gather ninety-six poets of various persuasions both within and outside Movement influence and yet not even apologize for including only six women—Matthias began to review female poets hard to see from our shores, like Welshwoman Gillian Clarke, and the then little known Irish poet Eavan Boland. He judged Boland's sequence 'Outside History' as 'unparalleled in recent Irish poetry' (in a review that included Seamus Heaney), and Clarke's 'Letters from a Far Country' important not least for 'its concern for the history and experience of women'—for 'as [was then] the case with modern English poetry, Anglo-Welsh poetry does not seem to have produced many poems of merit written by women about the lives of women'.[40] (We simply could not see, in 1985, that such poems *were* produced in feminist and experimental circles; most clearly on view for us, beyond *The Bloodaxe Book of Contemporary Women Poets: Eleven British Writers*—a fine intervention published that year, but largely treating older poets—was Carol Rumens' 'post-feminist' anthology that advocated abandonment of gendered experience.) Many American readers have noted how male-dominated the British and Irish scene and their anthologies look to us, but few have actually retrieved female poets' work for our attention. Kinnahan would continue Matthias's project, if with a difference, looking further into the experimental realm than Matthias has tended to go. But in one way or another, many of us have continued reading like him—so as to broaden the view from the USA.

IV

And that has indeed happened, rather dramatically, in the last two decades. There are many reasons for this. Certainly the globalizing tendencies that I noted at the outset of this chapter are among them. But we've also entered another era of reading one another, if this time with long-running British and Irish experimental poetries suddenly prioritized rather than repressed, given the emerging dominance in academe of America's own avant-garde. I credit both developments for the extraordinary success of, for example, a large conference/festival I ran in 1996, which focused on small press writing and

---

[39] Matthias, *Reading Old Friends*, 272.
[40] Matthias, *Reading Old Friends*, 255.

introduced numerous 'unrepresented' poets overseas to American poets and readers.[41] (Among other things, the event revealed an avant-garde Irish tradition impossible for us to see before, scattered as it was between poets writing independently of one another; after the conference it began to hold its own spin-offs in Ireland, and several invitees—Trevor Joyce, Maurice Scully, Catherine Walsh, and Randolph Healy—appeared in Tuma's groundbreaking OUP anthology five years later.[42]) Electronic communication in the forms of poetry centres, poetics chatlines, and blogs as they were just then emerging and becoming central to our 'trade' as poets and critics meant that such an event had long-term effects; it continued in electronic discussions and debates, and its featured small press books were made available from distributors accessible online. (Indeed, *so* much suddenly was—including poems—that 'selling books', as Paterson put it, rapidly became only one indicator of a poet's impact or visibility.) By the end of the century Salt Publishing appeared, which printed cheaply on demand and could afford to make a wide range of writers easily available to Americans; its astonishingly swift success (until the recent cuts to arts funding) spoke volumes about changed relations. The millennium had also prompted academics to redefine 'postmodernism' as a literary era, and we didn't believe the claim that had been made by, say, the 1982 Penguin anthology that *it* was showcasing postmodern writing overseas. (This was one of many attempts to, as British critic Ian Gregson writes, 'lower the profile of most postmodernist poetry'[43] by co-opting its terms.) Both outside and inside academe, then, Americans began catching up with British poetry again—but in a very different mix, and with better understanding of its complicated history after the war.

So the *new* story goes. I realize this is a 'glass half full' reading of the state of things; even Tuma, so central in facilitating our renewed interest, reproduced the 'glum thesis' that 'Americans have lost sight of British poetry' in his first book published near the end of the decade.[44] This was his moment to rehearse the old story, as we all have at one point or another—my own turn having been taken two years before him, in the Introduction to *Contemporary British Poetry: Essays in Theory and Criticism* (SUNY Press) which, like millennial critical anthologies published overseas, strove to bring transatlantic critics together again in the study of 'new British poetry'. But the stumbling point, from our point of view (which mirrored Perloff's earlier) was a lack of vibrant critical debate to enter. Tuma argued that what little serious critical discourse there was seemed perpetually to be discussing the same poets; and without it, 'British poetry is destined to remain...invisible nearly, and therefore extremely hard to learn about in the United States'. This statement seems inadvertently ironic since Tuma *himself* emerged as

---

[41] See Romana Huk (ed.), *Assembling Alternatives: Reading Postmodern Poetries Transnationally* (Middletown, Conn.: Wesleyan University Press, 2003).

[42] He also, with William Walsh, anthologized these poets and others in the American journal *Talisman* 18 (Fall 1998), 93–135.

[43] Ian Gregson, *Contemporary Poetry and Postmodernism: Dialogue and Estrangement* (London: Macmillan, 1996), 214.

[44] Keith Tuma, *Fishing by Obstinate Isles: Modern and Postmodern British Poetry and American Readers* (Evanston, Ill.: Northwestern University Press, 1998), 2.

a major force in making the work visible, like transatlantic readers Matthias and Davie before him. Matthias reviewed his book as 'the best possible introduction for American readers to a range of British poetries and poetic histories long neglected here';[45] it was groundbreaking in its careful reading of not only Bunting but Mina Loy and lesser known figures such as Joseph Gordon Macleod and Lynette Roberts, as well as later experimental poets, among them Peter Riley, Allen Fisher, and Kamau Brathwaite. It's true that initially I'd objected in a review to his naming much British work 'late modernist' (rather than 'postmodernist') given its 'continuities' with past writing, which seemed too swayed by the old story to me. But odd things are happening to that story; the twenty-first-century adoption of (or 'signifying on') the term 'late modernist'—even 'Modernist' again—by experimental British poets themselves has destabilized both our terminology and our assumptions about 'postmodern' relations with the past.

Which is itself evidence of the re-growth of 'serious critical discourse' overseas. I might date it back to the poetically-attuned British journal *Textual Practice* (Routledge), which put us back on the same page in 1987; soon afterwards small-press journals began to redress the balance between poetries (*Parataxis* in Cambridge, *fragmente* in Oxford, *Object Permanence* in Glasgow, increasingly interesting *Poetry Wales*, etc.). By the mid-1990s revisionary collections of essays appeared, too, such as *Contemporary Poetry Meets Modern Theory* (1991) and *New British Poetries: The Scope of the Possible* (1993), alongside poetics talks series in London, new university 'centres' for the study of poetry, and a sudden blossoming of conferences countrywide. Women's poetry was accumulating powerful new critics, and producing evidence of its 'ubiquitousness', too, in (for instance) Linda France's *Sixty Women Poets* (1993). Raced writing was also finding new critical voices and journals, such as *Wasafiri*. Though the New Gen phenomenon didn't reflect them, fine fights about aesthetics were gearing up—between, say, France's criteria for inclusion in her anthology: 'form that communicates itself... unequivocally to a reader',[46] and Maggie O'Sullivan's in her international anthology of 'linguistically innovative' women's poetry: 'explorati[ion]' that 'cannot be read in familiar ways'.[47] And by the late 1990s, as Irish Studies programmes began multiplying stateside, new Irish critics such as Alex Davis and Dónal Moriarty were attending to, for example, the long-neglected modernist work of Denis Devlin and Brian Coffey—in whose poetry Samuel Beckett had once famously rooted 'the nucleus of a living poetic in Ireland'.[48]

Not all of this was easy to see from stateside. But given the Internet, 'out of sight' no longer meant 'out of mind'. And in the same year Tuma's book appeared, Wesleyan University Press published the first American anthology with a wide-ranging selection

---

[45] Matthias, *Who was Cousin Alice?*, 232.

[46] Linda France (ed.), Introduction to *Sixty Women Poets* (Newcastle upon Tyne: Bloodaxe Books, 1993), 16.

[47] Maggie O'Sullivan (ed.), 'To the Reader', *Out of Everywhere: Linguistically Innovative Poetry by Women in North America & the UK* (London and Benhall Green: Reality Street Editions, 1996), 9.

[48] Samuel Beckett (alias: Andrew Belis), 'Recent Irish Poetry', *Bookman* (Aug. 1934), 235–6 (236).

of the unrepresented British and Irish writers we longed to see: *Other: British and Irish Poetry Since 1970*. Three years later we had Tuma's own larger and more comprehensive *Anthology of Twentieth-Century British and Irish Poetry* (OUP), perhaps the most important intervention in the last decade; its success to date—selling between 400 and 600 copies per year—suggests its importance in university classrooms as well. Its first-ever inclusion of both expected mainstream *and* less familiar experimental figures in its charting of poetry across the century caused a grand stir, given that it was redefining 'the tradition' *tout court*. Yet I would suggest that its arguments are less radical than we might think, because as Simon Armitage and Robert Crawford's surprisingly revisionary tome of an anthology in 1998—*The Penguin Book of Poetry from Britain and Ireland since 1945*—illustrated, with its fairly even-handed inclusion of particularly earlier experimental figures, a rapprochement *has* been occurring, slowly but surely. New critical surveys—by Peter Childs, for example, and Sarah Broom—also make this clear, alongside collections such as *Contemporary Women's Poetry* (Macmillan, 2000), a special issue of the *Yale Journal of Criticism* on 'British Poetry After Modernism' (2000), and *Poetry and Contemporary Culture* (Edinburgh University Press, 2002). But Tuma's anthology galvanized the defensive anxiety we hear in 2004 (from not only Paterson and Simic but also from *Poetry*, which produced a special issue featuring 'Thirteen British Poets' that largely mirrored their choices) for two reasons, I think. First, it's published by OUP (albeit its New York branch), which remains authoritative in poetry, despite its controversial closing of the Oxford Poets series. That it should sponsor a revision of poetic history suggests that more than a brief revival of the 'Revival' is occurring; indeed, the year after its publication, *Poetry Review* experienced its *second* takeover by editors sympathetic to experimental work: David Herd and Robert Potts. Secondly, the anthology's emphasis on experimental figures in its latter half is a reversal of the usual practice, whereby anthologies finish off—like the Armitage/Crawford tome—with no experimental figures at all, in order to secure, perhaps, poetry's future directions. It's no doubt more upsetting to the present mainstream to find itself sidelined than excluded altogether—in which case such collections were, in the past, simply marginalized. But *that* isn't likely to happen to an OUP anthology.

So one might say that the last two decades of transatlantic conversation about British poetry have been characterized, ironically, by both unremarked rapprochement *and* rather voluble high anxiety; by returns to expansiveness *and* retrenchment to protectionist definitions of 'Britishness'. But as new books on poetry's broad spectrum proliferate, and even-handed 'companions' and handbooks (like this one) multiply fruitfully, and home-grown journals devoted to critical writing on the avant-garde spring up—like *Journal of British and Irish Innovative Poetry*—and even books on teaching such writing appear from established presses with new initiatives, like *Teaching Modernist Poetry* (2010) in Macmillan's 'Teaching the New English' series, wilful transatlantic ignorance of what an *inclusive* view yields of 'new poetry' overseas will become harder to defend. For the moment, some Americans continue as they were, no doubt threatened by the continuing ubiquity and encroachments of 'other' kinds of poetry over here. So 'over there', they like to think—as of old—modernism *still* 'never happened'.

Coda

In 2009, rising poetry critic Stephen Burt of Harvard University delivered a *PN Review* lecture entitled 'Transatlantic Disconnections, or, the Poetry of the Hypotenuse'. It antagonized American readers of British poetry given his surprisingly late repetition of the old story—which is to say: his apparent lack of awareness of all the work that I've only had time to gesture at in this chapter. It infuriated Anania, a long-time reader of British poets. In his retort (*PN Review 193*, 35/5), Anania half-rightly argues (as I have here) that '[t]he "transatlantic disconnection" of Burt's title is dependent on Burt's excluding from essential British-ness the British poets Americans are most likely to have read'. But he's also half-wrong; Burt reads across mainstream/avant-garde lines, as I've suggested many Americans do, including in his model of 'British-ness' experimentalists Prynne, Denise Riley, Tony Lopez, Robert Sheppard, and Peter Riley (and not dismissively, as Anania claims). That Burt 'forgets' American readers before him is best explained by his *greater* allegiance to the work which, as I've said, we've indeed not read enough lately: post-Movement poets; New Gen and 'Next Gen' (2004) poets; *New British Poetry*. Yet he attempts to extend what he sees in such poems to the avant-garde as well: 'a consciousness of the literary and cultural past',[49] which he argues makes it impossible for the poet to work, as in America, 'all alone'. And as he finds, say, Denise Riley's poems 'attend[ing] to imagined listeners', performing 'the lyric person' overwritten by the 'echoes of older metres' and legends and texts I find myself agreeing, in part. He extends, in other words, what Brown argued, and what Simic and Gioia suggested earlier about British poetry as 'public speech', and celebrates, therefore, what he concludes only it can do: provide new 'model[s] of sustainable relations' between people (and, in his 'ecocritical' argument, between them and the forgotten Earth).

Anania scorns Burt's findings and his titular image—which speaks back to Perloff's earlier sense of the irreparable rift between our poetic languages. It pictures poet and poem at the triangle's right angle; at the second, 'the spoken language of the present'; and at the third, the poetry of the past. Burt argues that such connections are weak in US poetry and continuingly strong in British poetry—which is why, he claims, quoting Davie, it remains hard for Americans to 'hear' UK work. Anania rightly deconstructs the image's assumptions about that 'past' for poets, arguing that it 'only seems singular when it is under the control of a culturally dominant present'. He's also annoyed by the idea, which travels to Burt from Davie, that for the British 'the writing of poems is a public and social activity'. Instead he asserts that '[w]e propose readers to ourselves because it would be lonely without them, but they are fictions'. Yet Burt's image of the American writer working alone appears affirmed in this remark.

Is this just another iteration of the old story, or is something else going on here? I think it's a little of both, and that the latter has to do with new anxieties about the location, task,

---

[49] Stephen Burt, 'Transatlantic Disconnections, or, The Poetry of the Hypotenuse', *PN Review 190*, 36/2 (Mar. 2010), 20–9 (22).

and audience for new century poetry that cry out for transatlantic debate. We've long since arrived at a threshold of some kind; with the 'postmodern' moment apparently over, and the authority of its poetics indefinitely shifted, what rules in our oxymoronic 'post-avant' moment in the US is a 'hybridized', overtly depoliticized aesthetics evident in new anthologies like Norton's *American Hybrid* (2009)—though also in UK ones, like Bloodaxe's *Identity Parade* (2010). A conspicuous return to 'lyric' dominates these and many new anthologies' introductions and selections (as well as the US critical world, its 'new lyric humanism'). As even Juliana Spahr suggests, in *American Women Poets in the 21st Century: Where Lyric meets Language* (2002), this involves the aestheticization of earlier modes of radical intervention and renewals of lyric writing disinclined toward Language-poetry-like collective efforts. And yet post-9/11 terror and war crimes, escalating environmental concerns (like those that inform Burt's analysis), economic disasters, and now occupation movements simultaneously put pressure on any new retreat to lyric isolation in the old style; therefore we also find key critic Charles Altieri arguing that Spahr and other American poets are currently 'revers[ing] the Modernist expulsion of rhetoric from lyric practice', and 'exploring how poetry might take on more overt social responsibilities'.[50] *Are* Americans writing 'all alone', then, as Burt would have it, or (and?) shifting towards those rhetorical modes of public address that modernism overseas never banished from lyric practice? How might their thus-far poorly theorized return to lyric compare with, for example, what British poet-critic John Wilkinson named 'political lyric' when speaking of the UK's newest avant-garde, which absorbed its tradition's foregoing experiments in performance writing, suffered no allergy to collective formation, and continues in highly articulate terms to process 'lyric poetry as a declaratively political practice'?[51] Have the theoretical tables turned? Where are 'we' in understanding even this seemingly square-one word in poetics, 'lyric'? What can it possibly mean transatlantically anymore—and make possible for poets writing either across eroding mainstream/avant-garde lines *or* towards future radical interventions within widening conceptions of community?

I, of course, have my own 'view' of the matter. But more *dialogue* is what we need.

Select Bibliography

Altieri, Charles, 'The Place of Rhetoric in Contemporary American Poetics: Jennifer Moxley and Juliana Spahr', *Chicago Review*, 56/2–3 (Autumn 2011), 127–45.
Barry, Peter, *Poetry Wars: British Poetry of the 1970s and the Battle of Earls Court* (Cambridge: Salt Publishing, 2006).
Beckett, Samuel (alias: Andrew Belis), 'Recent Irish Poetry', *Bookman* (Aug. 1934), 235–6.
Brown, Merle E., *Double Lyric: Divisiveness and Communal Creativity in Recent English Poetry* (London: Routledge & Kegan Paul, 1980).

---

[50] Charles Altieri, 'The Place of Rhetoric in Contemporary American Poetics: Jennifer Moxley and Juliana Spahr', *Chicago Review*, 56/2–3 (Autumn 2011), 127–45 (127).

[51] John Wilkinson, *Lyric Touch* (Cambridge: Salt Publishing, 2007), 126.

Burt, Stephen, 'Transatlantic Disconnections, or, The Poetry of the Hypotenuse', *PN Review* 190, 36/2 (Mar. 2010), 20–9.

Caddel, Richard and Quartermain, Peter (eds.), *Other: British and Irish Poetry since 1970* (Hanover, NH: Wesleyan University Press, 1998).

Davie, Donald, *With the Grain: Essays on Thomas Hardy and Modern British Poetry*, ed. Clive Wilmer (Manchester: Carcanet Press, 1998).

France, Linda (ed.), *Introduction to Sixty Women Poets* (Newcastle upon Tyne, Bloodaxe Books, 1993).

Forbes, Peter, 'Talking About the New Generation', A Poetry Review Special Issue: The New Generation Poets, *Poetry Review*, 84/1 (Spring 1994), 4–6.

Gascoyne, David, 'The State of Poetry' issue, *Agenda*, 27/3 (1989), 30–5.

Gilbert, Sandra M., 'Common Wealth', *Poetry*, 184/3 (June–July 2004), 227–34.

Gioia, Dana, *Barrier of a Common Language: An American Looks at Contemporary British Poetry* (Ann Arbor: University of Michigan Press, 2003).

Gregson, Ian, *Contemporary Poetry and Postmodernism: Dialogue and Estrangement* (London: Macmillan, 1996).

Hofmann, Michael and Logan, William, 'A Conversation on British and American Poetry', *Poetry*, 84/3 (June–July 2004), 212–20.

Huk, Romana (ed.), *Assembling Alternatives: Reading Postmodern Poetries Transnationally* (Middletown, Conn.: Wesleyan University Press, 2003).

Matthias, John, *Reading Old Friends: Essays, Reviews, and Poems on Poetics 1975–1990* (Albany, NY: State University of New York Press, 1992).

Matthias, John, *Who Was Cousin Alice? And Other Questions* (Exeter: Shearsman Books, 2011).

Milne, Drew, 'Neo-Modernism and Avant-Garde Orientations', in Nigel Alderman and C. D. Blanton (eds.), *A Concise Companion to Postwar British and Irish Poetry* (Oxford and Chichester: Wiley-Blackwell, 2009), 155–75.

Mottram, Eric, 'Introduction: A Treacherous Assault on British Poetry', in Gillian Allnutt, Fred D'Aguiar, Ken Edwards and Eric Mottram (eds.), *The New British Poetry* (London: Paladin, 1988).

Norbrook, David, 'What Happened to MacDiarmid?', *London Review of Books*, 8/18 (23 Oct. 1986), 24–6.

O'Sullivan, Maggie (ed.), 'To the Reader', *Out of Everywhere: Linguistically Innovative Poetry by Women in North America & the UK* (London and Benhall Green: Reality Street Editions, 1996).

Paterson, Don and Simic, Charles (eds.), *New British Poetry* (Saint Paul, Minn.: Graywolf Press, 2004).

Perloff, Marjorie, Introduction: 'The Two Poetries: the Postwar Lyric in Britain and America', a special issue of *Contemporary Literature*, 18/3 (Summer 1977), 263–78.

Perloff, Marjorie, 'One of the Two Poetries', *PN Review* 19, 7/5 (May–June 1981), 47–51.

Sherry, Vincent (ed.), *Poets of Great Britain and Ireland since 1960* (Detroit: Gale Research, 1985).

Stevenson, Randall, *The Oxford English Literary History*, xii. 1960–2000: The Last of England? (Oxford: Oxford University Press, 2004).

Tuma, Keith, *Fishing by Obstinate Isles: Modern and Postmodern British Poetry and American Readers* (Evanston, Ill.: Northwestern University Press, 1998).

Tuma, Keith, 'Ed Dorn and England', *The Gig*, 6 (July 2000), 41–54.

Vendler, Helen, *Soul Says: On Recent Poetry* (Cambridge, Mass. and London: Harvard University Press, 1995).

Wilkinson, John, *Lyric Touch* (Cambridge: Salt Publishing, 2007).

CHAPTER 31

AUDIENCE AND AWKWARDNESS: PERSONAL POETRY IN BRITAIN AND NEW ZEALAND

ANNA SMAILL

Perhaps the first thing that will strike a reader of contemporary New Zealand poetry, if seeking to compare it to its counterpart in Britain, is its casual speaking voice. The events that motivate New Zealand poetic utterance are, on first glance, offhand and everyday; the subject matter defiantly prosaic, matter-of-fact. 'Then Murray Came' by Jenny Bornholdt is a poem that typifies the down-to-earth, domestic flavour characteristic of much contemporary New Zealand poetry:

It was the morning for
selling the car, but
when I went out to start it,
it wouldn't go. Greg went
to get petrol on the bike. I
rang the A. A. Then Ray
arrived. I said *I'm sorry*, he
said *don't worry* and looked at
the car and at the wheels and
in the boot and said *she's a lovely
old thing*.[1]

---

[1] Jenny Bornholdt, 'Then Murray Came', in Andrew Johnston and Robyn Marsack (eds.), *Twenty Contemporary New Zealand Poets: An Anthology* (Manchester: Carcanet Press, 2009), 131–2.

Another example, Geoff Cochrane's poem 'Impersonating Bono', describes a walk the speaker takes with a sister visiting from Australia. The poem is painstaking in its record of the details of personal experience:

Our jaunty tour takes in
the carpeted mall, the TAB Dad ran,
the library in which you once worked.
In Paper Plus, we score a couple of Little Golden Books.[2]

Both of these examples are taken from Carcanet's recent *Twenty Contemporary New Zealand Poets: An Anthology* (2009), a useful collection not only in its presentation of a strong cross-section of New Zealand poetry, but in its intention to introduce this national poetry to an audience of British readers. That British poetry is widely read in New Zealand means a comparable text for New Zealand readers is not easy to find. However, a parallel exists in Don Paterson and Charles Simic's *New British Poetry* (2004), which attempts to bridge a related literary gap; introducing the work of contemporary British poets to an American audience. The triangulation of New Zealand, British, and American readerships here speaks of a complex interaction of attention and influence. In light of this chapter, the most important point to note is that, where American and New Zealand poetries have a strong historical connection with British poetry through their very different colonial pasts, in the twentieth and twenty-first centuries, New Zealand and British poets are more likely to read and feel the influence of American voices. Drawing on these anthologies, this chapter will examine the respective first-person speakers of New Zealand and British personal poetry, how they filter American influence, and how they might still speak to each other across a significant cultural and geographic divide.

In immediate contrast to the examples above, the first-person speaking voice of British poetry seems characterized by greater confidence and polish, more complex syntax, and a closer connection with traditional form and metre. This voice can be heard, for example, in Glyn Maxwell's poem 'Helene and Heloise', which captures and explores the aesthetic resonances of childhood memory in a courtly diction and metre:

So swim in the embassy pool in a tinkling breeze
The sisters, *mes cousines*, they are blonde-haired Helene and Heloise,
One for the fifth time up to the diving board,
The other, in her quiet shut-eye sidestroke
Slowly away from me though I sip and look.[3]

In moving away from such formal polish, the intimacy of New Zealand poetry's voice and its focus on the domestic sphere is frequently understood by critics as a reflection of

---

[2] Geoff Cochrane, 'Impersonating Bono', in Johnston and Marsack (eds.), *Twenty Contemporary New Zealand Poets*, 169–70.
[3] Glyn Maxwell, 'Helene and Heloise', in Don Paterson and Charles Simic (eds.), *New British Poetry* (St Paul, Minn.: Graywolf Press, 2004), 129–32.

the influence of American writers, and particularly the so-called 'confessional' school.[4] In the 1960s, the wider availability of American poetry offered a liberating example, encouraging New Zealand writers to abandon the fixed forms associated with the British literary establishment and to turn away from the nationalist cultural project that had dominated poetry since the 1930s. As Bill Manhire states:

> This idea of the poem as conversation, as intimate address from writer to reader, has been very important in American poetry. I think you can see signs of it in the work of several New Zealand writers since the 1960s. James K. Baxter's *Jerusalem Sonnets* are a clear example.[5]

Alongside these new precedents for personal and intimate address, the American influence also galvanized a growing scepticism about language's referential capacity, and the assumption of authority tied to the speaking voice. Donald M. Allen's anthology, *The New American Poetry: 1945–1960*, was enormously influential, in particular on the group of poets loosely based around Auckland University (including Ian Wedde, Alan Brunton, Alan Loney, and Murray Edmond). For these writers, attuned to counter-culture movements and pop-cultural influence, American poetry offered new models for a relationship with language that involved exploration, performance, and play.[6]

British poetry of the same period also reveals the influence of American writing, and contemporary British poets are just as likely to question the naïve assumption of transparent self-expression in a speaking voice. However, it's possible to see that the 'I' in British poetry works in a different way to deflect such assumptions. As in Glyn Maxwell's poem quoted earlier, traditional formal and rhetorical techniques are frequently foregrounded, as if to highlight the organizing principles behind poetic utterance and draw attention to their artificiality. The frequent use of multiple, deft, often surreal, personae in contemporary British poetry works in a similar way to disturb the integrity of first-person experience, as well as offering a challenge to the self-reflective, reticent speakers that characterized the formal, highly crafted poetry of the 1950s. The first-person speaker of these poems is often dramatically amplified via myth or history—a tactic resulting in skewed yet recognizable speakers that build on, while effectively distancing themselves from, the poets' own experience. Intricate and polished personae occur in the work of poets as diverse in style as Simon Armitage, Carol Ann Duffy, Ian Duhig, James Fenton, Robin Robertson, and Jo Shapcott. As good an example as any of this mode, Michael Donaghy's 'Shibboleth' is a dreamlike vignette that establishes character and drama with great economy. The

---

[4] See Terry Sturm, 'New Zealand Poetry', in Neil Roberts (ed.), *A Companion to Twentieth-Century Poetry* (Oxford: Blackwell Publishing, 2001), 293–303 (300).

[5] Bill Manhire, *Doubtful Sounds: Essays and Interviews* (Wellington: Victoria University Press, 2000), 73.

[6] Sturm, 'New Zealand Poetry', 301.

poem's speaker, a Second World War GI, explains how cultural minutiae might weed out potential 'infiltrators':

One didn't know the name of Tarzan's monkey.
Another couldn't strip the cellophane
From a GI's pack of cigarettes.[7]

The disparity between the voices of these two contemporary poetries reflects cultural differences that are not addressed through the critical narrative of American poetic influence on New Zealand writers. Critics often describe the trajectory of this influence as a swift about-face, in which all New Zealand poetry preceding the 1960s was 'as well-behaved and as predictable as most British poetry' and all poetry following it liberated and irreverent.[8] However, it's possible to see that the seeds have long been planted for New Zealand poetry's focus on the particularities of individual experience, on domestic and ostensibly anti-poetic subject matter, and on the priority of capturing an individual voice and idiom. It might be more useful to ask why the specific elements of American poetry—its close, collusive, and 'impure' voice—were so congenial to a generation of New Zealand writers.

Donald Davie explains the tonal divide between British and American poetries as in part a function of American poets' isolation: 'For the English poet the writing of poems is a public and social activity, as for his American peers it is not.'[9] The inward focus Davie attributes to American poets is reinforced by geography; social isolation is exaggerated by the country's sheer size. It is arguable that the intimate voice of New Zealand poetry is shaped by a similar awareness of the function of poetry. New Zealand's isolation is certainly increased by its geographical position. However, the shaping effect of New Zealand's relative distance from the cultural centres of Europe—diminished of course by twenty-first-century travel and communications—must also be placed against a different factor, the possibility for a relative intimacy of cultural reference and understanding. Though New Zealand is a multicultural and economically stratified society, two demographic factors aid this possibility. The first is its relatively small population. At a 2010 estimate New Zealand's population was 4.3 million, a size that, when ranked with the twenty-six other OECD countries, places it above only Ireland, Luxembourg, and Iceland.[10] The second factor, though not always a social and economic reality, is New Zealand's ideal of classlessness. This pervasive cultural myth is strongly based in New Zealand's colonial past: many immigrants to the country were motivated by the prospect of leaving behind the class distinctions and values associated with Britain and

---

[7] Michael Donaghy, 'Shibboleth', in Paterson and Simic (eds.), *New British Poetry*, 47.

[8] Johnston and Marsack, 'Introduction', in Johnston and Marsack (eds.), *Twenty Contemporary New Zealand Poets*, 11.

[9] Donald Davie, *The Poet in the Imaginary Museum: Essays of Two Decades* (New York: Persea Press, 1977), 289.

[10] R. G. Mulgan (updated by Peter Aimer), *Politics in New Zealand* (1997; 3rd edn., Auckland: Auckland University Press, 2004), 20.

Europe. More recently allied to New Zealand's sense of itself as egalitarian and liberal is its perceived success as a bicultural society—a culture that equally recognizes the values and political rights of Maori and Pakeha (New Zealanders of predominantly European descent). Adherence to this perception can result in a downplaying of real difference and thus a perpetuation of racial marginalization. However, these ideals are not without some potency. New Zealand government policy stresses biculturalism and emphasizes the rights of Maori as the indigenous landholders and signatories of the Treaty of Waitangi. A commitment to classlessness is revealed in New Zealand's expectations of university attendance and homeownership, along with taxation policy. As Mulgan points out, 'the idea of egalitarianism, though not firmly based in social and economic fact [...] may nonetheless have been politically influential'.[11]

That the belief in a shared cultural experience is central to New Zealand identity suggests an insight into the informal nature of its poetic voice. New Zealand poetry frequently explores this breed of social propinquity, even while examining and challenging its limits. Bill Manhire is, for example, able to extrapolate confidently from his own observation to a wider truism of New Zealand experience when explaining his well-known poem 'Zoetropes'. Playing on the flash of familiarity afforded a travelling New Zealander when glimpsing a stray 'Z' in a block of text, 'Zoetropes' captures a 'little burst of hope replaced by an extended sense of loss'. 'All New Zealanders who travel' know it, Manhire writes, 'it's the Kiwi way'.[12] We can see Jenny Bornholdt playing on a similar assumption of intimacy in 'Then Murray Came'. The poem's flurry of first names and definite articles assumes a familiarity with context and detail, as well as playing somewhat wryly on that other New Zealand truism: that everybody knows everyone else. Similarly, in 'Impersonating Bono', Cochrane understands that a reference to the TAB (the Totalizator Agency Board—a state-run gambling agency), and Paper Plus (an ubiquitous stationery chain), will be immediately clear to a New Zealand reader.

Speaking from a place in which shared experience and mutual understanding might be possible obviates a certain amount of explanation. Accordingly, New Zealand poets are more inclined than their UK counterparts to rely on an image-based shorthand for specific emotive effects. That their readership can be trusted to catch specific aesthetic and emotional associations with objects of culture—the bathos, for example, of passing the TAB that one's father used to own, or the rather 'Kiwi' experience of having a personal relationship with one's AA driver—potentially relieves New Zealand poets from establishing emotional connection via more forceful rhetorical devices.

A further characteristic of New Zealand poetry's casual, confidential tone is its inclusive approach to seemingly anti-poetic subject matter and its determination to draw together formal and informal registers. Bill Manhire, New Zealand's inaugural Poet Laureate and arguably most influential contemporary voice, discusses New Zealand poetry in terms of its mixing 'pure and impure' words, its tendency to concoct 'a text

---

[11] Mulgan, *Politics in New Zealand*, 41.
[12] Bill Manhire, 'Note', *A Calendar of Modern Poetry: PN Review 100*, 21/2 (1994), 125.

which is a sort of conversation between words from different languages', adding that 'Many of New Zealand's best poets are code-switchers'.[13] Ian Wedde's introduction to *The Penguin Book of New Zealand Verse* (1984) established similar terms, tracing contemporary New Zealand poetry's development via its increased juggling of 'hieratic' and 'demotic' registers.[14] Code-switching and register-crossing is, of course, also present in contemporary British poetry. However, it's possible to see different agendas and effects in the use of the demotic in these two poetries. The casual, playful tone of New Zealand poetry's experiments with register can again be understood in relation to the country's egalitarian self-image, whereas collisions of dialect in British poetry often present a concerted attack on cultural boundaries. In Britain, where as Tom Leonard argues, language can be 'considered the possession of a particular class, a form of property which like other forms of property need[s] protection',[15] such register-crossing potentially has more at stake.

Tony Harrison's work, for example, is famous for drawing a phonetically rendered Leeds accent and idiolect into strict iambic pentameter, as in the *School of Eloquence* sequence. This juxtaposition implies Harrison's mastery of establishment tools in response to a fierce sense of cultural and class-based exclusion. As Sarah Broom notes, 'many of Harrison's poems [...] put [their] eruditon on display as a kind of taunting gesture towards the school-teachers and other authorities who relegated him to "the comic bits" '.[16] His work also addresses an alienation from the working-class community increasingly enforced by his grammar school and university education. This division is captured in the poem 'Me, Tarzan', in which a scholarship boy's homework thwarts him from joining his friends: '*Ah bloody can't ah've gorra Latin prose*'.[17]

In this light, it's interesting to compare Harrison's work with one of New Zealand poetry's most committed code-switchers, the Maori poet Hone Tuwhare (1922–2008). A deeply political writer, Tuwhare addresses issues of class and cultural marginalization in his work. However, where a clash of registers in Harrison's poetry works to maintain a sense of cultural division, Tuwhare often attempts to hold oppositions in a form of balance. Tuwhare's poem 'Dear Cousin' is both a dinner invitation to the cousin of the title, and a loose meditation on sensual pleasure versus spiritual pursuit. Playing on the inherent contrast between the high-culture associations of poetry and the immediacy of a personal speaking voice, Tuwhare's elegant three-line stanzas accommodate his customary oratorical rhythms alongside demotic language and slang ('What do you reckon, Cous?', 'throw our hand in') and shift between English and Maori ('whaariki',

---

[13] Bill Manhire, *Doubtful Sounds*, 18.

[14] Ian Wedde and Harvey McQueen (eds.), *The Penguin Book of New Zealand Verse* (Auckland: Penguin Books, 1985), 29.

[15] Quoted in Keith Tuma, *Fishing by Obstinate Isles: Modern and Postmodern British Poetry and American Readers* (Evanston, Ill.: Northwestern University Press, 1998), 4.

[16] Sarah Broom, *Contemporary British and Irish Poetry: An Introduction* (Hampshire: Palgrave Macmillan, 2006), 15.

[17] Tony Harrison, *Selected Poems* (2nd edn., Harmondsworth: Penguin Books, 1987), 116.

'kamokamo, riwai'[18]). Tuwhare's erudition and his status as a poet do not, however, involve separation from the poem's addressee. Where for Harrison, education and literacy is divisive—as 'Book Ends' has it: 'what's still between's | not the thirty or so years, but books, books, books'[19] —for Tuwhare, the sensuality of poetry offers a leap of inclusive recognition; the poet and his cousin's shared appreciation for boiled fishbrains allows him to conclude 'we're both brainy buggers'.

As a liking for fishbrains might correlate with intellectual superiority, the poem also seeks to hold together the tendencies towards both innocence and violence, bodily appetite and religious capacity:

because I know that you are also

a devout man—deeper than any prayer can
grab you—I will simply say: go for it.
And we'd crack a bottle or three together[20]

These contradictions are allowed to simmer together like the shared stew of 'puha, | kamokamo, riwai, brisket-on-the-bone', a useful objective correlative for the poem's linguistic and cultural melting pot.

In this, Tuwhare's poem exemplifies another characteristic of contemporary New Zealand poetry: its resistance to the pull of closure. In a significant number of poets' work, we can see a determination that tonally diverse and emotionally opposed elements should be allowed to coexist without necessarily reaching towards a definitive aesthetic conclusion. Of course, an awareness of the problematic authority inherent in the click of closure has reached the level of postmodern truism. Contemporary British poetry also resists neat narrative closure. However, it's possible to note that it enacts this resistance from within the shaping constraints of extended metaphor and traditional form.

An example here is Sujata Bhatt's often-anthologized poem 'Muliebrity'. The poem circles a strong personal memory—that of seeing a young girl gathering cow-dung on the road to Radhavallabh temple in India. Crucially, 'Muliebrity' foregrounds, and self-consciously rejects, a common tendency in contemplative personal poetry—the reliance on a representative metaphor that will rise above individual meditation and observation. The speaker emphatically resolves that she will not 'use' the girl 'for a nice image' and, in order to avoid this tendency, seeks to prolong the open-ended nature of observation and description.[21] The speaker focuses on concrete detail (the precise location of the girl's position on the main road) and an immersion in sensory particularity ('the smell of cow-dung and road-dust and wet canna lilies...'). However, the poem

---

[18] Respectively, the terms refer to a woven mat used to cover the floor, and to the stew's ingredients of squash and potato.

[19] Harrison, *Selected Poems*, 126.

[20] Hone Tuwhare, 'Dear Cousin', in Johnston and Marsack (eds.), *Twenty Contemporary New Zealand Poets*, 31.

[21] Sujata Bhatt, 'Muliebrity', in Paterson and Simic (eds.), *New British Poetry*, 22.

ultimately cannot resist breaking its own injunction and using the girl to afford an element of closure. The poem ends with a description of 'the power glistening through her cheekbones | each time she found a particularly promising | mound of dung—'. By showcasing the underlying aesthetic contradiction between the girl's ostensibly degrading chore and the 'greatness | and the power' that the speaker sees 'glistening through her cheekbones', the poem seeks to provide an unexpected lesson—the possibility that 'dung' might be associated with 'promise'. The poem's title employs a similar tactic. 'Muliebrity' is an ungainly, even ugly, word and thus unexpected as a synonym for femininity. This contradiction does not, however, undermine the title's, or the poem's, impulse towards definition.

A related approach is taken by Jamie McKendrick in 'Six Characters in Search of Something', a poem that details an anecdote told about a man whose father, after generously offering his stick as protection for another lone traveller, is eaten by a polar bear. The poem is incidental and light-hearted, and rounds to the following end:

There may be a moral in this story
for the man, his son, the man he met,
for my friend, for me, or even for the bear,
but if there is it's better left unsaid.[22]

Here again, the poem and title perform an attempt to resist closure. Yet in spite of this, McKendrick still manages to achieve resolution in the neat anecdotal capture of irony as well as through a careful use of form and metre. As in Bhatt's poem, the denial of closure becomes a form of conclusion and resonance in its own right.

It's possible to see that New Zealand poets resist resolution in a different way to their British counterparts. Bernadette Hall's 'Snow Falling', for example, similarly foregrounds and struggles against the potentially meaningless nature of personal experience. The poem addresses the 7/7 Underground bombings in London, and the speaker's personal loss in the tragedy. Its movement is fragmentary and associative, built out of discursive prose that is loosely contained in balanced couplets. As the poem ponders the nature of grief it attempts to gain meaning through metaphor—rough analogies for the movement through personal loss are presented via a description of the transformative process by which water changes into snow, and attention to the persistence of seasonal change. A further analogical relationship is sketched between the helplessness of grief and the way in which an orang-utan observed at the Auckland zoo resists its keeper's attempts at capture. The animal is observed hiding from the tranquillizer dart by placing his head in a sack: 'eventually he picked the barb up and handed it | back, you might almost say ruefully, to his keeper'.

However, a key difference is that, while Bhatt's and McKendrick's poems both deny the possibility or understanding of a listener—Bhatt is 'unwilling [...] to explain to anyone' and McKendrick concludes that any moral 'is better left unsaid'—Hall's is addressed to

---

[22] Jamie McKendrick, 'Six Characters in Search of Something', in Paterson and Simic (eds.), *New British Poetry*, 134–5.

an unnamed second person who has an intimate knowledge of the poem's context. As a result, its lines resemble fragments of an ongoing conversation: 'Did I tell you that since her death the only people | I can bear to read are the beautiful Czechs?' And though the speaker makes repeated attempts at analogy, the parallels remain personal and provisional. The poem closes:

Snow's falling. I'm still looking for her face
in the crowd, the point where the bright body

kicks in, where spring enters like a dancer,
and summer, and Merv will come over

with a plate of strawberries from his garden.[23]

Though we have been lead to a possible understanding, via the listed appositive clauses, of the poem's closing image, it does not ultimately offer resolution, remaining suspended between winter and summer, as between the experience of grief and the hope of its release. Merv and his strawberries cannot be made to function as a wider symbol; they remain irreducibly themselves in a way that Sujata Bhatt's cow-dung digging girl does not.

The narrative of American influence also potentially underplays the deeper and more gradual historical movements that shape New Zealand poetry and distinguish it from its British counterpart. Allen Curnow's *The Penguin Book of New Zealand Verse* (1960) is largely understood as the first attempt to document and articulate the development of New Zealand's national literature. In his introduction to this anthology, Curnow assesses the poetry written in 1840–1920, the period immediately following colonization, and dismisses the majority due to its cultural reliance on British poetry. He criticizes this poetry's inaccurate reflection of colonial experience, and identifies a stridency or sentimentality that typically accompanied 'standard rhymed genuflexions to Empire and colonial Destiny'.[24] The critical apparatus that Curnow draws up here is significant. The criterion by which he salvages a handful of poems from the colonial period is the same he brings to bear in his choice of poets from 1930 onwards, representatives of what he calls the first distinct phase of New Zealand's literary culture. Curnow prizes observational accuracy and favours a dispassionate attitude over sentiment. A focus on personal vision rather than representative or communal experience is also clear. It's possible to see that diffidence, restraint, and a tendency to withhold judgement—to observe and describe rather than to proclaim—quickly become an aesthetic precedent. Although Marsack and Johnston are quick to dismiss the ongoing influence of this 'laconic style' on the talky, register-crossing poetry of their 2005 anthology, an element of the distinctively matter-of-fact, understated flavour can be traced in poets as different as Brian

---

[23] Bernadette Hall, 'Snow Falling', in Johnston and Marsack (eds.), *Twenty Contemporary New Zealand Poets*, 163–4.
[24] Sturm, 'New Zealand Poetry', 294.

Turner ('A drain | is real, no argument | there') and Glenn Colquhoun ('I drive a car that is falling apart. | There is bog in the body. | There is rust in the doors').[25]

Crucially, also, Curnow drew attention to the problematic relationship between language and experience that governs Pakeha New Zealanders writing in English. As Curnow describes it in his own poem, 'The Unhistoric Story', the first colonial experience was 'something different, something nobody counted on'. This experience of difference would have to be negotiated with a new literature, but also a new relationship between language and the land, one potentially fraught with 'a special awareness' of semantic problems, and 'conscious pains and anxieties over words and meanings'.[26] Curnow's critical stance thus involved a keen awareness of language's detachability from experience. Though the collection came under critical fire in subsequent decades for its insistence on an essential 'reality' that preceded experience, there was disingenuousness and a provision for multiplicity in Curnow's sense of the relationship between language and landscape, an acknowledgement that perceptions of reality will always be multiple and inherently fictive:

> In making a first really comprehensive anthology of my country's verse, I have found myself piecing together the record of an adventure, or series of adventures, in search of reality—of which New Zealand has been the scene, containing the deserts and dragons as well as the forests and fountains and fine prospects.[27]

This early sense of linguistic contingency and rhetorical capability prefigures an ongoing focus in New Zealand poetry on the materiality of language, its collapse as a transparent vehicle for expression. As Bill Ashcroft notes, the post-colonial experience instigates and exaggerates the epistemological questions that we associate with post-structural, and subsequently postmodern, thought. In the post-colonial environment,

> unease with the 'gulf' between imported language and local world became in time a radical questioning of the relationship between language and the world, an investigation into the means of knowing rather than into what is, or can be, known.[28]

A further continuity with Curnow's vision is New Zealand poetry's emphasis on the role of the poet as an observer and measurer of relationship. The nationalist project largely ignored a more significant relationship shaping the colonial environment—that between Pakeha settlers and indigenous Maori culture. It also brought with it a strong teleological imperative: the promise that at some point Pakeha culture and imagination would successfully colonize this landscape. However, it's interesting to see that Curnow's

---

[25] Johnston and Marsack, 'Introduction', 11; Brian Turner, 'Drain', 90; Glenn Colquhoun, 'Bred in South Auckland', in Johnston and Marsack (eds.), *Twenty Contemporary New Zealand Poets*, 193.
[26] Allen Curnow, *The Penguin Book of New Zealand Verse* (Harmondsworth: Penguin Books, 1960), 60.
[27] Curnow, *Penguin Book of New Zealand Verse*, 17.
[28] Bill Ashcroft, Gareth Griffiths, and Helen Tiffin, *The Empire Writes Back: Theory and Practice in Post-Colonial Literatures* (New York: Routledge, 2002), 137.

selection criteria emphasizes poets' representation of individual tension in relation to their cultural identity. This tension, he explains, stems from the need to look continually back towards an inherited cultural tradition, as well as remaining responsive to the exigencies of a new and unexpected environment.[29]

Contemporary New Zealand poetry demonstrates, to a large extent, a relaxation of the anxiety attendant on this dual gaze. However, New Zealand poetry still insists on a constant examination and evaluation of relationships—between individual and culture, between language and landscape, between here and there. Ian Wedde's introduction to the later Penguin anthology focuses on poets' responsiveness to what he calls the 'grid of intersections' that makes up an informed awareness of New Zealand culture. He measures poetic success largely in terms of a confidence in steering amongst criss-crossing cultural, social, and historical networks. Thus, David Eggleton's poem 'Painting Mount Taranaki' is singled out for praise due to its deft navigation of cultural and linguistic maps: 'Its language is a confident if erratic blend of vernacular, lyric, and "high demotic"; this confidence allows for mobile and ironic cross-currents animating the texture and depth of the language throughout.'[30] In many ways, then, the development of New Zealand literature has prioritized a keen awareness of and constant evaluation of relation. Even where such evaluation is not immediately obvious, the long-lasting effect of this constant measuring is a self-reflexiveness when it comes to language, and a certain ironic detachment from cultural allusions, physical objects, and even personal experience.

Allen Curnow's poem 'The Skeleton of the Great Moa in the Canterbury Museum, Christchurch' is often quoted in discussions that evaluate New Zealand's current state of poetic confidence. The poem looks forward to a point at which the struggle to define New Zealand's cultural position vis-à-vis Britain and an inherited literary tradition is over, and an awaited New Zealander is able to stand on his or her own two feet. Curnow predicts: 'Not I, some child, born in a marvellous year, | Will learn the trick of standing upright here.'[31]

If we take the child as a figure for the nation and for cultural confidence, it's more striking that, rather than learning how to stand upright, children figure frequently in contemporary New Zealand poetry as a sign of absence. Ian Wedde's poem 'To My Sons', for example, suggests the paradoxical nature of home when your birth country is defined by travel and departure:

Home's where you're always going, it's the place you've just
Left, where your father takes all the photographs
In the unfinished dwelling of the tribe [...]

---

[29] Curnow, *Penguin Book of New Zealand Verse*, 59–60. As Sturm notes, Curnow's 'emphasis on inward, unresolved tensions fits closely Stephen Slemon's argument that "ambivalence of emplacement"—outside the "illusion of a stable self|other, here|there binary division"—is "the 'always already' condition of Second-World settler and post-colonial literary writing"', 'New Zealand Poetry', 298.

[30] Wedde and McQueen (eds.), *The Penguin Book of New Zealand Verse*, 24, 40.

[31] Allen Curnow, 'The Skeleton of the Great Moa in the Canterbury Museum, Christchurch', in Wedde and McQueen (eds.), *The Penguin Book of New Zealand Verse*, 199.

[. . .] It's great to be home
Again, say our wandering sons, as they wave goodbye.[32]

Lost children are a casual aside in Gregory O'Brien's poem 'Whole Forgotten Days': 'some of the children got so lost they actually found themselves | *in suburbs*'. And children are repeatedly lost or stolen in Bill Manhire's work. In 'Miscarriage', for example, the speaker wakes at dawn to find his daughter's place empty: 'Where had she gone? | Was she lost in the headlines?'; in 'The Writer', children are 'stolen [. . .] by sleep, by the night and its darkness [. . .] by their own first lies'.[33]

The recurring image of loss or erasure can be seen as a simple response to the fact that foreign travel remains a rite of passage for young New Zealanders. Just as New Zealand is 'prone to disappearing when you are away from it', as Bill Manhire states, those who leave New Zealand also undergo a form of disappearance.[34] However, this factor in itself points to a wider truth of New Zealand's cultural position. Although New Zealand has become far more confident in the process of defining its own culture and history without external reference points, international experience, recognition, and educational and career opportunities still exert a strong pull. Thus, while these domestic disappearances function on a literal level, they can also be seen to speak more widely of New Zealand's ongoing view of its geographic position and its relation to the cultural centres of Europe and America.

If New Zealand poetry can't be described as having turned a fully upright back on the sense of distance that inheres in its relationship to these cultural centres, it's useful to posit a different metaphor, one that might open a further understanding of this poetry's continued development. In the brief introduction to the selection of his work in the Carcanet anthology, Manhire writes that he 'started writing poems out of a deep shyness and social awkwardness, and because words could sound magical'. Stepping past the idea of poem as social defence mechanism, he elaborates further on the characteristic of 'awkwardness' as it applies to poetry:

> [A]wkwardness [. . .] can give a poem peculiar worth—so that the apparently finished thing thrives inside its own sense of incompleteness, keeping faith with the clumsy world it came from. Awkwardness guarantees a kind of authenticity. The stumble, like the presence of bad special effects in a movie, makes us feel human.[35]

Here it's important to be aware of Manhire's sleight of hand. There is, of course, a real difference between unintentional awkwardness, or gaucheness without self-awareness

---

[32] Ian Wedde, 'To My Sons', in Johnston and Marsack (eds.), *Twenty Contemporary New Zealand Poets*, 64–5.

[33] Gregory O'Brien, 'Whole Forgotten Days', in Johnston and Marsack (eds.), *Twenty Contemporary New Zealand Poets*, 119; Bill Manhire, *Collected Poems* (Wellington: Victoria University Press, 2001), 150; Bill Manhire, *Lifted* (Wellington: Victoria University Press, 2005), 26.

[34] Manhire, *A Calendar of Modern Poetry*, 125.

[35] Bill Manhire, 'Note', in Johnston and Marsack (eds.), *Twenty Contemporary New Zealand Poets*, 69.

(bad special effects in a movie), and a willingness to allow, admit, and even cultivate aesthetic awkwardness. The concept moves beyond the clumsy stumble to suggest a drawing together of elements that are difficult to reconcile—the tonally jarring or emotionally opposed. This begins to have immediate resonance with the characteristics of New Zealand poetry examined earlier—its ease with the demotic voice, as well as its habit of crossing registers and evading closure. As Manhire further defines this quality, we can see the term expanding, along with its potential relevance for discussion of the poetic sensibility of a country as a whole: 'Sometimes awkwardness is there in other ways. I love the [...] way in which the mundane can both call up and undermine the lyrical.'[36] The casual first-person voice of so much contemporary New Zealand poetry enacts the very awkwardness Manhire describes here, in both evoking and undercutting the purity of lyric. In fact, lyric speech provides a useful final lens for examining the difference between contemporary British and New Zealand poetries and their relationship to audience.

John Stuart Mill famously defined poetry as a form of expression that is completely unconscious of a listener, and which the reader, therefore, must overhear.[37] In his subsequent discussion of lyric, Northrop Frye picks up on Mill's description of poetry as that which is overheard. However, he also specifically emphasizes the element of pretence involved in lyric's relationship with an audience, its potential for performativity: 'The lyric poet normally pretends to be talking to himself or to someone else [...] The poet, so to speak, turns his back on his listeners.'[38] Thus, as a form, lyric is essentially ambivalent about its audience: even when presented as a solitary expression of individual meditation, it remains reliant on the very readers it turns its back on. When lyric makes use of apostrophe, the poet's pretence potentially operates on two levels. The disavowal of its readers is mirrored by the ambivalence underlying the act of address—lyric address suggests a deep desire for the appearance of that which is addressed, yet the precondition of this address is solitude. As Ann Keniston notes, lyric apostrophe illustrates a fundamental paradox:

> Lyric is, and must remain, the utterance of a single voice. Should the nightingale or skylark or Nature or Presences or dead son or father suddenly respond, the poem would lurch out of lyric and into drama. While lyric desires that the other appear, it also desires its own perpetuation and so requires the continued absence of the addressee.[39]

While all lyric partakes in an essential contradiction, not all lyric is apostrophic or draws attention to the act of utterance. As discussed earlier, the lyric speakers of

---

[36] Manhire, 'Note', 69.

[37] John Stuart Mill, 'What is Poetry?' in *Essays on Poetry*, ed. F. Parvin Sharpless (Columbia: University of South Carolina Press, 1976), 12.

[38] Northrop Frye, *Anatomy of Criticism: Four Essays* (Princeton: Princeton University Press, 1957), 249–50.

[39] Ann Keniston, '"The Fluidity of Damaged Form": Apostrophe and Desire in Nineties Lyric', *Contemporary Literature*, 42/2 (Summer, 2001), 294–324 (301).

contemporary British poetry often complicate and challenge the status of subjectivity via the self-reflexive use of traditional form and the development of highly crafted personae. However, they do not typically disturb the primary contract between a poem's speaker and its reader. That these poems orchestrate particularized personal detail in a performative fashion (as in the example from Glyn Maxwell), or sidestep it altogether (as in that from Michael Donaghy), suggests their determination to communicate with and to entertain a wide general readership. Their first-person speakers are not typically threatened by the possible absence of a specific addressee, a fact that speaks of a greater confidence in their overhearing audience.

In distinction to this, New Zealand lyric has tended to emphasize the tentative and fallible, the inherently *awkward*, nature of lyric address itself. Epistolary poems, for example, have a strong tradition in New Zealand poetry, from Ursula Bethell's 'Response'—ostensibly a letter written to a friend in England—through James K. Baxter's sequences 'Pig Island Letters' and 'Jerusalem Sonnets' to, more recently, Dinah Hawkens's 'Writing Home' sequence. These poems are all sustained by the illusion of personal proximity that a letter entails—we write as if the individual is listening to us in spite of mutual distance; when a letter is read, it sustains the illusion of a speaking voice—yet in foregrounding the process of communication in this way, they also underscore absence.

In the 1960s and 1970s New Zealand poets increasingly employed an intimate first-person lyric that addressed an autobiographically specific second person and seemed almost to intentionally snub a wider audience. As John Newton comments on the work of Ian Wedde and Murray Edmond: 'Th[e second-person] pronoun seems to point neither to the reader, nor to someone who might yet stand in for the reader, but to an intimate other listening *inside* the poem, while the general reader shrinks to a distant third party.'[40] This particularity of context works in a similar way to the accumulation of proper nouns and autobiographical detail employed by Jenny Bornholdt and Geoff Cochrane in the works already discussed. On one level it points to a self-assured framework of New Zealand cultural reference; however it also suggests an ambivalent relationship with a wider audience, rather than the confident interdependent relationship described by Northrop Frye.

The work of Bill Manhire represents a further development in New Zealand lyric. Manhire's poetry has typically involved an oblique, detached first-person speaker who navigates the distance between his own experience and the presence of a shadowy, always just-out-of-reach second person. Communication and connection with the other of this poetry has the tendency to blur and shatter, even as it sustains the promise of intimacy. Where the I/You address of much of the New Zealand poetry of the 1960s and 1970s relies on a specific relationship, and thus excludes the reader, the anonymity and inaccessibility of Manhire's addressees paradoxically work to increase

---

[40] John Newton, 'The Old Man's Example: Manhire in the Seventies', in *Opening the Book: New Essays in New Zealand Writing* (Auckland: Auckland University Press, 1995), 162–87 (168).

the flexibility and plurality of his lyric address. His own description of this process is useful:

> In my own writing, I'm struck by the frequency with which I use the word *you*. It's an odd, shifty pronoun: it can refer directly to the reader; it can signify a specific figure within the poem, even the writer of the poem; or it can do the generalizing job that the English 'one' does. I'm never quite sure how the word operates in my poems—sometimes it seems to shift between the various possibilities, rather than opting for any single one of them—but it's certainly there.[41]

The poem 'Good Looks' from the 1982 collection of the same title, for example, reveals how the denial of access and communication can be potentially fertile. The poem stages a meeting in which the speaker and a nameless addressee 'talk and talk till silence interrupts' and the latter retreats into 'distance'.[42] We gradually learn that this discussion is illusory, as the poem's addressee is unconscious, possibly dead: 'What did I think of, thinking | you would wake?' However, this withdrawal begins to suggest a benign, familiar space that erases distinction and even allows the possibility for a kind of strained mutuality, a place where 'there is no special relief | because there is no special pain'.

The possibility that poetic utterance might continue in the face of, and even be sustained by, absence is made more explicit in Manhire's 2005 collection *Lifted*. The collection's epigraph, from John Ashbery's poem 'This Room', echoes the knowledge at the heart of 'Good Looks'. Ashbery's speaker continues in spite of confirmed absence: 'Why do I tell you these things? | You are not even here'.

It's possible to argue that the specific paradoxes of lyric and lyric address offer an analogical relationship with the complexities of New Zealand's own geographic position and its relationship with a poetic audience. As discussed earlier, absence and isolation are preconditions for lyric, yet simultaneously the very conditions that lyric address attempts to undo. New Zealand's poetic reflects this suspended state: on one hand, its contemporary poetry suggests a confident freedom from the British tradition in its cultural self-referentiality; on the other, it remains tuned to the threats of distance and absence. Similarly, New Zealand poets insist on an intimate and particularized first-person voice, yet this voice is potentially prey to solipsism and disintegration, and often betrays doubt about the wider significance of its utterance.

In this light it is interesting to compare Bill Manhire's poem 'Kevin' with 'Prayer' by Britain's current Poet Laureate, Carol Ann Duffy. Both lyrics occupy a similar emotional territory, exploring ideas of personal loss and reflecting doubt about the possibility for human communication. Via a series of unnamed characters, Duffy's poem describes moments of solitude or even despair that might be redeemed in chance occurrences of grace and memory, moments in which 'although we cannot pray, a prayer | utters itself'.[43]

---

[41] Manhire, *Doubtful Sounds*, 73.
[42] Manhire, *Collected Poems*, 89.
[43] Carol Ann Duffy, *New Selected Poems* (London: Picador, 2004), 129.

As a mode of address, prayer is inherently problematic—a form of communication that typically persists without hope of reciprocation. Duffy's poem further removes the possibility for dialogue by redefining prayer as a random instant of personal recognition and relief. Such moments might use or suggest language but they do not function linguistically, rather they chime with emotion or memory. For the poem's isolated characters, prayer might be located in the sound of a train, a neighbour summoning their child, or, finally, the familiar repeated place names of the BBC shipping forecast: 'Inside, the radio's prayer—| Rockall. Malin. Dogger. Finisterre'.

The poem suggests, however, that the failure of address has its own emotional potency. As is made clear in the opening lines, these cathartic instances can only occur at those points when 'we cannot pray'. Although each individual character is isolated and each experience singular—a lonely lodger in a Midlands town; a woman observed with her head in her hands—they are allowed to become representative of general human experiences of loneliness and loss.

Manhire's poem 'Kevin' similarly highlights the failure of direct communication while also suggesting that this failure might open deeper possibilities for communion. The poem addresses the Kevin of the title:

I don't know where the dead go, Kevin.
The one far place I know
is inside the heavy radio. If I listen late at night,
there's that dark, celestial glow,
heaviness of the cave, the hive.[44]

As for Duffy, the radio in Manhire's poem suggests a one-sided form of communication. The poem's speaker is cast as a permanent listener, unable to reply to the radio's impersonal dispatches. That these voices are disembodied suggests the great distance they have travelled from their origins. (The speaker's consequent understanding that the world inside the radio is a 'far place' becomes more literal considering New Zealand's reliance on international broadcasts.) The poem makes a further logical connection between distance and absence: the speaker does not know where the dead go, but, since they are also inaccessible and unable to respond, it follows that they might also occupy the radio's remote interior world.

In a way that parallels the realizations of Duffy's poem, a measure of comfort is gained in spite of, and perhaps as a result of, absence and exclusion. For Manhire's speaker, the radio's continual voice softens and blurs the condition of isolation, providing a form of companionship. It suggests the warmth, darkness, and enclosure of a cave, as well as a place of swarming, undifferentiated togetherness, a place where we can't distinguish between bodies—the hive.

In spite of the similarities between these two poems, the way in which each frames the encounter with doubt and failure is revealing of an understanding of subjectivity,

---

[44] Manhire, *Lifted*, 79.

as well as a relationship to their respective poetic audiences. Duffy's poem presents a self-possessed reflective speaker who is confident enough in her audience to immediately conjure a 'we' and an 'us'. The final lines tellingly rely on the significant place in collective British consciousness held by the BBC shipping forecast, a place made clear in the number of allusions it garners in literature and other media.[45] Though each individual portrait of loss or despair in Duffy's poem is potentially self-implicating, each draws on a privileged access and insight into the characters' personal background and experience. The ability of Duffy's speaker to comment on behalf of the poem's characters paradoxically allows a shoring-up of her lyric autonomy. The poem ultimately works to uphold the lyric convention of the powerful speaker who, in a moment of personal meditation, turns away from her audience.

In contrast, Manhire's poem enacts the fallibility of communication from within its diffident first-person voice. The poem's use of apostrophe draws attention to the problematic nature of lyric address and thus of lyric itself. There is no assurance here that Kevin is able to hear, let alone to reply; like those voices that emerge from the radio, he is remote, unresponsive, even perhaps one of the dead himself. In insisting on the limitations of first-person address, the poem eschews lyric's tendency to confer distinction on the speaker through a universal emotive uplift; likewise, what mutuality it extends can only come at direct cost to personal individuation. Thus, the radio's voice offers comfort and communality, but entering its world becomes synonymous with death and disintegration: 'Eventually we all shall go | into the dark furniture of the radio'.

Manhire essentially reverses lyric convention by casting the poem's speaker as the permanent, excluded listener who must always overhear the confident voice of the radio. Rather than a unifying cultural reference point, as it is for Duffy, the radio's utterance provides an ambivalent challenge to the lyric preconditions of silence, singularity, and isolation. This voice is endlessly present, endlessly duplicated, and aesthetically indiscriminate: even after the listener is 'lifted' (a metaphor that suggests death, transcendence, rebirth), the radio will continue 'dirtying' the lyric silence with 'some terrible breakfast show'.

What comes to light in this examination of lyric address is a useful distinction between contemporary poetry in New Zealand and the United Kingdom. Where British poets tend to present a confident, polished first-person voice that sacrifices intimacy in favour of breadth of reference and representativeness, New Zealand poets more frequently highlight the flawed and awkward nature of first-person address. This emphasis of lyric awkwardness is suggestive of New Zealand's continued ambivalence towards loss and absence, and the still active presence of New Zealand's colonial past, as well as its global position as a small island. It also presents a possible analogue for the ambivalent relationship New Zealand poets might have to their own national poetic audience,

---

[45] An obvious example is Seamus Heaney's sonnet 'The Shipping Forecast', but the forecast appears in several films, books, and comedic parodies, as well as in the lyrics of bands including Blur, Radiohead, and The Prodigy.

an audience that is intimate and proximate, but—in part as a result of these characteristics—cannot command for poetry the public and social role that it asserts in the United Kingdom. Paradoxically, for a poetry that may speak to a closer shared experience, New Zealand poetry is more hesitant than its British counterpart in laying claim to representative pronouncement. In the intimacy of this poetic voice there is a concomitant hesitation to move from individual to universal experience.

In reading Bill Manhire's work, we can see that the trope of awkwardness provides a fertile space for future development, however, not only in terms of an increased ease in straddling multiple registers and cultures, but in an ability to hold oppositions and mutualities in arrested balance, to retain a footing in the colonial past while endeavouring to shape a responsive poetic present. In fact, from a British perspective, it's possible to see a telling physical description of New Zealand's geographical location enshrined in the word Manhire chooses to describe this aesthetic quality. The Middle English etymology of 'awk' from Old Norse 'afugr'—meaning 'the wrong way round, upside down' rather quickly conjures the antipodes, as a place where, in St Augustine's words, 'men walk with their feet opposite ours'.

Select Bibliography

Ashcroft, Bill, Griffiths, Gareth, and Tiffin, Helen, *The Empire Writes Back: Theory and Practice in Post-Colonial Literatures* (New York: Routledge, 2002).
Broom, Sarah, *Contemporary British and Irish Poetry: An Introduction* (Hampshire: Palgrave Macmillan, 2006).
Curnow, Allen, *The Penguin Book of New Zealand Verse* (Harmondsworth: Penguin, 1960).
Davie, Donald, *The Poet in the Imaginary Museum: Essays of Two Decades* (New York: Persea Press, 1977).
Duffy, Carol Ann, *New Selected Poems* (London: Picador, 2004).
Frye, Northrop, *Anatomy of Criticism: Four Essays* (Princeton: Princeton University Press, 1957).
Grossman, Allen, *The Long Schoolroom: Lessons in the Bitter Logic of the Poetic Principle* (Ann Arbor: University of Michigan Press, 1997).
Harrison, Tony, *Selected Poems* (2nd edn., Harmondsworth: Penguin Books, 1987).
Johnston, Andrew, and Marsack, Robyn (eds.), *Twenty Contemporary New Zealand Poets: An Anthology* (Manchester: Carcanet, 2009).
Keniston, Ann, '"The Fluidity of Damaged Form": Apostrophe and Desire in Nineties Lyric', *Contemporary Literature*, 42/2 (Summer, 2001), 294–324.
Manhire, Bill, 'Note', *A Calendar of Modern Poetry: PN Review 100*, 21/2 (1994), 125.
Manhire, Bill, *Doubtful Sounds: Essays and Interviews* (Wellington: Victoria University Press, 2000).
Manhire, Bill, *Collected Poems* (Wellington: Victoria University Press, 2001).
Manhire, Bill, *Lifted* (Wellington: Victoria University Press, 2005).
Mill, John Stuart, 'What is Poetry?', in *Essays on Poetry*, ed. F. Parvin Sharpless (Columbia: University of South Carolina Press, 1976).
Mulgan, R. G. (updated by Peter Aimer), *Politics in New Zealand* (1997; 3rd edn., Auckland: Auckland University Press, 2004).

Newton, John, 'The Old Man's Example: Manhire in the Seventies', in *Opening the Book: New Essays in New Zealand Writing* (Auckland: Auckland University Press, 1995), 162–87.

Paterson, Don, and Simic, Charles (eds.), *New British Poetry* (St Paul, Minn.: Graywolf Press, 2004).

Sturm, Terry, 'New Zealand Poetry', in Neil Roberts (ed.), *A Companion to Twentieth-Century Poetry* (Oxford: Blackwell Publishing, 2001), 293–303.

Tuma, Keith, *Fishing by Obstinate Isles: Modern and Postmodern British Poetry and American Readers* (Evanston, Ill.: Northwestern University Press, 1998).

Wedde, Ian, and McQueen, Harvey (eds.), *The Penguin Book of New Zealand Verse*, (Auckland: Penguin, 1985).

PART V
RESPONSIBILITIES AND VALUES

CHAPTER 32

SPEECH ACTS, RESPONSIBILITY, AND COMMITMENT IN POETRY

MAXIMILIAN DE GAYNESFORD

Work on a theory of speech acts prompted by J. L. Austin can be used to transform debate in philosophy about the nature and value of poetry. This may seem a surprising claim. Austin is notorious, after all, for declaring that poetry is not 'serious'.[1] Leading philosophers, who have taken up his suggestions about the way we do things with words, use the same terms to describe poetry.[2] The charge seems obnoxious, repellent in its tone of boisterous disregard, of blanket contempt. So it is natural to assume that Austin, and those he has influenced, are averse to poetry, or at least unreceptive to it, and hence that their work on speech acts must be incapable of contributing usefully to philosophical debate on poetry.[3] But this would be a mistake.[4] The purpose of this chapter is to offer some ways to avoid making it, to become resistant to the temptation to make it.

Four questions lie at the heart of these issues: (1) How might speech act theory transform the way philosophical debate about poetry has been organized? (2) Is there evidence in poetry to support the proposed transformation of debate? (3) What objections

---

[1] J. L. Austin, *How To Do Things With Words* (2nd edn.), ed. J. O. Urmson and M. Sbisà (Oxford: Oxford University Press, 1975), 104, 22, 9.

[2] e.g. P. F. Strawson, 'Intention and Convention in Speech Acts', in *Logico-Linguistic Papers* (London: Methuen, 1971), 149–69, esp. 149. John Searle, *Speech Acts* (Cambridge: Cambridge University Press, 1969), esp. 57 n. 1. Kendall Walton shows the influence of this discussion in *Mimesis as Make-Believe* (London: Harvard University Press, 1990), esp. 5, 85, 103.

[3] Christopher Ricks, 'Austin's Swink', in *Essays in Appreciation* (Oxford: Oxford University Press, 1996), 262.

[4] See my 'The Seriousness of Poetry', *Essays in Criticism*, 59 (2009), 1–21; 'Incense and Insensibility: Austin on Poetry', *Ratio*, 66 (2010), 69–83; and 'How Not to Do Things with Words', *British Journal of Aesthetics*, 51 (2011), 1–19.

are there to such a transformation, and can they be answered? (4) What are the implications and consequences of such a transformation? Each question is the subject of a section in what follows. The final section draws the elements together and shows how they help explain characteristic forms of anxiety about the roles of poets in contemporary culture.

I

Philosophy has proceeded under a problematic assumption, at least since Plato and Aristotle made debate about the nature and value of poetry rigorous and systematic: that the business of poetry is to state or describe states of affairs, and that it must do so either truly or falsely, or at least in a way that purports to be either true or false.

At one end of the spectrum defining this debate, some claim that poetry consists of statements and descriptions that are or must be false. Poetic utterances straightforwardly fail to correspond to anything we can regard as reality. (Here and throughout I use 'poetic utterance' to mean what is said by forms of words in poetry when uttered on a particular occasion; so the same lines of poetry may furnish the material for innumerable poetic utterances.) At best, they misrepresent the way things are for the sake of pleasure and delight. At worst, they distort the way things are for the sake of some nefarious purpose. In either case, they are a kind of ingenious nonsense of which we should be careful. Thus Plato dismisses the poets from his ideal city because he thought their work 'as imitative as it could possibly be', and because he thought imitation far from the truth: it is 'a kind of game and not something to be taken seriously'.[5] Similarly, Gottlob Frege claims that poets express thoughts but do not put them forward as true; this is because, in poetry, 'the requisite seriousness is lacking [*der dazu nötige Ernst fehlt*]'.[6] Francis Bacon, John Locke, and Jeremy Bentham hold versions of these views.[7]

At the other end of the spectrum, some claim that poetry consists of statements and descriptions that are, or at least on occasion can be, true. Perhaps poetic utterances do indeed represent the way things are. Or if they do not match up with the world of sense-experience, perhaps there is nevertheless a super-sensible or transcendent reality to which they do correspond. Or perhaps the truth of poetic utterance is dependent instead on accurately representing only certain elements of ordinary reality: the contents of certain experiences, for example, or the feeling of certain emotions. Or perhaps the truth of poetry is a matter of the poet's sincerity: it is truthful in so far as it accurately

---

[5] Plato, *Republic*, book X, 602b7–8, tr. G. M. A. Grube, rev. C. D. C. Reeve, in *Plato: Complete Works*, ed. John M. Cooper (Indianapolis: Hackett Publishing Company, 1997), 971–1223 (1206).

[6] Gottlob Frege, 'Der Gedanke' (1918), in *Logische Untersuchungen*, ed. G. Patzig (Göttingen: Vandenhoeck & Ruprecht, 1993), 30–53 (36).

[7] Bacon, *The Advancement of Learning*, ix. Locke, *An Essay Concerning Human Understanding*, III. x. 34. Bentham, *The Rationale of Reward*, 253–4.

represents or captures the state of the poet's mind. Or perhaps the truth of poetry is dependent on an ontology of fictional worlds: poetic utterances are true in that they assert of a fictional world that it is a certain way, and, within a game of make-believe, the fictional world is indeed that way. Aristotle, William Wordsworth, John Stuart Mill, Matthew Arnold, and Kendall Walton hold versions of these views.[8]

Towards the centre of this spectrum, some claim that poetry consists of statements and descriptions that only purport to be true or false. In fact, they are neither. Poetic utterances are the expression of feelings, perhaps, not assertions about reality. Or if such utterances are more than expressive, they nevertheless fall short of presenting propositions for affirmation or denial. What they present instead are objects for aesthetic contemplation. Samuel Taylor Coleridge (on some occasions), I. A. Richards, and A. J. Ayer hold versions of these views.[9]

But the assumption on which this debate-defining spectrum rests—that poetry is a matter of statements and descriptions which are, or purport to be, true or false—may itself be false. That this is so becomes clear when we consider verses like these, with which Chaucer prepares to conclude his *Troilus and Criseyde*:

O moral Gower, this book I directe
To the and to the, philosophical Strode,
To vouchen sauf, ther need is, to correcte,
Of youre benignites and zeles goode.
And to that sothfast Crist, that starf on rode,
With al myn herte of mercy evere I preye,
And to the Lord right thus I speke and seye:[10]

These lines are laced together with a series of verbal phrases, 'I directe...', 'I preye...', 'I speke and seye...'. These phrases are of a character that commonly occurs in both poetic and non-poetic utterance. The sentences in which they occur do not express commands or wishes or questions or exclamations, and it may seem tempting to classify them in the grammatical category of statements. But this would be a grave mistake. And it is Austin's work on the occurrence of phrases with this character in ordinary non-poetic uses of language that shows us why.[11]

First, the one uttering each such phrase is not thereby *stating* that he is doing what he would be said to be doing in uttering it. (Here and elsewhere I shall use '(poetic) uttering' to mean the action whereby a (poetic) utterance is produced.) Nor is he thereby

---

[8] Aristotle, *Poetics* 1448a25–8; 1448b25–7; 1449a32–7; 1449b25, trans. I. Bywater, in *The Complete Works of Aristotle: The Revised Oxford Translation*, ed. J. Barnes (Princeton: Princeton University Press, 1984), 2316–40. Wordsworth, Preface to *Poems* (1815). Mill, *Autobiography*, 106–7. Arnold, 'The Study of Poetry', in *Essays in Criticism*, 2nd ser. (London, 1898), 48. Walton, *Mimesis as Make-Believe* (Cambridge, Mass.: Harvard University Press, 1990), 35–43.

[9] Coleridge, *Biographia Literaria*, ii. 10–11, 104. Richards, *Science and Poetry* (London, 1926), 56–9. Ayer, *Language Truth and Logic* (1936; repr. London: Penguin, 1971), 27–8.

[10] *Troilus and Criseyde* V.1856-1862 in *The Riverside Chaucer* 3rd edition reissue, ed. Larry D. Benson et al (Oxford: Oxford University Press, 2008) p. 585

[11] *How To Do Things With Words*, *passim*; particularly Lecture I.

describing his doing of what he would be said to be doing. He is simply *doing* it—directing his book to another, praying, speaking and saying, as the case may be. To use Austin's phraseology: *in* uttering certain things, he *does* certain things; or again, things are *done* in being *said*.

Second, what statements make of interest about themselves is primarily a matter of their truth values: whether what one is stating to be the case accords with what is indeed the case, whether it is a statement of fact, for example. But it is unclear that the sentences these verbal phrases compose have truth-values at all, let alone that it is primarily in terms of truth that we assess them. What utterance of these sentences makes of interest about themselves is primarily a matter of their doings: what actions one would be performing in uttering them, what, for example, one would thereby be doing or causing to be done.

Now it is not irrelevant to ask of such an utterance whether what is said to have been done is in fact done. And in that way, the question of truth can be made to re-enter. But it does so in a secondary and indirect manner that distinguishes an utterance of this particular sort from statements. It is because such an utterance purports to do things that we can ask—amongst other things—whether what purports to have been done has truly been done. And it is not of such an utterance itself that we ask 'is it true?'. The sentence we directly consider, on such an occasion, is a sentence *about* such an utterance, a secondary sentence that has the form 'That utterance did in fact do what it purported to do'. And there is no difficulty in asking of this secondary sentence 'is it true?' because it is, after all, a bona fide statement.

If action rather than truth is made basic to poetic utterance, and if descriptions and statements are no longer treated as paradigm instances of poetry, philosophical debate will proceed against a radically different spectrum of possible positions. At one end will be those who would affirm that those responsible for poetic utterances do things in saying what they thereby say. We will present evidence in support of this position in the next section of this chapter. At the other end of the spectrum will be those who would claim that those responsible for poetic utterances are incapable of doing what they say in saying what they do. We will examine objections from this part of the spectrum in the third section. Finally, towards the centre of the action-dependent spectrum, will be those who would claim that it is incorrect either to affirm or deny that those responsible for a poetic utterance are capable of doing things in saying what they say. They may say, for example, that in these special circumstances, something is indeed 'done' in the saying, but it is nevertheless not what those responsible purport to be doing in saying it. Or they may say that, if anything at all is 'done' in these circumstances, it is done only in a weak sense: the action of those responsible is not fully performed, not wholly brought off. We will look at a version of this position, which appears to be Austin's, in the fourth section.

To orientate debate towards action in this way is not to ignore the issue of truth altogether. We have already seen one reason why this is so. It is always relevant to ask of any uttering which also purports to be a doing whether it is true that the thing said to be being done is indeed being done. It is an important fact about using words to make promises, for example, that there are circumstances in which one does not make a promise in uttering the words 'I promise to do such-and-such' (when one is obviously joking, for example). But the proposed approach to philosophical debate about poetry treats relations to truth as secondary. Settling whether it is true that something is in fact done in some particular poetic utterance is dependent on settling a logically prior issue, basic to the nature of utterances as such: namely, whether it is *possible* for things to be done in poetic utterance, and if so how.

So Austin's revisionist approach to utterances in general may be illuminating where his comments on poetry in particular are not. Poetry is not exclusively concerned with making statements or offering descriptions that are (or purport to be) either true or false. Moreover, those parts of poetry which do consist of statements or descriptions nevertheless fall into the same general category as the lines from Chaucer's *Troilus*: they are all utterances which are primarily to be regarded in terms of action, of what they do.

II

We should explore the evidence that those responsible for poetic utterances may indeed do things in saying things. One might attempt this by showing how all the speech acts found in non-poetic utterances may also be found in poetry. But this would require far more space than is available here. It would also be comparatively unambitious. For there is an alternative: to concentrate on showing how one particular type of speech act is variously instantiated in poetry. This approach enables us to use poetry to sharpen our understanding of the type. We would also be open to the possibility that there are kinds of speech act, or ways of achieving such acts, which are peculiar to poetic utterance. So this second approach is ambitious and enables an additional result: to demonstrate ways in which philosophy stands to benefit from the study of poetry.

The particular type of speech act we shall concentrate on is the most striking: that exemplified by the verses from Chaucer's *Troilus*. Call it, then, the 'Chaucer-Type'. If Austin had been prepared to admit poetic utterances as speech acts, he would have classified these verses as 'Explicit Performatives', a type that he treated as uniform, homogenous, and readily identifiable by a common defining characteristic: that what one does in uttering such sentences is explicit in what one says.[12]

As Austin recognized, this is a special type of speech act. Most are not of this sort, even if we hesitate to say that there is a useful sense in which *all* utterance is 'performative'. For example, there are numerous ways to make a promise that do not involve uttering the word 'promise'. In most ordinary circumstances, saying 'I will be there', or 'You will have your money by the end of the month' is to do just what one does in saying 'I promise...'. Subsequent theorists have suggested that the special type of speech act exemplified by

---

[12] *How To Do Things With Words*, 32.

the lines from Chaucer should be further subdivided: for example, into cases where the act done in uttering the words is dependent on convention (over and above the role convention plays in giving words their meaning), and those where it is not.[13] But what is not commonly appreciated is that even if we concentrate on the latter sort, instances of this type are various, distinct, and dependent on shifting arrangements of complex criteria for their identification. It is evidence from poetry that helps reveal this.

If we consider Chaucer's verses, three features stand out as characteristic of this type of speech act. First, what plays the decisive role is a verbal phrase in the first person singular present indicative active ('I directe...', 'I preye...', 'I speke and seye...'). Second, unless circumstances are special, the action associated with the utterance is peculiarly self-guaranteeing: what is done is done in the uttering of the sentence, hence what is done is guaranteed to have been done by the utterance itself. Third, the verb used is a word for what the speaker can be reported as having done in uttering the sentence. In consequence, the whole sentence to which the verbal phrase contributes is peculiarly self-referential: it is not just that the utterance does something in saying something; precisely what it does is named and made explicit in the very act of uttering it.

Instances of the Chaucer-Type—with its three features of verbal form, self-guarantee, and self-reference in place and explicit—are not uncommon in modern poetry. Yeats was fond of the form. 'I call on those that call me son ... To judge what I have done' ('Are You Content?').[14] 'I sing what was lost and dread what was won' ('What Was Lost').[15]

I say that Roger Casement
Did what he had to do.
He died upon the gallows,
But that is nothing new.[16]

Geoffrey Hill employs the Chaucer-Type frequently in his later poetry. *Oraclau: Oracles* is sewn together with instances: 'Let me propose'; 'Let us, I beg'; 'I elegize'; 'I write'; 'I allude'; 'I do | Acknowledge'; 'I recommend'; 'I admit'; 'I wish'; 'I argue'; 'I recuse' ('Your Calvinisms gnaw me').[17]

Kathleen Raine uses the form in her 'Short Poems 1994':

All I have known and been
I bequeath to whoever
Can decipher my poem.[18]

---

[13] See Geoffrey Warnock's distinction between 'Mark I performatives' and 'explicit performatives': 'Some Types of Performative Utterance', in Isaiah Berlin et al. (eds.), *Essays on J. L. Austin* (Oxford: Oxford University Press, 1973), 69–89. See also Max Black 'Austin on Performatives', in K. T. Fann (ed.), *Symposium on J. L. Austin* (London: Routledge and Kegan Paul Ltd, 1969), 401–11.

[14] W. B. Yeats, *Collected Poems* (2nd edn., London: Macmillan, 1950), 370.

[15] Yeats, *Collected Poems*, 359.

[16] Yeats, 'Roger Casement', *Collected Poems*, 351.

[17] Geoffrey Hill, *Oraclau: Oracles* (Thame: Clutag Press, 2010) 20 (7); 128 (43); 31 (11); 43 (15); 62 (21); 74 (25); 82 (28); 93 (31); 100 (34); 136 (46); 110 (37).

[18] *The Collected Poems of Kathleen Raine* (Ipswich: Golgonooza Press, 2000), 343.

Very often poets are producing instances of the Chaucer-Type when they use verbal forms like 'I plead', 'I dedicate', 'I thank', 'I welcome', 'I bid farewell', or their equivalents. This is not always unambiguous. Such forms may mean 'I [hereby] plead' (dedicate, thank, etc.), in which case they are of the Chaucer-Type. But the same forms may also be used in a purely descriptive way, as in 'I [tend to] plead', or 'I [habitually] thank'. J. H. Prynne's 'Thoughts on the Esterházy Court Uniform' contains lines that are ambiguous because they fit either option:

How can we sustain such constant loss.
I ask myself this, knowing that the world
is my pretext for this return through it,[19]

Is the speaker hereby asking himself this question, or is he describing himself as one who asks himself this question? There may be an urgency about these lines, which suggests the former; the lack of a question mark at the end of the first line may suggest the latter. The sense teeters uncomfortably between the options, making a considerable difference to how we read the poem.

Minimal departures from the basic type frequently occur, these instances being, nevertheless, sufficiently close to count as variants. For example, it is common enough to separate the elements by detaching content (e.g. what is said) from form (e.g. 'I say'), as in 'The Way My Mother Speaks' by Carol Ann Duffy:

I say her phrases to myself
in my head
or under the shallows of my breath,
restful shapes moving.
The day and ever. The day and ever.[20]

Wider variants occur. On occasion, for example, an element is omitted altogether. The first-person form disappears, for example, in certain sorts of praise in verse. Hopkins's 'Pied Beauty' opens with an example: 'Glory be to God for dappled things'.[21] If the sense of the first words is to be paraphrased as 'I give glory...' (rather than 'Let glory be given', another possibility), then the lines count as a close variant of the Chaucer-Type of doings-in-sayings. For the first person is then implicit, and what is done is both explicitly named (hence it is self-referential) and done in the uttering (hence it is self-guaranteeing). The same may be said of conventional expressions of salutation or leave-taking: as in Basil Bunting's 'Against the Tricks of Time':

Farewell, ye sequent graces,
Voided faces, still evasive![22]

---

[19] J. H. Prynne, *Poems* (2nd edn., Tarset: Bloodaxe Books, 2005), 99.
[20] Carol Ann Duffy, *The Other Country* (London: Anvil Press, 1990), 54.
[21] Gerard Manley Hopkins, *The Major Works,* ed. Catherine Phillips, revised (Oxford: Oxford University Press, 2002), 132.
[22] Basil Bunting, *Complete Poems* (Newcastle upon Tyne: Bloodaxe Books, 2000), 188.

On occasion, what is done is not named. This means that the whole cannot be considered explicitly self-referential. Austin Clarke's 'A Curse' offers a complex example:

Black luck upon you Seamus Mac-an-Bhaird
Who shut the door upon a poet
Nor put red wine and bread upon the board.[23]

To gain the sense of this, we have to supply that which makes it a variant of the Chaucer-Type. So the title-suggested paraphrase 'I curse you...' makes explicit the first-person actor and the name of the act being done, an act that is—at least ostensibly—done in the uttering. ('Ostensibly' is meant to reflect the complexity of the occasion. What is 'ostensibly' being done in what is being said may not be being done at all, either because the utterance is ironic, or because the uttering takes place in the peculiar context of staged fiction. We will review other examples of similar complexities in the next section.)

Sometimes, the verbal form is future rather than present, as in Christopher Smart's *Jubilate Agno*:

For I will consider my Cat Jeoffry.
For he is the servant of the Living God duly and daily serving him.
For at the first glance of the glory of God in the East he worships in his way.[24]

Since uttering 'I will consider...' in circumstances such as these just is to perform the act of considering, the utterance manages to be a doing-in-saying. The verbal form playing the decisive role is both first-personal and self-referential (the act done is named in the uttering itself), but it is not itself self-guaranteeing. To utter 'I will consider' may be—indeed usually is—merely to announce one's intention to do so. It is the context in which this form occurs that makes the utterance as a whole an act of considering.

Sometimes the verbal form is past rather than present, as in Geoffrey Hill's 'September Song':

(I have made
an elegy for myself it
is true)[25]

The sense of these lines, in context, suggests that the utterance is meant to be a doing-in-saying—as opposed to a mere description of what has been done. But there is evidently a tight restriction on the kinds of circumstance in which uttering 'I have made an elegy' could count as performing the act of making an elegy. Again, the verbal form is first-personal and self-referential without being guaranteeing. Again, it is context that turns the phrase to its performative use.

---

[23] Austin Clarke, *Collected Poems*, ed. R. Dardis Clarke (Manchester: Carcanet Press, 2008), 112.
[24] Fragment B, ll. 695–7, in Ricks (ed.), *The Oxford Book of English Verse*, 286.
[25] Geoffrey Hill, *King Log* (London: André Deutsch, 1968), 19.

These last examples do not sit quite happily, perhaps, as mere variants of the Chaucer-Type. But they are not sufficiently distant to count as exemplifying a new type altogether.

Greater departures are apparent in 'Mabel Kelly' by Austin Clarke:

He sees the tumble of brown hair
Unplait, the breasts, pointed and bare
    When nightdress shows
    From dimple to toe-nail,
All Mabel glowing in it, here, there, everywhere.[26]

The poem as a whole does what the decisive verbal form says it does: it 'shows' Mabel Kelly, makes her stand displayed. So we may regard the utterance as self-referential, but in an extended sense. It is the whole poem, rather than the sentence containing the verbal phrase itself, which does what that phrase says. There are other significant departures also: the verbal form is not first-personal, and it is not self-guaranteeing. To utter 'When nightdress shows...' is not necessarily, or thereby, to show anything.

Much the same may be said of Seamus Heaney's 'The Grauballe Man'.[27] It seems intended that the corporeal figure which 'lies [perfected in my memory]' should also, by the poem's deep description, lie before the reader's mind and memory.

There are occasions of the converse sort, where the first-person singular form is retained but differences in other features nevertheless distance the utterance considerably from the Chaucer-Type. It is then sometimes possible for utterances in poetry to do more than what they say. Tennyson's unfinished poem 'Reticence' is an example:

Latest of her worshippers,
I would shrine her in my verse!
Not like Silence shall she stand,
Finger-lipt, but with right hand
Moving toward her lips, and there
Hovering, thoughtful, poised in air.[28]

The poem may be said to treasure and venerate its subject in the restrained way that is proper to reticence; hence, in an established sense of this rare verb, the one responsible for the utterance does indeed 'shrine' reticence in verse.[29] But although the decisive phrase is first-person singular, it is subjunctive and conditional in form, expressing a desire or intention ('I *would* shrine her'). And although the utterance is self-referential, since what is done is named in the uttering itself, it is nevertheless not self-guaranteeing. For to say 'I shrine such-and-such'—still less to say 'I would shrine such-and-such'—is not necessarily, or thereby, to shrine it.

---

[26] Clarke, *Collected Poems*, 295.
[27] Ricks (ed.), *The Oxford Book of English Verse*, 661.
[28] *The Poems of Tennyson*, ed. Christopher Ricks (2nd edn., London: Longman, 1987), iii. 628–9.
[29] *Oxford English Dictionary*, 'to shrine': sense 3.

If reticence is indeed shrined here, that is an achievement of the whole verse, rather than of the particular sentence in which the decisive phrase occurs. Moreover, what is thus done, by the one uttering the lines, is what (so it is said) that same utterer merely desires or intends to do. So the whole utterance achieves a particular end in the act of expressing the desire or intention to achieve that end. Hence what is done goes beyond what is said. In short, by departing from features defining the Chaucer-Type of 'doing-in-saying', and thus complicating the relationship between what is said and what is done, some utterances in poetry can do more than what they say.

The Tennyson example clearly takes us a considerable distance from examples of the Chaucer-Type. But, like all the cases discussed in this section, it retains the aspect of self-reference: something is done in what is uttered, and what is done is explicit, named in what is uttered. Hence, if we retain the standard practice of speech act theorists who distinguish 'Explicit' from 'Implicit' Performatives by appeal to this aspect, we will feel compelled to collapse the Chaucer and Tennyson examples into a single type. What we have begun to appreciate, however, is that a considerable number of distinctions separate the types manifest in these examples, that each distinction marks a step taking one progressively away from one case and towards the other, and that this is not a purely formal, abstract point: for each one of these steps, we can find a substantial, concrete realization in poetry.

It is possible that what poetry has to teach us about the varied class otherwise known as 'Explicit Performatives' could have been gained from the study of non-poetic uses of language alone. But two final examples suggest that there are ways of performing actions in uttering sentences in poetry that are peculiar to poetry. If this is correct, it opens up new perspectives: there are types of speech act which a theory of such acts could only discover by the study of poetry.

Some speech acts are dependent on the syntax of enjambment, which is a phenomenon peculiar to poetry. (We cannot say it is *unique* to poetry because signwriters, for example, can achieve effects by the way they lay out prose. But it is to poetry we should look for the full complement of such effects.) In Douglas Dunn's poem 'Arrangements', for example, the line break acts like a corner to be turned, thus enabling the utterance to do precisely what it says: 'And here I am, closing the door behind me, | Turning the corner on a wet day in March'.[30] Enjambment makes the utterance performative: I am hereby | Turning the corner. The occasion clearly belongs to the basic Chaucer-Type, with its three essential features. The verbal form playing the decisive role is first-person singular present indicative active; given the enjambment, what is done is guaranteed to have been done by the utterance itself; and the verb used is a word for what the speaker can be reported as having done in uttering the sentence.

Some speech acts are dependent on metre, also a phenomenon peculiar to poetry. In Tennyson's poem 'Crossing the Bar', for example, there is another 'turn', but this time

---

[30] Douglas Dunn, *Elegies* (London: Faber & Faber, 1985), 17.

from the iambic to the trochaic. Again, the requisite word appears ('turns' this time), making the utterance name precisely what it does:

But such a tide as moving seems asleep,
    Too full for sound or foam,
When that which drew from out the boundless deep
    Turns again home.[31]

In fact, there are two turnings here. Tennyson's sentence describes one in performing another, and the turning performed is the turning dependent on metrical change.[32] Evidently this occasion does not belong to the basic Chaucer-Type: the decisive verbal phrase is not first-personal in form. But the occasion is closely related to this basic type, and in ways that we have seen variously exemplified: given the role metre plays, the utterance is both self-guaranteeing and self-referential.

So poetic utterances can indeed be speech acts, and explicitly so. Chaucer-Type cases are sufficient to show this, though they are just one amidst a range of types. Philosophy stands to benefit from the recognition that this is so. Theorists can use poetry to add to what is known about speech acts from the study of non-poetic uses of language alone. First, there are distinctions that the study of poetry enables the theorist to appreciate fully. Second, there are types of speech act, or at least ways of achieving such acts, which a theorist could only discover and identify by studying poetry.

III

The proposal is that those responsible for poetic utterances may indeed do things in saying what they thereby say. Difficulties and objections can be divided into three groups: those that relate primarily to the action (the putative doing); those that relate primarily to the deed (the thing putatively done); and those that relate primarily to the agent (the one responsible for the putative doing). We shall address each in turn.

First, then, it is natural to wonder whether what we have so far taken to be 'actions' should indeed count as such. We tend to think of actions as interventions in the world, events that make a difference, occasions in which some kind of change is caused or brought about. And we treat as paradigmatic of the term 'action' instances like opening windows, throwing balls, standing up, blowing one's nose. All these actions can be regarded as movements, and all are, or at least involve, movements of the body. But most of the cases of 'action' in poetry reviewed so far are not movements of any sort, let alone bodily movements: someone 'directs' a poem to another, or asks a question, or greets Matrimony, or bids farewell, or considers a cat, or describes a woman, or wonders. It is beside the point, of course, that speaking can be regarded as a bodily movement; we are

[31] *The Poems of Tennyson*, iii. 253.
[32] See my 'Speech Acts and Poetry', *Analysis* 70 (2010), 1–3.

not asking whether producing speech is an action, but whether certain things we do *in* speaking—directing, asking, greeting, for example—count as actions.

If these worries pose an objection, it is to the theory of speech acts as a whole, rather than to the claim that uttering in poetry can count as a form of action. For it is speech act theory which claims that the relevant verbs—together with a host of others (to warn, urge, advise, plead, veto, propose, promise, consent, affirm, deny, revise, etc)—do indeed name actions, even though they do not name movements, bodily or otherwise. Furthermore, we may wonder whether the objection itself is sound. For the theory of speech acts has grounds for regarding as forms of action what these verbs name. We are happy, after all, to affirm that warning and urging and advising, and so on, are all things that we 'do' as agents. Finally, we may question the assumption which lies behind the objection: that bodily movements are the paradigm of actions. We may do so while acknowledging that actions are interventions in the world which bring about change. This is because bodily movements are evidently not the only way of intervening in the world, and perhaps not even the only standard way. Taken together, these remarks suggest a natural way to handle the initial objection. We should distinguish, just as Austin does, between 'ordinary physical actions' and 'the special nature of acts of saying something'.[33] Poetic uttering can then be regarded as a species of the latter group.

But this does not make the issues concerning action disappear entirely. Some of the cases we have reviewed do in fact use verbs which would ordinarily imply some sort of movement, perhaps even bodily movement: to 'display' articles for dressing, for example, to 'turn' oneself home, to 'shrine' another person. And this might immediately suggest that we have straightforward evidence that poetic uttering can indeed be a form of action, even using the paradigm-based account of what an action is. In fact, however, these cases are more contentious still. For the fact that all these 'movements' take place in poetry ('I would shrine her in my verse') may seem to undermine their claim to being genuinely accounted *movements* at all. Of course, it may be said in reply that this response simply begs the question. But that does not resolve the larger issue: whether poetic uttering can be deemed a genuine action at all, even if of a form that sets it apart as belonging to a special group, 'acts of saying something'. It may be said, for example, that it is only in a limited, non-standard, attenuated, or simply metaphorical sense that poetic uttering can be accounted a form of action. This raises significant issues within the philosophy of action, and one that has yet to receive its share of attention.

Suppose that poetic utterings may indeed count as doings, and of the type we call 'action'. Then a second set of difficulties arises: what we are to make of the corresponding deeds, those things that are thereby done. The main issues here turn on how we should count such deeds, and how we should locate them in time and space. These questions turn out to be related at a deeper level.

The answers may seem straightforward in the Chaucer case. In producing the utterance—'O moral Gower, this book I directe | To the and to the, philosophical

---

[33] *How To Do Things With Words*, 112; cf. 111–15.

Strode'—Chaucer 'directs' his work to others. What is done thereby is done once and for all, on the particular occasion and in the particular place of his producing the utterance. But this is not always the case; indeed, it is perhaps the exception. In the lines quoted from Smart's *Jubilate Agno* ('For I will consider my Cat Jeoffry'), it is more plausible to think that the deed corresponding to the action named in the verse is done, not once in the spatio-temporal location of its initial production, but on as many occasions and in as many locations as there are repetitions of the utterance.

Sometimes the possibility of such repetition is made explicit. A familiar instance occurs at the conclusion of Yeats's 'Easter 1916':

I write it out in a verse—
MacDonagh and MacBride
And Connolly and Pearse
Now and in time to be,
Wherever green is worn,
Are changed, changed utterly:
A terrible beauty is born.[34]

The passage begins with a Chaucer-Type phrase ('I write it out in a verse'), denoting what is presumably a one-off event. But this leads straight into a declaration of—commitment to—the essentially repeatable character of the general type of which this particular action is an instance: stating that those named are changed utterly. Instances of this general type are performed in each repetition of the utterance, not just 'wherever green is worn'.

Other cases appear more difficult, hovering uneasily between the unrepeatable one-off instance and the innumerably repeatable occasion. Poets exploit this indeterminacy. For example, in *The Triumph of Love*, Geoffrey Hill writes: 'So—Croker, MacSikker, O'Shem—I ask you: | what are poems for?'[35] Something is done here: namely, a question is asked. But it is unclear whether this question was asked once and for all (as Chaucer 'directed' his poem), or whether it continues to be asked on as many occasions as the utterance is repeated (as in Yeats's 'Easter 1916'). The directness of the question and its naming of addressees speak for the former; but the weight of the question and its resonance within the poem speak for the latter. This is a difficulty for the interpretation of the poem, of course, and of a sort that poets may seek to build into reception of their poetry. It is not a problem for the overall claim that poetic utterances may count as actions.

The third set of difficulties relates primarily to agency. Actions are by agents. So if a poetic uttering is to count as an action in some context, we expect an answer to an identity question of the form 'who is the agent of that context?' But it is a truism that poetry

---

[34] Yeats, *Collected Poems*, 205.
[35] Geoffrey Hill, *The Triumph of Love* (New York: Houghton Mifflin, 1998), 82. This instance has its ancestor in Chaucer: 'That I axe, why that the fifthe man | Was noon housbonde to the Samaritan?' (*The Wife of Bath's Prologue*, ll. 21–2).

frequently, intentionally, by design, and with calculation, makes that question difficult, or even impossible, to answer. Poets are praised, after all, for the 'generosity of [their] ventriloquism'.[36] So it can be difficult to say whether the agent of the context is the poet, or a guise the poet has taken, or a fictional person who speaks for the poet, or a fictional person quite removed from the poet, or some thing that is not a 'person' at all, or some complex made up of all or none of these.

The difficulties run deeper still. Perhaps we should not simply assume, in the special conditions set by the context of poetry, that the identity question is a good question, one that could have an answer (i.e. whether or not any answer it could have is something we might discover or come to know). For if it is not exactly a truism, it is certainly a familiar thought, that we somehow miss the point of particular poems if we insist that there must be some fact of the matter, whether discoverable or not, about which particular individual is responsible for any poetic utterance.

These issues arise even, perhaps especially, when poetry contains uses of the first-person term. Most of the examples we have used, being examples of the 'Chaucer-Type', not only contain uses of that term but turn on them. It might seem that, here at least, the identity question creates no difficulties. For we might suppose that, in using 'I', the poem indicates that it is appropriate to raise the identity question. Moreover, we might think that the use of 'I' gives us directions on how to answer that question: if we identify the referent of the use of 'I', we will know who the agent of the content is. But this simply postpones resolution of the original problem. For it is at least equally difficult to say whether the referent of the use of 'I' is the poet, or the poet's guise, or a fictional person, or some complex made up of all or none of these. And it is at least equally legitimate to ask whether the corresponding identity-question is a good one. There may be good reason to reject the assumption that, in the special context of poetry, there must be some fact of the matter, discoverable or not, about who is referred to by the use of 'I'.

If poetry does indeed resist application of these identity questions, we are owed an explanation why. The most robust vindication would be this: that poetry resists application of the notion of agency altogether. But if this is correct, then evidently we could not regard poetic utterings as speech acts, or indeed any species of action. So this may be too robust a vindication. A plausible alternative is to claim, not that poetry resists application of these identity questions exactly, but that it simply resists attempts to answer them, making the issues arising—intentionally, by design, and with calculation—difficult or impossible to resolve. This weaker way of framing the point still leads to a distinctly sceptical conclusion. For if a poetic uttering resists attempts to identify its agent, and actions are by agents, then it is plausible to conclude that the uttering resists attempts to have itself identified as an action.

We can respond to objections of these sorts in various ways. Perhaps the context of poetry is special enough to justify making the connection between action and agency

---

[36] Lowell on Browning in his 'After Enjoying Six or Seven Essays on Me', *Collected Poems*, ed. Frank Bidart and David Gewanter (London: Faber & Faber, 2003), 989–92 (992).

looser than in the normal case. If this is correct, then it would be possible to regard poetic uttering as a form of actions without assuming that the identity questions have an answer, let alone one that we could provide. But this response is less robust than it might appear. Once action-in-poetry is made an exception to the general case, there is a risk of attenuating the sense in which poetry can be accounted 'action' at all.

Another way of responding is to claim that, in many cases at least, the identity question is applicable, and indeed readily answerable. Chaucer himself, for example, seems a good candidate for the agent and referent of 'I' in the verses quoted from his *Troilus*. Who else could it be who 'directs' his book to 'moral Gower' and 'philosophical Strode'? And where the identity question is not easily answered, the very difficulties we experience may indicate that it is nevertheless applicable.

The lines quoted from Geoffrey Hill's *The Triumph of Love*—'I ask you: | what are poems for?'—may provide an instance of this. The poem artfully exploits the play between a poet's voice and the voice of the person who is that poet. This can make it seem equally uncomfortable either to attribute the thoughts expressed directly to Hill himself or not to do so. But this difficulty seems integral to the way the poem works itself out. Far from making the identity questions inapplicable, Hill raises them to the status of a key puzzle, one we must grapple with if we are to grasp the poem at all. And if the identity questions are therefore at least applicable, then there is no reason to doubt the exercise of agency here. What is done in the uttering of this poem is genuinely done; questions are raised, for example. And this is so, not in spite of the fact that the identity of the agent remains unsettled, but precisely because the poem makes the question of identity a puzzle.

So the claim that poetic uttering can count as a form of action, a speech action, raises difficulties. Some of these difficulties are of a sort that any theory of speech acts faces quite generally (for example, what is an action if these utterings are to be accounted actions?). Some are of a sort that is particular to the case of poetry (for example, how many doings are there here, where and when do they take place, who exactly is responsible for them?). But none of these difficulties amount to objections to the overall claim. Rather, they set an agenda for the interpretation of specific poems, a list of questions that interpretations must resolve to count as satisfying. And this agenda proves an essential device. For where these difficulties arise, they direct the attention to the very issues the poem itself is trying to raise.

IV

If poetic uttering can indeed count as a form of speech act, we are free to transform philosophical debate so that it turns on action rather than truth. This gives prominence to two related notions: responsibility and commitment. Since this is the most significant consequence of transforming the debate, it is worth dwelling on two issues: why responsibility and commitment must play a leading role, and how they can do so in the context of poetry.

The reason why these notions must play a leading role depends on the nature of the transformed debate: the fact that what will matter fundamentally is not whether what is said is true, and if it is true whether it is aptly said, and if it is aptly said whether it was right to have said it, but rather whether what is said is done, and if it is indeed done, whether it is done well, and if it is indeed done well, whether it was good to have done it.

Consider the lines from Smart's *Jubilate Agno*. In the transformed debate, we are pressed to ask whether, in uttering them, the speaker does indeed manage to 'consider' his cat Jeoffry. This is the basic, and primarily pragmatic, question. Perhaps there was no real intention to do what the words claim to do. If so, the deed may nevertheless be done, by accident, perhaps, or by mistake. Or perhaps there was an attempt that fails to come off.

If the deed is done, and it was intended to be done, we are pressed to ask primarily aesthetic questions, concerning the manner in which the speaker carried out this action. Was this manner pleasing? Were the words apt, well ordered, suited to their task? Or is there something botched about the performance? Was it carried off, but in a way that is ugly, bumbling, lazy?

Finally, in the transformed debate, we are pressed to ask questions that are primarily moral. Was the action carried off in uttering these words right or good? Was it dutiful, or fitting, or virtuous to have performed this action? Or was this action wrong, or evil, or malicious? Was it tactless, or insensitive, or cruel to have performed it?

The criteria of evaluation will change accordingly. For if what is at issue is the truth in what is said, then those who produce poetic utterances will be judged primarily in relation to their epistemic standing. Did they have reason to say what they did? Did their statements rest on evidence, on argument, on reasoning? But if what is at issue is the action in what is said, those who produce poetic utterances will be judged primarily in relation to their responsibility. Who is it that actually performed this action and is thus answerable for it? What were their immediate and underlying intentions in doing so? Are they accountable for the ways in which the action was carried out, for its consequences?

These questions can be asked at each of the three levels previously identified. So we will ask of Chaucer, for example, whether it was indeed he who intentionally and voluntarily 'directed' his *Troilus* to Gower and Strode, or whether he was somehow constrained to do so. This is a primarily pragmatic question. We will also ask primarily aesthetic questions: for example, what he meant by choosing precisely these words rather than any others to perform this action. Finally, we will ask whether Chaucer is to be praised or blamed for making these persons the recipients of the book. This is a primarily moral question.

Each of these questions of responsibility rests in their turn on issues of commitment. Did the person who performed this action really mean to do what in fact they did? Did they realize what obligations would be laid on them by doing this? Did they accept, consent to, or undertake these obligations? For if the answer to any of these questions is 'No', then we may refuse to hold the person responsible for what was done, or at least qualify their responsibility, at each of the three levels: pragmatic, aesthetic, moral.

For example, when Hill writes 'I ask you: | what are poems for?', we will question whether the speaker is genuinely committed to what asking a question plausibly requires. Does he take up a position of inquiry; is he open to possible answers; does he make himself receptive and sensitive to evidence? If the speaker utters these words as a mere rhetorical device, he is not committed in these ways. And if he is not committed to asking a question, we may deny that he is responsible for asking one, on the grounds that no question can have been asked. So this is one clear indication of the pivotal role that commitment and responsibility play in a transformed, action-orientated debate. Where commitment and hence responsibility are absent, it is plausible to deny that the relevant action has even been performed.

This leads directly to the second issue: whether responsibility and commitment can indeed be present in poetic utterance, and, if so, how. That there should be doubt about this might seem strange. There may be particular instances where it is unclear who exactly is responsible for a poetic utterance, or whether there is a genuine attempt by the persons responsible to commit themselves. But some would deny that responsibility and commitment are ever possible in the particular context that is poetry.

For example, Austin declared that poetry is not 'serious' for precisely this reason. He took the view that, when produced in the poetic context, 'any and every utterance' is '*in a peculiar way* hollow or void'.[37] In his proprietary usage, an utterance is 'void' when the speaker fails outright to do what he tries to do in saying it (I say 'I veto this bill', for example, but lack the requisite authority). An utterance is 'hollow', in his sense, when the speaker succeeds in doing what he tries to do, but there is nevertheless something improper about the action: it is not fully consummated or implemented (I say 'I bet you £5 that such-and-such an event will occur', for example, but have no intention of paying the forfeit).[38] So if Austin is correct, when anyone produces an utterance in poetry which contains a 'commissive' verb, one that is apt to make a commitment, the act named is not brought off: what is said is not done. Moreover, the requisite intention is lacking: no real attempt is being made to bring off what is said. Poets are free to use commitment-apt verbs, but the utterances they thereby produce neither succeed in making commitments nor attempt to do so. Thus there is nothing for which those who produce poetry might be held responsible. In the poetic context, language is only ever 'on holiday'. And for this reason, poetry is not to be regarded as 'serious'.[39]

But this position is untenable. To undermine it, we need not argue that poetry is always, or indeed usually, responsible, committed, and thus 'serious'. We need only produce examples of commitment-apt utterances in poetry where there is a genuine attempt to make that commitment, and where that commitment is indeed made. The Chaucer example will suffice, perhaps. For it seems evident that he is responsible for his act, and committed to what it entails, in producing the poetic utterance which 'directs'

---

[37] *How To Do Things With Words*, 22.
[38] *How To Do Things With Words*, 12–45.
[39] See my 'How Not To Do Things With Words', *British Journal of Aesthetics*, 51 (2011), 31–49.

his poem to Gower and Strode. So it is possible to be both responsible and committed in poetry.

This holds true in a wider sense than that which Austin wanted to deny. For poets need not use commissive verbs to commit themselves responsibly. They do so whenever they are serious in their use of language. For to be serious is to acknowledge what is required if one is to be taken seriously: a commitment to be reasonably clear about what one means, to be willing to explain what one says, to account for what one claims. And it is not only possible but actual that poets commit themselves responsibly in these various ways (for example, in essays, reviews, manifestos, interviews).

This is just as well, since responsibility and commitment are essential to any vindication of poetry as 'serious'. Unless one is capable of doing what one says, one cannot be serious in saying what one does. And to be capable of doing what one says requires being able to commit oneself in saying it. So those responsible for poetic utterances must be able to count as such in a deeper sense than mere causal efficacy. It must be possible and actual for them to commit themselves in saying what they do. Hence it must be possible and actual for them to be, and to be held to be, responsible in what they say.

V

If poets are indeed capable of responsibility and commitment in making poetic utterances, we would expect indications of anxiety about their role in contemporary culture. This is just what we find in prose commentaries by contemporary poets.[40] It is also what we discover embedded in contemporary poetry. These latter instances are of more direct relevance to the issues at hand: enactments of anxiety at responsibility and commitment offer one final type of action that poems can perform. There is space enough to identify just two salient issues.

One concerns what it is possible for a poem to achieve. These lines from Kathleen Raine were quoted as an example of the Chaucer-Type:

All I have known and been
I bequeath to whoever
Can decipher my poem.[41]

But there are complications. For the act of bequeathing to be genuinely and successfully performed, it must be possible for someone to inherit 'all I have known and been'. And it must be possible for a poem—indeed *this* poem—to be the instrument of this bequeathing. If this is not possible, it must be because either of two things are the case. Either there is something hollow about the speaker's act, or her attempt to perform it

---

[40] e.g. Dennis O'Driscoll, *Stepping Stones: Interviews with Seamus Heaney* (London: Faber & Faber, 2008).

[41] 'Short Poems 1994', *The Collected Poems of Kathleen Raine*, 343.

fails altogether.[42] The first possibility implies that the speaker lacks commitment. The second possibility absolves the speaker from responsibility.

There is a way to resolve this tension. Perhaps the real significance of these lines lies not in a bequeathing by one person to another, but in what that bequeathing signifies: a particular revelation of the speaker about herself, that she is such that all she has really known and truly been can be—and is—bequeathed in and through this very poem. This would be consistent with the achievement of the act, and hence with the ascription of commitment and responsibility to the speaker.

This resolution, which preserves the capacity of a poem to achieve things, comes at a price. In order for the poem to succeed in committing the speaker, making her responsible for what she says, we have to reconfigure what the poem acts on: in this case, the speaker's own self. A price of this sort may seem too high, and we might distrust those who are willing to pay it. This would itself be a cause of anxiety about the poet's role. But there may be a deeper cause: not the price of success, but success itself.

This is the second salient issue: whether it is desirable for a poem to achieve. Roy Fisher raises it in 'It is Writing':

Because it could do it well
the poem wants to glorify suffering.
I mistrust it.

I mistrust the poem in its hour of success,
a thing capable of being
tempted by ethics into the wonderful.[43]

To express mistrust at achievement in poetry by means of poetry is itself an achievement of poetry. 'The wonderful' into which poetry is tempted includes the thought that ethics could 'tempt'. To point this out is ethical and hence to succumb to the temptation. In these various ways, the poem is encompassed, quite knowingly, by the very dangers it identifies. This gives it the authentic feel of anxiety, a condition which is essentially, and self-consciously, self-undermining.

But the poem leaves one crucial aspect unexplored. It bothers Fisher that 'what the poem wants' is to do what poetry can do well. This seems to be his diagnosis for a familiar complaint: that poetry glorifies suffering, turns it into 'the wonderful' ('it could do it well'). But what is it about the 'hour of success' that makes poetry 'capable of being tempted by ethics'?

Perhaps we have the resources for an answer, at least in part. In successful poetic utterances, poets perform acts of responsibility and commitment. This places their actions deep in ethics, the realm of what is owed and what ought to be done. And perhaps it is by this that poets are 'tempted'. For it is an easy step—but a step nonetheless—from

---

[42] What Austin calls failures of 'abuse' and 'misfire' respectively in *How To Do Things With Words*, Lecture II.

[43] Roy Fisher, *The Long and the Short of It: Poems 1955–2005* (Tarset: Bloodaxe Books, 2005), 221.

recognizing that what one does is constrained by ethical considerations, to supposing that what one does must direct itself towards achieving ethical ends. It is a plausible diagnosis: that the reason why a poem might end up glorifying suffering is that it aims at ethical ends rather than suffering, looking beyond one to achieve the other. Reason indeed to be anxious about what it is possible for a poem to achieve.

So, in summary, there are good grounds to extend Austin's analysis of speech acts in ordinary language to the case of poetry. Chaucer-Type cases are just one of many ways to show that those responsible for poetic utterances may indeed do things in saying things. Philosophical debate about poetry might helpfully be made to turn on action and what is done with words, rather than on truth and what congruity there is between what is said and what is the case.

Evidence can be ordered to this effect. Examples of poetic utterances reveal underlying distinctions in the way poetry does things with words. The addition of new categories of actions, some peculiar to poetry, reveal ways in which philosophy can increase knowledge of language use by attending to poetry.

Objections can be dealt with. For it seems that, when we analyse the problems into those primarily concerning the action, the agent, and the thing done, the analysis of speech acts in ordinary language can indeed be extended to the use of language in poetry.

These implications can be welcomed. For responsibility and commitment come to the fore when philosophical debate about poetry turns on action rather than truth. Poets are capable of both in making poetic utterances. So we can vindicate poetry as a 'serious' use of language while aligning suitably sensitive criticism with the concerns of philosophy.

These implications can also be feared. Responsibility and commitment place familiar burdens and constraints on those enjoined. This gives reason for what we find evidence of: anxiety about the poet's role in contemporary culture.

But the upshot is positive. Austin thought that philosophical debate about language would bring about a 'revolution in philosophy', 'the greatest and most salutary in its history' if it were made to turn on action rather than truth.[44] It may yet be possible to achieve results that match his hopes, at least in modest form, in the study of poetry.[45]

Select Bibliography

Austin, J. L., *How To Do Things With Words* (2nd edn.), ed. J. O. Urmson and M. Sbisà (Oxford: Oxford University Press, 1975).
Black, Max, 'Austin on Performatives', in K. T. Fann (ed.), *Symposium on J. L. Austin* (London: Routledge and Kegan Paul Ltd, 1969), 401–11.
Basil Bunting, *Complete Poems* (Newcastle upon Tyne: Bloodaxe Books, 2000).
Clarke, Austin, *Collected Poems*, ed. R. Dardis Clarke (Manchester: Carcanet Press, 2008).

---

[44] *How To Do Things With Words*, 3.
[45] For critical comments on earlier versions, I am most grateful to Peter Robinson.

Duffy, Carol Ann, *The Other Country* (London: Anvil Press, 1990).
Dunn, Douglas, *Elegies* (London: Faber & Faber, 1985).
Fisher, Roy, *The Long and the Short of It: Poems 1955–2005* (Tarset: Bloodaxe Books, 2005).
Frege, Gottlob, 'Der Gedanke' (1918), in *Logische Untersuchungen,* ed. G. Patzig (Göttingen: Vandenhoeck & Ruprecht, 1993), 30–53.
Gaynesford, Maximilian de, *I: The Meaning of the First Person* Term (Oxford: Oxford University Press, 2006).
Hill, Geoffrey, *King Log* (London: André Deutsch, 1968).
Hill, Geoffrey, *The Triumph of Love* (New York: Houghton Mifflin, 1998).
Hopkins, Gerard Manley, *The Major Works,* ed. Catherine Phillips, revised (Oxford: Oxford University Press, 2002).
O'Driscoll, Dennis, *Stepping Stones: Interviews with Seamus Heaney* (London: Faber & Faber, 2008).
Prynne, J. H., *Poems* (2nd edn., Tarset: Bloodaxe Books, 2005).
Ricks, Christopher, *Essays in Appreciation* (Oxford: Oxford University Press, 1996).
Ricks, Christopher (ed.), *The Oxford Book of English Verse* (Oxford: Oxford University Press, 1999).
Searle, John, *Speech Acts* (Cambridge: Cambridge University Press, 1969), esp. 57 n. 1.
Strawson, P. F., 'Intention and Convention in Speech Acts', in *Logico-Linguistic Papers* (London: Methuen, 1971), 149–69.

CHAPTER 33

'IS A CHAT WITH ME YOUR FANCY?': ADDRESS IN CONTEMPORARY BRITISH POETRY

NATALIE POLLARD

In speaking to immediately present companions and estranged auditors, long dead historical figures and wayward critics and readers, contemporary poets repeatedly employ the plain-speaking accents of address. Everyday speech-styles intertwine with formally and syntactically playful registers. In the work of the Scottish poet W. S. Graham, for instance:

Is a chat with me your fancy? Now in the dark
Give me the password. Wince me your grip for O
The times are calling us in and the little babes
Are shouldering arms in the cause of the Future Past.
[...]
Finish here of Yours Truly. Please please CUT.

    The titles are finished
    It was a way
    Of speaking towards you.

Maybe we could have a word before I go,
As I usually say. I mean there must be some
Way to speak together straighter than this,
As I usually say.[1]

Graham's address buttonholes *you* directly, even as it emphasizes the mediations of the printed page. At first glance, *I* is Graham himself, addressing his friend, the St Ives

---

[1] W. S. Graham, 'Wynter and the Grammarsow', *New Collected Poems*, ed. Matthew Francis (London: Faber & Faber, 2004), 187. Subsequently referred to as *NCP*.

School painter Bryan Wynter. The conversation seems to take place in private, hence the need for a lyric 'password', and the speaker's plea not to be kept 'in the dark'. Yet Graham's address is worldly too. Talk of 'titles', 'the times', and the need to find the right 'way | Of speaking' to auditors, makes clear the speaker's alertness to readers as a plural 'you' listening at the margins. The lines deploy a range of typographical styles, spliced editorial commentary, provisional annotations and instructions, as if Graham let us glimpse, offstage, the hand of a tinkering editor-figure, or an authorial double rearranging the lyric material.

Speaking to *you* is often intimate and conspiratorial. Frequently, it marks out particular, personally known recipients (in Graham's case, Wynter), as if address were exclusive contact. Yet to say *you* on the printed page is also to engage with a larger public body of unspecified reading and editorial listeners. As Graham's lyric knows, the play between these different audiences gestures towards verbal slippage and disorder: 'CUT', 'Wince me your grip', 'Please please', 'Finish here'. Graham's archly familiar tone ('Is a chat with me your fancy?', 'we could have a word') is interlaced with talk of codes, aporia, uncertainty, and grammatical skirmishes. Even as this address holds itself before us as an unpremeditated attempt to 'have a word before I go', Graham is also testing out words' capacity to negotiate listeners, and wielding lyric power over his readership. These are lines that showcase address's public intimacies.

Graham's lines offer an excellent example of how contemporary poetry alerts 'you' to the perplexities that structure an everyday 'chat with me'. The poet's wish 'to speak towards you' is troubled by the difficulty of finding 'some | Way to speak together straighter than this, | As I usually say'. Haunting Graham's quotidian labours with the bent nature of straight talking is Beckett's line from *Endgame*: 'No one that ever lived ever thought so crooked as we'.[2] The directness of the late twentieth-century address moves with the modernist awareness that part of what drives literature's moving utterance is recognition of its everyday ineptness ('as I usually say'). Touchingly 'crooked' attempts to talk straighter, fail better, or address *you* with unmediated lyric speech are part of our means of 'speaking together', of making contact in spite (or because) of what Graham once called 'the obstacle of language' which waylays *I*s and *you*s.[3]

'Really, it is not I who am writing this crazy book,' James Joyce said of *Finnegans Wake*, 'it is you, and you, and you, and that man over there, and that girl at the next table.'[4] Joyce's playful emphasis of *your* part in the writing act is itself an address to a private *you* (his friend Eugène Jolas) that finds its tongue rooted in everyday social acts and impulses: 'this', 'that man', 'that girl'. Both in and out of the literary text, address taps the quotidian immediacy of deixis: it makes deft ontological observations about the

---

[2] Samuel Beckett, *Endgame (1958)*, in *The Complete Dramatic Works* (London: Faber & Faber, 1986), 97.

[3] Graham, 'Malcolm Mooney's Land' (1970), 'Have I not been using the obstacle of language well?', *NCP*, 153.

[4] See 'Eugène Jolas, Memoir of Joyce, 1927', in Robert H. Deming (ed.), *James Joyce: The Critical Heritage*, i. 1907–1927 (London: Routledge & Kegan Paul, 1970), 384.

instabilities of identity and the limitations and breakthroughs of language. In contemporary poems, as well as in Joyce, to say *you* is to surround oneself with recognizable objects, events, and persons: 'that man over there', 'that girl at the next table'.[5] At the same time, address makes clear to listeners that *you* is not merely material to be used in the text, or a passive recipient waiting to be spoken to, but is actively *writing the author in*. For Joyce 'it is not I who am writing [...] but you'. For Graham: 'I think I am beginning to have nearly | A way of writing down what it is I think | You say'.[6] These acts of address *shape* poetic speakers and readers. They structure how we speak on the published page and 'over there' at the next table. To address an interlocutor is not to engage in an opaque or exclusive act. This is what the ordinariness of saying *you*—to each reader, to an assembled audience body, to fellow writers, to the nation, to one's personal friends (say, Bryan Wynter or Eugène Jolas)—demands we recognize.

Admittedly, speaking to others in poems remains a slippery business. *I* and *you* are not fixed characters but pronominal positions, across which a peculiarly changeable succession of speaking and listening voices is played: 'you is transferrable [...] | To you and you and you' the English poet C. H. Sisson writes, at once disconcerted by *your* precariously alterable presence, and brilliantly making music out of that flux with and for *you*:

O, 'I' and 'you' are two conceptions
Neither of which is justified;
Neither 'you' by 'I', nor it cannot be,
'I' by 'you' exactly.[7]

When Alice Notley observes that ' "I am life a | thousands a walking millions nuances walking as | one" ',[8] or Wallace Stevens wonders 'How is it I find you in difference, see you there | In a moving contour, a change not quite completed? || You are familiar yet an aberration', they too speak clearly of the paradoxes of address, of its ability to communicate incommunicably alterable identities to listeners. Each of these poets addresses *you* directly ('You are familiar', 'To you'), and also points out that *you* are so 'nuanced' as to remain elusive. The interlocutor is both on the page, and 'not quite' there: 'an aberration', 'conception', 'a moving contour [...] not quite completed'.[9]

---

[5] See J. H. Prynne, 'double glazing | and gracious sashcords', 'No Song No Supper' (1987), *Poems* (Tarset: Bloodaxe Books, 2005), 343; Don Paterson, 'bell-wire and 40W bulbs', 'The Alexandrian Library', *Nil Nil* (London: Faber & Faber, 1993), 33; Kathleen Jamie, 'well-meaning bees | [...] remind me again, | of my father... whom, Christ, | I've forgotten to call', 'The Buddleia', *The Tree House* (London: Picador, 2004), 27

[6] Graham, 'A Note to the Difficult One' (1975), *NCP*, 206.

[7] C. H. Sisson, 'The Garden of the Hesperides' (1980), *Collected Poems* (Manchester: Carcanet Press, 1998), 255–7.

[8] Alice Notley (1981), in Mary Margaret Sloan (ed.), *Moving Borders: Three Decades of Innovative Writing by Women* (Jersey City, NJ: Talisman House, 1998), 193–4.

[9] Wallace Stevens, 'Notes Toward A Supreme Fiction', *Collected Poems* (London: Faber & Faber, 1984), 406.

This sense of lyric address as rooted public speech *and* an intangible multiplicity of voices is found across the diverse range of Anglo-American and Continental European poets writing today—from Paul Muldoon to Carol Ann Duffy; John Ashbery to Czeslaw Milosz; Linton Kwesi Johnson to Susan Howe. I want to focus here, for the sake of concision, on address in contemporary English and Scottish poetry, and I'll draw on the work of W. S. Graham, Geoffrey Hill, Don Paterson, Douglas Dunn, Tony Harrison, Anne Stevenson, and J. H. Prynne in particular. Other poets could have served as well, but this range of quite different writers shows how, as Anne Stevenson put it, contemporary British poetry offers both 'a wordlife running from mind to mind', and a recognition that '[t]he way you say the world is what you get'.[10] Underlining how intimate and civic responsibilities are carried in the lyric tongue, and how identities and allegiances are forged in speaking to and for others, the poetry of Scottish *makar* and Cambridge don, Faber author and edgy outsider exemplify how lyric address is part of the carrying stream of tradition. In speaking to *you* the poet discovers that 'our word is our bond', an addressed, historically weighted bond.[11]

That remark comes from Geoffrey Hill's essay of the same title, which insists that the lyric tongue is bound to the iterations of earlier writers. More specifically, Hill's title is indebted to the ordinary language philosopher J. L. Austin, whose mid-century lectures, *How To Do Things With Words*, identified in language certain *illocutionary* acts: performative utterances in which speaking *is* a form of action, and make clear that we can be held to—and ensnared by—what we say.[12] Hill's fresh insistence that 'our word is our bond' reinscribes as well as revisits Austin's earlier argument, exemplifying the performed historical weight of the contemporary poet's verbal world, and unearthing the historico-archaeological inflections of Austin's argumentation: 'If we stir the soil about the roots of [...] these locutions we unearth seventeenth-century shards.'[13] (Austin was, of course, also bound to Hippolytus, who coined the phrase: 'our word is our bond'.) When Hill asks, in *The Triumph of Love*, 'What remains? You may well ask. Construction | or deconstruction? There is some poor | mimicry of choice, whether you build or destroy | But the Psalms—they remain; and certain exultant', he carries this sense of logopoeic bond into lyric form.[14] So too, the Cambridge poet J. H. Prynne, identifies a comparable sense of poetic bond with *you* when he combines intimate and historical addresses: 'We are a land | hammered by restraint, into | a too Cycladic past. It is | the battle of Maldon binds | our feet: we tread | only with that weight & the empire | of love', 'you | must know, I will tell | you, this, love, is | the world'.[15] Such work re-sounds

---

[10] Anne Stevenson, 'Making Poetry', *Collected Poems* (Tarset: Bloodaxe Books, 2004), 17; Stevenson, 'Saying the World', *Collected Poems*, 18.

[11] Geoffrey Hill, 'Our Word is Our Bond' (1983), in *Collected Critical Writings*, ed. Kenneth Haynes (Oxford: Oxford University Press, 2009), 146–69 (168). Subsequently referred to as *CCW*.

[12] See Hill's example from Austin: 'If you are a judge and say "I hold that..." then to say you hold is to hold', *CCW*, 147. Austin, *How To Do Things With Words*, ed. J. O. Urmson and Marina Sbisà (Cambridge, Mass.: Harvard University Press, 1975), 8.

[13] Hill, *CCW*, 147.

[14] Hill, *The Triumph of Love* (1998; New York: First Mariner, 2000), 23:12.

[15] Jamie, 'The Queen of Sheba', *Waterlight*, 85; Prynne, 'Song in Sight of the World', *Poems*, 76–7.

past acts of verbal mastery with present *you*s, interweaving contemporary idioms with a culture's changeable literary-historical voicings. *You* is a nexus of contemporary and historical, private and public, lyric and economic articulations. There is a public *you* behind or beyond the intimate addressee.

This distinctive form of publicly poly-vocal lyric address arises differently again in the work of the Dundonian poet, academic, and publisher Don Paterson. In a poem from his early volume, *God's Gift to Women*, Paterson's ear is closely attuned to historical and philological bonds, even as he delivers seemingly private addresses to a longed-for *you*:

CANDLEBIRD

after Abbas al-Ahnaf, c.750

If, tonight she scorns me for my song,
You may be sure of this: within the year
Another man will say this verse to her
And she will yield to him for its sad sweetness.

' "Then I am like the candlebird," ' he'll continue,
After explaining what a candlebird is,
' "Whose lifeless eyes see nothing and see all,
Lighting their small room with my burning tongue;

His shadow rears above hers on the wall
As hour by hour, I pass into the air."
Take my hand. Now tell me: flesh or tallow?
Which I am tonight, I leave to you.'

So take my hand and tell me, flesh or tallow.
Which man I am tonight I leave to you.[16]

Speaking plainly in the here-and-now, Paterson secures *your* attention through a startlingly direct address: 'So take my hand', 'tell me', 'you may be sure of this'. *I* speaks with intimacy and immediacy, even as it situates its auditors publicly, economically and historically. 'Candlebird' is written 'after Abbas Ibn Al-Ahnaf', the medieval Arabic poet whose *ghazals* won him his place as favourite at the court of Harun Al-Rashid.[17] Like the source text, which sings of the tortuous demands of patronage and love in the Abbasid lyric tradition, Paterson creates a disturbing negotiation of courtly customs, panegyric, love poetry, contemporary audience-manipulation, and economic patronage. The apparently personal voice of the lyric present is shaped by the violent interlocutive contexts of the past. 'Candlebird' directs us to the resonance of praise and barter. It summons the patron–client system of medieval Arabic cultural life, where poems were commissioned, composed, and performed as part of a system of social exchanges predicated on duty, gift-giving, mutual obligation with wealthy, powerful *you*s. This

---

[16] Paterson, 'Candlebird', *God's Gift to Women* (London: Faber & Faber, 1997), 55.
[17] Abbas Ibn Al-Ahnaf, *Birds Through an Alabaster Ceiling: Three Abyssinian Poets*, trans. G. B. H. Wightman (Harmondsworth: Penguin Books, 1975).

contemporary address sounds in the ears and on the tongues of trans-historical *I*s and *you*s, opening a complex echo-chamber of past and present audience demands, medieval and modern speakers, listeners and patrons.

Paterson's address reminds us of the insistently public demands of poetry through the ages, which is inscribed (however intimately) by the desires of audiences, publishers, and readerships. Arresting temporal progression through the immediacy of the second person, his interlocutions underline the fathomless depths and abysses of everyday contact with loved and commissioning *you*s. Lyric address might be intimate hand-to-hand, eye-to-eye touch, but that tactility is coupled with public requirement: the artwork achieves worldly success by being passed between multiple receiving hands, ears, and speaking tongues. The poet's private speech—now and in the lyric past—is packaged, disseminated, circulated, discussed, and valued and revalued by a plurality of demanding recipients (and lovers).

By opening us to lyricism's cross-currents of voices, address demands acknowledgement of poetry's rich participation in the carrying stream of tradition, and of the politics that govern that flow and flux. To voice, and hear another say, *you* is to be tuned in to the diverse cultural registers that comprise the present, and the medley of speaking and listening voices that structure lyric interlocutions. Paterson arrests readers with that inheritance. Many of the poems in the early volumes, and in *Landing Light*, show how texts across the ages insist that *you* 'listen': they accost readers, purchasers and audiences. Buttonholing his inattentive, penny-pinching ancient Greek audience in the guise of Simonides, Paterson's speaker in 'The Reading' wields the second person as promise and threat: 'your coupons, my rapt listeners | I'll have nailed by the end of this poem'.[18] *I* then brings the roof down on his *you*. Comparably belligerent, 'A Talking Book' rounds on its audience, accusing *you* of 'not taking this seriously enough'.[19] Again, the speaker is not without cause: these are listeners that must be reminded to 'shake yourself awake' and 'stay patient'. In Paterson, the need to secure *your* attention is closely allied with coercive lexicons—on both sides of the printed page: 'the poet hears his voice | suddenly forced, like a bar-room singer's', 'You don't know it quite yet, but this whistling noise | is your call-up'.[20] They flag up how address is often bound to the pressing financial and institutional pressures placed on poets today. One implication is that the demands of audiences and institutions in the contemporary poetry industry might be seen as analogous to those made in much earlier literary periods—in early modern, ancient Greek, or medieval Arabic patronage systems. Paterson's movingly direct lyric addresses refuse to shy from documenting the demands of the poetry industry and of viewers/listeners: he addresses them. And in his response to these *you*s, his work repeatedly takes up the combative public accents of the lyric page and stage.

---

[18] Paterson, 'The Reading', *Landing Light* (London: Faber & Faber, 2003), 25–7. Subsequently referred to as *Light*.

[19] Paterson, 'A Talking Book', *Light*, 28–33.

[20] Paterson, 'Poetry', *The Eyes* (London: Faber & Faber, 1999), 28; Paterson, 'The Alexandrian Library', *Light*, 49.

This combination of tonal directness, forcefulness, and historical attunement manifests across a diverse range of poetry written today—lyrics with quite divergent aesthetic, political, social, and formal agendas. In Tony Harrison, for instance, address goes hand in hand with the urge to rebuke the literary establishment in 'my own name and voice', encouraging fellow listeners to tell bourgeois *you*s 'where to go'.[21] Harrison's poem 'Them & [uz]' angles its interlocutions, with pointed truculence, towards a particular group of antagonists:

So right, yer buggers then! We'll occupy
your lousy leasehold Poetry.

I chewed up Littererchewer and spat the bones
into the lap of dozing Daniel Jones,
dropped the initials I'd been harried as
and used my *name* and own voice: [uz] [uz] [uz],
ended sentences with by, with, from,
and spoke the language that I spoke at home.
RIP RP, RIP T. W.
I'm *Tony* Harrison no longer you!

You can tell the Receivers where to go
(and not aspirate it) once when you know
Wordsworth's *matter/water* are full rhymes,

'[Y]er buggers', 'I'm [...] no longer you', 'RIP T. W.', 'you can tell the Receivers [...] when you know'. The *you*s of Harrison's poem make contact both with their declared addressees—the cultural custodians that prompted the young Loiner poet into abandoning 'the language that I spoke at home'—and all those who read, and may be incited by, his lines. 'Them & [uz]' uses address to speak to the young Harrison encouragingly—'You *can* tell'—rousing him (and others in his position) to speak out, as the older poet is unafraid to: 'I'm *Tony* Harrison no longer you!' At the same time, the lines wield address upon the youthful poet-figure, occupying the mocking voice of the 'Receivers': ' "Poetry's the speech of kings. You're one of those | Shakespeare gives the comic bits to" ', '*E-nun-ci-ate!*' This address is multiple and determinedly slippery. It enacts no-nonsense voicing, and fluctuates between readerly and critical audiences, past and present, persuasion and critique, invitation and argumentation. We find many possible *you*s. The slippery facets of address (changing speakers, a shifting between *I* and *you*—'I'm [...] no longer you'—and its faltering between talking about and talking to) are bound to, and dependent on, the particulars of the public listening and speaking world of 1970s British class-conscious culture.

Such lyricism is alert to how literary and everyday language is shaped by *your* collective soundings and re-soundings. It calls to another using 'my own voice', even as it implements that voice as dialect and dialectic, as heckling communal speech. (It's a technique that is not dissimilar to Tom Leonard's address to bourgeois audiences from 'wanna yoo scruff', in 'The Six O Clock News' ('yi canny talk | right', 'belt up'), as well as the defiant railing of an

---

[21] Tony Harrison, 'Them & [uz]', *Selected Poems* (New York: Random House, 1987), 122–3.

authoritarian 'y'u' in Linton Kwesi Johnson's 'Forces of Victory', though clearly its politics are very different).[22] These are poems that use the immediacy of saying *you* to demand that readers attend to Receivership and reception, class, gender, economics, politics, community and inheritance, privilege, power, and nationhood.

In each of these writers, poetic address is part of general public intelligibility, a huge common vocabulary; akin to what Stanley Cavell once called 'agreement in valuing'.[23] The dominant lexicons and demands of the publishing and editing world co-opt the published literary object, as do the 'caught habits of language' that Graham thought inflected quotidian speech. Yet poets riff off these demands and inflections, demanding closer engagement with disturbing moments of ellipsis, fragmentation, rupture, and verbal breakdown.[24] Saying *you* enables a lexical sportiveness that is sharp and playful, engaging and precariously shape-shifting. Poetry's alterable interlocutors and auditors, readers and writers, contexts and histories take shape in familiar language, in seemingly unremarkable conversational modes. Such address demands *your* scrutiny of the politics of everyday speech, and of the ways class, identity, nationhood and belonging emerge in 'ordinary' *I–you* relations.

Address has become key to a number of contemporary poets who wish readers to attend to the long-standing power structures and aesthetic impulses that articulate contemporary depictions of identity, entitlement, and inheritance. Harrison is among them. So is the Scottish working-class poet Douglas Dunn, albeit with quite different historical and political inflections. Dunn has repeatedly employed barbed address forms to demand *you* attend to the politics of ordinary speech. His poems place speakers within the muddle of conflicted verbal registers they depict: a savage cacophony from which the regional, national, and personal identities of *I* and *you* struggle into shape. In Dunn's mock-dated, mock-located poem, 'Gardeners (England, Loamshire, 1789)', address is collectively voiced by those labourers who tend the gardens of the country house: speaking in unison, they brutally wield the second-person pronoun upon the lord who owns the land.[25] The poem is part of Dunn's 1979 volume *Barbarians*, a series of country-house poems drawing on the pastoral forms of Jonson and Marvell, and its addresses weave together historico-political and economic enterprise and the language of immediate, personal requirement:

> We know
> Our coarser artistries will make things grow.
> Others design the craftsmanship we fashion

---

[22] Tom Leonard, 'The Six O Clock News', in *Intimate Voices: Selected Work, 1965–1983* (London: Vintage, 1984), 88; Linton Kwesi Johnson, *Forces of Victory* (Island Records, 1979): the poem uses address to assert the right of the black community to occupy public space as part of the Race Today Collective, and responds to the belligerent policing (listen especially to Track 3, 'Sonny's Lettah'). See also Carol Ann Duffy's *Standing Female Nude* (London: Anvil Press, 1985). Each might be seen as implementing what Ian Gregson calls 'the desire to give voice to those who are habitually spoken *for*'. See *Poetry and Postmodernism: Dialogue and Estrangement* (Basingstoke: Macmillan, 1996), 99.

[23] Stanley Cavell, *The Claim of Reason* (Oxford: Oxford University Press, 1979), 94.

[24] Graham, *NCP*, 162.

[25] Douglas Dunn, *Barbarians* (1979), in *Selected Poems 1964–1983* (London: Faber & Faber, 1986), 105–6. Subsequently referred to as *DSP*.

To please your topographical possession.
A small humiliation—Yes, we eat,
Our crops and passions tucked out of view
Across a shire, the name of which is you,
[...]

Townsmen will wonder, when your house was burned,
We did not burn your gardens and undo
What likes of us did for the likes of you;
We did not raze this garden that we made,
Although we hanged you somewhere in its shade.[26]

Dunn's address combines the tone of conversational address to a familiar, intimately-beheld *you* ('To please your [...] passion', 'Yes, we eat'), and the dangerously repressed grudging of long-buried class resentment: 'What likes of us did for the likes of you', 'a shire, the name of which is you'. The threat of violent response ghosts the rhetoric of 'our' tidy efficiencies of 'craftsmanship', 'fashion', and 'design', and of workers' swallowed rage at their enforced enslavement to *your* polite dictates: 'tucked out of view', 'to please your [...] possession | A small humiliation'.

In Dunn, the suppressed violence of address is run alongside the literary-historical power of saying *you*. His ear is attuned especially to the early modern period, where addresses to patrons were key in fashioning (and preserving) political realities, reputations, places, and eras. For Dunn, saying *you* continues to be bound to representations of England's national, economic, and political realities; to what he calls in 'In the Grounds', 'England's art of house and leaf'.[27] In Dunn, as in Jonson and Marvell, Milton and Herrick, the lyricist can foreground the violent impulses written into artistic depictions of nation, landscape, and power—in 'shire', 'garden', and nation—and cunningly bring these into public recognition through the poet's commissioned tongue: 'Our coarser artistries will make things grow'. Like the gardener's hand, the poet's tongue is made to speak from the position of an addressed 'coarseness' that possesses threateningly fecund power. *I* and *you* can create or 'raze this garden'. Compliment and criticism are intertwined and sharply focused through this rallying cry of address. Using the second person to accost accountable addressees, Dunn's interlocutions demand readers attend to the power structures and aesthetic impulses that structure contemporary depictions of language, regional identity, entitlement, and inheritance; English and Scottish, master and serf, patron and poet. In Dunn as in Harrison, historically weighted, no-nonsense address draws *your* attention to poetry's opening onto, and active involvement in, constructing, economic, and social spheres.

Contemporary lyric address insists we recall art's long-standing role and function in shaping our cultural climate, and consider poetry's deployment of the economic,

[26] Dunn, 'Gardeners', *DSP*, 105-6.
[27] Dunn, *DSP*, 101.

institutional, philosophical, conversational, historical, political lexicons that structure speech.[28] Today, speaking to *you* is often held to be asocial; an interiorized or private lyricism conducted directly to a loved one or close friend, rather than to political or historical figures, dominant social groups, or publishing, editorial, or commissioning bodies.[29] But as we've seen, to address *you* is not to create a privileged space free from the competing discourses and concerns that inflect our language: it's to probe the politics of deploying lyricism's apparently unmediated voice. In so doing, poets repeatedly interlace communicable lyric speech to *you* with the out-of-reach, the unsayable, and the formally dislocated. Saying *you* fuses the touchingly intimate language of speaker to listener—often associated with the 'spontaneous' lyricism of Romantic discourse and the apostrophic tradition of personal, apolitical voicing—with the entrenchedly public circumstances of utterance. It attends to the *you* that speaks to England or Scotland, forging a nation, the *you* that sings to patrons in medieval or early modern culture, hungry for status or power, the *you* that addresses editors, publishers, book-buying readerships, and assembled audiences at poetry readings, and the *you* that is solicited from billboards, in magazines, and from television sets. Contemporary British address, like that of classical, metaphysical, and Romantic poetry, flags up the politics (and economics) of speaking privately in public places—whether on the published pages of one's *Collected Works*, in the *Guardian*, at the *London Review of Books*, or as Poet Laureate. These are literary innovations that rely on re-sounding the voices of past masters, and on reworking present styles of speaking to *you*—with all the attendant gaps, dislocations, frustrations, pastiches of traditions, and cacophonous interlocutions. Such work draws attention to the constructed and continually regenerated linguistic relationships between the identities of readers and writers, authors and audiences, gentle and ungentle purchasers.

What poets as different as Paterson and Graham, Dunn and Hill, Stevenson and Prynne have in common is their polyphony of address. It's a trait reminiscent of modernist poets, who, before them, used aporia, fragmentation, and cacophony to trouble

---

[28] In so doing, these poets remind us that the notion of address as cut off from the public sphere is a relatively recent phenomenon. In the early modern period, for instance, lyrics were commonly addressed to wealthy patrons/monarchs, and performed a pivotal civic function: address established and maintained the existing networks of power relations (as well as offering sly critique). In Marvell, Herrick, Milton, Jonson, address is part of political, personal, and national negotiation. See Heather Dubrow, *The Challenges of Orpheus: Lyric Poetry and Early Modern England* (Baltimore: Johns Hopkins University Press, 2007) and Terry Walker, *Thou and You in Early Modern English Dialogues* (Amsterdam: John Benjamins, 2007).

[29] See Mark Smith, 'Apostrophe, or the Lyric Art of Turning Away', *Texas Studies in Literature and Language* 49/4 (Winter 2007), 411–37; Barbara Johnson, *Persons and Things* (Cambridge, Mass.: Harvard University Press, 2008), 5–8; Alan Richardson, 'Apostrophe in Life and in Romantic Art: Everyday Discourse, Overhearing, and Poetic Address', *Style*, 36/3 (Fall 2002), 363–85; Ann Keniston, *Overheard Voices: Address and Subjectivity in Postmodern American Poetry* (New York: Routledge, 2006). Anne Stevenson, *Poems 1955–2005* (Tarset: Bloodaxe Books, 2005). Geoffrey Hill, *Speech! Speech!* (London: Penguin Books, 2000), 92:4. Subsequently referred to as *SS*.

the notion of art as well-honed self-expression. Pound, for instance, made much use of the energetic plurality of saying *you*:

Mistress of many tongues; merchant of chalcedony
I am Geryon twin with usura,
You who have lived in a stage set.[30]

In Pound's address, artist and artwork meet and mingle in the world of everyday correspondence, information, and gesture. *I* takes shape from a medley of past and present voices. That 'stage set' emphasizes the poem as a site of performance, theatricality, and spectatorship, where *I* conducts affairs with *you* as part of poetry's incorrigibly social theatre. Pound's public traffic includes merchants, speculation, semi-precious gemstones (chalcedony, a form of quartz, comes in three different forms) as well as usury. Such address transgresses the apparent privacy of saying *you*, wielding it as an outward-directed principle of plurality. In Pound, the self is not only 'twin', but emergent as the multiple-formed figure of Geryon. Meanwhile, *you* is subject to slippage between 'many tongues', voices, auditions, and 'staged' roles.

In modernist and in contemporary poetry, these slippages of roles and personas raise nagging epistemological and ethical questions—even as address's intimately chameleon nature is celebrated for emphasizing the very ordinary multiplicity of identities encountered on the street, in the bar, at the theatre, lecture hall, office, or across the kitchen table. In the work of the English poet-scholar and Oxford professor of poetry Geoffrey Hill, address is used to emphasize how poetry participates in an energetically poly-vocal theatre of public words that are tried out, inhabited, and delivered to *you* at the line of speech: 'a galaxy of voices | leaping static'. Hill's late volume, *Speech! Speech!* both gets a kick out of delivering hostile addresses to invading 'trite' and 'fake' *you*s, and depicts a textual space tyrannized by interfering interlocutors, as though the poem were forced to host a range of meddling, uninvited discourses:

> I will
match you fake pindaric for trite
violence, evil twin. Here I address
fresh auditors: suppose you have gone the full
distance. Take up—ón line—the true nature
of this achievement. [...][31]

Like the irascible address of Pound's Canto 1—'Lie quiet, Divus'—Hill's lines register the authorial 'will' to rebuff threatening textual inhabitants, commanding its audience to 'Take up—ón line—the true nature | of this achievement'. Yet Hill's language also gets a kick out of the disparate energies of doublings and twinnings that arise in competing with *you* for control of the lyric medium, and even encourages new forms of

---

[30] Ezra Pound, *The Cantos of Ezra Pound* (New York: New Directions, 1996), Canto 51, 250.
[31] Hill, *SS*, 92:46.

competition: 'Take up', he commands, directing antagonists to new 'ón line' media that they might use to sing his praises. Simultaneously showcasing his verbal ingenuity, that phrase also instructs antagonists to stay 'in line', punning on the ease with which the lyric exchange could turn nasty, be out of line. The poet-figure's one-upmanship with 'you' creates a curious parity with its addressee(s) as the *I* strives to outdo *your* lyric invasions and fakeries: 'I will | match you', 'evil twin', 'fake Pindaric for trite | violence'. *I* and *you* switch positions, so that the poem sings *with* its *you*, in a co-authored succession of 'violently' interrupting rebuttals. Such address delights in vigorously addressing antagonistic auditors.

>   I want. You want.
> You want I should write. Write what | I ask.
> Like, write this down, maybe. BEHOLDEN |
> I love it. Tell me | when were we ever
> nót beholden? And yes, righteousness
> sticks át it if unrecognized. Steadfast
> witnesses you might have called us [...][32]

Speaking to *you* in this way stages a disconcerting range of invading languages and lexicons that co-opt the lyric space. Note the staccato, improvisatory syntax of 'I want. You want', 'Write what', 'Like, write this down, maybe'. Simultaneously, Hill performs an act of powerful co-option. If his lines present a testy, messy tussle between lyric *I*s and *you*s, authorial and readerly presences, they also masterfully bend *your* ear: 'Tell me', 'yes'. Probing the ground over which different poetic interlocutors enact literary takeover bids, Hill implements his own, putting to work the cultural weight that certain lexicons have attained; making masterful music that demands readerly attention: 'BEHOLDEN', 'righteousness', 'witnesses'. Like Paterson's currents of quotation and italicization in 'The Candlebird', or Dunn's interlocutions in 'The Gardeners', Hill's address tunes into poetry's capturing of the dissonant registers and competitive accents that situate contemporary writing, and also the literary politics of speaking to *you* in 'chaotically' multi-vocal English.

I've been suggesting that, in speaking to *you*, contemporary poets redeploy innovative, cacophonous urges akin to those which animated modernist poetry's determination to 'make it new'; and are alert to the culpabilities of writers and audiences in that enterprise. True, Harrison and Dunn attend to the poly-vocalism of the speaking subject in a quite different—less thoroughgoing 'late modernist'—way from that of Graham or Hill. If the former are invested in holding on to the voice of a coherent speaking subject (which is interrupted or threatened by particular social groups), the latter wrong-foot the notion of a coherent poet-figure or recipient, through a succession of role swapping *I*s and *you*s. This pronominal pirouetting, like Joyce's, showcases the dangers as well as the delights of texts being written 'not by me', but by 'you, and you, and you'.

---

[32] Hill, *SS*, 18:9.

I want to turn to a poem by Anne Stevenson, which I think will help us to distinguish between one kind of poetic voicing and another. Stevenson's 'Invocation and Interruption (*i.m. Ted Hughes*)' initially appears to break with the notion that a single, isolated voice can sustain lyric address.[33] The lyric begins by hailing Hughes, the past master being commemorated. Stevenson's *I* speaks *to* and *in* another's voice, both appropriating tradition and being appropriated by it:

*Gigantic iron hawk
coal-feathered like a crow,
tar-coated cave bird,
werewolf, wodwo,*

*you've flown away now,
where have you flown to?*

was how this poem began [...]

It's at this point that Stevenson's elegized addressee—'Hughes'—interrupts and hijacks the poem. *You* (Hughes) turns the tables on the apparently empowered all-perceiving poetic *I*, delivering a riposte to the living writer who attempts to memorialize the dead:

'Please don't imagine I have
flown anywhere,' said the silence [...]
[...]
'The underworld was always a metaphor,
the life after life in which poets
are remade by their interpreters.
I'm better off here with
Sylvia and Otto, Coleridge and Ovid.
Nothing can hurt us;
we're immune to our reputations.
As for you and the others—
you'd best be getting on
with getting on.

On the one hand, Stevenson's lines enact rather than merely describe 'Interruption'. The poetic utterance is commandeered by the dead literary master it addresses. The deceased Hughes, cast as a *you* who, in speaking back to Stevenson's living *I*, invades the poem under construction and speaks in her stead. Even as the poet-figure uses Hughes's voice for its own ends, *you* inveigles itself into the speech of the lyric *I*. This is a composite and combatively dialogic poetic text. It's reminiscent of Hill's competitive voicings in *Speech! Speech!* in so far as it emanates not purely from a set-apart *I*, but from a movement between speaker and interlocutor. The resulting sound-effect

---

[33] Stevenson, *Poems 1955–2005*, 389.

depends on *your* impinging interruptions, hecklings, cross-rhythms, and trans-historical communications.

On the other hand, Stevenson's lyric remains anchored to the semblance of the focal consciousness of the speaker, which the poem envisages as 'disrupted' and 'interrupted' by the *you* it attempts to address. Although the poem *is* a conversation that demonstrates an *I* violently appropriated by *your* voice—and although it stages forms of address rather darker than gentle communication between well-matched interlocutors—the lyric implies that *you* rudely trespasses into the space that should be marked out for soliloquy. Stevenson's poem casts its speaker less as a constructed persona, created out of slippages between possible voices and registers, than as a fixed character: the 'Anne Stevenson' of the title page. In that respect, the address shies from the very polyphony it stages. Only a single species of interruption is made, and the reader and poet are implicitly part of a cultural 'we' that ultimately remains stable, albeit stirred and shaken. Stevenson's lyricism has much more in common with the speaking and listening voices employed by Harrison and Dunn. Her staging of 'interruption' works quite differently from the ways in which the notion of consistent voicing is sent up through the flux of colliding voices in Pound—and later in the work of poets such as Hill, Graham, and Prynne.

'It has mostly been my own aspiration, for example, to establish relations not personally with the reader, but with the world and its layers of shifted but recognisable usage; and thereby with the reader's own position within this world' writes Prynne.[34] In his essay 'Reader's Lockjaw', he proposes that lyric language should be 'related to clearly marked tones of common speech but derived from placings to one side of that speech; not placed inside individual embarrassment or at the ticket barrier of a class station but not immune to either; not touching into "literary" culture but admitting, even so, the pull of such *de luxe* ambition'.[35]

Prynne's remarks might put one in mind of Hill's argument that, in the creative act, 'the genius of language alienates us from itself. [...] It is [...] like being brushed past, or aside, by an alien being'.[36] In both, physical positioning ('brushed aside'; 'not placed inside'; 'alienates') is key in conducting responsible address. It's possible to be too close for comfort to *you*, and to exploit that proximity in order to showcase unalienated 'genius'. For both, 'the genius of language' and the 'clearly marked tones of common speech' need to be present in the most moving poems—but they should not be used to court worldly success with *you*. Instead, address should alert us to the tempting 'pull of such *de luxe* ambition', and to the poet's susceptibility to being winsome with readerships. Both Hill and Prynne often make recourse to a kind of necessary alienation in speaking to *you*: they achieve an ethics of address in 'establish[ing] relations not

---

[34] J. H. Prynne, private letter to Peter Riley, 15 Sept. 1985. See also Riley's pamphlet, *Reader* (London, 1992).

[35] J. H. Prynne, 'Reader's Lockjaw', Review of Paul St Vincent (later revealed as E. A. Markham), *Perfect Bound*, 5 (1978), 73–7. See [http://jacketmagazine.com/20/pbs.html#sjpb].

[36] Hill, 'A Postscript on Modernist Poetics' (2005), in *CCW*, 566.

personally', and in speaking at odd angles, 'to one side' and 'aside from' violent urges for comprehension and lyric genius.

'Homing in acutely at the side of others and being jostled by them, makes for compound ironies' writes Prynne, for whom 'lockjaw' is often much in mind, in the poems.[37] His lyrics are continually alert to the constraints on those participating in and being addressed by poetic speech. Such acuteness is at play in *Bands Around The Throat*, which plays on words' forceful constrictions of readerly and writerly voices. Poetry's glittering displays are associated with violence and throttling: 'at the neckline the word you give then | is padlocked by voiceprint, by neat cement'.[38] Masterful lyric utterance is on the one hand a crowning triumph that 'you give' listeners. On the other, it silences non-routine dialogue between *I*s and *you*s, leaving the language 'padlocked' with nothing new to say and no fresh way of saying it. Too 'neat' a verbal precision is akin to ornamented violence: 'padlocked [...] by neat cement'. Speaking to *you* questions to what extent lyric speech can resist exhibiting this aesthetic power, and in what respects poetry uses the intimately everyday accents of address to dazzle and co-opt listening *you*s. Could lyric language move sensuously and directly, with the accents of intimate 'common speech'—or would this be too close to a padlocked 'punishment routine'? In staging addresses, can poetry both resist conscripting *you* for its own ends, and avoid passively reflecting the values of those listening and participating recipients it seeks to delight?

In Prynne's later lyric sequence, *Down Where Changed*, 'placings to one side' of our daily language world—between immediately recognizable, plain-speaking usages, and redeployed clichés—are tested out, resisted, and subjected to subterfuge. Here, common idioms arrive at odd angles to each other, spatially and semantically, down the page. 'The rail is interfered with | it is cut up already' the poem informs *you* matter-of-factly.[39] The lines issue two apparently direct statements, in the simple present tense of information giving: 'is', 'is'. Deploying a briskly informative tone and idiom—'cut up', 'on the road ahead', 'no more to it'—the lines move as though useful data is being imparted to *you*: 'I'm telling you'. However, as is quickly apparent: 'telling you makes, really | no odds at all':

The rail is interfered with
it is cut up already
libel on the road ahead

telling you makes, really
no odds at all. That bend
is too bad, magnanimous

like a hot-air balloon
over the stupendous balkans
or privately dabbing your finger

---

[37] Prynne, 'Reader's Lockjaw', 73-7.
[38] Prynne, 'Punishment Routines', *Bands Around the Throat* (1987), in *Poems*, 350.
[39] Prynne, *Down Where Changed* (1979), in *Poems*, 296.

you do, that rail's done
as a praline, softly
in the airy open

there's no more to it
so out of true
the rail is sundered

I'm telling you.

One can't fasten on any particular incident that has taken or is about to take place here: perhaps a car or train crash up ahead; maybe an accident that *you* cannot avert; or an analogy for the colliding 'rails' of the artistic process itself: 'that rail's done'? Nor can we know or step inside the consciousness of any single *I* or *you*. What emerges is unspecified danger, imprecise agency, attempted warning, risk-taking, bet-making, *your* culpability and incomprehension, and semantic and temporal impenetrability. These mingle with the direct language of address, and the well-modulated aural rightness of the enjambed lines, and their insistent final full rhyme: 'true', 'I'm telling you'. The lines try out an instance of aurally predictable lyric mastery even as they reject it semantically: 'so out of true', 'sundered'. They make us feel that we might *get* not getting it. What it is that's 'so out of true' is not clear, but the no-nonsense tone of 'no more to it' and the emphatic final rhyme flag up someone's desperation for certainty to be arrived at—especially when certainty must be dismissed—and of a rhetorical tool-kit being brought out to assert 'it'.

    Prynne's lyric appears to be an act of intimate address to a 'you'. The act of 'telling you' makes recourse to a language in which responses are 'privately', 'softly' delivered. Yet at the same time, the lyric combines the hostile accents of drunken bravura with the overemphatic present continuous tense: 'I *am* telling you' (i.e. 'you're not hearing me'; 'it's not working'). The companionable act of 'telling you' what it might help *you* to know has mutated into the finger-stabbing helplessness of 'I'm telling you', with all its intimate truculence and frustration at not being 'rightly' received. This address stages what Prynne might call an ambition to clutch after the straws of 'truth' to persuade *you* of something: an intimate power strategy. (Compare the abrupt, accusatory rudeness of the next lyric in the sequence, which addresses *you*: 'shut yer face', 'Their follies are | as now, your pride's excuse'.)[40] To what extent does this savvy deployment of matter-of-fact speech, almost Larkinesque lyric directness, and a range of everyday idioms and clichés, enable Prynne masterfully to hold our attention whilst riddling our sense of who *I* and *you* are, and of what could be at stake in 'telling' *you* about the sundered rail? Might Prynne's poetry gain power over readers precisely by withholding orienting contexts for its address? To what extent can the attempt to preserve a correct distance from the 'clearly marked tones of common speech', and to enact lyricism's appropriate 'placings to

---

[40] Prynne, *Poems*, 297.

one side of that speech; not [...] inside individual embarrassment' and cultural custodianship risk encouraging a perverse gratification in lyric mystification?

'Language, ah now you have me', wrote W. S. Graham, in his 1976 poem of that name:

Please speak for me between the social beasts
Which quick assail me. Here I am hiding
In the jungle of mistakes of communication.[41]

Like Prynne, Graham knows that humbly confessing to *you* failures of expression simultaneously enables the poet to deploy winsomely 'ordinary' speech. Graham's address, too, is reminiscent of Larkinseque straight-talking: 'ah', 'now you have me', 'speak for me'. His lines issue a collusive appeal that charms *you* into sympathy with *I*'s confession of all-too-familiar communicative ineptitude. Yet in Graham as in Prynne, recognizing poetry's self-interested deployment of the common tongue provides the ground for closer scrutiny of lyricism's verbal manipulations, and of the perils of speaking for, and with, listening *you*s. These are addresses that test out late modernist linguistic anxieties: fears about being spoken for and by language, and of words as 'social beasts' that waylay or 'assail' *I*s and *you*s. They underline our *longing* to be caught up, and caught out, in that shared verbal 'jungle'. 'Please', the voice begs. Its act of hiding announces: 'Here I am'. *I* and *you* are imperilled and delighted by their graceful articulation of the linguistic contacts and contexts that are most threatening.

Such addresses surprise us into hearing the old sounds of cliché anew. They enact art's fresh use of platitude in speaking to—or willingly delivering themselves into the hands of—that half-antagonistic, half-inviting auditor, language: 'now you have me'. In making sport with the coercive undertones of being 'had' (cheated, taken for a ride) by common idiom, Graham is also asking to be gathered to cliché's bosom, just as his deixis hands *I* into *your* possession. By these lights, saying *you* is a tantalizingly social act, for the poet's words don't merely reach out to interlocutors, but are actively shaped by and through them.

In Graham and Prynne, such linguistic mutuality indicates an oscillation between innovation with and enslavement to 'common' sense, between speaking plainly and in received tongues, between creativity and glibness:

So what you do is enslaved non-stop
to perdition of sense by leakage
           into the cycle: one man's meat
better late than never. [...][42]

In speaking to *you*, Prynne's address plays out temporal, physical, and verbal constraint. '[N]on-stop' and 'better late than never' hint at impatient tussling for lyric space and greater haste. On the heels of that truism, 'better late than never' interrupts 'one man's

---

[41] Graham, *NCP*, 207-8.
[42] Prynne, *The Oval Window* (1983), in *Poems*, 323.

meat is another man's poison', as if there were insufficient time even to complete clichés in this 'non-stop' verbal 'cycle'. Such fast-paced trade keeps 'poison' out of the lyric space, but that 'perdition of sense by leakage'—and the circulating contaminated 'meat' in the system—indicate a toxicity that cannot be held at bay, which imperils bodily and mental 'senses'.

Like Graham's, Prynne's address conducts a mischievous punning on idiomatic speech. Deploying and disrupting quotidian language, it demands attention to historical and etymological contexts. Casual asides are historically bound, as in Hill, for whom words are bonds with past and present *you*s. These complexities are constraints, verbal bands around the throat, which reveal to *you* to the weightedness of 'common language's' logopoeic affiliations. Yet they also point out, with intimate urgency, how the artist's language is tempted to adorn itself inappropriately, and risks commandeering those it speaks with and to.

'I read Austin [...] as affirming that I am abandoned *to* them, [my words] as to thieves or conspirators, taking my breath away', wrote Stanley Cavell.[43] To mean what I say to *you* is to assume responsibility for the implications of that saying, even though these implications will mutate, and take new shape in the mouths of different *you*s. To be verbally responsible is to commit to a language that moves beyond I's single-handed capacity to control: it is 'As if to write toward self-knowledge is to war with words, to battle for the very weapons with which you fight'.[44] Each of the quite different poets we've considered uses address to battle with the ethical and cultural pressures of literature's philological and historical power. Some insist that, as part of that struggle, the poet must turn his weapons upon himself, on his own acts of intimate and public address, and on his acts of verbal witness, broadcast, and circulation. From one direction, this differentiates the speech of Prynne or Graham, say, from that of Harrison or Stevenson, whose interlocutions might be accused of commandeering the common idiom of address to rail against established custodians of power whilst neglecting their *own* verbal culpabilities (and manipulations of power) in their critique. But then we might say this of Hill or Prynne, too. Prynne's, Hill's, and Graham's scrutiny of the aggressiveness of language's historical and etymological force has much in common with the social concerns of Harrison, Dunn, and Stevenson. In each of these formally very different contemporary poets one finds oneself bound to judge how ordinary language's verbal clout can bar or enable the route to innovative expression, and to responsible public interaction with different kinds of *you*s.

---

[43] Stanley Cavell, *Philosophical Passages: Wittgenstein, Emerson, Austin, Derrida* (Oxford: Wiley-Blackwell, 1995), 64.

[44] Stanley Cavell, *The Claim of Reason: Wittgenstein, Skepticism, Morality, and Tragedy* (Oxford: Oxford University Press, 1999), 352.

Select Bibliography

Abbas Ibn Al-Ahnaf, *Birds Through an Alabaster Ceiling: Three Abyssinian Poets*, trans. G. B. H. Wightman (Harmondsworth: Penguin Books, 1975).
Austin, J. L., *How To Do Things With Words*, ed. J. O. Urmson and Marina Sbisà (Cambridge, Mass.: Harvard University Press, 1975).
Beckett, Samuel, *Endgame* (1958), in *The Complete Dramatic Works* (London: Faber & Faber, 1986).
Cavell, Stanley, *The Claim of Reason* (Oxford: Oxford University Press, 1979).
Cavell, Stanley, *Philosophical Passages: Wittgenstein, Emerson, Austin, Derrida* (Oxford: Wiley-Blackwell, 1995).
Cavell, Stanley, *The Claim of Reason: Wittgenstein, Skepticism, Morality, and Tragedy* (Oxford: Oxford University Press, 1999).
Deming, Robert H. (ed.), *James Joyce: The Critical Heritage*, i. *1907–1927* (London: Routledge & Kegan Paul, 1970).
Dunn, Douglas, *Selected Poems 1964–1983* (London: Faber & Faber, 1986).
Harrison, Tony, *Selected Poems* (New York: Random House, 1987).
Hill, Geoffrey, *Speech! Speech!* (London: Penguin Books, 2000).
Hill, Geoffrey, *Collected Critical Writings*, ed. Kenneth Haynes (Oxford: Oxford University Press, 2009).
Graham, W. S., *New Collected Poems*, ed. Matthew Francis (London: Faber & Faber, 2004).
Jamie, Kathleen, *The Tree House* (London: Picador, 2004).
Johnson, Barbara, *Persons and Things* (Cambridge, Mass.: Harvard University Press, 2008).
Johnson, Linton Kwesi, *Forces of Victory* (Island Records, 1979).
Keniston, Ann, *Overheard Voices: Address and Subjectivity in Postmodern American Poetry* (New York: Routledge, 2006).
Leonard, Tom, *Intimate Voices: Selected Work, 1965–1983* (London: Vintage, 1984).
Paterson, Don, *Nil Nil* (London: Faber & Faber, 1993).
Paterson, Don, *God's Gift to Women* (London: Faber & Faber, 1997).
Paterson, Don, *Landing Light* (London: Faber & Faber, 2003).
Pollard, Natalie, *Speaking To You: Address in Contemporary British Poetry* (Oxford: Oxford University Press, 2012).
Pound, Ezra, *The Cantos of Ezra Pound* (New York: New Directions, 1996).
Prynne, J. H., *Poems* (Tarset: Bloodaxe Books, 2004).
Richardson, Alan, 'Apostrophe in Life and in Romantic Art: Everyday Discourse, Overhearing, and Poetic Address', *Style*, 36/3 (Fall 2002), 363–85.
Sisson, C. H., *Collected Poems* (Manchester: Carcanet Press, 1998).
Sloan, Mary Margaret (ed.), *Moving Borders: Three Decades of Innovative Writing by Women* (Jersey City, NJ: Talisman House, 1998).
Smith, Mark, 'Apostrophe, or the Lyric Art of Turning Away', *Texas Studies in Literature and Language* 49/4 (Winter 2007), 411–37.
Stevens, Wallace, *Collected Poems* (London: Faber & Faber, 1984).
Stevenson, Anne, *Collected Poems* (Tarset: Bloodaxe Books, 2004).
Stevenson, Anne, *Poems 1955–2005* (Tarset: Bloodaxe Books, 2005).
Waters, William, *Poetry's Touch: On Lyric Address* (Ithaca, NY and London: Cornell University Press, 2003).

CHAPTER 34

'THERE AGAIN': COMPOSITION, REVISION, AND REPAIR

PETER ROBINSON

'Rien ne m'a plus étonné chez les poètes', Paul Valéry wrote, 'et donné plus de regrets que le peu de recherche dans les compositions' (Nothing in poets has more amazed me, or caused me more regret, than the little study they have given to composition).[1] Not all critics believe they should compensate for this regrettable state, as Martin Stannard illustrates when suggesting that commentary on variants is 'a sort of inventive practical criticism which tries to re-imagine the creative process' which 'can be stimulating', but 'does not help the textual critic: it is not comprehensive and it is not objective'.[2] Believing that poems are not completed but abandoned, Valéry illustrates the preservation, after abandonment, of the first-personal reviser's viewpoint:

> Une fois publié, un texte est comme un appareil dont chacun se peut servir à sa guise et selon ses moyens: il n'est pas sûr que le constructeur en use mieux qu'un autre. Du reste, s'il sait bien ce qu'il voulut faire, cette connaissance trouble toujours en lui la perception de ce qu'il a fait.
>
> (Once published, a text is like an apparatus that anyone may use as he will and according to his ability: it is not certain that the one who constructed it can use it better than another. Besides, if he knows well what he meant to do, this knowledge always disturbs his perception of what he has done.)[3]

---

[1] Paul Valéry, 'Au sujet du "cimetière marin"', avant-propos to Gustave Cohen, *Essay d'explication du Cimitière marin* (Paris: Gallimard, 1958), 27; trans. from 'Concerning "Le Cimitière marin"', in *The Art of Poetry*, trans. Denise Folliot (Princeton: Princeton University Press, 1958), 149.

[2] Martin Stannard, in his edition of Ford Madox Ford, *The Good Soldier* (New York: Norton, 1995), 191.

[3] Valéry, 'Au sujet du "cimetière marin"', 33; trans. from *The Art of Poetry*, 152.

Yet do an author's manuscript drafts give access to traces of such a first-personal viewpoint? Are they signs of what the poet 'meant to do' before arriving at the published text, at what has been written? Uncertainty about how to answer such questions forms along the divide of first- and third-person points of view and perhaps along the further dilemma that the poet appears capable of occupying both, while the reader might only be able to occupy one. Yet in this light the first-person viewpoint of the poet is simultaneously privileged and out-of-bounds, and poets will have had experience of such simultaneous prestige and irrelevance.

Yet poets don't even know what they think when they see what they say; rather, they can think with what they find they have said, on a par with any other reader, because they too are interpreting the words as poetry readers and because they will want to remove from their experience of the poem any strictly first-personal reflections (or want to bracket them out), so as to be able to read the work *as if it had been written by someone else*. They want to transform the first-personal point of view into a third-personal one, or, at least, to act as writers with that in mind. When we read others' manuscript drafts, or their transcriptions, we need not try to reconstruct what we think were the thought processes of the composing poet *in medias res*. The poet may not even have had any such distinguishable or detachable or thoroughly articulated thought processes, because he or she was too busy doing the writing. The poet will have rationales, but will not be rationalizing them at the same time as exercising them. We can read each draft as readers, such as the poet also was, and then, by interpreting each state of the work to the best of our ability, understand the changes to have been made according to principles which are not occulted or only personal to the poet, but held culturally in common. We can reason out the poet's implicit rationale for any particular change. What follows from understanding processes of composition in such a light is that the relation between the prestige and irrelevance of the poet's first-personal viewpoint alters. The creative process is not, *pace* Martin Stannard, intangibly subjective, to be dubiously recovered by third-personal speculation. It is as understandable and interpretable as any other writing, and equally in the same terms by poet and not-poet. The only thing that the poet can mean by what has been written is what others can understand by it, and this must include all the intermediate drafts as well.

Here I look at literary value and the contemporary poet at work, the poet as the poem's first reader, in the light of subsequent readers evaluating the poem or reviewing its working drafts. Three convictions shape the discussion, and I express them now: aesthetic response in readers is not *caused* by the poem, as is suggested by the word 'response', an active involvement on the part of that reader, one which will vary from person to person, and within the same person at different times; formed words are repositories of values, but those values are activated in and by use, their being combined and in reading what is thus composed; and in the case of art objects—poems here—the value they may show is attributed by such acts of reading, responding, and commenting (including those performed by the poet as first reader). It follows that to disagree about a putative evaluation is to redescribe the object with a counter-evaluation. Descriptions can be detached from their accompanying values, but only in the light of other acts of value-bearing description. The revising poet is engaged in both activities, often simultaneously, though not in this case redescribing but rather 'rescribing'.

Evaluation 'functions regulatively, and it controls how and whether the artist should go on',[4] Richard Wollheim writes, and a poet makes innumerable such evaluations during composition. Not only do decisions to 'go on' require judgements of value, they depend upon values in those judgements. The subsequent attribution of value to the poem by reader and literary-critical uses depends upon, but isn't determined by, the composing poet's evaluative activities. The relation of 'depends upon' to 'not determined by' again points to how reader's responses to a poem are occasioned by its words but not caused by them, a view adapted from Wittgenstein's conversations on aesthetics.[5] I offer an account of the relationships between the evolving work and the evaluating poet by means of the interrelated viewpoints already indicated, namely the first-person viewpoint of a poet composing a poem and the third-person view of a reader experiencing the poem or reflecting on processes in the textual remains of such a poet's work.

These two viewpoints turn out to be less distinct than might be expected, as is underlined by a remark of Lucian Freud's: 'I begin to think a picture is finished when I have the sensation I am painting someone else's picture.'[6] Though there is a difference in the apparent certainty or assurance about the kinds of speculation that can be made from first- or third-person viewpoints, the criteria for speculation are not—and, I suspect, cannot be— entirely different. Experienced poets are only too aware of the risk of projective illusion in the stages of making, and their testing evaluative activities are involved in establishing a sense of the work whose value is as little dependent upon wishing and hoping as possible. The poet's reading is thus the invoking of at best a third-person-like perspective. Value in these interdependent activities of writing and reading poetry engages with ethical values at three levels: in the events, or putative events, themselves; in their representations; and, related, in the actions performed by the poet at work. The values in these three levels can all be in fruitful, or mutually confounding, tension.

While textual scholars don't tend to speculate about authors' actions; literary critics prefer not to be participant-observers; and poets have been reluctant to play the role of their own anthropologists or moral psychologists.[7] Let me begin, then, by sketching

---

[4] Richard Wollheim, *Art and Its Objects* (2nd edn., Cambridge: Cambridge University Press, 1980), 229. See my 'Wittgenstein's Aesthetics and Revision', in John Roe and Michele Stanco (eds.), *Inspiration and Technique: Ancient to Modern Views on Beauty and Art* (Bern: Peter Lang, 2007), 261–76.

[5] Wittgenstein told Moore that to 'ask "Why is this beautiful?" is not to ask for a causal explanation', G. E. Moore, *Philosophical Papers* (New York: Collier Books, 1966), 301. See the height-of-a-door discussion in Ludwig Wittgenstein, *Lectures and Conversations on Aesthetics, Psychology and Religious Belief*, ed. Cyril Barrett (Oxford: Blackwell, 1966), 13–14, and Frank Cioffi, *Wittgenstein on Freud and Frazer* (Cambridge: Cambridge University Press, 1998), 50ff., Severin Schroeder, '"Too Low!": Frank Cioffi on Wittgenstein's *Lectures on Aesthetics*', *Philosophical Investigations*, 16/4 (Oct. 1993), 261–79, and P. M. S. Hacker, *Wittgenstein: Connections and Controversies* (Oxford: Oxford University Press, 2001), 74–8.

[6] Cited in Martin Gayford, *Man with a Blue Scarf: On Sitting for a Portrait by Lucian Freud* (London: Thames & Hudson, 2010), 141.

[7] But see W. H. Auden and Karl Shapiro in *Poets at Work* (New York: Harcourt, Brace, 1948), Anne Stevenson, Don Paterson, et al. in Tony Curtis (ed.), *How Poets Work* (Cardiff: Seren, 1996); and commentary on 'process' and 'product' in Philip Horne, 'Rights and Wrongs of Revision', ch. 2 in *Henry*

two large and puzzling questions. The first is whether the awareness that something is awry in a draft poem occurs with an accompanying intuition about what can be done to improve the work, to remove the fault, or whether, rather, the critical awareness of a problem and a sense of possibility pointing towards its solution are entirely independent, or, indeed, whether either can occur without the other being present at all. Stravinsky reports experiencing 'a sort of terror when, at the moment of setting to work and finding myself before the infinitude of possibilities that present themselves, I have the feeling that everything is permissible to me' and he adds that 'if nothing offers me any resistance, then any effort is inconceivable'.[8] Without critical doubts coinciding with intuitions about what to do, such terror would occur not only starting out but at every moment of composition. Purposive action requires a reduction from such infinities of possibility, one enabling poets to distinguish between making progress and thrashing about.

Rather the contrary might be said of the *mot juste*, because if there is only one right word, and you fear you haven't found or can't find it, composition will grind to a halt without an adjunct sense of possibilities for improvement. As a retrospective acknowledgement, a reason for stopping making changes, the *mot juste* notion can doubtless play a role. The evidence of the draft stages of the poem that follow may not point unequivocally towards my preferred sense that, in revising, critical insights occur with intuitions about what can be done to make improvements. The poet at work has a repertoire of techniques, and techniques for reading the writing techniques, which produce critical insights with their application. The application of technique need not be a response to a sense of something wrong. Rather the sense of something wrong may rise with the application of the technique.

Rubbish Theory would suggest that an appropriate way to integrate these possibilities might be to recognize how purposive action is not possible without some version of my preferred idea, but that the process of revision will also inescapably include 'the results either of impulse or random experimentation, and, even if this were not so, there would always be accidents'. Yet such accidents will equally need to be responded to rationally and accommodated with the value-sustaining project of the work in progress, so that 'first-time accidents may be perceived to have beneficial results and we are able, thanks to them, to enjoy benefits which otherwise would have remained unknown to us'—from which, Michael Thompson, the founding exponent of Rubbish Theory concludes: 'Such happy accidents form an important part in creativity.'[9] For a poet in mid-vocation

---

James and Revision (Oxford: Oxford University Press, 1990), 20–46, Christopher Ricks, *Decisions and Revisions in T. S. Eliot: The Panizzi Lectures 2002* (London: British Library and Faber & Faber, 2003), 71–2, and Sally Bushell, *Text as Process: Creative Composition in Wordsworth, Tennyson, and Dickinson* (Charlottesville: University of Virginia Press, 2009).

[8] Igor Stravinsky, *Poetics of Music*, trans. Arthur Knodell and Ingolf Dahl (Cambridge, Mass.: Harvard University Press, 1970), 63.

[9] Michael Thompson, *Rubbish Theory: The Creation and Destruction of Value* (Oxford: Oxford University Press, 1979), 148.

process and product may thus interact to give a dynamic trajectory to the learning experience of writing, and help reinforce the facilitating assumption that a stylistic repertoire is open-ended and responsive to new occasions for poems.

A second set of questions involves the relationship between the *in medias res* instinctual and practice-based decision-making that poets perform when at work, and the values that these actions may or may not exhibit. Do readers—the first of whom is the poet—attribute such values? Or are they rationally drawn from the evidence of those actions? If the decisions are locally made, without conscious calculation of their consequences and implications, what distinguishes these actions from 'random experimentation' or 'accident'? The evidence of actions performed, the artwork, would constitute a set of entirely unpredictable discoveries whose values are to be attributed in reading and rereading? Here I'm inclined to assume this last, but remain jealous of the idea that the poet's decisions are meaningful and value bearing, even when, in the heat of composition, no such meanings and values were consciously intended.[10] There again, unpredictable combinations of such possibilities may occur in practice.

Valéry also describes how 'une œuvre toujours ressaisie e refondue prenne peu à peu l'importance secrete d'une enterprise de réforme de soi-même' (a work perpetually resumed and recast gradually takes on the secret importance of an exercise in self-reform),[11] an insight necessary but not sufficient to what follows, since for self-reform to be real it must include reform of relations with others. These others may be both the subjects of writing and readers. Let me then suggest that the finished poem is a set of decisions, of word choices, that are believed by the first-personal poet as initial third-personal reader to be capable of sustaining value attribution in the reception process. Yet how did those capacities for value sustenance in the art object get there? Creative decisions, including the decision to stop making changes, must be contributing the first moves in that reception process, performing trial ascriptions of value, from an at best third-person-like perspective—ascriptions which editors, critics, and readers are then invited to confirm, contradict, and variously develop from the offering of the work for publication and critical reception. Such provisional publication in little magazines contributes to trial value ascription, to which the living poet, because in a shared evaluative situation, may continue to respond.

The poem I've chosen to explore, 'There Again', begun in summer 1979, exists in two published states. Accepted in a two-verse version by Stephen Romer for the Paris-based magazine *Twofold*,[12] the earlier text duly appeared in November 1980. A three-verse

---

[10] In experiencing art 'background knowledge must include beliefs about a work's history of production and the specific processes of art that went into its making', Richard Wollheim, 'Correspondence, Projective Properties, and Expression', in *The Mind and Its Depths* (Cambridge, Mass.: Harvard University Press, 1993), 156.
[11] Valéry, 'Au sujet du "cimetière marin"', 7; trans. from *The Art of Poetry*, 140.
[12] Peter Robinson, 'There Again' and 'Cleaning', *Twofold*, 2 (Nov. 1980), 6–7.

version, first collected in *This Other Life* (1988), was published by *Poetry Wales* some seven years after the *Twofold* appearance.[13] Unchanged, it then appeared in a *Selected Poems* (2003):

1

Our witnesses were just visible views,
mountains north-west of Milan,
as lightning flashes at four in the morning
revealed taut power lines,
and by crash barriers, puddled verges
encroached on hard shoulder;
a cloud burst dissolving the distances
softened reddish clay earth—
the predictable returns of windscreen wipers
like mitigating circumstances.

2

Yet seeing the muzzle of an automatic weapon,
(his other hand fumbling
with your tricky brooch) I nearly relive
the taste sour breath has
harsh against your expressionless face,
and the unutterable humbling
my being there couldn't relieve.

3

Driven into a landscape without choices—
where no law was applicable
but his common sense's
wanting an object, you would serve.
And wait was all I had to do.
Because the first thing's to survive,
you said you'd bear the consequences,
whatever he demanded, giving me
occasion to revise or think again
how in that lay-by, and alive,
we viewed each other differently.[14]

The poem revisits a sexual assault witnessed by the poet at gunpoint upon his companion in Italy. Its occasion included situations and states of mind multiply 'shameful or degrading or frightening', and by no means only for the poet. The phrase is from

---

[13] Peter Robinson, 'There Again', *Poetry Wales*, 22/2 (1987), 82.
[14] Peter Robinson, *This Other Life* (Manchester: Carcanet Press, 1988), 27, and Robinson, *Selected Poems 1976–2001* (Manchester: Carcanet Press, 2003), 40–1.

Wollheim's exploration in 'The Sheep and the Ceremony' of how creative process 'can depreciate or impoverish' a work:

> First of all, the work of art may insufficiently, too imprecisely, fit the internal states that it is supposed to reflect, and, if this happens, not just any old how, but along a particular dimension, in that something felt to be shameful or degrading or frightening, something (to go back to an earlier thought) whose outward manifestation could not be easily contemplated, fails to get externalized, then the artist, in making the work of art, not only fails to acquire self-knowledge, he strenuously attains to self-error.[15]

Wollheim observes that 'it is no small mark of the austerity, of the high seriousness, of art that, while there are several ways in which the activity of making the work can detract from its significance, there is only one way in which it can add to it'. Perhaps this painful truth mirrors the fact that completeness is a single state, while errors or mistakes can occur all over a work, and any one will detract from that single completeness.

Wollheim outlines the one way that artistic activity may add to the significance of a work:

> It can add to it only when the activity constitutes a process of self-knowledge—with all that that implies: for self-knowledge invariably brings in train self-change, self-reparation. And the creative activity can become a process of self-knowledge when the work of art reflects with sufficient precision some complex constellation of inner states which the artist seeks to externalize.

Such self-knowledge, achieved, I would suggested, by means of that externalizing process, must then become an invitation to knowledge and self-change in the reader, and the writer as first reader. Of the ways in which the creative activity may detract from the work's significance, I began by citing Wollheim's first. The second occurs when the work seems to achieve a successful surface, but 'the increment of self-knowledge that might reasonably be expected of the creative process does not occur, and the reason why is to do with the spirit in which the work was undertaken'. This happens because 'the artist may wish to triumph over what the work could show him; he may want to disown it, or treat it as the belonging of another; he may make it serve his designs upon the spectator, to lure him or scandalize him'. The dangers outlined are at issue in what follows, and I return to reader relations in my conclusion.

The composition of 'There Again' occurred at various interrupted points over approximately three and a half years from early summer 1979 through to winter 1982–3. I am looking at a poem written almost thirty years ago. Reflections upon the decisions made are, strictly speaking, reflections on decisions I can see have been made. Looking back at manuscripts I had not read for as many years, the process of discussing the work appears like a reconstruction of decisions such as that performed when articulating a narrative for

---

[15] Wollheim, 'The Sheep and the Ceremony', in *The Mind and Its Depths*, 11–13.

the work of someone else.[16] The distinction between first- and other-person perspectives on experience as regards attribution of authority is inseparable from the matter of 'There Again'. This is because this worst thing that happened to me didn't happen to me. The sequence of events that produced this not so unusual situation is described in a 1998 interview.[17]

Attempts at bringing what had happened into perspective were conducted in the terms of poetic composition. The relations of public and private spheres related to my doing this, and were in play both in the writing of the poems, in revision, publication, and their reception. They are revived and in play again in my discussing the drafts here. The challenge this series of events sets to the writing of lyric poetry is that the key experience is not being suffered by the first person, or, put another way, the material from which the poem's lines might be spun is also first-personal recall of another's experience. The events the poem articulates are themselves equivocal between first- and third-person perspectives. Wollheim's reflections on self-knowledge, self-change, and reparation in the process of making art, and of the dangers of damage to the outcome in an array of unhappy motivational attitudes, scandalizing and the like, are equally relevant. The equivocal nature of the perspectives on experience highlights issues about knowledge, change, or reparative value in the work for others beyond the composing poet, the benefit of these forms for others also inscribed within them.

'There Again' emerged slowly from passages in various draft poems, uncompleted and unpublished. Two such draft poems bear directly upon the eventual outcome of 'There Again', as does a third, which attempts to develop materials for 'Vacant Possession', a title used for various drafts poems behind the published text of that name.[18] Writing these earliest drafts was an imagined revisiting, reviewing, or revising, of the prompting series of occasions. Reworking such attempts begins so early in the creative process, at least for me, that it is difficult to distinguish between composition and revision. One of these first efforts is a draft poem of five six-line stanzas. The first includes: 'unbroken clouds dissolved | in sepia drips, where there was | nothing I could do but wait | in the want of daylight'. The second verse prefigures lines in 'A September Night' and 'Vacant Possession'. In the third verse, the storm comes through in 'under rain and thunder | flashed behind forked pylons'. A fourth with revisions reads:

Stupidly ['Private' *written above*] the [*changed to* 'that'] meaningless
violence ~~death~~ threatened ['s' *added*] us ['you' *written above*], a man
with a gun, ~~like dirty rain~~ and I spectate.
The grass verge, without choices,
dropp~~ed~~ ['s' *added*] across hard shoulder
to fields that night obliterates.

---

[16] See my 'Bernard Spencer's "Boat Poem"', *English*, 58/224 (Winter 2009), 318–39.

[17] For the poem and its occasions, see Peter Robinson, *Talk about Poetry: Conversations on the Art* (Exeter: Shearsman Books, 2006), 40–4 and 74–5. For values in its close, see Eric Griffiths, 'Blanks, misgivings, fallings from us', in Adam Piette and Katy Price (eds.), *The Salt Companion to Peter Robinson* (Cambridge: Salt Publishing, 2007), 72–3.

[18] Robinson, *This Other Life*, 33, and Robinson, *Selected Poems*, 44.

Hesitations over pronoun-use and the privacy of the violence are already present. The last verse contains both the phrases 'the counterpane', first published title for 'A September Night'[19] and, as its concluding phrase, 'the vacant possession'. This attempt brings, blinking into the light, more matter than its lines can focus. Two pages later is a fair copy of 'Death is about my Age':[20]

Even asleep your eyelids press
anxious against a release
into waking, a distance
inside your skin, inviolate
and nothing I could do but wait
in the want of daylight.

Private, that meaningless
violence threatened you, a man
with a gun, and I spectate.
The grass verge, without choices,
dropped across hard shoulder
to fields that night obliterates.

Not to be victims of our own
short histories, special, so alone,
home's creased in the counterpane.
<u>Exemplary</u> confessions, we can't
sell what we have never owned,
our senses, the vacant possession.

Line 2 of verse 3 contains a first indication of the phrase 'not specially alone, alive' in the completed version of 'Cleaning'. The poem is then abandoned, memories of phrases from it being carried over into four of the eventual seven poems in the published sequence.

This notebook contains a further poem that attempts to locate the event in an Italian landscape. 'After Giovanni Bellini' exists in two pencil drafts, then an ink fair copy with red and green revisions. Then follows a pencil rewrite in eight unrhymed, more coherently rhythmical tercets. These eight verses, halved by an asterisk, evoke Bellini's *Madonna and Child in a Meadow* (National Gallery, London), and then shift to the events seeking articulation:

A grass verge, car pulled up there,
dropp~~ed~~ ['s' *added*] across hard shoulder
to fields the blue obliterates.

---

[19] Peter Robinson, 'The Counterpane', *Granta*, NS 2 (1980), 112; Robinson, *This Other Life*, 30, and Robinson, *Selected Poems*, 42.

[20] The title is from Donald Davie's 'After an Accident', *Collected Poems*, ed. Neil Powell (Manchester: Carcanet Press, 2002), 165.

Turned from his windscreen,
the driver, ~~undoing~~ ['unclasping' *inserted*] her blouse,
breathes hard and enters her.

His fist grips a small black gun
pointing to the back~~seat~~, ['at' *inserted*] someone
~~lying there~~ who
watched, ~~there~~ doesn't move,

who suffered this to happen,
['and' *inserted*] prayed for the attention
of that infant's love.

Here the violent acts infect the clumsy phrasing. Such efforts at finding a rhythm are a primitive sign of the need to transform into poetry the brutal blankness of the minimally narrated events. The appearance of rhythm and poetic form is itself equivocal between imposing upon these events and bringing them into salience and significance, an equivocation instantiating the conflicting impulses to leave well alone or work imaginatively and creatively with it. Further, the character of the responsibility for enduring this experience is not properly attributed to those present. The first-person speaker needs to take responsibility, while avoiding speaking about another person's experience of being sexually assaulted. These conflicted obligations impede the poem's addressing its materials in the collaboration between memory and creative work.

'There Again' begins to emerge in drafts of a sonnet and a three-quatrain poem:

Sheet lightening [*sic*] flares
brief parallel lines, the shutters
of this frontroom where I sleep,
like interference on a screen.

I'm waiting for the thunder
and count out the distance
there, and back to where she ran
wet from the downpour, fear, love.

Grass verge slipped beyond the shoulder
to obliterated vistas, dirty rain
pushed away by windscreen wipers.

Because it seems important to survive
she surrendered to his threat,
let the car roof's texture float.

The octave of this would-be sonnet adopts the flashing of an Italian summer storm to get back to the haunting memories. The failure of these verses can be summed up in the phrase 'downpour, fear, love', where the flicker in the last word between the nominal and vocative uses of 'love' is frustrated because the nominal use fails to pick out remotely appropriate senses. The same could be said for anything metaphorical in 'downpour'. Yet the sestet finds words that would prove important in approaching the eventual poem. Here are the beginnings of the 'puddled verges' and the 'hard shoulder'. The 'just visible views' are waiting to be found in the 'obliterated vistas', while the 'windscreen wipers' that will eventually appear 'like mitigating circumstances' have made their debut. The first line of the final tercet has the first and last words of the eventual final reading ('Because the first thing's to survive'), but the phrase conjoining them is woefully inadequate to its occasion. That it 'seems important to survive' might be a miscued understatement, while that present-tense verb 'seems' jars as I read it.

Similar things can be said for the lyric, which brings in the 'mountains' and 'landscape…without choices', the 'cracked red | clay' and returns to the 'verges', the now 'hard shoulder', the 'obliterated vistas', and the 'dirty rain…windscreen wipers':

Lake mountains were etched
against storm clouds, (the) night sky;
not paying at the toll booth
he made gains, and did us down.

In a landscape, cracked red
clay and without choices, grass verges
dropped across hard shoulder
to obliterated vistas.

Our deaths—the dirty rain
swept away by windscreen wipers—
in drenched grasses, we were alive
and saw each other differently.

The detail 'in drenched grasses' where 'we were alive' places the moment when we changed in each other's eyes at a different point in the sequence of events. The idea that we 'saw each other differently' is a retrospective attribution of meaning to that moment, indicated in revision by the word 'viewed', which, echoing the 'witnesses' and 'views' in the poem's opening, makes a formal reconstruction of significance, not a report on what happened.

The line that would close the first published stanza 1 appears elsewhere in a draft of 'Vacant Possession' now reduced to five numbered tercets. While the first two contain lines that form the opening of the eventually published poem, the third is entirely unused in the published sequence, and the fourth reads 'Evenings under the lamp she relives | discomfort in her stomach, and his eyes | my being here won't relieve.' Here is the association of 'relive' and 'relieve' being brought into proximity, though the pronominal subjects of the verbs will have to be redistributed and the character of their application nuanced. The fifth stanza contains key lines for 'Cleaning': 'roughly imagined, she has been | taken as though insubstantial. | You punish in yourself another's want.' The material emerged thus as a tangle of glimpsed contextual details, observations, and reflections that could not be integrated into a single poem, or simply distributed into separate occasions. The parts of the experience had to be separated out, and apportioned into constructed part-occasions joining together distinct points in the reiterating times of the events and their aftermaths. The association of the words 'relive', 'relieve', 'survive', and 'alive' aren't produced by a moment of verbal wit. Rather, the words appear in different drafts and are combined by subsequent acts of association and condensation alighted on in the processes of rereading, reflecting, and of self-criticism.

One manuscript and a typescript contain versions of the first-published text. A transcription of the manuscript shows the first appearance of the literal and idiomatic title phrase, with two attempts at how it might best be sounded:

THERE AGAIN
AND
~~NOT~~ THERE AGAIN

Our witnesses were rain obscured views
to the west of Milano, broken cloud
dissolved against the distances,
cracked clay earth,
the sodden grass verge
slid beyond crash-barriers
and as if at the point of his gun, I relive
that sickening in my stomach,
his eyes' ['hand's' *added*] unfigured ['tender' *added to* 'un'] want
hard against her expressionless face
my being there couldn't relieve.

Driven in ['to' *added*] a landscape without choices,
where no law was applicable
but his common sense's [*full stop deleted*]
['demanding to be served' *inserted*]
['and' *inserted*] ~~To~~ wait was all I was to do [*comma and dash deleted*] --
because the first is to survive
she said she'd bear the consequences
of his desires, giving me
occasions to revise or think again
how in that lay-by, and alive,
we viewed each other differently.

The typescript appears to be derived from this draft. There is a pencil change of 'hand's' to 'mouth's', a reading that appears in the *Twofold* text. However, the memory of Milton's 'They also serve who only stand and wait',[21] coarsened in this dragging of his 'serve' into the 'served' of sexual services, is not yet revised to the reading in the publication, where 'demanding to be served' has been changed to 'wanting an object, she would serve'.

---

[21] John Milton, 'When I consider how my light is spent', *The Poetical Works*, ed. H. C. Beeching (Oxford: Oxford University Press, 1938), 85.

In the *Twofold* publication, the poem was published alongside 'Cleaning' in its definitive version. Here is the first published version of 'There Again':

Our witnesses were rain-obscured views
to the west of Milan, some broken cloud
dissolved against the distance
into cracked clay earth,
the sodden grass verge
slid beyond crash barriers
and as if at the point of his gun, I relive
that sickening in my stomach,
his mouth's untender want
hard against her expressionless face
my being there couldn't relieve.

Driven into a landscape without choices—
where no law was applicable
but his common sense's
wanting an object, she would serve
and wait was all I was to do
because the first is to survive,
she said she'd bear the consequences,
whatever he demanded, giving me
occasion to revise or think again
how in that lay-by, and alive,
we viewed each other differently.

This poem shows four contributions that provided memorable phrases around which its difficult matter could emerge. The first is Bernard Spencer's 'On the Road',[22] about travelling in Europe with a loved woman and celebrating the plenitude of a passing moment. This 'There Again' borrows his two-stanza form for evoking and reflecting on the contribution a woman's presence had made. The second is César Vallejo's 'Piedra negra sobre una piedra blanca' (Black Stone on a White Stone) which provides a prompt for my opening: 'son testigos | los días jueves y los huesos húmeros, | la soledad, la lluvia, los caminos...'[23] (witnesses are | the Thursdays and the humerus bones, | the loneliness, the rain, the roads...). The association of words linking my first 'just visible views' to the last line's 'we viewed' was helped by Vallejo.

The opening of the second stanza adapts from Shakespeare's *The Rape of Lucrece*, lines 544–6: 'a wildernesse where are no lawes, | To the rough beast, that knowes no gentle right, | Nor ought obayes but his fowle appetite'. This passage first appears as an epigraph to a few texts of 'With Detail from Memory', the poem eventually entitled 'From a

---

[22] Bernard Spencer, 'On the Road', *Complete Poetry, Translations & Selected Prose*, ed. Peter Robinson (Tarset: Bloodaxe Books, 2011), 136.

[23] César Vallejo, 'Black Stone on a White Stone', *Poemas Humanos/Human Poems*, trans. Clayton Eshleman (London: Jonathan Cape, 1969), 116–17.

Memory'.[24] I had associated it with the last line of Milton's sonnet ('They also serve who only stand and wait') and this had come about by back formation from the fact of having to 'wait', and then to reflection upon the possible applications of the word 'serve', sharing out the verbs of Milton's line between the two of us. 'There Again' acknowledges being eternally indebted to the bravery and cool-headedness of the young woman, figuratively expressing this through an audible indebtedness to other poetry. These associations of texts with an event provide prompts for particular phrases or lines, and lend the idea of a potential artistic representation to the array of detail, so aptly summed up by Vallejo's 'witnesses' which are only circumstances, his 'loneliness' matching our being alone in being together, his 'rain' our thunderstorm, and his 'roads' our Italian autostrada or *tangentiale*.

But debts have to be properly repaid. I recall a sharp sensation of dissatisfaction produced by reading the text of 'There Again' in its first magazine printing, and suspect that the feeling may have either occurred or been associated with a conversation I had about the two magazine poems soon after publication. The dissatisfaction may then have had two adjunct contexts: the presence of another poem from the projected sequence that had come off better and made the other look unfinished, and the sense of a public critical context in which its inadequacies would be measured according to another's criteria. Thus an actual third-person critical perspective is beginning to establish itself as helping define the point of arrival for a first-personal work of imaginative exploration. From such experiences derives the reflection that a composing poet is attempting to convert a first-personal reading of what has been written into an independently existing third-personal view, stably available to readers. Understanding the drafts is not, then, an attempt to reconstruct the ineffable mental processes of someone else, but to see how that person's work moves towards thoroughly available reading experiences.

Surviving manuscript and typescript evidence suggests that the revising of the poem from the two- to three-stanza text was slow and unsure. In February 1981, I took up a temporary lectureship at the University of Wales in Aberystwyth. The poems related to these events were among the unfinished business I took with me. A typescript (on the office typewriter) still has the third-person pronouns in the second verse, which have then been overwritten in black ink with second-person pronouns: 'Our witnesses were rain-obscured views' is adjusted to read 'For witnesses we had unfamiliar views'. For 'cracked clay earth, | the sodden grass verge', I attempt 'cracked clay earth | and darkness, the sodden grass verge'; and there is an abortive manuscript draft of these lines at the foot of the revised typescript. However, 'that sickening in my stomach' becomes 'in ~~your~~ stomach', 'hard against her expressionless face' becomes 'your expressionless face'. In the second verse 'she would serve' and 'she said she'd bear the consequences' have third-person pronouns replaced with second persons: 'you would serve', and 'you said you'd bear'. This change, adopted in all subsequent drafts, I return to later.

---

[24] Robinson, *This Other Life*, 29, and Robinson, *Selected Poems*, 41–2.

Three further drafts of the two-stanza poem with various adjustments to the phrasing are followed by a pencil version in a green notebook written during summer 1981—a draft with three verses. The first title is written to the right and arrowed to signify an alternative for the sequence, a title from the Italian for the crime the man was accused of, not 'stupro' (rape) but 'violenza privata'. A handwritten fair copy of the new second verse appears beside that draft:

There again—at the point of his gun,
reconjuring the sudden fear
half undressed, so you relive
that sickening in the stomach,
his other hand's fumbling
with a tricky broach, the sour taste
of drunk breath's untender want
harsh against your expressionless face
and now the unutterable humbling
my being there couldn't relieve.

A subsequent typescript has the first verse revised almost to completion and the opening of the second verse revised by borrowing lines from the already completed and published poem 'The Counterpane' (later retitled 'A September Night'):[25]

THERE AGAIN

Our witnesses were just visible views,
mountains north-west of Milan,
as lightning flashes at four in the morning
revealed taut power lines
and, by crash barriers, puddled verges
encroached on hard shoulder;
a cloud burst dissolving the distances
softened reddish clay earth,
the ~~steady~~ ['squeaky' *inserted*, ~~'usual'~~ *and* 'predictable' *in margin*] returns of
　windscreen wipers
like mitigating circumstances.

Tonight's not warm, and waking
['I listen to the rhythm of the falling rain
as ~~if~~ though it were only wet weather is making' *added in ink*]
you snuggle beneath the bed's counterpane.
Is it only bad weather is making
me remembering the muzzle of a gun, ['an automatic weapon,' *added*]
his other hand's fumbling
with your tricky broach, ~~as~~ ['now' *added above*] I nearly relive

---

[25] Robinson, 'The Counterpane', *Granta*, 112.

th~~at~~ ['e' *added*] taste ~~his~~ sour breath has
harsh against your expressionless face,
and th~~e~~ ['at' *added*] unutterable humbling
['which' *added*] my being there couldn't relieve. [*question mark added, but deleted*]

Driven into a landscape without choices—[*dash deleted*]
where no law was applicable
but his common sense's
wanting an object, you would serve [*full stop changed to colon*]
['~~and wait was all I had to do~~' *added*]
~~B~~because the first thing is to survive ['thing's' *added, comma after* 'survive' *deleted*]
you said you'd bear the consequences [*comma added and dash deleted*]
~~(whatever he demanded)~~, giving me [*dash before* 'giving me' *deleted*]
occasions to revise or think again
how in that lay-by, and alive,
we viewed each other differently.

This text derives from a pencil manuscript draft, the only one, surviving in a white-covered notebook dated on its first page '1 Nov 1982'. The draft appears on page 7, helping date these revisions. 'Tonight's not warm, and waking' is a self-quotation, while 'I listen to the rhythm of the falling rain' is a near-quotation from a song by The Crystals. In the right margin there is an attempt to rephrase this opening so as to muffle the citations: 'Here beside you, still, half-waking, | I listen to the rhythm the ~~falling~~ ['steady' *added*] rain'. These lines, which in any case repeat 'A September Night', do not survive beyond this typescript.

However, though the poem is now almost complete, the typescript-remains at this point suggest a final hesitation. A further typescript exists in which the idea of numbering the stanzas is introduced, but the poem reverts to a two-stanza text, with an addition to the circumstantial details of the first verse trying to convey the lost material: 'he stopped his car, took advantages | of you, unforeseen, without warning'. The middle verse had been adapted as the third for a draft of the next poem in the sequence, one attempting to evoke a scene from the trial in Milan:

Seeing the muzzle of an automatic weapon,
his other hand fumbling
with your tricky broach, I nearly relive
the taste sour breath has
harsh against your expressionless face,
and the unutterable humbling
my being there couldn't relieve.

This poem, 'A Trial', in its final draft without this verse, was published in *This Other Life* then cut from the sequence for *Selected Poems*.[26] 'There Again' will be effectively

[26] Robinson, *This Other Life*, 28.

complete once the third verse above is numbered '2' and placed back in the middle of its poem. There is a further surviving typescript, made on a typewriter dating it to some time after July 1982, and with last adjustments before the making of the final typescript on an early computer attached to a laser printer, which reveals that the only revision to the poem made on the proofs of *This Other Life* in 1987 was the removal of a comma reintroduced after 'survive' in the third verse.

Rereading the first published version of 'There Again', I am struck by the inadequacy of the pronominal choices. Yet it may be that the capacity to shift pronominal perspectives, to apportion experience pronominally to the three protagonists, with attempts at appropriate emphases, and to shift between simple present and simple past tenses, was what the writing of these poems had to find as a necessary repertoire of techniques. The distinctness of pronoun uses in the first published 'There Again' produces a false flatness and stability in the narration of experience, one which misattributes the experiences for reasons that, though not necessarily wrong, are impeding the truths the poem is attempting to access. This shows in the poem's first word 'Our'. The very idea that the views are 'Our witnesses', shared, may not be wrong in itself, but sounds amiss when followed first by 'and as if at the point of his gun, I relive | that sickening in the stomach' and then, the grammar states, 'I relive…his mouth's untender want | hard against her expressionless face'. This now sounds simply not true, and probably not even possible. I can 'relive' the feelings in my own stomach at the time these events happened, but I can't in the same way, as suggested by the two things being governed by the same verb, relive 'his mouth' on 'her face'. However much I might want to imagine myself into that close suffering, nevertheless the grammar is attempting to abolish a distance, a separateness of experience, which cannot be wished away. This may be sensed from the turn of the last line in the first stanza 'against her expressionless face | my being there couldn't relieve'. But if the enjambment catches that fact too, the intuition does not track back up the stanza, rearticulating the relationships in that light. Rather, the intuition is stifled by the inapposite pronominal use.

Something similar occurs when this triangulation of 'his' with 'she' and 'I' is followed through in the not-far-from-definitive second verse. Yet this text is itself so near and yet so far, for, in 'she would serve | and wait was all I was to do | because the first is to survive', the placement of the rapist's immediate victim in the third person imitates the disposing of her as he did, while the move onto 'I' waiting, however accurate from the first-person narrative viewpoint, seems to rush selfishly onto *my* suffering. The flow of the syntax gives a false impression of who instigated what in the series of events. Whereas 'she' does not rhyme with 'do', the second person 'you' does, so in the revised stanza there is an insistent sequence of 'you…all I had to do…you said you'd bear'. This draws attention to the immediate victim's acts of endurance, keeping her vocatively central to the events, displacing the 'I' viewpoint towards the edge of its narrative. The first-person pronoun isn't stressed in the iambic 'And wait was all I had to do', but it is terminally stressed in the contrastive 'giving me | occasion to revise'.

This triangle sounds wrongly and untruly configured if the poem tells the story of 'he' and 'she' and 'I', with the other two equally third-person, instead of 'he' and 'you' and 'I'. This poem and the entire sequence shy away from making him an active subject, a 'he', presumably because this would attribute to him a coherent subject position from which he is willing his actions, a behaviour that this writing wasn't able to contemplate. Starting from 'Our witnesses were just visible views' the poem has to get to 'we viewed each other differently', another shared first-person plural: the use of the second person for the immediate victim enables this trajectory. What is being shared, though, is not shared because of what has happened, but because of endangered attachments that might survive it. So the intimacy of the 'I' and 'you' relationship flows into the 'we' of the last line, and occasions the chill within that intimacy, the 'viewed each other differently'—which was already there and expressed by the 'I' and 'she' relationship. The revision of the pronouns is, I think, the key creative decision, and the other improvements of accuracy and fidelity flow from it. These are among the reasons why I want to suggest that the deleted *pentimenti* of literary texts do contribute to the completed work's value. What's edited out shadows what remains, an absent presence made manifest in studying a poem's drafts.

The pronominal triangle of the protagonists mediates the relationship between the poem and its readers, who are an implicit 'you', singular or plural, throughout. They too are being timorously invited to 'nearly relive' things that they didn't live in the first place, so the positioning of the 'I' at a distance from the central event, is an equivalent for the positioning of readers at a further distance. The triangulation of aggressor, victim, and witness (he, you, and I) is shadowed across that other triangulation of poem, readers, and poet (it, you, and I). The revising poet slowly recognizes how disturbances within the first are unhelpfully disturbing the latter. Wollheim had noted the danger of luring or scandalizing the reader.[27] Because of what 'you', his victim, underwent, the things that we may 'nearly relive' and that 'my being there couldn't relieve', 'you', both victim and reader, are 'giving me' (a near-rhyme with 'survive' and 'alive' added to the 'serve' sequence) the 'occasion to revise'. The work of the poem depends on the uninvited endurance of another person undergone for our survival, and the writing attempts to align itself with that experience. 'There Again' was published as the first in a series of emblematically reparative (self-reparative, and relationship-repairing) tributes to her courage.

Select Bibliography

Bushell, Sally, *Text as Process: Creative Composition in Wordsworth, Tennyson, and Dickinson* (Charlottesville: University of Virginia Press, 2009).

---

[27] For first-time responses, see Jane Davies, 'Reading in Reality: A Reading of "There Again" by Members of the Ridgeway Library Reading Group', in Piette and Price (eds.), *The Salt Companion to Peter Robinson*, 122–35.

Cioffi, Frank, *Wittgenstein on Freud and Frazer* (Cambridge: Cambridge University Press, 1998).
Gayford, Martin, *Man with a Blue Scarf: On Sitting for a Portrait by Lucian Freud* (London: Thames & Hudson, 2010).
Griffiths, Eric, 'Blanks, misgivings, fallings from us', in Adam Piette and Katy Price (eds.), *The Salt Companion to Peter Robinson* (Cambridge: Salt Publishing, 2007).
Hacker, P. M. S., *Wittgenstein: Connections and Controversies* (Oxford: Oxford University Press, 2001).
Milton, John, 'When I consider how my light is spent', in H. C. Beeching (ed.), *The Poetical Works* (Oxford: Oxford University Press, 1938), 85.
Moore, G. E., *Philosophical Papers* (New York: Collier Books, 1966).
Ricks, Christopher, *Decisions and Revisions in T. S. Eliot: The Panizzi Lectures 2002* (London: British Library and Faber & Faber, 2003).
Robinson, Peter, 'There Again', *Poetry Wales*, 22/2 (1987), 82.
Robinson, Peter, *This Other Life* (Manchester: Carcanet Press, 1988).
Robinson, Peter, *Selected Poems 1976–2001* (Manchester: Carcanet Press, 2003).
Robinson, Peter, *Talk about Poetry: Conversations on the Art* (Exeter: Shearsman Books, 2006).
Schroeder, Severin, '"Too Low!": Frank Cioffi on Wittgenstein's *Lectures on Aesthetics*', *Philosophical Investigations*, 16/4 (Oct. 1993), 261–79.
Spencer, Bernard, 'On the Road', in Peter Robinson (ed.), *Complete Poetry, Translations & Selected Prose* (Tarset: Bloodaxe Books, 2011), 136.
Stravinsky, Igor, *Poetics of Music,* trans. Arthur Knodell and Ingolf Dahl (Cambridge, Mass.: Harvard University Press, 1970).
Thompson, Michael, *Rubbish Theory: The Creation and Destruction of Value* (Oxford: Oxford University Press, 1979).
Wollheim, Richard, *Art and Its Objects* (2nd edn., Cambridge: Cambridge University Press, 1980).

CHAPTER 35

REPARATION, ATONEMENT, AND REDRESS

PIERS PENNINGTON

I

LOOKING back on his life from old age, and wondering about the consequences of his actions, W. B. Yeats finds in 'The Man and the Echo' (1939) that 'All that I have said and done... Turns into a question'.[1] As a playwright, as well as a poet, he is deeply interested in the reach of words, and the possibility of a connection between the performance of his drama in the Abbey Theatre and the Easter Rising of 1916 worries him first of all: 'Did that play of mine send out | Certain men the English shot?' he asks, two further questions about the relation between words and events following on from this one—but, tellingly, no answers. Yeats had excluded the poets of the Great War from his edition of the *Oxford Book of Modern Verse* (1936) for the Arnoldian reason that 'passive suffering is not a theme for poetry', but there is no escape from personal anguish in 'The Man and the Echo', only the quiet resignation of distraction.[2] For even though the poem suggests the greatest work to be 'that which cleans man's dirty slate', its writing brings the poet no closer to the fullness of resolution and lasting peace of mind which he ultimately desires: the few words repeated by the echo confirm there to be no way beyond this

---

[1] W. B. Yeats, 'The Man and the Echo', *Last Poems and Two Plays* (Dublin: The Cuala Press, 1939), 27–9.
[2] W. B. Yeats (ed.), *The Oxford Book of Modern Verse, 1892–1935* (Oxford: Oxford University Press, 1936), p. xxxiv. As Yeats explains, 'I have rejected these poems for the same reason that made Arnold withdraw his *Empedocles on Etna* from circulation'. Arnold set out his understanding of 'situations' from which 'no poetical enjoyment can be derived' in the Preface to his *Poems* (1853): 'They are those in which the suffering finds no vent in action; in which a continuous state of mental distress is prolonged, unrelieved by incident, hope, or resistance; in which there is everything to be endured, nothing to be done.'

particular impasse, while the closing intimation of a different kind of echo, the primal cry of a rabbit struggling for its survival, raises still more questions about causes and effects. W. H. Auden's elegy for Yeats, written after the poet's death in January 1939, provided a conclusive response: 'poetry makes nothing happen', he asserted in apostrophic address, describing the medium as 'A way of happening' instead.[3] These words have prompted countless pages of critical dispute, yet they appear to hold true for the feelings of remorse which Yeats expresses in 'The Man and the Echo'—not only because what Seamus Heaney calls 'the limitations of human existence' prevent him from making reparation, but also because the limitations of poetry do.[4]

Indeed, there is a fundamental difference between making reparation—'The action of making amends for a wrong or harm done by providing payment or other assistance to the wronged party' (*OED*, 'reparation, *n*', 3a)—and expressing remorse: where the latter is an essentially individual act, the former requires the presence of a second party, as one's 'payment or other assistance' has to be accepted by that second party in order for the action to be completed. The presence of such a second party is accordingly integral to the regulation of the great codes of human conduct: in the legal system, for instance, one makes reparation for a wrong before society as a whole, as determined by the letter of the law and the authority of the magistrate or the judge, while in theological understandings one ultimately makes reparation before the superlative authority of God. Inevitably there will be situations in life in which it is impossible to make reparation—most notably those involving the dead—but when it comes to poetry the limitations of the medium will always interpose a primary barrier: the singularity of a poem's speech, which can only incorporate the poet's representation of other voices, and not those other voices in their originality, ensures that any reparation which a poet desires a poem to make could only ever occur beyond its bounds, as part of the greater reality of the poet's life. In other words, poems which seek to make interpersonal reparation can fairly be said to approximate to the condition of elegy, being mostly, because inescapably, about the poet. The definition of 'making amends' which Peter Robinson outlines in his study of poetry and performativity takes this limitation into account, and suggests a means of negotiating it: 'Making amends doesn't mean putting things back the way they were before the bad event happened', but rather 'making some symbolic or emblematic acts and gestures that represent regret and the wish that what has befallen had not occurred', so 'changing the way the past is seen by altering the future through an act performed in the present'.[5] As this intimates, the expression of remorse can be understood as a performance

---

[3] W. H. Auden, 'In Memory of W. B. Yeats', *Another Time* (London: Faber & Faber, 1940), 107–10.
[4] Seamus Heaney, *The Redress of Poetry: Oxford Lectures* (London: Faber & Faber, 1995), 160: 'the consciousness of the poet is in full possession of both its creative impulse and its limiting knowledge', this being the knowledge 'that pain necessarily accompanies the cycles of life, and that failure and hurt—hurt to oneself and to others—persist disablingly behind even the most successful career'.
[5] Peter Robinson, *Poetry, Poets, Readers: Making Things Happen* (Oxford: Oxford University Press, 2002), 24. For a related meditation on 'the desire to make reparation' in 'circumstances in which no appropriate action is possible', see his earlier essay 'Reparation and "The Sailor's Mother"', in *In the Circumstances: About Poems and Poets* (Oxford: Oxford University Press, 1992), 1–23. Compare also the essays gathered under the heading 'Reparation' in Adam Piette and Katy Price (eds.), *The Salt Companion to Peter Robinson* (Great Wilbraham: Salt Publishing, 2007).

of reparative intent, and, in the context of poetry, the poet will always be shaping this performance with the presence of a different second party somewhere in mind: there may be no answers to Yeats's questions, but still he asks them before the collective witness of the community of readers.

As such, the publication of a poem will always be a real act, with real consequences, as Geoffrey Hill argues in his questioning of the philosopher J. L. Austin's understanding of performative utterances.[6] Austin suggested in *How To Do Things With Words* (1962) that for such utterances to be valid they have to be issued 'seriously' and 'in ordinary circumstances', meaning that they will be '*in a peculiar way* hollow or void if said by an actor on the stage or introduced into a poem'.[7] On this view, Yeats had nothing to worry about—but then his poem's expression of remorse would have been similarly weightless.[8] The italicized words, which stress what they do not fully explain, gesture towards one of the fundamental differences between everyday speech and the language of literary art, since meaning in the latter is generated by form as well as by content, not only by what is said but also by the way in which it is said, poetry being the medium which keeps this interplay most constant and pushes it to its furthest extremes. The resulting potential for tension between authenticity and artifice can be understood, as it is by Austin, to compromise the poet's sincerity and therefore to problematize the performance of such personal sentiments as the expression of remorse. Factoring in the separation between poet and speaker casts the tension in fresh light, however: even though Yeats's poem is much removed from everyday speech—being mostly shaped into lines of rhyming tetrameter—and even though its situation is largely fictional, this does not mean that he is not being serious in his attempt to come to terms with his actions and their possible consequences, because the construct of the poem's drama is authentic in its artifice. Indeed, it might be suggested that the effects which the medium allows the poet to exploit enable him to be serious in a way that everyday speech does not. Peter McDonald has argued that remorse for Yeats 'exists in the most intimate relation to the poetic impulse, and happens even in the textures of the poetry itself... through the structures of rhyme and repetition',[9] and this understanding of the deep interrelation of the voice's subjectivity and the medium's objectivity points to the especially disquieting power of 'The Man and the Echo', since the only answers to the speaker's questions are the echoes which are to be heard in the verse, aural reminders of the poet's engagement with another presence, if not another party.

---

[6] Geoffrey Hill, 'Our Word is Our Bond', in *Collected Critical Writings*, ed. Kenneth Haynes (Oxford: Oxford University Press, 2008), 146–69.

[7] J. L. Austin, *How To Do Things With Words* (2nd edn.), ed. J. O. Urmson and Marina Sbisà (Oxford: Oxford University Press, 1976), 9, 22.

[8] As Hill points out, 'the necessary consequence of admiring Austin's logic would seem to be that there is nothing to take up. "If said by an actor on the stage, or if introduced in a poem, or spoken in soliloquy" our ideal terms can have no actual consequences' (*Collected Critical Writings*, 151).

[9] Peter McDonald, *Serious Poetry: Form and Authority from Yeats to Hill* (Oxford: Oxford University Press, 2002), 25.

These questions about the poet's desire to right personal wrongs open up more general and suggestive questions about the medium's reparative potential. It is important, however, to bear in mind the subjectivity of critical statements on such themes. To take a related example, Michael Edwards asks in a recent essay whether spiritual belief is possible in poetry—not in terms of content, 'the assertion of religious platitudes, or novelties', but in terms of form, which is 'something other' than this. When he answers the question, he does so, revealingly, by means of analogy: like poetry, his religion 'turns on the same need...to engage intensely with the world and to see it and live it anew', which means that for the Christian poet 'his way of believing...will find a response in the way in which poetry works'.[10] The tenets of the belief can be accommodated by the medium, then, but they are by no means fundamental to it, the lack of direct connection between the two being a consequence of the critic's attempt to overlay a particular understanding onto what is—in formal terms, at any rate—an essentially neutral practice.[11] The three words brought together by this chapter's title are, as the dictionary reveals, closely interlinked, the first word appearing among the definitions given for the other two, which all coalesce around the shared sense of undertaking corrective action (*OED*).[12] But just as Yeats's desire to right his wrongs encounters insurmountable limitations, both Geoffrey Hill's understanding of atonement and Seamus Heaney's understanding of redress come up against a commensurate problem: for there is an important difference between the elaboration of such ideas in prose, as experiences observed and beliefs proclaimed by the poet, often from an implicitly compositional perspective, and the guarantee of their manifestation by poetry.[13]

II

Unusually, one of Geoffrey Hill's earliest poems, 'In Memory of Jane Fraser' (1953), was included in both his debut volume, *For the Unfallen* (1959), and his second collection,

---

[10] Michael Edwards, 'Believing in Poetry', *Literature & Theology*, 25/1 (Mar. 2011), 10–19 (10, 16, 17).

[11] But see Terry Eagleton's *The Ideology of the Aesthetic* (Oxford: Blackwell, 1990) for a sustained questioning of this view: 'The construction of the modern notion of the aesthetic artefact is...inseparable from the construction of the dominant ideological forms of modern class-society, and indeed from a whole new form of human subjectivity appropriate to that social order', and yet 'the aesthetic, understood in a certain sense, provides an unusually powerful challenge and alternative to these dominant ideological forms, and is in this sense an eminently contradictory phenomenon' (3).

[12] See especially 'atonement, *n*' sense 4a and 'redress, *n*' senses 1a, 1b, 2, and 4a.

[13] The two poets have often been considered together. See e.g. McDonald's chapter 'Three Critics: T. S. Eliot, Seamus Heaney, Geoffrey Hill' in *Serious Poetry* for a discussion of the prose, and for two more recent studies of the creative and the critical work see Stephen James, *Shades of Authority: The Poetry of Lowell, Hill and Heaney* (Liverpool: Liverpool University Press, 2007), and David-Antoine Williams, *Defending Poetry: Art and Ethics in Joseph Brodsky, Seamus Heaney, and Geoffrey Hill* (Oxford: Oxford University Press, 2010). The questions of 'atonement' and 'redress' are large topics in each poet's respective work, and further discussions are to be found throughout the secondary literature.

King Log (1968).[14] The most obvious difference between the two iterations is the subtitle which he added to the second, 'An Attempted Reparation', a note on the following page explaining that 'I dislike the poem very much and the publication of this amended version may be regarded as a necessary penitential exercise'. Otherwise, the only major change is to be found in the concluding line, which has been revised from 'And a few sprinkled leaves unshook' to 'Dead cones upon the alder shook', removing the invented 'unshook'. If there seems to be something of a disparity between the scale of the error and the weight of the language used to describe it, then the performance reveals just how permanent Hill understands the fact of the poetic record, and its reflection of the self, to be: the original mistake can never be undone, the 'reparation' merely 'attempted', and yet the 'necessary penitential exercise' still has to be undertaken, if only symbolically. This early realization of the limitations of publication snared the poet's imagination in a profound way, and exerted a lasting influence upon his work: not only is a similar occurrence detailed in the abandoned biography which Hill at one stage intended to accompany 'The Songbook of Sebastian Arrurruz',[15] but its memory is also to be felt throughout his foundational critical statement 'Poetry as "Menace" and "Atonement"'—in which Hill questions whether his 'comic sub-plot', his apprehension of 'empirical guilt' in the writing of poetry, is really only 'an anxiety about *faux pas*, the perpetration of "howlers", grammatical solecisms, misstatements of fact, misquotations, improper attributions', before concluding the piece with a final evocation of 'the shocking encounter with…irredeemable error in the very substance and texture of one's craft and pride'.[16]

First delivered in 1977, as Hill's inaugural lecture on becoming Professor of English at the University of Leeds, 'Poetry as "Menace" and "Atonement"' has been given a comparable prominence in its subsequent appearances in print, being the first essay in Hill's first book of essays, *The Lords of Limit* (1984), as well as opening the *Collected Critical Writings* (2008).[17] As the title intimates, the lecture's polarizing terms have their origins in the poet's creative practice, and it comes as no surprise when Hill describes 'menace' as being 'meanly experiential rather than grandly mythical'.[18] He makes the second of his terms work in a number of ways, but, once again, the predominant concern is the poet's relation to the medium. 'The poet will occasionally, in the act of writing a poem, experience a sense of pure fulfilment which might too easily and too subjectively be misconstrued as the attainment of objective perfection', he cautions near the beginning of the lecture, yet this vigilant scepticism of the subjective disappears when he turns his attention from poet to poem: for Hill, ultimately, 'the technical perfecting of a poem is an act

---

[14] Geoffrey Hill, *For the Unfallen: Poems 1952–1958* (London: André Deutsch, 1959), 23; *King Log* (London: André Deutsch, 1968), 69 (poem), 70 (note). Compare Andrew Michael Roberts, 'Error and Mistakes in Poetry: Geoffrey Hill and Tom Raworth', *English*, 56/216 (Autumn 2007), 339–61, esp. 345.

[15] See the notebooks for *King Log* in the Literary Papers and Correspondence of Geoffrey Hill, Brotherton Collection, particularly MS 20c Hill/2/1/7 and 2/1/8.

[16] Hill, *Collected Critical Writings*, 15, 9, 19.

[17] Compare also the 1983 sermon 'Thus my noblest capacity becomes my deepest perplexity', which takes its title from the epigraph (by Karl Barth) to 'Poetry as "Menace" and "Atonement"'.

[18] Hill, *Collected Critical Writings*, 17.

of atonement, in the radical etymological sense', which is to say, 'an act of at-one-ment, a setting at one, a bringing into concord, a reconciling, a uniting in harmony'.[19] This is a greatly abstracting definition, which refuses to deal in particulars of agency, and Hill requires it to be so because atonement, in his understanding, is something which only the poet is able to perceive. When he is taking issue with a statement made by Auden's editor Edward Mendelson, for instance, he approaches the question from a compositional perspective, arguing that 'the proof of a poet's craft is precisely the ability to effect an at-one-ment between the "local vividness" and the "overall shape", and that this is his truthtelling'.[20] But the subjectivity of such 'truthtelling' becomes apparent in the clarification which follows, even though Hill's careful phrasing tempers the agency involved, to encourage the suggestion of an objective event: 'When the poem "comes right with a click like a closing box", what is there effected is the atonement of aesthetics with rectitude of judgement', he states, quoting Yeats, as the passive construction 'what is there effected' constrasts with the individuality implicit in 'rectitude of judgement'.[21] In this regard, it is telling that no such hesitation occurs when Hill uses the term in a more general way. Discussing the writing of the Great War, for instance, he singles out a letter by Charles Sorley, one which is critical of Rupert Brooke: 'I even suggest that it atones for Brooke's "sentimental attitude"', he claims, finding that 'it brings together details and perceptions which the "sentimental attitude" has arbitrarily set apart and at odds', where the presence of 'even' admits the partiality of the perspective.[22]

Hill acknowledges 'my belief that a debate of this nature is committed to a form of mimesis' early in the lecture, and it could be argued that the subjectivity of his understanding remains implicit throughout.[23] Even so, Christopher Ricks has questioned the 'hopefulness' of the lecture's central premise: 'the word "atonement" obdurately will not return to its radical roots, to "at-one-ment"', he objects, pointing out that the latter is 'simply, and finally, and unanswerably, not a word in the English language'.[24] Ricks goes on to read the earlier work (up to 1978's *Tenebrae*) in terms of 'reconciliation', but the argument made by David-Antoine Williams in *Defending Poetry* intimates the poet's understanding of atonement to be part of a deeper imaginative concern with questions of equivalence, an awareness of distance becoming increasingly apparent in the later work.[25] At two points in the early essay 'Redeeming the Time' (1973), for instance, Hill draws attention to shortcomings caused by disjunctions between 'energy' and 'perception'—but celebrates the achievements of Wordsworth, who, in the 'Immortality' Ode, not only has 'the "recognition"' but also 'the "strategy" to match the recognition', and Hopkins, who 'in his choice of themes and methods... is attempting a correlative

---

[19] Hill, *Collected Critical Writings*, 3, 4.
[20] Hill, *Collected Critical Writings*, 12.
[21] Hill, *Collected Critical Writings*, 12.
[22] Hill, *Collected Critical Writings*, 13.
[23] Hill, *Collected Critical Writings*, 4.
[24] Christopher Ricks, *The Force of Poetry* (Oxford: Oxford University Press, 1984), 319, 321.
[25] This understanding informs the chaper on Hill ('A Question of Value', 161–217), even though it is largely conducted in terms of 'at-one-ment'—but see 166-8 for a related discussion.

pattern'.[26] The lecture's subsequent discussion of the meaning of 'assent' is conducted in related terms: 'From the depths of the self we rise to a concurrence with that which is not-self', Hill asserts, using the understanding to gloss some words of Ezra Pound—'The poet's job is to *define* and yet again define till the detail of surface is in accord with the root in justice'.[27] He returned to this passage from Pound's correspondence in a later interview (1981), having expressed his belief—developed from some words of Father Christopher Devlin—that 'there's a real sense in which every fine and moving poem bears witness to this lost kingdom of innocence and original justice'.[28] But if these appeals to 'justice' (even though they originate in others) raise questions about the subjectivity of their understandings, then Hill's invocation of Devlin's words in *Speech! Speech!* (2001) is characteristic of the scepticism which runs through his later poetry: not only does the caricatured description of 'axiomatic | redemption grafted to the condemned stock | of original justice' appear to register a criticism of contemporary society, but it also raises doubts about the idea of 'original justice', even as the enjambment intimates the poet to be holding on to it.[29]

As these lines suggest, the later poetry often finds Hill acknowledging the subjectivity of his perceptions. The implied situation of much of *Scenes from Comus* (2005) is revelatory in this regard, with the poet understanding 'imbalance' to be 'everywhere'—even in 'the tectonic plates | ripping Iceland apart'.[30] Late in the sequence he states that 'Our duty is to find | consonance in the disparities', but the poem which concludes the book's opening section encounters the difficulties of doing so, in the qualifying and questioning manner which is central to Hill's late style:

That weight of the world, weight of the word, is.
Not wholly irreconcilable. Almost.
Almost we cannot pull free; almost we escape
the leadenness of things.[31]

In his discussion of the poem's closing line—which repeats this opening line, excepting its change from 'That' to 'But'—Ricks points out a play of consonance and disparity: 'Weight of the world and weight of the word are distinguished without being distinct', he writes, arguing that 'Had the apothegm ended with *are*, they would have been differentiated', and wondering 'Are they one and the same, as *is* might insist?'.[32] He remains equivocal about the possibility of equivalence, answering the question 'Yes and no', but in both instances the poem's form works alongside the choice of verb to intimate its presence, each sentence being at one with the length of the line. Hill proceeds

---

[26] Hill, *Collected Critical Writings*, 92, 100, 102.
[27] Hill, *Collected Critical Writings*, 4.
[28] John Haffenden, *Viewpoints: Poets in Conversation with John Haffenden* (London: Faber & Faber, 1981), 99 (Pound), 88 (Devlin).
[29] Geoffrey Hill, *Speech! Speech!* (London: Penguin Books, 2001), 7.
[30] Geoffrey Hill, *Scenes from Comus* (London: Penguin Books, 2005), 63.
[31] Hill, *Scenes from Comus*, 57, 12.
[32] Christopher Ricks, *True Friendship: Geoffrey Hill, Anthony Hecht, and Robert Lowell under the Sign of Eliot and Pound* (New Haven and London: Yale University Press, 2010), 5.

to complicate this intimation at the poem's beginning: the qualifications in the second line register uncertainty as to what can be understood to be complete, 'irreconcilable' (which has Ricks in mind)[33] being tellingly positioned within the line, but at the end of a sentence, as the three instances of 'almost' are questioningly placed at points of boundary. The final repetition of this word introduces a number of further complications, the break between stanzas momentarily allowing 'escape' to float into the expanse of the page's space, before being grounded by 'The leadenness of things'—a movement which recalls the earlier critical understanding that 'Language gravitates and exerts a gravitational pull'.[34] These qualifications are absent from the concluding line, but the fact of its repetition ensures that they remain subtly implicit, as the change of 'That' to 'But' implies a certain resignation, the poet's awareness of the distance between his desire for equivalence and the difficulty of its assertion.

The later poetry also finds Hill interrogating such ideas at a more fundamental level, as he raises questions about language's ability to represent concepts. *The Triumph of Love* (1998), for instance, puns that 'Penitence can be spoken of, it is said, | but is itself beyond words',[35] while *The Orchards of Syon* (2002) is directly personal in its treatment of a similar thought: 'Even now I confess | difficulty in pronouncing | súch wórds | as absolution', Hill writes, the overtly printed lines playing with the medium's suggestion of speech.[36] When he returns to the idea of atonement in *A Treatise of Civil Power* (2007), he does so with a comparable scepticism, which is similarly rooted in the acceptance of subjectivity. 'In Framlingham Church' makes a final claim during the course of its brief meditation on the burial monument for Henry Howard, Earl of Surrey—one of the great innovators in English verse, who was sentenced to death by Henry VIII: 'Nothing atones ever', the poet states, being disappointed to find the 'ornate' tomb 'unsatisfactory', with its 'stiff | inaccurate pietas'.[37] But the recollection of a different kind of representation keeps the possibility of adequate memorial fleetingly alive:

Nothing atones ever, but for a moment,
Holbein's unfinished sketch perhaps, as if
the sitter could not wait for the rich detail [...]

Not only does this memory contrast with the reality of the tomb, but a further comparison is implied, since Holbein's 'unfinished sketch' can also be set against his completed portrait of Surrey,[38] and Hill's choice of the one over the other suggests the thinking of the lecture to be somewhere in mind: 'That commonplace image, founded upon the

---

[33] In confirmation of this, the poem goes on to refer to 'the learned readers of J. Milton'.
[34] Hill, *Collected Critical Writings*, 91. For an extended discussion of this understanding, see Robert Macfarlane, 'Gravity and Grace in Geoffrey Hill', *Essays in Criticism*, 58/3 (July 2008) 237–56.
[35] Geoffrey Hill, *The Triumph of Love* (London: Penguin Books, 1998), 8–9.
[36] Geoffrey Hill, *The Orchards of Syon* (London: Penguin Books, 2002), 10.
[37] Geoffrey Hill, *A Treatise of Civil Power* (London: Penguin Books, 2007), 22.
[38] For reproductions of Holbein's two sketches of Surrey, as well as the completed portrait, see Jane Roberts, *Holbein and the Court of Henry VIII: Drawings and Miniatures from the Royal Library, Windsor Castle* (Edinburgh: National Galleries of Scotland, 1993), 48–9.

unfinished statues of Michelangelo, "mighty figures straining to free themselves from the imprisoning marble"... seems more to embody the nature and condition of those arts which are composed of words.'[39] The image also seems to anticipate this late understanding of atonement, as the directly following 'De Necessitate' continues the previous poem's argument: 'But that was Holbein's way not Surrey's whim', it begins, making the movement of the two poems—from blunt statement to momentary possibility to realistic knowledge—work through various stages of the subjective perception of atonement, again with an accompanying sense of resignation.[40]

Indeed, the influence of Hill's earlier thinking continues to be felt in the essay 'Civil Polity and the Confessing State' (2008). When, for instance, he imagines a public figure admitting wrong and asking forgiveness, so 'bearing the burden of his guilt, publicly acknowledged and publicly received', it is hard not to think of 'In Memory of Jane Fraser' and the 'Attempted Reparation' of the poem's revision, as well as the lecture's subsequent concern with 'empirical guilt'.[41] The broader contours of 'Poetry as "Menace" and "Atonement"' can also be discerned, but there is an important difference between the poet's relation to the medium, on the one hand, and the medium's relation to society, on the other, and Hill comes up against this when he sets out the dichotomy of his argument in the first part of the essay: 'I have affirmed that "poetry is inextricably bound into the purpose of civil polity"', and yet 'I have also conceded my incapacity to suggest how any real "purchase"... of poetry on polity might be achieved'.[42] The subjective perception of the earlier understanding is simply not possible in this context, and Hill goes on to introduce a passage from Simone Weil—which he first quoted in 1971—with the statement that 'I have for many years regarded the following proposal... as crucial, as unequalled, in its definition of the only possible relation between poetry and politics'. But he does not define the nature of this relation, leaving it implicit in the words of Weil:

> Simultaneous composition on several planes at once is the law of artistic creation, and wherein, in fact, lies its difficulty.
> A poet, in the arrangement of words and the choice of each word, must simultaneously bear in mind matters on at least five or six different planes of composition... Politics, in their turn, form an art governed by composition on a multiple plane.[43]

Weil draws poetry into her discussion of 'political action' by stating that 'Politics have a very close affinity to art', and Hill's quotation picks out the similarity of multiple planes in order to intimate an equivalence between the two. Yet a reading of *The Need for Roots* raises the possibility that the poet desired a deeper connection: Weil believes 'concentration' to be

---

[39] Hill, *Collected Critical Writings*, 3.
[40] Hill, *A Treatise of Civil Power*, 22.
[41] Geoffrey Hill, 'Civil Polity and the Confessing State', *Warwick Review*, 2 (2008), 7–20 (12).
[42] Hill, 'Civil Polity and the Confessing State', 10.
[43] Hill, 'Civil Polity and the Confessing State', 11. For a recent discussion of Hill's understanding of the 'analogical relationship' between poetics and politics, see Michael Molan, 'Milton and Eliot in the Work of Geoffrey Hill', in Piers Pennington and Matthew Sperling (eds.), *Geoffrey Hill and His Contexts* (Oxford: Peter Lang, 2011), 81–105, esp. 98–105.

necessary for successful poetic composition, but when it comes to politics what is needed is, by contrast, a desire for 'justice'—the English word deriving from the Old French *justise*, one of whose meanings is 'uprightness' (*OED*).[44]

III

In its conviction that poetry is able to influence the public realm, Seamus Heaney's understanding of redress is similarly dependent upon a sense of equivalence. But, as a poet from Northern Ireland, whose career has long been conditioned by expectations surrounding public speech, Heaney is not primarily concerned to stress the medium's political aspects (although these are much discussed), choosing to set his account of its unique capacities against the backdrop of the situation. Once again, the critical understanding has its origins in the poet's creative practice, and 1984's *Station Island* collects a number of poems which anticipate the later arguments. 'Sandstone Keepsake', for instance, holds the issues in tension, being situated by a lough which divides the north from the south, and which overlooks an internment camp in County Derry. The speaker picks a stone from the shore in what he calls 'my free state of image and allusion', a description which remains ambiguous about the relation between the poetic and the political, before the poem concludes by raising questions about the act's significance: having been 'swooped on, then dropped by trained binoculars', Heaney sees himself in the closing lines as 'a silhouette... not about to set times wrong or right, | stooping along, one of the venerators'.[45] Further questions about the poet's role are prompted by 'Station Island', the sequence from which the volume takes its title. Named after an ancient site for pilgrimage—which involves a 'penitential vigil of fasting and praying', Heaney explains in his notes[46]—its twelve sections present a series of fictional encounters with figures from the poet's life and Ireland's past, as Heaney looks back and attempts to weigh up his actions. A specifically poetic regret emerges in the final encounter with James Joyce, whose ventriloquized speech advocates the singularity which 'Sandstone Keepsake' only gestures towards. 'What you must do must be done on your own', the shade advises: 'You lose more of yourself than you redeem | doing the decent thing.'[47]

The word 'straight' appears three times in this closing section,[48] and it is telling that Heaney returned to it a decade later, when he remembered taking some important steps

---

[44] Simone Weil, *The Need for Roots: Prelude to a Declaration of Duties Towards Mankind*, trans. Arthur Wills (London: Routledge and Kegan Paul, 1952), 206, 207.

[45] Seamus Heaney, *Station Island* (London: Faber & Faber, 1984), 20.

[46] Heaney, *Station Island*, 122.

[47] Heaney, *Station Island*, 92–4. 'The main tension is between two often contradictory demands: to be faithful to the collective historical experience and to be true to the recognitions of the emerging self', Heaney explains in 'Envies and Identifications: Dante and the Modern Poet', *Irish University Review*, 15/1 (Spring 1985), 5–19 (19).

[48] As pointed out by Neil Corcoran in *Seamus Heaney* (London: Faber and Faber, 1986), 167.

towards his artistic independence. Reflecting on the course of his career in 'Crediting Poetry', his Nobel Lecture of 1995, Heaney described how 'finally and happily, and not in obedience to the dolorous circumstances of my native place but in spite of them, I straightened up' and started to acknowledge 'the marvellous as well as the murderous'—where 'marvellous' chimes with the 'veneration' of 'Sandstone Keepsake', even if the poet was only 'stooping along' there.[49] 'Crediting Poetry' touches upon a number of the ideas which Heaney outlined as Professor of Poetry in the University of Oxford, and the ten lectures comprising *The Redress of Poetry* (also 1995) are similarly influenced by the idea of straightness. Discussing the definitions for 'redress' given by the dictionary, Heaney explains that even though many of the entries for the verb are now obsolete, 'I have...taken account of the first of these', which begins 'To set (a person or a thing) upright again' (*OED*).[50] But as well as developing the imagery of the poetry, the lectures also find Heaney developing his earlier critical insights, and the volume amounts to a comprehensive declaration of belief in the power of the art. Bernard O'Donoghue has suggested that a clarification in Heaney's thinking occurs between *Preoccupations* (1980) and *The Government of the Tongue* (1988), two books which are concerned to explore 'the poet's duties, private and public', and the possibility of 'free poetic imagination',[51] while Tim Kendall has argued that together the three volumes 'chart a continuity of interests and an increasing sophistication of argument'.[52] Most notably, the Oxford lectures develop the ideas of doubleness ('tension') which underpin *The Government of the Tongue*. Introducing the volume, Heaney draws upon his own experience in order to establish a distinction between 'art' and 'life', observing that 'both are often perceived to be in conflict', despite their shared contribution to the poet's 'formation'.[53] The passive construction disguises the subjectivity of the statement, but the partiality of the perspective becomes clear to see when Heaney suggests this conflict to be 'constantly and sympathetically suffered by the poet', who begins to feel that 'a choice between the two, a once-and-for-all option, would simplify things'.[54] Accordingly, the introduction proceeds to work its way out of this dilemma, coming down on the side of 'art' with a grand yet tentative statement which makes no claim to objectivity, as Heaney asserts his belief that 'poetry can be as potentially redemptive and possibly as illusory as love'.[55]

[49] Seamus Heaney, *Crediting Poetry* (Oldcastle: The Gallery Press, 1995), 20; repr. in *Opened Ground: Poems 1966–1996*, 447–67 (458). A number of critics have drawn attention to the celebratory tone of Heaney's Oxford lectures.

[50] Heaney, *The Redress of Poetry*, 15. Heaney repeats the definition in the closing lecture (192).

[51] Bernard O'Donoghue, 'Heaney's *ars poetica*: *The Government of the Tongue*', in Tony Curtis (ed.), *The Art of Seamus Heaney* (Bridgend: Seren, 2001), 181–90 (182). O'Donoghue goes on to draw attention to the doubleness of the title *The Government of the Tongue* (183), and a number of critics have made similar points about *The Redress of Poetry*.

[52] Tim Kendall, 'An Enormous Yes? *The Redress of Poetry*', in Curtis (ed.), *The Art of Seamus Heaney*, 229–39 (237).

[53] Seamus Heaney, *The Government of the Tongue* (London: Faber & Faber, 1988), p. xii.

[54] Heaney, *The Government of the Tongue*, p. xii.

[55] Heaney, *The Government of the Tongue*, p. xxii.

But these polarizing terms are not so readily separable as Heaney's argument requires them to be, and the Oxford lectures attempt a more nuanced treatment of the question—the paragraph which introduces *The Redress of Poetry* celebrating two poems which both embody 'the way consciousness can be alive to two different and contradictory dimensions of reality and still find a way of negotiating between them'.[56] When it comes to the more general discussion of the medium, though, these two dimensions can be understood as variations on 'art' and 'life', terms which are themselves redolent of the familiar distinction between 'form' and 'content', and the opening lecture finds Heaney maintaining his earlier belief by emphasizing the fundamentality of poetry's form. At times, he gestures towards the possibility of its autonomy: 'The felicity of a cadence, the chain reaction of a rhyme, the pleasuring of an etymology' occur to the poet 'in an area of mental operations which is cordoned off by and from the critical sense', as poetry's unique capacities spark different kinds of connection to those encouraged by syntax alone.[57] Elsewhere, Heaney's confidence in form is less explicitly stated. If, for instance, 'the redress of poetry' most obviously means 'affirming that which is denied voice'—in which case poetry is understood to be an 'agent for proclaiming and correcting injustices'—then such a concern for the message runs the risk of disregarding the medium's singularity: 'poets are in danger of slighting another imperative, namely, to redress poetry *as* poetry, to set it up as its own category', which is to say, 'an eminence established and a pressure exercised by distinctly linguistic means', where Heaney's understanding of 'distinctly linguistic means' has the form of poetry much in mind.[58] Yet this dimension will always be present, however strong a poem's message, as Heaney intimates when he goes on to argue that poetry which 'consciously seeks to promote cultural and political change' retains the potential to 'operate with the fullest artistic integrity', there being a tacit acknowledgement that the one does not preclude the other, that a poem's form can only be a complicating factor.[59]

This emphasis anticipates the key revelation which the lectures are concerned to articulate, as Heaney replaces his earlier understanding of opposition with a new belief in equivalence. 'Its projections and inventions should be a match for the complex reality which surrounds it and out of which it is generated', he suggests of poetry, such a 'match' occurring when 'the co-ordinates of the imagined thing correspond to those of the world that we live in and endure', a definition which is later given a more personal modulation as 'the co-ordinates of the imagined thing correspond to and allow us to contemplate the complex burden of our own experience', where the movement from 'the world' to 'our own experience' concedes the subjectivity of the claim.[60] But even though Heaney provides a demonstrative reading of George Herbert's poem 'The Pulley', which he at one point describes as 'a true paradigm of the shape of things, psychologically, politically, metaphorically, and, if one wants to proceed

---

[56] Heaney, *The Redress of Poetry*, p. xiii.
[57] Heaney, *The Redress of Poetry*, 5.
[58] Heaney, *The Redress of Poetry*, 2, 5-6.
[59] Heaney, *The Redress of Poetry*, 6.
[60] Heaney, *The Redress of Poetry*, 8, 10.

that far, metaphysically',[61] this later understanding is ultimately just as problematic as the earlier one: in the same way that the boundary between 'art' and 'life' can never be surely defined, so the dimensions of 'the imagined thing' and 'the world' (and 'our own experience') can never be gauged once and for all, meaning that the detail of the correspondence must remain ambiguous. Related questions are raised by the final lecture, delivered five years later, in which Heaney's intention is not only to work his various apprehensions of redress into a final statement of broader relevance, but also to acknowledge the informing context of the political situation. Having admitted that 'the unspoken background has been a Northern Irish one', he brings the lectures to their close by attempting to transfer his understanding of poetry's doubleness into the domain of lived experience, in final acquiescence to the creative frustration which he registered in the previous book: 'I wanted to affirm that within our individual selves we can reconcile two orders of knowledge which we might call the practical and the poetic', he declares in the concluding paragraph, before advancing a further variation on 'art' and 'life'—'to affirm also that each form of knowledge redresses the other and that the frontier between them is there for the crossing.'[62]

Despite its developing interest in figures of straightness, Heaney's poetry from this period is often sceptical about the possibility of redress. The title of this final lecture ('Frontiers of Writing') recalls the earlier poem 'From the Frontier of Writing' (1987), which marks an early attempt at manifesting something of the doubleness which is the criticism's concern. The poem begins with a strong impression of situation—'The tightness and the nilness round that space | when the car stops in the road', as the speaker describes the ordeal of approaching a checkpoint at which inspecting troops are both presently interrogative and distantly observant, in echo of 'Sandstone Keepsake'. Then, in the second half, the restrictions of realism give way to a sense of imaginative release: 'And suddenly you're through, arraigned yet freed', Heaney writes, the closing lines presenting the image of 'the posted soldiers flowing and receding | like tree shadows into the polished windscreen'.[63] Discussing the poem in his essay on Heaney's 'mutable redress', Stephen James argues that such an 'escape from a site of imposed, artificial control into liberated, natural elements...is made to serve a subtle but steadfast redressive function in Heaney's verse'.[64] Yet it is important to acknowledge the hesitation in this particular instance, since the closing presence of the 'polished windscreen' anchors the imaginary within the dimensions of the real, preventing fullness of transcendence by drawing attention to the means by which the vision is created. 'From the Frontier of Writing' comes up against the limitations of the conventional lyric, then, in its attempted movement from realism to imagination, but the distanced perspective of the lines of chorus which Heaney added to *The Cure at Troy* (1990)—his translation of *Philoctetes* by Sophocles—allowed him to make some more definite statements about the power of the art. If the protagonist is at one point instructed to 'Win by fair combat.

---

[61] Heaney, *The Redress of Poetry*, 10.
[62] Heaney, *The Redress of Poetry*, 191, 203.
[63] Seamus Heaney, *The Haw Lantern* (London: Faber & Faber, 1987), 6.
[64] James, *Shades of Authority*, 1512.

But know to shun | Reprisal killings when that's done', in lines which cannot but resonate with the context of Northern Ireland (as James goes on to note),[65] then the impersonality of the chorus gives other lines a generalizing authority, in something approaching the manner of critical writing: the assertion that 'No poem or play or song | Can fully right a wrong | Inflicted and endured' concedes a limitation which goes against the argument of the lectures, yet the following lines anticipating a time when 'justice can rise up | And hope and history rhyme' maintain a belief in the medium's potential, as this expressly poetic manifestation ('rhyme') activates the figure of uprightness once again ('rise up').[66]

Heaney's translation of *Beowulf* (1999) also illustrates the poet's difficulties in working his understanding of redress into the texture of his poetry, even though the concept is a fundamental component of the world view which the medieval poem records. The word 'redress' appears only a handful of times in the translation, but the questions of doubleness which Heaney broaches in his introductory essay reveal how deeply the contours of his critical thinking have influenced his apprehension of the poem.[67] Not only does he suggest that the process of translation drew him away from the 'unmoored speech' of the contemporary poetry which he was teaching at the time, and took him 'back to the first stratum of the language', but his analysis of the poem's structure provides the evidence for an earlier claim: 'woven from two such different psychic fabrics', these being the original poet's alternating sympathy with and distance from the poem's events, *Beowulf* 'perfectly answers the early modern conception of a work of creative imagination as one in which conflicting realities find accommodation within a new order'—where such a 'conception' is tellingly similar to the closing statement of the final lecture.[68] When the poet finally succeeds in finding a way of working his understanding into his poetry, in his elegy for Ted Hughes, 'On his Work in the English Tongue' (2001), he does so from a personal perspective, speaking very much as himself—as friend to Hughes, and translator of *Beowulf*. The elegy makes reference to Yeats at the beginning of its third section. 'Passive suffering: who said it was disallowed | As a theme for poetry?' asks Heaney in quiet challenge, presenting an excerpt from the translation as countering evidence in the following section (a recasting of the 'Father's Lament').[69] He mentions another writer still in the concluding lines, as the poem strikes a balance between elegiac and literary critical modes in order to celebrate poetry itself:

        Which is, as Miłosz says,
'A dividend from ourselves,' a tribute paid
By what we have been true to. A thing allowed.

---

[65] James, *Shades of Authority*, 159.

[66] Seamus Heaney, *The Cure at Troy: A Version of Sophocles' Philoctetes* (London: Faber & Faber, 1990), 79, 77. For a related discussion see *Defending Poetry*, 148.

[67] Seamus Heaney, *Beowulf* (London: Faber & Faber, 1999), 29, 51, 77. James discusses the 'double perspectives' of Heaney's translation in political and linguistic terms (*Shades of Authority*, 160–1), while Conor McCarthy writes in *Seamus Heaney and Medieval Poetry* (Cambridge: D. S. Brewer, 2008) about its crossing of boundaries and the 'dual perspectives' of its style (109–16).

[68] Heaney, *Beowulf*, pp. xxii, xvii. Compare *Seamus Heaney and Medieval Poetry*, 109–16, where McCarthy's focus is on translation and style, rather than redress.

[69] Seamus Heaney, *Electric Light* (London: Faber & Faber, 2002), 61–3.

These lines invoke the argument of the lectures by intimating that the presence of poetry is able to provide some kind of relief, with the etymology of 'allowed' bringing together the Latin senses 'to praise' and 'to place' (*OED*, 'allow, *v*'). Heaney characterized poetry as 'a space where anything can happen' in the first of his Oxford lectures, and the essay which introduces 'Anything Can Happen' (2002), his translation from Horace's *Odes* (1, 34), goes one step further, picking up the elegy's 'true' by suggesting the 'indispensable poem' to possess 'a soothsaying force, as if it were an oracle delivered unexpectedly and irresistibly'.[70]

IV

Despite the many differences between these understandings—which have only been touched upon here—some intriguing parallels are still to be discerned. Most obviously, there are a number of shared points of reference, intimating a common hinterland to these related concerns: both poets cite Wallace Stevens as an exemplary figure of belief in the power of creative imagination, for instance, as both poets invoke the work of Simone Weil, one of the great ethical writers of the twentieth century. Some more suggestive correspondences might also be ventured, such as the similarity between Heaney's use of redress (to mean upright) and Hill's definition of 'assent' in the inaugural lecture, which originates in his reading of a letter by Gerard Manley Hopkins. 'What the one says the other assents to by the roots and upwards from the level of the sea,' Hopkins writes of the speech of two gardeners. 'To assent by the roots is to become an entire embodiment of *assent*', Hill goes on to argue, furthering the notion when he quotes P. T. Forsyth: 'The man who does not rise to be a person...knows nothing of responsibility, of guilt, of sin.'[71] Heaney's understanding does not depend upon the language of theology, but the importance of 'Station Island' as a poetic turning point gestures towards the possibility of a link between the lasting influence of his Catholic upbringing and his conception of redress: 'the idea that your own travails could earn grace for others...was appealing', he recalled in interview, introducing his response by alluding to Yeats ('passive suffering') and concluding it by making reference to Hopkins. Heaney is not thinking about poetry here, but related ideas are at work when he describes the 'good' which it does as a 'kind of intervention'.[72]

---

[70] Heaney, *The Redress of Poetry*, 11; *Anything Can Happen: A Poem and Essay with Translations in Support of Art for Amnesty* (Dublin: Townhouse, 2004), 13.

[71] Hill, *Collected Critical Writings*, 103 (quoting Hopkins), 105, 19 (quoting Forsyth). 'He may "rise to be a person" in a society of aggregates and items', Hill suggests of the poet in the lecture's closing lines (19).

[72] Dennis O'Driscoll, *Stepping Stones: Interviews with Seamus Heaney* (London: Faber & Faber, 2008), 39, 388. 'Although the dominant connotations of the term "redress" are judicial or political, Heaney's use of the word frequently shades into the theological', writes Stephen James, citing an earlier instance of 'intervention' in Heaney's critical writing (*Shades of Authority*, 147–8).

Indeed, both poets are concerned to emphasize the reality of poetry's form. 'Taking poetry seriously can also mean taking poetry seriously as an authority', suggests Peter McDonald, who points out that 'poets have written, and often still write, poetry which has more resource, complexity, and imagination than they could themselves demonstrate as men and women', a statement which acknowledges that the creative endeavour can lead to insights as lasting as those gained from the different challenges presented by life—for reader as well as for writer.[73] Such an acknowledgement helps to cast fresh light on the ideas of equivalence which are to be found in both of these understandings, even if one strength of poetry's authority is its resistance to total definition. Hill's understanding of atonement can be seen to anticipate the focus on 'alienation' in his later thought, as Williams has suggested:[74] our relation to the poem is 'like being brushed past, or aside, by an alien being', Hill writes in 'A Postscript on Modernist Poetics', arguing in a later public conversation (with reference to R. P. Blackmur) that 'a true poem has got to end by adding to the stock of available reality', the result being that 'everything else in one's comprehension has to adjust itself slightly around it'.[75] Heaney makes a comparable suggestion when he is introducing his reading of 'The Man and the Echo' and the limitations which, in his argument, the poem transcends. 'When language does more than enough, as it does in all achieved poetry, it opts for the condition of overlife, and rebels at limit', he suggests, turning his attention to content—'the vision of reality which poetry offers should be transformative'—before returning to the originating poet: 'The truly creative writer, by interposing his or her perception and expression, will transfigure the conditions' and effect a fundamental change, the world being 'augmented' by such a 'reading' of it.[76]

The first of the definitions for 'value' given by the *OED* casts further light on these related ideas: 'Worth or quality as measured by a standard of equivalence'.[77] At the most general level, the weight of the poetic record, with its accumulation of individual expression, provides a lasting counterpoint to the dominant discourses of the day, testing the sureties of our being in language. More particularly, poets can approach their art with specifically reparative aims in mind, as demonstrated by Hill's elegies for the dead and Heaney's expressly political poems. But to discuss questions of reparation, atonement, and redress in anything other than a specific context will always be difficult, because these are fundamentally questions of reception, having to do with the presence of a

---

[73] McDonald, *Serious Poetry*, 5. As he goes on to write, 'the unique property of a real poem is its capacity to work against the grain of opinion, or in complex and guarded relation to it, so as to create an original order in which language overpowers the "weight of judgement or opinion" through an individual (and essentially unrepeatable) form'.

[74] Williams, *Defending Poetry*, 162–3, 214, 215.

[75] Hill, *Collected Critical Writings*, 566; Hill's conversation is quoted in Pennington and Sperling (eds.), *Geoffrey Hill and His Contexts*, 2–3. Compare T. S. Eliot: 'The existing order is complete before the new work arrives; for order to persist after the supervention of novelty, the *whole* order must be, if ever so slightly, altered'—'Tradition and the Individual Talent', *The Sacred Wood: Essays on Poetry and Criticism* (London: Methuen, 1920; repr. 1960), 50.

[76] Heaney, *The Redress of Poetry*, 158–9.

[77] Compare *Defending Poetry*, 165.

second party. Accordingly, what these critical understandings have in common is their subjectivity: we may be able to accept the premises and the nuances of these arguments, but when we read a poem by Yeats, for instance, or a poem by Auden, it is unlikely that such questions of atonement or redress will be much on our mind—unless, of course, these are questions which the poem or its context raise. With the same caveat, these questions may not be much on our mind even when we are reading a poem by Geoffrey Hill or by Seamus Heaney, unless we are reading the creative work in the light of the critical understanding. To be sure, whatever poetry makes happen, both in terms of particular meaning and metapoetic consequence, will always be deeply implicate with questions of interpretation, which only the second party of the reader can decide—and yet this means that poetry can participate in the work of reparation, atonement, and redress in all sorts of unpredictable ways.

Select Bibliography

Austin, J. L., *How To Do Things With Words* (2nd edn.), ed. J. O. Urmson and Marina Sbisà (Oxford: Oxford University Press, 1976).
Corcoran, Neil, *Seamus Heaney* (London: Faber and Faber, 1986).
Edwards, Michael, 'Believing in Poetry', *Literature & Theology*, 25/1 (Mar. 2011), 10–19.
Eagleton, Terry, *The Ideology of the Aesthetic* (Oxford: Blackwell, 1990).
Eliot, T. S., 'Tradition and the Individual Talent', *The Sacred Wood: Essays on Poetry and Criticism* (London: Methuen, 1920; repr. 1960).
Haffenden, John, *Viewpoints: Poets in Conversation with John Haffenden* (London: Faber & Faber, 1981).
Heaney, Seamus, *Station Island* (London: Faber & Faber, 1984).
Heaney, Seamus, 'Envies and Identifications: Dante and the Modern Poet', *Irish University Review*, 15/1 (Spring 1985), 5–19.
Heaney, Seamus, *The Haw Lantern* (London: Faber & Faber, 1987).
Heaney, Seamus, *The Government of the Tongue* (London: Faber & Faber, 1988).
Heaney, Seamus, *The Cure at Troy: A Version of Sophocles' Philoctetes* (London: Faber & Faber, 1990).
Heaney, Seamus, *Crediting Poetry* (Oldcastle: The Gallery Press, 1995).
Heaney, Seamus, *The Redress of Poetry: Oxford Lectures* (London: Faber & Faber, 1995).
Heaney, Seamus, *Beowulf* (London: Faber & Faber, 1999).
Heaney, Seamus, *Electric Light* (London: Faber & Faber, 2002).
Hill, Geoffrey, *For the Unfallen: Poems 1952–1958* (London: André Deutsch, 1959).
Hill, Geoffrey, *King Log* (London: André Deutsch, 1968).
Hill, Geoffrey, *The Triumph of Love* (London: Penguin Books, 1998).
Hill, Geoffrey, *Speech! Speech!* (London: Penguin Books, 2001).
Hill, Geoffrey, *The Orchards of Syon* (London: Penguin Books, 2002).
Hill, Geoffrey, *Scenes from Comus* (London: Penguin Books, 2005).
Hill, Geoffrey, *A Treatise of Civil Power* (London: Penguin Books, 2007).
Hill, Geoffrey, *Collected Critical Writings*, ed. Kenneth Haynes (Oxford: Oxford University Press, 2008).
Hill, Geoffrey, 'Civil Polity and the Confessing State', *Warwick Review*, 2 (2008), 7–20.

James, Stephen, *Shades of Authority: The Poetry of Lowell, Hill and Heaney* (Liverpool: Liverpool University Press, 2007).

Kendall, Tim, 'An Enormous Yes? *The Redress of Poetry*', in Curtis (ed.), *The Art of Seamus Heaney*, 229–39.

Macfarlane, Robert, 'Gravity and Grace in Geoffrey Hill', *Essays in Criticism*, 58/3 (July 2008), 237–56.

McCarthy, Conor, *Seamus Heaney and Medieval Poetry* (Cambridge: D. S. Brewer, 2008).

McDonald, Peter, *Serious Poetry: Form and Authority from Yeats to Hill* (Oxford: Oxford University Press, 2002).

Molan, Michael, 'Milton and Eliot in the Work of Geoffrey Hill', in Piers Pennington and Matthew Sperling (eds.), *Geoffrey Hill and His Contexts* (Oxford: Peter Lang, 2011), 81–105.

O'Donoghue, Bernard, 'Heaney's *ars poetica*: *The Government of the Tongue*', in Tony Curtis (ed.), *The Art of Seamus Heaney* (Bridgend: Seren, 2001), 181–90.

O'Driscoll, Dennis, *Stepping Stones: Interviews with Seamus Heaney* (London: Faber & Faber, 2008).

Ricks, Christopher, *The Force of Poetry* (Oxford: Oxford University Press, 1984).

Ricks, Christopher, *True Friendship: Geoffrey Hill, Anthony Hecht, and Robert Lowell under the Sign of Eliot and Pound* (New Haven and London: Yale University Press, 2010).

Roberts, Andrew Michael, 'Error and Mistakes in Poetry: Geoffrey Hill and Tom Raworth', *English*, 56/216 (Autumn 2007), 339–61.

Roberts, Jane, *Holbein and the Court of Henry VIII: Drawings and Miniatures from the Royal Library, Windsor Castle* (Edinburgh: National Galleries of Scotland, 1993).

Robinson, Peter, *Poetry, Poets, Readers: Making Things Happen* (Oxford: Oxford University Press, 2002).

Weil, Simone, *The Need for Roots: Prelude to a Declaration of Duties Towards Mankind*, trans. Arthur Wills (London: Routledge and Kegan Paul, 1952).

Williams, David-Antoine, *Defending Poetry: Art and Ethics in Joseph Brodsky, Seamus Heaney, and Geoffrey Hill* (Oxford: Oxford University Press, 2010).

Yeats, W. B. (ed.), *The Oxford Book of Modern Verse, 1892–1935* (Oxford: Oxford University Press, 1936).

CHAPTER 36

CONTEMPORARY POETRY AND BELIEF[1]

MICHAEL SYMMONS ROBERTS

IN an interview for *Paris Review* with Donald Hall in 1961, the great American modernist Marianne Moore was asked to explain why she saw so much common ground between the roles of poet and scientist: 'Do you think this is helpful to the modern poet?' asked Hall, adding that 'most people would consider this comparison a paradox, and assume that the poet and the scientist are opposed'. Moore's response is to set out the beginnings of an *ars poetica*:

> Do the poet and scientist not work analogously? Both are willing to waste effort. To be hard on himself is one of the main strengths of each. Each is attentive to clues, each must narrow the choice, must strive for precision. As George Grosz says, 'In art there is no place for gossip and but a small place for the satirist'. The objective is fertile procedure. Is it not? Jacob Bronowski says in the Saturday Evening Post that science is not a mere collection of discoveries, but that science is the process of discovering. In any case it's not established once and for all: it's evolving.[2]

When Moore (quoting Jacob Bronowski) speaks of poetry and science as 'a process of discovering', I take her to mean discovering something real, something true, and that whatever truth may be discoverable, and however complex and contradictory it may be, it exists and refers beyond the poem itself. This might seem obvious, but within three decades of Moore's interview, it was a commonplace in literary magazines and interviews with poets to hear a declaration (or read an implicit assumption) that there is no longer any possibility of discerning truth or meaning beyond the poem itself. The role

---

[1] This chapter draws on previous public lectures and articles by the author, including 'Poetry in a Post-Secular Age', *Poetry Review*, 98/4 (Autumn 2008), 69–75.

[2] Marianne Moore and Donald Hall, *Poets at Work*, ed. George Plimpton (Harmondsworth: Penguin Books, 1989), 98.

of the poet had shifted from truth-seeker to truth-maker. As Philip Blond outlines in his introduction to *Post-Secular Philosophy*, an essential aspect of postmodern thought 'is that now consciousness is thought to construct the phenomenal world'.[3]

This shift was, in part, a necessary corrective. When political and religious certainties are collapsing around you, how should a poet respond? One answer seemed to be to commit to nothing beyond the poem itself. Writing a poem no longer looked like a process of discovery, but a process of construction. In a world without meaning, the poem becomes its own sphere of meaning. The idea of poetry as an act of making was (and is) a necessary corrective too, a counterblast to the notion of the poem as mere self-expression. In this chapter, much of the discussion will centre on religious belief, but the collapse (and rediscovery) of the language of 'belief' in poetry extends to politics and science too, and scientific belief has been in the vanguard of the recovery.

In its effects on poetry, it is impossible to separate the collapse of religious and political certainties from the collapse of religious and political language. The Anglo-Welsh modernist poet and artist David Jones heralded the crisis in religious poetic language over fifty years ago, a crisis of dead or dying signs and symbols. Using the example of the word 'wood'—although it could just as easily be applied to blood, or water—he said:

> If the poet writes *wood*, what are the chances that the Wood of the Cross will be evoked? Should the answer be 'None', then it would seem that an impoverishment of some sort would have to be admitted. It would mean that that particular word could no longer be used with confidence to implement, to call up or to set in motion a whole world of content belonging in a special sense to the mythus of a particular culture and of concepts and realities belonging to mankind as such. This would be true irrespective of our beliefs or disbeliefs. It would remain true even if we were of the opinion that it was high time that the word *wood* should be dissociated from the mythus and concepts indicated. The arts abhor any loppings off of meanings or emptyings out, any lessening of the totality of connotation, and loss of recession and thickness through.[4]

As Jones himself pointed out, many readers in the 1950s may welcome the severing of the link between the English language and Christian iconography, but poets shouldn't. Atheist, agnostic, or believer, all should—Jones argued—feel a sense of loss when our language looks thinner. He wasn't suggesting that baptism or the Cross should be the primary reference for water or wood, but that they should keep a place among many connotations.[5]

In the notes to his epic poem *The Anathémata*, Jones describes a memory that became a touchstone in his poetic imagination. Thirty-five years before writing *The Anathémata*, he was staying in the Welsh borders, at Capel Y Ffin. On Christmas Eve, the water supply

---

[3] Philip Blond (ed.), *Post-Secular Philosophy: Between Philosophy and Theology* (London: Routledge, 1998), 9.
[4] David Jones, Preface to *The Anathémata* (London: Faber & Faber, 1952), 23–4.
[5] Jones, Preface to *The Anathémata*, 25.

to the house suddenly ran dry, and Jones and the writer René Hague set off to find the source of the mountain-stream that gave the house its water. Right at the source, they found that the stream had been deliberately blocked and diverted, so they *freed the waters*, and followed those waters back to Capel Y Ffin for Christmas Day. This image of 'freeing the waters' continued to resonate with Jones, and recurs in his work. It comes in *The Anathémata* as part of a passage rich in water metaphors, full of rivers and fountains and oceans, a passage which culminates in Christ's cry from the Cross, as set down in the Good Friday liturgy—'Sitio'—'I thirst'. In the preface to his epic poem, Jones writes: 'Water is called the *matter* of the Sacrament of Baptism. Is two of hydrogen and one of oxygen that *matter*? I suppose so. But a knowledge of the chemical components of this material water should, normally, or if you prefer it, ideally, provide us with further, deeper, and more exciting significances vis-à-vis the sacrament of water, and also, for us islanders, whose history is so much of water, with other significances relative to that.'[6] Jones believed that the artist, the poet, should be a maker of signs. Writing in 1951, he had seen the early stages of what Seamus Heaney has since called 'the big lightening, the emptying out' of our religious language, but even he may have been shocked by its pace. He saw the English language littered with dying signs and symbols, specifically the signs and symbols associated with our Judaeo-Christian past. The resultant impoverishment hasn't just affected poets, but readers too, and this has been borne out by the now common struggles of English teachers in schools and universities to provide the biblical and historical literacy necessary to make sense of Milton, Donne, Herbert, T. S. Eliot, and others.

But if Jones was right about the loss of a shared symbolic language, he may have been surprised by other aspects of these interesting times. For a start, this debate should be over. The Enlightenment project was meant to see off religion by now, but instead, many sociologists argue that it is secularism that's in retreat. Worldwide, the case is clear-cut. Christianity and Islam are growing very rapidly throughout the developing world, and a recent report placed the numbers of atheists worldwide at 3 per cent and falling. In Western Europe, it's more complicated. Most of our churches are as empty as ever, but in the last few years, a number of philosophers and sociologists (led by German philosopher Jurgen Habermas) have coined the term 'post-secular' to describe our current condition. People in the West may not be returning to organized religion, but they seem to be losing faith in organized secularism too. Was Jones half right? Is our language drained of religious significance, but our yearning for the metaphysical or religious as strong as ever? Has our language become more secular than we are?

In his book of essays, *Post-Secular Philosophy*, Philip Blond suggests that 'secular minds are only now beginning to perceive that all is not as it should be, that what was promised to them—self-liberation through the limitation of the world to human faculties—might after all be a form of self-mutilation'.[7] If he is right, then we might expect all kinds of writers—not just card-carrying religious believers—to be reflecting this dissatisfaction with a secular world-view. In his 2007 book *Partial Faiths*, John A. McClure

---

[6] Jones, Preface to *The Anathémata*, 16–17.
[7] Blond (ed.), *Post-Secular Philosophy: Between Philosophy and Theology*, 1.

examines the work of major American novelists including Don DeLillo, Thomas Pynchon, and Toni Morrison, and concludes that their work can fruitfully be read as a 'postsecular project'. McClure argues that certain common features can be traced across the field of post-secular texts:

> The partial conversions of postsecular fiction do not deliver those who experience them from worldliness into well-ordered systems of religious belief. Instead, they tend to strand those who experience them in the ideologically mixed and confusing middle zones of the conventional conversion narrative, zones through which the conventional protagonist passes with all possible haste, on his way to a domain of secure religious dwelling. And yet the postsecular characters deposited in these zones do not seem particularly uncomfortable there nor particularly impatient to move on to some more fully elaborated form of belief and practice.[8]

So where does this leave contemporary poets who want to explore or reflect something of this area of human struggle and experience we used to call 'religious'? Well, there's clearly a terminology problem. T. S. Eliot said he disliked the term 'religious poetry', pointing out that 'to many people religious poetry sounds like a variety of minor poetry. It seems to imply that the religious poet is not a poet who is treating the whole subject of poetry in a religious spirit, but... is leaving out what men and women consider their major passions, and thereby confessing to his or her ignorance of them.'[9] 'Sacred poetry' sounds untouchable, devotional, and precious. Metaphysical doesn't really work either. As a branch of philosophy, metaphysics is the study of reality from first principles, but (unlike poetry) it often isn't grounded in empiricism. And its association with a group of seventeenth-century poets carries connotations of style and form as well as subject. Perhaps this problem of terminology is part of the reason there haven't been many anthologies in this territory in recent years. Donald Davie tackled the problem with *The Oxford Book of Christian Verse*, but admitted in the introduction that 'we may as well admit that the very concept "Christian verse" is one that won't stand up to close scrutiny'.[10] R. S. Thomas had previously taken a different tack with *The Penguin Book of Religious Verse*, in which he said he was 'roughly defining religion as embracing an experience of ultimate reality, and poetry as the imaginative presentation of such'.[11]

But surely there are great opportunities here too. In the mid-1990s, working as a documentary film-maker for the BBC, I made a film about the (then incomplete) mapping of the human genome. So new was this science at the time that the metaphors, the whole descriptive language, were awaiting formulation. What did this sequence, represented by the letters ACTG, tell us about ourselves? Apart from attaching the word 'map' to

---

[8] John A. McClure, *Partial Faiths: Postsecular Fiction in the Age of Pynchon and Morrison* (Athens, Ga.: University of Georgia Press, 2007), 4.

[9] T. S. Eliot, 'Religion and Literature' (1935), in *Selected Prose* (Harmondsworth: Penguin Books, 1953), 34.

[10] Donald Davie (ed.), *The New Oxford Book of Christian Verse* (Oxford: Oxford University Press, 1981), p. xviii.

[11] R. S. Thomas (ed.), *The Penguin Book of Religious Verse* (Harmondsworth: Penguin Books, 1963), 9.

the process, the scientists had not settled on a descriptive language for all this. Some years later, when I was commissioned to write a poem about genetics for the anthology *Wild Reckoning*,[12] I went back to Sir John Sulston (who led the team that mapped the genome), and he still felt there was need for—and a lack of—a fuller dialogue with the culture (in particular the arts and media), a dialogue that would offer new ways of talking about this new science.

The collapse of religious language as any kind of common currency leaves us in a similar position with religious faith, ideas, and experiences now. The opportunity is there to find new terms, new metaphors. Of course, that opportunity was always there for poets, but now, when the old symbols are losing their purchase, the field is wide open. Poetry, like religion, begins and ends in silence. And poetry, like religion, must attempt to enter the great silence, the ineffable, or it is nothing more than 'verse'. It calls to mind Wittgenstein's insistence that he could imagine (and would like to see) a religion without doctrinal formulations, 'in which there is thus no talking'. As Fergus Kerr points out in his essay 'Metaphysics and Magic: Wittgenstein's Kink', there is plenty of evidence that Wittgenstein was as negative about religious and theological language as he was positive about the beliefs it sought to express: 'It is not just that he deplored philosophical attempts to provide rational foundations for religion—he clearly believed that *all* theorizing, and thus all theology and even doctrine, only undermined the religious feelings and practices for which he evidently had unbounded respect.'[13] The challenge for a contemporary 'poetry of belief' is to become the sort of language that opens on to the metaphysical, rather than shutting it down.

In May 1944, the young Dietrich Bonhoeffer wrote a heartbreaking letter, under the title 'Thoughts on the Day of the Baptism of Dietrich Wilhelm Rudiger', from Tegel Prison, Berlin. Less than a year later, he was murdered by the Nazis for his role in a failed plot to assassinate Adolf Hitler. In this letter to the first of a new generation of his family, Bonhoeffer expresses something of his growing sense that Christianity itself is entering a new stage, in need of a new response from the next generation:

> By the time you have grown up, the church's form will have changed greatly [...] It is not for us to prophesy the day (though the day will come) when men will once more be called so to utter the word of God that the world will be changed and renewed by it. It will be a new language, perhaps quite non-religious, but liberating and redeeming—as was Jesus's language; it will shock people and yet overcome them by its power.[14]

---

[12] 'To John Donne', in John Burnside and Maurice Riordan (eds.), *Wild Reckoning* (Lisbon: Calouste Gulbenkian Foundation, 2004).

[13] Fergus Kerr, 'Metaphysics and Magic: Wittgenstein's Kink', in Blond (ed.), *Post-Secular Philosophy*, 255.

[14] Dietrich Bonhoeffer, *Letters and Papers from Prison* (New York: Touchstone, 1953), 300.

Is Bonhoeffer's 'new language' possible in contemporary poetry? And, at the point where belief becomes politically active, will this 'new language' make any difference to the world into which it is spoken?

A few years ago, a hall of mirrors felt like an interesting place to be as a writer. Postmodernism had encouraged us to see the language as a vast field of signs pointing only at each other. This was a liberation from 'grand narratives' or 'meta-narratives' like religion or politics which claimed to explore ultimate values, truth claims, meaning. In their introduction to *The New Poetry* in the early nineties, its editors asserted that much of the 'new poetry' is about 'a realization that ideas of meaning, truth and understanding are in themselves fictions determined by the rhetorical forms and linguistic terms used to express them'.[15]

Again, the ground has shifted in the last decade. Politically and financially the world is a volatile place, and relativism will no longer do. Above all, perhaps, our exit from the hall of mirrors is driven by ecological concerns. Relativism simply collapses in this context. The climate is changing or it isn't. Species are dying out or they aren't. Humanity is responsible for this or we aren't. There's no possibility of global warming being true for you but not for me. The future of the planet—now such a powerful and urgent theme for many poets and critics—is nothing if not a grand narrative complete with meaning, truth claims, and ultimate values at stake. As Christian Wiman wrote in *Poetry Review*: 'You have to believe that poetry has some reach into reality itself—or you have to go silent.'[16]

One of the concerns about 'grand narratives' of any sort is that the poetry may be imprisoned or used by them. The myth of the uncommitted artist (free-spirited and unshackled from the burdens of political, religious, or personal commitment) was always an empty one. To be alive in the world is to have beliefs and commitments, and these extend at some level to politics and theology. But this myth has left us with a terror of the imagination in thrall to a belief. Surely this could limit the scope of the work, may even reduce it to a thin preconceived outworking of doctrine or argument? Yet this fear was always unfounded. The counter-examples are obvious, including great twentieth-century innovators such as Eliot, Jones, Auden, Moore, Berryman, and Bunting. In fact, the evidence points in the opposite direction. Many of the quantum leaps, the formal and thematic revolutions in twentieth-century poetry, came from poets working with (and attempting to explore) powerful religious and political belief systems. And there's an equivalent list in the other arts too (music's list would include Stravinsky, Schoenberg, Messiaen, Poulenc, Gubaidulina, Schnittke, Penderecki). The relationship between creative freedom and religious belief is far from limiting. T. S. Eliot famously said of William Blake that since he worked within no tradition, he had to invent a religion and world view as well as to write original poetry.[17] Eliot disapproved

---

[15] Michael Hulse, David Kennedy, and David Morley (eds.), *The New Poetry* (Newcastle upon Tyne: Bloodaxe Books, 1993), 24.

[16] Christian Wiman, 'Some Notes on Poetry and Religion', *Poetry Review*, 97/2 (Summer 2007), 73.

[17] T. S. Eliot, 'On Blake' (1920), in *Selected Prose*, 171.

of this, believing that innovation was best confined to the poetry, and that that aim was best achieved by writing within a solid framework, which for him was Anglo-Catholic, Conservative, and Royalist, but could equally be Protestant Nonconformist, politically radical, and republican—closer to Basil Bunting's framework.

So, if there are opportunities for poets in this post-secular age, how are they to be seized? There are many strategies, but one is to take up William Carlos Williams's famous maxim 'no ideas but in things'. For most contemporary poets, this is second nature. A poetry rooted in the concrete detail of shared experience can certainly express something of our shared religious longings and experiences. For me, the body is this kind of common ground. And in addition to its commonality it reaches into other rich areas of our culture, including genetics and bioethics. The body feels like particularly interesting and contested ground at the moment, because as a culture we don't know if we want to worship or deny it, subdue it or preserve it for ever. Of course, truth needn't be (perhaps ultimately isn't) propositional. It may be personal, as in an encounter with a personal God, mirrored in our relationships with each other. This means that love poetry, erotic poetry, and poetry that addresses the rifts and fractures in those relationships can also be a response to 'the religious'. In Christian theological terms, the 'concrete' is also the 'incarnational', and as such a proper place to engage with ultimate values.

Science is also rich territory for post-secular poetry. Far from being opposites, science and religion are at heart (as Marianne Moore argued) both concerned with truth and falsehood, both are grounded in narratives, and both search for meaning and purpose in the world. Both are also constantly shifting and contested. Above all, perhaps, science can—like theology—tell us extraordinary and moving things about ourselves. Some recent thinking in genetics attempts to explain the apparent difference between the human genome and that of apparently less developed and intelligent animals. Not only is our genome small in comparison, but various parts of it also appear to be inactive in us, but active in other creatures. Shouldn't the most complex and intelligent creatures have the most complex genome? It seems not. And this opens the door to a new story of our evolution as a series of genetic 'switchings off'. If our evolutionary ancestors were rooted to the earth and the seasons by the power of their genetic instincts, then what happens when you no longer have the instinct to build a particular shelter in a particular landscape at a particular time of year? A sudden freedom, mixed with a sense of loss and anxiety? Is this the source of humanity's abiding 'homelessness'? A loss of instinctive connection with the earth? If so, then surely it is also the source of our creativity. It calls to mind St Paul's words about the glorious (and terrifying) liberty of the children of God.

Science in poetry comes with its own concerns too. Science shifts. But even disproved scientific ideas can be profound, and true to elements of human experience in the context of a poem, as John Donne's poems continue to demonstrate. Needless to say, there are many other areas of concrete shared experience. One of the most fertile and urgent is the poetry of place, dwelling, and home—opening as it does onto our current ecological concerns. This concern with place has been a central part of British and Irish poetry for decades, and continues in the work of poets as diverse as Seamus Heaney, Alice Oswald, and John Burnside.

But William Carlos Williams can't have it all his own way. Another timely and powerful approach is to risk a greater reach, bigger statements, so there has never been a better time to ignore the workshop cliché 'avoid abstractions'. Rather than avoid them, reach for them and renew them, or change their terms of reference. Some of the more abstruse bits of doctrine can offer a language or image with rich potential for reinvention and retelling. Take the ascension. According to the New Testament, Jesus came back to his disciples after the resurrection, then (on the Mount of Olives, according to tradition), he withdrew into heaven, witnessed by his disciples. Exactly what they witnessed is not described, so it has remained a mysterious doctrine, allowing space for artists to make it new. Auden, in his poem 'Ascension Day 1964'[18] doesn't attempt to tell the original story, but fixes on its themes of departure and absence.

Will as we may to believe
That parting should be
And that a promise

Of future joy can be kept,
Absence remains
The factual loss it is:

The Welsh-language poet Saunders Lewis in his poem translated as 'Ascension Thursday'[19] describes the natural world on Ascension Day, in May, playing out the ascension on the hills outside a South Wales council estate: 'Look at them, at the gold of the broom and laburnum | And the glowing surplice on the hawthorn's shoulders'.

Denise Levertov, in her poem 'Ascension',[20] takes on the physicality of the original story, describing it with the language of science, theology, and psychology, her poem's staggered layout on the page evoking the sheer taut effort of the act:

Matter reanimate
    now must relinquish
itself, its
    human cells,
        molecules, five
senses, linear
    vision endured
        as Man

In a recent essay, the theologian and archbishop Rowan Williams spoke about two possible strategies by which contemporary poets can write about religious faith and experience. The first is—as many poets have attempted—to try to think or feel your way into someone else's religious sensibility. This reflects the growing influence of non-Christian

---

[18] W. H. Auden, *Collected Poems* (London: Faber & Faber, 1976), 743.
[19] Saunders Lewis, in *Twentieth Century Welsh Poems*, trans. Joseph Clancy (Llandysul: Gomer, 1982), 87.
[20] Denise Levertov, *A Door in the Hive* (Newcastle upon Tyne: Bloodaxe Books, 1993), 207.

religious traditions on poetry in English. The second, and to me the most fascinating, is the attempt to write into and around the gaps, the fractures, the silence. This will be a poetry in which the breakages and shortfalls of the language are significant. They will not always, indeed, and perhaps only rarely be about religious subject matter, but they will be written in an awareness of silence and tension. As Williams puts it: 'The articulation of that tension reveals the gap, the pulse, the rhythm.'[21] But in a parched poetic culture, how can the metaphysical, the theological, and the mystical be expressed or even approached? The most widely acceptable term at the moment seems to be 'spiritual'. Poetry can be 'spiritual' without being seen as 'religious'. Indeed, many would argue that *all* poetry is or should be spiritual. What is 'spiritual poetry'?

The Scottish composer James MacMillan—with whom I have been working as a librettist and collaborator for the last ten years—has written about the current dominance of 'spiritual' music on the classical scene. He is often grouped with John Tavener, Henryk Gorecki, and Arvo Part—all overtly Christian composers, all commissioned and performed by orchestras across the world, all at the height of their reputation. Does this mean that music is less hostile to the 'religious' than poetry? Less parched even? Well, it doesn't take much listening to John Tavener's music to realize that his central vision, the icon of his music, if you like, is that of Christ risen, ascended, glorified. A Russian Orthodox convert, he dislikes Western Christianity's focus (as he sees it) on the Cross. Tavener, like Part and Gorecki, has in his music explicitly turned his back on conflict, drama, suffering, on fallen-ness. One of the most striking aspects of James MacMillan's music is that the whole story is there, the whole drama. Christ could not have risen if he had not been crucified first. The battle is ultimately won, but it continues all around us. Truly religious art, truly Christian art—whether music or poetry—must surely live and draw creative breath from that tension, that struggle, that completeness in the midst of incompleteness. Spiritual music, like spiritual poetry, has come to mean a kind of one-dimensional heightened or transcendent experience without any sense of sacrifice or conflict. Even though it is often very accomplished and very beautiful, it has come to mean a flight from reality, an escape from the darkness. Spiritual poetry is a term almost entirely stripped of meaning.

So here I'm returning to the central question, to use Eliot's definition—how can a contemporary poet 'treat the whole subject of poetry in a religious spirit'? The philosopher John Milbank argues that 'Poetry is not fiction, but the most intense of real interventions'.[22] He elaborates that 'Of its essence, poetry makes, but it makes only to see further, and to establish something real in the world: real, because it further manifests the ideal and abiding. In this context it can be seen that its unavoidable detour via fiction is paradoxically a sign of its necessary humility: it must, in part, conjecture, since it cannot fully see and create in one simple intuition, like God himself.'[23]

---

[21] Rowan Williams, in public lecture at Manchester University, 1999.
[22] John Milbank, Introduction to *The Mercurial Wood* (Salzburg: University of Salzburg Press, 1997), p. xii.
[23] Milbank, Introduction to *The Mercurial Wood*, p. xiii.

I'm presuming that he means good poetry, or real poetry, or poetry that works. To borrow a word from another philosopher, Catherine Pickstock, it is possible to look at poems—and that movement or dynamic within poems—as 'liturgies'.[24] Pickstock uses the word liturgy to analyse our secular culture. She argues that secularism is not built on reason (as is often claimed), but is sustained by myths and rituals that alone secure a substantive emptiness. Just as there were once all-encompassing daily rituals that inculcated a sense of transcendence, so now there are equally all-encompassing rituals that inculcate a sense of a world without mystery, closed in upon itself. Thus, for Pickstock, the central task of philosophical theology becomes one of exposing and decoding these secular myths and rituals. Poems too are ritualistic, not read like most prose to follow a story or glean information. Poetry is incantatory, thrives on repetition, and is best learnt by heart. If, in this sense, poems too are liturgies, or parts of greater liturgies, then they can be liturgies of emptiness and banality, or liturgies of profundity, truth and meaning. Our choice is not between a seemingly narrow religious poetry or a postmodern writing free from cultural constraints and assumptions. Our choice is which liturgies we choose.

The Australian poet Les Murray has spoken of the defining characteristic of real, whole poetry as 'presence'. Perhaps this is another way of describing John Milbank's 'something real in the world: real, because it further manifests the ideal and abiding'.[25] For Murray, as for Milbank, this reality, this presence, is fundamentally theological. For Murray in particular, it has a sacramental sense, as a Catholic poet who believes in the real presence at the heart of the Mass. But if real poems are 'epiphanies'—a word now regularly used by secular critics to describe what poems can do—then they need to be hard-earned epiphanies.

David Jones, who had so acutely described the crisis of religious language in poetry almost half a century ago, did attempt to mark out a way forward too. As a poet, it was natural for him to look for this way forward by burrowing deep into the roots of the language itself. In an essay called 'Art and Sacrament', he said:

> I understand that more than one opinion has prevailed with regard to the etymology of the word *religio*, but a commonly accepted view is that a binding of some sort is indicated. The same root is in 'ligament', a binding which supports an organ and assures that organ its freedom of use as part of a body. And it is in this sense that I here use the word 'religious'. It refers to a binding, a securing. Like the ligament, it secures a freedom to function. The binding makes possible the freedom. Cut the ligament and there is atrophy—corpse rather than corpus. If this is true, then the word religion makes no sense unless we presuppose a freedom of some sort.[26]

If David Jones is right, then that image of the free-spirited and uncommitted artist is, and always has been, an illusion. Freedom is not absence. When I think of Jones's 'binding to make free', I think of a composer like Olivier Messiaen, whose technical and imaginative

---

[24] Catherine Pickstock, *After Writing: On the Liturgical Consummation of Philosophy* (Oxford: Blackwells, 1998).
[25] Milbank, Introduction to *The Mercurial Wood*, p. xiii.
[26] David Jones, 'Art and Sacrament', in *Epoch and Artist* (London: Faber & Faber, 1959), 158.

virtuosity underlie much of contemporary classical music—inspiring pupils such as Pierre Boulez. But Messiaen is a problem for the likes of Boulez, because his expansive creativity arose out of a very orthodox Christian faith. Postmodernist music critics try to cope with Messiaen by separating his music from his faith, which they regard as a bizarre personal idiosyncrasy. The Welsh poet Waldo Williams described his religion and his native language (he believed the two to be inextricably linked) as 'a great hall | between narrow walls'.[27] In other words, as with Messiaen, it was a radical freedom won through constraint, a 'binding to make free'.

And if religious poetry is a radical and liberating act, then how much more radical, and how much more liberating, is praise poetry. Those religious poets in the late twentieth century who found praise hard to write—great religious poets like John Berryman—have still found material in the often-frustrated desire to praise, the friction between presence and absence, praise and despair. This remains essential territory for many contemporary poets writing in English, including Geoffrey Hill, Kevin Hart, and Fiona Sampson. The leading Welsh-language poet Bobi Jones is a convert to that language from a Cardiff English-speaking family. He is also a convert to Calvinism. Both put him in the margins of contemporary Western culture, yet he has written a substantial body of work that makes clear his commitment to praise. In his own words: 'Praise continues, even at the deepest level, but it is praise under siege.'[28] In this Jones is by no means alone. The praise tradition in Welsh poetry is strong and deep-rooted. But the comparison with a literary tradition so close geographically, yet so utterly foreign to English is striking. A poem like Jones's love poem 'Shadow' seems—even in English translation—to come from a markedly different sensibility:

Beneath self-love consecration rises on the fruit that comes forth
Full are the grains: blithe of skin: the seed is wondrous.
Near the bank I struggle upon my knees to sip
Your miracle that bears fruit beneath a shadow.

In Bobi Jones's case,[29] praise is not so much a choice as a religious duty. As a Calvinist, the cultural mandate given to man by God in Genesis emphasizes man's purposeful activity on earth, to replenish and fructify it, but above all to praise, serve, and enjoy God for ever. That a contemporary poet might try to fulfil such a commandment is, depending on your personal beliefs, either crazy or revolutionary. It is certainly no longer a conformist choice. Bobi Jones himself, writing about his formation as a poet, has written about the society around him, and the choices he faced:

> Obviously, the aimlessness could not just be avoided: one could not flee the wilful incomprehensibility or the brainwashing onslaught on order and significant

---

[27] Waldo Williams, quoted in translation from his poem 'Pa Beth Yw Dyn' by Rowan Williams in a lecture given in New York, 2003.
[28] Bobi Jones, BBC Radio 3 interview for 'Daring the Depths' (first broadcast 1991).
[29] Bobi Jones, in *Twentieth Century Welsh Poems*, 200.

conceptualising: one could not just dump the ironic destruction of family life, the agnostic hatred of Welsh identity, and the whole artistic attempt to reflect or interpret this absurd world with over-modest fidelity. One could not go back. Indeed, my own work was something of an interpretation, but it was also an attempt to free itself without 'escape'. It was a deliberate re-orientation.[30]

'Freedom without escape', a binding to make free... Praise poetry is radical for a number of reasons—it's radical because is it is hard to write with authenticity, especially in a language so emptied of religious significance as English. It is radical because those who write it believe it is realistic. It is not merely optimistic, but as Bobi Jones expresses it, 'praise is the completest refusal I know of the absurd. And it unashamedly and pointedly has a direction'. Commenting on the plight of the religious poet writing in English, as compared to his own Welsh, he picked up on the 'fashionable dryness, which has not always been part of the tradition, and can be almost neurotic'. But Jones added that 'A dry ironic spell should not necessarily be a bad thing, as long as praise is not permanently inhibited, and as long as poets are permitted once more to stand on their heads'.[31]

So, is David Jones's image of walking to the source of that stream above Capel Y Ffin to free the waters still a resonant one half a century on? I think so, not least because, however parched our culture might become, there is still water in abundance. The stream has been diverted—perhaps wilfully—but it has not dried up. In the early 1990s, the poet and critic Jeremy Hooker asked (in an essay and a Radio 3 documentary) why poets were no longer 'daring the depths'.[32] He felt that, with notable exceptions, too much British poetry had become anecdotal, lacking in ambition. Now, two decades on, more poets are 'daring the depths' again. Meta-narratives are no longer seen as necessarily a danger to poetic freedom, and the myth of the uncommitted poet has been exposed as a fallacy. Poetry may well make nothing happen, as Auden famously declared, but poets are no longer afraid to try, and the potential 'happenings' are religious, political, and scientific. Interesting times...

Select Bibliography

Auden, W. H., *Collected Poems* (London: Faber & Faber, 1976).
Blond, Philip (ed.), *Post-Secular Philosophy: Between Philosophy and Theology* (London: Routledge, 1998).
Bonhoeffer, Dietrich, *Letters and Papers from Prison* (New York: Touchstone, 1953).
Davie, Donald (ed.), *The New Oxford Book of Christian Verse* (Oxford: Oxford University Press, 1981).
Hulse, Michael, Kennedy, David, and Morley, David (eds.), *The New Poetry* (Newcastle upon Tyne: Bloodaxe Books, 1993).
Jones, David, Preface to *The Anathémata* (London: Faber & Faber, 1952).

---

[30] Bobi Jones, 'Daring the Depths'.
[31] Jones, 'Daring the Depths'.
[32] Jeremy Hooker, BBC Radio 3 feature 'Daring the Depths' (first broadcast 1991).

Levertov, Denise, *A Door in the Hive* (Newcastle upon Tyne: Bloodaxe Books, 1993).

McClure, John A., *Partial Faiths: Postsecular Fiction in the Age of Pynchon and Morrison* (Athens, Ga.: University of Georgia Press, 2007).

Pickstock, Catherine, *After Writing: On the Liturgical Consummation of Philosophy* (Oxford: Blackwells, 1998).

Thomas, R. S. (ed.), *The Penguin Book of Religious Verse* (Harmondsworth: Penguin Books, 1963).

Wiman, Christian, 'Some Notes on Poetry and Religion', *Poetry Review*, 97/2 (Summer 2007), 73.

CHAPTER 37

THE LONELINESS OF THE LONG-DISTANCE POET

ANDREA BRADY

For poets writing in the 1970s and 1980s, the first-person pronouns were awkward. The sources of this discomfiture are many, and can only be sketched out here. They include theoretical developments: the death of the author, the formation of the subject by power, or the arbitrary nature of the linguistic sign. These ideas forced poets to re-evaluate the poetic representation of subjectivity, and the relationship between the author and the text. For many of the poets I discuss in this essay, challenges by structuralist and post-structuralist theory to notions of authenticity, communication, and personal feeling or perception were exciting, even liberating. But these challenges also demanded new textual strategies, combined with a vigilant scrutiny of the personal. Veronica Forrest-Thomson, for example, was deeply influenced by the so-called 'linguistic turn' in analytic philosophy, and regularly cited Ludwig Wittgenstein in her poems. Denise Riley's extensive philosophical writings draw on such disparate sources as Volosinov's assertion of the social nature of the sign, Lacan's description of the unconscious as being structured like a language, Althusser's theory of interpellation, and Deleuze's depiction of a polyphonic subjectivity, though she also reaches further back, finding in Hegel as well as the ancient myth of Narcissus an imperative to question the solidity of the 'I'. John Wilkinson's representation of subjectivity has been developed through psychoanalytic accounts of the psyche; his thinking about the relation between inner and outer realities is particularly indebted to the object relations school. For the other poets discussed here, including Douglas Oliver and John James, the debt to theory is less explicit, but the challenge is the same: to make poetry out of the subject's relation to its social, economic, and political formation, poems which reflect the brutal realities of that relation but also attempt to sketch out an escape route.

But more potent than academic developments such as deconstruction were the radical measures taken by the Right to deconstruct the welfare state. Neo-liberalist attacks on class solidarities in the late 1970s and 1980s transformed the subject of politics into an individual consumer. David Harvey articulates the view held by many leftist critics of late twentieth-century capitalism when he asserts that 'the narcissistic exploration of self, sexuality, and identity became the leitmotif of bourgeois urban culture'.[1] Poets who valued their Romantic inheritance and wished to explore the perceptions and archaeology of the self were also included in a wider cultural indulgence of the self that was used to fuel commodity capitalism in the post-industrial West. At the same time, the potential to identify with the masses—or to work for the good of a collective which surpassed the private needs of the individual—was being attacked from the Right and impeded by the ineptitudes of the Left. In the wake of the abortive revolutionary movements of 1968, and the fall of the Labour government following the 1978 'winter of discontent' (a crisis produced by stagflation, strikes by public sector unions, unemployment, and austerity measures imposed by the International Monetary Fund (IMF)), there was no viable political party with which left-leaning poets could identify. Coming to power in 1979, Margaret Thatcher led an assault on collectivism, demolishing trade unions, privatizing public assets, and undermining local authorities (most notably the Greater London Council) populated by leftist politicians. In a 1987 interview, Thatcher famously asserted that 'who is society? There is no such thing! There are individual men and women and there are families and no government can do anything except through people and people look to themselves first'.[2] Her politics and rhetoric of radical individualism appalled many poets, including Oliver, who portrayed Thatcher in *The Infant and the Pearl* (1985) as a ghostly televisual projection, her face a screen for traditional Tory assaults on 'the idle, the dull, the deprived, the drunks'.[3] She was also condemned by Ken Edwards, who described Thatcher's use of the royal 'we' as an expression of her will to power. Writing in 1991, Edwards identified 'a lack and a need' poised 'between the inauthentic, arrogated "we", on the one hand, and the flight from personal pronouns (singular to plural to impersonal), on the other'. This lack and need could be satisfied by accepting and working through 'the self', confronting 'its plural form, starting out of the fabric of contingency'.[4] For Edwards, the personal can be maintained as a site of ethical resistance to power—of authenticity—only when the contingent or provisional nature of the self (I) and the group (we) is acknowledged.

Many poets came to believe that the 'we' was an imperious and arrogant form, used to assert dominance in a variety of discourses, including colonialism, political conservatism, patriarchy, and capitalism. Denise Riley dreamed of falling from 'Anglo-Catholic clouds of drifting *we*'s high tones of feeling down | to microscopic horror':[5] the regal 'we' of a poetics of deep cultural assurance came to seem dogmatic or hieratic, as the

---

[1] David Harvey, *A Brief History of Neoliberalism* (Oxford: Oxford University Press, 2007), 47.

[2] Douglas Keay, Interview in *Woman's Own*, 23 Sept. 1987 [http://www.margaretthatcher.org/document/106689].

[3] Douglas Oliver, *Three Variations on the Theme of Harm: Selected Poetry and Prose* (London: Paladin and Grafton Books, 1990), 10.

[4] Ken Edwards, 'Grasping the Plural', in Denise Riley (ed.), *Poets on Writing: Britain, 1970–1991* (Basingstoke: Macmillan, 1992), 21–9 (21, 25).

[5] Denise Riley, 'Dark Looks', *Selected Poems, 1986–1993* (London: Reality Street Editions, 2000), 74.

confidence that 'we' spoke for any discernible 'us' faltered. That pronoun must be relinquished in recognition of the cultural and ethical marginalization of poetry, but Riley among others affirmed that the 'I' was also enfeebled by sentimental usage, identity politics, and bad narcissism. As Peter Middleton argued in 1983, 'Too much inclusiveness from the collective pronoun and there is a stink.' Middleton saw his contemporary poets as engaging in active opposition to 'that easy use of "we" by which oppressive forms enlist us all, contaminating that word so necessary to resistance'.[6] Held in balance with the poet's desire to articulate the experiences of his or her community, or to identify a potential collective which could resist the atomizing effects of liberal individualism, was the conscriptive 'we' used by the forces of political conservativism to identify, for example, a compulsory set of (English) values.

The arrogation of the first person by the forces of oppression took many forms. Wendy Mulford interrogated an 'I' contaminated by patriarchy and capitalism: 'Who was this "I" speaking? What was speaking me? How far did the illusion of selfhood, that most intimate and precious possession, reach? How could the lie of culture be broken up if the lie of the self made by that culture remained intact? And how could the lie of capitalist society be broken if the lie of culture were not broken?'[7] For Mulford, there is an implicit link between a poetic uncovering of the 'lie of the self' and liberation from capitalism. In *The ABC of Writing*, Mulford developed an alternative rhetoric of the self, whose multiplicity and provisionality originated in the specific activities of mothering:

> That practice of being *available*, as hands, lips, body, limbs from the earliest total presence to the later availability *at any time on demand* of ear, tongue, hands, *is* directive of *how* we listen, *how* speak, basic rhythm of attention and response. [...] Multiplicity that is not metonymic of privileged condition, not value to be sought as release from male bondage, of the single, erect, unified, but is condition of continuous struggle in daily, social experience. For a whole self, a whole work.[8]

For Mulford, the 'whole work' reflecting a 'whole self' is a goal to be achieved only through 'continuous struggle', including struggle within the home. *The ABC of Writing* combines intimate lyrics which depict domestic duty and care alongside meditations on the social and political landscape, violence, and the liberational as well as oppressive powers of art-making. Mulford's feminist politics are also apparent in her foregrounding of the (female) body in its procreative, sexual, and labouring reality as a means to overcome the powers of patriarchy, capitalism, and the superego.[9] Drawing on Continental theorizations both of embodiment and language, she replaces the autonomous lyric subject with an embodied, fragmented, and shared subjectivity.

---

[6] Peter Middleton, 'Breaking the Perspex: Recent Poetry of Wendy Mulford', *Many Review*, 1 (Spring 1983), 3–9.

[7] Wendy Mulford, 'Notes on Writing: A Marxist/Feminist Viewpoint', *Red Letters*, 9 (1979); repr. in Michèlene Wandor, *On Gender and Writing* (London: Pandora, 1983), 31–41 (31).

[8] Wendy Mulford, *The ABC of Writing and Other Poems* (Southampton: Torque, 1985), repr. in *and suddenly, supposing: selected poems* (Buckfastleigh: Etruscan Books, 2002), 60.

[9] Mulford, *The ABC of Writing and Other Poems*, repr. in *and suddenly, supposing*, 58.

Another poet who struggled against the confessional register of the lyric 'I' while still maintaining a passionate investment in embodied selfhood was John Wilkinson. He revealed that 'In all my writing I meet difficulty with the pronouns, both on top of things and obliterated, displaced, dispersed. Especially, I find it absurd to write "we"; by turns I dominate and succumb, or even in the same moment. And in this country, at this time, "we" has lost all possibility of adventure.'[10] But, like Edwards and all the other poets I discuss in this essay, Wilkinson did not believe that it was possible to retrieve that 'possibility of adventure' by excising personal reference, and specifically the authorial 'I', from poetry. He wrote in another essay that

> It can feel as though the lyric poetry of the twentieth-century has been harried past endurance by the problem of the first-person singular, the lyric 'I', variously by its pomposity, its frailty, its pretensions and its inadequacy. This cannot be evaded by extirpation of the cursed pronoun, for the depersonalised poem tends to then lay claim to an overweening authority. The first person plural tends to a presumption of common cause or sensibility with the smug or wheedling 'I', and the second person singular or plural to arraign the reader or society from the vantage of the arrogant 'I'.[11]

Although he recognizes the tendency towards domination implied in poems addressed to 'you', and the 'overweening authority' of first-person declarations, Wilkinson suggests that the 'I' is indestructible because it serves as a restraint on the poem's grandiose claims to universality.

There is a complex relation, for each of the poets mentioned so far, between the loss of poetry's power to voice a shared civic reality through an address to (or description of) any 'we' and the problems with self-assertion and narcissism implicit in 'I'-centred writing. This chapter will consider how poets responded to these political, theoretical, poetic difficulties, in part by looking at how they used loving address to fabricate elusive intimacies with the reader. This is, to be sure, an ancient strategy, but it became particularly significant in an era when poetry seemed to be an outmoded practice with almost no political potency and considerable problems in reaching a wide audience. Poets continued to write about love and desire as ways out of this (partly self-imposed) impasse, as a means to make contact with the reader, and to test the possibility of solidarity. Were the problems of love exemplary of the wider problem of alienation? Could love be an antidote to capitalism, or did it merely mitigate for the individual the general condition of harm? I will now briefly consider how four poets—Veronica Forrest-Thomson, Douglas Oliver, Denise Riley, and John James—might have answered these questions. Despite sharing much common ground, these poets developed distinct theories and practices in response to the challenges of maintaining a truth-telling and affective lyric self, in a time and place which seemed increasingly hostile to poetry of any description.

---

[10] John Wilkinson, 'Imperfect Pitch', in Riley (ed.), *Poets on Writing*, 154–72 (166).

[11] John Wilkinson, 'Frostwork and the Mud Vision', *The Lyric Touch* (Cambridge: Salt Publishing, 2007), 187.

Veronica Forrest-Thomson: 'Love is put to the ... *grammatical* test'

Veronica Forrest-Thomson's work is the most extreme example among the poets discussed here of the consequences for the poetic imagination of the so-called 'linguistic turn'. Her advocacy particularly of the thinking of Wittgenstein sometimes verged on the chauvinistic, as when she declared in a 'Contributor's Note' written in 1969 that poems reveal 'the impossibility of expressing, or even of experiencing, a non-linguistic reality'.[12] Nonetheless, in her brief writing career she began to discover an edge in the experience and expression of love that rasped against her ardent commitment to theory. Forrest-Thomson wrote frequently about love, as a situation that tested the durability of a selfhood which, she seems persuaded in her early poems, was a fiction of language. Her work reveals an intensifying ambivalence between the conviction that there is no extra-linguistic reality, and a playful recognition that language's autonomy is intruded upon by the impenetrable or unobliging nature of other people—in particular, of the beloved. Her poem 'Zettel' tests this ambivalence, using the expression of love as an example of a Wittgensteinian 'language-game | with pronouns'. Much is at stake in that game. It not only imperils the possibility of a true expression of loving feeling, but even the certainty of 'a living being' itself.

I love you.
—the language-game
with pronouns and
'Confucius he say':
The concept of a living being
has the same indeterminacy
as that of a language.
Love is not a feeling.
Love is put to the test
—the *grammatical* test.[13]

Who is the 'I' who can do this loving, the poem asks, either in the poem, or in real life? Put not to the test of an emotional ordeal, but to a grammatical test, love is a signifier whose nature cannot be determined by the actions or desires of any individual. It locks the lovers into an arbitrary relationship mediated by language rather than by bodies or psychic realities.

But the experience of unrequited love transforms Forrest-Thomson's playful erotic nominalism into a test of the reality of subjectivity itself. When love is not returned, the

---

[12] Veronica Forrest-Thomson, *Collected Poems and Translations* (London: Allardyce Barnett, 1990), 261.
[13] Forrest-Thomson, *Collected Poems*, 24.

loving self which is given to the beloved is also withheld. In 'Canzon, for British Rail Services', 'I' tell 'you' that

My self is at one remove
Because it has gone to you
Who will not display
The sense of me another,
Being bound in yourself
By my forlorn desire.[14]

Love estranges me from my self, makes that self into an object that can be traded, given and received, retained and hidden by the other. The circular form of the canzon brings Forrest-Thomson to a conclusion in which the emotional stasis of being 'bound in' by forlorn desire can be broken by a playful exchange of selves:

And yet I would not not love
If I could chose [sic] not to;
For I require to play
By hazarding myself
To you, my self, the other
Whom I always desire.[15]

The allegations of love and self are simultaneously offered and retracted; the poem is both a real invitation and a display of theoretical competence. Love is not declared; rather, it is not not declared, and that double negation allows the lover to risk both losing the self (by giving it to the other), and retaining the self (by claiming the other as her own) in a paradoxical state of 'required play'. In this witty, metaphysical poem, Forrest-Thomson transforms the ludic properties of Wittgensteinian language theory into a seductive trope. Love is an opportunity for play, but it also has the capacity to upset or resist play: 'It is always a wrong move | In the chess game of all we do; | It upsets the sparkling play'.[16] If love is no more than a 'sparkling' intellectual exercise in strategy, then there is every chance that the lover will be defeated. More than that: you 'cancel out my play | Being so much another'.[17] The otherness of the beloved resists assimilation, undermining the writer's self-aggrandizing claim to operate the mechanism of language that creates reality. Consequently, in an aching pun, ' "Pain stopped play" '.[18]

In her long poem on the subject of love, 'The Garden of Proserpine', Forrest-Thomson avers that love, 'however trite, is always interesting | At least to those in its clutches | and usually also to their readers'.[19] It is maddening folly, it 'kills people and the police

---

[14] Forrest-Thomson, *Collected Poems*, 102.
[15] Forrest-Thomson, *Collected Poems*, 103.
[16] Forrest-Thomson, *Collected Poems*, 102.
[17] Forrest-Thomson, *Collected Poems*, 103.
[18] Forrest-Thomson, 'Cordelia, or a Poem Should Not Mean, But Be', *Collected Poems*, 108.
[19] Forrest-Thomson, *Collected Poems*, 88.

can't do anything to stop it'; the only option 'Is to try to solve it'.[20] But the jingle which is Forrest-Thomson's solution—'I loved you and you loved me | And then we made a mess' etc.—is at best an ironic palliation of love's pains.[21] Like Denise Riley, Forrest-Thomson uses irony to resist self-aggrandizement and to show up the unoriginality of our most heartfelt statements: 'If I say "I love you" we can't but laugh | Since irony knows what we'll say'.[22] Irony is a rhetorical device which resists the lyric's claims to truthfulness and authenticity. It undermines 'the "I" which ascends', also known as 'the author...a mythical figure which the poem itself aims to create and which can only exist within the realm of artifice'. As a marker of the author as one element within the heterogeneity of the text, the 'I' can be subjected to formal challenge.

Forrest-Thomson described herself in 1976 as embarked on three quests: a quest for a style, a quest for a 'subject other than the difficulty of writing, and the quest for another human being. Indeed such equation of love with knowledge and the idea of style as their reconciliation is as old as the art itself, for the other person is the personification of the other, the unknown, and the external world and all one's craft is necessary to catch him'.[23] Love poetry integrates these three quests. But it also reveals the inadequacy of writing. Forrest-Thomson was forced by love—or enabled by it—to confront the resistance of the world to her theories. 'Sonnet' opens with the admission that 'My love, if I write a song for you | To that extent you are gone'.[24] The lover is a fugitive from the controlling tendencies of the writer; 'If I try to free myself by my craft | You vary as night from day.' Love forces the poet to temper her structuralist convictions, and recognize the potential for domination claimed by the language artist whenever language's monopoly on signification and reality are vaunted.

Douglas Oliver: 'gliding with love-like content'

Douglas Oliver filled his poetry with references to a self who shared his own history or characteristics: not in fulfilment of a confessional tendency, but out of a passion for politically engaged lyric. Oliver emigrated in 1982, living in the US and France in exile from Thatcher's Britain. In *Penniless Politics*, Will Penniless presents a conspicuously autobiographical predicament:

Give up my plumy fucker voice.
Learn situation. Having left an English dream

---

[20] Forrest-Thomson, *Collected Poems*, 89.
[21] Forrest-Thomson, *Collected Poems*, 90.
[22] Forrest-Thomson, 'Sonnet', *Collected Poems*, 91.
[23] Forrest-Thomson, Preface, *Collected Poems*, 264.
[24] Forrest-Thomson, *Collected Poems*, 91.

half-finished, come abroad
seeking a voice change
to find that my voice must
crack open like a snake's egg for,
being its old self, whole and ineffectual,
it takes part in the real only by irony.[25]

Oliver moves beyond the defensive irony characteristic of Forrest-Thomson, looking for a way to 'crack open' the poetic voice through attention to an international reality and through a remarkable range of verse forms.

Oliver's poetry consists largely of the poet putting himself in harm's way. It represents the limitations of the self without flinching, often attempting to delineate those limitations through contrast with unknowable others: women, non-European subjects, infants. Through love for these others, the lyric subject becomes more than himself: becomes capable of empathy, and an agent for effects that range beyond the harm intrinsic (in Oliver's view) to the poetic instant. In the Preface to his *Selected Poems*, Oliver declares that 'since 1969 I've had a life-project to widen my political attention by progression from one book to the next, going always outwards, and then drawing inwards by a movement of inclusive contraction. In such a way, I've tried to show that any political flaws in the public arena also reside in the "self"—in "myself"—and therefore inside the area of the poem-as-art too.'[26] The poem is an amalgamation of outwards and inwards, self and others, harm and harmlessness, held together by love. Oliver's desire to be open to voices outside himself is apparent in the early text *In The Cave of Suicession* (1974), in which the poet spent the night in a Derbyshire cave channelling the voices of an oracle through his typewriter. In *The Infant and the Pearl* (1985), the lyric subject is personally implicated in the brutal Tory politics and City greed. He cavorts with debutantes and finally finds himself as a backbench MP, confused by a lust for power into betraying his socialist politics. It is only the intervention of his father, and more significantly of 'Rosine', who 'in medieval guise' would 'denote Mercy, the divine *donum*; | secularized, she was Socialism', which relieves the lyric 'I's blindness and anguish.[27]

Didactic figures of this kind recur throughout Oliver's poetry, aiding the lyric subject in that movement from outwardness to inwardness, from a sense of the suprasensible reality of others to a recognition of the self's limits. For example, in *Salvo for Africa* (2000) the deep mysteries of 'A Woman in Ethiopia' show how narrow are the poet's experience, his memories 'trivial compared with these red hills of Ethiopia', and his ignorance: 'poverty has stages I shall never know'.[28] While this Ethiopian woman remains an icon of the limits of Oliver's project to 'imagine Africa', the leader of the SPIRIT party in *Penniless Politics*, a voodoo priestess called Emen, penetrates the white male in

---

[25] Douglas Oliver, *Penniless Politics: A Satirical Poem* (Newcastle upon Tyne: Bloodaxe Books, 1991), 25.
[26] Douglas Oliver, *Selected Poems* (Jersey City, NJ: Talisman House, 1996), 1.
[27] Oliver, *Selected Poems*, 61.
[28] Douglas Oliver, *A Salvo for Africa* (Newcastle upon Tyne: Bloodaxe Books, 2000), 31–2.

order to transform him. The party's founding moment is an act of lovemaking in which the Haitian 'Woman on Top' inseminates the 'immigrant Anglo-Scot' Will Penniless, 'squirting black womanly sperm into him, | remaking his mind and his tongue while he was still | asleep'.[29] The notion that political transformation can begin with a sexual awakening, the white male European subject being penetrated by the black female essence, is revisited in *Salvo for Africa*. There, 'The Mixed Marriage' counterpoises 'the real world's beauty' to the violent pretence of a video game. This 'real' woman locked inside a virtual world (like that of the poet's imagination) is suffering, 'starved, flinching | at bombs, or cackling with laughter'; and

I love her so truly she multiplies
into millions, warm, crowding, hungry
in their nations, as if her image were
jiggered by time-lapses into histories.
She waits for any sincere person
to penetrate this strangeness we've created
and to become flesh with her flesh.[30]

By 'loving' her, Oliver is able to encounter the 'millions' she represents; but of course the woman is merely a patient receptacle, an emblem of passivity and maternal inclusiveness. While the problems with this recurrent trope are obvious, it also demonstrates Oliver's desire for a mobile, passionate, and politically energizing intersubjectivity.

It is not only women who lead the lyric subject through his own limits. In *The Infant and the Pearl*, Rosine carries an infant known as 'Ignorance', the child with Down's syndrome who also recurs as a symbol of innocence and harmlessness throughout Oliver's writing. This child, modelled on Oliver's own son Tom who died in 1969, is a figure of joy and serenity, becoming 'all I desired, the divine | baby-being in non-being'.[31] He is 'an analogy for my own stupidity', 'a symbol for sweetness, "stupidity" and near-harmlessness'.[32]

> Joined to an energetic and mature cleverness, such sweetness may become a force for good. Loving that real baby as I tried and still try to do, failing to love him as I failed—once crucially—and still fail to do, I have an index of how vanity mars my good intentions and of how, proudly shunning my own mental inadequacy, I often cause harm.[33]

Loving the baby requires an acknowledgement of one's own 'vanity' and 'harmfulness': the baby becomes 'an area of almost no-harm like a clearing in the middle of harm'.

---

[29] Oliver, *Penniless Politics*, 17.
[30] Oliver, *Salvo*, 94–5.
[31] Oliver, *Selected Poems*, 56.
[32] Douglas Oliver, *The Harmless Building* (Brighton and Lincoln: Ferry Press and Grosseteste Review Books, 1973), 5.
[33] Oliver, *The Harmless Building*, 5.

Oliver made love and harm essential to both the ethics of poetry and his theory of prosody. In his autobiographical text *An Island That Is All the World*, Oliver claims to have learned from 'the harmlessness of Jains and the destructiveness of the boxer' to distinguish between the purity of a vowel sound and the destructive impact of a consonant in the poetic line.[34] This oscillation leads to a sense in reading poetry of something fleeting which cannot be captured, something which relates not only to the prosodic modulations of the verse but also to an ontology. In 'The boy knocked out', Oliver connects the poem's 'beat' to the opponent, caught by a punch

mid-mind
before the self has thought
to fill itself with the self
which is protection[35]

Oliver's text combines poetic and prose accounts of moments of paradoxical calm, when he perceived 'within me a steady, confident self, which I imagine to be the self I had often speculated about, the unconscious unity of everything we have experienced and incorporated throughout our length of days, an entity that persists, minutely changing, very minutely, as our conscious self goes through its wilder swings of mood'.[36] For Oliver, this calm centre where the self is revealed out of the immediacy of physical and psychic impressions is similar to the instant of poetic stress.

Oliver challenged the genera of 'modern linguistic philosophy' to which Forrest-Thomson was loyal, and which 'argue this large entity [of the self] out of all real existence'. Defending the self, Oliver found in these paradoxical moments of harm and harmlessness, violence and calm, the 'spiritual sources' for his poems. He denies the premise that

> we are trapped in the web of language, doomed, it seems, to disbelieve in the unity of self and of artistic forms: along with that, goes a loss of spirit. [Literary theorists] are dangerous guides in areas where the poem, on the other hand, can make evident to the simple-hearted: 'This happened—spirit entered language and simultaneously I perceived such and such sights, spoke such and such words.'[37]

For Oliver, a sense of the self as that which is occluded by consciousness and which partakes of the ephemeral experience of prosodic stress allows one to escape both the 'trap' set by the linguistic turn, as well as the potential solipsism of a poetics founded on selfhood. He construes an ethical rhythm for life from 'poetic melody'; prosody produces 'a repeatable vivid present', 'and it feels as if in that alone lie true knowing, true freedom, and true beginning of memory. Imagined poet and imagined reader meet there, in the poem, without the witchcraft of domination.'[38] So, although part of Oliver's theory of

---

[34] Oliver, *Three Variations on the Theme of Harm*, 70.
[35] Oliver, *Three Variations on the Theme of Harm*, 62.
[36] Oliver, *Three Variations on the Theme of Harm*, 45.
[37] Oliver, *Three Variations on the Theme of Harm*, 39.
[38] Oliver, *Three Variations on the Theme of Harm*, 75.

prosody is predicated on the notion of dramatic harm—the boxer's blow, in which interpersonal violence vanquishes consciousness—he also construes poetry as a meeting place for poet and reader, free of coercion. In another essay, he refines these thoughts, arguing that 'something is different about an instant filled and gliding with love-like content and one filled with cruelty. I suppose that in the first case the instant is filled with interpersonal union and in the second the content is the isolated self, triumphant.'[39] For all its limits, limits which Oliver himself recognized and even thematized within the poems themselves, his poetry represents an attempt to transcend the isolated and triumphant self and to achieve an intersubjectivity which could be the grounding of a transformative politics. Although Oliver recognizes the seductive potential of the power to harm, he asserts that poetry is a culmination of thought as love: 'The proper resolution of time's successive instants into its flow must surely be the love-like, life-full action of mind, brimming with unfulfilled potential, brimming also with honour and energy.'[40]

Denise Riley: 'cooled | to the grace of being common'

Over nearly four decades as a poet and philosopher, Denise Riley's writings about language, the self, history, poetics, politics and social life have consistently challenged the premise of individual autonomy on which liberal government is based. Her poetry ponders a question provoked by the depredations of Thatcherism: 'Where do I put myself, if public life's destroyed'?[41] The answer is resolutely not to take refuge in privacy and personality. However, the poet must admit that her work has become peripheral, and that response from the public may be infinitely delayed. Riley's poetry dramatically enacts the loneliness and insecurity of this position, one which reflects the sociological situation of poetry in late twentieth-century Britain as well as the guilty, harmful, and coercive aspects of an interpellated identity. However, rather than revelling in isolation, and succumbing to the potential elitism and quietism of that position, Riley wants to use language to imagine a genuine commonality which might be extended to political formations. She desires words

        cooled
to the grace of being common

so to achieve my great colourlessness
I dive into the broken brilliant world
and float in it unindividuated, whitely.[42]

---

[39] Douglas Oliver, 'Three Lilies', in Riley (ed.), *Poets on Writing*, 276–81 (280).
[40] Oliver in Riley (ed.), *Poets on Writing*, 282.
[41] Riley, 'Knowing in the Real World', *Selected Poems*, 53.
[42] Denise Riley, 'The ambition to not be particular speaks', *Dry Air* (London: Virago, 1985), 54.

The self can become 'unindividuated', not coloured and particular but 'white', by merging with a world whose reality is fragmented and 'broken'. To find the words which might address a commons, then, the poet must give up her attachment to the notion of a discrete self and seek an impersonal solidarity through the demotic quality of linguistic affect.

Like Oliver, Riley constantly returns to the relationship between language and personal, social and political harm or remediation, a relation which is centred on the subject. Her first book of poems, *Marxism for Infants* (1977), explored the possibility of autonomous self-definition amidst the constraints and generosities of the family. These assertions meshed with her classic feminist essay on childcare regimes in *War in the Nursery* (1983), a work of archival history which also showed Riley's debt to Foucault. There, Riley argues that there is a tendency to regard 'social' and 'intersubjective' as synonyms, 'as if the social was nothing more complex than a straightforward multiplication of what goes on between any two human beings'.[43] Since these early publications, Riley has consistently worked to piece together the complexities of the social without losing sight of the individual and its intimate interactions. Recognizing the power of imposed identities such as the category of 'women' (the subject of *Am I That Name?*, 1988), her writing also pauses in the moment of misrecognition, discomfort, and maladaptation, when the subject notices its difference from the subjective identity which has been imposed. As she writes in her poem 'Affections must not', 'inside a designation there are people permanently startled to bear it, the not-me against sociology'.[44] How we bear our designations, what we claim for ourselves in their place, has been central to Riley's theorization of identity and lyric selfhood.

One of the most startling designations for Riley seems to be that of 'writer'. Claiming that she writes in order to *eliminate* the incriminating marks of authorship, Riley argues that the awkwardness in saying 'I am a writer' only demonstrates a more general guilt in laying claim to any originality in language.[45] The provisional and echolalic voice of the 'I' in *Mop Mop Georgette* (1993) exemplifies this discomfort. In that book, confessions of need, lyric seductions of the reader, and attacks on the security of any pronouncement at times threaten the lyric subject with dissolution: 'but I do want to kill and die'.[46] While 'Dark Looks' declares that 'Who anyone is or I am is nothing to the work. The writer | properly should be the last person that the reader or the listener need think about', the testing of 'who I am' is absolutely central to *Mop Mop Georgette*'s lyric method.[47] As a consequence, the book also tests who 'you' are, and puts the relation between writer and reader under considerable strain. 'Wherever you are, be somewhere else', for example, begins with 'a body shot through, perforated', light and voices slipping through its

---

[43] Denise Riley, *War in the Nursery: Theories of the Child and Mother* (London: Virago, 1983), 20.
[44] Riley, *Selected Poems*, 20.
[45] Denise Riley, *Words of Selves: Identification, Solidarity, Irony* (Stanford, Calif.: Stanford University Press, 2000), 60.
[46] Riley, 'Cruelty without Beauty', *Selected Poems*, 71.
[47] Riley, *Selected Poems*, 74.

openings.[48] This seems to endorse familiar ideas of the subject as fragmented and insecure, held 'in a look until dropped like an egg on the floor'. It depends for its coherence on the (loving) regard of another, its entire reality determined extrinsically: 'whichever | piece is glimpsed, that bit is what I am'. At times, the poem seems to promise that dependence for identity on another might be a source of liberation: I am 'seen through, seen past, no name, just scrappy | filaments lifting and lifting over in the wind'. But it also threatens to obliterate me. These 'gothic riffs' of a self straining 'over a glacier overhanging blackness', looking perilously into the darkness of its own dissolution, then lead to a summation of the function of writing: 'To stare at nothing, just to get it right | get nothing right, with some faint idea of | this as a proper way to spend a life': is this the proper, the ethical way to live?[49] But the poem immediately retracts this account of writing. The poem is not a scrutiny of 'nothing', but an appeal:

> No, what
> I really mean to say instead is, come back,
> won't you, just all of you come back, and give
> me one more go at doing it all again but doing it
>
> far better this time round—the work, the love stuff—
> so I go to the wordprocessor longing for line cables
> to loop out of the machine straight to my head
>
> and back, as I do want to be only transmission—[50]

In this view, the poet is a cyborg fixed to the word processor, conduit for language rather than personality. Revision, or the composition of a new poem, is a way of retaining the reader in the 'loop' from poet to machine: the loop that is language. But her longing also eroticizes the relation between writer and reader. Riley makes the act of reading—skimming to the foot of the page—a gesture in an erotic relationship in which the poetic speaker is distinctly vulnerable. The poem dramatizes the speaker's own chagrin as she listens to her own efforts: '*The flower breaks open to its bell of sound | that rings out through the woods.* I eat my knuckles || hearing that.'[51] Judging its aesthetic effect, the poem regrets that 'I've only earned a modern, what, a flatness. | Or no, I can earn nothing, but maybe | some right to stop now and to say to you, Tell me.' The poem achieves nothing but a right to a response from you, the reader. But what should the reader tell it? Are 'you' required to tell your own truth, or to validate the poem's? Before 'you' can speak, however, comes a confession that even 'That plea for mutuality's not true'; 'I never have wanted || "a voice" anyway, nor got it.'

After these perseverations, the poem concludes: 'Stop now. Hold it there. Balance. Be beautiful. Try. |—And I can't do this. I can't talk like any of this. | You hear me not

---

[48] Riley, *Selected Poems*, 47.
[49] Riley, *Selected Poems*, 48.
[50] Riley, *Selected Poems*, 48.
[51] Riley, *Selected Poems*, 49.

do it'. The lyric subject is under extreme pressure to be balanced and beautiful, fixed in the reader's gaze; 'I' am incapable of doing or talking 'like any of this'. But, paradoxically, its confession of failure comes after it has, indeed, been talking like this. How can the reader—the 'you' who is privy to the subject's failure—hear something that is not happening? And what is the effect on our relation to the lyric 'I' of its confession? As the poem's failures double back on themselves, what is created is not so much a space for readerly interventions but a chronicle of impossibilities: of authentic speech, of the transfer of affect from 'I' to 'you', of sustainable lyric beauty. Rather than constructing a commons through exchange between reader and writer, the poem forecloses those exchanges with skittish impatience; the invitation to respond is always immediately retracted. A similar procedure is applied in 'A Shortened Set':

Are you alright I ask out there
straining into the dusk to hear.
I think its listening particles of air
at you like a shot.
You're being called across your work[52]

But there is no return of interest: 'Am I alright you don't ask me'. This failure of the reader to respond exacerbates the speaker's feeling of intense 'loneliness'. The plea for 'company | to crack my separate stupidity' then results in the melancholic definition of lyric as unheeded echo: 'You do that; love me; die alone'.[53] Writing is a lonely activity, in which the writer courts (and sometimes repels) the reader, but her energies are never requited and 'you' stay silent just when you are asked (commanded) to speak.

Admitting that 'describing myself, I set out the stall of my self, however reluctantly, as advertising', Riley asks, 'Can speaking the self ever be managed without flattery or abnegation?'[54] These poems represent an attempt, perhaps, to manage the self without flattering it or hiding it behind a tyrannical universalism. Their scrutiny of the self and of lyric quality is at times an impediment to the achievement of words 'cooled to the grace of being common'. But they can be taken as an attempt to inscribe in 'a social democracy of loneliness'[55] a different kind of lyric subject than we are accustomed to: one whose provisionality, fragmentation, and reliance on the reader's approving gaze are not merely fulfilments of French theories, but painful limits revealed by the lyric psychomachia. For Riley, the self can be managed only through rigorous scrutiny, irony, and a Stoic *ratio recta* which recognizes language to be both impersonal and affective. 'The intimacies between consenting to be a subject and undergoing subjection are so great that even to make demands as an oppositional subject may well extend the trap, wrap it furiously around oneself. Yet this is hardly a paralysing risk, if it's recognised.'[56] We cannot escape

[52] Riley, *Selected Poems*, 39.
[53] Riley, *Selected Poems*, 43.
[54] Riley, *Words of Selves*, 28.
[55] Riley, 'A Shortened Set', *Selected Poems*, 41.
[56] Denise Riley, *'Am I That Name?' Feminism and the Category of 'Women' in History* (Minneapolis: University of Minnesota Press, 1988), 112.

the trap of subjection, even by making demands; but we can find some room in it to move. While her emphasis is often on the negative—unease, bad words, guilt, anxiety, oppression, violence, racism, and sexism—as the fountain of identity, Riley writes optimistically at the end of *Words of Selves* that 'There is indeed an ethics of decentring, one that pertains to solidarity. The decentred subject need be no anaemic spectre of a conservative postmodernism, but the pulsating and elastic creature of a million circulating words, vulnerable to history while it speaks history'.[57] This subject is created in 'words', made by history but also able to speak its own history; not at the centre of its discursive universe, but freely at play within it, where 'meaning is flocking densely around the words seeking a way | any way in between the gaps, like a fertilisation'.[58]

John James: 'radio Babylon'

Like Riley, John James explores the challenges to constructing a practical, political solidarity while recognizing the limits of the poetic imagination in effecting any reconciliation between the particular and the general. Like Riley, he also vacillates between loving and violent, coercive, or even hateful identifications of other people who form the community from which his own, individual relationships are derived. In one of his more optimistic, New York School moments, James advises the reader (as a potential poet) to explore the city, spelling out the imaginative and existential rewards for an attitude of openness:

You will discover
particular people at a
particular time
& in a particular place
these people are the others
without whom you would not exist.[59]

Walking the city, the poet discovers and records 'the imprint made by others | all you others'.[60] Sociability gives access not only to the variety of others, but to the evidence of one's own existence, which depends on mutuality. The poet as a 'radio Babylon' channels all these particular voices into a babble of attitudes.[61] The poetry that results embraces collage, fragment, and repetition, both of emotional events and of found language. These devices create a dialectic between the speech and active presence of others, and the interpretive authority of the individual speaker, almost always designated as 'I' (but

---

[57] Riley, *Words of Selves*, 178.
[58] Riley, 'A Note on Sex and "the reclaiming of language"', *Selected Poems*, 11.
[59] John James, 'A Theory of Poetry', in Riley (ed.), *Poets on Writing*, 249.
[60] John James, *Toasting* (1979), repr. in *Collected Poems* (Cambridge: Salt Publishing, 2002), 174.
[61] John James, *Inaugural Address* (1979), in *Collected Poems*, 183.

sometimes as 'we') in his poems. Many of James's poems are also love lyrics, intermingled with representations of a politicized (alienated and/or revolutionary) civic landscape. This mixture conveys the potential for escape from the boredom of an isolated subjectivity, but also acknowledges 'the world, the variousness of that response'.[62]

Although many of James's poems celebrate the dignity of recreation, including talking and listening, they also tend to revel in the poet's violent distinctiveness from its others. The prominence of the poet is particularly apparent in his writings on landscape, which often trouble the fantasy of solidarity with the general through a (literally) prominent 'I'. 'The Conversation' depicts a climb up Snowdon. Near the summit, the speaker is struck by

this great volcanic frame of things in all
the revolutionary hope & practices
of women & of men does not remain unchanged
it too has its faults through which an exile voice can sing[63]

The physical landscape can be changed by revolutionary hope, theory, and praxis. It inspires an 'unashamed' reflection on 'might have been', which is a way of 'fixing on what was at last & wonder for just how much I am to answer | having to stop & stop again to write'.[64] Writing is a way of 'stopping', removing oneself from human movement, and—the poem goes on to imply—from his own class origins. It gives the speaker time to 'fix on what was', and to consider his own responsibilities. But the poem does not rest in a satisfied contemplation of revolutionary potential; the descent is mirrored by a despairing list of '7 burdens', including 'labour poverty debt disease & grief', 'waste & crass stupidity', 'continual strife at work & in the street | the want of pleasure & repose | & all that drinks away the sustenance of choice'. The poem hints of a 'new sense of strengthening regard for common things' as 'the land gave up a breath of gentler touch', but simultaneously there is 'the undertow of darkness | in the phones'.[65] James concludes with mixed feelings:

I see the millions I catch the language
which is the world of all of us
this only place in which we find our happiness or not at all
the end[66]

This is distinct from Forrest-Thomson's purist belief that it is impossible to experience a non-linguistic reality; it is much closer to Riley's discovery of an impersonal solidarity through linguistic affect. And, like Oliver empathizing with the 'millions' through a woman in a video game, James tunes in to the millions who share the language which

---

[62] John James, 'Narrative Graffiti', *Berlin Return* (1983), in *Collected Poems*, 223.
[63] John James, *Dreaming Flesh* (1991), repr. in *Collected Poems*, 296.
[64] James, *Dreaming Flesh*, 296.
[65] James, *Dreaming Flesh*, 297.
[66] James, *Dreaming Flesh*, 298.

creates a shared world; it is in that world, and by implication that language, that 'we' can find a shared happiness (though that is not guaranteed).

The relation of the poetic self to people as an abstracted communality, and to the landscape, is also regulated by the presence of companions. For example, in the first poem from *The Small Henderson Room* (1969), James describes a journey through the Severn Valley with a 'lady' in whose 'mutual presence | catastrophe may be averted'.[67] In 'the paroxysm of an embrace', I attain 'the intense & complete awareness of one | another as dream'; and I recognize that I am no more than 'an imagined creature', the product of the loving regard of the other. In many of James's poems, mutuality awakens the recognition that personal love can transform 'the entire world | into an erotic object'.[68] The beloved mediates between the universal and the particular, between the I and its others, producing both awareness and dream-vision; it reveals, in terms which would be familiar to John Wilkinson, the absurd grandiosity of the self (capable of turning the world into its object) and its transformative potential.

Distance from that beloved other is figured as physical space and liminal time in many of James's poems. Waiting, arrivals and departures, the time before or after the presence of an interlocutor, are common tropes in *Berlin Return*: 'I was leaving, love on the platform';[69] 'I know you will enter the room in 25 seconds';[70] 'you've just come back | I definitely love you';[71] 'I think about my friends | who are not here'.[72] The departure can trigger a return, the resumption of desire made more intense through separation: distance translated into closeness. But as in the poems by Forrest-Thomson, erotic desire for the absent or resistant object also reveals the self to be a strange object: 'Oh what a | great distance off | from the inviolable & | imaginary self', James writes in 'For the Safety of Lovers'—what is at a distance, estranged and estranging, is not only the beloved, who is sensed as the giving, receiving, and making of space; but also the speaker's own body (which is inflamed by 'poisons' and blistering with a rash).[73] But just as love induces a sense that the self is dispossessed of its duplicitous integrity, so it can also reconstruct the damaged self into a sense of wholeness and lightness. In 'Bad Thoughts', self-alienation, 'scattered griefs', and exhaustion are all remedied by 'the restful breast of your lover'.

By her let yourself be carried as far as the border
where to be cancelled itself is to revoke all endings
accept yourself & your heritage from which you have been
formed & passed from age to age

stay mysterious rather than be pure accept your
multifariousness your pluralism[74]

---

[67] James, *Collected Poems*, 53.
[68] John James, 'Talking in Bed', *Striking the Pavilion of Zero*, in *Collected Poems*, 113.
[69] James, *Collected Poems*, 196.
[70] James, *Collected Poems*, 203.
[71] James, *Collected Poems*, 235.
[72] James, *Collected Poems*, 237.
[73] James, *Dreaming Flesh*, 295.
[74] James, *Berlin Return*, 197–8.

Love is an inducement to be transported beyond the border of the subjective; and through that transport, to 'revoke all endings' and escape mortality.

Although James writes again and again of the conditions of personal intimacy, and in his most euphoric moments attributes to the commons the power to create the whole of subjectivity, he is sceptical about the possibility of a just and irenic community. In his early poem 'Inventory', James advocates a poetry of commitment, modelled on the communication between isolated prisoners: 'I would speak out not in solution, but cell to cell | as long as I remain unsevered from my purpose'.[75] And yet, there is a tension between the desire for 'closeness', 'not distanced', 'unsevered from my purpose', and the commitment to cellular isolation over 'solution'. James insists on retaining personal autonomy as separateness, combined with a desire for erotic intimacy which overcomes it. This tension is characteristic of his lyric mode, where images of loving subjects are also marked by gaps, apertures, and distances felt or imagined. The pattern is for no return, but only the ever-increasing distance between the present and the absent. The poem can be fabricated in that distance. Read in this way, the concluding lines of James's *Collected Poems* offer up the space of the untraversable distance to the reader as an invitation to make new work: 'the line knows where it's going | & we know we're going with it || I leave the rest to you | distance no object'.[76]

This chapter has referred to a group of different poets, writing and working in awareness of each other and publishing each other's work. Although I have highlighted what they share—a scepticism about the possibility of communication or the expression of social bonds which are free, pleasurable, and intimate; a recoiling from the imperial, patriarchal, or capitalist 'I'; an interest in renovating the forms of self-expression and intimacy, not by turning to domesticated confession but through challenging the capacities of language—I have not intended to suggest that their responses to the complex political, social, and theoretical conditions of the 1970s and 1980s were identical. Nonetheless, they did share a common cultural position on the margins of public discourse. That position is normally explained in terms of dissemination (small presses, little magazines, short print-runs) and intellectual obscurity (elitism). Before that marginalization is accepted as fact, however, the sociality represented by the exchange of books, letters, and research materials, the conviviality of readings and conferences and reading groups, should be considered as an alternative to the trope of poetic loneliness. Poets are enabled to voice their alienation, dismay, and violent resistance to what is now taken for the 'commons' by a communal network of publishers, editors, curators, and readers.

I have outlined how a range of experimental poets responded to the poetic, as well as political, challenge of speaking to or for their readers. These challenges were specific to the theoretical and historical conditions in which they were writing, but it could also be contended that they are definitive for lyric. Nietzsche described the lyric poet as one who, by 'a mystical process of un-selving', generates a world of images which are 'objectified versions of himself. Being the active centre of that world he may boldly speak in

---

[75] John James, *Trägheit* (1968), in *Collected Poems*, 50.
[76] John James, 'Idyll', *Schlegel Eats a Bagel* (1996), in *Collected Poems*, 365.

the first person, only his "I" is not that of the actual waking man, but the "I" dwelling, truly and eternally, in the ground of being'.[77] In similar terms, Adorno proclaimed that the lyric was elevated by 'immersion in what has taken individual form' to 'the status of something universal'.[78] The promise is that lyric poetry can achieve a kind of dignity, even when it is populated by a particular subjectivity: but only if its 'I' transcends particularity and articulates an objective and universal condition.

But how can personal love do this? Unselved and negated, the 'I' of contemporary experimental practice nonetheless generates through lyric objectification a world in its own image. The intimate pairing of the lover and the reader sacralize poetry as a form of relation that can overcome reification through its truthful intimacy (although its truth is always already constituted by the recognition of its futility). That use of love persists in the work of a younger generation, most conspicuously in that of Keston Sutherland, who has recently declared that

> The specific intention of much of my recent poetry has been to 'shatter the optimism of the bourgeois world', not only by means of satires against that optimism and its disguised material bases, but, just as importantly, by making a song of love whose power is deeply incompatible with the optimism of the bourgeois world, a song that tries to expose the forms and uses of specious universalism in professional politics and in everyday existence by turning love against them, even at the peril of love itself. Universalism must be forever reinvented by love. Love is the origin and enemy of universalism.[79]

Sutherland's poetry precipitates a reinvented universalism by addressing a 'you' who is simultaneously the particular beloved and the general reader. Embracing at once the revolutionary and lyrical history of the notion of universalism, Sutherland's paradoxical conclusion reveals the challenge of integrating love with politics, or a critical poetry with the bourgeois world.

Select Bibliography

Adorno, Theodor, 'On Lyric Poetry and Society', *Notes to Literature*, i, ed. Rolf Tiedemann, trans. Shierry Weber Nicholson (New York: Columbia University Press, 1991).
Edwards, Ken, 'Grasping the Plural', in Denise Riley (ed.), *Poets on Writing: Britain, 1970–1991* (Basingstoke: Macmillan, 1992), 21–9.

---

[77] Friedrich Nietzsche, *The Birth of Tragedy and The Genealogy of Morals*, trans. Francis Golffing (New York: Doubleday, 1956), 38–9.
[78] Theodor Adorno, 'On Lyric Poetry and Society', *Notes to Literature*, i, ed. Rolf Tiedemann, trans. Shierry Weber Nicholson (New York: Columbia University Press, 1991), 38.
[79] Keston Sutherland, 'Statement for the Helsinki Poetics Conference 2010', Helsinki, Aug. 2010 (unpublished paper).

Forrest-Thomson, Veronica, *Collected Poems and Translations* (London: Allardyce Barnett, 1990).
Harvey, David, *A Brief History of Neoliberalism* (Oxford: Oxford University Press, 2007).
Middleton, Peter, 'Breaking the Perspex: Recent Poetry of Wendy Mulford', *Many Review*, 1 (Spring 1983), 3–9.
Mulford, Wendy, 'Notes on Writing: A Marxist/Feminist Viewpoint', *Red Letters*, 9 (1979).
Nietzsche, Friedrich, *The Birth of Tragedy and the Genealogy of Morals*, trans. Francis Golffing (New York: Doubleday, 1956).
Oliver, Douglas, *The Harmless Building* (Brighton and Lincoln: Ferry Press and Grossteste Review Books, 1973).
Oliver, Douglas, *Three Variations on the Theme of Harm: Selected Poetry and Prose* (London: Paladin and Grafton Books, 1990).
Oliver, Douglas, *Penniless Politics: A Satirical Poem* (Newcastle upon Tyne: Bloodaxe Books, 1991).
Oliver, Douglas, *Selected Poems* (Jersey City, NJ: Talisman House, 1996).
Oliver, Douglas, *A Salvo for Africa* (Newcastle upon Tyne: Bloodaxe Books, 2000).
Riley, Denise, *War in the Nursery: Theories of the Child and Mother* (London: Virago, 1983).
Riley, Denise, *'Am I That Name?' Feminism and the Category of 'Women' in History* (Minneapolis: University of Minnesota Press, 1988).
Riley, Denise, *Words of Selves: Identification, Solidarity, Irony* (Stanford, Calif.: Stanford University Press, 2000).
Wandor, Michèlene, *On Gender and Writing* (London: Pandora, 1983).
Mulford, Wendy, *The ABC of Writing and Other Poems* (Southampton: Torque, 1985).

CHAPTER 38

CONTEMPORARY POETRY AND VALUE

PETER ROBINSON

I

As T. S. Eliot put it in the sentence with which I began my Introduction to this *Handbook*: 'There is one thing to be said for contemporary poetry that can't be said of any other, and that is that it is written by our contemporaries.'[1] Inviting an interest in poems of the present and recent past, Eliot's words contrast strikingly with Geoffrey Hill's at the conclusion to his 'Poetry and Value':

> A poem issues from reflection, particularly but not exclusively from the common bonding of reflection and language; it is not in itself the passing of reflective sentiment through the medium of language. The fact that my description applies only to a minority of poems written in English or any other language, and to the poetry written in Britain during the past fifty years scarcely at all, does not shake my conviction that the description I have given of how the uncommon work moves within the common dimension of language is substantially accurate.[2]

If this view of all poetry in every language is believed, then only a small amount of it is 'uncommon' and, presumably, little worth reading. Hill's conviction not only serves to dismiss the vast majority of world poetry from serious attention, it also dismisses from attention those who have written it, and those who have paid it any mind. Far from 'substantially accurate', I believe Hill's conviction to be mistaken, his application of it

---

[1] T. S. Eliot, a filmed remark on a BBC *Arena* profile shown on Thursday, 8 Oct. 2009.
[2] Geoffrey Hill, 'Poetry and Value', in *Collected Critical Writings,* ed. Kenneth Haynes (Oxford: Oxford University Press, 2008), 489.

unsupported and insupportable, and its cultural implications sorry. However, his assertion that a poem 'is not in itself the passing of reflective sentiment through the medium of language' may well be right, for there is likely to be no such 'reflective sentiment' existing in any mind prior to language so as to pass through the medium, whether into the poem or through it to a putative reader. My asserting this does not imply a capitulation to an assumption of the priority of language before sensory experience, which, in turn, is not to suppose that sensory experience does not require the learning of a language to be communicably structured. Yet in 'reflective sentiment' both adjective and noun indicate a state of conscious thought and location in culturally established forms of idea and emotion. These cannot be *passed through* the medium of language because they are already language. Hill's objection may then not be that the sentiment is being passed through the language, but that it is articulated in words he dislikes, commonplace or narcissistic words, before the writing of poems—the matter of the poem not then formed as he prefers by that poetic composition to whose transformative value he justly cleaves.

Hill's criticism of this false idea about the communicable priority of 'reflective sentiment' involves its adherents mistaking the role of the possessive pronoun in '*my* ideas' or '*my* feelings', where the pronoun distinguishes the noun, but not as regards unique possession: though *my* death is not *yours*, I do not *own* it. Being made of words, made thus communicable to others and the experiencing self, these 'ideas' or 'feelings' belong in the language and the history of the culture in which they are expressed. Hill is aware of complexity in first-person pronouns and possessives, articulating a similar point towards the close of 'Rhetorics of Value and Intrinsic Value':

> My language is in me and is me; even as I, inescapably, am a minuscule part of the general semantics of the nation; and as the nature of the State has involved itself in the nature that is most intimately mine. The nature that is most intimately mine may by some be taken to represent my intrinsic value. If it is so understood, it follows that intrinsic value, thus defined, bears the extrinsic at its heart.[3]

'My language', though, is both *not me*, in that I, like the ones J. Alfred Prufrock imagines, can say 'That is not what I meant at all',[4] and *me* in that if I say those words they come out of my mouth, even as they are also not mine in being Prufrock's companions' words if I am consciously alluding, and T. S. Eliot's too, and also in their 'belonging' to English (though there is no finite or single abstract object to do that possessing either). 'The nature that is most intimately mine', Hill writes, 'may by some be taken to represent my intrinsic value.' Some may imagine they can experience such intrinsic value from a person's intimate nature, though it is likely that words and actions are representing the nature whose value is at issue. Here I argue that there is no 'value' that is 'intrinsic' to such a 'nature' and can be 'taken' from it, for as well as the actions and their consequences,

---

[3] Hill, 'Rhetorics of Value and Intrinsic Value', in *Collected Critical Writings*, 477.
[4] T. S. Eliot, 'The Love Song of J. Alfred Prufrock', *Collected Poems 1909–1962* (London: Faber & Faber, 1963), 16, 17.

such as works of art, there need to be actions of evaluation for value to be present, and these cannot be intrinsic to the deeds or works or their putative values.

Hill asks, in the sentence immediately following the passage just cited, 'do I confuse intrinsic with mediated value?' His answer is that he does not confuse them; rather, he concedes that 'intrinsic value' is always accompanied by 'mediated value', though his subsequent reassertion of belief reconfigures 'extrinsic' or 'mediated' in the communication of 'intrinsic' value:

> It is simply not true to say that the intrinsic value of a line or phrase cannot be assayed and proven in close and particular detail. For the intrinsic value of the entire poem so to be established would require the significant detail to illumine and regulate the whole. I am left with no other course but to say that the great poem moves us to assent as much by the integrity of its final imperfection as by the amazing grace of its detailed perfection. At those points where the intrinsic value of the formal structure, by whatever means, is revealed to us, that value is on the instant mediated.[5]

But what is here called the 'intrinsic' value of a line or phrase may not be 'assayed and proven in close and particular detail', not least because changes in language use over time inevitably recalibrate relations between writings and their readers. This is also evident if we unbury the metaphor in 'assayed and proven', one which associates the line or phrase with 'aureate' metaphors for poetry, as in calling an anthology *The Golden Treasury*.[6] If you assay and prove the amount and purity of a lump of gold you do not fix its intrinsic value: you quantify its object-hood. This measured material existence is then attributed with exchange value, as fluctuations in the price of gold illustrate. The metaphor breaks down, as metaphors must, in that language is not composed of a single element that can have 'purity' of this material kind: hence the point of the aureate or purity metaphor, which includes gold's fetish value, in claiming it. There is also an ambiguity in the use of the word 'proven', equivocating between 'test' and 'demonstrate', where the former allows for experiential failure and the latter guarantees the coherent truth of what is shown. The 'detail' of a line can be discussed, qualities illustrated by speaking them or pointing to sonic and semantic characteristics, and the sceptical reader can be invited to experience it in the different light of other insights as to its worth; but that its features are to count for anyone as relevant or pertinent felicities requires their freely granted conviction and assent—invalidated if coerced.

When Hill moves on to describing the great poem as showing integrity of imperfection and the amazing grace of its perfection, there is (as so often) theology in his aesthetics. 'Amazing Grace', the hymn to which he alludes, continues 'how sweet the sound | That saved a wretch like me'. Yet there is a discrepancy between a line's being 'assayed and proven' to have what is here called intrinsic value, an activity that suggests effort and expertise, and the instantaneous communication of this value 'by whatever means'

---

[5] Hill, 'Rhetorics of Value and Intrinsic Value', 477.
[6] For disparaging comments on compulsively aureate poetic language, see Hill, 'Gurney's "Hobby"', in *Collected Critical Writings*, 432.

when 'the value is on the instant mediated'. The words 'instant mediated' may prove characteristically oxymoronic. The phrase 'by whatever means' acts as a veil upon the mystery: the 'means' by which this could happen is either by reading the work, or having it read and listening to it. The attention required to appreciate a poem is essential to these 'means', and may be elicited by its textures. It is an attention that has to be educated in the art of poetry and reading, because aesthetic form in words, one of poetry's constituents, is neither self-evident nor self-demonstrating. Hill acknowledges that value has to be 'mediated', but he undervalues what that mediation must involve and the consequences for value of its necessary presence. The value in a line of poetry is not intrinsic to it; this value is not able to communicate itself without activation *by* a reader or listener; and its being recognized as a value is not usually experienced 'on the instant', because it will have to sink in and be felt over time. To be struck by a line is to have the experience that value may be ascribable, and may occasion the wish to ascribe it by reporting on that experience. The gap between experience and ascription is essential to avoiding the suspicion of coercion or bedazzlement in judgement.

II

Hill writes of the 'fact' that his 'description applies only to a minority of poems written in English or any other language' and that this 'does not shake my conviction that the description I have given of how the uncommon work moves within the common dimension of language is substantially accurate'.[7] The application of such evaluative descriptions to works of art, to poems, cannot and does not issue in what is here called a fact. It is a judgement. Nor can he know whether his description is an accurate one only for 'a minority of poems written in English *or any other language*' (my emphasis), because no one has read enough to command the data, while the view that his limiting judgement characterizes the British poetry of the past fifty years arrives with scant evidence in his writings of appreciative or critical attention to what it judges.[8] The pronouncement bears a complex relation to two of Hill's key precepts, one drawn from F. H. Bradley, that '"to get within the judgement the condition of the judgement" is, so far as I can be said to understand it, the basic essential of all true criticism',[9] and the related idea from T. H. Green that 'to place ourselves "outside the process by which our knowledge is developed" is to conceive of an untenable "ecstacy", whereas to recognize our being within the process is to accept our true condition'.[10]

---

[7] Hill, 'Poetry and Value', 489.

[8] The index to *Collected Critical Writings* has few references to living persons, and barely any to contemporary poetry. A rare, uncollected exception turns out to prove the rule. See Geoffrey Hill, 'Il Cortegiano: F. T. Prince's *Poems* (1938)', *PN Review 147*, 29/1 (Sept.–Oct. 2002), 28–31.

[9] Hill, 'Eros in F. H. Bradley and T. S. Eliot', in *Collected Critical Writings*, 561. Hill extends aspiration to this impossibility into his primary vocation: 'Each true poem is required to bear within it the condition of the judgement that inspired it.'

[10] Hill, 'Our Word Is Our Bond', in *Collected Critical Writings*, 158.

Bradley allows that the 'more the conditions of your assertion are included in your assertion, so much the truer and less erroneous does your judgement become'. But, he adds, 'can the conditions of judgement ever be made complete and comprised within the judgement? In my opinion this is impossible.'[11] What Hill takes as a prerequisite for probity is—given the singular complexity and extent of the world when contrasted with (for instance) the limits of an individual's senses—exactly what Bradley believes to be impossible. Inability to command, or even illustrate attention to, the object being evaluated at the close of 'Poetry and Value' places its writer ecstatically outside the condition of judgement, according in this with Bradley's opinion, but not Hill's own understanding of it. Yet, that understanding of it being (according to Bradley) impossible, this 'ecstacy' becomes where we all are: standing out *in medias res*. To be 'within the process' and 'the condition' means having inevitably limited relations with that very 'condition'. The assurance of substantial accuracy in Hill's conviction about poetry appears, then, notwithstanding the displays of academic scruple, tactlessly misplaced.

He calls his judgement a fact because wanting to assert that 'the intrinsicality of value can be, ought to be, made viable in and for the contingent world, the domain of worldly power and circumstance'.[12] Attempts to characterize the art of poetry in theological terms, by which intrinsic value may be revealed in and can redeem a contingent world of exchange value, link the poetry of Eliot with that of Hill. Yet there may be no such viable redeemer or redeeming *in poetry*. Eliot does not appear to have countenanced it: in a 1927 review of I. A. Richards's *Poetry and Science* he stated that to say poetry could save us was 'like saying that the wall-paper will save us when the walls have crumbled'.[13] If Eliot's simile underestimates poetry's contribution to the bricks and mortar of culture, as equally the poetry of Jesus' utterances, Hill's criticism of Eliot's supposed capitulation to the consensus of his contemporaries is among the reasons for his needing to resist the earlier poet's strict separation here of poetry and religion.[14] Poetry can be involved in doing many things, but the actions it contributes to performing are a part of what we can hope to do as human beings in the contemporary settings of our continuing lives. We may, if facilitating circumstances and conditions are in place, repair or make amends, for instance, because this is a human-level activity in communicative exchanges that has been achieved both in and out of poetry. But redeeming in the sense intended by Eliot and probably Hill is a divine prerogative, one in which we might imagine that 'intrinsic value' is 'instantly mediated' in the poetic equivalent of a revelation.

Contesting John Ruskin's use of the phrase 'intrinsic value', Hill offers a critical redefinition of its use: 'Ruskin devotes many pages throughout his collected writings to establishing a density of evidence to justify his neologism "illth"; by contrast, "intrinsic value"

---

[11] F. H. Bradley, 'On Appearance, Error and Contradiction', in *Essays on Truth and Reality* (Oxford: Oxford University Press, 1914), 252–3, cited and discussed by Michael McKie, 'In Defence of Poetry', *Essays in Criticism*, 61/4 (Oct. 2011), 428–9.

[12] Hill, 'Poetry and Value', 488.

[13] T. S. Eliot, 'Literature, Science and Dogma', *The Dial*, 82 (Mar. 1927), 243.

[14] See e.g. Hill, 'Dividing Legacies', in *Collected Critical Writings*, 377–9.

is, I would have said, *not* rooted in its "meaning and history and uttermost significance". He then describes Ruskin as deploying the term to mean 'whatever we desire shall stand as the moral opposite of illth and collective national bad faith'.[15] Though Hill identifies why 'intrinsic value', as thus understood, has no referent outside our desiring its existence, and, in addition, why his own use of the term is vulnerable to such an accusation of polemical vagueness, he is unable entirely to give it up. He will later concede that 'intrinsic value [...] bears the extrinsic at its heart'—inevitably, in that the terms are paired for a relational contrasting of concepts. Collocating the terms doesn't confuse them, though; it reveals, as does their mutual definition by contrast, that neither term sufficiently defines the complex of what is happening in the promulgation of a perceived value.

Hill accuses Ruskin of not being able to substantiate his 'intrinsic value' in the history of usage,[16] accusing the Victorian social critic of succumbing to moral exasperation and polemical inexplicitness. Yet Ruskin did have a definition, if not a historically sanctioned one, for 'intrinsic value' when countering 'exchange-value', as has been pointed out by Michael McKie:

> But Hill misunderstands Ruskin's use of 'intrinsic value'. Ruskin was engaged in a debate with contemporary economists, and Mill in particular, concerning the nature of wealth and the use of supply and demand and exchange-value as the only measures of value. Against these assumptions, Ruskin argued that things can have an intrinsic value in so far as they support life, hence a sheaf of wheat has intrinsic value as food. The value is intrinsic because it exists whether the object possessing intrinsic value is used or exchanged or not.

He concludes that what 'in Ruskin's hands was precise and relevant to an important concern of his day [...] becomes in Hill's work a vague and misunderstood term of only totemic value'.[17] McKie further notes that Ruskin employed his term to claim the value as *there* prior to whether the object is used or not. Yet such a value is not 'intrinsic' to the object either, for the ability to adapt flora (as in the history of the lettuce) so as to produce nourishment requires processes of work, interpretation, and evaluation (as also when picking mushrooms), and imaginative flexibility (as when seeing a patch of nettles as the seasoning for a soup). Though it has been argued that labour adding value to naturally occurring matter is compatible with the intrinsic value in substances such

---

[15] Hill, 'Translating Value: Marginal Observations on a Central Question', in *Collected Critical Writings*, 388. For a tracking of Hill's reflections on value, see David-Antoine Williams, 'Geoffrey Hill: A "Question of Value"', in *Defending Poetry: Art and Ethics in Joseph Brodsky, Seamus Heaney, and Geoffrey Hill* (Oxford: Oxford University Press, 2010), 159–202.

[16] Not all language use important to Hill requires validation from the history of usage. Coleridge's formative distinction between 'Fancy' and 'Imagination' had no such prior authentication. For a discussion of why Hill 'requires Ruskin's intrinsic value to be rooted in previous usage', see Marcus Waithe, 'Hill, Ruskin, and Intrinsic Value', in Piers Pennington and Matthew Sperling (eds.), *Geoffrey Hill and His Contexts*, (Oxford: Peter Lang, 2011), 143–4.

[17] McKie, 'In Defence of Poetry', 426–7.

as water,[18] I would argue that even the value of naturally existing salt water (as in 'The Ancient Mariner'[19] or a tsunami wave) can exemplify a glut on the market, while the evident need to interpret or purify or build walls against such matter, as in Hill's own 'The Lowlands of Holland', pushes its supposed 'intrinsic' value yet further off.[20]

When McKie writes that what 'in Ruskin's hands was precise and relevant to an important concern of his day [...] becomes in Hill's work a vague and misunderstood term of only totemic value',[21] he suggests that the poet appropriates a misunderstood description of Ruskin's term, and then fails to provide what he, Hill, would regard as a legitimate definition in relation to his own art. But Hill himself had accused Ruskin of such a totemic use of the term, promulgated by what Marcus Waithe calls 'Ruskin's confidence that value can exist beyond the sphere of human estimation'.[22] When the poet writes that for Ruskin 'intrinsic value' is 'whatever we desire shall stand as the moral opposite of illth and collective national bad faith',[23] the indignation is not the Victorian sage's alone. This is why Hill writes in 'Poetry and Value' that 'intrinsicality of value can be, ought to be, made viable in and for the contingent world, the domain of worldly power and circumstance'.[24] But what if Hill's 'intrinsicality of value', value 'intrinsic' to certain poems, turns out to be what McKie calls it, namely a 'vague and misunderstood term of only totemic value'? The term, like the 'dissociation of sensibility' perhaps, while not empirically demonstrable, might still prove a useful conceptualization to enable illuminating thought. McKie's word 'totemic', though, suggests otherwise. Genealogical fictions, however unverifiable, provide a warrant for assertions believed to be true about the world—or they cannot be distinguished from delusions. If 'the intrinsicality of value' is impossible to verify, its totemic deployment may conceal, from Hill too, that his claims are a part of 'the domain of worldly power and circumstance', and a powerful part because so theologically inflected.[25] If he has brought the value of poetry into the domain of worldly power by asserting intrinsic value so powerfully, with the aid of theological analogies, he may have done what he set out to do; but that he depends upon the totemic for this power points to his doing it at the expense of failing to reserve intrinsic value and religious faith from that same illthy realm. What it was hoped would be a value *in* the world may appear no less *of* the world than what it had been set against.

[18] See Waithe, 'Hill, Ruskin, and Intrinsic Value', 142 and 145.
[19] 'Water, water, every where, | Nor any drop to drink', ll. 121–2 (1834 text) in Samuel Taylor Coleridge, *The Complete Poems*, ed. William Keach (Harmondsworth: Penguin Books, 1997), 171.
[20] 'Witness earth fertilized, decently drained, | The sea decent again behind walls', Geoffrey Hill, *Collected Poems* (Harmondsworth: Penguin Books, 1985), 47.
[21] McKie, 'In Defence of Poetry', 427.
[22] Waithe, 'Hill, Ruskin, and Intrinsic Value', 142.
[23] Hill, 'Translating Value', 388.
[24] Hill, 'Poetry and Value', 488.
[25] For an account of 'intrinsic value' appropriated to worldliness, see Henry James, *The Portrait of a Lady*, ed. Philip Horne (London: Penguin Books, 2011), 414–15.

III

Hill admits that 'intrinsic value' is something 'we are attempting to define': '"intrinsic value" is a form of technical integrity that is itself a form of common honesty'.[26] This places the value as a quality of the poet's and the critic's activity. Hill then makes a further attempt to define it, writing that another 'way of stating the claim is to say that the ethical and the technical are reciprocating forces and that the dimension in which this reciprocation may be demonstrated is the contextual'.[27] Here he attributes category-abstractions from activity ('the technical' and 'the ethical') with a 'force', moving from 'common honesty' to 'force' in the space of two paragraphs. Applied to the techniques of poetry, this suggests that the 'cut' in a caesura or the 'leap' in an enjambment or the 'turn' in a sonnet's *volta* are themselves 'forces'. Tempered and focused mental and physical action is employed in activating such 'cuts', 'leaps', and 'turns' when writing and reading poetry. Those mutually interdependent skills in action are not synonymous with Hill's 'dimension' that 'is the contextual', because he is intent on the 'demonstration' of an 'intrinsic' value in a text and its immediate historical as well as longer and larger context, which might extend to the whole world, while my concern is with qualities in the activities that must be present, and their mediating roles (in the times of composition and of subsequently being read) so that value may accrue.

'Value is in activity', as William Empson's poem title puts it, a work its editor explicates by citing the poet's 1935 review of John Laird's *An Enquiry into Moral Notions*: 'whether or not the values open to us are measurable, we cannot measure them, and it is of much value merely to stand up between the forces to which we are exposed'.[28] Value, which Empson claims may, like happiness, be perceived but not measured, is in activity—as when, for example, a poet writes: 'like a gleaner thou doest keep | Steady thy laden head across a brook' or evokes how 'the small gnats mourn | Among the river sallows, borne aloft | Or sinking'.[29] One indication that an activity has value is that it is cherished, as John Keats cherishes the act of the gleaner's living hand with the movement of his lines. But there is no force in the words *themselves*, or in their techniques of caesura and enjambment *as such*. The force, though that is not the appropriate word, is in the writing activity of a specific person at one moment in his life (September 1819 in Winchester),

---

[26] Hill, 'Poetry and Value', 481. He precedes this appeal to 'common honesty' with a passing denigration of some anonymous near-contemporaries, stating that Blake's energy and reason were 'demeaned to the level of marketable slogan' by 'Allen Ginsberg and his British counterparts [...] half a century ago'. Hill has continued to redefine his relations with a touchstone 'intrinsic value'. See e.g. 'Confessio Amantis', in Keble College, *The Record 2009*, 46 and 51.

[27] Hill, 'Poetry and Value', 482.

[28] William Empson, *The Complete Poems*, ed. John Haffenden (London: Allen Lane, 2000), 11, 158. 'Three Ethics', in William Empson, *Argufying: Essays on Literature and Culture*, ed. John Haffenden (London: Chatto & Windus, 1987), 571-2.

[29] John Keats, 'To Autumn', ll. 19-20 and 27-9, *The Complete Poems* ed. John Barnard (3rd edn., Harmondsworth: Penguin Books, 1988), 434, 435.

shaping those words in that exact way, and in the acts of understanding readers then reading (whoever, wherever, whenever). But the 'force', too, is not the value; rather, it is necessary to the activation of value. It may be objected that such 'force' is in English syntax as enjambed over a line ending; but while the poet cannot produce a unique enjambment of particular words without the present history of the language as used and of a poetic tradition, once again, only in the continuing ability to activate such qualities can they be alive, renovated by Keats, and by us as we bring to life his work by reading it, and, further, in our sustaining its forms by emulating them in the necessarily different terms of our own day. This is as true of poets writing as of a reader's willingness to reactivate a poem's characteristics in reciprocal work, by reading its words with a suitable amount of engagement, identification, and appropriate energy. The poet's commitment to writing those words, and our willingness to read them, are among reasons for doubting that unidirectional 'force' has a place in the reciprocation activating value in poetry.

The same can be said for the 'force' of 'the ethical' in Hill's formulation; it is, after all, by no means simple to account for what brings a person to behave ethically, to keep a promise, for example. The 'force', again, is not in the ethical pronouncement *itself* ('it is more blessed to give than to receive'), but in the activation of the ethical by an agent (an act of giving), its acceptance by an equally necessary act of receiving, and shared perceptions of the value in that process. Imagining that the value is intrinsic to the language or the human action or artefact appears to lie behind Hill's belief about what is contained in the *OED*'s word lists, definitions, and illustrative citations:

> Believing, as I have admitted I do, in the radically flawed nature of humanity and of its endeavours entails an acceptance of the fact that, in one way or another, our integrity can be bought; or our honesty can be maimed by some flaw of *technē*; at the same time, however, our cynicism can be defeated, our defeatism thwarted, by processes within the imagination that, as processes, are scarcely to be distinguished from those that discover and betray some flaw in our conceptual structure or hypothesized ideal. There are, indeed, various terms—'discover' and 'betray' are two of them, 'reduce' and 'invent' are others—that in themselves reveal this to be so. They are descriptive of *technē* and also imply moral deductions having to do with technicalities. The supporting evidence is preserved in and by the *Oxford English Dictionary* (*OED*).[30]

The *OED* here stands in the way of an immensely varied history of common usage that is then, in its lexicographical form, called as a witness against that history in a species of trial. Admitting that he believes in the 'radically flawed nature of humanity and of its endeavours', Hill finds himself compelled to state belief in a commonplace—if this is taken to mean that people display flaws in their day-to-day actions and that whatever they attempt is similarly likely to be imperfect in its outcomes. Belief seems too self-aggrandizing an attitude towards such a state of affairs, which needs acknowledging

---

[30] Hill, 'Poetry and Value', 481.

or accepting. But the word might be appropriate if he means that humanity is flawed *in principle* (as indicated by use of the word 'radically') and, as a consequence, all human endeavour is similarly flawed *in and to its roots*. So he believes in original sin. But, a manifestation of amazing grace, those 'processes within the imagination' can relieve us from the consequences of succumbing to this 'radically flawed nature'. Achieving 'intrinsic value', the poet is saved in his work from that nature's 'cynicism' and 'defeatism'.

This mysterious process of mitigation is then evidenced by words related to creative processes 'that in themselves reveal this to be so'. These words, however illustrative 'in themselves' of human qualities, cannot reveal the qualities *by* themselves. Yet it is only because words are implied to reveal these things as such that the *OED* may be wielded as a repository of 'supporting evidence'. The words Hill cites ('discover', 'betray', 'reduce', and 'invent') do not even reveal these things *in* themselves, but under an etymologically inflected descriptive interpretation. While the *OED* does provide a fossil record for social and ethical change in the society contemporary with recorded usage, this does not necessarily constitute supporting evidence for any one thesis or theory of history, philosophy, or theology. Rather it lists our implements for arguing those things—along with anything that anglophone human beings have needed to develop and articulate in and about their lives and cultures. This may be why W. H. Auden, no less a Christian, equally questionably, though contrastively, asserted that 'a dictionary is absolutely passive and may legitimately be read in an infinite number of ways'.[31]

The history of usage can provide supporting evidence for what Hill believes, but only under his interpretation, and it can provide counter-evidence too. What he believes it provides supporting evidence for is not *in* the words themselves, but in the ways people have used them for their purposes, including their interpretations of those uses. These uses, if written down, have then precipitated out as traces of meanings that can be picked up by later users with access to dictionaries, including obsolete ones in the case of revivalists. Yet, once again, these words and their meanings are only alive in so far as they are used by contemporaries, and the fact that words do have histories of changing usage instances the processes that can be seen to reveal human societies, including the fact that their futures are unpredictable. That the same will be true for the future meanings of words shows that it is not the meanings of the words that are at stake, but the meanings of their uses. The value, whether ethical or aesthetic, is then in their use and not in the words *in themselves*. Words in dictionaries are provided with succinct and often only approximate meanings, themselves interpretations of uses, which, after all, are derived from instances of use, and not the other way around, while the selection of the instances is itself subject to criticism, interpretation, and evaluation.[32]

---

[31] Cited in Charlotte Brewer, 'The Use of Literary Quotations in the *Oxford English Dictionary*', *Review of English Studies*, NS 61/248 (2009), 94.

[32] See Brewer, 'The Use of Literary Quotations', 93–125.

IV

Hill asserts in 'Translating Value' that in David Hume's appeal 'to the "durable admiration, which attends those works, that have survived all the caprices of mode and fashion, all the mistakes of ignorance and envy"' he is 'not saying that the value is conferred by the admiration, but that society will in the end be brought to recognize the value that has always been there'.[33] The citation taken from 'Of the Standard of Taste' does not express this quite as baldly as Hill represents it. The 'admiration' appears to be 'durable' because it has outlasted the 'caprices' and 'mistakes'. This admiration 'attends' the works in that it goes with them and supports them. It is affirmed to be a preferable valuing in that it overcomes and outlives 'mode and fashion' or 'ignorance and envy'. The admiration is justified by its appropriateness to its object, and by its surviving beyond the passing of less appropriate evaluations. While Hume does not say that the 'value is conferred by the admiration', something Hill notes, he also does not say that the value 'has always been there'. In the same paragraph, noting how 'though all the general rules of art are founded only on experience and on the observation of the common sentiments of human nature', he adds that nevertheless 'we must not imagine, that, on every occasion, the feelings of men will be conformable to these rules'. Hume then observes that at less propitious times the 'relation, which nature has placed between the form and the sentiment, will at least be more obscure; and it will require greater accuracy to trace and discern it'.[34]

The value is not in the object, but in what Hume calls the natural relation between form and sentiment, between an object and a feeling about it, one that can be concealed by contingent circumstance. He then comes to the conclusion that Hill cites as showing the benefit of evaluative tradition in such circumstances. It is thus this 'relation, which nature has placed between the form and the sentiment' that is referred to by 'its influence' in the following: 'We shall be able to ascertain its influence not so much from the operation of each particular beauty, as from the durable admiration, which attends these works.'[35] It is 'not so much from the operation of each particular beauty', not the work, but from good, lasting criticism which helps clarify the appropriate relation, the relation 'nature has placed between the form and the sentiment', and which we may come to identify in our response to the work. Hume is particularly concerned with this relation between object and feeling, because disagreement about 'each particular beauty' would appear non-negotiable (as if there were no accounting for taste); but there are grounds, he argues, for adjusting our *relations* with those beauties. The object need not change, but our relations with it can. Hill's interpretation of this is that the society is brought to see what was always there, as if without the mediation. Coming to appreciate an art object that previously repelled or left you indifferent is to have your *relation*

---

[33] Hill, 'Translating Value', 388. Hill cites David Hume, 'Of the Standard of Taste', in *Essays Moral, Political and Literary*, ed. Eugene F. Miller (Indianapolis: Literary Fund, rev. edn., 1988), 233.
[34] Hume, 'Of the Standard of Taste', 232–3.
[35] Hume, 'Of the Standard of Taste', 233.

to it changed. What you once disliked, you now admire, and that changes the role the object plays in your life because instead of neglecting it and allowing it to disappear from human attention, and, if sufficiently neglected, cease to exist, you try to maintain its lineaments, by scholarly preservation or reconstruction, for instance, and to keep it present in the light of esteem.[36]

Earlier in his essay, articulating ideas that he opposes, Hume had contrasted two false ideas of where beauty is to be found: 'Beauty' is said to be either a 'quality in things themselves' or it 'exists merely in the mind which contemplates them'.[37] His subsequent arguing for a natural relation between the form and the sentiment, a relation that can be obscured by contingencies and aided by long-standing traditions of evaluation ('durable admiration'), counters both these earlier assertions: it is neither in 'things themselves' nor only in 'the mind which contemplates'. Beauty is not, according to Hume, merely 'in the eye of the beholder', a proverb he alludes to, nor is it a 'real matter of fact', for if so there could be no acceptably variable views in aesthetic judgement. There is, further, no other way for appropriately perceived value to be promulgated than through such 'durable admiration'.

What alternative does Hill have to this complex relation? In his sentence quoted earlier he has an agent-less passive verb acting upon a generality so as to bring it to see what was intrinsic to a work: 'society will in the end be brought to recognize the value that has always been there'. But who is 'society'? Who or what will bring it to recognize this pre-existing value? When is 'the end'? Even if the value we are to recognize were allowed to be 'intrinsic', a word insufficiently accurate to the situation as Hume describes it, there is still no other way for the value to be made manifest than through the actions of persons, such as their 'admiration', and ones belonging to the society that is supposed in Hill's formulation to 'be brought'. Hume was concerned with the grounds for asserting that a 'taste' can have a 'standard' that may be recognized, and what held the taste to a standard for Hume was 'experience and the common sentiments of human nature'. We may like to believe that the value we appreciate by admiring it has 'always been there' in the object of our evaluation, but even that value had to be seen by someone, had to be picked out and applauded. Hill's disagreement with Hume about the value of John Bunyan's writings[38] points to the permanently contested situation of 'durable admiration' which, though time can make value seem permanent, has ever to be reaffirmed, sustained by further acts of admiration and criticism.

---

[36] Wittgenstein adds to Hume's insight the observation that this *relation* is not a causal one: the characteristics of the object do not causally produce feeling in the reader or observer. This is one of the reasons why the relation can be adjusted—by, for example, conversation in front of an artwork or at a reading group. See Ludwig Wittgenstein, *Lectures and Conversations on Aesthetics, Psychology and Religious Belief*, ed. Cyril Barrett (Oxford: Blackwell, 1966), 13–14. And see my 'Wittgenstein's Aesthetics and Revision', in John Roe and Michele Stanco (eds.), *Inspiration and Technique: Ancient to Modern Views on Beauty and Art* (Bern: Peter Lang, 2007), 261–76.

[37] Hume, 'Of the Standard of Taste', 230.

[38] See Hume, 'Of the Standard of Taste', 230–1, and Hill, 'Translating Value', 386–7.

Value is thus neither 'intrinsic' nor 'extrinsic', neither simply 'recognized' nor merely 'conferred'. Value is identified in the activity of evaluation, by picking out qualities from an array of phenomena, giving more weight or salience to some and less to others, and providing explanations and justifications for these weightings, inviting others to agree or to offer counter-explanations for a different experience. The title to the fourth section of Hill's *Collected Critical Writings* is 'Inventions of Value', an equivocating phrase that allows him to be referring to poems, 'Inventions', which he admires as 'of Value', while simultaneously suggesting that 'Value' is invented, with an implication of a value-conferral by the inventors. This equivocation also serves to embed necessary processes of evaluation in the processes of poetic composition which result in that identified value supposed to be intrinsic. Yet while he and we may like to hope that qualities of perception and argument will win out in the triumph over time of 'durable admiration', nothing guarantees that it will—beyond our efforts and determination to see the better judgement win through.

The Arts Council of England recently nodded towards both intrinsic and instrumental values, a binary opposition with which Hill begins 'Translating Value' when taking up A. C. Bradley's contrast between the 'intrinsic' and 'ulterior' value in his 'Poetry for Poetry's Sake' (1901), the latter term equivalent to 'instrumental'.[39] I. A. Richards in *Principles of Literary Criticism* (1924) similarly allows a sharing of values between the intrinsic, poetry for poetry's sake, as Bradley's title has it, and the 'ulterior', the socially useful, in support of, for instance, culture or religion.[40] This debate brings us back to the explanations and justifications for finding value in the weighting, the salience, of particular phenomena in a work of art. It might appear that there are two types of argument and justification: those that support the value of poetry in itself, and those that support its social usefulness. But there is no such distinction. The value that poems 'in themselves' may manifest is inextricable from, and can only be felt to have substance and meaning by, the roles they play in the lives of readers and writers. These roles cannot be detached from their lives in society. Just as there is no 'intrinsic' (nor, by that token, 'extrinsic') value, so, in poetry and the arts, there is no 'instrumental' value either. This does not, however, imply that we do not use poetry in our lives. We can't create the benefits to culture, religion, social cohesion, individual well-being, or other worthy end by writing or reading poetry *to get them*, but neither would we have reason to read poetry if we are hoping for nothing but 'poetry' from it. The minutest and most

---

[39] Art is 'intrinsically valuable' and also 'necessary for a successful economy, to our national prestige, to our mental health, to our social cohesion, to our sense of identity, to our happiness and to our well-being [...] Intrinsic and instrumental arguments all have their place'. 'Achieving Great Art for Everyone: A Strategic Framework for the Arts' (London: Arts Council England, 2011), 4. See Matthew Sperling's discussion of this passage in relation to public support for contemporary poetry publishing in 'Books and the Market: Trade Publishers, State Subsidies, and Small Presses', 191–212 above. See also Robert Hampson, 'Custodians and Active Citizens' and Rónán McDonald, 'The Value of Art and the Art of Evaluation' in Jonathan Bate (ed.), *The Public Value of the Humanities* (London: Bloomsbury Academic, 2011), 68–75 and 283–94.

[40] Hill, 'Translating Value', 384.

poetically technical of qualities, the timing of a cadence or a rhyme, for instance, can only be appreciated and admired as the bearer of values if these are understood as shaping matters beyond those technical operations. There is no autonomous domain of poetry that can stand against the world: poetry is in and a part of the world, the value it may bear remaining within the conditions and processes of life.[41]

Nietzsche in *On the Genealogy of Morals* (1887) mocks Kant's idea of the disinterested contemplation of autonomous and function-free art objects by asserting that his conception of beauty is centred not in the artist's activity but in the viewer's: '"That which pleases *without interest*", Kant has said, "is beautiful." Without interest! Compare this definition with that offered by a genuine "spectator" and artist—Stendhal, who once described the beautiful as *une promesse de bonheur.*'[42] Value accrues to works of art because we are interested by and in them, and Hill's artist's interestedness is everywhere apparent in his poetry and criticism.[43] Damaging to his argument for 'intrinsic' value, though, is its tacit withholding of responsibility from the necessary agents in the activities of writing and reading poetry. In his phrase about Hume's 'durable admiration', we recall, Hill wrote that 'society will in the end be brought to recognize the value that has always been there' in the work. He attributes this putative intrinsic value to the mysterious interaction of painstaking creative work and grace in inspiration. True, perhaps, but even here the conscious artist has to *accept* the grace of a given passage or work, has to decide to leave it alone, to preserve it, to try to publish it. Poets have, legitimately and necessarily, to value their own work sufficiently to think it worth making available to others. The poets are responsible for beginning those processes of discerning and weighing salience, and, in offering the work for publication they invite others to share that responsibility, to take it over, to carry it on through time as 'durable admiration'.

'*Intrinsic value* | I am somewhat less sure of', Hill writes in section LXX of *The Triumph of Love* (1998), and attempts a further definition of the phrase laid out as verse:

> *Intrinsic value*
> I am somewhat less sure of. It seems
> implicate with active virtue but I cannot
> say how, precisely. Partaking of both
> fact and recognition, it must be, therefore,
> in effect, at once agent and predicate:
> imponderables brought home
> to the brute mass and detail of the world;
> there, by some, to be pondered.[44]

---

[41] There is disagreement about whether Hill's poetry and criticism presuppose an autonomous aesthetic realm of poetic action, and his views about this too may have evolved in later years. Alex Pestell draws attention to a Kantian residue in Hill's thought, one derived from Coleridge, Green, and Bradley, in his as-yet-unpublished University of Sussex PhD thesis 'Geoffrey Hill: Poetry, Criticism and Philosophy' (Sept. 2011).

[42] Friedrich Nietzsche, *On the Genealogy of Morals: A Polemic,* trans. Douglas Smith (Oxford: Oxford University Press, 1996), 83.

[43] For Hill's belief in, and struggle with, 'disinterestedness', see 'Translating Value', 383.

[44] Geoffrey Hill, *The Triumph of Love* (Boston: Houghton Mifflin, 1998), 37.

This passage too is an attempt to preserve 'intrinsic value' in 'fact' while admitting the role of evaluation in 'recognition', linking thus 'value' in the thing and 'virtue' in the perceiver, but, once again, failing sufficiently to appreciate the role and necessity of that non-causal relation between the two. I once suggested in a footnote that it would require more time and space than then available 'to explain why he can neither be sure' of intrinsic value 'nor abandon the idea'.[45] Now, as we saw, McKie has Hill employing 'intrinsic value' as a 'term of only totemic value'. He turns against the poet himself Hill's criticism of Ruskin's reliance on 'whatever we desire shall stand' as a 'moral opposite'. The difference to be noted, though, in these two criticisms of the term's use is that while 'whatever we desire' is inextricable from value and evaluation, the 'totemic' points to a form of superstitious tribal hierarchy maintenance. Though what we may or may not desire is necessarily in the hands of those to whom it matters, the totemic is a means for arrogating power through the imposition of what are taken to be empty forms for worship. Hill cannot be sure of 'intrinsic value' because value is inextricable from 'whatever we desire', what we can argue for and against, while he cannot abandon 'intrinsic value' because depending on 'the value that has always been there' in the maintenance of esteem for and in poetry, an esteem not granted to be in the hands of none other than present and future readers.

The eighteenth part of Hill's 'Pindarics *after Cesare Pavese*' in *Without Title* (2006) returns to this projected quality that he is 'somewhat less sure of'. The section is headed with an epigraph from Pavese's *Il mestiere di vivere* in a 1980 English translation: 'Fundamentally the fine arts and letters did not suffer under fascism; cynically accepting the game as it was.'[46] In the 1990 Italian edition derived from Pavese's manuscript, this passage from 5 March 1948 reads more complexly: 'In fondo l'intelligenza umanistica—le belle arti e lettere—non patí sotto il fascismo; poté sbizzarrirsi, accettare cinicamente il gioco' (After all, humanistic intelligence—the fine arts and letters—did not suffer under Fascism; it was able to let itself go, cynically to accept the game).[47] Hill's first stanza sketches a further predicament for his 'intrinsic value' prompted by Pavese's 10 May 1941 remark that 'La banalità delle ideologie totalitarie corrisponde alla banalità della predicazione umanitaria che le ha provocate. Tolsoi, Ruskin, Gandhi, hanno creato...'[48] (The banality of the totalitarian ideologies corresponds to the banality of the humanitarian preaching that provoked them. Tolstoy, Ruskin, Gandhi, they have created...):

The nature it seems of that intelligence
is to be compromised. But, then, nothing is pure.
P. (Ces) blamed Ruskin for the fascist state.
Intrinsic value's at the root of this,
it can branch either way.

---

[45] Peter Robinson, *Poetry, Poets, Readers: Making Things Happen* (Oxford: Oxford University Press, 2002), 5n.
[46] Geoffrey Hill, *Without Title* (London: Penguin Books, 2006), 52.
[47] Cesare Pavese, *Il mestiere di vivere 1935–1950*, ed. Marziano Guglielminetti and Laura Nay (Turin: Einaudi, 1990), 348. The translations, here and later, are mine.
[48] Pavese, *Il mestiere di vivere*, 224.

However, Pavese doesn't exactly blame 'Ruskin for the fascist state', not only because it isn't Ruskin alone who is mentioned, but also because it is the quality of banality found by Pavese in those humanistic aspirations for human betterment. This would include for Hill, presumably, 'intrinsic value' as rhetorically ill-defined, in his view, by Ruskin—a term vulnerable to misappropriation, as it might be, by Ezra Pound who 'was a Ruskinian, so it works out', he continues, and 'so it | fits and sits fair to being plausible'. The poem then reasserts:

The presence of the intrinsic's not in doubt,
the modus is. Now cue for oxymoron
that sounds—rocks—as a Monteverdi choir
is expected to, in its joyous lament.
Intrinsic virtue's weighted by the elect;
is, first-last, for the people.[49]

These lines attempt thus to preserve 'intrinsic value' and the related 'virtue' not only for judgements about poetry, but also as a quality aligned not with totalitarian politics but a democratic culture given ballast and substance by 'the elect', who, like a benign dictatorship of the proletariat, must be understood to be working for the good of all. Yet the use of definite articles in these last two lines creates unhappily contrasted generalities, for 'the elect' is as prejudicially presumptuous as 'the people' is patronizingly undifferentiated.

Hill's lines respond to sentences that follow the epigraph in Pavese's 5 March 1948 entry:

> Dove il fascismo vigilò fu nel passaggio tra intellighentsia e popolo; tenne il popolo all'oscuro. Ora il problema è uscire dal privilegio—servile—che godemmo e non «andare verso il popolo» ma «essere popolo», vivere una cultura che abbia radici nel popolo e non nel cinismo dei liberti romani.[50]
>
> (Where Fascism kept watch was in the passage between 'intellighentsia' and people; it kept the people in the dark. Now the problem is to leave behind the—servile—privilege that we enjoyed and not 'go towards the people' but 'be people', to live a culture that has roots in the people and not in the cynicism of the freed Roman slaves.)

So Pavese distinguishes between 'going towards the people' and 'being people'—his comment as much a criticism of the false 'socialism' of the Fascist cult of the people, the collaborating of some (though by no means all) intellectuals with Fascism, and the proletarianizing of some post-war neo-realist art. But again we see Hill equivocally asserting ('joyous lament') the existence of the 'intrinsic' without any assurance about how it can make itself felt, and this leads him to the sorry state of having to reassert the value of his 'elect' ones for the benefit of 'the people', unable to allow 'people' (without

---

[49] Hill, *Without Title*, 52.
[50] Pavese, *Il mestiere di vivere*, 348.

the definite article) to do the electing by promulgating through their activities the values that, as Hume had pointed out and Hill misinterpreted, cannot exist without that eighteenth-century-style natural relation, which I have suggested requires at least an equal admixture of educational nurture and acculturation.

V

Hill's 'On Reading *Blake: Prophet Against Empire*' from *A Treatise of Civil Power* (2007), a poem in which the speaker is identified as its poet, illustrates further how Hill's later poetry has been tormented to distraction by its inability to accept, even-handedly, the role of the reader:

III

As to the sublime, don't take
my gloss on it. *The Spiritual Form
of Nelson Guiding Leviathan*: you behold
only the hero, the corpses, and the coils
of his victories, grandly weighed and spread.
For *a long age* you do not see the monster.

IV

The visual syntax so conducive to awe.
Which is why, in *Jerusalem*, he could
contradict and contain multitudes (I've
cribbed Whitman, you stickler—short of a phrase).
One poet is very like another and rejoices
in the final artifice. I mean great poets.

V

If *counting gold* is not *abundant living*
nothing else counts. That there are over-
flowing granaries of Imagination
stands neither here nor there. Money is fertile
and genius falls by the way. It doesn't—
but stays in its own room, growing confused

VI

as I suppose Will: Blake did, overwhelmed
by the spoiled harvest of *The Four Zoas*.[51]

---

[51] Geoffrey Hill, *A Treatise of Civil Power* (London: Penguin Books, 2007), 11–12.

The passage calls up Blake's allegorical painting which rebukes the cult of Nelson and his victories for its triumphal imperialism and collusion with slavery.[52] While 'The visual syntax so conducive to awe' may assume inherent, self-demonstrating qualities in the image, the word 'syntax' points to the interpretive work of reading required to appreciate its allegorical meaning and value, aided by the 'durable admiration' in David V. Erdman's study of poet and artist. Hill effectively underlines this relational process with his italicized allusion to Keats' *a long age*.[53] The passage addresses readers first implicitly, in the intent of its aphoristically curt phrases, and then explicitly in the parenthesis with its self-contradicting equivocations: '(I've | cribbed Whitman, you stickler—short of a phrase)'.

This calls upon 'Do I contradict myself? | Very well then I contradict myself, | (I am large, I contain multitudes.)'[54] Not addressing the reader with equanimity, Hill characterizes his (supposed) reader in prejudicial terms. Nor has he 'cribbed' from Whitman; he has alluded to some of the American poet's most familiar lines. Hill's Acknowledgements to the volume point out that a 'word or phrase in italics mostly, though not invariably, indicates a direct quotation'.[55] In his poem the reader is heckled as an ungenerous pedant, 'you stickler', the second-person pronoun a retort to an imagined accusation that Hill is muddling his poets. The word 'stickler' accuses the reader of failing to take Hill's words in the spirit in which they may have been meant, attributing to Blake an idea of Whitman's in 'Song of Myself'. Yet in such a face-off, who is the 'Accuser who is God of this World'?[56] Is it the evoked accusing reader, or the dramatized poet initiating the accusations by forestalling an objection to his unitalicized allusion? Readers, familiar with Whitman's words, could understand Hill's idea that Blake in *Jerusalem* could 'contradict and contain multitudes'. But the parenthetical address *prevents* such readers from unprejudicially understanding these words in that way.

This prevention allows Hill a further opportunity: it occasions his offered justification for taking the phrase from Whitman and applying it to Blake: 'One poet is very like another and rejoices | in the final artifice. I mean great poets.' The need to add what 'I mean' derives from the implication that *any and all* poets are 'very like' one another, which is why Hill qualifies the remark by saying it's only true of 'great' ones—a category in which, sympathetic readers will suppose, he does not presume to include himself. Blake and Whitman are imagined to be very like one another in that they both 'rejoice | in the final artifice', they resist capitulating to the social consensus by attending to

---

[52] 'The Spiritual form of Nelson guiding Leviathan, on whose wreathings are infolded the Nations of the Earth' (1809) is plate VIII in David V. Erdman, *Blake: Prophet against Empire* (2nd edn., New York: Dover, 1977), facing 327. For a discussion of the work, see 448–55.

[53] See 'Ode to a Nightingale', l. 12, Keats, *The Complete Poems*, 346.

[54] Walt Whitman, 'Song of Myself' (1891–2 edn.), *Poetry and Prose*, ed. Justin Kaplan (New York: Library of America, 1982), 246.

[55] Hill, *A Treatise of Civil Power*, unpaginated front matter.

[56] See William Blake, '[Epilogue]' to 'For the Sexes: The Gates of Paradise', *The Complete Poems* ed. Alice Ostriker (London: Penguin Books, 1977), 863.

their work in its realm of aesthetic completion. Again, there is not only little evidence for such an assertion, but it is unhelpful as regards understanding these poets' works or their reception. Blake's obscurity and neglect in his lifetime contrasts dramatically with, for instance, the cult of Whitman in old age. Similarly, the evidence of Whitman's revisions to 'Song of Myself' between 1855 and 1891–2, as Hill well knows, might illustrate no such rejoicing until very late in the day, while Whitman's writing his own early reviews indicates a poet committed to far more than the finality of his artifice. But such questionings as these can be subsumed into the melodrama of Hill's verses, because the remark about 'great poets' then gives way to a contrast between material riches and those of the Imagination, with its Coleridgean capital letter. The mundanely aureate then defeats genius—or it doesn't, no, it leaves him in his room confused, as Blake may have been. The assertion about great poets is then perhaps presented as an instance of this poet's own late-life confusion. The writer identifies with Blake, is a dupe of compulsive self-aggrandizing, and knows it, and so on in descending spirals of reflexivity.

The explicit relationship with the reader here, short-circuiting a reading of the allusion to Whitman as it might have been appropriately understood, is necessary for the precipitation of the poem into this spiral of affront about the treatment of poets. Though Erdman's writings retrospectively vindicate Blake's opposing his times, for the contemporary poet *in medias res* self-confusion may result in being treated similarly in life, the self-confusion compounded by the felt need for a counter-assertion of exclusive self-worth projected in the faulty aphorism about great poets being like one another. The movement of his poem re-enacts this isolating of the poet in confusion, as an exemplary mimicking of the contemporary poet's predicament. Had the poem been without this aside (and it is just one instance of innumerable such slanted remarks in Hill's work) the reader could have been left to respond unhindered to the allusion to Whitman and, in so being left, to countersign a relationship (an offer made in other parts of the poem, ones less fenced about with suspicion and mutual accusation). In striving to 'get within the judgement the condition of the judgement', meaning here a travesty of the poem's supposed reception within its composition, this parenthesis shorts its reading by attempting a presumed dramatization of that very process. For poets and poems to be 'in the process' requires them freely to let it happen; while further, as it now appears, what Hume meant by 'durable admiration' has for some decades begun to accrue to Hill's work, massively contradicting the isolate confusion staged in 'On Reading *Blake: Prophet Against Empire*'.[57]

Concluding his essay 'Isaac Rosenberg, 1890–1918', Hill observes of his subject's posthumous reputation:

> There must surely be more than one canon at any given time: a canon of general acceptance and a canon of intrinsic value. General acceptance presupposes general

---

[57] The secondary bibliography is now vast. See, for a start, Peter Robinson (ed.), *Geoffrey Hill: Essays on his Work* (Milton Keynes: Open University Press, 1985); Pennington and Sperling (eds.), *Geoffrey Hill and His Contexts*; and John Lyon and Peter McDonald (eds.), *Geoffrey Hill: Essays on his Later Work* (Oxford: Oxford University Press, 2012).

acceptability. Intrinsic value need not be generally acceptable. I see no reason in theory, however, to prevent a work from taking its rightful place in both canons.[58]

A moment's thought on whether the critical history and eventual general acceptance of works by Shakespeare, Jane Austen, Emily Brontë, Thomas Hardy, or T. S. Eliot presuppose their 'general acceptability' may reveal what must appear resentment towards the people reading who by their activity form canons. This chapter's discussion of Hill's difficulties with 'intrinsic value' may also give pause as to whether there can be 'a canon of intrinsic value'. However, the non-existence of intrinsic value does not produce the consequence that the debatable qualities of a poem cannot be perceived and promulgated by people. Moreover, no such works have a 'rightful place' in any canon, for the use down the ages of literary works is not a Kingdom of Heaven; those works have their place in the expressed experiences of living and once living readers. There is no reason, in theory or practice, why values such as those Ruskin and Hill have needed to call 'intrinsic', should not find general acceptance—because, as in the cases of those oeuvres cited above, general acceptance is not, in itself or in principle, a discredit, and because through the expression of readers' minds in imaginative and collaborative relation with such works these two supposed canons of Hill's are indistinguishable. What people find good may be neglected and forgotten, but it may also not be—if those who care resist its passage to oblivion.

Marcus Waithe notes that 'Hill's renunciations are also tinged by the elegiac, by a consciousness of mourning that expresses dissenting attraction to the intrinsic'.[59] This would appear the emotional consequence of an inability to trust to peoples' judgements in the process of being read over time. Such feelings also skew his pronouncement on 'poems written in English or any other language' and 'the poetry written in Britain during the past fifty years' with which I began. Poetry, and contemporary poetry within it, is not governed or judged by the instant revelation of intrinsic values that were always there. Poetry is a part of the humanly contested field of created values, values inextricable from ethical distinctions, many of them, in British and Irish poetry (though by no means all), learned in Christian teaching and tradition. Ethical standards such as those exemplified in acts of 'understanding' and 'forgiveness' may equally be applied to the life of art and poetry. 'Judge not that ye be not judged' continues to be, and should remain, a challenging aphorism for literary criticism. Good criticism explores, understands, and illuminates far more than it judges, and, as regards his view of the poetry written in Britain and Ireland during the last fifty years or so, Geoffrey Hill's judgement cannot be a fact and may not be accurate, not least because, being in the process and condition of judgement, he, like the rest of us, is not in a position to know.

---

[58] Hill, 'Isaac Rosenberg, 1890–1918', in *Collected Critical Writings*, 464.
[59] Waithe, 'Hill, Ruskin, and Intrinsic Value', 149.

SELECT BIBLIOGRAPHY

Brewer, Charlotte, 'The Use of Literary Quotations in the *Oxford English Dictionary*', *Review of English Studies*, NS 61/248 (2009).
Hill, Geoffrey, *The Triumph of Love* (Boston: Houghton Mifflin, 1998).
Hill, Geoffrey, *Without Title* (London: Penguin Books, 2006).
Hill, Geoffrey, *A Treatise of Civil Power* (London: Penguin Books, 2007).
Lyon, John and McDonald, Peter (eds.), *Geoffrey Hill: Essays on his Later Work* (Oxford: Oxford University Press, 2012).
Nietzsche, Friedrich, *On the Genealogy of Morals: A Polemic*, trans. Douglas Smith (Oxford: Oxford University Press, 1996).
Robinson, Peter (ed.), *Geoffrey Hill: Essays on his Work* (Milton Keynes: Open University Press, 1985).
Robinson, Peter, *Poetry, Poets, Readers: Making Things Happen* (Oxford: Oxford University Press, 2002).
Waithe, Marcus, 'Hill, Ruskin, and Intrinsic Value', in Piers Pennington and Matthew Sperling (eds.), *Geoffrey Hill and His Contexts* (Oxford: Peter Lang, 2011).
Whitman, Walt, 'Song of Myself' (1891–2 edn.), in Justin Kaplan (ed.), *Poetry and Prose* (New York: Library of America, 1982).

Index

Ackroyd, Peter 364, 371, 413n
Adcock, Fleur 84, 360
Adorno, Theodor 24, 112, 132, 725
Agamben, Giorgio 61n, 507–8
Agard, John 521, 583n
Agbabi, Patience 519, 521, 527, 529–31, 533
Agenda 82
Akhtar, Sascha Aurora 317
Albion Village Press 194
Aldington, Richard 26
Allen, Donald 235, 509, 580, 598
Allen, Woody 457
Allen and Unwin 144
Allott, Kenneth 2
Althusser, Louis 369, 707
Alvarez, Al 85, 95, 100, 102–6, 112, 116–7, 141, 578
Alvi, Moniza 325, 519, 527
Amis, Kingsley 94–5, 97–101, 103–4, 108, 421n
André Deutsch 8, 80, 101
Anedda, Antonella 548
Anvil Press 9, 80, 148, 192, 199–200, 534
Apollinaire, Guillaume 26, 544
Appiah, Kwame Anthony 403, 520n
Arc Publications 201–2, 534
Arendt, Hannah 501, 507–8, 510, 515
Aristotle 335, 618–9
Armitage, Simon 43–4, 252–3, 325, 546–7, 592, 598
Arnold, Matthew 98, 462–3, 498–501, 504, 506, 508, 515, 531–3, 619, 676
Arts Council 9, 179, 192, 199–202, 524, 534, 583, 739
Arvon Foundation 202, 324–5, 327, 329–30, 333
Ashbery, John 35, 86, 136, 271–2, 512, 542, 549, 555, 584, 610

Auden, W.H. 38–55, 98–100, 118, 178, 699, 705, 736
 'Ascension Day 1964' 701
 'On the Circuit' 202
 'Consider this and in our time' 40
 European reception 541, 544, 549
 'The Fall of Rome' 42
 'Homage to Clio' 51
 and Ireland 424–39
 'Journey to Iceland' 43–4
 'Letter to Lord Byron' 41
 Look, Stranger! 532
 'In Memory of W.B. Yeats' 13, 15, 38, 50, 677
 'New Year Letter' 42
 and Old English 343–4
 Poems 183–4
 'In Praise of Limestone' 504
 'September 1, 1939' 47, 499
 'The Shield of Achilles' 50–51, 82
 'Spain' 417
 'Stop all the clocks' 305–6
 In Time of War 44–5
 'Under Which Lyre' 49
Austin, J.L. 616, 619–21, 628, 633, 635n, 636, 641, 655, 678
Ayres, Gillian 274

Bacigalupo, Massimo 547–8
Bakhtin, Mikhail 341, 437, 562
Ballard, J.G. 390
Barker, George 21, 61, 426, 431
Barque Press 192–3, 195, 199–200
Barnett, Anthony 511–12
Barraclough, Simon 308–10, 312, 316, 319
Barrault, Michel 572
Barthes, Roland 175, 236, 414, 542
Baudelaire, Charles 26, 542

Baxter, James K. 598, 609
Beatles, The 173
Beauvoir, Simone de 164
Beckett, Samuel 26, 30, 435, 473, 524, 591, 639
Beer, Patricia 83–4, 147
Bell, Martin 144, 146
Bellini, Giovanni 297–300, 665
Benjamin, Jessica 156–8, 163, 170
Benjamin, Walter 267, 269, 279
Bennett, Louise 519, 522–3
Beowulf 258, 351–3, 546, 689
Berengarten, Richard 540, 550–1
Bergonzi, Bernard 94–6, 102
Bergvall, Caroline 267, 281–3, 317, 583n
Bernstein, Charles 499, 507, 576
Berry, James 519, 522, 534
Berryman, John 105, 199, 232, 424, 443, 699, 704
Betjeman, John 8, 178, 365, 410
Bhatt, Sujata 578n, 602–4
Bishop, Elizabeth 156, 158–61, 169, 421, 577
Blackmur, R.P. 231, 234, 691
Blacksuede Boot Press 184, 187
Blake, William 22, 54, 250, 307, 312, 342, 359–81, 385, 389, 549, 699, 743–5
  America 313
  'Auguries of Innocence' 305
  The Four Zoas 369, 743
  Jerusalem 359, 362, 365, 370, 743–4
  Milton 377
  A Vision of the Last Judgement 371
Blast 117, 175–6, 178, 408
Bloodaxe Books 8, 192, 199, 201, 206, 306, 325, 408, 534
Bloom, Harold 87, 157
Bloom, Valerie 519, 583n
Bök, Christian 210
Boland, Eavan 35, 424, 449, 465, 475, 477–8, 589
Bonhoeffer, Dietrich 698–9
Bonney, Sean 267, 277–81, 583n
Bornholdt, Jenny 596, 600, 609
Boyle, Charles 200, 202, 210–11
Bradley, A.C. 739
Bradley, F.H. 730–1, 740n

Brady, Andrea 192–3, 195, 199–200, 307, 390; *see also* Barque Press
Brathwaite, Edward Kamau 523, 525, 591
Breeze, Jean 'Binta' 261–2, 521, 583n
British Council 539, 549, 552, 556
Britten, Benjamin 43, 313
Brooks, Cleanth 231, 235–6
Brown, George Mackay 144–5, 558
Brownjohn, Alan 101, 205, 325, 330–1, 352
Bryce, Colette 152n, 160, 162–3
Buffoni, Franco 548
Bunting, Basil 21, 25–6, 207, 326, 412, 549, 699–700
  'Against the tricks of time' 623–4
  American reception 578, 582–4, 591
  Briggflatts 25, 33–4, 59–60, 122–3, 342, 544, 582
  Collected Poems 35
  'On the Flyleaf of Pound's Cantos' 126
  The Spoils 26, 61
Burnside, John 544, 549, 554, 559, 565–7, 700
Burt, Stephen 351–2, 576, 593–4
Byron, George Gordon Noel (Lord) 41–2, 204–5, 552

Caddel, Richard 59, 138–9, 266
Cage, John 65
Cannan, May Wedderburn 144, 147
Canongate 210, 534
Cape *see* Jonathan Cape
Cape Goliard 384
Capildeo, Vahni 127
Carcanet Press 8, 80, 148, 192, 199, 201, 206, 325, 534, 584
Carson, Anne 169
Carson, Ciaran 35, 443, 445, 464–8, 477
Carswell, Catherine 184
Carver, Raymond 549
Cash, Johnny 275
Catling, Brian 207, 369, 394
Caulfield, Patrick 513–4
Cavell, Stanley 645, 655
CB Editions *see* Charles Boyle
Celan, Paul 572
Cézanne, Paul 292, 295–6
Chadwick, Helen 164
Chatto and Windus 191

Chaucer, Geoffrey 41, 521, 535, 619, 621–7, 629–36
cheek, cris 360, 367, 583n
Churchill, Winston 375–7, 379
Circle Press 194
Clanchy, Kate 153n, 169, 562
Clare, John 324–5
Clark, Thomas A. 123, 562
Clark, Tom 177–8
Clarke, Adrian 196
Clarke, Austin 21, 624–5
Clarke, Gillian 152, 250, 589
Cleary, A.A. 147
Clemo, Jack 200
Clutag Press 198–9
Cobbing, Bob 177, 183, 186–7, 189–90, 196, 360, 385; *see also* Writers Forum
Cochrane, Geoff 597, 600, 609
Cocteau, Jean 103, 310
Coffey, Brian 26–7, 29–30, 426, 591
Coleridge, Samuel Taylor 78, 119–20, 162, 313, 619, 732n, 733n, 745
Collins, William 288
Conquest, Robert 22, 94–5, 101–3, 116–7, 200, 413, 577
Constable, John 293–6
Constantine, David 540, 553–4
Constantine, Helen 540
Cope, Wendy 147, 209, 325, 548
Cowper, William 78, 101, 258
Crane, Hart 103, 218
Crashaw, Richard 225–6
Crawford, Robert 256–7, 413, 559, 561, 571, 592
Creeley, Robert 178, 182, 582
Crichton Smith, Iain 558, 589
Critchley, Emily 126n, 319
Criterion, The 188, 204, 538
Cronin, Anthony 424
Crozier, Andrew 58, 61–5, 106–7, 119, 123–4, 488–9, 508–11; *see also* Ferry Press
Cuala Press 193
Curnow, Allen 604–6

Dante Alighieri 51, 53, 168, 372, 547
Danto, Arthur C. 131–3, 148
Darras, Jacques 542–4

Darwin, Charles 154, 429, 498
Daryush, Elizabeth 147
Davie, Donald 118, 140–7, 500–8, 510–15, 576–7, 580–2, 585, 587, 590, 599, 697
    Articulate Energy 513
    'Huntingdonshire' 503
    and the Movement 94–109
    'Poem as Abstract' 98
    Purity of Diction in English Verse 97–8, 103, 500–3
    'Remembering the Thirties' 47–8, 96
    The Shires 134–5
    Thomas Hardy and British Poetry 107, 412, 503–6
    'To a Brother in the Mystery' 103
Day Lewis, Cecil 38n, 205
Debord, Guy 10, 287
Deguy, Michel 541, 543–4
Delanty, Greg 545, 548
Deleuze, Gilles 276, 308, 366, 707
De Luca, Christine 52
De Man, Paul 236
Derrida, Jacques 236–7, 307, 466, 542
Deutsch *see* André Deutsch
Devlin, Denis 26–30, 34, 426, 591
Dickens, Charles 111–12, 153n, 353, 364
Dickinson, Emily 218, 224, 548
Didsbury, Peter 408, 414–21
Doce, Jordi 549
Donaghy, Michael 324, 333, 354, 598–9, 609
Donne, John 21, 232, 549, 561, 696, 700
Doolittle, Hilda *see* H.D.
Dorn, Edward 189, 501, 582
Doty, Mark 566
Downie, Freda 147
Dryden, John 98, 239, 376, 530
Duffy, Carol Ann 141, 145, 147, 306, 325, 535, 569–70, 579, 598, 641
    The Bees 207
    European reception 546n, 548, 554
    'Little Red Cap' 169
    'Originally' 246n
    'Prayer' 610–12
    'The Way My Mother Speaks' 623
Dugdale, Sasha 540, 552
Duhig, Ian 343, 350–3, 598
Dun, Aidan 360

Duncan, Andrew 79, 132, 193, 315, 413n, 416
Duncan, Robert 312
Dunmore, Helen 147
Dunn, Douglas 413–6, 418–9, 549
  'After Closing Time' 413
  'Arrangements' 626
  Barbarians 413
  'Gardeners' 46, 645–6, 649
  'Incident in the Shop' 413–4
  'Modern Love' 46
  The Silences 414
  Terry Street 408–9, 555
  'Window Affairs' 414
Durcan, Paul 35, 424, 545
Durrell, Lawrence 21
Dylan, Bob 4–5

Easdale, Joan 155–6
Edwards, Ken 194–6, 208, 360, 370, 384, 390, 708, 710; *see also* Reality Street Editions
Eggleton, David 606
Elgar, Edward 373–7
Eliot, T.S. 1–2, 5, 8, 21–2, 24–5, 39, 48, 98, 125, 126, 233–4, 323, 585, 696–7, 699, 727, 731
  European reception 541, 544, 547, 549
  Four Quartets 116, 118, 417
  'Hamlet and his Problems' 3, 162
  'The Love Song of J. Alfred Prufrock' 111, 728
  Old Possum's Book of Practical Cats 4, 209
  as publisher 4, 72, 81, 113, 202, 205–6
  'Tradition and the Individual Talent' 1, 112, 119, 121, 154, 538, 691n
  The Waste Land 26, 32, 40, 111–12, 114–6, 118, 204–5, 230, 309–11, 395, 544
  see also The Criterion
Emerson, Ralph Waldo 424, 581
Emin, Tracey 167–8
Empson, William 98, 100, 124, 126, 230–3, 237, 407, 418, 734
Encounter 178–9
English Intelligencer, The 61, 187
English Review, The 174–6
Enitharmon Press 9, 148, 194, 201–2
Enright, D.J. 94, 97, 101–4, 108, 205, 413, 577, 584
Enzensberger, Hans Magnus 540

Evaristo, Bernardine 519, 527, 535
Ezekiel, Nissim 250–1

Faber & Faber 9, 11, 123–4, 148, 192, 201–2, 209–11, 409, 534, 588, 641
  and Wendy Cope 209
  and T.S. Eliot 4, 202, 205–6, 209
  and Seamus Heaney 8, 11, 209
  and the Movement 101–2
  and F.T. Prince 80–1
  and Craig Raine 209, 211
  and Lynette Roberts 72, 113
Faber & Gwyer *see* Faber & Faber
Fantasy Press 95, 99, 101
Farley, Paul 209
Farrell, J.G. 435
Feaver, Vicki 84, 548
Feinstein, Elaine 144, 147, 187, 541, 586
Fenton, James 44–5, 197, 209–10, 425, 579, 598
Ferry Press 61, 188, 194
Finlay, Ian Hamilton 176, 179, 183, 187, 216, 578, 582; *see also Poor. Old. Tired. Horse.*, Wild Hawthorn Press
Fisher, Allen 123, 207, 366–70, 379, 384–6, 388–91, 393–405, 582, 591
Fisher, Roy 35, 107, 123, 133, 139, 207, 578
  and Ronald King 194
  City 183–4, 187, 189
  Collected Poems 1968 198
  A Furnace 240–44
  'It Is Writing' 420, 635
  'A Modern Story' 9, 326
  'Sets' 130–31, 133, 149, 325
  Standard Midland 326
  'Style' 264
  'Texts for a Film' 415
Fodor, Jerry 226–7
Ford, Ford Madox 31, 175–6, 184
Ford, Mark 542, 555
Forrest-Thomson, Veronica 124, 126, 509, 511, 585, 707, 711–14, 723
Fortnightly, The 175
Fortune Press 80, 97
Foucault, Michel 461, 465, 718
Frege, Gottlob 618
Freud, Lucian 659
Freud, Sigmund 23, 41, 49, 288, 315

Frost, Robert 53, 78, 162, 331, 335, 435, 438, 453
Fulcrum Press 35, 80, 86, 198, 384
Fuller, John 197–8, 425; see also Sycamore Press
Fuller, Roy 147

Galbraith, Iain 553–4
Gallet, René 543
Garioch, Robert 253–4, 259
Gascoyne, David 310, 540, 542–3, 586
Gautier, Théophile 108, 215, 542
Gawain and the Green Knight 240–4
Genet, Jean 236, 542
Gibbon, Lewis Grassic 184
Ginsberg, Allen 312–3, 362–3, 369, 381, 540, 734n
Gioia, Dana 576, 580–2, 585, 588
Goldsmith, Oliver 98, 101, 501
Gollancz see Victor Gollancz
Goethe, Johann Wolfgang von 424
Goodby, John 27, 58, 65–7, 474
Goodland, Giles 65
Gorman, Rody 563, 570–1
Grant, Michael 511
Graham, W.S. 107, 124, 304–5, 412, 645
  'Language, ah now you have me' 654–5
  'What is the language using us for?' 14
  'Wynter and the Grammarsow' 638–40
Graves, Robert 72, 101, 177, 552
Gray, Thomas 342, 388
Green, T.H. 731, 740n
Greig, Andrew 255–6, 264
Greenaway, Peter 314
Greenlaw, Lavinia 160–3, 169, 356–7, 390, 544, 554
Griffiths, Bill 207, 360, 384, 394
Groarke, Vona 545, 552
Grosseteste Review 188
Gunn, Neil 184
Gunn, Thom 38–9, 94, 97, 99, 100–2, 105, 108–9, 580

Hadfield, Jen 562–3
Hall, Bernardette 603–4
Hall, Donald 576, 580, 587, 694
Halsey, Alan 393–4

Hamburger, Michael 106, 264, 540, 553–4, 580
Hamilton, Ian 22, 101, 103, 106, 119, 410, 588
Hardy, Thomas 2–3, 35, 39, 104, 134, 388, 461, 501, 504–6, 513, 580
Harrison, Tony 248–53, 303, 306, 548, 555, 586–7, 649, 655
  'The School of Eloquence' 54–5, 601–2
  'Them & [uz]' 248–9, 644–5
  V 251–2
Harsent, David 119, 550
Hart, Kevin 704
Hartley, Anthony 99–101, 105
Hartley, George see Marvell Press
Hartnett, Michael 443–4
Harvey, David 708
Harwood, Lee 35, 394, 467
  'The Late Poem' 85–7
  The White Room 86
Hayward, John 200
H.D. 26, 32, 115, 184
  Helen in Egypt 314–5
  Trilogy 22–4
Heaney, Seamus 8, 107, 124, 141, 192, 201, 334–6, 355, 443, 461–3, 696
  on Auden 38, 48, 50–1
  Death of a Naturalist 10–11
  'Digging' 533
  European reception 544–9
  'The Grauballe Man' 625
  on Kavanagh 410–11, 430
  'Ministry of Fear' 249–50
  North 35, 257–8, 341–2, 350, 366
  'An Open Letter' 510n
  'Punishment' 417
  on redress 677, 679, 685–92
  'The Shipping Forecast' 612
  'Singing School' 329
Hecht, Anthony 425, 580
Hegel, G.W.F. 223, 236, 707
Heidegger, Martin 236, 291, 420, 485–6, 506–7, 542, 566–7, 585
Hendrix, Jimi 277
Hendry, J.F. 62–4, 586
Henri, Adrian 141
Herbert, George 687–8, 696
Herbert, W.N. 256, 571
Herbert, Zbigniew 540–1, 555

Hewitt, John 408, 424
Hill, Geoffrey 105, 119, 218–9, 374–6, 655, 679–84, 690–2, 704, 727–46
  'After Reading *Children of Albion*' 381
  American reception 577–8, 580, 585–6
  on Auden 50
  Canaan 375–81
  'Churchill's Funeral' 375–81
  'Dark-Land' 375
  European reception 543–4, 547–9
  'In Framlingham Church' 683–4
  'To the High Court of Parliament' 378
  King Log 216, 680
  on Larkin 417
  'In Memory of Jane Fraser' 679–80, 684
  Mercian Hymns 35, 122–3, 342–3
  The Mystery of the Charity of Charles Péguy 375
  'On Reading *Blake: Prophet Against Empire*' 743–5
  Oraclau/Oracles 622
  The Orchards of Syon 683
  'Pindarics' 379n, 741–3
  on F.T. Prince 87–91
  Scenes from Comus 682–3
  'September Song' 624
  'The Songbook of Sebastian Arrurruz' 680
  Speech! Speech! 647–51, 682
  A Treatise of Civil Power 198–9
  The Triumph of Love 199, 629, 633, 641–2, 683, 740–1
Hilson, Jeff 127
Hitchcock, Alfred 308, 318
Hobsbaum, Philip 11, 234
Hofmann, Michael 360, 542–3, 553–4
Hogarth Press 154, 204
Hoggart, Richard 165, 413
Holden, Molly 135, 139
Hollinghurst, Alan 91
Holloway, John 94, 99–102, 105, 109
Holub, Miroslav 335, 540–1, 570
Homer 30, 259, 372
Hooker, Jeremy 705
Hopkins, Gerard Manley 41, 304, 379, 501, 543, 623, 681–2, 690
Horace 28, 44, 424, 690
Horovitz, Michael 84–5, 106, 136, 139, 141, 362

Houédard, Dom Sylvester 216
Housman, A.E. 461
Houston, Douglas 408, 427
Howe, Sarah 170
Howe, Susan 641
Hudson, W.H. 57
Hughes, Langston 313
Hughes, Ted 117, 123–4, 366, 424, 650, 689
  American reception 580, 583
  Crow 145–6, 541
  'A Dream of Horses' 105–6
  and *Encounter* 178
  European reception 540–1, 544, 548–9
  and Faber & Faber 209
  'Hawk Roosting' 40
  Remains of Elmet 341–2
  and teaching 141, 323, 329–30, 334–5
  Wodwo 342
Hulme, T.E. 75, 115–6
Hume, David 737–8, 743, 745
Huyssen, Andreas 485–6

Infernal Methods 192
Ishiguro, Kazuo 390

Jackson, Andy 308
Jacob, Max 542
James, Henry 81, 733n
Jamie, Kathleen 183–4, 254–6, 333, 343, 347–9, 353, 567–8, 573, 640
James, Elizabeth 476
James, John 267, 275–7, 381, 464, 466–8, 707, 710, 721–4
Jameson, Fredric 481–3, 486
Jarman, Derek 303, 312–4
Jarniewicz, Jerzy 553–5
Jarrell, Randall 40, 234
Jennings, Elizabeth 48, 94, 97, 101, 106, 108–9, 147
Jennings, Humphrey 68–70
Jess-Cooke, Carolyn 317
Johnson, Linton Kwesi 259–61, 521, 525, 583n, 641, 645
Johnson, Samuel 98, 101, 202–3, 205
Jonathan Cape 8, 80, 192, 534
Jones, Bobi 704–5
Jones, Brian 335

Jones, David 21, 72–3, 125, 144–5, 342–3, 357, 367, 461, 582, 705
   The Anathémata 32–4, 122, 342, 345, 587, 695–6
   'Art and Sacrament' 703–4
   In Parenthesis 32, 342
   The Tribune's Visitation 35
Jones, Emma 158
Jones, Gavin 369
Jonson, Ben 323–4, 331, 645–6
Jouve, Pierre Jean 540
Joyce, James 30–2, 137, 176, 310, 421, 426–7, 473, 639–40, 685
Joyce, Trevor 126–7, 590

Kant, Emmanuel 288, 366, 482–5, 569, 740
Kavanagh, Patrick 28, 408–9, 411, 424–31, 434–5, 461
Kay, Jackie 169, 519, 534, 562, 588
Kelman, James 249, 257
Kelmscott Press 193
Kenner, Hugh 111, 576, 584
Kermode, Frank 584
Kettle, Arnold 216
Keynes, John Maynard 200
King, Ronald *see* Circle Press
Kinloch, David 571–3
Kinsella, John 207
Kinsella, Thomas 424, 546n, 548
Kipling, Rudyard 533, 552
Klein, Melanie 156, 288
Kociejowski, Marius 224
Kushner, Aleksandr 541

Lacan, Jacques 165, 707
Lake, Grace 197
Langland, William 376, 461
Langley, R.F. 114–6, 126, 287–8, 296–301
Larkin, Peter 123
Larkin, Philip 22, 78, 111–12, 116–7, 209, 462
   'Afternoons' 419
   'Ambulances' 52
   American reception 577–8, 580–1
   'Arrival' 82–3
   'At Grass' 105
   on Auden 48
   'Bridge for the Living' 410

   'Deceptions' 413, 417
   European reception 541, 549, 555
   'Here' 410
   and Hull 407–22
   'The Importance of Elsewhere' 412
   'I Remember, I Remember' 415
   'The Large Cool Store' 411–12
   The Less Deceived 12, 95, 407
   and the Movement 94–109
   The North Ship 97, 183–4, 186
   'Mr Bleaney' 46
   The Oxford Book of Twentieth-Century English Verse 141–9
   Selected Letters 409–10
   'Vers de Société' 422
   The Whitsun Weddings 102, 421
La Rose, John 522–3
Lasdun, James 543
Lawrence, D.H. 24–5, 62, 117–8, 532
Leavis, F.R. 50, 96, 99, 126, 235, 585–7
Leonard, Tom 247–50, 256–7, 579, 601, 644–5
Lessing, Doris 389–90
Levertov, Denise 586, 701
Lewis, Alun 72
Lewis, Gwyneth, 152n
Lewis, Saunders 33, 701
Lewis, Wyndham 24, 117–8, 176, 178
Lindsay, Vachel 312
Listener, The 131–49
Lochhead, Liz 562, 568, 588
Long, Richard 275–6
Longley, Michael 52, 409, 424, 443
   'Aschy' 53–4
   'Aubade' 447
   'Ceasefire' 30
   'Phemios and Medon' 258–9
Longville, Tim 61, 139n, 508–10
Lopez, Tony 511–15, 593
Lowell, Robert 91, 105, 167, 178, 234–5, 323, 424, 553, 577
   'To Elizabeth Bishop' 161
   'To Speak of the Woe that is in Marriage' 240
Loy, Mina 184, 591
Lucie-Smith, Edward 117, 119, 589
Lukács, Georg 24, 32
Lyotard, Jean-François 481–5

MacBeth, George 95, 99, 101, 205, 580
MacCaig, Norman 558
McCooey, David 308
McCullers, Carson 436–7
MacDiarmid, Hugh 21, 25, 31–3, 122, 253, 342, 588–9
MacDonald, Helen 123, 197
McDonald, Peter 48
McEwan, Ian 390
McGough, Roger 85, 139, 141, 409
MacGreevy, Thomas 26–8, 30, 34
McGuckian, Medbh 35, 443, 445–7, 467, 582
McGuinness, Patrick 74, 548
MacInnes, Mairi 2
McKendrick, Jamie 207, 547–8, 603–4
Mackey, Nathaniel 267–8, 280
MacLean, Sorley 558, 570, 588–9
McLuhan, Marshall 286–7
MacMillan, James 702
MacNeice, Louis 38–9, 43, 51–5, 424, 436, 549
McNeillie, Andrew *see* Clutag Press
MacPhee, Kona 317
MacSweeney, Barry 184, 187, 197, 361; *see also* Blacksuede Boot Press
McVety, Allison 327–8, 333
Madge, Charles 69
Magrelli, Valerio 547
Mahon, Derek 30, 409, 424–5, 430–5, 443, 447
  'After Nerval' 434
  'Beyond Howth Head' 431–3
  'A Disused Shed in Co. Wexford' 49, 434–5
  'Going Home' 414n
  'Heraclitus on Rivers' 433–4
  The Hudson Letter 49–50, 431
  'The Hunt by Night' 49
  'North Wind: Portrush' 433
  'Nostalgias' 414
  'The Snow Party' 42
Major, John 360
Mallarmé, Stéphane 26, 85, 127, 542
Malraux, André 501–2
Mandelstam, Osip 221, 335, 501
Manhire, Bill 598, 600–1, 607–13
Manson, Peter 127
Markham, E.A. 517, 520–8, 533, 651n

Marlowe, Christopher 533, 541
Marson, Una 519, 522
Marvell, Andrew 28, 78, 232, 407, 421, 645–6, 647n
Marvell Press 12, 95, 102
Marx, Karl 41, 203–4, 369
Matthias, John 576, 578, 580, 583, 587, 588–9, 591
Maxwell, Glyn 43–4, 597–8, 609
Melville, Herman 513
Menard Press 80, 148n
Mengham, Rod 58, 67–70, 542, 555
Merleau-Ponty, Maurice 112, 165, 274
Merrill, James 41n, 424
Messiaen, Olivier 699, 703–4
Mew, Charlotte 2, 162
Middleton, Christopher 178, 224–5, 544, 553–4, 580
Migrant Press/*Migrant*, 184, 187, 190
Milbank, John 702–3
Mill, John Stuart 608, 619, 732
Milton, John 28, 80, 116, 199, 202–5, 313–14, 426, 429, 530–1, 668, 670
Mirlees, Hope 2, 154–5
Mitchell, Adrian 135, 141
Montague, John 144, 424, 443, 447, 544–5, 548, 588
Montale, Eugenio 29, 421, 541, 547, 558
Montgomery, Stuart *see* Fulcrum Press
Moore, Alison 209
Moore, George 205
Moore, Marianne 2, 103, 156, 694, 699
Moore, Nicholas 197
Morgan, Edwin 123, 136, 304, 335, 558, 568
Morley, David 330–3, 343
Morris, Sharon 317
Morris, William 193–4; *see also* Kelmscott Press
Morrissey, Sinéad 468–71, 477
Morrison, Blake 47, 191–2, 204–5
Morrison, Toni 697
Morsman, Jeff 489
Motion, Andrew 12–13, 77–9, 87, 125, 145, 579
  'Anne Frank Huis' 46–7
  The Cinder Path 78–9
  'Close' 78

'It Is an Offence' 91–2
'Letter to an Exile' 46
The Motion Report 201
Mottram, Eric 117–8, 136, 361, 367, 582–5
Muir, Edwin 184, 349
Muldoon, Paul, 343, 424–5, 435–9, 467, 533, 548–9, 588, 641
  '7, Middagh Street' 42–3, 51–3, 425, 435–7
  'The Bangle (Slight Return)' 436, 438–9
  'The Frog' 53
  'Holy Thursday' 439
  'Lunch with Pancho Villa' 438
  'The Marriage of Strongbow and Aoife' 438
  and Nuala Ní Dhomhnaill 445, 447–59
  'Paris' 436
  Plan B 194, 439
  'The Plot' 438
  Quoof 545
  'Rune' 343
  'Sushi' 439
  'Yarrow' 122–3, 439
  'Yggdrasill' 343
Mulford, Wendy 184, 195–6, 361, 466–7, 709; *see also* Street Editions
Müntzer, Thomas 220–2
Murdoch, Iris 100
Murdoch, Rupert 207, 379
Murray, Les 579, 703

Nagra, Daljit 250–1, 264, 519, 527, 531–5
Nichols, Grace 523, 583n
Nicholson, Norman 144–5
Nicholson, William 178
NíChuilleanáin, Eiléan 443, 445–6, 448
NíDhomhnaill, Nuala 442–59
Nietzsche, Friedrich 724–5, 740
Notley, Alice 640

Oakes, Philip 95, 99, 101–2
O'Brien, Flann 193
O'Brien, Gregory 617
O'Brien, Sean 133, 139, 148, 333, 407–8, 416, 418–21
O'Callaghan, Conor 552
O'Casey, Sean 96
O'Donoghue, Bernard 198, 448, 463–5, 468, 477, 686

O'Hara, Frank 167, 277, 312–3, 424, 542, 549, 555
  Collected Poems 10
  'The Day Lady Died' 86
  'Personism: A Manifesto' 276
Oliver, Douglas 164, 244, 490, 707–8, 713–7, 722
Olsen, Redell 318–20
Olson, Charles 29, 61–2, 189, 366, 498
  Archaeologist of Morning 393
  The Maximus Poems 123, 363, 368, 505–6
Once 177–8
Oppen, George 64, 301, 402, 501
O'Rourke, Donny 559
Orwell, George 533
O'Sullivan, Leanne 545
O'Sullivan, Maggie 196, 361, 384–8, 393–4, 405, 591
Oswald, Alice 207, 552, 700
Ovid 239, 307, 650
Owen, Wilfred 45, 312–3
Owl, The 177
Oxford University Press 8, 22, 191, 198, 207–8, 592

Paladin 207–8, 393
Pasolini, Pier Paolo 310, 563–4
Pasternak, Boris 103, 501, 552
Paterson, Don 120, 332, 343, 560
  '00:00: Law Tunnel' 353
  'The Alexandrian Library' 353, 640n
  'Candlebird' 642–3
  'Correctives' 354
  as editor 206–8, 578–9, 583–4, 588, 590, 592, 597
  European reception 548, 552, 554
  The Eyes 568, 643
  God's Gift to Women 353–4, 642
  'Incunabula' 353–4
  Landing Light 353–4, 569, 643
  Nil Nil 353
  Orpheus 568–9
  'Phantom' 354–5
  Rain 354–5
  'The Reading' 643
  'A Talking Book' 643
  'The Wreck' 569

Patten, Brian 84, 141–7, 548
Paulin, Tom 42, 54, 259, 375, 409, 424, 579
Pavese, Cesare 741–2
Payback Press 534
Paz, Octavio 267–8, 549, 565
Peepal Tree Press 534
Penguin Books 136, 164, 198–9, 586, 589–90, 592, 606
Perfect Bound 5
Perloff, Marjorie 27, 576, 585, 587, 590, 593
Perril, Simon 307–8, 311
Perse, St-John 513
Peterloo Poets 148
Petit, Pascale 551
Picador 192, 196, 206–7, 209
Pickard, Tom 35
Pilinsky, János 540–1
Plath, Sylvia 35, 87–8, 158–60, 162, 240, 424, 435, 535, 544, 548
Plato 618
Poetical Histories 197–8
Poetry & Audience 180, 216
Poetry Book Society 4, 201–2, 209, 534
Poetry Review 176, 178, 181–2, 189, 551, 578, 583–5, 592
Poetry Society 176, 181, 202, 333, 583, 585
Pollard, Clare 166–9
Poor. Old. Tired. Horse. 176, 179, 187
Popa, Vasko 540–1, 550
Pope, Alexander 98, 204, 530
Porter, Peter 48, 117n, 207, 335, 546n
Potter, Sally 314, 316, 319
Potts, Kate 166, 169–70
Pound, Ezra 8, 22–4, 33–4, 91, 104, 122, 184, 218, 234, 503, 513, 546–7
  Cathay 115
  The Cantos 21, 31, 118–9, 126, 127, 286–8, 402, 542, 544, 648
  The Classic Anthology Defined by Confucius 21
  and Bob Dylan 4–5
  and Geoffrey Hill 682, 742
  Guide to Kulchur 538
  Hugh Selwyn Mauberley 108
  'Salutation the Third' 117
  and T. S. Eliot's *The Waste Land* 112, 114, 311, 331

Price, Jonathan 95, 99, 101
Price, Richard 133, 194, 562, 568
Prince, F.T. 80–92, 730n
Prynne, J.H. 29, 61, 75, 107, 112–16, 123–4, 126, 139, 192–3, 390–3, 413n, 640n, 651–5
  on Adrian Stokes 288–9
  American reception 579, 582, 585, 587, 593
  Aristeas 194
  'As Mouth Blindness' 113, 116
  Brass 392
  Down Where Changed 368, 652–3
  European reception 544, 548
  Fire Lizard 183–4, 187–8, 189
  Force of Circumstance 390
  'The Glacial Question, Unsolved', 120–22
  'The Holy City' 504
  A Night Square 194
  The Oval Window 489–493, 654–5
  To Pollen 193
  'Questions for the Time Being' 393
  'Song in Sight of the World' 641–2
  Sub Songs 116, 193
  'Thanks for the Memory' 391
  'Thoughts on the Esterházy Court Uniform' 623
  Triodes 193
  The White Stones 120, 504–6
  Wound Response 391

Rafat, Taufiq 250–1
Raine, Craig 113, 119, 123, 209–11
Raine, Kathleen 22, 147, 622–3, 634–5
Rakosi, Carl 61
Randell, Elaine 184, 187; *see also* Blacksuede Boot Press
Ransom, John Crowe 231–4, 580
Raworth, Tom 35, 136–8, 301, 384–6, 393–4, 544, 578
  'Envoi' 117–8
  'Eternal Sections' 385–6
  'How to Patronise a Poem' 118
  'That More Simple Natural Time Tone Distortion' 138
  The Relation Ship 137
  'Tracking' 81
  'West Wind' 486–8

Reading, Peter 343, 356–7, 360, 371–6, 378, 380–1, 546n, 549, 587
Reality Street Editions 194–6, 361
Redgrove, Peter 187, 546n
Reed, Henry 48, 81
Reed, Jeremy 312, 543
Reid, Alistair 468
Reid, Christopher 210–11, 407, 409
Resnais, Alain 309–310
Reverdy, Pierre 542
Rich, Adrienne 467–8
Richards, I.A. 99, 126, 230–1, 233, 237, 619, 731, 739
Ricks, Christopher 235, 577, 681–2
Riding, Laura 124
Riley, Denise 163–6, 196, 267, 283, 511, 593, 707–9, 713, 717–21
  'The Castalian Spring' 272–3
  'Dark Looks' 165, 708–9
  'Lure, 1963' 274, 276
  'Lyrical' 318
  Marxism for Infants 183–4, 717–8
  'A Misremembered Lyric' 166, 269–74
  Mop Mop Georgette 718–9
  'A Part Song' 274
  'Seven Strangely Exciting Lies' 361–2
  'A Shortened Set' 720
  'Song' 238–40
  'When It's Time To Go' 111–12
  'Wherever You Are, Be Somewhere Else' 164–5, 718–20
Riley, John 586–7 *see also* Grosseteste Review
Riley, Peter 123, 126, 191, 197–8, 288–92, 301, 467, 591; *see also* Poetical Histories
Rilke, Rainer Maria 44, 164, 424, 568
Rimbaud, Arthur 1–2, 26, 193, 542
Roberts, Lynette 2, 72–3, 113, 125, 591
Robertson, Robin 246–7, 343, 355–6, 548, 561–2, 568, 598
Robinson, Peter 43n, 137, 143n, 288, 301, 326, 543, 548, 568n, 657–74, 677
  'After Giovanni Bellini' 665–6
  'Cleaning' 669
  'Clear as Daylight' 381
  'Death is about my age' 665
  'From a Memory' 669–70
  'A September Night' 664, 671

'The Spelk' 246n
'There Again' 661–74
'A Trial' 672
'Vacant Possession' 664, 667
Rodker, John 61
Roethke, Theodore 234, 435
Romer, Stephen 543, 661
Rossetti, Christina 168
Roubaud, Jacques 266, 542
Routledge & Kegan Paul 101, 148, 191, 591
Rouzeau, Valérie 544–45
Rudolf, Anthony 87, 540, 543
Rumens, Carol 409, 421–2, 589
Ruskin, John 288, 379, 731–3, 741–2, 746
Rutherford, Maurice 421

Salt Publishing 35, 192, 208, 308, 590
Sampson, Fiona 152n, 181, 551–2, 704
Sanesi, Robert 541
Sansom, Ann 332–3
Sansom, Peter 322–3, 326, 332–3
Scannell, Vernon 95, 141
Schaeffer, Pierre 268–9
Schmidt, Michael 147, 181, 584–5; *see also* Carcanet Press
Sebald, W.G. 57, 314, 418
Secker & Warburg 8, 101–2, 191, 205
Selerie, Gavin 315–6
Self, Will 324, 407
Sexton, Anne 159–60, 167, 240, 323
Shakespeare, William 3, 52, 248, 314, 335, 426, 429, 501, 549, 644, 746
  Antony and Cleopatra 52
  Hamlet 3, 162
  Julius Caesar 163
  King Lear 52
  The Rape of Lucrece 669
  Sonnets 67, 232–3, 312, 530, 541, 552
Shapcott, Jo 153n, 163–4, 169–70, 207, 306, 361, 598
Shayer, Michael 184, 187; *see also* Migrant Press/*Migrant*
Shelley, Percy Bysshe 31, 123, 314, 335, 360, 487, 541
Shoestring Press 325
Silkin, Jon 216–9, 546n, 580, 587
Sillitoe, Alan 413

Simic, Charles 549, 576–8, 581, 584, 592, 597
Simms, Colin 58–61, 123
Simms, Jacqueline 207
Sinclair, Iain 112, 164, 194, 207, 360, 362–71, 369–71; *see also* Albion Village Press
   Conductors of Chaos 58, 196
   Dining on Stones 57
   Kodak Mantra Diaries 362
   Landor's Tower 365
   Lights Out for the Territory 58, 363
   Liquid City 136
   London Orbital 58, 365
   Lud Heat 35, 363–8, 379
   Suicide Bridge 365–6
   White Chappell, Scarlet Tracings 365
Sissay, Lemn 519, 527–9, 534
Sisson, C.H. 640
Sitwell, Edith 72
Skoulding, Zoë 152n, 468, 470–2, 475–7
Smart, Christopher 624, 629, 632
Smith, Ken 360, 586
Smith, Mikey 519
Smith, Simon 511
Smith, Stevie 77–85, 87–8, 91–2, 407
Smyth, Cherry 317
Snodgrass, W.D. 234, 580
Solnit, Rebecca 57
Spencer, Bernard 2, 38n, 664n, 669
Spender, Stephen 38–9, 47, 54–5, 62, 80–1, 100, 184
Spicer, Jack 507
Stainer, Pauline 343–7, 356, 579
Stallworthy, Jon 207
Stein, Gertrude 126,
Stevens, Wallace 2, 218, 232, 234, 548, 584, 640, 690
Stevenson, Anne 147–8, 158–60, 641, 648, 650–1, 655, 659n
Stevenson, Robert Louis 552, 572
Stimson, Nick 329–30
Stokes, Adrian 288–9, 292–3, 295–8, 301
Stopes, Marie 154
Street Editions 184, 195–6
Sturluson, Snorri 346, 351, 353
Sutherland, Keston 127, 192–3, 195, 725; *see also* Barque Press

Sutherland-Smith, James 551–2
Sweeney, Matthew 551
Sycamore Press 197–8
Szirtes, George 194, 548, 552

Tafari, Levi 262
Tait, Margaret 303–5
Tarn, Nathaniel 541, 544, 586
Tate, Allen 218, 231, 234, 580
Tavener, John 702
Tennyson, Alfred 78–9, 204–5, 625–7
Tessimond, A.S.J. 2
Thatcher, Margaret 280, 349, 360–2, 365–8, 370–1, 375, 379, 381, 419, 510, 518, 708, 713, 717
Thomas, Dylan 21–2, 65–7, 96, 118, 461, 541, 549
Thomas, Edward 78, 183–4, 314, 331, 388
Thomas, Keith 208
Thomas, R.S. 105, 461–2
Thwaite, Anthony 95, 101, 131–2, 138–41, 145–7, 205, 217–8
Times, The 117, 181, 374, 379
Tomlinson, Charles 21–2, 102–3, 107, 124, 288, 292–6, 301, 412, 541, 548–9, 584
Torrance, Chris 467
Tranströmer, Tomas 11
Treece, Henry 62, 97
Trigram Press 384
Turnbull, Gael 184, 187; *see also* Migrant Press/*Migrant*
Tuwhare, Hone 601–2

Upton, Lawrence 196, 384

Valéry, Paul 103, 538–9, 657, 661
Vallejo, César 669–70
Vendler, Helen 235, 576, 581–2
Victor Gollancz 101, 148
Virgil 51, 169

Wain, John 94–7, 99–102, 106, 108, 413
Wainwright, Jeffrey 215–228, 544, 546n
Walcott, Derek 313–4, 523, 534, 548–9
Walsh, Catherine 468, 472–5, 590
Warner, Sylvia Townsend 2, 157–8
Warnock, G.J. 95, 622n

Warren, Robert Penn 231, 580
Waterhouse, Andrew 343, 349–50, 354
Watkins, Vernon 541
Waugh, Evelyn 100
Wedde, Ian 598, 601, 606–7, 609
Weil, Simone 684–5, 690
Weissbort, Daniel 540
Wellek, René 134, 231
Wellesley, Dorothy 154
Welsh, Irvine 257
Wharton, Gordon 95, 101–2
Wheale, Nigel 192, 194, 195–6; *see also* Infernal Methods
Whigham, Peter 82
Whitman, Walt 218, 313, 743–5
Whyte, Christopher 559–60, 563–5, 570
Wicks, Susan 545
Wilbur, Richard 425
Wild Hawthorn Press 179, 183, 187
Wilkinson, John 58, 71–4, 125–6, 193, 276–7, 301, 594, 707, 710, 723
Williams, C.K. 35
Williams, Hugo 119
Williams, Oscar 580
Williams, Raymond 235
Williams, Rowan 701–2
Williams, Waldo 704
Williams, William Carlos 29, 118–9, 182, 221, 225, 577, 584
  'No ideas but in things' ('A Sort of a Song') 124, 416, 700–1
  Paterson 123, 127, 362–3
Wilson, Anthony 324, 328–333, 335–6
Wilson, Rab 562

Wiman, Christian 699
Winters, Yvor 147, 231
Wittgenstein, Ludwig 215, 225, 587, 589, 659, 698, 707, 711–12, 738n
Wollheim, Richard 297, 659, 661n, 662–4, 674
Woolf, Virginia 24–5, 151–5, 170, 314; *see also* Hogarth Press
Wordsworth, William 22, 40–1, 134, 162, 249, 388, 488–9, 513–4, 530, 548, 644, 681
  Lyrical Ballads 119–21
  The Prelude 292–3, 514
Writers Forum 177, 183–4, 186, 189–90, 196

Yeats, Jack B. 289–92
Yeats, W.B. 2, 24, 34, 52, 116, 118, 140, 681, 689
  'Are You Content?' 622
  and W.H. Auden 42–3, 44, 49, 425–6, 677
  'Easter 1916' 629
  European reception 548–9
  'Fisherman' 427
  'Leda and the Swan' 162
  'The Man and the Echo' 676–8
  and the Movement 97, 117
  'Roger Casement' 622
  'Under Ben Bulben' 329
  'What Was Lost' 622
  see also Cuala Press

Zephaniah, Benjamin 262–4, 306, 334, 519, 583n
Zukofsky, Louis 301, 363, 402